D1231638

50/-
$

A MIDDLE ENGLISH READER

THE MACMILLAN COMPANY
NEW YORK · BOSTON · CHICAGO
DALLAS · ATLANTA · SAN FRANCISCO

MACMILLAN AND CO., LIMITED
LONDON · BOMBAY · CALCUTTA
MADRAS · MELBOURNE

THE MACMILLAN COMPANY
OF CANADA, LIMITED
TORONTO

A MIDDLE ENGLISH READER

EDITED, WITH GRAMMATICAL INTRODUCTION
NOTES, AND GLOSSARY

BY

OLIVER FARRAR EMERSON, A.M., Ph.D.

PROFESSOR OF ENGLISH
IN WESTERN RESERVE UNIVERSITY

NEW AND REVISED EDITION

NEW YORK
THE MACMILLAN COMPANY

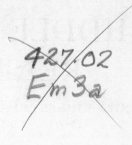

427.02
Em3a

First Edition 1905

New and Revised Edition, 1915

July Printing 1960

All rights reserved

PRINTED IN THE UNITED STATES OF AMERICA

PE
537
.E5

7.00

Blackwell's

23 mar 1966

PREFACE

THIS Reader is intended to serve as an introduction to the language and literature of the period concisely called Middle English, that is the centuries between 1100 and 1500. It consists of a Grammatical Introduction based on lectures to students beginning the study of Middle English; selections arranged on the basis of the great dialectal divisions of the language during the period, and accompanied by explanatory Notes; a Glossary which, in addition to the necessary general information of a lexicon, accounts for the forms of words on the basis of dialectal differences in Old and Middle English.

The arrangement of the book on the basis of a single dialect has seemed to be justified by the writer's experience with students during the last ten years. Whatever book has been used, the student has been first introduced to those selections best illustrating the chronological development of a single dialect, as the Midland, and only then to each of the others, with direct relation always to the one already mastered. This has not failed to insure a fairly accurate knowledge of the main features of each division of the language, rather than a confused conception of linguistic forms such as often results from reading selections without regard to dialectal differences. This method, it will be seen, is but following the best practice in reading Old English, or Anglo-Saxon. Indeed, the great advance in the latter study may be dated from the time when a grammar was prepared on the basis of texts representing a single dialect, West Saxon, in its purity, rather than a mixture of dialectal forms such as much Old English literature presents. The plan of Old English study, therefore, as well as experience in teaching, seems to justify some such arrangement as the present. The emphasis of the Midland dialect is owing to its fundamental importance in linguistic and literary history. Since Midland became the language of the most important literature as early as the middle of the fourteenth century, and the foundation of the standard language of modern times, it is that dialect which is most important to the student of both language and literature for at least six centuries. Besides, the apparent continuity of Southern

108447

English in its relation to West Saxon is apparent rather than real in any important sense. So thoroughly is the continuity broken by important phonetic and orthographic changes, wide-spread leveling of inflexions, and considerable differences in syntax, that it affords no decided advantage over Midland, even to the student fresh from Old English study. In any case the change to Midland must be made not later than the middle of the fourteenth century, and the student must then be led back to the beginnings of Midland English, in order fully to understand the language of Chaucer and those who follow him. There seems, therefore, no special advantage in emphasizing the Southern dialect as the descendant of West Saxon, though this may be done even with the present book if desired.

It is believed that a sufficient number of texts have been given, to represent adequately for the beginner each great dialectal division of the language. Kentish has been given least space, and is not separated from the rest of Southern English. This is owing partly to the limitations of an introductory book, partly to the relatively unimportant place of that dialect in both Old and Middle English. The Kentish selections chosen could be easily grouped together, however, and special emphasis of Kentish peculiarities will be found in the Notes upon them. On the other hand, the dialect of London is especially represented in order to illustrate the change from Southern to Midland, so important in relation not only to the language of Chaucer but also to Modern English. Owing, also, to necessary limitations of a single handbook texts from writers of the fifteenth century have not been used. To that century little introduction is necessary apart from such study of the earlier period as this book will permit.

As to the selections themselves, the purpose has been to present texts representing the dialects in their purity, together with as much of interest as is compatible with the first and most important consideration. Comparison with such lists as those by Morsbach, ' Mittelenglische Grammatik,' pp. 7–11, will show how fully this has been done. In fact, except for two or three selections from poetical romances, chosen on the score of interest along with a fair degree of purity, all texts may be relied upon as typical of the time and region to which they belong. When possible, texts or selections not found in other books have been used, so as to furnish a greater variety within the reach of student and teacher. In all cases the selections are of sufficient length to afford a fairly comprehensive view of the author or period. Partly because they would not be typical, partly owing to mixture of dialectal forms, some short pieces which might have been included on the score of interest have been omitted.

For each selection, the best manuscript from the standpoint of linguistic purity has always been followed. This is now more easily possible owing to the great number of well-edited texts accessible in printed form, but the manuscripts themselves have been examined when necessary to secure linguistic purity. It has not been thought necessary, however, to burden the pages of an introductory book with readings from less important texts, though references to these sometimes occur in the Notes. Finally, the selections chosen have been reproduced in their integrity in all essential particulars. Yet this does not mean that a mediæval punctuation has been preserved, or an irregular and meaningless use of capitals. To retain these, as has sometimes been done in beginners' books, is but to confuse the student without any measurable advantage. The footnotes give references to abbreviations expanded with regard to the forms of the particular dialect, and to manuscript readings not given in the text. These are usually errors of a careless scribe, or readings in which emendation seemed necessary. Regularization of orthography has not been attempted in general, but in the Midland selections, as those which will usually be first read, some slight assistance of this sort has been offered the beginner. All such forms, however, have been indicated in footnotes, so that they cannot mislead if they do not assist.

The Notes on each selection give such information as is known regarding the manuscript, its date, author, place of composition, and some account of the work from which the extract is made. This is followed by explanations of points in grammar, history, life of the times, and similar subjects when necessary. In all cases, use is made of critical articles in the various scholarly journals, and references are given to assist the student in independent examination when desirable.

The Glossary has been prepared on the basis of the Midland dialect, from which the greater number of selections have been made, but with inclusion in alphabetical order of all words not found in the Midland selections, and cross-references when necessary to the forms of other dialects. In the matter of cross-references, as in arrangement within the alphabet, the needs of the beginner have always been regarded as the most important in an introductory book. Thus the strictest alphabetic arrangement has been chosen in all cases. The ligature *æ*, though a simple sound rather than a diphthong at any time, has been placed after *ad* because the beginner will more easily find it there. He may then easily learn its real value, as he must in most other cases in which alphabetic arrangement gives no certain clue.

A word as to the Grammatical Introduction may not be out of place. In the incomplete state of the exhaustive treatment of Middle English grammar proposed by Morsbach, it would be impossible to expect so accurate a summary as may in future be written. The task was simpler, however, than it might seem. It was to present in systematic order the main grammatical facts of the Midland dialect, with such notes as would make possible an intelligent reading of the literature in the remaining divisions of the language. It need not be said that the writer is grateful, as all must be, for the part of Morsbach's grammar which has appeared. He has also made use of most special studies of the period, or of particular works, so far as they were important for the book in hand. But the arrangement of material is based upon the writer's presentation of the subject to students for some years.

The book is intended for those who have had some introduction to the study of Old English. This will be seen from the numerous references to Old English grammar, and to grammatical forms of the older period. It is needless to say that no minutely careful study of Middle English is possible without a fundamental knowledge of the earlier period. On the other hand, a reading knowledge of Middle English literature is easily possible with even a moderate attention to grammatical relationships, and it is hoped that the book may be of use to those who have not begun with the more fundamental study of earlier English.

It is impossible here to give credit to all books and monographs used in the preparation of the Reader. Mention in Introduction or Notes of articles and commentators is intended to imply grateful acknowledgement of indebtedness. Failure to mention others does not imply that the writer has not used them so far as seemed wise. Certainly it has been his purpose to weigh and consider practically all of the literature of the subject up to the time of going to press.

O. F. E.

CLEVELAND, *April* 15, 1904.

CONTENTS

PART I

THE MIDLAND DIALECT

PART II

THE DIALECTS OF THE NORTH, THE SOUTH, AND THE CITY OF LONDON

ABBREVIATIONS[1]

AF. Anglo-French.
AN. Anglo-Norman.
Ang. Anglian.
cogn. Cognate.
EETS. Early English Text Society.
eME. Early Middle English.
EMl. East Midland.
eMl. Early Midland.
eSth. Early Southern.
Goth. Gothic.
Icl. Icelandic.
infl. Influenced by.
Kt. Kentish.
Lat. Latin.
LG. Low German.
LL. Low Latin.
lME. Late Middle English.
lNth. Late Northern.
lOE. Late Old English.
lWS. Late West Saxon.
MDu. Middle Dutch.
ME. Middle English.
Merc. Mercian.
MHG. Middle High German.
Ml. Midland.

MLat. Middle Lat.
MLG. Middle Low German.
MnE. Modern English.
N.E.D. New English Dictionary.
NEMl. Northeast Midland.
NF. Norman French.
Nth. Northern.
NWMl. Northwest Midland.
OAng.[2] Old Anglian.
ODan. Old Danish.
OE. Old English (Anglo-Saxon).
OF. Old French.
OFris. Old Frisian.
OIr. Old Irish.
OKt. Old Kentish.
OM. Old Mercian.
ON. Old Norse.
ONth. Old Northern, Northumbrian.
OSw. Old Swedish.
SEMl. Southeast Midland.
Sth. Southern.
Teut. Teutonic, General Teutonic.
WMl. West Midland.
WS. West Saxon.
$<$ From, or derived from.

[1] The ordinary grammatical abbreviations are not included, since well-known or easily understood. Special abbreviations used in the glossary, together with a few diacritics, will be found in the note preceding that division of the book.

[2] Does not differ from Anglian, the dialect of the Anglian territory in Old English times. So Mercian and Old Mercian are the same.

GRAMMATICAL INTRODUCTION

THE LANGUAGE AND THE DIALECTS

1. By Middle English is meant that form of the language used in England between the years 1100 and 1500, that is English of the twelfth, thirteenth, fourteenth, and fifteenth centuries. At the first date, the language shows such considerable differences from Old English (Anglo-Saxon) as to warrant a new name. By the last date, all essential elements of Modern English had come into existence.

2. Middle English is not so homogeneous in form during the whole period as the Old English of literature (mainly West Saxon) on the one side, or as Modern English on the other. It is most homogeneous for the Midland dialect, with which this introduction especially deals, between 1200 and 1400, or normal Middle English as it will be considered. From 1100 to 1200, known as early Middle English, the language shows less of regularity, owing to more rapid changes from Old English, and to the gradual absorption of new elements in the vocabulary, as of Danish and French words. Besides, the scribes of this period were largely influenced by the traditional orthography and grammar of the language, so that literature of this time was largely a copy, with slight variations, of that properly belonging before 1100. From 1400 to 1500, late Middle English, the language was more rapidly approaching its modern form. This introduction, therefore, deals with Middle English proper, with notes on early and late forms, and on the different dialects.

NOTE 1.—Scholars differ somewhat as to the divisions of the ME. period. Sweet, 'History of English Sounds,' p. 154, makes the periods 1050 to 1150, 1150 to 1450, 1450 to 1500; Morsbach, 'Mittelenglische Grammatik,' p. 11,

gives the dates 1100 to 1250, 1250 to 1400, 1400 to 1500. As changes in
language are always gradual, exclusive divisions are naturally impossible.
Besides, chronological divisions must differ somewhat when different dialects are
taken as the basis, the language of the South being much more conservative
than that of the Midland or the North. For the South, the date 1250 is none
too late to close the first period, and early Southern, in notes on the dialects,
will include the years 1100 to 1250. For the other districts the date 1200 is
late enough for all practical purposes, so that early Midland and early Northern
will comprise the twelfth century, 1100 to 1200.

3. Some characteristics of Middle English, as compared with
Old English, may be briefly summarized. Middle English phonology shows a reduction to simple sounds of all OE. diphthongs,
and the formation of new diphthongs; widely-spread changes in
quantity of both long and short vowels; and the loss of the
consonant *h* in OE. initial combinations *hl*, *hn*, and *hr*. The
vocabulary shows large additions of foreign words, especially
Danish and French. The inflexions show a far-reaching leveling,
and later a loss of older inflexional endings. Finally, the syntax
is characterized by a marked tendency to a fixed order of words,
and by larger use of connective words to perform the functions
of the lost inflexions, as prepositions to join nouns and pronouns
to other elements, and of verbal auxiliaries to effect unions of
verbal elements.

4. Middle English embraces the great dialect divisions, Southern,
Midland, and Northern, corresponding in general to Southern,
Mercian, and Northumbrian of the OE. period. Northern, how-
ever, extended beyond the region of the older Northumbrian to
the Lowlands of Scotland on the north, to the north half of
Lancashire on the west, and probably to parts of Nottinghamshire
and Lincolnshire on the south. Southern included, as in Old
English, Kent and the region south and west of the Thames, with
Gloucestershire and parts of Hereford and Worcestershire. Mid-
land embraces the region between Northern and Southern from
Wales to the North Sea. Southern and Midland are again divided
into east and west divisions. The eastern division of Southern

includes Kent and a small part of the old West Saxon district; the western division all the remainder of Southern as already described. West Midland is bounded by Wales on the west, and the Danelaw on the east. East Midland includes the larger part of the older Mercia, together with East Anglia, Essex, and Middlesex. As the East Midland district contained the city of London, the center of national life from the middle of the twelfth century, the language of this division gradually became most important in the history of English, and formed the basis of the modern language of standard speech and of literature. For this reason, selections from East Midland are placed first in this book, and upon it this introduction is based. Unless otherwise stated, therefore, Middle English, as used in this book, will mean the Midland (mainly East Midland) dialect.

NOTE 1.—West Midland, in its purer examples, differs so slightly from East Midland, and is so scantily represented by texts uninfluenced by Southern on one side or Northern on the other, that it has been but sparingly represented.

NOTE 2.—The language of London, the seat of government after the beginning of Henry the Second's reign (1154), was largely Southern during the earlier part of the ME. period, as shown by the proclamation of Henry III in 1258 (see p. 226). It gradually lost its Southern character however, until, toward the end of the fourteenth century, it was essentially Midland. The importance of London English, in relation to the development of the literary language, has suggested devoting to it several special selections.

5. The differences between the different dialects will be best understood by a study of phonology and of inflexions in the following pages. Some of the more characteristic differences may be given here, especially of Midland with which we have most to do. Midland English, like Northern, is based on Old Anglian, and shows forms due to OAng. phonology and inflexion as compared with West Saxon. See Sievers, 'Angelsächsische Grammatik'[1] (Sievers-Cook, 'Grammar of Old English'), §§ 150–168, and notes under inflexions, as well as notes under § 16 f. of this Introduction. The most marked phonological differences between Old Anglian

[1] All references are to the third edition, and translation of same.

and West Saxon are the lengthening of OE. *a* before *ld*, the retention of Teutonic *ē* as a close sound (WS. *ǣ*); the monophthonging of Teutonic *au*, *eu* (WS. *ēa*, *ēo*) to *ē* before *c*, *h*, *g*; and the appearance of *ē* for WS. *īe* and *e* for WS. *ie*, the mutation of *ēa*, *ea*. Owing to these OAng. peculiarities, Midland English has *ǭ* for OAng. *ā* before *ld*, as for OE. *ā* in other situations, together with a far greater number of close *ē* sounds than Southern. Otherwise the clearest idea of Midland English may be gained by a clear separation from it of Northern and Southern dialects. Phonologically, Northern is distinguished by retention of OE. *ā* (OAng. *ā* before *ld* also) as *ā*; by the guttural quality of *k*, *g* sounds; by the use of *qu(w)* for OE. *hw*, when beginning a word or syllable; and by *s* for OE. *sc* in unstressed words and syllables, as *sal* 'shall,' *Inglis* 'English.' Southern is clearly marked by the retention of the quality of OE. *y* sounds (< *ŭ*, less commonly lWS. *ĭe*, *ў̆*), representing them by *u* (*ui*) under the influence of OF. orthography; and by the tendency of OE. *f*, *s*, *hw*, *þ*, to become *v*, *z*, *w*, voiced *þ*, initially and when following an unstressed prefix. The last consonantal changes, especially of *f*, *s* to *v*, *z*, are more fully represented in Kentish than in southwest Southern. Otherwise Kentish is distinguished by the use of *ě* for OE. *ў̆*, as in Old Kentish.

6. As to inflexion, by the last of the thirteenth century Northern had reduced almost all nouns to a single inflexional form, based on OE. strong masculines, and had completely leveled most inflexions of adjectives and adjective pronouns. The two preterit stems of OE. strong verbs had commonly been reduced to one, usually the singular. The OE. prefix *ge*, whether of past participles or other parts of verbs, had been wholly lost. Final unstressed *e* was no longer pronounced after the middle of the fourteenth century. On the other hand, Southern is distinguished by retaining the weak *en* plurals of nouns, and even by extending that ending in some cases; also by the retention of a larger number of inflexional forms of adjectives and adjective pronouns, and of *īe(n)*, *īe*, *īeð* in infinitive and present tense of OE. weak verbs of the second class; by the preservation of final unstressed *e*, in general, through the fourteenth century. In these particulars the Midland dialect agrees more commonly with Northern than with Southern, though southeast Midland agrees with Southern in many cases. The most distinctive mark of inflexion in the three dialects is that of the present indicative of verbs, the inflexional endings of which are as follows:—

Nth. Sg. 1. (*e*) or *es*: 2. *es*: 3. *es*.   Pl. 1, 2, 3, *es*, or *e*[1].

Ml.   1. *e*: 2. *est*: 3. *eþ(th)*:   ,,   *en*, later *e*.

Sth.   1. *e*, (*īe*)[2]: 2. (*e*)*st*: 3. (*e*)*þ(th)*   ,,   *eþ*, (*īeþ*)[2], *eth*(*īeth*)[2].

In addition, Northern is also peculiar in the use of the ending *and*(*e*) in the present participle, the usual loss of personal endings in the weak preterit, and the reduction of the two preterit stems in strong verbs to one, generally the singular. Midland and Southern agree in general in retaining the personal endings of weak preterits, and both preterit stems of strong verbs, while in the present participle Midland uses the ending *end*(*e*), later *inge*, seldom *and*(*e*), and Southern *inde*, later *inge*, seldom *ende*.

NOTE.—For a fuller statement of dialectal differences, see Morsbach, 'Mittelenglische Grammatik,' pp. 11–14; Kaluza, 'Historische Grammatik der englischen Sprache,' § 17, 204. Naturally not all works written in Middle English are equally valuable for the study of the language. Especially popular works, which were frequently copied, show a mixture in orthography as well as in dialect, owing to changes by different scribes. The purest texts are of course necessary to an understanding of the language as it actually existed, and from these most of the selections for this book have been made. For fuller lists of pure texts representing the different dialects, see Morsbach, as above, pp. 4–11, and Sweet, 'History of English Sounds,' pp. 154–6.

See also ' Die mittelenglischen Mundarten,' by Richard Jordan, 'Germanisch-Romanische Monatschrift,' ii. 124.

[1] When immediately before a personal pronoun.
[2] In verbs of OE. second weak conjugation.

ORTHOGRAPHY AND PRONUNCIATION

7. Middle English orthography is based on older English spelling, but shows marked influence of French orthography. The union of the two systems produced many apparent irregularities, some of the most important of which are as follows:

Vowels: The OE. digraph *æ*, when representing a long sound, was displaced by *e*, as in *hwẹ̄te* 'wheat.' The short OE. *æ* had already become *a*, pronounced as in *artistic*.

au interchanged with *a* before a nasal in closed syllables of French words, sometimes in those of English origin, as *aunswere* beside *answere*.

ie (*ye*) was used for long close *e* in late Middle English, as in *lief* 'dear,' *belief*, more naturally in French words as *mischief*.

o took the place of short *u* in proximity to *n*, *m*, *u* (*v*), *w*, to prevent confusion of manuscript forms, sometimes also in other places. Examples are *wonede* 'dwelt,' *icomen* 'come,' *wode* 'wood'; also late ME. *bote* 'but,' *corāge* 'courage,' where the use of *u* might have suggested the long sound.

ou (*ow*) for *ū*, sometimes *u*, as in *hōūs* 'house,' *cōūþe* 'known,' *cōw* for long *ū*, and *sorou*(*w*) 'sorrow' for short *u*.

v for *u*, especially in initial position, as *vnder* 'under.'

y and *i* are used interchangeably for OE. *i* or *y*, long or short. Especially before *n*, *m*, *u* (*v*), *w*, *y* commonly takes the place of *i* in late Middle English, to prevent confusion, as in the case of *o* for *u* above. It also takes the place of *i* in the diphthongs *ai*, *ei*, *oi*, *ui*, especially when final in syllable or word.

Consonants: There were even more variations from OE. usage in the case of consonants. In the first place, the OE. forms of *f*, *r*, *s*, *w*, now seldom preserved in printing OE. texts, gave way to French forms of those letters which are nearer to those used to-day. Besides,

c is used in early Middle English for *ts*, as in *blecen* for *bletsen* 'bless'; see also *tz*, *z*, for the same. Later *c* (*sc*) and *ce* were used for voiceless *s*, *ss*, as *alce* 'also,' *lescūn* 'lesson,' *fāce*.

ch is used for OE. palatal *c*, as well as for *ch* in French words; examples, *chirche* 'church,' *chāse*. When doubled, *cch* (*chch*) are written, as in *wicche* (*wychche*) 'witch.'

ct, *cht*, are sometimes written for *ȝt* (*ht*), as in *mycht* 'might.'

ff for capital *f* occurs in late Middle English.

g (the French form, our modern *g*) took the place of the guttural stop, as in *gold*, and *gg* (*g*) the place of OE. *cg*, as in *brigge* 'bridge.' *g* also occurred sometimes for French soft *g* (=*j*), as in *jugen* 'judge.'

ȝ (the English form of *g*) was used for the palatal spirant *g*(*gh*), as in *miȝt* 'might'; for OE. *g* (=*y*) initially, as in *ʒē* 'ye'; and sometimes in late Middle English for voiced *s*, as *sīdeʒ* 'sides,' by confusion with *z*.

gh (*ʒh*) for spirant *g* (*h*) in later Middle English, as in *might*, *miʒht* 'might'; the combination with *t* was also sometimes written *gth*, *ʒth*, as in *knigth* 'knight.'

gu occurs in late Middle English for the guttural stop of French words, as *guard*, and sometimes in English words before a palatal vowel, as *guest*, *guilt*, to avoid confusion with *g* (=*j*), as in *gest* 'jest.'

i (consonantal) was occasionally used for initial *ʒ* (=*y*), as in *iaf* 'gave'; also for *j*, as *ioy* 'joy.'

j initially in French words, as *jugen* 'judge,' in later Middle English.

k came to be used for *c* before *e*, *i*, and *n*, sometimes before *a*, *o*, *u*, the former because *c* before *e*, *i*, in French words was *s* in sound; examples are *kēpen* 'keep,' *king*, *kāre* 'care,' *kniʒt* 'knight.'

qu for OE. *cw*, as in *quēn* 'queen,' as well as for French *qu* (=*kw*), as in *quīte*; it was also occasionally used for *hw*, as in *quilk* 'which.'

sch, *sh*, *ss* for OE. *sc*, as in *schal*, *shal*, *ssal* 'shall.'

st. for *ht* sometimes, as *nist* 'night.'

th displaces *þ*, which had itself displaced *ð* almost entirely in early Middle English. But *þ* occasionally remained to modern times, especially in the forms *yē* (=*thē*), *yt* (=*that*), where *y* represents *þ* with an open top.

tz occasionally for *ts*, as in *bletzen* 'bless.'

u (consonantal), later *v*, for voiced *f*, as in *heuen*, *heven*, OE. *heofon* 'heaven.'

w was used in later Middle English for *u*, in *ou*, especially when final in word or syllable, as *cōw*, earlier *cū*, *cōu* 'cow.' *w* also rarely occurs for *v*.

y (consonantal) in later Middle English for earlier *ʒ* (=*y*); also for *þ* (*th*), through confusion with *þ* with open top, as already noted.

z occasionally for *ts*, as in *vestimenz* 'vestments'; rarely also for voiced *s*, as in *wēzele* 'weasel,' though common in Kentish.

NOTE 1.—In early Midland the older orthography prevails, as *æ* beside *a* and *e*, and the rune for *w*, as by Orm. A large number of the peculiarities already noted are also found. The most important orthography of the period is that of Orm, who indicated pronunciation with minute care, especially by the doubling of consonants, the relations of which will be discussed under 'Changes in Quantity.' Minuteness in other respects may be indicated from his use of separate signs for the stop *g*, as in *God*, the spirant as in ME. *ʒif* 'if,' and the MnE. *g* as in *singe*.

NOTE 2.—Nth. shows few distinctive peculiarities. Especially to be noted are the indication of length in the vowels *a*, *e*, *o*, by adding *i* (*y*) in late Nth. Thus *ai* (*ay*), *ei* (*ey*), *oi* (*oy*) correspond to ME. *ā*, *ē*, *ō*. Besides, *cht* and *ght* are used for the palatal spirant, as in *mycht* 'might'; *gh* for the palatal spirant in other situations, as *high, hight* 'promised'; *qu* regularly for OE. *hw*, as *quā* 'who,' *quīte* 'white.' Sth. shows the following peculiarities: *e*, in early Sth., for OE. *æ*; *ie* (*ye*) for long close *ē*, especially in Kentish; *oa* (*ao*) for long open *ǭ*, in early Sth.; *u* for OE *y* long and short, sometimes *ui* (*uy*) for OE. *ȳ*; *ue*, *u*, *oe* (*o*) for OE. *ēo*, less commonly for OE. *ē*, and occasionally for OE. *eo* (*e*); the same usage is also often found in West Midland; *sch*, *sh*, and *ss* were all used for *sh*, OE. *sc*.

8. Accents were sometimes used in early Middle English to indicate long quantity, or occasionally for emphasis. In a later time they were also sometimes employed to indicate that a final *e* or *y* was not silent, as in *plenté*. The breve (◡) was also sparingly used to indicate short quantity. The common means of indicating long quantity, however, whether of vowels or consonants, was by doubling the letter, as *good*, OE. *gōd* 'good,' *wicche* 'witch.' The doubling of vowels when long was increasingly common in later Middle English, and accounts for double vowels in many modern words. Cf. also the indication of long vowels by digraphs, as in the table under § 7.

9. Abbreviations are not uncommon in Middle English texts. Some of the most frequent are a macron over a vowel for following *n* or *m*, as *cō* for *com*, *hī* for *him*, *þīg* for *þing*; a curl above a letter, sometimes through the stem of it, for *er, re, ur*; a small undotted *i* above the line for *ri*; a roughly written *a* for *ra*. Certain common words were often abbreviated, as ꝫ, later *&* for *and*; *þt*, later *yt*, *þ*, *ð* for *that* (*thet*); *qd* for *quod* 'quoth'; *wt* for *wiþ, with*; *k̄* for *king*; *b̄* for *bishop*; *s'* for *sanct, sant, saint*; *ihc, ihu* for *Jēsus, Jēsu*. As such abbreviations admit of no misinterpretation, they are regularly expanded in all the texts of this book with no further notice than a single reference to the earliest. Even this has not been thought necessary except in case of abbreviations for words, as *and, that, king*, &c.

10. The following table shows the approximate pronunciation of the vowels and diphthongs of Middle English. The order chosen is that which represents essential relations of the sounds, as of pitch and physiological formation, rather than the merely conventional order of the alphabet. It will thus be possible to see at a glance the sounds which are closely related in fundamental characteristics and may therefore most easily interchange.

THE VOWELS

SHORT	LONG
i, as in h*i*t.	ī, as in mach*i*ne.
e, as in m*e*n.	ē (close), as in th*ey*, but without vanish.
	ę̄ (open), as in th*e*re, c*a*re.
a, as in *a*rtistic.	ā, as in *a*rt, f*a*ther.
o, as in n*o*t (not Italian a).	ǭ (open), as in l*o*rd.
	ō (close), as in n*o*, but without vanish.
u, as in f*u*ll [1].	ū ($\overline{ou}$), as in f*oo*l.

THE DIPHTHONGS

iu (iw), as *i + u*, or *ew* in f*ew*.
ei (ey), as *e + i* sounded together.
eu (ew), as *e + u*, later as *ew* in f*ew*.
ai (ay), as in *ai*sle, more nearly as *a* of m*a*n + *i*.
au (aw), as *ou* in h*ou*se, *ow* in c*ow*.
oi (oy), as in j*oy*.
ǫu (ow), as *o* in l*o*rd + *u*.
ou (ow), as *o* in n*o* + *u*.
ui (uy), rare, as *u + i*.

[1] The question of how far the quality of OF. *ü* in *plus* was actually adopted in the speech of the Midland and Northern districts, and how long it retained its purity, cannot be positively settled. It is agreed, however, that toward the end of the period this sound had fallen in with OE. short *u* or had become *iu*. From the small number of words with this OF. sound, and from their necessarily gradual adoption, it seems more than doubtful whether the pure French pronunciation ever existed on Midland (Nth.) soil, except as spoken by those who knew French. The exact quality of the vowel is naturally most important in rime, and the lack of significance of it for our purposes may be indicated by the fact that there is in this book but one rime, twice repeated, with this vowel. This is the rime, *Jēsu : vertu* (97, 17–18 ; 99, 3–4). For practical purposes, therefore, we shall disregard the French quality of this vowel and consider that from the first it had fallen in with OE. *u* and the ME. diphthong *eu (iu)*. Cf. Behrens, 'Franz. Sprache in England,' p. 118 ; Luick, 'Anglia,' xiv. 287.

11. Theoretically there are two sets of the diphthongs *ei*, *eu*, *ǫu* and *ou*, those with the first elements long or short, according as they developed from long or short vowels or diphthongs in Old English. Indeed, Orm distinguished them in his orthography (see § 71, n.), but otherwise they are not distinguished in written forms and can be separated only by a knowledge of their development from older English. As their later development also shows no separation, the distinction of long and short diphthongs in Middle English may be disregarded for all practical purposes. Besides, the distinction between *ǫu* and *ou*, *iu* and *eu*, was not long preserved, and that between *ei* and *ai*, which was frequently confused in Chaucer's English, as shown by his rimes, was lost in late Middle English. A new *ou* before *ʒt* (*ht*, *ght*), as in *ouʒt* (*ought*), developed during the period, but, as it often interchanges with *o* and has had a separate development from either of the *ou* diphthongs (compare English *ought*, *brought* with *know*, *grow*, *bow* in *rainbow*), it need not be pronounced diphthongic. The combination *ui* was never sufficiently common to merit consideration beside the other diphthongs. By a slight conventionalization for practical purposes, these nine diphthongs may thus be reduced to five at most. Those who wish to make more minute distinctions have but to refer to the historical basis of the sounds.

Note 1.—Early Midland English shows some considerable retention of OE. pronunciation, as of OE. orthography. Owing to many peculiarities of orthography, however, most words must be analysed in relation to their earlier and later forms in order to be sure of their pronunciation. See, for example, the passages from the *Chronicle* and notes thereon.

Note 2.—Nth. has no differences in pronunciation not sufficiently indicated by the spelling, as the retention of OE. *ā* as *ā*. Sth. has, in addition to the above, the sounds *e*, from OE. *æ*, as *a* in *man*; *ü*, from OE. *y*, with the older mutated sound, as in French *plus*; and *ǖ* (*ui*, *uy*), from OE. *ȳ*, as in French *lune*.

12. The consonants are in general pronounced like those of Modern English, except as already explained under orthography. In addition, doubled consonants are to be pronounced long, as in

sunne 'sun,' which differs from *sune* 'son'; *ch* was pronounced *tsh*,
as in *church* to-day, whether in English or French words; *h* has the
sound of German *ch* in *ich, auch*, except initially.   For other notes
see the Phonology under each consonant.

13. As to word-stress or accent, we must distinguish between
Teutonic words, that is those from Old English and Norse, with
a few from Low German, and the ever increasing number from
French.   The former, which make the basis of the speech, were
in general accented as in Old English— simple words on the first
syllable, compound words on the first syllable if nouns, adjectives,
or words derived from them, on the root syllable if verbs, or adverbs
formed from prepositional phrases.   Even in Old English, however,
the prefixes *ge, for*, usually *be*, and sometimes *un, al*, and the
borrowed *earce* 'arch,' were unstressed in nouns and adjectives.
In addition, during Middle English times, the prefixes *un, al*,
and usually *mis*, lost accent in nouns and adjectives, except in
almost, also, and *alway*(*s*), which have retained prefix stress to the
present time.   There was also a shifting of accent to the second
element of some nouns, as at present in *man·kind*[1], *Nor·thumbrian*,
a stress which was occasional in Old English, as shown by
Norþ·hymbron, 'Battle of Maldon' 266.   A similar shifting of stress
affected adjectives when in predicate rather than attributive position
as today in *thirteen*; compare 'he's *thir·teen*' with 'a ·*thirteen* year
old boy.'   In all such cases the stress can be certainly known only
from verse, where the metre will sufficiently indicate the position of
the accent.

14. New compounds in Middle English also followed the general
law of stress, as in ·*dōmesdai*, ·*sometīme*, ·*whōsǭ, tōˑfǭre, wiþ·ūten*.
Sometimes the root, sometimes the prefix syllable was stressed in
new compound adverbs, as *þērfǭre, þērof, intō, intil, upon*.   Secondary
stress, which was strong in Old English upon the second elements
of compounds, was still so in Middle English.   It is especially

---

[1] A turned period indicates stress on the syllable before which it is placed.

important for ME. metre, since this strong secondary stress was often elevated to a principal position in the line of verse. This is particularly true of certain syllables, wholly unstressed at present when next the principal accent, as *ande* (*ende*) *inge, ēre, nesse, schipe, līke* (*lȳ, līche*), *hood, dōm, ish, ȳ.*

15. Borrowed words of French origin vary in stress during the period, as they at first retain their original stress on the final syllable (except weak *e*) or tend to assume the Teutonic stress. Thus *rēsōun* 'reason' is variously accented, *rē·sōun* or *·rēsōun*, in Chaucer's verse. The following general principles may be set down. Old French nouns and adjectives tend to assume the Teutonic stress on the first syllable. Disyllables, or trisyllables with final weak *e*, when acquiring stress on the first syllable retain a strong secondary stress, corresponding to the original principal accent. Examples are *pítèe, prísoun, mánère.* Trisyllables, or polysyllables with weak *e*, which originally had secondary stress on some antecedent syllable, shift principal and secondary stress respectively. This brings principal stress on the first syllable, as in *chárìtè, émperòur, páradìs,* or sometimes on the second as *povértè, victórìe, religìun, condicìun.* In the latter cases a second shift of the principal stress may take place, as in *víctorìe, póvertè.* On the other hand, many nouns and adjectives, especially prefix compounds, never acquired stress on the initial syllable, as *acc·ount, aff·air, att·empt, con·dicīoun.* This may have been due to the fact that there was no secondary stress on the prefix in Old French, more often to the influence of the corresponding verb. Disyllabic OF. verbs, accented on the first syllable, fell in with uncompounded English verbs and suffered no change of stress, as *·preie*(*n*), *·suffre*(*n*). Polysyllabic verbs fell in with native compounds in retaining stress on the last syllable (except weak *e*(*n*)), as *esc·āpe*(*n*), *ass·aile*(*n*), or shifted it to a preceding secondary stress as *·punishe*(*n*), *dim·inishe*(*n*), *condicìone*(*n*). A further shift to prefix, perhaps under the influence of the corresponding noun, may take place, as in *cónfòrte*(*n*). The best guide to stress in Middle English is metre, but this, while

usually sufficient for itself, is no certain guide to the pronunciation of every word in prose.

NOTE I.—Following the principles above, and sometimes no doubt under the influence of analogy, OF. verbs fall in with Sth. verbs ending in *īe(n)*, as *carȳe(n), chastīe(n)*. In Midland and Nth. such OF. verbs in *ier* usually assume the common infinitive ending *e(n)*.

PHONOLOGY[1]

THE VOWELS OF STRESSED SYLLABLES

SHORT VOWELS

16. Middle English *a*, pronounced like Italian short *a* or unstressed *a* in *artistic,* is one of the commonest sounds, and occurs in English, Norse or Danish, and French words. It springs from:

1. OE. *a, ǫ* before a nasal except when lengthened, and *ā* when shortened: OE. *a* as in *asschen* 'ashes'; OE. *ǫ* as in *man, began (bigan)*; OE. *ā* as in *asken (axen)* 'ask,' *alderman*.

2. OE. *æ* (Merc. *e=æ*), and *ǣ* from Teut. *ai* by *i*-mutation, sometimes *ǣ* (Merc. *ē*, Gothic *ē*) by shortening: OE. *æ* as in *cat (kat)*; OE. *ǣ* from Teut. *ai* as in *agasten* 'terrify,' *ladder, fat*; OE. *ǣ* (Merc. *ē*) as in *bladdre* 'bladder,' *naddre (addre)* 'adder,' *dradde* 'dreaded' (cf. § 33).

3. OE. *ea* (Merc. sometimes *a*) before *r* + consonant, and *ēa* by shortening: OE. *ea* as in *harpe* 'harp,' *sharpe* 'sharp'; OE. *ēa* as in *chapman* 'merchant,' *chaffare* 'merchandise.'

4. ON. *a, ǫ* by *u*-mutation of *a* (ODan. *a*), and *ā* when shortened:

---

[1] In the following descriptive chapters on Middle English sounds the borrowed elements are treated with the native, as their considerable importance warrants. Attention is first given to the Teutonic element, Old English and Old Norse or Danish, and then to that derived from Old French. Differences between Mercian, on which the Midland dialect is based, and West Saxon are also noted. The notes are intended to cover, in order, first, early Midland English, next the principal variations of the dialects.

ON. *a* as in *carl, want, stac* 'stack'; ON. *ǫ* as in *adlen* 'gain', *bark* (of a tree); ON. *ā* as in *laten* 'let.'

5. OF. *a* as in *barge, Anne, cas* (later *cāse*) 'case.'

17. The principal sources of ME. *a* will be seen to be OE. *a, æ, ea*, and *ǫ* from *a* before a nasal, which all regularly become *a* in Midland English, as well as long OE. *ā, ǣ, ēa* when shortened. A large number of OF. words also belong here. Besides *a* from regular OE. *æ*, ME. *a* sometimes springs from OE. *æ* instead of *ę* by *i*-mutation of *a* (cf. Sievers, Gr. § 89). This usually appears in ME. in closed syllables before nasals, *ch* (*cch*), and *r*, as in *wanden* beside *wenden* 'wend,' *panis* (*pans*) beside *penis* (*pens*) 'pence,' *lacche* 'seize,' *macche* (less commonly *mecche*) 'match,' *barlȳ* (*barlic*, seldom *berlic*) 'barley.' As indicated, in most cases of this sort forms with *e* also appear; cf. § 19. OE. *ǫ* from *a* before a nasal, which was regularly lengthened before certain consonant groups (see § 72), sometimes appears as *a* by earlier shortening, especially in certain words as *land, hand, standen* 'stand,' *gangen* 'go,' *hangen* 'hang,' *answeren* 'answer.' West Midland, however, sometimes has *o* for *a* before nasals not causing lengthening, as in *mon* 'man,' but this was not common enough to be a distinguishing feature of the dialect. For OF. *a* before a nasal + cons., see § 56.

18. Certain forms with *a* corresponding to OM. *ē* (Goth. *ē*, WS. *ǣ*) require special mention. They occur before *r* in unstressed words, as *þar* beside *þēr* (Sth. *þę̄r*), *whar* beside *whēr* (Sth. *whę̄r*), *waren* beside *wēren* (Sth. *wę̄ren*) 'were.' Corresponding forms with long open *o* (*ǭ*), on the other hand, must have developed from eME. forms with *ā* existing beside the shortening here supposed. For these see § 43. Words with ME. *a* sometimes rime with *e* words, as if pronounced with *e*, at least dialectally. There would thus seem to be double forms of such words, as *was–wes, fast–fest, gadren–gedren* 'gather.' Rarely also *a* becomes *o*, as before *v* in *govel* 'tribute,' *hove* 'have,' and in *quoþ* (*quod*) 'quoth,' where it is probably due to lack of stress. Individual words which also show interchange of *a–e* are *masse–messe* (Nth. always *messe* by influence

of OF. *messe*) 'mass,' *gadeling–gedeling* less commonly, *tōgadre–tōgedre* (*tōgidre*). The word *Chester* (*-chester*) < OE. *ceaster* regularly has *e* in Ml., though *a* in Nth. *Doncaster*, &c. Forms with *e* are also common from shortening of OE. *ǣ* and Merc. *ē*, *ǣ*, as under § 19, 2 below.

NOTE 1.—In early Midland this sound was still represented by the older Mercian *æ* or *e*, as in *hæfden* (*hefden*) 'had,' *wæs* (*wes*) 'was,' *æfter* (*efter*) 'after.' The digraph *ea* is not found in the 'Chronicle' after 1132, but the Mercian variant *eo* once appears in *weorþ* for *wearþ*. Even before 1132, its interchange with OE. *æ* probably indicates that it was not diphthongic much after 1100. Orm never uses *ea*, and only exceptionally *æ* for short *a*.

NOTE 2.—Nth. agrees with Midland in almost every particular. Before a nasal, however, it has *a* for OE. *ǫ* (*ā* before consonant groups causing lengthening), except in *monȳ* beside *manȳ* 'many,' which is characteristically Northern. Sth., in the earliest period, generally shows *a* for OE. *a*, *e* (*æ*, *ea*) for OE. *æ*, *ea*, as for *ǣ*, *ēa* when shortened. Later all become *a*, as in Midland, except that Kentish, which had *e* for WS. *æ* in Old English, retains it regularly until late ME. times. For OE. *ea* Kentish uses, in the early period, *ia* (*ya*, *yea*). Minor variations are not noted here. For OE. *ǫ* from *a* before a nasal (except before consonant groups causing lengthening) Sth. has *a* in western Sth. and in Kentish, but often *o* in middle and southeast Sth. Before consonant groups causing lengthening, *ā* or *ǭ* are found in Kentish and southeast Sth. The London dialect has *a* with great regularity except before consonant groups causing lengthening, and even here in later ME. by shortening, as commonly in *land*, *England*, *hand*, &c.

19. Middle English *e*, an open sound like that in *men*, has the following origin.

1. OE. *e*, *ę* by *i*-mutation of *a*, *eo*, and *ē*, *ēo* by shortening: OE. *e* as in *west*, *helpen* 'help'; OE. *e* as in *men*, *bet*, *tellen* 'tell'; OE. *eo* as in *self*, *heven* 'heaven'; OE. *ē* as in *mette* (OE. *mētte*) 'met'; OE. *ēo* as in *fell* (OE. *fēol*) 'fell,' *derre* (OE. *dēorra*) 'dearer.'

2. OM. *e* (WS. *ie* by *i*-mutation of *eo*), *e* after a palatal consonant (WS. *ie*, later *y*), and when shortened *ē*, *ǣ* (Gothic *ē*, WS. *ǣ*, *ēa* after a palatal cons.), *ē* (WS. *ie* by *i*-mutation of *ēa*), and sometimes *ǣ* by *i*-mutation of Teut. *ai*: OM. *e* as in *wercen* (WS. *wiercan*) 'work'; OM. *e* as in *ʒelp* (WS. *ʒielp*)

'yelp,' *ӡeten* (WS. *ӡietan*) 'get'; OM. *ē*, *ǣ* as in *slepte* (WS. *slǣpte*) 'slept,' *shephērde* (WS. *scīephierde*) 'shepherd'; OM. *ē* as in *hersum* (WS. *hīersum*) 'obedient'; OE. *ǣ* as in *evere* 'ever,' *everӯ* (*everīch*, *everilk*), *enӯ* beside *anÿ̆*, *clensen* 'cleanse.'

3. ON. *e*, or *ę* by *i*-mutation of *a*: ON. *e* as in *þwert* 'thwart'; ON. *ę* as in *egg*, *eggen* 'egg or urge on,' *benk* 'bench.'

4. OF. *e* as in *dette* 'debt,' *serven* 'serve,' *defenden* 'defend.'

20. The principal sources of ME. *e*, in native words, are OE. *e*, *ę*, *eo* when remaining short, and OE. (Merc.) *ē*, *ēo* when shortened. Sporadically, *e* is found for OE. *i* and *y*, the former in open syllables and in connexion with labials, nasals, and liquids; the latter before liquids and nasals. Examples of the first are *smeten* 'smitten,' *resen* 'risen,' *clemben* 'climb,' *fenger* 'finger,' *wekked* 'wicked.' Such occasional rimes as *helle–stille*, *wille–telle*, *denne–wiþinne*, also point to the same fact. Sometimes this may be accounted for by confusion of forms, as in the verbs *springen* and *sprengen* 'cause to spring,' *swingen* and *swengen* 'cause to swing,' where the weak verbs with *e* have influenced the corresponding strong verbs with *i*. So perhaps *welcome* for *wilcome* by influence of *wel*; *þredde* for *þridde* 'third' by influence of *þree* 'three.' Unstressed position in the sentence may also account for some such *e*'s, as in *heder* for *hider* 'hither,' *here* for *hire* 'her.' Examples of *e* for *i* from OE. *y* are *ferst*, *cherche*, *dent*, *stent*, beside *first*, *chirche*, *dint*, *stint*. In a few OF. words, *e* springs from AN. *ē* (< OF. *ue*) by shortening in originally unstressed syllables, as *keveren* beside *coveren* 'cover,' *keverchēf* (*kerchēf*) 'kerchief.'

21. ME. *e* sometimes becomes *i* before dentals and palatals. Some cases which have been preserved to Modern English are *ridden* 'rid,' *rideles* 'riddle' with loss of final *s*, *hinge*, *lingren* 'linger,' *singen* 'singe,' *grinnen* 'grin,' *minglen* 'mingle.' In *þinken* 'think' (OE. *þęncean*), found in Midland and Nth. from the thirteenth century, there is no doubt confusion with *þinken* 'seem' (OE. *þyncean*). Sth. keeps *þenchen* (*þenken*), and Chaucer

separates the two except in preterit and past participle. Beside *e*
sometimes appear forms with *o* or *u* from OE. *eo* after *w*, as in
sword, worþ, worþi 'worthy,' *worþen* (*wurþen*) 'become.' So
swolwen (*swolhen*) is from a form with OE. *e* after *w*. This change
had no doubt begun in Old English as similar forms appear in that
period; cf. § 26. For *e* to *i* in unstressed prefixes cf. § 83.

NOTE 1.—Early Midland shows *æ* for *e*, less commonly *æo* for *eo*, as in *æten*,
bigæten for *eten, bigeten*, and *æorl* for *eorl*, in the 'Chronicle.' The 'Chronicle'
and Orm also have *eo* for OE. *eo* sometimes, as in *weorces* 'works,' *heom*
'them,' *weorþenn* 'worth, be,' *heoffne* 'heaven.'

NOTE 2.—The dialects in general agree with Midland. Early Sth. usually
preserves *eo*, though sometimes it becomes *o* or *e*, and occasionally *u* as in
dupe 'deep,' *mulk* 'milk.' Sth. also sometimes has *e* or WS. *ie* (later *y*) from
e by influence of a preceding palatal consonant. In all cases Sth. *e* must be
separated from Sth. *e* = *æ*, derived from OE. *æ, ea*, as already noted in § 18, n. 2.
Kentish has *ie* (*ye*) for OE. *eo*, as in *ierþe* 'earth,' *lyerne* 'learn.' Kentish
also retains OE *e* for *y*, so characteristic of this dialect in OE. times, thus
increasing greatly the number of *e*'s in literature of this district.

22. Middle English *i*, with a sound like that of *i* in *hit*, is
common in words from all sources. Its frequency is increased for
Midland English because it corresponds not only to *i* in English
and Danish words, but to older *y* by *i*-mutation of *u*, the latter
having become *i* in sound. On this account also the vowel is
represented by *i* or *y* at the pleasure of the writer. ME. *i* springs
from:

1. OE. *i*, *y* by *i*-mutation of *u*, and when shortened *ī* and *ȳ*:
   OE. *i* as in *smiþ* 'smith,' *his, writen* 'written'; OE. *y* as in
   king (*kyng*), *synne* 'sin,' *kissen* 'kiss'; OE. *ī* as in *fiftēne*
   'fifteen,' *wisdōm*; OE. *ȳ* as in *wisshen* 'wish,' *hydde*
   'hid.'

2. OM. *i* (WS. *io*), and *e* (WS. *eo*) before *ht*: OM. *i* as in *rihten*
   'make straight,' *brihte* 'bright,' *wiht* 'wight,' *milk*; OE.,
   OM. *e* as in *riht* 'right,' *kniht* 'knight,' *liht* 'light, easy,'
   fliht 'flight.'

3. ON. *i, y* by *i*-mutation of *u*, and *ī* or *ȳ* when shortened: ON.

i as in *skill, skin, twinne* 'twin'; ON. *y* as in *flitten* 'flit,' *biggen* 'build,' *kindlen* 'kindle'; ON. *ȳ* as in *imis* 'variously.'

4. OF. *i* as in *simple, prince, delivren* 'deliver,' *cilē* 'city.'

23. For *e* instead of *i*, from OE. *i, y*, see § 20. For forms with *u*, beside those with *y* by *i*-mutation of *u*, see § 28. One word, OE. *wīfman*, shows various forms, as *wimman, wimmen* by shortening, and by later change of *i* to *u* (written *o*) under the influence of preceding *w*, *womman, wommen*. Similar influence of *w* is seen in *woll(e)* 'will.' By Caxton's time, however, the forms of Modern English, with the sound of *u* in singular, *i* in plural, seem to have become established. OF. *ei, ui*, sometimes appear as *i* in unstressed syllables, as in *malisūn, werriōr* for original *ei*, and *angwys* 'anguish' for *ui* (§ 70).

NOTE 1.—The use of *i* for OE. *y* is found as early as 1121 in the 'Chronicle' and regularly later and in Orm. There is also early use of *y* for OE. *i*, showing conclusively the like character of the two sounds. Later, *y* is more generally used for OE. *ī, ȳ*.

NOTE 2.—Nth. agrees with Midland. Sth. shows *ü*, as in French *plus*, for OE. *y* by *i*-mutation of *u*, as already noted, § 5. Examples are *sünne* 'sin,' *fülde* 'filled,' *kün* 'kin,' *cüsse* 'kiss.' Sth. *ü* also appears for a late WS. *y* from *i, ie*, as in *wülle, wüten*, Ml. *wille, witen, ȝüt* for Ml. *ȝēt (ȝet)*. Kentish, on the other hand, which had levelled OE. *y* by *i*-mutation of *u* under *e*, still preserves the latter, except before palatal *ht, ng*, and in *king*. This accounts for such forms as *melle* 'mill,' *cherche* 'church,' *lest* 'lust,' *dent* 'dint,' in that dialect. The dialect of London probably agreed with Sth. in the earliest time, but by the last quarter of the fourteenth century usually has *i* for OE. *y*, though sometimes an *e* which is probably Kentish in origin. Chaucer frequently uses this Kentish *e* beside Midland *i* in rimes, though mostly in closed syllables.

24. Middle English *o*, with the sound of *o* (not Italian *a*) in Modern English, occurs in words from all sources. It corresponds to:

1. OE. *o*, or *ō* when shortened: OE. *o* as in *folk, bodiȝ (bodȳ)* 'body,' *cok* 'cock,' *on*; OE. *ō* as in *softe* 'soft,' *oþer* 'other.'

2. ON. *o*, *ō* when shortened: ON. *o* as in *lot* 'bow of the head,' *loft* 'upper room,' *odde* 'odd'; ON. *ō* as in *þoh* 'though.'

3. OF. *o* as in *apostle*, *potāge*, *offis* 'office,' *hostāge*.

25. Short *o* occasionally interchanges with *e* by *i*-mutation of *o*, as in *Wodnesday* beside *Wednesday*, *wolken* beside *welkin*, *sorwen* beside *serwen* 'to sorrow.' It also becomes *u* sometimes, by influence of preceding *b*, *m*, or *w*, as in *burd* for *bord* 'board,' *wurd* for *word*, *murþ* 'death' (cf. MnE. *murder*, OE. *morðor*). Probably an OE. interchange of *o* and *u* accounts for *plocken* 'pluck,' OE. *pluccian*: *knocken* 'knock,' OE. *cnocian*, *cnucian*; *þrostel* beside *þrustel* 'throstle,' OE. *þrostle*. For *o* beside *e* from OE. *eo* (*e*) see § 21.

NOTE.—In general early Midland and the dialects all agree. Early Sth., as in Layamon, occasionally uses *eo* for OE. *o* as in *heors* 'horse,' *beord* (*bēord*) 'board,' and individual writings, as those of Shoreham, show *ou* for *o*, as in *sourwe* 'sorrow.'

26. Middle English *u*, with the sound of *u* in *full*, is common in English, Danish, and French words. Its sources are:

1. OE. *u*, and *ū* when shortened: OE. *u* as in *under*, *sunne* 'sun,' *drunken* 'drunk'; OE. *ū* as in *us*, *buxom*, *buten*, (*bute*, *but*) 'but,' OE. *beūtan*, *būtan*.

2. OM. *u* (WS. *eo* by preceding palatal *g* (*ʒ*) and sometimes *sc*), as in *ʒung* 'young,' *schunen* 'shun.'

3. ON. *u*, and *ū* when shortened: ON. *u* as in *bule* 'bull,' *uglī* 'ugly'; ON. *ū* as in *scum*, *busken* 'prepare.'

4. OF. *u*, or *ü* in closed syllables: OF. *u* as in *purse*, *suffren* 'suffer'; OF. *ü* as in *juggen* 'judge,' *humble*.

27. Middle English *u* is often written *o* (seldom *ou*), especially in proximity to *n*, *m*, *u* (*v*), *w*, as already noted under orthography, § 7. This use of *o* for *u* accounts for such forms as *wolf*, *woll* 'wool,' *wode* 'wood,' *son*, *ton*, *come*, *love*, and many others which have remained to Modern English. Beside *dure* 'door,' as above, there is also a ME. *dōre* (*dǫǫre*) with lengthened vowel, probably from OE. *dor*, or some such form with *o* instead of *u*. OE. *eo* becomes *u* after *w* sometimes, as in *wurþen* 'become,' *wurþ, wurþī* 'worthy'; cf. § 21. So OF. *ui* becomes *u* occasionally as in *frut* 'fruit,' *frutestēre* 'fruiterer,' and in unstressed syllables *u* (beside *i* § 23) as in *biscut* (cf. §§ 61, 70).

28. Forms with *u* beside those with *i*, from OE. *y*, probably depend upon OE. forms with *u* beside others with mutation. Examples are *cluster*, OE. *cluster, clyster*; *brustel* beside *bristil, bluscen* 'blush,' *clucchen* 'clutch,' *dull* (*doll*) beside *dill* 'dull,' *rusche* beside *rische* (*rasche*) 'rush,' *mukel* (Sth. *muchel*) beside *mikel, shuttel* beside *schitel* 'shuttle.' In other cases analogy accounts for a form with *u* instead of *y*, as *hungren* influenced by the noun *hunger, sundrȳ* by the adjective *sunder*.

NOTE.—Early Midland and the dialects agree in general. From this *u* (OE., ON., OF. *u*) is to be separated of course Sth. *ü* from OE. *y*, as already explained under ME. *i*, § 23, n. 2. The writing of *o* for *u*, as above, is not found in early Midland, as the 'Chronicle' and Orm, and not until the last half of the twelfth century even in Sth. From the middle of the thirteenth century it becomes common.

LONG VOWELS

29. Middle English *ā*, with the sound of *a* in *art*, is limited in its occurrence, so far as Teutonic words are concerned, by the change of OE., ON. *ā* to *ǭ*, § 41. Long *ā* results from the lengthening of OE. and ON. short *a* under various conditions, and frequently appears in French words under similar circumstances. Its sources are as follows:

1. OE. *a* when lengthened, as in *dāle, gāte, blāde, nāme, gāmen* 'game, sport.'

2. ON. *a* when lengthened, as in *tāken* 'take,' *dāsen* 'daze.'

3. OF. *a* when lengthened, as in *fāce, grāce, plāce, āge, pāle* 'pale.'

30. The lengthening of the older short *a* occurs in open syllables (cf. § 73), or in OE. monosyllables with final consonant, most of which assumed in ME. an inorganic, final *e*. By reason of the latter change the unstressed syllable became open, and the *a* vowel subject to the lengthening which affected syllables originally open. OE. *a* before certain consonant combinations which caused lengthening in late OE., when remaining long, had of course become ME. *ǭ*, as in the case of original *ā*.

NOTE.—The dialects agree. In Nth. this newly lengthened *ā* fell in with *ā* from OE. *ā* (§ 43, n. 2). In lNth. *ā* is often written *ai* (*ay*), as noted under § 7, n. 2, and still later (the early fifteenth century) *ai* from whatever source sometimes shows monophthonging to *ā*, as *travāle* from *travaile*.

31. Middle English *ē*, written *e*, or later especially *ee*, represents two different sounds, which are of different origin and are, in general, kept distinct throughout the period. The first of these, called open *ē* and often designated at the present time by a tag below (*ę̄*), had the sound of the vowel in *there, care, bear*. The second, called close *ē*, had the sound of *ē* in *they*, or of the first element when *they* is pronounced with a diphthong. The dialectal differences, which are especially important in the case of these two *ē*'s, will be noted, as usual, under each of them. There are, in addition, occasional interchanges of sounds naturally so much alike, as shown by rimes, but these are probably due to dialectal confusion or the same poetic licence that is sometimes found in Modern English.

32. Middle English open *ē* (*ę̄*) develops from:

1. OE. *ǣ* (Merc. *ē* sometimes) by *i*-mutation of Teut. *ai*, *ēa* (except WS. *ēa* before *c*, *h*, *g*), and when lengthened *e* and *ę* by *i*-mutation of *a*, or *ea*: OE. *ǣ* as in *dę̄l* 'deal,' *hę̄len* 'heal,' *hę̄te* 'heat'; OE. *ēa* as in *dę̄d* 'dead,' *dę̄f* 'deaf,' *lę̄d* 'lead,' *bę̄m* 'beam,' *hę̄ved* 'head'; OE. *e* as in *brę̄ken* 'break,' *bę̄ren* 'bear'; OE. *ę* as in *stę̄de* 'stead,' *swę̄ren* 'swear'; OE. *ea* as in *ę̄rd* 'dwelling-place,' *ę̄rn* 'eagle.'

2. ON. *ǣ* by *i*-mutation of Teut. *ai*, and when lengthened *e*, or *ę* by *i*-mutation of *a*: ON. *ǣ* as in *gę̄ten* 'guard,' *hę̄ben* 'mock'; ON. *ę* as in *nę̄ve* 'fist,' *skę̄ren* (beside *skerren*) 'scare.'

3. OF. $\bar{e}$ before *l*, AN. $\bar{e}$ by monophthonging of *ai*, *ei*, and OF. *e* when lengthened: OF. $\bar{e}l$ as in *naturēl* 'natural,' *condicionēl* 'conditional'; AN. $\bar{e}$ from *ai* as in *trēsōn* 'treason,' *rēsōn* 'reason,' *pēs* 'peace,' *ēse* 'ease,' *fētīs* 'shapely'; AN. $\bar{e}$ from *ei* as in *dēs* 'dais,' *encrēs* 'increase'; OF. *e* as in *bēste* 'beast,' *fēste* 'feast.'

33. The principal sources of Ml. $\bar{e}$ are OE. *e* of whatever origin when lengthened in open syllables (§ 73), OM. $\bar{æ}$, *ēa* though far less common than WS. $\bar{æ}$, *ēa*, and OF. or AN. $\bar{e}$. In a few cases OM. close $\bar{e}$ seems to have become open $\bar{e}$, though the exact circumstances under which this occurs are not easily made out, owing to the uncertainty as to certain rimes in long *e*. Thus, while keeping apart ME. open and close $\bar{e}$ as a rule, a poet may have allowed himself occasional impure rimes, as in every period of English. Less careful poets no doubt did this more frequently, so that it is impossible to formulate a principle except from a considerable number of cases in more than a single poet. Besides the rimes there is also Orm's significant use of *æ* ($= \bar{e}$) for certain words with OM. $\bar{e}$. From this and from rimes it seems likely that OM. $\bar{e}$ gave $\bar{e}$ after *w*, *l*, and *r*, as in *wēt* 'wet,' *wēpen* (later *wepen*) 'weapon,' *lēchen* 'cure,' *rēden* 'read, advise.' But not all such words, especially not all in which Orm uses *æ*, can have had open $\bar{e}$ in all cases in ME. The practice of this book is to rest the probable quality on the usual development of the OM. sounds, especially when confirmed by later English, though recognizing the possible variation in well established cases. Thus OE. $\bar{æ}$ from Teut. *ai* seems to give ME. $\bar{e}$ (beside $\bar{e}$) when final, as in *sē* 'sea.' Similarly the AN. $\bar{e}$ from *ai*, *ei* before *r* becomes ME. $\bar{e}$ (beside $\bar{e}$), as in *pōēr* 'power,' *dubonēre* 'debonair,' *gramēr* 'grammar.'

34. The AN. monophthonging of *ai*, *ei* took place especially before *s*, *t*, *d*, *v*, *s* + cons., a palatal + liquid cons., and sometimes before *r*. Even under such conditions diphthongic forms sometimes appear, as *aise* 'ease' beside $\bar{e}se$.

NOTE 1.—In early Midland the digraph *æ* was still used for open $\bar{e}$, as in the

'Chronicle' *sǣ* 'sea,' *ǣr* 'ere,' *ǣvre* 'ever.' Orm also regularly uses the digraph for open *ę̄*, as in *sǣ* 'sea,' *hǣte* 'heat,' from OE. *ǣ*, and in *dǣf* 'deaf,' *flǣt* 'floated,' &c., from OE. *ēa*, as well as for OM. *ē* sometimes; see § 33.

NOTE 2.—All the dialects agree, in general, with the usage above indicated. Early Sth. sometimes has *ēa*, probably a digraph rather than a diphthong, and *ǣ* beside *ę̄*. Sth., however, except Kentish and early Sth., has a much larger proportion of open *ę̄* sounds from WS. *ǣ*, *ēa*. Thus Sth. open *ę̄* springs from the following sources, in addition to the above:

WS. *ǣ*, Gothic *ē*, as in *bę̄ren* 'bore.'

WS. *ēa* by influence of preceding palatal cons., as in *gę̄r* 'year,' *gę̄fen* 'gave,' pl.

WS. *ēa* before palatal *c, g, h*, as in *hę̄h* 'high,' *ę̄ge* 'eye.'

WS. *ea* (*ēa*) before *l* + cons., as in *hę̄lde(n)*, Ml. *hǭlde(n)*<OM. *hāldan*.

Kentish and eastern Sth., together with a small district in the extreme north of middle Sth., agree with Midland and Nth. in the main. On the other hand, Kentish has *ēa*, *ȳa*, *yēa* for OE. *ēa*, the first element being a close *ē*, sometimes even *ī*. Kentish also has sometimes *īe* beside *ē* for WS. *īo*, *ēo*.

35. Middle English close *ē* is the development of:

1. OE. *ē*, *ē̆* by *i*-mutation of *ō*, *ēo*, and *e* or *eo* when lengthened in late Old English: OE. *ē̆* as in *hēr* 'here'; OE. *ē* from *ō* as in *grēne* 'green,' *sēken* 'seek,' *bēche* 'beech,' *fēt* 'feet'; OE. *ēo* as in *bē* 'bee,' *sēn* 'see,' *trē* 'tree,' *dēre* 'dear'; OE. *e, eo* as in *fēld* 'field,' *schēld* 'shield,' *ēnde* 'end,' *ērþe* 'earth.'

2. OM. *ē* cognate with various WS. sounds: OM. *ē* (WS. *ǣ*, Goth. *ē*) as in *bēre* 'bier,' *ēven* 'evening,' *bę̄ren* pt. pl. of *bę̄ren* 'bear,' *ʒēr* (*gēr*) 'year,' *ʒēven* 'gave'; OM. *ē* (WS. *ēo, ēa* before OE. *c, g, h*) as in *flēʒen-flēh* 'fly-flew,' *sēc* 'sick,' *hēh* 'high,' *nēh* 'nigh'; OM. *ē* (WS. *īe* by *i*-mutation of *ēa*), *ēo*, as in *hēren* 'hear, obey,' *nēd* 'need,' *stēren* 'steer'; OM. *ē* from earlier *e* (WS. *ie*, late *īe* by *i*-mutation of *ēa*) as in *ēlde* 'eld,' *ērve* 'heritage,' *dērne* 'secret.'

3. ON. *ē*, *ø̄* by *i*-mutation of *ō*, and *iu* (*io*): ON. *ē* as in *sēr* 'several'; ON. *ø̄* as in *slēh* 'sly,' *fēre* 'power,' *ēpen* 'cry, call' (cogn. OE. *wēpan* 'weep'); ON. *iu* (*io*) as in *mēk* 'meek,' *skēt* 'soon.'

4. OF. *ē*, and AN. *ē* by monophthonging of OF. *ie, ue*, some-

times of *ai*, *ei* (*ieu*): OF. *ē* as in *degrē* 'degree,' *compēr* 'compeer,' *procēden* 'proceed'; AN. *ē* from *ie* as in *grēf* 'grief,' *pēce* 'piece,' *manēre* 'manner,' *achēven* 'achieve'; AN. *ē* from *ue* as in *bēf* 'beef,' *pēple* 'people,' *mēven* 'move'; AN. *ē* from *ai*, *ei* (*ieu*) sometimes, as in *gramēr* 'grammar,' *pōēr* 'power,' *pardē* < OF. par dieu.

36. While the sources of close *ē* seem so various, they resolve themselves into a much smaller number if we consider the characteristic phonology of the Mercian dialect, in which this sound was especially frequent as compared with West Saxon. In fact the sources of far the larger number of words may be summed up as OM. *ē*, *ēo*, *ē* in late lengthenings, corresponding, however, to various WS. vowels, as *ē*, *ēo*, *ǣ*, *ēa*, early and late *ie* (*ȳ*). To these must be added the important OF. sources, from which come many words, and the less important ON. contingent.

37. The variation between ME. open and close *ē* has been noted in § 33. A few words with OE. *ēo* show *ō* instead of *ē* in Middle English by reason of a shifting of stress and absorption of the first element of the diphthong. Examples are OE. *hēo* 'she' which gives *ȝho* (*ȝō*, *hō*) beside *hē* (Sth. *hē*, *hā*), and OE. *sēo* 'she' which gives *scho* (*sho*) beside *schē* (*shē*). Similarly *ȝōde* (lNth. *ȝude*) from OE. *geēode*, and for *fower*, *trowen* see § 60. For words with *ei* from AN. *ē* < *ie* see § 53. To the AN. monophthongs of *ai*, *ei* may be added *verrē* (OF. *verai*), and *monē* (OF. *moneie*), beside the more common forms. Monophthonging in originally stressed syllables which have lost the stress are exemplified by *suden* (*suden*) 'sudden.' Besides forms with *ē* from AN. *ē* (OF. *ue*) occur others with *ō* (cf. § 45). In unstressed syllables this *ē* becomes short, as in *ceveren*, beside *coveren*, *keverchef*, 'kerchief.' Certain Romance words with *ē* (*ee*) beside (*eie*) forms (cf. § 53) depend upon Central French forms with *ē* (*ee*) beside AN. *eie*. Examples which belong here are *cuntrē* (*contrē*) 'country,' *jornē* 'journey.' In the case of ME. *dēȝen* (*deien*) 'die' the word may be from an OE. source, rather than from the ON. word with *ȝy* reduced to *ē* (cf. § 52). For ME. *e* for AN. *ē* (< OF. *ue*), by shortening in originally unstressed syllables, cf. § 20.

NOTE 1.—In early Midland *ēo* is occasionally used for OE. (Merc.) *ē* or *ēo*, as in 'Chronicle' *forðfēorde* (OE. *.fērde*) 'went forth, died,' *dēovles* (OE. *dēofles*) 'devils,' *prēostes* (OE. *prēostes*) 'priests.' Orm also sometimes uses *ēo* for OE. *ēo*, as in *prēost* 'priest.' It is probable, however, that this was rather traditional spelling in his time than the representation of a real diphthong.

NOTE 2.—Nth. agrees with Midland except for *ei* (*ey*) written for *ē* (§ 7, n. 2). Sth. differs in a number of important respects owing to a different development from older West Saxon and Kentish. Middle and western Sth., the old West Saxon district, shows the following peculiarities :

> *e* [*ę̄*], seldom *ü*, rarely *i*, for WS. *ie* by *i*-mutation of *e* or *a* before *l* or *r* + cons., or of *ea*, *eo* not before a palatal cons.
>
> *ĕ* or *ɫ*, seldom *ŭ*, for WS. *ĭe* after a palatal cons.

Kentish and eastern Sth. differ from Midland and Sth. in having :

> *ē* from WS. *ȳ*, for WS. *ǣ* of whatever origin, and for WS. *ĭe* after a palatal cons.
>
> *ēa*, *ȳa*, *yēa* (close *e* with obscure second element), for WS. *ea* before *l* or *r* + cons.
>
> *ĭe* beside *ē* for WS. *ĭo*, *ĕo* by *u* or *o*-mutation.

The Katherine group, representing the northern part of middle Sth., agrees with Midland in having *ē* for WS. *ǣ* = Gothic *ē*, but *e*, *ea* for Ml. *a* before *r* in unstressed words ; also *ē* for WS. *ĭe* by *i*-mutation of *ēa* and *ēo*. In addition it has :

> *ā* for WS. *ea* before *l* + cons.
>
> *ēa*, *ǣ*, *ē* (open or close *ē*) for WS. *ie* by *i*-mutation of *ea* before *l* or *r* + cons.
>
> *i* for WS. *ie* by *i*-mutation of the *eo* breaking.

38. Middle English *ī*, with the sound of *i* in *machine*, corresponds in Teutonic words to older *ī* and to *ȳ* by *i*-mutation of *ū*. In addition to these two principal sources it occurs in many words of French origin. Like short *i*, as already noted (§ 22), it is written *i* or *y*, with a growing tendency toward *y* in late Middle English. In detail the origin of ME. *ī* is as follows:

1. OE. *ī*, *ȳ* by *i*-mutation of *ū*, and *i* or *y* when lengthened ; OE. *ī* as in *wīs* 'wise,' *līf* 'life,' *fīve* 'five,' *wrīten* 'write'; OE. *ȳ* as in *brīd* 'bride,' *hȳde* 'hide,' *fīr* 'fire'; OE. *i* as in *wild*, *chīld*, *fīnden* 'find'; OE. *ȳ* as in *kīnd* 'kind.'

2. ON. *ī, ȳ* by *i*-mutation of *ū*; ON. *ī* as in *tīþende* 'tidings,' *þrīven* 'thrive'; ON. *ȳ* as in *sīte* (*sīt*) 'pain,' *-bī* in *Grimesbī* 'town.'

3. OF. *i* when lengthened, as in *crīen* 'cry,' *prīme* 'prime,' *delīt* 'delight,' *bīble* 'Bible.'

39. There seems to be no evidence of lengthening of ON. *i, y* in Middle English, such words as *skinden* 'hasten,' *kindlen* 'kindle' preserving their short vowels. This would perhaps indicate that such words entered the language after the OE. lengthening before *nd* had taken place, though the examples are too few to make this certain. In a few cases OF. *ei* becomes *ī* in a syllable which loses principal stress, as *werrīen* 'make war,' falling in with OF. verbs in *ier* (ME. *īen* sometimes) as *carrȳen* 'carry.'

NOTE 1.—Early Midland shows no special peculiarities.

NOTE 2.—Nth. agrees with Midland. Sth., which preserves the older mutated sound of *ȳ* as already mentioned (§ 11, n. 2), used for it *ü* (*üi*) under the influence of French orthography. Examples are *hüren* (*hüiren*) 'hire,' *für* (*füyr*) ' fire,' *küþen* ' make known.' With this *ü* from OE. *ȳ* in Sth. also fell in, in some cases, a French *u*, with the sound of *u* in French *lune* to-day. This was easily possible owing to the similarity of the two sounds in Sth., but in Midland, which had not preserved the older mutated sound of OE. *ȳ*, this French *ü* finally associated itself with the diphthong *eu* (*iu*); see § 60. As already noted under close *ē* (§ 37, n. 2), Kentish has *ē* for OE. *ȳ* in accordance with older Kentish.

40. Middle English *ō*, like ME. *ē*, represents two different sounds of different origin and development. The first, open *ō* designated by *ǭ*, had the sound of *o* in *lord*. The second, close *ō*, was pronounced like *o* in *no*, or like the first element when *no* is pronounced with a diphthong. These two sounds are usually kept apart in Middle English rimes, and in general have maintained a separate development to Modern English.

41. Middle English open *ō* (*ǭ*) springs from :

1. OE. *ā*, and when lengthened *ǫ* from *a* before a nasal or *o* in open syllables : OE. *ā* as in *tǭ* 'toe,' *ǭþe* 'oath,' *stǭn* 'stone'; OE. *ǫ* as in *lǭng* 'long,' *strǭng*, *sǭng*; OE. *o* in *hǭse* 'hose, trousers,' *pǭke* 'bag,' *þrǭte* 'throat,' *befǭre* (*bifǭre*) ' before.'

2. OM. *ā* (WS. *ea*, *ēa*) from *a* before *ld*, as in *ǭld*, *bǭld*, *cǭld*.

3. ON. *ā*, and when lengthened *ǫ* from *a* + nasal or *o* in open syllables : ON. *ā* as in *lǭte* 'countenance,' *brǭþe* 'violent,' *rǭþen* 'counsel, explain' ; ON. *a* as in *wrǫng*, *wǫnd* ' rod '; ON. *o* as in *bǭle* ' stem of a tree,' *scǭre* ' score.'

4. OF. *o* when lengthened in open syllables, and AN. *o* + *rie* (OF. *oire*): OF. *o* as in *rǭse*, *nǭble*, *restǭren* 'restore'; AN. *orie* as in *glǭrie* (*glǭrȳ*), *stǭrie* (*stǭrȳ*), *memǭrie* ' memory.'

42. The principal sources of ME. open *ǭ* are OE. *ā*, and when lengthened in open syllables OE., OF. *o*. Special note should be taken of the small group of words with OM. *ā* from *a* before *ld*, since WS. forms could not possibly account for the MnE. words *old, bold*, &c. In the few possible cases OE. *ā*, preceded by a cons. + *w*, early developed *ō* (< *ǭ*) under the influence of *w*, as in *twō* 'two,' *swōpen* 'swoop.' Preceding *w* alone did not affect the change (cf. Hempl, ' Jour. of Germ. Phil.' I, 14). In the case of *sǭ* which seems to have open *ǭ* more commonly in Midland, we may perhaps assume a late OE. *sā* with loss of *w*.

43. In § 18 attention was called to certain words with ME. *ǭ*, eME. *ā* (see the strong preterits like *bǭren* 'bore'), where we expect Ml. *ē* (OM. *ē*, WS. *ǣ*). These may possibly represent an OM. *ā* beside *ē* or from *ē*, may be due to analogy or to Norse influence, such forms having *ā* in Old Norse. Norse influence certainly seems probable, though see the discussion in Björkman, ' Scand. Loan-words in Mid. Eng.,' p. 84.

NOTE 1.—In early Midland OE. *ā* often remains as in 'Chronicle' *āþes* 'oaths,' *stānes* 'stones.' Orm, too, writing in northeast Midland not far from the northern border, has *ā* regularly as in Nth. From the beginning of the thirteenth century *ǭ* was the rule.

NOTE 2.—In Nth., as already noticed (§ 5), OE. *ā* remained *ā* through the period and is thus a distinguishing feature of that dialect. In early Sth., *ā* is still written, though beside *ǭ*, *oa* (*ao*). From the thirteenth century *ǭ* (*oa*) are regular, as in ' Ancren Riwle.' The change of *ǭ* to *ō* after cons. + *w*, noted above for Midland, was very late in Sth., probably not taking place until 1400.

44. Middle English close *ō* springs from:

1. OE. *ō*, or *ō* from *o* before certain consonant combinations: OE. *ō* as in *dōm* 'doom,' *gōd* 'good,' *cōk* 'cook'; OE. *o* as in *gōld*, *bōrd*, *wōrd*.

2. ON. *ō* as in *bōne* 'prayer, boon,' *bōþe* 'booth,' *crōk* 'crook.'

3. OF. *ō* (AN. *ū*), *o* rarely, AN. *ō* from OF. *ue* sometimes: OF. *ō* as in *trẹ̄sōn* 'treason,' *barōn, condiciōn*; OF. *o* as in *pōvre* (*pōre*) 'poor,' *fōl* 'fool'; AN. *ō* from *ue* as in *mōven* 'move,' *prōven* 'prove,' *dōlen* 'grieve,' *pōple* 'people.'

45. OF. words in *ō*, especially before *n*, beside AN. forms with *ū* (cf. § 46) are common in early Middle English. Forms with AN *ō* from OF. *ue*, by monophthonging, occur beside those with *ē* already noted (§ 35). In unstressed syllables this AN. *ō* becomes *o*, as in *coveren* 'cover.'

NOTE 1.—Early Midland and the dialects agree in general. In late Nth. this sound is frequently written *u*, indicating a change in the direction of French *eu* in *peu*, the sound of Scotch *u* in *gude* 'good.'

46. Middle English *ū*, with the sound of the vowel in *boot*, is found in words from all sources. Under the influence of French spelling it is often written *ōu* (*ōw*), but this orthography never indicates a diphthong in the case of this vowel. The sources of ME. *ū* are:

1. OE. *ū*, and *u* when lengthened: OE. *ū* as in *fūl* 'foul,' *hūs* 'house,' *ōut*, *lōud*, *hōw*; OE. *u* as in *wūnde* 'wound,' *grūnd* (*grōund*) 'ground.'

2. ON. *ū*, and *u* when lengthened: ON. *ū* as in *būn* 'ready, prepared,' MnE. 'bound,' *skūten* 'project,' *drūpen* 'droop'; ON. *u* as in *lūnd* 'nature, disposition.'

3. AN. *ū* as in *crōune* 'crown,' *dōute* 'doubt,' *avōwen* 'avow,' *mōunt, acōunt, flōur* 'flower,' *preciōus*.

NOTE 1.—Early Midland has no special peculiarity, except that *ū* is never written with French *ou*, but regularly with the English symbol.

NOTE 2.—There is general agreement in the dialects with regard to ME. *ū*. In the thirteenth century the French *ou* came to be used for ME. *ū* first in Sth., where it was especially necessary to distinguish this sound from *ū* (*ü*) for OE.

ȳ. Later it spread to other dialects, and in late Middle English became the rule. For Sth., in the earlier period especially, ME. *u* must be carefully separated from *ū* (*ü*) for OE. *ȳ*. For Sth. *u* from French *u*, with the sound in French *lune*, see § 10, footnote.

THE DIPHTHONGS

47. As has been shown (§ 3), the OE. diphthongs became monophthongs in Middle English. Their place was supplied by certain new diphthongs formed from certain combinations of OE. vowels and following consonants. The change probably began in late Old English, and was certainly completed in the early Middle English period. The formation of the new diphthongs follows the accompanying scheme :

1. An OE. palatal vowel, *ǣ, ĕ, ĕa, ĕŏ* + a palatal *h* or *g* became *ai, ei*.

2. An OE. guttural vowel, *ă, ŏ* + guttural *h* or *g* became *au, ou*.

3. An OE. palatal vowel, *ǣ, ĕ, ĕa, ĕŏ, ĭ* + *w*, and occasionally medial *f* (i. e. *v*) when developing into *w*, became *eu*.

4. An OE. guttural vowel, *ă, ŏ* + *w*, and occasionally *f* as above, became *au, ou*.

48. As the vowels of these formulæ were long or short, two sets of diphthongs resulted in the earliest period. This is proved by the orthography of Orm, who doubles the second element of the diphthong in all cases when the first is short. On the other hand, long and short diphthongs were not otherwise distinguished in their written form or in their later development, so that they need not in general be separated. A more essential distinction, especially in the *ou* diphthongs, is the quality of the first element, which was either open or close according as it developed from OE. *ā* and *o*, or from OE. *ō*. Even these can be distinguished only by knowing their origin in Old English. The diphthongs naturally developed most readily in the case of a following *w*, as in *soule*, OE. *sāwle* 'soul,' *growen*, OE. *grōwan* 'grow.' They next appear when *g* (*h*) are final, medial between vowels, or between vowel and voiced consonant, as in *saide*, OE. *sægde* 'said,' *drawen*, OE. *dragan* 'draw.'

Only occasionally do they appear from a vowel and a medial f (v), as in *hawk*, OE. *hafoc* 'hawk.' Before OE. *ht*, sometimes before final or medial *h* when still preserved, a parasitic *i* or *u* developed in later ME., as in *eighte* 'eight,' *draught* 'draught,' *nought*, *wrought*, and these diphthongs have usually had a somewhat different development from others. Diphthongs are also occasionally formed by the development of a parasitic vowel before other palatal consonants than *h* and *g*, as in *bleinte*, OE. *blencte* 'blenched,' *meinde*, OE. *mengde* 'mingled,' *aische*, OE. *asce* 'ashes,' *fleisch*, OE. *flæsc* 'flesh.'

49. To these diphthongs of OE. origin must be added some from other languages, especially Danish and French. These usually associated themselves with those of English origin, as will be seen from the following sections, but in the case of OF. *oi* (*ui*) a new diphthong was added to the language.

NOTE.—When it is said above that the OE. diphthongs became monophthongs in Middle English, it should be remembered that in Kentish the older diphthongs were preserved to a late period. These have been noted already under § 37, n. 2. The consonants *g* and *h* do not immediately disappear on the formation of the diphthong, which is probably due to the formation of a parasitic vowel before the consonant. This accounts for such forms as *deigen* 'die,' in 'Gen. and Ex.' The consonant *h* appears especially when in conjunction with *t*. For a late monophthonging of *ei* and *ou* sometimes, see §§ 54, 69.

50. Middle English *ai*, in the earliest times, had the sound of the diphthong in *high*. As *ai* came to rime with *ei* in late ME., its pronunciation probably assumed the sounds *a* (as in *man*)+*i* in the course of its development. It springs from :

1. OE. *æg*, as in *dai* (*day*), *mai* (*may*) 'may,' *sayde* ' said.'
2. ON. *ag* (*ǫg*) rarely, as in *gainen* (ON. *gagna*), *kairlíc* (Orm *kaȝȝerrleȝȝc*) if from Norse *kǫgur* as Brate 'Nord. Lehnworter,' p. 46.
3. OF. *ai*, as in *payment*, *paien* 'satisfy, pay,' *bitraien* 'betray.'

51. Attention has been called to the development before OE. *ht*, no diphthong appearing as early as in other cases. In *miȝt*, *niȝt*, OE. (Merc.) *mæht*, *næht*, *i* resulted from the influence of the following palatal. There could therefore be no diphthongization in these cases. OF. *ei* appears as *ai* from the twelfth century, so that the number of *ai* forms is considerably increased in this way.

NOTE 1.—In early Midland the first element of the diphthong is written *æ* or *a*, and the last element *g* sometimes. Thus the 'Chronicle' has *dæi* (*dæg*) 'day.' Orm writes *daȝȝ* 'day,' *maȝȝ* 'may,' in accordance with his usual spelling of the diphthong. He also has *mahht, nahht*, 'might, night.' In 'Genesis and Exodus' *migt, nigt* appear beside *magt, nagt*.

NOTE 2.—INth. *ai* becomes *ā* (§ 30, n. 1). Early Sth. has *ei* for Midland and Nth. *ai*, as in *dei* 'day,' *mei* 'may,' in accordance with its usual use of *e* for OE. *æ*. Sth. also developed the diphthong *ei* before *ht*, sometimes *h*, much earlier than the other dialects, as in *eihte* 'eight.'

52. Middle English *ei*, with the sound of *e + i*, comes from:

1. OE. *eg*, or *ęg* from *ag*, *āg* from Teut. *aig*, and *ēg* from *ōg* by *i*-mutation: OE. *eg* as in *wei* (*wey*) 'way,' *pleien* 'play'; OE. *ęg* as in *eiȝe* (*eie*) 'fear, awe'; OE. *āg* as in *feie* 'fay,' *clei* 'clay,' *kei* 'key'; OE. *ēg* as in *feien* 'join,' *wreien* 'accuse.'

2. OM. *ēg* corresponding to various WS. vowels: OM. *ēg* (WS. *āg*, Goth. *ēg*) as in *grei*(*y*) 'gray'; OM. *ēg* (WS. *ēag, ēog*) as in *fleien* 'fly,' *dreien* 'endure'; OM. *ēg* (WS. *īeg* by *i*-mutation of *ēag*) as in *beien* 'bend.'

3. ON. *ei* (*æi*), and *øy* (*ey*) by *i*-mutation of Teut. *au*: ON. *ei* as in *reisen* 'raise,' *beiten* 'bait,' *þei* 'they'; ON. *øy* (*ey*) as in *ay* 'aye,' *cairen* 'go, return,' *traist* 'strong, confident.'

4. AN. *ei* as in *preien* 'prey,' *streit* 'strait,' *peinten* 'paint,' *kweynte* 'quaint,' *aqueyntaunce*.

53. While these sources seem to be various they are, in reality, very few. Thus ME. *ei* springs from OE. (Merc.) *ęg* (*āg*) from whatever source. The principal foreign sources are ON. and OF. *ei* diphthongs, which are responsible for a considerable number of *ei* words. In a few native words *ei* develops from *e* under the influence of a following palatal consonant or consonant combination. Here belong *fleisch* beside *flesch* (OE. *flǣsc*) 'flesh,' *weisch* (*weis*) beside *wesch* 'wash,' *leincte* beside *lengten* (*lenten*) 'spring,' *bleincte*

(*bleinte*) < *blencen* 'blench,' *dreincte* (*dreinte*) < *drencen* 'drench.'
Some AN. words have a diphthong *ei* (*e*), (*ai*) where OF. forms
have *ē* (*ee*); examples are *contraie* (*contray*) 'country,' *jorneie*
(*jornay*) 'journey.' Cf. § 37. In the case of words with OE.
ǣg by *i*-mutation of Teut. *aig* (see 1 above), we should expect ME.
ai by early shortening of *ǣ*. Either this did not take place in the
few words belonging here, or more probably the open *ǣ* quality
was changed to close *ē* under the influence of the following *g*. In
a few cases *ei* (*ey*) springs from AN. *ē* (OF. *ie*) as *maynteynen*
'maintain,' *susteynen* 'sustain,' perhaps by analogy of words ending
in *ei*(*ai*)*ne*, for example *atteinen* 'attain.' Beside AN. forms in
ei (*ai*) occur cognates from Central French in *oi*; see § 64.

54. For early confusion between OF. *ei* and *ai* words see § 51.
ON. words with *ǿy* also usually appear in Middle English with *ai*,
perhaps indicating early change of quality from *ei* to *ai*. There is
a tendency in late ME. to confuse all *ei*'s and *ai*'s as already noted
under *ai* (§ 50). This is shown even as early as Chaucer, who
sometimes rimes *ei* and *ai*. Besides, ME. *ei*, more especially in the
southeast Midland as shown by Chaucer's usage, occasionally
becomes a monophthong *ī*, by palatalization of the first element
and contraction. Examples are *flīen* 'fly,' *drīen* 'endure,' *dīen*
(*dȳen*) 'die,' *sȳe* 'saw.' A similar change took place in late Middle
English in such words as *heigh*, *neigh*, *sleight*, by which they
acquired the long *ī* which later became the Modern English
diphthong *ai*.

NOTE 1.—Early Midland has *ei*, as in 'Chronicle' *eie* 'awe,' OE. *ege*. Orm
writes *eȝȝ* for *ĕi*, *eȝ* for *ēi* in accordance with his usual orthography.

NOTE 2.—Nth. writes *ai* even in the earliest texts (last half of the thirteenth
century) for *ei* (except for *ei* from OE. *ĕg*⟨*h*⟩), as in *þai* 'they,' *ay* 'aye,' *raise*,
pray 'prey,' *paint*. *Ei* from OE. *ēg*⟨*h*⟩ does not become *ī* in Nth.; cf. Scotch
dee, *ee*, 'die, eye.' In lNth. *ei* became *ē*. Sth. does not differ from Midland,
except that the palatalization of *ei*, from *eg*, to *ī* does not seem to occur.

55. Middle English *au*, a diphthong with the pronunciation of
that in *house*, is of common occurrence in both native and foreign
words. In general it develops from OE. *a* + *w* or *g* when final or

medial in voiced company, while it also appears in many words borrowed from Old French. In detail, its sources are:

1. OE. *aw* or *eaw*, *āw* or *ēaw* when shortened, and rarely *afo* (*eafo*) by vocalization of *f* (=*v*): OE. *aw* or *eaw* as in *clawe* ' claw,' *raw, straw, awel* ' awl' ; OE. *āw* or *ēaw* as in *tawen* (OE. *tāwian*, perhaps *tawian*) ' prepare,' *aunen, taunen* (OE. **ēawnian *ætēawnian*) ' show ' ; OE. *afo* (*eafo*) as in *hauk* (OE. *heafoc, hafoc*) ' hawk,' *nauger* (OE. *nafogar*) ' auger,' and OE. *afl* as in *craulen* (OE. *craflian*) ' crawl.'

2. OE. *ag, ahh*, and *aht*, or when shortened *āht* (*āht*): OE. *ag* as in *drawen* (earlier *drāʒen*) ' draw,' *gnawen* 'gnaw '; or *ahh*, as in *lauʒhen* 'laugh,' *lauhte* ' laughed '; OE. *āht* (*āht*) as in *auhte* (*auʒte*) 'aught,' *tauhte* (*taugte, tauʒte, tauʒhte*) ' taught.'

3. ON. *ag* as in *lawe* 'law,' *awe, felawe* 'fellow.'

4. OF. *au*, as in *cause, pause, applauden* 'applaud,' *assault*.

56. As already noted the diphthongs which develop from *ag* (*h*) appear later than those from *aw* (cf. § 48). In Romance words, *au* from OF. *a* before a nasal+cons. (except *nk* and *n*+the stop *g*) appears in Middle English from the thirteenth century. The exact quality of this sound is not clear, but it seems not to have been a strict diphthong like OF. *au*, and was more probably an open *o* sound like that of OE. *ǫ* from *a* before a nasal, varying with *a* as the interchangeable orthography would indicate. Its development during the period is different under different circumstances. It falls in with ME. *a* as in *sample, champiŏn, chance, branch*, and in unstressed syllables as *servant, coūntenance* ; with ME. *ā* as in *chāmber, chānge, dānger, grānge, strānge* ; and with ME. *au* or *ou* before *ht* as in *daunt, vaunt, paunch, staunch, lawn* with loss of final *d*. A similar *au* appears from OF. *ave* before a nasal, as in *aunter* beside *aventure* ' venture, adventure,' *paraunter*, probably *laundēre* ' laundress.' Cf. Behrens, ' Franz. Sprache in England,' p. 77, Luick, ' Anglia,' XVI, 479 f.

NOTE 1.—In early Midland, as in the other dialects, the change of *g* to *w* had not been carried out. Thus Orm writes *draȝhenn* for OE. *dragan* 'draw,' *laȝhe* 'law.' The change was not completed, perhaps, until the beginning of the fourteenth century.

NOTE 2.—In early Sth., OE. *g*, which became vocalized to *w*, was written *h*, as in *drahen* 'draw,' but the diphthongic change was completed by the beginning of the thirteenth century, as in 'Ancren Riwle' *drawen* 'draw.' In Kentish, however, *aȝ* for OE. *ag* is found as late as the middle of the fourteenth century; cf. 'Ayenbite of Inwit.' The earliest Nth. texts, the last half of the thirteenth century, also show the change complete. In Nth. before *ht*(*hh*) no *au* diphthong develops, but the *au* diphthong is otherwise increased by the addition of *au* from OE. *āw*, *āg*, since in Nth. OE. *ā* remained *ā* (§§ 5, 43, n. 3). In Kentish also, OE. *āw* frequently remained *āw*, beside *ou*, and only later fully developed *ou* in all cases.

57. Middle English *eu* (*ew*) represents two slightly different sounds as the first element was open or close *e*. This gave a slightly different pronunciation to the two through the period, but they became one in early Modern English, when the first element of each had assumed the sound of *i*.

58. Middle English *eu*, with the sound of open *e* + *u* as in *fool*, has its principal sources in OE. *e* (*eo*), or *ǣ* (*ēa*) + *w*. In detail these are as follows:

1. OE. *ew* (*eow*), *ęw* (*ęow*) from Teut. *aw* by *i*-mutation, *ǣw*, *ēaw*, are rarely *ef* (=*ev*): OE. *ew* (*eow*) as in *sewen* 'sew'; OE. *ęw* (*ęow*) as in *ewe*; OE. *ǣw* as in *mew* 'sea bird,' *lewed* (*lewd*) 'lay, lewd'; OE. *ēaw* as in *dew*, *hewen* 'hew,' *fewe* 'few'; OE. *ef* as in *ewte* (OE. *efete*) 'newt.'

2. OF. *eau* in originally unstressed syllables as in *beautē* (*beutē*) 'beauty,' *lewtē* 'loyalty.'

NOTE 1.—In early Midland OE. *ǣw* (*ēaw*) was written *æu*(*w*), as in 'Chronicle' *fæu* 'few,' Orm *dæw* 'dew,' *shæwen* 'show.' The consistent use of *æ* for OE. *ǣ* (*ēa*) shows that the first element of the diphthong was still long.

NOTE 2.—Nth. does not differ from Midland. Early Sth. has *ea* many times, as *sheau*(*w*)*en* 'show,' *leawede* 'lewd.' Kentish also has *ēa* (*yea*) for OE. *ēa*; see § 34, n. 2.

59. Middle English *eu*, with the sounds of close *e* + *u* (*fool*), has its principal sources in OE. *ēow*, OM. *ēw* (*ēow*), less commonly OE. *īw* and OF. diphthongs of similar quality. It springs from:

1. OE. *ēow*, sometimes *īw*: OE. *ēow*, as in *ew* (*yew*) 'yew,' *hrewen* 'rue,' *chewen* 'chew,' *brewen* 'brew,' *knew* 'knew,' *grew* 'grew'; OE. *īw*, as in *steward* beside earlier *stiward*, *Tewesdai* beside *Tiwesdai* 'Tuesday.'

2. OM. *ēw* (*ēow*) corresponding to different WS. diphthongs: OM. *ēw* (WS. *āw*, Goth. *ēw*), as in *bilewen* 'betray'; OM. *ēow* (WS. *īew*, *īw* by *i*-mutation of *ēow*), as in *hewe* 'hue,' *newe* 'new'; OM. *ēow* (WS. *īw*), as in *spewen* 'spew,' *clewen* 'ball of thread, clue.'

3. OF. *eu* (*ieu*), and sometimes *ü*, *üi*: OF. *eu* (*ieu*), as in *Jew* 'Jew,' *Hebrew*, *sewen* 'sue,' *curfew*, *rewle* 'rule'; OF. *ü*, especially when final or before a vowel, as in *virtew* 'virtue,' *crewel* 'cruel'; OF. *üi* rarely, as in *frewte* 'fruit,' *seute* 'suit.'

60. Here belong many preterits of reduplication verbs with OE. *ēow*, as *hew* 'hewed,' &c. To these, in later English, a few were added by analogy, as *drew*, *slew*, ME. *drōh* (*drou*), *slōh* (*slou*). Words with OE. *īw* were largely reduced in number for Mercian by their appearance in that dialect with *ēow*. Perhaps on this account early ME. *stiward* becomes *steward*. OF. words with *ü* (*üi*) sometimes show a like phonology. On the other hand, words with ME. *eu* from OF. *eu* (*ieu*) sometimes have *iu* beside *eu*, as in *riwle* 'rule,' *Juus* = *Jiues*. Beside forms with *eu* (*ew*) OE. *ēow* gives *ow* sometimes, by absorption of the first element of the diphthong, as in *trowen* 'trust, believe,' *trowð* (*trouthe*) 'truth,' *fower* 'four.' In ME. *ōu* (*ōw*, *ȝōu*) 'you' OE. *ēow* has become *ū*, perhaps earlier *ou* as a diphthong.

NOTE 1.—In early Midland, OE. *ēow* is sometimes written beside the new diphthong. Thus Orm writes *neowe* 'beside,' *newe* 'new.'

NOTE 2.—Early Sth. preserves *eo*, as in *treowe* 'true,' in accordance with § 37, n. 1. Otherwise the dialects are in general agreement with Midland.

61. Middle English *iu* is rare in native words and later falls in with *eu* (see above). That it developed in later ME. times from OF. *ü* (*üi*) when lengthened is certain (cf. Luick, 'Anglia,' XIV, 287).

How early this came about depends upon the question how far
OF. *ü* was adopted in its purity in Middle English (cf. § 10, footnote). We shall here assume that OF. *ü* (*üi*) were diphthongal
from the first, or practically so. Middle English *iu* has therefore
the following origin:

1. OE. *īw* as in *stiward*, later *steward*, *Tiwesniȝht* 'Tuesday
    night.'
2. OF. *ü* and *üi* (AN. *ü* sometimes): OF. *ü* as in *rude, huge,
    usen* 'use,' *accusen* 'accuse,' *pursuen* 'pursue,' *nature, mẹsure*
    'measure,' *duk* 'duke,' *pur* 'pure,' *vertu* 'virtue'; OF. *üi*
    (AN. *ü* sometimes) as in *frut* (*fruit*), *sute* (*suite*), *anui*
    'annoy,' *nuisance.*

62. Confusion with the ME. diphthong *eu* has been noted under
that combination. OF. *ui* also becomes *oi* as in the following
section. On the other hand some words with *ew* appear with *iu* (*iw*)
as *riwle* 'rule,' or, in unstressed syllables, *u* (=*iu*?) as in *construe(n)*
'construe,' Sth. *asunīen* 'excuse.'

NOTE.—In Nth. and NWMl. OF. *ü* sometimes becomes *ū*, as in *Lōūk*
'Luke,' regularly in the ending *ure*, as *armōūr* 'armor.'

63. Middle English *oi*, with the sound of the diphthong in *coy*
but with close *o* as the first element, is almost exclusively of romance
origin. It springs from:

OF. *oi* (i.e. *ǫi*), *oi* (AN. *ui*, sometimes *ei*), and AN. *oi+l, n*
(OF. *o*): OF. *oi*, as in *joie* 'joy,' *choice, cloister, noise*; OF.
oi (AN. *ui*), as in *destroien* 'destroy,' *Troye* 'Troy,' *vois*
'voice,' *crois* 'cross,' *moiste* 'moist'; OF. *oi* (AN. *ei* sometimes), as in *quoynte* (*coint*) 'happy, gay,' *quointise* 'skill,'
point, enointen (*anointen*) 'anoint,' *joint, coin*; AN. *oi+l, n*
(OF. *o*), as in *soile* 'soil,' *spoilen* 'spoil,' *despoilen* 'despoil,'
oil, joinen 'join,' *Burgoine.*

64. Attention has already been called to AN. *ei* (*ai*) for OF. *oi*
in some words, accounting for such MnE. forms as *acquaint, quaint*.
Nth. *aquynt* 'acquainted' shows monophthonging of AN. *ei*. Beside
forms with *oi* from *ui* may be mentioned the rare *froit*, beside *fruit*

(*frut*) 'fruit.' ME. *jewel* (*juel, jouel*) has perhaps been influenced by OF. *ju, jeu* 'game.' ME. *boie* 'boy' is certainly of ultimate Teutonic origin, and possibly from an unrecorded OF. word. In *broiden*, pret. pl. and pp. of OE. *bregdan*, *oi* develops naturally perhaps from OE. *og* before *d* (§ 179). For *ui* beside *oi* see §§ 61, 70.

65. Middle English *ou*, like *eu*, represents two different diphthongs which, however, came together in late Middle English, and were not always distinct in the earlier ME. period. The two sounds differ, as one had open, and the other close *o* for its first element.

66. Middle English *ǫu*, with the sound of open *ǫ + u* (*fool*), has its principal sources in OE. *ow, og* and *ā + w* or *āg*, while some Norse words with *au* have ranged themselves with these. Its sources, in detail, are:

1. OE. *āw, āg(h), āht*: OE. *āw*, as in *sowen* 'sow,' *blowen* 'blow,' *crowen* 'crow'; OE. *āg(h)*, as in *owen* 'owe,' *dou* (*doh, dogh*) 'dough'; OE. *āht*, as in *ouʒt* 'ought,' *ouʒte* 'ought' (vb.).

2. OE. *ow, og* (*h, hh*), *oht*, and when shortened *ōh* or *ōht*: OE. *ow*, as in *tow* 'coarse flax'; OE. *og* (*h, hh*), as in *bowe* 'bow of the archer,' *flowen* 'flown,' *trouʒ* (*troh, trogh*) 'trough,' *couʒ* (*cogh*) 'cough,' *couʒen* (OE. *cohhettan*) 'cough'; OE. *oht*, as in *douʒter* 'daughter,' *bouʒt* 'bought'; OE. *ōh* as in *touʒ* (*toh, togh*) 'tough'; OE. *ōht*, as in *souʒt* 'sought,' *fouʒten* 'fought' (pp.).

3. ON. *og, ōh* when shortened, and *ou* (*au*): ON. *og*, as in *lowe* 'fire'; ON. *ōh*, as in *þou* (*þoh, þouʒ*) 'though'; ON. *ou* (*au*), as in *nout* 'cattle,' *routen* 'roar,' *rouste* 'voice.'

67. In a few cases double forms appear, as OE. *āht* becomes short (cf. § 55) or remains long until OE. *ā* had become ME. *ǭ* as in 1 above.

NOTE 1.—In early Midland the diphthongs had not yet developed in the case of *og, āg, oht*, as already noted in § 56, n. 1. Orm thus writes *aʒhen* 'owe,' OE. *āgan*.

NOTE 2.—The dialects agree in general. In Nth., as OE. *ā* remains, OE. *āw*, *āg* become *au*, not *ou*. Nth. *ah*, *aht* also do not develop a diphthong. The same is true in Kentish of OE. *āw* which remains *au*, though later becoming *ou*; see § 56, n. 2.

68. Middle English *ou*, with the sound of *ō + u* (*fool*), is of infrequent occurrence. It is from

OE. *ōw*, as in *growen* 'grow,' *flowen* 'flow,' *stowen* 'stow.'

69. This diphthong, which occurs in no large number of words, assumed the quality of *ǫu* in the fourteenth century, as shown by rimes of Chaucer, and has since had a similar development. For *ou* from OE. *ōh*, see § 66. In a few words ME. *ou* (probably close *o*) springs from OE. *ēow* by absorption of the first element of the diphthong, as in *foure* (OE. *fēower*) 'four,' *trowen* (OE. *trēowian*) 'believe.' This may also explain *ū* ($\overline{ou}$, $\overline{zou}$) from OE. *ēow* 'you,' but if so the diphthong soon became *ū*, as shown by rimes.

70. A Middle English *ui*, occurring in Romance words, may represent OF. *üi*, which soon became ME. *iu* (cf. § 61) or in unstressed syllables *u(i)* as noted in §§ 23, 27. Otherwise ME. *ui* represents OF. *ui*, which has a diphthongal sound approximating ME. *oi*, with which it varies in early texts and by which it is finally displaced (§ 63). Examples are *destruien* 'destroy,' *fuisōn* 'abundance,' *Burguine* 'Bourgogne.' After *k* (*c*) this OF. *ui* sometimes became *kwi*, as in ME. *quylte* 'quilt,' Nth. *aquynt* 'acquainted.' Perhaps a similar change also accounts for *anguis* 'anguish,' which sometimes seems to have stress on the last syllable. In originally unstressed syllables this OF. *ui* became *u* or *i* as noted in §§ 23, 27.

NOTE.—A Sth. *ui* (*üi*) rarely springs from CE. *ȳ + g* as in 'Ancren Riwle' *druie* (<OE. *drȳge*) 'dry,' but the quality of the diphthong is uncertain. Cf. Sweet, 'Hist. of Eng. Sounds,' § 717.

VARIATIONS IN VOWEL QUANTITY

71. As compared with Old English, Middle English shows important variations of vowel quantity. Some of these are extensions of changes which were operative in late OE. times: see Sievers, 'Gr.,' §§ 120–125 and notes to §§ 150–168; Bülbring,

'Altenglisches Elementarbuch,' § 284 f. Others belong to the Middle English period, and affect not only a great number of English words, but also those borrowed from Norse and French. The best criteria for the variations in quantity of ME. vowels are, (1) the orthography of Orm; (2) the doubling of vowels and consonants, and the use of two symbols for a single sound, as *ey* for *i*, *ui* (*y*) for *u*, *ea* for *e*; (3) the occasional use of accents or other signs for vowel length; (4) the rimes in Middle English poetry, and other metrical evidences as of syncope, apocope, &c.; (5) the relation of ME. vowels to the course of their development in the modern period. Reference may be made especially to Morsbach, 'Mittelenglische Grammatik,' pp. 65–92 ; Sweet 'History of English Sounds,' §§ 392, 616–640.

NOTE.—Orm, to whom special reference is made above, undertook to indicate pronunciation with minute exactness by doubling consonants and the second elements of short diphthongs, as well as by the occasional use of the accent and the breve. The most striking feature, the doubling of consonants, has led some to believe that Orm intended to indicate consonant length, while others think vowel length alone was intended. In any case, however, Orm's orthography is of practical value mainly in determining vowel quantity. Thus, vowels followed by doubled consonants are invariably short, as in *staff, gladd, inn, allderrmann, asskenn, clennsenn* ; those followed by a single consonant in closed syllables are long, as in *bāld* 'bold,' *fēld* 'field,' *chīld, gōld, grūnd* 'ground.' The quantity of vowels followed by a single medial consonant is indeterminate by Orm's orthography, but in these cases, as in closed syllables, Orm uses accents to show original length in many words, and the breve to show original short quantity in something like a third of the examples. Those who believe that Orm intended to indicate vowel length only, explain his failure to double the consonant after a short medial vowel because such doubling would have produced confusion between such words as *sune* 'son' (OE. *sunu*) and *sunne* 'sun' (OE. *sunne*), the difference between which was still important. In the case of diphthongs, the first vowel is short when the second element is doubled, as in *clawwess* 'claws,' *knewwe* 'knew,' *trowwenn* 'trow' ; otherwise long, as in *cnāwen* 'know,' *sāwle* 'soul,' *sāwen* 'sow.' The two views above are supported by Trautmann ('Anglia,' 7, 'Anzeiger,' 94, 208), Ten Brink ('Chaucer Gr.,' §§ 96–97), Effer ('Anglia,' 7, 'Anzeiger,' 167) for the first; Sweet ('Hist. of Eng. Sounds,' § 616 f.), Morsbach ('Mitteleng. Gr.,' § 15, anm. 2–3) for the second, with which most scholars agree. On Orm's marks of quantity, cf. Deutschbein, 'Archiv,' cxxvi–vii.

LENGTHENING

72. It may be assumed, in accordance with the evidences of lengthening in late Old English, that OE. long vowels and diphthongs remained long in open syllables and before a single final consonant, except as shown hereafter; and that original OE. short vowels and diphthongs had become long before certain consonant groups made up of a liquid or nasal and a voiced consonant, as *ld, rd, rl, rn, rþ, mb, nd, ng, nǧ* (= *ng* as in *strange*), though probably not *rm*. Original short vowels were also sometimes long in monosyllables, especially when final. Some examples of original short vowels with long quantity at the beginning of ME. times are *hwā* (*hwō*) 'who,' *hē* 'he,' *bī* 'by,' *nū* 'now'; *wēl* 'well,' Scotch 'weel[1],' *hōl* 'hole'; *ǭld* (*ald*) 'old,' *cǭmb, ēnde* 'end,' *bīnden* 'bind,' *hōrd* 'hoard,' *gōld, sūnd* 'sound as of body,' *būnde* 'bound.'

NOTE 1.—Lengthening had not taken place in Old English before consonant groups made up of a liquid or nasal and a voiceless consonant. In French words, however, *u* before *nt, ns* (*nce*), shows similar lengthening in ME., as in *cōunt, mōunt, ōunce, flōunce,* &c.; so also OF. *e* before *st* in some words, as *bēst* 'beast,' *fēst* 'feast.' Lengthening before *lt* in *cǫlt, bǫlt, mǫlten,* and before *lst* in *bǫlster* occurred in late Middle or early Modern English.

NOTE 2.—Sporadic shortening occurs very early, as in Orm's *tenn* 'ten,' *annan* 'anon,' while in late ME., the fifteenth century, it was more common, especially before dental consonants, as *rĕd, drĕd* 'dread,' *lĕt* 'permit,' *wĕt, hŏt* (OE. *hāt*), *brĕth* 'breath,' *dĕth* 'death,' *nŏne*.

73. During the Middle English period OE. short *a, e, o* were lengthened in open syllables, as in *rāke* 'rake,' *nāme, schāme* 'shame,' *wēfen* 'weave,' *mēle* 'meal,' *hōpen* 'hope,' *hǭse* 'hose, trousers.' Examples of Norse words showing similar lengthening are *tāken* 'take,' *dāsen* 'daze,' *scēren* 'scare'; French words, *fāce, grāce, cēsen* 'cease,' *apēlen* 'appeal,' *rǭse, clǭsen* 'close.' Lengthening did not take place, however, when the following syllable was weak, as *ī* (*ȳ*) in *penȳ* 'penny,' *hevȳ* 'heavy,' *bodȳ*. When the following syllable consists of a short vowel and *l, r, n,* or *m,* in French words *le,* &c.,

---

[1] Cf. Horstmann, 'Anglia, Beiblatt,' xiii, 16.

the lengthening sometimes occurred, sometimes not. It would be resisted naturally by the strong tendency to syncopation of *e*, especially in inflexional forms ; but some cases of certain lengthening are *wēsele* 'weasel,' *ēven*, *nāvele* 'navel,' *crādel* 'cradle,' *ōver*, *stōlen*. Borrowed words follow the same rule, lengthening sometimes taking place, sometimes not. Some French words with certain lengthening are *stāble*, *tāble*, *nōble*.

74. Lengthening of OE. short vowels in open syllables did not affect OE. *i*, *u*, or *o* for *u*, as in *hipe* 'hip,' *ʒiven* 'given,' *sune* (*sône*) 'son,' *numen* 'taken,' *cômen* 'come.' But English words which had developed forms with *e* for OE. *i* (*io*) show lengthening of *e*, as in *clēven* 'cleave, adhere' (OE. *cliofian*), *lēnen* 'lean' (OE. *hlionian*), *wēke* 'week' (OE. *wiocu, weocu*). In all these cases the ME. forms with *e* no doubt rest on OE. forms with *e* (*eo*), as often in Mercian. On the other hand, *i*, *u* in French words are long in open syllables in ME., as are *a*, *e*, *o*. Examples are *crīen* 'cry,' *bible* 'Bible,' *brībe*, *desīren* 'desire,' *avōw*, *prōw*, *crōune* 'crown.' In these cases perhaps OF. *i*, *u*, because of their close quality, associated themselves with English *ī*, *ū*, rather than with *ĭ*, *ŭ*, and thus assumed long quantity.

NOTE 1.—Lengthening of OE. short vowels in open syllables does not, in general, belong to the twelfth century, though there are some evidences that it may have begun in this period. It was clearly operative in the first half of the thirteenth century, and by the middle of the century was complete. In accordance with this principle OE. vowels in open syllables are not marked long in early Midland or Southern selections, even though the phonology seems to imply lengthening in some cases. Northern selections are all later than the change indicated, and therefore show lengthening in all cases.

NOTE 2.—Later shortening no doubt accounts for such forms as show short vowels in Modern English, as *rot*, *knock*, *crack*, *lap*, ME. *rōten*, *knōken*, *crāken*, *lāpen*. Sometimes also analogy accounts for the change, as in MnE. *sweat*, vb. by analogy of the preterit with short vowel, ME. *swette*.

75. Compensatory lengthening also occurred in Middle English, as in the case of the *i*, *u* vowels, by the vocalization of a following consonant. Examples are *Ī* from *ic* (*ik*), *stīe* 'sty' (OE. *stigu*, early ME. *stīge*), *rīe* 'rye' (OE. *ryge*), *stīle* (OE. *stigel*), *fūel* (*fowel*) 'fowl' (OE. *fugel*), *sōw* (OE. *sugu*) 'sow.'

SHORTENING

76. At the close of the Old English period, OE. long vowels and diphthongs, whether in simple or compound words, were usually shortened before long, that is doubled, consonants and before consonant groups, except those which had caused lengthening of short vowels and therefore preserved the quantity of long vowels (§ 72). Examples under the various heads are as follows:

(*a*) Before long, that is doubled, consonants, *lĕdde* 'led,' *sprĕdde* 'spread,' *hătte* 'called,' *fĕll*, *hĭdde* 'hid,' *hătter* 'hotter.'

(*b*) Before more than two consonants, *hĕrcnen* 'hearken,' *ĕrnde* 'earned,' *lĕrnde* 'learned.'

(*c*) Before two consonants, not those groups which preserved long quantity, *fĭlþe* 'filth,' *hĕlþe* 'health,' *kĕpte* 'kept,' *slĕpte* 'slept,' *lăst*, *brĕst* 'breast,' *sŏfte* 'soft,' *sŏhte* 'sought,' *tăhte* 'taught,' *lĭht* 'light,' *lĭhten* 'make light,' *drŭhþe* 'drought,' but dialectal 'droughth,' *lĭttle*, *Wĕdnesday*, *clĕnsen* 'cleanse,' *brĕmmil* (*brĕmbel*) 'bramble,' *slŭm(e)ren* (*slŭmbren*) 'slumber,' *ever*, *everȳ*.

(*d*) Before two or more consonants in compounds, *chăpman* 'merchant,' *Ĕdward*, *shĕphĕrde*, *wĭsdōm*, *fĭftȳ*, *gŏshawk*, *clĕnlȳ* 'cleanly,' *hŭsbonde* 'husband,' *hŭswif* 'hussy, housewife.'

NOTE 1.—The short vowel is often replaced by the long under the influence of analogy. Thus, in inflexional forms, the shortened vowel of the genitive singular and the plural, as *dĕvles*, is replaced by the long vowel of the nominative-accusative singular, *dēvel*, becoming *dēvles*. On the other hand, the short vowel of the genitive and plural sometimes replaced the long in the nominative-accusative, as in *mŏþer*, *brŏþer*, *ŏþer* 'mother, brother, other.' For a similar reason there is variation in quantity in compounds, as *sŭþdāle* 'south part,' *sōþfast* 'soothfast,' *hŏmward* 'homeward,' *mēknesse* 'meekness,' *wīslȳ* 'wisely,' with long vowels by analogy of the uncompounded *sūþ*, *sōþ*, *hōm*, *wīs*.

NOTE 2.—Variations in quantity are also found before certain consonant groups, as *st*, before which the long vowel often remains, as in *gāst* (*gōst*) 'ghost,' *prēst* 'priest,' *Crīst* 'Christ,' *lēste* 'least.' But if a third consonant follows *st*, the vowel is regularly short, as in *wrăstlen* 'wrestle,' *crĭstnen* 'christen,' *thĭstle*, *fŏstren* 'foster,' *blŏstme* 'blossom,' yet *ēstren* 'easter.' Modern

English shows many cases of shortening, as *hest, breast, fist, list, dust, rust.* Before OE. *sc*, ME. *sh* (*sch*), a long vowel is preserved by Orm in *flēsh*, though not in *wesh* 'washed.' Short vowels are common before *sh*, as in Modern English *flesh, mesh, wish, rush.*

77. Long vowels and diphthongs were sometimes shortened when one or more syllables with strong secondary stress followed the accent. Examples are *hăliday* 'holiday,' *hĕring* 'herring,' *stĕrop* 'stirrup,' *nŏþing* 'nothing,' *fĕlawe* 'fellow' (ON. *fēlagi*). Before the syllable *ī* (*ȳ*) there is variation, shortening occurring sometimes as in *rĕdȳ* 'ready,' *sŏrȳ* 'sorry,' *ănȳ* (*ĕnȳ*) 'any,' while in other cases the long vowel is retained, as in *īvȳ, wērȳ* 'weary,' *grēdȳ* 'greedy,' *hōlȳ.*

NOTE.—Here also analogy may counteract the operation of the rule, as in such words as *frēdōm, rīdĕre* 'freedom, rider,' where the long vowel is due to the influence of the uncompounded words *frē, rīden* 'free, ride.'

78. Before the consonant groups which usually preserved vowel length (§ 72), original short vowels remained short or were shortened, when followed immediately by (*a*) another consonant, as in *hŭndred, chĭldren*; (*b*) a syllable having strong secondary stress, as in *wŭrþi* 'worthy,' *ĕrþlȳ* 'earthly'; (*c*) a syllable made up of a short vowel and *l, r, n* (though not usually inflexional *n*), or *m*, as in *gĭrdel, wŭnder, ălderman, sĕlden* (*sĕldom*) 'seldom.' In cases under (*c*) frequent syncope of the short vowel before the liquid or nasal is presupposed, so that shortening would be due to the same influence as in cases under (*a*). In some words two of the above influences were operative at the same time, as in *wĭlderness, ălderman.* Inflexional *en* did not usually affect the preceding vowel, but the vowel remained long when *n* was dropped.

79. The vowels *i, u*, before *ng*, though long in early ME. as shown by the orthography of Orm, were short from the middle of the thirteenth century, as in *þĭng* 'thing,' *tŭnge* 'tongue.' Many cases of shortening before consonant groups also appear, especially in later Middle English. Shortening is most common before *ng, rn, rl, rþ*. Some examples of these are Orm's *ȝerrne* beside *ȝērne* 'desire,' *turrnenn* 'turn.'

Note.—Analogy doubtless accounts for many forms, as *frend* ' friend,' by influence of *frendly̆, frendship*.

THE VOWELS OF SYLLABLES WITHOUT PRINCIPAL STRESS

80. In syllables bearing strong secondary stress, Middle English vowels usually retain the quality of their Old English originals, as *fredōm, Godhę̄d, handsum*. The same is usually true of prefixes, as in *arīsen* ' arise,' *forlǭren* 'forlorn,' *upbę̄ren* 'upbear' (cf. *lō*, § 82). On the other hand, in suffixes and prefixes *o* and *u* before a nasal sometimes suffer change in quality, the first becoming *a* or *u*, the second *i*, partly no doubt under the influence of analogy. Thus the suffix *ung* (*lung*) of OE. nouns became *ing* (*ling*) in Middle English, and the prefix *on*, except the privative prefix, became *an* (*a*). The privative prefix *on*, as in OE. *onlūcan* ' unlock,' became *un*, perhaps under the influence of the negative *un* so commonly used. The greatest change in vowel quality from Old to Middle English, however, is in the case of inflexional endings. In these every OE. unstressed *a*, *o*, or *u* become *e*, a far reaching change which affected all classes of words.

Note 1.—The change of OE. *a*, *o*, *u* to *e* is often carried out in early Midland, as in ' Chronicle ' and ' Ormulum,' but not so fully as later.

Note 2.—Nth. shows complete change of *ung* (*lung*) to *ing* (*ling*), and of the privative prefix *on* to *un*, but otherwise the prefix *on* usually remains *on* (*o*). The change of vowel quality in inflexional endings has not affected the Nth. present participle, which ends in *and*(*e*). In early Sth. the suffix *ung* (*lung*) sometimes remains unchanged, but later regularly appears as *ing* (*ling*), as in other dialects. The other changes in vowel quality already mentioned are carried out, and in addition the ending of the present participle has become *inde* in most cases before the further change to *inge*, § 163.

81. Owing to the changes in stress many syllables in Romance words which formerly bore principal stress retain a strong secondary accent (cf. § 15). These also usually retain their original quality. In a few cases already mentioned in the preceding sections, certain changes in quality do appear, *ēre* instead of *ę̄re* from OF. *aire* (§ 33), *werrīen* beside *werreien* (§ 39), *eu* instead of *ęu* in *beutē* ' beauty' (§ 58), but it is not certain that such changes may not be due to

some other influence, as the following *r* in the first case. Similarly
Romance nouns in *-ion*, which occasionally seem to show variation
between *-ōn* and *ǫn*, may have suffered by the same influence. The
OF. prefixes *des*, *en*, *mes* often appear as *dis*, *in*, *mis*, the latter no
doubt partly under the influence of OE. *mis*. Examples are
distroien, inclǫsen, mischeef 'destroy, inclose (enclose), mischief.'
OF. initial *e* sometimes becomes *a* as in *ascāpen* 'escape,' *anointen*
'anoint,' *asunīen* 'excuse.'

82. The second elements of compounds, when containing a long
vowel or diphthong, usually retain original length under strong
secondary stress, as *Alfrẹd, barfōt* 'barefoot.'   The same is often
true of suffixes bearing secondary stress, as *hǭd, hẹd* which are
regularly long, and *dōm, ẹre, lẹs, līke* (*līche*) which are sometimes
short, however.   The length is proved by doubling of vowels, as in
hood, heed, doom, lees, and the occasional shortening by such spellings
of the suffixes as *dam, less*. Prefixes with original long vowels show
shortening in Middle English, as *arīsen* 'arise,' *tofǫre* 'before,'
from OE. prefixes *ā* and *tō*.   In the case of *tō-* the spelling clearly
indicates occasional shortening, as well as variation in quality;
cf. *tegadere* (*gidere*), *teday* 'together, today.'   Yet these are on
the whole rare forms, and the probability is that the prefix *tō-* was
associated with the preposition-adverb *tō* and was usually regarded
as long.   The same is true of vowels in words unstressed in the
sentence, as *an* (*a*), *but* (*bot*), *anȳ* (*enȳ*), *nat* (*not*), *þoh* (though), *us*,
sholde, wolde, wel beside *wēl*, &c.

NOTE.—In early Midland the long quantity is retained, as shown by Orm's
orthography in *hād, dōm, lēs* 'less,' *wīs* 'wise,' *rēde, līk* (*like*) 'like,' often
ẹre, though the latter is sometimes short.   So also *ī* (*ȳ*), from OE. *ig*, as in
hālī3, bodī3, and the second elements of compounds as *æd*(*d*)*mōdnesse*, where
mōd is long as indicated by the single *d* following the vowel.   Shortening of
vowels in words unstressed in the sentence is also shown in Orm's *butt, uss,*
þohh, ann(*a*), &c.

83. Other changes in unstressed syllables are those called syncope,
apocope, aphæresis, elision, contraction, the occurrence of which
follows general laws that may be briefly summarized.   To begin

with, every vowel or diphthong, whether medial or final, makes a syllable except as noted hereafter. But unstressed syllables, that is those without principal or secondary stress, often show syncope of medial *e*. Thus, after an accented syllable, medial *e*, whatever its origin, is syncopated, as in *chirche* 'church,' *hevne* 'heaven,' *lernde* 'learned,' *ōpnen* 'open.' In many such cases, however, the syncopated *e* is restored by analogy of unsyncopated forms, as *chireche*, *hevene*, *lernede*, *ōpenen*. The same is true of medial *e* between a principal and secondary stress, as *trewlȳ*, *sēmlȳ*, *Englōnd*, beside *trewelȳ*, *sēmelȳ*, *Engelōnd*. Syncope of any other vowel than *e* is rare, though *i* in the suffixes *iȝ*, *ish* is sometimes lost.

NOTE.—Early Midland shows the same syncope in many cases, as in Orm's *effne*, *errnde*, *gaddrenn*, *heffne*, *oppnenn*, &c., while in other forms the loss has not occurred.

84. Medial *e* is sometimes syncopated or partially lost in certain endings. Syncopation frequently occurs before final *r*, *l*, *n*, as in *silv(e)r*, *hung(e)r*, *striv(e)n*, *līt(e)l*. It is especially common between a vowel or liquid and *n*, as in the past participles *drawn*, *slayn*, *born*, *torn*. In past participles of weak verbs, the ending *ed* shows similar syncopation sometimes, owing to such a change in Old English (Sievers, 'Gr.,' § 406), though unsyncopated forms also occur. Syncopation seldom occurs in the endings *est*, *eþ* (*eth*) of the present indicative; in *es* (*is*) of the genitive singular, the nominative plural, and the adverb; in *en* of the infinitive, the plural of verbs, and in other forms except the past participle of strong verbs; in *ed* of preterit singular and plural, and *er*, *est* of comparative and superlative in adjectives. Syncope often occurs in words unstressed in the sentence, as *arn* for *āren* 'are,' *wiln* (*woln*) for *willen* (*wollen*) 'will.'

NOTE 1.—In early Midland syncope is less common except in the verbal endings *est*, *eþ(eth)*, in which it is sometimes found. Compare Orm's *seȝȝst* 'sayest,' *seȝȝþ* 'sayeth.'

NOTE 2.—In addition to general agreement with Midland, Nth. shows syncope in *es* of nouns and verbs. Sth., while also showing general agreement with Midland, differs in a much more frequent syncopation of *e* in the *est*, *eþ* (*eth*) verbal endings, as in Old English.

85. When medial *e*, of whatever origin, is followed by a syllable with another unstressed *e*, syncope or apocope often takes place. This gives rise to double forms, such as *apel*, *aþ(e)le* 'noble'; *adys*, *ad(e)se* 'adze'; *ever*, *ev(e)re* 'ever'; many also in inflexion, as *loved*, *lov(e)de* 'loved'; *hevens*, *hev(e)nes* 'heavens.' In the last half of the fourteenth century, apocope of *e* is preferred in preterits of weak verbs, the latter thus agreeing with the past participle. Upon this apocope and consequent agreement between preterit and past participle, rests the regularity of Modern English forms.

NOTE 1.—In early Midland the same variation between syncope or apocope also occurs, as in Orm's *heffne* 'heaven,' *aþell* 'noble,' but *lufede* 'loved.'

NOTE 2.—In Nth. the final *e* is usually silent or has suffered apocope. Sth. seems to prefer syncope of medial *e*. Chaucer makes frequent use of both forms for the same word, no doubt for metrical purposes.

86. Apocope of final *e* is common in Middle English, and materially affects the spoken forms of words, whether indicated or not by the orthography. It occurred earliest in polysyllables after a strong secondary stress, as in *almess*, OE. *ælmesse* 'alms'; *lafdiȝ* (*lēvdiȝ*), OE. *hlǣfdige* 'lady'; and in inflected forms of such words as *drinking*, *wurþiȝ* 'worthy,' *twentiȝ* 'twenty.' On the other hand, some such words occasionally assumed an inorganic *e* in the nominative by analogy of other forms, instead of suffering apocope in the latter, as *tiþende* 'tidings,' *twīfālde* 'twofold.' Similar apocope often occurred in words not bearing principal stress in the sentence, as in pronouns, unstressed adverbs and conjunctions, and auxiliary verbs. Examples are *mȳn*, *hir*, *swich* (*such*), *whan*, *þan* (*than*), *shul*, *myȝt*, beside forms with *e* in which the spelling is often merely traditional. Total or partial apocope, that is slurring, also occurs in poetry when unstressed *ne*, *þē* (*thē*), *a* precede words beginning with a vowel, as proved by the metre.

NOTE 1.—In early Midland, syncope is already clear from such cases as Orm's *laffdīȝ*, *drinnkinng* and others; unstressed words as *an*, *all*, *mīn*, *þīn*; and such evidences of elision as *þarrke* 'the ark.'

NOTE 2.—In the earliest Nth. apocope has taken place even more commonly than in other dialects; compare § 6. Sth. is far more conservative, with the exception of Kentish, which does not differ from Midland.

87. After syllables bearing principal stress, final *e*, of whatever origin, tends to disappear in Middle English, sometimes through analogy, later especially through general weakening. At the beginning of the period, the beginning of the thirteenth century, final *e* is usually retained except as already noted. About 1300 it remains or disappears at the pleasure of the writer, as shown by poetry, and in late Middle English, that is about the middle of the fifteenth century, it is wholly lost. Texts written in the northeast Midland district show disappearance of final *e* before those of the southeast Midland.

NOTE 1.—In early Midland final *e* was still preserved as a rule, though lost in words not bearing sentence stress, and in some inflexional forms as the dative of nouns.

NOTE 2.—In Nth. final *e* was wholly lost by the middle of the fourteenth century, a century before it disappeared entirely in Midland. It remained longest in the adjective inflexion, less commonly in nouns and verbs. In Sth., except Kentish, final *e* was kept somewhat longer than in Midland, though sometimes silent in the fourteenth century. In Kentish it is generally kept as late as the middle of the fourteenth century. In the dialect of London it is also retained somewhat longer than usually in Midland, as shown by the writings of Chaucer, in which, though often silent, it may still form a syllable for metrical purposes at the pleasure of the writer.

88. Elision of weak final *e* occurs before a word beginning with a vowel or weak *h*, that is *h* in unstressed words as *hē*, *him*, or those with French *h*. Examples are numerous in poetry, as indeed they are rarely found in Old English verse. The commonest OE. elision, that of *e* in the negative *ne*, remains to Middle English in such forms as *nas* for *ne was*, &c. In Middle English also *e* of *þē* (*thē*) is often elided. This is shown by such early Midland forms as *þemperīce* 'the empress' in the 'Chronicle,' and *þarrke* 'the ark' in the 'Ormulum.' Common also is elision of *o* in unstressed *tō*, as in *toffrenn* 'to offer,' *tunnderrgān* 'to undergo' from the 'Ormulum.' Rarely the *e* of the pronouns *mē*, *þē* (thee) also suffers elision, as in *þhalighte* 'thee alight,' *dō mendȳte* 'do me endyte.'

89. Aphæresis, that is loss of an initial vowel (or syllable), some-times occurs in unstressed words or syllables. Examples in un-stressed words are *hēt* for *hē it, wast* for *was it.* So also the un-stressed vowel has disappeared in *rīsen* from OE. *ārīsan* 'arise,' *taunen* from OE. *ætēawnian* 'show,' *twīten* from OE. *ætwītan* 'twit.' Similarly *i* (*y*) from OE. *ge* usually suffers aphæresis in Northern and Midland, though often not in Southern. Old French *e* before *sc* (*sk*), *sp*, *st* is often lost as in *spȳen* 'espie, spy,' *spōuse, stāt* 'state,' *stǫrīe* (*stǫrȳ*), *scāpen* 'escape.' Aphæresis of *a, e* under other circumstances also occurs sometimes, as *prentys* 'apprentice,' *semblee* 'assembly,' *nuien* (*noien*) 'annoy,' *pistle* 'epistle.' Aphæresis of an unstressed syllable in Romance words occurs in *sample* < *en-sample, buschment* < *embuschment, fenden* < *defenden, sport* < *desport, struien* < *destruien.*

90. Contraction of vowels brought together by vocalization of a medial consonant sometimes occurs. Examples are *dēl* for *dēvel, ēl* for *evel, yēde* (*yōde*) from OE. *ge-ēode, whēr* for *wheþer, ǫr* (*or*) for *ouþer* 'or,' *ēr, nēr* for *ever, never.*

The Consonants

91. The Middle English consonant system may be best exhibited by a table such as the following:

	Stops.		Continuants.				
			Spirants.				
	Voice-less.	Voiced.	Voice-less.	Voiced.	Semi-vowels.	Liquids.	Nasals.
Labials	*p*	*b*	*f*	*v*	*w*		*m*
Dentals	*t*	*d*	{ *þ* *s* *sh*	*þ* *z*		*l* *r*	*n*
Palatals	*k'*	*g'*	*ȝ'(h)*	[*ȝ(h)*]	*ȝ, y*		
Gutturals	*k*	*g*	*ȝ'*	*ȝ*			*ŋ*

To these must be added the breath consonant *h*, and the combinations *hw* (MnE. *wh* as in *what*), *ch* (=*tsh*) as in *church*, *g, j* (=*dzh*) as in *wāge, judge*.   *x* is but a sign for *ks*.

NOTE.—The pronunciation of most of the consonants is the same as in Modern English. The palatal stops *k′, g′* are pronounced as in *kid, get*, compared with the guttural stops in *cot, got*. The voiced *þ* (ð, *th*) is sounded as in *the*. *Sh* (*sch*) represents the simple consonant sound in *she*, no voiced variety being found in Middle English. The palatal spirant ȝ (*h*) has the sound of *ch* in Ger. *ich*, the voiced ȝ (medial and only in early Middle English) may be pronounced as *y* in *yet*. The guttural spirants represent respectively the Ger. *ch* in *auch*, and *g* in *sagen*. ŋ represents the sound of *n* before *k* or *g*.

92. The general relations to the Old English consonant system may be briefly summarized; compare also a table similar to the above in Sievers, 'Gr.,' § 170. In the first place, most consonants in Middle English correspond to similar ones in Old English on the one side, and in Modern English on the other. Especially is this true of the semi-vowels, liquids, and nasals, as well as of the dental and labial stops and spirants. The most radical changes that have taken place have affected the palatal and guttural stops and spirants. In addition to this there are of course some minor changes within the limits of each consonant, which will be noticed as they occur. Owing to the general similarity between the Old, Middle, and Modern English consonant systems, however, it seems best here to presuppose knowledge of the Old English system, and to consider mainly those changes that are necessary for an understanding of Middle English proper. In considering the consonants, the order will be that of the table above, the stops first, and next the various classes of continuants, spirants, semi-vowels, liquids, and nasals [1].

---

[1] This order is chosen as best exhibiting the essential character of the consonants on the physical, rather than the physiological side. The physiological terms, as guttural, palatal, &c., and the descriptive terms, as semi-vowels, liquids, &c., are also freely employed because of their long acceptance and their general value.

THE STOPS

93. The Middle English voiceless and voiced stops of labial and
dental varieties, *p–b*, *t–d*, correspond so nearly with those of Old
and Modern English that little space need be given to them. Each
is a stable consonant in the main, and subject only to such changes
as may affect any consonant at different times; see § 112 f.
It is worthy of note that the voiceless labial *p*, which was rare
initially in Old English, became common owing to the great number
of French words introduced in Middle English. The geminated
labial *b*, when medial as in a few OE. words, was replaced by *v*
under the influence of the numerous forms in which *v* (OE. medial *f*)
occurred in Old English. Examples are *hāven*, OE. *habban* 'have,'
liven, OE. *libban* 'live,' *hęven*, OE. *hebban* 'heave.' For *d* under
grammatical change see § 116.

NOTE.—The dialects in general agree. In late Nth., final unstressed *d* was
often unvoiced to *t*, and this has remained to modern Scotch. In Sth. geminated
bb as above was not replaced by *v*. Early Sth. shows unvoicing of final unstressed *d* as in *asket* 'asked,' *tōwart* 'toward,' *inempnet* 'named,' but later *d*
was restored by analogy of other forms.

94. The ME. voiceless palatal stop *k* (as in *kid*) springs from
the OE. guttural stop *c* (*k*), from Norse *k*, and in a few words from
OF. *c* (= *k*). It occurs initially before the OE. palatal mutated
vowels *ę*, *ē* < *ō*, sometimes *ǣ*, usually before the OE. guttural *ў* (from
ŭ) which had become palatal *ī* by unrounding, before *e*, *i* in words
from Norse (rarely Old French), and sometimes by analogy of
guttural vowels in allied forms. Examples of native words are
ME. *kemben* 'comb,' *Kent*, *kēne* 'keen,' *kei* (OE. *cǣge*) 'key,'
kichen (OE. *cycene*) 'kitchen,' *kīte* (OE. *cўta*) 'kite.' A considerable number of Norse words also occur, as *ketel* 'kettle,' *kevel* 'bit,
clamp, gag,' *kide* 'kid,' *kindlen* 'kindle,' *kirke* 'church.' On the
other hand, OF. words with palatal *k* are limited by rare occurrence of OF. *c* (= *k*), except before gutturals, but compare AN.
forms with *e* < *ē* by monophthonging of OF. *ue* (§ 35, 20), which
account for ME. *keveren* beside *coveren* 'cover,' and *keverchef*

(*kerchef*). Here belong also ME. *kenet* 'hound,' *kenel* 'kennel,' *kitōn* 'kitten.' By analogy of guttural *k* in pret. pl. and past participle, the palatal stop *k* (*c*) took the place of ME. *ch* in the present of *kerven* 'carve.' Medially the ME. palatal stop *k* appears as above, as well as before OE. *a, o, u*, which had become ME. *e* in unstressed syllables (§ 80). Examples are *tāken, māken, āker* 'acre.' By analogy of the indicative present third singular of certain verbs as *sēkeþ, wirkeþ*, palatal *k* often appears in the infinitive and other present forms, as *sēken, wirken*. In *chiken* 'chicken,' *īsikel* 'icicle,' the *k* is doubtless due to the OE. inflected forms, as *cycnes, īsikles* in which OE. *c* would remain *k*. The combination *s* + palatal *c* (= *k*) always indicates borrowing, as in *skil* 'reason,' *skin, skēre* 'clear.'

NOTE.—The examples of palatal *c* (*k*) are increased for the Nth. dialect by the lack of palatalization of OE. *c* to *ch* (§ 110, n. 2). Examples are *mikel* 'much,' *swilk* 'such,' *līk* 'like,' *sēk* 'seek,' *wirk* 'work,' and many others. For Nth. *s* < OE. *sc*, cf. § 102, n. 2.

95. The voiced palatal stop *g* springs from OE. guttural *g* before *ӯ* which had become palatal *ī* by unrounding, from OF., ON. *g* before palatal vowels, and is sometimes due to analogy of allied forms with guttural *g*. Examples of initial *g* in native words are *gilden* 'gild,' *gilt*, 'guilt,' *girden* 'gird'; in those from Old French, where *g* represents earlier *gu, gīle* 'guile,' *gimelot* (*gimbelet*) 'gimblet,' *gilerne* 'guitar'; in Norse, *gēre* 'gear,' *gēren* 'do, make,' *gil* 'gill of a fish,' *gest* 'guest,' the last supplanting the native English word. Analogy of *g* in preterit and past participle accounts for *geven* (*given*) 'give' beside English *ʒeven* (*ʒiven*) and *ginnen, beginnen* 'begin,' while *geten* beside *ʒeten* 'get' is of Norse origin. Medially, palatal *g* appears in the combination *ng* (= *ŋ* + *g'*) before palatal vowels, as *singen* (OE. *singan*) 'sing,' *gengen* (ON. *genga*) 'go,' *genge* (ON. *gengi*) 'company.'

96. The Middle English guttural stops *c* (*k*)–*g* correspond to OE. (ON.) guttural stops *c*–*g* in Teutonic words, or to similar sounds in Old French. Both guttural stops occur before consonants and the guttural vowels *ă, ŏ̝, ŏ, ŭ.* For the stops *c (k)–g* which occur before OE. *ĕ, y̆,* sometimes *ǣ* when due to mutation, see § 94, and for OF. *ch* before *a, au,* see § 110. The guttural *c* (*k*) also appears in the combination *x* (=*ks*), *qu* (=*kw*), *nc* (*k*) =*ŋ + k,* and the stop *g* in the combination *ng* (=*ŋ + g*), occasionally in gemination (*gg*). Guttural *c* (*k*) initially in Teutonic words may be illustrated by *clŏ̄þ* 'cloth,' *cāre (kāre), cŏ̄ld, cŏ̄le* 'coal,' *cumen* (*cómen*) 'come,' and in Romance words by *crȳen* 'cry,' *cas (cāse)* 'case,' *colūr* 'colour,' *cūrs (cōūrs)* 'course.' In Romance words the stop *c* (*k*) before *a, au* indicates learned origin or Norman-Picard dialect, in which vulgar Latin *k* did not become *ch* (as in Central French). Examples are *cas (cāse), cause, cāge, carpentēr,* and the doublets *catēl, cachen* 'catch,' *calīce, carité,* beside OF. *chatel, chācen, chalīce, charité* (cf. § 110). Medially the guttural stop *c* (*k*) appears before a guttural vowel in syllables having principal or secondary stress, and finally after a guttural vowel. Between a guttural and palatal vowel, the stop must have varied between guttural and palatal quality as it belonged to the syllable with one vowel or the other. The combination *s +* guttural *c* (*k*) always indicates borrowing, either from Norse as in *scŏ̄wl, scull, bask,* Old French as in *scŏrn, scūren,* 'scour' *scŏ̄ute* 'scout,' or other minor sources.

NOTE.—In Nth. the number of guttural *k*'s is increased by the fact that OE. *c* did not become *ch* in that dialect (§ 94, n.). Examples are *caf* 'chaff,' *calk* 'chalk.' For the combination *sk* < OE. *sc* in unstressed words, see § 102, n. 2.

97. The guttural stop *g* initially may be exemplified by *grēne* 'green,' *galle* 'gall,' *gŏ̄ld, gŏd* 'good,' *gume* 'man' in Teutonic words, and *glŏ̝rīe, governen* 'govern,' *gŏ̄ute* 'gout' in Romance. In Teutonic words borrowed by vulgar Latin initial *w* became *gu* (=*gw*), and this combination became guttural *g* in Old French, as in ME. *garde, garisŏn, regard,* while remaining *w* (except before *i*) in Anglo-Norman, and therefore appearing in the doublets *warde, warisŏn, reward* (§ 106). Before *i, g* < Teut. *w* appears in *gīden* 'guide,' *gīse* 'guise,' *gīle* 'guile,' *begīlen* 'beguile.' Medially and finally guttural *g* occurs under the same circumstances as guttural *k* above. In a few cases ME. guttural *g* represents late OE. geminated, that is long *g* (*gg*), as in *dogge* 'dog,' *frogge* 'frog,' *hogge* 'hog,' *stagge* 'stag.' Usually, however, medial or final guttural *g* implies borrowing, as in *draggen* 'drag,' *big*, *egg*, *legg* from Norse. ME. *sugre*, beside *sucre* 'sugar,' shows voicing of OF. *c* to *g*. ME. *garden* represents Picard *garden*, beside OF. *jardin*.

THE SPIRANTS

98. The spirants *f–v* (*f*) in Teutonic words occurred under the same conditions as in Old English and to-day. The voiceless *f* appears initially in a stressed syllable, as in *fader* 'father,' *befðren* 'before'; medially when preceding a voiceless consonant or in gemination (*ff*), as in *shaft*, *offren* 'offer'; finally, as in *wulf*, *self*. In Romance words *f* was regularly voiceless and retained this quality whether in stressed or unstressed syllables. Examples of Romance words in which *f* appears contrary to the rule in Teutonic are *còmfort*, *trufle*.

99. The voiced spirant *v* (sometimes written *f*) in Teutonic words springs from OE. (ON.) *f* in voiced company, as *ðver*, *given* (*ʒiven*, *yiven*) 'give'; occasionally also in inflected forms with final *f* in nominative singular, as *stäves* from *staf* 'staff,' *calves* from *calf*. To these were added in Middle English many *v*'s, both initial and medial, from Old French. As initial *v* did not occur in Teutonic words, except rarely in those borrowed from the Sth. dialect, Midland words with initial *v* or with *v* beginning a stressed syllable are of Romance origin, as *vīne*, *devīne*.

NOTE 1.—In early Middle English *f* was still written for *v*, as in the OE. period; cf. *iäfen* (= *ʒäven*), *hðfen* 'have,' &c.

NOTE 2.—Nth. agrees with Midland. In Sth. the number of initial *v*'s was largely increased by the voicing of initial *f*, as in *vader* 'father,' *vihten* 'fight.' Cf. Kt. selections especially.

100. The spirants *þ* (*ð*, *th*), voiceless and voiced without distinction of written sign, occurred in Teutonic words under exactly the

same circumstances as *f–v*, and need not be especially illustrated.
While in Modern English some borrowed words have the voiceless
th, the voiced and voiceless spirants usually indicate Teutonic origin.
In late Middle English *th* came to be written for OF. *t* (*th* = *t*),
as in *thẹatre, thẹorie, thẹme, thrọne, authọur* 'author,' and these were
doubtless still pronounced with *t* until, in Modern English, they
acquired the spirant sound by influence of the spelling.   There is
no evidence that initial *þ* (*th*) had become voiced in pronominal
words, as *þē, þat, þis, þū*, &c., or final *þ* in unstressed *wiþ*.   Initial
unstressed *þ* in pronominal words often becomes *t* after *d, t,* sometimes *s* by back assimilation, as in *and tat* 'and that,' *at tat* 'at
that,' *is tat* 'is that.'   Occasionally ME. *þ* interchanges with the
voiced stop *d* in medial position, as *cōude* beside *cōuþe* 'could,'
afōrden 'afford,' and finally in the preterit *quod* 'quoth.'   After
a voiceless spirant, *f, s, ʒ* (*h*), ME. *þ* becomes *t*, as in *þefte* 'theft,'
leste (OE. *lǣs þē*) 'lest,' *heiʒte* 'height.'

NOTE.—Nth. agrees with Midland.   The parallel voicing in Sth. of initial
f, s, sometimes *wh* (*hw*) to *w*, implies voicing of *þ* in similar position, but the
orthography gives no evidence of it.

101. The spirants *s*, voiced and voiceless, but usually without
distinction of written sign, are parallel to *f–v* in their occurrence in
Teutonic words.   The voiced spirant is usually written *s, z* ordinarily indicating *ts* in Middle English.   *z* is found, especially when
final in unstressed syllables, as in WMl. forms like *sīdez* 'sides,'
indicating the voicing of *s* in this position.   Both spirants were
largely increased from Old French sources.   OF. voiceless *s*
(written *s* (*sc*) *ss*, or *c* before *e, i*) occurs in all positions and need
not be especially illustrated.   Medial OF. *iss* usually became ME.
isch (*issh*) as in *finischen* (OF. *finir, finiss-*) 'finish,' *perischen*
'perish,' *anguische* 'anguish.'   OF. voiced *s* is found in such words
as *prisūn* 'prison,' *trẹsōn* 'treason.'   In *citesen* 'citizen' the voiced
spirant has been inserted, perhaps by analogy of similar *sen* (*zen*)
forms.   For Picard *ch* in words with OF. *c* = *s* cf. § 110.

NOTE.—In general Nth. agrees with Midland, but note Nth. *s* for Ml. Sth.

sch (*sh*), § 102. For OF. *sīre* Nth. has *schir* sometimes. Teutonic initial
s was voiced in Sth., as shown especially by initial *z* in the Kentish ' Ayenbite
of Inwit.'

102. The Middle English spirant *sch* (*sh*) is a characteristic
ME. sound springing from OE. *sc* in all positions. Examples are
schaft (*shaft*) ' shaft,' *schort* (*short*), *asche* ' ash,' *Englisch*, *fisch*
(*fish*)   From such strictly English words with ME. *sch* (*sh*) are to
be separated the Norse and OF. borrowed words with *sc* (*sk*); but
medial OF. *iss* gave ME. *isch* (*ish*) as already noted.   In the pronoun *schē* (*scho*, *sho*) ME. *sch* springs from OE. *s*+*y* (< *e*) in unstressed *sēo* (*seō*) from OE. *sēo*. In *asken* ' ask ' (OE. *ascian*, *axian*),
sk probably represents a late metathesis of *x*.   *Scotland*, *Scottisch*,
scōl ' school,' are doubtless learned forms, the first two influenced
by the Nth. *Scot*, the last by OF. *escole* or mediæval Latin *scola*.
There was no corresponding voiced spirant in Middle English.

NOTE 1.—In ' Chronicle,' *sc* is still written for ME. *sch* (*sh*), but Orm writes
sh after long, *ssh* after short vowels.

NOTE 2.—Nth. agrees with Ml. in the main, but OE. *sc* in unstressed words
and syllables became *s*, as in *sulen*, *sal*, *suld*, ' schulen, shall, should,' *Inglis*,
' English,' *Scots* ' Scotch.' In Sth., sometimes Ml., *ss* (*s*) are written for the
spirant sound.

103. The Middle English palatal spirants ȝ (*h*)–ȝ (ȝ*h*), voiceless
and voiced without much distinction of signs, are exclusively of
Teutonic origin and of limited occurrence.   They cannot occur
initially because the corresponding OE. palatals *c*, *g* had become
ME. *ch*, and the semivowel ȝ (*y*) respectively.   They are also
limited, in medial and final position, by their vocalization to form
diphthongs (§ 47), or *ī*, *ū* (§ 75).   While this vocalization was
probably complete in early Middle English, as shown by the spelling of Orm (§ 71, n.), the signs were still sometimes written as *hēh*
(*hēg*, *hēȝ*) ' high,' *leȝen* (*leȝhen*) ' lay.'   Otherwise the voiceless spirant
ȝ (*h*) is found only medially in the OE. combinations *ht*, *hþ*, which
both became ȝ*t*, written also *ht*, *gt*, *ct*, ȝ*ht*, *ght*, less commonly ȝ*th*,
gth, *cth*.   Examples are *riȝt* (*riht*) ' right,' *kniȝt* (*kniht*) ' knight,'
driȝten (*drihten*) ' lord,' and *heȝte* (*heȝt*, *hiȝt*) ' height,' *siȝte* ' sight,'

with change of *þ* to *t* in accordance with § 100. ME. *ȝt* is sometimes written *st* by confusion of these high-pitched palatal sounds.
The OE. combination *rhþ* had become *rþ*, as in *mirþe* 'mirth,' and
such forms as ME. *fē* 'money, fee,' spring from OE. forms which
had lost the final *h*, as *fēo* beside *feoh*; cf. also ME. *þur* beside
þurȝ (*þurh*) 'through.' The voiced palatal spirant *ȝ* (*ȝh*) is found
medially as above until fully vocalized after vowels to form diphthongs, after *r* or *ĭ* to *ī*, as *mirīe* (OE. *myrge, myrige*) 'merry,' *birīen*
(OE. *byrgan*) 'bury,' *sīþe* (OE. *sigeþe*) 'scythe,' *drīe* (OE. *drȳge*)
'dry.' Finally in stressed syllables the voiced spirant had probably
become unvoiced, but in unstressed *iȝ* (OE. *ig*) the voiced spirant
also became *ī*, as in *bodī* (*bodȳ*), *hǭlī* (*hǭlȳ*). ME. *belī* (OE. *belg,
belig*) no doubt comes from the form with parasitic *i*, compared
with that with *g* which gave *w* after *l* as in ME. *belwe* (*belou*) 'bellows.'

NOTE 1.—In early Ml. the voiceless spirant is still spelt *h* as in Old
English, and the voiced spirant *g*, *ȝh* as in Orm.

NOTE 2.—The dialects agree in general, though in Nth. OE. *ht* remained
guttural as in Northumbrian. Sth. has a larger number of palatal spirants,
owing to the larger number of palatal vowels in that dialect, as *leȝhen* (*liȝhen*)
from WS. *hliehan*, beside Ml. *lahhen* (*lauhwen, lauwen*) from OM. *hlæhhan*
'laugh.' Sth. also retains *ī* from OE. *ig* in the present tense of OE. weak
verbs of the second class (§ 6).

104. The Middle English guttural spirants *ȝ* (*h*, *ȝh*)*-ȝ* (*ȝh*),
voiceless and voiced without much distinction of signs, are also
of Teutonic origin and of as limited occurrence as the palatal
spirants. They cannot occur initially because not so appearing in
Old English, OE. guttural spirant *g* having become a guttural stop
before ME. times. While occurring in medial and final position
they later became vocalized after vowels to form diphthongs (§ 47),
or the voiced spirant became *w* after *l* or *r*, after *ŭ* was absorbed
(§ 75). The voiceless *ȝ* remained voiceless throughout the period
only in the OE. combination *ht*, as in *taȝte* (*tauhte*) 'taught,'
douȝter 'daughter,' *fouȝten* 'fought,' *þouȝt* 'thought.' When final
it remained voiceless until finally vocalized in the preceding diphthong which had been formed (§ 66). Examples are *þoh* (*þouȝ*)

'though,' *slōh* (*slou3*) 'slew,' *þurh* (*þur3*) 'through.'   The OE.
medial voiceless guttural *hh* became voiced and developed as the
voiced guttural through *3h* to *w*, as in *lau3en* (*lauwen*) 'laugh,'
cou3en (*couwen*) 'cough.'   The preterit singular *saw* has its *w* from
the plural *sawen* (OE. *sāwon*), and *þorw* (*þorow*) developed from
þoru3 beside *þur3*.   The medial voiced spirant *3* remained as *3* (*3h*)
until vocalized after vowels to form diphthongs, after *ŭ* to strengthen
the preceding vowel, after *l*, *r*, to *w*.   Examples are *dra3en* (*drawen*)
' draw,' *ō3en* (*ōwen*) ' owe,' *fu3el* (*fūel*, *fōwel*) < OE. *fugel* 'fowl,'
fol3en (*folwen*) 'follow,' *sor3e* (*sorwe*) < OE. *sorh*, f., 'sorrow.'
When final, the original voiced spirant had become voiceless and
fell in with that sound as above.   Examples are *dou3* 'dough,'
plou3 'plow.'   Such forms as ME. *schō* 'shoe' rest upon the forms
which had lost final *h* in Old English, as *scō* beside *scōh* (cf. § 103).

NOTE 1.—In early Ml. *h* was still written for the voiceless guttural, and
g (*gh*, *3h*) for the voiced : cf., however, *halechen* for more regular *hal3en*
(*halwen*) 'saints', *halechede* for later *hal3ede* (*halwede*) 'hallowed' of 'Chronicle.'

NOTE 2.—The dialects agree.

THE CONSONANT *H* AND ITS COMBINATIONS

105. The ME. breath consonant *h*, essentially a spirant of
palatal or guttural character, occurs in general as in Old and
Modern English, that is only in initial position, or initially in the
second element of compounds.   It had been regularly lost, however,
from the OE. initial combinations *hl*, *hr*, *hn*, as in *lēpen*, 'leap,'
ring, *nute* ' nut,' and sometimes also initially in unstressed words as
it for OE. *hit*.   In unstressed syllables it regularly disappeared as
in *fostrild* < OE. **fōstorhild* 'nurse.'   OF. *h*, in words of Teutonic
origin, falls in with OE., ON. *h*, as in *hardī*, *harneis* 'harness.'   In
words of Latin origin *h*, though frequently written by scribes, was
not pronounced.   This accounts for the double forms *eremite–
hermit*, *abit–habit*, *onōur–honōur*.   The OE. combination *hw* was
retained in Middle English, though early written *wh* as by Orm,
sometimes with the characteristic Nth. *qu* as in 'Genesis and Exodus.'

Occasionally *wh* (*hw*) is reduced to *h*, as in *hō* for *whō* (§ 106). In OE. *hēo* initial *h* became *ʒh*, as in *ʒhē*, *ʒhō* ' she.'

NOTE.—Nth. agrees with Ml. as to *h*, but uses *qu* (*quh*) for *wh*, showing a strengthening of the original *hw* to *kw*. Sth. shows a more frequent loss of initial *h*, as in *ā* for OE. *hē*, *hēo*, and *abben* ' have.' In Kt. the orthography *lh*, *nh* for OE. *hl*, *hn*, perhaps indicates a retention of the original combinations.

THE SEMIVOWELS, LIQUIDS AND NASALS

106. The ME. semivowel *w*, which appears only in Teutonic words, though a few are from Romance sources, springs from OE. *w*, though limited by its vocalization to form diphthongs (§ 47). To words with OE., ON. *w* were added a few from Anglo-Norman which had retained an original Teut. *w* instead of the usual OF. *gu*. Examples of the latter are *waiten* ' wait,' *wāfre* ' wafer,' *wāge*, *walop*, *werre* ' war,' *werreien* (*werrīen*) ' make war.' Teut. *w* was not retained before *i* and hence an OF. *g* appears in such words as in § 97. In Teut. words *w* disappears between an initial consonant and a following *o* (*u*), as in *tō* beside *twō* ' two,' *þǫng* beside *þwǫng* ' thong,' *sōte* beside *swōte* ' sweet,' *hō* beside *whō* (*hwō*) ' who.' In *sǭ*, *alsǭ*, the disappearance of *w* was earlier than in the other words, perhaps as early as late Old English (cf. § 42). *w* also disappears initially in a few unstressed words of common breath groups, as *nas* for *ne was*, *nēre* for *ne wēre*, *nille* for *ne wille*, *nǫt* for *ne wǫt*, *God ǫt* (*God wǫt*). OE. *cw*, ON. *kv* (=*kw*) were generally written *qu*, under French influence, and with them fell in OF. words with *qu* together with a few with OF. *c* (=*k*)+*ue*, *ui* as *quēre* ' choir,' *squiēre* (*squīre*), *squirel*. For AN. *queint*, *aqueinten* see § 53. Similarly *gu* (=*gw*) springs from OF. *g*+*ue*, *ui* in *anguische* ' anguish.'

NOTE.—The dialects agree, but Nth. also has *qu* (*quh*) for OE. *hw*, and *w* was preserved in *twā*, *quā*, &c. in which OE. *ā* had not become *ǭ* (*ō*).

107. The ME. semivowel *ʒ* (*y*) is exclusively of Teutonic origin, and springs from the OE. semivowel *g* as in *ʒēr* ' year,' *ʒǫke* ' yoke,' *ʒung* (*ʒòng*) ' young,' or the OE. palatal spirant *g* as in *ʒēlden* 'yield,' *zērd* (*zard*) 'yard.' Before *i*, OE. *g* is sometimes vocalized as in *icchen* (OE. *gyccean*) 'itch,' *Ipswich* (OE. *Gipeswīc*), *Ilchester* (OE. *Gifelceaster*), and in unstressed *īsikel* (OE. *īsgicel*) 'icicle.' Similarly in the OE. unstressed prefix *ge* also became *i* (*y*), though regularly preserved only in Sth.   ME. *z* sometimes develops initially before a palatal vowel as in *zork* (OE. *Eoforwīc*), *zōū* (*yōū*) from OE. *ēow*, the latter perhaps by influence of *zē* (*yē*) 'ye.'

108. The ME. liquids *l*, *r*, do not differ in general from their Teutonic or OF. originals.   In OE. words *l* disappears before and after *ch*, as in *swich*, *such* (OE. *swilc*) 'such,' *which* (OE. *hwilc*), *ēch* (OE. *ǣlc*) 'each,' *müche* beside *müchel* (OE. *mycel*), *wenche* beside *wenchel* (OE. *wencel*).   The combination *rld* sometimes becomes *rd* in *werde* 'world.'   The OE. metathesis of *r* remains in Middle English, and some new examples of metathesis appear as *fresch*, *preschen* 'thresh.'   Double forms of some OF. words are found, owing to OF. double forms as *marbre–marble, purpre–purple*.

NOTE.—In Nth., *l* before *k* does not disappear as before the corresponding *ch* in the other dialects ; cf. *swilk, quilk* 'such, which.'

109. The ME. nasals *m*, *n*, *y* (=*n* before *k* or *g*) do not differ from their Teutonic and OF. originals, so far as preserved.   OE. final unstressed *m* in inflexional endings had become *n* in late Old English.   ME. final unstressed *n* in similar position or in unstressed words tends to disappear throughout the period.   This affects especially the *en* of verbal endings, and such unstressed words as *an* (*a*), *ǭn* (*ǭ*), *nǭn* (*nǭ*), *būten* (*bute, but*) 'but.'   Some stressed words show a similar loss at times, as *morwe*(*n*), *gāme*(*n*), *maide*(*n*), *ǭpe*(*n*), *seve*(*n*).

NOTE.—In Nth. infinitives no final *n* was received from OE. times. This indicates the beginning of the tendency to lose inflexional *n*, a tendency that was more pronounced and rapid than in Ml., far more than in Sth.

THE AFFRICATIVE COMBINATIONS

110. The ME. combination *ch*, as in *church* (*tsh*), occurs in native and Romance words.   In native words it springs from the OE.

palatal stop *c* (*cc*) before palatal vowels, as initially in *chirche, chīld, cheste, cherl, cherren* ' turn,' *chēse* ' cheese,' *chaf* ' chaff ' ; medially in *wrecche* ' wretch,' *spēche* ' speech.' After a palatal vowel OE. *c* became ME. *ch* when final in unstressed words and syllables, as in *ich* 'I,' *which, swich* 'such,' *Ipeswich* ' Ipswich'; sometimes in stressed words as *lich* ' body,' *pich* ' pitch,' *French*, owing to inflected forms with OE. *c* in medial position or possibly in some cases to analogy of corresponding verbal roots. By analogy also *ch* appears in *chōsen*, pp. for OE. *coren*. On the other hand *ch* is replaced by the palatal stop *k* in the infinitive and other present forms of some verbs by analogy of the pres. 3rd sg., which had no *ch* ; examples are *sēken* beside *sēchen* ' seek,' *wirken* (*wirchen*) ' work.' In Romance words *ch* appears before *a, au* in those from Central French, before *e, i* in those from the Picard dialect, beside NF. *c* (*k*) for the former and *c* (=*s*) for the latter. Examples are *charme, charge, chaunge, chaumbre, prēchen* 'preach,' *aprōchen* 'approach,' *cherischen* 'cherish,' *chisel, chimeneie* ' chimney.' For doublets with NF. *c* (=*k*) beside OF. *ch*, and OF. *c* (=*s*) beside Picard *ch*, see §§ 96, 101. For OE. *s* + palatal *c*, see § 102.

NOTE 1.—In 'Chronicle,' *c* is still written for OE. *c*, but Orm uses *ch* which continues to prevail.

NOTE 2.—As Old Northumbrian suffered no palatalization of OE. *c*, Nth. has *c* (*k*) in place of Ml. Sth. *ch*; cf. *caf* ' chaff,' *calk* ' chalk,' *mikel, ik* ' I,' *quilk* 'which,' *swilk* ' such,' *sēk* ' seek,' *wirk* ' work' (§ 94, n.). Sth., on the other hand, shows a greater number of *ch* forms, owing to the greater number of palatal spirants in West Saxon ; cf. Sth. *chēld* (*chald*) ' cold ' from WS. *ceald*, with Ml. Nth. *cōld* from OAng. *cāld*, and *mūchel* with *ch* after an original guttural vowel.

III. The ME. voiced combination *g* (*j*), as in *judge* (*dzh*), corresponding to the voiceless *ch* above, occurs also in native and Romance words. In native words it springs only from the OE. voiced palatal stop *g* in gemination (*cg*) or in the combination *ng* (=*n* + *dzh*). Examples are *briğğe* 'bridge,' *eğğe* 'edge,' *heğğe* 'hedge,' *senğen* (*singen*) ' singe,' *crinğen* ' cringe.' As the OE. combinations *cg, ng* could not occur initially, most such words with *ğ*, *j* (=*dzh*) are of Romance origin. OE. *cg* (*cge*) in the present tense of verbs was displaced by analogy of the 3rd sg. in which *ǧ* (=*dzh*) had not developed (cf. § 165). Examples are *seien* (*seyen*) 'say,' *leien* 'lay,' *bȳen* 'buy.' In Romance words ME. *ǧ*, *j* represents OF. *ǧ*, *j*, as in *gentil* 'gentle,' *general, geant* (*gīant*) 'giant,' *joie* 'joy,' *jęlous* 'jealous,' *engīn* 'engine,' *chargen* 'charge,' *juggen* 'judge,' *cāge, plegge* 'pledge.' In proper names with initial *I* (*J*) in the MSS. it becomes difficult to determine accurately, especially in Biblical names, whether they are from Old French or adopted directly from Latin with initial *I=Y*. It seems safe to assume that OF. Biblical names only gradually displaced the OE. and Latin, such words as *Jēsus, Jǫhan* (*Jǫhn*), *Jāmes, Jordan, Jerusalem* being adopted before the more unusual as *Jōsēph*; cf. Orm's *Josæp*, and *Iōsēp* (*Iōsēph, Ōsēp*), *Iācōb* (*Ācōb*) in 'Genesis and Exodus.'

NOTE.—Nth. shows no palatalization of OE. *cg, ng* and the voiced guttural stop therefore appears, as in *brig* 'bridge,' *lig* 'lie,' *big* 'buy,' *meng* 'mingle, disturb.' Sth. retains the voiced affricative in verbs, as *seǧǧen* 'say,' *büǧǧen* 'buy.'

GENERAL CHANGES AFFECTING CONSONANTS

112. Certain general changes which affect consonants more or less regularly may best be treated together. The most important of these for Middle English, Vocalization, has already been explained as it affected the voiced spirants *ȝ* (*h*), rarely *v*, and the semivowel *w* in the formation of diphthongs (§ 47). Similarly the voiced spirant *ȝ* after *ĭ, ŭ* was completely vocalized, causing compensatory lengthening when the preceding vowel was not long (§ 75); cf. also the vocalization of *ȝ* in the suffix *iȝ* (§ 103). Attention has also been called to the vocalization of the initial vo.celess spirant *ȝ* (=*y*) in § 107. Other consonants are more stable, but medial *v* is also vocalized in *hāst, hadde*, and in OF. *pōvre* (*pōre*) 'poor.' The final voiceless *f* suffers the same change in the OF. ending *if*, as in *bailȳ* beside *bailif, jolȳ* beside *jolif*. Medial *k* is completely vocalized in *māde* from *makede*, and *d* in *dīst* for *didest*. The ME. ending *we*, from OE. *we*, *ge*, during the period vocalizes to a syllable written *ou* (*ow*), as in *sorow* < earlier *sorȝe* (*sorwe*). Virtual vocalization in breath groups accounts for such forms as *nille* (*ne wille*), *nas* (*ne was*), *nǫt* (*ne wǫt*), § 106. The opposite tendency, Consonantizing, rarely occurs, and then only initially, as *ȝork* (OE. *Eoforwīc*) 'York,' *ȝōw̄*, § 107.

NOTE.—Nth. carries the vocalization of *k*, *v* still further, as in *tā* 'take,' *tān* 'taken,' *mā* 'make,' *hā* 'have,' *gīs* 'gives,' and allied forms.

113. Voicing and Unvoicing. The most noteworthy voicing of consonants in Middle English is the regular shift of initial *f*, *þ*, *s*, to *v*, voiced *þ*, *z* in Sth. English. In Ml. the most common shifting was that of *s* to *z* in unstressed inflexional syllables of late Middle English, as indicated by the occasional spelling with *z*. OE. medial *hh* must also have become voiced before developing into the second element of the diphthongs, § 104. Besides these, voicing is rare, as perhaps of OE. *c* (*k*) to *g* in **bedgen, beggen* if from OE. *bedician*, and OF. *c* to *g* in *sugre* 'sugar,' *graunten* 'grant.' OF. *t* became *d* in *jupardȳ*, *dīamaund* 'diamond,' *waraund* 'warrant.' Unvoicing of *d* to *t* occurs frequently in preterits of weak verbs ending in *ld*, *rd*, *nd*, *vd*, as *bilte* 'built,' *girte* 'girded, girt,' *wente* 'went,' *lefte* 'left,' and sometimes in past participles, as *nempnet* 'named,' *glifnit* 'glanced,' § 93 n. Unvoicing of initial OF. *b* to *p* appears in *putten* (OF. *bouter*), *purse*, *pudding* (OF. *boudin*).

114. Assimilation and Dissimilation. Assimilation is common, as in all periods. Thus *f* becomes *m* before *m*, as in *wimman* (*wumman*) from OE. *wīfman*, *lemman* from OE. *lēofman*; *n* becomes *l* in *elle* < *elne* 'ell,' *mille* < *milne* (OE. *mylen*, *myln*). By partial assimilation the dental nasal *n* becomes the labial nasal *m* before a labial, as *hemp*, OE. *henep*, *brimstǭn* < ON. *brennistān*, *noumpīre* < OF. *nonpere*, *comfort* < OF. *confort*. Assimilation also accounts for the disappearance of *h* in *mirþe* < OE. *myrhþe* 'mirth,' and *c*, *g* before *þ*, *t* or *d* in *lenten* (*leinten*) < *lengten* 'spring, lent,' *strenþe* (*streinþe*) < *strengþe*, *dreinte* < *drencte* 'drenched,' *meinde* < *mengde* 'mingled.' *þ* in the combination *rþf* is assimilated and disappears in *Norfolk*, and *þ* is assimilated to *f* in *Suffolk*, to *s* in *Sussex*, OE. *Norðfolc*, *Sūðfolc*, *Sūð Seaxan*. The stops are more stable, but *t* is assimilated to *s* in *blessen* < OE. *bletsian*, *best* < *betst*, *last* <*latst*, *Essex* < *East Seaxan*; *d* becomes *s* in *gossip*, *gospel* < *Godsib*, *Godspel*, and *n* by back assimilation in *winnow* < *windwian*. Back assimilation after *d*, *t* (*s*) also accounts for *atte* < *at þē*, *and tat* < *and þat*, *is tat* < *is þat*, *wǭst ū* < *wǭst þū* (§ 100). It is virtual assimilation also, when such a form as *such* results from *swilch* through *swuch*. Dissimilation has often been limited to such substitution of *l* for *r* as in OF. *purple* < *purpre*. So ME. *pilgrim* for *pelerin*. But a spirant has also been dissimilated to the corresponding stop, as *þ* to *t* in the combination *f, s, ʒ* (*h*) +*þ*. Examples are *pefte* < OM. *þēfþe* (WS. *þiefþe*), *leste* < OE. *þȳ lǣs þe*, *nostrils* < *nosepirles*, *siʒte* < OE. *gesihþ*, *heiʒte*, OM. *hēhþu* (WS. *hiehþu*), *sleiʒte* < ON. *slǣgþ*, 'sleight,' (cf. § 100). A voiced spirant *þ* after the continuant *r*, especially before *r*, *n* (*en*), has become the voiced stop *d* as in *murdre* < OE. *morþor*, *afŏrden* < OE. *aforðian*, *burdene* beside *burþene* < OE. *byrþen*.

NOTE.—In the dialects such examples as Nth. *s* from OE. *sc* in unstressed words and syllables must be set down to assimilation; cf. § 102, n. 2.

115. Metathesis is occasional in Middle English. Thus *sk* in the verb *asken* (OE. *acsian*, *axtan*) probably springs from a late metathesis of *ks*, since OE. *sc* would have given *sch* (*sh*). Metathesis of *r* appears in *fresch* 'fresh,' *þreschen* 'thresh,' but probably depends on OE. forms in *gras*, *rinnen* (*rennen*) 'run.'

116. Substitution. One consonant seems to be substituted for another, though the cause is not clearly apparent, in *cōūde* < *cōūþe* 'could,' *quod* < *quoþ* (OE. *cwæð*). In the latter *ð* must first have become voiced in the breath group between vowels, and the substitution in both cases may be due to the preference for a stop between continuants. By analogy of forms without grammatical change (Sievers, 'Gr.,' § 233), consonants due to this influence are regularly replaced by their originals, but a few forms remain, as the verb *sēþen–soden* (pt. and pp.), or the past participles used as adjectives, *lǭren* (*lorn*), *forlǭren* (*forlorn*), *cǭren* (*ycǭren*) 'chosen.'

117. Ecthlipsis. The loss of a consonant through assimilation has been illustrated. The most common case of loss under other circumstances is that of final unstressed inflexional *n*, mentioned in § 109. Under a similar influence final *n*, which is not inflexional, is also lost in some cases. Examples are *a*(*n*), *ǭ*(*n*), *morwe*(*n*), *seve*(*n*), *ǭþe*(*n*), *tǭ*(*n*) 'toe.' OF. final *t* also disappears in *plai*(*t*) 'plea,' *peti*(*t*) 'petty.'

118. Addition. A stop consonant is frequently added finally in word or syllable after a continuant, the kind of stop depending upon the preceding, and its voiceless or voiced character on the following sound. Thus the labial *p* intrudes after *m* at the close of the syllable in *nempnen* 'name,' *emptȳ*, *dampnen* 'condemn,' *solempne* 'solemn,' *tempten* 'tempt,' the first two from native, the last from Romance sources. Similarly before a vowel or voiced consonant *b* is intrusive after *m* in *þumbe* (OE. *þūma*), *crumbe* (OE. *cruma*), *schambles* (OE. *sceamol–sceamles*) 'shambles,' *brembel* 'bramble,' *þimbel* 'thimble,' *slumbren* 'slumber.' The voiceless dental *t* is added at the close of the syllable after the dental *s* in *listnen* 'listen,' *glistnen* 'glisten,' *behest* (OE. *behǣs*), *anჳēnst* 'against,' *bitwixte*, and finally after the dental nasal *n* in the French derived *tiraunt*, *fęsaunt* 'pheasant,' *parchment*, *pāgeant*. The voiced *d* is added after *n*, *l* in voiced company, as *þunder*, *kindrẹd*, *expōunden*, *jaundīce*, *alder* (OE. *alra*) 'of all,' and after final *n* in *sōund*, *riband*, no doubt because of more frequent use before a vowel or voiced consonant. Less commonly a liquid *l*, *r* is added after a stop or spirant, as in *principle* (OF. *principe*), *manciple*, *syllable*, *chronikle*, *philosǭphre* (OF. *philosophe*), *provendre* (OF. *provende*). *N* (*ỹ*) has also been added in *niჳtingāle*, *messengēr*, *passengēr*. By incorrect breaking of the breath group an initial *t* has been added in *tǭ* < *þat ǭ*(*n*), *tōþer* < *þat ōþer*, an *n* in *newt* < *an ewt*, *nǭnes* (*nǭnce*) < *þen ǭnes*.

INFLEXIONS

Introductory

119. As compared with Old English, most changes in the inflexion of Middle English words may be summed up under the one head of simplification of forms.   This simplification, too, far from being exceptional in the history of language, has taken place naturally and gradually under the influence of phonetic change and analogy. How far it had gone during the period may be briefly shown. The noun, in general, had come to have but a single form for all plural cases, and usually but two forms for the singular ; the strong adjective and adjective pronoun but one form in the singular, and one in the plural ; the verb also shows a reduction in the number of personal endings and in the number of tense and mode forms.   The former influence, phonetic change, had made dissimilar inflexional endings indistinguishable ; the latter influence, analogy, had caused the substitution of more common forms for the less common, until they had wholly displaced the latter.   Both influences were strong in late Old English, and their strength was no doubt increased by the unusual linguistic conditions after the Conquest.   From this time, for a considerable period, English was less frequently the language of government and of a national literature, while to a less extent it was influenced by the use of Anglo-Norman on English soil and by the gradual introduction of new words from foreign sources.

NOTE.—This is not intended to imply that there was any considerable influence of the foreign language on English inflexions. Not a single inflexional form in the English of common people to-day cannot be accounted for by influences within English itself, and foreign influence should be assumed only beside the native, or when the latter fails to explain the phenomenon. While inflected tense and mode forms were reduced in number as mentioned above, it must be remembered that the compound forms with auxiliaries were increasing.

120. Specifically the most general phonetic change affecting

inflexions from Old to Middle English was the weakening
in unstressed inflexional endings to *e*, as in most other unstres.
syllables (§ 80), and their consequent union with *e* already common
in inflexion. This had followed upon the late OE. weakening of
unstressed inflexional *m* to *n*, as in the dative plural of nouns,
adjectives and disyllabic pronominal forms. Except in the earliest
period also, all words show syncopation of final *e* before words
beginning with a vowel or *h*, and frequent loss of final unstressed
n. These were followed during the period by the total loss of final
unstressed *n* in inflexional endings, and in late Middle English by
final unstressed *e*, whether belonging to the inflexion or the stem.
Owing to these phonetic changes, which obliterated many of the
differences between the different genders—for example the only
difference between weak masculines and feminines in nouns and
adjectives—the distinctions of grammatical gender in nouns,
adjectives, and adjective pronouns was quickly lost. The most
general analogical change was the substitution of the more common
for the less common form. Specifically it may be pointed out that
in the noun the accusative is probably the case-form of greatest
frequency and therefore of greatest influence, and in the adjective
and adjective pronoun, owing to the loss of grammatical gender,
the neuter prevailed over masculine or feminine. In the personal
pronouns, the more frequent use of the dative had almost obliterated
the accusative before the close of Old English. In verbs, the third
person of the indicative was more common than the other present
forms and prevailed in its root over the others (§ 165). In the
strong verbs the four stems tended to become three, either the
preterit singular prevailing over the plural, or the preterit plural
and past participle, when alike, prevailing over the singular preterit.

NOTE.—It is significant of the influence of accusative and oblique case forms
that nouns adopted from Norse appear in the stem form found in the accusative singular, and nouns and adjectives from Old French almost invariably have
the form of the OF. oblique case singular rather than the nominative singular.
Cf. § 136.

121. That grammatical gender had about disappeared in early Middle English is clear from the loss of feminine forms for the adjective and the pronoun (except the personal), and the almost entire loss of inflexional forms based on feminine and neuter originals in Old English. Even when inflexional forms which belong to older feminines or neuters are preserved, as an occasional genitive singular and a plural in *e*, and some neuter plurals without ending, there is little reason to suppose that they were regarded as connected with grammatical gender. They are more probably forms which had not yet fully assumed the common inflexion, based on that of masculine nouns. As an added evidence of the loss of grammatical gender, it may be noted that no foreign-derived noun assumed grammatical gender in English. When grammatical gender disappeared, natural gender took its place, as in Modern English. One of the earliest evidences of this is the assumption of natural gender by such words as *wife*, *maiden*, which were neuter in Old English, and *woman*, *lēfman* 'leman' which were masculine.

NOTE.—As usual, what is said above applies to the Midland dialect. In Nth., the loss of inflexional final *n* had taken place even in OE. (Sievers, 'Gr.,' § 276, anm. 5; § 354, 2, 363, 1, 365, 2), as indeed the inflexions had been simplified in other respects. The result is that Nth. shows greater simplification than Midland even in the earliest period. Sth., on the other hand, was somewhat more conservative than Ml. It retains a greater number of inflexional forms, especially in the earliest period, as also some distinctions of grammatical gender. Even in Sth., however, natural gender begins to prevail over grammatical, as shown by feminine pronouns referring to such words as *wumman*, *lēofman* 'woman, leman.' Further details of dialectal usage will be given under inflexions of nouns, pronouns, &c.

THE NOUN

122. Most Middle English nouns are inflected in one of two ways, according as they do or do not end in weak *e* in the nominative singular. Both these declensions are based on the forms of OE. masculine strong *o* (*a*)-stems, as shown by the plural in *es* (OE. *as*). These OE. masculines were assisted in their

influence, as in genitive singular, by similar neuter stems, which
did not differ in inflexion except in the nominative-accusative plural.
The normal endings of these two declensions are as follows:

		I.	II.
Singular,	N. A. V.	—	*e*
	G.	*es (s)*	*es*
	D.	— *(e)*	*e*
Plural,	N. A. G. D.	*es (s)*	*es*

123. Instead of *es, is (ys)* also occurs occasionally, especially in
Northern. Forms in parentheses are less common. In addition,
there are occasional forms, based on the retention of older inflexional
endings, which are so uncommon as not to be considered normal
in any sense. Such are plurals without ending, based on the OE.
neuter plural of long stems, and those in *en (e)*, based on the
OE. weak declension. The first usually belong to declension I,
the second to declension II, and will be treated under those heads
(§§ 127, 132).

NOTE 1.—Early Midland, as represented in the 'Chronicle' and Orm, differs
mainly in the somewhat more common retention of older forms, as of dative
singular in *e*, and of plural forms without ending or with *en (e)*. In the
selection from the 'Chronicle,' out of the first twenty-one plurals of different
words, sixteen have *es (s)*, three have no ending, one has *en*, and one *e*. This
does not include two umlaut plurals, which of course belong under § 133.

NOTE 2.—In Nth. of the earliest times from which a literature is preserved,
these two declensions have largely become one, owing to the loss of final *e*, the
change being completed by the middle of the fourteenth century. Nth. also
commonly shows syncopation of *e* in the plural, less commonly in the genitive
singular. A Nth. genitive without ending, especially in proper names, sometimes occurs. Sth., on the other hand, preserves many plurals in *en*, based on
the OE. *an* of weak nouns, while there are some other peculiarities, as follows.
The dative singular of declension I more commonly preserves *e*, and the
genitive plural sometimes has forms in *e* or *ene*. Nouns of declension II,
besides having *en* in N. A. D., have *en (ene)* in the genitive plural. Texts
differ considerably in these respects, and plurals in *en* are gradually replaced
by *es (s)* forms. For instance, out of thirteen different plurals in the selection
from the 'Poema Morale,' ten end in *es*, two in *en*, one in *e*. In the 'Juliana'
selection, out of the first twenty different plurals, eleven have *es (s)*, eight *en*,

one no ending. In the selection from 'Robert of Gloucester,' out of the first twenty-four plurals, nineteen have *es* (*e*), three *en*, and one no ending.

124. The First declension includes nouns ending in a consonant or in any vowel except unstressed *e*. It may be illustrated by *dōm* 'doom,' *dai* 'day,' *trē* (*trew*) 'tree,' *tǭken*, as follows:

SINGULAR

N. A. V.	*dōm*	*daȝ, dai*	*trē* (*trew*)	*tǭken*
G.	*dōmes*	*daȝes, daies*	*trees, trewes*	*tǭknes*
D.	*dōm*[*e*]	*daȝ*[*e*], *dai*[*e*]	*trē, trewe*	*tǭken* (*tǭkne*)

PLURAL

N. A. G. D.	*dōmes*	*daies* (*dawes*)	*trees, trewes*	*tǭknes* (*tǭkenes*)

125. To this declension belong most OE. *o* (*a*)-stems and long *wo*-stems; long masculine and neuter *i*- and long masculine *u*-stems, which had in Old English assumed the inflexion of *o*-stems in the main; some OE. *ā*-stems which had not assumed, from the accusative and other oblique cases, inorganic *e* in the nominative; and some anomalous nouns, as those having mutation, which had become regular by the loss of their anomalous inflexion. The few OE. *ā*-stems which did not assume inorganic *e* may have become masculine or neuter in Old English, as ME. *rērd* (*reord*) 'speech,' beside *rērde* (*reorde*). Special mention should be made of OE. feminine long *i*- and long *u*-stems, which had no inflexional final *e* in the accusative singular and show some variation between declensions I and II in Middle English. Their appearance without final *e* may be due to the influence of the accusative singular, possibly to change of gender and resulting change of inflexion, as in *wiȝt* 'creature,' *flōr* 'floor,' *werld*, *hand* (*hǫnd*). Those with final *e* may have assumed it in Old English (cf. Sievers, 'Gr.,' § 269, anm. 1), as *nēde*. Here belong OE. feminine long stems ending in a vowel, as *sē̜* 'sea,' *tǭ* 'toe,' *bē* 'bee,' *slǭ* 'sloe,' whether originally strong or weak. Such words, as all others ending in a long vowel, assume *s* only in gen. sing. and the plural.

126. It is impossible in a single table, except a very complex one, to represent all variations due to ME. orthography or other causes. The most prominent may be briefly mentioned. The ending of the genitive singular, as of the plural, is sometimes *is* (*ys*). Loss of *e* in the dative singular, common even in early ME., is increasingly frequent until that case becomes like the nominative-accusative, as in Modern English. In certain expressions, however, an OE. dative singular in *e* still survives. Examples are *on līve* (< *līf*) 'alive,' *tō bedde, tō wedde* 'for a pledge,' *for fēre* 'for fear.' Disyllabic stems in *el, en, er* often show syncopation of the root *e* when assuming an inflexional ending, as in *tōken* above [1]. Even when the spelling shows retention of the stem vowel, syncopation is usually to be assumed for the spoken form. Syncopation, often loss of inflexional *e*, occurs in polysyllables accented on the first syllable, as *pilgrimes, rivēres* (pronounced as if spelled *pilgrims, rivērs*) beside *humours, pilōurs* (*pelēr*) 'robbers.' The orthographic variations of words with new diphthongs, as *daȝ* (*dai*), are numerous, but will be clear by reference to the phonology. Thus 'Genesis and Exodus' has *dai* (*dei*), *dages* (*daiges, dais*) 'day, day's, dayes,' and a plural *dawes* is also found, based on the development of OE. *ag* to *aw* (§ 55). The latter has usually been displaced by a plural based on the singular, where OE. *æg* became ME. *aȝ* (*ai*). Occasionally, however, a new singular *daw* develops from the plural *dawes*. Stems ending in *f, þ, s* show voicing of these consonants before a vocalic ending, as in genitive (sometimes dative) singular and the plural. Only in case of *f* to *v*, however, is the voicing indicated orthographically.

127. Beyond those noted above, there are but few exceptions to the regularity of the common plural form. The most important is a plural without ending in the case of certain OE. neuters, or in words that have associated themselves with them. Examples are *folk, þing* 'thing,' *gēr* 'years,' *swīn* 'swine,' *hors* 'horses,' *shēp*

---

[1] Cf. Sievers, 'Gr.,' § 244.

'sheep,' *dēr* 'deer,' *nēt* 'neat cattle,' *wēpen* 'weapons.' Most of these gradually adopted the usual *es* (*s*) ending, though a few remain uninflected in the plural to modern times. Occasionally words which were not OE. neuters, as *fugel, fish* 'fowl, fish,' are uninflected in the plural when used in a collective sense, as in Modern English. Variation in the plural of the root finals *f, þ, s* has been noticed in the preceding paragraph.

128. Foreign derived words were adopted in the stem form or that of the accusative singular or oblique case when that differs from the stem. Thus ON. words do not appear with the nominative inflexional *r*, but with the accusative singular as *od* 'point,' *bol* (*bōle*) 'tree-trunk,' *bark, garþ* 'yard,' *Orm*, ON. *oddr, bolr, bǫrkr, garðr, Ormr.* Similarly, where the OF. oblique case singular differs from the nominative, the former is regularly adopted, as in OF. *degrē, castel* (*chastel*), *dōl* (*dēl*) 'grief' < OF. *degrez, castels* (*chastels*), *duelz.* The apparent exceptions, so far as OF. words are concerned, probably represent differences in OF. usage as *tempest, poverte,* beside *tempestē, povertē.* Only in *armes* 'arms' was an OF. plural directly borrowed, and this the more easily because it agreed exactly with ME. plurals in *es.* Borrowed words generally assume the native inflexion in its entirety. Thus ON., OF. words regularly assume native endings, as the gen. and pl. *es* (*s*), though OF. nouns ending in *s* often remain uninflected as *cas* 'case,' *pas* 'pace, pass,' and proper names as *Ēnēas, Prīamus, Pērs* 'Pierce.' Occasionally other borrowed words, especially Biblical names, remain uninflected in the genitive singular, as *Adam soule, Dāvid lǫnd,* following mediæval Latin usage.

NOTE 1.—In early Midland some further traces of inflexion are found, as in the nom.-acc. pl. in *as* in the 'Chronicle' occasionally, and a gen. pl. in *e*, a dat. in *e* (*on*) rarely ; cf. *wintre*, OE. *wintra* 'winters.' So Orm has a similar genitive in such expressions as *allre kinge king* 'king of all kings,' *dēofle follc* 'folk of devils.'

NOTE 2.—As already indicated (§ 123, n. 2), Sth. is much more conservative in inflexions than Midland or Nth., and retains many older forms, as *e*, in the dat. sg., *e, ene* (*en*) in gen. pl., *en* in dat. pl. Many nouns, also, which belong to declension I in Ml., have assumed *en* in the plural in Sth., and hence belong to declension II. This is especially true of OE. short stem neuters and *ā*-stems.

129. The Second declension includes all nouns with final unstressed *e* in the nominative-accusative singular, and may be illustrated by *ēnde* (*ende*) 'end,' *helpe* 'help,' *soule* 'soul,' *þewe* ' habit, custom,' as follows :

Singular, N. A. V.	*ēnde*	*helpe*	*soule*	*þewe* (*þeuwe*)
G.	*ēndes*	*helpes*	*soules*	*þewes*
D.	*ēnde*	*helpe*	*soule*	*þewe*

Plural, N. A. G. D.	*ēndes*	*helpes*	*soules*	*þewes*

130. Here belong most OE. *jo* and short *wo*-stems; the majority of *ā* (*jā*, *wā*)-stems ; short and many long feminine *i*-stems ; short *u*-stems ; the great body of weak nouns, which had early lost final *n* ; and such others as had assumed inorganic *e* in the nominative singular. OE. feminines (sometimes masculines) ending in *g* (*h*), by influence of the oblique cases, assume *ȝe*, later *we*, as *sorȝe* (*sorwe*) 'sorrow,' *furȝe* (*furwe*) ' furrow,' *arwe* ' arrow,' while side by side a form with final *ȝ* (*h*) may exist, as *furȝ* (*furh*). OE. nouns ending in *f* assumed *ve* of the oblique cases, as *lēve* ' permission,' *glōve* ' glove.' OE. neuter *wo*-stems had no *w* in the nom.-acc. sg. or pl. and so do not assume it in Middle English, as *mēle* 'meal,' *smēre* ' ointment,' *tēre* ' tar.' OE. short feminine *wa*-stems assume *we* from the oblique cases, as *schadwe* ' shadow,' *sinwe* ' sinew,' and long stems show double forms sometimes, as *mēde, mēdwe* ' mead, meadow,' corresponding to forms with or without *w* in Old English. ME. *schāde* is possibly from OE. *scead* neut., and not *sceadu* the *wā*-stem. OE. short neuters with *e* from *u* in nom.-acc. pl. sometimes assumed *e* in the singular, as *blāde* ' blade,' *dāle, bēde* ' prayer,' *hōle* ' hole,' *dōre* ' door,' *ȝōke* ' yoke,' and a few masculines which may have become feminines, as *sēle* (OE. *seolh*) ' seal.' ME. *mēre* (*mare*) 'mare' is from OM. *mere* (WS. *miere*), not OE. *mearh*, masc. OE. masculines ending in *cg* acquired inorganic *e*, perhaps under the influence of the greater number of such words which were feminine. Some original weak nouns have a plural in *en*, but, for the Midland dialect, are not sufficiently numerous to warrant treatment in a separate declension. Even when they have *en* plurals, *es* plurals are often found side by side with them.

131. A so-called genitive singular in *e* rarely occurs, but such forms may be better explained as essentially compounds. Examples are *helle pīne* 'hell punishment,' *chirche dure* 'church door,' *rōde cross* 'rood-cross.' All such words have originally, or have assumed, inorganic *e* in the nominative, so that the form is merely the uninflected one which so commonly enters into compounds, whether marked by a sign of union or not. In the dative singular, *n* is rarely added, more especially in rimes with forms regularly ending in *n*. As these occur mainly in south-east Midland texts of the earliest time, they may be due to the influence of the Sth. dialect, in which this peculiarity is more common (see Note 2 below), or they may be connected with the influence of the plural *en* forms.

132. The most important peculiarity of the plural is the retention of *en* (*n*) forms from the OE. weak declension, and the extension of this occasionally to nouns not originally weak. The whole number of such nouns is relatively small, and they decrease throughout the ME. period, until the only relics left in MnE. are *oxen*, rarely *eyen* in poetry, and *brethren, children, kine*, to which this ending has been extended. Examples in 'Gen. and Ex.' are *wunnen* 'customs,' *fēren* 'companions'; in 'Bestiary,' *willen* 'wishes,' *ēgen* 'eyes.' 'Gen. and Ex.' also shows the extension of this *en* to OE. strong nouns, as *cōlen* 'coals,' *treen* (*trēn*) beside *trees* 'trees,' *mēten* 'meats,' *stēden* 'places,' *sunen* beside *sunes* 'sons.' Owing to its early date and its south-east Midland dialect, the number of such forms in this poem is greater than in others, especially in rime, where the usage can hardly be relied on as showing the forms of ordinary speech. More rarely still, plurals in *e* are found, as in 'Gen. and Ex.' *elne* 'ells,' *senwe* 'sinews,' *fēre* 'companions.'

Note 1.—In early Midland a gen. sg. in *e* is occasional, as in Orm's *sāwle* 'soul's,' *frōfre* 'comfort's,' *asse* 'ass's,' *wicche* 'witch's.' Probably in all these cases the intrusion of *s* was resisted by the close connexion with the following noun. Rarely also, gen. plurals in *e* are also found, as Orm's *sāwle* 'souls',' *shaffte* 'creatures''; compare the retention of *en* in true compounds, as *Sunenn-daȝȝ* 'Sunday,' *uhhtennsang* 'early morning song.' Plurals in *en* are also somewhat more common in this period, as *halechen* 'saints' in the 'Chronicle,' *wawenn* 'walls,' *hallghenn* 'saints,' *ēȝhne (ehne, ehhne)* 'eyes' in 'Ormulum.' Orm also has occasional *e* plurals, as *hallfe* 'halves,' *shaffte* 'creatures.'

Note 2.—Nth. is even more radical than Midland in giving up the old weak plurals in *en*, but a few still appear in 'Cursor Mundi,' as *oxen, eien* 'eyes,' *ēren* beside *ēres* 'ears.' Occasionally no inflexion occurs, as in *heven blis, heven king*, which are essentially compounds. In other respects Nth. does not differ markedly from Ml. except as noted in § 123, n. 2. Sth. retains many more relics of the OE. declension, as a gen. sg. in *e*, and a dat. in *en* in case of many OE. weak nouns. Indeed *en* sometimes intrudes itself into the singular nominative-accusative forms. In the plural, forms in *en, e*, rarely *a*, are especially common in the earliest period, as also genitives in *ene (en), e*, and datives in *en*. All such forms gradually grow less frequent, and are almost entirely replaced in late Sth. by regular forms.

ANOMALOUS NOUNS

133. A few nouns belonging to minor declensions in Old English show some peculiarities of inflexion. They include nouns with mutation as the distinctive feature, nouns of relationship, and those with original stems in *nd, os (es)*. Those of the first subclass are declined as follows :

Singular,	N. A.	*fōt*	*man*	
	G.	*fōtes*	*mannes*	
	D.	*fōt(e)*	*man, manne*	
Plural,	N. A. D.	*fēt*	*men*	
	G.	*fētes (fōte)*	*mennes (manne)*	

134. Few examples of these mutation nouns are found in Middle English, since most of them had already lost all traces of mutation and had ranged themselves with the regular classes. It is difficult therefore to be certain of all forms, but there is a clear correspondence in the singular with the nouns of declension I. In the

piural, the distinguishing feature is a nominative-accusative-dative
with mutation but no ending. For the genitive plural, Orm has
menness once, beside *manne.* An old genitive plural *fōte* occurs
after a numeral, as *twel fōte* 'twelve feet' (dialectally to-day 'twelve
foot'), 'Havelok,' 1054. Other nouns having mutation plurals are
gōs 'goose,' *mūs* 'mouse,' *lūs* 'louse,' *kū* (*cōw̄*) the plural of which,
kȳn 'kine,' has assumed *n* by analogy of *en* forms. A few nouns
have uninflected plurals without mutation, as *mōneþ* (OE. pl. *mōneð*)
in *twelve monthe* 'twelvemonth,' *niht* in such expressions as *seven
niht* 'seven nights, sennight.' ME. *brēch*, 'breech, breeches,'
preserves the mutation plural of OE. *brōc*, and becomes singular.

NOTE 1.—Early Midland has a few other mutation nouns, as Orm's *gāt*
'goat,' *gǣt* 'goats,' an old feminine.

NOTE 2.—Nth. does not differ from Midland, except in greater regularity of
forms. Thus *kū* (*kōu*) 'cow,' has the regular mutation plural *kī* (*kȳ*) without
the *n* of Ml. and Sth. usage. Sth. has a greater variety of forms, as gen. pl.
monne, monnene (*en*), dat. *monnen.* So also *fōten* as gen. pl., and *brēchen*
(*brēches*) a pl. of *brēch* 'trousers.'

135. The nouns of relationship are declined as follows:

Singular, N.A.V.   *fader* 'father'   *brōþer* 'brother'
          G.   *fader, fadres*   *brōþer, brōþres*
          D.   *fader*   *brōþer*

Plural, N.A.G.D. *fadres*   *brēþren, brēþere*

The genitive singular without ending persists through the ME.
period, though the form in *es* also occurs from the earliest time.
The older mutated dative has entirely disappeared. Like these
nouns are declined *mōder, dohter* (*doȝter, douȝter*) 'daughter,' *sister,*
the last from Norse *syster* and the regular Midland form.

NOTE 1.—Early Midland, as Orm, has uninflected forms more commonly,
with the mutated form of *brēþre* in plural nom., acc., and gen. Orm also uses
susstress 'sisters,' from the OE. rather than the Norse form of the word.

NOTE 2.—Nth. prefers the uninflected form of the gen. sg., and the plural in
es (*s*) except for *brōþer* which has pl. *brēþer* for all cases. The mutated
dehteres occurs sometimes, beside the more common *dohteres* 'daughters.' Sth.
has both inflected and uninflected gen. sg., but prefers *en* plurals in the earlier

period, as *brōþeren* (*brēþeren*), *dohtren*, *sustren*. The native English *suster* from OE. *sweoster* (*swuster*), rather than the Norse form of the word, is common in Sth. as in Chaucer.

136. Here may be mentioned the remnants of the OE. *os, es* stems, *chīld, lamb*, the only words that show peculiar forms. The natural developments of the OE. plurals, *chīldru, lambru*, were *chīldre, lambre*, and these are often found in Midland. Later they both assumed the *en* ending, first in Sth., later in Midland, though at the same time *lamb* acquired a regular plural *lambes*. In the North *childre* (*childer*) remained the plural form, and *lambre* gave place entirely to *lambes* (*lambis*). In Sth. another word of this class, *calf*, followed *chīld* in adding *en*(*n*) to the older plural in *re*, as *calveren* 'calves.'

137. Of stems in *nd*, only *frĕnd, fĕnd* 'friend, fiend' preserve peculiarities, and these only in the earlier part of the period. In that period uninflected plural forms are found, as *frĕnd, fĕnd* 'friends, fiends.' These were soon displaced by the regular *frĕndes, fĕndes*. For the quantity of *frend*, see § 79, n.

THE ADJECTIVE

138. The adjective has lost all trace of its OE. inflexion except for an ending *e*, which is added to those not originally ending in a vowel, to form the plural, the weak form after a demonstrative or possessive pronoun, or rarely a dative case. So far as this trace of the older inflexion is found, adjectives in Middle English are declined in one of two ways, as they do or do not end in unstressed *e*. The weak form of the adjective is used after a possessive or demonstrative pronoun, including the definite article, and in the vocative. In either case, if the adjective follows the noun without the repetition of the demonstrative (definite article), it remains uninflected.

I. **Strong**

Singular	*wīs*	*manī*	*lītel*	*frē*
Plural	*wīse*	*manī* (*manīȝe, manīe*)	*lītel* (*lītle*)	*frē*

Weak, Sg. and Pl.

wīse   manī (manīe)   lītel   frē

II. Strong and Weak

Singular *grēne*
Plural   *grēne*

139. To declension I belong *o* (*a*)-stems, including polysyllables
and short *jo*-stems, except a few which have assumed inorganic *e*;
long *wo*-stems with vowel preceding *w*; and long *u*-stems which
had gone over to the *o*-stems in OE. times. Monosyllables ending
in a vowel, and usually polysyllables, are uninflected. The
participle is also regularly uninflected, as often in Old English.
Relics of older inflexion appear in *aller* (*aldre*), OM. *alra* (WS.
ealra) 'of all,' both alone and in compounds as *alderbest* (*alþerbest*);
and in occasional dative phrases, as *of nȳne gōde, of harde grāce*.
In the latter part of the period the adjective tends to lose all trace
of inflexion, as shown by poëtry, especially when far removed from
the noun. This is but preliminary to the total loss of final *e* in
adjectives as in other words. Adjectives belonging to declension II
are virtually inflexionless. Here belong OE. long *jo*-stems; short
wo-stems; *i* and *u*-stems, except such as had taken the inflexion of
OE. *o*-stems. Short *wo*-stems, ending in *u* with *w* in oblique case
forms, usually end in *we* in Middle English, as *calwe* 'callow,' *falwe*
'fallow,' *salwe* 'sallow,' *ȝelwe* 'yellow,' but sometimes forms ending
in *e* alone are also found, as *ȝāre* beside *ȝarwe* 'ready' (Shake-
speare's *yare*), *nāre* beside *narwe* 'narrow.' OE. adjectives ending
in palatal *h* (*g*) lose the final consonant as a rule, those with
guttural *h* (*g*) develop forms in *ȝe* (*we*) from the oblique cases, as
noh–nowe 'enough,' *woh* (*wouȝh*)–*wowe* 'bad,' *sorful–soruful* 'sorrowful,' *walwe* (OM. *walg*, WS. *wealg*) 'sickly,' *arh*(*ȝ*)–*arwe*
'cowardly.' OE. adjectives ending in *f* regularly change *f* to *v*
before *e*.

140. Most borrowed words fall into the same classes as the corresponding native adjectives and are similarly inflected. Thus OF. adjectives not ending in a vowel assume the plural and weak *e*, as do native words, but OF. polysyllables which have acquired the Teutonic accent on the first syllable remain uninflected. The OF. *seint* often appears as *seinte*, but not exclusively before feminines. It is probable that both forms were adopted without regard to the OF. distinction of gender, though *seinte* would more naturally occur with certain feminines, as *Seinte Mārīe* (116, 15); but cf. *Seint Mārīe* (118, 2), *Seinte Powel* (200, 19). A few OF. adjectives with OF. *s* plurals are found, as in *plāces delitābles* 'delectable places,' *goodes temporelles* 'temporal goods,' but these are mainly in prose translated pieces, rarely poetry and that of the more learned poets, so that they can hardly have been living forms among the people.

NOTE 1.—Early Midland shows a somewhat fuller retention of older forms, though in the 'Chronicle' from the year 1132 there is no variation from what is given above.

NOTE. 2.—In Nth. the two declensions tend to become one by the loss of final unstressed *e*, as in nouns. The plural *e* of declension I has generally disappeared, and many adjectives ending in unstressed *e* have lost this ending, and have fallen in with those without *e*. Even the ending *e* of weak forms is not regularly preserved after a demonstrative. In early Sth. some further traces of OE. inflexions are still found, as a genitive singular in *es*, especially when the adjective stands without a substantive, but also in some other cases as *summes weies* 'some ways' in the 'Juliana' selection. So *bōþen* 'both,' with *en*, but such forms are rare. The distinction between strong and weak forms of adjectives not ending in unstressed *e* is generally preserved, as in declension I above.

COMPARISON

141. The adjective is compared by the addition of the endings *re* (later *er*) for comparative, *est* for superlative, from the OE. endings *ra*, *ost* (*est*) by regular vowel changes. At the same time comparison by use of the adverbs *mōre*, *mōst* begins to be used, especially with polysyllables. Long root syllables show shortening in comparative and superlative, in accordance with § 76, as *grēt–gretter*, *swēte–swetter*, but analogy of the positive often restores the long vowel. Adjectives from Old French are compared like native words, with a tendency to use the adverbial comparison with polysyllables. As to inflexion, comparatives could not assume *e* after *re*, and did not usually after the later *er*; superlatives like *best*, *mǭst*, *first* were regularly inflected, as well as those with secondary stress upon the superlative ending, for example *sēmlīest*, but most superlatives remain uninflected.

142. As in Old English, a few adjectives are irregular in comparison. Thus *ǭld*, *lǭng*, *strǭng* still retain mutated comparatives, as *elder–eldest*, *lenger–lengest* 'longer–longest,' *strenger–strengest* 'strong–strongest.' Some adjectives have forms of comparison with different roots from the positive, as *gōd* 'good,' *bettre (betre)–best*; *ivil (ēvil)*, *werse (worse, wurse)–werst (worst, wurst)*; the corresponding Norse forms are also found, as *ille–werre*, the former of which has remained to Modern English; *michel (mikel, muchel, much)*, *mōre (mǭ)–mǭst (mēst)*; *lītel (līte)*, *lesse (lasse)–lēst* 'least.' Forms of comparison based on adverbs, sometimes prepositions, are *fer* 'far,'–*ferre (ferrer)* 'farther,' dialectal *farer–ferrest* 'farthest'; *fōre*, *first*; *ǭver*, *ǭverest*; *utter*, *utterest*; *upper*, *uppest*. In *nerre* 'nearer,' *ferrest* 'furthest,' new forms of comparison have been based on older comparatives. The OE. superlative suffix *mǣst* appears as *mēst*, *mast* and *mǭst*, the latter finally prevailing.

NUMERALS

143. Most numerals are adjectives in function, though often uninflected. The older use as nouns with a following genitive disappeared entirely, except in sporadic cases, as *twel fōte* 'twelve feet' ('Havelok,' 1054), where the expression is a mere survival without syntactical significance for Middle English. The cardinal numerals are as follows, though no attempt is made to give every variant even of Midland: *ǭn (ǭ)* 'one'; *twō (tweyne, tweye)* 'two, twain'; *þrē (thrē)* 'three'; *foure (fowre)* 'four'; *fīf (fȳve)* 'five';

sex (*sexe, sixe*) 'six'; *seven* (*sevene, seve*) 'seven'; *eȝte* (*eghte, eighte*) 'eight'; *niȝen* (*nīne*) 'nine'; *tēn*; *enleven* (*elevene, eleve*) 'eleven'; *twelf* (*twelve*); *þrettēne* (*þrittēne*) 'thirteen'; *fourtēne*; *fiftēne* (*fyftēne*); *sextēne* (*sixtēne*); *seventēne*; *eȝtēne* (*eghtēne, eightēne*); *niȝentēne* (*nīnetēne*); *twentī* (*twentȳ*); *þrittī*; *fourtī*; *hundred*; *þousen* (*þousende*) 'thousand.' The ON. form *hundreþ* is found beside the English *hundred,* and from OF. the new numeral *miliūn* (*milliōun*) 'million' was adopted. Counting by the score (ON. *skor* ME. *skǫre*) is of Norse origin, as the word itself implies by its form.

144. The numeral *ǭn* 'one' sometimes has the old genitive *ǭnes* in early texts, and a plural of the same form in the expression *for þē nǭnes* 'for the nonce.' Plurals of the adjective form, *ǭne, nǭne, alǭne, nǭ ǭnes,* also occur rarely. Such forms as *fīve, sixe, twelve* usually occur when standing alone or after a substantive, as well as in the plural. Two or three Old French numerals are rarely found, as *cinq, sis* 'five, six' in Chaucer. In early Midland the weakened forms of the first numeral, *an* (*a*), are common as an indefinite article, and these are found throughout the period as in Modern English. Owing to the tendency to drop inflexional *n* in unstressed syllables such forms as *seve* 'seven,' *eleve* 'eleven' result.

NOTE I.—Early Midland has other inflexional forms of the first and second numerals, as Orm's *āness* 'one's,' *ēnne,* acc. masc.

NOTE 2.—Nth. forms naturally differ in phonology, as *ān* (*ā*), *twā, aht* (*aght*) 'eight,' but these differences will be easily understood. Nth. has lost all forms of inflexion for the numerals, except as in other adjectives; see § 138. Nth. also has some Norse forms which are less common in Midland, as *twin, þrin, hundreþ* 'two, three, hundred.' Sth., especially early Sth., preserves the gen. masc. and fem. *ǭnes, anre* (*āre*), the latter also as dat. fem.; the acc. masc. and fem. as *anne, ane.* Sth. also has a gen. and dat. pl. of OE. *twēgen,* 'two,' as *tweire, twam.* These, however, soon give place to regular forms.

145. The ordinal numerals are *firste* (*forme, firme*), *ōþer* and later *secōunde, þridde* (*þirde*), *ferþe* (*fourþe*), *fifte, sexte* (*sixte*), *ṣeveþe* (*sevende, sevenþe*), *eȝteþe* (*eȝtende, eighteþe*), *niȝeþe* (*niȝende,* *nīnþe*), *tēʒþe* (*tigþe, tēnde, tēnþe*), *endlefte* (*ellefte, ellevend, elevenþe*), *twelfte, þretēþe* (*þretēnde, þretēnþe*), &c. Ordinals with *ende*, as *sevende*, are sometimes Mercian in origin, sometimes perhaps Norse. Old English *ōþer* is finally displaced by *secōunde* from Old French, though remaining pronominal as always. The ordinals regularly end in *e*, owing to their position as weak adjectives after *þē* ' the.'

NOTE.—In Nth. the forms with *ende* (*end, and, ind*) prevail, while in Sth. these are rare except in Kentish.

146. Multiplicatives are formed with the suffix *fǭld*, OMerc. *fāld* (WS. *feald*), as *ǭnfǭld* ' onefold.' The multiplicative idea, however, is expressed in various other ways, as by words meaning ' times ' and by various adverbs. Distributives are *ǭn and ǭn* ' one and (by) one,' *twō and twō*, &c. Adverbs also, as *betwēn*, frequently express a distributive idea.

THE PRONOUNS

147. As to function, pronouns are either substantive, adjective, or both, and this distinction is important in understanding their inflexions in Middle English. Those that are wholly or mainly adjective in function, as possessives, demonstratives, and most indefinites, followed adjectives in their simplification to two forms, one for the singular and one for the plural. Those pronouns that are wholly or mainly substantive in function, as the personal, interrogative, and inflected relative, preserve, as their peculiar feature, an accusative-dative, generally based on an original dative and differing in form from the nominative. But the genitives of the personal pronouns have largely lost any substantive function, as of a substantive in oblique case, and their adjective functions are supplied by the possessives based upon them, together with new third personal possessives from the genitives of the so-called pronoun of the third person. The latter, therefore, though given in the inflexion, are enclosed in parentheses to indicate their more restricted use.

148. The Personal Pronouns proper are inflected as follows :—

	FIRST		SECOND	
	Sing.	Plur.	Sing.	Plur.
N.	*Ic* (*Ik, Ich*) *Ī*	*wĕ*	*þŭ* (*þōu, thōu*)	*ȝĕ* (*yĕ*)
G.	(*mȳn*)	(*ŭre, ōure*)	(*þin*)	(*ȝure, ȝōure, yōure*)
D. A.	*me*	*ŭs* (*ōus*)	*þĕ* (*thee*)	*ȝŭw* (*ȝōu, yōu*)

149. It is scarcely necessary to give all orthographic variations of these and the other personal pronouns. *Ic* (*Ik*), *Ī*, though without capitalization in the manuscripts, are the normal Midland forms, as also *ȝŭre, ȝŭw* (*yōure, yōu*) with initial *ȝ* (*y*) by analogy of *ȝĕ* (*yĕ*), and a vowel due to shifting of accent from the first element of the diphthong in OE. *ēower, ēow*, owing to constant use in unstressed position in the sentence. The form *þŭ*, owing to similar unstressed position and to assimilation, often becomes *tŭ* (*ŭ, ōu*) when immediately following a verb ending in *t*, as *shalt tŭ* (*ŭ, ōu*) for 'shalt thou.' For *tē* from *þē*, see §§ 100, 114. Dual forms are rarely found in the earliest texts, as *wit-unc, gunker–gunc* 'we two,' 'you two,' in 'Genesis and Exodus'; but these so soon disappear as to be quite irregular, and not deserving of a place in inflexion.

NOTE 1.—Early Midland does not differ materially. For *ȝure, ȝuw*, the earliest 'Chronicle' has *iūre*, suggesting the older Northumbrian form *iurre* (Sievers, 'Gr.,' § 332, anm. 4). Orm also has *ȝure, ȝuw*, showing the early addition of initial *y*.

NOTE 2.—Nth. does not differ from Midland. In Sth. *Ich* is the normal form for the first person. This is sometimes united with a following *wulle* (*wŏlle*) 'will,' as *ichulle* (*ichŏlle*) 'I will,' though each word is preserved separate in this book. Sth. also preserves genitive and accusative forms of the second personal pronoun without initial *y*, as *ēower* (*ōwer*) 'your,' *ēow* (*ōw, ōu*) 'you.' Besides, dual forms, which are almost unknown in Midland, are occasionally found.

150. The so-called third personal pronoun has the following forms:—

SINGULAR

Masc.		Neut.	Fem.
N. *hĕ̆*		*hit, it*	*schĕ̆, shĕ̆ (shŏ̆), hēo (hĕ̆, hŏ̆)*
G.	(*his*)		(*hire, hir, here, her*)
D.		*him*	*hire (hir), here (her)*
A. *him* [*hin*]		*hit, it*	*hire (hir)*

PLURAL

N.	*hĭ (hy̆, hĕ̆), þei (þey, þai, þay)*
G.	(*here, hire, þeire, þeir, þair*)
D.A.	*hem, þem (þeim, þaim)*

151. The genitives of the third personal pronoun, under the influence of possessives formed from the same case of the first and second personal pronouns, became possessives also, as shown by their inflexion in Middle English. The old masculine accusative singular, *hine* (*hin*), occurs rarely in early texts, as 'Genesis and Exodus'; but with this exception the masculine and neuter forms are quite regular. Those of the feminine singular nominative, on the other hand, are numerous, as they are based on OE. *hēo* or on the OE. demonstrative *sēo*, from which the prevailing form develops. The former appear as *gĕ̆* (*ghĕ̆*) in 'Gen. and Ex.,' *gĕ̄* in 'Best.,' *hĕ̆o* (*hĕ̆*) in 'Flor. and Blanch.,' *hyē* (*hĕ̆*) in 'Adam and Eve.' Forms based on the latter appear first in the 'Chronicle' as *scæ̆, sgĕ̆* (*=syĕ̆*), *schĕ̆* in 'Gen. and Ex.,' *schĕ̄* (*shĕ̆, schēo, shŏ̆*) in other Midland texts until, about 1300, they prevail over the others. The earliest plurals are based on the OE. plurals *hĭ–here–hem*. The prototype of the Modern English *they*, based on the Norse demonstrative which is first found in Orm, occurs once as *þei* in 'Gen. and Ex.' In general, however, it is not until the beginning of the fourteenth century that the nominative *þei* (*þai, they*) becomes common, and not until late ME. that all forms with initial *th* (*þ*) prevail. Chaucer, as representative of London English, has *thei* (*they*), but *here–hem*. In some early texts, as 'Gen. and Ex.' *hit* (*it*) is plural as well as singular, and another plural *his* (*is, es*), perhaps based on the singular masculine or from Sth., is also found.

152. As in Old English, the personal pronouns are used reflexively, both alone and in combination with *self*. But such forms as *mīself*, *þȳself*, based on weak forms of the dative-accusative, or possibly combinations of the possessives and *self* used substantively, occur as early as the fourteenth century, and in Sth. a century earlier.

Note 1.—In early Midland the early use of *scǣ* 'she,' in the 'Chronicle,' and *þeȝȝ* (*þeȝȝre*), *þeȝȝm* 'they-their-them,' in Orm are the most important variations.

Note 2.—Nth. regularly has the fem. *schǒ* (*scǒ*), acc. *hir*, as also the plural forms with *þ, þai* (*þei*), *þair* (*þeir*), *þaim* (*þaime, þām, þāmę*), but with an occasional *ham* 'them.' Sth. has preserved the masc. acc. *hine* beside the dat. *him*, and the fem. *hēo* (*hǎ, hě, hǐ, hue*). Variants for masc. *hě* are also *hǎ* (*ǎ*). The plural forms are based on those of OE., as nom. acc. *hǐ* (*hii, hue, hēo*), *here* (*hire, heore, hueore, hor*), *heom* (*ham, huem, hem, hom*). Sth. also has a plural *hise* (*is*) 'them,' beside *hǐ*, &c. As reflexives, Nth. has occasional forms with the genitive instead of the dative-accusative, as *yōurself, þairself*, which seem to be unknown in Sth.

153. The Possessive Pronouns are *mīn* (*mī, mȳ*), *þīn* (*þī, thȳ*), *his, hire* (*hir*), *ūre* (*ūr, ōur*), *ȝūre* (*ȝūr, yōure, yōur*), *here* (*her, hire, hir*) with *their* (*þeir*) in late ME. These are declined like adjectives, with plurals in *e* when the singular does not end in that vowel. The weakened forms *mī, þī*, occur only before words with initial consonants. The predicate and absolute forms are *mīn, þīn, his, here, ūre, ȝūre, here*, with plurals in *e*. Late forms in *s* are *ūres, ȝūres, heres*, but these do not appear in the earlier part of the period. Some texts also show forms with *n*, as *ōuren, ȝūren, heren* occasionally. The dual possessives *uncer, incer* appear only in the earliest period.

Note 1.—Early Midland (Orm) shows *þeȝȝrs*, the earliest absolute form in *s*, though perhaps due to Nth. influence.

Note 2.—Nth. works frequently show absolute forms in *s*, as *hers, ūrs, yōurs, þairs*, while they are unknown in Sth.

154. The Demonstrative Pronouns, like adjectives with which they agree in use, retain at most only singular and plural forms without distinction of gender. They are three in number, two from OE. masculine and neuter *sĕ* (late OE. *þĕ*) and *þæt* 'the,' 'that,' and one from the OE. neuter *þis* 'this.' The first, (*þē*) (*thē*), is invariable and is used as a definite article ; the others are declined as follows :—

Sing. *þat* (*þet, that*)   *þis* (*þys, this, thys*)
Plur. *þǫ* (*þa, thǫ*)   *þise* (*þis, this(e)*), *þēse* (*þēs, thēs(e)*), *þǫs*.

155. A relic of the OE. dative plural *ðǣm* remains in the expression *for þē nǭnes = for then ǭnes* 'for the nonce,' with final *n* from *m* transferred to the beginning of the next word. In a similar way final *t* of *þat* is sometimes transferred to a word beginning with a vowel, as *þē tǫ, þē iǒþer* (earlier *þet ǫ, þet ōþer*) ' the one, the other' ; 'tother' is still dialectal English. For *tē, tat, tǫ* from *þē, þat, þǫ* after words ending in *d, t,* sometimes *s*, see §§ 100, 114. In the later period only *atte = at þē* ' at the ' remains. A relic of the OE. instrumental *þȳ* appears in *forþī*, and as *þē*, in *þē mǭre* and similar expressions. Occasionally *ȝon, ȝǫnd* (*yon, yǫnd*) < OM. *gon* (WS. *geon*) are also found as demonstratives.

NOTE 1.—Early Midland shows *þā* for *þǫ*, in accordance with § 43, n. 1. The 'Chr.' once has *þās* 'these,' the OE. form, under the year 1132.

NOTE 2.—Nth. has *þaas* (*þās*) beside the more common *þā* (*þaa*) as plural of *þat*, as well as Norse *þir* (*þeir, þēr*), and *þiis* (*þēs*) for the plural of *þis*. Sth., especially early Sth., shows a much fuller retention of OE. forms. Masc. are N. *þē*, G. *þes* (*þē*), D. *þēn* (*þē*), A. *þēne* (*þē*) ; Neut. N. A. *þet* (*þē*), G. *þes* (*þē*), D. *þēn* (*þē*) ; Fem. N. *þēo* (*þē*), G. D. *þēr* (*þē*). Plural N. A. *þēo* (*þē*), G. *þēo, þē* (*þēr*), D. *þēo, þē* (*þēn*). Also Masc. N. *þēs*, G. *þisses*, D. *þisse*, A. *þisne* ; Neut. N. A. *þis*, G. D. as masc. ; Fem. N. A. *þēos*, G. D. *þisse*. Plural N. A. G. *þēos*, D. *þēos, þissen*.

156. The pronoun of identity, *ilc* (*ilk, ilche, īche, ȳche*), is declined like an adjective. The demonstrative *þē* and *ilk* (*ilke*) often unite by elision of *e*, as *þilke* (*þilche*). The intensive *self* also appears as *selve, selven*.

NOTE 1.—Nth. has *ilk, ilke* invariably ; Sth. *ilch, ilche*, later *īch*.

157. The Relative Pronoun of Middle English, which is used universally and in all periods, is *þat* 'that.' Beside it OE. *þe* is found for a time, but soon disappears altogether. These are both indeclinable. In the fourteenth century others appear, as *which*, pl. *whiche* (which), and the genitive *whōs* (*whōse*) dative *whōm* come to be used; also compound relatives as *þat hē, þat his*, &c., *þē which, which þat, þē which þat.*

NOTE 1.—In early Midland *þe* is common beside *þat*.

NOTE 2.—Nth. has *þat* alone in the earliest texts. Sth. uses *þe, þet*, later *þat*, and retains *þe* much longer than in Midland. In the early fourteenth century Sth. also has *whan* (*wan, wanne, wane*) 'whom, what,' evidently from OE. *hwām* by weakening of *m*.

158. The Interrogative-Indefinite Pronouns are *whō (hō), whilc (hwilc, which), wheþer (hweþer, whether)* ' who, which, whether.' The first is declined as follows, without distinction of number:

Masc.-Fem.	Neut.
N. *hwō (wō, whō, hō)*	*hwat (wat, what)*
G.	*hwōs (wōs, whōs, whōse)*
D.	*hwōm (wōm, whōm)*
A. *hwōm (wōm, whōm)*	*hwat (wat, what)*

159. The others are declined like adjectives, though *whether* is usually uninflected. Compound forms are also found, as *hwō sȳ, hwōse* 'whoso,' &c. Some Midland texts, as ' Genesis and Exodus,' have the spelling with *qu* for *hw (wh)* which is especially characteristic of Nth. Thus *quō, quōm (quam), quat, queþer*, &c.

NOTE 1.—Early Midland shows the earliest use of *wh* for OE. *hw*, as regularly in Orm, a spelling which is not established until the last half of the fourteenth century.

NOTE 2.—In Nth. the spelling with *qu* for *hw* prevails with few exceptions. Nth. uses *sum* as well as *swā* in compound forms, as *quāsum, quatsum*. Sth. variants are *hwoa* beside *hwō*, and occasional forms with *a*, as *hwas, hwam (hwan), hwase*, 'whoso.' Sth. also has *hwuch, hwuþer*, for *hwich, hweþer*, by influence of the preceding consonant on the vowel.

160. Other indefinites are *al* 'all'; *anī (anȳ, ǭnȳ, enȳ)* ' any '; *aȝt (auȝt, ought)* 'aught'; *naȝt (naught, nought)* 'naught'; *bǭthe* 'both'; ēlch (ēch, ę̄che) 'each'; aiþer (eiþer, ouþer) 'either'; naiþer (neiþer, nouþer) 'neither'; everilc (everich, everī) 'every'; everīwhēr (whēre) 'everywhere'; manī 'many'; man, (men, me) 'man, one, they'; ǫn 'one'; nǫn 'none'; ōþer 'other'; sum (som) 'some'; swilc (swich, such) 'such'; wiht (wight) 'wight.' Compound forms are also common, as everilcǫn (everichǫn) 'everyone,' manī an(a) 'many a,' sumdę̄l 'somedeal,' sumkin 'some-kind,' sumwat 'somewhat,' &c.

161. The indefinites are in general declined as adjectives, but a few special forms must be mentioned. An old genitive plural of al, aller (alder, alþer) is found occasionally, and in one or two compounds as a stereotyped form, as yōure aller cost 'cost of you all,' and alderbest 'best of all,' alder first 'first of all'; bōthe 'both' sometimes has a plural bōthen in imitation of nouns in en; a genitive of ōþer, ōþres 'other's' also occurs.

NOTE.—Nth. has allirs, bāþir (bāþirs) 'of all, of both,' instead of aller, bōþe (bōþen) above; also sāme 'same,' slīke (slīc, slī) 'such,' both Norse forms peculiar to Nth. texts or those influenced by Nth. Nth. also retains quōn 'few,' from OE. hwōn. Sth. retains many inflexional forms from OE. times, such as have been mentioned already under § 140, n. 2. In addition, Sth. has some plurals formed under the influence of the en nouns, as bōþen 'both,' ōþeren 'others.' Other forms of special peculiarity are Sth. enī, ei 'any'; nenne, acc. sg. of nǫn 'none'; summes, pl. of sum 'some.'

THE VERB

162. With the exception of the few anomalous forms, verbs belong to two classes as in Old English, the weak distinguished by a preterit tense with dental suffix, the strong by one with change of root vowel[1]. As in Old English, also, the verb has both inflected and compound forms, the latter made up by the use of verbs originally independent but weakened to the force of auxiliaries, as

[1] The distinction between gradation and original reduplication verbs need not be here regarded, since the distinguishing feature remaining to Middle English is a change of root vowel, though sometimes owing to contraction of original reduplication.

in Modern English. The inflected forms, all belonging to the active voice, are two tenses, a present and preterit; two modes, an indicative and subjunctive, or subjunctive-optative since it has the uses of both; an infinitive, and two participles, a present and a past. The compound forms are four indicative tenses, a future and three perfects, present, past and future; a present and past optative, or potential, with auxiliaries *may*, *can*, &c.; a present perfect infinitive and participle; and a passive with all the modes and tenses of the active, both inflected and compound.

163. The normal inflexional endings of the verb may be seen in the following scheme:

Inflexional Endings of the Verb

	Weak	Strong		Weak	Strong
	PRESENT		INDICATIVE	PRETERIT	
Sing. 1.	*e*		*ede, de (te)*	–
2.	*est*		*edest, dest (test)*	*e (–)* [2]
3.	*eþ (eth)*		*ede, de (te)*	–
Pl. 1, 2, 3.	*e(n)* [1]		*ede(n), (ed), de(n), te(n)*	*e(n)*

SUBJUNCTIVE

Sing. 1, 2, 3.	*e*		*ede, de (te)*	*e*
Pl. 1, 2, 3.	*e(n)*		*ede(n), de(n), te(n)*	*e(n)*

IMPERATIVE

Sing. 2. *e*	–	
Pl. 2. *eþ (eth), e*	*eþ (th), e, –*	

INFINITIVE

e(n) |

PARTICIPLES

ende (ande), inge | *ed (d, t)*   *e(n), (e)n*

[1] Loss of final *n* in all *en* forms grows increasingly common through the period. For dialectal peculiarities, see § 166, notes.

[2] Loss of final *e* is most common in this inflexional form.

164. So far as inflexional endings are concerned, a single class of weak verbs resulted from the three weak classes of Old English. In the present tense the endings of the weak and strong verbs are the same, but for slight differences in the imperative. Syncope and apocope of *e* are sometimes found, more commonly in the latter part of the period. Loss of final *n* also grows more common through the period, thus reducing the number of forms, while final *e* is regularly silent in late Middle English. The second and third person singular of the present indicative, occasionally the plural imperative, sometimes have *es* (*s*), the characteristic Nth. forms. Assimilation and simplification in the consonants of the third singular are occasional, as *fīnt* beside *fīndeþ*, *sit* beside *sitteþ*. Verbs ending in a vowel naturally show contraction with the vowel of the ending, as *see, sēst, sēþ* 'see, seest, seeth.' The imperative plural ending is reduced to *e*, or lost altogether when immediately followed by its pronoun. The prefix *i* (*y*), OE. *ge*, in the past participle is rarely found.

165. Analogy played an important part in the development of inflexional endings. Thus OE. verbal stems in *r* which retained *i* from the Teutonic *jan* ending, whether weak or strong, and verbs of the second weak class in *īan* (*īgean*) regularly lost *i* (*ī*) in all forms in which it occurred. Their infinitives came to end in *en* as in the case of other OE. verbs in *an*, and *e* in the 1st sg. pres., *en* in the plural and *eþ* in the imp. pl. Examples are *hēren* (OE. *herian*) 'praise' for the OE. first weak class, *swēren* (OE. *swerian*) 'swear' the only strong verb, and *wunen* (OE. *wunian*) 'dwell' for the second weak class. But OE. verbal stems in *rgan* (*rgīan*) retain *ī* from palatal *g* (*ig*), as *birīen* 'bury.' Similarly OE. verbal stems in *cg*, *bb*, whether weak or strong, lost those combinations in the present and assumed those of the third *sg.*, as *seien* for *seggen* (OE. *secgan*) 'say,' *liȝen, līen* (OE. *licgan*) 'lie, recline,' *hāven* (OE. *habban*) 'have,' *hēven* (OE. *hebban*) 'heave, raise.' OE. *libban* 'live,' however, gave way before OE. *lifīan* of the second weak class in preterit and past participle, the present of both verbs falling together by reason of both the above changes. For grammatical change in strong verbs see § 172.

166. The verb *hāven* 'have,' the only relic of the third weak conjugation which has not become regularized, has the following peculiarities: present *hāve, hast* (*has*), *haþ* (*hath*); pl. *hāven* (*hāve*); preterit, *hafde* (*haved, hadde, had*). *Māken* 'make' shows a similar loss of medial *k*, and *clōþen* 'clothe' of medial *þ*, as *māked* (*māde*), *cladde* 'clad.'

NOTE 1.—Early Midland differs mainly in a somewhat fuller preservation of OE. forms. Analogical changes, also, had not been fully carried out, Orm having *habben, libben, seğğen, leğğen* from OE. forms with *bb, cg*.

NOTE 2.—Nth. agrees with Midland in the main, but the endings of the present indicative are characteristic, as 1 *e* (-, *es*) ; 2, 3 *es* ; pl. 1, 2, 3 *es* (*e* when followed immediately by the personal pronoun). The infinitive has no final *n* and often no *e* remaining, as *bīnd* 'bind,' for Ml. *bīnde*(*n*). Syncopated forms of the present are exceedingly rare ; the preterit of the weak verb has, in general, lost its personal endings ; the present participle ends in *and* (*e*), and the prefix of the past participle, *i* (*y*), OE. *ge*, is wholly lost. Sth. retains OE. weak verbs of the second class with infinitives in *īe*(*n*) and the following endings in the indicative present ; Sg. 1 *īe* (*ī, ȳe, ȳ*) ; Pl. 1, 2, 3 *īeþ* (*īeth*). OF. verbs in *ier* and sometimes those in *eier* or *er* fall in with this characteristic Sth. class. Sth. also often has infinitives in *īen* from OE. *ian* after *r*, and present stems with *ğğ* < OE. *cg*, *bb* < OE. *bb*. In the second and third persons *es* (*s*) for *s* is unknown ; syncopated forms are very common, as also those with assimilation and simplification of consonants ; the present participle ends in *inde* (seldom *ende*), later *inge* ; the prefix *i* (*y*) of the past participle is often retained. All other verbs have *eþ* (*eth*) in the plural. The London dialect seldom retains the prefix *i* (*y*), OE. *ge*, of the past participle, as in Midland, but Chaucer makes extensive use of it in poetry, no doubt for metrical reasons ; see any glossary of Chaucer under *y* (*i*).

THE WEAK VERB [1]

167. The weak verb in Middle English may be divided into two classes, distinguished by a preterit tense ending of *ed* (*e*) or *de* (*te*).

---

[1] Weak verbs are placed first because they are the most numerous class in all periods of English, and hence represent regularity in forms as compared with all other classes. Besides, this arrangement brings together all minor divisions, as strong, preterit-present, and the four anomalous verbs.

The first, with preterit in *ede*, includes verbs of the OE. first weak class with original short stems, except those ending in *d* or *t*; most verbs of the OE. second weak class by weakening of OE. *ode* to *ede*; strong verbs with short stems, when becoming weak by analogy; and such borrowed verbs as have ranged themselves with them because of similar formation.

168. Verbs of the second class in Middle English are distinguished by a preterit tense-ending *de*, or *te* after stems ending in a voiceless consonant. To this class belong polysyllabic verbs of the OE. first weak class, together with those having original long stems, or short stems ending in *d* or *t*, and those with mutation only in the present (Sievers, 'Gr.' § 407); the small number belonging to the OE. third weak class; some verbs of the OE. second weak class which have lost the connecting vowel of the preterit ending; strong verbs with long stems, when becoming weak by analogy; and such borrowed verbs as have ranged themselves with them because of similar formation, especially long stems.

169. The past participles of both classes usually end in *ed*. Certain verbs of class II, however, have *d* or *t* without connecting vowel, as those with mutation only in the present, and the few originally belonging to OE. class III. Besides, some verbs ending in *d*, *t*, have past participles without ending, by reason of earlier syncopation of *e* and simplification of the resulting consonant group, as *fed*, *set*. A few others, as those ending in a vowel or liquid, also have past participles in *d*; for example, *flēn* 'flee'–*fled*, *hēren* 'hear'–*herd*.

170. Some irregularities naturally occur. In addition to the cases in which *te* regularly belongs to the preterit and *t* to the past participle, those endings are sometimes found after consonants voiced in the present but becoming voiceless in the other forms after syncopation of the connecting vowel *e*; examples are *lōsen–loste–lost* 'lose–lost,' *clēven–clefte–cleft* 'cleave–cleft.' Some verbs ending in a liquid + *d* change *d* to *t* in preterit and participle, as *wēnden–wente–went*, *bilden–bilte–bilt* 'build–built,' *gīrden–girte–girt* 'gird–girt.' This last change is far less common in Nth. Some verbs differ in present and preterit by reason of special phonetic changes, as *blenchen* 'blench, blanch'–*bleinte–bleint*, *mengen* 'mingle'–*meynte–meynt*, § 48. In § 165 attention was called to the development of OE. palatal *g* after *r* as in *birīen* 'bury'; when OE. guttural *g* followed *l*, *r* it regularly became *ʒ* later *w*, as in *folʒen* (*folwen*) 'follow,' *borʒen* (*borwen*) 'borrow.'

171. Borrowed verbs, with few exceptions, assumed the inflexion of the weak verb, following one of the two classes above, according as they agreed with one or other in phonetic peculiarities. ON. weak verbs were easily received without much change, yet such verbs ending in *ja*, *va* (=*wa*) follow their presents without those endings in English. Examples are *eggen* < ON. *eggja*, *gēren* < *gǫrva*. Verbs from OF. sources almost invariably became weak in Middle English. In general their forms depend upon the form of the OF. present stem, as ME. *chanten* < *chanter*, *plainen*, *responden* < *plaindre*, *respondre*, but *rendren*, *battren* 'render, batter' < *rendre*, *batre*; *mōven* < *movoir*; *aisen* (*ēsen*), *chāsen* (*cachen*) < *aisier*, *chasier* (Picard *cachier*) 'ease, chace, catch'; but *marīen* 'marry,' *carīen* 'carry,' *replīen* 'reply,' *studīen* 'study,' *denīen* 'deny.' The present stem is especially important as accounting for ME. verbs in -*ischen* (*issen*) from the OF. pres. pl. in *iss-*, infinitives in *ir*, as *finischen* < *finir* 'finish,' *florischen*, *nurischen*, *punischen*, *rejoissen* 'rejoice,' *traissen* (*betraissen*) beside *traien* (*betraien*) 'betray,' *obeischen* (*obeissen*) beside *obeien* 'obey.' Double forms in OF. account for certain peculiarities in ME. verbs, as the two forms *clāmen*, *claimen* 'claim.' A few verbs are formed from OF. past participles used as adjectives, as *clōsen*, *peinten* 'paint,' *fainten* 'faint, feint' beside *feinen* 'feign,' *enointen* (*anointen*) 'anoint'; cf. OF. *clore–clos*, *peindre–peint*, *feindre–feint*, *enoindre–enoint*. In late Middle English other verbs were similarly formed from OF. or Lat. perfect participles first adopted as adjectives; cf. *creāt* 'created,' *desolāte* 'desolated' and the verbs from them. The greater number of borrowed verbs assumed the forms of class I, but some, especially

those ending in a vowel, took the preterit *de* of class II ; examples
are *crīen* ' cry '–*crȳde, payen* ' pay '–*payde.* By analogy of *lacchen–
lauʒte–lauʒt* ' seize,' and others of its class, OF. *cacchen* ' seize,
catch' formed its preterit and participle as *caughte–caught.*

NOTE.—Nth. agrees with Ml. Sth. retains infinitives in *īen* from OF. verbs
in *ier,* the latter falling in with OE. weak verbs of the second class in that
dialect.

THE STRONG VERB

172. This class, as in Old English, includes gradation verbs, and
those with original reduplication, the former including several minor
divisions. The most noticeable change in strong verbs during
ME. times is that many of them have become weak by analogy of
the great weak class. On the other hand, a very few new ones
appear, owing to borrowings from Norse and to rare analogical
formations. Strong verbs also show a tendency toward the reduction of the two preterit stems of most OE. strong verbs to one,
but this tendency was not fully carried out until modern times.
It results naturally from the fact that even in Old English the
preterits of reduplication verbs, of those of class VI, and some of
class V had the same stem vowel in both singular and plural.
The reduction of the four OE. stems to three was further influenced
by the similar vowel in preterit plural and past participle of verbs
belonging to class I and most of class III, and by the regularizing
of consonants in verbs originally having grammatical change.

NOTE.—In this reduction of preterit stems the dialects differ markedly. Nth.
has lost one stem, usually the plural, almost entirely. Sth. retains both forms
as a rule. Midland stands between the two in this respect, though agreeing
more nearly with Sth. through most of the period. With this general statement, dialectal differences in the various classes need not be noted, except in
special cases. Differences due to the different phonologies of the dialects have
been sufficiently exemplified in the part on Phonology.

173. The inflexional endings of strong verbs have been shown
in § 163. The preterit second singular is often without ending.
There are also few peculiarities of strong stems not already noted.

Attention has already been called to the change in present stems ending in *cg*, and those which retained *i* after *r* in Old English, § 165. Variations originally due to mutation in second and third singular present indicative have also disappeared by the influence of the unmutated forms, though mutation was never so common in the Anglian dialects as in West Saxon (Sievers, 'Gr.' § 371, anm. 5 f).

NOTE.—Nth. seldom preserves the *e* of the second person preterit indicative, while in Sth. it is not uncommon. Sth. also preserves OE. *cg* of verb stems as *ğğ* (= *dzh*) more commonly than Midland.

174. Gradation verbs belong to six sub-classes, as in Old English, with the following vowels in their various stems,—the present, preterit singular, preterit plural, and past participle respectively[1]:

1. $\bar{\imath} - \bar{\varrho} - i\,(\bar{\varrho}) - \imath$
2. $\bar{e}\,(\bar{u}) - \bar{\xi} - \bar{\varrho}\,(\bar{\xi}) - \bar{\varrho}$
3. $i\,(e) - a\,(\breve{\varrho}) - u\,(ou, \breve{\varrho}) - \bar{\varrho}, u\,(ou)$
4. $\bar{\xi} - a - \bar{e}, \bar{\xi}\,(\bar{\varrho}) - \bar{\varrho}\,(u)$
5. $\bar{\xi}\,(i) - a\,(\bar{e}, \bar{\xi}) - \bar{e}, \bar{\xi} - e\,(i)$
6. $\breve{a}\,(\bar{\xi}, o) - \bar{o} - \bar{o} - a\,(\bar{a}, \bar{\xi}, o)$

175. Verbs of class I are exemplified by *driven* 'drive'–*drǭf*–*driven* (*drǭf*)–*driven*; *writen* 'write'–*wrǭt*–*writen* (*wrǭt*)–*writen*; *riden* 'ride'–*rǭd*–*riden* (*rǭd*)–*riden*. The introduction of the preterit singular vowel in the plural is especially to be noticed as suggesting the Modern English form. The verb *stīȝen* (*stīen*) 'ascend' has a pret. *steiȝ* as if from OE. *stēah of the second class or possibly from Norse. To verbs which regularly belong here from OE. times must be added two borrowed verbs, *riven* 'rive' from Norse, and *striven* 'strive' from French, the latter with strong forms by analogy. The weak verb *chiden* 'chide' also shows strong forms as early as the thirteenth century; compare *chidden*, a past participle, in 'Gen. and Ex.' 1927.

---

[1] The order of these sub-classes is unimportant, except that sub-classes 1–5 develop from the Teutonic *e–a*, and 6 from *a–ō* gradation series. In England the reduplication verbs are sometimes called class I, and the above are then given in the order 6, 4, 5, 3, 1, 2. Streitberg, followed by Kaluza, adopts the new order 5, 4, 3, 1, 2, 6.

176. Of the contract verbs belonging to this class, only *þēn* (*thee*) 'thrive, prosper,' and *wrēn* (*wrīen*) 'cover, conceal' seem to be preserved. Even in Old English, too, these had been influenced by verbs of class II, so that some of their forms still correspond with those of that class. The first has preterit sing. *þēg*, pret. plur. and past part. *þǭgen*, later *þowen*; the second, pret. sing. *wrēȝ* (*wreigh*), pret. plur. and past part. *wriȝen* (*wreȝen*).

NOTE.—Early Ml. and Nth. retain *ā* in pt. sg. in accordance with §§ 5, 43.

177. Class II early adopted a preterit plural with the stem vowel *ǭ*, by analogy of the past participle, though occasionally the vowel of the preterit singular was introduced into the plural. Examples of verbs which are fairly regular are *shēten* 'shoot'–*shḛt*–*shǭten* (*shḛt*)– *shǭten*; *chēsen* 'choose' –*chḛs*–*chǭsen* (*chḛs*)–*chǭsen*, the latter with *s* instead of *r* in preterit plural and past participle by analogy of the remaining stems (OE. *curon–coren*). A form with *ū* in the present is *shūven* 'shove'–*shḛf* (*shḛf*)–*shǭven*–*shǭven*; with change of consonant due to Verner's law, *sēþen* 'seethe'–*sḛþ*–*sǭden*–*sǭden*; *lēsen* 'lose'–*lḛs* (*las*)–*lḛsen*, (*lǭst*)–*lǭren*; *flēgen* (*flȳen*) 'fly'–*flḛg* (*flei*)– *flǭgen* (*flowen*)–*flǭgen* (*flowen*). *Bēden* shows influence of *bidden* (class V) in forms and meaning.

178. Weak forms are found beside the strong in some cases, as *crēpen* 'creep'–*crepte–crept*, beside *crēp* (*crōp*)–*crǭpen–crǭpen*, and *lēsen* 'lose'–*lǭste–lǭst* beside the strong forms above. The contract verb *flēn* (OE. *flēon*) 'flee' has the same preterit as *flēgen* (*flȳen*) 'fly,' and there is in other respects much confusion between the two. The other contract verb, *tēn* 'draw,' has preterit *tḛh* (*tei*) and past part. *tǭgen* (*towen*).

NOTE.—Grammatical change disappears during the period except in *sēþen* 'seethe,' though past participles sometimes preserve the original consonant when used mainly as adjectives.

179. Class III consists of two subdivisions as the present stem has *e* or *i*, the latter before a nasal as in Old English. Both classes show occasional intrusion of the vowel of the singular preterit into the plural. Verbs with *e* in the present stem are exemplified by *helpen* 'help'–*halp* (*holp*)–*holpen*–*holpen*; *swellen* 'swell'–*swal*–*swollen*–*swollen*. A few show peculiarities due to lengthening in accordance with § 72, as *zelden* (*yelden*) 'yield'–*zǭld* (*zāld*)–*zǭlden* (*yǭlden*)–*zǭlden* (*yǭlden*). The verb *fizten* 'fight' has *i* from original *e* in the present stem, according to § 22, 2; its remaining principal parts are *fazt* (*faught*)–*fozten* (*foughten*)–*fozten* (*foughten*). The verb meaning 'to become' (OE. *weorðan*, North. *worþan*) early appears as *wurþen* (*worþen*)–*wurþ* (*worþ*, *warþ*)–*wurþen* (*worþen*)–*wurþen* (*worþen*) without change of *þ* to *d* in the last two forms, and with *u* (*o*) in all stems, by influence of preceding *w* (§ 25). Similarly OE. *swelgen* appears as *swelzen* (*swelwen*, *swolwen*) 'swallow,' and develops a weak past participle *swolzed* (*swolwed*). Here also may be mentioned *bresten* 'burst' with preterit singular *brast* and *brost* (compare § 76, *n.* 2). OE. *bregdan* becomes *breiden* (*brēden*)–*breid*–*broiden*–*broiden*.

180. The more numerous subdivision, with *i* in the present stem before an original nasal + consonant, is exemplified by *winnen* 'strive, win'–*wan*–*wunnen*–(*wǒnnen*)–*wǒnnen*; *drinken* 'drink'–*drank*–*drǒnken*–*drǒnken*; *springen* 'spring'–*sprang* (*sprǭng*)–*sprǒngen*–*sprǒngen*, the latter with *ǭ* in preterit singular, beside *a*, according to § 17. The *o* of preterit plural and past participle is of course orthographic for *u* (§ 27). A few verbs have lengthened vowels in all forms, as *finden* 'find'–*fǭnd* (*fānd*)–*fǭnden* (*foūnden*)–*foūnden*, the only others of this sort being *binden*, *grinden*, *winden* 'bind, grind, wind.' The verb *rinnen* 'run' has a present, in *e*, as *rennen*, with the remaining forms regular. Similarly *brennen* 'burn' has *e* in the present, though like several others belonging to this class it has become weak. The preterit of *ginnen* 'begin' is frequently used as a preterit auxiliary in such expressions as *gan gǭ* 'went, did go.'

NOTE.—In late Nth. *begin* developed a weak pret. *begoūþe* by analogy of *coūþe*. The pret. *gan* also appears as *can*, as sometimes in Ml.

181. Class IV is a small class, as in Old English, and it early

shows a tendency to the introduction of the vowel of the past
participle into the preterit plural, occasionally the preterit singular.
Verbs which are most nearly regular are *stęlen* ' steal '–*stal–stēlen–
stōlen*; *shēren* ' shear '–*shar–shēren–shōren*. With *o* forms as above,
bęren ' bear '–*bar* (*bǭr*, *bēr*)–*bēren* (*bǭren*)–*bōren*; *bręken* ' break '–
brak–brēken (*brǭken*)–*brǭken*. Quite irregular, as in Old English,
are *nimen* (*nĕmen*, perhaps Norse) ' take '–*nam* (*nōm*)–*nōmen* (*nāmen*,
nam)–*numen*, and *cumen* (*cŏmen*) ' come '–*cam* (*cōm*)–*cōmen* (*cāmen*)–
cumen (*cŏmen*).

182. To this class, which originally contained *brękan* ' break '
irregularly, several others of class V began to attach themselves by
assuming past participles with the vowel *o* beside *e*. Examples are
given under the class to which they originally belonged.

NOTE.—For *ǭ* (eMl. Nth. *ā*) instead of *ē* (Sth. *ę̄*) in the pret. pl. of this and
the following class, see §§ 18, 43.

183. Class V, also a small class in Old English, is made smaller
during Middle English by the tendency of verbs originally belonging here to assume forms of class IV, and thus range themselves
with that class by analogy. Examples of those that still belong
here in all their forms are *mēten* ' mete,'—*mat–mēten–meten*; *ęten*
' eat '–*ēt* (*at*)–*ēten–eten*. Verbs with original *i* in the present stem
(Sievers, ' Gr.' §§ 391–3) are exemplified by *sitten* ' sit '–*sat–sēten–
seten*. The verb *ʒiven* (*ʒeven*), with *i* from original *e*, has preterits
ʒaf–ʒēven, past participle *ʒiven* like the infinitive; besides, its
initial *ʒ* gradually gives way to *g*, under the influence of Norse
geve ' give,' as also in ME. *ʒeten* ' get ' by influence of Norse *gete*.
Irregular, by reason of the final consonants of the stem, is *liǧǧen*,
later *līen* ' lie, recline,'–*lay–leyen–leyen*, with analogical present
(§ 165). *Bidden* shows influence of *bēden* (class II) in forms and
meaning. The preterit *quoþ* (*quoth*, *quod*), alone remaining from
OE. *cweðan* ' say,' perhaps has its vowel *o* by lack of stress in the
sentence (§ 18). The only contract verb retained, *sēn* ' see,' has
also various forms for its remaining principal parts, as *sey* (*saw*,

saugh)–seyen (sāwen, sǭwen, sayen)–seyen (sēn, sogen, sowen). Verbs which have been influenced by class IV are as follows:—

wrēken ' avenge,'*–wrak–wrēken–wreken (wrǭken).*

spēken ' speak,'*–spak–spēken (spāken, spǭken)–spǭken (speken).*

wēven ' weave,'*–waf–wēfen–wǭven (weven).*

drēpen ' kill '*–drap (drǭp)–drēpen (drāpen)–drǭpen.*

ȝeten ' get '*–ȝat (yǭt)–ȝēten–ȝeten (ȝūten).*

NOTE.—Contrary to the rule, change of *s* to *r* by Verner's Law remains in *was–wēren*, originally belonging here but defective and associated with *bēn* ' be.'

184. Class VI seems to present greater irregularities than in Old English, owing to various phonetic causes. Most verbs have lengthened vowels in present and past participle, as *fāre–fōr–fōren –fāren, forsāken* ' forsake '*–forsōk–forsōken–forsāken.* To these have been added *tāken* ' take '*–tōk–tōken–tāken* from Norse. Verbs with mutated presents suffer various changes. A new form with unmutated *a* appears in *shāpen* ' shape '*–shōp–shōpen–shāpen,* sometimes in *stappen* beside the prevailing *steppen,* which soon acquires weak forms as well. The infinitive of *laȝhen (lauȝen, lauhwen)* ' laugh '*–lōh (lough)–lowen–loghen (lowen)–lauȝhen (laughen)* must also have been influenced by the past participle (cf. Orm's *lahhȝh-enn.* OE. *sceððan* ' injure ' gave place to *skāþen* ' scathe ' < ON. *skaða,* a weak verb. On the other hand, *swēren* ' swear ' and *hēven* ' heave,' have retained present stems in *e* (*ē*), but have been influenced by verbs of class IV. Their principal parts are *swēren–swǭr (swar)–swǭren (swēren)–swǭren (swǭrn)* ; *hēven–hǭf (haf)–hǭfen–hǭven.* Verbs with stem in OE. *g* have forms like *draȝen (drawen)–drōȝ (drouȝ)–droȝen (drowen)–draȝen (drawen).* As in Old English *standen* ' stand ' has *n* in the present and past participle only. ME. *waxen* ' grow,' originally belonging here, has fallen in with the reduplication verbs, and *waschen* ' wash ' has both preterits, *wōsch (wēsch, weisch).* By analogy of verbs of this class, *quāken* ' quake,' a weak verb, has acquired a strong preterit *quōk.*

185. Contract verbs, *slǭn (slēn)* ' slay ' and *flǭn (flēn)* ' flay ' have the following principal parts : *slōn (slēn)–slōg (slug, slough, slow)–*

slōgen (*slowen, slugen, slagan*)–*slawen* (*slayen*); *flōn* (*flēn*)–*flōgh* (*flow*)–*flowen–flawen* (*flain*).

186. Verbs with original reduplication are regular in having in the preterit *ē*, from OE. *ē, ēo*, or *ew* from OE. *ēow*, while the vowels of the present and past participle differ considerably owing to various phonetic changes of OE. originals. Examples of these with preterits in *ē* are *fallen* 'fall'–*fēl* (*fil*)–*fallen*; *lēten* 'let, allow'–*lēt* (*lat*)–*lēten* (*laten*); *hǫlden* 'hold'–*hēld–hǫlden*. Those with preterits in *ew* are exemplified by *blowen* 'blow as the wind'–*blew–blowen*; *growen* 'grow'–*grew–growen*; *hewen* 'hew'–*hew–hewen*. The last example shows how the distinctive forms of Old English became one in Middle English, after which the verb frequently became weak. The verb *hǫten* 'call, promise' (OE. *hātan*) has two preterits depending on the two OE. forms *heht* and *hēt*, as *hiht* (*hight, highte*) and *hēt*. At the same time *hihte* became present as well as past, and the OE. passive *hatte* 'am called' became a past. The OE. contracts *fōn* 'seize,' *hōn* 'hang,' soon gave way before new infinitives *fangen, hangen* under the influence of the past participles, while a weak *fangen* was adopted from ON. *fanga* and OE. *hangian* became Ml. *hangen*. Many of the reduplication verbs also have weak forms, as *slepte, wepte, walkede, dradde,* 'dreaded.'

THE PRETERIT-PRESENT VERBS

187. The preterit-present verbs show no exceptional changes from OE. times beyond the loss of some of their number, and of certain forms, as the infinitive. The more important forms in the several classes of strong verbs to which they originally belonged are as follows :—

I. Two verbs *ǭȝen* (*owen*) 'owe, have' and *witen* 'know'; inf. *ǭȝen* (*owen*); pres. indic. *owe, owest, oweþ* (*oweth*)–*owen*; pres. subj. *owe–owen*; pret. *aȝte* (*ǭȝte, aughte, oughte*); inf. *witen*; pres. indic. *wǭt, wǭst, wǭt–witen* (*wǭt*); pres. subj. *wite*; imp. *wite*; pres. part. *witende* (*witinge*); pret. *wist* (*wiste*); past part. *wist*.

NOTE.—Early Ml. has *wāt*, *āȝen*; Nth. *āgh* (*awe*) in inf. and pres. indic., *aght* in pret., in accordance with their phonologies. Negative forms of *witen* are *niten-nǫt* (Nth. *nāt*) *-niste*, &c. Sth. has *wüten*, *nüten*, &c., from lWS. *wytan*, *nytan*.

III. Three verbs, *cunnen* ' be able, can ' and *durren* ' dare,' *þurven* ' need '; inf. *cunnen* (*cónnen*); pres. indic. *can* (*con*), *canst*, *can* (*con*)*–cunen* (*cunnen*) ; pres. subj. *cunne* (*cónne*)*–cunnen* (*cónnen*); pret. *cūþe* (*cōuth*, *cōuthe*, *cōude*).

Inf. *durren* (*duren*); pres. indic. *dar*, *darst*, *dar–dor* (*dar*); pres. subj. *durre* (*dóre*)*–durren* ; pret. *durste* (*dorste*, *dirste*).

Inf. *þurven* ; pres. indic. *þarf*, *þarf*(*t*), *þarf–þurven* ; pres. subj. *þurve–þurven* ; pret. *þurfte* (*þorfte*, *þorte*)*–þurften*.

NOTE.—Nth. has no such forms as *con*, *cónne*.

IV. Pres. indic. *shal*, *shalt*, *shal–shullen* (*shul*, *shól*, *shal*) ; pres. subj. *schule–schulen* ; pret. *sholde* (*schulde*, *schold*, *scholde*).

NOTE.—Nth. has *sal-suld* in accordance with its phonology. It also retains pres. indic. *mon* ' remember, have in mind, must,' *-mune* ; pres. subj. *mune* ; pret. *mónd* (*munde*).

V. Inf. *muȝen* (*mōwen*); pres. indic. *mai*, *miht* (*mai*, *mayest*), *mai–mōwen* (*mōw*, *may*); pres. subj. *mōwe–mōwen* ; pret. *miȝte* (*mihte*, *mighte*, *moughte*).

NOTE.—Nth. has only pres. *mai*, pret. *might* (*moght*).

VI. Pres. indic. *mōt*, *mŏst*, *mōt–mōten* (*mŏst*) ; pres. subj. *mōte–mōten*; pret. *mŏste* (*muste*).

188. In the earlier part of the period relics of several other preterit-presents are also found, as *dugen* ' avail ' (class II), *unnen* ' grant ' (class III); *munen* ' be mindful ' (class IV), but these soon disappear, though a pres. and pret. of *munen* occur in Nth. (see above). Relics of the old strong past participles of these verbs are found in the adj.-adv. *wis* (*iwis*) ' certain, certainly,' and the adj. *owen* (eMl. Nth. *āȝen*, *āgen*) ' own.'

THE ANOMALOUS VERBS

189. Four verbs are quite anomalous in the number and character of their forms. They are *bēn (bē)* 'be,' *willen* 'will,' *dōn* 'do,' *gǭn* 'go.' These have the following forms :—

1. *Bēn (bē)* 'be.' Pres. indic. *am, art (ert), is (es)*, and *bē, bēst, bēþ*; plur. *arn (āre), bēn (bē)*; pres. subj. *bē*, plur. *bēn (bē)*; pret. *was, wēre (wǭre, was), was*; plur. *wēren (waren, wǭren)*; pret. subj. *wēre–wēren (wǭren)*; imp. *bē–bēþ (bēth)*; past part. *bēn (bēnę)*.

NOTE 1.—In early Midland, as Orm, sometimes a little later also, the present forms *bēst, bēoþ*, pl. *sinden*, are found, and *sī* as pres. subj.

NOTE 2.—Nth. has for present indic. sg. *am, ert (art, es), is (es)*; pl. *er (ar, ern, es)*; also third sg. *bēs*, pl. *bēn (bēs)*; pret. sg. *was (wes)*, pl. *wēr (wēre, wāre, weir, was)*. Sth. has pres. indic. second sg. *ert*, pl. *bę̄oþ (bēþ, bǖþ)*; subj. *bēo*, pl. *bēon*; pret. *was, wę̄re, was*, pl. *wę̄ren*; imp. *bēo–bēoþ*; inf. *bēon*; past part. *ibēon (ibēn, ybēn)*. Early Sth. also has the gerund, or inflected infinitive *bēonne*.

2. *Willen* 'will.' Pres. indic. *wil (wol), wilt (wolt), wil (wol)*; plur. *wiln (wil, woln, wol)*; pres. subj. *wile (wole)*; pret. *wolde (wilde), woldest (wost, wilde), wolde (wilde, walde, welde)*; plur. *wolden (wold, welde)*. A negative form, *nillen* 'will not' also occurs.

NOTE.—Nth. has pres. indic. sg. and pl. *wil (will, wille, wel)*; pret. *wald (wild, weld)*. Sth. uses pres. indic. *wüle (wülle, ich ülle, ich olle = ich wulle), wült, wüle*; pl. *wülleþ*; pres. subj. *wüle–wüllen*; pret. *wolde*.

3. *Dōn (dō)* 'do.' Pres. indic. *dō, dōst, dōþ (dōth)*; plur. *dōn*; subj. *dō–dōn*; imp. *dō–dōþ (dōth)*; pres. part. *dōende (dōinge)*; pret. *dide (dēde)*; past part. *dōn (dō)*.

NOTE.—Nth. has pres. indic. *dō, dōs (dōse, duse)*; pl. *dō (dōse, dōn)*; pres. subj. sg. and pl. *dō*; imp. *dō–dō (dōs)*; pret. *did (dēd)–did (dide)*; pres. part. *dōand*; past part. *dōn (dune)*. Sth. has pres. indic. *dō, dēst, dēþ*; pl. *dōþ (dōth)*; pret. *düde*; pres. part. *dōnde*; past part. *idōn*.

4. *Gǭn (gǭ)* 'go.' Pres. indic. *gǭ, gǭst, gǭþ (gǭth)*; plur. *gǭn*;

pres. subj. *gǭ–gǭþ* (*gǭth*); pres. part. *gǭend* (*gǭing*). The preterit is supplied by a different root, in the earlier period by *ȝēde* (*ȝōde, ȝēde*), OE. *geēode*, later by *wente–wenten* from *wēnden* 'wend, go.'

NOTE.—Nth. has inf. *gān* (*gā*); pres. indic. *gā, gās* (*gāse, gais*), *gās* (*gāsc, gais*); pl. *gās*; pres. subj. *gā–gā* (*gān*); imp. *gā–gā* (*gān*); *gā* (*gās, gaes, gais*); past part. *gān* (*gāne, gain*); pret. supplied by *went*. Sth. has inf. *gǭn*; pres. indic. *gǭ, gēst, gēþ* (*gēth*); pl. *gǭþ* (*gǭth*); pres. subj. *gǭ–gǭn*; pret. *ēode* (*ȝēde, ȝōde*).

THE ADVERB

190. Many adverbs in Middle English do not differ from their Old English forms, except for phonetic changes common to them with other words. They are based on adjective, substantive, and pronominal roots, and are both simple and compound. Simple adverbs, based on adjectives, end in *e*, *lĭke* (*lĭ, lȳ̆*), *inge* (*linge*). Those of the first class include adverbs which retain OE. *e*, or have *e* from *a* by weakening, as *sōfte* 'softly,' *sōþe* 'in truth,' *sōne* (OE. *sōna*) 'soon'; those of the second, adverbs which ended in *līce* in OE., and many which assumed this ending in Middle English, as *hārdlīke* (*hārdlĭ*) 'hardly,' *sōþlīke* (*sōþlĭ*) 'soothly'; to the third, those ending in *inga, enga, unga* (*linga, lenga, lunga*) in Old English, as *allunge* 'wholly.' During the period those of the first class gradually lost final *e*, and thus had the same form as the corresponding adjectives. With them came to be associated many adverbs from Old French which had the same form as the corresponding adjectives, as *just, verȳ, quīte*. The second adverbial ending, *lĭke*, was gradually weakened until it became confused with the adjective ending *lĭ* (*lȳ̆*), OE. *lic*, which henceforth came to be the distinctive adverbial ending and was greatly extended in its use with both native and foreign words. The third ending above is least frequent of all, and was not extended in the ME. period.

191. Adverbs, formed from the oblique cases of adjectives or substantives in Old English, also remain in Middle English. These are most commonly genitives in *es*, the masculine-neuter ending,

as *elles* 'else,' *unwāres* 'unawares,' *daies* 'by day,' *nihtes* 'by night,'
nēdes 'needs.' This ending was considerably extended in its use
in Middle English, as to adjectives otherwise ending in *e, inge*
(*linge*), and to nouns without regard to original gender. Old
accusatives are *lītel, līt* 'little,' *firn* 'formerly,' *ful* 'fully,' *ʒenōh*
(*enough, anough*). Old datives are *sōre, seldom, whīlom*, relics of
OE. dative-instrumental singulars or plurals. Neither of these
last two case-forms was frequently used in forming ME. adverbs,
and many formed in OE. gradually disappeared.

192. Pure pronominal adverbs are *þǭ* 'when,' *þus* 'thus,' *hū* (*hōu*)
'how,' *whȳ* 'why,' *þan* (*þen*), *whan* (*when*). Adverbs of place,
based on adjective or pronominal roots, commonly have the ending
en, from OE. *an*, as in case of those signifying 'where' or 'whence.'
Examples of adverbs signifying 'place where' are *innen* (*inne*) 'in,
within,' *ūten* (*ūte*) 'out,' *fǭren* (*fȳrn, fǭre*) 'before'; of those signifying 'place from which' *hennen* (*henne*) 'hence,' *hwennen* (*hwenne,
whenne*) 'whence,' *ēsten* (*ēste*) 'from the east.' To this class was
added also some Norse forms, as *hepen* 'hence,' *þepen* 'thence.'
On the other hand, some of these adverbs have *es* instead of *en* in
late Midland by extension of the *es* ending, as already mentioned
above. A few adverbs denoting 'place whither' end in *der*, originally comparative, as *hider* 'hither,' *þider* 'thither,' and perhaps by
influence of these *ʒonder*.

193. Compound adverbs are frequent, some being of OE. origin,
some of Middle English formation. As belonging to the former,
those ending in *līke* might be counted, although this had become
a well-established adverbial ending in OE. Better examples are
those ending in *ward*, OE. *weard*, as *upward, sūþward* 'southward,'
and *mēle*, OM. *mēlum*, as *dropmēle* 'drop by drop.' To these
were added in Middle English many ending in *ful, dēl*, 'part,' *tīme,
whīle, way, wīse*, and others. Still other compound adverbs are
made up of a prefix, the relic of an older preposition, and a noun
or pronoun, as *besīde, away, adūne* 'adown,' *forþī* 'because,' *þerin*
'therein,' *þērof* 'thereof.' Such adverbs as *alway* (*always*), *sum-*

time, sumwhīle, are made up of an indefinite pronoun and a noun, and such as *within, withōūten (withōūte)* of two adverbs.

NOTE 1.—In early Midland adverbs differ little from the later time except as they conform somewhat more nearly to OE. forms.

NOTE 2.—The principal variations of the dialects are as follows. Nth. shows the loss of final *e* in most adverbs, so that adjectives and corresponding adverbs are invariable as a rule. The ending *līke* was early weakened to *lĭ* (*lў̆*), and in its place Norse -*leiki* is sometimes found, as *hardlaike* 'hardly.' The ending *inge (linge)* frequently becomes *inges (linges)*, and the *es* ending is otherwise extended, as to numeral adverbs *ānes* 'once,' &c. The Norse adverbs of place are much more common, as *heþen* 'hence,' *queþen* 'whence.' Among compound adverbs, Nth. uses the Norse suffix *gāte* 'way, manner,' as in *algāte* 'always,' *þusgāte* 'in this manner,' while forms like *ūtwith* 'without,' *forwith* 'before,' are more common. The preposition *on,* when becoming a prefix, remains *on (o),* as in *obove* 'above,' *onān* 'anon,' *onlīve (olīve)* 'alive.' Sth. retains the *e* ending, even where wholly lost in other dialects, as in the numeral adverbs *ǣne* 'once,' &c. The Sth. form of OE. *līce* is *līche,* which is not weakened to *lĭ* (*lў̆*), and *inge (linge)* does not become *inges (linges)*. The ending *en (e)* is more extended in its use. Norse forms are not found, and OE. *on,* when becoming a prefix, is weakened to *an (a)* as in *alīve, abōūt, anǫn.*

194. The comparative and superlative of the adjective may be used as an adverb without change. In addition, a few adverbs not derived from adjectives have comparative endings. A few monosyllabic adverbs with mutation remain from OE. times, as *bet* 'better,' *ǣr (ǣre)* 'ere,' *leng* 'longer'; compare Sievers, 'Gr.' § 323.

THE PREPOSITION.

195. Little need be said of Middle English prepositions, since they present no serious difficulties, and show few changes not easily understood from the ordinary changes in phonology. Most OE. prepositions were preserved in Middle English, and some few were added from other sources, as Norse. Thus *frǭ* 'from' is derived from Norse *frā,* as is probably *umb (um),* cognate with OE. *ymbe* 'around.' Some few prepositions altered their meaning, as *wiþ* 'with,' which more commonly meant 'against' in Old English. In Middle English it ordinarily came to mean 'with,' doubt-

less through use in such expressions as *fight with*, in which it could have either signification. When this came to be true, *mid* in the latter meaning gradually disappeared. Simple prepositions from OF. were adopted in certain phrases, as *par amūr, par fai, paraventure* (*paraunter*), and certain OF. words came to be used as prepositions; examples are *rūnd* 'round,' *except, maugrē* 'in spite of,' *sāve, acordaunt*, later *acording*. Compound prepositions and preposiional phrases became common in Middle English, as *aȝein* (*again*), *aȝeines, amǭng, alǭng, besīde, nēȝhǭnd* (*nērhǭnd*) 'near at hand, near,' *tōward, ūttāken* 'except.' OF. words were also united in these phrases as *bi cause of, be rę̄son of, in regard of, arǭund, according tō*.

NOTE.—It is naturally impossible to separate dialects on the basis of prepositions only, but some prepositions seem almost peculiar to certain dialectal divisions. Thus Nth. uses *at* and *til* (*intil, until*) for *tō* and *untō, amēl* (*omēl, emēl, imēl*) for *betwēn*, and *wiþ* more commonly instead of *mid*. Sth. has *an* (*a*) for *on, tō, untō*, and *med* for *wiþ*.

THE CONJUNCTION

196. Old English conjunctions in general remain in Middle English, subject to such changes as were natural to their phonetic forms. Among those deserving special mention are *eiþer* (*eiȝþer*) 'either,' *ouþer* (*ǭþer, or*) 'or,' *siþen* (*siþenes, siþe, sith, seþe*, &c.) 'since,' Nth. *sin, sen*. Among correlative conjunctions, *þē . . . þē* remain from OE. *þ̄y : . . þȳ* with different vowel by analogy of *þē*; but OE. *swā . . . swā* gave place to *alswǭ . . . ase*, or *as . . . as*. From OE. correlatives and preceding indefinite pronouns also arose the new correlatives of Middle English, as *eiþer* (*ǭþer*) . . . *or, neiþer* (*nǭþer*) . . . *nor*, in which *or, nor* are weakened forms of the indefinite *ǭþer*, OE. *āhwǣðer, āwðer*. The common negative of Middle English is *ne*, which often suffers apocope of *e* and unites with the following word as in Old English. The OE. *nā*, from *ne + ā*, remained sometimes in *nǭ*, as to-day in *no better, no more of it* but at the same time a new negative *nat* (*not*), based on OE.

nāwiht ' naught,' came into use and gradually supplanted both of
the others in most situations. Sometimes both *ne* and *nat* (*not*)
were used in the same sentence. In Middle English also, the
Norse negative *nei* (*nay*) was adopted, as was also the affirmative *ei*
(*ay*) beside the OE. affirmative *ȝes* (*ȝis, yes*).

THE INTERJECTION

197. Middle English interjections come from Old English, as *lọ̄*,
ọ̄ (*ọ̄h*), *wọ̄*, with the weak forms *la*, *a* (later perhaps *lā, ā, āh*), *wa*
(*walawa*). From Norse came *wei* (*wai*) ' woe,' *weilawei* (*wailawai*),
and *hō*; from Old French *alas, fȳ*. The adoption of foreign
interjections is probably mainly of literary origin.

SYNTAX

WORD ORDER

198. The order of words in early Middle English prose follows
that of the older language in the freedom of word-position. This
is especially true of the verb, which may appear at the end of the
clause, that is after object or modifiers, or before the subject
(inverted order). Examples of the first in principal clauses are:
oc Crīst it ne wolde (1, 8); *and tē Lundenisce folc him underfēng*
(2, 8); *and tē king it besæt* (2, 13); *and hī tōgædere cōmen* (2, 16).
Subordinate clauses with final verb are even more common: *þe þēr
wǣron* (1, 6); *þā hē nān mọ̄r ne mihte* (1, 7); *ðat hē mīlde man was*
(2, 27). The verb precedes the subject even more frequently than
it ends the clause. Compare *cōm Henrī* (1, 1); *was it noht* (1, 8);
warth þē king dẹ̄d (1, 18); *and forþī him luveden God and gōd men*

'and because God and good men loved him' (4, 27); and in
subordinate clauses, *þā wiste þē kīng* (1, 6); *þā þēstrede þē dai*
(1, 14); *þā diden hī alle wunder* (2, 28). The subjunctive inverted
appears in *come þou* 'if thou shouldst come' (52, 8); *wēre hē
never sǭ hǭlȳ man* 'if he were, &c.' (74, 11). Poetical usage
naturally shows metrical inversion, and some greater liberties are
taken than in the modern period. As Middle English develops, the
order of the modern language more and more appears.

NOTE.—In syntax, as in versification, there are few strongly marked
dialectal peculiarities. Sth. is most conservative, Nth. most radical. For
example, early Sth. tends to preserve the older word order. Nth., as later in
development, shows the modern order; compare Rolle of Hampole, p. 143 f.

199. Other peculiarities of word order are not numerous. In
the early time the appositive sometimes follows the noun, as in
Henrī kīng and *Henrī abbot* (1, 1); *Stēphnes kīnges* (4, 28); *þē
kīnges sune Henrīes* (5, 13). When the last usage gave way to
a phrase for the appositive, it also follows, as in *þē kīnges suster of
France* (7, 1). The predicate modifiers may precede the verb, as
in *gōdman hē wes* (2, 3); *pais hē makede men* (2, 4); *manī þūsend
hī drāpen mid hünger* (3, 18). The adjective sometimes follows the
noun in prose, but perhaps usually under foreign influence, as in
ȝātes everlastand (101, 24); *lufe ynesche* (144, 14); *þē hert sorowful
and mēke* (102, 23). It is common for the relative to be separated
from the antecedent, as in *ǣvre man . . . þe mihte* 'every man who
might' (2, 1); *Tēobāld . . . þe was abbot* (5, 17). The final position
of the adverb, which later, as preposition, preceded the relative, is
usual, as in *hē þat al his trīst is tō* 'he in whom is all his trust'
(51, 15). In *alle hī* (2, 29), *alle hē* 28 20 the order is the reverse
of what is now possible.

200. Middle English syntax is loose compared with that of
to-day. This is shown by the unnecessary repetition of the subject,
not only as in *wan þē gǭst it scholde gǭ* (48, 5); *þē bodī it seide*
(52, 9); *þē wreche peoddare mǭre noise hē mākeð* (198, 27); but
also in such cases as *wanne hē is ikindled stille līð þē lēun* (14, 8),

instead of 'when born the lion lies still'. So the appositive is sometimes loosely used instead of a closer syntax, as in *Rogingham þē castel* (4, 22); *Vaspāsian hys tȳme* (220, 7); *Vaspāsian þē emperor hys tȳme* (220, 17).

THE NOUN, ADJECTIVE, AND PRONOUN

201. The oblique cases of the noun retain some older uses. Thus the objective genitive persists, as in *for ūre Drihtines luve* 'for the love of our Lord' (4, 31); *nāness kinness shaffte* (12, 32). So the genitive of inanimate things, as in *tē sēes grūnd* 'the bottom of the sea' or 'the sea bottom' (19, 23). The adverbial genitive remains in the phrases *here þankes . . . here unþankes* 'according to their pleasure . . . according to their displeasure', or 'willingly and unwillingly' (6, 31–32). The dative without *to* appears more freely, as in *tē king iaf ðat abbotrīce ān prīōr* 'to a prior' (1, 9); *þē wǣrse hī wǣron him* 'to him' (5, 20); *sais us* 'says to us' (149, 19). It is used adverbially after certain verbs, as *and benam him al* 'and took away from him all' (5, 21); *hē bitagte Iōsēp his ring* (24, 11); *us sal bēn hard* 'it shall be hard for us' (27, 11). It is used as an old instrumental in *þat God himselve ran on blōde* 'on which God himself ran with blood' (78, 3); *al his wlite wurð tēres wēt* 'with tears' (28, 32). It expresses time in which, as in *þis gēar* (1, 1); *þis gēare* (2, 18). The accusative without preposition denotes duration of time, as in *þā nigentēne wintre* (3, 21); *nigentēne wintre* (4, 9). Two accusatives occur with certain verbs, as in *al ðat hē cūthe āxen him* (5, 19).

202. The adjective syntax is chiefly distinguished by frequent use as a noun. Compare *for hēvīe* 'for heaviness' (35, 20); *for nō newe* 'for no new love' (37, 14); *hidinges* 'hiding places' (233, 22). The definite form (§ 138) occurs after a demonstrative or possessive pronoun, a noun in the possessive, in direct address, and when used substantively. The last use is illustrated by the examples above. Other examples of the definite form are *tē*

Lundenisce folc (5, 33); *þē þridde wīse* (8, 15); *þiss Englissche bōc* (13, 22).

203. The pronoun syntax differs from to-day in several particulars. It may be omitted as subject or object, as in *ðat him brǣcon alle þē limes* 'that they broke', &c. (3, 13); *wēnde tō begǣton* 'they thought to get' (7, 2); *wrythen tō ðat* 'twisted them so that' (3, 8). Again, the subject may be repeated in a pronoun, as *wan þē gōst it scholde gō* (48, 5); *þē bodī it seide* (52, 9). Lack of concord between pronoun and antecedent is not uncommon: *give wē ilk ān þāre langāge* 'if we give each one *their* language' (134, 5).

204. The personal pronoun is used reflexively, as in *mē nogt wēren* 'not protect myself' (22, 19); *hē lutten him* 'they bowed themselves' (25, 3). The plural of the second person is first used as a singular in *but gē wið us sēnden Benjamin* (27, 16). Yet the singular remains the rule long after the time of this selection. The genitive of the personal pronoun is used objectively, as in *her nouþer* 'neither of them' (6, 16); *ūre nōn* 'none of us' (28, 6). The dative without a preposition is used much more freely than at present: as indirect object in *gūr silver is gū brogt agōn* (28, 4); as dative of advantage or disadvantage in *ðat him brǣcon* 'that they broke for them' (3, 13); *annd fōrþedd tē þin wille* 'and accomplished for thee thy will (8, 18); *what hire wēre* 'what was to her = the matter with her' (36, 19). An accusative for the genitive appears in *wart it war* 'became aware of it' (5, 12).

205. The demonstrative is sometimes used for the possessive, as in *als thē ēom wes* 'as his uncle had been' (2, 20); *alle þē limes* 'all their limbs' (3, 13). It is also omitted where necessary at present, as in *ǣvric man sōne rǣvede ōþer þe mihte* 'the other' (2, 1). It is used as an indefinite in *wiþ þat hē māde* 'with that which he made', OE. *wiþ þat þat hē macode* (67, 16); *þat understāndes þat Ī tell* (134, 8). The relative pronoun is frequently omitted, as in *Martin was gehāten* 'who was called Martin' (1, 11). It precedes its antecedent, as in *that þey receyve in forme of brēd*, *hyt is Goddes body* (122, 5). The nominative-accusative is used for a dative in *þat bērs of bāret bē ful irk* 'to which', &c. (150, 2). The relative may refer to a genitive antecedent, as in *in his ward ... þat māked him* 'in the custody of him who made him' (67, 28–29); *þaire wyll þat aghte it* 'the will of them that owned it' (147, 13)

THE VERB AND OTHER PARTS OF SPEECH

206. The verb does not always agree with its subject, especially if the latter follows, as in *wes al unfrið and yvel and rǣflāc* (2, 10); *cōm tō Flǫrīs writ and sǫnde* (46, 28). The copula is sometimes omitted, as in *wēl mē* 'well is to me' (32, 3). The impersonal verb is common, as in *unnc birrþ* 'it behooves us two' (8, 26); *him līkede* 'it pleased him' (14, 16); *hem drempte* 'it came to them in vision' (21, 13); *mē wǫre lēvere* 'it were pleasanter to me' (22, 21). Change from indirect to direct discourse or the reverse often occurs, as in passages at 27, 15–16; 29, 12 f.; 82, 14 f. The auxiliary of the passive for intransitive verbs is still the verb to be, as in *dērðe is cumen* 'dearth has come' (30, 25); *hē bēn cumen* (35, 8); *hū hit is went* (42, 19).

207. The inflected tenses are still used with general force, the present for present and future, the preterit for all past time. Thus the preterit is a past perfect in *þā was þē king strengere þanne hē ǣvert ēr was* 'had been' (7, 23). On the other hand the compound tenses are also common, and make more explicit the time relations. The preterit tense is also used as a present in clauses of unreality, as in *hū ðǫ him līkede ... migte nevre divel witen* 'may the devil never know' (14, 16–17).

208. The subjunctive is common in both subjunctive and optative senses. Examples are *fāre hē* 'if he go' (16, 26); *ðū it sǫge* 'if thou shouldst see it' (19, 4); *ȝyf þōu hade wolde* 'if thou hadst wished' (102, 20); *wāre Henrī king* 'Henry should be king' (7, 16); *þat ōþer deide befǫre* 'that the other should die before [him]' (45, 2); *hāve hē* 'may he have' (77, 29).

209. The infinitive without *to* is common, as in *unnc birrþ bāþe þannkenn* (8, 26); *dēde hem wassen* 'made them wash' (29, 3); *dōn bē* 'made to be' (34, 13); *wēnde hir fīnde* 'thought to find' (40, 29). The infinitive as a verbal complement still persists, especially in Southern, as in *þẹr cōm . . . līðen* 'there came . . . going' (191, 1-2); *whan Arður cume līðen* 'when Arthur may come' (191, 10). Occasionally a participle is used as a noun, perhaps under Latin influence, as in *þē sēchand hym* 'the [ones] seeking him' (101, 19).

210. Certain uses of adverbs and prepositions may be noted. Thus *sǭ . . . sǭ* are correlative, as in *al sǭ briht sǭ it wēre day* (83, 2); and *so* for *as* in *al is man sǭ is tis ẹrn* (16, 13). The preposition *toward* is divided, as in *tō Gode ward* (16, 21); *tō ðē hevene ward* (18, 9).

NOTE.—Nth. sometimes uses *til* (*till*) for Ml., Sth. *tō*, as in *tō cum þē till* 'to come to thee' (140, 2); *till ēnd* 'to the end' (141, 3). So also Nth. is characterized by the use of *at* for *tō*, as in *noght at hīde* 'nought to hide' (158, 5).

VERSIFICATION

211. Like modern English verse Middle English poetry is accentual, and the metrical stress regularly coincides with the principal or secondary stress of the word as usually pronounced. Yet ME. verse shows considerable variety of form. There are in this book examples of the older alliterative line, the Latin septenarius or line of seven stresses without rime, the same with rime, the four and five stressed couplets, and several stanza forms. All lines but the alliterative are prevailingly iambic.

212. The alliterative line is of complicated structure, its principal features being two half-lines of two principal stresses each, but without syllabic regularity. The half-lines are usually bound together by alliteration of the stressed syllables, one in each half-line, two in the first and one in the second, or two in each. Besides, there may be assonance in the final stressed syllables of

the half-lines, or rime with more or less frequency. A good
example of a verse matching the Old English scheme is,

> Welle hḗg is tat hil   ðat is hevenrīche (14, 14).

But the alliterative syllable of the second half-line is often on the
second, rather than the first principal stress, as in

> Bī wilc weie sǭ hē wille   to dḗle niðer wēnden (14, 3).

Again, the alliteration may fail altogether in the second half-line,
as in

> Ǭðer dūst ǭðer deu   ðat hē ne cunne is fīnden (14, 6).

On the other hand, there may be two alliterative syllables in the
second half-line, as in

> Fī́gteð wið ðis wirm   and fāreð on him fīgtande (17, 21).

Crossed alliteration of the forms *abab* or *abba* may also occur, as

> Drāgeð dūst wið his stert   ðēr hē dūn steppeð (14, 5);
>
> Ǭðer ðurg his nḗse smel   smāke ðat hē negge (14, 2).

213. Rime sometimes appears in the alliterative line at the end
of each half, as in

> In a stǭn stille hē lai   til it kam ðē ðridde dai (15, 12);

or two lines may be bound together into a couplet, as in

> His hǭpe is al tō Gode ward,   and of his luve hē lēteð,
>
> Ðat is tē sunne sikerlīke,   ðus his sigte hē bēteð (16, 21–22).

Again, a couplet may rime finally and in its first half-lines, as

> And tus hē neweð him, ðis man,   ðanne hē nimeð tō kirke,
>
> Ǭr hē it biðenken can   hise ēgen wēren mirke (16, 15–16).

Occasionally rime may appear as a tag to the preceding line, as at
the bottom of page 14. The rime may entirely supersede alliteration as a binding force for the half-lines, and couplet structure
results as on pages 15 and 19; compare also the selection from
Layamon's *Brut* at p. 181. On the other hand alliteration has
remained an occasional adjunct of all rimed verse; see § 218.

214. The septenarius without rime appears in the selection from the *Ormulum* (p. 18), and its couplet structure in the *Poema Morale* (p. 176) and Gloucester's *Chronicle* (p. 203). The first is stilted verse, the stress of the word not corresponding to the metrical stress, as in *aftterr* (8, 13, and 20), *unnderr* (8, 17). In these and other cases we probably are to see the substitution of the trochee for the iamb, so common in modern verse. Orm's lines are invariably of fifteen syllables each. In other poems the first unstressed syllable may be omitted, as in

Ich æm élder þen ich wes ā wíntre and ā lǫ́re (176, 1);

or after the cesural pause, as in

Wēl láte ic hábbe mē bipóht, bute mē Gód dō mílce (176, 8).

Robert of Gloucester is considerably less regular in his verse structure, often omitting the fifteenth syllable (feminine ending) as well as the first, and occasionally unstressed syllables within the line, as well as sometimes misplacing accents.

215. The four-stressed line is normally of eight syllables, as the five-stressed is of ten. But any such line may have an extra unstressed syllable at the end, as in

And hāveð démpt Iōsḗp tō bāle (21, 2);
As ríot, hásard, stýwes and tavérnes (237, 3).

Besides, a stressed syllable at the beginning of the line may do duty for the whole of the first foot, as in

Cūpen hē lḗt fílle of flūres (35, 15);

or for the first after the cesural pause, as in

Þē duc þat þē ring fúnde (44, 13).

As in modern verse a trochee may appear for the first iamb, or for the first after a cesural pause, the latter as in

Þē Ádmiral þǫ́, wél him bitíde (46, 9).

216. The loss of unstressed syllables has already been treated in §§ 80–90. In addition, final unstressed *e* is elided in poetry

before a vowel or weak *h*. Sometimes it is also dropped before
a consonant, as in

> Mē drempt(e) als ic̀ was wun(e) tō dōn (22, 2).

Contraction and slurring in other cases will be clear from the
principles given above.

217. Perfection in rime is naturally a gradual development. In
the earliest verse even assonance is sometimes sufficient, as in

> Đē kínges kúppe is hadde on hónd ;
>
> Đe beríes đōrínne mē đugte ic wróng (21, 27-28).

Rime in the consonant and not the vowel of the syllable may be
found, as in *Effraym—hem* (24, 23-24). So rime of long and
short vowels is not unusual, as in *wīn—đĕrin* (22, 3-4); *sperd—ḗrd*
(22, 29-30); *Chanaan—forđan* (24, 27-28). Rime words also
differ in the quality of the vowel, especially open *ē*'s and *ō*'s often
riming with the corresponding close vowels. Examples are *spĕd—
frigtihę̄d* (26, 29-30); *lę̄den—đēden* (29, 13-14); *ę̄n—Pharaōn*
(23, 29-30); *gǭn—Symeōn* (26, 3-4).

218. Alliteration has always been an ornament of English
poetry. When it ceased to be the regular binding feature of the
half-lines in alliterative verse, it continued as an occasional adjunct
of the poetic line. In short lines, two or three stressed syllables
may be bound together by this head-rime. In longer lines, four
syllables may begin with the same consonant, or with the same or
different vowels. Examples will be easily found in every selection.

INDEX

The numbers refer to paragraphs.

I. THE MIDLAND DIALECT

A. EARLY EAST MIDLAND

I. THE PETERBOROUGH CHRONICLE

1132. Ðis gēar cōm Henrī Kīng tō þis lānd. Þā cōm Henrī abbot and [1] wreide þē muneces of Burch tō þē kīng forþī ðat [2] hē wolde underþēden ðat mynstre tō Clunīe, swā ðat tē kīng was wēl nēh bepaht and sende efter þē muneces. And þurh Godes milce and þurh þē Biscop [3] of Seresberī and tē Biscop of Lincol and tē ōþre 5 rīce men þe þēr wǣron, þā wiste þē kīng ðat hē fēorde mid swic-dōm. Þā hē nān mōr ne mihte, þā wolde hē ðat his nefe sculde bēn abbot [4] in Burch, oc Crīst [5] it ne wolde. Was it noht swīthe lāng þērefter þat tē kīng sende efter him and dide him gyven up ðat abbotrīce [6] of Burch and faren ūt of lānde; and tē kīng iaf ðat 10 abbotrīce ān prīōr of Sanct [7] Nēod, Martin was gehāten. Hē cōm on Sanct Pētres messedei mid micel wurscipe intō thē minstre.

1135. On þis gǣre fōr sē Kīng Henrī [7a] over sǣ æt tē Lammasse. And ðat ōþer dei þā hē lai an slēp in scip, þā þēstrede þē dæi over al lāndes and ward þē sunne swilc als it wāre thrē niht āld mōne, 15 and [8] sterres abūten him at middæi. Wurþen men swīðe ofwundred and ofdrēd, and sǣden ðat micel þīng sculde cumen hērefter, swā dide; for þat ilc gǣr warth þē kīng dęd, ðat ōþer dæi efter Sanct Andrēas massedæi on Normandī. Þā wes tręsōn ā [9] þās lāndes, for

---

[1] ꝛ as often.   [2] ð only, as usually.   [3] ᵬ.   [4] abᵬ.   [5] Xpist, as usually.   [6] abᵬrice.   [7] S', as always.   [7a] H'.   [8] an.   [9] westre sona.

ǣvric man sōne rǣvede ōþer þe mihte.   Þā nāmen his sune and
his frēnd and brohten his līc tō Englelānd[1] and bebirīeden[2] in Rędinge.   Gōd man hē wes and micel æie wes of him.   Durste nān
man misdōn wið ōðer on his tīme.   Pais hē makede men and dēr[3].
Wuāswā bāre his byrthen, gōld and sylvre, durste nān man sei tō 5
him naht būte gōd.

Enmāng þis was his nefe cumen tō Englelānd, Stēphne de Blais,
and cōm tō Lundene ; and tē Lundenisce folc him underfēng and
senden æfter þē ærcebiscop, Willelm[4] Curbuil, and halechede him
tō kīnge on midewintre dæi.   On þis kīnges tīme wes al unfrið 10
and yfel and rǣflāc, for agēnes him risen sōna þā rīce men þe
wǣron swikes, alrefyrst Baldwin de Redvērs, and hēld Execestre
agēnes him ; and tē kīng it besæt, and sið ðan Baldwin acordede.
Þā tōcan þā ōðre and hēlden her castles agēnes him, and David
Kīng of Scotlānd tōc tō werrīen him.   Þā, þohwethere þat, here 15
sāndes fēorden betwyx heom, and hī tōgædere cōmen and wurðe
sæhte, þoþ it lītel forstōde.

1137.   Ðis gǣre fōr þē Kīng[6] Stēphne[7] ofer sǣ tō Normandī and
thēr wes underfāngen, forþī ðat hī wēnden ðat hē sculde bēn alswic
alse thē ęom wes, and for hē hadde gēt his tresōr ; ac hē todęld it 20
and scatered sotlīce.   Micel hadde Henrī Kīng gadered gōld and
sylver, and nā gōd ne dide me for his sāule tharof.

Þā þē Kīng Stēphne tō Englalānd cōm, þā makod hē his gadering æt Oxenefōrd and þar hē nam þē biscop Rogēr of Sereberī, and
Alexander Biscop of Lincol and tē Cancelēr Rogēr, hise neves, and 25
dide ælle in prisūn til hī iāfen up here castles.   Þā thē swikes undergǣton ðat hē mīlde man was and softe and gōd, and nā justīce ne
dide, þā diden hī alle wunder.   Hī hadden him manrēd maked and
āthes sworen, ac hī nān trēuthe ne hēolden ; alle hī[7] wǣron forsworen and here trēothes forloren, for ǣvric rīce man his castles 30
makede and agǣnes him hēolden, and fylden þē lānd ful of castles.
Hī swencten swȳðe þē wrecce men of þē lānd mid castelweorces.

---

[1] Englel, as usual.   [2] bebiriend.   [3] dær.   [4] Willm, as usual.
[5] k, as often.   [6] Steph., as usual.   [7] he.

Þā þē castles wāren maked, þā fylden hī mid dēovles and yvele
men. Þā nāmen hī þā men þe hī wēnden ðat anī gōd hefden,
bāthe be nihtes and be dæies, carlmen and wimmen, and diden
heom in prisūn efter gōld and sylver, and pīned heom untellendlīce
pīning. For ne wāren nǣvre nān martyrs swā pīned alse hī wǣron; 5
me hēnged ūp bī thē fēt and smoked heom mid fūl smoke; me
hēnged bī thē þūmbes ōther bī thē hēfed, and hēngen brynīges on
her fēt; me dide cnotted strēnges abūton here hǣved and wrythen
tō ðat it gǣde tō þē hǣrnes. Hī diden heom in quarterne þar
nadres and snakes and pades wǣron inne, and drāpen heom swā. 10
Sume hī diden in crūcethūs, ðat is in ān cæste þat was scort and
nareu and undēp, and dide scærpe stānes þērinne and þrēngde þē
men þǣrinne ðat him brǣcon alle þē limes. In manī of þē castles
wǣron lof and grin, ðat wǣron rachentēges ðat twā ōþer thrē men
hadden onōh tō bæron ōnne; þat was swā maced, ðat is fæstned 15
tō ān bēom, and diden ān scærp īren abūton þē[1] mannes throte
and his hals, ðat hē ne myhte nōwiderwardes, ne sitten ne līen ne
slēpen, oc bǣron al ðat īren. Manī þūsend[2] hī drāpen mid
hūnger[3].

Ī ne can ne Ī ne mai tellen alle þē wunder, ne alle þē pīnes ðat 20
hī diden wrecce men on þis lānd; and ðat lastede þā nigentēne[4]
wintre wīle Stēphne was kīng, and ǣvre it was werse and werse.
Hī lǣiden gǣldes[5] on thē tūnes ǣvre um wīle and clepeden it
tenserīe. Þā þē wrecce men ne hadden nān mōre tō gyven, þā
rǣveden hī and brendon alle thē tūnes ðat, wēl þū myhtes faren all 25
a dæis fare, sculdest thū nēvre fīnden man in tūne sittende ne lānd
tiled. Þā was cōrn dǣre and flēsc[6] and cǣse and butere, for nān
ne was ō þē lānd. Wrecce men sturven of hūnger; sume iēden
on ælmes þe wāren sum wīle rīce men; sume flugen ūt of lānde.
Wes nǣvre gǣt māre wreccehēd on lānd, ne nǣvre hēthen men 30
werse ne diden þan hī diden; for ōwer sithon ne forbāren hī
nouther circe ne cyrceiǣrd, oc nāmen al þē gōd ðat þarinne was
and brenden sythen þē cyrce and al tegædere. Ne hī ne forbāren

---

[1] þa. [2] þusen. [3] hungær, as often. [4] xix. [5] gæildes. [6] flec

biscopes [1] lānd, ne abbotes [2], ne prēostes, ac rǣveden munekes and clerkes and ǣvric man ōther þe ǫwer myhte. Gif twā men ǫþer ðrē [3] cōman rīdend tō ān tūn, al þē tūnscipe flugen [4] for heom; wēnden ðat hī wǣron rǣvęres. Þē biscopes and lęred men heom cursede ǣvre, oc was heom naht þarof for hī wēron al forcursed [5] and forsworen and forloren. Warsæ me tilede, þē ērthe ne bar nān cōrn, for þē lānd was al fordōn mid swilce dǣdes and hī sǣden openlīce ðat Crīst slēp and his halechen. Swilc and māre þanne wē cunnen sǣin wē þolęden [6] nigentēne [7] wintre for ūre sinnes.

On al þis yvele tīme hēold Martin abbot his abbotrīce twentī [8] wintre and half gǣr and ehte [9] dǣis mid micel swinc, and fānd þē munekes and tē gestes al þat heom behōved; and hēold mycel caritēd in thē hūs, and þoþwethere wrohte on þē circe and sette þartō lāndes and rentes, and gōded it swȳthe and lǣt it rēfen, and brohte heom intō þē newæ mynstre on Sanct Pētres mæssedæi mid micel wurtscipe. Ðat was *anno ab incarnatione Domini mcxl, a combustione loci xxiii.* And hē fōr tō Rōme and þǣr wæs wæl underfāngen fram þē Pāpe Eugenīe, and begæt thare privilegies, ān of alle þē lāndes of þē abbotrīce [10] and ānōþer of þē lāndes þe līen tō þē circewīcan ; and, gif hē lēng mōste liven, alse hē mint tō dōn of þē hōrderwȳcan. And hē begæt in lāndes þat rīce men hafden mid strengthe : of Willelm Malduit þe hēold Rogingham þē [11] castel, hē wan Cotingham and Ęstūn ; and of Hugo of Waltevile hē wan Hyrtlingberī [12] and Stanewīg and sixtī [13] solidi [14] of Aldewingle ǣlc gǣr. And hē makede manīe munekes and plantede wīniærd and makede manī weorkes, and wende þē tūn betere þan it ǣr wæs, and wæs gōd munec and gōd man and forþī him luveden God and gōde men.

Nū wē willen sægen sum dęl wat belamp on Stēphnes Kīnges tīme. On his tīme þē Iudēus of Norwīc bohton ān Cristen [15] cīld beforen Ęstren and pīneden him alle þē ilce pīning ðat ūre Drihten was pīned ; and on lāng Frīdæi him on rōde hēngen for ūre Drihtines luve, and sythen byrīeden him. Wēnden ðat it sculde

---

[1] ð.   [2] aðð.   [3] iii.   [4] flugæn.   [5] forcursæd.
[6] þolenden.   [7] xix.   [8] xx.   [9] viii.   [10] þabbotrice.   [11] þæ.
[12] Hyrtlingb.   [13] lx.   [14] soł.   [15] Xpisten.

bēn forholen, oc ūre Dryhtin atȳwede ðat hē was hālī martyr[1];
and tō munekes him nāmen and bebyrīed him hēglīce in þē minstre,
and hē maket þur ūre Drihtin wunderlīce and manīfældlīce miracles,
and hātte hē Sanct Willelm.

1138. On þis gǣr cōm David, Kīng of Scotlānd[2], mid ormēte 5
fǣrd tō þis lānd ; wolde winnan þis lānd, and him cōm tōgǣnes
Willelm Ēorl of Albamar, þe þē kīng hadde[3] betȩht Evorwīc, and
tō ōther ǣvest[4] men mid fæu men and fuhten wid heom, and
flēmden þē kīng æt tē Standard and slōghen swīthe micel of his
gēnge.   10

1140. On þis gǣr wolde þē Kīng Stēphne tæcen Rodbert Ēorl of
Gloucestre, þē kīnges sune Henrīes, ac hē ne myhte for hē wart it
war. Þērefter in þē lēngten þēstrede þē sunne and tē dæi abūton
nōn-tīd dæies þā men eten, ðat me lihtede cāndles tō æten bī ; and
þat was ðrētēne *kalendas Apriles*[5]. Wǣron men swȳthe ofwundred. 15
Þērefter fordfēorde Willelm Ærcebiscop of Cantwarberī[6], and tē
kīng makede Tēodbāld ærcebiscop þe was abbot in thē Bec.

Þērefter wǣx swȳthe micel werre betwyx þē kīng and Randolf
Ēorl of Cæstre, noht forþī ðat hē ne iaf him al ðat hē cūthe āxen
him, alse hē dide alle ōthre, oc æfre þē māre hē iaf heom, þē wærse 20
hī wǣron him. Þē ēorl hēold Lincol agǣnes þē kīng and benam
him al ðat hē āhte tō haven ; and tē kīng fōr þider and besætte him
and his brōther Willelm de R[om]are[7] in þē castel. | And tē æorl
stæl ūt and fērde efter Rodbert Ēorl of Gloucestre and brohte him
þider mid micel fērd ; and fuhten swȳthe on Cāndelmasse dæi 25
agēnes heore lāverd and nāmen him—for his men him swyken and
flugen[8]—and lǣd him tō Bristowe, and diden þar in prisūn and
[fe]teres. Þā was al Englelānd styred mār þan ǣr wæs, and al
yvel wæs in lānde.

Þērefter cōm þē kīnges dohter Henrīes þe hefde bēn emperice in 30
Alamanīe and nū wæs cūntesse in Angou, and cōm tō Lundene
and tē Lundenissce folc hire wolde tæcen and scǣ flēh and forlęs

---

[1] mr.   [2] Scotl.   [3] adde.   [4] ævez.   [5] xiii k̄. April.   [6] Cantwarð.
[7] R. . . are ; bracketed letters or words are conjectural.   [8] flugæn.

þar micel. Þerefter þē biscop of Wincestre, Henrī þē kīnges brōther Stēphnes, spac wid Rodbert Ēorl and wid þe emperice[1], and swōr heom āthas ðat hē nẹvre mā mid tē kīng his brōther wolde hālden, and cursede alle þē men þe mid him hēolden, and sǣde heom ðat hē wolde iiven heom ūp Wincestre, and dide heom cumen þider. Þā hī þǣrinne wǣren, þā cōm þē kīnges cwēn mid al hire strengthe and besǣt heom, ðat þēr wǣs inne micel hūnger. Þā hī ne lēng ne muhten þolen, þā stāli hī ūt and flugen; and hī wurthen war widūten and folecheden heom and nāmen Rodbert Ēorl of Gloucestre, and ledden him to Rōvecestre and diden him þare in prisūn; and tē emperice flēh intō ān minstre. Þā fēorden þē wīse men betwyx þē kīnges frēond and tē ēorles frēond, and sahtlede swā ðat me sculde lēten ūt þē kīng of prisūn for þē ēorl, and tē ēorl for þē kīng; and swā diden.

Sithen þerefter sahtleden þē kīng and Randolf Ēorl at Stanfōrd, and āthes swōren and trēuthes fǣsten ðat her nouþer sculde beswīken ōther. And it ne forstōd naht, for þē kīng him sithen nam in Hamtūn þurh[2] wicci rǣd, and dide him in prisūn; and efsōnes hē lēt him ūt þurh wǣrse rēd, tō ðat forewarde ðat hē swōr on hālidōm and gȳsles fānd þat hē alle his castles sculde iiven ūp. Sume hē iaf ūp and sume ne iaf hē noht, and dide þanne wǣrse þanne hē hēr[3] sculde.

Þā was Englelānd swȳthe todẹled. Sume hēlden mid tē kīng and sume mid þē emperice; for þā þē kīng was in prisūn þā wēnden þē ēorles and tē rīce men þat hē nẹvre māre sculde cumen ūt, and sǣhtleden wyd þē emperice[1] and brohten hire into Oxenfōrd and iāven hire þē burch. Þā þē kīng was ūte, þā hērde ðat sǣgen and tōc his fēord and besǣt hire in þē tūr; and me lǣt hire dūn on niht of þē tūr mid rāpes, and stal ūt and scǣ flēh and iǣde on fōte tō Walingfōrd. Þǣrefter scǣ fērde over sǣ and hī of Normandī wenden alle frā þē kīng tō þē Ēorl of Angæu, sume here þankes, and sume here unþankes; for hē besǣt heom til hī a-iāven ūp here castles, and hī nān helpe ne hæfden of þē kīng.

---

[1] þemperice, as usually.   [2] þurhc, as in next clause also.   [3] hær.

Þā fērde Eustace þē kīnges sune tō France and nam þē kīnges
suster of France tō wīfe; wēnde tō begæton Normandī þǣrþurh.
Oc hē spedde lītel, and be gōde rihte for hē was ān yvel man, for
warese hē [cōm hē] dide māre yvel þanne gōd. Hē rę̄vede þē
lāndes and læide mic[ele gēlde]s on; hē brohte his wīf tō Englelānd 5
and dide hire in þē caste[l on Can]teberī[1]; gōd wimman scǣ wæs
oc scǣ hedde lītel blisse mid him. And Crīst ne wolde ð̄at hē
sculde lānge rīxan, and wærd dę̄d and his mōder beien.

And tē Ēorl of Angæu wærd dę̄d and his sune Henrī tōc tō þē
rīce. And tē cwēn of France tōdǣlde frā þē kīng and scǣ cōm tō 10
þē iunge Ēorl Henrī, and hē tōc hire tō wīve and al Peitou mid
hire. Þā fērde hē mid micel fǣrd intō Englelānd and wan castles;
and tē kīng fērde agēnes him mid micel māre fērd. And
þoþwæthere fuhten[2] hī noht, oc fērden þē ǣrcebiscop and tē wīse
men betwux heom and makede ð̄at sahte ð̄at tē kīng sculde bēn 15
lāverd and kīng wīle hē livede, and æfter his dæi wāre Henrī kīng;
and hē hēlde him for fader and hē him for sune, and sib and sæhte
sculde bēn betwyx heom and on al Englelānd. Þis and tē ōthre
forwardes þet hī makeden swōren tō hālden þē kīng and tē ēorl
and tē biscop and tē ēorles and rīce men alle. Þā was þē ēorl 20
underfāngen æt Wincestre and æt Lundene mid micel wurtscipe,
and alle diden him manrēd and swōren þē pais tō hālden; and hit
ward sōne swȳthe gōd pais, swā ð̄at nę̄vre was ę̄re[3]. Þā was þę̄
kīng strengere þanne hē ǣvert ę̄r[4] was; and tē ēorl fērde over sǣ
and al folc him luvede, for hē dide gōd justīse and makede pais. 25

1154. On þis gǣr wǣrd þē Kīng Stēphne dę̄d and bebyrīed þēr
his wīf and his sune wǣron bebyrīed æt Favresfēld; þæt minster hī
makeden. Þā þē kīng was dę̄d þā was þē ēorl beiōnde sǣ, and ne
durste nān man dōn ōþer būte gōd for þē micel eie of him. Þā
hē tō Englelānd cōm þā was hē underfāngen mid micel wurtscipe, 30
and tō kīng blētced[5] in Lundene on þē Sunnendæi beforen midwinter dæi, and hēld þǣr micel cūrt. Þat ilce dæi þat Martin,
abbot[6] of Burch, sculde þider faren, þā sǣclede hē and ward dę̄d,

---

[1] teb.   [2] fuhtten.   [3] here.   [4] her.   [5] bletcæd.   [6] abƀ.

fowre *nonas Januarias*[1], and tē munekes innen dæis cusen ōþer of
heom sælf, Willelm de Waltevile is gehāten, gōd clerc and gōd
man, and wæl luved of þē kīng and of alle gōde men. And o[n
circ]en[2] byrīeden þē abbot[3] hēhlīce, and sōnc þē cosan abbot[4]
fērde and tē muneces [mid him tō] Oxenfōrde tō þē kīng, [and hē] 5
iaf him þat abbotrīce[4a]. And hē fērde him sōn[e to Linc]ol and
wæs þ[ær blētced tō] abbot ær hē hām cōme, and [sithen] was
underfāngen [mid mic]el [wurtscipe at] Burch, mid [mice]l processiūn. And swā hē was alswā at Ramesæie, and at Torneie[5], and
at . . . , and Spallding[6], and at S . l . bares, and . . . , and [nū is] 1
abbot, and fa[ire] haved begunnon. Cristus[7] him un[ne gōd
ēndinge].

II. THE DEDICATION TO THE ORMULUM

Nū, brōþerr Wallterr, brōþerr mīn affterr þē flæshess kīnde,
Annd[8] brōþerr mīn ī Crisstenndōm þurrh fulluhht annd þurrh trowwþe,
Annd brōþerr mīn ī Godess hūs ʒēt[9] ō þē þridde[10] wīse,   1
Þurrh þatt witt hafenn tăkenn[11] bā ān reʒhellbōc tō follʒhenn,
Unnderr kanunnkess hād annd līf swā summ Sannt Awwstīn sette ;
Icc hafe dōn swā summ þū badd annd fōrþedd tē þīn wille,
Icc hafe wennd inntill Ennglissh goddspelless hallʒhe lāre[12],
Affterr þatt little witt þatt mē mīn Drihhtīn hafeþþ lēnedd.   2
Þū þohhtesst tatt itt mihhte wēl till mikell frame turrnenn,
Ʒiff Ennglissh follc, forr lufe off Crīst, itt wollde ʒērne lērnenn
Annd follʒhenn itt annd fillenn itt wiþþ þohht, wiþþ wōrd, wiþþ dēde ;
Annd forrþī ʒerrndesst tū þatt icc þiss werrc þē shollde wirrkenn,
Annd icc itt hafe fōrþedd tē, acc all þurrh Crīstess hellpe,   2
Annd unnc birrþ bāþe þannkenn Crīst þatt itt iss brohht till ēnde.

---

[1] iiii Nᵒ. Iañ.   [2] All bracketed words are conjectural.   [3] þaþþ.
[4] aþ.   [4a] aþþrice.   [5] Torn'.   [6] Spall'.   [7] Xpus.   [8] ꜣ, as usually.
[9] ʒet, with double accent.   [10] þride.   [11] The breve, as usual when
in MS.   [12] lāre.

Icc hafe sammnedd ō þiss bōc þā goddspelless nēh alle
Þatt sinndenn ō þē messebōc inn all þē ʒēr att messe ;
Annd aʒʒ affterr þē goddspell stannt þatt tatt tē goddspell mēneþþ,
Þatt mann birrþ spellenn tō þē follc off þeʒʒre sāwle nēde ;
Annd ʒēt [1] tær tēkenn māre inōh þū shallt tæronne fīndenn,   5
Off þatt tatt Crīstess hallʒhe þēd birrþ trowwenn wēl annd follʒhenn.
Icc hafe sett hēr ō þiss bōc amāng goddspelless wōrdess,
All þurrh mēsellfenn, maniʒ wōrd þē rīme [2] swā tō fillenn ;
Acc þū shallt fīndenn þatt mīn wōrd, eʒʒwhær þær itt iss ēkedd,   9
Maʒʒ hellpenn þā þatt rēdenn itt tō sēn annd t' unnderrstanndenn [3]
All þess tē bettre, hū þeʒʒm birrþ þē goddspell unnderrstanndenn.
Annd forrþī trowwe icc þatt tē birrþ wēl þolenn mīne wōrdess,
Eʒʒwhær þær þū shallt fīndenn hemm amāng goddspelless wōrdess ;
For whāse mōt [4] tō læwedd follc lārspell off goddspell tellenn,
Hē mōt [4] wēl ēkenn maniʒ wōrd amāng goddspelless wōrdess.   15
Annd icc ne mihhte nohht mīn ferrs aʒʒ wiþþ goddspelless wōrdess
Wēl fillenn all, annd all forrþī shollde icc well offte nēde
Amāng goddspelless wōrdess dōn mīn wōrd, mīn ferrs tō fillenn.

    Annd tē bitæche icc off þiss bōc, hēh wīkenn alls itt sēmeþþ,
All tō þurrhsēkenn illc ān ferrs, annd tō þurrhlōkenn offte,   20
Þatt upponn all þiss bōc ne bē nān wōrd ʒēn Crīstess lāre,
Nān wōrd tatt swīþe wēl ne bē tō trowwenn annd tō follʒhenn.
Witt shulenn tredenn unnderr fōt [4] annd all þwerrtūt [4] forrwerrpenn
Þē dōm off all þatt lāþe flocc þatt iss þurrh nīþ forrblēndedd,
Þatt tæleþþ þatt tō lofenn iss þurrh nīþfull mōdīʒnesse.   25
Þeʒʒ shulenn lætenn [5] hæþeliʒ off unnkerr swinnc, lēf brōþerr,
Annd all þeʒʒ shulenn takenn itt onn unnitt annd onn īdell,
Acc nohht þurrh skill, acc all þurrh nīþ, annd all þurrh þeʒʒre
    sinne.
Annd unnc birrþ biddenn Godd tatt hē forrʒife hemm hēre sinne ;
Annd unnc birrþ bāþe lofenn Godd off þatt itt wass bigunnenn,   30
Annd þannkenn Godd tatt itt iss brohht till ēnde þurrh hiss hellpe ;

----

[1] ʒet, with double accent.   [2] rīme.   [3] tunnderrstanndenn.
        [4] vowel with double accent.   [5] lætenn.

Forr itt ma33 hellpenn alle þā þatt blīþelīke itt hērenn,
Annd lufenn itt annd foll3henn itt wiþþ þohht, wiþþ wōrd, wiþþ
dēde.

Annd whāse wilenn shall þiss bōc efft ōþerr sīþe wrītenn,
Himm bidde icc þatt hē't [1] wrīte [2] rihht, swā summ þiss bōc himm
tǣcheþþ,

All þwerrtūt [1] affterr þatt itt iss uppō þiss firrste bīsne,   5
Wiþþ all swillc rīme [3] alls hēr iss sett, wiþþ all se fele wōrdess;
Annd tatt hē lōke wēl þatt hē ān bōcstaff wrīte [2] twi33ess
E33whær þǣr itt uppō þiss bōc iss wrītenn ō þatt wīse.

Lōke hē wēl þatt hē't [1] wrīte swā, forr hē ne ma33 nohht elless
Onn Ennglissh wrītenn [4] rihht tē wōrd, þatt wite hē wēl tō sōþe. 10

Annd 3iff mann wile wītenn whī icc hafe dōn þiss dēde,
Whī icc till Ennglissh hafe wennd goddspelless hall3he lāre,
Icc hafe itt dōn forrþī þatt all Crisstene follkess berrhless
Iss lāng uppō þatt ān, þatt te33 goddspelless hall3he lāre
Wiþþ fulle mahhte foll3he rihht þurrh þohht, þurrh wōrd, þurrh
dēde.   15

Forr all þatt æfre onn ērþe iss nēd Crisstene follc tō foll3henn
Ī trowwþe, ī dēde, all tǣcheþþ hemm goddspelless hall3he lāre;
Annd forrþī whāse lērneþþ itt annd foll3heþþ itt wiþþ dēde,
Hē shall onn ēnde wurrþī bēn þurrh Godd tō wurrþenn borr3henn.
Annd tǣrfore hafe icc turrnedd itt inntill Ennglisshe spǣche, 20
Forr þatt Ī wollde blīþelī3 þatt all Ennglisshe lēde
Wiþþ ǣre shollde lisstenn itt, wiþþ herrte shollde itt trowwenn,
Wiþþ tūnge shollde spellenn itt, wiþþ dēde shollde itt foll3henn,
Tō winnenn unnderr Crisstenndōm att Godd sōþ sāwle berrhless.
Annd 3iff þe33 wilenn hērenn itt, annd foll3henn itt wiþþ dēde, 25
Icc hafe hemm hollpenn unnderr Crīst tō winnenn þe33re berrhless.
Annd Ī shall hafenn forr mīn swinnc gōd lǣn att Godd onn ēnde,
3iff þatt Ī, forr þē lufe off Godd annd forr þē mēde off heffne,
Hemm hafe itt inntill Ennglissh wennd forr þe33re sāwle nēde.
Annd 3iff þe33 all forrwerrpenn itt, itt turrneþþ hemm till sinne, 30

---

[1] het, vowel with double accent.   [2] wrīte.   [3] rīme.   [4] wrītenn.

Annd Ī shall hafenn addledd mē þē Lāferrd Crīstess āre,
Þurrh þatt icc hafe hemm wrohht tiss bōc tō þeȝȝre sāwle nēde,
Þohh þatt teȝȝ all forrwerrpenn itt þurrh þeȝȝre mōdīȝnesse.

Goddspell onn Ennglissh nemmnedd iss gōd wōrd, annd gōd
    tīþennde,
Gōd errnde, forrþī þatt itt wass þurrh hallȝhe goddspellwrihhtess 5
All wrohht annd wrītenn uppō bōc off Crīstess firrste[1] cōme,
Off hū sōþ Godd wass wurrþenn mann forr all mannkinne nēde,
Annd off þatt mannkinn þurrh hiss dǣþ wass lēsedd ūt[2] off helle,
Annd off þatt hē wisslīke rās þē þridde daȝȝ off dǣþe,
Annd off þatt hē wisslīke stāh þā siþþenn upp till heffne, 10
Annd off þatt hē shall cumenn efft tō dēmenn alle þēde,
Annd forr tō ȝēldenn īwhillc mann affterr hiss āȝhenn dēde.
Off all þiss gōd uss brinngeþþ wōrd annd errnde annd gōd tīþennde
Goddspell, annd forrþī maȝȝ itt wēl gōd errnde bēn ȝehātenn.
Forr mann maȝȝ uppō goddspellbōc gōdnessess fīndenn seffne 15
Þatt ūre Lāferrd Jēsu Crīst uss hafeþþ dōn onn ērþe,
Þurrh þatt hē comm tō manne annd þurrh þatt hē warrþ mann
    onn ērþe.
Forr ān gōdnesse uss hafeþþ dōn þē Lāferrd Crīst onn ērþe
Þurrh þatt hē comm tō wurrþenn mann forr all mannkinne nēde.
Ōþerr gōdnesse uss hafeþþ dōn þē Lāferrd Crīst onn ērþe 20
Þurrh þatt hē wass ī flumm Jorrdān fullhtnedd forr ūre nēde ;
Forr þatt hē wollde uss waterrkinn till ūre fulluhht hallȝhenn,
Þurrh þatt hē wollde bēn himmsellf onn ērþe ī waterr fullhtnedd.
Þē þridde gōd uss hafeþþ dōn þē Lāferrd Crīst onn ērþe
þurrh þatt hē ȝaff hiss āȝhenn līf wiþþ all hiss fulle wille 25
Tō þolenn dǣþþ ō rōdetrē sacclǣs wiþþūtenn wrihhte,
Tō lēsenn mannkinn þurrh hiss[3] dǣþ ūt[2] off þē dēfless wālde.
Þē fērþe gōd uss hafeþþ dōn þē Lāferrd Crīst onn ērþe
Þurrh þatt hiss hallȝhe sāwle stāh frā rōde dūn till helle,
Tō tǎkenn ūt[4] off hellewā þā gōde sāwless alle 30

---

[1] fisste.   [2] vowel with double accent.   [3] his.   [4] vowel with double accent.

Þatt haffdenn cwemmd himm ī þiss līf þurrh sōþ unnshaþiʒnesse.
Þē fīfte gōd uss hafeþþ dōn þē Lāferrd Crīst onn ērþe
Þurrh þatt hē rās forr ūre gōd þē þridde daʒʒ off dǽþe,
Annd lēt[1] tē posstless sēn himm wēl inn hiss mennisske kīnde ;
Forr þatt hē wollde fesstenn swā sōþ trowwþe ī þeʒʒre brēstess   5
Off þatt hē, wiss tō fulle sōþ, wass risenn upp off dǽþe,
Annd ī þatt illke flǽsh þatt wass forr uss ō rōde naʒʒledd ;
Forr þatt hē wollde fesstnenn wēl þiss trowwþe ī þeʒʒre brēstess,
Hē lēt[1] tē posstless sēn himm wēl, well offte sīþe onn ērþe,
Wiþþinnenn daʒʒess fowwerrtīʒ frā þatt hē rās off dǽþe.   10
Þē sexte gōd uss hafeþþ dōn þē Lāferrd Crīst onn ērþe
Þurrh þatt hē stāh forr ūre gōd upp inntill heffness blisse,
Annd sennde siþþenn Hāliʒ Gāst till hise lērninngcnihhtess,
Tō frōfrenn[2] annd tō bēldenn hemm tō stanndenn ʒæn þē dēfell,
Tō gifenn hemm gōd witt inōh off all hiss hallʒhe lāre,   15
Tō gifenn hemm gōd lusst, gōd mahht, tō þolenn alle wāwenn
All forr þē lufe off Godd, annd nohht forr ērþlīʒ loff tō winnenn.
Þē seffnde gōd uss shall ʒēt[1] dōn þē Lāferrd Crīst onn ēnde
Þurrh þatt hē shall ō dōmess daʒʒ uss gifenn heffness blisse,
ʒiff þatt wē shulenn wurrþī bēn tō fīndenn Godess āre.   20

Þuss hafeþþ ūre Lāferrd Crīst uss dōn gōdnessess seffne,
Þurrh þatt tatt hē tō manne comm tō wurrþenn mann onn ērþe.
Annd ō þatt hallʒhe bōc þatt iss apokalypsīs nemmnedd
Uss wrāt[1] tē posstell Sannt Johān, þurrh Hāliʒ Gāstess lāre,   24
Þatt hē sahh upp inn heffne ān bōc bisett wiþþ seffne innseʒʒless,
Annd sperrd swā swīþe wēl þatt itt ne mihhte nān wihht oppnenn[3]
Wiþþūtenn Godess hallʒhe Lāmb þatt hē sahh ēc inn heffne.
Annd þurrh þā seffne innseʒʒless wass rihht swīþe wēl bitācnedd
Þatt sefennfāld gōdleʒʒc þatt Crīst uss dide þurrh hiss cōme ;   29
Annd tatt nān wihht ne mihhte nohht oppnenn þā seffne innseʒʒless
Wiþþūtenn Godess Lāmb, þatt comm forr þatt itt shollde tācnenn
Þatt nān wihht, nān enngell, nān mann, ne nāness kinness shaffte,

---

[1] vowel with double accent.   [2] frofren.   [3] opnenn, but oppnenn
regularly.

Ne mihhte þurrh himmsellfenn þā seffne gōdnessess shǣwenn
Ō mannkinn, swā þatt it mannkinn off helle mihhte lēsenn,
Ne gifenn mannkinn lusst, ne mahht, tō winnenn heffness blisse.
Annd all all swā se Godess Lāmb, all þurrh hiss āȝhenn mahhte,
Lihhtlīke mihhte annd wēl inōh þā seffne innseȝȝless oppnenn,   5
All swā þē Lāferrd Jēsu Crīst all þurrh hiss āȝhenn mahhte,
Wiþþ Faderr annd wiþþ Hālīȝ Gāst, ān Godd annd all ān kīnde,
All swā rihht hē lihhtlīke inōh annd wēl wiþþ alle mihhte
Ō mannkinn þurrh himmsellfenn þā seffne gōdnessess shǣwenn,
Swā þatt hē mannkinn wēl inōh off helle mihhte lēsenn,   10
Annd gifenn mannkinn lufe annd lusst, annd mahht annd witt annd
        wille,
Tō stanndenn inn tō cwēmenn Godd tō winenn heffness blisse.
Annd forr þatt hālīȝ goddspellbōc all þiss gōdnesse uss shǣweþþ,
Þiss sefennfāld gōdleȝȝc þatt Crīst uss dide þurrh hiss āre,
Forrþī birrþ all Crisstene follc goddspelles lāre follȝhenn.   15
Annd tǣrfore hafe icc turrnedd itt inntill Ennglisshe spǣche,
Forr þatt Ī wollde blīþelīȝ þatt all Ennglisshe lēde
Wiþþ ǣre shollde lisstenn itt, wiþþ herrte sholde itt trowwenn,
Wiþþ tūnge shollde spellenn itt, wiþþ dēde sholde itt follȝhenn,
Tō winnenn unnderr crisstenndōm att Crīst sōþ sāwle berrhless.   20
Annd Godd allmahhtīȝ ȝife uss mahht annd lusst and witt annd wille
Tō follȝhenn þiss Ennglisshe bōc þatt [1] all iss hālīȝ lāre,
Swā þatt wē mōtenn wurrþī bēn tō brūkenn heffness blisse.
        Am[ǣn].   Am[ǣn].   Am[ǣn].
Icc þatt tiss Ennglissh hafe sett, Ennglisshe menn tō lāre,   25
Icc wass þǣr þǣr Ī crisstnedd wass Orrmīn bī name nemmnedd;
Annd icc, Orrmīn, full innwarrdlīȝ wiþþ mūþ annd ēc wiþþ herrte
Hēr bidde þā Crisstene menn þatt hērenn ōþerr rēdenn [2]
Þiss bōc, hemm bidde icc hēr þatt teȝȝ forr mē þiss bede biddenn,
Þatt brōþerr þatt tiss Ennglissh writt allre ǣresst [3] wrāt [4] annd wrohhte,
Þatt brōþerr forr hiss swinnc tō lǣn sōþ blisse mōte [5] fīndenn.   31
        Am[ǣn].

---

[1] þat.   [2] rēdenn.   [3] allrǣresst.   [4] vowel with double accent.   [5] mōte.

B. MIDLAND OF THE THIRTEENTH AND FOURTEENTH CENTURIES

I. THE BESTIARY

THE LION'S NATURE

Ðe leūn stant on hille;   and[1] hē man hunten hēre,
Ǭðer ðurg his nęse smel   smāke ðat hē negge,
Bī wilc weie sǭ hē wile   tō dęle niðer wēnden,
Alle hise fētsteppes   after him hē filleð;
Drāgeð dūst wið his stert   ðēr hē dūn[2] steppeð,   5
Ǭðer dūst ǭðer deu,   ðat hē ne cunne is fīnden;
Drīveð dūn tō his den   ðar hē him bergen wille.

  An ōðer kīnde hē hāveð.   Wanne hē is ikindled
Stille līð ðē leūn,   ne stireð hē nout of slēpe,
Til ðē sunne hāveð sinen   ðrīes him abūten;   10
Ðanne reiseð his fader him   mit tē ręm ðat hē mākeð.

  Ðē ðridde lāge hāveð ðe leūn;   ðanne hē līeð tō slēpen
Sal hē nevre lūken   ðē lides of hise ēgen.

SIGNIFICATION

  Welle hēg is tat hil   ðat is hevenrīche;
Ūre Lǫverd is tē leūn   ðe liveð ðēr abuven;   15
Hū[3] ðǭ him līkede   tō ligten hēr on ērðe,
Migte nevre divel witen,   ðǭ hē bē dērne hunte,
Hū hē dūn cōme,   ne hū[3] hē dennede him
In ðat defte meiden,   Mārīe bī nāme,
    Ðe him bar tō manne frāme.   20

---

[1] ɟ, as usually.   [2] he steppeð.   [3] wu.

Ðǫ ūre Drigten dęd was,   and dolven alsǫ his wille was,
In a stǫn stille hē lai   til it kam ðē ðridde[1] dai;
His fader him filstnede swǫ   ðat hē rǫs frǫ dęde ðǫ,
                    us tō līf hǫlden.

Wākeð sǫ his wille is,   sǫ hīrde for his fōlde;   5
Hē is hīrde, wē bēn sēp;   sīlden hē us wille
If wē hēren tō his wōrd   ðat wē ne gǫn nǫwor wille.

The Eagle's Nature

        Kiðen Ī wille ðē ęrnes kīnde
        Alsǫ ic it ō bōke rędē;
        Hū[2] hē neweð his gūðhęde,   10
        Hū hē cumeð ūt of ēlde,
        Siðen hise limes arn unwēlde,
        Siðen his bęc is al tōwrǫng,
        Siðen his fligt is al unstrǫng,
        And his ēgen dimme.   15
        Hēreð hū[2] hē neweð him;
        A welle hē sēkeð ðat springeð ai,
        Bǫðe bī nigt and bī dai;
        Ðērǫver hē flēgeð and up hē teð
        Til ðat hē ðē hevene sēð,   20
        Ðurg skīes sexe and sevene,
        Til hē cumeð tō hevene.
        Sǫ rigt sǫ hē cunne
        Hē hǫveð in ðē sunne;
        Ðē sunne swīðeð[3] al his fligt,   25
        And oc it mākeð his ēgen brigt,
        Hise feðres fallen for ðē hęte,
        And hē dūn mide tō ðē węte
        Falleð in ðat wellegrūnd,
        Ðēr hē wurðeð[4] heil and sūnd,   30

---

[1] dridde.   [2] wu.   [3] swideð.   [4] wurdeð.

And cumeð ūt al newe,
Ne wēre his bẹc untrewe.
His bẹc is gēt biforn wrǫng,
Ðog hise limes sinden¹ strǫng,
Ne maig hē tilen him nǫn fōde   5
Himself tō nǫne gōde.
Ðanne gǭð hē tō a stǫn,
And hē billeð ðēron,
Billeð til his bẹc bifǫren²
Hāveð ðē wrengðe forlǫren;   10
Siðen wið his rigte bile
Tākeð mẹte ðat hē wile.

SIGNIFICATION

Al is man sǫ is tis ẹrn,   wulde gē nū listen³
Ǫld in hise sinnes dērn   ǫr hē bicumeð cristen.   14
And tus hē neweð him, ðis man,   ðanne hē nimeð tō kirke;
Ǫr hē it biðenken can   hise ēgen wēren mirke;
Forsākeð⁴ ðǫre Sātanas   and ilk sinful dēde,
Tākeð him tō Jēsu⁵ Crīst   for hē sal bēn his mēde,
Lēveð on ūre Lǫverd Crīst   and lẹreð prēstes lǫre;
Of hise ēgen wẹreð ðē mist   wīles hē drecheð ðǫre.   20
His hǫpe is al tō Gode ward,   and of his luve hē lēteð⁶,
Ðat is tē sunne sikerlīke,   ðus his sigte hē bēteð;
Nāked falleð in ðē funtfat,   and cumeð ūt al newe,
Būten a lītel; wat is tat?   his mūð is gēt untrewe;
His mūð is gēt wēl unkūð   wið paternoster and crēde.   25
Fāre hē norð or ⁷ fāre hē sūð,   lẹren hē sal his nēde;
Bidden bōne tō Gode   and tus his mūð rigten,
Tilen him sǫ ðē sowles fōde   ðurg grāce off ūre Drigtin.

---

¹ senden.   ² biforn.   ³ listlen.   ⁴ forsaket.   ⁵ ihu.
                ⁶ lereð.   ⁷ er.

The Serpent's Nature

An wirm is ō werlde   wēl man it knoweð,
Neddre is tē nāme ;   ðus hē him neweð
Ðanne hē is forbrǫken [1],   and in his ēlde al forbroiden [2].
Fasteð til his fel him slākeð   tēn daies fulle,
Ðat hē is lęne and mainlęs   and ivele mai gangen ;   5
Hē crēpeð cripelande forð,   his craft hē ðus kīðeð,
Sēkeð a stǫn ðat a ðirl is on,   narwe būten hē nēdeð him,
Nimeð unnęðes ðurg,   for his fel hē ðēr lēteð.
His flęs forð crēpeð,   walkeð tō ðē water ward,
Wile ðanne drinken.   Oc hē speweð ǫr al ðē venim   10
Ðat in his brēst is bred   frǫ his bīrde tīme ;
Drinkeð siðen inōg,   and tus hē him neweð.

    Danne ðē neddre is   of his hīd nāked
And bāre of hīs brēstatter,
If hē nāked man sē   ne wile hē hīm nogt neggen,   15
Oc hē flēð frǫ him   als hē frǫ fīr sulde.
If hē clǫðed man sē   cǫf hē waxeð,
For up hē rigteð him   rędī tō dęren,
Tō dęren er tō dęd māken,   if hē it muge fōrðen.
Wat if ðē man war wurðe   and węren him cunne,   20
Figteð wið ðis wirm   and fāreð [3] on him figtande ?
Ðis neddre siðen   hē nēde sal
Mākeð sēld of his bodī   and sīldeð his hęved ;
Lītel him is of hise limes,   būte hē līf hǫlde.

Signification

    Know Cristene man   wat tū Crīst higtest,   25
Atte kirkedure   ðar ðū cristned wēre.
Ðū higtes tō lēven on him,   and hīse lāges luvīen,
Tō hēlden wit herte   ðē bǫdes of hǫlī kirke [4].

---

[1] forbroken and forbroiden.   [2] forwurden.   [3] freð.   [4] krke.

If ðū hāvest is brǫken,   al ðū forbrēdes [1],
Forwurðes and forgelwes   ēche līf tō wǫlden;
Ēlded art frǫ ēche blis   sǫ ðis wirm ō werld is.
Newe ðē forðī [2]   sǫ ðē neddre dōð,
It is tē nēd.   5

Feste ðē of stędefastnesse,   and·ful of ðewes,
And help ðē pōvre men   ðe gangen abūten.
Ne dēme ðē nogt wurðī [3]   ðat tū dure lōken
Up tō ðē hevene ward;   oc walke wið ðē ērðe,
Mīldelīke amǫng men.   Nǫ mōd ðū ne cune,   10
Mōd ne mannes uncost;   oc swīc of sineginge,
And bōte bid tū ðē ai,   bǫðe bī nigt and bī dai,
Ðat tū milce mōte hāven   of ðīne misdēdes.

Ðis līf bitǫkneð ðē stī   ðat tē neddre gangeð bī,
And tis is ðē ðirl of ðē stǫn   ðat tū salt ðurg gǫn: 15
Lēt ðīn filðe frǫ ðē   sǫ ðē wirm his fel dōð;
Gǫ ðū ðan tō Godes hūs   ðē godspel tō hēren,
Ðat is soule drink,   sinnes quenching.

Oc ǫr sei ðū in scrifte   tō ðē prēst sinnes tīne,
Fēg ðē ðus of ðī brēstfilðe [4]   and feste ðē forðward   20
Fast at tīn herte   ðat tū firmest higtes.
Ðus art tū ging and newe,   forðward bē ðū trewe.
Nēdeð ðē ðē devel nogt,   for hē ne mai ðē dęren nogt;
Oc hē fleð frǫ ðē   sǫ neddre frǫ ðē nākede.
On ðē clǫðede ðē neddre is cǫf,   and tē devel cliver on sinnes; 25
Ai ðē sinfule   bisetten hē wile,
And wið al mankin   hē hāveð nið and win.
Wat if hē lęve hāve   of ūre Hevenlǫverd
For tō dęren us   sǫ hē ūre eldere ǫr dēde?
Dō wē ðē bodī in ðē bāle   and bergen ðē soule,   30
Ðat is ūre hęved gēvelīc,   hēlde wē it wurðlīc.

---

[1] forbreðes.   [2] fordi.   [3] nog wurdi.   [4] filde.

The Whale's Nature

Cēthegrande is a fis
Đē mǭste ðat in water is;
Đat tū wuldes seien gēt,
Gef ðū it sǭge wan it flēt,
Đat it wēre an eilǭnd [1]   5
Đat sēte on [2] ðē sęsǭnd.

  Đis fis ðat is unrīde,
Đanne him hungreð hē gāpeð wīde;
Ūt of his ðrǭte it smīt an ǭnde,
Đē swetteste ðing ðat is ō lǭnde.   10
Đērfǭre ōðre fisses tō him drāgen,
Wan hē it fēlen hē āren fāgen;
Hē cumen and hǭven in his mūð,
Of his swike hē arn uncūð.

  Đis cēte ðanne hise chāveles lūkeð,   15
Đise fisses alle in sūkeð;
Đē smāle hē wile ðus biswīken,
Đē grēte maig hē nogt bigrīpen.

  Đis fis wuneð wið ðē sęgrūnd,
And liveð ðēr evre heil and sūnd,   20
Til it cumeð ðē tīme
Đat storm stireð al ðę sę,
Đanne sumer and winter winnen.
Ne mai it wunen ðērinne,
Sǭ drōvī is tē sęes grūnd,   25
Ne mai hē wunen ðēr ðat stūnd,
Oc stireð up and hǭveð stille.
Wīles ðat [3] weder is sǭ ille,
Đē sipes ðat arn on sę fordriven,—
Lǭð hem is dęð [4], and lēf tō liven,—   30

---

[1] a neilond.   [2] one.   [3] ðar.   [4] ded.

Bilōken hem and sēn ðis fis,
An eilǫnd hē wēnen it is.
Ðērof hē āren swiðe fāgen,
And mid here migt ðartō hē drāgen
Sipes on festen,   5
And alle up gangen.
Of stǫn mid stēl in ðē tunder
Wēl tō brennen on[1] ðīs wunder,
Warmen hem wēl and ēten[2] and drinken.
Ðē fīr hē fēleð and dōð hem sinken,   10
For sōne hē dīveð dūn tō grūnde;
Hē drēpeð hem alle wiðūten wūnde.

SIGNIFICATION

Ðis devel is mikel wið wil and magt,
Sǫ wicches hāven in here craft;
Hē dōð men hungren and hāven ðrist,   15
And manī ōðer sinful list,
Tolleð men tō him wið his ǫnde,
Wōsǫ him folegeð hē fīndeð sǫnde.
Ðǫ arn ðē little in lēve lāge,
Ðē mikle ne maig hē tō him drāgen;   20
Ðē mikle, Ī mēne ðē stēdefast
In rigte lēve mid flēs and gast.
Wōsǫ listneð develes lǫre,
On lengðe it sal him rewen sǫre;
Wōsǫ festeð hǫpe on him,   25
Hē sal him folgen tō helle dim.

[1] one.   [2] heten.

II. THE STORY OF JOSEPH

Putifar trewiðˇ hise wīves[1] täle,
And hāveðˇ[2] dempt Iōsēp tō bāle;
Hē bad bēn sperd faste[3] dūn,
And hǫlden harde in prisūn.
An lītel stūnd quīle hē was ðˇēr,   5
Sǫ gan him luven ðˇē prisunēr,
And him ðˇē[4] chartre hāveðˇ bitagt
Wiðˇ ðˇǫ prisūnes tō liven in agt[5].

Or for misdēde, or for onsāgen,
Ðǫr wǫren tō ðˇat prisūn drāgen   10
Ǫn ðˇat ðˇē kinges kuppe będ,
And ǫn ðˇe māde ðˇē kinges bręd.
Hem drempte dręmes bǫðˇen ō nigt,
And hē wurðˇen swīðˇe sǫre ofrigt.
Iōsēph hem servede ðˇǫr on sēl   15
At here drink and at here mēl;
Hē herde hem mūrnen, hē[6] freinde forquat;
Harde dręmes ǫgen awǫld ðˇat.
Ðǫ seide hē tō ðˇē butelēr[7],
'Tel mē ðˇīn dręm, mī brōðˇer dēr[8];   20
Queðˇersǫ it wurðˇe softe or strǫng,
Ðē reching wurðˇ on God bilǫng.'

'Mē drempte ic stōd at a wīntrē
Ðat hadde[9] waxen buges ðˇrē;
Ǫrest it blōmede, and siðˇen bar   25
Ðē berīes rīpe, wurðˇ ic war.
Ðē kinges kuppe ic[10] hadde on hǫnd;
Ðē berīes ðˇǫrinne mē ðˇugte ic wrǫng,

---

[1] wiwes.   [2] haved.   [3] fast.   [4] de.   [5] hagt.   [6] he hem
[7] butuler.   [8] her.   [9] adde.   [10] kinges ic.

And bar it drinken tō Phāraōn,
Mē drempte, als ic was wune tō dōn.'
    'Good is,' quaðð Iōsēph, 'tō drēmen of wīn,
Heilnesse and blisse is ðerin;
Ðrē daies bēn gēt for tō cumen,   5
Ðū salt bēn ūt of prisūn numen,
And on ðīn offis¹ set agēn.
Of mē ðū ðenke² ðan it sal bēn;
Bēd mīn ernde³ tō Phāraōn,
Ðat⁴ ic ūt of prisūn wurðe dōn;   10
For ic am stọlen of kīnde lọnd,
And wrigtelẹslīke⁵ họlden in bọnd.'
    Quað ðis brẹdwrigte, 'Liðeð nū mē:
Mē drempte ic bar brẹadlẹpes ðrē,
And ðọrin brẹad and ōðer mẹten   15
Quilke bēn wune ðē kinges tō ẹten;
And fugeles hāven ðọron lagt,
Ðọrfọre ic am in sorge and agt⁶,
For ic ne migte mē nogt wẹren,
Ne ðat mẹte frọ hem bẹren.'   20
    'Mē wọre lēvere,' quad Iōsēph,
'Of ẹddī drẹmes rechen swēp;
Ðū salt, after ðē ðridde dei,
Bēn dō on rōde, weilawei!
And fugeles sulen ðī fleis tōtẹren,   25
Ðat sal nọn agte mugen ðē wẹren.'
    Sōð wurð sọ Iōsēph seide ðat.
Ðis butelēr Iōsēph sōne forgat;
Twō gēr siðen was Iōsēph sperd
Ðọr in prisūn wiðūten ẹrd.   30
Ðọ drempte Phāraōn king a drẹm
Ðat hē stōd bī ðē flōdes strẹm,

---

¹ offiz.   ² ðhenke.   ³ herdne.   ⁴ ða.   ⁵ her wrigteleslike.
                          ⁶ hagt.

And ðeðen[1] ūtcōmen sevene[2] nẹẹt,
Everilc wēl swīðe fẹt and grẹt ;
And sevene lẹne after ðǭ,
Ðe dēden ðē sevene fette wǭ.

Ðē lẹne hāven ðē fette freten ;   5
Ðis drẹm ne mai ðē king forgeten.
An ōðer drẹm cam him bifǭren :
Sevene ẹres[3] wēxen fette of cōrn[4],
On an busk ranc and wēl tīdī,
And sevene lẹne rigt ðǭrbī,   10
Welkede and smāle and drugte numen,
Ðē rance[5] hāven ðǭ ǭvercumen ;
Tōsāmen it smiten and on a stūnd
Ðē fette ðrīsten tō ðē[6] grūnd.

Ðē king abraid and wōc in ðogt[7],   15
Ðēs drẹmes swēp ne wǭt hē nogt ;
Ne was nǭn sǭ wīse[8] in al his lǭnd
Ðe kūde undōn ðis drẹmes bǭnd.

Ðǭ him biðogte[9] ðat butelēr
Of ðat him drempte in prisūn ðēr,   20
And of Iōsēph in ðē prisūn,
And hē it tǭlde ðē king Phāraūn.
Iōsēph was sōne in prisūn ðǭ sogt[10],
And shāven and clad and tō him brogt.
Ðē king him bad bēn hardī and bǭld,   25
If hē can rechen ðis drẹmes wǭld ;
He tǭld him quat him drempte ō nigt,
And Iōsēp rechede his drẹm wēl rigt.

'Ðis twō drẹmes bǭðen bēn ǭn,
God wile ðē tawnen, King Phāraōn.   30
Ðǭ sevene[11] gēr bēn gēt tō cumen,
In al fulsumhẹd sulen it bēn numen,

[1] ðeden.   [2] vii, as throughout this passage.   [3] eares.   [4] coren.
[5] ranc he.   [6] ðrist hem to ðo.   [7] ðhogt.   [8] so wis man.   [9] biðhogte.
[10] hogt.   [11] vii, as usual.

And sevene ōðere sulen after bēn,
Sǫrī and nēdful men sulen is sēn.
Al ðat ðise firste[1] sevene māken
Sulen ðis ōðere sevene rospen and rāken.
Ic rēde ðē, King, nū hēr bifǫren,   5
Tō māken lāðes and gaderen cōrn[2],
Ðat ðīn folc ne wurð undernumen
Quan ðǫ hungrī gēre bēn forðcumen.'

King Phāraōn listnede hise rēd,
Ðat wurð him siðen sēlī spēd.   10
Hē bitagte Iōsēp his ring,
And his bēge of gōld for wurðing,
And bad him al his lǫnd bisēn,
And under him hēgest for tō bēn;
And bad him wēlden in his hǫnd   15
His folc, and agte, and al his lǫnd.

Ðǫ was under him ðanne Putifar,
And his wīf ðat hem sō tōbar.
Iōsēph tō wīve his dowter nam,—
Ōðer is nū ðan[3] ēr[4] bicam;   20
And ghē ðēr him twō childer bar,
Ǫr men wurð of ðat hunger war,
First Manassēn and Effraym;
Hē luveden God, hē gēld it hem.

Ðē sevene fulsum gēres fāren,   25
Iōsēp cūðe him bifǫren wāren;
Ðan cōrn[2] wantede in ōðer lǫnd,
Ðǫ was ynug[5] under his hǫnd.

Hunger wēx in lǫnd Chānaan,
And his tēne[6] sunes Iācōb forðan   30
Sente intō Ēgipt tō bringen cōrn[2];
Hē bilēf at hǫm ðe was gungest bǫren.

---

[1] first.   [2] coren.   [3] quan.   [4] ear.   [5] ðo ynug.   [6] x.

Ðē tēne [1] cōmen, for nēde sogt,
Tō Iōsēp, and hē ne knewen him nogt.
And ðǭ [2] hē lutten him frigtīlīke,
And seiden tō him mīldelīke,
'Wē bēn sǭndes, for nēde driven   5
Tō bigen cōrn ðǭrbī tō liven.'

   Iōsēp hem knew al in his ðogt [3],
Als hē lēt hē knew hem nogt.
'It sēmeð [4] wēl ðat gē spīes bēn,
And intō ðis lǫnd cumen tō sēn;   10
And cume gē for nǫn ōðer ðing
But for tō spīen ūr lǫrd ðē king.'

   'Nai,' hē seiden everilc ǭn,
'Spīes wēre wē never nǫn,
Oc alle wē bēn ǭn faderes sunen;   15
For hunger dōð us [5] hider cumen.'

   'Oc nū ic wǫt gē spīes bēn,
For bī gūre bēring men mai it sēn.
Hū sulde ǭn man [6] pōvre forgeten,
Swilke and sǭ manīge sunes bigeten?   20
For sēldum bitīd self anī king
Swilc men tō sēn of hise ofspring.'

   'A, lǫverd, mercī, gēt is ðǭr ǭn,
Migt hē nogt frǭ his fader gǭn.
Hē is gungest, hǭten Beniamin,   25
For wē bēn alle of Ēbrisse kin.'

   'Nū, bī ðē feið ic ǭg tō King Phāraōn,
Sule gē nogt alle heðen [7] gǭn
Til gē mē bringen Beniamin,
Ðē [8] gungeste brōðer of gūre [9] kin.'   30
For ðǭ was Iōsēp sǭre fordrēd
Ðat hē wǭre oc ðurg [10] hem forrēd.

---

[1] x.   [2] ðog.   [3] ðhogt.   [4] semet.   [5] doðes.   [6] husuld suld oninan.
[7] eðen.   [8] ða.   [9] ɼore.   [10] ðhurg.

Hē dēde hem bīnden, and lę̄den dūn
And spę̄ren faste in his prisūn;
Ðē ðridde dai hē lēt hem gǭn,
Al but ðē tǫn brōðer Symeōn;
Ðis Symeōn bilę̄f ðǭr in bǫnd   5
Tō wedde under Iōsēpes hǫnd.

  Ðēs ōðere brēðere sōne onǭn
Tōken lę̄ve and wenten hǫm.
And sōne hē wēren ðę̄ðen [1] went,
Wēl sǭre ɦē hāven hem biment,   10
And seiden hem ðan ðǭr bitwēn,
'Wrigtful wë in sorwe bēn,
For wē sinīgeden quīlum ǫr
On ūre [2] brōðer michil mǭr
For wē werneden him mercī,   15
Nū drēge wē sorge al forðī.'
Wēnde here nǭn it on his mōd,
Oc Iōsēp al it understōd.

  Iōsēpes men ðǭr quīles deden
Al sǭ Iōsēp hem hadde [3] beden;   20
Ðǭ brēðere seckes hāven hē filt,
And in everilc ðē silver pilt
Ðat ðōr was paied [4] for ðē cōrn [5],
And būnden ðē mūðes ðǭr bifǭren.
Oc ðē brēðere ne wisten it nogt,   25
Hū ðis dēde wurðe wrogt;
Oc alle hē wēren ǭverðogt,
And hāven it sǭ tō Iācōb brogt,
And tǫlden him sǭ of here spēd;
And al hē it listnede in frigtīhę̄d.   30
Quan men [6] ðǭ seckes ðǭr unbǫnd,
And in ðē cōrn [5] ðǭ agtes fǫnd,

---

[1] ðeden.   [2] hure.   [3] adde.   [4] paid.   [5] coren.
                          [6] and quan.

Alle hē wǫren ðanne sǫre[1] ofrigt.
Iācōb ðus him bimēneð origt,
'Wēl michel sorge is mē bicumen,
Ðat mīn twō childre āren mē fornumen.
Of Iōsēp wǫt ic ēnding nǫn,   5
And bǫndes bēn leid on Symeōn;
If gē Beniamin frǫ mē dōn,
Dēað[2] and sorge mē sēgeð on.
Ai sal Beniamin wið mē bilēven[3]
Ðǫr quīles ic sal on werlde liven.'   10
Ðǫ quað Iudas, 'Us sal bēn hard,
If wē nǫ hǫlden him nǫn forward.'
    Wēx dērðe, ðis cōrn[4] is gǫn,
Iācōb eft bit hem fāren agǫn;
Oc hē ne duren ðē weie cumen in,   15
'But gē wið us sēnden Beniamin.'
Ðǫ quað hē, 'Quan it is nēd,
And ic[5] ne can nǫ bettre rēd,
Bēreð ðat[6] silver hǫl agǫn
Ðat hem ðǫrof ne wante nǫn,   20
And ōðer silver ðǫr bifǫren
For tō bigen wið ōðer cōrn[4];
Fruit and spīces of dēre prīs
Bēreð ðat man ðat is sǫ wīs.
God unne[7] him ēðemōded[8] bēn,   25
And sēnde mē mīn childre agēn.'
    Ðǫ nāmen hē forðweie rigt,
Til hē bēn intō[9] Ēgypte ligt.
And quanne Iōsēp hem alle sag
Kīnde ðogt in his herte lag[10].   30
Hē bad his stiward gerken his[11] mēten,
Hē seide hē sulden wið him ēten[12].

---

[1] ðanno sori.   [2] dead.   [3] bilewen.   [4] derke ðis coren.   [5] no ic
in MS.   [6] dat.   [7] hunne.   [8] eðimodes.   [9] ben cumen into.   [10] ðhogt
... was.   [11] is.   [12] alle eten.

Hē ledde hem alle tō Iōsēpes birī,
Her nǫn hadden ðǭ lǫten mirī.

'Lǫverd,' hē seiden ðǭ everilc ǫn,
'Gūr silver is gū brogt agǫn;
It was in ūre seckes dōn,   5
Ne wiste ūre [1] nǫn gilt ðǭron.'

'Bēð nū stille,' quad ðē stiward, [2]
'For ic nū hāve mīn forward.'

Ðǭr cam ðat brōðer Symeōn
And kiste his brēðere ǫn and ǫn;   10
Wēl fagen hē was of here cōme,
For hē was numen ðǭr tō nǫme.
It was undren tīme or mǭre,
Hǫm [2a] cam ðat riche lǫverd ðǭre;
And al ðǭ brēðere [3] of frigtī mōd,   15
Fellen biforn ðat lǫverdes [4] fōt,
And bedden him riche present
Ðat here fader him hadde [5] sent.
And hē lēvelīke it understōd,
For alle hē wēren of kīnde blōd.   20

'Liveð,' quad hē, 'ðat fader gēt
Ðat ðus manīge sunes bigat?'

'Lǫverd,' hē seiden, 'gēt hē liveð,'—
Wǫt ic ðǭr nǫn ðat hē ne biveð,—
'And ðis is gunge Beniamin   25
Hider brogt after bǫdewōrd ðīn.'

Ðǭ Iōsēp sag him ðǭr bifǫren,
Bī fader and mōder brōðer bǫren,
Him ǫverwente his herte onǫn;
Kīnde luve gan him ǫvergǫn.   30
Sōne hē gēde ūt and stille hē grēt,
Ðat al his wlite wurð tēres wēt.

---

[1] ur.   [2] quad stiward.   [2a] om.   [3] briðere.   [4] louerdis.   [5] hi adde.

After ðat grot he weis his[1] wliten.
And cam ðan in and bad hem eten.
Hē dēde hem wassen, and him bifọren
Sette[2] hem as hē wēren bọren ;
Gēt hē ðogte[3] of his faderes wunes,   5
Hū hē sette at ðē mete hise sunes.
Of everilc sọnde, of everilc wīn,
Mọst and best hē gaf Beniamin.
In fulsumhẹd hē wurðen glāðe,
Iōsēp ne ðoht ðọrof nọ scāðe,   10
Oc it him līkede swīðe wēl.
And hem lẹrede and tagte wēl,
And hū hē sulden hem best lẹden
Quane hē cōmen in unkīnde ðēden ;
'And al ðē bettre sule gē spēden,   15
If gē wilen gū wið trewðe[4] lẹden.'
   Eft on morwen quan it was dai,
Ọr ọr ðē brēðere fērden awai,
Here seckes wọren alle filt wið cōrn[5],
And ðē silver ðọrin bifọren ;   20
And ðē seck ðat agte Beniamin
Iōsēpes cuppe hid was ðọrin.
And quan hē wēren ūt tūne went,
Iōsēp hāveð hem after sent.
   Ðis sọnde hem ọvertākeð rāðe,   25
And bicalleð of harme and scāðe ;
'Unsēlī men, quat hāve gē dōn ?
Gret unselhðe[6] is gū cumen on,
For is it nogt mīn lọrd forhọlen
Ðat[7] gūre ọn hāveð his[1] cuppe stọlen.'   30
   Ðọ[8] seiden ðē brēðere sikerlīke,
'Up quām ðū it fīndes witterlīke,

---

[1] is.   [2] and sette.   [3] ðhogte.   [4] treweiðe.   [5] coren.   [6] unselðehe.
[7] ða.   [8] ð.

Hē bē slagen [1] and wē agēn driven
Intō ðraldōm, evermǫr tō liven.'
Hē gan hem ransāken ǫn and ǫn,
And fǫnd it ðǫr sōne anǫn;
And nam ðǫ brēðere everilk ǫn   5
And ledde hem sorful agǫn,
And brogte hem bifǫr Iōsēp
Wið rewelī lǫte, and sorwe and wēp.

Ðǫ quat Iōsēp, 'Ne wiste gē nogt
Ðat ic am o wēl [2] witter ðogt?   10
Mai nogt lǫnge mē bēn forhǫlen
Quatsǫevere on lǫnde wurð stǫlen.'

'Lǫverd,' quad Iudas, 'dō wið mē
Quatsǫ ðī wille on werlde bē,
Wiððan ðat ðū friðe Beniamin.   15
Ic ledde him ūt [3] on trewthe mīn
Ðat hē sulde eft [4] cumen agēn
Tō hise fader, and wið him bēn.'

Ðǫ cam Iōsēp swilc rewðe upon,
Hē dēde alle [5] ūt ðē tōðere gǫn;   20
And spac unēðes, sǫ hē [6] grēt,
Ðat alle hise wlite wurð tēres wēt.
'Ic am Iōsēp, drēdeð gū nogt,
For gūre helðe ǫr hider brogt.
Twō [7] gēr bēn nū ðat dērðe [8] is cumen,   25
Gēt sulen fīve [9] fulle bēn numen,
Ðat men ne sulen sowen ne shęren,
Sǫ sal drugte ðē fēldes dęren.
Rāpeð gū tō mīn fader agēn,
And seið him quilke mīn blisses bēn;   30
And dōð him tō mē cumen hider,
And gē and gūre orf al tōgider.

---

[1] he slagen.   [2] wol.   [3] ledde ut.   [4] ef.   [5] halle.   [6] e.
[7] to.   [8] derke.   [9] v.

Of lewse gōd in lǫnd Gersen
Sulen gē sundrī rīche bēn.'
Everilc hē kiste, on ilc hē grēt,
Ilc here was of his[1] tēres wēt.

Sōne it was King Phāraōn kid 5
Hū ðis newe tīðing wurð bitid;
And hē was blīðe, in herte fāgen,
Ðat Iōsēp wulde him ðider drāgen,
For luve of Iōsēp migte hē tīmen.
Hē bad cartes and waines nimen, 10
And fechen wīves and childre and men,
And gaf hem ðǫr al lǫnd Gersen,
And hēt hem ðat hē sulden hāven
Mǫre and bet ðan hē kūde crāven.

Iōsēp gaf ilc here twinne srūd, 15
Beniamin mǫst hē māde prūd;
Fīf wēden best bar Beniamin,
Ðrē hundred plātes of silver fīn.
Alsǫ fẹle ōðre ðǫrtil
Hē bad bēn in his faderes will; 20
And tēne[2] asses wið sẹmes fest,
Of alle Ēgyptes welðe[3] best,
Gaf hē his brēðere wið herte blīðe,
And bad hem rāpen hem hǫmward swīðe;
And hē sǫ dēden wið herte fāgen; 25
Towārd here fader hē gunen drāgen,
And quane hē cōmen him bifǫren
Ne wiste hē nogt quat hē wǫren.

'Lǫverd,' hē sẹiden, 'Israēl,
Iōsēp ðīn sune grēteð ðē wēl, 30
And sēndeð ðē bǫde ðat hē liveth;
Al Ēgipte in his wille[4] cliveð.'

[1] is, as often.　　[2] x.　　[3] welðhe.　　[4] wil.

Iācōb abraid, and trewĕð [1] it nogt
Til hē sag al ðat welðe brogt.
'Wēl mē,' quað hē, 'wēl is mē wēl
Ðat ic hāve [2] abiden ðus swilc [3] sēl.
And ic sal tō mīn sune fāre,   5
And sēn ọ̄r ic of werlde chāre.'
Iācōb [4] wente ūt of lọ̄nd Chānaan,
And of his kīnde wēl manīe a man.
Iōsēp wēl faire him understōd,
And Phāraōn ðogte it ful good;   10
For ðat hē wēren hīrdemen
Hē bad hem bēn in lọ̄nd Gersen.

Iācōb was brogt bifọ̄ren ðē king
For tō geven him his blissing [5].
'Fader dēre [6],' quað Phāraōn,   15
'Hū fẹ̄le gēr bē ðē on?'
    'An hundred gēr and ðrittī [7] mọ̄
Hāve ic hēr drogen in werlde wọ̄;
Ðog ðinkeð mē ðọ̄roffen fọ̄
Ðọ̄ [8] ic is hāve drogen in wọ̄,   20
Siðen ic gan on werlde bēn,
Hēr ūten ẹ̄rd, mankin bitwēn.'
Sọ̄ ðinkeð [9] everilc wīse [10] man
Ðe wọ̄t quọ̄rof mankin bigan,
And ðe of Adames gilte muneð,   25
Ðat hē hēr ūten ẹ̄rdes [11] wuneð.

Phāraōn bad him wurðen wēl
In softe reste and sēlī mēl;
Him and hise sunes in reste dēde
In lọ̄nd Gersen on sūndrī stẹ̄de.   30
Siðen ðọ̄r was mād ọ̄n sitē [12]
Ðe was ihọ̄ten [13] Ramesē

---

[1] trewed.   [2] ave.   [3] swil.   [4] acob.   [5] bliscing.   [6] derer.
[7] xxx.   [8] ðog.   [9] ðinked.   [10] wis.   [11] herdes.   [12] scite.   [13] yeten.

Iācōb on līve wunede ðēr [1]
In reste fulle fowrtēne [2] gēr;
And God him lēt bifọren sēn
Quilc tīme hise ēnding sulde bēn.

Hē bad Iōsēp his lēve sune 5
Ọn ðing [3] ðat off hē [4] wēl mune,
Ðat quan it wurðe [5] mid him dōn,
Hē sulde him birīen in Ēbrōn;
And witterlīke hē it hāveð [6] him seid
Ðē stẹde ðọr Ābraham was leid. 10
Sọ was him lēf [7] tō wurðen leid
Quọr Hālī [8] Gāst stille hadde seid
Him and hise eldere fer ẹr [9] bifọren,
Quọr Jēsu Crīst wulde bēn bọren,
And quọr bēn dẹad, and quọr bēn grāven; 15
Hē ðogt wið hem reste tō hāven.

Iōsēp swōr him al sọ hē bad,
And hē ðọrof wurð blīðe and glad.
Ọr ðan hē wiste off werlde fāren,
Hē bad hise kīnde tō him chāren, 20
And seide quat of hem sulde bēn;
Hālī Gāst dēde it him seen.
In clẹne ēnding and hālī [8] līf,
Sọ hē forlēt ðis werldes strīf.

Iōsēp [10] dēde hise līch faire gẹren, 25
Wassen, and richelīke smẹren,
And spīcelīke swēte smāken;
And Ēgipte folc him biwāken
Fowertī [11] nigtes and fowertī [11] daiges;
Swilce [12] wọren Ēgipte laiges [13]. 30
First nigen [14] nigt ðē līches bẹðen,

---

[2] ðor.   [2] xiiij.   [3] ðhing.   [4] offe.   [5] wurð.   [6] aveð.
[7] lif.   [8] ali.   [9] ear.   [10] osep.   [11] xl.   [12] swilc.   [13] lages.
[14] ix.

And smēren, and wīnden and biquēþen.
And wāken is siðen fowertī[1] nigt;
Ðē men sō dēden ðe hadden[2] migt.
And Ēbrisse folc hadden[2] an kire,
Nogt sōne delven it wið ȳre,   5
Oc wassen it and kēpen it rigt,
Wiðūten smērles sevene nigt,
And siðen[3] smēred ðrittī[4] daiges.
Cristene folc hāveð ōðer laiges;
Hē bēn smēred ðōr quīles hē liven,   10
Wið crisme and olīe, in trewðe given[5];
For trewðe and gōde dēdes mide
Dōn[6] bēn ðan al ðat wechdēde.
Sum ōn, sum ðrē, sum sevene[7] nigt,
Sum ðrittī[4], sum twelve[8] mōneð rigt,   15
And sum everilc wurðen gēr,
Ðōr quīles ðat hē wunen hēr,
Dōn for ðē dēde chirchegōng,
Elmessegifte, and messesōng,
And ðat is on ðē weches stēde;   20
Wēl him mai bēn ðat[9] wēl it dēde.
Ēgipte folc hāveð[10] him wāked
Fowertī[1] nigt and fēste māked,
And hise sunes ðrittī daiges,
In clēne līf and hālī[11] laiges.   25
    Sō wōren forð tēn[12] wukes gōn,
Gēt hadde[13] Iācōb birīgeles nōn.
And Phāraōn King cam bōde bifōren,
Ðat Iōsēp hāveð his fader swōren.
And hē it him gatte ðōr hē wēl dede,   30
And bad him nimen him fēres mide,

[1] xl.   [2] adden.   [3] siden.   [4] xxx.   [5] geven.
[6] ðon.   [7] vii.   [8] xii.   [9] dat.   [10] aveð.   [11] ali.
[12] x.   [13] adde.

Wēl wǭpnede men and wīs of hēre,
Ðat[1] nǭ man hem bī weie dēre[2].
Ðat bēre is led, ðis folc is rad,
Hē fōren abūten bī Ādad.
Ful sevene nigt hē ðēr abiden,   5
And bimēning for Iācōb deden.
Sǭ lǭnge hē hāven ðeðen numen,
Tō flum Jurdan ðat hē bēn cumen,
And ǭver Phāran til Ēbrōn;
Ðǭr is ðat līche in birīele dōn.   10
And Iōsēp intō Ēgipte went
Wið al his folc ūt wið him sent[3].

III. FLORIS AND BLAUNCHEFLUR.

Þē portēr þoȝte what tō rēde;
Hē lēt flūres gadere on þē mēde,
Cūpen hē lēt fille[4] of flūres   15
Tō strawen in þē maidenes būres.
Þat was his rēd tō helpe him sǭ,
Hē lēt Flǭrīs[5] on þat ǭn cūpe gǭ.
Tweie[6] gegges þē cūpe bēre,
And for hēvīe wrǭþ hī wēre;   20
Hī bēden God ȝive him yvel[7] fīn
Þat sǭ manīe flūres dide[8] þērin.
Tō þē chaumbre þēr hī scholde gǭ
Ne ȝēden hī ariȝt nǭ;
Tō anōþer chaumbre hī bēn[9] agǭn,   25
Tō Blauncheflūres chaumbre nǭn.
Þē cūpe hī sette tō þē grūnde,
And gǭn[10] forþ and lēte[11] hire stūnde[12].

---

[1] dat.   [2] deren.   [3] wid al ... snt.   [4] fulle.   [5] Floriz, as often.
[6] twei.   [7] vuel.   [8] dude, as often.   [9] beoþ.   [10] goþ, as often.
[11] letez.   [12] stonde.

Ǭ maiden cōm and wōlde
þē flūres handlen and bihǫlde;
Flǫrīs wēnde hit wēre his swēte wiȝt,
Ūt of þē cūpe hē lēp ariȝt,
And þat maide for þē drēde   5
Bigan tō crīe and tō grēde.
Þǭ niste¹ Flǫrīs what tō rǫde
For þē fērlīch þat hē hadde;
Intō þē cūpe hē sterte aȝē²
And wiþ þē flūres hidde hē³.   10
Þis maide þoȝte anǫn riȝt
Þat hit was Flǫrīs, þat swēte wiȝt,
For here chaumbres niȝe⁴ wēre,
Sēlde was þat hī tōgadere nēre,
And ofte Blaunchefflūr hire hadde itǫld   15
Hū hēo was fram him isǫld.

Nū maidenes cōmen in tō hire lǫpe,
Wēl fiftēne in ǫn hǫpe,
And axede hire what hire wēre,
And whī hēo mākede suche bēre.   20
Wēl hēo was biþoȝt and wharc
Tō fīnden hem answare:
'Tō þē cūpe,' hēo sǫde, 'ich⁵ cōm and wōlde
Þis flūres handlen and bihǫlde;
Þēr fliȝte⁶ ūt a buterflīȝe,   25
Are ich wiste on mīn īȝe,
Sǭ sǫre ich was offērd of þan
Þat ich lūde⁷ crīe bigan.'
Þis ōþere lōȝen and hadde glēo,
And gǫn aȝēn and lēten⁸ bēo.   30
   Clārīce hatte þat maide hēnde;
Tō Blaunchefflūr hēo⁹ gan wēnde

---

¹ nuste.   ² aȝe, from MS. A.   ³ he hudde him.   ⁴ niȝ.   ⁵ ihc, and
always.   ⁶ fliste.   ⁷ lude, not in MS.   ⁸ leteþ.   ⁹ blaunchefflures chaumbre heo.

And sęde, 'Swēte Blauncheflūr,
Wilt ū sēo a wēl fair flūr?
Hit ne grew noȝt on þis lǫnde,
Þat flūr þat ich bringe þē tō hǫnde.'
'Away, Clārīs[1],' quaþ Blauncheflūr, 5
'Hō þat luveþ paramūr,
And haþ þērof joye mai luve flūres;
Ac ich libbe in soreȝe in þis tūres,
For ich wēne, wiþūte[2] gabbe,
Þat þē Admiral mē wile[3] habbe. 10
Ac þilke day ne schal nevre bē,
Ne schal me nevere atwīte mē
Þat ich bēo of luve untrewe,
Ne chaunge luve for nǫ newe,
Ne lēte þē ǫlde for nǫ newe bē, 15
Sǫ dōþ Flǫrīs on his contrē;
Ac þeȝ Flǫrīs forȝete[4] mē,
Ne schal ich nevre forȝete þē.'

 Clārīs iherde þēs ille reuþe
Of trewnesse and of trewþe; 20
Þē tęres[5] glide of hire lēre:
'Blauncheflūr,' hē sęde, 'gōde isēre,
Lēve swēte Blauncheflūr,
Cum and sē a wēl fair flūr.'

 Tōgedere hī gǫn nū iwis, 25
And Flǫrīs haþ iherd al þis;
Ūt of þē cūpe hē lēp anǫn,
And tō Blauncheflūr hē gan gǫn.
Eiþer ōþer sōne ikneu,
Bǫþe nūþe hī chaungen[6] heu; 30
Tōgadere wiþūte wōrd hī lēpen,
Klepte and kiste[7], and ēke wēpen[8];

---

[1] Clariz, occasionally. [2] biþute, as often. [3] wule, as occasionally.
 [4] forȝe. [5] tieres. [6] chaungeþ. [7] keste. [8] weopen.

Here kissinge [1] ilęste a mīle,
And þat hem þuʒte lītel whīle.

Þǭ [2] Clārīce bihēld [3] al þis,
Here cūntenaunce and here blis;
Seide Clārīce tō Blauncheflūr,   5
'Knowest ū oʒt ʒēte o [4] þis flūr?
A lītel ęr þū noldest hit sē,
Nū ne miʒte hit lēte fram þē.
Hē mōste kunne michel [5] of art
Þat þū woldest ʒeve þērof part.'   10
'Certes,' quaþ Blauncheflūr tō Clārīs,
'Þis is mīn ǭʒene swēte Flǭrīs.'

Nū bǭþe twō þēs swēte þinge [6]
Crīe [7] hire mercī al wēpinge,
Tō þē Admiral þat hem ne wreie   15
For þenne wēre here soreʒe neie [8].
Clārīce hadde of hem pitē:
'Nǭþing,' hēo sęde, 'ne dūte ʒē,
Ne dūte ʒē namǭre [9] wiþalle
Þat hit wēre tō mē bifalle.   20
Hęle ich wille and nǭþing wreie
Ower beire cumpaignīe.'

Clārīce hem haþ tō bedde ibroʒt
Þat was of pal and selc iwroʒt;
In bedde hēo broʒte hem adūn,   25
And hire [10] self wende hem fram.
Þǭ Flǭrīs first [10a] spęke bigan:
'Ūre Lǭverd,' hē sęde, 'þat mākedest man,
Þē ich þonke [11], Godes sune,
Þat ich am tō mī lēof icume.   30

---

[1] kessinge.   [2] þǭ, not in MS.   [3] biheold.   [4] o, not in MS.
[5] muchel, as occasionally.   [6] þinges.   [7] crieþ.   [8] niwe.
[9] nammore.   [10] hure, as occasionally.   [10a] furst.   [11] þonki.

Mī lēof, nū ich habbe þē fūnde[1],
Of al mī cāre ich am unbūnde.'
  Nū aiþer haþ ōþer itǫld
Of here soreȝe and cāre cǫld,
þat hī hadde ifūnde bǫ   5
Siþþe hī wēre idęld atwǫ.
Nū hī cleppen[2] and kisse[3],
And māken tōgadere michel blisse;
If þēr was aȝt bute kiste[4],
Swēte Blaunchef_lūr hit wiste.   10
Nǫn ōþer hevene hī ne będe
Bute evre swiche[5] līf tō lęde.
  Ac lǫnge ne miȝte hī hem wite
þat hī nēren underȝete,
For[6] þē Admiral hadde such a wune,   15
Ęch[7] moretīd þēr mōste cume
Twō maidenes wiþ michel honūr
Up[8] intō þē hēȝeste tūr,
þat wēre feire and swīþe[9] hēnde;
þat ǫn his hęved for tō kēmbe,   20
þat ōþer[9a] bringe tōwaille and bācin
For tō wasse his hǫnden in.
Swiche him serven[10] a day sǫ faire,
Ā moreȝe mōste anōþer peire.
  Ac męst wēre wuned[11] intō þē tūr   25
Maide Clārīs and Blauncheflūr.
  Clārīce, joie hire mōt bitīde,
Arǫs up in þē moreȝentīde,
And haþ cleped[12] Blauncheflūr
Tō gǫ wiþ hire intō þē tūr.   30
Quaþ Blauncheflūr, 'Ich am cominge,'
Ac hēo hit sęde al slēpinge.

---

[1] ifunde.   [2] cleppeþ.   [3] cusseþ.   [4] custe.   [5] swich.   [6] vor.   [7] ehc.
[8] up, not in MS.   [9] suþe.   [9a] not in MS.   [10] serveþ.   [11] iwuned.   [12] icluped.

Clārīs cōm intō þē tūr;
þē Admiral axede Blauncheflūr.
'Sīre, al niȝt at hire [1] bōke
Heo haþ [2] þēron irad and lōke,
And þēron będe [3] hire oresūn   5
Þat God þat þǫlede passiūn
þē hǫlde, Sīre, lǫnge alīve;
And nū hēo is aslēped swiþe
Þat hēo ne mai come tō þē.
'Is þat sōþe [4]?' sęde hē.   10
Hēo sęde, 'ȝē, Sīre, withūte lęsing.
'Hēo is,' hē sęde, 'a swēte þing,
Wēl aȝte ich willen hire tō wīf
þat sǫ ȝērne biddeþ mī līf.'

Ā moreȝe þǫ Clārīs arīst   15
Blauncheflūr hēo atwīst
Þat hē mākede sǫ lǫnge demēre [5].
'Arīs,' hēo sęde, 'and gǫ wē ī fēre.'
Quaþ Blauncheflūr, 'Ich come anǫn.'
Ac Flǫrīs cleppen hire bigon,   20
And hēo [6] him alsǫ unwīse,
And felle [7] aslēpe one þis wīse.

Þǫ Clārīce tō þē pilēr cōm,
And þē bācin of gōlde nōm
Tō bęre wiþ hire intō þē tūr,   25
Hēo lōkede after Blauncheflūr.

Þǫ Clārīce cōm intō þē tūr,
Hē axede after Blauncheflūr:
'Sīre, ich wēnde hire fīnde hēre,
Hēo [8] was arise are ich wēre;   30
Nis hēo noȝt icume ȝete?'
Quaþ hē, 'Hēo dūteþ mē tō lite.'

---

[1] heo set at hire.   [2] and haþ.   [3] ibede.   [4] soþ.   [5] demure.
    [6] he.   [7] feolle.   [8] he.

Hē clēpede[1] tō him his chaumberlayn,
And hēt him gō wiþ alle mayn
For tō wite whī hēo ne cōme[2]
Tō his hęste swiþe[3] sōne.

Forþ hē wende sōne anōn,   5
Tō hire chaumbre þat hē cōm.
In hire bedde hē fǫnd twǫ,
Wēl faste iclept[4], aslēpe bō
Neb tō neb, and mūþ tō mūþ;
Sōne wēre here soreȝen[5] cūþ.   10

Tō þē Admiral sōne hē teȝ
And tǫlde him what hē iseȝ.
Þē Admiral hēt his swērd bringe;
Iwite hē wolde of þis[6] þinge.
Forþ hē wende wiþ al his mayn,   15
Hē and his chaumberlayn;
In þē bed hē[7] fǫnd tweie,
Ȝit was þē slēp in here eie.
Hē lēt adūn þē clǫþes caste
Binēþen here breste;   20
Bī here breste hē knew anōn
Þat ǫn was maide and þat ōþer mon[8].

Þē children awǫke þǫ anōn,
And sēȝe þē Admiral bifǫre[9] hem gǫn
Wiþ his swērd al adrāȝe;   25
Sǫre hī bēn offērd, and wēl māȝe.
'Seie,' quaþ þē Admiral, 'belamȳ,
Hō mākede þē sǫ hardȳ
For tō come intō mī tūr,
And tō ligge bī Blauncheflūr?'   30
Hī crīen[10] him mercī bǫþe swiþe
Þat hē ȝive hem first of līve.

---

[1] clupede.   [2] cume.   [3] suthe, as occasionally.   [4] iclupt.   [5] soreȝ'en.
[6] þus.   [7] heo.   [8] a mon.   [9] bevore.   [10] cries.

After his barnāge hē haþ isent[1]
Tō awrēke him wiþ jugement,
And lēt hem þē whīle bīnde faste
And intō prisōn bēn icaste.
His palais þat was sō faire ibild[2]   5
Of ērles and barōns it was ifild.
Up hē stōd amōng hem alle,
Bī semblaunt wēl wrōþ wiþalle:
'Lōrdinges,' hē sēde, 'wiþ michel honūr
ȝē habbe iherd of Blauncheflūr,   10
Hū ich hire boȝte apliȝt
For seve sīþe of gōld hire wiȝt;
Tō hire was mī mēste wēne
For tō habbe tō mī quēne.
Nis noȝt ȝōre þat in[4] ich cōm,   15
And fōnd hire wiþ hōredōm[5],
mē tō schāme and deshonūr
In hire bedde on mī tūr.
Ich habbe ȝōū tōld hū hit is went;
Awrēkeþ mē wiþ jugement.'   20
    Þanne spak a frēo burgeis
Þat was hēnde and curteis:
'Sīre, are hī bēo tō dēþe[6] awrēke,
Wē mōte ihēre þē children spēke;
Hit nēre noȝt elles riȝt[7] jugement   25
Wiþūten answare tō acūpement.'
    Þē king of Nubīe sēde þō,
'Forsōþ, ne schal hit noȝt gō sō;
Hit is riȝt þureȝ alle þing
Felōns inome hōndhabbing   30
For tō suffre jugement
Wiþūte answare ōþer acūpement.'

[1] isend.   [2] ibuld.   [3] ifuld.   [4] ine.   [5] hordom.
[6] diþe.   [7] rist.

After þē children nū me senden[1];
Hem tō bērne fīr me tenden[2].
Seide Flǫrīs tō Blauncheflūr,
'Of ūre līf nis nǫ sucūr,
Ac mīn is þē gilt[3], and þē unmęþ   5
Þat þū for mē schalt þǫlīe dęþ;
Ac if kīnde[4] hit þǫlīe miȝte
Ich oȝte deie twȳe wiþ riȝte,
Ǫ dęþ for þē, ǫn ōþer for mē,
For þis þū þǫlest nū for mē.   10
For if Ī nēre intō þis tūr icume,
Wiþ mireȝþe þū miȝtest hērinne wune.'

Hē drōȝ forþ a rīche ring
His mōder ȝaf him at his parting:
'Hāve þis ring, lemman mīn,   15
Þū miȝt[5] nǫȝt deie whīle[6] hē is þīn.'
Þē ring hē hāveþ forþ araȝt
And tō Blauncheflūr bitaȝt.
'Þē ring ne schal nevre aredde mē,
For dęþ ne mai ich sē on þē.'   20
Þē ring hēo wolde aȝē ręche
And tō Flǫrīs him bitęche;
Ac for al þat hēo miȝte dō,
Hē him nolde aȝēn ifō,
And þē ring bī ǫne stūnde   25
Fēl adūn tō þē grūnde.
A duc stūpede and him upnōm,
And was þērof wēl blīþe mon.

Nū þēs childre forþ me bringe[6a]
Tō here dōm al wēpinge,   30
Ac þēr nas nǫn sǫ stirne[7] mon
Þat hem lōkede upon,

---

[1] sendeþ.   [2] tendeþ.   [3] guld.   [4] cunde.   [5] ne miȝt.
[6] þe while.   [6a] bringeþ.   [7] sturne.

Þat nolde þ̣o swīþe fāȝe [1]
Þat jugement wēre wiþdrāȝe;
For Flọ̄rīs was sọ̄ fair ȝongling,
And Blauncheflūr sọ̄ swēte þing,
Of men and wimmen þat bēn [2] nūþe,   5
Þat gọ̄ and sē [3] and spẹ̄ke [4] wiþ mūþe,
Ne bēn sọ̄ faire in here gladnesse
Sọ̄ hī wēre in here sorīnesse.
Ac þē Admiral was sọ̄ wrọ̈þ and wōd
Hē quākede for grāme þēr hē stōd,   10
And hēt hem bīnde wẹl faste
And intō þē fīre caste.

    Þē duc þat þē ring fūnde
Cōm tō þē Admiral and rūnde,
And al tọ̄gadere hē gan him schewe   15
Of þat þē children wēre biknewe.
Þē Admiral lēt hem aȝēn clẹ̄pe,
For hē wolde wiþ Flọ̄rīs spẹ̄ke.
'Sīre,' quaþ Flọ̄rīs, 'forsōþ ich telle
Þū noȝtest noȝt þat maide quelle;   20
Of al þis gilt ich am tō wīte,
Ich oȝte deie and hēo gọ̄ quite.'
Quaþ Blauncheflūr, 'Aquel þū mē,
And lēt Flọ̄rīs alīve bē;
ȝif [5] hit nēre for mī luve   25
Hē nēre noȝt fram his lọnde icome.
Quaþ þē Admiral, 'Sọ̄ ich mōte gọ̄,
ȝē schulle deie tọ̄gadere bọ̄;
Mīself ich wille mē awrẹ̈ke,
Ne schulle ȝē nevre gọ̄ ne spẹ̄ke.'   30

    Flọ̄rīs forþ his nekke bẹ̈d,
And Blauncheflūr wiþdrāȝe him ȝēt;
Blauncheflūr bid forþ hire swire [6],
And Flọ̄rīs aȝēn hire gan tire.

---

[1] suþe faȝe.   [2] buþ, as occasionally.   [3] seoþ.   [4] spekeþ.   [5] ȝef.   [6] swere.

Neiþer ne miȝte þēre þǫle
Þat ōþer deide bifǫre.

Þǫ þē Admiral, þeȝ hē wrǫþ wēre,
Þēr hē chaungede his chēre;
For eyþer[1] wolde for ōþer deie,   5
And hē[2] seȝ manī wēpinge[3] eie,
And for hē luvede sǫ muche þat mai,
Al wēpinge hē turned away.
His swērd fēl of his hǫnd tō grūnde,
Ne miȝte hē hit hǫlde þilke[4] stūnde.   10

Þē duc þat here ring hadde,
For hem tō spēke wille hē hadde:
'Sīre Admiral,' hē sēde, 'iwis
Hit is þē wēl lītel prīs
Þis feire children for tō quelle;   15
Ac betere hit is þat hī þē telle
Hū hē cōm intō þī tūr
Tō ligge þēr bī Blaunchefflūr.
His engīn whan þū hit wite
Þē betere wiþ ōþer þū miȝt þē wite.'   20

Alle þat herde wōrdes his
Bisēchen[6] þat hē graunte[5] þis.
Hē hēt him telle his engīn,
Hū hē tō Blaunchefflūr cōm in,
And hō[5a] him radde and help þartō.   25
'Þat,' quaþ hē, 'nelle ich nevre dō
For þing þat me mai mē dō,
Bute hit hem bēo forȝive alsō.'
Alle þē ōþere bisēchen[6] þis,
And of þē Admiral igranted is.   30

Nū ōrd and ēnde hē haþ hem tōld[7];
Hū Blaunchefflūr[8] was fram him sōld[9],

----

[1] he seȝ þat eyþer.   [2] for he.   [3] wepinde.   [4] þulke.   [5] graunti.
[5a] to.   [6] bisecheþ.   [7] itold.   [8] blacheflur.   [9] isold.

Hū[1] hē was of Spaygne a kinges sone
For hire luve þider[2] icume,
Tō fǭnden wiþ sume ginne
Hū hē miȝte hire awinne ;
And hū, þureȝ þē cupe and þē[3] gersume,   5
Þē portēr was his man bicume,
And hū hē was in a cūpe ibǭre.
Alle þēs ōþere lowe þērfǭre[4].

Þē Admiral þǭ, wēl him bitīde,
Þat chīld hē sette[5] bī his sīde ;   10
And haþ forȝive his wraþþe bǭ,
Flǭrīs and Blauncheflūr alsǭ,
And sẹde wiþ him hī scholde bē
Þē beste of al his mainē.

And Flǭrīs hē mākeþ stǭnde upriȝt,   15
And þer hē dubbede him tō kniȝt.
Nū bǭþe tōgadere þēs childre for blisse
Falle[6] tō his fēt, hem tō kisse ;
Hē lēt hem tō ǭne chirche bringe,
And spūsen hem wiþ ǭne gōld ringe.   20
Þureȝ þē rēd of Blauncheflūr
Me fette Clārīs adūn þē[7] tūr.
Þē Admiral hire nam tō quēne ;
Þilke fẹste was wēl brēme,
For þēr was alle kinnes[8] glēo   25
Þat miȝte at enī brīdale[9] bēo.

Hit nas þērafter nǭþing lǭnge
Þat þēr cōm tō Flǭrīs writ and sǭnde,
Þat þē king his fader was dẹd
And þat hē scholde nimen his rẹd.   30
Þanne seide þē Admirail[10],
'If þū dōst bī mī cōnsail,

---

[1] and hu.   [2] þuder.   [3] þures þe.   [4] þervore.   [5] set.
[6] falleþ.   [7] of þe.   [8] kunnes.   [9] briddale.   [10] Admiral.

Bilēf wiþ mē, and wēnde naȝt hǫm;
Ich wille ȝeve þē a kinedōm
Al sǭ lǫng and al sǭ brǭd,
Alsǭ evre ȝēt þī fader bǭd [1].'
    Ac Flǭrīs nolde for nǭ winne,   5
Lēvere him wēre wiþ his kinne.
Þē Admiral hē bid godday,
And þonkede Clārīs þat faire may,
And tō hire hē haþ iȝōlde
Twentī pūnd of rēde [2] gōlde;   10
And tō Dārīs þat him sǭ taȝte
Twentī pūnd hē araȝte,
And alle þat for him diden ei dēl
Hē ȝēld here whīle swīþe wēl.
Hē bitaȝte hem alle God Almiȝte,   15
And cōm hǫm when hē miȝte.
Hē was king wiþ michel honūr,
And hēo his quēne Blaunchefłūr.
    Nū ȝē hāven [3] iherd þane ēnde
Of Flǭrīs and his lemman hēnde,   20
Hū after bāle comeþ bōte.
God lēve þat us sǭ mōte,
Þat wē him mōte lov͞e sǭ
Þat wē mōte tō hevene gǭ. Amēn.

IV. THE DEBATE OF THE BODY AND THE SOUL

ALS Ī lay in a winteris nyȝt [4]   25
  In a drōupening [5] bifǭr þē day,
Forsōþe [6] Ī sauȝ a sellȳ syȝt [7],
  A bodȳ on a bēre lay,

---

[1] ibod.   [2] pond of ride.   [3] habbeþ.   [4] nyt.   [5] droukening.
        [6] vorsoþe.   [7] syt.

Þat hāvede bēn a mōdȳ knyȝt
  And lītel[1] served God tō pay[2];
Lọren hē hāved þē līves lyȝt,
  Þē gọst was ōute and scholde away.

Wan þē gọst it scholde gọ,   5
  It[3] biwente and withstōd,
Bihẹld[4] thē bodȳ þēre it cam frọ
  Sọ serfullī with drẹdlī mōd;
It seide, 'Weile and walawọ!
  Wọ worþe þī fleys, þī fōule blōd.   10
Wreche bodī wȝȳ līst ōu[5] sọ,
  Þat ȝwīlene wēre sọ wīlde and wōd?

' Þōu þat wēre woned tō rīde
  Heyȝe on horse in and ōut,
Sọ kweynte[6] kniȝt ikūð[7] sọ wīde,   15
  As a lȳūn fērs and prōud,
Ȝwēre is al þī michele prīde,
  And þī lēde þat was sọ lōud?
Ȝwī līst ōu þēre sọ bāre ō sīde[8]
  Ipricked in þat pōre schrōud?   20

' Ȝwēre bēn þī wurðlī[9] wēdes,
  Þī somers with þī rīche beddes,
Þī prōude palefreys and þī stēdes?
  Þat þōu abōut[10] in dester leddes?
Þī faucōuns þat wēre wont[11] tō grēde,   25
  And þīne hōundes þat þōu fedde[12]?
Mē þinkeþ God is þē tō gnēde,
  Þat alle þīne frēnd bēon frọ þē fledde.

---

[1] lutel.   [2] payȝ.   [3] yt, as often.   [4] biheold.   [5] listouȝ.
[6] koweynte.   [7] knit ikud.   [8] bareside   [9] murdli.   [10] haddest.
[11] nouȝt.   [12] ledde.

'Ȝwēre bēon þī castles and þī tōūres,
    Þī chaumbres and þī rīche halles
Ipeynted with sǭ rīche flōūres,
    And þī rīche rǭbes alle?
Þīne cōwltes and þī covertōūres,   5
    Þī cendels and þī rīche palles?
Wreche, ful derk[1] is nōū[2] þī bōūr;
    Tōmoruwe þōu[3] schalt þērinne falle.

'Ȝwēre bēn þīne cōkes snelle,
    Þat scholden gǭn tō[4] greiþe þī mēte   10
With spēces swēte for tō smelle,
    Þat þōu nevere wēre[5] fol of frēte,
Tō dō þat fōūle fleys tō swelle
    Þat fōūle wormes scholden ēte?
And þōu hāvest þē pīne of helle   15
    With glotonȳe mē bigēte. . . .'

'For God þē schōp[6] aftir his schaft[7],
    And gaf þē bǭþe wyt and skil;
In þī lōking was Ī laft
    Tō wisse aftir þīn oune wil.   20
Ne tōc Ī nevere wychecraft,
    Ne wist Ī ȝwat was gōd[8] nǭr il,
Bote as a wretche dumb and daft[9],
    Bote as tōū taugtest mē[10] þērtil.

'Set tō serven þē tō quēme   25
    Bǭþe at ēven and at morn[11],
Siþin Ī was þē bitauȝt tō ȝēme,
    Frǭ þē tīme þat þōu was born.
Þōu þat dēdes cōūþest dēme
    Scholdest habbe bē war biforn   30

---

[1] wrechede it is.   [2] nouȝ, as often.   [3] þouȝ, as often, but always printed þou.   [4] to, from Auch. MS.   [5] werere.   [6] schop þe.   [7] schap.
[8] guod, as often.   [9] mad.   [10] me, not in MS.   [11] morwen.

Of mī folȳe, as it sēme[1];
Nōu wiþ þīselve thōu art forlorn.'

Þē gast it seyde, 'Bodī bē stille!
Ȝwō haþ lēred þē al þis wite
Þat givest mē þēse wōrdes grille,   5
Þat līst þēr bollen as a bite?
Wēnest ōu, wretche, þoȝ thōu fille
Wiþ þī foule fleisch[2] a pite,
Of alle dēdes thōu didest ille
Þat þōu sọ̄ liȝtlī[3] schalt bē quite?   10

'Wēnest ōu nōu tō[4] gete þē griþ
Þēr þou līst rọ̄ten in þē clay?
Þey þōu bē rọ̄tin pile and piþ,
And blowen wiþ þē wīnd away,
Ȝēt[5] schalt ōu come wiþ lime and lyþ   15
Agein tō mē on dōmesday,
And come tō cōūrt and Ī þē wiþ
For tō kēpen ōūre harde pay.

'Tō tẹ̄che wēre[5a] þou mē bitauȝt;
Ac ȝwan þöu þouȝtest of þē quẹ̄d,   20
Wiþ þī tēþ þē brīdel þou lauȝt,
Þou dīst al þat Ī þē forbẹ̄d.
Tō sinne[6] and schāme it was þī drauȝt,
Til untīd and til wikkedehẹ̄d;
Inouȝ Ī stōd ageyn and fauȝt,   25
Bot ai þou nōme þīn oune rẹ̄d.

'Wan Ī þē wolde tēme and tẹ̄che
Ȝwat[6a] was yvel and ȝwat was gōd,
Of Crīst ne kirke was nọ̄ spẹche,
Bote renne abōūte and breyde[7] wōd;   30

---

[1] semet.   [2] fleichs, as often.   [3] litli.   [4] to, from Auch. MS.
[5] ȝeot.   [5a] ȝwere.   [6] sunne, as usually.   [6a] ȝwat not in MS.   [7] breyd.

Inʊuȝ Ī miȝte preye and pręche,
　Ne miȝte Ī nevere wēnde þī mōd
Þat þōu woldest God knoulęche,
　But dōn al þat þīn herte tō[1] stōd.

'Ī bad þē þenke on soulenēdes[2],　　　　　5
　Matines, masse, and ēvesǫng;
Thōu mōstist first dōn ōþere dēdes[3],
　Þōu seidist al was īdel gǫng.
Tō wode and water and fēld thōu ēdest,
　Or tō cōūrt[4] tō dō men wrǫng;　　　　10
Bote for prīde or grettore mēdes[5]
　Lītel[6] þōu dīst[7] gōd amǫng.

'Hō may mǫre traysōn dō,
　Or his[8] lǫverd betere engīne,
Þan hē þat al his trīst is tō,　　　　　15
　In and ōūt[9] as oune hȳn?
Ay seþþe þōu was þriven and þrǫ,
　Miȝtis did[10] Ī alle mīne,
Tō porveie[11] þē rest and rō,
　And þōu tō bringe mē in pīne.　　　　20

'Nōū mōūwe þē wīlde bęstes renne
　And līen under līnde and lęf,
And fōūles flīe bī fēld and fenne,
　Siþin þī false herte clęf.
Þīne eiȝene are blīnde and connen nouȝt kenne,　25
　Þī mōūth is dumb, þīn ęre is dęf;
And nōū sǫ lǫþlī[12] þōu līst grerne,
　Frǫ þē comeþ a wikke węf.

[1] to, not in MS.　　[2] soulenede.　　[3] dede.　　[4] cour.　　[5] mede.
[6] lutel.　　[7] dust.　　[8] is, as in next line.　　[9] ouȝt.　　[10] miʋis ded.
[11] porveȝe.　　[12] lodli.

'Ne nis nǫ lȩvedī briȝt on blē,
  Þat wēl wēre woned¹ of þē tō lēte,
Þat wolde lȳe a niȝt² bī þē
  For nouȝt³ þat men miȝte hem bihēte.
Þou art unsēmlȳ for tō sē,   5
  Uncomlī for tō kissen swēte⁴;
Þou ne hāvest frēnd þat ne wolde flē,
  Come þou stertlinde in þē strēte.'

Þē bodī it seide, 'Ic seyȝe,
  Gast, þou hast wrǫng iwys   10
Al þē gilt⁵ on mē tō leyȝe,
  Þat þou hast lorn þī mikil blis.
Wēre was Ī bī wode or weyȝe,
  Sat or stōd or dide ouȝt mys,
Þat Ī ne was ay under þīn eyȝe?   15
  Wēl þou wǫst þat sōth it is⁶.

'Wedir Ī ēde up or doūn,
  Þat Ī ne bar þē on mȳ bac,
Als þīn as frǫ toūn tō toūn,
  Alse þou⁷ me lēte hāve rap and rac?   20
Þat toū ne wēre and rēde⁸ roūn
  Nevere did Ī þing ne spac;
Hēre þē sōþe sē men mowen
  On mē þat ligge sǫ⁹ blǫ and blac.

'For al þē wīle þou wēre mī fēre   25
  Ī hadde al þat mē was nēd,
Ī miȝte spȩke, sē and hēre,
  Ī ēde and rǫd and drank and ēt.
Lǫþlī chaunged¹⁰ is mȳ chēre
  Sin þē tȳme þat þou mē lēt;   30

---

¹ iwoned.   ² niȝth.   ³ nouȝth.   ⁴ cussen suwete.   ⁵ wyt.   ⁶ ys.
    ⁷ als se þouȝ.   ⁸ red.   ⁹ here so.   ¹⁰ lodli chaunched.

Dẹf and dumb Ī ligge on bēre,
　　Þat Ī ne may sterin hand ne fēt.

'Ī scholde hāve bēn dumb as a schēp,
　　Or as an ouwe or as a swȳn
Þat ēt and drank and lai and slēp,　　　　　　5
　　Slayn, and passid al his pīn;
Nevere of catẹl nome[1] kēp,
　　Ne wyste wat was water ne wȳn,
Ne leyn in helle þat is sǫ dēp,
　　Ne wēre þē wit þat al was þīn.[2]'　　　　　10

Þē gast it[3] seide, 'Is nǫ dōute;
　　Abōuten, bodī, þou mē bar;
Þou mōstist nēde, Ī was wiþōute
　　Hānd and fōt, Ī was wēl war.
Bote as tōu bēre mē abōute　　　　　　　　15
　　Ne miȝt Ī dō þē lẹste char;
Þǫrfǫre mōst Ī nēde lōute,
　　Sǫ dōth þat nǫn ōþer dar.

'Of ǫ wymman born and bredde,
　　Bodȳ, wēre wē bōþe twǫ;　　　　　　　20
Tōgidre fostrid fayre and fedde
　　Til þou cōupist spẹke and gǫ.
Softe þē for love Ī ledde,
　　Ne dorst Ī nevere dō þē wǫ;
Tō lēse þē sǫ sǫre Ī dredde,　　　　　　　25
　　And wēl Ī wiste tō gete[4] nā mǫ.

For mē þou woldest sumwat dō
　　Wȝīle þou wēre ȝong a lītil first,
For frēndes eyȝe þat þē stōd tō,
　　Þē wīle þou wēre bẹtin and birst;　　　　30

---

[1] he ne.　　[2] nevere ne wist of al þat was tin.　　[3] yt, as often.　　[4] getin.

Oc wan þōū wēre þriven and þrǫ,
  And knewe hunger, cǫld and þirst,[1]
And ȝhwilk was eyse, rest and rō,
  Al þīn oune wil þōū dīst.

'Ī saw þē fair on fleysch and blōd   5
  And al mī love on þē Ī kest;
Þat þōū þrīve mē þouȝte gōd,
  And lēt þē hāven rō and rest.
Þat māde þē sǫ stirne[2] of mōd,
  And of werkes sǫ unwrest;   10
Tō fiȝte with þē ne was nǫ bōt
  Mē þat þōū bar in þī brest.

'Gloterīe and lecherīe,
  Prīde[3] and wicke coveytīse,
Nīþe and ǫnde and envīe   15
  Tō God of hevene and alle hise,
And in unlust for tō lȳe,
  Was tī wone in alle wīse[4];
That Ī schal nōū ful dēre abȳe,
  A, weyle! sǫre may mē grīse.   20

'Þōū was warned hēr bīfǫre,
  ȝwat wē[5] bǫþe scholden hāve;
Īdel tāle hēld tōū þat þǫre
  Þōū sauȝ fęle dūn[6] in grāve.
Þōū dīst al þat þē werld þē bad,   25
  And þat þī fleys þē wolde crāve;
Ī þǫlede þē and dide[7] as mad
  Tō bē maister and Ī þī cnāve.'

'Iwēnest[8] þōū, gǫst, þē geyned ouȝt[9]
  For tō quite þē wiþal,   30

[1] virst.   [2] sturne.   [3] prude.   [4] waste wane non of þise.
[5] we, not in MS.   [6] bi dun.   [7] dide, not in MS.   [8] iweneste.   [9] out.

Þou þat was sō worþlī[1] wrouȝt,
To seye Ī māde þē mȳ þral?
Did[2] Ī nevere on līve nouȝt,
Ī ne rafte ne Ī ne stal
Þat first[3] of þē ne cam þē þouȝt;   5
Abȳ it þat abȳȝe schal!

Ȝwat wist Ī wat was wrǫng or riht[4],
Wat tō tāke or ȝwat tō schone,
Bote þat þou pottest in mī siȝht[5]
Þat al þē wisdōm scholdest cone?   10
Ȝwanne þou mē tauȝtist ǫn untiȝht[6],
And mē gan þēroffe mone,
Þanne did[2] Ī al mȳ miȝht[7]
Anōþer tīme tō hāve mȳ wone.

'Oc haddist þou, þat Crīst it ōuþe,   15
Given mē honger, þirst[8] and cǫld,
And þou witest mē þat nǫ gōd cōuþe,
In bismere ȝwan Ī was sǫ bǫld,
Þat Ī hadde undernomen in ȝōuþe
Ī hāvede hǫlden ȝwan Ī was ǫld[9],   20
Þou lēt mē reykin north and south
And hāven al my wille on wǫld.

'Þou scholdist for nǫ līf ne lǫnd[9a],
Ne for nǫn ōþer worldes winne,
Hāve soffrid mē tō lein ǫn hǫnd,   25
Þat hāvede tornd tō schāme or sinne[9b]
Oc for Ī þē sǫ eise fǫnd,
And þī wretche wit sǫ þinne[10],
Þat ay was wrīþinde as a wǫnd,
Þērfǫre[11] cōuþe Ī nevere blinne.   30

---

[1] wordli. [2] dud. [3] furst. [4] rith. [5] pottist . . . siȝth. [6] untiȝth.
[7] miȝth. [8] vurst. [9] I havede holden old. [9a] for lond. [9b] sunne,
as occasionally. [10] with so þunne. [11] þefore.

' Tō sinne þoū wistist was mȳ kīnde,
        As mankinne it is al sǫ,
And tō þē wretche world sǫ mīnde,
        And tō þē fēnd þat is ūre[1] fǫ.
Þoū scholdest ęr hāve late mē bīnde   5
        Wan Ī misdēde, and dōn mē wǫ ;
Ac ȝwanne þē blīnde lat þē blīnde,
        In dīke hē fallen bǫþe twǫ.'

Thǫ bigan þē gǫst tō wēpe,
        And seide, ' Bodī, allas, allas,   10
Þat Ī þē lovede evere ȝēte,
        For al mī love on þē Ī las.
Þat toū lovedest mē þoū lēte[1ᵃ],
        And mādest mē an hoūve of glas ;
Ī dide al þat þē was sēte,   15
        And þoū mȳ traytōr evere was.

' Þē fēnd of helle þat hāveþ envīe[2]
        Tō mankinne[3], and evere haþ had,
Was in us as is a[4] spīe
        Tō dō sum gōd ȝwan Ī þē bad.   20
The werld hē tōc tō cumpaynīe[5],
        Þat manī a soule hāved forrad ;
Þey þrē wisten þī folȳe,
        And māden[6], wretche, þē al mad.

' Ȝwan Ī bad þē reste tāke,   25
        Forsāke sinne ay and ǫǫ,
Dō penaunce, faste and wāke,
        Þë fēnd[7] seide, ' Þoū schalt nouȝt sǫ,
Þus[8] sōne al þī blisse forsāke,
        Tō liven ay in pīne and wǫ !   30

---

[1] ore, as often.   [1ᵃ] le.   [2] enviȝe.   [3] mankune.   [4] as a.   [5] cum-
paniȝe.   [6] madin.   [7] fe.   [8] þos.

Joye [1] and blisse Ī rēde þou māke,
And þenke tō live ȝēres mǭ.

'Ȝwan Ī bad tē lęve prīde,
  Þī manīe mes, þī rīche schrōud,
Þē false world þat stōd bisīde,
  Bad þē bē ful quoynte and prōud;
Þī fleysch with rīche rǫbes schrīde,
  Nouȝt als a beggare in a clōut [2],
And on heiȝe horse tō rīde
  Wiþ mikel meynē in and ōut [3].

'Ȝwan Ī bad þē ęrlīche tō rīse,
  Nim of [4] mē þī soule kēp,
Þou seidest thōu miȝtest ā nǫne wīse
  Forgǫn þē mirīe [5] morweslēp.
Wȝan ȝē hadden set yōur sīse,
  ȝē [6] þrē traytōurs, sǫre Ī wēp;
Yē ladde mē wiþ ȝōure [7] enprīse,
  As þē bochēre [8] dōþ his schēp.

'Ȝwan ȝē [9] þrē traitōurs at ǭ tāle
  Tōgidere wēren agein mē sworn,
Al ȝē māden trotevāle
  Þat Ī hāved seid biforn.
Ȝē ledde mē bī dōune and dāle
  As an oxe bī þē horn,
Til þēr as him is browen bāle
  Þēr his þrǫte schal bē schorn.

'For love þī wille Ī folewede al,
  And tō mīn oune dęth Ī drouȝ,
Tō foluwe þē þat was mī þral,
  Þat evere wēre false and frouȝ;

5

10

15

20

25

30

---

[1] ioyȝe.   [2] clouȝt.   [3] ouȝt.   [4] on.   [5] murie.   [6] þe
[7] wid oure.   [8] boþelere; Auch. MS. bucher.   [9] ȝe, not in MS.

Þōu it dīst and Ī forhal,
 Wē wisten[1] wēl it was wouȝ ;
Þērfǭre mōte wē kēpe ūre fal,
 Pīne and schāme and sorewe inouȝ.

' Þeiȝ alle þē men nōu under mōne   5
 Tō dēmen wēren sete on benche,
Þē schāmes þat us schullen bē dōne
 Ne schulden[2] halven dẹ̄l biþenche[3].
Ne helpeþ us nǭ bẹ̄de ne bōne,
 Ne may us nōu nǭ wȳl tōwrenche ; 10
Hellehōundes comen[4] nōu sōne,
 Forþī ne mōuwe wē noyþer blenche.'

Ȝwan þat bodī say þat gast[5]
 Þat mǭne and al þat soruwe māke,
It seide, ' Allas, þat mī līf hath last, 15
 Þat Ī have lived for sinne sāke.
Þat mīn herte[6] ne hadde tōbrast[7],
 Ȝwan Ī was fram mī mōder tāke ;
Ī miȝte hāve bēn in ērþe kast[8],
 And leiȝen and rǭted[9] in a lāke. 20

' Þanne hāved Ī nevere lerned
 Ȝwat was yvil[10], ne ȝwat was gōd,
Ne nǭ þing with wrǭnge[11] ȝernd,
 Ne pīne þǭled as Ī mōt,
Ȝwēre nǭ seint miȝte bẹ̄ren ūre[12] ernde 25
 Tō him þat bouȝte us with his blōd,
In helle ȝwanne wē bēn bernd[13]
 Of sum mercī tō dōn us bōt.'

' Nay, bodī, nay[14], nōu is tō lāte
 For tō preien[15] and tō prẹ̄che, 30

---

[1] wistin. [2] schuldin. [3] biþenke. [4] cometh. [5] gost.
[6] herte anon. [7] toborste. [8] kest. [9] ileiȝen and iroted. [10] uvilne.
[11] wrong. [12] is. [13] brend. [14] nay, from Auch. MS. [15] preiȝe.

Noū þē wayn is atte ¹ ȝāte,
  And þī tonge haþ leid þē spēche.
Ǭ poynt of ūre pīne tō bāte,
  In þē world ne is nǭ lēche;
Al tegidere wē gǭn ǭ gāte,   5
  Swilk is Godes harde wrēche.

'Ac haddest þoū a lītel ēr,
  Ȝwīle us was līf tōgidre lent,
Þǭ þat was sǭ sēk and sēr,
  Us schriven and þē devel schent,   10
And laten renne a reulȳ tēr,
  And bihiȝt amendement,
Ne þorte us hāve friȝt ne fēr,
  Þat God ne wolde us blisse have sent ².

'Þey alle þē men þat bēn ō lȳve ³   15
  Wēren prēstes, messes for ⁴ tō singe,
And alle þē maidenes and þē wȳve ⁵
  Wydewes, hǭndene for tō wringe,
And miȝte sweche ⁶ fȳve
  Als is in werld of alle þinge,   20
Siþin wē ne moūwen us selven ⁷ schrīve,
  Ne schulde us intō blisse bringe.

'Bodī, Ī may nǭ mǭre dwelle,
  Ne stǭnde for tō spēke with þē;
Hellehoūndes hēre Ī ȝelle,   25
  And fēndes mǭ þan men moūwe sē,
Þat cōmen tō fette mē tō helle,
  Ne may Ī nǭȝwēr ⁸ from hem flē;
And þoū schalt comen with fleys and felle
  Ā dōmesday tō wone ⁹ with mē.'   30

¹ ate.   ² his blisse us sent.   ³ iyves.   ⁴ for, not in MS.
⁵ wyves.   ⁶ suweche.   ⁷ sulven.   ⁸ noweder.   ⁹ wonie.

Ne hāvede it nōū ẹ̄r þē wōrd iseyd,
    It ne wiste ȝwider it scholde gǭ;
In abrēken at a breid
    A þōūsend develene and ȝēt mǭ.
ȝwan thei hadden[1] on him leyd   5
    Here scharpe cloches alle þǭ,
It was in a sǭrī pleyt,
    Reulīche toyled tō and frǭ.

For thei wēren ragged, rōūe and tayled,
    With brǭde bulches on here bac;   10
Scharpe clauwes, lǭnge nayled,
    Nǭ was nǭ lime withōūte lac.
On alle halve it was asayled
    With manī a devel fōul and blac;
Mercī crīende lītel[2] availede   15
    ȝwan Crīst it wolde sǭ harde wrac.

Some þē chaules it tōwraste[3]
    And ȝǭten in þē lẹ̄d al hǭt,
And bēdin him tō drinke faste,
    And shenke abōūten him abrǭt[4].   20
A devil kam þēr atte[5] laste
    Þat was maister, wēl Ī wǭt;
A colter glowende in him hē þraste
    Þat it þoruȝ þē herte smǭt[6].

Gleyves glowende some setten   25
    Tō bac and brest and bǭþe sīdes,
Þat in his herte þē poyntes mettin,
    And māden him þǭ wōūndes wīde,
And seiden him fol wēl hē lette
    Þē herte þat was sǭ fol of prīde;   30

---

[1] haddin.   [2] lutel.   [3] towrasten.   [4] senke abouten him
a brod.   [5] ate.   [6] herte it smot.

Wēl hē it hadde þat men him hette [1],
  For mǫre scholde it bitīde.

Worþlī [2] wēdes for tō wēre
  Þei seiden þat hē lovede best;
A develes cǭpe for tō bēre,   5
  Al brennynde on him was kest,
With hǫte haspes imād tō spēre
  Þat streite sat tō bac and brest;
An helm þat was lītel [3] tō hēre
  Kam him, and [4] an hors al prest.   10

Forth was brouȝt þērewith a brīdel,
  A corsed devel als a cǭte,
Þat grislīche grennede and ȝēnede wīde,
  Þē leyȝe it lēmede of his þrǫte;
With a sadel tō thē midsīde   15
  Fol of scharpe pīkes schǫte,
Alse an hechele on [5] tō rīde;
  Al was glowende, ilke a grǫte.

Upon [6] þat sadil hē was sloungen,
  As hē scholde tō þē tornement;   20
An hundred devel on him dongen
  Hēr and þēr þan hē was hent;
With hǫte spēres þoruȝ was stongen,
  And wiþ oules al tōrent;
At ilke dint þē sparkles sprongen   25
  As of a brǫnd þat wēre forbrent [7].

Ȝwan hē hadde riden [8] þat rǫde
  Upon þē sadil þēr hē was set,
Hē was kast dōun as a tǫde,
  And hellehōundes tō him wēre let [9]   30

---

[1] bihette.   [2] wordli.   [3] lutel.   [4] anon him kam.   [5] onne.
  [6] Opon.   [7] forbrend.   [8] reden.   [9] led.

Þat broiden out þǫ pēces brǫde,
  Als hē tō helle ward was fet;
Thēr alle þē fēndes fēt it trǫde,
  Men miȝte of blōd foluwe þē tred.

Hē bēden him honten[1] and blowen,   5
  Crīen on Bauston and Bewis,
Þē ratches þat him wēre woned tō[2] knowen
  Hē scholden sōne blowe þē prīs;
An hundred develes, on[3] a rowe,
  With stringes him drowen, unþanc his,   10
Til hē kōme tō þat lǫþlī[4] lowe
  Þēr helle was, Ī wǫt tō wis.

Ȝwan it kam tō þat wikke won,
  Þē fēndes kasten swilk[5] a ȝel,
Þē ērþe it ǫpenede anǫn,   15
  Smǫke and smoþer up it wēl[6];
Bǫþe of[7] pich and of[7] brimstǫn[8],
  Men myȝte fīf mīle hāve þē smel.
Lǫverd, wǫ schal him bē bigǫn
  Þat haþ þēroffe þē tenþe dęl!   20

Ȝwan þē gǫst þē sōþe isey,
  Wȝider[9] it scholde, it kaste a crī,
And seide, ' Jēsu[10] that sittest on hey,
  On mē, þī schāp, nōu hāve mercī.
Ne schōpe þōu mē þat art sǫ slyȝ?   25
  Þī cręature al sǫ was Ī
Als man þat sittes þē sǫ nȳȝ,
  Þat þōu hāvest sǫ wēl dōn bȳ.

' Þōu þat wistest al biforn[11],
  Wȝī schōpe þōu mē tō wrǫþer hęle,   30

---

[1] hontin.   [2] te.   [3] ratches on.   [4] lodli.   [5] suwilk.
[6] wal.   [7] of, from Auch. MS.   [8] brumston.   [9] wȝide.   [10] Ihu,
as usual; Crist added, but incorrectly for metre.   [11] bifor.

Tō bē þus togged and tōtorn[1],
    And ōþere tō hāven al mī wẹle?
Þọ þat scholden bē forlọrn,
    Wretches þat tōu miȝtest spẹle,
A, weile, wȝī lēst ōu hem bē born,   5
    Tō ȝeve þē fōule fénd sọ fẹle?'

Agein him þē féndes gonnen crīe[2],
    'Caitif, helpeþ þē nā mọre
Tō calle on Jēsus ne Mārīe,
    Ne tō crīe Crīstes ọre.   10
Lọren þōu hāvest thē cumpainȳe,
    Þōu hāvest served us sọ ȝọre;
Þarfọre nōu þōu schalt abȳe
    As ōþere þat lēven on ūre lọre.'

Þē fōule féndes þat wēren fayn,   15
    Bī top and tail hē slongen hit,
And kesten it with myȝt and mayn
    Dōun intō thē develes pit,
Þēr sonne ne schal nevere bē seyn;
    Hemself hē sonken in þērmit;   20
Þē ērþe himself[3] it lēk aȝeyn,
    Anọn þē donge it was fordit.

Wȝan it was forth, þat fōule lọd
    Tō hellewel ọr it wēre day,
On ilk a hēr a drọpe stōd   25
    For friȝt and fér þēr as Ī lay;
Tō Jēsu Crīst with mīlde mōd
    Ȝērne Ī kalde and lōkede ay,
Ȝwan þọ féndes họt and wōd[4]
    Cōme tō fette mē away.   30

_____
[1] totoren.   [2] criȝe.   [3] hem sulf.   [4] hot fot.

Ī þonke him þat þǫlede dēþ,
  His michele [1] mercī and his ǭre,
Þat schīlde mē fram manī a quęd,
  A sinful [2] man as Ī lai þǫre.
Þǭ alle sinful Ī [3] rēde hem ręd   5
  Tō schrīven hem and rewen sǫre;
Nevere was sinne idōn sǫ gręt
  Þat Crīstes mercī ne is wēl mǫre.

V. ADAM AND EVE

Ēve haþ Seþ yladde
Tō Paradȳs as Adam badde.   10
And [4] Ēve drouȝ hir fram þē ȝāte,
Schē ne [5] durst nouȝt lōke in þērate,
Schē durst nouȝt schewe God hir fāce,
Bot lēte Seþ abīde grāce.
And Seþ in þilke stęde,   15
Sǫre wēpeand, in hǫlȳ będe,
Hē abǫd þēr alle stille
Godes mercī and Godes wille.
  Þurch [6] þē vertu of Godes miȝt
Þēr cōm adoūn an āngel briȝt,   20
And seyd tō Seþ in þis manēre [7],
Þat hē miȝt wiþ ęren hēre:
' God þat al þē warld haþ wrouȝt
Sēnt þē wōrd, þoū biddest for nouȝt,
Ęr þē terme [8] bē ygǫn   25
Of fīve þoūsende winter and ǫn,
And fīve and twentī winter and mǭ.

---

[1] muchele.   [2] sunful, as also in next line.   [3] þo þat sunful ben.
[4] ꝛ, as often   [5] no, as always.   [6] þurth.   [7] maner.   [8] term.

Ēr þat terme[1] bē agǭ,
And God þat is ful of miȝt
Bē intō ērþe yliȝt,
And hāve ynomen kīnd of man,
And bāþed in þē flom Jordan;   5
Þan schal Adam and Ēve his wiif
Bē anoint wiþ oyle of liif,
And alle þǭ þat after hem comen
Þat have cristendōm[2] ynomen.
Gǭ tel Adam þī fader þis,   10
Þat nǭn ōþer grāce þēr nis;
And tō grayþe him bid him hȳȝe[3],
His terme neiȝeþ þat hē schal dȳe.
And when þē bodī þat haþ dōn sinne,
And þē soule schal parten atwinne,   15
Riȝt whan þat tīme schal bē,
Miche mervayl ȝē schullen ysē.
Sǭ seyþ[4] mī Lǭrd þat alle haþ wrouȝt,
And biddeþ þat ȝē ne drēde nouȝt,
For nouȝt þat ȝē schul hēre ne sē;   20
Sǭ hē sent ȝōū wōrd bī mē.'
    Ēve and Seþ her waye nōme,
And went aȝain[5] as þai cōme,
And tōld Adam þē tīding
Þat him sent þē Hevenking;   25
And Adam hēld up bǭþe his hǭnd,
And þonked God of alle his sǭnd.
Adam his eiȝen unfēld,
And seþþen his sone hē bihēld
And seyd, 'Mercī, swēte Jēsus[6],   30
Whō haþ wōunded mī sone þus?'
    'Bī God, Adam,' quaþ Ēve,
'Hē þat is abōut tō grēve

---

[1] term.   [2] ciristendom.   [3] heyȝe.   [4] seyt.   [5] oȝain.   [6] Ihus, as usual.

Ōure soules bōþe niȝt and day,
As michel as ever hē may,
Þat is þē fēnde, þat is our fō,
Þat haþ ōus brouȝt intō þis wō.
Hē cōm and mette[1] wiþ ōus tway   5
As wē ȝēden in þē way,
And went tōward Paradȳs ;
Þus hē bōt him in þē viis.'
'Ō wē, Ēve,' quaþ Adam þō,
'Þōu hast ywrouȝt michel wō !   10
Alle þat after ōus bē bōre,
Alle schal curssen ōus þērfōre ;
And alle þat after ōus liven,
Bōþe ā morwe and ēke an ēven,
Schul bē bisȳ tō bēre þē wō   15
Þat is ywākened of ōus twō.
Þērfōre, Ēve, telle alle þīne childer
Bōþe þē ȝonger and þē elder,
Þat þai bē fīled of ōur sinne,
And bid hem ēch ōn[2] biginne   20
Niȝt and day mercī tō crīe.
Mī tīme is comen, Ī[3] schal dȳe.'

    Þus Adam bad Ēve his wiif
Tēchen his childer after his liif,
Hōu þai schuld anōn beginne   25
Tō crīen mercī for her sinne.
    And þō hē hadde ytauȝt hem þus,
As þē bōke telleþ ōus,
Hē knēled adōun in his bēde,
And dȳed anōn in þat stēde.   30
And as þē āngel hadde yseyd,
Alle þē liȝtnisse was yleyd[4] ;

---

[1] mett.   [2] ichon.   [3] y.   [4] aleyd.

Sonne and mōne lorn her liȝt
Sexe [1] days and sexe [1] niȝt.

Ēve bigan tō wēpe and crīe,
Þǫ schē [2] seyȝe Adam dȳe ;
And Seþ māde rewelī mǫn,　　　　　　　5
And fēl dōun on his fader anǫn,
And as it telleþ in þē bōk [3]
In his armes his fader hē tōk,
And ful bitterlīche hē wēpe.

And God Almiȝtī þērof tōke kēpe,　　　10
And sent adōun an āngel briȝt
Þat seyd tō Seþ anǫn riȝt,
'Arīse and lēte þī sorwe bē,
And wiþ þīne eyȝen þōu schalt sē
God, þat al þē warld schal glāde,　　　15
What hē wil dō wiþ þat hē māde.'

God þat sit in heven heyȝe
Tōk Adam soule, þat Seþ it seiȝe,
And bitōk it Seynt [4] Miȝhēl,
And seyd : 'Hāve, lōke þis soule wēl,　20
And put it in sorwe and þesternisse,
Out of joie [5] and alle liȝtnisse,
Til fīve þōusend winter bēn agǫ,
Twō hundred and eiȝte and twentī mǫ,
Frǫ þē tīme þat hē ēte　　　　　　　25
Of þat appel him þouȝt sǫ swēte.
Sǫ lǫnge [6] for his gilt,
In his ward hē schal bē pilt,
Þat māked him mīn hēste [7] brēke ;
Sǫ lǫnge ich wil bēn awrēke　　　　　30
On him and alle his blōd ēke,
Mī comandment for hē brēke.

---

[1] sex.　　　[2] he.　　　[3] boke.　　　[4] seyn.　　　[5] ioie, as always.
[6] long, as often.　　　[7] hest.

And whan þat terme is agǭ,
Tō joie schal turn al his wǭ;
And afterward þan schal hē
Sitten in þilke selve sē
Þat Liȝtbern sat, mīn āngel briȝt,   5
Ēr prīde was in his hert aliȝt.'

    Þus seyd Jēsus þat sitt an heyȝe,
And seþþen intō heven hē steiȝe.
Fram þē tīme þat cas fēl
Þat curssed Kaim slouȝ Abēl,   10
Til Adam dȳed upon mōld,
As swēte Jēsus Crīst it [1] wōld,
Ȝēte lay Abēl above ērþe;
Til Jēsus Crīst,—herd mōt hē wērþe—
Bad his āngels þat þai schōlde   15
Birȳ þē bodīs under mōlde.

    Þē āngels al wiþōuten chẹst
Dēde anǭn Godes hẹst.
Intō [2] clǭþes þē bodī þai fēld;
Ēve and hir children stōde and bihēld   20
Riȝt in þilke selve stẹde,
And hadde wonder what þai dēde,
For þai ne hadde ar þan
Never sēn birȳ nǭ man.

    Þan seyd an āngel þēr hē stōde,   25
Tō Ēve and tō al hir brōde:
' Tāke ȝēme hōw wē dō,
And hēr afterward dō sō.
Birīeþ alle sǭ þat dȳen
As ȝē sē wiþ ȝōure ȳȝen [3];   30
Þat wē dōn þis bodīs hēre,
Dōþ ȝē in þē selve manēre.'

---

[1] it, not in MS.   [2] ito.   [3] ȝoụr eyȝen.

Þǭ þē āngels had seyd þus
Þai wenten oȝain tō swēte Jēsus,
Tō heven þēr þai formast wēre,
And lẹved Ēve and hir children þēre.

Sex days after Adam was dẹde,   5
God Almiȝtī an āngel bẹde
Gǭ tellen Ēve, Adames wiif,
Þē terme was comen of hir liif.

Þǭ Ēve wist schē schulde[1] dȳe,
Schē clẹped forþ hir progenīe,   10
Bǭþe þē ȝonger and þē eldre,
Hir childer and hir childer childre,
And sayd þat alle miȝten hēre :
' Þǭ ich and Adam, mī fēre,
Brēken Godes comandement[2],   15
Anǭn his wrẹþe[3] was ysent
On ōus and on ōur progenīe ;
And þērfǭre mercī ȝē schul crīe,
And bǭþe bī day and ēke bī niȝt
Dōþ penance bī al ȝōur miȝt.   20
And þōu, Seþ, for anī þing
Ich comand þē on mī blisceing
Þat þī fader liif bē write,
And mīn alsǭ, everī smite,
Frǭ þē bigining of his liif   25
Þat hē was māked, and ich his wiif,
And hōu wē wēre fīled wiþ sinne,
And what sorwe wē[4] hān lived inne,
And in whiche manēr þat þōu seye
Rẹdilīche wiþ þīne eyȝe   30
Þī fader soule tō pīne sent,
For hē brak Godes comandement[2].

---

[1] schuld.   [2] comandment.   [3] wretþe.   [4] whe-

Alle þis lōke þat þōū wrīte
As wēle as þōū kanst it dīte,
Þat þǭ þat bē nōw ȝong childre
Mai it see, and her elder,
And ōþer þat hēreafter bē bǭre,   5
Hōū wē hān wrouȝt hēre bifǭre,
Þat þai mowe tāken ensaumple of ōūs,
And amenden aȝain [1] Jēsus.'

Þǭ Ēve hadde þus yseyd,
And hir erand on Seþ yleyd,   10
Schē knēled adōūn and bad hir będe;
And riȝt in þilke selve stęde,
Þat alle hir kin stōden and seyȝe
Whēre, schē dȳed biforn her eyȝe.

Anǫn riȝt as Ēve was dęde,   15
Her children tōken hem tō rēde,
And bēren hir þilke selve day
Untō þē stęde þēr Adam lay,
And birīed hir in þilke stęde,
Riȝt as þē āngels dēde   20
Þat birīed Adam and Abēl;
Þērof þai tōken hēde ful wēl.
And þǭ schē was in ērþe ybrouȝt,
Þai wēre sǭrī in her þouȝt,
And wōpen and māde miche wǭ.   25
Þǭ Adam and Ēve was agǭ,
Bǭþe an ēven and ā morwe
Þai wōpen and māde miche sorwe.

And at þē foure [2] dayes ēnde,
Jēsu [3] māde an āngel wēnde,   30
And seyd þēr þai wēpen sǭre:
'Dōleþ sex days and na mǭre;

---

[1] oȝain.   [2] four.   [3] Ihu.

Þē seven day rest of ȝōūre[1] sorwe,
Bōþe an ēven, and ā morwe.
For God þat alle þē warld haþ wrouȝt,
And alle þē warld māde of nouȝt,
As him þouȝt it wold[2] bē best,   5
Þē seven day hē tōke rest.
And anōþer þing witterlȳ.
It bitōkneþ þē day of mercī;
Þē seven day was Sonenday[3],
And þat day schal bē dōmesday,   10
And alle þē soules þat wēle hāve wrouȝt
Þat day schul tō rest bē brouȝt.'

Þō[4] þē āngel hadde his erand seyd
Þat God Almiȝtī[5] hadde on him leyd,
Intō heven þē way hē nam,—   15
Þai wist never whar hē bicam.

Seþ anōn riȝt bigan
Of Adam þat was þē forme man,
Al tōgider hē wrōt his liif,
As Ēve hade beden, Adames wiif,   20
As telleþ þē bōke þat wēle wōt,
In stōn alle þē letters hē wrōt,
For fīr ne water opon mōld
Never grēven it ne schōld.

Þō Seþ hadde writen Adames liif,   25
And Ēves þat was Adames wiif,
Riȝt in þilke selve stēde
Þēr Adam was won tō bide his bēde,
In þilke stēde þē bōk hē leyd,
As wīse men ēr þis hān seyd[6],   30
Þēr Adam was won tō biden his bēde,
And lēved it in þilke stēde;

---

[1] ȝour.   [2] wald.   [3] sononday.   [4] to.   [5] almiȝten.
[6] yseyd.

And þēr it lay alle Nōēs flōde,
And ne hadde nouȝt bot gōde.

Lǫng after Nōēs[1] flōd was gǫ,
Salamōn þē king cōm þǫ
Þat was heir[2] of Dāvid lǫnd;   5
And Adames liif þēr hē fǫnd,
And al in stǫn writen it was,
And damāged[3] nǫn letter þēr nas.
For alle þat Salamōn cōuþe
Þink in hert or spęke wiþ mōuþe,   10
Qn wōrd hē ne cōuþe wite.
Of alle þat ever was þēr write,
Hē ne cōuþe ǫ wōrd understǫnd
Þat Seþ hadde writen wiþ his hǫnd.
And Salamōn þat was wiis   15
Bisouȝt þē King of Paradȳs,
Þat hē schulde[4] for his miȝt
Sēnde him grāce fram heven liȝt,
Þat hē miȝt hāve grāce tō wite
What þing wēren þēre ywrite.   20

   God—yblisced mōt hē wērþe—
Hē sent an āngel into ērþe
Þat tauȝt Salamōn everī smite,
Alle Adames liif ywrite,
And seyd tō Salamōn ywis: 25
'Hēre, þēr þis wrīteing is,
Riȝt in þis selve stęde,
Adam was wont tō bid his będe.
And hēre þōu schalt a temple wirche
Þat schal bē clęped hǫlī chirche,   30
Þēr men schal bid hǫlȳ będe
As Adam dēde in þis stęde.'

---

[1] nes.   [2] air.   [3] damaghed.   [4] schuld.

And Salamōn þē king anǭn
Lēte rēren a temple of līme and stǭn,
Þē firste[1] chirche under sonne
Þat ever in warlde[2] was bigonne.

Nōw hāve ȝē herd of Adames liif,   5
And of Ēve þat was his wiif,
Whiche liif þai ladden hēre on mōld,
And seþþen diden as God wōld.

And þǭ Adam in ērþe was dēd,
For sinne þat cōm of her sēd,   10
God sent Nōēs flōd
And adrenched al þē brōd[3];
Swiche[4] wrēche God ynam[5]
Of alle þat of Adam cam,
Sāve Nōē[6] and his wiif   15
Þat God hadde graunted liif,
And his children þat hē hadde
Tō schip wiþ him þat hē ladde.

Of Nōē seþþen and of his childer
Wē bēþ ycomen al tōgider.   20
And seþþen þai lived[7] in swiche sinne
Þat for þē liif þai liveden inne
Sodom and Gomore, þat wēr þǭ
Swīþe nǭble citēs twǭ,
Bǭþe sonken intō helle,   25
As wē hēre clerkes telle.
And anōþer nǭble citē,
Þat was yhǭten Ninivē,
Was in þilke selve cas;
Bot as þē prophēte Jǭnas   30
Bad for hem bī[8] day and niȝt,
Tō swēte Jēsu ful of miȝt,

---

[1] first.   [2] warld.   [3] blod.   [4] swich.   [5] nam.
[6] noee, as in l. 19.   [7] leved.   [8] bi, not in MS.

And māde bōþe king and quēne,
And alle þat ōþer pōple bidēne,
In her bedes hē māde hem wāke,
And hard penaunce hē dēde hem tāke.
And þọ þai wēre tō penaunce pilt   5
God forȝaf hem here [1] gilt;
Þus Ninivē sāved was
Þurch bisēkeing of Jọnas.

    Ȝēte after Nōes flōd,
Al þat cōm of Nōēs [2] blōd,—   10
Wēre [3] hē never sọ họlȳ man,—
For þē sinne þat Adam bigan,
Þēr mōst nọn in heven com,
Ẹr God hadde his cōnseyl nome
Tō liȝten in þē virgine Mārīe,   15
And on þē rōde wolde [4] dȳe,
For tō biggen ōus alle frē,—
Yherd and heyed mōt hē bē.

    Nōw hāve ȝē herd of swēte Jēsus,
As þē bōke [5] telleþ ōus;   20
Of þē warld hōū it bigan,
And hōū hē māde of mōlde [6] man.
Jēsu þat was nomen wiþ wrọng,
And þọled manī paines strọng
Among þē Jewes þat wēre felle,   25
Tō bring Adam ōut of helle,
Ȝif ōus grāce for tō winne
Þē joie þat Adam nōw is inne.

---

[1] her.   [2] noees.   [3] weren.   [4] wald.   [5] bok.   [6] mold.

VI. HAVELOK THE DANE

In þat tīme, sǫ it bifelle,
Was in þē lǫnd[1] of Denemark
A rīche king, and swȳþe stark;
þē[2] nāme of him was Birkabeyn.
Hē hāvede manī knict and sweyn;   5
Hē was fayer[3] man, and wicht[4],
Of bodī hē was þē beste knicht[5],
þat evere micte lẹden ūt[6] hẹre,
Or stēde on[7] rīde, or handlen spẹre.
þrē children hē hāvede bī his wīf,   10
Hē hem lovede sǫ his līf;
Hē hāvede a sone and[8] douhtres twǫ,
Swīþe fayre, as fēl it sǫ.
Hē þat wile nǫn forbẹre,
Rīche ne pōvre, king ne kaysẹre,   15
Dẹth him tōk þan hē best wilde[9]
Liven; but hyse dayes wēre filde[10],
þat hē ne moucte nǫ mǫre live
For gōld[11] ne silver, ne for nǫ gyve.

Hwan hē þat wiste, rāþe hē sende   20
After prēstes fer and[12] hēnde,
Chanōūnes gōde and monkes bǫþe,
Him for tō wisse and tō rǫðe[13];
Him for tō hoslen, and tō[14] shrīve,
Hwīl his bodī wēre on līve.   25
Hwan hē was hosled and shriven,
His quiste māked and for him gyven,

---

[1] lon.   [2] þ.   [3] fayr.   [4] wicth.   [5] knicth, as often.
[6] uth.   [7] onne.   [8] and, not in MS.   [9] bes wolde.   [10] fulde.
[11] gol.   [12] an, as occasionally.   [13] rede.   [14] hoslon an forto.

Hise knictes dēde hē alle site,
For þoru hem hē wolde wite
Hwō micte yēme hise children yunge,
Til þat hē kōuþen spēken wiþ [1] tunge;
Spēken and gangen, on horse rīden,   5
Knictes and [2] sweynes bī here sīden.

Hē spōken þēroffe, and chǫsen sōne
A rīche man þat [3] under mōne
Was þē trewest þat hē wēnde,
Godard, þē kinges oune frēnde;   10
And seyden hē mouchte [4] hem best lōke,
Yif þat hē hem undertōke,
Til hise sone mouhte [5] bēre
Helm on hēved, and lēden ūt hēre,
In his hand a spēre stark,   15
And king bēn māked of Denemark.

Hē wēl trowede þat hē seyde,
And on Godard handes leyde,
And seyde, 'Hēre bitēche Ī þē
Mīne children alle þrē,   20
Al Denemark and al mī fē,
Til þat mī sone of ēlde [6] bē.
But þat ich wille, þat þōu [7] swēre
On auter and on messegēre,
On þē belles þat men ringes,   25
On messebōk þē prēst on singes,
Þat þōu mīne children shalt wēl [8] yēme,
Þat here [9] kin bē ful wēl quēme,
Til mī sone mōwe bēn knicht [10],
Þanne bitēche him þǫ his richt [11],   30
Denemark and þat þērtil lǫnges,
Casteles and tūnes, wodes and wǫnges.'

---

[1] wit.   [2] an, as occasionally.   [3] was.   [4] moucthe.   [5] mouthe, as often.
[6] helde.   [7] þo.   [8] we.   [9] hire.   [10] knicth.   [11] ricth.

Godard stirt up, and [1] swōr al þat
Þē king him bad, and siþen sat
Bī thē knictes þat þēr wāre,
Þat wēpen alle swiþe sāre
For þē king þat deide sōne.   5
Jēsu [2] Crīst þat māked mōne
On þē mirke niht [3] tō shīne,
Wite his soule frǫ hellepīne,
And lęve þat it mōte wone
In henerīche with Godes sone.   10

Hwan Birkabeyn was leyd in grāve,
Þē ērl dēde sōne tāke þē knāve,
Havelok, þat was þē heir [4],
Swanborow his sister, Helflēd þē tōþer,
And in þē castel dēde hē hem dō,   15
Þēr nǫn ne micte hem comen tō
Of here kyn, þēr þei sperd wǫre [5].
Þēr hē grēten ofte sǫre,
Bǫþe for hunger and for kǫld,
Ǫr hē wēren þrē winter ǫld [6].   20
Fēblelīke hē gaf hem clǫþes,—
Hē ne yaf a note of hise ǫþes;
Hē hem clǫþede riht [7], ne fedde,
Ne hem ne dēde rīchelīke bedde [8].
Þanne Godard was sikerlike   25
Under God þē mǫste swike
Þat evre in ērþe shāped was,
Withūten ǫn, þē wike Judas.
Hāve hē þē malisūn tōday
Of alle þat evre spēken may!   30
Of pātriark, and of pǫpe,
And of prēst with loken cǫpe;

---

[1] an.   [2] Ihu, as always.   [3] nith.   [4] eir.   [5] were.   [6] hold.
[7] rith, as often.   [8] bebedde.

Of monekes and hermītes bǫþe,
And of þē lēve hǫlī rōde
Þat God himselve ran on blōde!
Crīst warīe him with his mōuth;
Warīed worþe[1] hē of norþ and sūth,   5
Offe alle men[1a] þat spēken kunne,
Of Crīst þat māked[2] mōne and sunne!

Þanne hē hāvede of al þē lǫnd
Al þē folk tilled intil his hǫnd,
And alle hāveden sworn[3] him ǫth,   10
Rīche and pōvre, lēf and lǫth,
Þat hē sholden hise wille frẹme,
And þat hē shulden him nouht[4] grẹme,
Hē þouhte[5] a ful strǫng trẹcherȳ,
A traysōn and a felōnȳ,   15
Of þē children for tō māke,—
Þē devel of helle him sōne tāke!
Hwan þat was þouht[6], onǫn hē ferde
Tō þē tōur þēr hē wǫren sperde,
Þēr hē grēten for hunger and cǫld.   20
Þē knāve, þat was sumdẹl bǫld,
Kam him ageyn, on knēs him sette,
And Godard ful ſeyre hē þēr grette.
And Godard seyde, 'Wat is yū?
Hwī grēte yē and goulen nōu?'   25

'For us hungreth swīþe sǫre,'
Seyden hē wiþūten[7] mǫre;
'Wē ne hāve tō ẹte[8], wē ne hāve
Hērinne neyther kniht[9] ne knāve
Þat yeveth us drinken, ne nǫ mẹte   30
Halven dẹl þat wē mōun ẹte.
Wǫ is us þat wē wēren born!

---

[1] wrþe.   [1a] man.   [2] maude.   [3] sworen.   [4] nouth, as often.
[5] þouthe.   [6] þouth.   [7] wolden.   [8] hete ne.   [9] knith.

Weilawei, nis it nǫ cōrn
Þat men micte māken of brȩd?
Us[1] hungreth, wē āren ney dȩd.'
   Godard herde here wā,—
Thēroffe yaf hē nouht[2] a strā,—   5
But tōk þē maydnes bǫthe sāmen,
Al sǫ it wēre upon his[3] gāmen,
Al sǫ hē wolde with hem leyke,
Þat wēren for hunger grēne and bleike.
Of bǫþen hē karf on twō here þrǫtes,   10
And siþen karf[4] hem al tō grǫtes.
Þēr was sorwe, wōsǫ it sawe,
Hwan þē children bī þē[5] wawe
Leyen and sprauleden in þē blōd.
Havelok it saw, and þēr[6] bī stōd: 15
Ful sǫrī was þat sēlī knāve,
Mikel drēd hē mouhte[7] hāve,
For at hise herte hē saw a knīf
For tō rȩven him hise lȳf.
But þē knāve[8] þat lītel was,   20
Hē knēlede bifǫr þat Judas.
And seyde, 'Lǫverd, mercī nōu!
Manrēde, lǫverd, bidde Ī[9] yōu;
Al Denemark Ī wile yōu yive[10],
Tō þat forward þū late mē live.   25
Hēre Ī[11] wile on bōke swȩre
Þat nevre mǫre ne shal Ī bȩre
Ayēn þē, lǫverd, shēld[12] ne spȩre,
Ne ōþer wepne[13] that may yōu dȩre.
Lǫverd, hāve mercī of mē;   30
Tōday Ī wile frǫ Denemark flē,
Ne nevere mǫre comen ageyn.

---

[1] þs.   [2] nouth.   [3] hiis.   [4] karf, not in MS.   [5] þ.   [6] þe.   [7] mouthe.
[8] kave.   [9] biddi.   [10] yeve.   [11] hi.   [12] shel.   [13] wepne bere.

Swēren Ī wole þat Birkabeyn [1]
Nevere yēte mē ne gat.'
  Hwan þē devel herde [2] þat
Sumdēl bigan him for tō rewe,
Withdrow þē knīf þat was lewe   5
Of þē sēlī children blōd.
Þēr was mirācle fair and gōd,
Þat hē þē knāve nouht ne slou,
But for rewnesse him wiþdrow [3].
Of Havelok [4] rewede him ful sōre,   10
And þoucte hē wolde þat hē dēd wōre,
Buten [5] þat hē nouht wiþ [6] his hēnd
Ne drēpe him [7], þat fūle fēnd;
Þoucte hē, als hē him bī stōd
Stārinde alsō [8] hē were wōd,   15
'Yif Ī [9] late him līves gō
Hē micte me wirchen michel wō;
Grith ne get Ī [9] nevere mō,
Hē may mē [10] waiten for tō slō.
And if [11] hē wēre brouct of līve,   20
And mīne children wolden thrīve,
Lōverdinges after mē
Of al Denemark micten hē bē.
God it wite, hē shal bēn dēd,
Wile Ī tāken nōn ōþer rēd;   25
Ī shal dō casten him in þē sē [12],
Þēr Ī wile þat hē drenched [13] bē;
Abōuten his hals an anker gōd,
Þat hē ne flēte in þē flōd.'
Þēr anōn hē dēde sēnde   30
After a fishēre þat hē wēnde
Þat wolde al his wille dō,

---

[1] bircabein.   [2] hede.   [3] witdrow.   [4] avelok.   [5] but on.   [6] wit.
[7] him nouth.   [8] als.   [9] y.   [10] me, not in MS.   [11] yf.   [12] she.
[13] drench.

And sōne anǫn hē seyde him tō,
'Grim, þōū wǫst þū art mī þral;
Wilt ū[1] dōn mī wille al
Þat Ī wile bidden þē,
Tōmorwen Ī[2] shal māken þē frē,   5
And aucte þē yeven and rīche māke.
With þan þū wilt þis chīld tāke,
And lẹden him with þē tōnicht,—
Þan þōū sēst þē mōneliht[3],—
Intō þē sẹ and dōn him þrinne[4],   10
Al wile Ī tāken[5] on mē þē sinne.'

   Grim tōk þē chīld and bǫnd him faste
Hwīl þē bǫndes micte laste,
Þat wēren of ful strǫnge[6] līne.
Þǫ was Havelok in ful strǫng pīne;   15
Wiste hē nevere ẹr[7] wat was wǫ.
Jēsu Crīst, þat mākede tō gǫ
Þē halte, and þē dōumbe spẹke[8],
Havelok, þē of Godard wrẹke[9].

   Hwan Grim him hāvede faste bōunden,   20
And siþen in an ǫld clǫth wōunden[10],
A kevel of clūtes, ful unwraste,
Þat hē mouhte[11] spẹke ne fnaste
Hwēre hē wolde him bẹre or lẹde,—
Hwan hē hāvede dōn þat dēde,   25
Hwan þē swike him hāvede bede[12]
Þat hē shulde him forth lẹde[13]
And him drenchen[14] in þē sē,—
Þat forwarde mākeden hē,—
In a pǫke, fūl and blac,   30
Sōne hē caste him on his bac,

---

[1] wilte.   [2] I, not in MS.   [3] se mone lith.   [4] þerinne.   [5] wile
taken.   [6] strong.   [7] her.   [8] speken.   [9] wreken.   [10] wnden.
[11] mouthe.   [12] he þede.   [13] lede, not in MS.   [14] drinchen.

And bar him hǭm tō hise clęve;
And bitaucte him Dāme Lęve,
And seyde, ' Wite þou þis knāve,
Al sǭ thou with mē[1] līf hāve.
Ī shal dreinchen him in þē sē;   5
For him shole wē bēn māked frē,
Gōld hāven ynou and ōþer fē;
Þat hāveþ[2] mī lǭverd bihǭten mē.'

    Hwan Dāme Lęve[3] herde þat,
Up shē stirte and nouht[4] ne sat,   10
And caste þē knāve sō harde adoūn[5]
Þat hē þēr crakede hise croūne[6]
Ageyn a gręt stǫn, þēr it lay;
Þǭ Havelok micte sei, ' Weilawei,
Þat evere was Ī kinges bęrn!'   15
Þat him ne hāvede grīp or ęrn,
Leoūn or wulf, wulvine[7] or bęre,
Or ōþer bęst þat wolde him dęre.
Sǭ lay þat chīld tō middelnicht[8],
Þat Grim bad Lęve bringen lict,   20
For tō dōn on hise[9] clǫþes:
' Ne thenkest[10] ū nowt of mīne ǭþes
Þat ich hāve mī lǭverd swǭren?
Ne wile Ī nouht bē forlǫren;
Ī shal bęren him tō þē sē,   25
Þou wǫst þat it bihōves[11] mē,
And Ī shal drenchen him þērinne;
Rīs up swīþe and gǭ þū binne,
And blou þē fīr and liht[12] a kandel.'

    Als shē shulde hise clǫþes handel   30
On for tō dōn, and blawe þē[13] fīr,

---

[1] mi.   [2] havet.   [3] Lęve, not in MS.   [4] nouth.   [5] adoun
so harde.   [6] hise croune he þer crakede.   [7] wlf wlvine.   [8] nicth.
[9] his.   [10] thenkeste.   [11] Þat hoves.   [12] lith, as often.   [13] þer.

Shē saw þērinne a liht ful shīr,
Al sǫ briht [1] sǫ it wēre day
Aboūte þē knāve þēr hē lay.
Of hise moūth it stōd a stēm,
Als it wēre a sunnebēm;   5
Al sǫ liht was it þērinne,
Sǫ þēr brenden cerges inne.
' Jēsu Crīst!' quat [2] Dāme Lēve,
' Hwat is þat liht in ūre clēve.
Rīs [3] up Grim and lōke wat it mēnes,   10
Hwat is þē liht [4] as þoū wēnes?'
Hē stirten bǫþe up tō thē knāve,—
For man shal gōd wille hāve,—
Unkeveleden him and swīþe unboūnden,
And sōne anǫn upon [5] him fūnden,   15
Als hē tirneden of his serk,
On his riht [6] shuldre a kynemerk,
A swīþe briht [1], a swīþe fair.
' Godd ǫt,' quath Grim, ' þis is [7] ūre eir
þat shal bēn [8] lǫverd of Denemark;   20
Hē shal bēn king strǫng and stark,
Hē shal hāven in his hand
Al [9] Denemark and Engeland.
Hē shal dō Godard ful wǫ,
Hē shal him hangen or quik flǫ;   25
Or hē shal him al quic grāve,
Of him shal hē nǫ mercī hāve.'
þus seide Grim and sǫre grēt,
And sōne fēl him tō þē fēt,
And seide, ' Lǫverd, hāve mercī   30
Of mē, and Lēve þat is mē bī!
Lǫverd wē āren bǫþe þīne,
þīne chērles, þīne hīne.

---

[1] brith.   [2] wat.   [3] sir.   [4] lith.   [5] upon, not in MS.   [6] rith.
[7] is, not in MS.   [8] ben, not in MS.   [9] a.

Lǫverd, wē sholen þē wēl fēde,
Til þat þū cone rīden on stēde,
Til þat þū cone ful wēl bẹ̄re
Helm on hẹved, shēld and spẹ̄re;
Ne [1] shal nevere wite sikerlike,   5
Godard, þat fūle swike.

Þoru ōþer man, lǫverd, than þoru þē
Shal [2] Ī nevere frēman bē.
Þōu shalt mē, lǫverd, frē māken,
For Ī shal yēmen þē and wāken;   10
J'oru þē wile Ī frēdōm hāve.'

Þǭ was Havelok a blīþe knāve;
Hē sat him up and crāvede brẹd,
And seide, 'Ich am neye [3] dẹd,
Hwat for hunger, wat for bǫndes   15
Þat þū leidest on mīn hǫndes,
And for þē [4] kevel at þē laste,
Þat in mī mōuth was þrīste [5] faste;
Ī [6] was þērwith [7] sǭ harde prangled
Þat Ī was þērwith neye [3] strangled.'   20

'Wēl is mē þat þū mayht [8] ẹ̄te;
Godd ǫt [9],' quath Lẹ̄ve, 'Ī [6] shal þē fẹ̄te.
Brẹd and chēse, butere and milk,
Pāstees and flaunes, al with swilk
Shole wē sōne þē wēl fēde,   25
Lǫverd, in þis mikel nēde;
Sōth it is þat men seyth [10] and swẹ̄reth,
Þēr God wile helpen, nouht [11] ne dẹ̄reth.¹

Þanne shē [12] hāvede brouht [13] þē mẹ̄te,
Havelok anǫn bigan tō ẹ̄te   30
Grūndlīke, and was ful blīþe;
Cōuþe hē nouht [11] his hunger mīþe.

---

[1] he ne.   [2] sal.   [3] ney.   [4] þe, not in MS.   [5] þrist.   [6] y.
[7] þewith, as in next line.   [8] mayth hete.   [9] goddoth.   [10] seyt.
[11] nouth   [12] sho.   [13] brouth.

A lǫf hē ēt[1], Ī wǫt[2], and mǭre,
For him hungrede swīþe sǭre.
Þrē dayes þēr biforn, Ī wēne,
Ēt hē nǭ mēte, þat was wēl sēne.
Hwan hē hāvede ēten and was fed,   5
Grim dēde māken a ful fayr bed;
Unclǭþede him and dēde him þērinne,
And seyde, 'Slēp, sone, with michel winne,
Slēp wēl faste and drēd þē nouht[3],
Frǭ sorwe tō joye art þū brouht[4].'   10
    Sōne sǭ it was liht[5] of day,
Grim it undertōk þē wey
Tō þē wicke traitour Godard,
Þat was Denemarkes[6] stiward,
And seyde, 'Lǫverd, dōn ich hāve   15
Þat þōu mē bēde of þē knāve;
Hē is drenched in þē flōd,
Aboūten his hals an anker gōd.
Hē is witerlīke dēd,
Ēteth he nevre mǭre brēd;   20
Hē līþ drenched in þē sē:—
Yif mē gōld and[7] ōþer fē,
Þat Ī[8] mōwe rīche bē,
And with þī chartre māke mē[9] frē,
For þū ful wēl bihēt it[10] mē   25
Þanne Ī laste[11] spak with þē.'
Godard stōd, and lōkede on him
Þorūtlīke[12] with eyne grim,
And seyde, 'Wilt ū noū[13] bēn ērl?
Gǭ hǭm swīþe, fūle dritchērl;   30
Gǭ hēþen and bē everemǭre
Þral and chērl, as þōu ēr wǭre;

---

[1] het. [2] y woth. [3] nouth. [4] brouth. [5] lith. [6] denemak a.
[7] and, not in MS. [8] y. [9] me, not in MS. [10] bihetet. [11] last.
[12] Joruthlike. [13] nou, not in MS.

Shalt ū hāve[1] nǫn oþer mēde.
For lītel Ī shal[2] dō þē lẹ̄de
Tō þē galwes, sǫ God mē rēde,
For þou hāves dōn a wicke dēde,
Þou maiht[3] stǫnden hēr tō lǫnge,   5
Bute þou swiþe hẹþen[4] gǫnge.'

  Grim thoucte tō lāte þat hē ran
Frǫ þat traytōur, þat[4a] wicke man,
And þoucte, 'Wat shal mē tō rǫþe[5]?
Wite him[6] onlīve, hē wile us bǫþe[7]   10
Heye hangen on galwetrē.
Betere us is of lǫnde tō flē,
And berwen bǫþen ūre līves,
Mīne[8] children and mīne wīves.'
Grim sǫlde sōne al his cōrn,   15
Shēp wiþ[9] wolle, nẹ̄t[10] wiþ[9] hōrn,
Hors and swīn, and gǫt[11] wiþ bẹrd,
Þē gees, þē hennes of þē yẹrd,—
Al hē sǫlde þat ouht douhte[12],
Þat hē evre selle moucte,   20
And al hē tō þē penī drou.
Hise ship hē greyþede wēl inow;
Hē dēde it tẹre and[13] ful wēl pike
Þat it ne dōutede sǫnd ne krike;
Þērinne dide a ful gōd mast,   25
Strǫnge cābles and ful fast,
Ǫres gōde, and ful gōd seyl;
Þērinne wantede nouht[14] a nayl
Þat evere hē sholde þērinne dō.

  Hwan hē hāved it[15] greyþed sō,   30
Havelok þē yunge hē dide þērinne,

----

[1] shal have.   [2] shal, not in MS.   [3] mait.   [4] eþen.   [4a] þa.   [5] rede.
[6] he him.   [7] wile beþe.   [8] and mine.   [9] wit, as in next line.
[10] neth.   [11] and got, not in MS.   [12] outh douthe.   [13] an.   [14] nouth.
[15] et.

Him and his wīf, hīse sones þrinne,
And hise twō doutres þat faire wǭre;
And sōne dēde hē leyn in an ǭre,
And drou him tō þē heye sē,
þēre hē miht alþerbeste¹ flē.   5
Frǭ lǫnde wǭren hē bote a mīle,
Ne wēre nevere but ane hwīle,
þat it ne gan² a wīnd tō rīse
Out of þē north men calleth bīse,
And drǭf hem intil Engelǫnd,   10
þat al was siþen in his hǫnd,
His, þat Havelok was þē nāme;
But ǭr hē hāvede michel shāme,
Michel sorwe and michel tēne;
And siþe³ hē gat it al bidēne,   15
Als yē shulen nōū forthwar lęre⁴,
If⁵ that yē wilen þērtō hēre.

In Humber Grim bigan tō lēnde,
In Lindeseye riht⁶ at þē north ēnde;
þēr sat his⁷ ship upon þē sǫnd,   20
But Grim it drou up tō þē lǫnd.
And þēre hē māde a lītel cǫte
Tō him and tō al⁸ hise flǫte;
Bigan hē þēre for tō ęrde⁹,
A lītel hūs tō māken of ērþe,   25
Sǭ þat hē wēl þǭre wēre
Of here herboru herborwed þēre:
And for þat Grim þat plāce auhte¹⁰,
þē stęde of Grim þē nāme lauhte¹¹;
Sǭ þat Grimesbī it¹² calle¹³   30
þat þēroffe spęken alle,
And sǭ shulen men callen it ay
Bitwēne þis and dōmesday.

---

¹ mith alþerbest. ² bigan. ³ þrie. ⁴ here. ⁵ yf. ⁶ rith. ⁷ is.
⁸ al, not in MS. ⁹ erþe. ¹⁰ aute. ¹¹ laute. ¹² it, not in MS. ¹³ calleth alle.

VII. ROBERT MANNING'S HANDLYNGE SYNNE
THE TALE OF PERS THE USURER

Ōkerērs and kauersyns,
As wykked þey āre as Sarasyns.
Whōsǭ myȝt prēve whych þey wǭre,
Wēre þey lewed or wēre þey lǫre,
Þey shulde nat come in[1] Crȳstys hērde,   5
Ne come in cherche ne chyrcheȝērde.
Nǭþelḛs, þurgh þys skylle
Þey mōwe bē sāved, ȝyf þat þey wylle
Lḛve þat synne and dō nǭ mǭre,
And dō at hǫlȳ cherches lǫre;   10
And ȝyve aȝeyn þat yche þyng
Þat þey hāve tāke in ōkeryng;
Ȝyf þey mōw nat aȝēn hyt ȝyve,
Helpe þē pōre men þērwyþ[1a] tō lyve
Largelȳ and wyþ gōde wylle,   15
And þey mōwe peyse here dēdys ylle.
A gōde ensample mōw ȝē hēre,
Of Pērs þat was a tollēre;
And Ī[2] shal telle ȝōw as quyk
Hōw hē was bǭþe gōde and wyk.   20
Seynt Jǫne[3] þē aumenēre
Seyþ Pērs was an ōkerēre,
And was swȳþe coveytōus,
And a nygun and avarōus,
And gadred penes[4] untō stǫre   25
As ōkerēres[5] dōne[5a] aywhǭre.

[1] yn, as always.   [1a] þerwt, as always.   [2] y, as always.   [3] Ione.
[4] pens.   [5] okerers.   [5a] doū.

Befyl hyt sǭ upon a day
Þat pōre men sāte in þē way,
And spred here hatren on here barme
Aȝēns þē sonne þat was warme,
And rekened þē custome hōūses ęch ǭne [1]   5
At whych þey had gōde, and at whyche nǭne [2];
Þēre þey hadde gōde þey preysed weyl,
And þēre þey hadde noght, never a deyl.
As þey spāk of manȳwhat,
Cōme Pērs forþ in þat gat;   10
Þan seyd ęch ǭne þat sate and stōde,
'Hēre comþ Pērs þat never dyd gōde.'
Ęch ǭne seyd tō ōþer jangland,
Þey tōke never gōde at Pērs hand;
Ne nǭne pōre men never shal hāve,   15
Cōūde hē never sǭ weyl crāve.
Ǭne of hem began tō sey,
'A wājōūr [3] dar Ī wyþ ȝōw ley
Þat Ī shal hāve sum gōde at hym,
Bē hē never sǭ gryl ne grym.'   20
Tō þat wājōūr þey graunted alle,
Tō ȝyve hym a ȝyft, ȝyf sǭ myȝt befalle.
Þys man upsterte and tōke þē gāte
Tyl hē cōm at Pērs ȝāte.
As hē stōde stylle and bǭde þē quęde,   25
Ǭne cōm wyþ [4] an asse charged wyþ bręde;
Þat yche bręde Pērs had boght,
And tō hys hōūs shuld hyt bē broght.
Þǭ hē sagh Pērs come þēr wyþal [5],
Þē pōre þoght, nōw aske Ī shal: 30
'Ī aske þē sum gōde pur charytē,
Pērs, ȝyf þȳ wylle [6] bē.'

---

[1] oun, as regularly.   [2] noun, as always.   [3] waiour, as in l. 21.   [4] wt,
as usually. So also in compounds.   [5] wtalle.   [6] wyl.

Pērs stōde and lōked on hym
Felūnlȳche wyþ yȝen grym.
Hē stoūped dōwn tō sēke a stǭne,
But, as hap was, þan fǭnde hē nǭne.
For þē stǭne hē tōke a lǭſe,   5
And at þē pōre man hyt drǭſe.

    Þē pōre man hente hyt up belȳve,
And was þērof ful fērlȳ blȳþe.
Tō hys ſelawes [1] faste hē ran
Wiþ þē lǭſe, þys pōre man.   10
'Lǭ,' hē seyde [2], 'what Ī hāve
Of Pērs ȝyft, sǭ God me sāve.'
'Nay,' þey swōre bȳ here þryſt,
'Pērs ȝāve never swych a ȝyft.'
Hē seyd, 'Ȝē shul weyl undyrstǭnde   15
Þat Ī hyt had at Pērs hǭnde;
Þat dar Ī swēre on þē halȳdōm
Hēre befǭre ȝōw ēch ǭn [3].'
Grēte merveyle had þey alle
Þat swych a chaunce myȝt hym befalle.   20

    Þē þridde day,—þus wryte hyt is [4],—
Pērs ſyl in a grēte syknes;
And as hē laye [5] in hys bedde,
Hym þoght weyl þat hē was ledde
Wyþ ǭne þat aſtyr hym was sent   25
Tō come untō hys jugement [6].
Befǭre þē Juge [7] was hē broght
Tō ȝēlde acōunte hōw hē hadde wroght.
Pērs stōde ful sǭre adrad,
And was abashed as amad [8];   30
Hē sagh a ſēnde on þē tǭ partȳ
Bewreyyng hym ful felūnlȳ.

---

[1] felaws.   [2] seyd.   [3] echone.   [4] ys, as always.   [5] ley.
[6] iugement.   [7] iuge.   [8] a, not in MS.

Alle hyt was shewed hym befǫre
Hōw hē had lyved syn hē was bǫre,
And nāmelȳ everȳ wykked dēde
Syn fyrst hē cōūde hymselve [1] lęde:
Whȳ hē hem dyd and for what chęsūn, 5
Of alle behōveþ hym ȝēlde [2] a ręsōūn.
On þē tōþer [3] partȳ stōde men ful bryȝt
Þat wulde hāve sāved hym at here myȝt,
But þey myght nǫ gōde fȳnde
Þat myȝt hym sāve or unbȳnde. 10
Þē seyre men seyd, 'What is tō rēde?
Of hym fȳnde wē nǫ gōde dēde
Þat God is payd of, but of a lǫfe
Þē whych Pērs at [4] þē pōre man drǫfe.
Ȝyt ȝāve hē hyt wyþ nǫ gōde wylle, 15
But kast hyt after hym wyþ ylle;
For Goddys love ȝāve hē hyt noȝt,
Ne for almesdēde hē hyt had þoght.
Nǫþelęs, þē pōre man
Had þē lǫfe of Pērs þan.' 20
Þē fēnde had leyed [5] in balaunce
Hys wykked dēdes and hys myschaunce;
Þey leyd þē lǫfe aȝēns hys dēdys,—
Þey had noȝt elles, þey mōte nēdys,—
Þē hǫlȳ man telleþ us, and seys 25
Þat þē lǫfe māde ęven peys.
Þan seyd þēse seyre men tō Pērs,
'Ȝyf þōū bē wȳs, nōw þōū lęres
Hōw þys lǫfe þē helpeþ at nēde
Tō tylle þȳ soule wyþ almesdēde.' 30
    Pērs of hys slēpe gan blynke,
And grętlȳ on hys dręme gan þynke,

---

[1] hymself. [2] to ȝelde. [3] touþer. [4] a. [5] leyd.

Syghyng wyþ mōrnyng chēre
As man þat was in grẹ̄te wẹ̄re,
Hōw þat hē acōūped was
Wyþ fēndes fẹ̄le for hys trespas,
And hōw þey wulde hāve dampned hym þēre,   5
3yf mercȳ of Jēsu[1a] Crȳst ne wēre.
Alle þys in hys herte hē kast,
And tō hymself hē spak at þē laste,
Þat 'For a lọ̄fe in ẹ̄vyl[1] wylle
Halpe mē in sọ̄ grẹ̄te perel,   10
Moche wulde[2] hyt helpe at nēde
Wyþ gōde wyl dō almesdēde.'
Frọ̄ þat tȳme þan wax Pērs
A man of sọ̄ feyre manērs,
Þat nọ̄ man my3te[3] in hym fȳnde   15
But tō þē pōre bọ̄þe mēke and kȳnde;
A mȳlder man ne my3t nat bē,
Ne tō þē pōre mọ̄re of almes frē,
And reuful of herte alsọ̄ hē was
Þat mayst þōū hēre lẹ̄re in þys pas.   20

    Pērs mette, upon a day,
A pōre man bȳ þē way
As nāked as hē was bọ̄re,
Þat in þē sẹ̄ẹ had alle lọ̄re.
Hē cōme tō Pērs þēre hē stōde,   25
And asked hym sum of hys gōde,
Sumwhat of hys clọ̄þing,
For þē love of Hevenekyng.
Pērs was of reuful herte,
Hē tōke hys kyrtyl of as smert,   30
And dēd hyt on þē man above,
And bad hym wẹ̄re hyt for hys love.

---

[1] eveyl.   [1a] Ihu, as always.   [2] wlde.   [3] my3t.

Þē man hyt tōke and was ful blȳþe;
Hē ȝēde and sǫlde hyt as swȳþe.

Pērs stōde and dyd behǫlde
Hōw þē man þē kyrtyl sǫlde,
And was þērwyþ fērlȳ wrǫþe   5
Þat hē sǫlde sō sōne hys clǫþe.
Hē myȝt nǫ lēnger for sorow stand[1],
But ȝēde hǫme ful sǫre grētand,
And seyd hyt was an ēvyl sȳgne,
And þat hymselve[2] was nat dȳgne   10
For tō bē in hys preyēre;
Þērfor nolde hē þē kyrtyl wēre.

Whan hē hadde ful lǫng grēte,
And a partȳ þērof gan[3] lēte,—
For comūnlȳch after wēpe   15
Fal men sōne on slēpe,—
As Pērs lay in hys slēpyng,
Hym þoght a feyre swevenyng.
Hym þoght hē was in hevene lyȝt,
And of God hē had a syght   20
Syttyng in hys kyrtyl clad,
Þat þē pōre man of hym had;
And spak tō hym ful mȳldelȳ,
'Whȳ wēpest þōu and art sǫrȳ?
Lǫ Pērs,' hē seyd, 'þys is þȳ clǫth;   25
For hē sǫlde hyt, wēre þōu wrǫth.
Know hyt weyl, ȝyf þat þōu can,
For mē þōu ȝāve hyt þē pōre man;
Þat þōu ȝāve hym in charytē,
Everȳ deyl þōu ȝāve hyt mē.'   30

Pērs of slēpe ōute breyde,
And þoght grēte wunder and seþen seyd[4],

---

[1] stande.   [2] hymself.   [3] began.   [4] seyd.

' Blessyd be alle pōre men
For God Almyȝtȳ loveþ hem;
And weyl is hem þat pōre āre hēre,
Þey āre wyþ God bōþe lēfe and dēre,
And Ī shal fonde bȳ nyȝt and day   5
Tō bē pōre, ȝyf þat Ī may.'
Hāstlȳ hē tōke hys kateyl
And ȝāve hyt tō pōre men ęche deyl.

   Pērs kalled tō hym hys clerk
Þat was hys nǫtarȳe, and bad hym herk:—   10
'Ī shal þē shewe a pryvytē,
A þyng þat þōu shalt dō tō mē,
Ī wyl þat þōu nǫ man hyt telle;
Mȳ bodȳ Ī tāke þē hēre tō selle
Tō sum man as in bǫndāge,   15
Tō lyve in povert and in servāge;
But þōu dō þus Ī wyl bē wrǫth,
And þōu and þȳne shal bē mē lǫth.
Ȝyf þōu dō hyt, Ī shal þē ȝyve
Tēn pōund[1] of gōld wel wiþ tō lyve;   20
Þǫ tēn pōund Ī tāke þē hēre,
And mē tō selle on bǫnde manēre,
Ī ne recche untō whōm,
But ǫnlȳch hē hāve þē crystendōm.
Þē raunsūn þat þōu shalt for mē tāke,   25
Þarfǫre þōu shalt sykernes māke
For tō ȝyve hyt blȳþelȳ[2] and weyl
Tō pōre men everȳ deyl,
And wyþhǫlde þērof nǫ þyng
Þē mōuntouns of a ferþyng.'   30

   Hys clerk was wǫ tō dō þat dēde,
But ǫnlȳ for manās and for drēde.

---

[1] pownd, as in next line.   [2] bleþely.

For drēde Pērs māde hym hyt dō[1],
And dēde hym plyghte hys trouthe þērtō.
Whan hys clerk had māde hys ǭthe,
Pērs dēde on hym a fōule clǭthe;
Untō a cherche bǭþe þey ȝēde   5
For tō fulfylle hys wyl in dēde.
Whan þat þey tō þē cherche cōm,
'Lǭrde,' þoght þē clerk, ' nōw whōm
Myȝt Ī fȳnde, þys yche sēle,
Tō whōm Ī myȝte[2] selle Pērs wēle?'   10
    Þē clerk lōked everȳwhēre,
And at þē last hē knew whēre
A rȳche man was[3] þat ēr had bē
Specyal knowlych ever betwē,
But þurgh myschaunce at a cas   15
Alle hys gōde ylǭre was;
Ȝōle, þus þat man hyghte,
And knew þē clerk wēl bē syghte.
Þey spak of ǭlde aqueyntaunce,
And Ȝōle tǭlde hym of hys chaunce.   20
' Ȝē,' seyde þē clerk, ' Ī rēde þōu bȳe
A man tō dō þȳ marchaundȳe,
Þat þōu mayst hǭlde in servāge
Tō restǭre weyl þyn dammāge.'
    Þan seyd Ȝōle, ' On swych chaffāre   25
Wulde Ī feyn mȳ sylver wāre.'
    Þē clerke seyd, ' Lǭ, ǭne hēre,
A trew man and[4] a dubonēre[5],
Þat wyl serve þē tō pay
Peyneble, al þat hē may.   30
Pērs shalt þōu calle hys nāme,
For hym shalt þōu hāve moche frāme.

---

[1] *ll.* 1–6, not in Harleian MS., but supplied from Bodl. MS. 415.   [2] myȝt.
[3] was, not in MS.   [4] an.   [5] dubonure.

Hē is a man ful grācyōus
Gōde tō wynne untō þȳn hōus,
And God shal ȝyve þē hys blessyng,
And foysyn in alle þyng.'

Þē clerk ȝāve alle hys raunsūn   5
Tō þē pōre men of þē tōun,—
Plenērlȳ alle þat hē tōke
Wyþhēlde hē nat a ferþyng nōke.
Þē emperōure sent hys messagēres
Alle abōute for tō sēke Pērs,   10
But þey ne myȝte[1] never hēre
Of rȳche. Pērs, þē tollēre,
In what stẹ̄de hē was nome,
Ne[2] whydyrward hē was become;
Ne þē clerk wuld telle tō nọ̄ne   15
Whydyrward þat Pērs was gọ̄ne.

Nōw is Pērs bycome brȳche,
Þat ẹ̄r was bọ̄þe stōute and rȳche.
Alle þat ever anȳ man hym bad[3],
Pērs dyd hyt wyþ herte[4] glad.   20
Hē wax sọ̄ mȳlde and sọ̄ mēke,
A mȳlder man þurt nọ̄ man sēke;
For hē mēked hymself ọ̄verskyle
Pottes and dysshes for tō swyle[5].
Tō grẹ̄te penaunce hē gan hym tāke,   25
And moche for tō fast and wāke,
And moche hē loved þọ̄lmōdnesse
Tō rȳche, tō pōre, tō mọ̄re, tō lesse.
Of alle men hē wuld hāve dōute,
And tō here byddyng mēklȳ lōute;   30
Wulde þey bydde hym sytte or stande,
Ever hē wulde bē bōwande.

---

[1] myȝt.   [2] no, as in next line.   [3] do bad.   [4] hert.   [5] swele.

And for hē bāre hym sǭ mēke and scfte,
Shrewes mysdēde hym ful ofte,
And hēlde hym folted or wōde
For hē was sǭ mȳlde of mōde.
And þey þat wēre hys felawes [1]   5
Mysseyd hym mǭst in here sawes;
And alle hē suffred here upbreyd,
And never naght aȝēns hem seyd [1a].

Ȝōle, hys lǫrde, wēl undyrstōde
Þat al hys grāce and hys gōde   10
Cōm hym [2] for þē love of Pērs,
Þat was of sǭ hǫlȳ manērs.
And whan hē wyst of hys bōuntē,
Hē kalled Pērs in pryvytē :
'Pērs,' hē seyd, 'þōu wēre wurþȳ   15
For tō bē wurscheped mǫre þan Ī,
For þōu art weyl wyþ Jēsu,
Hē sheweþ for þē grēte vertu ;
Þarfǫr Ī shal māke þē frē,
Ī wyl þat my felaw þōu bē.'   20
Þartō Pērs graunted noght
Tō bē frēman as hē besoght ;
Hē wulde bē as hē was ǫre
In þat servāge for evermǫre.
Hē þanked þē lǫrde mȳldelȳ   25
For hys grēte curteysȳ.

Syþþen Jēsu, þurgh hys myȝt,
Shewed hym tō Pērs syȝt,
For tō bē stalworþe in hys fǫndyng,
And tō hym hāve lovelǫngyng.   30
'Bē nat sorowful tō dō penaunce,
Ī am wiþ þē in everȳ chaunce ;

---

[1] felaus. [1a] seyde. [2] hym, not in MS.

Pērs, Ī hāve mȳnde of þē,
Lǭ hēre þē kyrtyl þōu¹ ȝāve for më,
Þērfǭr grāce Ī shal þē sēnde
In alle gōdenesse weyl tō ēnde.'

    Byfyl þat serjauntes² and squyērs   5
Þāt wēre wunt tō serve Pērs
Went in pylgrymāge, as in kas,
Tō þat cuntrē þēre Pērs was.
Ȝōle ful feyre gan hem kalle,
And preyd hem hǭme tō hys halle.   10
Pērs was þēre þat yche sēle,
And everȳch ǭne hē knew hem wēle.
Alle hē served hem as a knāve
Þat was wunt here servȳse tō hāve.
But Pērs nat ȝyt þey knew,   15
For penaunce chaunged was hys hew;
Nat forþȳ þey behēlde hym fast,
And oftyn tō hym here yȝen þey kast,
And seyde³, 'Hē þat stonte hēre
Is lȳche tō Pērs þē⁴ tollēre.'   20
Hē hydde hys vysege al þat hē myȝt
Ōut of knowlych of here syȝt;
Nǭþelẹs þey behēlde hym mǭre
And knew hym weyl, al þat wēre þǭre,
And seyd, 'Ȝōle, is ȝone þȳ pāge?   25
A rȳche man is in þȳ servāge;
Þē emperǭure bǭþe fer and nēre
Haþ dō hym sēche þat wē fȳnde hēre.'
    Pērs lestned, and herd hem spẹ̄kyng,
And þat þey had of hym knowyng;   30
And pryvylȳ awey hē nam
Tyl hē tō þē portēr cam.

---

¹ kyrtyl þat þou.   ² seriauntes.   ³ seyd.   ⁴ þe, not in MS.

Þē portēr had hys spēche lǫre,
And hēryng alsǫ, syn hē was bǫre ;
But þurgh þē grāce of swēte Jēsu
Was shewed for Pērs feyre vertu.
Pērs seyd, ' Late mē furþe [1] gǫ.'   5
Þē portēr spak and seyde [2] ' ʒǫ.'
Hē þat was dęf, and dōūmbe alsō,
Spak whan Pērs spak hym tō.
Pērs ōūte at þē ʒāte wente,
And þedyr ʒēde þēre God hym sente.   10
Þē portēr ʒēde up tō þē halle,
And þys merveyle tǫlde hem alle,
Hōw þē squylēr of þē kechyn,
Pērs, þat haþ woned hēreyn,
Hē asked lęve ryʒt nōw lāte,   15
And went furþ ōūt at þē ʒāte.
' Ī rēde ʒōw alle, ʒeveþ gōde tent,
Whederward þat Pērs is went ;
Wyþ Jēsu Crȳst hē is pryvē,
And þat is shewed weyl on mē,   20
For what tȳme hē tō mē spak,
Ōut of hys mōūþ mē þoghte [3] brak
A flamme of fȳre bryght and clēre ;
Þē flaumme māde mē bǫþe spęke and hēre,
Spęke and hēre nōw bǫþe Ī may,   25
Blessed bē God and Pērs tōday.'
Þē lǫrde and þē gestes alle,
Ǫne and ōþer þat wēre in halle,
Had merveyle þat hyt was sō,
Þat hē myʒte swych myrācle dō.   30
Þan as swȳþe Pērs þey soght,
But al here sēking was for noʒt.

---

[1] furþ.   [2] seyd.   [3] þoght.

Never Pērs þey ne foūnde,
Ny3t ne day, in nǭ stoūnde,
For hē þat tōke Ennok and Ēlȳ
Hē tōke Pērs þurgh hys mercȳ,
Tō reste wyþoūtyn ēnde tō lẹde,
For hys mēknes and hys gōde dēde:
    Tāke ensample hēre of Pērs,
And parteþ wyþ þē pōre, 3ē ōkerērs,
For 3o͞w shal never come joye[1] wyþynne,
But 3ē lẹve fyrst þat synne,
And 3yve tō almes þat yche þyng
Þat 3ē hāve wune wyþ ōkeryng.
No͞w wyþ God lẹve wē Pērs;
God 3yve us grāce tō dō hys manērs.

VIII. THE WEST MIDLAND PROSE PSALTER

Psalm I.

Blesced bē þē man þat 3ēde nou3t in þē co͞unseil of wicked, ne
stōde nou3t in þē waie of sin3ẹres, ne sat nau3t in fals jugement.
2. Ac his[2] wylle was in þē wylle of o͞ure Lǭrd, and hē schal þenche
in his[2] lawe bǭþe daye and ny3t. 3. And hē schal bē as þē trē
þat is[2] sett bȳ þē ērnynges of waters, þat schal 3eve his frut in his[2]
tȳme. 4. And his[2] lẹf schal nou3t fallwen, and alle þynges þat þē
ry3tful dōþ schal multiplīen. 5. Nou3t sǭ bēn þē wicked, nou3t sǭ;
as a po͞udre þat þē wȳnde casteþ fram þē fāce of þē ērþe[3]. 6.
Forþi ne schal nou3t þē wicked arīse in jugement, ne þē sinniẹrs in
þē cōnseyl of þē ry3tful. 7. For o͞ure Lǭrd knew þē waie of þē
ry3tful, and þē waye of synnẹrs schal perissen.

---

      [1] ioye.   [2] hiis.   [3] þerþe.

Psalm XXIII.

Ōur Lǫrd governeþ mē, and nǫþyng shal defailen tō mē ; in þē stę̄de of pasture hē sett mē þēr. 2. Hē norissed mē up water of fyllyng ; hē turned mȳ soule fram þē fēnde. 3. Hē lad mē up þē bistiȝes of riȝtfulnes for his nāme. 4. For ȝif þat ich hāve gǫn amiddes of þē shadowe of dę̄þ, Ī [1] shal nouȝt dōuten ivels, for þōu 5 art wyþ mē. 5. Þȳ disciplīne and þȳn amendyng conforted mē. 6. Þōu mādest radī grāce in mȳ siȝt oȝayns hem þat trublen mē. 7. Þōu mākest fatt mȳn hę̄ved wyþ mercȳ ; and mȳ drynk, mākand drunken, is [2] ful clēre. 8. And þȳ mercī shal folwen mē alle daies of mī līf. 9. And þat ich wonne in þē hōus of ōur Lǫrd in lengþe 10 of daies.

Psalm XXIV.

1. Þē ērþe is our Lǫrdes and his plentē ; þē world and ich ǫn þat woneþ þērinne. 2. For hē bigged it up þē sę̄ę̄s, and māde it rę̄dī up þē flōdes. 3. Whō shal clīmben intō þē mōuntein of ōur Lǫrd, ǫþer whō shal stǫnde in his hǫlȳ stę̄de? 4. Þē innocent in 15 hǫnde and of clę̄ne hert, þat ne tōke nouȝt his soule in īdelnesse and ne swōre noȝt in gilerī tō his neȝbūr. 5. Hē shal tāke bliscyng of ōur Lǫrd, and mercȳ of God his helpe. 6. Þis is [4] þē biȝetyng of þē sēchand hym, sēchand þē fāce of God of Jācob [3]. 7. Ǭpeneþ ȝōur ȝātes, ȝē princes of helle, and bēþ ȝē lifted, ȝē everlastand ȝātes, 20 and þē kynge of glǫrīe shal entre. 8. Which is hē, þat kyng of glǫrīe? Þē Lǫrd strǫnge and miȝtful, þē Lǫrd myȝtful in batail. 9. Ǭpeneþ ȝōur ȝātes, ȝē princes of hevene, and bēþ ȝē lifted, ȝē ȝātes everlastand, and þē kynge of glǫrīe shal entren. 10. Which is hē, þat kynge of glǫrīe? Þē Lǫrd of vertu, hē is [4] kynge of 25 glǫrīe.

Psalm LI.

1. Hā mercȳ on mē, God, efter þȳ mychel mercȳ. 2. And efter þē mychelnes of þȳ pitēs, dō way mȳ wickednes. 3. Wasshe [5]

---

[1] y, and always.   [2] ys, and occasionally.   [3] God Iacob.   [4] his.
[5] whasshe.

mē mọre of mȳ wickednes, and clense mē of mȳn synne. 4. For ich knowe[1] mȳ wickednes, and mȳ synne is evermọre oȝains me. 5. Ich hāve synned tō þē alọn, and ich hāve dōn ivel tōfọre þē, þat ōu bē māde ryȝtful in þȳ wōrdes, and þat ōu ọvercum whan þōu art juged.   6. Sē, for ich am conceived in wickednesses, and mȳ mōder conceived mē in synnes.   7. Sē, for þōu loved sōþenes; þē uncerteyn þynges and pryvē of wisdōm þōu māde tō mē apert.   8. Þōu sprengest mē, Lọrd, wyþ þȳ mercȳ, and Ī shal bē māde clẹne; þou shalt purifīe mē, and Ī shal bē māde whȳte[2] up snowe.   9. Þou shalt ȝeve joie and gladnes tō mȳn hēryng[3], and þē mȳlde dēdes of mȳ hert shul glāden.   10. Turne þȳ fāce fram mȳn synnes[4], and dō oway al mȳn wickednes.   11. Ha, God, māke in mē clẹne hert, and newe þōu a ryȝt gọst in mȳn hert. 12. Ne putt mē nouȝt fram þȳ fāce, and ne dō nauȝt oway fram mē þȳn họlȳ gọst.   13. Ȝelde tō mē gladnes of þȳn helpe, and conferme mē wyþ þȳn họlȳ gọst.   14. Ī shal tẹchen þē wicked þȳn wayes, and þē wicked shul bēn converted tō þē.   15. Ha, þōu God, God of mȳn helþe, deliver mē of sinnes[5], and mȳ tunge shal glāden þȳ ryȝtfulnes.   16. Lọrd, þōu shalt ọpen mȳn lippes, and mȳ mōuþe shal tellen þȳn hẹryyng.   17. For ȝyf þōu hade wolde, ich hade ȝeven sacrifīce; forsōþe þōu ne shalt nouȝt delīten in sacrifīces. 18. Trubled gọst[6] is sacrifīce tō God; þōu, God, ne shal nouȝt despīsen þē hert sorowful and mēke.   19. Dō blisfullīch, Lọrd, tō þȳ chọsen in þȳ gōde wille, þat þē gōde bē confermed in hevens. 20. Þan shalt ōu tāke sacrifīce of ryȝt servīce, and honōurs; hii shul þan setten gōdenesses tōfọre þy thrọne.

Psalm XC.

1. Lọrd, þōu art māde socōur tō ōus fram kȳnde tō kīnde.   2. Tōfọre þat þē mōunteins wēre māde, ọþer þē ērþe[7] wēre fourmed and þē werld þōu art God, fram þē world untō þē world wyþōuten ẽnde.   3. Ne turne þōu nouȝt intō mīldnes; and þōu seidest, ȝẽ

---

[1] knewe.   [2] whyȝte.   [3] beryng.   [4] synmes.   [5] sines.   [6] god.   [7] þerʃe.

childer of men, turneþ ȝou.   4. For a þousand ȝeres bēn tōſǭre
þӯn eȝen as ȝisterdai þat is passed.   5. And þē kēpyng ō nyȝt,
þat for nouȝt bēn had, shul bē her ȝēres.   6. Passe hē as gresse in
þē mornyng; floriſche hē in þē mornyng and passe; ſalle hē at
ēven [1], and harden and wax hē drīe.   7. For wē failed in þӯn īre, and 5
wē bēn disturbed in þӯn vengeaunce.   8. Þou laidest ōur wicked-
nesse in þӯ siȝt; ōur world is in liȝtyng of þӯ chēre.   9. For alle
ōur daies faileden, and wē failed in þӯn ӯre.   10. Ōur ȝeres shul
þenchen as þē lob, þē daics of ōur ȝēres in þē seventī ȝēre.   11.
Forſōþe ȝyf eȝṭī ȝēre bēn in myȝtes, þē mǭre ǭver hem shal bē 10
travail and sorowe.   12. For mīldnes comeþ [2] þēron, and wē shul bē
wiþnumen.   13. Whō knew þē myȝt of þӯn īre, and tō tellen þӯ
wraþe for þӯ drēde?   14. Māke sǭ þӯn helpe knowen, and þē lǭred
of hert in wisdōme.   15. Lǭrd, bē þou turned untō nōu, and bē
þou bidlīch up þӯ servantes.   16. Wē bēn fulfild ērlīch of þӯ 15
mercӯ, wē shul glāden and delīten in alle ōur daies.   17. Wē
glāded in þē daies in which þou lowed us, for þē ȝēres in which wē
seiȝen ivels.   18. Lōke tō þӯ servauntes and tō þӯn werkes, and
dresce her sones.   19. And þē shӯnyng of ōur Lǭrd God bē up us,
and dresce up us þē werkes of ōur hǭndes, and dresce up us þē 20
werkes of ōur hǭndes [3].

Psalm XCI.

1. Hē þat woneþ [4] in þē helpe of þē heȝest, hē shal dwelle in þē
defens of God of heven.   2. Hē shal saie tō ōur Lǭrd, Þou art
mӯ tākēr and my refut; mī God, Ī shal hǭpen in hym.   3. For
hē deliverd mē fram þē trappes of þē fēndes, and fram asper wōrd 25
of men.   4. And hē shal shadow þē wyþ hys shulderis, and þou
shalt hǭpe under hys feþers.   5. Þē sōþenes of hym shal cumpas
þē wyþ shēlde, and þou ne shalt nouȝt dōute of þē drēde of nyȝt;
6. Of temptācioun waxand in daie, fram nēde gǭand in derknes,
fram þē cūrs of þē fēnde bryȝt shӯnyng.   7. A þousand temptā- 30
cioūns shul ſallen fram þī [5] sӯde, and tēn þousandes fram þӯ ryȝt

---

[1] heven.   [2] com.   [3] last clause repeated.   [4] whoneþ.   [5] þe.

half; þē devel, forsōþe, ne shal noȝt comen tō þē.   8. Þou shalt
sē, forsōþe, wyþ þȳn eȝen, þou shalt sē þē ȝēldyng of synȝērs.
9. For þou, Lǫrd, art mȳn hǫpe, and þou setted þȳ refut alderheȝest.   10. Yvel ne shal nouȝt com tō þē, and turment ne shal
nouȝt com nēre þy tabernācle.   11. For hē sent tō his aungels of
þē, þat hii kēpe þē in alle þȳn waies.   12. Hii shul bēre þē in
hǫndes þat tou ne hirt nouȝt, peraventure, þȳ gǫst wyþ vīces.
13. Þou shalt gǫn up queintīs [1] and gōdenes, and þou shalt defoule
þē fēnde and helle.   14. For hē hǫped in mē, and Ī shal deliver
hym; Ī shal defēnden hym, for hē knew mȳ nāme.   15. He crīed
tō mē and Ī shal hēre hym; ich am wyþ hym in tribulācioun,
Ī shal defend him and glǫrifīen hym.   16. Ī shal fulfillen hym
wyþ lengþe of daies, and Ī shal shewe hym mīn helþe.

Psalm CIII.

1. Ha, þou mȳ soule, blisce our Lǫrd; and alle þynges þat bēn
wyþinnen mē, blisce hys hǫlī nāme.   2. Ha, þou mȳ soule, blisce
our Lǫrd; and ne wille þou nouȝt forȝete alle his ȝēldeinges.
3. Þē which is mercīful tō alle þīn wickednesses; þē which hēleþ [2]
alle þy sēkenisses.   4. Þē which ransounneþ þȳ līf fram dēᵹþ; þē
which crouneþ þē wyþ mercȳ and pitēs.   5. Þē which fulfilleþ þȳ [3]
desīre in gōdes [4]; þȳ ȝengþe shal bē māde new as of an ērne.
6. Our Lǫrd is dōand mercīes and jugement tō alle þē suffrand
wrǫnge.   7. Hē māde hys waies knowen tō Mōysēs; hē did tō þē
childer of Israēl her willes.   8. Our Lǫrd is ryȝtful and mercīāble,
and of lǫnge wille and michel mercīāble.   9. Hē ne shal nouȝt
wraþþe him wyþouten ēnde, nē hē ne shal nouȝt menācen wyþouten
ēnde [5].   10. Hē ne did nouȝt tō us efter our synȝes, ne hē ne ȝēldeþ
nouȝt tō us efter our wickednes.   11. For efter þē heȝt of heven
fram ērþe hē streinþed [6] hys mercȳ up hem þat drēden hym.   12. Hē
māde fer fram us our wickednes, as þē ēste departeþ fram þē west.

---

[1] quenitis.   [2] helþe.   [3] þe.   [4] goddes.   [5] last clause from Dublin MS.
[6] MS. possibly streinþed; Dublin MS. strengþid.

13. As þē fader has mercȳ on his childer, our Lǫrd is mercīāble of hem þat drēden hym; for hē knoweþ ūr[1] faintes. 14. Hē recorded þat wē bēn pōuder[2]. Man is as hai; hys daies bēn as flōure of þē fēld; sǫ hē shal florissen. 15. For gǫst shal passen in hym, and hē ne shal nouȝt dwelle, and hē ne shal nǫ mǫre knowen his stȩde. 16. Þē mercȳ of ūr Lǫrd is forsōþe fram wyþōuten ēnde untō wyþōuten ēnde[3] up hem þat drēden hym. 17. And his riȝtfulnes is untō[4] chīld of childer tō hem þat[5] kēpen his testament. 18. And hii bēn remembraunt of his comaundements[6] tō dōn hem. 19. Oūr Lǫrd shal diȝten his sȩte in heven, and his kyngdōme shal lǫrdship alle. 20. Ha, alle his āngeles, miȝtful of vertu, dōand his wōrde, tō hēre þē voice of hys wōrdes, blisceþ ōūr Lǫrd. 21. Ha, alle his vertu, blisceþ ōūr Lǫrd; ȝē his ministris, þat dōn hys wille, blisceþ[7] ōūr Lǫrd. 23. Ȝē alle werke of ōūr Lǫrd, blisceþ ōūr Lǫrd in alle stȩdes of his lǫrdship; ha, þōū my soule, blisce[8] ōūr Lǫrd.

5

10

15

IX. THE EARL OF TOULOUSE

ALL they assentyd tō the sawe,
They thoght hē spake rȩsōn and lawe.
  Then answeryd þē kyng wyth crōwne,
'Fayre falle thē for thȳn avȳse.'
Hē callyd knyghtys of nǫbyll prȳce,
  And badd them bē rȩdȳ bōwne
For tō crȳe thorow all þē lǫnde,
Bǫthe be sȩȩ and be sǫnde,
  If[9] they fȳnde mōwne
A man þat is[10] sǫ moche of myght,
That for þat lādȳ dar tāke þē fyght;
Hē schall hāve hys waresōūn[11].

20

25

---

[1] knowe and erasure in MS.; our, from Dublin MS.   [2] prude.   [3] unto wyþouten ende, from Dublin MS.   [4] into.   [5] þa.   [6] comaundementȝ.   [7] blisced.   [8] blische.   [9] yf, as always.   [10] ys, as always.   [11] wareson.

Messangērys, Ī[1] undurstǫnde,
Crȳed thorow all þē lǫnde
    In manȳ a rȳche cytē,
If anȳ man durste prōve hys myȝt
In trewe quarell for tō fyght,   5
    Wēle avaunsed schulde hē bee.
The Ērle of Tolōūs[2] herde[3] þys telle,
What anger thē lādȳ befelle,
    Thēreof hē thoghte[4] grēṭe pytē.
If hē wyste that schē had ryght,   10
Hē wolde aventure hys lȳfe tō fyght
    For that lādȳ free.

For hur hē mōrned nyȝt and day,
And tō hymselfe can hē say
    Hē wolde aventure hys lȳfe: 15
'If Ī may wytt þat schē bē trewe,
They þat hāve hur accused schull rewe,
    But they stynte of thēr strȳfe.'
The ērle seyde, 'Bī[5] Seynte Jǫhn,
Intō[6] Almayn wyll Ī gǫǫn   20
    Whēre Ī hāve fǫmen rȳfe;
Ī prey tō God full of myght,
That Ī hāve trewe quarell tō fyȝt,
    Ōut of wǫ tō wynne þat wȳfe.'

Hē rǫde on huntyng on a day,   25
A marchand mett hē bī þē way,
    And asked hym of whens hē was.
'Lǫrde,' hē seyde, 'of Almayn.'
Anǫn thē ērle can hym frayne
    Of that ilke[7] cāse.   30

---

[1] y regularly.   [2] Tullous, sometimes Tollous.   [3] harde.   [4] thoght.
[5] be, as always.   [6] ynto.   [7] ylke.

' Whērefǫre is yōure [1] emperes
Put in sǭ grę̄te dystress,
    Telle mē for Goddys grāce;
Is schē gyltȳ [2], sǭ mōte thōu thē?'
' Nay, bī hym þat dȳed on tree,   5
    That schōpe man aftur hys fāce.'

Then seyde the ērle wythōute [3] lett,
' When is thē day sett,
    Brente that schē schulde bee?'
The marchande seyde, ' Sikerlyke [4],   10
Ę̄ven thys day thrē wyke,
    And thērfǭre wǭ is mee.'
Thē ērle seyde, ' Ī schall thē telle,
Gōde horsys Ī hāve tō selle,
    And stēdys twō or thrē.   15
Certys myght Ī selle þem yāre,
Thidur [5] wyth thē wolde Ī fāre
    That syghte [6] for tō see.'

Thē marchand seyd wyth [7] wōrdys hēnde,
' Intō thē lǫnde if yē wyll wēnde,   20
    Hyt wolde bē for yōure prōwe;
Thēre may yē selle þem at yōur wylle.'
Anǫn thē ērle seyde hym tylle,
    ' Sȳr, herkyn tō mē [8] nōwe;
Thys jurney [9] wylt þōu wyth mē dwelle   25
Twentȳ pōunde [10] Ī schall thē telle
    Tō mēde, Ī māke a vōwe.'
Thē marchand grauntyd hyt [11] anǫn.
Thē ērle seyde, ' Bī Seynt Jǫhn,
    Thȳ wylle Ī alōwe.'   30

---

[1] yowre, as often.   [2] gylte.   [3] wtowte, as often.   [4] sekyrlyke.
[5] thedur.   [6] syght.   [7] wyth, not in MS.   [8] herkyn me.   [9] yurney.
[10] pownde.   [11] hyt, not in MS.

Thē ērle tǫlde hym in þat tȳde,
Whēre hē schulde hym abȳde,
  And hǫmeward wente hee.
Hē busked hym þat nǫ man wyste
For mikyll[1] on hym was hys tryste.   5
  Hē seyde, 'Sȳr, gǫ wyth mee.'
Wyth them they tōke stēdys sevyn,—
Thēre wēre nǫ ſayrer[2] undyr hevyn
  That anȳ man myght see.
Intō Almayn þey can rȳde;   10
As a corsur of mikyll[3] prȳde
  Hē sēmyd for tō bee.

Thē marchand was a trewe gȳde;
Thē ērle and hē tōgedur can rȳde
  Tyll they cāme tō that plāce.   15
A mȳle besȳde thē castell,
Þēre thē emperōūre can dwelle,
  A rȳche abbey thēr was;
Of the abbot lẹve they gatt
Tō sǫjorne[4] and māke þēr horsys fatt;   20
  That was a nǫbyll cās.
The abbot was the lādȳes ẹme,
For hur hē was in grẹte wandrẹme,
  And moche mōrnyng hē mās[5].

Sǫ hytt befelle upon a day   25
Tō churche thē ērle tōke þē way,
  A masse for tō hēre.
Hē was a feyre man and an hȳe;
When thē abbot hym sȳe,
  Hē seyde, 'Sȳr, come nēre.   30

---

[1] mekyll.   [2] fayre.   [3] coresur of mekyll.   [4] soyorne.   [5] mase.

Syr, when thē masse is dōne,
Ī pray you ę̄te wyth mē at noone,
   If yōūre wylle wēre.'
Thē ērle grauntyd all wyth gāme;
Afǫre mę̄te they wysche all sāme,   5
   And tō mę̄te they wente in fēre.

Aftur mę̄te, as Ī yōū say,
Intō an orchard þey tōke þē way,
   Thē abbot and thē knyght.
The abbot seyde and syghed sāre,   10
'Certys, sȳr, Ī lyve [1] in cāre
   For a lādȳ bryght;
Schē is accusyd, my herte is wǫǫ,
Thērfǫre schē schall tō dę̄the gǫǫ
   All agayne thē ryght;   15
But schē hāve helpe, verrament,
In a [2] fȳre schē schall bē brente
   Thys day sevenyght.'

Thē ērle seyde, 'Sǫ hāve Ī blysse,
Of hyr mēþynkyþ grę̄te rewþe hyt is,   20
   Trewe if that schē bee.'
Thē abbot seyde, 'Bī Seynt Poule,
For hur Ī durre [3] ley mȳ soule
   That nevyr gyltȳ [4] was schē.
Soche werkys nevyr schē wroght,   25
Neythyr in dēde nor in thoght,
   Sāve a rynge sǫ free
Tō þē Ērle of Tolōūs schē gaſe [5] wyth wynne,
In ę̄se of hym and for nǫ synne;
   In schryſte thus tǫlde schē mē.'   30

---

[1] leve.   [2] a, not in MS.   [3] dar.   [4] gylte.   [5] ȝaſe hyt.

Thē ērle seyde, 'Syth hyt is sǫǫ,
Crȳste wrẹke hur of hure[1] wǫǫ,
    That boght hur wyth hys bloode.
Wolde yē sekyr mē, wythout fayle,
For tō hǫlde trewe coūnsayle,   5
    Hyt myght bē for yoūre gōde.'
The abbot seyde bī bōkes fẹle
And hys[2] professyōn, þat hē wolde hẹle,
    And ellys hē wēre wōde.
'Ī am hē þat schē gafe the rynge   10
For tō bē owre tǫkenynge,
    Now hẹle[3] hyt for the rōde.

Ī am comyn, lēfe syr,
Tō tāke thē batayle for hyr,
    And[4] thēretō stǫnde wyth ryght;   15
But fyrste mȳselfe Ī wole hur schrȳve,
And if Ī fȳnde hur clẹne of lȳve,
    Then wyll mȳ herte bē lyght.
Lēt dyght mē in monkys wēde
Tō þat plāce men[5] schulde hyr lẹde,   20
    Tō dẹthe tō bē dyght;
When Ī hāve schryvyn[6] hyr, wythout fayle
For hur Ī wyll tāke þē[7] batayle,
    As Ī am trewe knyght.'

Thē abbot was nevyr sǫ gladd,   25
Nēre for joie[8] hē waxe madd,
    Thē ērle can hē kysse;
They māde merȳ[9] and slewe cāre
All that sevenyght hē dwellyd þāre,
    In myrthe, withoūte[10] mysse.   30

[1] hur.   [2] and be hys.   [3] heyle.   [4] and, not in MS.   [5] þat men.   [6] schrevyn.
    [7] þe, not in MS.   [8] yoye.   [9] mere.   [10] wythout.

That day þē[1] lādȳ schulde bē brent
Thē ērle wyth thē abbot wente
  In monkys wēde, ywys;
Tō thē emperōur hē knēlyd blȳve
That hē myght þat lādȳ schrȳve;   5
  Anǫn receyved[2] hē is.

Hē examyned hur wyttyrlȳ,
As hyt seythe in thē stǫrȳ;
  Schē was wythōute gylte.
Schē seyde, 'Bī hym þat dȳed on tree,   10
Trespas was nevyr nǫne in mē
  Whērefǫre Ī schulde bē spylte,
Sāve ǫǫnys, wythōute lęsynge,
Tō thē Ērle of Tolōus Ī gafe a rynge;
  Assoyle mē if thōu wylte.   15
But þus mȳ destanȳe is come[3] tō ēnde,
That in þys fȳre Ī muste bē brende;
  Thēre Goddys wylle bē fulfyllt[4].'

Thē ērle assoyled hur wyth hys hǫnde,
And syþen pertelȳ hē can upstǫnde,   20
  And seyde, 'Lǫrdyngys, pęsc!
Yē that hāve accused þys lādȳ gente,
Yē bē worthȳ tō bē brente.'
  That ǫǫn knyght māde a ręęs:
'Thōu carle monke, wyth all þȳ gynne,   25
Thowe yōure abbot bē of hur kynne,
  Hur sorowe schalt thōu not cęęs;
Ryght ʒǫ thōu woldyst sayne
Thowe all yōure covent had bī hyr layn,
  Sǫ āre yē lythyr and lęęs.'   30

[1] þat þe.   [2] resceyved.   [3] comyn.   [4] fulfyllyt.

Thē ērle answeryd wyth wōrdys free,
'Sȳr, that ǫǫn Ī trowe thōu bē
   Thys lādȳ accused has.
Thowe wē bē men of relygyōn,
Thōu schalt dō us but rę̄sōn   5
   For all thē fāre thōu mās;
Ī prōve on hur thōu sayst not ryght,
Lǭ, hēre mȳ glōve wyth þē tō fyght,
   Ī undyrtāke thys cāse;
As[1] false men, Ī schall yōu kenne   10
In redde fȳre for tō brenne,
   Thērtō God gyf mē grāce.'

All þat stōden in that plāce,
Thankyd God of hys grāce,
   Wythōute anȳ fayle.   15
Thē twō knyghtys wēre full wrǫthe;
Hē schulde bē dedd, þey swę̄re grę̄te ǭthe,
   But hyt myght not avayle.
Thē ērle wente thēre besȳde,
And armyd hym wyth mekyll prȳde,   20
   Hys enemȳes tō assayle.
Manlȳ, when they tōgedur mett,
They hewe thorow helme and basenet,
   And marryd[2] manȳ a mayle.

They ridyn[3] tōgedur wythōut lakk,   25
That hys ǫǫn spę̄re on hym brakk,
   That ōthyr faylyd thǫǫ.
Thē ērle smǫte hym wyth hys spę̄re,
Thorow thē bodȳ hē can hym bę̄re,
   Tō grōunde can hē gǫǫ.   30

---

[1] os.   [2] martyred.   [3] redyn.

That sawe that ōþer[1], and ſaste can flee;
Thē ērle ǫvyrtōke hym undur a trē,
   And wroght hym mikyll[2] wǫǫ;
Thēre þys traytōur can hym ʒēlde[3]
As[4] recrēaunt in thē fēlde[5],   5
   Hē myght not flē hym frǫǫ.

Befǫre thē emperōure they wente,
And thēre hē māde hym, verrament,
   Tō telle for the nǫǫnys.
Hē seyde, 'Wē thoghte[6] hur tō spylle   10
For schē wolde not dō ōwre wylle,
   That worthȳ is in wǫnys[6a].'
Thē ērle answeryd hym then,
'Thērſǫre, traytōurs, yē schall brenne
   In thys fȳre bǫthe at ǫnys.'   15
The ērle anǫn them[7] hente,
And in thē fȳre hē þem brente,
   Flēsche, felle, and bǫǫnys.

When þey wēre brent bǫthe twǫǫ,
Thē ērle prevelȳ can gǫǫ   20
   Tō that rȳche abbaye.
Wyth joye[8] and processyōun
They ſett thē lādȳ intō thē tōwne,
   Wyth myrthe as[4] Ī telle may.
Thē emperōure was full gladd;   25
'Fette mē thē monke,' anǫn hē badd,
   Whȳ wente hē sǫ awaye?
A byschoperȳke Ī wyll hym gyve[9],
Mȳ helpe, mȳ love, whȳll Ī lyve[10],
   Bī God that owyth thys day.'   30

---

[1] odyr.   [2] mekyll.   [3] ʒylde.   [4] os.   [5] fylde.   [6] thoght.
[6a] wonnys.   [7] hym.   [8] yoye.   [9] geve.   [10] leve.

Thē abbot knēlyd on hys knee,
And seyde, 'Lǫrde, gǫne is hee
  Tō hys owne lǫnde;
Hē dwellyth wyth the Pǫpe of Rōme,
Hē wyll bē glad of hys cōme,   5
  Ī dō yōu tō undurstǫnde.'
'Sȳr abbot[1],' quod thē emperōure,
'Tō mē hyt wēre a dyshonōure,
  Soche wōrdes Ī rēde thōu wǫnde;
Anǫne, in hāste, that Ī hym see,   10
Or thōu schalt nevyr hāve gōde of mē,
  And thērtō hēre mȳn hǫnde.'

'Lǫrde,' hē seyde, 'sythe hyt is sǫǫ
Aftur hym þat Ī muste gǫǫ,
  Yē muste make mē seurtē;   15
In cāse hē hāve byn yōure fǫǫ,
Yē schall not dō hym nǫ wǫǫ;
  And then, al sǫ mōte Ī thee,
Aftur hym Ī wyll wēnd[2],
Sǫ that yē wyll bē hys frēnd,   20
  If yōure wylle bee.'
'Ȝys,' seyde thē emperōure full fayne,
'All mȳ kynne þogh hē had slayne,
  Hē is welcome tō mee.'

Then spake thē abbot wōrdys free,   25
'Lǫrde, Ī tryste nōw on thee,
  Yē wyll dō as[3] yē say[4];
Hyt is Sȳr Barnard of Tolōus,
A nǫbyll knyght and a chyvalrōus,
  That hath dōne thys jurnay[5].'   30

---

[1] abbot, not in MS.   [2] wynde.   [3] os.   [4] sey.   [5] jurney.

'Nōw certys,' seyde thē emperōūre,
'Tō mē hyt is grēt dyshonōūre;
    Anǭn, Sȳr, Ǐ thē pray,
Aftur hym þat thōū wēnd¹,
Wē schall kysse and bē gōde frēnd²,   5
    Bī God that owyth thys day.'

Thē abbot seyde, 'I assente.'
Aftur thē ērle anǭn hē wente,
    'And seyde, 'Sȳr, gǭ wyth mee.
Mȳ lǫrde and yē, bī Seynt Jǫhn,   10
Schull bē māde bǭthe at ǫǫn,
    Goode frēndys for tō bee.'
Thērof þē ērle was full fayne.
Thē emperōūre came hym agayne
    And sayde, 'Mȳ frēnde sǭ free,   15
Mȳ wrathe³ hēre Ǐ thē forgyve;
Mȳ helpe, mȳ love, whȳll Ǐ lyve,
    Bī hym that dȳed on tree.'

Tōgedur lovelȳ can they kysse;
Thēreof all men had grēte blysse,   20
    Thē rǭmaunse tellyth sǫǫ,
Hē māde hym steward of hys lǫnde,
And sēsyd agayne intō hys hǫnde
    That hē had rafte hym frǫǫ.
Thē emperōūre livyd⁴ but yērys thrē;   25
Be elexiōn⁵ of thē lǫrdys free
    Thē ērle tōke they thǫǫ,
And⁶ māde hym thēr emperōūre,
For he was styffe in stōūre
    Tō fyght agayne hys fǫǫ.   30

---

¹ wende.   ² frende.   ³ wrath.   .   ⁴ levyd.   ⁵ alexion.
                ⁶ they.

He weddyd þat lādȳ tō hys wȳſe ;
With joye[1] and myrthe þey ladd þēr lȳſe
  Twentȳ yēre and three.
Betwēne þem had þey chyldyr fyſtēne[2],
Doghtȳ knyghtys all bedēne,
  And sēmelȳ on tō see.
In Rōme thys geste cronyclyd is[3]
A lay of Bretayne callyd ywys[4],
  And evyr mǫre schall bee.
Jēsu[5] Crȳste tō hevyn us brynge,
Thēre tō hāve ōwre wonnyng ;
  Amēn, amēn, for charytee.

X. GILD OF THE HOLY TRINITY AND OF
SAINT WILLĪAM OF NORWICH

IN þē[6] nāme of þē Fader and Sone and Hǫly Gǫst, thrē
persones, ǭ God in Trinitē, and in þē worschipe[7] of ōure Lavedȳ,
Seynte Mārīe his dēre mōder, and of Seynt William þē hǫlȳ
innocent and dīgne marter, and alle halewyn : in þē yēr of ōure
Lǫrd Jēsu[8] Crȳst a thōusande thrē hundred seventȳ and sexe,
peltyērs and ōþere gōd men begunne þis gylde and þis bretherhǫd
of Seynt Willyam, þē hǫlȳ innocent and marter in Norwyche ; and
alle þis ordenaunces undirwriten[9], al þē bretheren and systeren
schulyn hēlden and kēpen upen here pōwēr.

At þē fyrste alle þē bretheren and systeren thus hān behǫten,
þat þey everȳ yēr, on þē Sunday next[10] aftyr þē fęst of Seynt Pēter

---

[1] yoye.   [2] xv.   [3] geste ys cronycglyd ywis.   [4] callyd hyt ys.
[5] Jhu.   [6] þ appears as y except where printed th.   [7] worchepe, and always.
[8] jhesu.   [9] undirwreten.   [10] nexst.

and Powel, in worschipe of þē Trinitē and of ōure Lēvedȳ and Seynt William and alle halwen, schullen offeren tō flōūred candelys afǫrn Seynt Willyams tōūmbe in þē mynstre of þē Trinitē, and everī of hem offeren an halpenȳ at þē messe and hēren al þē messe. And qwōsǫ bē absent, þanne hē schal payen tō Seynt 5 Williams lyhte[1] thrē pōūnd of wax; and it schal bēn reysed and gadered bī þē alderman and his felas. Alsǫ a knāve chȳld innocent, schal[2] bēren a candel þat day, þē wyghte of tō pōūnd, led betwyxen tō gōde men, tǫkenynge of þē glǫryōūs marter.

Alsǫ it is ordeyned þat nǫ man schal bēn excusyd of absence 10 at þat messe, but it bē for þē kynges[3] servīse, or[4] for strǫnge sēkenesse, or[4] twentȳ mȳle dwellynge frǫ þis cytē[5], þat hē ne schal payen þē peyne of thrē pōūnd of wax. And qwōsǫ schal bēn excused for any ōþer schyl, it schal bēn at þē aldermannes wyl and at þē cumpanȳ. 15

Alsǫ alle þē bretheryn and systeryn hān ordeyned[6] and graunted for anȳ ordenaunce þat is mād or schal bēn mād amǫnges hem, þat þey schal sāve þē kynge hys ryhte[7], and nǫn prejudȳs dōn ageyn his lawe in þēs ordenaunce.

Alsǫ it is ordeyned, þat everȳche brōþer and syster of þis gylde, 20 ērlȳ on morwe aftyr þē gyldeday, schal hēryn a messe of rēquiem for allē þē brethere soules and systeren soules of þis gylde, and for alle crystene soules, at Seynt Williams auter in þē mynstre of þē Trynytē in Norwyche, and offeren a ferthynge. And qwōsǫ bē wāne, schal paye a pōūnd of wax. And qwan þē messe is dōn, 25 bī[8] her aldermannes asent þey schal alle tōgedere gǫn tō an in, and everȳ man þat haþ anȳ[9] catelle of þē gilde leyn it dōūn; and ordeynen þēr of here lȳkynge bī[8] comōūn assent, and chēsen offycēres for þē nexte yēr. And qwō fayle schal payen three pōūnd of wax. And eyghte[10] men of þē aldermannes chēsynge, 30 on þē gyldeday, schulen chēsen an alderman and tō felas, and a somonōr for þē nexte yēr.

---

[1] lythe. [2] schal, not in MS. [3] kyngges. [4] er, as always. [5] syte.
[6] hordeyned. [7] rythe. [8] be, as always. [9] ony. [10] viii.

Alsǫ it is ordeyned, in þē worschipe of þē Trinitē and of ōure Lę̄vedȳ Seynt Mārīe, and of Seynt William and of alle halwyn, þat qwat brōther or syster bī Goddis sǫnde falle in mischēfe or mysę̄se, and hāve nout tō helpen hemselfe, hē schal hān almesse of everī brōþer and syster everȳ woke, lestende his myschēfe, a ferthynge; of qwyche ferthynges hē schal hān fourtēne pens[1], and þē remenaunt gǫn tō catelle. But if it bē his folȳ, hē schal nout hān of þē almes[2].

Alsǫ it is ordeyned bī comōun assent, qwōsǫ bē chǫsen in offys and refuse it, hē schal paye tō Seynt Wylliams lyhte[3] thrē pōund of wax, and up peyne of his ǫthe.

Alsǫ if anȳ[4] brōther or syster deye, hē schal hān of þē gylde foure torches, and foure pōre men cladde, abōuten his cors; ande everȳ brōther and syster schul[5] offeren at his messe, and hēryn al pē messe and bȳden his enterynge, and at messe offeryn a ferthynge, and an halpenȳ ʒeven tō almes for þē[6] soule; and ʒeven tō a messe a penȳ, þē qwyche schal[7] bē gaderyd bī þē alderman and hise felas tō dōn for þē soule and for alle crystene. Alsǫ if any brōþer or syster deye sevene mȳle frǫ þē citē, þē alderman and ōþer sevene bretheryn at his exequīses schul[8] wēnde in fēre tō þē cors, and ordeynen and dōn for þē soule as for ǫn of þē bretheren.

Alsǫ it is ordeyned bī comōun assent, þat þēse bretheren, in worschipe of þē Holy Trinytē and Seynt William, schul ę̄tyn tōgeɑere on þat day at here comōun cost. And qwōsǫ bē somōuned tō dōn semblē or tō congregācioūn beforn þē alderman and þē bretheryn and come nout, hē schal paye a pōund of wax tō þē lyht[9]. Alsǫ it is ordeyned bī comōun assent þat nǫ brōþer ne syster in þis gilde schal bē reseyvet but bī þē alderman and twelve bretheryn.

Alsǫ it is ordeyned bī comōun assent þat þē comōun belleman schal gǫn thurghe þē citē oɴ þē gildeday after nōne, and recomandyn al þē brethere soules and systeres of þē gilde bī nāme,

---

[1] xiiij d.   [2] elmes.   [3] lythe.   [4] ony.   [5] schul, not in MS.   [6] ʒe.
[7] schal, not in MS.   [8] exequises schul, not in MS.   [9] lyt.

and alle˙ crystene soules; and seyn þat a messe of rēquiem schal
bēn seyd ęˉrlȳ on þē morwen, bī prīme day, in memorīe of þē soules
and alle crystene, and somoūnyn alle þē bretheryn and systeryn
þat þey bēn at þē messe at þē auter of Seynt William at þat tȳme
of prīme, up þē peyne of thrē poūnd of wax.   5

XI. JOHN MYRC'S INSTRUCTIONS FOR
PARISH PRIESTS [1]

God seyth hymself, as wryten wē fȳnde,
That whenne þē blȳnde lędeth þē blȳnde
Intō þē dyche þey fallen bǫǫ,
For þey ne sēn wharebȳ tō gǫˉ.
Sǫˉ fāren prēstes now bȳ dawe;   10
They bēth blȳnde in Goddes lawe,
That whenne þey scholde þē pēpul rēde,
Intō synne þey dō hem lęde.
Thus þey hāve dō now fulle ʒǫˉre,
And alle is [2] for defawte of lǫre;   15
Wharefǫˉre, þoū prēste curatoūre,
ʒef þoū plęse thȳ Sāvyoūre,
ʒef thow bē not gręte clerk,
Lōke thow mōste on thys werk;
For hēre thow myʒte fȳnde and [3] rēde   20
That þē behōveth tō conne nēde,
How thow schalt thȳ paresche pręˉche,
And what þē nēdeth hem tō tęche;
And whyche þoū mōste þȳself bē,
Hēre alsǫˉ thow myʒte hyt sē,   25

---

[1] Latin title reads, 'Propter presbiterum parochialem instruendum.'   [2] ys,
as often.   [3] &, as often.

For luytel is worthȳ þȳ pręchynge
ȝef thōw bē of ęvuyle lyvynge.

Prēste, þȳself thow mōste bē chāst,
And say þȳ serves wyþōwten hāst,
That mōwthe and herte acorden ī fēre,   5
ȝef thōw wole that God þē hēre.
Of hǫnde and mōwþe þōu mōste bē trewe,
And gręte ǫþes thōw mōste eschewe[1];
In wōrde and dēde þōu mōste bē mȳlde,
Bǫthe tō mon and tō chȳlde.   10
Dronkelęc and glotonȳe,
Pruyde and slouþe and envȳe,
Alle þōw mōste putten away
ȝef þōw wolt serve God tō pay.
That þē nēdeth, ęte and drynke,   15
But slę þȳ lust for anȳ thynge.
Tavernes[2] alsǫ thōw mōste forsāke,
And marchaundȳse þōw schalt not māke;
Wrastelynge and schōtynge and suche gāme[3]
Thōw myȝte not use wythōwte blāme;   20
Hawkynge, huntynge, and dawnsynge,
Thōw mōste fǫrgǫ for anȳ thynge.
Cuttede clǫthes and pȳked schōne,
Thȳ gōde fāme þey wole fordōne.
Marketes and feyres Ī thē forbēde,   25
But hyt bē for thē mǫre nēde.
In honeste clǫthes thōw mōste gǫn,
Baselard ne[4] bawdryke węre þōw nǫn;
Bęrde and crōwne thōw mōste bē schāve,
ȝef thōw wole thȳ ordere sāve.   30
Of męte and drynke þōw mōste bē frē,
Tō pōre and rȳche bȳ thȳ degrē.

---

[1] enchewe.   [2] taverneſ.   [3] maner game.   [4] ny.

Ӡērne thow mōste thȳ sawtēre rēde,
And of thē day of dōme hāve drēde ;
And evere dō gōde aӡeynes ēle[1],
Or elles thow myӡte not lyve wēle.
Wymmones serves thow mōste forsāke,   5
Of ēvele fāme leste they thē māke ;
For wymmenes spēche that bēn schrewes,
Turne ofte away gōde thewes.

From nȳse jāpes and rybawdȳe,
Thow mōste turne away þȳn ȳe ;   10
Tuynde þȳn ȳe þat thow ne sē
Thē cursede worldes vanytē.

Thus thys worlde þow mōste despȳse,
And hǫlȳ vertues hāve in vȳse ;
Ӡef thow dō þus, thow schalt bē dēre   15
Tō alle men that sēn and hēre.

Thus thow mōste alsǫ prȩche[2],
And thȳ paresche ӡērne tȩche ;
Whenne ǫn hath dōne a synne,
Lōke hē lȳe not lǫnge thēreynne,   20
But anǫn that hē hym schrȳve,
Bē hyt husbande, bē hyt wȳve,
Leste hē forӡet bȳ lentenes day,
And ōute of mȳnde hyt gǫ away.

. . . . .

Alsǫ thow mōste thȳ God pay,   25
Tȩche thȳ paresch þus and say.
Alle that bēn of warde and ēlde,
Þat cunnen hemself kēpe and wēlde,
They schulen alle tō chyrche come,
And bēn ischryve alle and some,   30
And bē ihoseled wythowte bēre
On asterday alle ī fēre ;

[1] evele.   [2] Subtitle, ' Quid et quomodo predicare debet parochianos suos.'

In þat day bȳ costome,
Ȝē schule bē hoselet alle and some.
Tẹche hem þenne, wyth gōde entent,
Tō belēve on that sacrament ;
That þey receyve in forme of brẹd,   5
Hyt is Goddes bodȳ þat soffered dẹd
Upon the họlȳ rōdetrē,
Tō bȳe ōwre synnes and make us frē.
Tẹche hem þenne, never þē later,
Þat in þē chalȳs is but wȳn and water   10
That þey receyveth for tō drynke,
After that họlȳ hoselynge.
Thērfọre warne hem þōw schal
That þey ne chewe þat hōst [1] tō smal,
Leste tō smale þey dōne hyt brẹke,   15
And in here tēth hyt dō stẹke ;
Thērefọre þey schule wyth water and wȳn
Clanse here mōwþ that noȝt lẹve þerin :
But tẹche hem alle tō lēve sāde [2],
Þat hyt þat is in þē awter māde,   20
Hyt is verrē Goddes blōde
That hē schedde on þē rōde.
Ȝēt þōw mōste tẹche hem māre,
Þat whenne þey dōth tō chyrche fāre,
Þenne bydde hem lẹve here monȳ wōrdes,   25
Here ȳdel spēche and nȳce bōrdes,
And put away alle vanytē,
And say here paternoster and āvē [3].
Ne nọn in chyrche stọnde schal,
Ne lẹne tō pylēr, ne tō wal,   30
But fayre on knēus þey schule hem sette,
Knēlynge dōun upon thē flette,

---

[1] ost.   [2] sadde.   [3] here ave.

And pray tō God wyth herte mēke
Tō ʒeve hem grāce and mercȳ ēke.
Soffere hem tō māke nō bēre,
But ay tō bē in here prayēre;
And whenne þē gospelle irēd bē schalle,   5
Tẹ̄che hem þenne tō stǫnde up alle,
And blesse hem[1a] feyre, as þey conne,
Whenne *gloria tibi* is bygonne.
And whenne þē gospel is idōne,
Tẹ̄che hem eft tō knēle dōwne sōne;   10
And whenne they hēre thē belle rynge
Tō that hǫlȳ sakerynge,
Tẹ̄che hem knēle dōwne, bǫþe ʒonge and ǫlde,
And bǫþe here hǫndes up tō hǫlde,
And say þenne in þys manēre,   15
Feyre and softelȳ, wythōwte bēre;
'Jēsu[1], Lǫrd, welcome þōw bē,
In forme of brẹd as Ī þe sē;
Jēsu, for thȳ hǫlȳ nāme,
Schēlde mē tōday frǫ synne and schāme;   20
Schryfte and hōwsele, Lǫrd, graunte[2] mē bǫ
Ẹ̄r that Ī schale hennes gǫ,
And verrē contrycyōne of mȳ synne,
That Ī, Lǫrd, never dȳe thēreinne.
And as þōw wēre of a may ibǫre,   25
Sofere mē never tō bē forlǫre,
But whenne þat Ī schale hennes wēnde,
Grawnte mē þē blysse wythōwten ēnde.   Amēn.'
Tẹ̄che hem þus, ǫþer sum ōþere þynge,
Tō say at thē hǫlȳ sakerynge.   30
      Tẹ̄che hem al. ǫ, Ī thē pray,
That whenne þey walken in þē way

And sēne þē prēste agayn hem comynge,
Goddes bodȳ wyth hym bērynge,
Thenne wyth grēte devǭcyōne,
Tēche hem þēre tō knēle adōwne.
Fayre ne fowle, spāre þey noghte　　　　　　5
Tō worschype hym þat alle hath wroghte.
For ryȝt[1] glad may þat mon bē
Þat ǭnes in þē day hym[2] sē;
For sǭ mykyle gōde dōþ þat syȝt,—
As Seynt Austyn tēcheth aryȝt,—　　　　　10
Þat day þat þow sȳst Goddes bodȳ
Þēse benefȳces schalt þou hāve sycurlȳ:
Mēte and drynke, at thȳ nēde,
Nǭn schal þē þat day bē gnēde;
Īdele ǭthes and wōrdes alsǭ,　　　　　　15
God forȝeveþ thē bǭ;
Soden dēth that ilke[3] day
Thē dar not drēde wyþowte nay;
Alsǭ þat day, Ī thē plyȝte,
Þow schalt not lēse þȳn ȳesyȝte,　　　　　20
And every fōte þat þou gǭst þenne,
Þat hǭlȳ syȝt for tō sēne,
Þey schule bē tǭlde tō stǭnde in stēde
Whenne thow hast tō hem nēde.

Alsǭ, wythynne chyrche and seyntwarȳ,　　　25
Dō ryȝt thus, as Ī thē say;
Sǭnge and crȳ and suche fāre,
For tō stynte þow schalt not spāre;
Castynge of axtrē and ēke of stǭn,
Sofere hem þēre tō use nǭn;　　　　　　30
Bal and bāres and suche play,
Oute of chyrcheȝorde put away.

---

[1] ryȝt, not in MS.　　　[2] may hym.　　　[3] ylke.

Coūrte hǫldynge, and suche manēr chǫst,
Out of seyntwarȳ put þow̄ mōst;
For Crȳst hymself tēcheth us
J'at hǫlȳ chyrche is hys hōw̄s,
Þat is māde for nǫ þynge el!es   5
But for tō praye in, as þē bōke telles;
Þēre þē pēpulle schalē geder withinne,
Tō prayen and wēpen[1] for here synne.

Tēche hem alsǫ welle and greythe,
How̄ þey schule paye here teythe.   10
Of alle þynge that dōth hem newe,
They schule teythe welle and trewe;
After þē costome of þat cuntraye,
Everȳ mon hys teythynge schale paye,
Bǫthe of smale and of grēte,   15
Of shēp and swȳn and ōþer nēte.
Teyþe of huyre and of hǫnde
Gǫth by costome of þē lǫnde.
Ī hǫlde hyt but an ȳdul þynge
Tō spēke myche of teythynge,   20
For þaȝ a prēste bē but a fonne,
Aske hys teyþynge welle hē conne.

Wychecrafte and telynge,
Forbēde þou hem for anȳ þynge;
For whōsǫ belēveth in þe fay   25
Mōte belēve thus bȳ anȳ way,
That hyt is a sleghþe of þē dēl
Þat mākeþ a bodȳ tō cache ēl;
Þenne syche belēve hē gart hem hāve,
Þat wychecrafte schale hem sāve,   30
Sǫ wyth charmes[2] and wyth tele
Hē is ibroȝte aȝeyn tō hele.
Þus wyth þē fēnde hē is iblende,
And hys bylēve is ischende.

---

[1] to wepen.   [2] chames.

PART II

THE
DIALECTS OF THE NORTH, THE SOUTH, AND THE CITY OF LONDON

THE NORTHERN DIALECT

I. PROLOGUE TO THE CURSOR MUNDI

MAN yērnes [1] rīmes for tō hēre,
And rōmans rēd on manēres sēre :
Of Alisaundur þē conquerōūr,
Of Julȳ Cēsar þē emparōūr,
O Grēce and Troy þē strānge [2] striif   5
Þēre manȳ thosand lēsis þēr liif;
Of Brut, þat bērn bāld of hand,
Þē firste [3] conquerōūr of Ingland;
O Kyng Arthōūr þat was sō rīke,
Quām nōn in hys tīm was līke ;   10
O fērlȳs þat hys knyhtes [4] fell
Þat aunters sēre Ī hēre of tell,
Als Wawān, Cai, and ōþer stābell
For tō wēre þē rōnde tābell;
Hōw Charles Kyng and Rauland faght,   15
With [5] Sarazins wald þai nā saght;
Of Tristrem and hys leif Ysote,
Hōw hē for here becōm a sote;

---

[1] yhernes.   [2] strang.   [3] first.   [4] knythes.   [5] wit (wyt), as usual.

O Iǫneck and of Ȳsambrāse,
O Ydoine and of Amadāse,
Stǫrīs als o sēre kin thinges
O princes, prelātes, and o kynges,
Sānges sēre of selcūth rīme, 5
Inglis, Frankys, and Latīne ;
Tō rēde and hēre ilk ǫn is prest
Þē thynges þat þām līkes best.
Þē wīs man wil o wisdōm hēre,
Þē foul hym draws¹ tō folȳ nēre ; 10
Þē wrāng tō hēre o right is lāth,
And prīde wyth buxsumnes is wrāth ;
O chastitē has lichūr lēth,
On charitē ai werrais wrēth ;
Bot be þē fruit may scilwīs sē 15
O quat vertu is ilk a trē.
Of al kyn fruit þat man schal fȳnd
Hē fettes frǫ þē rōte his kȳnd ;
O gōde pērtrē coms gōde² pēres,
Wers trē, wers fruit it bēres. 20
   Þat Ī spēke o þis ilke trē
Bytākens man, bōth mē and þē ;
Þis fruit bitākens alle ōure dēdis,
Bōth gōde and ille quā rightlȳ rēdis.
Ūr dēdis frǫ ūr hert tās rōte, 25
Quedur³ þai bē worthī bāle or bōte ;
For be þē þyng man drawes till
Men schal him knaw⁴ for gōd or ill.
A saumpul hēr be þām⁵ Ī say
Þat rāges in þāre rīot ay ; 30
In rīot and in rigolāge
Of all þēre liif spēnd þai þē stāge,

¹ draghus.   ² god.   ³ dur.   ⁴ kaw.   ⁵ þaem.

For now is hālden nǫn in cūrs
Bot quā þat luve can paramūrs.
Þat folȳ luve, þat vanitē,
Þām līkes now nān ōþer glē;
Hit neys bot fantum for tō say   5
Tōday it is, tōmoru away.
Wyth chaunce of dęd or chaunge [1] of hert,
Þat soft began has ēndyng smart;
For wen þow traistest [2] wēnis at bē,
Frǫ hir schalt þou, or scho frǫ þē.   10
Hē þat stīthest [3] wēnis at stānd,
Warre hym, his fall is nexst his hānd;
Ār hē swā brāthlȳ don bē broght
Wydur tō węnde ne wāt hē noght,
Bytwixand his luf haf hym ledd   15
Tō slī mēde als hē forwith bedd [4];
For þan sal mēde withōuten [5] mere
Bē mette for dēde or bettur or were.

  Forþī blisce Ī þat paramōur
Quen Ī hāve nēde mē dōs socūre;   20
Þat sāves mē first in ērth [6] frā syn
And hevenblys mē helps tō wyn.
For þof Ī quīlum haf bēn untrew,
Hyr luve is ay ilīke [7] new;
Hir luve scho [8] hāldes lęle ilīke,   25
Þat swetter es þan honȳ o bīke.
Swilk in ērth [6] es fūndun nān,
For scho es mōdur and maiden;
Mōder and maiden never þē lesse
Forþī of hir tōk Crīst his flesse.   30
Quā trulȳ loves þis lemman,
Þis es þē love bēs never gān;

---

[1] chaunce.   [2] traistes.   [3] titthest.   [4] bedd, not in MS.   [5] witoten.
[6] herth.   [7] ilik.   [8] sco.

For in þis love scho failes never,
And in þat tōþer scho lastes ever.
Of swilk ān suld ȝē matēr¹ tāke,
Craftȳ þat can rīmes māke,
Of hir tō māk bāth rīm and sāng   5
And luve hir swēte sun amāng.
Quat bōte is tō sette traveil
On þyng þat may not avail,
Þat es bot fantum o þis werd²
Als ȝē hāve sēne inogh and herd?   10
Matēr fȳnd ȝē large and brāde,
Þof rīmes fẹle of hir bē māde;
Quāsā will of hyr fayrnes³ spell,
Fīnd hē sal inogh tō tell.
Of hir gōdnes and hir treuthēde,   15
Men may fȳnd evermār tō rēde;
Ō reuth³ᵃ, ō love, and charitē,
Was never hir mak, ne never sal bē.
Lavedī scho es o lẹvedīs all,
Mīld and mēk withōuten gall,   20
Tō nēdī neghest on tō call,
And raises synful quen þai fall.
Til al ōure bāle ai for tō bēte
Ōure Lāuerd has māde þat maiden swēte⁴;
Þārbī man mai hir helping kenn,   25
Scho praies⁵ ai for sinful menn;
Quā menskes hir, þai mai bē bāld;
Scho sal þām ȝēld a hundrethfāld.
   In hir wirschip wald Ī bigyn
A lastand warc apon tō myn,   30
For tō dō man knaw hir kyn
Þat us⁶ sclī wirschip cum tō wyn.

---

¹ mater, dim in MS.   ² warld.   ³ hy farnes.   ³ᵃ reut.   ⁴ suette.
                    ⁵ prais.   ⁶ hus.

Sumkins jestes for tō scaw,
Þat dōne wēre in þē ālde [1] law,
Bitwix þē āld law and þē new
Hōw Crīstes [2] brith bigan tō brew,
Ī sal yōw schew with mȳn entent   5
Brēflī of aiþere testament.
Al þis werld, ọ̄r þis bōk blin,
With Crīstes help Ī sal ọ̄verrin,
And tell sum gestes principāle,
For alle may nā man hāve in tāle [3].   10
Bot forþī þat nā werc may stand
Withōuten grūndwall tō bē lastand,
Þārfọ̄r þis werc sal Ī fūnd
Apon a selcūth stedfast grūnd,
Þat es þē hālȳ trinitē   15
Þat all has wroght with his beutē.
At him self first Ī sette mī merc,
And sithen tō tell his handewerc [4];
O þē āngels first þat fell,
And sithen Ī will of Adam tell,   20
Of hys oxspring, and of Nōē,
And sumquat of his sunes [4a] thrē;
Of Ābraham and of Ȳsaāc
Þat hālȳ wāre withōuten māke.
Sythen sal Ī telle [5] yōw   25
Of Jācōb and of Ēsaū;
Þār neist sal bē sythen tāld
Hōw þat Jōsēph was boght and sāld;
O þē Juus and Mōysēs
Þat Goddis folk tō lẹ̄de him chẹ̄s,   30
Hōw God bigan þē law hym gyfe,
Þē quilk thē Juus in suld life;

---

[1] hald.   [2] Crist.   [3] talle.   [4] hand werc.   [4a] sunus.   [5] tell.

O Saul þē kyng and o Dāvī,
Hōw þat hē faght again Golī;
Sithen o Salamōn þē wīs,
Hōw craftīlīk hē did justīs;
Hōw Crīst cōm thoro prophecī,   5
Hōw hē cōm his folk tō bii.
And hit sal bē redd yuu þanne
O Jōachim and of Sānt Anne[1],
O Māre als, hir doghter mīld,
Hōw scho[2] was born and bare a chīld;   10
Hōw hē was born and quen and wāre,
Hōw scho him tō þē temple bar;
O þē kynges þat him soght,
Þat thrē presandes til him broght;
Hōw þat Herōde kyng, with wogh,   15
For Crīstes[3] sāk þē childer slogh;
Hōw þē chīld tō Ēgypte fled
And hōw þat hē was theþen ledd.
Þār sal ȝē fīnd sumkyn dēdis
Þat Jēsus[3a] did in hys barnhēdis;   20
Sithen o þē Baptist Jōhan
Þat Jēsu[4] baptīst in flum Jordan;
Hōw Jēsus, quen hē lāng had fast,
Was fōndid with þē wikke[4a] gāst;
Siþen o Jōnes[5] baptīsyng,   25
And hōw him hefdid Herōd Kyng;
Hōw þat Jēsu Crīst him selve
Chēs til him apostels twelve,
And ōpenlīk bigan tō prēche
And alle þat sēk wāre tō lēche,   30
And did þē merācles suā riif
Þat þē Juus him hild in striif;

---

[1] sant tanne.   [2] sco, as in l. 12.   [3] crist.   [3a] Ih's, as usual.   [4] Ihu
[4a] wik.   [5] Ions.

Syþen hōw þat hālȳ Drightin
Turned watur intō wȳn[1],
O fīve thossand men þat hē
Fedd wyth fīve lāves and fisses thrē.
Of a man sal ȝē sithen fīnd   5
Ðat hē gāve sight, and born was blīnd;
O þē[2] spōusebrȩk womman
Þat þē Iuus dempt tō stān;
Hōw hē hȩled ǫn al unfēre
Þat sēke was thritte and aght yeir;   10
Hōw þē Magdalēn with grēte
Cōm for tō was ōur Lǫrde fēte,
Of hir and Martha þat was fūs
Abote þē nēdes of þāre hūs;
O Lāzar dȩd, laid under lām,   15
Hōw Jēsus raised his līcam;
Hōw Juus Jēsu oft umsette
And for his sermon thrālī thrette;
Hōw þai schēd his blisced blōde
And pīned him opon þē rōde.   20
With Crīstes[3] will þan sal Ī telle
Hōw hē siþen hāred helle;
Hōw Juus with þēr grȩt unschill
Wēnd his uprīsyng tō dill;
Hōw hē uprais, hōw hē upstey,   25
Manȳ man onstad and sey;
Hōw hē þat ō myght es māst
Send intill ērth his hālȳ gāst;
O twelve apostlis sumkyn gest,
Bot hōw þai endid at þē lest.   30
Hōw ōur Lȩvedī endid and yāld
Hir sēlȳ saul, hit sal bē tāld:

---

[1] vyn.   [2] þe, not in Cotton, but in all other MSS.   [3] crist.

O þe hālī croice, hōw it was kyd
Lāng efterward þat it was hid;
Of Antecrīst cōm, þat sal bē kēne,
And o þe drērī days fivetēn
Þat sal cum forwith dōmesday.   5
Sythen of þe dōme yōw sal I say,
Þan of ōure Lẹvedī murnand mōde
For hir sune scho sagh on rōde.
Þe laste rẹsūn of all þis ron
Sal bē of hir concepciōn.   10

   Þis āre thē matērs redde on raw
Þat I thynk in þis bōk tō draw,
Schortlȳ rīmand on þe dēde
For manī er þai hērof tō spēde.
Notful mē thinc it wāre tō man   15
Tō knaw himself hōw hē began;
Hōw hē[1] began in werld tō brẹde,
Hōw his oxspring began tō sprẹde;
Bāth ō þe first and ō þe last
In quatkin cūrs þis werld es past.   20
Efter hālȳ kyrces[2] stāte
Þis ilke bōk it es[3] translāte,
Intō Inglis tong tō rēde
For þe love of Inglis lēde,
Inglis lēde of Ingeland[4],   25
For þe commūn at understand.

   Frankis rīmes hēre I redd
Comūnlīk in ilk a sted[5];
Māst es it wroght for Frankis man,
Quat is for him nā Frankis can?   30
Of Ingeland[4] þe nāciōn,
Es Inglis man þār in commūn;

---

[1] he, not in MS.   [2] kyrc.   [3] ilk bok is es.   [4] Ingland.   [5] ilk sted.

Þē spēche þat man with māst may spēde,
Māst þārwith tō spęke wār nēde.
Selden was for ānī chance
Praised Inglis tong in France;
Give wē ilk ān þāre langāge,   5
Mē think wē dō þām nǫn ōutrāge.
Tō lauid Inglis [1] man Ī spell
Þat understāndes þat Ī tell,
And tō þǫǫ spęke Ī alþermāst
Þat won in unwarces tō wāst   10
Þair liif in trofel and truandīs,
Tō bē wāre with þat self and wīs
Sumquat untō þat thing tō tent,
Þat al þār mōde might with amend.
Ful il hā þai þat spēnding spēnd,   15
Þat fīndes nā frute [2] þārof at ēnd.
Slī wōrd and werc sum wē til heild,
Traistlī acōuntes [3] sal wē yeild;
Þārfǫr dō draw þām hiderward
Þat o þē pardōn will hā part;   20
Tō hēre and hāld sal hā pardōn
O plight with Crīstes [4] benisūn.
Nōw o þis prǫloug wil wē blin [5],
In Crīstes [4] nām ōur bōk begin;
Cūrsur o World man aght it call,   25
For almāst it ǫverrennes all.
Tāk wē ōur biginning þan
Of him þat al þis werld bigan.

---

[1] laud and Inglis.   [2] fro.   [3] armites, but meaningless.

[4] crist.   [5] b.

II. THE DEATH OF SAINT ANDREW

Saint Andrew, Crīstis apostil dēre,
Whīls hē went in þis werld hēre,
Ful mekill folk in sēre cuntrē
Tō cristen trouth convertid hē ;
And at þē last, sǭ it byfell,   5
In a cetē whǭre hē gun dwell.

A dōmesman in þat cetē was,
And his nāme was cald Ēgēas;
A man þat lifed in maumetrȳ
And in fals goddes, ful of envȳ.   10
Hē gederd tōgedir bǭth bǭnd and[1] frē,
Rīche and pōver of ilk cuntrē,
And bad þai suld māk sacrafīse
Untō his goddes of mekil prīse;
And whōsǭ wold noght ofrand māke,   15
Grǣte vengeance wold hē on þām tāke.

Þē folk ful fast þan þeder soght
And tō þǭ warlaus wirschip wroght.
And sōne when Saint Andrew herd tell
Of þat fōul fāre hōw it bifell,   20
Þedir ful playnlī gun hē pas,
And þus sayd[2] unto Ēgēas:
'Sen þōu covaytes þat folk þē ken
Als dōmesman ǭver al ōþer men,
Þan suld þōu knaw in dēde and stevyn   25
Þī dōmesman, þat es God in hevyn,
Þat sal þē dēme efter þī dǭde.
Him for tō knaw nōw wār it nēde;

---

[1] &, as often.   [2] he sayd.

Hē es þī God and ǫver all mightī,
And all ōþer er fals maumetrī;
Him for tō honūre evermǫre þē awe
And verrailȳ for þī God him knawe,
And draw þī hert frǫ dēvils oway,   5
Þat lędis tō pīne þat lastes ay.'

Ēgēas þan answerd ogayne :
'Þīr wurdes,' hē sayd, 'er all in vayne,
And nǫthing suth þou tels mē till
Þat may Ī prōve bȳ propir skill;   10
For, whīls ʒōwre God þat ʒē on call
Pręchid þē pōple in ērth ǫverall,
And tęchid his men þat with him dweld
Tō pręche þē sāme þat þou hēre teld,
Omāng þē Jews[1] hēre tāne was hē   15
And nayled and hānged high on trē;
And had hē bēne God, als þou says,
It had noght bēne sǫ, by nǫ ways.
Þārfǫre Ī say, þīr wurdes er vayne.'

Saint Andrew þan answerd ogayne :   20
'And þou kōuth klērelȳ knaw and sē
Þē vertu of þat ilk hālȳ trē
Þat nāmed es þē cros in lānd,
Þan wald þou wit and understānd
How Jēsu[2] Crīst, mȳ maystir frē,   25
Bī ręsonāble caus of charitē,
And for petē þat hē had in mȳnde
Of þē gręte meschēvys of mankȳnde,
Payn of þē cros hē put[3] him till,
Noght mawgrē his, bot with his will.'   30

Ēgēas þan untō þis thing
Answerd als in gręte hęthing;

---

[1] Iews.   [2] Ihu, as usual.   [3] putted.

Hē sayd, 'Hōw may þou say þīr sawes,
Sen þat þīself þē suth wēle knawes?
At þē first tīme bitrayd was hē,
And thurgh āne of his awin mẹnȝē,
And sethin tākin with Jewes[1] kēne,   5
And būnden and led furth þām bitwēne
Tō Cayfas hall þē graythest gāte,
And frọ þeþin untō Sir Pīlāte;
Þọre was hē dēmid on cros tō hāng,
Als þē Jews ordāned[2] þām omāng.   10
Maugrē his þai gun him spill,—
Hōw prōves þou þan it was his will?'
    Saynt Andrew says, 'His will it was,
Þat may Ī prōve wēle ọr Ī pas;
Of his mẹnȝē mīself was āne[3]   15
In þē sāme tīme when hē was tāne[4],
And bifọr þē time hē was bitrayd
Untō us all sāmyn þus hē sayd,
Hōw hē suld for mans syns bē sāld[5],
And suffer paynes ful manȳfālde[6]   20
And dȳ on þē cros right als þou tels,
For hẹle of mans sauls and for noght[7] els,
And on þē thrid day ful right uprīse.
Þīr wurdes hē tọlde us on þis wīse;
Þārfọre Ī tell þē in þis stẹde,   25
Þat with his will hē sufferd dẹde.'
    Ēgēas þan thoght grẹte dispīte,
And tō Saint Andrew said hē tīte:
'Þou hāves lẹrd[8] of a symple skōle,
Þī prẹching prōves þīself a fōle;   30
For, whethir it wār his will or nọne,
Þou grauntes þat hē on cros was dōne,

---

[1] Iews.   [2] ordand   [3] one.   [4] tone.   [5] sold.   [6] manyfolde.
[7] nght.   [8] lerid.

And hāngid hē was als Ī said āre;
And þārfǫre lęve þat lūrdans lāre
And untō mȳ goddes offrand māke,
Or els Ī sall for þī God sāke
Ger hāng þē right on swilk a trē   5
Als þōu sais suld sǫ honōrde bē.
For fōuler dęde may nǫ man hāve,
Þārfǫre on þē Ī vōuche it sāve.'

Saint Andrew þan, withōuten īre,
Said, 'Sertis þat es mȳ mǫste desīre.   10
Ī wold bē wurthī for his sāke
Opon a cros mȳ dęde tō tāke;
Þārtō ever sal Ī rędī bē
For anȳ payn þōu may dō mē.'

Ēgēas þan, with gręte envȳ,   15
Sent efter al his turmentrȳ,
And bad þām smertlȳ þām omāng
Ordān a cros him for tō hāng,
And fest þārtō bǫth hēnd and fēte
Þat nǫne of þām with ōþer mēte.   20
'Festes him with nǫne nayles, Ī rēde,
Tō ger him hāstilī bē sǫ dęde,
Bot bīndes him tō with rāpes strāng
Sǫ þat hē may bē pȳned lāng.'

Tō dō his biding wār þai bayne;   25
A cros þai māde with al þaire maine,
And hāndes on him þan fast þai fest,
Tō dō him payne þai wār ful prest.
Þai led him thurgh þat cetē
Tō þē stęde whāre hē suld[1] hānget bē.   30
And al þē folk þat dweld obōut[2]
Gedird tōgyder in ful gręte rōut,

---

[1] he, not in MS.   [2] þare obout.

And al þus said þai þām omāng :
'Allas, þis wirking es al wrāng ;
What has þis rightwīs man dōne ill
þat ȝē on þis wīse will him spill?
þis nǫbill man þat never did mis   5
Ful saklęs suffers hē all þis ;
Ful saklęs bēse hē dōne on rōde,
And saklęs sall men spill his blōde,
For hē has ever bēne blīth and glad
Tō mēnd al men þat mistēr had.'   10

   Saint Andrew þan þē puple praid,
And al þus untō þām hē sayd :
'Wēndis ogayn, all Ī ȝōw pray,
And lettes mē noght of joy[1] þis day ;
Desturbes noght nōw mī passiōun,   15
For untō blis it mākes mē bōun.'
And sōne when Saint Andrew bihēlde
þē cros bifǫr him in þē fēlde,
Untō God māde hē his prayēre,
And untō þē cros on þis manēre   20
Hē crīed and sayd with ful high voice :
'Hayl bē þōu, hālȳ and bliscèd croyce,
þat haloud es and glǫrifīde[2]
With Crīstes membris on ilk a sīde ;
And honōurd es þōu with his bānes   25
Wēle better þan with precius stānes.
With joyful[3] hert Ī cum tō þē,
Sǫ þat þōu gladlī resayve mē,
Discīple of him withōuten pēre
þat hānged on þē, mī mayster dēre.   30
Nōw es þōu rędī mē on tō hāng,
þat Ī in hert hāve covayt lāng ;

---

[1] ioy.   [2] ever glorifide.   [3] ioyful.

Ī hāve þē lufde with hert and will,
And covayted ever tō cum þē till.'
Bifǫr þē cros þan knēlid hē dōune,
And þus hē māde his orisōune :
'Ā, nǭbil cros of grēte bōuntē,   5
Frǫ ērthlī men resayve nōw mē,
And ȝēlde mē tō mȳ maister gōde [1]
Sǭ þat hē **may**, with mīlde [1a] mōde,
Bȳ þē resayve mē, þat hē wroght,
Als hē thurgh þē frǫ bāle mē boght;   10
Nō better bēde Ī hāve tō byd.'
His ǭvermāst clǭthes þan of hē did;
Tō þē turmentōurs hē gun þām bēde,
And bad þai suld dō furth þaire dēde.

þē turmentōurs, when þis was sayde,   15
Tōke his bodī with bitter brayde;
Untō þē cros þai gun it bēnd,
And festid ful fast bǭthe fēte and hēnd;
And all his bodī ful fast þai bānd
Als Ēgēas had þām comānd.   20
When hē was būnden sǭ on brēde,
þai lēte him hing and hǭme þai ȝēde.
Folk gederd ful faste [2] him obōut,
Of al þat cuntrē in grēte rōut;
Hē hēld his ēghen up untō hevin,   25
And þus hē sayd with joyful stevin:
'Ī sē mī Lǫrd God Alwēldand [3],
And in his sight nōw hēre Ī stand.'
Opon þē cros þǫre quik hē hāng
Twō days, prēchand þē puple omāng;   30
þat was ful lāng swilk payn tō fēle,
Bot with Crīst was hē confort wēle.

---

[1] gude.   [1a] mild.   [2] fast.   [3] god and alweldand.

Twentī thoūsand folk wār þāre [1]
Tō hēre him prẹche, with hertes sāre [2].
When þē first day till ēnd was went,
Al þat puple by ǫne assent
Til Ēgēas hoūs [3] fast þai ryn,   5
And said al quik þai suld him brin,
Bot if hē tīte gert tāk him doūne
Þat hānged was ogayns rẹsoūne.
'Hē es a rightwīs man,' þai say,
'And wēle has dōne bǫth night and day;   10
A gude tẹcher ever has hē bēne,
And mǫre suthfast was never sēne,
And swilk a man, sir, for sertayne
Suld noght suffer sǫ hard payne;
Þārfǫre, bot hē bē tāne doūn sōne,   15
In ẹvil tȳme þat dēde was dōne.'

  Ēgēas drēd þē puple wrāke,
And doūn hē hight him for tō tāke;
And furth hē went with þām in hī,
Bǫth hē and al hys turmentrī.   20
Þē folk thrāng efter al on a thrum;
And when Saint Andrew saw þām cum,
Of þaire cumyng hē was noght paid,
And untō Ēgēas þus hē sayd:
'Whārtō cums þoū untō mē,   25
Bot þoū wald trow in Jēsu frē,
And lẹve þī maumetes mǫre and les
And pray tō Jēsu of forgifnes?
If þoū will noght on þis wīse dō,
Ryn fast ǫr vengeance cum þē tō.   30
Þoū gettes nǫ force ne nǫ fuysoūne
Tō negh my bodī ne tāk it doūne;

---

[1] þore.   [2] sore.   [3] hows.

Mī Lǫrd will lēn tō mē þat lāne
Þat quik sall Ī noght dōun bē tāne.'
    Þan turmentūrs, with ēgir mōde
Went tō him, als þai wār wōde.
Þai rugget at him with ful grēte bir,   5
Bot nǫthing might þai of him stir[1];
Þaire armes and hāndes sōne in hī
Als þai wār hērdes, wēx þai drī;
Als þai kest up þaire armes him till,
Als drȳ stykkes þan stōde þai still.   10
    Saint Andrew þan māde his prayēre
Tō mightȳ God on þis manēre.
Hē said, 'Lǫrd, if it bē þī will,
In þis stęde lēt mē hing still,
Þat nǫne hāve pōwer mē tō fell   15
Dōun of þis cros þat Ī on dwell,
Untō þat tȳme þīself vōuche sāve
Tō þē blis of hevin mē for tō hāve;
Bot lat mē hing still als Ī dō,
Til tȳme þōu tāk mī saul þē tō.'   20
When þis was said, þār cōme a light
Dōun frǫ þe hevyn with bęmis bright,
And umbilappid his bodī abōut.
Þē folk þārfǫre had mekil dōut;
Þai might noght luke for mekil light   25
Untō his bodī, sǫ was it bright.
And als þē light was alþirmāste,
Tō God in hevyn hē gaf þē gāste.
    Ēgēas was ful drēdand þan,
And for fērde fast hǫme hē ran;   30
Bot in þē way, ǫr hē cōme hāme,
Hē sufferd dęd with mekel[2] schāme.

---

[1] of stir.   [2] mykel.

Sǫ sudan sorous wār tō him sent,
Als wurthī was, tō wǫ hē went.
Saint Andrew saul with āngell stevyn,
And with þat light was lift [1] to hevyn
Whǫre hē lēndes in ay lastand blis;   5
Alwēldand God þeder us wis.

Ēgēas had a wurthlī wīfe
Þat lufed Saint Andrew in his life;
For him scho ordānd a monument,
And berid his bodī with trew entent.   10
And of his grāve, als men might sē,
Sprāng· up oyle ful fayre plentē
Þat medcyn was tō mǫre and les,
Þat þeder soght for sēre sēkenes.
And bȳ þat oyl, als says þē bōke [2],   15
Al þat cuntrē ensaumple tōke;
For, when it sprāng on sīdes sēre,
Þan hǫpid þai for tō hāve gude ȝēre
Of cōrn and fruyt and ōþer thing;
And when þai saw it skarslī spring,   20
Þan hǫpid þai tō hāve skant of cōrn,
And of fruyt, als Ī sayd biforn.

III. TREATISES OF RICHARD ROLLE OF HAMPOLE

I. On the Nature of the Bee.

THĒ bee has thrē kȳndis. Āne es þat [3] scho es never ȳdill, and
scho es noghte with thaym þat will noghte wyrke, bot castys
thaym ōwte and puttes thaym awaye. Anōthire es þat, when scho 25
flȳes, scho tākes ērthe in hyr fēte [4] þat scho bē noghte lyghtlȳ
ǫverheghede in the ayere of wȳnde. Thē thyrde es that scho

---

[1] lifted.   [2] buke.   [3] þ, as often.   [4] fette.

kēpes clēn and bryghte hire wynges. Thus, ryghtwȳse men þat
lufes God āre never in ȳdillnes: for[1] owthire þay ere in travayle,
prayand or thynkande or rēdande or ōthere gude dōande, or
withtākand[2] ȳdill mene, and schewand thaym worthȳ tō bē put
frā þē ryste of hevene for thay will noghte travayle hēre. Þay 5
tāke ērthe, þat es þay hālde þāmselfe vīle and ērthelȳ that thay bē
noghte blawene with þē wȳnde of vanytē and of prȳde. Thay kēpe
thaire wynges clēne; that es, þē twā commandemēntes of charytē
þay fulfill in gud concyens, and thay hāfe ōthyr vertus unblēndyde
with þē fylthe of syne and unclēne luste. Aristotill sais þat þē bees 10
āre feghtande agaynes hym þat will drawe þaire honȳ frā thaym;
swā sulde wē dō agaynes dēvells þat afforces tham tō rēve
frā us þē honȳ of pōvre lȳfe and of grāce. For many āre þat never
kane hālde in[3] þē ordyre of lufe ynesche þaire frēndys, sybbe or fremede, bot outhire þay lufe þaym ōvermekill or thay lufe þām ōverlyttill, 15
settand thaire thoghte unryghtwȳselȳ on thaym, or þay lufe thaym
ōverlyttill yf þay doo noghte all as þey wolde till þāme. Swylke
kane noghte fyghte for thaire honȳ, forthȳ þē dēvelle turnes it tō
wormes, and mākes þeire saules oftesȳthes full bitter in angwys
and tēne, and besȳnes of vayne thoghtes and ōþer wrechidnes; 20
for thay āre sō hevȳ in ērthelȳ frenchype þat þay may noghte flee
intill þē lufe of Jēsu[4] Crīste, in þē wylke þay moghte well forgaa
þē lufe of all crēatūrs lyfande in ērthe. Whārefōre, accordandlȳ,
Arystotill sais þat some fowheles āre of gude flyghyng, þat passes
frā ā lānd tō anōthire. Some āre of ill flyghynge for hevȳnes of 25
bodȳ and for þaire neste es noghte ferre frā þē ērthe. Thus es it
of thaym þat turnes þām tō Godes servȳs. Some āre of gude
flyghynge for thay flȳe frā ērthe tō hevene, and rystes thaym thāre
in thoghte, and āre fedde in delīte of Goddes lufe and has thoghte
of nā lufe of þē worlde. Some āre þat kan noghte flȳe frā þis 30
lānde, bot in þē waye late theyre herte ryste, and delȳtes[5] þaym in
sēre lufes of mene and womene, als þay come and gaa, nōwe āne

---

[1] ff for cap f, as occasionally.   [2] wttakand; wt, as often for with.
[3] in, not in MS.   [4] Ihu, as always.   [5] dalyttes.

and nōwe anōthire. And in Jēsu Crīste þay kan fȳnde nā swettnes; or if þay ānȳ tȳme fēle oghte it es swā lyttill and swā schorte, for ōthire thoghtes þat āre in thaym, þat it brynges thaym till nā stābylnes. Or þay āre lȳke till a fōwle þat es callede strucyo, or storke, þat has wenges and it may noghte flȳe for charge of bodȳ. 5 Swā þay hāſe undirstāndynge, and fastes and wākes and sēmes hālȳ tō mens syghte, bot thay may noghte flȳe tō luſe and contemplācyōne of God, þay are ſǫ chargede wyth ōthyre affeccyōns and ōthire vanytēs.

II. A Notabill Tretys off the Ten Comandementys Drawene by Richerde the Hermyte off Hampull.

Thē fyrste comandement es, 'Thȳ Lǫrde God þou[1] sall lōute 10 and til hym ānelȳ þou sall serve.' In this comandement es forbǫden all mawmetrȳse, all wychecrafte and charemynge, thē wylke may dō nā remedȳ till ānȳ sēknes of mane, woman, or bēste, for þay erre þē snarrys of þē dēvelle bȳ þē whilke hē afforces hym tō dyssayve manekȳnde. Alswā in þis comandement es forbǫdyn tō 15 gyffe trouthe till sorcerȳe or till dyvȳnynges[2] bȳ stērnys, or bȳ drēmys, or bȳ ānȳ swylke thynges. Astronomȳenes byhāldes þē daye and þē hōure and þē poynte þat man es borne in, and undir whylke sȳgne[3] hē es borne, and þē poynte þat hē begynnes tō bē in, and bȳ þīre sȳgnes[4] and ōþer þay saye þat that[5] sall befall þē 20 man aftyrwarde; bot theyre errōwre es reprōffede of hālȳ doctōurs. Hālȳ crosses men sall lōwte for thay āre in sȳgne[3] of Crȳste crucyfīede. Tō ymāges[6a] es þē lovynge þat es till thaym of whaym þai[6] are þē ymages; for þat entent ānelȳ þai[6] are for tō lōwte. Thē tōthire comandement es, 'Þou sall noghte tāke þē nāme 25 of God in vayne.' Hēre es forbǫdene āthe withōwttene chēsōn. Hē þat nevenes God and swēris fals, dispȳses[7] God. In thrē manērs mane may syne in swērynge; that es, if hē swēre agayne

---

[1] þ. [2] dyvynyngeȝ. [3] syngne. [4] syngnes. [5] þay say that; repetition of preceding. [6] þaire [6a] ymageȝ. [7] despyse.

his concyence, or if hē swēre be Crȳste wondes or blude, that es evermāre grȩt syne þofe it be sōthe that hē swēris, for it sōūnes in irreverence [1] of Jēsu Crȳste. Alsọ, if hē com agaynes his āthe, noght fulfilland þat hē has sworne. Thē nām of God es tākyn in vayne one manȳ manērs,—with herte, with mōūthe, with werke. With herte tākes false crystyn mene it in vayne, þat rescheyves þē sacrement withōwttene grāce in sawle. With mōūthe es it tāne in vayne with all āthes brȩkynge; of new prȩchynge þat es vanytē and undevọcyōne; prayēre when wē honōūr God with ōūre lippes and ōūre hertys erre ferre frā hym. With werke ypocrittes tākes Goddes nām in vayne, for they feyne gud dēde withōwttene, and þey erre withōwtten charytē and vertue and force of sawle tō stānd agayne all ill styrrynges. Thē thirde comandement es, 'Um-bethynke thē þat thōū halowe þī halȳdaye.' This comandement may be tākyn in thrē manēres: firste [2], generallȳ, þat wē sesse of all vȳces; sithen, specialī, þat wē sesse of alle bodīlī werkis [3] þat lettys devọcyōne tō God in prayenge and thynkynge; thē thyrde es specyall, als in contemplaytȳfe men þat departis þaym frā all werdlȳ thynges swā þat þey hālȳ [4] gyfe þaym till God. Thē fyrste manēre es nēdfull us tō dō, thē tōthire wē awe tō dō, thē thirde es perfeccyōne; forthī, one þē halȳdaye men awe, als God byddys, tō lȩfe all syne and dō nā werke þat lettis thaym tō gyffe þaire herte tō Godd, thatt þay halowe þē daye in ryst and devọcyōne and dēdys of charytē.

Thē ferthe comandement es, 'Honōūre thȳ fadyre and þī mōdyre.' That es, in twā thynges, þat es bodȳlȳ and gāstelȳ: bodȳlȳ, in sustenance, þat þay be helpede and sustaynede in þaire ēlde, and when þay are unmyghttȳ of þaymeselfe; gāstelȳ, in reverence and bōūxomnes þat þay say tō þām nā wōrdes of myssawe, ne un-honestē, ne of displȩsance unavȳsedlȳ, bot serve þāme mēkelȳ and gladlȳ and lawlȳlȳ þat þay may wyne þat Godde hyghte tō swylke bārnes, þat es, lānde of lyghte. And if þay be dēde, þaym

---

[1] irrevence.   [2] ffirste.   [3] 'sithen . . . werkis,' from Arundel MS. 507.   [4] hally.

awe tō helpe þaire sawles with almousdēdes and prayērs. Thē
fifte comandement es, þat 'Thōu slaa nā man, nowthire with
assente, ne with wōrde or fāvōur.' And alsǭ hēre es forbǭden
unryghtwȳse hurtynge of ānȳ persōne. Thay are slāḡrs gāstelȳ
þat will noghte feede þē pōver in nēde, and þat defāmes men, 5
and þat confoūndes innocentys. Thē sexte commandement es,
'Thōu sall bē nā lichoūre.' Þat es, thou sall hāve nā man or
womane bot þat þou has tāken in fourme of hālȳ kyrke. Alswā
hēre es forbǭdene all manēr of wilfull pollusyōne, procurede one
ānȳ manēr agaynes kȳndlȳ oys or ōþer gātes. 10

Thē sevende comandement es, 'Thōu sall noghte dō nā thyfte.'
In þē whylke es forbǭden all manēre of withdraweynge of ōþer
men thynges wrāngwȳselȳ agaynes þaire wyll þat aghte it, bot
if it wēre in tȳme of māste nēde when all thynges erre comōne.
Alsǭ hēre es forbǭdene gillerȳ of weghte or of tāle, or of mett 15
or of mēsure, or thorow ōkyre or vīolence or drēde, als bēdells
and forestērs duse, and mynystyrs of þē kynge, or thurghe extorcyōne as lǭrdes duse. Thē aughtene commandement es, that
'Thōu sall noghte bēre false wyttnes agaynes thī neghteboūre,'
als in assȳs or cause of matremoyne. And alsǭ lȳenges ere for- 20
bǭden in þis commandement, and forswērynge. Bot all lȳenges
āre noght dēdlȳ syn, bot if þay noye till som man bodȳlȳ or
gāstelȳ. The nȳnde commandement es, 'Thōu sall noghte covayte
þē hoūs or ōþer thynge, mǭbill or immǭbill, of þī neghtbōur with
wrānge.' Ne þou sall noghte hāld ōþer mens gude if þou may 25
ȝēlde thaym, ellis þī penance sāves þē noghte. Thē tēnd comandement es, 'Thōu sall noghte covayte þī neghteboūrs wȳefe, ne his
servande, ne his mayden, ne mǭbylls of his.' Hē lufes God þat
kēpis thīre commandements for lufe. His neghteboūr hym awe
tō lufe als hymselfe, þat es, till þē sāme gude þat hē lufes hym- 30
selfe tō, nā thynge till ill; and þat hē lufe his neghtboūr saule
māre þan his bodȳ, or ānȳ gudes [1] of þē worlde.

---

[1] gudeȝ.

IV. A METRICAL HOMILY—THE SIGNS OF
THE DOOM

Tōday Sain Lōūk telles us,
In ōūr godspel, þat Jēsus
Spac of þing þat es tō com,
And nāmelīc of þē dai of dōm.
Tākning hē saide [1] sal bē dōn   5
Bāthe in þē son and in þē mōn,
And in þē stērnes al bidēn;
And folc sal þọl wandrẹþ and tēn,
For folc sal dwīn [2] for din of sē
And for bāret þat þan sal bē.   10
Ọ̄ver al þis werd bēs rẹdnes,
Wandrẹ̄þ and uglīnes,
For mihtī gāstes of þē hevin
Sal bē afrayed of þat stevin;
Þan sal Crīst cum þat men may sē   15
In maistrī and in grẹt pōūstē.
Quen þis bigines for tō bē,
Lōkes up and yē may sē
Þat yōūr bīing and yōūr prīs
Ful nēr cumen tilward yōū es.   20
Himself ōūr bīing hē es [3] calde,
For hē boht us quen hē was salde.

    Quen Crīst hāvid said þis grimlī sau,
An ensampel gan hē schau,
And said, 'Quen yē sē lẹfes spring,   25
And þīr trēs froit forþe bring,

---

[1] said.   [2] duin.   [3] es, not in MS.

Þan wāt ȝē [1] wēl þat somer es nēr;
Als may yē wit on þat manēr,
Quen yē sē þīr tākeninges in land,
Þat Crīst es ful nēr cumand.
For hevin and ērþe sal passe [2] þār,
Bot mȳ wōrd passes never mār ';—
Als quā sai, þing þat Ī yōu telle
Ne mai nā miht fordō ne felle.—
' Quen þis werld þat Ī mād of noht
Sal bē gāne and til ēnd broht,
Þan sal mī wōrd bē sōþefast,
For mī kinrīc sal ever last.'
Þis es þē strenþe of ōur godspel.
Als man wiþ [3] Inglis tung may tel.

Þē maister on þis godspel prēches,
And sais þat Crīst þārin us tēches
For tō forsāk þis werdes winne,
Ful of wrechedhēd and sinne;
For Crīst sais us hōu it sal ēnd,
And warnes us ful fair als frēnd.
Hē telles us tākeninges snelle,
Þār hē biginnes his godspelle,
And sais, 'Kinrīc sal rohlȳ rīse
Igain kinrīc and ger men grīse,
For bāle sal ger þīr bērnes blēde,
And māk in lānd hunger and nēde;
Þis bāle sal bāld bāret breu,
And fel mikel of þis werdes gleu.'
Slīc wōrdes said Crīst of þīr wers
Þat folc in werd ful derfe ders [4];
For quatkin wer sal fal in land,
Til pōver folk es it sārest schouand.

5

10

15

20

25

30

---

[1] we.   [2] pas.   [3] wit, as usual.   [4] derf deres.

Þat felis wēl nōū hālī kirk
Þat bērs¹ of bāret bē ful irk;
For it and pōver men hāvis bāþe
Of wer and wandrēþ² al þē schāþe.
Þis bāret pinnes pōver prīde,   5
Als þai wēl wāt þat walkes wīde,
Bot werdes ahte³ and hey tūres
Gētes þīr citē men frā stūres;
Forþī rīche men hāvis ay iwis,
Inohe of mēt and drinc and blis,   10
Bot pōver þōles þē bāret,
Þat hāvis defaut of clāþe and mēt.
And forþī warnes Jēsus bāþe,
Rīche and pōver, of þaire⁴ schāþe,
Þār hē schaues in ōūr godspelle   15
Tākeninges þat bird ōūr prīde felle.

   Hē sais tākeninges sal bē dōn
Bāþe in þē sone and in þē mōn;
Þē sun sal turn intil mirknes,
As sais Jōël, þat bērs witnes   20
Of Crīst þat þīr tākeninges us schaues
In ōūr godspelle wiþ grislī sawes.
For mōn, hē sais, sal turned bē
Intil blōd þat folk sal sē;
Quen sun and mōn sal þusgāt turn,   25
Þan sal þē sinful sāre⁵ scurn,
For þan may þai wit witerlȳ
Þat Crīst sal com tō dēm in hī.
Bot gōde⁶ men sal nāþing drēd,
For þan sal þai bē seker of mēd,   30
In þat blisful lānd þat þai
Sal ever lif in gāmen and play.

---

¹ Camb. MS. reads aght.   ² wandreht.   ³ haht.   ⁴ þair.
⁵ sar.   ⁶ god.

And Crīst in ōūr godspel forþȳ
Confortes us ful mīldelī,
And bides us lōk til grouand trēs;
For quen men lẹ̄ves on þaim sees,
Men wāt þat ful nēr es somer comand,   5
And riht swā mai wē understand,
Quen wē sē þīr tākenis cume,
Þat nērhand es þē dai of dōm.

Bot for Crīst spẹ̄kes of tākeninge,
Þat tīþand of þis dōm sal bringe,   10
Forþī es gōd þat Ī yōū telle
Sum þing of þīr tākeninges snelle.
Sain Jerōm telles þat fiftēn
Fērlī tākeninges sal bē sēn
Bifǫr þē day of dōm, and sal   15
Ilk ān of þaim on sēr dai fal.
Þē firste [1] dai sal al þē sē
Boln and rīs, and heyer bē
Þan ānī fel of al þē lānd,
And als a felle up sal it stānd;   20
Þē heyt þārof sal passe þē felles
Bī sextī fōt, als Jerōm telles;
And als mikel þē tōþer day
Sal it sattel and wīt away,
And bē lauer þan it nōū esse   25
For water sal it haf wēl lesse.
Þē þride dai, mersuīne and qualle,
And ōþer grẹ̄te [2] fises alle,
Sal yel and māk sā reuful bēr
Þat soru sal it bē tō hēr.   30
Þē fērþe day, freis water and sē
Sal bren als fīr and glouand bē.

---

[1] first.   [2] gret.

Þē fifte[1] day, sal grese[2] and trēs
Suẹ̄t blōdī deu þat grislī bēs.
Þē sexte day, sal dōūn falle
Werdes werks, bāþe tōūrs and halle.
Þē sevend day, sal stānes grẹ̄t
Tōgider smīt and brēmlȳ bẹ̄te.
And all þē ērthe, þē achtande day,
Sal stir and quāc and al folc slay[3].
Þē neynde[4] day, þe felles[5] alle
Bē mād al ẹ̄vin wiþ ērþe salle.
Þē tēndᵉ[6] day, sal folc up crēp,
Als wōde[7] men, of pittes dēp.
Þē elleft day, sal bānes rīse
And stānd on grāves þār men nōū līes.
Þē tuelfte[8] day, sal stērnes falle.
Þē þretēnd day, sal men[9] dey alle,
Wiþ ōþer dẹ̄de[10] men tō rīse,
And com wiþ þaim tō grẹ̄t asīse.
Þē ſaurtēnd day, at a schift,
Sal bāþe brin, bāþe ērþe and lift.
Þē fifetēnde day, þai bāþe
Sal bē mād newe and fair ful rāþe;
And alle dẹ̄de[11] men sal rīse,
And cum bifọ̄r Crīst ōūr justīse.

Þan sal Crīst dēm als king ful wīs,
And ger þē sinful sāre grīse;
Sā grislī sal hē tō þaim bē,
Þat þaim wār lēver þat þai moht flē
Frā þat dōm þat hē sal dēm
Þan al þis werd; sā bēs hē brēm

---

[1] fift.　　[2] greses.　　[3] Small reads slay.　　[4] neynd.　　[5] fels
[6] tend.　　[7] wod.　　[8] tuelft.　　[9] quek men.　　[10] ded
[11] al ded.

Till þaim þat sinful cumes þār;
And forþī sal þai grēte¹ sār,
And say 'Allas, þat wē wār born,
Schāmlīc hāf wē us self forlorn.'
Þan salle þair wike dēdes alle   5
Stānd and þaim igaines² kalle,
And wiþ þair tākening bēr witnes
Of þair sin and þair wiknes.
Of mikel soru sal þai telle,
For Sātenas wiþ fēres felle,   10
Tō bīnd þaim hē sal bē ful snelle,
And brēmlī drawe³ þaim till helle;
Þār þai sal evermāre duelle,
And wāfullīc in pīnes welle,
And ēndelēs of soru telle.   15

Þis bēs þair dōm þat hēr in sin
Ligges, and wil þair sin noht blin;
Bot wald þai þink on dōmesdai,
Þaim birde⁴ lēf þair plihtful play.
Allas, allas, quat sal þai say   20
Bifōre⁵ him, þat mihtful may,
Quen al þē men þat was and esse
Sal sē þair sines māre and lesse,
And all þē āngeles of þē hevin,
And mā fēndes þan man mai nefen?   25
Igainsawe may þār nān bē,
Of þing þat alle men may sē.
Of þis ōpenlīc schauing
Hāvis Godd schawed manȳ tākning⁶;
Of a tākning⁷ Ī hāf herd telle,   30
Þat salles wēl til ōur godspelle.

---

¹ gret.   ² igaines þaim.   ³ draw.   ⁴ bird.   ⁵ befor.
⁶ taking.   ⁷ taking that.

A blak munk of an abbaye
Was enfermēr, als Ī herd say[1];
Hē was hālden an hālī man
Imānge his felaus everilk ān.
An cloyster monk loved him ful wēl, 5
And was til him ful special,
For rīvelīc tōgider drawes
Faiþful frēndes and gōd felaẃes[2].

Fel auntōūr þat þis enfermēr
Was sēk, and hē þat was him[3] dēr 10
Cōm tō māk him glad and blīþe,
And his lufrēdene til him tō kīþe;
Hē asked him hōū hē him felid,
And hē his stāt alle til him telld,
And said, 'Ful harde[4] fēl Ī mē, 15
Tō dẹde Ī drawe als yē mai sē.'

His felau was for him sārȳ,
And praied him ful gērn forþīe,
Þat yef Godd did of him his wille
Þat hē suld scheu his stāt him tille. 20
Þis sēke monk hiht tō com him tō,
Yef hē moht gete lẹf þartō;
'Ī sal,' hē said, 'yef Ī may,
Com tō þē, my stāt tō say.'

Quen þis was sayd hē deyed sōn, 25
And his felau asked his bōn,
And prayed Godd, for his mercȳe,
Þat hē suld schew him ọpenlȳ,
Ọþer wākand or slēpand,
Of his felaẃe[5] sum tīþand; 30
And als hē lay apon a niht,

---

[1] of all i herd say; Camb. MS. als i herd say. [2] faithe lufreden god
felawes; Camb. MS. faithefulle frendes & felaus. [3] til him. [4] hard.
[5] felaw state; Camb. MS. omits state.

His felaw cōm wiþ lēmes liht,
And tāld him bāþe of hevin and helle.
And hē prayed hē suld him telle
His stāte; and hē said, 'Wēl fār Ī,
Þoru þe help of ōur Lẹ̄fdī; 5
War scho nafd[1] bēn, Ī hāfid gān
Tō won in helle wiþ Sātan.'
His felau þoht hērof fērlȳ,
And asked him quārfọr and quī,
And sayd, 'Wē wēnd alle wēl þat þou 10
Hāved bēn an hālī man til nōu;
Hōu sal it fār of us kaytefes
Þat in sin and folī lyfes[2],
Quen þou þat led sā hālī līfe
Was dēmed till helle[3] for tō drīfe?' 15
Quen þis was said, þē dẹd ansuerd
And tāld his felaw hōu hē ferd;
And said, 'Sōn, quen Ī gaf þē gāste,
Till mȳ dōm was Ī led in hāste,
And als Ī stōd mȳ dōm tō hēr 20
Bifọr Jēsus, wiþ drērī chēr,
Of fēndes hẹrd ic manī upbrayd,
And a bōc was bifọr mē layd
Þat was þē reuel of Sain Benēt,
Þat ic hiht tō hāld and gēt. 25
Þis reul þai gert mē raplī rēde;
And als Ī rēd, sār gan Ī drēde,
For ọverlōp[4] moht Ī māc nān,
Bot of þē clauses everilk ān
Yāld ic accōunt, hōu Ī þaim hēld, 30
And mȳ consciens gan mē mēld.
It schawed þār ful ọpenlȳe
Þat Ī led mī līf wrāngwīslīe;

---

[1] ne hafd.   [2] lyes.   [3] tille hell.   [4] Camb. MS. overlepe.

For in þē reul es manī pas
Þat þan igain mē casten was,
Quarþoru almāst hāved Ī þāre
Bēn dēmid til helle for tō fāre.
Bot for Ī lufed wēl ōur Lēfdȳe   5
Quīl Ī lifd, ic hafd forþīe
Ful gōd help þār, þoru hir mercȳ.
For scho bisoht Crīst inwardlīe
Þat Ī moht in purgātorīe
Clens mī sin and mī folȳe.   10
Forþi hōp Ī tō fār ful wēle [1],
For mī soru sal sōn kēle;
Forþī, mȳ frēnd, Ī praie [2] þē,
Þat þōu ger felaus prai for mē.'
Quen þis was said, awai hē went,   15
And his felawe ful mikel him ment,
And efter þis siht manī a dai
Gert hē for his sawell prai.

    Þis tāle [3] haf Ī tāld yōu
Tō schaw on quat manēr and hōu   20
Wē sal bē dēmed, and yēld acōunt
Quat ōur sinnes mai amōuṇṭ;
For al sal com tō rōunge iwis,
Þar þat hēr mistākin isse
Bī þē lēste [4] īdel þoht,   25
For þār forgifnes bēs riht noht.
Þan sal wē bȳe þē sines dēre
Of quilke wē er noht schriven hēre;
Yef wē bē hēr of sines schriven,
Þār hāvis Godd us þaim forgiven,   30
Forþī birdd us ōur sin hēr bēte
Wiþ schrift of mōuþe and wōnges wēte.

---

[1] welle.   [2] prai.   [3] tal.   [4] lest.

For schrift of mouþe es medecīne
Þat schīldes man frā hellepīn,
For if wē schrīf us clẹn of sinne
Wiþ penans¹, dẹd wē sal hāf winne,
And mai bē siker on dōmesdai   5
Tō wīnd intil þat blisful plai,
Þar Crīst sal ever mār bē king;
For his mercī hē þider us bring. Amēn.

V. THE SONGS OF LAWRENCE MINOT

I.

Līthes and Ī sall tell ȝow tyll
Þē bataile of Halidon Hyll.   10

Trew king þat sittes in trọne,
    Untō þē Ī tell my tāle,
And untō þē Ī bid a bōne,
    For þou ert bute of all my bāle.
Als þou māde midelẹrd and þē mōne,   15
    And bēstes and fowles grẹte and smāle,
Unto mē sēnd þī socōre sōne
    And dresce mȳ dēdes in þis dāle.

In þis dāle Ī droupe and dāre
    For dērne² dēdes þat dōne mē dẹre;   20
Of Ingland had mȳ hert grẹte cāre
    When Edward founded first tō wẹre.
Þē Franche men wār frek tō fāre
    Ogaines him with schēld and spẹre;
Þai turned ogayn with sīdes sāre,   25
    And al þaire pomp noght worth a pẹre.

¹ penanz.   ² dern.

A pẹre of prīse es mọre sumtȳde
   Þan all þē bọste of Normandȳe[1].
Þai sent þaire schippes on ilk a sīde
   With flesch and wīne and whẹte and rȳe;
With hert and hānd, es noght at hīde,   5
   For tō help Scotland gan þai hȳe;
Þai fled and durst nọ dēde abīde[2],
   And all þaire fāre noght wurth a flȳe.

For[3] all þaire fāre þai durst noght fight,
   For dẹdes dint had þai slīke dōut;   10
Of Scotland had þai never sight
   Ay whīls þai wār of wōrdes stōut.
Þai wald hāve mẹnd þām at þaire might
   And besȳ wār þai þāre obōut;
Nōw God help Edward in his right,—   15
   Amēn,—and all his rẹdȳ rōwt.

His rẹdȳ rōut mōt Jēsu[4] spēde.
   And sāve þām bọth bȳ night and day;
Þat Lọrd of hevyn mōt Edward lẹde,
   And maintẹne him als hē wēle may.   20
Þē Scottes nōw all wīde will sprẹde;
   For þai hāve failed of þaire pray;
Nōw er þai dāreand all for drēde,
   Þat wār bifọre sọ stōut and gay.

Gai þai wār, and wēle þai thoght   25
   On þē Ērle Morrē and ōþer mā;
Þai said it suld ful dēre bē boght
   Þē lānd þat þai wār flēmid frā.
Philip Valays wōrdes wroght,
   And said hē suld þaire enmȳs slā;   30
Bot all þaire wōrdes was for noght,
   Þai mun bē met if þai wār mā.

Normondye.   [2] habide.   [3] ffor.   [4] Ihu, as usual.

Mā manāsinges ȝit hāve þai māked,
  Mawgrē mōt þai hāve tō mēde;
And manȳ nightes als hāve þai wāked
  Tō dęre all Ingland with þaire dēde.
Bot, loved bē God, þē prīde es slāked   5
  Of þām þat wār sǫ stōut on stēde;
And sum of þam es lęvid all nāked
  Noght fer frǫ Berwīk opon Twēde.

A lītell frǫ þat forsaid tōune,
  Halydon Hill þat es þē nāme,   10
Þāre was crakked manȳ a crōwne
  Of wīlde [1] Scottes and als [2] of tāme.
Þāre was þaire banēr born all dōune,
  Tō māk slīke bǫste þai wār tō blāme;
Bot neverþēlęs ay er þai bōune   15
  Tō wait Ingland with sorow and schāme.

Shāme þai hāve als Ī hēre say;
  At Dondē nōw es dōne þaire daunce,
And wēnd þai mōst anōþer way
  Ęvyn thurgh Flandres intō France.   20
On Filip Valays [3] fast crī þai,
  Þāre for tō dwell and him avaunce;
And nǫthing list þām þan of play
  Sen þām es tīde þis sārȳ chance.

Þis sārȳ chaunce þām es bitid,   25
  For þai wār fals and wonder fell;
For cursed caitefes er þai kid
  And ful of tręsōn, suth tō tell.
Sir Jǫn þē Comyn had þai hid,
  In hālȳ kirk þai did him qwell;   30
And þārfǫre manȳ a Skottis brīd
  With dōle er dight þār [4] þai mōst dwell.

----

[1] wild.   [2] alls.   [3] Valas.   [4] þat.

Þāre dwelled ōure king, þē suth tō saine,
    With his męnʒē a lītell whīle ;
Hē gaf gude confort on þat plaine
    Tō all his men obōut a mȳle.
All if his men wār mekill of maine,   5
    Ever þai dōuted þām of gīle ;
Þē Scottes gaudes might nǫthing gain,
    For all þai stumbilde at þat stīle.

Þus in þat stōwre þai left þaire līve
    Þat wār bifǫre sǫ prōud in pręse ;   10
Jēsu[1a], for þī wōundes fīve,
    In Ingland help us tō hāve pęse.

II.

Nōw for tō tell ʒōw will Ī turn
    Of þē[1] batayl of Banocburn.

Skottes ōut of Berwīk and of Abirdēne,   1
At þē Bannok burn wār ʒē tō kēne ;
Þāre slogh ʒē manȳ saklęs, als it was sēne,
And nōw has King Edward wrǫken it, Ī wēne.
    It es wrǫken, Ī wēne, wēle wurth þē whīle,
    Wār ʒit with þē Skottes, for þai er ful of gīle.   2

Whāre er ʒē, Skottes of Saint Jǫhnes tōune?
Þē bǫste of ʒōwre banēr es bętin all dōune ;
When ʒē bǫsting will bēde, Sir Edward es bōune
For tō kindel ʒōw cāre and crak ʒōwre crōwne.
    Hē has crakked ʒōwre crōune, wēle worth þē whīle ;   2
    Shāme bitȳde þē Skottes, for þai er full of gīle.

Skottes of Striflin wār stērn[2] and stōut,
Of God ne of gude men had þai nǫ dōut ;

[1a] Ihu, as usual.   [1] no þe in MS.   [2] steren.

Nōw hāve þai, þē pelērs, priked obōūt,
Bot at þē last Sir Edward rīfild þaire rōūt;
He has rīfild þaire rōūt, wēle wurth þē whīle,
Bot ever er þai under bot gaudes and gīle.

Rughfute riveling, nōw kindels þī cāre,   5
Bẹ̄rebag with þī bọ̄ste, þī biging es bāre;
Fals wretche and forsworn, whider wilt ōū fāre?
Busk þē untō Brughes[1] and abīde þāre;
    Þāre, wretche, salt ōū won and wērȳ þē whīle,
    Þī dwelling in Dondē es dōne for þī gīle.   10

Þē Skotte[2] gāse in Burghes and bẹ̄tes þē strētes,
All þise Inglis men harmes hē hētes;
Fast mākes hē his mọ̄ne tō men þat hē mētes,
Bot fọ̄ne frēndes hē fīndes þat his bāle bētes:
    Fune bētes his bāle, wēle wurth þē whīle,   15
    Hē uses all thrẹ̄ting with gaudes and gīle.

Bot manȳ man thrẹ̄tes and spẹ̄kes ful ill
Þat sumtȳme wār better tō bē stānestill;
Þē Skot in his wōrdes has wīnd for tō spill,
For at þē last Edward sall hāve al his will: 20
    Hē had his will at Berwīk, wēle wurth þē whīle;
    Skottes broght him þē kayes, bot gẹ̄t for þaire gīle.

III.

How Edward þē King cōme in Braband
And tōke homāge of all þē land.

God þat schōpe bọ̄th sẹ̄ and sand,   25
Sāve Edward, King of Ingeland[3],
Bọ̄the[4] bodȳ, saul and līfe,
And grante him joy withōwten strīf;

[1] Brig.   [2] skottes.   [3] Ingland.   [4] both.

For manī men tō him er wrāth [1]
In Fraunce and in Flandres bāth [2];
For hē defendes fast his right,
And þārtō Jēsu grante him might,
And sǫ tō dō bǫth night and day,   5
Þat yt may bē tō Goddes pay.

   Ōure King was cumen, trewly [3] tō tell,
Intō Brabant for tō dwell.
Þē kaysēr Lowis of Bavēre,
Þat in þat lānd þan had nō pēre,—   10
Hē, and als his sones [4] twā [5]
And ōþer princes manȳ mā [6];—
Bisschoppes and prelātes wār þāre fęle
Þat had ful mekill werldlȳ węle,
Princes and pōple, āld and ȝung [7],   15
Al þat spac with Duche tung,—
All þai cōme with gręte honōwre
Sir Edward tō sāve and socōure,
And proferd him, with all þayre ręde,
For tō hāld þē Kinges stęde.   20
Þē duke of Braband first of all
Swōre, for thing þat might bifall,
Þat hē suld, bǫth day and night,
Help Sir Edward in his right,
In tōun, in fēld, in frith and fen;   25
Þis swōre þē duke and all his men,
And al þē lǫrdes þat with him lēnd,
And þārtō hēld þai up þaire hēnd.
Þan King Edward tōke his rest
At Andwerp, whāre him līked best;   30
And þāre hē māde his monē playne
Þat nǫ man suld say þāre ogayne;

---

[1] wroth.   [2] both.   [3] trely.   [4] sons.   [5] two.
[6] mo.   [7] ȝong.

His monē þat was gude and lēle
Left in Braband ful mekill dēle;
And all þat lānd untill þis day
Fārs þē better, for þat jornay.

When Philip þē Valays[1] herd of þis,   5
Þarat hē was ful wrǫth iwis;
Hē gert assemble his barōunes,
Princes and lǫrdes of manȳ tōunes.
At Pariss tōke þai þaire cōunsaile,
Whilk pointes might þām mǫste availe;   10
And in all wīse þai þām bithoght
Tō stroy Ingland and bring tō noght.

Schipmen sōne wār efter sent
Tō hēre þē Kinges cumandment,
And þē galaies men alsā[2]   15
Þat wiste[3] bǫth of węle and wā[4].
Hē cumand þan þat men suld fāre
Till Ingland, and for nǫthing spāre
Bot brin and slā bǫth man and wīfe
And chīlde, þat nǫne suld pas with līfe;   20
Þē galay men hēld up þaire handes
And thanked God of þīr tīþandes.

At Hamton, als Ī understānd,
Cōme þē galayes[5] untō lānd,
And ful fast þai slogh and brend,   25
Bot noght sǫ mekill als sum men wēnd;
For, ǫr þai wēned wār þai mett
With men þat sōne þaire laykes lett.
Sum was knokked on þē hęvyd
Þat þē bodȳ þāre bilęvid;   30
Sum lay stāreand on þē stērnes,
And sum lay knǫked ōut þaire hērnes;

---

[1] Valas.   [2] also.   [3] wist.   [4] wo.
[5] gaylayes.

Þan with þām was nǫne ōþer glē,
Bot ful ſain wār þai þat might flē.
Þē galay men, þē ſuth tō say,
Mōst nēdes turn anōþer way;
Þai ſoght þē ſtremis fer and wīde   5
In Flandres and in Sẹland syde.

   Þan saw þai whāre Cristōfer ſtōde
At Aremōūth [1], opon þē flōde [2];
Þan went [3] þai þeder all bidēne,
Þē galayes men with hertes kēne,   10
Aght and fourtī [4] galays and mā [5],
And with þām als wār tarettes twā [6],
And ōþer manȳ of galiǫtes,
With grẹte noumber of smāle bǫtes;
All þai hǫved on þē flōde   15
Tō ſtẹle Sir Edward mennes [7] gōde.
Edward ōūre King þan was noght þēre,
Bot sōne when it cōme tō his ẹre
Hē sembled all his men full still,
And said tō þām what was his will.   20
Ilk man māde him rẹdȳ þen;
Sǫ went þē King and all his men
Untō þaire schippes ful hāstilȳ,
Als men þat wār in dēde doghtȳ.
Þai ſānd þē galay men grẹte wāne [8],   25
A hundereth ever ogaynes āne [9];
Þē Inglis men put þām tō wẹre
Ful bāldelȳ [10] with bow and spẹre;
Þai slogh þāre of þē galaies men
Ever sextȳ ogaynes tēn,   30
Þat sum ligges ȝit in þat mīre,
All hẹvidlẹs withōūten hīre.

---

[1] armouth.   [2] flude.   [3] wen.   [4] viii and xl.   [5] mo.   [6] two.
[7] mens.   [8] wone.   [9] one.   [10] baldly.

Þē Inglis men wār armed wēle
Bōth in ȳren and in stēle;
Þai faght ful fast, bōth day and night,
Als lānge [1] als þām lasted might;
Bot galay men wār sō manȳ   5
Þat Inglis men wēx all werȳ;
Help þai soght bot þāre cōme nāne [2],
Þan untō God þai māde þaire māne [3].
Bot sen þē tīme þat God was born,
Ne a hundreth ȝēre biforn,   10
Wār never men better in fight
Þan Inglis men, whīls þai had myght.
Bot sōne all maistrī gan þai mis;
God bring þaire saules untill his blis,
And God assoyl þām of þaire sin   15
For þē gude will þat þai wār in. Amēn.

Listens nōw, and lēves mē,
Whōsō lifes þai sall sē
Þat it mun bē ful dēre boght
Þat þīr galay men hāve wroght.   20
Þai hōved still opon þē flōde,
And rēved pōver men þaire gōde [4];
Þai robbed and did mekill schāme,
And ay bāre Inglis men þē blāme.
Nōw Jēsus [5] sāve all Ingeland [6],   25
And blis it with his hālȳ hand. Amēn.

---

[1] lang.   [2] none.   [3] mone.   [4] gude.   [5] Ihc.   [6] Ingland.

VI. BARBOUR'S BRUCE—THE PURSUIT OF
KING ROBERT

Hōw Jǫhn of Lorne soucht þē gud Kyng Robert Bruce wyth
þē sleuth hūnd.

Þē kyng tōward þē wōd[1] is gāne,
Wērȳ, forswat, and will of wayn;
Intill þē wōd soyn enterit hē,
And hēld him[2] dōūn tōward a valē
Quhār throu þē wōd a wattir ran.　　　　　　5
Þiddir in gręt hȳ went[3] hē þan
And begōūth tō[4] rest hym þair,
And said hē mycht[5] nǫ forþirmār.
His man' said, 'Schir[6], þat may nocht[7] bē;
Abȳde ȝhē heir, ȝē sal soyn sē　　　　　　10
Fiffe[8] hundreth ȝarnand ȝōū tō slā,
And þai ār sęle agānis us twā;
And sen wē may nocht deill wyth mycht,
Help us all þat wē may wyth slycht.'
Þē kyng said, 'Sen þat þōū will swā,　　　　　　15
Gā furth and Ī sall with þē gā.
Bot Ī hāf herd oftsīþys[9] say,
Þat quhā endlāng a wattir ay
Wald wayd a bowdraucht, hē suld ger
Bāth þē sleuthhūnd and his lędar　　　　　　20
Tȳne þē sleuth men gert him tā;

---

[1] vod; v for w is common, and occasionally w for v.　　[2] him, not in MS.
[3] wend.　　[4] for to.　　[5] myᵗ, as often.　　[6] s, and an abbreviation, written
Schir in other places.　　[7] noᵗ, as often.　　[8] v, as often.　　[9] oftsiss.

Pruf wē gif it will dō nōw swā,
For wār ʒon dēvill hūnd away
Ī roucht nocht of þē layff, perſay.'

   As hē devīsit þai hāf dōne,
And enterit in þē wattir sōne   5
And hēld on endlāng it þar way;
And syne tō þē lānd ʒeid þai
And hēld þair way as þai had ẹre.
And Jọhn of Lōrn, with grẹt effẹre,
Cōm with his rōut richt tō þē plăce   10
Quhār þat his fīfe men slāne was.
Hē mẹnyt þāme quhen hē þaim saw,
And said, eſtir a lītill thraw,
Þat hē suld venge in hȳ þār blude;
Bot ōþir wayis þē gammyn ʒude.   15
Þair wald hē māk nọ mair duelling,
Bot furth in hȳ followit þē king.
Richt tō þē burn þai[1] passit ar;
Bot þē sleuthhūnd maid stynting þār,
And wāveryt lāng tȳme tō and frā   20
Þat hē nā certāne gāt cōuth gā.
Till at þē last þan Jọhne of Lōrn
Persāvit þē hūnd þē sleuth had lorn,
And said, 'Wē hāf tȳnt þis travāle[2];
Tō pas forþir may nocht avāle,   25
For þē wōde is bāth braid and wȳde
And hē is weill fer be þis tȳde.
Þārfọre Ī rēde wē turn agāne,
And wāst nọ mair travāle in vayn.
With þat relȳit[3] hē his mẹnʒhē,   30
And his way tō þē họst tuk hē.

   Þus eschāpit þē nọbill kyng;
Bot sum men sais þis eschāping[4]

---

[1] þame.   [2] travell, but cf. l. 29.   [3] releyt, as at 169, 5.   [4] enchaping.

Apon āne ōþir manēr it fell
Þan throu þē wāding; for þai tell
That þē kyng a gud archēr had,
And quhen hē saw his lǫrd swā stad,
That hē wes left swā ānerlȳ,   5
Hē ran on fut alwayis hym bȳ
Till hē intill þē wōd wes gāne;
Þan said hē till hymself allāne,
Þat hē arest rycht þair wald mā
Tō luk gif hē þē hūnd mycht slā.   10
For gif þē hūnd mycht lęst[1] on līf,
Hē wist full weill þat þai wald drīf[2]
Þē kyngis trass till þai hym tā;
Þan wist hē weill þai wald him slā.
And for hē wald his lǫrd succōūr,   15
Hē put his līf in aventūr,
And stud intill a busk lurkand
Quhīll þat þē hūnd cōm at his hānd,
And with āne arrow soyn hym slew
And throu þē wōd syne hym withdrew.   20
Bot quheþir his eschāping[3] fell
As Ī tāld first, or nōw Ī tell,
Ī wat it weill withōut lęsyng,
At þat būrn eschāpit þē king.

Þē king furth has his wayis tāne,   25
And Jǫhne of Lōrne agāne is gāne
Tō Schir Āmēr, þat frā þē chass
With his men þan repārit wass,
Þat lītill sped in þair chassing;
For thow[4] þat þai maid following   30
Full ęgirlȳ, þai wan bot small;
Þair fais neir eschāpit all.

---

[1] left?   [2] rif.   [3] enchaping.   [4] how.

Men sais Schir Thomas Randale þan,
Chassand, þē kyngis banēr wan,
Quhārthrou in Yngland wyth þē kyng
Hē had rycht grēt prīce and lovyng.
Quhen þē chāsēris relȳit wār,   5
And Jōhne of Lōrne had met þaim þār,
Hē[1] tāld Schir Āmēr all þē cass,
Hōw þat þē king eschāpit was,
And hōw þat hē his fiff men slew
And syne hē tō þē wōd hym drew.   10
Quhen Schir Āmēr herd þis, in hȳ
Hē sānyt hym for þē fērlȳ,
And said, 'Hē is grētlȳ tō priss,
For Ī knaw nāne þat liffand is
þat at myscheif can help hym swā;   15
Ī trow hē suld bē hārd tō slā,
And hē wār bōdyn all ēvynlȳ.'
On þis wiss spak Schir Āmerȳ.

   And þē gud kyng hēld furth his way,
Hē and his man, ay quhīll þat þai   20
Passit throu þē forest wār.
Syne in a mure þai enterit ār,
þat wes bāth hee and[2] lāng and[3] braid;
And ōr þai half it passit had,
þai saw on sȳde thrē men cumand   25
Līk tō lichtmen and wāverand.
Swērdis þai had and axis als,
And āne of þāme apon his hals
A mekill būndyn weddir bāre.
þai met þē kyng and halsit þār;   30
And þē kyng þāme þār halsing ȝald
And askit þāme queheþir þai wald.

---

[1] and; he, in MS. E.   [2] no 'and' in MS.; E has &.   [3] &, as occasionally.

Þai said, 'Robert þē Bruce þai socht,
Tō meit with hym gif þat þai mocht;
Þair duelling with hym wald þai mā.'
Þē kyng said, 'Gif þat ȝhē will swā,
Hāldis furth ȝōur way with mē   5
And Ī sall ger ȝōw soyn hym se.'
Þai persāvit be his spękyng,
And his effęr, hē wes þē kyng,
And chāngit contenanss and lāt,
And hēld nocht in þē first estāt[1];   10
For þai wār fayis tō þē kyng,
And thoucht tō cum intō scōwkyng,
And duell with hym quhīll þat þai saw
Þār tȳm, and bryng hym þan of daw.
Þai grantit till his spēk forþī;   15
Bot þē kyng, þat wes wittȳ,
Persāvit weill bē þair hāvyng[2]
Þat þai lufit hym in nā thing.
Hē said, 'Fallowis, ȝhē man all thrē,
Forthir aquynt quhīll þat wē bē,   20
All be ȝōurself forrōuth us[3] gā,
And on þē sammyn wiss wē twā
Sall fallow ȝōw behȳnd weill neir.'
Quod þai, 'Schir, it is nā mysteir
Tō trow intill us ānȳ ill.'   25
'Nāne dō Ī,' said hē, 'bot Ī will
Þat ȝhē gā forrōwth us[4], quhīll wē
Bettir with ōþir knawyn bē.'
'Wē grant,' þai said; 'sen ȝē will swā,'
And furth apon þair gāt gan[5] gā.   30

    Þus ȝeid þai till þē nycht wes neir,
And þan þē formāst cumin weir

---

[1] stat.   [2] awyng.   [3] us, not in MS.   [4] forrow us.   [5] can.

Till a wāst husbandis hōūss, and þār
Þai slew thē weddir at þai bār,
And slew fȳre for tō rǫst þār mēt,
And askit þē kyng gif hē wald ēt
And rest hym till þē mēt wār dicht.   5

Þē kyng, þat hungrȳ wes Ī hicht,
Assentit tō þair spēke in hȳ;
Bot hē said, hē wald ānerlȳ
Betuyx hym and his fallow bē
At a fȳre, and þai all thrē   10
In þē ēnd of þē hōūss suld mā
Ane ōþir fȳre; and þai did swā.

Þai drew þāme in þē hōūsis ēnd,
And half þē weddir till hym sēnd;
And þai rǫstit in hȳ þair mēt,   15
And fell rycht frēklȳ¹ for till ēt.

  Þē kyng weill lāng hē fastyt² had,
And had rycht mekill travāle māde;
Þārfǫr hē ēte richt ēgyrlȳ.

And quhen hē ētyn had hāstelȳ,   20
Hē had tō slēpe sā mekill will
Þat hē mycht set nā let þārtill;
For quhen þē vānys fillit ār,
Þē bodȳ worþis hēvȳ evirmār,
And tō slēpe drawis hēvȳnes³.   25

Þē kyng þat all fortravalit wes,
Saw þat hym worthit slēp neidwais;
Till his fostir brōþir hē sais,
'May Ī trāst þē mē tō wākk⁴,
Till Ī a lītill slēpyng tāk?'   30
'ȝhā, Schir,' hē said, 'till Ī may drey.'
Þē kyng þan wynkit a lītill wey⁵,

---

¹ frakly.   ² fastyn.   ³ hevynas.   ⁴ walk ; lk = kk.   ⁵ we.

And slēpit nocht, bot ynkurlȳ
Gliffnit [1] oft up suddanlȳ [2];
For hē had drēde of þā [3] thrē men,
Þat at þē tōþir fȳre wār þen;
That þai his fayis wār hē wyst,　　　　　5
Þārfǫr hē slēpit as fōul on twist.

　　Thē kyng slēpit bot lītill [4] þan,
Quhen sic a slēpe fell on his man
Þat hē mycht not hāld up his ē,
Bot fell on slēpe and routit hē.　　　　　10
Nōw is þē kyng in grȩt perill [5],
For slēpe hē swā a lītill quhīle,
Hē sall bē dȩd forōuten drēd;
For þē thrē trātōuris tuk gud hēde
Þat hē on slēp wes, and his man.　　　　15
In full grȩt hȳ þai raiss up þan,
And drew þair swērdis hāstelȳ,
And went tōwārd þē kyng in hȳ
Quhen þat þai saw he slēpit swā,
And slēpand thoucht þai wald hym slā.　　20
Till hym þai ʒeid a full grȩt pass,
Bot in þat tȳm, throu Goddis grāce,
Þē kyng blenkit up hāstelȳ,
And saw his man slēpand him bȳ,
And saw cumand þē trātōuris thrē.　　　25
Delyverlȳ on fut gat hē,
And drew his swērd out and þāme met;
And as hē ʒeid, his fut hē set
Apon his man weill hȩvalȳ.
Hē wāknyt [6], and raiss all desalȳ;　　　30
For þē sleip masterit hym swā
That, ǫr hē gat up, āne of þā [7]

---

[1] and gluffnyt.　　　[2] suddandly.　　　[3] þai, as also in l. 32.　　　[4] litill.
[5] perell.　　　[6] walknyt.　　　[7] þai.

Þat cōm for tō slā þē kyng
Gāf hym a strāke in his rȳsyng,
Swā þat hē mycht help hym nō mair.
Þē kyng sō strātlȳ stad wes þair,
That hē wes never ȝeit swā stad ;   5
Nā wār þē armyng þat hē had,
Hē had beyn dēd forōutyn weyr.

Bot nocht forþī on sic maneir
Hē helpit hym swā in þat bargāne,
Þat þā¹ thrē trātōuris hē has slāne,   10
Throu Goddis grāce and his manheid.
His fostir brōþir þair wes dēd ;
Þan wes hē wounder will of wayn,
Quhen hē saw hē wes left allāne.

His fostir brōþir mēnyt hē,   15
And waryit all þē tōþir thrē,
And syne his way tuk hym allāne
And rycht tōward his trist is gāne.

   Þē kyng went furth, wrāth and angrȳ,
Mēnand his man full tendirlȳ,   20
And hēid his way all hym allāne,
And richt tōward þē hōuss is gāne
Quhār hē set trist tō mēte his men.
It wes weill lāt of nycht be þen ;
Hē cōm soyn in þē hōuss, and fānd   25
Þē gud wīf on þē bynk sytand.
Scho askit hym soyn quhat hē wes,
And quhene² hē cōm, and quhār hē gais.
'A travalland man, dāme,' said hē,
'That travalys heir throu þē cuntrē.'   30
Scho said, 'All þat travaland ere,
For saik of āne, ār welcom hēre.'

¹ þai.   ² quhyne.

Thē kyng said, 'Gud dāme, quhat is hē
Þat garris ȝow̄ hāve sic specialtē
Till men þat travalis?' 'Schir, perfay,
Quod þē gud wīf, 'Ī sall ȝow̄ say;
Gud Kyng Robert þē Bruce is hē,   5
Þat is rycht lǫrd of þis cuntrē.
His fayis hym hāldis now̄ in thrāng,
Bot Ī thynk tō sē, ǫr oucht lāng,
Hym lǫrd and kyng ǫvr al þē lānd,
Þat nā fayis sall hym withstānd.'   10
'Dāme, lufis þou̅ hym sā weill?' said hē.
'Ȝhā, Schir,' scho said, 'sā God mē sē.'
'Dāme,' said hē, 'lǫ, hym hēre þē bȳ,
For Ī am hē.' 'Sā ȝhē suthlȳ?'
'Ȝhā, certis, dāme.' 'And quhār ār gāne   15
Ȝou̅r men, quhen ȝē ar þus allāne?'
'At þis tȳme, dāme, I hāve nǫ mā.'
Scho said, 'It may nǫ wiss bē swā;
I hāve twā sonnys wicht and hārdȳ,
Þai sall becum ȝou̅r men in hȳ.'   20

As scho devīsit, þai hāve dōne;
His sworn men becōm þai sōne.
Þē wīf gart soyn hym syt[1] and ęt;
Bot hē had schort quhīl at þę męt
Sittyn, quhen hē herd gręt stampyng   25
Abou̅t þē hou̅s; þan, but lettyng,
Þai stert up þē hou̅s tō defend.
Bot soyn eftir þē kyng has kend
Jāmes of Dou̅glas; þan wes hē blīth,
And bad oppyn þē dures swīth,   30
And þai cōm in, all at þai wāre.
Schir Edward þē Bruce wes þāre,

[1] set.

And Jāmes alsuā [1] of Dōuglas,
Þat wes eschāpit frā þē chas
And with þē kyngis brōþir met.
Syne tō þē trist þat þāme wes set
Þai sped þāme with þair cumpanȳ,   5
That wār āne hundreth and fyftȳ,
And quhen at þai has seyn þē kyng,
Þai wār joyfull of þair mētyng,
And askit hōw hē eschāpit was;
And hē þaim [2] tāld all haill þē cass,   10
Hōw þē fiff men hym presit fast,
And hōw hē [3] throu þē wattir past,
And hōw hē met þē thēvis thrē,
And hōw [4] hē slēpand slayn suld bē,
Quhen hē wāknyt [5] throu Goddis grāce;   15
And hōw his fostyr brōþir was [6]
Slayne, hē tāld þāme all hāleȳ.
Þan lovyt þai God all comōnlȳ,
Þat þair lōrd wes eschāpit swā.

[1] als.   [2] hym; þaim, MS. E.   [3] ye.   [4] how, not in MS.
[5] valknyt.   [6] ded wes; next line then reads, ' þus all he tald þame
halely.'   MS. E reads 'was slayne.'

THE SOUTHERN DIALECT, INCLUDING KENTISH

I. THE POEMA MORALE, OR MORAL ODE

Icʜ æm elder þen ich wes ā wintre and ā lǫre;
Ic wǣlde mǫre þanne ic düde, mī wit āh tō bēn mǫre.
Wēl lānge ic habbe chīld ibēon ā wēorde and [1] ęch ā dęde;
Þęh ic bēo ā wintre ēaɪ̈. tō [2] ȝyng Ī eom ā ręde.
Unnüt līf ic habb ilæd, and ȝyet mē þincþ ic lęde;   5
Þanne ic mē biþenche, wēl sǫre ic mē adręde.
Męst al þat ic habbe ydōn ys īdelnesse and chilce;
Wēl late ic habbe mē biþoht, būte mē God dō milce.
Fele ȳdele wōrd ic habbe iqueden, syðð̄en ic speke cūþe,
And fale ȝunge dęde idō þe mē ofþinchet nūþe.   10
Al tō lōme ic habbe agült, ā weorche and ęc ā wōrde;
Al tō müchel ic habbe ispend, tō lītel yleid an hōrde.
Męst al þet mē līcede ǣr, nū hit mē mislīcheð [3];
Þe mychel folȝeþ his ywil, him sülfne hē biswīkeð.
Ich mihte habbe bet idōn, hadde ic þǫ yselþe;   15
Nū ic wolde ac ic ne mei, for ēlde ne for unhelþe;
Ȳlde me is bistolen on ǣr ic hit awyste;
Ne mihte ic isēon before mē for smēche ne for miste.
Ǣrwe wē bēoþ tō dōne gōd, and tō yfele al tō þrīste;
Mǫre æie stent man of manne, þanne hym dō of Crīste.   20
Þe wēl ne dēþ þē hwīle hē mei, wēl oft hit hym scæl ruwen;
Þænne hȳ mowen sculen and rīpen þęr hī ǣr sēowen.
Dōn ęc tō gōde wet ȝē muȝe, þē [4] hwīle ȝē būþ ā līfe;
Ne hopīe nǫ man tō müchel tō chīlde ne tō wīfe;

---

[1] &, as often.   [2] tu.   [3] mislichet.   [4] þa.

Þe him selve forȝüt for wīfe, ǭðer for chīlde,
Hē sceal cume an üvele stede, būte him God bēo mīlde.
Sēnde ǣch sum gōd biforen him, þē hwīle hē mei to heovene¹;
Betere is ān elmesse bifore þenne bēon æfter seovene.
Ne bēo þē lēovre þene þē sülf, þī mei ne ðī māȝe,   5
Sot is ðe is ōðres mannes frēond betre þene his āȝe.
Ne hopīe wīf tō hire were, ne wer tō his wīfe;
Bēo for him sülve ǣvrich man, þē hwīle hē bēo alīve
Wīs is þe him sülfne biþencð, þē hwīle hē mōte libbe,
For sōne wülleð him forȝite þē fremde and þē sibbe.   10
Þe wēl ne dēþ þē hwīle hē mei, ne sceal hē hwenne hē wolde;
Manīes mannes sāre iswinch habbeð oft unhōlde.
Ne scolde nān man dōn ā fürst, ne slāwen wēl tō dōne;
For manī man bihāteð wēl, þe hit forȝitet sōne.
Þē man ðe siker wüle bēon tō habbe Godes blisse,   15
Dō wēl him sülf þē hwīle hē mei, ðen haveð hē mid iwisse.
    Þēs rīche men wēneð bēo siker, þurh walle end þurh diche;
Hē dēð his ā sikere stede, þe sent tō heveverīche;
For ðę̄r ne ðierf bēon ofdrȩ̄d of fūre ne of þēove;
Þę̄r ne mei hī binime ðē lāðe ne ðē lēove;   20
Þar ne þærf hē habbe kare of wȳfe ne of chīlde.
Þider wē sēndet and sülf bereð tō līte and tō sēlde;
Þider wē scolden draȝen²and dōn wēl oft and wēl ȝelōme,
For þę̄r ne sceal me us naht binime, mid wrancwīse dōme.
Þider wē scolden ȝeorne draȝen, wolde ȝē mē ilēve,   25
For ðę̄re ne mei hit binimen ēow þē kīng ne sē irēve.
Þet betste þet wē hedde, þüder wē scolde sēnde,
For þę̄r wē hit mihte fīnde eft, and habbe būte ēnde.
Hē þe hēr dēð enī gōd, for habbe Godes āre,
Eal hē hit sceal fīnde ðę̄r, and hundredfȩalde māre.   30
Þē ðe ehte wile hȩalden wēl, þē hwīle hē mei is³ wȩalden,
ȝive is for Godes luve, þenne dēð hē is wēl ihȩalden.

¹ hevene.   ² draȝan.   ³ his, as twice in next line.

Ūre iswinch and ūre tilðe is oft iwuned tō swīnden ;
Ac ðet wē dōð for Godes luve, eft wē hit sculen afīnden.
Ne sceal nān üvel bēon unboht, ne nān gōd unforȝolde ;
Üvel wē dōð eal tō michel, and gōd lesse þenne wē scolde.
Þē ðe mę̄st dēð nū tō gōde, and ðē þe lę̄st tō lāðe,
Æiþer tō lītel and tō michel sceal ðinche eft him bāðe.   5
Þę̄r me sceal ūre weorkes weȝen beforen Hevekinge,
And ȝieven us ūre swinches līen, æfter ūre ę̄arninge.
Ę̄vre ę̄lc man mid þān ðe haveð mei biggen heverīche,
Þē ðe māre hefð and ðē þe lesse, bāþe mei ilīche ;
Eal sę̄ mid his penīe sę̄ ðē ōðer mid his pūnde ;   10
Þet is [1] ðē [2] wunderlukeste ware ðe ænī man ǣvre fūnde.
And þē ðe māre ne mei dōn mid his gōd iþanke,
Eal sę̄ wēl sę̄ ðe haveð gōldes feale manke [3] ;
And oft God kan māre þanc ðan ðe him ȝivet lesse ;
Eal his weorkes and his weies is milce and rihtwīsnesse.   15
Līte lāc is Gode lēof, ðe cumeð of gōde iwille,
And ę̄ðlę̄te müchel ȝive ðenne ðē heorte is ille.
Hevene and ēorðe hē oversihð [4], his ę̄ȝen bēoð swǭ brihte ;
Sunne, mōne, dei, and fūr bið þūstre tōȝę̄anes his lihte.
Nis him naht forhole ni hūd, swā michel bið his mihte ;   20
Nis hit nā swā dūrne idōn, ne ā swā þūstre nihte.
Hē wāt hwet dēð and ðenchet ealle quike wihte,
Nis nā hlāvord swilc sę̄ is Crīst, nā kīng swilch ūre Drihte.
Heovene and ēorðe and eal þet is biloken is in his hande,
Hē dēð eal þet [2] his wille is, ā wetere and ā lande.   25
Hē makede fisces in ðē sę̄, and fuȝeles in ðē lüfte ;
Hē wīt and wę̄aldeð ealle ðing and hē scōp ealle ȝesceafte.
Hē is ōrd abūten ōrde, and ēnde abūten ēnde ;
Hē āne is ǣvre en ę̄lche stede, wēnde þę̄r þū wēnde ;
Hē is buven us and bineoðen, biforen and bihīnde ;   30
Þē ðe Godes wille dēð, eiðer hē mei him fīnde.
Ę̄lche rūne hē ihūrð and hē wāt ealle dę̄de ;

---

[1] his.   [2] ð, as often.   [3] marke.   [4] ove sihð.

Hē ðurhsihð ęalches mannes ðanc whet sceal us tō ręde.
Wē þe brekeð Godes hęse, and gültet swā ilōme,
Hwet scule wē seggen ǭðer dōn æt ðē müchele dōme?
Þā ða luveden unriht, and üvel līf ledde,
Hwet scule hī segge ǭðer dōn ðęr engles bēoð ofdredde?   5
Hwet scule wē beren biforen us [1], mid hwān scule wē cwēmen [2],
Wē þe nævre gōd ne düden þē hevenlīche dēmen?
Þęr scule bēon dēofles swā vele ðe wülleð us forwrēȝen;
Nabbeð hī nāþing forȝyte of eal þat hī isęȝen.
Eal þet wē misdüde hēr, hit wülleð cūðe ŀǭre,   10
Būten wē habbe hit ibet ðē hwīle wē hēr węre.
Eal hī habbet an heore iwrite þet wē misdüde hēre;
Þęh wē hī nüste ne isęȝen [3] hī węren ūre ivēre.
Hwet sculen hōrlinges dō, þē swikene, þē forsworene?
Wī swā fele bēoð iclüped, swā fewe bēoð icorene?   15
Wī, hwī węre hī biȝite, tō hwān węre hī iborene,
Þe scule bēon tō dīeðe idēmd and ȝvre mā forlorene?
Ęlch man sceal him ðęr biclüpīen and ęch sceal him dēmen;
His āȝe weorc and his iðanc tō witnesse he sceal tēmen;
Ne mei him nā man eal swā wēl dēmen nᴜ swā rihte,   20
For nān ni cnāwað him swā wēl būte āne Drihte.
Ęlc man wāt him sülf betst, his weorch and his iwille;
Hē ðe lęst wāt hē seið ofte męst, ðē ðe hit wāt eal is stille.
Nis nān witnesse eal sę müchel sę mannes āȝe heorte;
Hwāsę segge þet hē bēo hāl, him self wāt betst his smeorte.   25
Ęlc man sceal him sülf dēmen tō dīeðe ǭðer tō līve;
Þē witnesse of his weorc tō ōðer, ðis him sceal drīve.
Eal ðet ȝvre ęlc man hafð idō süððe hē cōm tō manne,
Swilc hit sī ā bōc iwriten hē scal iðenche ðenne;
Ac Drihte ne dēmð nānne man æfter his biginninge,   30
Ac al his līf sceal bēo swich sę büð his ēndinge;
Ac ȝif þē ēnde is üvel eal hit is üvel, and gōd ȝif gōd is þenne.
God ȝyve þet ūre ēnde bēo gōd and wit þet hē us lenne.

---

[1] us, not in MS.   [2] cweman.   [3] ni seȝen.

Þē man þe nele dō nā gōd, ne nẹvre gōd līf læden,
Ǣr dīeð and dōm cume æt his dure hē mei sāre adrẹden
Þet hē ne muȝe ðenne bidde āre, for hit itīt ilōme ;
Forþī [1] hē is wīs ðe bēot and bẹat, and bit beforen dōme.
Þenne dẹað is æt his dure, wēl late hē biddeð āre ;   5
Wēl late hē lẹteð üvel weorc þe hit ne mei dōn nā māre.
Sünne lẹt þē and þū naht hīre, þanne þū is [2] ne miht dōn nā māre [3];
Forþī, hē is sot þe swā abīt tō habbe Godes āre [4].
Þẹhwheðer wē hit ilēveð wēl, for Drihte sülf hit sẹde,
Ā whilche tīme sẹ ẹvre ðē man ofðinchet his misdẹde,   10
Ọ̄ðer later ọ̄ðer raðe, milce hē sceal imēten ;
Ac ðē þe nafð naht ibet, wēl müchel hē sceal bēten.
Manī man seið, ' Hwā recþ of pīne ðe sceal habbe ēnde?
Ne bidde ich nā bet bēo ilūsd ā dōmesdei of bēnde? '
Lütel wāt hē hwet is pīne, and lītel hē icnāweð,   15
Hwilc hẹte is ðẹr sāule wuneð, hū biter wīnde þẹr blāweð;
Hedde hē ibēon ðẹr ānne dei, ọ̄ðer twā bare tīde,
Nolde hē for æl middenẹard ðe ðridde þẹre abīde.
Þet habbet isẹd þe cōme ðanne, þe it [5] wiste mid iwisse,
Üvel is pīnīe seove ȝẹr for seove nihtes blisse,   20
End ūre blisse þe ēnde hafð for ēndelīese pīne.
Betere is wọ̄rī weter idrunke þene atter imēng mid wīne ;
Swūnes brẹde is swüðe swēte, swā is of wīlde dēore,
Ac al tō dūre hē hī biȝð ðe ȝifð þẹrfore his [5ª] sweore.
Ful wāmbe mei lihtlīche speken of hunger and of festen [6];   25
Swā mei of pīne þe naht nāt hū pīne sceal alẹsten.
Hedde he is [7] afānded sume stūnde, hē wolde eal segge ōðer;
Ẹ̄ðlẹte him wẹre wīf and chīld, suster, and feder and brōðer;
Ẹvre hē wolde inne wā hēr and inne wāwe wunīen
Wið ðān þe mihte hellepīne biflēon and biscunīen.   30
Ẹ̄ðlẹte him wẹre eal woruldwele and eal ēorðlīche [8] blisse.
For tō ðē müchele mürcðe cume ðis mürhðe mid iwisse.

---

[1] ði ; cf. l. 8.   [2] þus.   [3] no more.   [4] hore ; couplet from Egerton E.
[5] þ.   [5ª] is.   [6] and festen.   [7] his.   [8] eordliche.

II. ARTHUR'S LAST BATTLE—FROM LAYAMON'S BRUT

Þā cōm þēr in āre tīden   ān oht mon rīden,
And brohte tīdinge   Arthūre þān kīnge
From Mōdrēde [1] his suster sune ;   Arðūre hē wes wilcume
For hē wēnde þat hē brohte   boden swīðe gōde.
Arðūr lai alle lǫnge niht   and spac wið þēne ȝeonge cniht ;   5
Swā naver nulde hē him sügge   sōð hū hit fērde.
Þā hit wes dæi ā marȝen   and duȝeðe gon stūrīen,
Arðūr þā up arās   and strehte his ærmes ;
Hē arās up and adūn sat   swülc hē wēore swīðe sēoc.
Þā axede hine ān væir cniht,   'Lāverd, hū havest þū ivaren
    tōniht ? '   10
    Arðūr þā andswarede—   ā mōde him wes unēðe—
' Tōniht ā mīne slēpe,   þēr ich læi on būre,
Mē imætte ā sweven ;   þērvore ich ful sārī æm.
Mē imętte þat mon mē hōf   uppen āre halle ;
Þā halle ich gon bistrīden   swülc ich wolde rīden ;   15
Alle þā lǫnd þa ich āh,   alle ich þēr oversah,
And Walwain sat bivoren mē,   mī swēord hē bar an hǫnde.
Þā cōm Mōdrēd [2] faren þēre   mid unimēte volke ;
Hē bar an his hǫnde   āne wīax strǫnge ;
Hē bigon tō hewene   hardlīche swīðe ;   20
And þā pǫstes forhēou alle   þa hēolden up þā halle.
Þēr ich iseh Wenhevēr ēke,   wimmonen lēofvest mē ;
Al þēre müche hallerōf   mid hire hǫnden [3] hēo tōdrōh.
Þā halle gon tō hælden,   and ich hæld tō grūnden,

---

[1] Moddrede, as often, but less commonly than the form with one d.
[2] Moddred.   [3] hondeden.

Þat mī riht ærm tōbrac;   þā seide Mōdrẹd 'Have þat.'
Adūn vēol þā halle   and [1] Walwain gon tō valle,
And fēol ā þẹre ēorðe;   his ærmes brẹken [2] beine.
And ich igrāp mī swēord lēofe   mid mīre leoft hǫnde,
And smæt of Mōdrẹdis hafd   þat hit wǫnd ā þēne vẹld;   5
And þā quēne ich al tōsnaðde   mid dēore mīne swēorde [3],
And seoððen [4] ich hēo adūn [5] sette   in āne swarte pütte;
And al mī volc rīche   sette tō flẹme,
Þat nüste ich under Crīste   whar hēo bicumen wẹoren.
Būten mī seolf ich gon [6] atstǫnden   uppen āne wǫlden,   10
And ich þẹr wǫndrīen agon   wīde ȝēond þān mōren,
Þẹr ich isah grīpes   and grislīche fuȝeles.
Þā cōm ān güldene lēo   līðen over dūne,
Dēoren swīðe hēnde   þa ūre Drihten makede [7].
Þā lēo mē orn foren tō   and ivēng mē bī þān midle,   15
And forð hire gun ȝeongen   and tō þẹre sǣ wēnde;
And ich isæh þā [8] ūðen   ī þẹre sǣ driven,
And þē lēo ī þān vlōde iwende   wīde mid mē [9] seolve.
Þā wit ī sǣ cōmen,   þā ūðen mē hire binōmen;
Cōm þẹr ān fisc līðe   and fereden mē tō lǫnde;   20
Þā wes al ich wẹt   and wērī of sorȝen and sēoc.
Þā gon ich iwakīen,   swīðe ich gon tō quakīen;
Þā gon ich tō bivīen   swülc ich al für burne.
And swā ich habbe al niht   of mīne swevene [10] swīðe iþoht,
For ich wāt [11] tō iwisse   agān is al mī blisse;   25
For ā tō mīne līve   sorȝen ich mōt drīȝe.
Wāle, þat ich nabbe hēre   Wenhavēr mīne quēne!'
    Þā andswarede þē cniht,   'Lāverd þū havest unriht;
Ne sculde me navere sweven   mid sorȝen arecchen.
Þū ært þē riccheste mon   þa rixleoð on lǫnden,   30
And þē alre wīseste   þe wuneð under weolcne.

---

[1] &, as occasionally.   [2] brekeen.   [3] sweorede.   [4] seoððen.
[5] adum.   [6] gond.   [7] make.   [8] þæ.   [9] me, not in MS.
[10] sweuenene.   [11] what.

Ȝif hit wēore ilimpe,   swā nülle hit ūre Drihte,
Þat Mōdrēd þīre suster sune   hafde þīne quēne inume,
And al þī kinelīche lǫnd   isæt an his āȝere hǫnd
Þe þū him bitahtest   þā þū tō Rōme þohtest,
And hē hafde al þus idō   mid his swikedōme,   5
Þen[1] ȝēt þū mihtest þē awreken   wurðlīche mid wēpnen,
And æft þī lǫnd hālden   and wālden þīne lēoden,
And þīne fēond fallen   þe þē üfel unnen,
And slǣn heom alle clane   þet þēr no bilaven nāne.'
    Arðūr þā andswarede,   aðelest alre kīnge,   10
' Lǫnge bið ǣvere   þat no wēne ich nǣvere,
Þat ǣvere Mōdrēd mī mæi,   þat mon is mē lēofvest[2],
Wolde mē biswīken   for alle mīne rīchen,
No Wenhavēr mī quēne   wākīen on þonke ;
Nülleð hit biginne   for nāne weorldmonne.'   15
    Æfne þān wōrde forðriht   þā andswarede þē cniht :
' Ī sügge þē sōð, lēofe kīng,   for ich æm þīn underling,
Þus hafeð Mōdrēd idōn ;   þīne quēne hē hafeð ifōn,
And þī wünlīche lǫnd isæt   an his āȝere hǫnd.
Hē is kīng and hēo is quēn[3] ;   of þīne küme nis nā wēne, 20
For no wēneð hēo navere tō sōðe   þat þū cumen aȝain from Rōme.
Ich æm þīn āȝen mon,   and iseh þisne swikedōm ;
And ich æm icumen tō þē seolven   sōð þē tō süggen.
Mīn hafved bēo tō wedde   þat isæid ich þē habbe
Sōð būten lēse   of lēofen þīre quēne,   25
And of Mōdrēde þīre suster sune,   hū hē hafveð Brütlǫnd þē
        binume.'
    Þā sæt hit al stille   in Arðūres halle ;
Þā wes þēr sǣrīnesse[4]   mid sēle þān kīnge ;
Þā wēoren Brüttisce men   swīðe unbālde vor þǣn.
Þā ümbe stünde   stefne þēr stürede ;   30
Wīde me mihte ihēren   Brütten ibēren,

---

[1] þe.   [2] half line supplied from text B, but with the forms of A.
[3] que ; probably intended for quē=quen.   [4] særinæsse.

And gunne tō tellen   ā feole cünne spellen
Hū hēo wolden fordēme   Mōdrẹd and þā quēne,
And al þat [1] moncün fordōn   þe mid Mōdrẹd hēolden.

  Arðūr þā cleopede,   hēndest alre Brütte,
' Sitteð adūn stille,   cnihtes inne halle,   5
And ich ēou telle wülle   spelles uncūðe.

Nū tōmærȝe þenne hit dæi bið,   and Drihten hine sēnde,
Forð ich wülle būȝe   in tōward Brüttaine ;
And Mōdrẹd [2] ich wülle slān [3]   and þā quēn forberne,
And alle ich wülle fordōn   þa biluveden þēn swikedōm.   10
And hēr ich bilẹofven wülle   mē lēofvest monne,
Howel minne lēofve mæi   hexst of mīne cünne,
And half mīne vērde   ich bilæfven ā þissen ærde
Tō hālden al þis kinelọnd   þa ich habbe ā mīre họnd.
And þenne þās þīng bēoð alle idōne,   aȝān ich wülle tō Rōme, 15
And mī wünlīche lọnd bitæche [4]   Walwaine mīne mæie,
And ivōrþe mī bēot seoððe [5]   bī mīne bare līfe ;
Scullen alle mīne fēond   væisīð [6] makeȝe.'

  Þā stōd him up Walwain   þat wes Arðūres mæi,
And þās wōrd saide ;   þē ēorl wes abolȝe :   20
' Ældrihten Godd,   dōmes wāldend,
Al middelærdes mūnd,   whī is hit iwurðen
Þat mī brōðer Mōdrẹd   þis morð hafveð itimbbred ?
Ah tōdæi ich atsake hine   hēre bivoren þissere duȝeðe,
And ich hine fordēmen wülle   mid Drihtenes wille ;   25
Mī seolf ich wülle hine anhōn   haxte alre warīen ;
Þā quēne ich wülle mid Goddes laȝe   al mid horsen tōdraȝe.
For ne bēo ich navere blīðe   þā wīle hā [7] bēoð alīve,
And þat ich habbe mīne æm   awræke mid þān beste [8].'
Brüttes þā answarede   mid bāldere stefne,   30
' Al ūre wẹpnen sünden ȝarewe ;   nū tōmarȝen wē scullen varen.'
  Ā marȝen þat hit dæi wes,   and Drihten hine senden,

---

[1] Þ, as occasionally.   [2] moddred.   [3] scaln.   [4] bitatæche.
[5] seodðe.   [6] wæisið.   [7] a.   [8] berste.

Arðūr[1] vorð him wende   mid aðelen his folke;
Half hē hit bilǣfde,   and half hit forð ladde.
Forð hē wende þurh þat lǭnd   þat hē cōm tō Whitsǫnd;
Scipen hē hǣfde sōne,   monie and wel idōne;
Ah fēowertēne niht fulle   þēre lǣi þā vērde   5
Þēos wederes abīden,   wīndes bidēlde.

  Nū was sum forcūð kempe   in Arðūres fērde ;
Anǣn swā hē dēmen iherde   of Mōdrēdes dēðe[1a],
Hē nōm his swein aneoste   and sende tō þissen lǫnde,
And sende wōrd Wenhavēren   heoū hit was iwurðen,   10
And hū Arðūr wes on vōre   mid mūclere fērde,
And hū hē wolde taken on,   and al hū hē wolde dōn.
Þā quēne cōm tō Mōdrēd   þat was hire lēofvest monnes
And tālde him tīdende   of Arðūre þān kīnge,
Hū hē wolde taken an,   and al hū hē wolde dōn.   15
Mōdrēd[2] nōm his sǫnde   and sende tō Sexlǫnd
After Childrīche—   þē kīng wes swīðe rīche—
And bǣd hine cume tō Brütaine;   þērof hē brūke sculde.
Mōdrēd[2] bad Childrīche,   þēne strǫnge and þēne rīche,
Wīde[3] sēnden sǫnde   ā fēouwer half Sexlǫnde,   20
And bēoden þā cnihtes   alle þat hēo biȝeten mihte,
Þat hēo cōmen sōne   tō þissen kinedōme[4],
And hē wolde Childrīche   ȝeoven of his rīche
Al biȝēonde þēre[5] Humbre,   for hē him scolde helpe
Tō fihten wið his ǣme,   Arðūre þān[6] kīnge.   25
  Childrīch bēh sōne   intō Brütlǫnde.
Þā Mōdrēd hafde his fērde   isomned of monnen,
Þā wēoren þēre itālde   sixtī þūsende
Herekempen harde   of hēðene volke,
Þa hēo wēoren icumen hidere   for Arðūres[7] hærme,   30
Mōdrēd tō helpen,   forcūðest monnen.
Þā þē vērde wes isōme   of ǣlche moncünne

---

[1] arðu.   [1a] ðeðe.   [2] modrǣd.   [3] weide.   [4] kinedone.   [5] þerere.
[6] arðuren, but cf. l. 14 and often.   [7] ardures.

Þā hēo wẹoren þẹr on hẹpe   ān hundred[1] þūsende,
Hẹðene and Cristene,   mid Mōdrẹde kīnge.

Arður lai at Whitsǫnd;   fēouwertēne niht him þuhte tō lǫng.
And al Mōdrẹd wüste   wat Arður þǣr wolde;
Ælche dai him cōmen sǫnde   from þās kīnges hīrede.   5
Þā ilomp hit an ǫne tīme   müchel rein him gon rīne,
And þē[2] wīnd him gon wēnde   and stōd of þān æstēnde;
And Arður tō scipe fūsde   mid alle his vērde,
And hehte þat his scipmen   brohten hine tō Romenel[3],
Þẹr hē þohte up wēnde   intō þissen lǫnde.   10
Þā[2] hē tō þẹre havene cōm,   Mōdrẹd him wes avorn on[4];
Ase þē dæi gon lihten[5]   hēo bigunnen tō fihten
Alle þēne lǫnge dæi;   monī mon þẹr dẹd læi.
Summe hī fuhten ā lǫnde,   summe bī þān strǫnde;
Summe hēo letten ūt of scipen   scerpe gāren scrīþen.   15
Walwain biforen wende   and þēne wæi rūmde,
And slōh þẹr aneuste   þeines elleovene;
Hē slōh Childrīches sune,   hē was þẹr mid his fader icume.
Tō rest ēode þā sunne;   wæ wes þā monnen.

Þẹr wes Walwain afslæȝe,   and idōn of līfedaȝe,   20
Þurh ān ēorle Sexisne—   særī wurðe his sāule.
Þā wes Arður særī   and sorhful an heorte forþī;
And þās wōrd bodede,   ricchest alre Brütte:
'Nū ich ileosed habbe   mīne sweines lēofe.
Ich wüste bī mīne swevene   whæt sorȝen mē wẹoren ȝeveðe.   25
Islaȝen is Āngel þē kīng   þe wes mīn āȝen dēorling,
And Walwaine mī suster sune—   wā is mē þat ich was mon
    iboren.
Up nū of scipen bilīve,   mīne bēornes ohte.'
Æfne þān wōrde   wenden tō fihte
Sixtī þūsend anǫn   sēlere kempen,   30
And brẹken Mōdrẹdes trume,   and wēl nẹh him seolve wes inome.
Mōdrẹd bigon tō flēon   and his folc after tēon;

---

[1] hunddred.   [2] þæ   [3] romerel.   [4] auorn on.   [5] lihte.

Fluȝen vēondlīche,   feldes beoveden ęke;
ȝurren þā stānes   mid þān blōdstręmes.
Þęr węore al þat fiht idōn,   ah þat niht tō raðe cōm;
ȝif þā niht nęore,   islaȝen hī węoren alle.
Þē niht heom tōdęlde   ȝeond slades and ȝeond¹ dūnen;   5
And Mōdręd swā vorð cōm   þat hē wes at Lundene.
Iherden þā burhweren   hū hit was al ifaren,
And warnden him inȝeong   and alle his folke.
Mōdręd þeone wende   tōward Winchestre²,
And hēo hine undervēngen   mid alle his monnen.   10
And Arður after wende   mid alle his mahte,
Þat hē cōm tō Winchestre   mid müchelre vērde,
And þā burh al birǣd;   and Mōdręd þęrinne abēod.
   Þā Mōdręd isǣh   þat Arður him wes swā nęh,
Ofte hē hine biþohte   wæt hē dōn mahte.   15
Þā ā þęre ilke niht   hē hehte his cnihtes alle,
Mid alle heore iwępnen   ūt of burhȝe wēnden,
And sǣide þat hē weolde   mid fihte þęr atstǫnden.
Hē bihehte þęre burȝewere   aver māre frēo laȝe,
Wið þān þā hēo him heolpen   at hęȝere nēoden.   20
Þā hit wes dæiliht   ȝaru þā wes heore fiht.
   Arður þat bihedde,   þē kīng wes abolȝe;
Hē lette bēmen blāwen   and bēonnen men tō fihten;
Hē hehte alle his þeines,   and aðele his cnihte
Sōn somed tō fihten,   and his vēond³ avallen,   25
And þē burh alle fordōn,   and þat burhfolc ahōn.
Hēo tōgadere stōpen   and stürnlīche fuhten.
   Mōdręd þā þohte   what hē dōn mihte;
And hē düde þęre,   alse hē düde elleswhare,
Swikedōm mid þān mǣste;   for avere hę düde unwraste;   30
Hē biswāc his ivēren   bivoren Winchestren,
And lette him tō cleopīen   his lēofeste anān cnihtes,
And his lēoveste frēond alle   of allen his folke,

---

¹ ȝeon.   ² winchastre.   ³ veod.

And bistal from þān fihte—   þē fēond hine āȝe—
And þat folc gōde lette   al þēr forwurðe.
Fuhten alle dæi;   wēnden þat heore lāverd þēr læi,
And wēore heom aneoste   at müchelere nēode.
Þā hēold hē þēne wai   þat tōuward Hamtone lai,   5
And hēolde tōuward havene,   forcūðest hæleðe;
And nōm alle þā scipen   þa þēr oht wēore,
And þā stēormen alle   tō þān scipen nēode [1],
And fērden intō Cornwalen,   forcūðest kīngen ā þān daȝen.
    And Arður Winchestre,   þā burh bilai wēl faste;   10
And al þat moncün ofslōh—   þēr wes sorȝen inōh—
Þā ȝeonge and þā ālde,   alle hē aquālde.
Þā þat folc wes al dēd,   þā burh al forswēlde,
Þā lette hē mid alle   tōbreken þā walles alle.
Þā wes hit itīmed þēre   þat Merlin seide whīle: 15
' Ærm wurðest þū Winchæstre,   þæ ēorðe þē scal forswalȝe.'
Swā Merlin sæide,   þē wīteȝe wes mære.
    Þā quēn [2] læi inne Eouwerwīc,   næs hēo nævere swā sārlīc;
Þat wes Wenhavēr þā quēne,   færȝest wimmonne.
Hēo iherde süggen   sōðere [3] wōrden,   20
Hū ofte Mōdrēd flah,   and hū Arður hine bibah;
Wā wes hire þēre whīle   þat hēo wes on līfe.
Ūt of Eouerwīke   bī nihte hēo iwende,
And tōuward Karliūn tühte   swā swīðe swā hēo mahte.
Þider hēo brohten bī nihte   of hire cnihten tweiȝe;   25
And me hire hafd biwēfde   mid āne hālī rifte,
And hēo wes þēr münechene,   karefullest wīfe.
Þā nüsten men of þēre quēne   war hēo bicumen wēore,
No feole ȝēre seoððe   nüste hit mon tō sōðe,
Whaðer hēo wēore on dēðe,   and hū hēo henne wende [4],   30
Þā hēo hire seolf wēore   isunken in þē watere.
    Mōdrēd wes ī Cornwale   and somnede cnihtes feole;
Tō Īrlǫnde hē sende   aneoste his sǫnde;

---

[1] neodde.   [2] qñe.   [3] soððere.   [4] half line from B.

Tō Sexlǫnde hē sende   aneouste his sǫnde;
Tō Scotlǫnde hē sende   aneouste his sǫnde;
Hē hehten heom tō cume alle anān   þat wolde lǫnd habben,
Ꝺðer seolver ǫðer gōld,   ǫðer[1] ahte ǫðer[1] lǫnd;
On ælchere wīsen   hē warnede hine seolven,   5
Swā dēð ælc witer mon   þā nēode cumeð uvenan
    Arðūr þat iherde,   wrāðest kīnge,
Þat Mōdrẹd wæs ī Cornwale   mid müchele monweorede,
And þẹr wolde abīden   þat Arðūr cōme rīden.
Arðūr sende sǫnde   ȝēond al his kinelǫnde,   10
And tō cumen alle hehte   þat quic wes on lǫnde,
Þā tō vihte oht wẹoren,   wẹpnen tō beren;
And whāswā[1a] hit forsẹte   þat þē kīng hēte,
Þē kīng hine wolde ā fōlden   quic[2] al forbernen.
Hit lǣc tōward hīrede   folc unimẹte,   15
Rīdinde and ganninde   swā þē rein falleð[3] adūne.
Arðūr fōr tō Cornwale   mid unimẹte[4] fērde.
Mōdrẹd þat iherde,   and him tōȝeines hēolde
Mid unimẹte folke,—   þẹr wẹore monīe væie.
Uppen þẹre Tambre[5]   hēo tühten tōgadere;   20
Þā stüde hatte Camelfōrd,   evermāre ilast þat ilke wēorde;
And at Camelfōrde wes isomned   sixtī þūsend,
And mā þūsend þẹrtō;   Mōdrẹd wes heore ælder.
    Þā þiderwārd gon rīde   Arðūr þē rīche,
Mid unimẹte folke,   væie þah hit wẹore.   25
Uppe þẹre Tambre   hēo tühte tōsomne;
Heven heremarken,   hālden tōgadere;
Luken swēord lǫnge,   leiden ō þē helmen;
Für ūt sprengen;   speren brastlīen;
Scēldes gonnen scanen;   scaftes tōbrẹken;   30
Þẹr faht al tōsomne   folc unimẹte.
Tambre wes on flōde   mid unimẹte blōde;
Mon ī þān fihte nǫn þẹr ne mihte   ikennen nenne kempe,

---

[1] oder.   [1a] wahswa.   [2] quid.   [3] rim falled; B. ren falleð.   [4] unite.   [5] **Tanbre.**

Nǭ hwā düde würse nǭ hwā bet,   swā þat wiðe wes imenged ;
For ǣlc slōh adūn riht,   węore hē swein, węore hē cniht.
Þęr wes Mōdręd ofslaȝe   and idōn of līfdaȝe,
And alle his cnihtes   islaȝe [1] in þān fihte.
Þęr wēoren ofslaȝe   alle þā snelle,
Arðūres hīredmen [2],   hęȝe and lowe [3],
And þā Brüttes alle   of Arðūres bōrde,
And alle his fosterlinges   of feole kinerīches,
And Arðūr forwūnded   mid walspęre brāde ;
Fiftēne hē hafde   fēondlīche wūnden ;   1c
Mon mihte ī þare laste   twā glōven iþraste.
Þā nas þęr nā māre   ī þan fihte [3a] tō lāve,
Of twā hundred þūsend monnen   þa þęr leien tōhauwen,
Būten Arðūr þē kīng āne,   and of his cnihtes tweien.

   Arðūr wes forwūnded   wunder āne swīðe.   1[
Þęr tō him cōm ā cnave   þē wes of his cünne ;
Hē wes Cadōres sune,   þē ēorles of Cornwaile [4] ;
Constantīn hehte þē cnāve,   hē wes þān kīnge dēore.
Arðūr him lōkede on   þęr hē lai on fōlden,
And þās wōrd seide   mid sorhfulle heorte :   2c
'Constantīn [5] þū art wilcume,   þū węore Cadōres sone ;
Ich þē bitache hēre   mīne kinerīche,
And wite mīne Brüttes ā   tō þīnes līfes [6] ēnde,
And hāld heom alle þā laȝen   þa habbeoð istǫnden ā mīne daȝen
And alle þā laȝen gōde   þa bī Uðeres daȝen stōde.   25
And ich wülle varen tō Avalūn,   tō vairest alre maidene,
Tō Argante þęre quēne,   alven swīðe scēone,
And hēo scal [7] mīne wūnden   makīen alle isünde,
Al hāl mē makīen   mid haleweiȝe drenchen ;
And seoððe [8] ich cumen wülle   tō mīne kinerīche,   3c
And wunīen mid Brütten   mid müchelere wünne.'

---

   [1] Gap in text A ; first part of line supplied from B.   [2] Ardures heredmen.
[3] and lowe supplied from B.   [3a] fehte.   [4] Corwaile.   [5] Costǣtin.
[6] þines lifes.   [7] slal.   [8] sceðe.

Æfne þān wōrden   þēr cōm of sē wēnden
Þat wes ān sceort bāt līðen,   scēoven mid ūðen,
And twā wimmen þērinne   wunderlīche idihte;
And hēo nōmen Arðūr anān,   and aneouste hine vereden,
And softe hine adūn leiden,   and forð gunnen līðen [1].   5
Þā wes hit iwurðen   þat Merlin seide whīlen,
Þat wēore unimēte care   of Arðūres forðfare;
Brūttes ilēveð ʒēte   þat hē bēo [2] on līve,
And wunnīe [3] in Avalūn   mid fairest alre alven;
And lōkīeð evere Brūttes ʒēte   whan Arðūr cume [4] līðen.   10
Nis naver þē mon iboren,   of naver nāne būrde icoren,
Þe cunne of þān sōðe   of Arðūre süggen [5] māre;
Bute whīle wes ān wīteʒe,   Merlin [6] ihāte;
Hē bodede mid wōrde—   his quides [7] wēoren sōðe—
Þat ān Arðūr sculde ʒēte   cum Anglen tō fülste.   15

III. THE LIFE OF SAINT JULIANA

IN ūre Lāverdes luve þe is Feader of frumschaft, ant on his dēorewurðe sunes nome, ant ō þēs hālī gāstes þet [8] glīdeð of ham bāðen, alle lewede men þet understōnden ne mahen Latīnes lēdene līðin and lüstnin āne meidenes līflāde, þet is of Latīn iturnd intō Englisch þet tē līfhālī Lēfdī in heovene luvīe us þē māre, ant of þis 20 līhinde līf lēade us, wið hire erndunge þe is icoren of Crīst, intō þē ēche of heovene.

Þēos meiden ant tis martir wes Juliāne inempnet in Nichomēdes burh, ant [9] of heðene cün icumen, ant hire fleschlīche feder wes Affrican ihāten, of þē heðene mēst. Þēo þet Cristene wēren 25 ꝑerflīche hē [10] drōh ham tō dēaðe; ah hēo, as þēo þet tē heovenlīch feder luvede, lēafde al hire aldrene lahen ant bigon tō luvīen þēne

---

[1] hine līðen.   [2] bon.   [3] wunnien.   [4] cumē = cumen.   [5] sugen.
[6] Mærlin.   [7] quiðes.   [8] þ, as usual; expanded þet in accordance with ꝼorms in text.   [9] ꞇ, as often; ant only form in the piece.   [10] he not in MS.

livīende Lāverd, þē luſsum Godd þat wisseð ant wēldeð al þet is on worlde ant al þet iwraht is.

Þā wes bī þon tīme, as rēdunge[1] telleð, Maximian, þe mōdī keisēr ine Rōme, hēinde ant herīende hͤͤᵭene mawmets wið unmēð müchel hīrd and undühtī duheðe, ant fordēmde alle þēo þe on Drihtin bilēfden. Þēs Maximian luvede ān hēh mon of cünne ant ēke rīche of rente, Elewſius wes ihāten, ant wēren as feolahes þurh[1a] müche frēontſchipe. Þis meidenes feder ant hē wēren swīðe wēl tōgederes. As hē ſum chere iſeh hire ūtnume feir ant frēolīche ӡuheðe[2], hē fēlde him iwūndet þet, wiðūten lēchnunge of hire, libben hē ne mahte. Affrican wiste wēl þet hē wes frēoboren, ant þet him walde bicumen ā frēoboren bürde, ant ӡettede him his dohter; and hēo[2] wes sōne ihͦndsāld al hire unwilles. Ah hēo trüste on him þat ne trukeneð nā mon þet trüsteð trēowlīche on him, ant euch deis dei ēode tō chirche tō lēornen Godes lāre, ӡēornlīche tō witen hū hā mahte best witen hire unweommet and hire meiðhād wiðūten mān of monne. Elewſius, þe luvede hire, lͦnge hit him þuhte þet tis dēde nēre idōn þet hēo ibroht wēre þurh wedlāc tō bedde. Ah, as hā wēnde hire summes weis tō witene, ſende him tō ſeggen þet nalde hā lihten ſwā lāhe, ne nēhlēchen him for nān livīende mon, ͤr þen hē wēre under Maximian hēhest in Rōme, þet is hēhrēve. Sōne sͦ hē iherde þis, hē biӡet et tē keiſer þet hē ӡettede him rēve tō bēonne as þet hē iӡīrnd hefde; and hē, as me þā luvede, lette lͤaden him intō cure þet[3] tē rīche riden in, ant tuhen him ӡont tē tūn from strēte tō strēte. And al þē cur wes bitild þet hē wes in wið purpre, wið pal, and wið ciclatūn ant dēorewurðe clāðes, as þē þet hēh þing hefde tō hēden. And þā hē hefde þis idōn, hē ſende hire tō ſeggen þet hē hefde hire wil iwraht, ant hēo ſchulde his würchen.

Juliāne þē ͤdīe, Jēsu[4] Crīstes lēovemon, of his blisfule luve bālde hire ſeolven, ſende him tō onſwere bī ān of hire ſͦnden: 'Elewſius, wite þū hit wēl irͤadī, wraððī sͦ þū wraððī, nͦ lengre nül ich hit heolen þē; ӡef þū wült lͤaven þē lahen þet tū līst in, ant lēven in

---

Godd Feder ant in his dēorewurðe Sune ant ī þē Hālī Gāst, ich
ülle wēl neomen þē; ȝef þū nült nō, þū art wūndī of me, ant ōðer
luve sēch þē.' Þā þē rēve iherde þis hē wreððede him swīðe, ant
hire feder cleopede ant fēng on tō tellen him hū his dohter drōh
him from deie tō deie, ant efter þet hē wēnde tō habben his iwil sō   5
hā him þis wōrd süllīche sende. 'Bī þet ilke Godd,' quoð hire
feder, 'þet mē is lāð tō gremīen, bēo hit sōð þat tū seist, tō wrāðer
hēale seide hā hit, ant nū ich ülle ō grēat grome al bitēachen hire
þē tō würchen þī wil ant al þet tē wēl līkeð as mit tīn āhne.' Ant
me cleopede hire forð bivoren hire feder, ant hē fēng feire tō fōndin   10
his dohter: 'Mī dēorewurðe dohter, hwērfore vorsakest ū þī sȳ ant
tī selhðe, þē weolen ant tē wünnen þet walden awakenin ant waxen
of þī wedlāc þet ich þē tō rēade? For hē is inōh lāverd, Elewsius,
ine Rōme, ant tū maht bēon lēafdī, dohter, ȝef þū wēl wült.'
Juliāne þē ēadīe onswerede him ant seide as þēo þet ine Godd hire   15
hope hefde, ' ȝef hē wüle lēven an God Almihtī, þenne mei hē
speoken þerof [1a] ant inōh raðe spēden; ant ȝef hē nüle nawt, ne schal
wīven on mē, wīve þēr his wil is.' Þā hire feder iherde þis, þā fēng
hē tō swerien: 'Bī mī kinewurðe lāverd Apollō, ant bī mī dēore
lēafdi Dīane, þet ich müche luvīe, ȝef þū hāldest hēron ich ülle   20
lēoten dēor tōteoren ant tōlūken þē, ant ȝeoven þī flēsch tō [1]
fuheles of þē lüfte.' Juliāne him onswerede ant softelīche seide,
'Ne wēn þū nawiht, lēove feder, þet tū affēare mē swā, for Jēsu
Crīst Godes sune, þet ich on lēve ant luvīe as Lāverd lufsumest on
līve, þah ich bēo forbernd ant tōloken limēl, nül ich hēr onont   25
būhen þē nawiht.' Þā fēng eft hire feder [2] on wið olhnunge tō
fōndin ȝef hē mahte eis weis wēnden hire heorte, ant seide hire
lufsumlīche þet ne schulde hā nāne wünne lihtlīche wilnin þet hē
ne schulde wēlden, wið þet hā walde hire þonc wēnden. 'Nai,'
quoð þet meiden, 'schuld ich dōn mē tō him þat is alle dēovlen   30
bitaht ant tō ēche dēð idēmet, tō furwurðen wið him world abūten
ēnde, for his wedlākes weole ōðer for enī wünne? Forsōð, ich hit
segge, unwurð is hit mē. Ich ülle þet hē hit wite wēl, ant tū ēke

---

[1a] þrof.   [1] to supplied from Bodl. MS.   [2] feder not in MS.

mid him, þet ich am iweddet tō ān þet ich ülle trēowlīche tō hālden, ant wiðūten lēs luvīen, þe is unlīch him ant alle worldlīch men ; ne nüll ich him nowðer lēaven ne līhen for weole ne for wünne, for wā ne for wünne þet ʒē mahen dōn mē.'

Þā fēng hire feder tō[1] wreððen swīðe fērlīch, and swīðe hōker-līche freinede, ' Me hwet is hē, þēs were þet tū art tō iweddet, þet tū hāvest wiðūten mē þīne luve ilēnet, for hwām þū lētest lūtel of þet tū schuldest luvīen ?   Ne ich never þet ich wite nes wið him icnāwen.'   ' For Gode,' quoð þet meiden, ' þīn harm is þē māre ; nāwt forþi þet tū navest ofte iherd of him ʒare, þet is Jēsu, Godes sune þe, for tō lēsen moncün þet forloren schulden bēon, lette his dēorwurðe līf on rōde.   Ne ich ne seh him never, þet mē sāre for-þüncheð ; ah ich him[2] luvīe ant lēve as on lāverde, ne schal mē firsin him from nowðer dēovel ne mon.'   ' For mī līf,' quoð hire feder, ' þē schal lāðin his luve, for þū schalt bēon ibēaten mid besmes swā bittre þet tū wummon wēre schal tō wrāðer[2ᵃ] hēale iwurðen.'   ' Swā müche,' qvoð hā, ' ich iwurðe him þē lēovere, sō ich dervre þing for his luve drēhe.   Þet tī wil is, würch nū.'   Ant hē hēt hatterlīche strüpen hire steortnaket, ant bēten hire swā lüðere þet hire lēoflīche līch liðerī al ō blōde.   Ant swā hā düden sō lüðere þet tē blōd ʒēt adūn of þē ʒērden.   Ant hēo bigon tō ʒeien, ' Bēaten sō ʒē bēaten, ʒē Bēliales büdeles, ne mahe ʒē nowðer mī luve ne mīn bilēave lütlen tōward him, mī lufsum lēof, mī leovinde[3] Lāverd ; ne nüll ich lēaven ōwer rēad þēt forrēadeð ōw seolven, ne ōwer mix mawmets[4] þet bēoð þēs fēondes fetles heien ne herīen, for tēone ne for tintreow þet ʒē mahen timbrin.'   ' Nā,' quoð hē, ' is it swā ?   Hit schal sutelin sōne, for ich ülle bitēachen mislīch þī bodī tō Elewsium, þē rīche rēve ī Rōme, ant hē schal forswelten ant forrēden þē efter his[5] wille, wið alles cünnes pīnen.'   ' ʒē,' quoð þis meiden, ' þet mei Crīst wēlden, for ne mahe ʒē nawt dōn mē būte hwet hē wüle þeavīen ōw, tō müchelin mī mēde ant tē mürðe þet līð tō meiðhādes menske ; for ever sō ʒē māre merrið mē hēr, sō mī crūne bið brihtre ant fehere.   For ich ülle blīðelīche

---

[1] te.   [2] ichim.   [2ᵃ] wraðel.   [3] leowinde.   [4] mawmex.   [5] es.

drēhen evereuch derf for mī dēore Lāverdes luve, ant softe mē
biˈ euch derf hwen ich him servī, þah þū mē tō Elewsium willes
bitęache. Ne ʒeve ich for inc nowˈer, þet ʒē mē mahen harmen;
for sǫ ʒē māre mē hēr harmeþ, sǫ māre ʒē mē helpeˈ seovevāld tō
heovene. Ant ʒef ʒē mē dōˈ tō dęaˈe, hit biˈ mē dēorewurˈe, ant   5
ich schal þērþurh blīˈe bicumen intō ēndelęse blissen, ant ʒē schulen,
wrecches,—a wei, ōwer wurˈes þet ʒē iboren wēren—sinken tō
wrāˈer hęale ōw tō þē bale bitter dēope intō helle.'

Hire feder Affrican, þurh þis bittre tēone bitahte hire tō Elewsium,
þē lūˈere rēve, ant hē lette bringen hire bivoren him tō his hēh   10
seotel as hē set in dōme as rēve of þē burhe. . . . Ant set þet bale-
fule bęast as ān bürst bār þet grūnde his tuskes, ant fēng on tō
fęmin ant te grispatīen ō þis mēoke meiden, ant þohte on hwücche
wīse hē mahte hire awēlden. Ant lette fecchen ā feat and wiˈ pich
hit füllen ant hęaten hit walm hāt, ant hēt warpen hire þērin[1] hwen   15
hit wōdelukest weolle. As me düde hire þērin[1], hā cleopede tō
Drihtin ant hit cōlede anān, ant warˈ hire as wünsum as ever enī
wlech weter þet wēre iwlaht te baˈīen, ant lēop wallinde hāt up
aʒein þēo ilke þet hit hefden iʒarket ant forscaldede of ham seolven
fiftī ant tēne, ant fordüde fiftī al itālde. Þā þē rēve iseh þis, hē   20
rende his clāˈes ant tōc him seolven bī þē top, ant fēng tō fiten his
mawmets[2] ant lasten his lāverd. ' Swīˈe,' quoˈ hē, ' ūt of mīn
ēhsihˈe, þet ich ne sēo hire nā māre ęr þē bodī wiˈ þē būc bēo
isundret from hire hęavet.'

Sōne as hā þis iherde, hā herede Godd in heovene ant warˈ   25
swīˈe gled, for þet hēo iwilnet hefde. Me ledde hire ant[3] lēac[4]
forˈ, ant hēo wes ęˈlūke. As hā stutte ō þē stüde þēr hā schulde
dęˈ drēhen, þā cōm þē ilke Bēlial of helle þet hā hefde ibęaten
hire bihīnden, ant gon tō ʒeien, ' Ā, stalewurˈe men, ne sparīe ʒē
nāwiht, hā haveˈ us alle scheome idōn; schēndeˈ hire nūˈen ant   30
ʒēldeˈ hire ʒarew borh, ne studgī ʒē nęaver.' Juliāne þē ędīe
openede hire ēhnen ant lōkede tōward him, ant tē bali blenchte ant
braid him aʒeinward as ān ischoten arewe. ' Wumme þet ich libbe,'

---

[1] þrin.   [2] mawmez.   [3] Supplied from Bodl. MS.   [4] hleac.

quoð hē, 'þā ich bēo nū nān ilaht, ant ȝef hā keccheð mē nū ne fīnd Ī
nę̄aver lēche; igrīpe hā mē ę̄nes, ne gā Ī nę̄aver eft māre.' Ant
lę̄ac him aȝeinward as ā beore, þet unwiht, ne mahte him nawt letten.
As hā schulde stūpen ant strecchen forð þē swire, hā bed first ant
fēng ōn þus tō lę̄aren þēo þet þēr wēren, ant þus seide: 'Lüsteð
mē, lēove men, ant līdeð āne hwīle.   Biwēpeð ant birēowseð ōwer
sünnen, ant lasseð wið sōð schrift ant wið dēdbōte; lę̄aveð ōwer
unlahen ant büldeð ōwer bōldes uppon trēowe staðele þet ne drēdeð
nā wīnd ne nā weder nowðer.   Lōkeð þet tē heovenlīch Lāverd bēo
gründwal of al þet ȝē würcheð, for þet stǫnt studelfast, falle þet
falle[1].   Cleopeð ȝēorne tō Godd in hālī chirche þet hē ȝeove ōw
wit wēl for te dōnne, ant strenge ōw wið his strencðe aȝein þēn
strǫnge unwiht þet sēkeð[2] ever ant aa ōw for te swolhen.   Lüsteð
writen lāre ant luvīeð þērefter[2a]; wēl is him þet wākeð wēl in þis
lütle hwīle, ant witeð wēl him seolven ant heortelīche sīkeð ofte
for his sünnen.   Þis world weint awei as weter þet ēorneð, ant as
imet sweven aswīndeð hire mürhðen; ant al nis būten a lę̄s wīnd
þet wē livīeð.   Lę̄aveð þē lę̄ase ant luvīeð þē sōðe, for wē schulen
lēten þis lif nüte we nę̄aver hwenne, ant reope wē of þet rīpe sēd
þet wē sēowen.   Swiðe ich bisēche ōw þet ȝē bidden for mē,
brēðren ant sustren.'   Ant cüste ham ā cos of pę̄s, alle as hā stōden,
ant bihēold uppard ant hēhede hire stefne: 'Lāverd Godd Almihtī,
þū luvest trēowe bilēave; ne lę̄f þū tō þīn ifān þīn ilīcnesse, ah
underfēng mē tō þē, ant dō mē in þīn englene hīrd wið meidenes
imę̄ane.   Ich aȝeove tō þē mī gāst, Drihtin.'   Ant wið þet ilke,
beide ant dę̄f düvelunge dūn tō þēr ēorðe, sōne bihę̄fdet; ant þē
ę̄dīe engles, wið hire sāwle, singinde sīhen tōward heovene.

Soððen sōne þērefter cōm ā sēlī wummon, Sophīe inempnet, bī
Nicomēdes burh ō rāde tōward Rōme, of hēh cün akennet, ant
nōm þis meidenes bodī ant ber hit in ā bāt, biwūnden dēorlīche
in dēorewurðe clāðes.   As hā wēren in wettre, cōm ā steorm ant
drāf ham tō lǫnde intō Campaine; ant þēr lette Sophīe, from þē
sę̄a ā mīle, setten ā chirche ant dōn hire bodī þērin[3] in stānene

---

[1] þet fall-, from Bodl. MS.   [2] seleð.   [2a] þrefter.   [3] þrin.

þruh hēhlīche as hit dēh halhen¹ tō dōnne. Þē rēve, þā hē herde
þis, bigon te rowen efter for te rēaven hit ham, ant ī þē sēa¹ᵃ
senchte; for þēr arisen stormes starcke ant strǫnge, ant brēken
þē schipes bōrd, adrenchten on hare þrittuðe sum ant þērtō ēke
fowre, ant warp ham adriven tō þē lǫnde, þēras wīlde dēor limēl 5
tōluken ham, ant tē unsēlī sawlen suncken intō helle.

Þus þet ēdīe meiden wende þurh pīnen tō heovenlīche wünnen,
in þē nomecūðe burh Nicomēde hātte, ō þē sixtēnðe dei of
Feoverēles mōneð, þē fortēnde kālende of Mearch þet cumeð efter.
Hēo us erndi tō Godd þē grace of him seolven, þet rixleð in 10
þrēohād, ant þah is ān untwēamet. Iheret ant iheiet wurðe hē
him āne as hē is wurðe, ant ever āh te bēonne, world abūten ēnde.
Amēn.

IV. THE ANCREN RIWLE, OR RULE OF NUNS

OF SPEECH

SPELLUNGE and² smecchunge bēoð ine mūðe bǫðe, ase sihðe is ī
þēn eien; auh wē schullen lēten smecchunge vort tet wē spēken of 15
ōwer mēte, and spēken nū of spellunge and tērefter of herrunge, of
bǫ imēne sume cherre ase gǫð tōgederes.

On alre ērest hwon ȝē schulen tō ōure parlūres þürle, iwiteð et
ōwer meiden hwǫ hit bēo þet³ is icumen, vor swüch hit mei bēon þet
ȝē schulen asunīen ōu; and hwon ȝē alles mōten vorð, creoiseð ful 20
ȝēorne ōur mūð, ēaren, and eien, and tē brēoste ēke, and gǫð forð
mid Godes drēde tō prēoste. On ērest siggeð '*confiteor,*' and

---

¹ deh alhen.　　¹ᵃ sea from Bodl. MS.　　² ꝛ, as usual.　　³ ꝥ, as often.

þęrefter ' *benedicite* ', þet hē ouh tō siggen ; hercneð his wōrdes and
sitteð al stille þet, hwon hē parteð vrom [1] ōu, þet hē ne cunne ōwer
gōd ne ōwer üvel nouðer, ne hē ne cunne ōu nouðer blāmen ne
preisen. Sum is sǫ wēl ilęred ǭðer sę̄ wīs iwōrded þet hēo wolde
þet hē wüste hit þe sit and spękeð tōuward him and ʒēlt him wōrd
aʒein wōrd, and bicumeð meister þe schulde bēon ancre, and
lęareð him þet is icumen tō lęren hire ; wolde bī hire tāle sōne
bēon mit tē wīse icūd and icnowen. Icnowen hēo is wēl, vor þurh [1a]
þet ilke þet hēo wēneð tō bēon wīs ihǫlden hē understont þet hēo
is sot, vor hēo hunteð efter prīs and keccheð lastunge. Vor ɛt tē
laste hwon hē is iwend awei, ' Þēos ancre,' hē wüle siggen, ' is of
müchele spęche.' Ēve hēold ine Paraïs lǫnge tāle mid tē neddre
þet tǫlde hire al þet lescūn þet God hire hefde ilęred and Adam of
þēn epple; and sǫ þē vēond þurh hire wōrd understōd anǫn riht
hire wǫcnesse and ivǫnd wei tōuward hire of hire vorlǫrenesse.
Ūre Lęfdī, Seinte Mārīe, düde al anōðer wīse, ne tǫlde hēo þēn
engle nǫne tāle, auh askede him þing scheortlīche þet hēo ne kūðe.
ʒē, mīne lēove süstren, voleweð ūre Lęfdī and nout þē kakele Ēve.
Vorþī ancre, hwatsę̄ hēo bēo, alsę̄ müchel ase hēo ever con and
mei, hǫlde hire stille. Nabbe hēo nout henne künde. Þē hen
hwon hēo hāveð ileid ne con būten kakelen. And hwat biʒit hēo
þęrof? Kumeð þē cǫve anǫn riht and ręveð hire hire eiren, and
fręt al þet of hwat hēo schulde vorð bringen hire cwike briddes.
And riht alsǫ þē lüðere cǫve dēovel berð awei vrom þē kakelinde
ancren and vorswoluweð al þē gōd þet hēo istrēoned habbeð, and
schulden ase briddes bę̄ren ham up tōuward heovene ʒif hit nę̄re
icakeled. Þē wreche peoddare mǫre noise hē mākeð tō ʒeien
his [2] sǫpe, þen a rīche mercēr al his dēorewurðe ware. Tō sume
gǫstlīche monne þet ʒē bēoð trüstī [3] uppen, ase ʒē muwen bēon of
lüt, gōd is þet ʒē asken ręd, and salve þet hē tęche ōu tōʒeines
fǫndunges, and ine schrifte schęaweð him gif hē wüle ihēren ōwer
gręste and ōwer lǫdlukeste sünnen, vorþī þet him arēowe ōu and
þurh þē birēounesse crīe Crīst inwardlīche mercī vor ōu, and habbe

---

[1] vrorm.   [1a] þ, as often.   [2] is.   [3] strusti.

ōu ine mūnde and in his bōnen. '*Sed multi veniunt ad vos in vestimentis ovium, intrinsecus autem sunt lupi rapaces*'; 'Auh witeð ōu and bēoð iwarre,' hē seið, ūre Lǫverd, 'vor monīe cumeð tō ōu ischrūd mid lǫmbes flēose and bēoð wōde wulves.' Worldlīche men ilēveð lūt[1], religiūse ʒēt lesse; ne wilnīe ʒē nout tō müchel hore kūðlęchunge. Ēve wiðūte dręde spec mit tē neddre; ūre Lęfdī was ofdręd of Gābriēles spęche.

Wiðūte witnesse of węopmon ǭðer of wummon þet ōu muwe ihēren, ne spęke ʒē mid nǫne monne ofte ne lǫnge; and þauh hit bēo of schrifte ī þēn ilke hūse ǭðer þęr hē muwe isēon tōuward ōu, sitte þē þridde, būte ʒif þē ilke þridde ōðer stūnde[2] trukīe. Þis nis nout vor ōu, lēove sustren, iseid, ne vor ōðer swūche; nowt, forþī þē trēowe is mislēved, and tē sākelęase ofte bilowen vor wone of witnesse. Me ilēveð þet üvel sōne, and tē unwreste blīðelīche līeð on þe gōde. Sum unisęlī, hwon hēo seide þet hēo schrǫf hire, hāueð ischriven hire al tō wundre. Vorþī owen þē gōde ever tō habben witnesse vor twǫ ancheisūns; nomelīche, þet ǫn is þet tē ontfule ne muwen līen on heom sǫ þet þē witnesse ne prēove heom valse, þet ōðer is vor tē ʒiven þē ōðre vorbīsne, and binime þē üvele ancre þet ilke unisęlī gīle þet ich of seide.

Ūt of chircheþürle ne hǫlde ʒē nǫne tāle mid nǫne monne, auh bęreð wurðschipe þęrtō vor þet hǫlī sacrament þet ʒē isēoð þęrþurh; and nimeð ōðerhwūles ōwer wummen tō þē hūses þürle, þēo ōðre men and wummen tō þe parlūrs þürle spęken būten vor nēode, ne ouwe ʒē būten et þēos twǫ þürles.

Sīlence evere et tē męte, vor ʒif ōðre religiūse dǭʒ hit ase ʒē wēl wūteð ʒē owen bivǫren alle; and ʒif enī hāveð dēore gist, dō hire meiden ase in hire stüde tē gledīen hire vēre, and hēo schal habben lęave tō ǫpenen hire þürl ęnes ǭðer twīes and mākīen sīgnes tōuward hire of ǫne glede chēre. Summes kurteisīe is nǫðelęas iturnd hire tō üvele; under semblaunt of gōd is ofte ihęled sünne. Ancre and hūses lęfdī ouh müche tō bēon bitwēonen. Everiche Vrīdeie of þe ʒēr hǫldeð sīlence, būte ʒif hit bēo

---

[1] hit.   [2] stude.

duble fęste, and teonne hǫldeð hit sum ōðer dai ī ðē wike; ī ðēn
Advent and ī ðē Ümbridawes, Wodnesdawes and Frīdawes; ī ðē
Leinten þrēo dawes, and al þē swīwike¹ vort nōn of Ẹstre ęven.
Tō ōwr meiden ʒē muwen þauh siggen mid lūt wōrdes hwatsę ʒē²
wülleð; and ʒif enī gōd mon is of feorrene ikumen, hercneð his
spęche and onswerīeð mid lūt wōrdes tō his askunge.

Müche fōl hē węre þe muhte tō his owene bihōve, hweðersę hē
wolde grīnden grēot ǫðer hwęte, ʒif hē grūnde þet grēot and lefde
þēne hwęte. Hwęte is hǫlī spęche, ase Seint Anselme seið. Hēo
grīnt grēot þe chęofled. Þē twǫ chēoken bēoð þē twǫ grīnstǫnes;
þē tunge is ƒē cleppe. Lōkeð, lēove süstren, þet ōuwer chēoken
ne grīnden never būte soulevōde, ne ōur ęaren ne hercnen never
būte soulehęale; and nout ǫne ōur ęaren auh ōwer eieþürles
tūneð aʒein īdel spęche, þet tō ōu ne cume nǫ tāle, ne tīðinge of þē
worlde.

Ʒē ne schulen vor nǫne þinge ne warīen, ne swęrien būte ʒif ʒē
siggen witterlīche ǫðer sikerlīche, ǫðer summe swüche wīse; ne ne
pręche ʒē tō nǫne mon, ne³ nǫ mon ne askī ōu ręad ne cōunsail,
ne ne telle ōu. Ręadeð wummen ǫne. Seinte Powel vorbęad
wummen tō pręchen—'*Mulieres non permitto docere.*' Nenne
węopmon ne chastī ʒē, ne ne etwīteð him of his unðęau, būte ʒif hē
bēo þē ǫverkūðre. Hǫlīe ǫlde ancreꝑ muwen dōn hit summes
weis, auh hit nis nout siker þing, ne ne limpeð nout tō þē ʒunge.
Hit is hore meister þet bēoð ǫver ōðre iset and habbeð ham tō
witene; ancre nāveð tō witene būten hire and hire meidenes.
Hǫlde everīch his owene mestēr and nout ne ręavīe ōðres. Monī
mon wēneð tō dōn wēl þet hē dēð al tō cwęade; vor, ase ich ęr
seide, under semblaunt of gōde is ofte ihęled sünne, and þurh
swüch chastīement hāveð sum ancre aręred bitwēonen hire and
hire prēost ǫðer a valsinde luve ǫðer a müche weorre.

Seneca seide, '*Ad summam volo vos esse rariloquos, tuncque pauci-
loquos*'; þet is, ' Þē ēnde of þē tāle,' seið Seneke thē wīse, ' ich ülle
þet ʒē spęken sēlde, and þeonne būten lūtel.' Auh monī pünt hire

---

¹ swiðwike.   ² No ʒe in MS.   ³ ne ne.

wōrd vor tē lẹ̄ten mọ̄ ūt, as me dēð water et tẹ̄r mülne clūse; and
sọ̄ düden Jōbes frēond þet wẹ̄ren icumen tō vrōvren him, sẹ̄ten
stille alle seoveniht, auh þeo hēo hefden[1] alles bigunne vor tō
spẹ̄kene þeone kūðen hēo nevere astünten hore cleppe. Gregorȳ[2]:
'*Censura silencii nutritura est verbi.*' Sọ̄ hit is ine[3] monīe, ase 5
Seint Gregorīe seið, 'sīlence is wōrdes fostrild and bringeð forþ
chẹ̄afle.' An ōðer half ase hē seið, '*Juge silencium cogit celestia
meditari,*'—'Lọ̄ng sīlence and wēl iwüst nēdeð þē þouhtes up
tōuward þẹ̄r heovene.' Al sọ̄ ase ȝē muwen isēon þet water hwon
me pünt hit, and stoppeð bivọ̄ren wēl sọ̄ þet hit ne muwe adūne- 10
ward, þeonne is hit inēd aȝein vor tō clīmben upward; and ȝē al
þisses weis pündeð ōwer wōrdes and forstoppeð ōuwer þouhtes,
ase ȝē wülleð þet heo clīmben and hīen tōuward heovene and nout
ne vallen adūneward, and tōvlēoten ȝēond tē wōrld ase dēð
müchel chẹ̄afle. Auh hwon ȝē nēde mōten spẹ̄ken, a lüte wiht 15
lēseð up ōuwer mūðes flōdȝeten, ase me dēð et tẹ̄r mülne, and
lẹ̄ted adūn sōne.

Of Domestic Matters

Hit ne limpeð nout tō ancre of ōðer monne elmesse vor tō
mākīen hire large. Nolde me lauhwen ane beggare lūde tō bise-
mare þet bēde men tō fẹ̄ste? Mārīe and Marthe bọ̄ðe hēo wẹ̄ren 20
sustren, auh hore līf sundrede. Ȝē ancren habbeð inumen ōu tō
Mārīe dọ̄le, þet ūre Lọ̄verd sülf herede. '*Maria optimam partem
elegit.*' 'Marthe, Marthe,' cweð hē, 'þū ert ine müchele bāret;
Mārīe hāveð ichọ̄sen betere, and ne schal hire nọ̄ðing binimen hire
dọ̄le.' Hūswīfscipe is Marthe dọ̄le, and Mārīe dọ̄le is stilnesse and 25
reste of alle worldes noise, þet nọ̄ðing ne lette hire vor tō ihēren
Godes stefne. And lōkeð hwat God seið, þet nọ̄ðing ne schal
binimen ōu þeos dọ̄le. Marthe hāveð hire mestēr; lẹ̄teð hire
iwurðen, and sitte ȝē mid Mārīe stọ̄nstille et[4] Godes fēt and
hercneð him ọ̄ne. Marthe mestēr is vor tō vēden and schrüden 30

---

[1] þeo hefden, heo above line.   [2] Greg.   [3] īne.   [4] ed.

pōvre men, ase hūselẹ̄fdī: Mārīe ne ouh nout vor tō entremẹ̄ten
hire þẹ̄rof, and ʒif ei blāmeð hire God sülf ọ̄veral wẹ̄reð hire þẹ̄rof,
ase họ̄lī writ witneð. An ōðer half, nọ̄n ancre ne ouh for tō nimen
būte gnēdelīche þet hire tō nēodeð. Hwarof þeonne mei hēo
mākīen hire large? Hēo schal libben bī elmesse ase neruhlīche
ase hēo ever mei, and nout gederen vor tō ʒiven hit eft. Hēo nis
nout hūsewīf, auh is a chirche ancre. ʒif hēo mei sparīen enī
pōvre schrẹ̄aden, sēnde ham al dērnelīche ūt of hire woanes; under
semblaunt of gōde is ofte ihẹ̄led sünne. And hwū schulen þēos
rīche ancren þet bēoð ēorðetilien, ọ̄ðer habbeð rentes isette, dōn tō
pōvre neihebōures dērnelīche hore elmesse? Ne wilnen nout for
tō habben wōrd of ọ̄ne large ancre, ne vor tō ʒiven müchel, ne bēo
nọ̄n þē grẹ̄dīure vor tō habben mọ̄re. Bēo [1] grẹ̄dīnesse rōte of
hire bitternesse; alle bēoð þē bōwes bittre þet of hire springeð.
Bidden hit vor tō ʒiven hit nis nout ancre rihte. Of ancre
kurteisīe, and of ancre largesse, is ikumen ofte sünne and schẹ̄ome
on ēnde.

Wummen and children þet habbeð iswunken vor ōū, hwatsẹ̄ ʒē
sparīeð on ōū mākīeð ham tō ẹ̄tene; nenne mon bivọ̄ren ōū būte
ʒif hē habbe nēode, ne lāðe ʒē tō drinken nout. Ne ʒīrne ich þet
me telle ōū hēndī ancren. Et gōde vrēond nimeð al þet ʒē habbeð
nēode hwon hēo bēodeð hit ōū; auh for nọ̄n bọ̄de ne nime ʒē nout
wiðūten nēode, leste ʒē kecchen þēne nọ̄me of gederinde [2] ancren.
Of mon þet ʒē mislēveð ne nime ʒē nouðer lesse ne mọ̄re, nout sọ̄
müche þet bēo a rōte gingivre. Müchel nēode schal drīven ōū vor
te bidden out; þauh ẹ̄dmōdlīche schẹ̄aweð tō ōwer lēoveste
vrēond ōwer miseise [3].

ʒē, mīne lēove sustren, ne schulen habben nọ̄ bẹ̄st būte kat ọ̄ne.
Ancre þet hāveð eihte þüncheð bet hūsewīf, ase Marthe was, þen
ancre; ne nọ̄ne weis ne mei hēo bēon Mārīe mid griðfulnesse of
heorte. Vor þeonne mōt hēo þenchen of þē kūes foddre, and of
hēordemonne hüire, olühnen þēne heiward, wārīẹn hwon me pünt
hire, and ʒelden þauh þē hermes. Wāt Crīst þis is lọ̄dlīch þing

---

[1] þeo.   [2] gederindde.   [3] meseise.

hwon me [1] mākeð mǫne in tūne of ancre eihte. Þauh ȝif enī mōt
nēde habben kū, lōke þet hēo nǫne monne ne eilīe, ne ne hermīe,
ne þet hire þouht ne bēo nout þēron ivestned.   Ancre ne ouh
nout tō habben nǫ þing þet drawe ūtward hire heorte. Nǫne
cheffare ne drīve ȝē ; ancre þet is chēapild, hēo chēapeð hire soule   5
þē chepmon of helle.   Ne wite ȝē nout in ōure hūse of ōðer monnes
þinges, ne eihte, ne clǫðes ; ne nout ne undervō ȝē þe chirche vesti-
ments [2], ne þēne calīs [3], būte ȝif strencðe hit makīe, ǫðer müchel eie,
vor of swüche witunge is ikumen müchel üvel oftesīðen. Wiðinnen
ōwer woanes ne lēte ȝē nenne mon slēpen. Ȝif müchel nēode mid   10
alle mākeð brēken ōwer hūs, þē [4] hwüle þet hit ever is ibrǫken lōke
þet ȝē habben þērinne mid ōu ǫne wummon of clēne līve, deies and
nihtes.

V. ROBERT OF GLOUCESTER'S CHRONICLE—HOW THE NORMANS CAME TO ENGLAND

Müche haþ [5] þē sorwe ibē ofte in Engelǫnde,
As ȝē mōwe hēr and ēr ihüre and [6] understǫnde,   15
Of monī bataile þat haþ [5] ibē, and þat men þat lǫnd nōme.
Verst, as ȝē habbeþ [7] ihürd, þē emperōurs of Rōme,
Süþþe Saxons and Englisse mid batayles strǫnge,
And süþþe hii of Denemarch þat hülde it al sǫ lǫnge ;
Atte laste hii of Normandī, þat maisters bēþ ȝüt hēre,   20
Wonne hit and hǫldeþ ȝüt, ich olle [8] telle in wüch manēre.

   Þǫ Willam bastard hürde telle of Haraldes swikelhēde,
Hōu hē hadde [9] ymad him king and mid süch falshēde,—
Vor þat lǫnd him was bitāke, as hē wēl wüste,
Tō wite hit tō him wēl and hē wēl tō him trüste ;—   25

----

me me. [1]   vestimenz. [2]   caliz. [3]   þeo. [4]   aþ. [5]
&, as often. [6]   abbeþ. [7]   icholle = ich wulle. [8]   adde. [9]

As þē hēnde hē düde verst, and messagērs him sende,
Þat hē understōde him bet his[1] dę̄de vor tō amende,
And boȝte on þē grę̄te ǭþ þat hē him hadde[2] ę̄r ydō
Tō wite him wēl Engelǭnd and tō spōūsī his[1] doȝter alsǭ,
And hūlde him þę̄rof vorewarde, as hē bihēt ę̄k þē kinge ;   5
And bote hē düde bitīme hē wolde sēnde him ōþer tīdinge,
And sēche him ōūt ar twelfmonþe, and his[1] riȝtes winne,
Þat hē ne ssolde habbe[3] in al Engelǭnd an hērne tō wite him inne.

Harald him sende wōrd þat folīe it was tō trüste
Tō süch ǭþ as was idō mid strengþe, as hē wēl wüste ;   10
Vor ȝif a maide treuþe ipliȝt tō dō an fōle dę̄de
Al ǭne privelīche, wiþōūte hire frēndes rę̄de,
Þülke vorewarde wę̄re vor noȝt ; and watloker it aȝte hēr,
Þat ich swōr an ǭþ þat was al in þī pōēr,
Wiþōwte cōnseil of al þē lǭnd, of þing þat mīn noȝt nas ;   15
Þę̄rvǭre nēde ǭþ iswǭre, nēde ibrǭke was.
And ȝif þōū mē wolt sēche in Engelǭnd ne bē þōū noȝt sǭ stürne ;
Siker þōū bē þōū ne ssalt mē fīnde in nǭne hürne.

Þǭ Willam hürde þat hē wolde susteinī his[1] tricherīe,
Hē lēt ofsēnde his[1] kniȝtes of al Normandīe   20
Tō cōnseilī him in þis cas, and tō helpe him in süch nēde ;
And hē gan of hor porchas largelīche hom bēde,
As hii fōūnde süþþe in Engelǭnd, þǭ it iwonne was ;
Þē betere was tōward him hor herte vor þis cas.

Þē Duc Willam his[1] wille amǭng hom alle sę̄de,   25
Þat four þinges him mā̄de mę̄st biginne þülke dę̄de :
Þat Godwine, Haraldes fader, tō dę̄þe lę̄t idō[4]
Sǭ vīllīche Alfrę̄d his[1] cosīn, and his[1] felawes alsǭ ;
And vor Harald hadde[2] his[1] ǭþ ibrǭke þat hē swōr mid his[1] riȝt hǭnd,
Þat hē wolde tō his[1] bihōfþe[5] witīe Engelǭnd ;   30
And vor Seint Edward him ȝef Engelǭnd alsǭ ;
And vor hē was next of his[1] blōd and best wurþe þę̄rtō,

---

[1] is, as often.   [2] adde.   [3] abbe.   [4] do.   [5] biofþe.

And vor Harald nadde nǫ riȝt bote in falshȩde;
Þēs þinges him māde mȩst biginne þülke dȩde.

And vor hē wolde þat alle men iseye his [1] trewehȩde,
Tō þē Pǫpe Alisandre hē sende in süch cas him tō rȩde.

Haraldes falshȩde þǫ þē Pǫpe ysey þȩre,— 5
And parauntre me him tǫlde mǫre þan sōþ wȩre,—
Þē Pǫpe asoilede and blessede Willam and alle his
Þat intō þis bataile mid him ssolde iwis,
And halwede his [1] banēr þat me atvǫre him bȩre.
Þǫ was hē and alle his gladdore þan hii ȩr wȩre. 10
Sǫ þat þis duc hadde [2] aȝēn hervest al ȝāre
His barōns and kniȝtes mid him vor tō fāre.

Tō þē hāvene of Sein Walrī þē duc wende þǫ,
Mid þē men þat hē hadde [2] and abide mǫ.

After hervest þǫ hor ssipes and hii al preste wȩre, 15
And wȳnd [3] hom cōm after wille hor seiles hii gonne arȩre,
And hiderward in þē sȩ wēl glad þēn wei nōme,
Sǫ þat bisīde Hāstinge tō Engelǫnd hii cōme;
Hom þoȝte þǫ hii cōme ā lǫnd þat al was in hor hǫnd.
As sōne as þē Duc Willam his [1] fōt sette ā lǫnd, 20
Ǫn of his [1] kniȝtes gradde, 'Hǫld vaste, Willam, nōu
Engelǫnd, vor þȩr nis nǫ king bote þōu;
Vor siker þōu bē Engelǫnd is nōu þīn iwis.'
Þē Duc Willam anǫn vorbȩd alle his
Þat nǫn nȩre sǫ wōd tō robbȳ, ne nǫ manēr harm dō þȩre 25
Upe þē lǫnd þat his [4] was, bote hom þat aȝēn him wȩre.
Al an fourtēne niȝt hii bilȩvede þȩr abōute,
And cōnseilede of batayle and ordeinede hor rōute.

King Harald sat glad ynou at Euerwīk at tē mȩte,
Sǫ þat þȩr cōm a messagēr ar hē hadde [2] iȝȩte, 30
And sȩde þat Duc Willam tō Hāstinges was icome,
And his [1] banēr hadde [2] arȩrd, and þē contreie al inome.

---

[1] is.   [2] adde.   [3] wynd, not in MS.; supplied from MS. B and
others.   [4] it.

Harald anǫn mid grę̄te herte corāgeūs ynou,
As hē of nǫ mon ne tǫlde þüderward vaste hē drou.
Hē ne lę̄t noȝt clüpīe al his[1] folc, sǫ willesfol hē was,
And al for in þē ōþer bataile him vēl sǫ vair cas.

þǫ Duc Willam wüste þat hē was icome sǫ nei,   5
A monek hē sende him in messāge and düde as þē sley:
þat lǫnd þat him was iȝive þat hē ssolde him up ȝēlde,
Ǫþer come and dereynī þē riȝte mid swērd in þē vēlde.
ȝif hē sę̄de þat hē nadde nǫne riȝte þę̄rtō,
þat, upe þē Pǫpes lōkinge of Rōme, hē ssolde it dō,   10
And hē wolde þę̄rtō stǫnde al wiþōute fiȝte,
Wę̄r Seint Edward hit him ȝaf, and wę̄r hē hadde[2] þę̄rtō riȝte.
Harald sende him wōrd aȝēn þat hē nolde him tāke nǫ lǫnd,
Ne nǫ lōkinge of Rōme, bote swērd and riȝt hǫnd.
þǫ hit ōþer ne miȝte bē, eiþer in his[1] sīde   15
Cōnseilede and ȝarkede hom bataile vor tō abīde.

þē Englisse al þē niȝt bivǭre vaste bigonne tō singe,
And spende al þē niȝt in glotonīe and in drinkinge.
þē Normans ne düde noȝt sǫ, ac crīede on God vaste,
And ssrive hom, ę̄ch after ōþer, þē wule þē niȝt ylaste, 20
And ā morwe hom lę̄t hoselī mid mīlde herte ynou.
And süþþe þē duc wiþ his[1] hǫst[2a] tōward þē bataile drou,
An stōunde hē gan abīde, and his[1] kniȝtes rę̄de:
'ȝē kniȝtes,' hē sę̄de, 'þat bēþ of sǫ nǫble dę̄de,
þat nę̄re nevere ǭvercome, ne ȝōure elderne naþemǫ,   25
Understǫndeþ of þē kynge[3] of France þat ȝōure elderne düde
sǫ wǫ,
Hōu mī fader in Paris amidde his[1] kinedōm,
Mid prōwesse of ȝōure faderes mid strengþe him ǭvercōme.
Understǫndeþ hōu ȝōure elderne þē king nōme alsǫ,
And hēld him vorte hē hadde[2] amended þat hē hadde[2] misdò; 30
And Richard þat was þǫ a chīld iȝǫlde Normandīe,
þat was duc hēr bivǭre, and þat tō süch maistrīe

---

[1] is.   [2] adde.   [2a] ost, as always.   [3] kunde; other MSS. kynge.

Þat at ēche Parlement þat hē in France wēre,
Þat hē wēre igürd wiþ swērd þē wule hē wēre þēre,
Ne þat þē King of France ne his sō hardī nēre,
Ne nōn atte Parlement þat knīf ne swērd bēre.

Understōndeþ ēk þē dēdes þat þulke Richard düde alsō,   5
Þat hē ne overcōm noȝt kinges alōne, ac wēl mōre þērtō,
Ac hē overcōm þē dēvel and adoūn him caste,
Tōgadere as hii wrastlede, and bōnd his[1] hōnden vaste
Bihīnde at his[1] rügge; of süch prōwesse ȝē þenche,
Ne ssāme ȝē noȝt þat Harald, þat evere was of lüþer wrenche,   10
And bivōre ȝoū was vorswōre, þat hē wolde mid his[1] taile
Turne his[1] wōmbe tōward us and his[1] fāce in bataile.

Understōndeþ þē swikedōm þat his[1] fader and hē wroȝte,
And hii þat mid him hēre bēþ, þō hii tō dēþe broȝte
Sō vīllīche Alfrēd mī cosīn, and mȳ künesmen alsō.   15
Hoū miȝte in enȳ wīse mōre ssāme bē idō?
Monīe þat düde þulke dēde ȝē mōwe hēr isē;
Hoū lōnge ssolle hor lüþer hēved above hor ssoldren bē?
Adraweþ ȝoūre swērdes, and lōke wō may dō best,
Þat me isē ȝoūre prōwesse fram ēst tō þē west,   20
Vor tō awrēke þat gentil blōd þat sō vīllīche was inome
Of ūr künesmen, vor wē mōwe wēl, ūr tīme is noū icome.'

Þē duc nadde noȝt al isēd, þat mid ērnest grēt
His folc quiclīche tō þē bataile sscēt.
A swein þat hēt Taylefēr smōt vorþ bivōre þēr,   25
And slou anōn an Engliss mon þat a banēr bēr,
And eftsōne[2] anōþer baneūr, and þē þridde almēst alsō,
Ac himsülf[3] hē was aslawe ar þē dēde wēre ydō.

Þē verst ēnde of his[1] hōst bivōre Harald mid süch ginne
Sō þikke[4] sette þat nō mon ne miȝte come wiþinne,   30
Wiþ strōnge targes hom bivōre þat archērs ne düde hom noȝt,
Sō þat Normans wēre nei tō groūnde ibroht.

---

[1] is.   [2] ef sone; other MSS. eft sone.   [3] hom sulf.   [4] þilke.

Willam biþoȝte an quointīse, and bigan tō flē vaste,
And his [1] folc vorþ mid him as hii wēre aghaste [1ᵃ],
And flōwe ǭver an lǫnge dāle and sǫ up an hey.
Þē Engliss hǫst was prōut ynou þǭ hē þis isey,
And bigonne him tō sprēde, and after þēn wey nōme.　　　　　5
Þē Normans wēre above þē hül, þē ōþer upward cōme,
And biturnde hom above al ēselīche, as it wolde bē donward,
And þē ōþere binēþe ne miȝte noȝt sǫ quiclīche upward,
And hii wēre bivǭre al tōsprad þat me miȝte bitwēne hom wēnde.
Þē Normans wēre þǭ wēl porveid abōute in ēche ēnde　　　10
And stǫnes adonward slonge upe hom ynowe,
And mid spēres and mid flǫn vaste of hom slowe,
And mid swērd and mid ax vor hii þat upward nōme.
Ne miȝte nǭ wille habbe [2] of dünt as hii þat donward cōme,　　14
And hor vantwarde was tōbrōke þat me miȝte wiþinne hom wēnde;
Sǫ þat þē Normans vaste slowe in ēch ēnde
Of þē Englisse al vor noȝt, þat þē valeie was nei
As hei ifüld mid dēde men as þē dōune an hei.
Þē ssētare donward al vor noȝt vaste slowe tō grōunde,
Sǫ þat Harald þoru þen eie issǭte was dēþes wōunde;　　　20
And a kniȝt þat isei þat hē was tō dēþe ibroȝt,
And smǫt him as hē lay binēþe, and slou him as vor noȝt.
Fram þat it was ā morwe þē bataile ilaste strǫng,
Vorte it was hei mid ǭvernōn, and þat was somdēl lǫng.
Monī was þē gōde dünt þat Duc Willam ȝef ā day;　　　25
Vor þrē stēdes hē slou under him as me say,
Vorpriked and vorarned abōute, and vorwōunded alsǫ,
And debrused aȝēn dēde men ar þē bataile wēre idō;
And ȝüt was Willames grāce þülke day sǫ gōd
Þat hē nadde nǭ wōunde warþoru hē ssedde [3] an drǫpe blōd.　　30

　　Þus, lǭ, þē Englisse folc vor noȝt tō grōunde cōm,
Vor a fals king þat nadde nǭ riȝt tō þē kinedōm,

---

　　　[1] is.　　　[1ᵃ] agaste.　　　[2] abbe.　　　[3] ssedde.

And cōme tō a nywe lǫverd þat mǫre in riȝte was ;
Ac hor nǫþer, as me may isē, in pur riȝte nas.
And þus was in Normannes hǫnd þat lǫnd ibroȝt iwis,
Þat an aunter ȝif evermǫ keveringe þḗrof is.
Of þē Normans bēþ heye men þat bēþ of Engelǫnde   5
And þē lowe men of Saxons, as ich understǫnde,
Sǫ þat ȝē sēþ in eiþer sīde wat riȝte ȝē habbeþ [1] þḗrtō ;
Ac ich understǫnde þat it was þoru Godes wille ydō.
Vor þē wule þē men of þis lǫnd pur hēþene wēre,
Nǫ lǫnd ne nǫ folc aȝēn hom in armes nēre ;   10
Ac noū sūþþe þat þet folc avēnge cristendōm,
And wel lūte wūle hūlde þē biheste þat hē nōm,
And turnde tō sleuþe and tō prūte, and tǫ lecherīe,
Tō glotonīe, and heye men mūche tō robberīe,
As þē gǫstes in a visiōn tō Seint Edward sēde,   15
Wū þḗr ssolde in Engelǫnd come sūch wrecchēde
Vor robberīe of heie men, vor clerken hōrdōm,
Hoū God wolde sorwe sēnde in þis kinedōm.
    Bitwēne Michelmasse [2] and Sein Luc ā Sein Calixtes day,
As vēl in þülke ȝēre in a Saterday,   20
In þē ȝḗr of grāce as it vēl alsǫ
A þoūsend and sixe and sixtī þis bataile was idō.
Duc Willam was þǫ ǫld nȳne and þrittī ȝḗr,
And ǫn and þrittī ȝḗr hē was of Normandīe duc ḗr.
Þǫ þis bataile was ydō Duc Willam lēt bringe   25
Vaire his [3] folc þat was aslawe an ērþe þoru alle þinge.
Alle þat wolde lēve hē ȝef þat his [3] fǫn an ērþe broȝte ;
Haraldes mōder vor hire sone wēl ȝērne him bisoȝte
Bī messagērs, and largelīche him bēd of hire [4] þinge
Tō grantī hire hire sones bodī an ērþe vor tō bringe.   30
Willam hit sende hire vaire inou wiþoūte enȳ þing warevǫre,
Sǫ þat it was þoru hire, wiþ grēt honoūr ybǫre,

---

[1] abbeþ.   [2] misselmasse.   [3] is.   [4] ire.

Tō þē hōūs of Waltham, and ibroȝt an ērþe þēre
In þē hōlī rōde chirche þat hē lēt himsülf rēre,
An hōūs of religiōn, of canōns ywis.
Hit was þēr vaire an ērþe ibroȝt, as it ȝūt is.

Willam, þis nōble duc, þō hē hadde[1] idō al þis,   5
Þēn wey hē nōm tō Londone, hē and alle his,
As king and prince of lōnde wiþ nōbleye ynou.
Aȝēn him wiþ vair processiōn þat folc of tōūne drou,
And undervēng him vaire inou as king of þis lōnd.

Þus cōm, lō, Engelōnd intō Normandīes hōnd;   10
And þē Normans ne cōūþe spēke þō bote hor owe spēche,
And spēke French as hii düde at hōm[2], and hor children düde alsō
    tēche,
Sō þat heie men of þis lōnd þat of hor blōd cōme
Hōldeþ alle þülke spēche þat hii of hom nōme;
Vor bote a man conne French[3] me telleþ[4] of him lüte.   15
Ac lowe men hōldeþ tō Engliss, and tō hor owe spēche ȝüte.
Ich wēne þēr ne bēþ in al þē world contreyes nōne
Þat ne hōldeþ tō hor owe spēche, bote Engelōnd ōne.
Ac wēl me wōt vor tō conne bōþe wēl it is,
Vor þē mōre þat a mon can þē mōre wurþe hē is.   20

VI. OLD KENTISH SERMONS

ON THE CALMING OF THE SEA.

'Ascendente Ihesu in naviculam, secuti sunt eum discipuli eius.
Et ecce motus factus est magnus in mari ita, ut operiretur fluctibus.
Erat autem illis ventus contrarius.'

Wē rēdeth ī þē hōlī godspelle of tōdai þat ūre Lōrd Jēsu[5] Crīst
yēde ōne tīme intō ane ssipe and hise[6] decīples mid him intō þē

---

[1] adde.   [2] om.   [3] Frenss.   [4] telþ.   [5] ihu.   [6] ise.

see. And sǭ hī wēre in þǭ ssipe, sǭ arǭs a grēat tempeste of wīnde; and ūre Lǫrd was ileid him don tō slēpe ine þǭ ssipe ę̄r þane þis tempeste arǫǫs. Hise decīples hedde grēt drēde of þise tempeste, sǭ awākede hine and seiden tō him, 'Lǫrd, sāve us; for wē perisset.' And hā wiste wēl þet hī ne hadde nocht gōde 5 belēave ine him, þǭ seide tō hem, 'Wat drēt yū, folk of litle belīave?' Þǭ arǫs up ūre Lǫrd and tōk þane wȳnd and tǭ see, and al sǭ rāþe hit was stille. And alse þǭ men þet wēren in þǭ ssipe hedde iseghe þǭ mirācle, sǭ awondrede hem michel.

Þis is sī vaire mirācle þet þet godspel of teday us telþ; þerefǭre 10 sal ūre belīave bīe þē betere astrengþed ine swiche Lǫrde þet siche mirācle mai dō, and dōþ wanne hē wile. Ac hit is us nȳede þet sē þet sucūrede hem ine þā peril, þet us sucūrī ine ūre nīedes, þet wē clę̄pīe tō him þet hā us helpe. And hē hit wille dō blēþelīche, yef wē him bisēcheth mercī mid good iwille, al sǭ 15 himselven seith bī þē Hǭlī Writes, '*Salus populi ego sum, et cetera;*' 'Ic[1] am,' hā seiþ, 'hēlēre of þē folke; wanne hī tō mē clę̄pīeth[2] ine hire sorghen and ine hire nīedes, ic hī sucūrī, and beneme hem al here ēvel withūte ēnde.' Grēde wē tō him mercī sikerlīche, yef sē devel us wille acumbrī þurch senne, þurch prēde, ǭþer þurch anvīe, 20 ǭþer þurch wrēþe, ǭþer þurch ōþer manēre of dīadlīche senne; grēde wē tō him mercī, and sigge wē him, 'Lǫrd, sauve us, þet wē ne perissi,' and þet hē us delivrī of alle ēveles, and þet hā yef us swiche werkes tō dōne in þise wordle, þet þǭ saulen of us mōte bīen isauved ā dōmesdai, and gōn tō þǭ blisce of hevene. *Quod* 25 *ipse prestare dignetur, etc.*

ON THE PARABLE OF THE VINEYARD.

'Simile est regnum celorum homini patrifamilias qui exiit, primo mane, conducere operarios in vineam suam.'

Ūre[3] Lǫrd God Almichtī tō us spę̄keþ ine þǭ hǭlī godespelle of teday, and us sēaweth one forbisne þet, yef wē willeth dōn his

---

[1] hic; so in next line also.   [2] clepiedh.   [3] Hure.

servīse, þet wē sollen habbe þǭ mēde wēl grīat ine hevene. For sǭ seyth ūre Lǭrd ine þǭ godspelle of tōdai, þet ǭn goodman was þat ferst ūtyēde[1] bī þē moreghen for tō hēre werkmen intō his winyarde, for ane penȳ of forewerde; and al sǭ hē hedde imad þise forewerde, sǭ hā sente hī intō his wynyarde. Sǭ hā dede at 5 undren, and at midday alsǭ. Þǭ, þat hit was ayēn þan ēven sǭ hā kam intō þē marcatte, sǭ hē fǭnd werkmen þet wēre īdel. Þǭ seyde hē tō hem, ' Wee bīe yē īdel?' And hīe answerden and seyde, ' Lǭrd, for wē ne fǭnden tedai þat us hērde.' ' Gǭþ nū,' hā seide, sē gōdeman, ' intō mīne wynyarde, and ic[2] þat richt is yū 10 sal yeve.' Þǭs yēde intō þise wynyarde mid þǭ ōþre. Þǭ þet hit was wēl ēven[3], þǭ seide þē Lǭrd tō his sergant, ' Clēpe þǭ werkmen, and yēld hem here travail, and agyn tō hem þat cōmen last, and gǭ al tō þǭ ferste; yef everiche of hem ane penȳ.' Sē sergant dede þēs Lǭrdes commandement, sǭ paide þǭ werkmen and 15 yaf everich ane penȳ. And sǭ hī seghen, þǭ þet bī þē morghen waren icomen, þet hī þet waren last icume hedden here everīch ane penȳ, þǭ wēnden hī mǭre habbe. Þǭ gruchchede hī amēnges hem, and seyden : ' Þǭs laste ǭn ūre habbeþ itravailed, and þū his mākest velaghes tō us þet habbeth al deai ibȳe ine þīne wynyarde, 20 and habbeth[4] iþǭled þē berdene of þǭ pīne, and of þǭ hēte of al þǭ daie.' Þǭ answerede sē gōde man tō ǭn of hem: ' Frēnd,' hā seide, ' Ī ne dō þē nǭǭn unricht. Wat forþingketh þat ic[5] dō mīn iwil.' And alsǭ ūre Lǭrd hedde itǭld þise forbisne, sǭ hē seide efterward, ' Sǭ sulle þǭ verste bīe last, and þǭ laste ferst; sēle bīeþ 25 iclēpede ac feawe bīeþ icornee.'

Nū ihēreþ þē signefiance. Þēs gōdeman betǭckneþ God Almichtī, ūre Lǭrd. Sē winyard betǭckneþ þē servīse of ūre Lǭrd. Þē werkmen betǭckneþ alle þǭ þet dōþ Crīstes servīse. Þǭ tīdes of þē daie betǭckneþ þē tīme of þis world. Bīe þē morghen 30 ihērde ūre Lǭrd werkmen intō his winyarde þǭ hā sente þē patriarches at ē begininge of þis wordle[6] ine his[7] servīse, þet

---

[1] uutyede.   [2] hic.   [3] hi wel even.   [4] habbeþ.   [5] hic.
[6] wordl.   [7] is.

þurch gōde belēavee him servede and sēden his tēchinge tō alle þǭ
þet hī hedden hit tō siggen. Alsǭ, at undren and at midday,
ihērede hē werkmen intō his winyarde þǭ hā sente be þǭ tīme þet
Mōysēs was and Aarōn; and ī þē tīme of his prophētes dede hē
manī gōd man intō his servīse þet, þurch grīate luve tō him, hēlden   5
and deden his servīse. Tōyēnes þan ēven, God Almichtī ihīerde
werkmen intō his winyarde þǭ þat hē ā last of þis wordle naam flēs
and blōd ine þē maidene Seinte Mārīe, and sēawede ine þis world.
Þǭ fǭnd hē men þet al day hedden ibē īdel; wērefǭre hē fǭnd þet
hēþen folk, þet be þǭ tīme þet was igǭ, hedden ibē ūt of Godes   10
belīave and of his luve, and of his servīse. Hī ne hedden nocht ibē
īdel for tō dōne þǭ develes werkes; ac þērefǭre seith þet godspel
þet hedden ibē īdel, þǭ þet hī nedden bilēved ane God Almichtī,
ne him lovīe, ne him servī. For al þat is ine þis wordle þet man is,
bote yef hā luvīe God Almichtī and him servī, al hit him may   15
þenche forlǭre and īdelnesse. Þǭ arēsūnede ūre Lǭrd þē pāens be
hise apostles, wērefǭre[1] hī hedden ibē sǭ lǭnge īdel, þǭ þet hī ne
hedden ibē in his servīse. Þǭ answerden þē pāens, þet nǭn ne
hedden ihērd hii; þet is tō sigge, þet hī ne hedden never te iheed
prophēte, ne apostle, ne prēchūr, þet hem sēawde, ne hem tachte,   20
hū hī[2] solden ine Gode belēve, ne him servī. ' Gǭþ,' ā seide, ūre
Lǭrd, ' intō mīne winyarde, þet is intō[3] mīne belēave, and ic[4] yū
sal yēve yūre penī, þet is heverīche blisce.' Þǭ hēþen men yēden
be þā daghen intō Crīstes servīse. And wē, þet of hem bīeþ icume
and habbeþ cristendōm underfǭnge, bīeþ ientred intō Crīstes ser-   25
vīse; þērefǭre wē sollen habbe ūre penī, þet is þē blisce of hevene,
al sǭ wēl ase þǭ þet cōmen bī þē morghen. For al sǭ wē hǭpīeþ
for te habbe heverīche blisce, ase þǭ patriarches and þǭ prophētes
and þǭ apostles and þǭ gōde men þet hwīlem ine þis world God
Almichtī serveden.   30

Sǭ as wē hābeþ iseid of dīvers wordles, þet God Almichtī dede
werkmen intō his winyarde, sǭ wē mōwe sigge of þǭ ēlde of
everiche men. For God Almichtī dēþ werkmen intō his winyarde

---

[1] vrefore.   [2] i.   [3] inte.   [4] hic.

bī þē morghen wanne hā clēpeþ of swiche þēr bīeþ intō his servīse
ine here chīldhẹ̄de, wanne hī of þis world wēndeþ beswọ̄ þet hī ne
be ine nọ̄ dīadlīch senne.　At undren hā sent men intō his winyarde, þet ā turneþ intō his servīse of āge of man.　At middai,
wanne þē dai is al þēr họ̄test, betọ̄kned þọ̄ men of þryttī[1] wyntre,
ọ̄þer of furtī, for þē nāture of man is of grēater strengþe and of
grēater hēte ine þọ̄ āge.　Sọ̄ ēven bitọ̄ckneþ ēlde of man, þet is sē
ēnde of þē līve.　Ūre Lọ̄rd dēþ werkmen intō his winyarde agēnes
þọ̄ ēven, wanne fẹ̄le ine here ēlde wēndeþ ūt of here senne intō
Crīstes servīse.　Al[2] sọ̄ solle hī habbe þọ̄ blisce of hevene ase þọ̄
þet ferst cōmen intō þē winyarde[3].　Nocht forþan for þise grīate
būntē þet ūre Lọ̄rd yefþ ne solde nọ̄ man targī for tō wēnde tō
God Almichtī, ne him tō servī; for alsọ̄ seid þet Họ̄lī Writ þet nọ̄n
ne wọ̄t þane dai of his dīaþe, for man mai lọ̄nge lives wēne, and
ofte him legheþ sē wrench.

　　Nū, gōde men, yē habbeþ iherd þet godspel and þē forbisne.　Nū
lōkeþ yef yē bīeþ withinne þọ̄ winyarde, þet is yef[4] yē bīeþ ine
Godes servīse, yef yē bīeþ withūte dīadlīche senne, yef yē hātīeþ[5]
þat hē[6] hāteþ, yef yē luvīeþ þet hē luveþ, and dōþ þet hē họ̄t; and
bute yē dō, yē bīeþ ūt[7] of his winyarde, þet is ūt of his servīse.
And yē dōþ þet ūre Lọ̄rd họ̄t, sọ̄ yē ofserveþ þane penī, þet is
heverīche blisce, yē ofserveþ þet good þet nọ̄on herte ne may
iþenche, ne nọ̄on ȳare ihēre, ne tunge telle þọ̄ blisce þet God halt
alle þọ̄ þet hine luvīeþ.　Þider, Lọ̄rd, grantī us tō cumene.　*Quod
ipse prestare dignetur per, etc.*

---

[1] xxx.　　　[2] as.　　　[3] winyyarde.　　　[4] þet yef.　　　[5] hatied.
　　　　　　　　[6] he he.　　　[7] hut.

VII. THE AYENBITE OF INWIT, OR REMORSE
OF CONSCIENCE

Vor to Lyerny Sterve.

Onnēaþe sterfþ [1] þet ylȳerned ne heþ. Lȳerne tō sterve, þanne
sselt [2] þōu conne libbe; vor nǫn wēl libbe, ne ssel conne, þet tō
sterve ylȳerned ne heþ, and þē ilke arȝȝt is yclēped wrechche þet
ne can libbe, ne ne dar sterve. Yef þōu wylt libbe vrīlīche, lȳerne
tō sterve gledlīche. Yef þōu mē zayst, hōu me hit ssel lȳernȳ, ich   5
hit wyle þē zigge an hāste. Þōu sselt ywyte þet þis lȳf ne is bote
dȳaþ, vor dȳaþ is a wēndinge and þet ēch wǫt; and þērvǫre me
zayþ of ane manne hwanne hē sterfþ, 'Hē wēnt,' and hwanne hē
is dȳad, 'Hē is ywent.' Þis lȳf alswǫ ne is bote a wēndynge
vorzōþe, vorzōþe a wēndinge wēl ssort; vor al þet lȳf of ane   10
manne, þaȝ hē levede a þōusond yēar, þet ne ssolde bȳ bote ǫnlēpȳ
prikke tō þē zyȝþe of þē ōþre lȳve þet evre wyþōute ēnde ssel
ylēste, ǫþer ine zorȝe ǫþer ine blisse wyþōute ēndynge. Þis ōus
wytnesset wēl þē kyng, þē ērl, þē prince, þē emperōur, þet þē
blysse of þē wordle hedden zomtȳme, ac [3] nōu ine helle wēpeþ and   15
grēdeþ, yelleþ and zorȝeþ: 'A, allas [4], hwet is ōus worþ ōure pōuēr,
worþsippe, nǫblesse, richesse, blisse, and bǫst? Al hit ys ywent
wēl raþre þanne ssed, ǫþer voȝel vlȳinde, ǫþer quarēl of arblaste.
And þōus gēþ al ōure lȳf. Nōu wē wēre ybǫre, and an hāste dȳad;
ne al ōure lȳf nes naȝt bote a lȳte prikke, nōu wē bȳeþ ine zorȝe   20
wyþōute ēnde. Oure blisse is ywent intō wǫp, ōure karoles intō
zorȝe; gerlǫndes, rǫbes, playinges, messinges, and alle guodes bȳeþ
ōus yfayled.' Zuyche bȳeþ þǫ zǫnges of helle ase þē wrītinge ōus

[1] sterf.   [2] Margin, Note wel þerne capitele.   [3] ac, not in MS.
[4] Margin, þe zang of helle.

telþ, ōus vor tō ssewȳ þet þis lȳf ne is bote a wēndynge wēl ssort; and þis wordle ne is bote a wēndynge, and libbe ne is bote a wēndynge. Þanne ne is libbe bote sterve, and þet is zōþ ase paternoster; vor hwanne þou begonne libbe, an hāste þou begonne tō sterve; and al þīn ēlde, and al þīne tīme þet ys yguo, þē dȳaþ þe heþ ywonne and halt. Þou zayst þet þou hest zixtī yēar; þē dȳaþ hise heþ, and neveremǭ his nele þē yēlde. Þērvǭre is þet wyt of þē wordle folȳe, and þē clerk, zȳinde, ne yzyȝþ naȝt; day and niȝt mākeþ ǭ þing, and þē mǭre þet hit mākeþ þē lesse zuǭ knāweþ; alneway sterveþ, and hī ne conne sterve, vor day and nyȝt þou sterfst, as ich þē habbe yzēd.

Yēt eft ine ōþre manēre ich þē tēche þise clergīe, þet þou conne wēl libbe and wēl sterve. Nōu yhȳer and onderstand. Þē dȳaþ ne is bot a tōdēlinge of þē zaule and of þē bodȳe, and þet ēch wēl wǭt. Nōu ōus tēkþ þē wȳse Cātōun : ' Lȳerne wē,' zayþ hē, ' tō sterve; tōdēle wē þane gǭst of þē bodīe ofte.' Þet deden þē mēste wȳse of þise philosǫphes þet þis līf zuǭ moche hāteden, and þē wordle zuǭ moche onworþede, and zuǭ moche wylnede lȳf naȝt dȳeadlīch þet hī westen þe hare wylle; ac hit nes ham naȝt worþ, vor hī ne hedden nǭn grāce ne þē belēave of Jēsu Krīst. Ac þē hǭlȳ men þet lovīeþ God and ylēveþ þet, of þrī dȳeaþes habbeþ þē tway ypased. Vor þēr is dȳaþ tō zenne [1], and dȳaþ tō þē wordle; nōu abȳdeþ þane þridde dȳeaþ, þet is þē tōdiȝtinge of þē zaule and of þē bodīe. Betwēne ham and Paradȳs ne is bote a lȳte wǭȝ þet hȳ agelteþ be þenchinge and be wylnynge. And yef þet bodī is of þis half, þē herte and þē gǭst is of ōþer half. Þēr hȳ habbeþ hyre blēvinge, as zayþ Saynte Paul, hire sǭlās, hire blisse, and hire confort, and alle hire lostes. And þērvǭre hȳ hātȳeþ þis lȳf, þet ne is bote dȳaþ, and wylneþ þane dȳaþ bodylīch; vor þet is damezēle Bȩreblisse, þet is [1a] þē dȳaþ þet alle þē halȝen corōuneþ and dōþ intō blisse. Dȳaþ [2] is tō guode men ēnde of alle kwēade, and gāte and inguoynge of alle guode. Dȳaþ is þē strēam þet tōdēlþ dȳaþ and lȳf. Dȳaþ is of þis half, līf of ōþre half. Ac þē wȳse of þise

---

[1] Margin, Note wel þri dyaþes.   [1a] is, not in MS.   [2] Margin, Hwet is dyaþ.

wordle, þet of þis half þē strēme yzȳeþ zuǭ briȝte, of ōþer half hī
naȝt ne yzēþ, and þērvǭre his clēpeþ þe wrītinge fōles and yblent;
vor þerne dȳaþ hī clēpīeþ lȳf, and þane dȳaþ, þet is tō þē guoden
beginnynge of līve, hī hit clēpīeþ þan ēnde. And þērvǭre hȳ
hātȳeþ zuǭ moche þane dȳaþ, vor hī nyteþ hwet hit is, ne of   5
ōþer half þē strēame ne habbeþ naȝt yblēved and naȝt ne wǭt þet
ōut ne gēþ.

Þanne yef þōu wylt ywyte hwet is guod and hwet is kwēad, guo
ōut of þī zelve, guo ōut of þē wordle, līerne tō sterve. Tōdēl þīne
zaule vram þē bodȳe be þoȝte; zēnd þīne herte intō þē ōþre wordle,   10
þet is tō hevene, intō helle, intō purgātorīe, þēr þōu sselt[1] yzȳ hwet
is guod and hwet is kwēad. Ine helle þōu sselt[2] yzī mǭ zorȝes
þanne me moȝe devīsȳ, ine purgātorīe mǭ tormens þanne me moȝe
þǭlȳe, ine Paradȳs mǭre blisse þanne me moȝe wylnȳ. Helle þē
ssel tēche hōu God awrēkþ dȳadlȳch zenne; purgātorīe þē ssel   15
sēawȳ hōu God clenzeþ vēniel zenne; ine hevene þōu sselt yzȳ
ǭpenlīche hōu virtues and guode dēdes bȳeþ heȝlīche yǭlde. Ine
þis þrī þinges is al þet is nȳed, wel tō wytene hōu me ssel conne
libbe and wēl sterve. Nōu lōke eftzōne a lȳte and ne tȳene þē
naȝt tō þise þrī þinges, vor þet þōu lȳernest tō hātȳe zenne.   20
Voryet þī bodȳ ǭnes a day; guo intō helle ine þīne libbinde, þet
þōu ne guo ine þīne stervinge. Þis dēþ ofte þē hǭlī man and þē
wȳse. Þēr[3] þōu sselt yzȳ al þet herte hāteþ and bevlȳȝþ, and
defaute of alle guode, ynoȝ of alle kwēade, vēr bērnynde, brenstǭn
stinkinde, tempeste brayinde, vōule dȳevlen, honger and þorst þet   25
me ne may naȝt stǭnchī, dȳverse pīnes and wēpinges and zorȝes mǭ
þanne herte moȝe þenche, ne tonge telle, and evre ssel ylēste
wyþōute ēnde. And þērvǭre is þē ilke zorȝe wēl yclēped dȳaþ
wyþōute ēnde. And hwanne þōu yziȝt þet hit behōveþ zuǭ dȳere
abegge ǭnlēpȳ dȳadlīch zenne, þē woldest þē raþre lēte bē vlaȝe   30
quik þanne þōu dorstest tō ǭnelēpī dȳadlīche zenne consentī.

Efterward[4] guo intō purgātorīe þēr þōu sselt yzī þē pīnes of þē

---

[1] sselelt.   [2] ssel.   [3] Margin, þe pines of helle.
[4] Margin, Of Purgatorie.

zaules þet hȳer hedden vorþenchinge, ak nēre naȝt vollīche yclenzed.
Nōu hī dōþ þēr þē lēvinge of hare penonce alhwet þet hī bȳeþ
briȝte and clēne ase hī wēren at ē poynt and at ē tīme hwanne hī
yēden ōut[1] of þē welle of cristninge. Ac þē ilke penonce ys wēl
grislīch and hārd; vor al þet evre þōleden þe hōlȳ martires, ōþer 5
wyfmen þet travayleþ of chīlde, of zorȝe ne ys bote a beþ ine chāld
weter tō þē reward of þē fornayse hwērinne bērneþ þe zaules alhwet
hī bȳeþ yclenzed, ase gōld al yclenzed[2] ine þē vēre.   Me ne vīnt
lesse þanne yclenzed, vor þet vēr is of zuyche kēnde, al þet hit
vīnt ine þē zaule of gelte, of dēde, of spēche, of þoȝte þet ȝērneþ tō 10
zenne ōþer līte ōþer moche, al vorbērnþ and clenzeþ.   And þēr bȳeþ
ypunissed and awrȩke alle vȩnyal zennes, þet wē clȩpīeþ lītle zennes,
þet wē dōþ ofte, and smāle fōle þoȝtes, wōrdes ȳdele, trufles, scornes,
and alle ōþre ȳdelnesses, alhwet hī bȳ worþe tō guo intō hevene hwēr
ne gēþ in naȝt bote hit bȳ riȝt briȝt.   þet ilke vēr drēdeþ þō þet bȳ 15
hare myȝte ham lōkeþ vram dȳadlīch zenne, and lōkeþ hōlȳlīche
hare herten and hare bodȳes and hare mōuþes and þē vīf wyttes
vram alle zenne, and zuō libbeþ ase hī ssolden ēche daye tō dōme
come tōvōre God.   And þȩrvōre þet nōn ne may libbe wyþōute
zenne ; vor, ase zayþ Salomōn, 'Zeve zīþe a day valþ þē guode 20
man.'   And þērvōre, be hōlȳ ssrifte and be tȳeares and be bēnes,
hī dōþ hare miȝte ham zelve tō arēre and tō amendī; and ham
zelve zuō dēme þet hī onderstōnde tō volȝī þane laste dōm, vor hwō
hīer him dēmþ zōþlīche him ne worþ nōn hēde tō bȳ vorlōre at ē
daye of dōme.   And þus me lȳerneþ kwēad tō knāwe and tō bevlȳ, 25
and alle zennes tō hātȳe, grat[3] and smal, and onderstōnde þē hōlȳ
drēde of God þet is beginnynge of guod līf and of alle guode.

Ac hit ne is naȝt ynoȝ tō lēte þē kwēades bote me lȳernȳ þet
guod tō dōne, and bote yef me zēche þē virtues, vor wyþōute ham
nōn ariȝt wēl ne leveþ.   þanne yef þōu wylt lȳernȳ wēl tō libbe be
virtue, lȳerne zuō, ase ich þē habbe yzēd, tō sterve.   Tōdēl þine
gōst vram þine bodȳe be þoȝte and be wylninge; guo ōut of þise
wordle stervinde ; guo intō þē lōnde of þē libbynde þēr nōn ne

---

[1] ouot.   [2] ychenzed.   [3] and grat.

sterſþ [1], ne yēaldeþ, þet is ine Paradȳs.　Þēr me lȳerneþ wēl tō libbe
an wyt and [2] corteysȳe, vor þēr ne may guo in nǭ vyleynȳe ; þēr is
blisfolle [3] velaȝrēde of God and of āngles and of halȝen ; þēr opwexeþ
alle guodes, vayrhēde, richesse, worþssippe, blisse, virtue, love, wyt,
joye, wyþōute ēnde ; þēr ne is nǭn ypocrisȳe, ne bāret, ne blǭndinge,　5
ne discord, ne envȳe, ne honger, ne þorst, ne hēte, ne chęle, ne
kwēad, ne zorȝe, ne drēde of vȳendes, ac alneway fęstes and kinges
brēdales, zǭnges and blisse wyþōute ēnde.　Þē ilke blisse is zuǭ grat
þet hwǭ þet hedde ytāke þērof ennelēpī drǭpe of þē lēste þinge þet
þēr ys, hē ssolde bȳ of þē love of God zuǭ dronke þet al þē blisse　10
of þise wordle him ssolde bȳ drēde and wǭ ; rychesses, dong ;
worþssipes, vōulhēde, and þē ilke.　Tō grēate love þet hē ssolde
habbe tō come þēr, him ssolde, bȳ an hondred þōuzen zīþe, þē
mǭre hardīlīche hātȳe zenne and lovīe virtues þet is al þē drēde of
helle hwērof ich habbe bevǭre ispeke ; vor love is mǭre stranger　15
þanne drēde.　And þanne is þet lȳf vayr and oneste, þanne me
bevlȳȝt þet kwēad and me dēþ þet guod, naȝt vor drēde vor tō bȳ
yspild, ac vor þē wylnynge of hevene and vor þē love of God and
vor þē grēate clennesse þet virtue heþ and guod lȳf.　And þē ilke
þet love lēdeþ, hē zēkþ raþre, and lesse him costneþ, þanne him　20
þet serveþ God be drēde.　Þē hāre ȳernþ, þē grȳhond hym volȝeþ,
þē ǭn be drēde, þē ōþer be wylnynge ; þē ǭn vlȳȝþ, þē ōþor hyne
drȳfþ.　Þē hōlȳ man ȳernþ ase grīhond þet habbeþ al day hare
ēȝe tō hevene, hwēr hī yzȳeþ þē praye þet hī drīveþ ; and þērvǭre
hȳ voryeteþ alle ōþre guodes, ase dēþ þē gentyl hond hwanne　25
hā zȳþ his praye tōvǭre his ēȝen.

Þis is þet lȳf of þē wēl lovīynde of gentil herte and affayted, þet
zuǭ moche lovȳeþ virtue and hātȳeþ zenne þet, yef hī wēren zykere
þet me ne ssolde his conne ne God ne ssolde his awręke, ham ne
daynede naȝt tō dō zenne ; ac al hare þenchinges and al hare　30
wyllis hire herten clenlīche lōkī and agrayþī þet hī bȳ worþī tō
habbe þē blisse of Paradȳs, hwēr nǭ cherl ne ssel come in, ne
vals, ne þȳef, ne prōud, vor þē worse ssolde bȳ þē velaȝrēde.

---

[1] sterf.　　[2] and wyt an.　　[3] Margin, Of þe blisses of paradis.

VIII. TREVISA'S TRANSLATION OF HIGDEN'S POLYCHRONICON

Book I, Chapter LVIII. The Inhabitants of Britain.

Brytōns wonede fürst in þis ȳlǭnd þē ȝẹ̄r of Hēlȳ þē prēost
eyȝtetēne; of Silvius Posthumus, King of Latȳns, enleuene; after
þē tākyng of Troye þrē and fourtȳ ȝẹ̄re[1]; tōfǭre þē büldynge of
Rōme foure hondred and twǭ and thrytȳ.   Hȳ[2] cōme hyder and[3]
tōk here cōurs fram Armorȳc þat[4] nōw ys þē ōþer[5] Brytayn; hȳ
hǖld lǭng tȳme þē sōuþ contrays of þē ȳlǭnd.   Hyt byfül afterward
in Vespāsian hys tȳme, Duk of Rōme, þat þē Pictes ōut of Scitia[6]
schipede intō occean, and wẹ̄re ydryue abōute wiþ þē wȳnd and
entrede intō þē norþ cǭstes of Īrlǭnd, and fǭnd þẹ̄r Scottes and
prayede for tō hāue a plāce tō wonȳ ynne, and myȝte nǭn gete;
for Ȳrlǭnd, as Scottes seyde, myȝte noȝt susteyne bǭþe pēople.
Scottes sende þē Pictes tō þē norþ sȳdes of Britayn, and byheet
ham help aȝēnes þē Britons þat wẹ̄re enemȳes ȝif hȳ wolde arȳse,
and tōk ham tō wȳues of here douȝtres apon süch condiciōn : ȝif
dōuteful whǭ scholde hāue ryȝt for tō bē kyng, ā scholde rāþer
chēose ham a kyng of þē mōder sȳde þan of þē fader sȳde, of þē
wymmen kyn rāþer þan of þē men kyn.   Yn[7] Vespāsian þē
emperōr[8] hys tȳme, whan Mārius Arvirāgus hys sone was kyng of
Britōns, ǭn Rodrīc, Kyng of Pictes, cōm ōut of Scitia and gan tō
destruye Scotlǭnd.   Þanne Mārius þē kyng slouȝ þis Rodrīc and
ȝaf þē norþ partȳ of Scotlᶒnd, þat hatte Cathenēsia, tō þē men þat
wẹ̄r ycome wiþ Rodrīc and wẹ̄re ǭvercome wiþ hym, for tō wone

---

[1] ȝere not in MS.   [2] Beda, libro primo, before sentence as authority
for statement; so in other cases of authorities.   [3] &, as often.   [4] þt, as
usual.   [5] þoþer.   [6] Scicia, as always.   [7] Gaufridus before sentence.
[8] þempor, with abbreviation for ur, or.

ynne. Bote þēos men hadde nǫ wȳves, ne nǫn myȝte habbe of þē
nācīōn of Britōns; þērfǫre hȳ seylede intō Ȳrlǫnd, and tōk ham
tō[1] wȳves Ȳryschmen doȝters, at þat covenaunt þat þē mōder blōd
scholde bē put tōfǫre yn successiōn of heritāge. Nǫþelēs[2] Servius[3]
super Vergilium seiþ þat Pictes būþ Agatirses þat hadde som wonyng 5
plāces abōute þē wateres of Scitia, and ā būþ yclēpud Pictes
bycause of peyntyng and smyttyng of wondes þat būþ ysēne on her
bodīes; for hȳ hadde muche flem, and wēr ofte boistōuslȳch ylete
blōd and hadde menȳ wondes ysēne on here bodȳ, sǫ þat hȳ sēmede
as hyt wēre men ypeynt wiþ wondes; þērfǫre ā wēre yclēpud 10
Pictes, as hyt wēre peynted[4] men. Þēose men and þē Gǫtes būþ
al ǫn pēople; for whanne Maximus þē tīraunt was awent ōut of
Britayn intō Fraunce for tō occupīe þē empere,[5] þanne Gratiānus
and Valentiniānus, þat wēre brēþeren[6] and felowes of þē emperōr,
brouȝte þēose Gǫthes ōut of Scitia wiþ grēt ȝeftes, wiþ flatryng and 15
fair byhestes, into þē north contrays of Britayn, for ā wēr stalworþ
and strǫng men of armes, and sende ham bȳ schipes tō werre apon
þē Britōns þat wēr þǫ nāked and baar, wiþōute knyȝtes and men
of armes. And sǫ þēoves and brībōrs wēr ymad men of lǫnd and
of contray, and wonede in þē norþ contrayes and būlde þēr cītēs 20
and tōunes. Carausius[7] þē tīraunt slouȝ Bassiānus bȳ help and
trēsōn of þē Pictes þat cōme in help and socōur of Bassiānus, and
ȝaf þē Pictes a wonyng plāce in Albānia, þat ys Scotlǫnd. Þar
þay wonede lǫng tȳme afterward, ymelled wiþ Brytōns. Þanne
seþþe[8] þat Pictes occupīede rāþer þē norþ sȳde of Scotlǫnd, hyt 25
sēmeþ þat þē wonyng plāce þat þis[9] Carausius ȝaf ham ys þē sōuþ
sȳde of Scotlǫnd þat strechcheþ fram þē þwartǫver wal of Rōmayn
work tō þē Scottysch sē, and conteyneþ Galway and Lodovīa,
Lodway. Þērof Bēda, *libro tertio, capitulo secundo*, spēkeþ in þis
manēre: Ninian, þē hǫlȳ man, convertede þē sōuþ Pictes; after- 30
ward þē Saxons cōme and māde þat contray lǫnge tō Brenicia, þē
norþ partȳ of Norþumberlǫnd, fortō þat Kynādius, Alpīnus hys

---

[1] two. [2] Giraldus. [3] Sirvius. [4] peyntud. [5] þempere, as in next line.
[6] breþeron. [7] Gaufridus. [8] seþthe. [9] þes.

sone, kyng of Scotlǫnd, put o͞ut þē Pictes and māde þat contray
þat ys bytwēne Twēde and þē Scottysch sę lǫnge tō hys kyngdōm.
Afterward[1] lǫng tȳme þē Scottes węr ylad bȳ Duk Reuda and
cōme o͞ut of Ȳrlǫnd, þat ys þē propre contray of Scottes, and wiþ
love ǫþer with strengthe māde ham a plāce fast bȳ þē Pictes, in þē
norþ sȳde of þat arm of þē sę þat brękeþ intō þē lǫnd in þē west
sȳde, þat departede in ǫld tȳme bytwēne Britōns and Pictes. Of
þis Duk Reuda þē Scottes hadde þē nāme, and węr yclęped
Dalreudīnes, as hyt węre Reuda hys part, for in here spēche a part
ys yclęped dāl. Þē[2] Pictes myȝt hāve nǫ wȳves of Britōns, bote
þay tōk ham wȳves of Ȳrisch Scottes and byȝēode ham fair for tō
wonȳ wiþ ham, and grauntede ham a lǫnd bȳ þē sęsȳde þar þē sę ys
narow; þat lǫnd no͞w hatte Galway. Ȳrisch[3] Scottes lǫndede at
Argail, þat is Scottene clyf, for Scottes lǫndede þare for tō harmȳe
þē Britōns ǫþer for þat plāce ys next tō Ȳrlǫnd for tō cōme alǫnd
in Britayn. And[4] sǫ þē Scottes, after Britōns and Pictes, māde
þē þridde manēr pēople wonyng in Bretayn.

Þanne after þat cōme þē Saxons, at þē prayng of þē Britōns, tō
helpe ham aȝęnes þē Scottes and þē Pictes. And þē Britōns węr
yput o͞ut anǫn tō Wāles, and Saxons occupīed þē lǫnd lȳtel and
lȳtel, and eft mǫre and mǫre, streyȝt anǫn tō þē Scottysch sę; and
sǫ Saxons māde þē furþe manēr of men in þē ȳlǫnd of Britayn.
For[5] Saxons and Angles cōme o͞ut of Germania; ȝet som Britōns
þat woneþ nyȝ clępeþ ham schortlȳch Germans. Nǫþelęs, abo͞ute
þē ȝęr of o͞ure Lǫrd eyȝte hondred, Egbertus, kyng of West Saxon,
comaundede and heet clępe al men of þē lǫnd Englyschmen.
Þanne[6] after þat þē Dānes pursued[7] þē lǫnd abo͞ute an twǫ hondred
ȝęr, þat ys tō męnyng fram þē forseyde Egbert hys tȳme anǫn tō
Seint Edward hys tȳme, and māde þē syfte manēr pēople in þē
ȳlǫnd, bote hȳ failede afterward. At tē laste cōme Normans under
Duk William and suduwede Englyschmen, and ȝet hǫldeþ þē lǫnd;

---

[1] Beda, libro quinto, capitulo quinto.   [2] Giraldus, distinctio prima.
[3] Marianus.   [4] Beda.   [5] Beda, libro quinto, capitulo quinto.
[6] Alfridus.   [7] pursuwed.

and hȳ māde þē syxte pēople in þē ȳlǭnd.   Bote in þē fürste Kyng
Henrȳ hys tȳme cōme menȳ Flemmyngs and fēng a wonyng plāce
for a tȳme bysīdes Mailrǭs, in þē west sȳde of Engelǭnd, and māde
þē seveþe pēople in þē ȳlǭnd.   Nǭþelęs, bȳ hęste of þē sāme kyng,
ā węr yhǭve þennes and yput tō Haverfōrd hys sȳde, in þē west 5
sȳde of Wāles.   And sǭ now in Brytayn Dānes and Pictes faileþ
al out, and fȳf nāciōns woneþ þęrynne : þat büþ Scottes in Albānia,
þat ys Scotlǭnd; Britōns in Cambria, þat ys Wāles, bote þat Flemmyngs woneþ yn West Wāles; and Normans and Englyschmen
ymelled yn al þē ȳlǭnd.   For hyt ys nǭ dōute in stǭrȳes how [1] and 10
in what manēre þē Dānes węr yputt away and destroyed out of
Britayn; now hyt ys tō declāryng how þē Pictes [2] węr destruyd and
faylede.

   Britayn [3] was somtȳme occupīed with Saxons, and pęs was ymād
and ystābled wiþ þē Pictes.   Þanne þē Scottes þat cōme wiþ þē 15
Pictes sȳe þat þē Pictes þey węre [4] lęęs þan þē Scottes, and węr
nǭbler of dędes and bettre men of armes þan węr þē Scottes, þanne
þē Scottes turnde tō here künde tręsōns þat hȳ useþ ofte, for in
tręsōn ā passeþ ōþere men and büþ traitours as hyt węr bȳ künde.
For þay prayde tō a feste al þē gręte of þē Pictes, and weytede here 20
tȳme whanne þē Pictes węr at ęse and merȳ, and hadde wēl ydronke [5],
and drouȝ out nayles þat hüld up þē holouȝ benches under þē
Pictes, and þē Pictes sodeynlȳch and unwar fēl ǭver þē hammes
intō a wonder pütfal.   Þanne þē Scottes fül on þē Pictes and slouȝ
ham. and lefte nǭn alȳve ; and sǭ of þē twey pēople þē better 25
werriour was hǭlȳch destruyd.   Bote þē ōþer [6], þat büþ þē Scottes
þat węre wēl unlȳch tō þē Pictes, tōk profyt bȳ þat fals tręsōn ; for
ā tōk al þat lǭnd and hǭldeth hyt ȝet hedertō, and clępeþ hyt Scotlǭnd after here oune nāme.   Þat tȳme, þat was in Kyng Edgar
hys tȳme, Kynādius, Alpīnus hys sone, was lędar of Scottes, and 30
werrede in Picte lǭnd and destruyde þē Pictes; hē werrede six

---

[1] houȝ.   [2] Pittes, as also in l. 15.   [3] Giraldus, distinctione prima,
capitulo septimo decimo.   [4] awere.   [5] ydrongke.   [6] þoþer.

sȳþes in Saxon, and tōk al þē lǫnd þat ys bytwēne Twēde and þē
Scottysch sę̄ wiþ wrǫng and wiþ strengthe.

CHAPTER LIX.   ON THE LANGUAGES OF THE INHABITANTS.

As hyt ys yknowe hōū3 menȳ manēr pēople būþ in þis ȳlǫnd, þę̄r
būþ alsǫ of sǫ menȳ pēople lǫngāges and tonges; nǫþelę̄s Walschmen and Scottes, þat būþ no3t ymelled wiþ ōþer nāciōns, hǫldeþ
wēl ny3 here fürste lǫngāge and spę̄che, bote 3ef Scottes þat wę̄re
som tȳme confederat and wonede wiþ þē Pictes drawe somwhat
after here spę̄che. Bote þē Flemmynges, þat woneþ in þē west sȳde
of Wāles, habbeþ yleft here strānge spę̄che and spę̄keþ Saxonlȳch
ynow. Alsǫ Englysch men, þey3 hȳ hadde fram þē bygynnyng þrē
manēr spę̄che, sōūþeron, norþeron, and myddel spę̄che, in þē
myddel of þē lǫnd, as hȳ cōme of þrē manēr pēople of Germānia,
nǫþelę̄s, bȳ commyxstiōn and mellyng fürst wiþ Dānes and afterward
wiþ Normans, in menȳe þē contray lǫngāge ys apeyred, and som
useþ strānge wlaffyng, chyteryng, harryng and garryng, grisbittyng.
Þis apeyryng of þē bürþtonge ys bycause of twey þinges. Ǫn ys,
for chyldern in scōle, a3ēnes þē usāge and manēre of al ōþer
nāciōns, būþ compelled for tō lę̄ve here oune lǫngāge and for tō
construe here lessōns and here þinges ā Freynsch, and habbeþ
sūþthe þē Normans cōme fürst intō Engelǫnd. Alsǫ gentilmen
children būþ ytau3t for tō spę̄ke Freynsch fram tȳme þat ā būþ
yrokked in here crādel, and conneþ spę̄ke and playe wiþ a chīld
hys brouch; and uplǫndysch[1] men wol lȳkne hamsylf tō gentilmen, and fǫndeþ wiþ grę̄t bysȳnes for tō spę̄ke Freynsch for tō bē
mǫre ytǫld of.

Þys[2] manēre was moche yused tōfǫre þē fürste moreyn, and ys
seþthe somdę̄l ychaunged. For Jǫhan[3] Cornwal, a mayster of
gramēre, chayngede þē lǫre in gramērscōle and construcciōn of
Freynsch intō Englysch; and Richard Pencrych lurnede þat manēre
tę̄chyng of hym, and ōþer men of Pencrych, sǫ þat nōw, þē 3ę̄r of

---

[1] oplondysch.   [2] Trevisa, indicating addition by translator.   [3] Iohan.

ōure Lǫrd a þōusond þrē hondred foure scǭre and fȳve, of þē
secunde Kyng Richard after þē conquest nȳne, in al þē gramēr-
scōles of Engelǫnd childern lẹ̄veþ Frensch and construeþ and
lurneþ an Englysch, and habbeþ þērbȳ avauntāge in ǫn sȳde and
desavauntāge yn anōþer. Here avauntāge ys, þat ā lurneþ here   5
gramēr yn lasse tȳme þan childern wẹr ywoned tō dō ; disavauntāge
ys, þat nōw childern of gramērscōle conneþ nǭ mǭre Frensch þan
can here lift heele, and þat ys harm for ħam and ā scholle passe þē sẹ̄
and travayle in strānge lǫndes, and in menȳ caas alsǭ. Alsǭ gentilmen
habbeþ nōw moche yleft for tō tẹ̄che here childern Frensch.   10

Hyt sēmeþ a grẹt wonder hōū ¹ Englysch, þat ys þē bürþtonge of
Englysch men and here oune lǫngāge and tonge, ys sǭ dȳvers of sōūn ²
in þis ȳlǫnd ; and þē lǫngāge of Normandȳ ys comlyng of anōþer
lǫnd, and haþ ǫn manēr sōūn ² among al men þat spẹ̄keþ hyt arȝt in
Engelǫnd. Nǭþelẹ̄s ³, þẹr ys as menȳ dȳvers manēr Frensch yn þē   15
rẹm of Fraunce as ys dȳvers manēre Englysch in þē rẹm of
Engelǫnd. Alsǭ, of þē forseyde Saxon tonge, þat ys dẹled ā þrē
and ys abyde scarslȳch wiþ fēaw uplǫndysch men, and ys grẹt
wondur ; for men of þē ẹst wiþ men of þē west, as hyt wẹre undur
þē sāme partȳ of hevene, acordeþ mǭre in sōūnyng of spẹ̄che þan   20
men of þē norþ wiþ men of þē sōūþ. Þẹrfǭre hyt ys þat Mercii,
þat būþ men of myddel Engelǫnd, as hyt wẹre partenērs of þē ēndes,
understǫndeþ betre þē sȳde lǫngāges, norþeron and sōūþeron, þan
norþeron and sōūþeron understǫndeþ eyþer ōþer. Al ⁴ þē lǫngāge
of þē Norþhümbres, and specialȳch at Ȝork, ys sǭ scharp, slyttyng 25
and frǫtyng and unschāpe, þat wē sōūþeron men may þat lǫngāge
unnẹ̄þe understǫnde. Ȳ trowe þat þat ys bycause þat ā būþ nyȝ tō
strānge men and āliens þat spẹ̄keþ strāngelȳch, and alsǭ bycause
þat þē kynges of Engelǫnd woneþ alwey fer fram þat contray ; for
ā būþ mǭre yturnd tō þē sōūþ contray, and ȝef ā gǭþ tō þē norþ   30
contray ā gǭþ wiþ grẹt help and strengthe. Þē cause whȳ ā būþ
mǭre in þē sōūþ contray þan in þē norþ may bē betre cōrnlǫnd,
mǭre pēople, mǭre nǫble cytēs, and mǭre profytāble hāvenes.

¹ houȝ.   ² soon.   ³ Trevisa.   ⁴ Willelmus de Pontificalibus, libro tertio.

THE DIALECT OF LONDON

I. THE ENGLISH PROCLAMATION OF HENRY THIRD

HENRĪ [1], þurȝ Godes fultume King on Engleneloande, Lhoaverd on Ȳrloande, Duk on Normandī, on Aquitaine, and Ēorl on Anjow, sēnd igrētinge tō alle hise hōlde, ilǣrde and ilȩ̄awede, on Huntendoneschīre : þæt witen ȝē wēl alle þæt wē willen and unnen þæt þæt ūre rǣdesmen alle, ǭþer þē moare dǣl of heom þæt bēoþ ichǭsen þurȝ us and þurȝ þæt loandes folk on ūre künerīche, habbeð idōn and shullen dōn in þē worþnesse of Gode and on ūre trēowþe, for þē frȩ̄me of þē loande þurȝ þē besiȝte of þan tōfǭreniseide rȩ̄desmen, bēo stȩ̄defǣst and ilȩ̄stinde in alle þinge abūten ǣnde.   And wē hoaten alle ūre trēowe in þē trēowþe þæt hēo us ǭȝen, þæt hēo stȩ̄defǣstlīche hȩ̄alden and swȩ̄rien tō hȩ̄alden and tō wȩ̄rien þǭ isetnesses þæt bēon imākede and bēon tō mākīen, þurȝ þan tōfǭreniseide rǣdesmen, ǭþer þurȝ þē moare dǣl of heom alswǭ alse hit is bifǭren iseid; and þæt æch [2] ōþer helpe þæt for tō dōne bī þan ilche ǭþe aȝȩ̄nes alle men riȝt for tō dōne and tō foangen.   And noan ne nime of loande ne of eȝte whȩ̄rþurȝ þis besiȝte muge bēon ilet ǭþer iwersed on ǭnīe wīse.   And ȝif ǭnī ǭþer ǭnīe cumen hēr onȝȩ̄nes, wē willen and hoaten þæt alle ūre trēowe heom hȩ̄alden dȩ̄adlīche ifoan.   And for þæt wē willen þæt þis bēo stȩ̄defǣst and lȩ̄stinde, wē sēnden ȝew þis writ ǭpen, iseined wiþ ūre sȩ̄ȩl, tō hālden amanges ȝew ine hōrd.   Witnesse us selven æt Lundene þane eȝtetēnþe day on þē monþe of Octǭbre, in þē twǭ and fowertiȝþe ȝȩ̄are of ūre crūninge.   And þis wes idōn ætfǭren ūre iswǭrene rȩ̄desmen, Bonefāce Archebischop on Kante-

---

[1] Henr'.   [2] æhc.

büri [1], Walter [2] of Cantelow, Bischop on Wirechestre, Sīmōn [3] of
Mūntfort, Ēorl on Leirchestre, Richard [4] of Clāre, Ēorl on Glow--
chestre and on Hurtſord, Roger [5] Bigod, Ēorl on Northſolke
and Marescal on Engleneloande, Perres of Savveye, Willelm [6] of
Fort, Ēorl on Aubemarle, Jōhan [7] of Plesseiz, Ēorl on Warewīk,   5
Jōhan [7] Geffrees sune, Perres of Mūntfort, Richard [4] of Grey,
Roger [5] of Mortemēr, Jāmes of Aldithelē [8a], and ætſōren ōþre inoӡe.

And al on þō ilche wōrden is isend intō ævrīche [8] ōþre schīre
ōver al þære kūnerīche on Engleneloande, and ēk intel Īrelōnde.

II. ADAM DAVY'S DREAMS ABOUT EDWARD II

Tō ōure Lōrde Jēsu [8b] Crīst in hevene   10
Ich tōday shewe mȳne swevene,
Þat ich mette in ōne niӡht [9]
Of a kniӡht of mychel miӡht ;
His nāme is ihōte Sir Edward þē Kyng,
Prince of Wāles, Engelōnde þē faire þing.   15
Mē mette þat hē was armed wēl
Bōþe wiþ ȳrne and [10] wiþ stēl,
And on his helme þat was of stēl
A corōune of gōld bicōm hym wēl.
Biſōre þe shrȳne of Seint Edward hē stood,   20
Myd glad chēre and mȳlde of mood,
Mid twō kniӡttes armed on eiþer sīde
Þat hē ne miӡht þennes gōo ne rīde.
Hetilīch hii leiden hym upon
Als hii miӡtten myd swērde [11] dōn.   25

---

[1] Kant' bur.'   [2] Walt.'   [3] Sim.'   [4] Ric.'   [5] Rog.'
[6] Will.'   [7] Ioh.'   [8] ævrihce.   [8a] Aldithel.   [8b] Ihu, as usual.
[9] niӡth ; so ӡth to ӡht in all words.   [10] &, as often.   [11] swerd.

Hē stood þēre wēl swīþe stille,
And þǫled al tōgedres her wille;
Ne strǫok ne ȝaf hē aȝeinward
Tō þilk þat hym wēren wiþerward.
Wōūnde ne was þēre blōdȳ nǫn,
Of al þat hym þēre was dōn.

After þat me þouȝht onǫn,
As þē tweie kniȝttes wēren gǫn,
In eiþer ēre of ōure kyng,
Þēre sprǫnge ōut a wēl fāre þing.

Hii wēxen ōut sǫ briȝht sǫ glēm
Þat shȳneð of þē sonnebēm.
Of dīvers colōures hii wēren
Þat cōmen ōut of bǫþe his ēren;
Foure [1] bēndes alle bȳ rewe on eiþer ēre
Of dīvers colōurs, rēd and whīte als hii wēre;
Als fer as mē þouȝht [2] ich miȝht see
Hii spredden fer and wȳde in þē cuntrē.

Forsōþe mē mette þis ilke [3] swevene—
Ich tāke tō witnesse God of hevene—
Þē Wedenysday bifǫre þē decollāciōūn of Seint Jǫn,
It is mǫre þan twelve mōneþ gǫn.
God mē graunte sǫ heveneblis,
As mē mette þis swevene as it is.
Nōw God þat is Hevenekyng,
Tō mychel joye tōurne þis mētyng.

Anōþer swevene mē mette on a Tiwesniȝht,
Bifǫre þē fēst of alle halewen, of þat ilk kniȝht,
His nāme is nempned hēre bifǫre;—
Blissed bē þē tȳme þat hē was bǫre;
For wē shullen þē day see,
Emperōur ychǫsen hē worþe of cristientē.
God us graunte þat ilke [3] bōne,

---

[1] ffoure; ff = F, as occasionally.   [2] þou.   [3] ilk.

Þat þilke[1] tȳdyng hēre wē sōne
Of Sir Edward ōūre dērworþ kyng.
Ich mette of hym anōþere fair mētyng:
Tō ōūre Lǫrde of hevene ich telle þis,
Þat mȳ swevene tōūrne tō mychel blis.   5
Mē þouȝht hē rǫǫd upon an asse,
And þat ich tāke God tō witnesse;
Ywonden hē was in a mantel gray;
Tōward Rōme hē nōm his way.
Upon his hevede sat an gray hure,   10
It sēmed hym wēl amēsure.
Hē rǫǫd wiþūten hǫse and shō,
His wone was nouȝht sǫ for tō dō;
His shankes sēmeden al bloodrēde;
Mȳne herte wēp for grēte drēde.   15
Als a pilgryme hē rǫǫd tō Rōme,
And þider hē cōm wēl swīþe sōne.
  Þē þride[2] swevene mē mette ā niȝht
Riȝht of þat dērworþe kniȝht;
Þē Wedenysday ā niȝht it was   20
Next þē day of Seint Lucīe bifǫre Cristenmesse.
Ich shewe þis, God of hevene,
Tō mychel joye hē tōūrne my swevene.
Mē þouȝht þat ich was at Rōme,
And þider ich cōm swīþe sōne;   25
Þē Pǫpe and Sir Edward, ōūre kyng,
Bǫþe hii hadden a newe dubbyng.
Hure gray was hēr clǫþing;
Of ōþere clǫþes seiȝ ich nǫþing.
Þē Pǫpe ȝede bifǫre, mȳtred wēl faire iwys,   30
Þē Kyng Edward cōm corōūned myd grēt blis;
Þat bitǫkneþ hē shal bē
Emperōūr in cristianetē.

   [1] þilk.   [2] þrid.

Jēsus Crīst, ſul of grāce,
Graunte ōure kyng in everȳ plāce
Maistrīe of his wiþerwynes,
And of alle wicked Sarasynes.

Mē met a swevene on worþingniȝht,   5
Of þat ilche dērworþe kniȝht;
God ich it shewe, and tō witnesse tāke,
And sǭ shīlde mē frǭ synne and sāke.

Intō an chapēl ich cōm of ōur Lęſdȳ;
Jēsus Crīst, hire lēve son, stood bȳ;   10
On rōde hē was, an lovelīch man
Als þilke¹ þat on rōde was dōn.

Hē unneiled his hǭnden twǭ,
And seide wiþ þē kniȝht hē wolde gǭ:
'Maiden and mōder and mȳlde quēne,   15
Ich mōte mȳ kniȝht tōday sēne.

Lēve mōder, ȝive mē lęve,
For ich ne may nǭ lenger bilęve;
Ich mōte conveye þat ilke kniȝht
Þat us haþ served day and niȝht;   20
In pilerināge hē wil gǭn,
Tō bēn² awręke of ōure fǭn.'

'Lēve son, ȝōure wille sǭ mōte it bē,
For þē kniȝht bǭþe day and niȝht haþ served mē,
Bǭþe at ōure wille wēl faire iwys,   25
Þęrſǭre hē haþ served hevenerīche blis.'

God þat is in hevene sǭ briȝht,
Bē wiþ ōure kyng bǭþe day and niȝht.
Amēn, amēn, sǭ mōte it bē;
Þęrtō biddeþ a paternoster and an āvē.   30

    Aḍam þē marchal of Stretford-atte-Bowe,
Wēl swīþe wīde his nāme is yknowe,
Hē hymself mette þis mętyng.

---

¹ þilk.   ² bien.

Tō witnesse hē tākeþ Jēsu, hevenekyng ;
On Wedenysday in clẹ̄ne leinte,
A voice mē bẹ̄de Ī ne shulde nouȝht feinte ;
Of þē swevenes þat hēr bēn write,
Ī shulde swīþe dōn mȳ lọ̄rde kyng tō wite.   5
Ich answerde þat Ī ne miȝht for derk gọ̄n.
Þē vois mē bad gọọ, for liȝht ne shuld ich faile nọ̄n,
And þat Ī ne shulde lette for nọ̄þing,
Þat ich shulde shewe þē kyng mȳ mẹ̄tyng.
Forþ ich went swīþe onọ̄n,   10
Ẹ̄stward as mē þouȝht ich miȝht gọ̄n ;
Þē liȝht of hevene mē cōm tō,
As ich in mȳ waye shulde gọ̄.
Lọ̄rd, mȳ bodȳ ich ȝelde þee tō,
What ȝōure wille is wiþ mē tō dō.   15
Ich tāke tō witnesse God of hevene,
Þat sōþlīch ich mette þis ilche swevene ;
Ī ne reiche what ȝee myd mȳ bodȳ dō,
Als wisselīch Jēsus of hevene mȳ soule undergọ̄.

Þē Þursday next þē bẹ̄ryng of ōure Lẹ̄fdȳ,   20
Mē þouȝht an aungel cōm Sir Edward bȳ ;
Þē aungel bitook Sir Edward on họ̄nde,
Al blēdyng þē foure forþer clawes sọ̄ wẹ̄re of þē Lọ̄mbe.
At Caunterbirȳ, bifọ̄re þē heiȝe autere, þē kyng stood,
Yclọ̄þed al in rẹ̄de murrē[1] ; hē was of þat blee rẹ̄d as blood. 25
God, þat was on gōde Frīday dōn on þē rōde,
Sō turne my swevene niȝht and day tō mychel gōde.
Tweye poynts[2] þẹ̄re bēn þat bēn unshewed
For mē ne worþe tō clerk ne lewed ;
Bot tō Sir Edward ōure kyng,   30
Hym wil ich shewe þilk mẹ̄tyng.
Ich telle ȝōu, forsōþe wiþōuten lẹ̄s,
Als God of hevene maide Mārīe tō mōder chẹ̄s,

[1] m're.   [2] poyntz.

Þē aungel cōm tō mē, Adam Dāvȳ, and sēde,
'Bot þōu, Adam, shewe þis, þee worþe wēl yvel mēde.'
Ī shewe ȝōu þis ilk mētyng,
As þē aungel it shewed mē in a visiōun ;
Bot þis tōkenyng bifalle, sō dooþ mē intō prisōun.
Lōrde, mȳ bodȳ is tō ȝōure wille [1] ;
Þeiȝ ȝee willeþ mē þērfōre spille,
Ich it wil tāke in þōlemōdenesse,
Als God graunte us heveneblisse ;
And lēte us nevere þērof mysse,
Þat wē ne mōten þider wēnde in clennesse.
Amēn, Amēn, sō mōte it bē,
And lēte us nevere tō ōþere waye tee.
Whōsō wil spēke myd mē, Adam þē marchal,
In Stretforþe-Bowe hē is yknowe and ōvere al ;
Ich ne shewe nouȝht þis for tō hāve mēde,
Bot for God Almiȝttīes drēde,
       For it is sooþ.

III. THE FIRST PETITION TO PARLIAMENT IN
ENGLISH

Tō [2] thē mōȯst nōble and [3] worthīest lōrdes, mōȯst ryghtful and
wȳsest Cōnseille tō ōwre līge Lōrde thē Kyng, compleynen, if it lȳke
tō yōw, thē folk of thē Mercerȳe of London as [4] a membre of thē
sāme citee, of manȳ wrōnges subtiles and alsō ōpen oppressiōns ydō
tō hem bȳ lōnge tȳme hēre bifōre passed. Of which ōon was, whēre
thē elecciōn of mairaltee is tō bē tō thē frēmen of thē citee bī gōde
and paisible avȳs of thē wȳsest and trewest, at ō day in thē yēre
frēlīch,—thēre, noughtwithstōndyng thē sāme frēdam or fraunchīse,

---

[1] willelle.   [2] T.   [3] ȝ, as usual.   [4] as not in MS.

Nicholus [1] Brembre wyth his upbęręrs propǫsed hym, thē yęre
next after Jǫhn [2] Northampton mair of thē sāme citee with strǫnge
hǫnde as it is ful knowen, and thourgh debāte and strenger partȳe
ayeins thē pęęs bifǫre purveyde was chǫsen mair, in destrucciōn
of manȳ ryght. For in thē sāme yēre thē forsaid Nicholus, withōuten   5
nēde, ayein the pęęs māde dȳverse enarmynges bī day and ęke bī
nyght, and destruyd thē Kynges trewe lȳges, som with ǫpen
slaughtre, somme [3] bī false emprisōnementz; and some fledde thē
citee for fęęre, as it is ǫpenlīch knowen.

And sǫ ferthermǫre for tō susteyne thise wrǫnges and manȳ   10
ōthere, thē next yęre after thē sāme Nicholus, ayeins thē forsaide
frēdam and trewe commūnes [4], did crȳe ǫpenlīch that nǫ man
sholde come tō chēse her mair but such as węre sompned, and
thǫ that węre sompned węre of his ordynaunce and after his avȳs.
And in thē nyght next after folwynge hē did carȳe grēte quantitee   15
of armūre tō thē guyldehalle, with which as wēl straungērs of thē
contree as ōthere of withinne węre armed on thē morwe ayeins
his owne proclamāciōn, that was such that nǫ man shulde bē
armed; and certein busshmentz węre laide that, when freemen of
thē citee cōme tō chēse her mair, bręken up armed crȳinge with   20
lōude voice ' Slę, slę,' folwyng hem; whęrthourgh thē pēple for fęęre
fledde tō hōuses and ōther hīdynges [5], as in lǫnde of werre adradde
tō bē dęd in commūne [6].

And thus yet hiderward hath thē mairaltee bēn hǫlden as it
węre of conquest or maistrȳe, and manȳ ōthere offices als, sǫ that   25
what man, pryvē or apert in special that hē myghte wyte grocchyng,
pleyned or hēlde ayeins anȳ of his wrǫnges or bī puttyng forth of
whǫmsǫ it węre, węre it never sǫ unprēnāble, węre apęched and it
węre displęsyng tō hym Nicholus, anǫn was emprisōned and, though
it węre ayeins falshęde of thē lęęst officēr that hym lüst meyn-   30
teigne, was hǫlden untrewe līgeman tō ōwre Kyng; for whǫ

---

[1] Nichol, generally with a curl indicating us.   [2] John, with crossed h.
[3] some, with macron over m.   [4] coes, with curve over o.   [5] nges.
[6] coe, with curve over o.

Long Serv. Strvt.

reprōved such an officēr, maynteigned bȳ hym, of wrǫnge or elles, hē forfaited ayeins hym Nicholus and hē, unworthȳ as hē saide, represented thē Kynges estāt. Alsǫ if anȳ man bicause of servȳce or ōther lęveful comaundement apprǫched a lǫrde, tō which lǫrde hē, Nicholus [1], dradde his falshęde tō bē knowe tō, anǫn was   5 apęched that hē was false tō thē cōnseille of thē citee and sǫ tō thē Kyng.

And yif in general his falsenesse wēre ayeinsaide, as of us tōgydre of thē Mercerȳe or ōthere craftes, or ǫnȳ cōnseille wolde hāve tāken tō ayeinstande it, or,—as tȳme [2] ōut of mȳnde hath   10 bē used,—wolden companȳe tōgydre, hōw lawful sǫ it węre for ōwre nēde or profite, we [3] węre anǫn apęched for arrȳsęrs ayeins thē pęęs, and falslȳ manȳ of us of [4] that yēt stǫnden endīted. And wē bēn ǫpenlīch disclaundred, hǫlden untrewe and traitōurs tō ōwre Kyng; for thē sāme Nicholus sayd bifǫr mair, aldermen,   15 and ōwre craft bifǫr hem gadred in plāce of recorde, that twentȳ or thirtȳ [5] of us węre worthȳ tō bē drawen and hanged, thē which thyng lȳke tō yōwre worthȳ lǫrdship bȳ an ęven juge tō bē prōved or disprōved thē whether that trowthe may shewe; for trouthe amǫnges us of fewe or elles nǫ man manȳ day dorst bē   20 shewed; and nought ǫǫnlīch unshewed or hidde it hath bē bȳ man nōw, but alsǫ of bifǫre tȳme thē mǫǫst profitāble poyntes of trewe governaunce of thē citee, compīled tōgidre bī lǫnge lābōur of discrēte and wȳse men, wythōut cōnseille of trewe men,—for thei sholde nought bē knowen ne contynued,—in thē tȳme of Nicholus Exton, mair, ōuterlīche węre brent.

And sǫ fer forth falsehęde hath bē used that oft tȳme hē, Nicholus Brembre, saide, in sustenaunce of his falshęde, ōwre līge lǫrdes wille was such that never was such, as wē suppǫse. Hē saide alsǫ, whan hē hadde disclaundred us, which of us wolde yēlde hym false tō his Kyng, thē Kyng sholde dō hym grāce, cherise hym, and bē good Lǫrde tō hym: and if anȳ of us alle,

---

[1] Nich, with curl indicating abbreviation.   [2] tȳme, not in MS.   [3] we, not in MS.   [4] of, not in MS.   [5] xx or xxx.

that wyth Goddes help hāve and shulle bē foūnden trewe, was sǫ hārdȳ tō profre prōvyng of hymself trewe, anǫn was comaunded tō prisōne as wēl bī thē mair that nōw is, as of hym, Nicholus Brembre, bifǫre.

Alsǫ, wē hāve bē comaunded ofttȳme, up ōwre līgeaunce, tō 5 unnēdeful and unlẹveful dīverse dōynges, and alsǫ tō wythdrawe us bī thē sāme comaundement frǫ thynges nẹdeful and lẹfful, as was shewed whan a companȳe of gōde women, thẹre men dorst nought, travailleden bārfōte tō ōwre līge Lǫrde tō sēche grāce of hym for trewe men as they suppǫsed; for thanne wẹre such proclamāciōuns 10 māde that nǫ man ne woman sholde apprǫche ōwre līge Lǫrde for sēchyng of grāce, and ǫvermanȳ ōthere comaundementz alsǫ, bifǫre and sithen, bī suggestiōn and informāciōn of suche that wolde nought her falsnesse had bē knowen tō ōwre līge Lǫrde. And, lǫrdes, bȳ yōwre lẹve, ōwre lȳge Lǫrdes comaundement tō 15 symple and unkonning men is a grẹt thyng tō bēn used sǫ fami- lerlīch withoūten nēde; for they, unwȳse tō sāve it, mōwe lyghtlȳ thẹr ayeins forfait.

Forthȳ, grāciōuse lǫrdes, lȳke it tō yōw tō tāke hēde in what manēre and whẹre ōwre līge Lǫrdes pōwēr hath bēn mysused bȳ 20 thē forsaid Nicholus[1] and his upbẹrẹrs, for sithen thise wrǫnges bifǫresaide hān bēn used as accidental or comūne[2] braunches oūtward, it sheweth wēl thē rōte of hem is a ragged subject or stok inward, that is thē forsaid brēre or Brembre, thē whiche comūne[2] wrǫnge uses, and manȳ ōther if it lȳke tō yow, mōwe bē 25 shewed and wēl knowen bī an indifferent juge and mair of ōwre citee; thē which wyth yōwre ryghtful Lǫrdeship ygraunted for- mǫǫst pryncipal remedȳe, as Goddes lawe and al rẹsoūn wole, that nǫ dōmesman stǫnde tōgidre juge and partȳe, wrǫnges sholle mǫre ǫpenlīch bē knowe and trouth dor apẹre. And ellis as 30 amǫnge us, wē konne nought wyte in what manēre withoūt a moch gretter disẹse, sith thē governaunce of this citee stāndeth, as

---

[1] Nich⁵.   [2] coe, with curve over o.

it is bifǫr saide, and wēle stānde, whil vittaillērs bī suffraunce
presumen thilke stātes upon hem; thē which governaunce, of bifǫr
this tȳme tō moche folke yhidde, sheweth hymself nōw ǫpen,
whether it hath bē a cause or bygynnyng of dyvysiōn in thē citee
and after in thē rewme, or nǫ.

Whērfǫre for grettest nēde, as tō yōw mǫǫst worthȳ, mǫǫst
ryghtful, and wȳsest lǫrdes and Cōnseille tō ōwre līge Lǫrde thē
Kyng, wē bisēche mēkelīch of yōwre grāce [1] corecciōn of alle
thē wrǫnges bifǫresayde, and that it lȳke tō yōwre lǫrdeship tō
bē grāciōus mēnes tō ōwre lȳge Lǫrde thē Kyng, that suche
wrǫnges bē knowen tō hym, and that wē mōwe shewe us and sith bēn
hǫlden suche trewe tō hym as wē bēn and owe tō bēn. Alsǫ wē
bisēche untō yōwre grāciōus lǫrdeship that if anȳ of us, in special
or general, bē apēched tō ōwre līge Lǫrde or tō his worthȳ Cōnseille bī comūnyng with ōthere, or apprǫchyng tō ōwre Kyng, as
wyth Brembre or his abettōūrs with anȳ wrǫnge wytnessebēryng,
as that it stōde ōtherwȳse amǫnges us hēre than as it is nōw
prōved it hath ystǫnde, or anȳ ōther wrǫnge suggestiōn by which
ōwre līge Lǫrde hath ybē unlēēffullīch enfourmed, that thanne
yōwre worshipful lǫrdship bē such that wē mōwe come in answer
tō excuse us; for wē knowe wēl, as forbȳ moche thē mǫre partȳe
of us and as wē hǫpe for alle, alle suche wrǫnges hān bēn unwytyng
tō us or elles entērlīch ayeins ōwre wille.

And, ryghtful lǫrdes, for ǫǫn thē grettest remedȳe with ōthere
for tō ayeinstǫnde manȳ of thilke disēses afǫresaide amǫnges us,
wē prayen wyth mēkenesse this specialīch, that the statut ōrdeigned
and māde bī parlement, hǫlden at Westmynstre [2] in thē sexte yēre
of ōwre Kyng nōw regnynge, mōwe stǫnde in strengthe and bē
execut as wēl hēre in London as elleswhēre in thē rewme, thē
which is this :

Item, ordinatum est et statutum, quod nec in civitate Londonie
nec in aliis civitatibus, burgis, villis, vel portubus maris, per totum
regnum predictum, aliquis vitallarius officium judicale de cetero

---

[1] gracious, changed to grace.   [2] westmystre.

habeat, exerceat, neque occupet quovis modo, nisi in villis ubi alia persona sufficiens ad hujus statum habendus repperiri non poterit, dumtamen idem judex pro tempore quo in officio illo steterit ab exercicio vitallarii, sub pena forisfacture victualium suorum sic venditorum, penitus cesset et se abstineat, per se et suos omnino 5 ab eodem, et cet.

IV. CHAUCER'S CANTERBURY TALES

The Tale of the Pardoner

In Flaundres whīlom was a compaignȳe
Of yonge folk that haunteden folȳe,
As rīot, hasard, stywes and tavernes,
Whēreas with harpes, lutes and gyternes   10
They daunce and pleyen at dees bǭthe day and nyght,
And ēten alsǭ, and drynken ǭver hir myght;
Thurgh which they doon thē devel sacrifīse
Withinne that develes temple in cursed wīse
Bȳ superfluytee abhomynāble.   15
Hir ǭthes been sǭ grēte and sǭ dampnāble
That it is grislȳ for tō heere hem swēre,
Ōure blissed Lǭrdes bodȳ they tōtēre;
Hem thoughte þat Jewes rente hym noght ynough,
And ēch of hem at ōtheres synne lough.   20
And right anǭn thanne cōmen tombestēres
Fētȳs [1] and smale, and yonge frutestēres,
Syngēres with harpes, baudes, wāferēres,
Whiche been thē verray develes officēres,
Tō kyndle and blowe thē fȳr of lecherȳe,   25
That is annexed untō glotonȳe.

---

[1] ffetys; ff for F, as often.

Thē hǫǫlȳ writ tāke Ī tō mȳ witnesse,
That luxurīe is in wȳn and dronkenesse.
Lǭ, hōw þat dronken Looth unkȳndelȳ
Lay bȳ hise doghtres twǭ unwitynglȳ.
Sǭ dronke hē was hē nyste what hē wroghte.   5
Herōdes, whǭ sǭ wēl thē stǫrīes soghte,
Whan hē of wȳn was repleet at hise fęęste,
Right at his owene tāble hē yaf his hęęste
Tō slęęn thē Baptist Jǫhn, ful giltelęęs.
Senek seith ęęk[1] a good wōrd, dōutelęęs;   10
Hē seith hē kan nǭ difference fȳnde
Bitwix a man that is ōut of his mȳnde
And a man which that is dronkelewe,
Bot that woodnesse, fallen in a shrewe,
Persevereth lenger than dooth dronkenesse.   15
    Ǭ glotonȳe, ful of cursednesse;
Ǭ cause first of ōure confusiōn,
Ǭ original of ōure dampnāciōn,
Til Crīst hadde boght us with his blood agayn!
Lǭ, hōw deere, shortlȳ for tō sayn,   20
Aboght was thilke cursed vileynȳe;
Corrupt was al this world for glotonȳe.
Adam ōure fader, and his wȳf alsǭ,
Frǭ Paradȳs tō lābōur and tō wǭ
Węre dryven for that vīce, it is nǭ dręde;   25
For whīl þat Adam fasted, as Ī ręde,
Hē was in Paradȳs, and whan þat hē
Ęęt of thē fruyt deffended on the tree,
Anǭn hē was ōutcast tō wǭ and peyne.
Ǭ glotonȳe, on thee wēl oghte us pleyne!   30

    .   .   .   .

Thise rīotōures[2] thrē, of which Ī telle,
Lǫnge ęrst ęr prīme rǫng of anȳ belle,

---

[1] eek, not in MS.; Corp. MS. eek good wordes.   [2] riotours.

Wēre set hem in a taverne tō drynke;
And as they sat they herde a belle clynke
Biforn a cors was carīed tō his grāve.
That ọọn of hem gan callen tō his knāve,
'Gọ bet,' quod hē, 'and axe rẹ̄dīlȳ   5
What cors is this þat passeth heer forbȳ,
And looke þat thōu report his nāme weel.'

    'Sire,' quod this boy, 'it nēdeth never a dẹẹl,
It was mē tọọld ẹ̄r yē cam heer twọ hōures;
Hē was, pardee, an ọld felawe of yōures,   10
And sodeynlȳ hē was yslayn tōnyght,
Fordronke, as hē sat on his bench upryght.
Thẹ̄r cam a privee theef men clẹ̄peth dẹẹth,
That in this contree al the pēple slẹẹth,
And with his spẹ̄re hē smọọt his herte atwọ   15
And wente his wey withōuten wōrdes mọ.
Hē hath a thōusand slayn this pestilence,
And maister, ẹ̄r yē come in his presence,
Mē thynketh that it wēre necessarīe
For tō bē war of swich an adversarīe;   20
Bēth rẹdȳ for tō meete hym everemọọre,—
Thus taughte mē mȳ dāme, Ī sey namọọre.'

    'Bȳ Seinte Mārīe,' seyde this tavernēr,
Thē chīld seith sooth, for hē hath slayn this yẹẹr,
Henne ọver a mīle withinne a grẹẹt villāge,   25
Bọthe man and womman, chīld and hȳne and pāge;
Ī trowe his habitāciōn bē thẹ̄re.
Tō been avȳsed grẹẹt wysdōm it wēre,
Ẹ̄r that hē dide a man a dishonōur.'

    'Yẹ̄, Goddes armes,' quod this rīotōur,   30
'Is it swich peril with hym for tō meete?
Ī shal hym sēke bȳ wey and ẹẹk bȳ strēte,
Ī māke avōw tō Goddes digne bọnes!
Herkneth, felawes, wē thrē been al ọnes,

Lat ęch of us hǫlde up his hande til oother
And ęch of us bicomen ōtheres brōther,
And wē wol slęęn this false traytōur dęęth.
Hē shal bē slayn which þat sǫ manȳe slęęth,
By Goddes dignitee, ęr it bē nyght.'   5

Tōgidres hān thise thrē hir trouthes plight
Tō lyve and dȳen ęch of hem for oother,
As though hē węre his owene ybǫren[1] brōther.
And up they stirte, al[2] dronken in this rāge,
And forth they gǫǫn tōwardes that villāge   10
Of which thē tavernēr hadde spǫke biforn ;
And manȳ a grislȳ ǫǫth thanne hān they sworn,
And Crīstes blessed bodȳ they tōrente,—
Dęęth shal bē dęęd, if that they may hym hente.

Whan they hān gǫǫn nat fullȳ half a mīle,   15
Right as they wolde hān troden ǫver a stīle,
An ǫǫld man and a pōvre with hem mette.
This ǫlde man ful mēkelȳ hem grette
And seyde thus, ' Nōw, lǫrdes, God yōw see.'
Thē prōūdeste of thise rīotōures[3] three   20
Answerde agayn, ' What, carl, with sǫrȳ grāce
Whȳ art ōw al forwrapped sāve thȳ fāce ?
Whȳ lyvest ōw sǫ lǫnge in sǫ gręęt āge ? '

This ǫlde man gan looke in his visāge
And seyde thus : ' For Ī ne kan nat sȳnde   25
A man, though þat Ī walked intō Ȳnde,
Neither in citee nor in nǫ villāge,
That wolde chaunge his youthe for mȳn āge ;
And thęrfǫre moot Ī hān mȳn āge stille
As lǫnge tȳme as it is Goddes wille.   30
Ne dęęth, allas, ne wol nat hān mȳ lȳf ;
Thus walke Ī lȳk a restelęęs kaitȳf,
And on thē grōūnd, which is mȳ moodres gāte,

[1] yborn.   [2] and.   [3] riotours.

Ī knokke with mȳ staf bọthe ẹrlȳ and lāte,
And seye, "Leeve mooder, lẹẹt mē in!
Lọ, hōw Ī vanysshe, flessh and blood and skyn;
Allas, whan shul mȳ bọnes been at reste?
Mooder, with yōw wolde Ī chaunge mȳ cheste   5
That in mȳ chāmbre lọnge tȳme hath bē,
Yẹ, for an heyre clōwt tō wrappe mē."
But yet tō mē shē wol nat dō that grāce;
For which ful pāle and welked is mȳ fāce.
But, sīres, tō yōw it is nọ curteisȳe   10
Tō spẹken tō an ọld man vileynȳe,
But hē trespasse in wōrd or elles in dẹde.
In họọlȳ writ yē may yourself wēl rẹde,
Agayns an ọọld man, họọr upon his hẹẹd,
Yē sholde arīse; whērfọre Ī yeve yōw rẹẹd,   15
Ne dooth untō an ọọld man nọọn harm nōw,
Namọọre than þat yē wolde men did tō yōw
In āge, if that yē sọ lọnge abȳde;
And God bē with yōw whẹre yē gọ or rȳde,—
Ī moote gọ thider as Ī hāve tō gọ.'   20

'Nay, ọlde cherl, bȳ God thōu shalt nat sọ,'
Seyde this oother hasardōur anọn;
'Thōu partest nat sọ lightlȳ, bȳ Seint Jọhn!
Thōu spak right nōw of thilke traytōur dẹẹth,
That in this contree alle ōure freendes slẹẹth;   25
Hāve heer mȳ trouthe, as thōu art his espȳe,
Telle whẹre hē is or thōu shalt it abȳe,
Bȳ God and bȳ thē họọlȳ sacrement.
For soothlȳ thōu art ọọn of his assent
Tọ slẹẹn us yonge folk, thōu false theef.'   30

'Nōw, sīres,' quod hē, 'if þat yē bē sọ leef
Tō fȳnde dẹẹth, turne up this crōked wey,
For in that grọve Ī lafte hym, bȳ mȳ fey,
Under a tree and thẹre hē wole abȳde;

Noght for yōure bǫǫst hē wole him nǫthyng hȳde.
Sē yē that ǫǫk?   Right thēre yē shal hym fȳnde;
God sāve yōw, þat boghte agayn mankȳnde,
And yōw amende.'   Thus seyde this ǫlde man;
And everīch of thise rīotōures [1] ran   5
Til hē cam tō that tree, and thēr they fōunde
Of flǫryns fȳne of gōld, ycoyned rōunde,
Wēl nȳ an eighte [2] busshels, as hem thoughte.
Nǫ lenger thanne after dēēth they soughte,
But ēch of hem sǫ glad was of that sighte,   10
For þat thē flǫryns been sǫ faire and brighte,
That dōun they sette hem bȳ this preciōus hoord.
Thē worste of hem hē spak thē firste wōrd.

 'Bretheren,' quod hē, 'taak kēpe what Ī seye,
My wit is grēēt though þat Ī bōurde and pleye.   15
This trēsōr hath fortune untō us yeven
In myrthe and joliftee ōure lȳf tō lyven,
And lightlȳ as it comth sǫ wol wē spēnde.
Ey, Goddes preciōus dignitee, whǫ wēnde
Tōday that wē sholde hān sǫ fair a grāce?   20
But myghte this gōld bē carīed frǫ this plāce
Hǫǫm tō mȳn hōus, or elles untō yōures,—
For wēl yē wǫǫt þat al this gōld is ōures,—
Thanne wēre wē in heigh felicitee.
But trewelȳ bȳ daye it may nat bee;   25
Men wolde seyn þat wē wēre thēves strǫnge,
And for ōure owene trēsōr doon us hǫnge.
This trēsōr mōste ycarīed bē bȳ nyghte
As wīselȳ and as slȳlȳ as it myghte.
Whērfǫre Ī rēde þat cut among us alle   30
Bē drawe, and lat sē whēr thē cut wol falle;
And hē þat hath thē cut with herte blīthe
Shal renne tō thē [3] tōwne, and that ful swīthe,

---

[1] riotours.   [2] viij.   [3] the, not in MS.

And brynge us brẹẹd and wȳn ful privelȳ.
And twǫ of us shul kēpen subtillȳ
This trẹsōr wēl, and if hē wol nat tarīe,
Whan it is nyght wē wol this trẹsōr carīe
Bȳ ǫǫn assent, whẹreas us thynketh best.'   5
    That ǫǫn of hem thē cut broghte in his fest,
And bad hem drawe and looke whẹre it wol falle;
And it fil on thē yongeste of hem alle,
And forth tōward thē tōun hē wente anǫn.
And al sǫ soone as that hē was gǫn,   10
That ǫǫn of hem[1] spak thus untō that oother:
    'Thow knowest wēl thou art mȳ sworne[2] brōther;
Thȳ profit wol Ī telle thee anǫn.
Thou wǫǫst wēl that ōure felawe is agǫn,
And heere is gōld and that ful grẹt plentee,   15
That shal departed been amǫng us thrē;
But nathelẹẹs, if Ī kan shāpe it sǫ
That it departed wẹre amǫng us twǫ,
Hadde Ī nat doon a freendes torn tō thee?'
    That oother answerde, 'Ī nǫǫt hou that may bē;   20
Hē wǫǫt how that thē gōld is with us tweye;
What shal[3] wē doon, what shal wē tō hym seye?'
    'Shal it bē cōnseil?' seyde thē firste shrewe,
'And Ī shal tellen in a wōrdes fewe
What wē shal doon and bryngen it wēl abōute.'   25
    'Ī graunte,' quod that oother, 'ōute of dōute,
That bȳ mȳ trouthe Ī shal thee nat biwreye.'
    'Now,' quod thē firste, 'thou wǫǫst wēl wē bē tweye,
And twǫ of us shul strenger bē than ǫǫn.
Looke, whan þat hē is set, thou[4] right anǫn   30
Arȳs as though thou woldest with hym pleye,
And Ī shal rȳve him thurgh thē sȳdes tweye

---

[1] of hem, not in E. MS.; all others have the words.   [2] sworn.   [3] wha l.
[4] that; Harl. MS. thou.

Whīl that thōu strogelest with hym as in gāme,
And with thȳ daggere looke thōu dō thē sāme;
And thanne shal al this gōld departed bē,
Mȳ deere freend, bitwixen mē and thee.
Thanne may wē bǭthe ōure lustes all fulfille,   5
And pleye at dees right at ōure owene wille.'
And thus acorded been thise shrewes tweye
Tō slęęn thē thridde, as yē hān herd mē seye.

   This yongeste, which þat wente untō thē tōun,
Ful ofte in herte hē rolleth up and dōun   10
Thē beautee of thise flǫryns newe and brighte.
' Ǭ Lǫrd,' quod hē, ' if sǭ węre þat Ī myghte
Hāve al this tręsōr tō myself allǭne,
Thęr is nǭ man þat lyveth under thē trǭne
Of God that sholde lyve sǭ mürȳe as Ī.'   15
And atte laste thē feend, ōure enemȳ,
Putte in his thought þat hē sholde poysōn beye,
With which hē myghte slęęn hise felawes tweye;
Forwhȳ thē feend fǭǫnd hym in swich lyvynge,
That hē hadde lęve hym [1] tō sorwe brynge,   20
For this was ōutrelȳ his fulle entente
Tō slęęn hem bǭthe and nevere tō repente.
And forth hē gǫǫth, nǭ lenger wolde hē tarīe,
Intō thē tōun untō a pothecarīe,
And preyde hym þat hē hym wolde selle   25
Som poysōn þat hē myghte hise rattes quelle;
And ęęk thęr was a polcat in his hawe
That, as hē seyde, hise cāpōns hadde yslawe;
And fayn hē wolde wręke hym, if hē myghte,
On vermyn þat destroyed hym bȳ nyghte.   30

   Thē pothecarīe answerde, ' And thōu shalt hāve
A thyng that, al sǭ God mȳ soule sāve,
In al this world thęr is nǭ cręāture,

----
[1] hem ; all others hym or him.

That ęten or dronken hath of this confiture
Noght but thē mōntance of a cōrn of whęte,
That hē ne shal his līf anǫn forlęte;
Yę, sterve hē shal, and that in lasse whīle
Than thōū wolt gǫǫn apaas nat but a mīle,⁣   5
This poysōn is sǫ strǫng and vīolent.'

This cursed man hath in his hōnd yhent
This poysōn in a box, and sith hē ran
Intō the nexte strēte untō a man,
And borwed of¹ hym large botels thrē,⁣   10
And in thē twǫ his poysōn pōūred hē ;
The thridde hē kepte clęne for his drynke²,
For al thē nyght hē shoope hym for tō swynke,
In cariynge of thē gōld ōūt of that plāce.
And whan this rīotōūr with sǫrȳ grāce⁣   15
Hadde filled with wȳn hise gręte botels thrē,
Tō hise felawes agayn repaireth hē.

What nēdeth it tō sermōne of it mǫǫre ?
For right as³ they hadde cast his dęęth bifǫǫre,
Right sǫ they hān hym slayn, and that anǫn.⁣   20
And whan þat this was doon, thus spak that ǫǫn :
' Nōw lat us sitte and drynke and māke us merīe,
And afterward wē wol his bodȳ berīe.'
And with that wōrd it happed hym, par cas,
Tō tāke thē botel thęr thē poysōn was,⁣   25
And drank and yaf his felawe drynke alsǫ ;
For which anǫn they storven bǫthe twǫ.
But certes Ī suppǫse that Avycen
Wrǫǫt nevere in nǫ canōn, ne in nǫ fen,
Mǫ wonder signes of empoisōnyng⁣   30
Than hadde thise wrecches twǫ ęr hir ēndyng.
Thus ended been thise homycīdes twǫ,

---

¹ of, from Harl. MS.   ² owene drynke ; all other MSS. drynke.
³ so as; all others as.

And ęęk thē false empoysōnēre alsǫ.

Ǫ cursed synne of alle cursednesse!

Ǫ traytōurs homycīde, ǫ wikkednesse!

Ǫ glotonȳe, luxurīe, and hasardrȳe!

Thōu blasphēmōur of Crist, with vileynȳe   5

And ǫthes gręte of usāge and of prīde,—

Allas mankȳnde,—hōw may it bitīde

That tō thȳ Cręatōur, which þat thē wroghte

And with his preciōus herteblood thee boghte,

Thōu art sǫ fals and sǫ unkȳnde, allas!   10

Nōw, goode men, God foryeve yōw yōure trespas,

And wāre yōw frǫ the synne of avarīce.

NOTES[1]

PART I

THE MIDLAND DIALECT

This part contains specimens of the several varieties of this dialectal division, but especially of East Midland, as that upon which later English is especially based. Only two selections represent West Midland, the 'Prose Psalter' (p. 100) and the 'Instructions to Parish Priests' (p. 119), as that dialect in its purity does not materially differ from East Midland. More important is the distinction of Early East Midland from that of the thirteenth and fourteenth centuries, which may be regarded as normal Middle English in this dialect. Early East Midland, represented by the first two selections, shows the language in a transition state. For example, OE. *ā* still remains *ā*, the characteristic lengthening of OE. *e, a, o* in open syllables had not taken place, and other less significant changes already mentioned in the Grammatical Introduction.

A. EARLY EAST MIDLAND

I. THE PETERBOROUGH CHRONICLE

The last part of the 'Chronicle,' from 1080 to its close, occurs only in Laud MS. 636 of the Bodleian Library, Oxford. The whole has been frequently edited, as by Thorpe and Earle, before the latter's edition was re-edited by Plummer, 'Two of the Saxon Chronicles Parallel' (1892–9). Selections are found in Morris ('Specimens,' I, 9) and Zupitza ('Übungsbuch,' p. 57, Schipper 75).

---

[1] These Notes are intended to give, in methodical manner, some account of MSS. and editions; time and place of composition, as well as author if known; character of the work, relation of the extract to the whole, and metrical relations, if poetry; source of derived material, when known; bibliography of more important monographs; explanations of words, phrases, allusions, and other difficulties. General works of reference are not mentioned in connexion with each selection, for teachers will naturally refer to Ten Brink's 'History of English Literature,' Morley's 'English Writers,' Brandl's 'Mittelenglische Litteratur' in Paul's 'Grundriss der Germanischen Philologie,' and Körting's 'Grundriss der Geschichte der Englischen Litteratur.' Cross-references to the texts are by page and line, the Notes to each page of text being arranged in a single paragraph.

Written at Peterborough, Northampton, the part chosen includes all that is written in the hand of the last continuator, who gives a summary of Stephen's reign immediately after his death in 1154. The selection therefore represents Northeast Midland (NEMl.) of the middle of the twelfth century. See Behm, 'The Language of the Latter Part of the Peterborough Chronicle' (1884); H. Meyer, 'Zur Sprache der jüngeren Teile der Chronik von Peterborough' (1889).

The 'Chronicle,' as the most important source for the history of the period, cannot be too highly regarded. Especially valuable is this contemporaneous account of Stephen's reign, since it is more detailed than most of the other entries and more vividly narrated. On the other hand the order of events is not chronological, as shown by Plummer (as above), II, 307.

As to language, the orthography of this selection is less regular than most others of the book. It shows the unstable condition of the written form when English was less commonly used in literature, as well as some orthographic influences of older works. Special peculiarities of orthography are *ǣ* for OM. *ā*, *ēa*, rarely *ēo*; *e* for OM. *e* (*æ*), especially in unstressed syllables; *ēa* for OM. *ē*, as in *gēar*; *ēo* for OM. *ē*, *ēo*, rarely *ēa*; *ēo* (*ǣo*) for OM. *ēo*, rarely *ēa*. Among consonants the most important peculiarities are *ch* for the OE. medial spirant *g* in a few words; *g(i)* for the OE. initial palatal spirant *g*; *t* initially for OE. *þ* (*ð*) in pronominal words when immediately following a final *d* or *t*; *w* for OE. *hw*, as in *warsæ*. The vocabulary shows a larger French element than the selections immediately following, partly owing to the number of terms connected with government and the church. The inflexions, which have been thought quite irregular, will fall into fairly definite schemes. Noun plurals in *es(s)* prevail, though a few OE. neuters with long stems still remain without ending. Adjectives have almost wholly lost oblique case forms. Verbs show somewhat more irregularities, but are fast tending to the simplicity of normal Middle English. The syntax of the period is also comparatively simple. On the other hand, the inverted order of subject and predicate is common, and the construction according to sense with collective nouns occasional. The title *kīng* (l. 1) is still an appositive and follows the personal name, or the personal name is in apposition with *kīng* (l. 13). The most striking single construction, from the standpoint of Modern English, is the double genitive, as *Stēphnes Kīnges* (4, 28), *þē kīnges sune Henrīes* (5, 12); yet these are quite in accord with OE. usage and the appositive noted above. Subjunctive forms of the verb are naturally much more frequent than in English of to-day.

Page 1, l. 1. **Henrī Kīng.** Henry I, who had come to the throne in 1100. **Henrī abbot.** Henry of Poitou, abbot of St. Jean d'Angely, from which he was expelled in 1131, to the great rejoicing of the monks who had been under him. He was related to Henry I and the Count of Poitiers, and had been a monk at Cluny or Clugni (1, 3) in Burgundy. This monastery was at the height of its prosperity in the twelfth century, some 2,000 religious houses throughout Europe acknowledging allegiance to it. **2. Burch.** That is Borough of St. Peter, Peterborough, a name which supplanted the earlier Medeshamstede. A Benedictine abbey of St. Peter had been founded in 655 by Oswy, King of Northumbria, and Peada, the first Christian King of Mercia. Plundered by the Danes in 870, it was re-established in 966 by Athelwold, Bishop of Winchester, who also changed its name. **3. tē.** For *þē*, after a word ending in *t* or *d*. **5. Biscop of Seresberī.** Roger of Salisbury and Alexander of Lincoln, his nephew. **6. þ϶.** Note the retention of the OE. relative particle in early Middle English, though soon to be replaced by *þat*. **hē.** The abbot Henry. As in Old English, pronouns are often lacking in explicit reference. So *hē ... hē ... his* of the next line refer to the same Henry. **10. iaf.** This form, among others, shows how completely OE. palatal spirant *g* had assumed the quality of MnE. *y*. Cf. *iāfen* (2, 26), *iēden* (3, 28). **11. Sanct Nēod.** St. Neot's in Huntingdonshire. The MS. abbreviation for St. gives us no hint as to whether the OE. noun form, *sanct*, or *sant* (cf. Orm's *sannt*) was actually used. It is doubtless too early for the OF. form *saint* with a diphthong. **12. Sanct Pētres messedai.** June 29, the feast of St. Peter and St. Paul in commemoration of their martyrdom; really the date of reburial of their supposed remains in 358 A.D. **14. þā pēstrede.** Henry I left England, never to return, on Aug. 1 (Lammas), 1133. The eclipse occurred on the next day, but Henry did not die until Dec. 1, 1135 (1, 18). Perhaps the traditional bringing together of these two dates accounts for the wrong dating of Henry's departure from England. **15. wāre.** 'Might be'; subjunctive preterit singular. For other forms with *ā* in pret. pl. cf. *nāmen* (2, 1), *drāpen* (3, 18), *wāren* (3, 29), *forbāren* (3, 31), *stāli* (6, 8). **16. sterres abūten.** The copulative verb omitted as often. **18. ðat ōþer dæi.** 'The second, or next day,' *ōþer* being used with ordinal force as in Old English. St. Andrew's day is Nov. 30, and Henry died on Dec. 1. Andreas, a borrowed word ending in *s*, takes no ending in the genitive. **19. þā wes trēsōn.** The MS. reading was long a puzzle, and various emendations were suggested before the present editor pointed out the true reading in 'Mod. Lang. Notes,' VII, 254. This was adopted by Plummer in a note to this passage (II, 307). Incidentally this is the first example so far discovered of the French word *treason* in English.

Page 2, l. 2. Rēdinge. Henry I had founded an abbey at this place, no doubt the reason for his burial there. **10. midewintre dæi.** That is Christmas day, but authorities give the date variously, as Dec. 22, 24, 25, 26, the latter being St. Stephen's day. The name midwinter day is Teutonic, and antedates the Christianization of Britain. With the Conquest, Christmas (*Crīstes mæsse*) came to be used. **12. Baldwin de Redvērs.** The rebellion really belongs to the year 1136, as also the compact with David, King of Scotland. This Baldwin, first Earl Redvers (Rivers), died in 1155. **18. fōr ... tō Normandī.** The journey was in March, the return (1, 23) in December. **20. gēt.** Plummer says past participle of a weak verb *geten* 'get,' but this is not likely on several accounts. The word is the adverb *gēt* (OM. *gēt*, WS. *gīet*) 'yet,' as given in the glossary to Morris's 'Specimens,' I; cf. for the same word 16, 3; 29, 5. The treasure which Stephen yet had, and for which they received him so gladly, was about £100,000. **23. gadering æt Oxeneford.** This was in June, 1139. Bishop Roger was justiciar, or chief justice, and regent in the king's absence. Roger, the chancellor, was nephew only by courtesy. **25. hise neves.** The plural form of the pronoun shows that the OE. genitive *his*, from *hē*, had developed a possessive pronoun, with inflexion, as *mīn* and *þīn* had done in the older period.

Page 3, l. 3. be nihtes ... be dæies. The force of the OE. adverbial genitive is apparently not felt, and the adverbial relation is more clearly indicated by a prepositional phrase. **carlmen and wimmen.** 'Men and women.' The word *man* was general in its meaning, and probably on this account the more distinctive *carlmen* was employed. **6. me henged.** 'They hanged (them) up by the feet,' &c. The indefinite *me*, an old singular, implies a plural, as indicated by the verbs *hĕngen* (l. 7) and *wrythen* (l. 8). **11. crū-cethūs.** The context sufficiently explains the meaning of this term. The first part is apparently Lat. *cruciatus*; for the quantity of *ū* cf. *crūc* in Pogatscher, 'Die griechischen, lateinischen und romanischen Lehnworte im Altenglischen.' **14. lof and grin.** This must be regarded as still a crux. The MS. reads *lof ⁊ grī*, which suggested to Thorpe *lǭþ and grim*, 'loathsome and grim,' as the names of the instruments, *lǭþ* being for OE. *lāð*. The use of the two names then accounted for the plural verb. On the other hand, the use of two adjectives in this way for an instrument would presuppose a singular verb, besides being unsatisfactory in other ways. **rachentēges.** Really a compound of OE. *racente* 'chain' and OM. *tēh(g)*, WS. *tēah(g)* 'fetter,' but the relation of the parts of the compound had probably been lost. **ǭþer.** To be carefully distinguished from *ōþer*, OE. *ōþer*. *Ǭþer*, OE. *āghwæðer*, soon became ME. *ǭr, or*, and MnE. *or*. **15. bæron.** This form for the infinitive *beren* is paralleled by *æten = eten* (5, 14), *begæten = begeten* (7, 2). While not marked long here they probably represent sporadic cases of lengthening of *e* in an open syllable, a change which was not regularly carried out until the thirteenth century. **21. ðat lastede.** This proves conclusively that the account was not written until the close of Stephen's reign. Cf. also the reference to Martin's abbacy (4, 10 f.) lasting to Jan., 1155. **23. ǣvre um wīle.** 'Ever from time to time,' OE. *ǣfre ymbe hwīle*. The form *um* is Old Norse, cognate with OE. *ymbe*; cf. *umstund* in 'Cursor Mundi.' **24. tenserīe.** First explained by Mr. Round and Mr. Toynbee in the 'Academy,' July 11, 1892. It is a NF. form based on LL. *tensarium*, 'a generic term for certain irregular taxations'; the latter is from *tensare*, 'to protect, exact tribute for protection.' **31. ǭwer sithon.** 'Everywhere thereafter, or afterwards.' The first word is OM. *āhwēr*, WS. *āhwǣr*.

Page 4, l. 3. tūnscipe flugen. Notice the construction according to sense; *tūnscipe* is a grammatical singular, a logical plural, and the verb agrees with the latter, as often. **6. warsæ**, perhaps -sǣ. OM. *hwēr* (*hwar*?), WS. *hwǣr*, and *sǣ* from older *swǣ*. **8. Crīst slēp.** In interpreting Christ's sleeping in the ship during the storm (Matt. viii. 24), the ME. 'Metrical Homilies' (ed. by Small, p. 135) explain that the ship is the church:

'And Crist þarin gasteli slepes,
Quen he þoles god men and lele
Wit wic(ce) men and fals(e) dele,
þat betes þaim wit dede and word
Als se bare betes on schipbord.'

11. fānd. 'Provided for.' Still used in dialectal English in which a country labourer is engaged for 'so much and found,' that is, so much pay in addition to board and lodging. **14. lǣt it rēfen.** 'Let roof it, caused it to be roofed.' **17. fōr tō Rōme.** This event, though placed under the year 1137, could not have taken place until 1145, since Eugenius did not become pope until that year. Cf. note to 3, 21. **18. privilegies.** The OF. form is *privilege*, so that *ie* is here not long, unless it shows influence of OF. words in *ie*. **20–21. circewīcan . . . hörderwȳcan.** That OE. *wīce* had acquired final *n* in the nominative is clear from Orm's use, so that these examples can hardly be assumed to be weak datives. **22. Rogingham þē castel.** 'The castle of Rockingham.' **24. solidi.** The MS. abbreviation is expanded as a Lat. plural, since the word was hardly English. The words **ǣlc gǣr**, inserted above the line by the writer of the MS., were bracketed by Morris as if not in the MS. ('Specimens,' I), and this led to the proposal of *solidatas*, 'a measure of land,' as the true reading ('Mod. Lang. Notes,' VII, 134). The correct reading of the MS. shows that a sum of money is intended. **25. wīniǣrd.** Plummer notes, on Bede ('Hist. Eccles.,' Bk. I, ch. i), that vine-growing was formerly common in England, especially in some of the monasteries. **28. Stēphnes Kīnges.** Each word is made genitive in form as in Old English. The MnE. group genitive has not yet developed; cf. *þē kīnges sune Henrīes* (5, 12), *þē kīnges dohter Henrīes* (5, 30). **29. On his tīme.** The death of William of Norwich, afterwards St. William, is placed in 1144 and 1146 by different chroniclers. Plummer says, 'The charge against the Jews of using the blood of murdered gentiles, especially Christian children, for ritual purposes is as old as the time of Josephus'; see his 'Contra Apionem,' II, 8. Cf. the similar story in Chaucer's 'Prioress's Tale.' **31. lāng Frīdæi.** The term occurs occasionally in OE. *langa Frigadæg* (*Frigedæg*), and is common in Old Norse as *langifrjādagr.*

Page 5, l. 2. and tō munekes. 'And those monks.' Editors have seemed to think *to* an unusual form, but it is a natural development of OE. *þā* after a final *d*; cf. 5, 8. **8. ǣvest,** MS. **ǣvez.** The MS. *z* is an OF. spelling, usually of *ts*, but here of *st.* **9. æt tē Standard.** The battle was fought at Northallerton, Yorkshire. Its name comes from the fact that banners of St. Cuthbert of Durham, St. Peter of York, St. John of Beverley, and St. Wilfred of Ripon were fixed upon a pole in a four-wheeled cart and placed in the centre of the English army. **12. wart it war.** 'Became aware of it.' **13. þēstrede þē sunne.** This date of March 20, 1140 (l. 15), is shown to be correct by the table of eclipses. **16. Willelm, Ǣrcebiscop.** The Willelm Curbuil mentioned at 2, 9. **24. Rodbert Ēorl of Gloucestre.** Robert was a natural son of Henry I and hence half-brother of Matilda, whose claims to the throne he vigorously espoused. **26. heore lāverd.** That is, King Stephen; so *him* of l. 27. Stephen was taken prisoner Feb. 2, 1141. **30. kīnges dohter Henrīes.** This was Æthelīc (Adelaide) of earlier references, the daughter of Henry I, who was given in marriage to Henry V of Germany. On her coronation, July 25, 1110, her name was changed to Matilda. At her husband's death, 1126, she returned to England, and her father caused homage to be done to her as his successor. This was reason enough for her enmity toward Stephen. Soon after she was given in marriage to Geoffrey of Anjou. She reached England in 1139 and was chosen Lady (the name Queen was not used for her) in 1141. In June of the same year she fled from London. **32. scǣ.** This is especially noteworthy as the earliest use of the form which became MnE. *she.*

Page 6, l. 1. biscop of Wincestre. Henry of Blois, formerly abbot of Glastonbury. **8. stāli hī.** Preterit plural with loss of final *n* when immediately followed by a subject pronoun. In Old English this occurred only in the case of the first and second persons, but it seems to have been extended to the third person in ME. times. Cf. 25, 11, 14. **14. swā diden.** The exchange was made in 1141. The next year came the reconciliation with

Randolph, earl of Chester.   **26. brohten hire intō Oxenfōrd.**   This was in March or May, 1141, the chronicler doubling back in his narrative to tell of the divided state of England.   Matilda was besieged in Oxford during October or November, 1142, and she escaped to Wallingford in December. She did not go over sea (l. 30) until the early part of 1147.   **27. þā hērde ðat sægen.**   'Then heard he that saying'; *sægen* is OE. *segen* (*sægen*), 'saying, assertion,' and not an infinitive (OE. *secgan*) as usually interpreted. Confusion has resulted from the form of the infinitive in 4, 28.   **30. hī of Normandī.**   This happened between 1141 and 1144.

Page 7, l. 1.   **fērde Eustace.**   Stephen's son Eustace married Constance, sister of the French king, in February, 1140.   He died (l. 8) in August, 1153, his mother May 3, 1152.   **2. tō wīfe.**   The OE. dative remains longest in such expressions as this, though finally displaced by the invariable nom. dat. acc. form; cf. *tō wīve* (24, 19), *tō wīf* (40, 13).   **9. his sune Henrī.** Henry succeeded to the dukedom of Anjou on the death of his father, Sept. 7, 1151.   In March, 1152, Eleanor was divorced from Louis VII, and she married Henry (l. 11) in May of the same year.   **tōc tō þē rīce.** 'Succeeded to the kingdom.'   The OE. idiom was *fōn tō*, and *fōn* had now been displaced by *taken*, from ON. *taka.*   **12. þā fērde hē.**   This was in January, 1153, and in November peace was made (l. 15).   **16. wāre.** Pret. subj., 'should be.'   Cf. l. 15.   **27. þæt minster.**   Stephen and his queen had founded the religious house at Feversham, Kent, and the minster had been completed in 1148.

Page 8, l. 1.   **innen dæis.**   Some number is perhaps omitted before *dæis.* **cusen.**   The OE. *curon* had already given way to a form with *s*, by analogy of the present and preterit singular.   So with the past participle *cosan = cosen* in l. 4.   **9. Ramesæie . . . Torneie . . . Spallding.**   These are Ramsey (Huntingdonshire), Thorney (Cambridgeshire), and Spalding (Lincolnshire), all in the neighbourhood of Peterborough.   The other places named cannot be made out with certainty.

II. THE DEDICATION TO THE 'ORMULUM'

The 'Ormulum' is preserved in Junius MS. 1 of the Bodleian Library, not improbably the MS. of Orm himself.   It has been edited by White (1852), and this revised by Holt (1878), though a more scholarly edition is still much needed. Selections occur in Morris ('Specimens,' I, 39), Mätzner ('Sprachproben,' I, 3), Sweet ('First Middle English Primer,' 43), Zupitza ('Übungsbuch,' 7, Schipper, 99).   An indispensable collation of the MS. was printed by Kölbing in 'Englische Studien,' I, 1.   Of the author nothing is known beyond what is given in this Introduction (see various notes).   The 'Ormulum' was composed in the neighbourhood of Lincoln about 1200, and the language therefore represents the Northeast Midland of that period.   Orm's language, in relation to orthography and vowel quantity, is discussed in the Grammatical Introduction (§ 71, note).   Besides may be noted Callenberg, 'Layamon u. Orm nach ihren Lautverhältnissen verglichen' (1876); Sachse, 'Das unorganische e im Ormulum' (1881); Brate, 'Nordische Lehnwörter im Ormulum' in Paul u. Braune's 'Beiträge,' X, 1; Kluge, 'Englische Studien,' XXII, 179.

The name of the work is given by the author (Preface, l. 1): þiss boc is nemmnedd Orrmulum, forrþi þatt Orrm itt wrohhte. Ormulum is clearly a diminutive, after the Latin, of the author's name. The book consists of an introduction, called dedication and preface, paraphrases intended to cover the gospels read in the church during the year, and homilies upon them. Of these paraphrases and homilies only about one-eighth were completed, or at least remain in MS., but these extend to nearly ten thousand long lines. The work has little literary value, as it is prosaic in the extreme, but is especially valuable for the light which it throws on the language of the time. The metrical form is that of the long line of fifteen syllables with cæsura after the eighth, but without rime or regular alliteration. The metrical flow is iambic, and the metre is clearly based on the Latin septenarius. With the addition of rime this metre became the MnE. quatrain of alternate eight and seven syllables, the long line being broken at the cæsural pause. On the other hand, Menthel, following Trautmann, tries to connect Orm's verse with that of Otfried, 'Zur Geschichte des Otfriedischen Verses in England' (Anglia, VIII, Anzeiger, 49). The sources of the 'Ormulum' have been shown to be principally Bede and Gregory the Great; cf. Sarrazin, 'Über die Quellen des Ormulum' (' Englische Studien,' VI, 1).

As to language, the peculiarities of Orm's orthography have been discussed in the Grammatical Introduction. Here may be added Orm's *ǣ* for OE. *ǣ*, sometimes OM. *ē*, the exact limits of the use not having been accurately made out; the use of *ʒ* or *w* for the second element of a true diphthong (cf. *þeʒʒ* ' they,' *Awwstin* for OF. *Austin*), as well as for OE. *ʒ* or *w*; *f* for OE. medial *f = v*; *g* in *gōd* ' good' distinguished from *g* in *strānge*, though no example occurs in our selection ; *sh(ssh)* for OE. *sc*, beside *sk* for ON., OF. *sk (sc = sk)*. The poetical form naturally gives special assistance in regard to language, as in accent of words, and elision of final *e* (occasionally other vowels) before a vowel or weak *h*. Orm's vocabulary is characterized by a large Norse element and a smaller OF. element than in the 'Chronicle.' His inflexions are exceedingly simple, and the syntax, at least of this selection, requires no special explanation other than an occasional note.

Page 8, l. 13. brōþerr mīn. Probably not blood-relationship in the restricted sense, but rather that in which Philemon is desired to receive Onesimus as ' a brother in the flesh,' Philem. 16. Cf. Henrici, ' Otfrid's Mutter und Orm's Bruder' (' Zeitschrift f. Deutsches Alterthum,' XXII, 231). **14. Annd.** The MS. sign (ꝛ) is thus expanded in accordance with occasional forms of the word in the 'Ormulum.' Of course there can be no question of the shortness of the vowel in this unstressed word. **15. ī Godess hūs.** In the religious house of which they were both canons, it would seem from l. 17. **16. witt.** The dual forms of the pronouns are rare except in the earliest period. **17. Unnderr.** While the rhythm of Orm's lines is prevailingly iambic, a trochee instead of an iamb often occurs at the beginning of the line, or immediately after the cæsura; cf. *Affterr* (l. 20), *eʒʒwhǣr* (9, 13), and following the cæsura *offlerr* (l. 13), *goddspelless* (l. 19). Those who suppose that these words are given iambic stress assume that Orm did violence to the natural accent of words, instead of following a frequent custom in all English iambic rhythm. **swā summ Sannt Awwstīn sette.** That is, St. Augustine, the great patron of the monastic life. The more explicit rule actually followed by Augustine monks was that of St. Benedict

(Benet), based on the brief directions in the writings of St. Augustine.
19. Ennglissh. The substantive *English* seems already to have become
established, since it never occurs with final *e* in Orm, while the adjective
appears with or without *e*, as in l. 22, where *Ennglissh ffolc* is practically
a compound, and at 10, 20.   **hallʒhe lāre.** The adjective is in the weak
form after a genitive, as shown by Sachse (mentioned above).   **20. Drihhtīn.**
According to Orm's manner of indicating vowel quantity the *i* of the last
syllable is long, though the word represents OE. *drihten*; cf. Morsbach, § 67,
Anm. 4.   **21. þohhtesst tatt.** The rule that initial *þ* of pronominal words
becomes *t* after *t* or *d* is followed absolutely in Orm, as shown by Blackburn
('Amer. Journal of Philology,' III, 46). See also note on 9, 11.   **22. lufe**
off. Elision of weak *e* occurs regularly before a vowel or weak *h* ; see Gram.
Introd.   **26. unnc birrþ.** 'It becomes (behooves) us both.'

Page 9, l. 1. **þā goddspelless nēh alle.** The Latin texts given by Orm
after the 'Dedication' show that he followed, in general, some gospel
harmony of his time.   **2. sinndenn.** This form is less common in Midland, except in the early period. It is displaced by *are(n)*, found in the
Anglian district in OE. times; cf. 'Vespasian Psalter' *earon*, Nth. *aron* (*un*),
and Sievers, 'Angelsächsische Grammatik,' § 427.   **4. sāwle nēde.** This
might almost be written as a compound. Such examples scarcely prove
retention of the OE. feminine genitive, with gender signification, at least for
Midland and Northern.   **7. āmāng.** Orm's orthography gives no clue to
the length of the first *a*, but the constant appearance of *a* instead of *o* (= *ǭ*)
in later texts seems conclusive proof of shortness; cf. *amǭng*, 18, 10.
10. t'unnderrstanndenn. Occasional elision of other vowels than weak *e*
occurs in the 'Ormulum'; cf. *he't*, 10, 4.   **11. þess tē bettre.** The change
of initial *þ* to *t* in pronominal words occurs after *s* in only a few such expressions as the above.   **þeʒʒm.** This form, with the nominative *þeʒʒ* (l. 26)
and genitive *þeʒʒre* (l. 4), shows that Orm's dialect had already begun to use
the ON. forms of the pronoun, a change which had not been fully accomplished
in Southeast Midland in Chaucer's time.   **16. ferrs.** OE. *fers*, from
Lat. *versus*, soon to give way to OF. *vers*.   **17. wēl . . . well.** Both forms
occur in Orm. Holthausen has shown ('Anglia Beiblatt,' XIII, 16) that *wēl* is
the prevailing form in both stressed and unstressed positions, and is used in
independent positions, while *well* is employed when modifying an adjective or
adverb. There are some exceptions even to this rule.   **annd all forrþī.**
'And therefore (*all forrþī*) I was compelled, full often of necessity, to put
(*dōn*) my word among the words of the gospel, to fill my verse.'   *Nēde* is an
adverb, and *shollde* has the old sense of ' was obliged, had to.'   **19. wīkenn.**
This OE. *n*-stem has acquired final *n* in the nominative singular, contrary to
the usual rule. Cf. the compounds *circewīkan*, *hōrderwȳcan* (4, 21–22).
26. lǣtenn. 'Think, judge,' less common meanings of OM. *lētan*, WS.
lǣtan, but common in Old Norse.

Page 10, l. 6. **fele wōrdess.** Note the early use of *fele* (OE. sb. *feola*)
as an adjective, and cf. German *viel*.   **24. att Godd.** 'From God'; cf.
'at the hands of,' a relic of this use in modern English.   **30. ʒiff þeʒʒ all**
forrwerrpenn itt. The same thought is to be found in Ælfric's 'Homilies,'
II, 528 : Gif we for synfullum mannum gebidda∂, and hi ∂ære ∂ingunge un-
wur∂e synd, ne beo we swa∂eah bedælede edleanes þæs godan willan, ∂eah
þe we ∂am forscyldegodan ge∂ingian ne magon. 'If we pray for sinful men

and they are unworthy of the intercession, yet we shall not be deprived of the reward of good intention, though we may not be able to mediate for the guilty.'

Page 11, l. 7. all mannkinne nēde. *Mannkinne* is an OE. genitive plural, which has not yet taken the invariable plural ending *es*, perhaps because it was felt to be part of a compound. The form *mannkinness* is also found in such expressions. **21. flumm Jorrdān.** Owing to the regular appearance of the two words in this order Kluge assumes that both are of OF. origin. While I have followed Kluge here, the whole subject of Scripture proper names in English needs fuller investigation. In Middle English the lack of certainty with regard to Latin or French origin of such names particularly affects names beginning with MnE. *J*, since they are written with *I* or *J* indiscriminately. **26. dæþþ.** The doubling of *þ* would indicate shortness of the vowel, but the latter is marked long in accordance with the more common writing *dæþ*; cf. l. 8. **wiþþūtenn wrihhte.** 'Without merit or desert,' so 'undeservedly.'

Page 12, l. 6. wiss tō fulle sōþ. 'Certainly, in full truth.' *Wiss* is OE. *gewiss*, strengthened by *tō fulle sōþ.* **18. seffnde.** The OE. *seofeðe* has already been displaced by the analogical form on the basis of the cardinal, as in MnE. *seventh.* **25. þatt hē sahh.** Cf. Rev. v. 1 f. **32. nāness kiness shaffte.** Note the genitive inflexion of both adjective and noun. The uninflected adjective is more common, but the inflected form remains in certain expressions.

Page 13, l. 4. all all swā se. The doubling of *all* for emphasis is not uncommon in Orm. **26. Orrmīn.** Mätzner regarded the name as formed on the Latin model, but Zupitza ('Guy of Warwick,' note to l. 9529, EETS., Extra Series, 25–26) makes it a diminutive of Orm on the French model; cf. *Awwstīn*, 8, 17. Orm's name is believed to be from ON. *ormr*, cognate with OE. *wyrm* 'worm, serpent.' **30. allre ǣresst.** The MS. gives clear evidence, as in some other cases, of elision.

B. MIDLAND OF THE THIRTEENTH AND FOURTEENTH CENTURIES

I. THE 'BESTIARY'

The 'Bestiary,' from which these selections are taken, is found in Arundel MS. 292 of the British Museum. It has been edited by Wright ('Altdeutsche Blätter,' II), by Wright and Halliwell ('Reliquiae Antiquae,' I, 208), by Morris ('An Old English Miscellany,' EETS. 49, 1), by Mätzner ('Sprachproben,' I, 55), and a selection by Morris ('Specimens,' I, 133). The language of the 'Bestiary' is that of the Southeast Midland (SEMl.) during the first half of the thirteenth century.

The poem consists of more or less fanciful descriptions of thirteen animals, with allegorical interpretations of their supposed characteristics. The first twelve sections are based on the Latin 'Physiologus' of Theobaldus, an Italian monk of the eleventh century, the thirteenth upon Alexander Neckam's 'De Naturis Rerum.' The 'Physiologus' of Theobaldus is printed by Morris as an appendix to 'An Old English Miscellany.' Fragments of an older 'Physiologus' occur in Old English poetry. The metrical forms of the 'Bestiary' are various. The first and third selections are in long unrimed lines with some attempt at alliteration. The second, with exception of the first line, breaks up into rimed couplets of four (occasionally three) stresses. The 'Signification' of the Eagle, however, shows long rimed lines with the first half-lines frequently riming together also. If the latter feature were perfectly carried out we should have a four-line stanza riming *abab*. The metre of the fourth is similar to the first part of the second, but all show many irregularities in detail. These metrical forms are especially interesting in relation not only to the alliterative line of Old English, but also to the rimed couplet of four stresses which was soon to be so common in England.

As to language, all Old English diphthongs have become simple vowels, and the new diphthongs are appearing; OE. *ǣ* is no longer used; the change of OE. *ā* to *ǭ*, and the lengthening of vowels in open syllables, have taken place; in other words typical East Midland is before us. Special peculiarities in orthography are OF. *c = s* initially; *g* for *g* in *gōd*, 'good,' and for *ʒ* in *liʒt*, 'light,' or *ʒ = y* in *gē*, 'ye'; *s (ss) = sh*; *ð* always for OE. *ð* or *þ*.

Page 14, l. 1. lēūn stant. Both *lēūn* and *līūn* occur in Middle English as in Old French, the latter finally prevailing. Contractions like *stant = standeþ* are more common in SEMl. than in NEMl., and still more common in Southern. hille. No doubt dative of *hil* (l. 14), though possibly from the OE. *hylle* f., beside *hyll* m. and. 'If'; it translates Lat. *si* of Theobaldus, introducing the subjunctive *hēre*. The Latin also shows that the first half-line is a separate sentence, not immediately connected with the next as usually punctuated. **4.** fētsteppes. Note that the plural in MnE. compounds of mutation nouns, except *man*, loses all trace of mutation. **5.** dūn. The addition of this word, though not corresponding exactly to anything in the Latin, seems justified by the context and especially by l. 18. It was first added by Morris. **6.** hē. Refers to 'hunter,' implied in *hunten* (l. 1). **9.** līð. With this contracted form compare *līeð* in l. 12. **16.** Hū. Both *hū* and *wū* are found in the selections, and represent OE. *hū* and *hwū* respectively, the latter commonly becoming *wū* in Sth. English. For convenience they have been regularized throughout the selection on the basis of the first form, the more common Midland variety. **17.** divel. This form shows conclusively that shortening of OE. *dēofol* had taken place, since only *dēvel* could have become *divel*. The latter is still common in dialectal English. **18.** dennede him. 'Made a resting-place for himself.' The Latin is:

'Viscera Marie tibi, Christe, fuisse cubile,'

and OE. *denn* is glossed 'cubile.' **19.** defte. 'Mild, gentle, meek.' OE. *gedæft*, whence MnE. *daft* by a change of meaning similar to that of 'simple,' 'innocent.' MnE. *deft*, from the same root if not the same word, has acquired the sense 'skilful' through 'easy,' a natural development from 'mild.' **20.** tō manne frāme. 'To the profit of men.' *Manne* is a relic of the OE. gen. pl. *manna*. Such a genitive plural is preserved only in certain expressions, and probably the folk-mind regarded combinations like *manne frame* as essentially compounds.

Page 15, l. 3. dę̄de = dę̄þe, with *d* from voiced *þ*. *Ded* for *death* still exists in English dialects. Cf. 122, 6 for the word in rime. **5. hīrde.** The strict Ml. form is *hę̄rde*, MnE. (shep)herd. *Hīrde* doubtless comes from WS. *hīerde*; cf. *sīlden = shilden* (l. 6) for Ml. *shę̄lden*, MnE. *shield.* **15-16. dimme . . . him.** The rimes of the ' Bestiary ' are sufficiently irregular so that the extra syllable of the first line does not seem remarkable. As *dimme* is pl. we assume the word was disyllabic, though compare 20, 26. **21. skīes sexe and sevene.** Referring to the traditional view of the heavens, based on the Ptolemaic system. **25. Dē sunne swīðeð.** The Lat. reads *Tunc sibi sol ambas accendit fervidus alas.*

Page 16, l. 2. **Ne wēre.** ' If his beak were not '; *wēre* pt. subj. **15 kirke.** A distinctly Nth. or NEMl. form, perhaps used for rime. **16. Ǫr.** Distinguish from *or*, ' or '; this is ON. *ār* cognate with OE. *ēr*, ' ere.' **21. tō Gode ward.** This is a not uncommon order of words in OE., though *tōweard* (*tōward*) also occurs. Cf. *tō ðē water ward* (17, 9). **lēteð.** ' Thinks '; this makes a perfect rime with *bēteð* and gives a good meaning. The MS. reading *lēreð = lę̄reð* is an imperfect rime in both vowel and consonant. **22. tē sunne sikerlīke.** The allegory here may be illustrated by an OE. ' Treatise on Astronomy' attributed to Ælfric (' Popular Treatises on Science,' Wright, p. 3), in which this passage occurs : ' Seo sunne getacneð urne Hælend Crist, se ðe ys rihtwisnesse sunne, swa swa se witega cwæð, *Timentibus autem nomen Domini orietur sol iustitiae, et sanitas in pennis eius* :—ðam mannum þe him ondrædað Godes naman þam arist rihtwisnysse sunne, and hælþe is on hyre fiðerum.' The sun betokens our Saviour Christ, who is the sun of righteousness, as the prophet said : ' Upon the men who fear God's name shall arise the sun of righteousness, and health is in his wings.' The prophecy is in Mal. iv. 2.

Page 17, l. 3. **forbrǫken.** Note the MS. reading in footnote. Some emendation is clearly necessary, and I suggest that in the text as better preserving the alliteration. **7. narwe būten.** The Latin original makes the passage clear :

> ' Querit angustum lapidis foramen ;
> Vix movens sese veniensque tandem
> Inde pertransit spoliatque carnem
>   Pelle vetusta.'

Thus *narwe* refers to *ðirl*. ' He seeks a stone in which (*ðat . . . on*) is a hole, narrow, but he forces himself (moves through with difficulty) for,' &c. **24. lītel him is.** ' Little (advantage) will be to him from his limbs '; ' he shall have little advantage,' &c. **25. higtest.** Note the shorter form *higtes* in the next line.

Page 18, l. 5. **It is tē nēd.** A half-line is lost as shown by the alliteration. **6. ful of ðewes.** It seems best to regard *ful* as imperative of OE. *fullian*, ' become full.' Otherwise, we must supply the imperative of the verb to be, or take *ful* as an adjective and omit *and* at beginning of the next line. The Latin gives no assistance. **31. Dat is ūre hę̄ved gēvelīc.** ' That is like our head.' The full sense is shown by the Latin, where our head refers to Christ :

> ' Vis novus vitam sine fine dignam,
> Semper illesum caput est habendum,
> Hoc caput, dico, quod habes in ipso
>   Principe Christo.'

hēlde wē. ' Incline we to,' ' if we incline to.' But *hēlde* might be a Sth. form for Ml. *hǫlden*, WS. *healdan* (*hēaldan*), OM. *haldan* (*hāldan*).

Page 19, l. 3. **seien.** Note the early development of a Midland infinitive based on the present indicative 3rd singular. Sth. *seggen,* OE. *secgan,* still remains for some time. **4. sǫge.** Pret. subj. 3rd sing., early ME. *ságe* ; cf. note on l. 15, and Siev. § 391, anm. 7. **9. it smīt.** 'It thrusts out.' *Smīt = smīteð.* **23. sumer and winter winnen.** 'Fair weather and storm strive together.' The Lat. has *Si sit tempestas cum vadit, vel venit estas.* **28. ꝺat,** MS. ꝺar. The emendation was suggested by Mätzner ('Sprachproben,' I, 69).

Page 20, l. 10. **dóꝺ hem sinken.** 'Maketh them to sink.' **13. ꝺis devel.** The whale was so commonly used as a figure for the devil that the English writer begins at once with ' This devil,' not following the Latin assertion of similarity : *Viribus est zabulus quasi cetus corpore magnus.* This was common interpretation of such Scripture passages as Ezek. xxxiii. 2 ; Isa. xxvii. 1 ; Job xli. 1. **18. wōsǫ him folegeð.** Note how the indefinite *wōsǫ* approaches relative force by the repetition of the subject (at first the clause) in *hē.* The next step was to place *hē* before *wōsǫ* or *whō,* when *wōsǫ* becomes wholly relative to *hē* as an antecedent. **22. gast.** A short secondary form of OE. *gást* occasionally occurring.

II. THE STORY OF JOSEPH

The 'Genesis and Exodus,' from which this selection is taken, is found in MS. 444 of the Library of Corpus Christi College, Cambridge. It was edited by Morris in EETS. 7 (1865) and reprinted with corrections in 1874. Specimens are found in Mätzner ('Sprachproben,' I, 75), Morris ('Specimens,' I, 153), Zupitza ('Übungsbuch,' 81), Wülker ('Lesebuch,' I, 1). As in the case of the preceding selection, with which this has much in common, the language of the 'Genesis and Exodus' is of the southern portion of the East Midland, and the poem was composed in the first half of the thirteenth century. A single author, otherwise unknown, is believed to have composed the whole poem ; cf. Fritzsche, 'Ist das altenglische Story of Genesis and Exodus das Werk eines Verfassers,' 'Anglia,' V, 43. Notes are to be found in 'Anglia,' VI, Anz. 1 ; XV, 191 ; XXII, 141 ; 'Englische Studien,' II, 120 ; III, 273 ; XVI, 429 ; XXII, 292 ; 'Archiv für neuere Sprachen,' XC, 143 ; 'Mod. Lang. Notes,' I, 65.

The poem consists of a paraphrase of the Scripture story, mainly based on the 'Historia Scholastica,' composed by Petrus Comestor between 1169 and 1175. As usual in such cases the treatment is free, many parts of the Bible story being omitted and many additions of mediæval legend and interpretation being added. The metre is the rimed couplet of four stresses with iambic movement, but with the syllabic irregularity so common in the period. Thus the line often ends with an unstressed syllable after the principal stress, and as often lacks an unstressed syllable at the beginning. In the latter case the first stressed syllable forms a monosyllabic foot. Alliteration of the stressed syllables is sometimes found, though without the regularity of alliterative verse. Our selection includes lines 2037–2490, covering Genesis xxxix. 19 to l. 14, though with large omissions. Another version of the story of Joseph may be read in 'Cursor Mundi' (EETS. 57, 59), beginning at l. 4037, and the part corresponding to our selection at l. 4417. The latter is much fuller and more dramatic, while also showing some interesting variations upon the story.

The language of the poem is similar to that of the ' Bestiary,' with which its
orthography agrees so thoroughly that in general no further remarks are
necessary. A few cases of OE. diphthongs occur, as at 22, 14–15, but similar
words are so frequently written with simple vowels as to prove that the older
forms did not represent true diphthongs. Otherwise the most noticeable
orthographic peculiarity is *qu* for OE. *hw*, as in *quīle* (21, 5), perhaps through
Nth. influence. The language of the poem is treated by Morris in the
Preface to his edition, by Hilmer in ' Die Sprache von Genesis und Exodus'
(1876), and by Fritzsche as above.

Page 21, l. 1. Putifar trewið. The form of Potiphar's name is that of
the Latin original, as are most of the other Scripture names in Genesis.
2. Iōsēp. The form here and the rimes at 22, 21–22 and 30, 7–8 prove
conclusively that the Latin, not OF. form of the word is meant. **3. sperd.**
Orm's *sperrd* (12, 26) shows the shortness of the vowel. Metrically the word
is disyllabic, and might be written *sperred*; though compare 22, 29–30.
6. prisunēr. Note that this is not the MnE. word 'prisoner.' **13. hem
drempte.** Impersonal uses of the verb were still common, as in OE.,
though soon to disappear; see Kellner, ' Hist. Outlines of Eng. Syntax,' § 151.
15. on sēl. Lines 15–16 paraphrase *Ioseph . . . ministrabat eis* of the Vulgate
and Petrus Comestor, but the above words were added to imply regularity of
the service. **17. hē freinde,** MS. hē hem freinde. The MS. reading is
impossible metrically, unless *hē hem* are to be read as *he'm*. The text follows
Kölbing, ' Eng. St.,' III, 305. **18. Harde drēmes.** ' Unpleasant (harde)
dreams have that power,' that is, to make people mourn. **27–28. hǫnd . . .
wrǫng.** Note the assonance instead of rime. **28. mē ðugte.** Morris says
ðugte = ðogte, corrected by Egge in ' Mod. Lang. Notes,' I, 66. ME. *ðuʒte,*
' seemed,' and *ðoʒte,* ' thought,' later fell together under *þouʒte,* MnE. *thought.*

Page 22, ll. 3–4. win . . . ðerin. Many imperfect rimes in the poem
show differences in vowel quantity. With rimes of long and short *i* cf. those
at 28, 25–26; 29, 7–8; 30, 15–16; 31, 17–18; 34, 4–5; see also 35, 21–22.
10. Ðat, MS. ðā. Morris suggested the emendation. **21. quad =
quað,** ' quoth.' For the change cf. Gram. Introd., §§ 100, 116. **25. fleis,
fleish.** For the diphthong see Gram. Introd. Cf. *weis* (29, 1). **26. agte.**
' Possessions, wealth,' not ' care' as Morris. The line means ' that no wealth
may protect thee.' Cf. *ðō agtes* (26, 32). This addition to the Scripture
narrative is not found in Petrus Comestor, but occurs in ' Cursor Mundi,'
l. 4493.

Page 23, ll. 7–8. bifǫren . . . cǫrn, MS. coren. The MS. reading makes
a good eye-rime, but it is doubtful whether *cǫrn* was disyllabic in pronunciation. Better assume *biforn* (*bifǫrn*) for *biforen*. **12. Ðē rance,** MS. ðe ranc
he. The emendation makes *rance* the correct plural, and leaves *sevene lēne* as
the more direct subject of *hāven ǫvercumen*. **13. it smiten.** ' They smote.'
Morris regards it as a neuter plural form, but perhaps this use is derived
from that of *it* as introducing plural verbs in OE. **14. ðrīsten tō ðē,**
MS. ðrist hem to ðo. The emendation seems justified by the syntax. The
plural *ðrīsten* is required and *ðē fette* must be object of it. Cf. the Latin:
*Septem spicae plenae pullulabant in culmo uno, aliaeque totidem iuxta orie-
bantur tenues, et percussae uredine, et devorabant priores.* **29–30. ǫn . . .
Phāraōn.** The NF. form of Pharaoh should rime with long close *ō,* as it

does at 22, 1–2, 9–10. Cf. 32, 15–16, and the OF. *Phāraūn* at 23, 21–22. **30. tawnen.** See the explanation of the form in the Glossary, and cf. MnE. *twit* for a similar initial *t* from OE. *æt* in a compound word.

Page 24, l. 8. gēre. The noun *gēr* = *ʒēr*, 'year,' appears with the plural *gēr* at 23, 31, *gēre* here, and *gēres* in l. 25. So most OE. neuters gradually assumed the *es* ending of masculines.   **17. ꝧanne Putifar.** Confusion in the names Potiphar and Potiphera of our Bible is easy from the Lat. forms Putiphar and Putiphara. It was then easy to make Asenath the daughter of Joseph's old master, as here. Hebrew tradition explained Joseph's marriage of a foreign woman by saying that Job's second wife was Dinah, daughter of Jacob (Gen. xxxiv), from whom a daughter was born and became the mother of Asenath (Petrus Comestor). Moslem tradition gave a romantic turn to the story by making Joseph marry Zuleekha, wife of Potiphar, after the latter's death (Weil's 'Biblical Legends,' 97 f.).   **20. Oꝧer is nū.** 'Another (condition) is now than had happened before.'   **24. Hē luveden God.** 'They (the sons of Joseph) loved God, he (God) repaid it to them.'   **29. Hunger wēx.** The 'Cursor Mundi' shows an interesting addition, probably from Hebrew tradition. Joseph, after threshing, casts the chaff upon the Nile, where Jacob, who casually walked by that river (geography did not trouble many mediæval writers), found it, and sent his sons along the Nile to Egypt to buy corn.   **29–30. Chānaan . . . forꝧan.** Another qualitative rime, as *Chanaan* seems to be disyllabic in 'Genesis,' though trisyllabic in 'Cursor Mundi,' as in Latin. Cf. 32, 7–8.

Page 25, l. 1. for nēde sogt. Morris defined *sogt* as 'reconciled,' associating it with OE. *sæht*, but it is the past participle of *sēken* in the less common sense of 'attacked, driven.'   **8. als.** A connective of *knew* (l. 7) and *lēt* (l. 8), *als* must mean 'yet' or 'though,' not 'also' as Morris. Cf. Egge, 'Mod. Lang. Notes,' I, 66, and Kock, 'Anglia,' XXV, 321.   **11. cume gē.** Note the form without ending before *gē*, as in OE. Cf. l. 28, and with *wē* in similar position, l. 14. Morris and Mätzner change *cume* to *came*, but this is surely unnecessary, since the action is regarded as present in time.   **16. dōꝧ us**, MS. dōꝧes. Mätzner suggested *dōꝧ us*, though retaining the MS. reading. The change is simple and satisfactory. Kock ('Anglia,' XXV) interprets *dōꝧes* as equivalent to *dōꝧ'e's = dōꝧ hē* (Jacob) *us*, but Mätzner's suggestion seems better.   **19. Hū sulde.** This addition to the Scripture is in Petrus Comestor: *Impossibile est enim viro idiotae tales filios esse, cum etiam regibus talis filiorum copia valde est difficilis.* The first part of the line was emended by Morris 'ani man,' but MS. *oninan = ʒn man.*   **32. Đat hē wǭre.** Kölbing shows ('Eng. St.,' III, 305) that *hē* refers to Joseph, not to Benjamin as Morris had assumed. He compares Petrus Comestor: *Timebat enim ne forte et in illum aliquid deliquissent.* This is added to explain Joseph's imprisonment of his brothers.

Page 26, l. 4. ꝧē tōn. The *t*, originally a part of *ꝧet (ꝧat)*, seems to have become an integral part of the following word, and is so printed. Cf. *tōpere* (30, 20), which still remains in dialectal English.   **6. Tō wedde.** 'For security,' 'as a pledge.' The frequent occurrence of OE. *wed* n. in this dative phrase no doubt accounts for the retention of the OE. dative form. Cf. *tō wive* (24, 19).   **12. Wrigtful wē.** 'Deservedly we are,' translating *Merito haec patimur, quia peccavimus in fratrem nostrum.*   **19. deden . . . beden.**

The rime assumes that both *dēden* and *deden* must have occurred in speech. This seems better than assuming *dēden . . . beden*. **24. ͨ͡ōr bifͻren.** Cf. Egge ('Mod. Lang. Notes,' I, 66): 'I take *in* a local sense, "there before, at the top," referring to the mouth of the sacks.' **27. ͻverͨ͡ogt.** Morris suggests 'over-anxious,' but the word corresponds to *obstupefacti turbatique* of the Vulgate: *Et obstupefacti turbatique mutuo* (Gen. xlii. 28). 'Amazed, stupefied' are better. **31. Quan men,** MS. **and quan men.** *And* is omitted, as it seems to have been copied from the preceding line by mistake.

Page 27, l. 5. Of Iōsēp. 'Of Joseph I do not know the end,' paraphrasing the Vulgate, *Ioseph non est super*. **7–8. dōn . . . on.** Cf. rimes of long and short *i* in note to 22, 3–4. Perhaps the adverb *on* had long *ō*; see rimes at 28, 5–6; 29, 27–28. **8. sͤͅgeͨ͡.** Note the plural subject with singular verb; probably *dͤͅaͨ͡* predominated in the mind of the writer. **16. But gē.** Note the abrupt transition from indirect to direct discourse; also the use of the plural pronoun in addressing one person, the earliest instance in English. **17. Quan it is nēd.** Kölbing points out ('Eng. St.,' III, 306) that *quan* = 'if' here, the clause translating *Si sic necesse est*. **18. And ic ne.** Mätzner adds *ic* here as rightly. **25. ͤͨ͡ͅemōded.** Mätzner's emendation of MS. *eͨ͡imodes*, making the word agree with its form in l. 1584 of the poem. **28. bēn intō Ēgypte ligt.** Mätzner's reading of the line. He suggests that *cumen* of the MS. was originally a gloss of *bēn ligt*. **30. lag,** MS. **was,** making no rime. Morris's *ͨ͡ag* = OE. *ͨ͡ā* is impossible, and Mätzner suggests assonance. Koch's late suggestion of *stāg* = OE. *stāg* is equally impossible, as OE. *ā* has regularly become *ͻ* in 'Genesis.'

Page 28, l. 2. Her nͻn. 'None of them.' The objective use of the genitive plural; cf. *ūre nͻn* (l. 6) and *gūre ͻn* (29, 30). **7. ͨ͡ē stiward.** Mätzner's suggestion for *stiward* of the MS. Otherwise the pause after *stille* must do duty for the omitted unstressed syllable. **8. For ic.** This part of the steward's answer does not very well agree with the Latin of the Vulgate, though the probable meaning is 'I have my instructions.' **11–12. cōme . . . nͻme.** Such seems to be the rime. The first word is Orm's *cōme*, 'coming,' and the second OE. *nām* f. There may have been, however, an OM. *nͻm* showing the root of the pret. pl. of *niman*. **24. Wͻt ic.** 'I think none there did not tremble.' The line corresponds to the Vulgate, *Et incurvati adoraverunt eum* (Gen. xliii. 28). *Incurvati* was apparently understood in its metaphorical sense 'disturbed in mind, trembling,' rather than the literal 'bowing.' **32. wurͨ͡ tͤͅres wēt.** 'Was wet with tears.' The expression occurs with and without a preposition; cf. 30, 22, and 31, 4.

Page 29, l. 4. Sette hem, MS. **and sette hem.** The reading of the text seems simpler than retaining *and* at the beginning of this line and omitting it before *him* in the preceding. **12. And hem.** There is nothing in the Scripture or Petrus Comestor for these lines, as Kölbing pointed out. In 'Cursor Mundi' the same 'sarmun' occurs, and the brothers are especially warned against theft. **18. Ͻr ͨ͡r.** 'Before.' The doubling of the particle is not uncommon. **29. For is it nogt.** All reference to divination (Gen. xliv. 5, 15) is omitted by the English writer here and at 30, 10. Petrus Comestor adds, after paraphrasing Joseph's words about divining, *Forte ioco dictum est, nec est imputandum*. **30. ͨ͡at,** MS. **ͨ͡a.** Morris's emendation, which seems necessary. **32. Up quām.** A very early use of *quām*, 'whom,' as a relative pronoun. Such use appears first in the oblique cases, but is not established until Late Middle and Early Modern English.

Page 30, l. 1. **Hē bē slagen.** Mätzner's emendation from MS. reading *he slagen.*   **agēn.** ' Back,' not ' again,' as Morris.   ' There is no reference to an earlier state of slavery ' (Egge).

Page 31, l. 1. **lewse.** This seems to be the only form of the MS., occurring also at l. 1576. No doubt the form should be *lēswe,* OM. *lēs* (acc. *lēswe*), WS *lǣs,* connected with OE. *lesan-lǣs,* ' to glean.'   **Gersen.** The Lat. form is *Gessen,* which a copyist seems to have transformed by mistaking *s* for *r.* With this rime with long *e* cf. 31, 12–13; 32, 12–13, where the vowel is clearly short.   **9. For luve of Iōsēp migte hē tīmen.** The *him* of l. 8 and the *hē* here seem to refer to the father (30, 31), and the line means ' For (on account of) love of Joseph might he prosper.' The rime of *tīmen* here and in other places may indicate shortening. **19. Alsọ fẹle.** Kölbing suggested connecting with following rather than preceding line. It translates Petrus Comestor, *Et totidem* (referring to Benjamin's gift) *misit patri.*

Page 32, l. 3. **Wēl mē.** No verb is necessary in the exclamation. Cf. *wumme* (195, 33).   **6. And sēn.** Mätzner adds *him,* but it is unnecessary and adds an extra syllable to the line.   **8. manīe a man.** Note the early introduction of *a* to make the singular number clear, indefinites tending to lose their singular uses and forms.   **15. Fader dēre,** MS. **derer.** Mätzner's change. **20. ðọ̄,** MS. **ðog.** The copyist was influenced by the preceding *ðōg* just above; cf. Gen. xlvii. 9.   **23. Sọ̄ ðinkeð.** Kölbing ('Eng. St.,' III, 307) pointed out that the speech of Jacob ends with the preceding line, these words paraphrasing a comment of Petrus Comestor: *Peregrinationis dixit, quia sancti vitam hanc pro incolatu habent.*   **29. Him and hise,** MS. **he.** The change is Mätzner's.

Page 33, l. 2. **fowrtēne gēr,** MS. **xiiij.** The writer is in error, as the Vulgate reads *decem et septem annos.* That the error is not a copyist's is clear from the fact that ME. *seventēne* would be too long to replace *fowrtēne.*   **6. off hē,** MS. **offe.** Mätzner added *hē* after *offe,* and Schumann ('Anglia,' VI, Anz. 1) proposed the reading adopted.   **7. Ðat quan it wurðe.** Literally, ' that when it should be done with him,' an idiom easily understood to-day though not a literary form.   **16. hem.** Kölbing ('Eng. St.,' III, 307) would change *hem* to *him,* referring to *Crīst* (l. 14) only.   He quotes the comment of Petrus Comestor: *Cura fuit sanctis sepeliri in terra, qua sciebant Christum resurrecturum, ut cum eo resurgerent.* But surely the wish of Jacob twice repeated (Gen. xlvii. 30; xlix. 29) was to be buried with his fathers, and it is more likely that *hem* is correct. It would include Christ with *hise eldere* (l. 13).   **27. smāken.** Mätzner alters to *māken,* but the sense of *smāken* is clear; cf. 14, 2.   **28. biwāken.** The whole passage upon the burial customs occurs in Petrus, though with several slight differences.   **29–30. daiges … laiges.** For forms see Gram. Introd.

Page 34, l. 5. **delven it wið ȳre.** ' Bury it with iron (instrument).' The last two words add nothing of value, but no doubt the whole was a common expression in rime.   **12–13. mide … wechdēde.** Perhaps for *mide* we should

read *mede* (*mēde*?) with the vowel of ON. *með*, Dan. *med*. Cf. 34, 30–31.
21. **wēl** him. 'Well may it be with him (*tō him*) that has done well.'
30–31. dede... mide. Another rime which shows the short form of ME. *dede*,
if not indeed that which Orm regularly uses, *dide*.

III. 'FLORIS AND BLAUNCHEFLUR'

The story of 'Floris and Blauncheflur,' of which this selection forms a part,
is found in four MSS.: Gg. 4, 27, 2 of Cambridge University Library; Cotton
Vetellius D. III of the British Museum; Auchinleck MS. of the Advocates'
Library, Edinburgh; Trentham MS. of the Duke of Sutherland's Library.
Of these the first and best, so far as complete, was edited by Lumby, EETS.
14 (1866), and re-edited by Dr. G. McKnight in 1901. Other editions of
the poem are those by Hartshorne ('Ancient Metrical Tales' (1829)), Laing
(Abbotsford Club Publ. (1857)). A critical edition, with valuable introduc-
tion from a comparative standpoint, was made by Emil Hausknecht for the
'Sammlung englischer Denkmäler' of Zupitza in 1885. The Cambridge
MS. belongs to the middle, possibly the second quarter, of the thirteenth
century. The language is that of the Southeast Midland, with a considerable
number of strictly Southern forms, as shown by the footnotes. This direct
Southern influence points to a district farther south than that of the 'Bestiary'
or 'Genesis and Exodus.' Owing to the mixture of Southern with Midland
forms this selection does not represent the East Midland in its purity, but
is added largely because of its greater literary interest. The metre of the
poem is the rimed couplet of four, sometimes three, stresses.

'Floris and Blauncheflur' is a romantic tale, probably of Eastern origin,
and brought to the West in the twelfth century, perhaps by crusaders. The
English poem was freely translated and condensed from a French version,
and is one of the earliest of a long series of French romances in Middle
English literature. The main current of the story to the beginning of our
selection (l. 433 of Camb. MS., 847 of the Hausknecht text) is as follows.
Floris and Blauncheflur had become passionately attached as children. The
father of Floris, the king of Spain, disapproves of the union, and suggests
killing the maiden. In the original French version Blauncheflur is the
daughter of a Christian captive, and the father of Floris a Saracen. The
queen, mother of Floris, proposes sending him away, and this was done.
Blauncheflur is then sold to the 'Admiral' of Babylon for a marvellous cup,
a tomb is erected, and Floris, on his return, is told that she is dead. He is
so heart-broken that he attempts his life, and the king and queen reveal to
him the truth. Floris proposes to seek Blauncheflur, and the king gives him
the marvellous cup, the queen a magic ring. He has various adventures in his
search, and finally reaches Babylon. Here, by giving him the marvellous cup
and promising great wealth, Floris at last persuades the porter of the tower in
which Blauncheflur is confined to assist him. Then follows our selection.

The Southern forms in the original text have been largely replaced by those
of the Midland. This applies especially to those with *u*, OE. *y*, and inflexional forms, while some with *ēo* (*hēo*, 36, 16), which would probably not
be found as late as this text but for Southern influence, have been retained.
Besides these peculiarities, among vowels may be mentioned the rare use of

o for *u* (*ȝongling*, 44, 3), a usage to become much more common in the follow-ing selections. Among consonants, the regular use of *ȝ* for *y* initially and for a palatal and guttural spirant medially separates these sounds from the stop *g* (as in *go*), though the latter character is still used for *g = dȝ* (as in *jugement*, 42, 2). For the latter sound initially, OF. *j* also appears. OF. *c = s* is found as in *certes* (38, 11), *Clārīce* (38, 3), and *sch* for *sh*. Contrary to the practice of the last two texts *wh* represents OE. *hw*, as in Orm. Among inflexional forms, a few with the prefix *i = OE. ge* have been left, as perhaps properly belonging to SEMl., at least longer than to Ml. and Nth. English. A special treatment of the language occurs in Hausknecht's edition, with which cf. 'Eng. St.,' IX, 92, 'Anglia,' Anz., VIII, 150. For notes see 'Anglia,' I, 473 ; 'Eng. St.,' III, 99, 272, IX, 389.

Page 35, l. 15. **cūpen.** Hausknecht takes this as OF. *cupe*, not Sth. *cūpe* = OE. *cȳpe*, because of the form in the Auchinleck MS., *coupe* (*couppe*) = *cūpe*. The meaning is the same in either case. 19. **gegges.** The Trenth. MS. has *maydens*. 20. **for hęvīe.** A substantive use of the adjective, as in the colloquial 'for cold,' 'for hot.' 28. **lēte hire stŭnde.** *Hire* refers to the basket (*cūpe*), the SEMl. apparently agreeing with Sth. in preserving grammatical gender later than in Ml. and Nth.; cf. *hē* referring to *ring* (43, 16). The adverb *stŭnde*, MS. *stonde*, completes the rime and sense : 'and go forth and leave it (*hire*) at once.' It is easy to see how *stŭnde* was misunderstood for *stę̄nde*.

Page 36, ll. 1-2. **wŏlde ... bihŏlde.** Long *ō* in *wŏlde* is proved by occasional rimes like these, though the short form is equally clear from Orm's *wollde* ; cf. 23-24. Otherwise we must assume qualitative rimes only, in such cases. 7-8. **rę̄de ... hadde.** These two lines, with imperfect rime, are found only in Camb. MS. and are rejected by Hausknecht from his critical text. Perhaps we are to read *hę̄de* (OE. *hǣde < hæfde*). 9. **agē**, MS. **agen.** The MS. rime *agen ... him* is of course impossible. *Agē*, from Auch. MS., and a slight change in the following line, makes all right. Trenth. MS. reads :

> 'When he sawȝ it was not shee,
> Into þe lepe aȝen stert he.'

15-16. **itŏld ... isŏld.** The retention of the OE. prefix *ge-* as *i-*, occasion-ally found in Ml., is characteristic of Sth. English ; cf. *ifere* (37, 22). 16. **hēo.** Note the Sth. feminine of the pronoun, as well as the OE. diphthong *ēo*. 17. **lę̄pe.** An infinitive dependent upon *cōmen*, as Zupitza pointed out in 'Anglia,' I, 473 : 'Now maidens came running (leaping) in to her.' 19. **what hire wēre.** 'What might be to her,' that is, 'what was the matter with her?' a common idiom. 21. **Wēl hēo was biþoȝt.** 'She was very (well) con-siderate and (considered) where to find them answer'; or could *whare* be for *ware*, 'wary'? Trenth. MS. has :

> 'Clarys byþouȝt hur anoon ryȝt
> þat hit was Blauncheflur þe white,
> And gave þe maydens answere anoon.'

23. **ich**, MS. **ihc** always. This can hardly indicate the true Sth. form *ich* = *itf* (*ch* in *church*), but rather a SEMl. *ic* in which *c* (*k*) is shading out into a spirant like German *ch* in *ich*.

Page 37, l. 2. **Wilt ū.** Usually printed as one word, but in this book the identity of each word has been consistently preserved by separating even the reduced forms, as here.   **8. libbe.** Another form at least more common in the South. In Ml. and Nth. *bb* of the OE. infin. and ind. pres. 1st sing. has been replaced by *v*, by analogy of the 3rd sing. and the other forms of the verb. Cf. MnE. *have, tive,* and for a similar loss of *gg, lie* ('recline'), *buy, say, lay.*

Page 38, l. 3. **þọ.** This addition to the MS. line seems to be required by the metre, though not added by Hausknecht.   **6. o = of.** Theoretically we must assume a long *ō* as in *ō* from *on*, but partly to differentiate the two words I have used short *o* in this word, even in these early instances.   **22. Ọ̄wer beire.** An objective genitive, 'of you two.'   **25-26. adūn . . . fram.** An impossible rime. All other MSS. read *aroum (aroom, rown),* i. e. *arūm,* OE. *on(an), gerūm,* 'apart,' and no doubt this is the correct form, though giving assonance only with *adūn.*

Page 39, ll. 13-14. **wite . . . underȝete.** Correct rime form here requires *undergite,* not uncommon in Sth., or possible *wete < wite.* 'But they might not long guard them, that they should not be perceived,' or as we should say, 'They could not long prevent them from being perceived.'

Page 40, l. 4. **lōke.** So MSS., but syntax requires *lōked,* in which final *d* is rarely dropped.   **15-16. arīst . . . atwīst.** Mätzner explains the first as a contracted form of *arīseð* (Siev. 'Angelsächsische Gram.,' § 359, 8), and the second as an analogical preterit like OE. *wiste.* We should expect preterits in both cases from the form of the narrative, but no such preterit as *arīst* seems to be known.   **23. pilēr.** The pillar in which the water-pipes were concealed.   **28. Hē axede.** The pronoun refers to *Admiral,* which the other MSS. repeat here as in 40, 2.

Page 41, ll. 9-10. **mūþ . . . cūþ.** Perhaps we should read *mūþe* ds., *cūþe* pl. of the adjective.   **11. teȝ.** The short form belongs here, or the rime is qualitative only, as in ll. 21-22.   **19-20. caste . . . breste.** With *keste* for *caste,* a not uncommon ME. form, the rime would be correct; cf. 42, 3-4. *Breste* is an OE. neuter which has not yet acquired the *es* plural.   **30. ligge.** A characteristic Sth. form, the prevailing Ml. being *lie(n).* Cf. note on 37, 8.

Page 42, l. 30. **họndhabbing.** A legal expression handed down from OE. times, the original word being a participle *handhæbbende;* cf. 'Anc. Laws and Inst. of England,' I, Index, *hæbbendæ handa.*

Page 44, l. 32. **ȝēt.** This word has not been satisfactorily explained, but the best assumption seems to be that it is for *ȝēd(e),* with *wiþdraȝe* as an infinitive depending upon it : 'And Blauncheflur went (endeavoured) to withdraw him.'

Page 45, l. 2. **þat ōþer.** The line is too short metrically, and probably we should read *þat eiþer ōþer deide bifǫre* ; cf. 37, 29 and 45, 5.

Page 46, l. 1. **of Spaygne.** It looks as if this were originally a gloss which had been thrust into the line, perhaps because the beginning of the story is incomplete in all the English texts, and the connexion of Floris's father with the Saracens was lost sight of.

IV. 'DEBATE OF THE BODY AND THE SOUL'

The 'Debate of the Body and the Soul' is found in six MSS.: Auch. MS., Edinburgh; Laud MS. 108, and Vernon MS., both of the Bodleian; Digby MS. 102, Royal MS. 18 AX, and Additional MS. 22, 283 of the British Museum. Our text is from Laud MS. 108, which was edited by Th. Wright in 'Latin Poems commonly attributed to Walter Mapes,' by Mätzner ('Sprachproben,' I, 92), and by Linow in 'Erlanger Beiträge zur englischen Philologie,' in which the Laud MS. is accompanied by three others and an important introduction, together with appendices. The 'Debate' was written in the second half of the thirteenth century, and the Laud MS. represents East Midland in the main, of northern rather than southern variety, but with a considerable number of Sth. forms. The interest of the poem rather than the purity of the text has led to its inclusion here.

The 'Debate' is based on a motive common in Western Europe in the middle ages. It finds expression in Old and Early Middle English in an 'Address of the Soul to the Body.' The 'Debate' or 'Dialogue' between the two belongs to Middle English only; cf. Bruce, 'A Contribution to the Study of the Body and the Soul Poems in English' ('Mod. Lang. Notes,' V, 197). To the 'Debate' two poems bear close relation, the Latin 'Visio Fulberti (Philberti)' printed by Wright in the above-mentioned work, as by Méril in 'Poésies populaires latines antérieures au douzième siècle,' and an OF. poem 'Un Samedi par Nuit,' Anhang I, to Linow above. A modern version of the 'Debate' was made by Sir Theodore Martin in the 'Monk's Dream,' and one was printed by Prof. F. J. Child of Harvard for private circulation. The metre of the poem is an eight-line stanza made up of lines with four stresses and iambic movement, riming *abababab*, with the *b* rimes more exact than the others. The poem has been treated in relation to sources, language, metre, by Kleinert, 'Über den Streit zwischen Leib u. Seele' (1880), Heesch, 'Über Sprache u. Versbau' (1884), Linow as above, Kunze, 'Þe Disputisoun bitwen þe Bodi and þe Soule' (1892), Bruce as above.

Special peculiarities of language which appear for the first time are the new diphthongs *ei* (*ey*) and *au* (*ou*) before palatal and guttural *ȝ* (*g*) respectively, as *eiȝene* (51, 25), *sauȝ* (47, 27). The former occur rarely in 'Genesis and Exodus,' as already noted. Here also *o* = *u* commonly, and $\overline{ou}$ = *ū* almost invariably. Among consonants *ȝw* represents OE. *hw*, as in *ȝwīlene* (48, 12), and *ȝth* of the MS. = *ȝt* (*ȝht*). Owing to lateness of the MS. copy, rather than the poem, final *ȝ* is often omitted, or added to words to which it does not belong. These peculiarities, as scribal, have been placed in the footnotes. Strictly Sth. forms have also been placed in the footnotes, and attention will be called to some of Nth. origin. The much more frequent loss of final *n* in inflexional forms should be noted in this and the following selection.

Page 47, l. 26. drōupening. The MS. reading *droukening* can hardly be correct, as it must be connected with ON. *droukna,* 'to drown,' an inappropriate meaning. Auch. and Vern. MSS. have *droupening* (*droupnynge*), while Digby MS. has *derkyng,* as if the scribe had not understood the form before him.

Page 48, l. 2. tō pay. 'For pleasure, satisfaction.' The MS. *payȝ* seems to indicate that, at the time of the copy, *ȝ* had already shaded out into *i,* since it is here added to an OF. word to which it could not have belonged. Cf. similar forms in the foothotes. **5. gǫst it.** Such repetition of the subject in pronoun form, originally used for emphasis, came to be employed by the metrist to complete his line. Cf. Kellner, ' Hist. Eng. Syntax,' § 284, 286. **6. It, MS. yt.** Initial *y* for *i* has usually been replaced by the latter in these early selections, to reduce the number of variants, especially in initials. **18. lēde.** The changes of meaning and use in this word are especially interesting. First, ' Latin (tongue),' a borrowed adjective; next, ' discourse, speech, in Latin '; then, ' any tongue, language, speech '; here, ' speech in sense of voice,' perhaps ' boasting speech '; the word may also mean ' song of a bird.' **21. 3wēre bēn.** In Laud MS. this and the next stanza change places, all other MSS. giving the order of the text. The Auch. MS. also has another stanza between the two. **26. fedde, MS. ledde.** The other MSS. have *fed* (*feddes*). *Feddes* would agree in use with *leddes*, but would not rime with *fledde* (l. 28).

Page 49, l. 10. gǫn tō greiþe. So Auch. MS., which seems better metrically than *gǫn greiþe*, though the latter is the older syntax. Two forms have developed, that of Auch. MS., and *gǫ and greiþe* of Digby, a well-known form in colloquial and dialectal English. **16. mē bigēte.** At this point the Laud MS. lacks seventeen stanzas as compared with the Auch. text. Eleven of these continue the speech of the 'Soul' (see Linow, or a modernization), after which the 'Body' (Auch. MS.),

> ' Lift up his heved opon þe swere ;
>> As it were sike it gan to gron,
> And seyd, " Wheþer þou art mi fere,
>> Mi gost þat is fro me gon ? " '

The 'Body' admits that it must decay, and then turns upon the 'Soul' with a countercharge :

> 'Soule, 3if þou it me wilt atwite,
>> þat we schul be boþe yspilt,
> 3if þou hast schame and gret despite,
>> Al it is þine owhen gilt.
> Y þe say at wordes lite,
>> Wiþ ri3t resoun 3if þat ow wilt,
> þou berst þe blame and y go quite ;
>> þou scholdest fram schame ous have yschilt.

Then follow the stanzas at 49, 17. **14. swelle.** Note the new vowel which has developed in the MS. *suwelle,* and cf. *koweynte* (48, 15). **17. þē schōp, MS. schop þe.** The text is the reading of all the MSS. except Laud. If the poet intended to mark the contrast between *þē* (the 'Soul') and the 'Body,' the Laud MS. is correct. **22. gōd, MS. guod.** The MS. form is of Nth. origin, unless perhaps Kentish can be assumed to have influenced the Laud MS. **23. dumb and daft.** An example of the alliterative phrases, once so common, and still often preserved in poetry. Cf. *lime and lyþ* (50, 15), *tēme and tēche* (50, 27), *linde and lēf* (51, 22), *fēld and fenne* (51, 23). Under the influence of these phrases of OE. origin new ones have often been made, as *pile and piþ* (50, 13), where the first is OF., and *preye and prēche* (51, 1), where both words are of OF. origin. In *rest and rō* (51, 19) the second is ON., and in *þriven and þrō* (51, 17) both are of Norse origin. **24. mē þertil.** *Mē,* omitted in Laud, occurs in all other MSS. and is necessary to the metre.

Page 50, l. 3. **gast.** Both *gǭst* and *gast* occur in the poem, the latter riming with short *a*, as at 58, 13, so that it probably represents not Nth. *gǣst*, but a secondary form from OE. *gǣst.* Cf. Morsbach, 'Mitteleng. Gram.,' § 62, anm.   **22. dīst.** A somewhat unusual shortening of *dīdest.* Cf. the form in rime at 54, 4.   **28. Ʒwat was yvel.** Linow has the impossible reading *Ʒwat was wel* from a misunderstanding of Sth. *ūvel* of the MS. *Ʒwat* at the beginning of the line was suggested by Mätzner ; cf. 58, 22.

Page 51, l. 9. **ēdest.** The shorter and earlier *ēdes* would make the rime perfect. Cf. *leddes* (48, 24).   **13. Hō may.** This stanza, found at this place in Auch. and Digby MSS., occurs in Laud after 56, 16. As to sense it fits either place.   **18. MiƷtis did**, MS. **mittis ded.** Mätzner proposed the reading of the text. Pluralizing an abstract noun for emphasis was common in OE., and remained in the ME. period sometimes ; cf. Kellner, 'Hist. Eng. Syntax,' § 21.   **19. rō.** Though from ON. *rō(r)*, and so having close *ō*, it is possible the *ō* has become open under the influence of preceding *r*.   **20. mē in pīne.** Mätzner added *mē*, which occurs in all the other MSS.

Page 52, l. 3. **niƷt, niƷth.** This is the beginning in our texts of the spelling *Ʒth* = *Ʒt* (*Ʒht*). Cf. *hc* = *ch* in 'Floris and Blauncheflur.'   **8. Come þou.** 'If thou shouldst come.' Subjunctive in transposed clause, as in MnE. 'had I.'   **14. Sat or stōd.** That is, ' (Where) sat (I) or stod,' in ellipsis with the preceding line.   **21. þat tou ne wēre.** 'That thou were not (present) and advised course (counsel),' that is, 'Unless thou wert present,' &c., 'I never did,' &c.   **23. mōwen.** The shortened form *mōwn* is necessary for the rime ; cf. 78, 31.   **29. chaunged**, MS. **chaunched.** Mätzner suggested the change, which is obviously necessary.

Page 53, l. 7. **Nevere of catēl.** 'I should have ' from the first line is to be supplied. Then *nome* (= *nume*) is a past participle depending upon 'should have.'   **10. Ne wēre þē wit.** 'Were it not for the wit that was wholly thine.'   **18. Sǭ dōth.** 'As doth that (one) who dares no other (thing).'   **26. gete**, MS. **getin.** The change seems necessary for metre, and is proper owing to the many infinitives which have lost final *n*.   **30. bēgin and birst.** Mätzner connects the last word with *bersten*, ' burst, broken,' but the pp. in Ml. would be *bersted* regularly, while both form and meaning point to OE. *gebrȳsed* with syncopation of *e* and shortening of the vowel after metathesis.

Page 54, l. 4. **dīst.** So MS., although breaking the rime sequence. Perhaps *dirst*, 'durst,' connected with OE. *dy(r)ste*, found once in the Rushworth 'Matthew,' a Mercian text.   **13. gloterīe.** Altered by Linow and Mätzner to *glotonīe*, but a substantive of this form, with the same meaning as *glotonīe*, occurs in OF. works.   **22. wē.** Mätzner added to the text as necessary. So also *dide* in l. 27, though Mätzner uses the Sth. form *düde.*   **24. þou sauƷ.** It has been customary to add *þōƷ.* ' though,' at the beginning of this line, and Vern. and Digby MSS. so read. Auch. MS. reads :

'Litel hede tok þou of þat
            When þou seiƷe ded men in grave.'

This seems to indicate that the third line of the stanza refers to the fourth and not to the second, and I therefore keep the MS. reading. The 'Body' took no heed of the many dead seen in the grave, and thought no such fate could come to it.

Page 55, l. 6. Abȳ . . . abȳȝe. Note the double forms of the same verb, one without the spirant ȝ. **11. Ǫn untiȝht.** Mätzner says, 'only orthographically different from *an untiht* of Vern. MS.,' but *ǭn* implies greater emphasis on the word than would be implied by the article. **25. lein ǫn hǫnd.** Mätzner interpreted *lein* as 'conceal, hide,' and Linow regards *ǭn* as an adverb modifying *lein*, taking *hǫnd* as a direct object. I assume that MS. *on* is 'one,' and that the expression means 'lay a (one) hand,' i.e. 'initiate one hand that hath turned to shame and sin.'

Page 56, l. 7. ȝwanne þē blīnde. Cf. Matt. xv. 14. **12. las.** Mätzner assumes this is pret. of *lēsen = lẹ̄s* (OE. *lēosan = lēas*), 'lose,' when it must be accounted a shortened form, certainly not common. I propose the pret. of *lẹ̄sen = las* (OE. *lesan = læs*), 'gather, collect'; 'for all my love on thee I collected or centered.' The usual, but special sense of 'glean,' is not the only one, as shown by 'Elene' 1238, where *ic læs* is used intransitively. **23. þey.** Note the double forms of the pronoun *þey, hē* (l. 8) in this poem. **29. þus sōne.** The Auch. MS. reads *so ȝong*, 'so young,' and Vern. and Digby *þus ȝong*. There seems no sufficient reason for departing from the Laud reading.

Page 57, l. 4. mes. Note the plural without ending in an OF. word ending in *s*. With its meaning of 'messes, courses at table,' cf. OE. *sand* (*sǫnd*), ME. *sande* (*sǫnde*) from *send*. **12. Nim of mē.** Laud MS. reads *on*, all others *of*. *þī soule* is appositive, of course. **18. bochēre.** Both Laud and Vern. MSS. read *boþelere*, Auch. *bucher*, Digby, *bell-wether*. The Auch. reading is to be preferred. **21. trotevāle.** The origin of the word is obscure. Perhaps from OF. **trotevale*, with some such meaning as 'a trifling thing.' Halliwell quotes:

> 'Yn games and festys and at the ale
> Love men to lestene trotevale.'

Page 58, l. 20. in a lāke. 'In a lake.' The MSS. vary greatly, as if the passage were misunderstood. Auch. reads:

> 'And seþþen into a pit ycast
> Unto a nadder and a snake.'

Page 59, l. 1. þē wayn. Mätzner thinks the reference is to the wagon used for carrying the dead body, and cites Turner's 'Hist. of the Anglo-Saxons,' III, 84. **2. leid þē spẹ̄che.** 'Laid (aside) the speech.' Auch. MS. reads:

> And þe tong haþ lorn his speche,'

giving the sense clearly. The other MSS. agree with Laud. **9. þǭ.** Mätzner would change to *þōū*, 'thou.' The Auch. MS. gives the sense:

> 'When þou feldest þe sike and sere.'

Our line may be read, 'When that (the life) was so sick and sere.' **19. And miȝte.** 'And might five (times) such as there are in the world of all things,' that is 'five times as many things as there are in the world.'

Page 60, l. 4. A þōūsand develene. The plural *develene = Ml. devels* is another indication of Sth. influence in this poem. **10. With brǭde bulches.** In the middle ages devils were often pictured as having the most hideous deformities. **20. shenke abōūten.** Mätzner proposed the emendation.

Page 61, l. 12. a cǭte. Mätzner alters to *colte*, ' colt,' on the ground that the devil was often represented as a horse. I have preserved the MS. reading, assuming that if the word is for *colte* the *l* has already been lost, thus preserving the rime.   18. ilke a grǭte. Note the addition of *a* after *ilke*, to make the singular clear. Cf. note on 32, 8.   30. tǒ him wēre let, MS. led. Surely *led* is impossible in both rime and meaning; *let*, ' permitted,' fits both exactly.

Page 62, l. 6. Bauston (MS. Hauston) and Bewis. All but Laud MS. agree in using alliterative names : Auch. *Bausan and Beweviis*, Vern. *Bauson and Beufys*, Digby *Bauʒan and Beaufitz*. Can the original names in Laud be connected with those in the OF. romance ' Beuves d'Hanstone ' ?   30. tǒ wrǭþer hēle. *Wrǭþer* seems to be an old fem. dat. sing. which has become fossilized in this stereotyped expression.

Page 64, l. 5. þǭ alle sinful. The Laud line is too long metrically, and Vern., Digby agree in *alle synful*.

V. ' ADAM AND EVE '

The metrical ' Adam and Eve,' or ' Canticum de Creatione' as it has been called, occurs in Auchinleck MS. at Edinburgh, and Trinity College MS. 57 at Oxford. The former, from which our selection is taken, was edited by Laing for the Abbotsford Club (1857), and by Horstmann, ' Altenglische Legenden ' (1878), p. 139. Prose versions of the story are found in Vern. MS. (Horstmann's ' Legenden,' 1878, p. 120), Egerton MS. 876, Harl. MS. 4775, Bodl. MS. 596, both the latter having been edited by Horstmann for the ' Archiv für neuere Sprachen,' LXXIV, 345. The language of the poem is that of the SEMl. dialect, as shown by Bachmann in his excellent monograph ' Die beiden Versionen des ME. Canticum de Creatione,' and the time of writing about 1300.

The poem contains an apocryphal story of the fall of man, the repentance and penance of Adam and Eve, and their death. It is based on the ' Vitae Adae et Evae ' (see edition of W. Meyer, 1878). Just before the beginning of the selection Adam, in his last illness, has commanded Eve to go with Seth to Paradise, where they are to receive a message from God. They are met in the way by the devil, who bites Seth in the face before the latter commands him to be gone. Then they proceed on their journey as in the passage chosen. To the latter version, represented by the Trinity MS., was added the story of the cross tree, said to have grown from the seeds brought by Seth from Paradise and placed under Adam's tongue on his deathbed. Both stories also appear in ' Cursor Mundi,' l. 1237 f. The metre is the rimed couplet of four stresses, with occasional lines of three stresses and other irregularities.

The language shows fewer peculiarities than any selection so far. The MS. omits final *e* in a number of forms to which it must be restored on metrical grounds, probably indicating that the copyist's speech had lost this sound, though perhaps owing only to scribal carelessness. On the other hand, the metre proves that final *e* was beginning to disappear in many classes of words, as pronouns and other unstressed words. Bachmann also thinks that final *e* at the end of the line was wholly lost, but his position seems not to be demonstrated by the examples cited. See his monograph for a fuller treatment of language.

Page 64, l. 12. **ne**, MS. **no**. The MS. form can hardly be regarded as the emphatic negative *nǭ*, OE. *nā*, and must be an orthographic variant of unstressed *ne*; cf. *oʒain* of MS. at 65, 23. **13. Sche ne durst nouʒt.** Earlier in the poem Adam had told Eve to take Seth :

> 'For he haþ nouʒt trespast so miche
> As have we, sikerliche,
> þerfore he may þe balder be
> To speke wiþ Jhesu Crist þan we.'

20. an āngel briʒt. According to the Trinity version this is *Miʒhel*, 'Michael.' **21. manēre**, MS. **maner**. The MS. shows lack of final *e* in a number of places in which it must have been originally written or pronounced; cf. *term* (l. 25 and 65, 1), *mett* (66, 5), &c. **26. Of fīve þōusande.** That is, as is not very clearly told, until Christ's death and the 'harrowing of hell' during his three days in the grave. Cf. the various versions of the 'harrowing of hell' story in Old and Middle English, and 67, 23.

Page 65, l. 12. **hȳʒe**, MS. **heyʒe**. The change is fully justified by the rimes *crīe* . . . *dȳe* (67, 3–4), *dȳen* . . . *ȳʒen* (68, 29–30), *dȳe* . . . *progenīe* (69, 9–10). Such rimes as *heyʒe* . . . *seiʒe* (67, 17–18), *heyʒe* . . . *steiʒe* (68, 7–8) probably represent older forms still preserved by the scribe. **23. aʒain**, MS. **oʒain.** The MS. form may mean *oʒain*, but probably *o* is merely the weak vowel in unstressed syllable, and it is altered to reduce the number of variants, especially of initials.

Page 66, l. 9. **Ǭ.** This is the strong form of the OE. interjection *ā*, and accounts for MnE. *O* (oh). The weak form *A*, from which MnE. *ah* comes, occurs at 25, 23 and commonly. **11. ōus.** The regular spelling with *ou* indicates the preservation of long *ū* in this dialect, beside the short form, for which we have the authority of Orm's *uss*. On the other hand, rimes like *þus* . . . *ōus* (ll. 27–28), *ōus* . . . *Jēsus* (70, 7–8 and 74, 19–20) indicate the short form, though the written form is the same and has been retained. **13–14. liven** . . . **ēven.** Such a rime cannot be wholly reconciled in its stressed vowels, but rime of unstressed syllables were often regarded as sufficient; cf. *childer* . . . *elder* (ll. 17–18). **32. alle þē liʒtnisse.** In the 'Revelation of Moses' (above) the sun and moon fell down and prayed for Adam, and were 'black-looking, because they could not shine in the presence of the Light of the Universe, and for this reason their light was hidden'; Ante-Nicene Fathers, VIII, 565, 569.

Page 67, l. 7. **bōk**, MS. **boke.** Both forms appear in the poem, though the word is usually disyllabic. Here, however, a disyllable is impossible in perfect rime. **17. sit.** The contract form for *sitteþ*, as occasionally. **18. Adam soule.** A genitive without ending in proper names, especially Biblical names, is not uncommon, no doubt through the influence of the Latin Scriptures in which it so occurs; cf. *David lond* (72, 5).

Page 68, ll. 11–12. **mōld** . . . **wōld.** Perhaps *mōlde* . . . *wōlde*, the final *e* in each case being organic; but cf. *mōld* . . . *schōld* (71, 23–24). Such rimes seem to indicate long forms of *wōld(e)*, *schōld(e)*, beside the usual short ones; cf. note on 36, 1–2. **13. ʒēte lay Abēl.** There is no reference to this in the Trinity MS. version, but it occurs in the apocryphal 'Revelation of Moses,' Ante-Nicene Fathers, VIII, 570.

Page 69, l. 23. **fader liif bē write.** Petrus Comestor, following another tradition, says that Enoch invented letters and wrote certain books from which the death of Adam is known.

Page 71, l. 22. **In stǫn.** In the Trinity version Eve is represented as having been more explicit in her directions. Seth was to make ' tables tweye ' :

> ' Tweye of erthe and tweye of ston,
>
> . . . .
>
> For long er domesday falle,
> þis worlde shal ben fordon alle
> By water or by fere (fire).'

The stone pillars would thus resist water, and the earth the fire. This Hebrew tradition appears commonly. Petrus Comestor, following Josephus (ch. ii), says two such pillars of marble and tile were made by Tubalcain to preserve the knowledge of his arts ; ' Hist. Schol.,' Gen. xxviii, also ' Genesis and Exodus,' 461, ' Cursor Mundi,' 1533.

Page 74, l. 13. **com.** So the MS., as if final *e* were not preserved in the infinitive. Probably, however, we should read *come = cume*, to rime with *nome = nume*, since final *e* must certainly be added within the line as shown by the metre.

VI. ' HAVELOK THE DANE '

The poetic romance from which this selection is taken is found in Laud MS. 108 of the Bodleian, Oxford. It was edited by Madden for the Roxburghe Club (1828) ; by Skeat for the Early English Text Society, Ex.' Ser. 4 (1868), and re-edited for the Clarendon Press (1902) ; and by Holthausen in the Morsbach-Holthausen series of Old and Middle English texts (1901). A selection appears in Wülker (' Lesebuch,' I, 80), and Morris (' Specimens,' I, 222). The date of the poem is about 1300 (see Skeat's introduction for full discussion), and the dialect is probably that of Lincolnshire of that time, that is, NEMl. This original dialect, however, has been somewhat modified by different scribes, as so often in the case of popular poems. The metre is the rimed couplet, regularly of four stresses.

The complete poem consists of 3001 lines, and the story is as follows. An English king Athelwold had a daughter Goldborough, whom he entrusted at his death to the care of Earl Godrich of Cornwall, charging him to marry her to the fairest and strongest man he could find, and place the government of England in her hands. The Earl, resolving to seize England for his son, imprisoned Goldborough in the castle of Dover. Then our selection takes up the hero Havelok. To finish the tale, Havelok assisted Grim in his trade as a fisherman at Grimsby. When a famine came he left his foster-father, walked to Lincoln, and took service as a scullion to the Earl of Cornwall's cook. One day, at some games, Havelok showed his great strength, and Godrich determined to fulfil his oath by marrying Goldborough to the supposed menial. Havelok at first rebelled, but finally took Goldborough to wife and departed for Grimsby. At night, as Grim's wife had done before, Goldborough perceives the light from Havelok's mouth, and the royal cross on his shoulder. An angel also tells her of good fortune to come. At the same time Havelok has a dream that he possessed all Denmark and England.

They go to Denmark and, with many adventures, Havelok becomes king after Godard is defeated and hanged. He invades England, Godrich is made prisoner and burnt, and Havelok and Goldborough are crowned at London, reigning happily for sixty years. The source of the tale, though clearly Teutonic and English in characters and localities, is probably an OF. poem now lost, but the ancestor also of the OF. 'Lai d'Havelok,' as of the stories in Gaimar's 'Estorie des Angleis,' and in Manning's translation of Peter Langtoft's 'Chronicle.' For further particulars see the bibliography in Skeat's edition of 1902.

Peculiarities of orthography, it is believed, will no longer trouble the student. Some Nth. and some Sth. forms occur, as indicated in notes and footnotes. For the first time *y* is used for initial *ʒ* (OE. *g*, as usually printed), while *cht*, *ht* (MS. *cth*, *th*) are employed for OE. *ht*, ME. *ʒt*. That this *th* does not mean OE. *þ* would be clear from the scribe's using it for *t* in such words as *ūth = ūt*, 'out.'

Page 75, l. 1. **In þat tïme.** The time of the earlier part of the story when Goldborough was placed in charge of Godrich. The line preceding reads:

> 'Sa(y) we nou forth in ure (hure) spelle.'

2. **lǫnd**, MS. **lon.** Note omission of final *d* here, in *gǫld* (l. 19), and in *and* (l. 21). 6. **fayer**, MS. **fayr.** The word is disyllabic for metre. Morris and Skeat both add something to the line, but unnecessarily. 16-17. **wilde ... filde**, MS. **wolde ... fulde.** If the first MS. form is correct, *fulde* as a Ml. form must represent *fullede* (OE. *fullode*). It seems more probable that *fulde* = Sth. *fülde*, Ml. *filde*, in which case the true Ml. rime must be *wilde*. This would either be for *willede* (OE. *willode*), or better a new form on the basis of *wille(n)*, such as occurs in 'Cursor Mundi.' The latter seems to settle all difficulties. 23. **rǫpe**, MS. **rede.** The MS. form makes no rime, but the ON. form of Ml. *rēde(n)* is *rāða*, ME. *rǫʒe*, and makes perfect rime. Cf. 86, 9-10. 26. **hosleð.** Besides ME. *hūsle(n)*, *hōwsle(n)*, a shortened form occurs with *o = u*. 27. **and for him gyven.** For explanation cf. the statement at the death of Athelwold (l. 218):

> 'He made his quiste swiþe wel,
> And sone gaf it evere ilk del.'

He not only made his bequest but gave over his property as well.

Page 76, l. 9. **Was þē trewest.** Zupitza, 'Anglia,' I, 468, proposes, quite unnecessarily, the change of *þat* to *as.* *Wënde* here takes the accusative directly, as sometimes in OE. usage. 22. **ëlde**, MS. **helde.** The addition of *h* initially is common in words beginning with a vowel; cf. *hǫld* for *ǫld* (77, 20). 25-26. **ringes ... singes.** Both Nth. present indic. 3rd sing. *Men* is the weak indefinite form of *man*; cf. 84, 27.

Page 77, ll. 3-4. **wäre ... säre.** An example of Nth. forms which have been allowed to remain. The Ml. forms appear in 17-18, as one of them exists in the MS. *were ... sore.* 6. **Jësu Crist.** Holthausen says a mistake for God, and he even proposes a new line, in spite of 78, 7 and frequent other references of the same sort, as at 149, 9. All these are based on John i. 3, and the usual interpretation of 'word' as Christ. Cf. the use of that passage in Tatian's 'Diatessaron,' and Milton's 'Paradise Lost,' VII, 139. *Godes sone* (l. 10) does not interfere with this interpretation, since the two lines express

the ordinary prayer for the dead, and the inconsistency is only apparent.
13–14. heir . . . tōþer. Such a rime is certainly suspicious, and Holthausen
assumes an omission of two lines. On the other hand, the sense is complete,
and a form *hēr* from *heir* (cf. Behrens, 'Französische Sprache in England,'
p. 141, for similar forms) may be assumed, though still riming with an unstressed syllable.   **13. Havelok.**   The name has been traced to OE. *Anlaf*
(ON. *Olaf*) through Irish *Amlaib*, Welsh *Abloc*, AN. *Avelok* (*Havelok*).
This Anlaf was Olaf Sitricson, called Cuaran ' of the sandal.'   **14. Swan-**
borow . . . Helflēd. These names seem thoroughly English. The first may
be OE. *Swan*, 'swan,' or *swān*, 'herdsman,' by shortening in the compound,
and OE. *burh*, also found in *Goldborough* (l. 284). Helflēd is doubtless
Elflēd, WS. *Ælflēd*.   **22. yaf a note.**   Cf. the expression at 79, 5.
25–26. sikerlike . . . swike. With the short form of the ending *-like* cf. the
same rime at 84, 5–6.

Page 78, l. 3. þat God himselve. 'On which (þat . . . on) God himself
ran (with) blood.' For the use of *blōde* without a preposition cf. the similar
expression *tēres wēt*, 'wet with tears,' at 28, 32.   **23. grette.** Note the
clear indication in the rime of the shortening of OE. *grētte*.   **24. Wat is**
yū. Cf. the indirect form of the same question at 36, 19.

Page 79, l. 1. nis it nō cōrn. 'Is there no corn?' Note use of the
expletive 'it,' as in OE. syntax.   **29. wepne, MS. wepne bere.** The
latter is no doubt repeated from l. 27 above, but quite unnecessarily.

Page 80, l. 6. Of þē sēli. Note the plural ' children ' without distinctive
genitive ending.   **11. And þoucte.** Napier proposed to read *þouh*, 'nevertheless,' instead of *þoucte*, and Holthausen accepts. It may be easily read as
it stands, except that *nouht* (l. 13) must be assumed to have intruded from
the preceding line: ' And thought, he would that he [Havelok] were dead,
except that he would not kill him with his [own] hand, the foul fiend.'
The MS. *but on* here and at l. 962 of the poem Skeat has proper'y explained
as OE. *būton*.

Page 81, l. 10. þrinne, MS. þerinne. The shorter form is required for
the rime here and perhaps at 85, 7.   **21. And siþen.** Holthausen assumes
the loss of two lines to say that Grim put the gag in Havelok's mouth. This
is not necessary, as *in . . . woūnden* with the next two lines are quite explicit
enough as to what was done. If any emendation is to be made I suggest that
mūth might be added after *siþen in*.   **26. Hwan þē swike.** Most editors
have assumed that *hwan* was incorrect, perhaps repeated from the line above,
and have altered it to *þan* (Morris) or *as* (Holthausen and Skeat). It is
possible, however, to consider this as a second subordinate clause to *Sone hē*
caste (l. 31). L. 25 merely emphasizes the action begun in l. 20, before taking
up the next one. The last word of the line is also an emendation of the
MS. *heþede*. Morris reads *him gan bede*, omitting *havede* entirely. Holthausen
and Skeat change the line to *As þē swike him bad hē yēde*, but this seems to
anticipate the action in ll. 30–32. Zupitza's explanation of *heþede* as *ēþede*,
based on OE. *āð*, is highly improbable if not quite impossible. The punctuation will make the passage clear.

Page 82, l. 2. Lēve. The word rimes with open *ę̄* words, but this does not especially assist in its etymology. 4. **Al ꜱǭ thoū.** Holthausen, followed by Skeat, alters to

'Also thou wilt mi lif save (nou save),'

but it seems to me the slight emendation of *mī* to *mē* is sufficient. Grim commands his wife to watch Havelok as she values her own life, and then explains the rewards to follow. 11. **sō harde adoūn . . . crakedꝫ hise croūne.** The change, suggested by Morris, is unquestionably right, final *e* in *croūne* not being pronounced. 16. **þat him.** Prof. Browne ('Mod. Lang. Notes,' VII, 134) makes the lament end with l. 18, at the same time suggesting the change of *dẹre*, 'injure,' to *nẹre*, 'save, deliver.' No emendation is necessary, however, as Havelok laments not only that he is a king's son, but that wild beasts do not have him rather than such inhuman people. Holthausen makes *him* refer to Grim, but surely this is impossible. The peculiarity seems to be that the last part is quoted indirectly rather than in the first person. 31. **blawe.** Another Nth. form, equivalent to Ml. *blowe*.

Page 83, l. 10. Rīs up, MS. sir up. Morris's change is obviously right and generally accepted. 17. **kynemark.** As Goldborough sees it, this is later described (l. 1262) as follows :

'On his shuldre, of gold red
She saw a swiþe noble croiz.

Page 85, l. 14. Denemarkes stiward, MS. denemark a stiward. It seems clear that Godard is not *a stiward*, but *the stiward*, appointed by the king above all others. Instead of inserting *of* before Denemark (Holthausen), I prefer to think the genitive *s* has been lost in the initial of *stiward*.

Page 86, l. 9. Wat shal mē. 'What shall (be) to me for counsel.' So in l. 118 of the poem. 16. **shẹp . . . nẹt.** The MS. *shep, net, hors, swin,* might all be plurals without ending, as they are all OE. neuters. But they are more likely general singulars, as are the descriptive words *wolle, hōrn, bẹrd.* For this reason the omitted word *gǭt,* not *gẹt* (*gẹẹt*), the mutated plural (Skeat, Holthausen), is adopted. 21. **And al hē.** 'And he drew all to the penny,' i.e. obtained money instead of barter for his possessions.

Page 87, l. 4. sē. This word, with open *ẹ* in OE. dialects, invariably rimes close in Havelok ; cf. Ten Brink, 'Chaucers Sprache,' § 24 a. 15. **siþe, MS. þrie.** The MS. reading is meaningless, and some change must be made. I repeat *siþe* from *siþen* (l. 11) ; Holthausen and Skeat read *yete,* 'yet.' 24–25. **ẹrde . . . ẹrþe.** The MS. *erþe* in both lines is impossible, and the change of the first to *ẹrde* is probably the best that can be made. 30. **Grimesbī it calle, MS. calleth alle.** The change is Zupitza's and is generally accepted.

VII. ROBERT MANNING'S 'HANDLYNGE SYNNE'

THE TALE OF PERS THE USURER

The 'Handlynge Synne,' or 'Manual of Sins,' is found in Harleian MS. 1701 of the British Museum, and Bodleian MS. 415. It was edited by Furnivall for the Roxburghe Club (1862) and has appeared in a new edition for the Early English Text Society. A selection occurs in Morris ('Specimens,' II, 50). Our selection is from the Harleian MS. as edited by Furnivall, and includes lines 5555 to 5946. The author, Robert Manning, was born at Brunne or Bourn near Market Deeping in Lincolnshire about 1260, and died about 1340. In 1303, while living at Brimwake in the hundred of Kesteven, he translated this work, as he tells us in the prologue. The language therefore represents NEMl. of the early fourteenth century.

Manning's work is translated from the French 'Manuel des Pechiez' of William of Waddington. It treats the seven deadly sins and seven sacraments, the twelve requisites of a good confession, and the twelve graces resulting therefrom. In illustration of various points such tales as this of Pers are introduced. In this case, as usually, the translation follows the OF. tale with slight variations. The metre, as so commonly at this time, is the rimed couplet of four stresses.

Like the last selection, the language of this contains some Nth. forms. The use of *y*, long and short, for *i* is exceedingly common. An occasional Nth. *ei* (*ey*) represent Ml. Nth. *ē*, an orthographic peculiarity which also grows more frequent. Final *e* is more generally lost in pronunciation than in previous selections, but is often written where it must have been silent, and even added where it never belonged historically. It is probably silent at the end of the line in most cases. A medíal *e* which is necessary for the metre has often been omitted. Among consonants *gh* appears for *ʒ* before *t*, as in MnE. spelling. Some of these are no doubt connected with the fact that the MS. is later than the time of Manning, that is about 1360.

Page 88, l. 1. kauersyns. Though used as a general name, as in OF., the word was originally more specific, since it is derived from the Provence town of Cahors, early noted for its usurers. Dante ('Inferno,' XI, 50) connects Cahors with Sodom, and Matthew of Paris has a chapter near the beginning of his 'History' on the extortions of these usurers. The word *kauersin* has been generally missed by the dictionaries, or wrongly glossed as 'hypocrite.' **2. wykked.** Note how early ME. *wikke* has assumed excrescent *d* after the analogy of adjectives and participles ending in *ed*. **5. nat.** This is probably a retention of OE. *naht*, rather than an early unrounding of *o* in *noht*. **18. Pērs.** Here, and often elsewhere, to be read as a disyllable. Perhaps we should print *Pēres* (cf. *pens, ōkerērs = penes, ōkerēres,* ll. 25, 26), but I have preferred to leave the MS. forms with this note. **21. Seynt Jȝne.** This St. John, the Almoner, was patriarch of Alexandria in the seventh century.

Page 89, l. 2. sāte. Evidently a Nth. form if the vowel is long, or possibly a new formation on the basis of the singular. **7–8. weyl ... deyl.** Examples of the Nth. use of *ei* (*ey*) for *ē*. **25. bȳde þē quēde.** 'Awaited the evil (man).'

Page 90, l. 1. Pērs stōde. Cf. 85, 27–28, thought by Skeat to have suggested this passage. It was probably a rather common expression in one form or another at the time. **5–6. lȳfe ... drȳfe.** A good example of the addition of final *e* where it could not have been pronounced, a practice increasingly common in later Middle English. **22. fyl.** A shortened preterit of *fallen = fēl*, with *e* become *i* (*y*). **24. Hym þoghte.** Note the confusion which has already taken place between ME. *þuʒte* and *þoʒte.* **30. abashed as amad, MS. as mad.** Morris suggested *a mad*, 'a maid,' but the correct form is the shortened pp. of *amǣden*, OE. *gemǣdan.*

Page 91, l. 28. nōw þou lẹres. 'Now thou shalt learn how this loaf shall help you at need, (and how) to improve thy soul with alms-deeds.' Note the present 3rd sing. in *-es* and *-eþ* side by side.

Page 92, ll. 29-30. herte ... smert. Another indication of the loss of final *e* from the spoken language of this region; cf. also *breyde ... seyd* (93, 31-32).

Page 93, l. 14. And a partȳ. 'And began in part, or in some measure, to leave off.'

Page 94, l. 31. Hys clerk was wǭ. In OE. syntax clerk would require a dat. after *was*, but the loss of distinctive ending for that case made a noun in such position seem the subject, and this syntax has prevailed in MnE. usage.

Page 95, l. 10. Tō whǒm. Note the clear use of *whom* as a relative. 17. ȝōle. The etymology is uncertain, but I have assumed its connexion with ON. *jōl*, OE. *gēol*, ' yule,' still found in MnE. *Yule.*

Page 96, l. 7. Plenērlȳ alle þat. Cf. Havelok, ll. 819-20 :
    ' Al þat he þerfore tok
    Withheld he nouht (nouth) a ferþinges nok.'
From some such resemblances between the two poems it is believed that Manning may have known the Havelok, another Lincolnshire work.

Page 98, l. 19. stonte = stǭndeþ. The contracted form is less common in Ml. and Nth. than in Sth. English. 25. ȝone. The OM. demonstrative *gon*, WS. *geon*, which is only dialectal in MnE., though the root occurs in *yonder*, OM. **gonre.*

Page 99, l. 13. squylēr. Though OF. in immediate relation to English, it is based on a Teutonic root which appears in MnE. *swill*, OE. *swilian*, 'to wash,' as at 96, 24. 23. A flamme of fȳre. A frequent attendant of supernatural manifestations, and probably connected in the mediæval mind with the pentecostal fire, Acts ii. 3. Havelok is known to be of royal birth by a similar token (83, 1-7).

VIII. THE WEST MIDLAND PROSE PSALTER

The translation of the Psalms from which our selection is taken is found in Additional MS. 17,376 of the British Museum and in MS. A 4, 4 of Trinity College, Dublin. On the basis of the former it has been edited from both MSS. by Karl Bülbring (Part I, EETS., 97), and Bülbring has been followed here. The language is almost pure West Midland, and belongs to the first half of the fourteenth century. This 'Psalter' was formerly attributed to William of Shoreham, with whose poems it occurs in the MS., but such authorship is impossible, as Shoreham's poems are Kentish and there is no trace of Kentish in this version; cf. Konrath, ' Beiträge zur Erklärung u. Textkritik des William von Shoreham' (1878). A WMl. selection is added to show how closely that dialect agreed with EMl. in most particulars.

This 'Psalter' is a close, though sometimes mistaken rendering of the Latin text, presumably the Italic version of the Scriptures. Some interesting examples of mediæval rendering and interpretation are given in the notes. For these and other peculiarities it may be compared with Hampole's earlier Nth. version (ed. by Bramley, 1884), and with the Wiclifite version (ed. by Forshall and Madden). It will be seen that the verse division is not quite the same as in our modern Bible, but the original numbering of the Psalms has been made to correspond with our own.

As already stated in the Grammatical Introduction the West Midland does not differ materially from East Midland, and this is especially true of the present selection, in its phonology. As to orthography, we may note *c* (*ce*) for *s* in OF. words; *ck* = *kk* (*wicked*, 100, 23), *sc* for *ss* (*blesced*, 100, 15). The one striking peculiarity of inflexion is the use of -*and*(*e*) in the present participle. Rarely, too, *is* = *es* appears in the plural of nouns.

Page 100, l. 16. **sinȝȩres**. The word is based on the root of OE. *syngian*, not the sb. *synne*; but note the variants, *sinniȩrs* (l. 23), *synnȩrs* (l. 25). 19. **frut**. The OF. diphthong *ui* is usually preserved in stressed syllables, but other cases of its appearance as simple *u* (= *iu*) are well known. 20. **fallwen**, MS. **fallen** with *w* in later hand. As the Lat. is *defluit* it is not impossible that the translator thought *fallen*, 'fall, fail, pass away,' a good rendering. 22. **as a pōudre**. The connective has been omitted; cf. the Lat. *sed tamquam*. 24. **ōure Lǫrd knew**. The translator has taken Lat. *novit* for a preterit, as in other places (103, 12; 104, 10). On the other hand, *cognovit* is translated *knoweþ* at 105, 2.

Page 101, l. 2. **water of fyllyng**. Lat. *aquam refectionis*, and Dub. MS. *water of fulfillyng*; MnE. Bible, *still waters*. No doubt *fyllyng* is used in the sense of 'fulfilling, restoring,' and is thus a good rendering of *refectio*. 3. **hē turned ... fram þē fēnde**. The Lat. is *animam meam convertit*, and the addition is probably due to some commentator. 4. **For ȝif þat ich hāve gǫn**. Lat. *nam etsi ambulavero*, and the translator has mistaken the fut. perf. for the perf., or had a different text before him. 8. **þou mākest fatt**. A literal rendering of the Vulg. *Impinguasti in oleo caput meum*. 15. **innocent in hǫnde**. Lat. *innocens manibus*; Dub. MS. *clene of hondes and clene of hert*. 19. **þē sēchand hym**. The translator uses the English participle exactly as the Latin: *Haec est generatio quaerentium eum, quaerentium faciem Dei Iacob*. 20. **princes of helle**. *Of helle* here and *of hevene* in verse 9 are additions to the original in accordance with mediæval interpretation, as referring to Christ when 'harrowing hell,' and later ascending to heaven. This is based on the apocryphal 'Gospel of Nicodemus,' which was closely followed in English versions of the 'harrowing of hell' story.

Page 102, l. 9. **whȳte up snowe**. The Lat. reads *super nivem dealbabor*, and the translator has not perceived that *super* means 'beyond, more than,' not 'up.' 29. **fram þē world**. A good example of the OE., ME. use of *world* in sense of time, as in *world without end*.

Page 103, l. 2. **þē kēpyng ō nyȝt**. 'And the watching (*kēpyng*) at night that avails not (*for nouȝt bēn had*) shall be their years'; Lat. *Custodia in nocte, quae pro nihilo habentur, eorum anni erunt*. Our modern version is based on a different text. 9. **þenchen as þē lob**. Lat. *anni nostri sicut* *aranea meditabuntur,* and the verb has been translated *þenchen,* 'think,' not *þinchen,* 'seem.' This is natural since *meditor* properly meant 'to think,' and only in mediæval times acquired the passive sense 'to seem.' **in þē seventī ȝēre.** The Lat. *dies annorum nostrorum in ipsis, septuaginta anni* evidently puzzled the translator. He has left *in ipsis* untranslated and the syntax of the phrase is not clear. **10. þē mōre ōver hem.** 'The more (years) beyond, or in addition to them,' another slavish rendering; cf. Lat. *amplius eorum.* **14. bē þou turned.** *Untō nou* perhaps translates *usque* of the Vulgate with possibly some other word. 'Be thou turned until now,' though not clear, seems to be the meaning. **19. dresce her sones.** 'Direct their sons,' translating literally Lat. *dirige filios eorum.* So the first part of the verse translates *Respice in servos tuos et in opera tua,* where the modern version has a different reading. **25. trappes of þē fēndes.** Lat. *de laqueo venantium,* the latter being interpreted as 'devils,' according to the commentary attributed to Jerome, ' Breviarium in Psalmos ' (Migne's ' Jerome,' VII). See my article on ' Some of Chaucer's Lines on the Monk,' ' Modern Philology,' I, 105. **asper word.** Lat. *verbo aspero,* where our version has 'noisome pestilence,' a different reading. **29. temptacioūn waxand.** Lat. *a sagitta volante,* familiar in our ' arrow that flieth.' With the application of the whole passage to man's contest with the devil, *sagitta* has been understood in the figurative sense of ' temptation.' **30. fram þē cūrs.** There are various readings of the original, as often. The Vulgate has *ab incursu et daemonio meridiano,* the last words being regarded as a reference to Lucifer. **þoūsand temptācicūns.** Lat. merely *cadent . . . mille,* and the translator assumes a connexion with the preceding and adds *temptācioūns* implied in *þē cūrs.*

Page 104, l. 1. þē devel. The translator refers the subject of the verb, unexpressed in Latin, back to *fēnde* in verse 6. **17. þē which.** The earliest use in our selections of this compound relative ; cf. ' Chaucers Sprache,' § 254. **21. is dōand.** A translation of Lat. *faciens.* **28. streinþed.** The MS. is not clear, but seems to have been corrected to read as in the text.

Page 105, l. 2. *faintes.* The Vulgate reads *figmentum.* **3. þat wē.** The OE. Vespasian text reads *quod pulvis sumus,* not *quoniam* as the Vulgate, and the former was probably before our translator.

IX. 'THE EARL OF TOULOUSE'

This poetic romance is found in four MSS., Cambridge Ff II, 38; Ashmole 45 and 61 of the Bodleian Library ; and Thornton MS. A 5 of Lincoln Cathedral Library. The first of these, represented in our selection also, was edited by Ritson, ' Ancient English Metrical Romances,' III, 93 (1802, revised by Goldsmid, 1885), and a so-called critical edition from all the MSS. was made by Lüdtke for Zupitza's ' Sammlung englischer Denkmäler ' in 1881. The poem was composed in the NEMl. district about the middle of the fourteenth century, although the MS. belongs to the fifteenth century, and therefore shows a later orthography than the time of composition.

The poem consists of 1,224 verses arranged in twelve-line stanzas, riming *aabccbddbeeb.* The first two verses of each triplet have four stresses, the last three stresses. Our selection begins with l. 895 and continues to the end. The earlier part tells how Earl Barnard made war upon the Emperor Diocletian, because the latter had deprived him of territory. Earl Barnard was successful, and, among other captives, takes Sir Trylabas of Turkey, whom he agrees to free if he will obtain for the earl a sight of the beautiful Empress Beulybon (Beaulyoun, Beaulilion). Trylabas arranges the meeting in the presence of others, Barnard appears as a hermit, and, on leaving, is given by the empress some coin and a ring. About the same time two knights are enamoured of the empress and, on her refusal to comply with their base wishes, contrive to make her appear guilty of adultery, of which they accuse her to the emperor. He condemns her to be burned alive, unless, as suggested in 'parliament' just before the opening of our selection, some one shall be found to support her innocence in combat with her accusers. The favour which this proposition meets is shown by the first line of the passage chosen. The story is believed to have historical foundation in the life of the Empress Judith, wife of Louis I (778-840). A romance based on this historical foundation became widely reproduced in Spain, Italy, France and other countries; see Lüdtke's excellent Introduction, 61 f. The immediate source of the English poem, the 'Lay of Bretayne,' mentioned in the last stanza, is unknown.

As already noted the orthography is late. For example, $\overline{ou}$ ($\overline{ow}$) is always used for long $\bar{u}$, *th* for earlier $\not{p}$, *ght* often for $\not{3}t$, and *wh* for OE. *hw*. On the other hand, *sch* for *sh* still prevails. Besides, *y* is used with great frequency for *i*, both alone and in the diphthongs *ai, ei*, and occasionally for *e* in unstressed syllables. The doubling of long vowels is also common.

Page 105, l. 18. **hē spake.** The 'olde knyght' who had proposed the trial by combat to decide the guilt of the empress. 24. **be sẹẹ and be sọnde.** An alliterative expression for the whole world, quite common in Middle English; cf. 161, 25.

Page 106, l. 14. **can = gan.** This weak form with voiceless initial is more common in Nth. English.

Page 107, l. 4. **Sọ mōte thọu thē.** 'So may thou prosper,' that is, ' as you hope to prosper.' 27. **māke a vowe.** The last two words represent OF. *avou*, ' vow,' but they became separated so as to suggest ' a vow' as here. We still say *make avowal*, and *an avowal*.

Page 108, l. 24. **mās.** Another form which suggests the Nth. dialect or a district near it. 29. **When thē abbot.** The shortness of the verse suggests an omission, as of *did* after *abbot*; cf. Ashmole MS. 45.

Page 109, l. 23. **durre**, MS. **dar.** Lüdtke reads *dare* as a disyllable, but surely that is not a likely form. One MS. reads *durste*, but I assume a subjunctive form as more probable.

Page 112, l. 22. **Manlȳ.** One MS. reads *manfully*, which shows the content of the word.

Page 114, l. 9. **Soche wōrdes.** 'I advise [that] thou shouldest alter such words.' *Wọnde* is subjunctive preterit of desire, from *winde(n)*. Note the preterit in a clause of unreality; cf. *Introd.* § 207. 10. **Anọne in hāste.** Note the absence of the verb in the clause as representing the abrupt manner of address.

Page 116, l. 4. **chyldyr fyftēne.** So Havelok and Goldborough have fifteen children, all kings and queens. **7–8. geste eronyclyd is . . . callyd ywis.** Some change is necessary, as shown by footnote readings, and I have adopted that of Lüdtke.

X. GILD OF THE HOLY TRINITY AND OF SAINT WILLIAM
OF NORWICH

This selection is from a MS. in the Public Record Office, London, Bundle CCCX 116, as edited by Lucy Toulmin Smith in 'English Gilds' (EETS., 40), p. 29. The 'Return' was made in January 1389, and the language is the East Midland of Norfolk, the descendant of East Anglian of Old English times.

These 'Returns' concerning the gilds had been ordered by a Parliament held at Canterbury in 1388. The extract is an account of the formation of the gild and the statutes under which the brotherhood was constituted. It is preceded in the MS. by a recital, in Latin, of the king's writ to the sheriff of Norfolk, and followed by two Latin sentences saying that no other statute had been established, and that the property of the gild consisted of four pounds, four shillings, 'et non plus nec minus.' The whole is endorsed 'Fraternitas Sancte Trinitatis ac beati Willelmi Innocentis et martiris in Norwico.' It is similar to other 'Returns,' and is chosen as a prose piece of sufficient length to represent one part of the EMl. dialect.

Few peculiarities of language need be mentioned. *Th* now interchanges with *þ*, written with open top and resembling *y*. *Qw* = OE. *hw* occurs as in Ml. occasionally (cf. 'Genesis and Exodus'), in Nth. commonly. For a special treatment of the language see Schultz, 'Die Sprache der English Gilds' (1891).

Page 116, l. 13. **In þē nāme.** This is immediately preceded by the Latin word *Constitutiones*. **15. Seynt William.** For the account of his martyrdom see the passage in the 'Chronicle' at 4, 28. Note the modern form of the name as compared with Willelm of the 'Chronicle.' **18. gylde.** The form of this word with initial guttural stop is not English, since OM. *gēld*, WS. *gield*, became Ml. *ʒēld*, Sth. *ʒild* or *ʒīld* respectively, and the Ml. form would have become MnE. *yield*; cf. the corresponding verb, the sb. *yield* applied to crops, and Chaucer's *yeldhalle* (MSS. *yeldehalle, yeldhalle, ʒeldehall, ʒildehalle*). The ME. form with guttural stop must therefore show external influence, probably that of ON. *gildi*; cf. MDu. *ghilde*. **20. systeren.** Note the extension of the OE. weak plural ending under the influence of constant association with *bretheren*. **21. upen here pōwēr.** 'According to their power, or ability.' This meaning does not seem to belong to OE. *uppan*, but is easily derived from it. **23. þē fēst of Seynt Pēter and Powel.** That is June 29. The Sunday after is then the *gyldeday* of 117, 21 f.

Page 117, l. 2. **tō.** This form of OE. *twā*, ME. *twō*, but with loss of *w*, is exactly parallel to *sǭ* from OE. *swā*, though I have assumed close *ō* in *tō* owing to a later disappearance of *w*. **14. þē aldermannes wyl.** The alderman, a master or president of the gild, was regularly chosen each year on the gildday, as indicated at l. 30. Other 'Returns' speak of wardens who have charge of the property. **15. at þē cumpanȳ.** Note the genitive without ending, no doubt as the last word of the clause. **18. săve þē kynge hys ryhte.** 'Preserve (save) to the king his right,' probably not 'Preserve the king's right.' **27. anȳ.** The MS. *ony* may indicate *ǫnȳ*, but the prevailing short *a* seems to show that this *o* is short also. **leyn it doūn.** Dependent upon *schal* above, which would be repeated in MnE. usage.

Page 118, l. 7. But if it bē. The gild laid great stress upon character, and every member was in some sense responsible for every other. **24. at here comōun cost.** 'At the cost of them all, or in common'; cf. Chaucer's well-known *at our aller cost*, Prol. to 'Cant. Tales,' I, 799.

XI. JOHN MYRC'S 'INSTRUCTIONS FOR PARISH PRIESTS'

These 'Instructions' are preserved in three MSS., Cotton Claudius A 11 in the British Museum, and Douce MSS. 60,103 in the Bodleian. The first and best was edited by Peacock for the Early English Text Society, 31 (1868), and from this have been selected ll. 1–76 and 234–371. The writer was a canon of Lilleshall, Shropshire, and is supposed to have written the work about 1400. The extract therefore represents WMl. of that time, though the MS. is of the early fifteenth century.

The title gives a good idea of the general character of the work. A note at the end tells us that it was translated from Latin, but its source is not definitely known. It is similar to many other mediæval treatises, the prior of Mirc's own house having written a more complete 'Manuale Sacerdotis.'

The language will present few difficulties after the previous selections have been read. We meet for the first time *uy* for OE. *ȳ*, Ml. *ȳ* (*ī*), Sth. *ū*.

Page 119, l. 10. dawe. Really a new singular based on the plural *dawes*, OE. *dagas*, and preserved in only a few phrases. **11. bēth.** Note the Sth. plural of the verb, as occasionally; cf. the Ml. plurals *fallen* (l. 8), *sēn* (l. 9), *fāren* (l. 10).

Page 120, l. 14. serve God tō pay. 'Serve God to his pleasure.' **23. Cuttede clǫthes and pyked schōne.** For the first we should say 'slashed,' that is, with long narrow openings to show the rich lining beneath. The shoes called *pyked* were long and pointed ones, used first in the reign of William Rufus, and often prohibited to the clergy by local councils. **27. honest clǫthes.** Note the old meaning of *honest*, 'honourable, suitable, according to law and custom.' **28. Baselard.** A short sword much worn in the fourteenth and fifteenth centuries, but not allowed to priests. They often failed to obey the prohibition, as shown by the following lines quoted by Peacock from the 'Plowman's Tale':

> 'Bucklers brode and swerdes long
> Baudrike with baselardes kene,
> Such toles about her necke they hong;
> With Antichrist soche priestes been.'

Cf. also 'Piers Plowman,' III B, 303. **30. thȳ ordere.** Mirc's order was a branch of the canons regular of St. Austin, taking its name from the city of Arras, where they were first established. The branch had been transplanted to England by Richard de Belmeis about 1145.

Page 121, l. 25. **Alsọ thōw.** The passage omitted relates to shriving of women, marriage and childbirth, and is of less general interest than that which follows.   30. **ischryve.** The retention of the OE. prefix *ge* as *i* is distinctly Sth., and is probably here indicative of Sth. influence, though it occasionally occurs in Ml., when it cannot certainly be attributed to Sth. influence.   32. **asterday.** A natural shortening of OE. *ēasterdæg*, but usually resisted by the influence of the uncompounded *ēaster*, 'Easter,' so that the two agree in MnE.

Page 122, l. 10. **but wȳn and water.** Peacock says : ' After communion it was the custom for the laity to drink unconsecrated wine, to assist them in swallowing the eucharistic wafer.' At this time it was not customary to give the cup to the laity.   32. **Knēlynge dōun.** Peacock notes this as evidence that there were no pews or benches in the churches.

Page 123, l. 11. **thē belle.** The so-called sanctus bell (*sance-*, *saucebell*) hung in mediæval churches, says Peacock, on the east gable of the nave outside the church. It was rung to permit those not present to join in the devotion. A hand-bell was also sometimes used, as to-day in Catholic churches. All these were ordered to ' be utterly defaced, rent and abolished' in 1576.

Page 124, l. 10. **As Seynt Austyn.** Peacock says not in St. Augustine's writings, though possibly in some work once attributed to him.   25. **seyntwarȳ.** The reading of Douce MSS. *chirchhay*, ' churchyard,' restores the rime, and is no doubt correct. In explanation of the MS. reading Peacock says : ' In mediæval documents belonging to this country (England) *sanctuarium* and its equivalents in English almost always mean churchyard.' As bearing this out cf. *seyntwarȳ* (125, 2), where the Douce MSS. have *chyrchyerd*, very likely the correct sense here also.   27. **Sǫnge and crȳ.** Peacock mentions that the Douce MS. 103 has a note in a somewhat later hand, which reads : ' danseynge, cotteyng, bollyng, tenessyng, handball, football, stoilball, and all manner other games out cherchyard.'   29. **Castynge of axtrē.** The axletree was sometimes used instead of the bar or the stone; cf. Strutt's ' Sports and Pastimes of the Middle Ages,' p. 140.   31. **Bal and bāres.** The former may be one of several games of ball. The latter is Base or Bars, or Prisoner's bars, the name being due to the practice of staking out the ' base.' Cf. for both Strutt, as above.

Page 125, l. 1. **Cōurte hǫldynge.** Peacock notes that the use of churches and churchyards for secular purposes was not uncommon, citing local histories for particular instances.   14. **Everȳ mon.** No doubt *ȝche*, occurring in one of the Douce MSS., is the correct reading.   23. **Wychecrafte.** In the service of excommunication, given in Douce MS. 60, reference is especially made to witchcraft. **telynge.** Cf. ' Ancren Riwle ' (ed. Morton), p. 208 : ' Sigaldren and false teolunges, levunge on ore and of swefnes, and alle wicchecreftes . . . nis hit þe spece of prude þet ich cleopede presumciun ?' *Telynge* is connected with OE. *tilian*, ' to strive, labour,' and may be equivalent to ME. *experiment*, ' sorcery,' as in a passage in Douce MS. 60 : ' All þat maken experimentes or wichecrafte or charmes.' Cf. also 145, 11.

PART II

THE DIALECTS OF THE NORTH, THE SOUTH, AND THE CITY OF LONDON

This Part is designed to illustrate the Northern and Southern dialects, and London English as it gradually changed from Southern to Midland. Northern is placed first, as most closely allied to Midland, and examples are here given of Northern English in the more distinctive sense, as well as of Middle Scotch which is based upon it. As there are few available selections until the end of the thirteenth century, no division of 'Early' Northern need be made.

I. PROLOGUE TO THE 'CURSOR MUNDI'

The 'Cursor Mundi' is preserved in various MSS., of which Hupe (EETS., 99, p. 62*; 101, p. 113*) describes no less than ten. Four of these, Cotton Vesp. A III of the British Museum, Fairfax 14 of the Bodleian, Göttingen MS. Theol. 107 r at the University of Göttingen, and Trinity College MS. R3, 8 at Cambridge, were edited by Morris for the 'Early English Text Society' (57, 59, 62, 66, 68, 99, 101). The purest of these completer texts is the Cotton above, of which our selection includes lines 1 to 270. The poem was written about 1300 (Hupe thinks as early as the last half of the thirteenth century) in a region placed by Murray as near Durham, and by Hupe in North Lancashire, owing to forms that suggest Ml. influence, as the words with *p̄* instead of Nth. *ā*, OE. *ā*. These indicate that the MS., if not the author, belongs to a region affected by the Ml. change. No author is known, but Hupe argues for a certain John of Lindberghe, whose name appears in the Göttingen MS., though usually assumed to be that of a scribe.

The 'Cursor Mundi' is a poetical history of the Hebrew and Christian world based on various sources, the Scriptures, the 'Historia Scholastica' of Petrus Comestor, the apocryphal books of the New Testament, and others; see Hænsch's 'Inquiry into the Sources,' EETS., 99, p. 1*. Some notes to our selection from the ME. 'Genesis and Exodus' show the common basis of the two, but the 'Cursor Mundi' is much fuller in all respects. Especially are the legendary portions interesting, as reflecting the credulous character of the mediæval mind. The metre, as will be seen, is the common rimed couplet of four stresses.

As to language, the mixture of Ml. *p̄* with Nth. *ā* from OE. *ā* has been mentioned. Otherwise the vowel phonology is simple. Among the peculiarities of consonants are the use of *s* in unstressed syllables for OE. *sc*, as

Inglis, Ml. *Englisch* (127, 6); *suld*, Ml. *schuld, schold* (129, 3); *sc = sk*, as in *scaw* (130, 1); *qu* for OE. *hw*, as sometimes in Ml.; *th* beside *þ*; *ght* for *ȝt* regularly.

Page 126, l. 3. Alisaundur. The widespread romances relating to most of these heroes are well known, as those of Alexander, Brutus, Arthur, Charlemagne (Charles King, l. 15), Tristrem (l. 17), Amadas (127, 2). **6. lēsis.** The form is clearly pres. pl., but perhaps we should read *lēs*, preterit with *thousand* as a collective sing. On the other hand, the only pret. form recorded by Kellner in his excellent glossary is *lest*, ' lost.' The pres. pl. could be explained as used in vivid narration. **9. sǭ.** Note this among many examples of strict Ml. forms, beside those of the North. **13. Wawān, Cai.** More commonly *Gawain, Kay*, as in Malory's 'Morte D'Arthur.' **ōper stābell.** 'Other brave ones.' **17. Ysote.** Hupe, in his critical text, changes to *Ysoud*, spoiling the rime in both vowel and consonant. With so many final *d*'s becoming *t*'s it is not strange that this name should have suffered the same alteration.

Page 127, l. 1. Ioneck . . . Ysambrāse. The first is one of the principal characters in the French romance ' Yonec.' The second is the subject of a romance in 'Thornton Romances,' p. 88. **2. Amadāse.** The romance of Sir Amadace is found in Robson's 'Three Metrical Romances,' Camden Society (1842), based on the OF. romance of 'Idoine and Amadas.' **6. Inglis.** The regular Nth. form of the adjective and substantive. Note change of *e* to *i* before the nasal as in the MnE. form, though we still write *E*. **10. draws.** The MS. form *draghus* is common in the Lancashire dialect (cf. *draȝeȝ* in 'Sir Gawain and the Green Knight,' l. 1,031), but a monosyllabic form is necessary for the metre. **15. scilwīs sē.** Hupe adopts *ilk wiis* for *scilwīs*, considering the latter a mistake for *slīwis*, but the change is wholly unnecessary. *Scilwīs* is used substantively, and the line means ' but by the fruit may wise (men) see.' **25. tās.** Both *tās* and *mās* for *tākes* and *mākes* are common in Nth.

Page 128, l. 7. chaunge of hert. The reading of Gött. and Trin. MSS., while Fairfax has a different expression, *or elles of hert*. **9. at bē.** Note the Nth. use of *at* with the infinitive for Ml. and Sth. *tō*. Modern English has a contraction of the Nth. form in *ado = to do*. **10. Frǭ hir schalt pōu.** The reference is to *folȳ, vanitē* of l. 3. **16. hē forwith bedd.** The MS. has *he hym forwit* (= *forwith*), but no rime word. The other MSS. vary greatly. I take *bedd* as a shortened form of *bēd*, ' offered, announced, threatened,' and the meaning of the passage to be, beginning with l. 13: 'Ere he shall be brought down so violently he knows not whither to turn, until his love has led him to such reward as he before announced.' **17-18. mere . . . were.** The other texts have *let* (*lett*), ' hindrance,' and this, together with the rime, suggests a noun not recorded for OE. but connected with OAng. *merran*, WS. *mierran*, ' hinder, mar.' *Mere* would thus represent OAng. *merre*, which occurs in Trin. MS. 24,802. The rime with *were = werre*, ' worse,' would then be perfect. Kaluza, in his glossary, translates ' harm, trouble' without explanation. **23. þof.** The OE. guttural spirant *h* (*g*) has become the labio-dental spirant *f*, as in MnE. *laugh, cough, tough*, and a few others. **32. þē love bēs never gān.** ' The love (that shall) be never gone,' that is, ' shall never perish.'

Page 129, l. 3. **matēr tāke.** *Matēr* added by Morris from the other MSS.　　7. **Quat bōte is.** Morris would insert *hit*, 'it,' after *is*, as in Trin. MS., but *bōte* may be disyllabic and the line complete.　　9. **werd, MS. warld.** The MS. reading must be a scribal alteration, as shown by the rime and the reading of the other MSS.　　19. **lavedī ... lẹvedīs.** Double forms of the word appear in two of the four MSS.

Page 130, l. 1. **scaw.** Such a form beside *schew* (l. 5) indicates scribal alteration or that both forms were found in the dialect of the poet.　　10. **hāve in tāle.** 'Have in tale,' that is, 'relate, be able to tell.'　　21. **Oxspring.** The other MSS. have *osprĭnge* (*hosprĭng*), indicating that *x* in the word probably represents *s*.　　26. **Ēsaū.** The word is regularly trisyllabic in the poem, as in Lat. and OF.　　29-30. **Mōysēs ... chẹs.** The same rime occurs once in 'Genesis and Exodus,' though *Mōysēs* usually rimes with close *ē*.

Page 131, l. 7. **redd yuu.** *Reddynn* of Morris is impossible, and the MS. must have been misunderstood.　　20. **þat Jēsus did.** The account is based upon the apocryphal 'Childhood of Jesus,' so literally accepted in the middle ages.

Page 132, l. 6. **þat.** 'To whom.' Without change of form *þat* is nom. dat. or accus.; though when dat. or accus. a preposition-adverb often follows the verb.　　12. **Lōrdǝ fēte.** All the other MSS. have a genitive in *es* (*is*). On the other hand, the genitive without ending is common in Nth. English. Cf. *lẹvedī* (133, 7).　　23. **unschill.** Morris notes as equivalent to *unscill*, that is, *sch = sc*.　　26. **onstad and sey.** Hupe reads *onstand and sey*. But a preterit *stad* appears in rime with *badd*, 'bade,' at l. 5,541, as well as a past participle *stad* (*stadd*) in several places. These indicate that *onstad* is probably correct, based on ON. *steðja-staddi*. The line means 'many a man was present and saw.'　　31. **Hōw ōur Lẹvedī ēndid.** The 'assumption' of the Virgin, believed to have occurred on August 15, and still celebrated in some countries.

Page 133, l. 4. **þē drērī days fivetēn.** A full account of these days occurs in the selection from 'Metrical Homilies,' beginning on p. 148.　　7. **ōure Lẹvedī murnand mōde.** This theme was often treated by mediæval poets, and frequently in English with such titles as 'Compassio Mariae,' 'Lament of Mary,' &c. In the 'Cursor Mundi' it is found at l. 23,945.　　14. **er.** Cf. note on 9, 2. The form preserves the original vowel of the root, which has become *a* in later English under the influence of *r*.　　23. **Intō Inglis tong.** The passage is interesting as showing the national spirit which produced a literature for Englishmen, notwithstanding the period of French influence following the Conquest, and the dominance of Latin as the language of learning.

Page 134, ll. 13-14. **tent ... amend.** The rime was probably perfect with *t* in both words, as final *d* so often became *t* in Nth. Cf. the past participles in *et* (*it*) for *ed* (*id*) in Burns.　　15. **Ful il hā þai.** Morris reads *il-ha*[*yl*], 'ill luck,' and Hupe follows him. But surely our text is complete and makes admirable sense, while with the reading of Morris another verb must be supplied.　　17. **sum wē til heild.** 'As we incline to.'　　18. **acōuntes, MS. armites.** The MS. reading seems impossible if the word means 'hermits.' *Acōuntes* is from Fairfax MS.

II. THE DEATH OF SAINT ANDREW

The story of Saint Andrew, of which this selection forms a part, belongs to the Northern collection of legends found in various MSS. ; see Horstmann, 'Altenglische Legenden,' Neue Folge, p. lx. That from which this is taken is Harl. 4,196 of the British Museum. Horstmann believed the collection was made in the diocese of Durham in the last quarter of the thirteenth century, though the MS. is of the fourteenth. The prevalence of Midland forms, however, indicates a region nearer the border of the Midland district; cf. Retzlaff, 'Untersuchungen über den nordenglischen Legendencyclus' (1888). The collection bears the marks of having been written by a single author, but nothing is known of him.

The legend of St. Andrew first appears in Old English times in the poem 'Andreas' of the eighth century, and in a prose version of the tenth century. Both these relate the story of Andrew's rescue of Matthew, but give no account of his death. The latter is told in the 'Acts and Martyrdom of Andrew'; see the translation in 'Ante-Nicene Fathers,' VIII, 511.

Page 135, l. 1. **Saint Andrew.** The story of Andrew, the first in the collection, is preceded by four introductory couplets, one of which tells us :

'Out of Latyn þus er þai draune,
Omang laud men for to be knaune.'

3. in sēre cuntrē. Tradition assigns Andrew's labours to Scythia, Greece, and Thrace, his martyrdom as here related to Petrae in Achaia. **5. sǭ.** Note the Ml. form as frequently. Only in rimes have these been replaced by those of strict Nth. English. **8. Ēgēas.** Called proconsul of Achaia in 'Acts and Martyrdom of Andrew.' His wife (143, 7) is called Maximilla. **18. war-laus.** Applied to the 'fals goddes' of l. 10, who were regarded as devils and often so called.

Page 136, l. 8. **þīr.** An ON. form of the plural demonstrative pronoun. **9. suth.** OE. *ō* shows change to *u* = *ü* (*iu*) as in Scotch *gude*, 'good.' In this text the change is only partially indicated, and perhaps is due wholly to the scribe of the later MS. **23. cros.** Kluge ('Eng. Etymol.,' 1898) explains this form beside *crois*, OF. *crois*, as borrowed from OIr. *cross*. **29. put, MS. putted.** The dissyllabic form makes the line too long, and I assume the unchanged preterit, occurring in Tib. MS. E VII and often in 'Cursor Mundi.'

Page 137, ll. 15-16. **āne ... tāne.** That *ā* is correct in both words is shown by the fact that *tāne* = *tāken* by contraction, and so has a vowel which never became ME. *ǭ*. The MS. forms with *ǭ* must therefore be purely scribal in origin. **28. tīte.** This adverb, of ON. origin, is still preserved in MnE. *tight*, with incorrect *gh*, which has been wrongly supposed to have come from OE. *þiht*; cf. 'run as *tight* as you can.'

Page 138, l. 8. **vǒuche it sāve.** From this phrase, with object after the adjective, has sprung our anomalous compound *vouchsafe.* **19. hēnd.** Note this ON. plural, used beside the English plural *handes.* Probably *hēnd* was associated in the folk mind with mutation plurals like *men.* **30. hē suld hānget.** The pronoun necessary to the sense is from Tib. MS. E VII. *Hānget* is the first in our selections of the common Nth. past participle in *et* (*it*) for Ml. Sth. *ed* (*id*).

Page 139, l. 23. and glōrifīde, MS. and ever glorifide.   The reading in the text is from Tib. MS. E VII.

Page 140, l. 13. Tō þē turmentoūrs.   Evidently in imitation of the taking of Christ's clothes at the crucifixion.   29. hǎng.   This preterit form is common in Nth., as in 'Cursor Mundi' for example.   It is probably a modification, by analogy of the present, of the old reduplicated preterit *hěng*. Beside this preterit, only the weak past participle *hǎnged* (*hǎnget*) seems to occur.

Page 141, l. 17. puple.   The *u* of this word is one of the numerous forms of OF. *ue*.   The AN. monophthong *ē* has become the standard modern form, but *pople*, *puple* and other forms occur in ME.   Note also the genitive without ending.

III. TREATISES OF RICHARD ROLLE OF HAMPOLE

The selections from the writings of Richard Rolle are from Thornton MS. A I, 17, preserved in the Library of Lincoln Cathedral.   They have been edited by Perry (EETS., 20), by Mätzner ('Sprachproben,' II, 120), and by Horstmann ('Richard Rolle and his Followers,' I, 184).   Hampole, where Rolle lived as a hermit, and from which he takes his name, is near Doncaster in South Yorkshire.   As the Thornton MS. was written about 1330-40 (Rolle died in 1349), these treatises represent the Northern dialect of the first half of the fourteenth century.

Rolle was a prolific writer of both prose and verse, Latin and English.   Some of his most important works in English are the 'Prick of Conscience' and the 'Mirror of Life' in verse, and a translation and exposition of the Psalms in prose.   The extracts give a good example of the religious character of all his writings, most of which are tinctured by the asceticism he exemplified in his life.

As to language Rolle's Treatises are pure Northern, for example, in the appearance of *ā* for OE. *ā* with no mixture of Ml. *ǭ*.

Page 143, l. 23. thrē kȳndis.   Cf. Pliny's 'Natural Hist.,' XI, 10, on which this is based.   26. fēte, MS. fette.   The MS. form perhaps indicates shortening of the vowel ; cf. *fotte = fōt* beside *fette = fēt* in 'Cursor Mundi.'

Page 144, l. 10. Aristotill sais.   The reference is to the so-called " Historia Animalium,' IX, 40.   14. kane hālde in þē ordyre of lufe ynesche.   The MS. lacks *in* and Mätzner supplies *of* instead, placing it after *ynesche*, but without improving the sense of the passage.   Perry in his edition solved the difficulty by translating *ynesche* as 'towards,' a wholly impossible rendering.   The meaning seems to be, ' For there are many that can never hold in the condition (*ordyre*) of tender love their friends,' &c.   For *lufe ynesche* cf. *hnesce lufu* in the Alfredian 'Past. Care,' 17, 11.   19. wormes.   Horstmann alters to *wormed = wermod*, 'wormwood,' but the change is too violent and quite unnecessary.   'Worms' was often used figuratively for that corruption characteristic of the devil's working.   Besides, though this is not conclusive, the alteration of OE. *wermod* toward *wormwood* does not appear until the fifteenth century.   24. Arystotill sais.   Cf. ' Hist. Anim.,' IX, 7 and 8.

Page 145, l. 4. strucyo or stork. As Mätzner points out, Rolle has confused the ostrich and the stork, the Latin name being the same for both. **12. mawmetrȳse.** Mätzner assumes this as a second form of *maumetrīe*, but the latter was used for 'idol' as well as 'idolatry,' and this seems merely a plural in the latter sense. Perhaps Rolle had in mind the *deos alienos* of the Vulgate. **thē wylke.** Note the voiced initial *w*, instead of the unvoiced *hw* (*qu*) of Nth.; cf. *þē whilke* (l. 14). **27. dispȳses, MS. dispyse.** Mätzner's alteration is adopted on account of the syntax. Horstmann retains the MS. reading without explanation.

Page 146, l. 1. wondes. For *o* for *u* (older *ū*) in such words cf. Morsbach, 'Mittelenglische Gram.,' § 125 b, and Heuser, 'Eng. St.,' XXVII, 353. **6. rescheyves.** The writing with *sch* must be assumed to represent *s*, as in some other Nth. forms. **8. āthes brękynge; of new pręchynge.** The punctuation of this passage has met with curious treatment by different editors. Without illustrating these at length, I understand there are three ways of taking the name of God in vain, false swearing, vain preaching, and prayer without the spirit. The difficulty is that Rolle, forgetting the exact connexion, has introduced the three clauses in three different ways. **13. ill styrringes.** 'Evil passions.' Even in Old English the word had acquired this metaphorical sense as applied to the mind, and it is so used several times by Rolle, as well as by other writers. **14. þī halȳdaye.** Mätzner suggests that *þī* should be *þē*, 'the.' But the text of John Gaytryge's sermon, which quotes Rolle, shows that the commandment is given a direct and personal application, and the MS. is therefore correct. **15. sesse.** This is OF. *cesser* in its exact form, while beside it is found ME. *cęse(n)*, MnE. *cease*. **16. sithen, specialī.** This second 'manner' is omitted in Thornton MS., but is supplied from Arundel MS. of John Gaytryge's sermon, quoting Rolle. **31. may wyne.** Perry wholly misunderstood the passage, and altered it. It is complete as it stands : ' That they may win that (which) God promised to such children, that is land of light.'

Page 147, l. 2. slaa = slā. The usual Anglian form of original *slahan*, WS. *slēan*. **10. oys.** A form peculiar to the Nth. dialect; cf. Jameson's ' Scottish Dict.' **24. neghtboūr.** The common occurrence of this form with excrescent *t* proves that it is a natural development in Nth.; it is still found in Scotch.

IV. A METRICAL HOMILY—THE SIGNS OF THE DOOM

The 'Metrical Homily' here chosen is from a MS. preserved in the Library of the Royal College of Physicians and Surgeons at Edinburgh, though also found in at least five different MSS. in Cambridge, Oxford, and London. A portion of this MS. was edited by John Small in 1862, and short extracts are given by Mätzner ('Sprachproben,' I, 278) and Morris ('Specimens,' II, 83). The collection was made about 1330—where is not known—and thus represents the Northern dialect of the first half of the fourteenth century.

The Homilies, of which this is one, became an important feature of literature, especially in the North. They consist of a paraphrase of the Scripture for the day, a homily interpreting it, and a legend or tale illustrating the subject. Gradually there grew up a series of these poetical homilies connected with the gospel story, as in the ' Ormulum,' or with the Scripture lessons assigned by the church, as in the collection from which our extract is taken. These followed the ecclesiastical year, beginning with Advent, our selection being that for the second Sunday in Advent. The metre is the common rimed couplet of four stresses.

Page 148, l. **1. Tōday.** The second Sunday in Advent, the gospel for which is Luke xxi. 25. The writing of *Louk* for *Luk* indicates a true long *ū*, as sometimes in Nth.; cf. Behrens, ' Franz. Sprache in England,' p. 118, ll. **bēs rędnes.** Based on Matt. xxiv. 29, probably associated with Joel ii. 10, 31 ; iii. 15, the second of which mentions that the sun shall be turned into blood. Cf. 150, 20–24.   **13. For mihtī gāstes.** The Vulgate has *nam virtutes coelorum movebuntur*, translated in our version ' the powers of the heaven shall be shaken.' The mediæval poet has taken *virtutes* to refer to one of the orders of angels, the ' virtues ' of Milton's ' Par. Lost,' V, 772.   **26. froit.** An occasional form of OF. *fruit* ; cf. Behrens, ' Franz. Sprache in England,' p. 159.

Page 149, l. **7. Als quā sai.** ' As any one may say.' The two lines are the poet's explanation, Christ's words ending with l. 6. The next lines seem to be put in direct form, though not based on any words of Christ.   **9. Quen þis werld.** Cf. note on 77, 6.   **12. For mī kinrīc.** No doubt based on Luke i. 33.   **15. þē maister.** The reference is not clear, unless intended for Jerome, mentioned at 151, 13.   **23. Kinrīc sal.** See Luke xxi. 10; Matt. xxiv. 8.   **27. sal bāld bāret.** Probably the true reading should be *bālde*, the adv., ' quickly.'

Page 150, ll. **11–12. bāret ... mēt.** Perhaps *met* is short here, as indicated by such spellings as *mett* in other Nth. texts.   **20. As sais Jōēl.** In three passages Joel mentions such signs, ch. ii. 10, 31 and iii. 15.

Page 151, l. **13. Sain Jerōm telles.** These ' signs of the doom,' attributed to Jerome, are not found in his works as printed, and probably belong to some work now lost. Jerome is said to have found them in a Hebrew MS., as in ' Cursor Mundi,' I, 22, 441 :

> ' Als Jeromme that well man trowes
> Telles he fand in the bok of Juwis.'

Page 152, l. **24. And cum.** This line is followed by thirty-three Latin verses on the signs, with the rubric : *Isti versus omittantur a lectore quando legit Anglicum coram laycis.*

Page 154, l. **1. A blak munk.** That is, one who wore a black habit, as a Benedictine ; cf. reference to ' Rule of Saint Benet ' (155, 24). A similar tale is told by Roger Wendover in his ' Chronicle ' under the year 1072.   **8. Faiþful frēndes.** The MS. clearly needs emendation, and the Camb. MS. seems to suggest the proper correction.   **13–14. felid ... telld.** The rime is no doubt monosyllabic, with shortening of the vowel of *fēld* (⟨ *feldd*), as in weak preterits of the first class.

Page 155, l. **28. ǫverlōp.** The strict English form would be *ǫverlēp* (Camb. MS. *overlepe*), and this one is probably of Scand. origin ; see Björkman, ' Scandinavian Loan-Words in Middle English,' p. 71. Cf. English *lope, elope.*

V. THE SONGS OF LAWRENCE MINOT

The 'Songs of Minot,' preserved in a single MS., Cotton Galba E IX of the British Museum, have been frequently edited. They are found in Ritson's 'Poems on Interesting Events in the Reign of Edward III' (1795, 1825), Wright's 'Political Poems' (1859), 'Quellen und Forschungen,' 52 (Scholle, 1884), and in Hall's 'Poems of Lawrence Minot' (1887). Extracts occur in Mätzner ('Sprachproben,' I, 320), Morris ('Specimens,' II, 126), Wülker ('Lesebuch,' I, 77). Nothing is known of the author but his name, and his probable connexion with the Minots of Yorkshire or Norfolk in the fourteenth century. The poems were clearly written at the time of the events they celebrate, so that they represent the Nth. dialect of about 1333 to 1352, somewhat modified by a Midland copyist ; or possibly Minot lived on the border of the two districts and used a mixed dialect. Cf. Scholle, p. vii ; Hall, p. xvii.

The 'Songs of Minot' represent the native political lyric which had been first written in England in the second half of the thirteenth century, beside Latin and Anglo-Norman poems of the same sort. The poet takes a religious-patriotic view of Edward's victories, with special emphasis of the attitude of Englishmen toward Scotchmen at this time. The poems chosen are the first three of the eleven preserved as a monument to Minot's genius. The metres of the poems are various, as indicated by the selections, and in this respect suggest the new metrical influences of the fourteenth century.

The language of Minot's poems, as already indicated, is a mixture of Northern and Midland, very likely due to a scribe. It has been especially investigated by Scholle and Hall, as by Bierbaum, 'Über Lawrence Minot und seine Lieder' (1876), and Dangel, 'Lawrence Minot's Gedichte' (1888).

Page 157, l. 9. Līthes. All but two of the poems are introduced by short couplets giving the general subject of the poem. A few of the main points of history leading up to the battle of Halidon Hill may be briefly given. Robert Bruce had gained the independence of Scotland by the treaty of Northampton (1328), but died the year after, leaving the throne to a son eight years old. Civil dissensions arising, Edward Balliol, claimant of the Scottish throne, headed an invading force of English barons who claimed estates in Scotland (1332). Edward III, who had opposed the expedition until its success in the crowning of Balliol at Scone, now obtained an acknowledgement of England's suzerainty and supported Balliol when driven from the realm. He personally appeared before Berwick, which had been garrisoned by Balliol's opponents, after Easter, 1333, and the battle chronicled resulted (July 19) from one of several unsuccessful attempts of the Scots to raise the siege. **11. trǫne.** The correct form of the word from OF. *trone*. Later, written *throne* in imitation of Lat. *thronum*, the *th* came to be pronounced like *th* from OE. þ. Cf. *author, authority, apothecary*. **18. dresce mȳ dēdes.** Perhaps in allusion to Ps. xc. 19 ; cf. 103, 19. **19. In þis dāle.** As in other of the ' Songs,' the first line of each stanza after the first repeats an emphatic word, sometimes a phrase, from the last line preceding. In the only departure from this (159, 9) *þat forsaid toune* takes the place of *Berwick* in l. 8. For such linking of stanzas cf. ' Pearl,' ' Aunters of Arthur,' and other poems of Northern or North-west Midland. **20. dērne, MS. dern.** Hall thinks MS. reading a mistake for *derv* (*derve*), ' terrible, injurious.' But OAng. *dērne*, WS. *dīerne*, means 'deceitful, evil' as well as 'secret,' and I see no reason to change the word, except to add *e* for metrical reasons. **23. þē Franche men.** This refers to a fleet of ten ships, armed and victualled by Philip VI of France (*Philip Valays* of 158, 29), which had been sent in aid of the Scotch besieged in Berwick, according to the French chronicler Nangis. These were defeated and the vessels destroyed by the English fleet at Dundee (1333). **26. noght worth a pēre.** A great number of such expressions are common in Middle and Modern English ; cf. Mätzner's 'Grammar,' II, 2, 128, and the expression at 158, 8.

Page 158, l. 2. þē bōste of Normandȳe. The French ships were armed with Norman sailors, between whom and those of the Cinque Ports there was long rivalry. This probably, rather than any traditional hatred of the Norman conquerors, accounts for the exultation over their defeat. **8. And all þaire fāre.** Note development in meaning of *fāre*, 'journey, going,' into 'behavior, boasting,' and cf. the same change in the word *gait*. **26. On þē Ērle Morrē.** A rising at Annan (Dec. 13, 1332), under John Randolph, Earl of Moray, and Archibald Douglas, Earl of Dunbar, had expelled Edward Balliol from the kingdom. **27. þai said.** The Scotch who had been expelled from the kingdom by Balliol and his English followers. **29. Philip Valays.** Note the form at 159, 21 and the MS. reading. See note to 157, 23.

Page 159, l. 7. all nākëd. The stripping of the dead is illustrated by Barbour's 'Bruce,' XIII, 459 f, in describing the battle of Bannockburn :

> 'And quen þai nakit spulȝeit war
> þat war slayne in þe battale þar,
> It wes, forsuth, a gret ferly
> Till se sammyn so feill dede ly.'

18. At Dondē. See note to 157, 23. **29. Sir Jōn þē Comyn.** John Comyn of Badenoch, killed by Robert Bruce in the church of the Minorites at Dumfries, Feb. 10, 1306. Comyn was Balliol's nephew and heir, and at his death Bruce definitely began the struggle for independence which ended at Bannockburn. For the Scotch use of *the* before a surname see note in Boswell's 'Tour of the Hebrides,' Sept. 6.

Page 160, l. 1. þāre dwelled. That is, before Berwick. **3. Hē gaf gude confort.** He encouraged them in a speech that lasted as long as it would take to go a mile. Examples in Mätzner ('Wörterbuch') show this to have been a common expression. *On þat plaine*, as Hall points out, is not appropriate to the hilly ground of the battle field, but as Minot was probably not present at the battle he uses the expression in a general sense. **13. Now for tō tell.** Evidently this is not a title in the strict sense, since Minot gives no account of Bannockburn. He regarded Halidon Hill as avenging the former defeat of the English, and in this sense is to treat *þē batayl of Banocburn*. **17. manȳ saklēs.** Hall quotes Barbour's 'Bruce,' XX, 173 f, where Bruce says :

> 'For þrou me and my warraying
> Of blud þar has beyne gret spilling
> Quhar many sakles men wes slayne.'

21. Saint Jōhnes tōun. This is Perth, occupied and fortified by the English after defeating the Scotch at Gaskmoor, or Dupplin Moor. A church in Perth is dedicated to St. John, and this accounts for the name ; cf. Froissart's use of

St. Jehanstone. **27. Striflin.** That is, Stirling, the Strevillyne of Barbour's 'Bruce.' Perhaps the allusion is to Wallace's most famous victory over the English, Sept. 11, 1297. The implication then is that Halidon Hill had wiped out the memory of that defeat also.

Page 161, l. 1. þē pilērs. Mätzner, Wülker, and Kölbing take this as meaning 'pillars,' either of state or boundaries of the country, but Hall is doubtless right in assuming connexion with OF. *pilleur* (AN. **pilēr*?), 'robber, raider.' **6. Rughfute riveling.** The riveling is a rough shoe made of raw hide tied round the ankle, and regarded as characteristic of the Scotch, who were thus called 'rough-footed.' So Skelton's 'Of the out yles the roughe foted Scottes,' I, 187. **Bērebag.** So called because the Scotch soldier carried his own baggage and was thus enabled to move more rapidly. **8. Brughes.** The MS. *brig* represents one pronunciation of the name; but Minot uses *Bruge* (*Brughes, Burghes*), all with *u*, and the last no doubt a scribal error for *Brughes*. The place was well known to Scotchmen in the fourteenth century. **11. bētes þē strētes.** Hall thinks imitated from OF. *batre les chemins,* 'to riot or revel in the streets,' but the idea of revelling seems hardly appropriate, and the words may mean no more than 'go about the streets persistently.' **23. Hōw Edward.** Out of the war with Scotland came the great Hundred Years' War with France, Scotland's ally. At the beginning of 1338 Philip attacked Agen in Gascony, still claimed by England, and Edward was forced to declare war. He crossed to Antwerp (162, 30) in July, in order to negotiate with his allies the princes of the Low Countries, and Lewis of Bavaria (162, 9), the German emperor.

Page 162, l. 3. his right. The claim to France, more or less fully acknowledged by the French king himself. The war on the part of France was virtually a struggle to free all French territory from English rule, an end accomplished at the close of the Hundred Years' War in 1451. **9. þē Kaysēr Lowis of Bavēre.** Louis IV, German king and Roman emperor from 1314 to 1347. Though he had been excommunicated by the pope, the electors, in the very month of Edward's departure for the continent, declared his power was derived from them and not from the church. The reception of Edward was by no means as flattering as Minot makes out. **31. māde his monē playne.** Louis had made Edward vicar-general of the empire, and he was empowered to coin money to pay his German auxiliaries. Jehan le Bel says he 'coined money in great abundance at Antwerp.'

Page 163, l. 23. at Hamton. On Oct. 4, 1338, the French from fifty galleys landed at Southampton, plundered the country, and burned the town on hearing that the English were gathering to oppose them. So rapidly did the country rise that some three hundred of the French were cut off from their ships.

Page 164, l. 7. þan saw þai. The poet has reversed the order of events, for the *Christopher* was taken by the French before the attack on Southampton (Froissart's 'Chronicle,' ch. 44). It was later recovered by Edward after the battle of the Swyn. **8. Aremoūth.** The word has gained an initial *y* in modern English, as also the river Yar, on which it is situated. **11. galays.** These were long narrow boats used by the Genoese and sailors of the Mediterranean. In 1337 Philip had engaged twenty such galleys of two hundred oars from Ayton Doria of Genoa, who was present at the attack on Southampton.   **12. tarettes.**   A large vessel like a galley, but commonly used for transport.   **13. galiōtes.**   These were similar to the galleys, but about half the size, each carrying a crew of one hundred men.   **17. Edward ōure King.**   Hall notes that no chronicler mentions the presence of Edward at the fight, and perhaps the poet has confused the ship *Edward* with the king, a suggestion of Sir Harris Nicolas in his 'History of the Navy,' II, 37.   **27. put þām tō wēre.**   Surely Hall is wrong in suggesting that this may mean 'put the enemy in distress.'   It is, as Skeat explains, 'prepared themselves for battle,' 'put themselves (in readiness) to war.'   **32. withowten hīre.**   Literally, 'without hire or recompense,' but idiomatically for a conquered and ignominious condition.   Similarly in Minot's 'Poems,' VII, 65–66 :

> 'Inglis men with site þam soght
> And hastily quit þam þaire hire ' ;

that is, vanquished them.

Page 165, l. 9. sen þē tīme þat God was born.   Often used to emphasize a situation by referring to a long time in general.   **26. with his hālȳ hand.**   The expression depends ultimately, doubtless, on the biblical use of the hand as a symbol of power and goodness.

VI. BARBOUR'S 'BRUCE'—THE PURSUIT OF KING ROBERT

The 'Bruce' occurs in two MSS., of which the better, so far as it is complete, is MS. G 23 in the Library of St. John's College, Cambridge. This was made the basis for the edition of Prof. Skeat for the Early English Text Society (Extra Series 12, 21, 29, 55), though the Edinburgh MS. had to be used for the first four books.   The 'Bruce' has been frequently printed, as by Hart (1616), Pinkerton (1790), Jamieson (1820) ; see also a list of editions in Skeat's 'Introduction,' p. lxvi.   Selections are found in Mätzner ('Sprachproben,' I, 371) and Morris ('Specimens,' II, 203).   The poem was completed in 1378, and therefore represents Northern of the last half of the fourteenth century, except for such differences as come from a later copyist, the MS. being a little more than a century younger than the original.   As Barbour was Archdeacon of Aberdeen from 1357 to his death in 1395, the Northern dialect here represented is that of the extreme North or Scottish English.   Of Barbour little is certainly known.   He first appears in 1357 as Archdeacon of Aberdeen, when he was granted a safeguard to study at Oxford.   From the responsible position he held at the time it is inferred that he was born about 1320.   He again visited England for study in 1364, and passed through it to France in 1365 and 1368.   He attained further honor in his own country, held a position in the king of Scotland's household, and was granted several sums of money by the king at different times.   According to Wyntoun's 'Chronicle' (about 1420), on the authority of which rests the ascription of the 'Bruce' to Barbour, he also wrote the 'Brut' and a genealogical poem called the 'Original of the Stuarts.'   Two other works formerly attributed to Barbour, the 'Siege of Troy' and a collection of 'Lives of Saints,' have been shown not to belong to him.

The 'Bruce' is a national epic, valuable alike for history and literature. It consists of some 13,500 lines, and covers the years 1286 to 1335. The passage chosen is a good example of the poet's power in vivid narration. Just before the selection begins, John of Lorn had sought to track the king with a hound, and five of his men had been slain by the king and his foster-brother. The latter then retreat before Lorn's approaching company to a wood near at hand.

As already noticed the MS. is younger than the work itself by a century, and this no doubt accounts for some differences in language, or at least in orthography. For example, the Northern use of *i* (*y*) after a long vowel to indicate length becomes more common. Compare such rimes as *gāne, wayn*; *pair, mār*; *agāne, vayn*; and such forms as *soyn*, 'soon,' *heir*, 'here,' *deill*, 'deal,' in the early lines. Perfect participles ending in *t* instead of *d* are also common.

Page 166, l. 7. **begŏūth.** Note this interesting example of analogy, formed on the model of *cŏuth*, preterit of *can*. This was perhaps assisted by the constant confusion, especially in Nth., of *can* and *gan*. **9. His man.** Really his foster-brother, as shown by 173, 15, and by references in Book VI of the poem. **10. Abȳde ȝhē heir.** 'If you abide here'; the subjunctive in condition.

Page 167, l. 9. **Jŏhn of Lŏrne.** John MacDougal of Lorn in Argyle-shire, son of Allaster of Lorn, and descendant of Somerled, Thane of Argyle and Lord of the Isles, who fell at Renfrew in 1164. See Scott's 'Lord of the Isles' and notes thereon.

Page 168, l. 11. **lĕst on līf.** 'Last, or remain, alive.' **27. Schir Āmēr.** Sir Aymer de Valence, Earl of Pembroke and leader of the English forces. He was a son of the half-brother of Henry III.

Page 169, l. 1. **Schir Thomas Randale.** Sir Thomas Randolph, Bruce's nephew, first fought with the latter until made prisoner at the battle of Methven. Then, submitting to the English, he even took part against Bruce as indicated here. Later, captured by Douglas, he was reconciled to his uncle and made Earl of Moray (Murray). He now distinguished himself by many exploits, especially the capture of Edinburgh. See note to 'Lord of the Isles,' VI, 1, and reference to his descendant John Randolph in Minot (158, 26). **9. And hŏw.** An adventure narrated in Book VI, 589 f. Five of Lorn's men had overtaken Bruce and his brother, but were all slain by the two, Bruce himself killing four. **17. And hē wār bŏdyn all ēvynlȳ.** 'If he were bidden or challenged (to fight) on even terms.' **19. And þē gud kyng.** This adventure is told with some alterations by Scott in 'Lord of the Isles,' III, 18 f. **26. Līk tŏ lichtmen.** Skeat explains as light-armed men; cf. *light-horse.*

Page 170, l. 14. **bryng hym þan cf daw.** 'Bring him then out of day,' that is, 'kill him,' a common ME. idiom.

Page 171, l. 3. **slew fȳre.** Skeat replaces *slew* of both MSS. by *strake*, 'struck,' on the ground that *slew* must have been repeated from the preceding line. On the other hand, *slew fire* is not uncommon (cf. the 'Bruce,' XIII, 26), and I prefer to keep the MS. reading. **10. At a fȳre.** 'At a fire,' with stress on *a* ' one.' The line might still be improved by an extra syllable, though the cæsural pause may account for its absence. **27. worthit.** A weak preterit of wurþe(n), ' be, become '; ' saw that sleep had become necessary to him.'

Page 172, l. 1. **And slēpit nocht.** Skeat reads *And slepit nocht [full] ynkerly, [Bot gliffnyt up oft] suddanly*, supplying the bracketed words from Edin. MS. With the different punctuation I have given the line, no syntactical alteration is necessary. **6. as foūl on twist.** Supposed to be indicative of readiness for any emergency; cf. MnE. ' with one eye open ' in similar connexion.

Page 173, l. 6. **Nā wār.** Pret. subj. ' and had [it] not been [for] the arming (armor),' &c. **18. his trist.** Bruce had divided his men into small bands when hard pressed, and had appointed a rendezvous for such as should not be taken. His party alone had been followed by the hound.

Page 174, l. 29. **Jāmes of Doūglas.** This Douglas, son of William who supported Wallace, had been the first to take up the cause of Bruce, and one of the most faithful. **31. at.** *At* for *þat* is especially common in Nth., though no doubt found in all dialects as a reduced form of the spoken language. **32. Edward þē Bruce.** The brother of Robert, fiery and head-strong. As Barbour says, thinking Scotland too small for him and his brother he tried to make himself king of Ireland, but lost his life in the attempt; cf. Book XVIII.

THE SOUTHERN DIALECT, INCLUDING
KENTISH

Southern English represents several somewhat different varieties. In our selections the first three pieces are of Early Southern, in which, as in Early Midland, certain changes of Old English forms had not yet taken place. The third of these pieces belongs to Southern of the so-called Katherine group (Morsbach, 'ME. Gram.,' § 3, anm. 2), that is, shows a Southern English with Midland peculiarities. This is due to the fact that the works of this group were written in a northern part of the Southern region near to Midland. Selections VI and VII represent Kentish English, the remaining pieces Southern of the normal type.

I. THE POEMA MORALE, OR 'MORAL ODE'

This characteristic bit of mediæval moralizing exists in six MSS., Digby A 4, Egerton 613 (two versions), and Jesus Coll. I Arch. I 29 at Oxford, Lambeth MS. 487 in London, Trinity Coll. MS. B 14, 52 at Cambridge. Not all of the MSS. are complete, and of the two groups into which they fall, the versions in Digby and Trinity Coll. MSS. are Kentish rather than Southern in the more restricted sense. Of the Sth. texts those of the Egerton MSS. are, on the whole, the best, and a selection from Egerton e is here taken. The poem has been edited at various times, as by Furnivall in 'Early English Poems and Lives of Saints,' p. 22; by Morris ('Old English Homilies,' I, 159, 288, II, 220); ('Specimens,' I, 194); ('An Old English Miscellany,' p. 58); by Zupitza ('Anglia,' I, 6); ('Übungsbuch,' p. 58); by Lewin in a critical edition (1881). The poem was written about 1170 in South Hampshire or Dorsetshire, and thus represents Southern of the middle district.

The 'Moral Ode' consists of 396 long lines of seven stresses, riming in couplets. As in the 'Ormulum,' with the metre of which it has close relations, the long line is divided into two parts by a cæsural pause after the fourth stress, so that each couplet might be printed in alternate lines of four and three stresses, riming *abcb*. Indeed this is the original of such a stanza in MnE. poetry, and this is the second stage in the development from the unrimed lines of Orm. The lines are often irregular in number of syllables, though many irregularities may be easily explained as due to lost inflexional or other elements, or to metrical peculiarities of Middle English. In content the poem begins with a penitential portion of eighteen lines in the first person, after which the moralizing becomes more general in character, and approaches that of a sermon in verse. The selection gives a good idea of the whole.

The language of the 'Ode' shows a mixture of early and late forms to some extent; cf. *ǭ* for OE. *ā* in the rimes of the first couplet, but *ā* usually.

Besides, *æ* (*e*) appear for WS. *æ*, *ea*; *ǣ*, *ēa* for WS. *ē*, *ēa*, beside *e* = *ę̄*; rarely *ēo* (*eo*) are found for WS. *ēo* (*eo*), and the former sometimes for WS. *ō*, as in *wēorde*, 'word.' These are in addition to the typical Sth. *ü*, *ü̃* for WS. *ȳ*, though occasionally *y*, as in *ȳlde*, *yfele*. As to inflexion, Southern is more conservative than Midland or Northern, and therefore longer retains Old English forms; there are also typical Southern peculiarities which have been already sufficiently mentioned in the Grammatical Introduction.

Page 176, l. 1. Ich. This is the characteristic Sth. form of the pronoun with *ch* as in *church* from OE. *c* after a palatal vowel. Note that both other forms also occur in the selection, *ic* (l. 2), *I* (l. 4).   **1–2. lǫre . . . mǫre.** A later Sth. rime modifying the earlier *lāre . . . māre*; cf. *māȝe . . . āȝe* (177, 5–6) and *āre . . . māre* (177, 29–30).   **3. habbe.** The Sth. dialect, with characteristic conservatism, retains such forms in case of verbs with different consonants in infinitive and 1st pers. pres. indic. from those in the remaining forms. Thus inf. *habbe(n)*, *libbe(n)*, *segge(n)*, and 1st pers. pres. indic. *habbe*, *libbe* (177, 9), *segge*. In the Anglian districts, on the other hand, under the influence of analogy, these have adopted the consonant of the other pres. forms, as *have(n)*, *live(n)*, *seie(n)*, 'have, live, say.' Cf. Gram. Introd., § 165.   **ibēon.** Note the characteristic Sth. prefix, a retention of OE. *ge* in reduced form. In this particular instance no OE. *gebēon* is known to literature, but it must have existed in speech at some time.   **7. chilche.** This difficult word, known only here, seems to have been formed from *child* (OE. **chilts* for *childs* f.), as OE. *milts*, ME. *milce* (*milche*?), is formed from *mild*. At least the meaning, 'childishness, puerility,' seems to fit the connexion fairly well.   **21. þe wēl ne dēþ.** The OE. relative particle *þe* was retained in Sth. much longer than in the other dialects.

Page 177, l. 6. ōðres. Note retention in early Sth. of the OE. inflexion of the adjective.   **12. Manīes mannes.** The line has met somewhat different interpretations, based especially on different conceptions of the words *iswinch* and *unhölde*. Morris ('Specimens,' I, 350) translates: 'Many a man's sore trouble often hath ungracious ones, i.e. a man often receives no return for his hard work.' In 'OE. Homilies' he translates quite freely: 'many kinds of sore trouble have often the infirm.' Lewin, opposing this quite rightly, finally proposes *manches Mannes sauer errungenen Gewinn haben oft die Widersacher*. The sense is 'Ungracious (or hostile) ones often obtain (have) the sore labor (or gain) of many a man,' and is probably based on Ps. xxxix. 6 and Luke xii. 20.   **13. dōn ā fürst.** Literally, 'put in time or respite,' and so 'put off, or delay.' The phrase occurs in several forms, *dō in firste* ('OE. Homilies,' I, 71); *dō . . . on frest* ('Havelok,' l. 1,337), printed by Skeat and Holthausen *onfrest*.   **21. of wȳfe ne of chīlde.** The imperfect rime *childe . . . selde* is at once suspicious, and it is not strange to find other MSS. with a different reading. The Lambeth reading *of ȝefe ne of ȝelde*, 'of gift nor of reward,' is probably the older form of the line.   **23. wēl oft and wēl ȝelōme.** A common phrase with two words for the same idea, in order to give it emphasis.   **26. sē irēve.** The prevalence of *þē* for OE. *sē* throws some suspicion on this expression. Digby MS. reads *ne his serreve*, 'nor his sheriff,' and Trin. MS. *ne ne scirreve*. Lewin reads *ne þe scirreve*.

Page 178, l. 12. And þē ðe māre. 'And the one who may do no more (may do) with his good intention as well as he that has many pieces (manke) of gold.' **14. kan māre þanc.** The phrase is OE. *cunnan þonc*, beside *witan þonc*, and it has survived in Scotch *con thanks*. Literally, 'to know thanks,' it is equivalent to 'feel (or express) gratitude, show favor.' 'And often God feels more gratitude to those who give less to him.' **19. biŏ.** The plural subjects are thought of as one and so take singular verb; cf. *děŏ . . . ŏenchet* (178, 22), where the verbs agree with *hwet*, not with *wihte*, the real subject.

Page 179, l. **3. scule wē.** Based on the OE. form when the verb was immediately followed by *wē* or *gē*. In Middle English it was extended to the third personal pronoun also; cf. *scule hē* (l. 6), but *Nabbeŏ hi* (l. 9). **8. vele.** Note this first case in our Sth. selections of initial *v* for older *f*. **28. cōm tō manne.** 'Came to man's estate.'

Page 180, l. **4. Ŏe bēot and bĕat, and bīt.** All texts give two verbs with initial *b*, indicating intentional alliteration, and Lambeth agrees with our text in its three forms *biet* and *bit* and *bet*. Three verbs that are possible in the place are OE. *bētan*, 'to amend,' *bedan*, ME. *bĕde(n)*, 'to pray,' *biddan*, 'to pray, beseech.' The line then means : 'therefore he is wise who repents and prays and beseeches before the judgement.' Lewin bases his text on the Trin. MS. reading, *þe bit and biȝet and bet*, though I cannot think with a better result in sense. The former are all contracts of the third singular present indicative. **7. Sünne lĕt þē.** 'Sin leaves thee and thou not it (or them), when thou art not able to do them any more.' *Hī* may be either sing. or pl., but *is* of the following clause seems to indicate that it was considered plural. Lewin alters *is* to *hi*, in order to agree with the former word. This line and the next, owing to omission and erasure, cannot be easily made out in the MS. **8. þe swā abīt.** 'Who so awaits,' that is as implied in the preceding line. **14. Ne bidde nā bet.** 'Should (I) not better pray to be loosed from bonds on doomesday?' Several MSS. have *ich (ic)* after *bidde*, and it has probably disappeared from our text. **20. Üvel is.** 'Evil is it to suffer seven years for seven nights' bliss.' *Üvel is* must be understood with the next line also. **32. For tō ŏē müchele mürcŏe.** 'For to come to the great bliss (of heaven) is happiness with certainty.'

II. ARTHUR'S LAST BATTLE—FROM LAYAMON'S 'BRUT'

Layamon's 'Brut' is preserved in two MSS. of the British Museum, Cotton Calig. A IX and Otho C XIII, from the former of which, the older, our selection is taken. Both texts were edited in 1847 by Sir Frederic Madden, and extracts are given in Mätzner ('Sprachproben,' I, 21), Morris ('Specimens,' I, 64), Zupitza-Schipper ('Übungsbuch,' p. 92). The poem is the work of a priest Laȝamon (later text Lawemon), but more commonly written Layamon, son of Leovenath, of Arnley in North Worcestershire, and was composed about 1200. The language therefore represents Southern of the Western division during the last of the twelfth and beginning of the thirteenth century.

The 'Brut' consists of some 16,000 long lines (a little less than 15,000 in the later MS.), or double the number of short lines as printed by Madden. These long lines are based on the older alliterative line and show frequent alliteration, though rime and assonance are also common in binding together the two half-lines. The metrical form is thus a combination of the old alliterative line and a rimed couplet of irregular character. Compare the similar lines of the 'Bestiary.' In content the poem is a legendary history of Britain from the destruction of Troy to the year 689 A.D. It is based on the Norman Wace's 'Roman de Brut,' which in turn has its source in Geoffrey of Monmouth's 'Historia Regum Britanniae.' Our selection begins with l. 13,996 (Madden, l. 27,992). Arthur, the world conqueror, resting after the great feast on the overthrow of the emperor of Rome, is summoned home by bad news as told in the passage chosen.

The language of the poem does not greatly differ from that of the 'Moral Ode.' It shows a similar mixture of older and later forms. OE. $\bar{a}$ still appears as $\bar{a}$, long and short $æ$ are not infrequent, and eo, $\bar{eo}$ are still preserved. The latter, eo, sometimes appears for Sth. $\bar{e}$, OE. $\bar{æ}$, as in $w\bar{e}ore$, unless indeed this is for Ml. $w\bar{e}re$ with close $\bar{e}$. Assuming the open quality of the first element, as indicating Sth. $\bar{e}$, the e is marked open ($\bar{e}$). Some Ml. forms certainly occur, as $h\bar{a}lden$ (183, 7), beside $h\bar{æ}lden$ (l. 1416). Among consonants the Sth. initial v for OE. f is more common than in the 'Moral Ode.' Inflexions show the usual Sth. conservatism. A special peculiarity of Layamon is the more frequent final n of inflexional forms, either retained from an older inflexion or often added where not original; cf. Stratmann, 'Anglia,' III, 552. Examples are $t\bar{i}den$, dsg. (181, 1); $d\bar{e}oren$, nsg. (182, 13); $cumen$, pr. subj. sg. (183, 21); $wari\bar{e}n$, gpl. (184, 26), perhaps from OE. gpl. in ena. In many cases inflexional en is a retention of OE. dpl. um. The vocabulary of Layamon is full of epic phrases from OE. poetry, so full as to imply some considerable acquaintance with OE. literature. For convenience of reference the line-numbering of Madden is always given in the notes, except of course when referring to our selection.

Page 181, l. 1. þā cōm þēr. Arthur is represented as being *inne Burguine*, 'in Burgundy,' when the news reaches him.　　āre. Note retention of inflexional forms in the pronoun, as $\bar{a}re$ = OE. $\bar{a}nre$; $þ\bar{a}n$ (l. 2) = $þ\bar{a}m$; $hine$ (l. 20); $\bar{a}ne$ (l. 29) f. asg.; $þ\bar{e}re$ (l. 23) = $þ\bar{e}re$.　　3. Mōdrēde. In setting out from England Arthur had left his kingdom in charge of Modred and Wenhavere (Guenevere), as told at l. 25,465 (Madden).　　6. Swā naver. 'Yet never would he,' the young knight. Only in a supernatural manner, through the vision, does Arthur find out the truth.　　17. Walwain, B text Waweyn. Better known as Gawain, nephew of Arthur and brother of Modred.　　22. Wenhevēr, B text *Gwenayfer*. The Welsh *Gwenhwyvar*, Eng. *Guenevere*. In Layamon she is simply an extremely fair woman, whose mother was of Roman birth and relative of Cador, Earl of Cornwall.　　24. tō hǣlden. The MnE. form has lost final d and appears as *heel*, 'to incline.' Layamon's word seems to be Midland $h\bar{e}lden$, a form which also appears in his text.

Page 182, l. 6. dēore mīne swēorde. This order of adjective and possessive is especially common in Layamon. Cf. the Elizabethan *dear my lord*.

Page 183, l. 20. quēn. The MS. *que* is probably for $qu\bar{e}$ = $qu\bar{e}n$, though the commoner form in Layamon is $qu\bar{e}ne$.　　21. cumen. The form is pres. subj. with excrescent n so common in Layamon. Cf. *þat Arður þider comen*, 'that Arthur thither should come,' ll. 27,078 and 19,110 (Madden).　　27. þā sæt hit. 'Then it remained all still.'

Page 184, l. 18. væisið, MS. wæisið. Madden suggested the change, required by the context and alliteration. Cf. *feieside makede* (l. 304) and *fæieside* (l. 26,040), in both cases alliterating with *f*. Here, of course, we must assume an earlier *f-f* alliteration, now become *f-v* or *v-v* by the regular Sth. change of initial *f* to *v*. **28. hā**, MS. **a.** The third personal pronoun, both masc. and fem., sometimes appears as *ā, hā*. **32. Ā marʒen þat hit.** So MS., but the correct reading is probably *þā*, 'when.' The B text has *þo*, 'when.' **and Drihten.** 'And the Lord had sent it (the day),' perhaps referring to its favorable character for an expedition.

Page 185, l. 3. **Whitsǫr.d.** Wissant, Pas-de-Calais, called *Hwitsand* in the 'Chronicle' under the year 1095. **17. Childrīche.** Childric was in those days an emperor of great authority in Alemaine, as we are told at l. 20,198. Arthur had already vanquished him when he came to Britain to assist Colgrim and Baldulf, as told in the lines following that quoted above.

Page 186, l. 9. **Romenel**, MS. **Romerel.** Romney in Kent without doubt. **11. avorn on**, MS. **avornon.** The phrase is an interesting example of the replacing of a worn-out form. *Avorn* is OE. *on foran*, the first part of which was no longer recognized in the reduced prefix *a*, and *on* was again added at the end. **26. Angel.** A king of Scotland whom Arthur had assisted to regain his kingdom. He had last led the foremost troop in the fight against 'Luces,' emperor of Rome. The name appears as *Aguisel* in Wace, *Augusel (Angusel?)* in Geoffrey of Monmouth, and is possibly Scotch *Angus*.

Page 187, l. 2. ʒurren þā stānes. 'The stones babbled with streams of blood.' 'Roar, resound' are too strong for *ʒurren*, which applied to the chattering of people, the whirring or singing of ropes when the ship met a storm; cf. *garring*, from the same root, at 224, 15. Such exaggerated descriptions of battle are common in Layamon, as in all early poetry. Cf. 189, 32.

Page 188, l. 1. þē fēond hine āʒe. 'May the devil take him.' **30. and hū.** The B text really reads *and ou ʒeo hinne ende*, with place for an initial in the last word. I have assumed the lost letter to be *w*, and have otherwise used the forms of the A text. **31. þā hēo hire seolf.** No doubt this is one of the alternatives beginning with *whaðer*, and we are to supply 'or whether' at the beginning of this line. The loss of the preceding half-line makes the connexion uncertain.

Page 189, l. 16. swā þē rein falleð, MS. rim falled. The change of *rim* to *rein* was suggested by Madden. Either this is a scribal error or perhaps the noun was influenced by the verb, which appears as *rine—rinde* in the 'Brut.' **20. Tambre.** The river Tamar between Devon and Cornwall. In Malory's 'Morte D'Arthur' the great fight is by the sea near Salisbury. **21. Camelfǒrd.** A Camelford, ford of the Camel, still exists in the north of Cornwall, but is naturally not connected with the Tamar river. Geoffrey of Monmouth says the battle took place near the 'river Cambula,' while Wace has *Camblan . . . a l'entree de Cornuaille, Tambre . . . en la terre de Cornoaille, Tamble,* &c. in different MSS. ('Brut,' l. 13,659). Confusion was easy because of the likeness between the MS. *c* and *t*, as well as by reason of the frequent interchange of *l-r*. Once in the 'Chronicle' *Camermuða* is found for *Tamarmuða*. The reference to the sea (191, 1) would imply a situation like that of Camelford in North Cornwall, and probably *Cambre* for *Tambre* is the correct reading of the preceding line.

Page 190, l. 11. ī þare lasten. 'In the least (of the wounds),' as mentioned in the line preceding.   **26. Avalūn.** Geoffrey of Monmouth twice speaks of the 'island of Avalon (Avallon),' and Wace follows with *en l'ile d'Avalon* ('Brut,' l. 9,516). In the passage corresponding to this Wace does not say an island, and Layamon also makes no specific reference to the situation of the place, except that Arthur reaches it by sea (191, 1). See discussions of the place in 'Romania,' Oct. 1898, and 'Mod. Lang. Notes,' XIV, 47.   **27. Argante.** Wace and Geoffrey of Monmouth make no mention of this personage. Malory names four, three queens and the Lady of the Lake.   **30. And seoððe.** Wace makes mention of the tradition that Arthur should come again, and Layamon, whose more dramatic treatment is seen in several places, puts it into the mouth of Arthur himself.

Page 191, l. 7. þat wẹore. 'That immeasurable trouble should come (be) after (of) Arthur's death.'

III. 'THE LIFE OF SAINT JULIANA'

The Middle English prose 'Life of St. Juliana' is preserved in two MSS., Royal 17 A 27 of the British Museum, and Bodleian MS. 34 at Oxford. Of these the first is the purest text, and from it our selection is taken. Both MSS. were edited for the Early English Text Society by Cockayne in 1872 (EETS., 51), and extracts from both are found in Morris ('Specimens,' I, 96). The work was written about 1200, the MSS. themselves being of the first half of the thirteenth century. It belongs to the northern part of the Southern district, and has certain Midland peculiarities. The language is therefore Sth. with Ml. coloring, as explained below.

The story of St. Juliana has already been told by Cynewulf in an Old English poem (cf. Garnett, ' The Latin and Anglo-Saxon Juliana,' Publ. of Mod. Lang. Ass., XIV, 279). It also appears, later than our prose version, in a poem of long rimed couplets (EETS., 51, 81) similar to those of the 'Moral Ode,' as also in an unpublished version ; cf. Horstmann, 'Altenglische Legenden,' p. xlvi f. As to the form of the present 'Life,' at once noticeable for its alliterative and rhythmical character, there is difference of opinion among scholars. Ten Brink speaks of the long alliterative line or the rhythmical alliterative prose (' Eng. Lit.,' p. 199). Einenkel undertook to prove that this work, together with the similar 'Lives' of St. Margaret (EETS., 80) and St. Katherine (EETS., 13), are in long alliterative lines. From this view Schipper dissents (' Grundriss der englischen Metrik,' p. 75), and I see no reason to print otherwise than as prose, though the alliterative and rhythmical elements will be clear to any reader. The source of the story is that found in the ' Acta Sanctorum' for Feb. 16.

The language of the ' Juliana,' like that of the prose ' Lives' of St. Katherine and St. Margaret, is a mixture of Sth. and Ml. ; cf. Morsbach, ' Mittelenglische Grammatik,' § 3, anm. 2; § 9, 1. The chief Ml. peculiarities are the close instead of open *ē* = Goth. *ē*, WT. *ā*, as in Mercian and the non-Wessex dialects, and the preservation of the *u* and *o* mutations in many cases. In other respects the dialect is Southern, as shown especially by *e* for OE. *æ*, Ml. *a*, and *ü*, *ü* for OE. *y*, *ȳ*. Besides may be noted the preservation of OE. *ā*, as in the preceding early Sth. selections, and the diphthongs *eo*, *ēo*, *ēa* (*ea*). The long diphthong *ēa*, used for OE. *ēa* or *ē* and certainly a mere graphic representation of ME. *ę̄*, has been marked *ę̄a*. No voicing of initial *f*, *þ*, and *s* is indicated by the orthography, but unvoicing of final *d* is common.

Page 191, l. 16. In ūre. This paragraph is preceded by the rubric: *Her cumseð þe vie of seinte iuliane and telleð of liflade hire*, 'Here commenceth the life of Saint Juliana, and (it) telleth of her manner of life.' **Feader.** The usual form is the Sth. *feder* = Ml. *fader*. **ant.** The usual form in this 'Life,' as in the others of the group, so that the sign for *and* is regularly expanded *ant*. **23. Nichomēdes burh.** Nichomedia in Asia Minor, founded by Nichomedes I. In the OE. 'Juliana' it appears as Commedia. **25. of þē hę̄þene mę̄st.** 'Greatest of the heathen.' Not in the Latin, and Bodl. MS. has a different reading: 'Affrican hehte, þe heande ꝛ heascede mest men þe weren cristene.' Egge ('Mod. Lang. Notes,' I, 138) connects with following clause, but I think not rightly. **26. dērflīche hē drōh**, MS. **derfliche droh.** The *hē*, subject of *drōh*, was probably lost by scribal confusion with *he* of the preceding word.

Page 192, l. 3. Maximian. Really Galerius Valerius Maximinus, made emperor in 308, and one of six to claim the title at that time. He renewed the persecution of the Christians after Galerius had published an edict of toleration, but was soon overthrown by Licinius and died in 314. Here he seems to have been confused with Maximian, contemporary emperor of the West, as in the OE. poem. Perhaps this is due to the frequent confusion of the Eastern and Western Roman empires, as shown also in the next note. **4. Rōme.** Of course Constantinople, or New Rome, in this place. **mawmets**, MS. **maumez.** The final *z* is unquestionably equivalent to *ts*, and I have not hesitated to expand it as if it were an abbreviation; cf. 195, 22 and note on 194, 25. **13. ihǫndsald.** 'Betrothed wholly against her will.' **24. as me þā luvede.** 'As they (me) then loved,' that is, as was the custom of the time. **intō cure þet**, MS. ꝛ. 'Into a chariot that the powerful rode in, or in which,' &c. Cockayne and Morris retain the MS. *and*, reading 'and ride into the kingdom.' I have assumed a phrase descriptive of the chariot, as *rīche* 'kingdom' seems inappropriate to a *rēve*. The Bodl. MS. has another descriptive phrase, *i cure up of fowr hweoles*, 'up into a chariot of four wheels.' **30. bālde hire seolven.** As it stands, *bālde* must be a past participle modifying *Juliane*. The Bodl. MS. has a sign for *and* before *sende*, making *bālde* and *sende* correlative, and this may be the correct reading. **32. wraðði sǭ.** 'Be angry as thou wilt.' Cf. a similar construction in the third pers. at 196, 10.

Page 193, l. 20. Ich ülle, MS. **ichulle.** The MS. form indicates that the two words were spoken in close association, as in the MnE. Sth. dialectal *chull*, 'I will.' **27. eis weis.** 'In any way (ways),' one of the few examples of the inflected adjective in this selection.

Page 194, l. 6. Me hwet. 'But what.' The conjunction *me*, 'but,' is found especially in Sth. texts, but apparently not in Old English or the Anglian

territory. This would argue for the Low German origin suggested for it.
16. wummon. Note the influence of the preceding *w* upon the original *i* from
ī in this word, causing it to become *u* as still preserved in the singular.
25. mix mawmets, MS. **mawmǝx.** Final *x* in the latter may be due to
scribal influence of the preceding word. **28. Elewsium.** Foreign derived
names retain their original inflexion as here, remain uninflected, or assume the
inflexion of English nouns, depending on the frequency of their usage.

Page 195, l. 8. ō̄w. A dative which seems redundant to-day, but no doubt
added force to the expression. It may be translated as a possessive, 'for your
evil fortune.'   **11. as rēve of þē burhe.** Since the 'Life' was too long to
use as a whole, the trial before Eleusius has been omitted and the account
resumed at the close of the tortures. The intervening part tells how Eleusius
is again struck with Juliana's beauty, and how she again repels his advances.
She is then beaten a second time, hanged by the hair, has boiling brass poured
over her, and is finally cast into prison. Here a supernatural visitor tempts her,
but she seizes him and makes him confess he is the devil. She binds him with
chains and drags him to the judgement seat of the prefect. She is torn to pieces
on a wheel of spikes, but is made whole by an angel, thus converting the
executioners. She is thrust into a great fire, but an angel quenches it. This
angers the prefect still more, and at this point the narrative is resumed.
31. ȝeldeð hire ȝarew borh. The speech differs here from that in the 'Acta
Sanctorum,' in which the devil speaks to Eleusius. *ȝarew borh* seems to be used
ironically, 'ready payment' as if for a debt, the Bodl. text reading 'ȝeldeð hire
ȝarow borh efter þat ha wurðe is.'

Page 196, l. 3. **unwiht.** Not found in OE. literature, but there is the
similar *untŷdre*, 'monster,' literally 'no child or offspring.'   **8. uppon trēowe
ɛtaðele.** Referring to Matt. vii. 24–27.   **24. underfēng.** Cf. with this imperative *onderfang* of Layamon ('Brut,' II, 168) and *undervong* of 'Anc. Riw.,'
p. 114.   **wið meidenes imēane.** No doubt alluding to Rev. xiv. 3–4.
Cf. 'Pearl,' l. 1,096 f.   **26. þē ēdie engles.** See, for an early instance of the
same, the account of the death of Chad in Bede, 'Eccl. Hist,' Bk. IV, ch. iii.
28. Cōm ā sēlī wummon. This incident, given in the Greek and Latin lives,
is omitted by Cynewulf. The name of the woman is variously given as Sophonia
(Sophronia) and Sophia, the latter by Symeon Metaphrastes the Greek martyro-
logist.   **32. from þē sēa ā mīle.** In the territory of Puteoli, as stated by
the first life in the 'Acta Sanctorum.' Later (the late sixth century) her remains
were transferred to Cumae for greater safety. Thence, in 1207, they were said
to have been taken to Naples, and various cities now claim them, as Brussels
for example.

Page 197, l. 1. **þē rēve.** In the 'Acta Sanctorum' no mention is made of
the reeve's pursuing Sophie, and twenty-four, not thirty-four, are destroyed by
the storm.   **4. þrittuðǝ.** Both MSS. have the form, though surely for *þrittī*,
'thirty,' it would seem.   **5. warp ham adriven.** 'Cast them, driven about,
on (to) the land.' The change from plural to singular in the verbs is also found
in the Bodl. MS. No doubt the general idea of storm was in the writer's mind.
8. þē sixtēnðǝ dei. This is the day on which the Romish church celebrates
her martyrdom, while the Greek church prefers Dec. 21.

IV. 'THE ANCREN RIWLE, OR RULE OF NUNS'

There are five MSS. of the 'Ancren Riwle,' Cotton Nero A XIV, Titus D XVIII, Cleopatra C VI in the British Museum, Corpus Christi Coll. MS. and Caius Coll. MS. 234 at Cambridge. Besides, a fragment of another MS. was recently discovered by Napier (' Jour. of Germ. Philology,' II, 199). The first of these, with collation of the second and third, was edited in 1853 for the Camden Society by Morton, and selections are found in Morris ('Specimens,' I, 110) and Mätzner ('Sprachproben,' II, 5). Our selection follows Morton's edition with such changes as are necessary by reason of Kölbing's collation with the MS. (' Jahrbuch für rom. und engl. Philologie,' XV, 180). The work was written about the beginning of the thirteenth century, in the middle part of the Southern district, since it mentions Tarente (Tarent-Kaimes or Kingston) near the Stour, in southwest Dorset. Morton suggested (Preface, p. xii) that its author may have been Rich. Poor, who was born at Tarente and died there in 1237. He was in turn bishop of Chichester, Salisbury, and Durham, and may have been a benefactor of the house since he was sometimes called its founder.

The ' Rule cf Nuns' is a free and not uninteresting treatment of monastic duties, prepared for three sisters of good family who had become nuns. It consists of a brief introduction and eight parts : of religious service ; keeping the heart ; of monastic life ; of temptation ; confession ; penitence ; love ; of domestic matters. Of plain and simple style, it contains numerous quotations from the Bible and the Church Fathers, with allusions to saintly lives but practically no legendary or moral tales. The first extract is from Part II (Morton, p. 64), dealing with each of the senses in turn ; the second from part VIII (Morton, p. 414).

The language of the ' Rule of Nuns' is a pure Southern, and in most respects represents the normal form of that dialect, as distinct from the Early Southern of the preceding selections. OE. $\bar{a}$ has now regularly become $\bar{o}$, the new diphthongs have developed, and the voicing of initial f to v is the rule. On the other hand, OE. $\bar{e}o$ (eo), $\bar{e}a$ ($\check{e}a$) still appear as in preceding texts. Occasionally $\bar{e}o$ of this text is equivalent to open $\check{e}$, so that it has in such cases been marked $\check{e}o$. Consonant peculiarities are not numerous. The most important is t for initial $þ$ after a word ending in t or d, as $vort$ tet (l. 15) for $vort$ $þet$; and $terefter$ (l. 16) for $þerefter$. Further see Wülker in Paul and Braune's ' Beiträge,' I, 209.

Page 197, l. 14. **Spellunge and smecchunge.** Note the retention of the *unge* ending of OE. nouns.

Page 198, l. 1. **þet hē ouh tō siggen.** Morton connects with preceding clause, but it belongs, as Mätzner shows, to the following. ' (To) that (which) he has to say, hearken to his words.' The peculiarity is in the repetition of ' his words.' **12. Paraïs.** Both this and *Paradīs* occur in OF. and ME. **22. þē cǫve**, MS. **coue.** The word here and in l. 24 has been somewhat variously read, as the MS. *u* may be *u* or *v*. Morton connects with OE. *ceo(h)*, ' chough,' but this should appear with ME. *ch* initially, to say nothing of the diphthong. Mätzner assumes a Netherland *kauwe* (*kauw*), which ought, it would seem, to give *caue*; cf. MnE. *caw*. Icl. *kofa*, ' young pigeon,' is also not easily connected with the word. To account for the form, and preserve the play upon the word, I assume OE. *cáf*, ME. *cǫve*, used in the first case as a substantive adj., 'the swift, the deceitful,' perhaps, 'the thief.' *Cumeŝ te ȝeape*, 'comes the cunning (one),' of Titus MS. shows the understanding of another scribe, and that he had no idea of the chough or any other bird.

Page 199, l. 1. **Sed multi veniunt.** Matt. vii. 15, the Vulgate for which is *Attendite a falsis prophetis, qui veniunt*. 7. **Gābriēles spēche.** The annunciation, Luke i. 29. 11. **ōˇer stūnde**, MS. **stude.** Morton's emendation is proved correct by the Latin text (Magd. Coll., Oxford), which conveys the same idea in positive form : *si tertius haberi possit*. 32. **Ancre and hūses lēfdī.** 'There ought to be much (difference) between an anchoress and a housewife.'

Page 200, l. 3. **swīwike, MS. swiˇðwike.** Mätzner suggested retaining the MS. reading as OE. equivalent for MLat. *hebdomeda maior*, though no such OE. word is known. On the other hand, we know that OE. *swigdæg*, 'day of silence.' was used for the three days of Holy Week between Thursday evening and Sunday morning ; cf. Ælfric's 'Homilies,' I, 218, 31 ; II, 268, 16. Besides, Titus MS. reads *swihende wike*, and Cleopatra MS. *swiwike*. The emendation therefore seems fully justified. The nuns are advised to make the whole week one of silence, rather than the customary three days. 9. **Ase Seont Anselme.** I have not found the original. 10. **chēofled = chēofleˇð.** Here, as occasionally in most texts, *ð* is replaced by *d* by scribal error ; cf. 201, 17. 20. **Mulieres.** 1 Tim. ii. 12 and 1 Cor. xiv. 34. Neither passage is followed verbatim, the former more nearly. 22. **þē ǫverkūˇðre.** Morton's omission of *þe* led Mätzner to a wrong understanding of the words. He rightly pointed out Morton's error in connecting this with the following sentence. 27. **ase ich ēr seide.** See 199, 31. 31. **Ad summam volo.** Morton has made the strange mistake of including *þet is* in the quotation as he translates it, and omitting *ich ulle*, &c. *þē ēnde of þē tāle* is of course a free rendering of *ad summam*.

Page 201, l. 5. **Censura.** I do not find the exact words here or in l. 7, but a discussion of silence with the figure of the water (201, 8) occurs in Gregory's 'Regulae Pastoralis Liber,' ch. 38 (Migne, 77, 53). 22. **Maria optimam.** Luke x. 42. The translation begins with the preceding verse.

Page 202, l. 15. **Bidden hit.** 'To ask (or beg) it, in order to give it away, is not the part (rihte) of an anchoress.' 19. **on ōu.** 'On yourselves,' that is, 'from your own wants.' **nenne mon.** That is, 'Let no man eat before you,' *mākīeˇð* of the preceding clause being understood with this also. 25. **Muche nēoðe.** That is, 'only much need.' 32. **heiward.** The hayward was the keeper of the cattle in the common field or pasture, and it was his duty to prevent trespass on cultivated ground. There was a similar officer of the manor or religious house. As the hayward could assess damages against the owner of cattle, a little flattery was evidently considered a good investment. **hwon me pūnt hirə.** 'When men impound her (the cow).'

Page 203, l. 1. **hwon me mākeˇð mǫne.** 'When they (me) make complaint in town of anchoresses' cattle.' Probably refers to formal complaint as before the town reeve.

V. ROBERT OF GLOUCESTER'S 'CHRONICLE'—HOW THE NORMANS CAME TO ENGLAND

This metrical 'Chronicle' is found in an earlier and later form. To the earlier belong the following MSS.: Cotton Caligula A XI, Harleian 201, Additional 19,677 and 18,631 of the British Museum, and Hunterian MS. at Glasgow; to the latter, Trinity Coll. MS. R 4, 26 at Cambridge, Digby 205 of the Bodleian, Univ. Library Ee 4, 31 at Cambridge, Lord Mostyn's Library 259, Pepysian Library, Magdalen Coll., Cambridge, 2,014, Sloane 2,027 of the British Museum, and Herald's Coll. MS., London. There are editions by Hearne (1724) based on the Harleian MS., and by Wright in the Rolls Series (1887) based on the Cotton MS. above. Extracts are found in Mätzner ('Sprachproben,' I, 155), Morris ('Specimens,' II, 1), Wülker ('Lesebuch,' I, 55). The name of the author is based on l. 11,748, which tells us that 'Robert þat verst þis boc made' saw the battle of Evesham (1265), but otherwise we know nothing of him. Stow first connected him with Gloucester, and this is at least probable. More recently Strohmeyer ('Das Verhältnis der Hds. der Reimchronik Roberts von Gloucester,' 'Archiv für neuere Sprachen,' LXXXVII, 217) shows that the 'Chronicle' is the work of three different authors, the first writing about the end of the thirteenth century lines 1-9, 137, the second (Robert of l. 11,748) lines 9,138-12,049, and a third writing and somewhat extending the later version. As the work mentions the canonization of St. Louis in 1297, it could not have been written before that event, and was probably composed about 1300 in Gloucester. The language is therefore Southern of that district about the last of the thirteenth century. Our selection is from Cotton Caligula A XI, the purest text, and consists of ll. 7,395-7,513 as printed by Wright above.

The 'Gloucester Chronicle' relates the history of England from the legendary Brutus to 1271. It contains about 12,000 long lines (12,600 in the later version), riming in couplets. As to the number of stresses the lines are sufficiently irregular to occasion considerable difference of opinion. They seem to be based on the line of seven stresses with cæsura after the fourth, but many lines occur with only six stresses. The sources of the poem are Geoffrey of Monmouth, Henry of Huntingdon, William of Malmesbury, and other chroniclers.

The language of the 'Chronicle' is some three-quarters of a century later than that of the 'Ancren Riwle.' The OE. diphthongs have entirely disappeared even from the orthography, and the language is therefore typical Southern in most respects. Among vowels there is a largely increased use of *o* for *u*. Among consonants the selection often shows loss of initial *h*, and a frequent voicing of *hw* to *w* which is parallel to some extent with that of initial *f* to *v*. Besides *ss* (*s*) regularly represents *sh*.

Page 203, l. 14. **haþ**. Note the unusually frequent omission of initial *h* in this text. **15. hēr and ēr.** Other MSS., as Harleian 201, read *her and þer*, 'here and there,' perhaps a better reading. On the other hand, *hēr* is constantly used, especially in the Chronicles, for ' now, at this time,' and *þēr* may be due to a scribal misunderstanding of *hēr* in this sense. **17. Verst.** Strict Sth. would require *vürst*, but *e* for *ü* is found in a few words in this writer. See *herne* (*hērne*) 204, 8 for Sth. *hürne*, but the latter in rime (204, 18), and cf. Morsbach, 'Mittelengl. Gram.,' § 133, anm. 2.

Page 204, l. 1. **As þē hēnde.** ' As the courteous one,' so ' politely, courteously.' 3. **þē grẹ̄te ọ̄þ.** See Freeman's ' Norman Conquest,' III, 91. 14. **þat was al.** The Harleian MS. reads *þo* after *þat*, ' that then was,' &c., but it seems no material improvement. 27. **Godwine.** The crime was attributed to Godwine, though committed by followers of Harold I. William now gives this as a reason for making war on Godwine's son Harold. 28. **Alfrẹ̄d.** The brother of Edward the Confessor, son of Æthelred II and Emma of Normandy, the latter sister of William the Conqueror's grandfather. *Cosīn* is therefore very freely used, as often in earlier English and sometimes to-day. On Alfred's return to England from Normandy in 1036 he was seized, his followers killed or enslaved, and his eyes torn out at Ely. 31. **Seint Edward.** Edward the Confessor, who had promised the throne to William, so the latter said. That he was ' next of his blōd ' (l. 32) was of course true.

Page 205, l. 13. **Sein Walrī.** This is St. Valéry at the mouth of the Somme, with *w* for OF. *v*, as in Wace's *Waleri.* 14. **and abide mọ̄.** We should expect a sing. pret. to agree with *wende, hadde,* but the construction certainly changes in the following clauses, and there is no reason to suppose it may not here. Otherwise we must assume an infin., with an omitted *tō* or *for tō* expressing purpose. 21. **Ọ̄n of his kniʒtes.** The well-known story of William's stumbling as he set foot on the land is here omitted entirely. The words of the knight therefore lose point.

Page 206, l. 2. **As hē of nọ̄ mon.** ' As if he took account of no man.' 4. **þē ōþer bataile.** The battle of Stamford Bridge, Yorkshire, September 25, 1066, in which Harold had defeated and killed King Harold of Norway. 10. **þat upe þē Pọ̄pes.** ' That he should rest (*dō*) it upon the judgement (*lōkinge*) of the Pope.' 13. **him tāke nọ̄ lọ̄nd.** ' Give or deliver him no land.' For this sense of *tāke(n)* see the use of *bitāke(n).* 12. **Wẹ̄r Seint Edward.** Morris suggests ' whether,' and Mätzner ' if ' for *wer.* But the meaning is rather ' notwithstanding, although.' 27. **mī fader.** Really his ancestor Rollo, first Duke of Normandy, in the early tenth century, or a hundred and fifty years before. 31. **Richard.** This was Richard the Fearless, who reigned from 943 to 996. The French king who was taken prisoner was Lewis (Louis) IV.

Page 207, l. 7. **hē overcōm.** There are numerous references to this story in the chroniclers. See also Uhland's poems on the subject. 31. **Wiþ strọ̄nge targes.** OE. poems often refer to making a ' war-hedge,' or close protection of overlapping shields before the men. No doubt this custom is intended here. **düde hom noʒt,** ' did them no harm.'

Page 208, l. 14. **nọ̄ wille habbe.** ' Have no chance (*wille*) of striking (*dünt*).' 17. **al vor noʒt.** A phrase of varying import, ' all in vain, all for nothing.' Here it seems to imply lack of resistance, and so ' easily.'

Page 209, l. 15. **gọ̄stes.** See Freeman's ' Norman Conquest,' III, 11. 19. **Seint Calixtes day.** October 14, when Pope Calixtus is supposed to have been martyred in 222. 31. **Willam hit sende hire.** This is a mistake. Harold's mother offered a large sum for the body, but William would not give it up and had it privately buried by the sea-shore, so that the grave could not be identified; cf. Ramsey, ' Foundations of England,' II, 35 f.

Page 210, 1. 20. Vor þē mǫre. This line shows that the writer had no strong feeling either for or against the conditions he mentions. The antipathy of the races had long passed away.

VI. OLD KENTISH SERMONS

These ' Sermons' are found in Laud MS. 471 of the Bodleian Library, Oxford, and were printed by Morris in ' An Old English Miscellany ' (EETS., 49), p. 26. They represent Kentish of about 1250, so that they really precede in time the previous selection, but are placed here to bring together the two specimens of Kentish in the book.

But five of these sermons are preserved, all brief and simple in plan. They are translations from the French of Maurice de Sully (d. 1196), the earliest French sermon writer to give up Latin for the vernacular. They all follow the same general plan of text, narrative, exposition, application, as exemplified in the fourth and fifth, here printed.

An outline of Kentish grammar is given by Morris in the Introduction to the volume quoted above, and more completely in the Introduction to ' Ayenbite of Inwit.' The characteristic mark of Middle Kentish is the retention of Old Kentish *e*, *ē* for non-Kentish *y*, *ȳ*; cf. *prēde* (211, 20), *ēveles* (211, 23). Besides, Kentish agrees with the non-Wessex dialects of Old English in having *ē* for T. *ē*, WT. *ā*, WS. *ǣ*, and *ē*, *īe* for *i*-mutation of OE. *ēa*, *ēo*, while it is itself peculiar in having *ē* for non-Kentish *ǣ* by *i*-mutation of *ā*. It has also the diphthongs *ȳa* (*īa*) beside *ēa*, for WS. *ēa* or lengthened *ea*, and *au* from OE. *āw*. The special treatise on Kentish of the Middle English period is by Danker, ' Die Laut- und Flexionslehre der mittelkentischen Denkmäler ' (1879).

Page 210, 1. 24. godspelle of tōdai. This is indicated by the Latin rubric, *Dominica quarta post octavam Epiphanie*, and the gospel is Matt. viii. 23 f. Apart from slight lack of verbal agreement with the Vulgate, the last clause is from Mark vi. 48, and no doubt suggests a gospel harmony as the basis.

Page 211, 1. 15. blēpelīche. This form of the word also appears regularly in ' Ayenbite of Inwit.' As the OE. word is *blīpelīce* not *blȳpelīce*, the first *e* may be short or lengthened from a short *e* which took the place of shortened *i*. 16. Salus populi. Hardly a quotation from any one passage of Scripture, certainly not from Christ's words. It may have come from one or more Psalms which were regarded as messianic; cf. Ps. xxxv. 3 ; and for the last part xviii. 6; 1. 15; lxxxvi. 7 ; cxviii. 5. 24. wcrdle. The prevailing form in Kt., as shown by the next selection. 25. Quod ipse prestare. An expression used as a benediction and closing, *qui vivit et regnat Deus per omnia secula seculorum*. But it has various forms. 29. godespelle. Lat. rubric, *Dominica in sexagesima* ; gospel, Matt. xiii. 24.

Page 214, 1. 13. nǫn man w—t. The preacher quotes very freely as before. Reference seems to be to the interpretation of such passages as Matt. xxiv. 36, 42; Luke xii. 19-20. 14. for man. A common proverb, cf. ' Ancren Riwle,' p. 338 ; ' Ayenbite of Inwit' (Morris), p. 129. A poem on long life (' Old Eng. Misc.,' p. 156) begins :

' Mon mai longe lives wene,
Ac ofte him lieð þe wrench.'

VII. 'THE AYENBITE OF INWIT, OR REMORSE OF CONSCIENCE'

This work, in the handwriting of the author, is contained in Arundel MS. 57 of the British Museum. It was edited by Stevenson in 1855 and by Morris for the Early English Text Society (No. 23) in 1866. Extracts appear in Mätzner ('Sprachproben,' I, 60), Morris ('Specimens,' II, 98), Wülker ('Lesebuch,' I, 112). The author gives his name as Dan Michel (Michael) of Northgate (Kent), tells us that he was an Augustine monk of Canterbury, and that he finished the 'Remorse of Conscience' in 1340. His language therefore represents Kentish of the first half of the fourteenth century, about three-quarters of a century later than the preceding selection, and a quarter of a century later than the 'Gloucester Chronicle.'

The work is a translation of 'La Somme des Vices et des Vertus' by Lorens, a Benedictine monk of the later thirteenth century. It treats of the ten commandments, the twelve articles of faith, the seven deadly sins, &c., with occasional illustrative tales, anecdotes, or lives of saints. It is strongly allegorical throughout, but the style is not as pleasing as that of the 'Ancren Riwle,' or as simple as that of the 'Kentish Sermons.' Our selection, 'How to learn to die,' is based on the text of Morris above (p. 70 f.), where it begins the more constructive teaching of the book. Special monographs on the work are by Varnhagen, 'Beiträge zur Erklärung und Textkritik' ('Eng. Stud.,' I, 379; II, 27); by Evers, dissertation with same title (1888); by Konrath, 'Die lateinische Quelle zu Ayenbite' ('Eng. Stud.,' XII, 459).

In Notes to 'Old Kentish Sermons' reference was made to the principal treatises on the Kentish dialect, and to important peculiarities. In the present selection are to be noticed *ēa* (*ȳa*, *ȳea*) for WS. *ēa* or lengthened *ea*, and *uo* for OE. ME. *ō* (*ọ̄*) sometimes; cf. *guodes* = *gōdes* (215, 22); *guo* = *gọ̄* (218, 32). Among consonants *z* is regularly written for voiced *s*, clearly indicating the voicing of the latter when initial as well as when medial between vowels.

Page 215, l. 18. raþre þanne ssed. The figure is a common one in Scripture; cf. 2 Chron. xxix. 15; Job viii. 9; xiv. 2; Ps. cii. 11; cix. 23.

Page 216, l. 15. þē wȳse Cātoūn. Presumably Dionysius Cato, whose 'Disticha' were so highly regarded in the middle ages. Nothing exactly like this occurs, but for contempt of death see 'Disticha' at I, 22, IV, 22.   **21.** þrī dȳeaþes. Another interpretation of the three deaths occurs in 'Old Eng. Homilies,' II, 169.   **29.** damezēle Bēreblisse. Explained in the following clause, 'death that crowns and places (*dọ̄þ*) in bliss all the saints.' For a name made in the same way cf. 161, 6.

Page 218, l. 7. tō þē reward of. 'In respect of or to.' *Reward* has the sense of 'regard,' the cognate word.   **20.** ase zayþ Salomōn. Prov. xxiv. 16, which reads in the Vulgate, *Septies enim cadet iustus, et resurget*.

Page 219, l. 2. þēr ne may guo in. Referring to Rev. xxi. 27; cf. l. 32.   **15.** mọ̄re stranger. The double comparative appears thus early.

VIII. TREVISA'S TRANSLATION OF HIGDEN'S 'POLYCHRONICON'

The English 'Polychronicon' of Trevisa is preserved in at least four MSS., St. John's Coll. H I at Cambridge, and Cotton Tiberius D VII, Harleian 1,900, Additional 24,194 of the British Museum. Of these the first was printed by Caxton in 1482, and with a later version (Harl. MS. 2261) was edited by Babington for the Rolls Series. Extracts from Trevisa are found in Mätzner ('Sprachproben,' II, 343), Morris ('Specimens,' II, 235), and Wülker ('Lesebuch,' II, 205). Our selection is from Cotton Tiberius D VII, a contemporary MS. in pure Southern. The translator, John Trevisa, was vicar at Berkeley, then canon at Westbury, Gloucestershire. He finished his translation in April 1387, as he tells us. The language is therefore Southern of Gloucestershire in the last half of the fourteenth century.

The 'Polychronicon' was originally written in Latin by Radulphus or Ranulphus Higden of Chester. As the name implies, the work is a sort of history of the world, brought down to the year 1342. This Trevisa translated freely, adding here and there, and extending to 1387. Besides this he is supposed to have translated other works, though these cannot be proved to be his with certainty.

As to language, Trevisa's Southern shows no voicing of initial *f*, *þ*, and *s*, so far as orthography is concerned, but otherwise well represents the dialect. The selection shows *ā* for *hā* (*ha*), beside *hī* (*hȳ*), in the plural of the third personal pronoun; cf. 'Juliana,' p. 191.

Page 220, l. 1. **þē ȝēr of Hēlȳ.** The mediæval historians were fond of such union of sacred and secular history, and it was natural to their annalistic form of historical writing. **7. Vespāsian hys tȳme.** That is 69-79 A.D. **Pictes ōut of Scitia.** This tradition appears in numerous chroniclers back to Bede. That the Picts entered Britain later than the Britons is probably true enough. Cf. 221, 6. **17. Yn Vespāsian.** Based on Geoffrey of Monmouth, as the footnote shows. This accounts for many statements of which authentic history gives no confirmation. **18. Mārius.** Geoffrey of Monmouth, 'Hist. Brit.,' IV, ch. xvii. Arviragus, his father, is mentioned in ch. xiii f, but neither is known to be historical, though Geoffrey connects them with the Roman emperors, as here. The same may be said of Rodric in the same line. **21. Cathenēsia.** The present Caithness doubtless.

Page 221, l. 4. **Servius.** The commentator on Virgil, who lived in the last of the fourth and beginning of the fifth century, the time of Jerome and Augustine. **5. Agatirses.** Cf. 'Aeneid,' IV, 146, where occurs *picti Agathyrsi*, giving rise to the comment of Servius. **12. Maximus.** The chronicler has here confused Magnus Clemens Maximus (383-388) with Maximus Tyrannus (408-411), as shown by the references to Gratianus and Valentinianus in l. 14. He has also mistaken the name Tyrannus for a descriptive title. Marius is mentioned, not by Geoffrey but by Gildas. **21. Carausius.** Mentioned by Geoffrey, 'Hist. Brit.,' V, ch. iii. **Bassiānus.** Better known as Caracalla. Geoffrey recounts the death of Geta as in battle between the brothers for supremacy in the empire. **27. þwartǫver wal.** The wall of Hadrian from Newcastle to Carlisle and the Solway Firth, here called the *Scottysch*, that is,

the Irish sea. So also at 222, 2 and 22.   **28. Lodovīa.** Trevisa seems
to have misread the Latin Lodoneya, which he should have translated by
'Lodonia (Loudonia), Loudon.'   **30. Ninian.** Bede gives the tradition
regarding Ninias or Nyniaa ('Eccl. Hist.,' III, iv), but his date cannot
be definitely fixed. He is said to have died in 432.   **31. Brenicia.** Berenicia,
founded according to Bede in 547 A.D.

Page 222, l. 3. Duk Reuda. In his edition of Bede, Plummer says the
northern portion of County Antrim, Ireland, was called Dal Riada, after an
ancient leader who is supposed to have died in 165 A.D. Thence the name
was transferred to Britain with an Irish colony.

Page 223, l. 2. Flemmyngs. In 1111 Henry I established a colony of
this people in Pembrokeshire, Southwest Wales.   **11. þē Dānes.** Reference
is doubtless to the massacre on St. Brice's day, 1002; cf. Freeman, 'Norm.
Conquest,' I, 182, 312 f, 634 f.

Page 224, l. 7. drawe somwhat. An early recognition, perhaps, of words
borrowed from the Celts.   **26. þys manēre.** This whole paragraph is an
addition to his original by Trevisa himself, and is naturally of greatest interest
as a contemporary account.   **þē fürste moreyn.** The great plague of
1348-9. A second occurred in 1361-2, a third in 1369, and some reckon a
fourth in 1375-6.   **27. Jǫhan Cornwal . . . Richard Pencrych.** Both
Cornishmen, as it would seem from their names. It is not improbable that they
were both at Oxford, as was Trevisa, for the name Master John Cornwall appears
in the records of Merton College, and the names Pencrych (Penkrissh) and
Pencrych Hall are also found. The latter was about opposite Nunne Hall,
where Cornwall taught. See Stevenson's article on the ' Introduction of English
in English Schools ' in ' An English Miscellany,' p. 421.

Page 225, l. 1. of þē secunde Kyng Richard . . . nȳne. The ninth
year of Richard II began June 22, 1385, so that this part must have been written
in the last half of that year.   **6. disavauntāge.** This shows that Trevisa
was not in the least prejudiced against French, when properly added to a knowledge of the mother tongue. Cf. Robert of Gloucester at 210, 19, 20.
11. grēt wonder. Trevisa was scarcely more in the dark than many a later
historian of our language. Of course the changes in spoken English were due
to an unconscious variation in different districts, while *þē lǭngāge of Normandȳ*
—that is French in general—was taught and learned, with some idea of a
normal or standard form. Had Trevisa been more widely acquainted with the
French as was Chaucer, he would have known that there was some variation as
spoken in England and on the continent; cf. what Chaucer says of the Prioress,
Prologue to 'Cant. Tales,' 124 f.   **28. bycause þat þē kynges.** Just what
influence Trevisa supposed the kings to have had is not clear, but the relation
of the capital city and the center of government to the development of a standard
language is well known.

THE DIALECT OF LONDON

The importance of the language of the capital city to the development of standard English has led to the placing of four selections from London English in this place. A comparison of these will show how the language gradually changed, in most particulars, from Southern to Midland.

I. THE ENGLISH PROCLAMATION OF HENRY III

This proclamation occurs in two MSS., one in the Public Record Office, London, and the other in the Bodleian Library, Oxford. The first of these was published by Rymer (1816), by Ellis in 'Transactions of the Philological Society' (1868), and by Mätzner ('Sprachproben,' II, 54). The second was printed in 'Memorials of Oxford' by J. Ingram (1837), and by Skeat in 'Transactions of the Philological Society' (1880-1). Our text follows the first. As indicated, the 'Proclamation' was issued Oct. 18, 1258, so that we have here the English of some London scribe in the middle of the thirteenth century.

This 'Proclamation' is the earliest in English, after the disuse of the latter in public documents following the Norman Conquest; cf. the author's 'History of the English Language,' ch. v. It was issued to confirm to the people the 'Provisions of Oxford,' a charter of rights which had been wrested from the king. As indicated at the end, a copy was sent to every shire in England and to Ireland. The copy we print indicates Huntingdonshire as its destination, as that of the Bodleian indicates Oxfordshire. The writ was issued in both French and English; cf. the French version in Ellis's edition. For the 'Provisions' themselves, which accompanied this Proclamation, see Stubbs's 'Select Charters'; Adams and Stevens's 'Select Documents of English Constitutional History,' I, 56.

The language of this selection shows the use of the OE. diphthongs *eo*, *ēo*, *ēa*, and the ligatures *æ*, *ǣ*, as in Southern texts of the same period; cf. the 'Ancren Riwle' with the Midland 'Genesis and Exodus.' To these are added the digraph *oa*, probably an early writing of ME. *ǭ* from OE. *ā*. In other respects the language shows a mixture of Southern and Midland, probably characteristic of London English of the time. True Southern forms are those with *u̇*, *ü̇* = OE. *ȳ*, those with the prefix *i* (OE. *ge*), and such verbal forms as *bēoþ*, *habbeð*, *mākīen*; besides these the older inflexional forms, as *þān* (OE. *þām*), *Gode*, *loande*, and the noun plurals in *en*, as *wōrden*. For a fuller consideration of the language of this 'Proclamation' cf. Morsbach, 'Schriftsprache,' p. 161.

Page 226, l. 1. þurȝ Godes fultume. For the OF. *par le grace Deu*, Lat. *dei gratia.* 3. sēnd = sēndeð. 4. witen ȝē. The subjunctive of mild command. willen and unnen. Note the present plurals in *en*, Ml. forms, and compare the Sth. *bēoþ* (l. 5), *habbeð* (l. 7).   **5. ūre rǣdesmen.** Reference is made no doubt to the Committee of Twenty-four, twelve elected by the barons and twelve by the king, who had drawn up the 'Provisions' in the Oxford session.   **24. Bonefāce.** No special note is necessary on these prominent men of the time. Thirteen sign here, sixteen the corresponding French translation. The same thirteen in the Oxford copy, in the same order, probably indicates, as Skeat emphasized from another circumstance, that all the copies were alike in this respect.

Page 227, l. 8. And al on. This part does not occur in the Oxford copy. It suggests that we may have before us the original, on which this note was made for general reference.   **9. þǣre küneriche.** Note the peculiar use of the feminine form of the pronoun with a noun originally neuter.

II. ADAM DAVY'S DREAMS ABOUT EDWARD II

This text is found in Laud MS. 622 at the Bodleian Library, Oxford, and was edited by Furnivall for the Early English Text Society (69) in 1878. The 'Dreams' were written between 1307 and 1327, probably soon after the accession of the king. Of Adam Davy, the author, little is certainly known beyond what he tells us in his verses; cf. the 'Dict. of Nat. Biography.' The 'Dreams' have no special literary value, but are important as exhibiting the language of the capital city. Their purpose was doubtless to obtain favor of the king. Certainly, that Edward II should be 'emperor in Cristendom' (229, 33) could hardly have been expected long after his troublous reign began.

The change of the language of London from a mixture of Southern and Midland toward pure Midland is very evident in this selection. The notable Sth. characteristics are wanting, as *ü*, *ǖ* for OE. *y*, *ȳ*, though the Sth. open *ę̄* (WS. *ǣ*, Merc. *ę̄*) still prevails. Similarly the indicative present plural of verbs ends in the Midland *en*, not Sth. *eþ* (*eth*). Forms with the Sth. prefix *i* (*y*), OE. *ge*, are not numerous. Even at the beginning of the fourteenth century, therefore, the language of London was closely approximating the Midland dialect of Chaucer.

Page 227, l. 15. Prince of Wāles. This title, coupled with that of king in the preceding line, shows that the 'Dreams' relate to Edward II, the first to possess the former title and the only one of the Edwards of the fourteenth century to be both prince and king.   **20. Seint Edward.** Edward the Confessor, commemorated on Jan. 5, though the title might apply to the second Saxon king of that name.

Page 228, l. 21. þē decollācioūn of Seint Jǫn. The beheading of John is commemorated on Aug. 29.   **28. þē fęst of alle halewen.** All Saints' day, Nov. 1.

Page 229, l. 21. þē day of Seint Lucīe. That is, Dec. 13.

Page 230, l. 5. worþingniȝht. This has not been identified, but would seem, from the chronological order followed, to fall between All Saints and Lent. The only analogous compound in OE. is *dægweorþing*, 'celebration, festival,' but this does not assist us unless *worþingniȝht* could be some very important festival as, perhaps, the 'Purification of the Virgin,' Feb. 2.

Page 231, l. 2. **in clẹne leinte.** Already the old word for (OE. *lengten*) has been specialized to the clerical use, as in modern English. 20. **þē bẹryng of ōur Lẹfdȳ.** The birth of the Virgin Mary, commemorated on Sept. 8. 29. **For mē ne worþe.** 'On account of me,' 'nor shall be (shewed) to learned or unlearned.'

III. THE FIRST PETITION TO PARLIAMENT IN ENGLISH

This 'Petition' is preserved in a MS. of the Public Record Office, London. It was printed, quite imperfectly, in 'Rolls of Parliament,' III, 225, and later by Morsbach in 'Neuenglische Schriftsprache,' p. 171. As it bears the date 1386, the language is London English of the last quarter of the fourteenth century. Apart from its linguistic value the 'Petition' is highly interesting as giving us a most vivid conception of municipal politics in early London. The language presents few peculiarities, and these will be readily understood from the previous readings. The sentence structure hardly suggests one accustomed to the pen, and the document may easily have been composed by some clerk of the Mercery.

Page 232, l. 21. **as a membre.** One of the twelve great Livery Companies of the city, and having an important place in the government. 22. **wrọnges subtiles.** Note the OF. adjective following the noun and taking the plural form, no doubt a documentary usage rather than one colloquially common at the time. 24. **is tō bē tō.** 'Is to be by' or 'belongs to,' as we should say. 25. **at ọ day.** The Anglo-French text reads: *chescun an le jour de Seint Edward le Roy,* that is, Jan. 5 ; cf. note on 227, 20.

Page 233, l. 1. **Nicholus Brembre.** A member of the Grocers' Company and chief supporter among the people of Richard II, Brembre became mayor in 1383-4 by forcible means as narrated. In 1386 he secured the election of his accomplice Nicholas Exton (234, 25), and he himself became a councillor of the king. In the next year he was charged with treason and fled to Wales. He was brought back and hanged in London in 1388. 2. **Jọhn Northampton.** Also called Comberton. He was leader of the faction supporting Wyclif and itself supported by John of Gaunt. Elected mayor in 1381, for two years he was imprisoned in 1384 by Brembre, but was released in 1387 and fully restored to London citizenship in 1390. 13. **her mair.** While the preceding *nọ man* is sing., it implies the pl. and accounts for the plural pronoun. 14. **of his ordynaunce.** The Anglo-French text reads: *par son assent,* 'of his assent or party,' explaining the passage. 15. **grẹte quantitee of armūre.** This passage is a wonderful revelation of the political methods sometimes employed at this time in the freest and most powerful city of England. 17. **of withinne.** Those of the city, besides the 'straungẹrs of the contrē.' 27. **of whọmsọ it wẹre.** 'Of whatsoever it might be.' The *whọm* is dat.-acc., the older dat. of the neuter *what.* 28. **and it wẹre.** 'If it were.' Morsbach adds (*if*) after *and,* but this seems unnecessary as shown by the punctuation.

Page 234, l. 10. **tȳme ōut of mȳnde.** That *tyme* was omitted by mistake is clear from the Anglo-French text, *del temps dount nulle memoire* *ne court.*   **11. wolden.** A subject *wē,* which may have been omitted by the scribe, is implied in 'thē Mercerȳe or ōthere craftes' above. Or perhaps the writer intended another construction connected with the clause beginning *as* (l. 8).   **17. thē which thyng lȳke tō yōwre.** 'Which (*thē which thyng*) may it please your worthy lordship to be proved or disproved, that truth may show which of the two (*thē whether*) (is correct).' Here and several times the word *lordship* is an abstract, used instead of the plural but implying all the lords in council.   **24. for thei.** 'So that (for) they should not be known or continued,' equivalent to 'lest they should be known and continued.'   **25. Nicholus Exton.** Made mayor in 1386 by Brembre and his party. As here accused, he is said to have publicly burnt a book of good customs called the 'Jubilee.' This event marks the revival of the party of Northampton in the city.   **30. which of us ... thē Kyng sholde dō hym.** Note the anacoluthon. Brembre made a charge of being false to the king, and then offered immunity to any who would admit the charge, hoping thus to gain a good witness for his case.   **32. and if anȳ.** Note the indicative in the condition, perhaps in emphasis of the reality of the case.

Page 235, l. 3. thē mair that now̄ is. That is, Exton, mentioned above. **8, thēre men.** 'Where men,' implying also ' because.'   **13. bī suggestiōn.** This seems to imply that the offer by Brembre (234, 30) had been accepted by some, who had thus shielded themselves from punishment in other particulars. **16. tō bēn used.** The sense is : 'your lord's command is too great a thing to be used familiarly among or toward simple men, lest they, because of their ignorance in obeying it (*unwȳse tō sāve it*),' &c.   **24. brēre or Brembre.** To understand the play upon the name it must be remembered that our word *bramble* had, in both Old and Middle English, a form *brember.* For this period cf. *brember-flour* (Harl. MS. of Chaucer) for *brembel-flour* of the received text.   **27. thē which.** 'Which being granted by your lordship'; that is, what is implied in that clause (l. 29).   **30. as amōng us.** 'Among ourselves.'

Page 236, l. 2. vittailērs. Brembre's party 'had its strength among the . . . grocers, then dominant, and the fishmongers, whose monopoly it upheld against the claims of the populace.'—'Dict. of Nat. Biog.,' Brembre. **28. in thē sexte yēre.** That is, in 1384.

IV. CHAUCER'S 'CANTERBURY TALES'

It is needless to give details regarding the Chaucer MSS., or the numerous editions of his works. The extract is from the Ellesmere MS. as reprinted by the Chaucer Society, except for the few changes indicated in the footnotes. Nor is it necessary to say much of place and language, since every detail of this sort is so easily accessible. It will be generally admitted that the 'Pardoner's Tale' represents London English, in the last decade of the fourteenth century, that is, somewhat later than the time of the last selection.

For the originals of the story, so far as known, see the account in Skeat's 'Chaucer,' III, 439 f. For Chaucer's language it is scarcely necessary to give special references, as to Ten Brink's 'Chaucer's Sprache und Verskunst' (trans. as the 'Language and Metre of Chaucer'), and the numerous introductory treatises giving two or three Tales with grammar, &c.

Page 237, l. 7. **In Flaundres.** The place was perhaps so indicated in the original form of the story which Chaucer used. **18. they tōtēre.** One of the best illustrative passages is from the 'Parson's Tale': 'For Cristes sake ne swereth nat so sinfully, in dismembringe of Crist by soule, herte, bones, and body. For certes it seemeth that ye thinke that the cursede Jewes ne dismembred nat ynough the preciouse persone of Crist, but ye dismembre him more.'

Page 238, l. 2. **luxurīe is** = luxurī 's. The Scriptural passage (Eph. v. 18) reads in the Vulgate *Nolite inebriari vino, in quo est luxuria.* As the passage is quoted by Innocent III in 'De Contemptu Mundi,' which Chaucer translated, he may have taken it from that source. **6. thē stōrīes.** Reference is to the 'Historia Scholastica' of Petrus Comestor, called 'clerke of the stories' in 'Piers Plowman,' B VII, 73, and 'maister of storyies' by Lydgate. The plural is used because each of several parts of the work is called 'Historia.' The clause then means 'whoso has well perused the stories. **10. Senek seith eek.** Tyrwhitt suggested Seneca's Epistles lxxxiii: *Extende in plures dies illum ebrii habitum; numquid furore dubitabis? nunc quoque non est minor, sed brevior?* **14. fallen in a shrewe.** 'Fallen on a shrew or evil person.' **18. Ō original.** The line is metrically complete without *O*, which may have intruded from the preceding lines. **22. Corrupt was.** Cf. the 'Parson's Tale,' § 70: 'This sinne (glottony) corrumped al this world, as is wel shewed in the sinne of Adam and Eve.' **30. Ō glotonȳe.** The original of this (Ecclus. xxxvii. 32) was quoted by Innocent III in 'De Contemptu Mundi.'

Page 239, l. 2. **a belle.** The custom of the time as shown by the direction of Myrc, 'Instructions for Parish Priests,' l. 1,964 :
'Make þy clerk before þe ȝynge,
To bere lyȝt and belle rynge.'
4. **That ōon of hem.** MnE. 'one of them' rather than 'the one'; *that* is the old demonstrative with *t* retained before a vowel. Cf. *thē tōn, thē tōther.* **17. this pestilence.** This shows that the story is placed in the time of one of the great plagues which swept western Europe, perhaps that of 1348-9, the worst of all. **34. al ōnes.** The usual expression is *at ōnes*, or *al at ōnes.*

Page 240, l. 19. **God yow see.** Cf. 'Cant. Tales' B 156, D 2,169; 'Troilus,' II, 85, *God you save and see.* While the corresponding OE. word seems not to have the meaning of 'protect,' that is found in the case of the corresponding ON. form. **26. Ynde.** Taken as an example of the far distant land. Sometimes Greece is used in the same way. **31. Ne dēeth.** As Prof. Kittredge pointed out, the next seven lines are imitated from the first elegy of Maximian; çf. Skeat's 'Chaucer,' v, 287.

Page 241, l. 5. **my cheste.** That in which his worldly belongings were kept; usually found in old times at the foot of the bed in the bed-chamber. **13. In hōolȳ writ.** Lev. xix. 32; in the Vulgate, *Coram cano capite consurge.* **17. did.** 'Should do'; subj. mode.

Page 242, l. 31. **thē cut.** The shortest, as in a fuller account of a drawing of cuts in the Prologue, 835-845.

Page 244, l. 6. **at o͞ure owene wille.** 'According to our own pleasure,' a common idiom.   **19. Forwhy̆ the͞ feend.** Cf. 'OE. Homilies,' II, 39 (EETS., 53): 'Swa giveð ure Drihten leve þe devle to ben on þe swinisshe men þe ihc er of spec, and on hem to wuniende and hem to drenchende, and of here wit to bringinde and to driven fram unrihtw to oðer, fram eðeliche laste to michele, fram synne to synne, fram ivele to ivele, and et tan ande hem drencheð on shameliche deðe and mid hem to helle ledeð.'

Page 245, l. 5. **go͡on apaas.** The first part of the last word is not the article, as sometimes explained, but *a = on.* The expression means go *on foot*, and is thus indicative of the time required for such travel.   **29. cano͞n . . . fen.** The work of Avicenna (Ibn-Sina) is called 'Book of the Canon in Medicine,' and one part in the Latin version is named *fen*, from Arabic *fann*.

Page 246, l. 11. **goode men.** The metre requires that these two words should be read as a compound of two syllables.

GLOSSARY

THE Glossary is arranged on a strictly alphabetical basis, except as follows :
initially, þ (ð) occurs after t, and ȝ just before y, with which it belongs in its
modern development; but medially þ (ð) are placed after tg, and ȝ with g after
f, since these positions are most natural to the modern reader. Each word is
given in its normal form, rather than in the form in which it happens to occur
the first time, as usually done in the so-called glossarial index. But words
tending to lose a final element (usually final e), even in normal Middle English,
are sometimes given in the shorter form. The great diversity of ME. spelling
makes frequent cross-reference necessary, and such references have been freely
given. Only in case of Orm's forms with extra doubling of consonants has
normalizing occasionally been practised ; though in rare cases forms with
medial y for i have not been given. Orm's forms, owing to their importance,
are designated by (O) after them.

The etymology is given so far as the immediate form and language from
which the word is derived. To attempt more would have been to increase
unwisely the size of the book. Yet when some considerable change in the form
of the word has occurred a hint of this is given. Thus OE. nouns (mainly
feminines) which have assumed inorganic e in the nominative-accusative, under
the influence of the oblique cases, are indicated by adding the OE. gender, as
f., m., neut. So the stem-forms of OE., OF. verbs, when differing from the
infinitive, are added to explain ME. forms. In case of all irregular verbs,
weak, strong, and minor classes, the OE. present and preterit-singular are
given. With strong verbs a number in parentheses indicates the class, according
to the numbering of the Grammatical Introduction. An (R) denotes reduplication verbs.

Common abbreviations need no explanation, as sb., substantive, vb., verb,
inf., infinitive, &c. The following may be explained : n., g., d., a., nominative,
genitive, dative, accusative ; ns., ds., etc., nom. sg., dative sg. ; wk., weak ; wkv.,
stv., ptprv., anv., weak, strong, preterit-present, anomalous verbs, as in the
Grammatical Introduction. For other abbreviations, see list at the beginning
of the book. All references to the text are to page and line.

The manner of marking quantity has been explained in the Grammatical
Introduction. In addition some few diacritics have been added in the Glossary
to assist in differentiating certain sounds. Thus c = ch is marked č ; g = j in
judge (dȝ), ǧ ; g = y initially in stressed syllables, ġ ; o = older English u, ó ;
OF. u = ü, short and long, ú. Medial or final e, when certainly silent, is
sometimes marked ẹ.

A.

ā, see ān, adj., an, prep. adv., hē.

a, see an, art.

a, ā, interj., OF. a, Lat. ah ; ah 25,
23 ; ā, 140, 5.

ā, aa, adv., OE. ā ; ever, 196, 13.

Aarōn, sb., Lat. Aaron ; Aaron, 213,
4.

abashed, pp. as adj., abassen < OF.
abaïr, 3 sg. abaïss- ; abashed, 90,
30.

20

GLOSSARY

abbeye, abbaye, *sb.*, OF. abbeie; *abbey*; abbey, 108, 18; abbaye, 113, 21.

abbot, *sb.*, OE. abbod, infl. by OF. abbat (?); *abbot*, 1, 1.

abbotrīce, *sb.*, OE. abbodrīce; *office of abbot*, 1, 10.

abeğğe(n), *wkv.*, Kt. = Ml. abiȝȝen (abīen); OE. ābycgan–bōhte; *buy, pay for, atone for*; *inf.* abegge, 217, 30.

Abēl, *sb.*, Lat. Abel; *Abel*, 68, 10.

abelȝe(n), *stv.*, OE. ābelgan–bealg (3); *grow angry, make angry*; *pp.* abolȝe, 184, 20.

abēod, *see* abīde(n).

abettour, *sb.*, OF. abettour; *abettor*; *pl.* abettours, 236, 16.

abhomynāble, *adj.*, OF. abominable; *abominable*, 237, 15.

abīde(n), abȳde(n), *stv.*, OE. ābīdan -bād(1) *abide, wait for*; *inf.* abȳde, 108, 2; *pr.* 3 *sg.* abȳdeþ, 216, 23; *pt. sg.* abǭd, 64, 17; *pt. pl.* abiden, 35, 5; abide, 205, 14; *pp.* abiden, 32, 4. Sth. 3 *sg.* abīt, 180, 8; *pt. sg.* abēod, 187, 13.

Abirdēne, *sb.*, *Aberdeen*, 160, 15.

aboght, *see* abȳe(n).

abolȝe, *see* abelȝe(n).

abote, abōute(n), *see* abūten.

above, *see* abuven.

Ābraham, *sb.*, Lat. Abraham; *Abraham*, 33, 10.

abreide(n),*stv.*, OE. ābregdan–brægd (3); *draw out, spring up, awake*; *pt. sg.* abraid, 23, 15.

abrēke(n), *stv.*, OE. gebrecan–bræc (4); *break*; *pt. pl.* abrēken, 60, 3.

abrǭt (MS. a brod), *adv.*, OE. on brād; *widely, profusely, abroad*, 60, 20.

absence, *sb.*, OF. absence; *absence*, 117, 10.

absent, *adj.*, OF. absent; *absent*, 117, 5.

abūten (abūton), abōuten, obōut, abóte, *prep. adv.*, OE. abūton < onbūton; *about*, 1, 16; 3, 8; a-bōuten, 53, 12; obōut, 138, 31; abóte, 132, 14; abōute, 222, 24.

abuten, *prep.*, OE. on-be-ūtan; *without*, 178, 28.

abuven, buven, *adv. prep.*, OE. abufan < onbufan; *above*, 14, 15; abóve, 92, 31; buven, 178, 30.

abȳde(n), abyden, *see* abīde(n).

abȳe(n), abȳȝe(n), *wk.*, OE. ābycgan -bohte; *pay for, atone for*, MnE. *abide* by confusion with ME. *abīden*; *inf.* abȳe, 54, 19, abȳȝe, 55, 6; *pr. sbj. sg.* abȳ, 55, 6; *pp.* aboght, 238, 21.

ac, oc, *conj.*, OE. ac, oc; *but*, 2, 20; acc (O) 8, 25; oc, 1, 8. Sth. ah, 184, 24; auh, 197, 15.

accidental,*adj.*, OF. accidentel (al?); *accidental*, 235, 22.

accordandlȳ, *adv.*, Nth. *pr. ppl.* of accorden (OF. accorder) + lȳ; *accordingly*, 144, 23.

account, *see* acounte.

accūse(n), *wkv.*, OF. acuser; *accuse*; *pp.* accused, 106, 17; accusyd, 109, 13.

achtande, *see* aughtēne.

acorde(n), *wkv.*, OF. accorder; *accord, agree, reconcile*; *pr. pl.* acorden, 120, 5; *pt. sg.* acordede, 2, 13; *pp.* acorded, 244, 7. Sth. *pr. pl.* acordeþ, 225, 20.

acounte, acount (account), *sb.*, OF. cunte (conte),infl. by *vb.* acunter; *account*, 90, 28; acount, 156, 21; account, 155, 30.

acoupe(n), *wkv.*, OF. encuper < enculper; *accuse, inculpate*; *pp.* acouped, 92, 3.

acumbrī(n), *wkv.*, OF. encombrer; *encumber*; Sth.*inf.* acumbrī, 211,20.

acūpement, *sb.*, OF. acoupement; *accusation*, 42, 26.

Ādad, *sb.*, Lat. Atad; *Atad*, 35, 4.

Adam,*sb.*, OE. Adam, Lat. Adamus; *Adam*; *gs.* Adames, 32, 25; Adam, 67, 18.

adle(n), *wkv.*, cf. dialectal Eng. ad-dle; cf. ON. öðlask; *gain*; *pp.* addledd (O), 11, 1.

admiral, admirail, *sb.*, OF. amiral, admiral, admirail; *amir, Saracen ruler*, 37, 10; admirail, 46, 31.

adonward, *see* adūnward.

adoūn, adrad, *see* adūn, adrēde(n).

adrāȝe(n), adrawe(n), *stv.*, OE. *ādragan–drōg (6); *draw out*; *imp. pl.* adraweþ, 207, 19; *pp.* adrāȝe, 41, 25.

adrēde(n), Sth. adrēde(n), *stv.*, OM. drēdan (WS. drǣdan)–drēd (R); *dread, fear*; *pp.* adrad, 90, 29. Sth. *inf.* adrēden, 180, 2; *pr.* 1 *sg.* adrēde, 176, 6.

adrenche(n), *wkv.*, OE. ādrencan; *drown, drench*; *pt. sg.* adrenched, 73, 12; *pt. pl.* adrenchten, 197, 4.

adrīve(n), *stv.*, OE. ādrīfan–drāf (1); *drive, drive away*; *pp.* adriven, .197, 5.

adūn, adoūn, *adv. prep.*, OE. of dūne; *down*, 38,25; adoūn, 82, 11.

adūneward, adònward, *adv.*, OE. on dūn,*f.*, + ME. ward; *downward*, 201, 10; adònward, 208, 11.

advent, *sb.*, OF. avent, advent; *advent*; *ecclesiastically, the period including the four Sundays before Christmas*, 200, 2.

adversarīe, *sb.*, OF. adversarie; *adversary*, 239, 20.

ǣch, æfne, *see* ēch, ēven.

ǣfre, *see* ēver.

ǣft, æfter, *see* eft, after.

æh, æie, *see* ac, eie.

æiþer, ǣlc, (ǣlch), *see* eiþer, ēch.

ǣlder, *sb.*, Sth. = Ml. alder; WS. ealdor; *chief, prince*, 189, 23.

ǣldrihten, *sb.* as *adj.*, OE. eal + drihten; *almighty*, 184, 21.

ælle, ælmes, *see* al, almes.

æm, ǣm, ǣnde, *see* bē(n), ēm, ēnde.

ænī, enī, *indef. prn.*, OE. ǣnig; *any*; ænī, 178, 12; enī, 46, 26. Sth. ei, 47, 13; *gs.* eis in *phr.*, eis weis, *in any way, by any means*, 193, 27. Cf. anī.

ǣorl, *see* ērl.

ǣr, ǣresst, *see* ēr.

ærcebiscop, *see* archebischop.

ǣrd, ǣre, ǣrm, *see* ērd, ēre, arm.

ært, ærwe, *see* bē(n), arȝ.

ǣstēnde, *sb.*, eME. for ēst-; OE. ēastende (ēnde); *east end*, 186, 7.

æt, æten, *see* at, ēte(n.)

ætfōren, *prep. adv.*, OE. ætforan; *before*, 226, 24.

ǣvest, *adj.*, OE. ǣfǣst; *loyal, trusty*, originally *pious*, 5, 8.

ǣvre, ǣvert, *see* ēver.

ǣvric, ǣvrich, *see* everilc.

afānde(n), *wkv.*, OE. āfandian; *try, tempt*; *pp.* afānded, 180, 27.

affaytīe(n), *wkv.*, OF. affaitier; *affect*; *fashion, prepare*; *adorn*; *tame, subdue*; *pp.* affayted, 219, 27.

affēare(n) = offēre(n), *wkv.*, OM. offēran, WS. offǣran; *frighten, frighten off*; Sth. *pr. sbj. sg.* affēare, 193, 23.

affeccyōn, *sb.*, OF. affeccion; *affection*; *pl.* affeccyōns, 145, 8.

afforce(n), *wkv.*, OF. aforcer; *force, try, attempt*; Nth. *pr. pl.* afforces, 144, 12.

Affrican, *sb.*, Lat. Africanus, OF. *African (?); *Africanus*, 191, 25.

affter, *see* after.

afīnde(n), *stv.*, OE. gefindan (fīndan) -fand (fǫnd) (3); *find, obtain*; *inf.* afīnden, 178, 2.

afōre(n), afōrn, *prep. adv.*, OE. on foran; *before*, archaic and dial. *afore*, 109, 5; afǫrn, 117, 3.

afraye(n), *wkv.*, OF. effraier; *frighten, startle*; *pp.* afrayed, 148, 14.

afslē̞(n), *stv.*, Sth. = Ml. ofslǫn (slē̞n) WS. slēan–slōh (6); *slay, strike down*; Sth. *pp.* afslǣȝe(n), 186, 20.

after, aftir (aftyr), efter, *prep. adv.*, OE. æfter; *after, afterward*; æfter, 2, 9; aftterr (O), 8, 13; aftir, 49, 17; aftyr, 90, 25; efter, 1, 4; after, *afterward*, 236, 6.

afterward, aftyrwardę, *adv.*, OE. æfterweard; *afterward, afterwards*, 68, 3; aftyrwardę, 145, 21.

agǣnes, *see* agēnes.

agā̇(n), *anv.*, eSth. = Ml. gǫn (agǫn); OE. āgān–ēode; *go*; *pp.* agān, 182, 25.

agānę, agānis, *see* agein, agaynes.

Agatirses, *sb.*, Lat. Agatirsis; *Agatirses*, 221, 5.

agaynę, *see* **agein.**

agaynes, aȝayns, agānis, igaines, *adv. prep.,* OM. on(an)gegn infl. by ON. īgegn; *again,* 144, 11; agānis, 166, 12; igaines, 153, 6; agayns, 241, 14; oȝains (oȝayns), 101, 7. **Sth.** ayeins, 233, 4.

āȝe, āȝere, *see* **ōȝen.**

agein,ageyn,agayne,aȝein(aȝeyn), *prep. adv.,* OM. on(an)gegn (WS. ongēn, gēan) infl. by ON. īgegn; *again,* 50, 16; ageyn, 50, 25; agaynę, 109, 15; aȝeyn, 63, 21; aȝain, 183, 21. **Nth.** ogayn, 129, 13; ogaynę, 136, 7; igain, 149, 24; agānę, 167, 28. **Sth.** aȝān, 184, 15.

aȝeinward, *adv.,* OE. ongegnward WS. ongēanweard; *backwards,* 195, 33.

agelte(n), *wkv.,* **Kt.** = Ml. agilte(n); OE. āgyltan; *be at fault;* *pr. pl.* agelteþ, 216, 25.

āȝe(n), āge(n), *see* **ōȝe(n).**

āge(n), āg(āgh), *ptprv.,* **eME., Nth.** = Ml. ōge(n), owe(n); OE. āgan–āhte; *have, owe, ought;* eME. *pr.* 1, 3 *sg.* āh, 176, 2; *pr. sbj. sg.* āȝe, 188, 1; *pt. sg.* āhte, 5, 22; agte, 29, 21; auhte, 87, 28. **Nth.** *pr.* 1, 3 *sg.* awe, 136, 3; *pr. pl.* awe, 146, 20; *pt. sg.* aght, 134, 25; *pt. pl.* aghte, 147, 13.

aȝē(n), agēn, ayēn, *adv.,* OE. on gēn < gegn; *back; again,* 88, 13; aȝē, 36, 9; agēn, 22, 7; ayēn, 79, 28.

agēnes (agēanes), aȝēnes, *adv. prep.,* OE. on gēn < gegn; WS. on gēan; *against;* agēnes, 2, 11; agēanes, 2, 31. **Nth.** ogayns, 141, 8. **Sth.** aȝēnes, 222, 19; onȝēnes, 226, 18.

aȝeve(n), aȝeove(n), *stv.,* OM. āge-fan–gæf (WS. giefan–geaf)(5); *give up, surrender;* *pt. pl.* aiāven, 6, 32. **Sth.** *pr.* 1 *sg.* aȝeove, 196, 25.

ageyn, aȝeyn, *see* **agein.**

aȝȝ, *see* **ai.**

aghast, *pp.* as *adj.,* OE. *āgāstan, cf. gāstan; terrified, aghast; pl.* aghaste, 208, 2.

āȝhenn, *see* **ōȝen,** *adj.*

aght. aht, *adj.,* **Nth.** = **Ml.** ehte, eiȝte, **ONth.** æhta; *eight,* 132, 10.

aght, aghte, *see* **aht, aȝē(n).**

aginne(n), agynne(n), *stv.,* OE. āginnan–gan (3); *begin; pt. sg.* agon, 182, 11; *imp. sg.* agyn, 212, 13.

agō(n), *pp.* as *adj.,* OE. āgān; *agone, gone;* agō, 65, 1.

agōn, *adv.,* OE. *ongān < ongagn; again,* 27, 19.

agrayþi(n), -e(n), *wkv.,* ME. a + ON. greiþa; *prepare;* Sth. *pr. sbj. pl.* agrayþī, 219, 31.

aȝt, *indef. prn.,* OE. āwiht, āwht, aht; *aught, anything,* 39, 9. Cf. oȝt.

agt = aht, *sb.,* OM. æht, WS. eaht, *f.; council, care,* 21, 8; 22, 18.

agte, ahte (ehte), aucte, *sb.,* OE. æht, *f.; possessions, property, power, money,* 22, 26; ahte, 189, 4; aucte, 81, 6. **Sth.** ehte, 177, 31; eȝte, 226, 16; eihte, 202, 29.

āgte, āhte, *see* **āge(n).**

agülte(n), *wkv.,* **Sth.** = Ml. agilte(n); OE. āgyltan; *be in fault; pp.* agült, 176, 11.

agyn, agynne(n), *see* **aginne(n).**

ah, āh (āhne), *see* **ac, āȝe(n).**

ahōn, *stv.,* OE. ahōn–hēng (R); *hang; inf.* ahōn, 187, 26.

aht, *see* **aght.**

ahte, *see* **agte.**

ai, ay, aȝȝ, *adv.,* ON. ei, cognate OE. ā; *ever,* 15, 17; aȝȝ (O), 9, 3; ay, 87, 32.

aiāven, *see* **aȝeve(n).**

aiþer, *see* **eiþer.**

akenne(n), *wkv.,* OE. ācennan; *beget; pp.* akennet, 196, 29.

al, *adj.,* OM. al, WS. eal; *all,* 2, 10; *pl.* al (for alle?) 1, 15; ælle, 2, 26; alle, 2, 28; *gpl.* allre (O), 13, 30. **Sth.** eal (eSth.), 177, 30; *gs.* alles, in *pl.r.* alles cünnes, *of every kind,* 194, 29; *ds.* allen, 187, 33; *fas,* alle, 181, 5; *gpl.* alre, 182, 31.

al, all, *adv.,* OAng. al, WS. eal; *wholly,* 3, 25; all if, *although,* 160, 5.

Alamanīe, *sb.*, OF. *Alamanie; Germany*, *Almaigne*, 5, 31.

Albamar, *sb.*, OF. Albemar, Albemarle, Fr. Aumale ; *Albemarle*, 5, 7.

Albānia, *sb.*, Lat. Albania ; *Albania*, 221, 23.

āld, *adj.*, eMe., **Nth.** for Ml. ọ̄ld ; OAng. āld, WS. eald ; *old*, 1, 15 ; 130, 2. eSth. ēald, 176, 4 ; *gpl.* aldrene, 191, 27. Cf. ọ̄ld.

alderheȝest, *adv.*, OM. alra (WS. ealra) + *superl. of* OM. hēh (WS. hēah) ; *highest of all*, 104, 3.

alderman, *sb.*, OM. alderman, WS. ealderman ; *alderman, chief of a guild*, 117, 7.

Aldewingle, *sb.*, *Aldwinkle* (Northampton), 4, 24.

Aldithelē, *sb.*, *Aldithley* ; James of, 227, 7.

aldrene, *see* āld.

alẹste(n), *wkv.*, OE. ālǣstan ; *endure, last*, 180, 26.

Alexander, *sb.*, OF. Alexandre ; *Alexander, Bishop of Lincoln*, 2, 25.

Alfrẹ̄d, *sb.*, OE. Ælfrẹ̄d ; *Alfred*, 204, 28.

alhwet, *conj.*, **Sth.** = Ml. alwhat ; OE. eal + hwæt ; *until*, 218, 2.

ālien, *sb.*, OF. alien, *adj.* ; *alien, foreigner ; pl.* āliens, 225, 28.

Alisandre, Alisaundur, *sb.*, OF. Alisandre ; *Alexander* ; Alisaundur, 126, 3 ; Alisaundre, 205, 4.

alīve, *adv.*, OE. on līve ; *alive*, 40, 7.

allānẹ, *see* alọ̄n.

allas, *interj.*, OF. alas, halas ; *alas*, 56, 10.

allen, *see* al.

alles, *adv.*, based on OE. eall ; *wholly, altogether*, 197, 20.

allmahhtīȝ, *adj.*, OM. ālmæhtig, WS. ealmihtig ; *almighty*, (O), 13, 21.

allọ̄ne, *see* alọ̄n.

allre, alls, *see* al, als.

almāst, *adv.*, **Nth.** = Ml. almọ̄st ; OAng. almǣst-māst ; *almost*, 134, 26.

Almayn, *sb.*, OF. Allemaigne, Alemaine ; *Almaigne, Germany*, 106, 20.

almes, *sb.*, OE. ælmesse, *f.* ; *alms*, 100, 11 ; eME. ælmes, 3, 29. **Sth.** elmesse, 177, 4.

almesdēde, almousdēde, *sb.*, OE. ælmesse + OM. dēd, WS. dǣd, *f.* ; *almsdeed, almsgiving*, 91, 18 ; *pl.* almousdēdes, 147, 1.

almẹst, *adv.*, OM. almǣst, WS. ealmǣst ; *almost*, 207, 27.

almichtī, *see* almiȝtī.

almiȝt, *adj.*, OM. almæht, (almiht) ; *almighty* ; almighte, 47, 15.

almiȝtī, almihtī, (almichtī), *adj.*, OM. almæhtig (almihtig) ; *almighty*, 67, 10 ; almihtī, 193, 16 ; almichtī, 211, 27.

almousdēde, *see* almesdēde.

alneway, alwey, *sb.*, OE. ealne + weg ; *always*, 216, 10 ; alwey, 225, 29.

alọ̄n (allọ̄ne), *adj.*, OM. al, WS. eal + ān ; *alone*, 102, 3 ; allọ̄ne, 244, 13. **Nth.** allāne, 168, 8.

alọ̄nd, *adv.*, OE. an (on) + land, lọnd ; *aland, on land*, 222, 15.

alōwe(n), *wkv.*, OF. allouer ; *allow* ; *pr.* 1 *sg.* alōwe, 107, 30.

Alpīnus, Alpȳnus, *sb.*, Lat. Alpinus ; *Alpinus*, 221, 32.

alrefyrst, *adj.*, OM. alra, WS. ealra + fyrst ; *first of all*, 2, 12.

als, alsẹ, *conj.*, OM. al swa ; *as*, 1, 15 ; alse, 2, 20 ; alsẹ, 52, 20 ; alls (O), 9, 19 ; *yet*, 25, 8 ; *also*, 127, 3.

alsọ̄ (sō), *adv.*, OM. al swā (*sā) ; WS. eall swā ; *also*, 15, 1 ; alswā (eME.), 8, 9. **Nth.** alsā, 163, 15. **Sth.** alswọ, 215, 9.

alswic, *adj. adv.*, OM. al (WS. eal) + swylc ; *such, wholly such*, 2, 19

alswọ, *see* alsọ̄.

alþerbeste, *adv.*, OM. alra, WS. ealra + beste ; *best of all*, 87. 5.

alþermāst, alþirmāstẹ, *adv.*, **Nth.** = Ml. alþermọst ; OAng. alra, (WS. ealra) + māst ; *most of all*, 134, 9 ; alþirmāstẹ, 142, 27.

alve, *sb.,* OE. æɪfen, *f.;* *fairy, elf;* *gpl.* alven, 190, 27.

alwayis, *adv.,* OAng. al(ne)weg + es; *always,* 168, 6.

alwēldand, *pr. ppl.* as *adj.,* OAng. alwēldan; *almighty,* 140, 27.

alwey, am, *see* alneway, bē(n).

amad, *pp.* as *adj.,* OE. gemǣdan; *driven mad, insane,* 90, 30.

Amadāse, *sb.,* OF. Amadace; *Amadace,* 127, 2.

amēen, *see* amēn.

amāng, imānge, *adv. prep.,* eME., Nth. = Ml, amǫng; OE. on gemang; *among,* 9, 7; 129, 6. Nth. omāng, 137, 10; imānge, 154, 4.

amanges, *adv.,* OE. on gemong; *among, amongst,* 226, 21.

amēn, amēen, *adv.,* Lat. amen; *amen, so be it;* amǣn (O), 13, 24.

amendement, *sb.,* OF. amendement; *amendment,* 59, 12.

amende(n), Sth. amendīe(n), *wkv.,* OF. amender; *amend, satisfy,* 70, 8; *pp.* amended, 206, 30. Sth. *inf.* amendī, 218, 22.

amendyng, *sb. pr. ppl.,* ME. amenden; *amending, correction,* 101, 6.

amēnges, *adv.,* OE. on gemǫng infl. by gemengan?; *among,* 212, 18.

Āmēr, Āmerȳ, *sb.,* OF. Aylmer; Aymer; *Sir Amer de Valence, Earl of Pembroke,* 168, 27; Amerȳ, 169,18.

amēsùre, *adj.,* OF. a mesure; *fitting, suitable,* 229, 11.

amidde, amiddes, *adv. prep.,* OE. on + midde; *amid, amidst,* 206, 27; amiddes, 101, 5.

amǫng, *adv. prep.,* OE. on gemang (-mǫng); *among,* 18, 10.

amǫnges, *adv.,* OE. on gemǫng; *among, amongst,* 117, 17.

amōūnte(n), *wkv.,* OF. amunter (amonter); *amount, rise to;* Nth. *inf.* amōūnt, 156, 22.

ān(ā), *adj.,* eME., Nth. = Ml. ǫn; OE. ān; *one, alone,* I, 11; 129, 3; ā, 144, 25; *ds.* ane, 87, 7. Sth. *as.* ānne, 180, 17; *fds.* āre < ānre, 181, 1; *fas.* āne, 191, 19; *wkns.* āne, *al ne,* 178, 30.

an(a), *indef. art.,* OE. ān 'one' in weak form; *an,* 17, 1, 7; a, 3, 26.

an(ā), ane, *adv. prep.,* OE. an, on; *on, in,* 1, 14; ā, 1, 19; ane, 213, 13.

anēen, anān, *see* anǫn.

ancheisūn, *sb.,* AN. encheisoun; *cause, reason;* *pl.* ancheisūns, 199, 17.

ancre, *sb.,* OE. ancra; *anchorite, nun,* 198, 6; *gs.* without ending, 202, 15; 203, 1. Sth. pl. ancren, 198, 25.

and, andę, *conj.,* OE. and, ǫnd; *and,* 1, 2; annd (O), 8, 14; andę, 118, 13; *if,* 14, 1. eSth. ant, 191, 16; end, 177, 17.

Andrēas, *sb.,* OE. Andrēas, Lat. Andreas, later displaced by OF. Andreu; *Andrew,* 1, 19.

Andrew, *sb.,* OF. Andreu; *Andrew,* 135, 1.

andswarīe(n), *wkv.,* Sth. = MJ. answere(n), (-sware(n)): OE. and (ǫnd)-swarian (swerian); *answer;* *pt. sg.* andswarede, 181, 11; *pt. pl.* answarede, 184, 30.

Andwerp, *sb.,* OF. Andwerp, Antwerp; *Antwerp,* 162, 30.

āne, ānne, *see* ān.

aneoste, aneouste, aneuste, *adv.,* OE. on + ōfest, ēfest; *quickly, in haste;* aneouste, 185, 9; aneoste, 188, 33.

ānerlȳ, *adv.,* based on OE. ān, or ON, einarðr?; *alone,* 168, 5.

Āngel, *sb.,* OE. Angel, Ǫngel; *Angel, name of one of Arthur's followers,* 186, 26.

ānġel(l), aunġel, *sb.,* OF. angel; *angel,* 64, 20; *pl.* aungels, 104, 5; āngelęs, 105, 11; āngles, 219, 3. Nth. *gs.* without ending, āngell stevyn *angel's voice,* or *music,* 143, 3.

anger, *sb.,* ON. angr; *anger, grief, distress,* 106, 8.

Angle (anġle), *sb.,* OE. Angle; *Angle, English;* *pl.* Anglis, 222, 23; Sth. *dpl.* anglen, 191, 15.

Anġou (Anjou), Anġæu, *sb.,* OF. Anjou; *Anjou,* 5, 31; Angæu, 7, 9; Anjow, 226, 2.

angwys, *sb.,* **Nth.** = Ml. anguische (anguisse); OF. anguisse; *anguish,* 144, 19.

anhō(n), *stv.,* OE. onhōn-hēng (R); *hang, crucify*; *inf.* anhōn, 184, 26.

anī, anȳ, ǫnī, *indef, prn.,* OE. ǣnig infl. by ān; *any,* 3, 2. **Nth.** ānȳ, 147, 10. **Sth.** ǫnī, 226, 17; *ds.* ǫnīe, 226, 17; *pl.* ǫnīe, 226, 18. Cf. ǣnī, enī.

Anjow, *see* **Anǵou.**

anker, *sb.,* OE. ancor; *anchor,* 80, 28.

annd, *see* **and.**

Anne, *sb.,* OF. Anne; *Anne,* 131, 8.

annexe(n), *wkv.,* OF. annexer; *annex, add*; *pp.* annexed, 237, 26.

anoint, *adj.,* OF. *pp.* enoint < enoindre; *anointed,* 65, 7.

anǫn, *adv.,* OE. an, ān; *at once, quickly, anon,* 36, 11; anǫn riht, *right at once, immediately,* 198, 14. eSth. anǣn, 185, 8; anān, 187, 32.

anōþǝr (eME. ānōþer), **anōthirę,** *adj., prn.,* OE. ān + ōðer, *another;* ānōþer, 4, 19; anōthirę, 143, 25.

ǎnre, *see* **ān.**

Anselme, *sb.,* OF. Anselme; *Anselm,* 200, 9.

answare, answer, onswere, *sb.,* OE. andswaru; *answer,* 36, 22; answer, 236, 21; onswere, 192, 31.

answere(n), *wkv.,* OE. andswerian (swarian); *answer*; *pt.sg.* answeryd, 105, 19; answerd (ansuerd), 136, 7; *pt. pl.* answerden, 212, 8. **Sth.** onswerīe(n); *imp. pl.* onswerīeð, 200, 6; *pt. sg.* onswerede, 193, 15.

ant, *see* **and.**

Antecrīst, *sb.,* Lat. antichristus, modified by OE. crīst; *Antichrist, gs.* without ending, Antecrīst cōm, 133, 3.

anvīe, *see* **envīe.**

apaas, *sb.,* OE. on (an, a) + OF. pas; *in pace, on foot, apace,* 245, 5.

apēche(n), *wkv.,* OF. empecher; *hinder, impeach*; *pp.* apēched, 233, 28.

apēre(n), *wkv.,* OF. aper- < aparoir; *appear*; *inf.* apēre, 235, 30.

apert, *adj.,* OF. apert; *open, manifest,* 102, 8.

apeyre(n), *wkv.,* OF. enpeirer; *impair*; *pp.* apeyred, 224, 14.

apeyryng, *sb.,* based on apeyre(n); *impairing,* 224, 16.

apliȝt, *adv.,* OE. on pliht; *on my faith,* 42, 11.

apokalypsīs, *sb.,* Lat. apocalypses; *apocalypse,* 12, 23.

Apollō, *sb.,* Lat. Apollo; *Apollo,* 193, 19.

apon, *see* **upon.**

apostel, apostil, apostle, *sb.,* OE. apostol; OF. apostle; *apostle,* 131, 28; apostil, 135, 1; apostle, 213, 20; *pl.* apostlis, 132, 29.

appel, *sb.,* OF. æppel; *apple,* 67, 26. eSth. *ds.* epple, 198, 14.

apprǫche(n), *wkv.,* OF. aprocher; *approach*; *pr. ppl.* apprǫchyng, 236, 15; *pt. sg.* apprǫched, 234, 4.

aquelle(n), *wkv.,* OE. ācwellan–OM. cwālde (WS. cwealde); *kill, quell*; *imp. sg.* aquel, 44, 23. **Nth.** *pt. sg.* aquālde, 188, 12.

aqueyntaunce, *sb.,* NF. aqueintance, OF. acointance; *acquaintance,* 95, 19.

Aquitaine, *sb.,* OF. Aquitaine; *Aquitaine,* 226, 2.

aquynt, *adj.,* **Nth.** = Ml. aqueint (aquaint); NF. *pp.* aqueint, OF. acoint; *acquainted,* 170, 20.

ār, ārę, *adv.,* **Nth.** = Ml., Sth. ǫr; ON. ār, cogn. with OE. ǣr; *ere,* 128, 13; ārę, 138, 1.

ar, arę, *adv.prep.* OE. ǣr, by shortening; *ere, before,* 68, 23; 204, 7; arę, 36, 26. Cf. ę̄r.

arǎs, *see* **arīse(n).**

araȝt, araȝte, *see* **arēchen.**

ārblaste, *sb.,* OF. arbaleste; *arbalist, cross-bow,* 215, 18.

archebischop, *sb.,* OE. arcebiscop; *archbishop,* 226, 24; eME. ærcebiscop, 2, 9.

archēr, *sb.,* OF. archier; *archer,* 168, 3.

āre, *see* **ān.**

ǣrę, arę, *see* ār, ar, bē(n).

āre, *sb.*, eME., Nth. = Ml. ǭre ; OE.
ār, *f.* ; *favor, grace*, 11, 1.

arecche(n), *wkv.*. OE. āreccan–reahte ;
expound, explain, 182, 29.

arēche(n), *wkv.*, OE. ārǣcan–rǣhte
(rāhte) ; *reach* ; *pt. sg.*, araȝte, 47,
12 ; *pp.* araȝt, 43, 17.

aredde(n), *wkv.*, OE. āhreddan ;
deliver, save ; *inf.* aredde, 43, 19.

Aremouth, *sb.*, earlier Eremouþ ;
Yarmouth on the Isle of Wight,
164, 8.

ǣre(n), *see* bē(n).

arēowe(n), *stv.*. eSth. = Ml. (a)re-
we(n) ; OE. *āhrēowan–hrēaw (2) ;
commiserate, repent ; *pr. sbj. sg.*
arēowe, 198, 32.

arēre(n), Kt. arēre(n), *wkv.*, OE.
ārǣran ; *raise, rear* ; *inf.* arēre,
205, 16 ; *pp.* arēred, 200, 29 ; arērd,
205, 32. Kt. *inf.* arēre, 218, 22.

arest, *sb.*, OF. arest ; *arrest, stoppage*,
168, 9.

arēsūne(n), *wkv.*, AN. araisuner ; *call
to account* ; *pt. sg.* arēsūnede, 213, 16.

aręwe, arrow, *sb.*, OE.earh, *f.* ; *arrow* ;
aręwe, 195, 33 ; arrow, 168, 19.

arȝ, *adj.*, OE. earh, *pl.* earge ;
cowardly ; *pl.* ærwe, 176, 19.

Argail, *sb.*. Argyle (?), 222, 14.

Argante, *sb.*, OF. Argante? ; *Argante*,
190, 27.

ariȝt, aryȝt, aryht, *adv.*, OE. on(an)
+riht ; *rightly, aright*, ariȝt, 35,
24 ; aryȝt, 215, 3.

arīse(n), *stv.*, OE. ārīsan–rās (1) ;
arise ; *pr.* 3 *sg.* arīst = arīseþ, 40, 15 ;
imp. sg. arīs, 40, 18 ; arīsę, 67, 13 ;
pt. sg. (eME. arās, 181, 8) ; arǭs,
39, 28 ; arǭǫs, 211, 3 ; *pt. pl.* arisen,
197, 3 ; *pp.* arise(n), 40, 30.

Aristotill, Arystotill, *sb.*, OF. Aristotle ; *Aristotle*, 144, 10, 24.

arm, *sb.*, OE. arm, earm ; *arm*, 67, 8.
eSth. ærm, 181, 8.

arm, ærm, *adj.*, OE. earm ; *poor*.
eSth. ærm. 188, 16 ; arm, 222, 6.

arme(n), *wkv.*, OF. armer ; *arm* ;
pt. sg. armyd, 112, 20 ; *pp.* armed,
227, 16.

armes, *sb. pl.*, OF. armes ; *arms*, 209,
10.

Armorȳc, *sb.*, OF. Armorique ; *Ar-
morica*, 220, 5.

armūre, *sb.*, OF. armure ; *armor*,
233, 16.

armyd, *see* arme(n).

armyng, *sb.*, OF. armer ; *arming* =
armor, 173, 6.

arn, *see* bē(n).

arǭs, arǭǫs, *see* arīse(n).

arrow, *see* aręwe.

arrȳsęr, *sb.*, based on OE. arīsan ;
ariser, revolter, 234, 12.

art, *sb.*, OF. art ; *art*, 38, 9.

Arðūr, Arthōūr, *sb.*, OF. Arthour ;
Arthur, 181, 8 ; *ds.* Arthūre, 181,
2 ; Arthōūr, 126, 9.

Arvirāgus, *sb.*, Lat. Arviragus ;
*Arviragus, mythical king of
Britain*, 220, 18.

aryȝt, aryht, *see* ariȝt.

as, *see* asse.

as, asę, *adv.*, OM. al swā, WS. eal
swā ; *as, so, also*, 29, 4 ; asę, 186,
12.

asayle(n), *see* assayle(n).

asę, asent, *see* as, assent.

asīse, assȳs, *sb.*, OF. assise ; *assize*,
152, 18 ; assȳs, 147, 20.

aske(n), Sth. askīe(n), *wkv.*, OE.
ācsian by late metathesis of cs (ks) ;
ask ; *inf.* aske, 89, 30 ; *pr.* 1 *sg.*
aske, 89, 31 ; *pr. sbj. pl.* asken,
198, 30 ; *pt. sg.* askede, 198, 17.
Nth. *pp.* askit, 171, 4. Sth. *pr.
sbj.* askī, 200, 18.

askunge, *sb.*, OE. ācsung, *f.* by late
metathesis ; *asking, request*, 200, 6.

aslawe, *see* aslē(n).

aslē(n), *stv.*, Sth. = Ml. aslǭ(n),
aslę̄(n) ; WS. āslēan–slōh(g), (6) ;
kill, slay ; *pp.* aslawe, 207, 28.

aslēpe, *adv.*, OE. on slēpe ; *asleep*,
40, 22.

aslēpe(n), *st. wkv.*, OM. *āslēpan
-slēp (WS. slǣpan), (R) ; possibly
OAng. geslēpa, *wkv.* ; *fall asleep,
be overcome of sleep* ; *pp.* aslēped,
40, 8.

asoile(n), *see* assoyle(n).

asper, *adj.*, OF. aspre; *harsh, cruel,*
103, 25.

assayle(n), *wkv.*, OF. assailer; *assail,
attack*; *inf.* assayle, 112, 21; *pp.*
asayled, 60, 13.

asse, *sb.*, OE. assa; *ass*, 31, 21; assę,
89, 26; as, 52, 19.

assemble(n), *wkv.*, OF. assembler;
assemble, come together, 163, 7.

assent, assentę, asent, *sb.*, OF.
assent, asent; *assent*, 141, 4;
assentę, 147, 3; asent, 117, 26.

assente(n), *wkv.*, OF. assentir;
assent; *pr.* I *sg.* assente, 115, 7;
pt. pl. assentyd, 105, 17. **Nth.** *pt.
sg.* assentit, 171, 7.

assoyle(n), asoile(n), *wkv.*, OF.
assoldre; *pr. st.* assoil-; *absolve*;
imp. sg. assoylę, 111, 15; *pr. sbj.*
assoyl, 165, 15; *pt. sg.* assoyled,
111, 19 : asoilede, 205, 7.

assȳs, *see* **asīse**.

asterday, *sb.*, OE. ēasterdæg by
shortening; *easterday*, 121, 32.

astrengþe(n), *wkv.*, OE.*āstrengðian,
or based on ME. strengþe;
strengthen; *pp.* astrengþed, 211,
11.

astronomȳen, *sb.*, OF. astronomien;
astronomer, astrologer, 145, 17.

astünte(n), *wkv.*, Sth. = Ml. astinten;
OE. āstyntan; *cease*; *inf.* astünten,
201, 4.

asunīe(n), *wkv.*, OF. essonnier,
essoigner; *excuse*; *inf.* asunīen,
197, 20.

aswīnde(n), *stv.*, OE. āswindan
(swīndan) - swand (swǭnd), (3);
vanish, pass away; *pr.* 3 *sg.*
aswīndeð, 196, 17.

at, *prep. adv.*, OE. æt; *to, at, from,
according to*; æt, 2, 24; at, 8, 9;
att (O), 9, 2; at ǭn, *at one, friendly,*
115, 11; att Godd (O), *from God,*
10, 27; at hym, *from him,* 89, 19.
Nth. at (used for tō), 128, 9. **Sth.**
et, 192, 23. *See also* **atte**.

at, *see* **þat**.

āth, āthę, *sb.*, eME., **Nth.** = Ml. ǭþ;
OE. āð; *oath*, 2, 29; āthę, 145, 26;
pl. āthas, 6, 3.

aðele, *adj.*, OE. æðel; *noble, generous*;
Sth. ds. aðelen, 185, 1; *superl.*
aðelest, 183, 10.

atsāke(n), *stv.*, OE. ætsacan-sōc (6);
deny, disown; eME. *pr.* 1 *sg.*
atsake, 184, 24.

atstǭnde(n), *stv.*, OE. ætstandan
(stǭndan)-stōd (6); *stand, stand
by*; *inf.* atstǭnden, 182, 10.

atte = at þe, *prep.* + *dem. prn.*, OE.
æt sē, lOE. þē; *at the, at,* 17,
26.

atter, *sb.*, OE. ātor, attor; *poison,
pus*, 180, 22.

atvǭre, *adv.*, Sth. = Ml. atfǭre; OE.
ætforan; *before*, 205, 9.

atwinne, *adv.*, OE. on(an) + ON.
twinnr; *in two, asunder*, 65, 15.

atwīst, *see* **atwīte(n)**.

atwīte(n), *stv.*, OE. ætwītan-wāt
(1); *blame, twit*; *pr.* 3 *sg.* atwīst =
atwīteþ, 40, 16; *pr. pl.* atwīte, 37,
12; *imp. pl.* etwīteð, 200, 21.

atwō, Sth. atwǭ, *adv.*, OE. an + twā;
in two, in twain, 39, 6. **Sth.**
atwǭ, 239, 15.

atȳwen, *wkv.*, OM. ætēwan (-īwan?),
WS. ætīewan (-ȳwan); *show,
appear*; *pt. sg.* atȳwede, 5, 1.

Aubemarle, *sb.*, OF. Albemarle,
Aubemarle; *Albemarle*, 227, 5.

aucte, *see* **agte**.

aughtene = aughtende, achtande,
adj, **Nth.** = Ml. ehteþe; OAng.
æhtoðe; *eighth*, 147, 18; achtande,
152, 7.

auh, auhte, *see* ac, āge(n).

aumenēre, *sb.*, OF. almonier, au-
monier; *almoner, dispenser of alms,*
88, 21.

aungel, *see* **ängel**.

aunter, auntour, *see* **aventūre**.

Austīn, Austyn, *sb.*, OE. Austīnus,
Lat. Augustīnus; *Augustine, Austin*;
Awwstīn (O), 8, 17; Austyn, 124,
10.

auter (awter), *sb.*, OF. auter, alter;
altar, 76, 24; awter, 122, 20; *ds.*
autere, 231, 24.

availe(n), avail(en), *wkv.*, OF. vaile
< valoir; *avail, profit*; *pt. sg.*

328 GLOSSARY

availede, 60, 15. Nth. *inf.* avail,
129, 8 ; avālę, 167, 25.
avalle(n), *wkv.*, Sth. = Ml. afallen ;
OM. ā fellan (WS. ā fiellan) by
confusion with fallan (WS. feallan)?
fell, cut down, destroy, 187, 25.
Avalūn, *sb.*, AN. Avalun ; *Avalun,
Avalon,* 190, 26.
avarīce, *sb.*, OF. avarice ; *avarice,*
246, 12.
avaroūs, *adj.*, OF. averous ; *avari-
cious,* 88, 24.
avaunce(n), *wkv.*, OF. avancer ; *advance* ; *inf.* avaunce, *pp.* avaunsed,
106, 6.
avauntāğe, *sb.*, OF. avantage ; *advantage,* 225, 4.
āvē, *sb.*, Lat. ave ; *ave, hail,* 122, 28.
avēnge, *see* avō(n).
aventūre (aunter), Nth. aventūr
(-oūr, -er), *sb.*, OF. aventure ;
adventure ; Nth. aventūr, 168, 16 ;
auntoūr, 154, 9 ; *pl.* aunters, 126,
12 ; an aunter, [*it is*] *a venture,*
209, 4.
aventūre(n), *wkv.*, OF. aventurer ;
adventure ; *inf.* aventure, 106, 11.
aver, *see* ever.
avō(n), *stv.*, Sth. = Ml. afōn ; OE.
āfōn-fēng (R) ; *receive, take* ; *pt.
pl.* avēnge, 209, 11.
avorn, *adv. prep.*, eSth. = Ml. afǫren
(forn) ; OE. on foran ; *before* ; avorn
on, *opposite,* 186, 11.
avōw, *sb.*, OF. *avou, cf. avouer, *vb.* ;
avow, vow, 239, 33. Cf. vōw.
Avycen, *sb.*, OF. Avycen ; *Avicen,
Avicenna,* 245, 28.
avȳs, avȳse, *sb.*, OF. avīs ; *advice,*
232, 25 ; avysę, 105, 20.
avȳse(n), *wkv.*, OF. aviser ; *advise* ;
pp. avȳsed, 239, 28.
awai, away, awey, awayę, *adv.*,
OE. on weg ; *away,* 29, 18 ; awey,
98, 31 ; oway, 102, 12 ; awayę,
143, 25. Nth. oway, 136, 5.
awāke(n), *stv.*, OE. *awacan-wōc
(6) ; *awake* ; *pt. pl.* awǫke, 41, 23.
awākene(n), *wkv.*, OE. awacnian ;
awaken, arise ; eME. *inf.* awakenin,
193, 12.

awākīe(n), *wkv.*, Sth. = Ml. a-
wāke(n) ; OE. āwacian ; *awake* ;
pt. pl. awākede, 211, 4.
awe, awei(y), *see* āge(n), awai.
awēlde(n), *wkv.*, OM. geweldan
(wēldan), WS. wieldan ; *rule, con-
strain* ; *inf.* awēlden, 195, 14.
awēnde(n), *wkv.*, OE. āwendan
(wēndan) ; *turn away* ; *pp.* awent,
221, 12.
awin, *adj.* < *pp.* Nth. = Ml. ǫwen ;
OE. āgen ; *own,* 137, 4.
awinne(n), *stv.*, OE. gewinnan-wann
(wǫnn) (3) ; *win,* 46, 4.
awite(n), *ptprv.*, OE. gewitan-wiste ;
know ; *pt. sg.* awyste, 176, 17.
awōke, *see* awāke(n).
awōld, *sb.*, OM. gewald (gewāld),
WS. geweald ; *power,* 21, 18.
awondrīe(n), *wkv.*, Sth. = Ml.
awundre(n) ; OE. āwundrian ;
amaze, surprise ; *pt. sg.* awondrede,
211, 9.
awręke(n), awrǣke(n), *stv.*, OE.
āwrecan-wrǣc (5) ; *drive away,
avenge* ; *inf.* awręke, 42, 2 ; (eME.
awreken, 183, 6) ; *pr.* 3 *sg.* awrękþ,
217, 15 ; *imp. pl.* awrękeþ, 42, 20 ;
pp. awręke, 67, 30 ; (eME. awrǣke,
184, 29).
awter, Awwstīn, *see* auter, Austīn.
awyste, *see* awite(n).
ax, *sb.*, OE. eax, *f.* ; *ax* ; *pl.* axis,
169, 27.
axe(n), eME. axen, Sth. axīe(n),
wkv., OE. ācsian (āscian) ; *ask* ;
eME. *inf.* āxen, 5, 19 ; *pt. sg.*
axede, 181, 10 ; *pt. pl.* axede, 36,
19.
axtrē, *sb.*, OE. eax + trēo, *perh.*
*eaxtrēo ; *axeltree,* 124, 29.
ay, ayeins, *see* ai, agaynes.
ayeinsaie(n), *wkv.*, OE. ongegn +
ME. saie(n), seie(n) ; *gainsay.
deny, *pp.* ayeinsaide, 234, 8.
ayeinstande(n), stǫnde(n), *stv.*,
OE. ongegn + standan-stōd (6) ;
stand against, withstand ; *inf.*
ayeinstande, 234, 10 ; ayeinstǫnde,
236, 26.
ayēn, *see* aȝēn.

ayerę, *sb.*, OF. air ; *air*, 143, 27.
aywhǫre, *adv.*, ON. ei + hvār, cogn.
  with OE, āhwēr, āwer, *everywhere*,
  88, 26.

B.

bā, *adj.*, eME., Nth. = Ml. bǫ ; OE.
  bā, *f.* of bēgen ; *both*, 8, 16.
baar, *see* bār, *adj.*
bac, *sb.*, OE. bœc ; *back*, 52, 18.
bācin, *sb.*, OF. bacin ; *basin*, 39, 21.
bad, badde, bæd, *see* bidde(n).
bæron, *see* bęre(n).
bal, *sb.*, OE. *bal ; *ball, ball playing*,
  124, 31.
balaunce, *sb.*, OF. balance ; *balance*,
  91, 21.
bāld, *adj.*, eME,, Nth. = Ml. bǫld ;
  OAng. bald, bāld ; *bold*, 126, 7.
  eSth. *fds.* bāldere, 184, 30.
bāldelȳ, *adv.*, OAng. bāldlīce ; *boldly*,
  164, 28.
bāldīe(n), *wkv.*, eME., Nth. = Ml.
  bǫlde(n) ; OM. baldian, bāldian,
  WS. bealdian ; *embolden, bear oneself bravely* ; Sth. *pp.* bālde, 192,
  30.
bāle, *sb.*, OE. bealu ; *bale, harm,
  calamity*, 18, 30.
balcful, *adj.*, eME. = Ml. bāleful ;
  OE. bealuful ; *baleful* ; *wk.* 195,
  11.
bali = bale, eME. = Ml. bāle ; *sb.*
  <*adj.*, OE. *bealo, *adj.* ; *baleful,
  evil one*, 195, 32.
bān, bānd *see* bǫn, bīnde(n).
banēr, *sb.*, OF. banere ; *banner*, 159,
  13.
baneūr, *sb.*, OF. baneur ; *standara-
  bearer*, 207, 27.
Banocburn, Bannok burn, *sb.*,
  Bannockburn, 160, 14 ; þē Bannok
  burn, 160, 16.
baptīs(e), *wkv.*, Nth. = Ml. bap-
  tīse(n) ; OF. baptiser ; *baptize* ; *pt.
  sg.* baptīst, 131, 22.
baptist, *sb.*, OF. baptiste ; *baptist* ;
  þē Baptist Jǫhan, 131, 21.

baptīsyng, *pr. ppl.* as *sb.*, *baptizing* ;
  Jǫnes baptīsyng, *John's baptizing*,
  131, 25.
bar(e), bāre *see* bęre(n).
bār, *sb.*, eME., Nth. = Ml. bǫr ; OE.
  bār ; *boar*, 195, 12.
bār, bāre, *adj.*, OE. bær ; *bare*, 17,
  14 ; baar, 221, 18.
bāre, *sb.*, OF. barre ; *bar* ; *pl.* bāres,
  124, 31.
bāre, *sb.*, ON. bāra = OE. bæra ;
  tidal wave, bore, p. 250.
bāret, *sb.*, OF. barat ; *debate, trouble,*
  148, 10.
bārfōt, *adj.*, OE. bærfōt ; *barefoot* ;
  pl. 235, 9.
bargāne, *sb.*, 1Nth. = Ml. bargaine ;
  OF. bargaine ; *bargain*, 173, 9.
barm, barmę, *sb.*, OE. bearm ; *bosom,
  lap* ; barmę, 89, 3.
bārn, *sb.*, OE. bearn ; *child*, 146, 32.
barnāgę, *sb.*, OF. baronage, barnage ;
  baronage, 42, 1.
Barnard, *sb.*, OF. Barnard ; *Barnard
  of Toulouse*, 114, 28.
barnhęd, -hēd, *sb.*, ONth. *barnhæd ;
  childhood, 131, 20.
barōn(ōun), *sb.*, OF. baron, AN.
  barun ; *baron* ; *pl.* barōns, 42, 6.
baselard, *sb.*, OF. baselarde ; *dagger*,
  120, 28.
basenet, *sb.*, OF. basinet ; *helmet,
  basinet*, 112, 23.
Bassiānus, *sb.*, Lat. Bassianus ; *Bassianus*, 221, 21.
bastard, *sb.*, OF. bastard ; *bastard*,
  203, 22.
batailę (batayle), batail (batayl),
  sb., OF. bataille ; *battle* ; batail,
  101, 22 ; bat019ylę, 110, 14 ; bataile,
  157, 10 ; batayl, 160, 14.
bāte(n), for abāte(n), *wkv.*, OF.
  abatre ; *abate, bate* ; *cast down,
  abolish* ; *inf.* bāte, 59, 3.
bāthe (bāth), *adj. prn.*, eME., Nth.
  for Ml. bǫþe ; ON. bāþir ; *both,
  also*, 3, 3 ; bāth, 129, 5. Sth. *dpl.*
  bāðen, 191, 18.
bāpe(n), Sth. bāðīe(n), *wkv.*, OE.
  baðian ; *bathe* ; *pp.* bāþed, 65, 5.
  Sth. *inf.* bāðīen, 195, 18.

baude, *sb.*, NF. *baude; *bawd*; *pl.*
baudes, 237, 23.

baudrike, *see* bawdrike.

Bauston, MS. Hauston, *sb.*, *Bauston*,
62, 6 [see note].

Bavēre, *sb.*, *Bavaria*, 162, 9.

bawdryke, *sb.*, OF. baldret, *baldrik;
baldrick, belt, 120, 28.

bayn, baynę, *adj.*, ON. beinn;
straight, prompt, 138, 25.

bē, be, *see* bē(n), bī.

bęast, *see* bęst.

bęat, bęate(n), *see* bēdę(n), bēte(n).

beautee, beutē, *sb.*, OF. beautē;
beauty, 244, 11 ; beutē, 130, 16.

bebirīe(n), *wkv.*, OE. bebyrgan
(byrigan) ; *bury* ; *pt. pl.* bebirīeden,
2, 2 ; bebyrīed, 5, 2 ; *pp.* bebyrīed,
7, 26.

Bec, *sb.*, OF. Bec ; *Bec* (Normandy),
5, 17.

bęc, *sb.*, OF. bec (lengthened) ; *beak*,
15, 13.

becume(n), *see* bicume(n).

bed(d), bedden, *see* bidde(n).

bed (bedde), *sb.*, OE. bedd ; *bed*, 41,
17 ; *ds.* bedde, 38, 23 ; *pl.* bedes,
74, 3.

Bēda, *sb.*, Lat. Beda ; *Beda, Bede*,
221, 29.

bedde(n), *wkv.*, OE. beddian ; *put to
bed* ; *inf.* bedde, 77, 24.

będe, eME. bede, *sb.*, OE. gebed ;
prayer, petition, MnE. *bead* ; bede,
13, 29.

bēde, będe, *see* bidde(n).

będell, *sb.*, OF. bedel ; *beadle*, 147, 16.

bēden, bēdin, *see* bidde(n).

będe(n), *wkv.*, OE. bedan ; *pray* ; *pr.*
3 *sg.* bęat = bęt, Ml. bętęþ, 180, 4.

bēde(n). *stv.*, OE. bēodan-bēad (2) ;
*offer, bid, announce, proclaim, com-
mand*; early confused with bidde(n),
pray, command; *inf.* bēde, 140,
13 ; *pr. sbj. sg.* bēde, 201, 20;
imp. sg. bēd, 22, 9 ; *pt. sg.* będ, 21,
11 ; będe, 69, 6 ; bedd, 128, 16 ; *pt.
pl.* bedden, 28, 17, clearly from
bidden in form ; *pp.* bǫdyn, 169, 17.
eSth. bēoden, 185, 21 ; *pr.* 3 *sg.*
bēodeð, 202, 22.

bədēne, *see* bidēne.

bee, *sb.*, OE. bēo ; *bee*, 143, 23.

befalle(n), *see* bifalle(n).

beforen, *see* bifǫren.

begæt, begæton, *see* biȝete(n).

bēȝe(n), *wkv.*, OM. bēgan, WS. bīe-
gan, bygan ; *bend*; *pt. sg.* beide,
196, 26.

bēge, *sb.*, OM. bēh(g) (WS. bēah),
m. ; *ring, collar, bracelet*, 24, 12.

begete(n), *see* biȝete(n).

beggare, *sb.*, based on begge(n) ;
beggar, 57, 8.

beginne(n), (begouth), *see* biginn-
ne(n).

beginnynge, *sb.*, OE. beginning, *f.*,
beginning, 218, 27.

bęh, *see* buȝe(n).

behǫte(n), *see* bihǫte(n).

behōve(n), *wkv.*, OE. behōfian ; *behoove, profit* ; *pr.* 3 *sg.* behōveþ, 91,
6 ; behōveth, 119, 21 ; *pt. sg.* behōved, 4, 12. Nth. *pr.* 3 *sg.* bihōves,
82, 26.

behȳnd, *see* bihinde.

beide, *see* bēȝe(n).

beien, *adj. pl.*, OE. bēgen ; *both, also*,
7, 8 ; *glp.* beire, 38, 22 ; beine,
182, 3.

beiȯnde, beire, *see* beȝȯnd, beien.

belamp, *see* belimpe(n).

belamȳ, *sb.*, OF. bel ami; *fair friend*,
41, 27.

bēlde(n), *wkv.*, OM. beldan, bēldan,
WS. bieldan ; *embolden, encourage*;
inf. bēldenn, 12, 14.

belēave, belīave, *sb.*, Kt. = Ml. belēve ; OE. *belēafe, gelēafe ; *belief*,
211, 6 ; belēavee, 213, 1 ; bilīave,
213, 11.

belēve, *see* bilēve(n).

Bēlial, *sb.*, Lat. Belial ; *Belial*, 194,
22.

belīave, *see* belēave.

belimpe(n), *stv.*; OE. belimpan-lamp
(lǫmp) (3) ; *happen*; *pt. sg.* belamp,
4, 28.

belle, *sb.*, OE. belle ; *bell*, 76, 25.

belleman, *sb.*, OE. bell + man : *bell-
man*, 118, 30.

belle(n), *stv.*, OM. bellan-ball (WS.

beall) (3) ; *roar, bellow, swell with rage* ; *pp.* bollen, 50, 6.

belȳve, bilīve, *adv.*, OE. be + life ; *quickly*, 90, 7 ; bilīve, 186, 28.

bēm, *sb.*, OE. bēam ; *beam* ; eME. bēom, 3, 16 ; *pl.* bēmis, 142, 22.

bēme, *sb.*, OM. bēme (WS. bīeme), *f.* ; *trumpet* ; *pl.* bēmen, 187, 23.

bē(n), *anv.*, OE. bēon-wæs ; *be* ; *inf.* bēn, 1, 8 ; bēo, 36, 30 ; bee, 106, 6 ; *pr.* 1 *sg.* am, 22, 11 ; 2 *sg.* art, 18, 22 ; 3 *sg.* is, 8, 2 ; ys, 176, 7 ; iss, 9, 9 ; *neg.* 3 *sg.* nis, 65, 11 ; (eME. *pr. pl.* sinndenn, 9, 2 ; sinden, 16, 4) ; *pr. pl.* āren, 19, 12 ; āre, 111, 30 ; arn, 15, 12 ; *pr. pl.* bēon, 48, 28 ; bēn, 105, 3 ; *pr. sbj. sg.* bē 9, 21 ; *pr. sbj. pl.* bē, 32, 16 ; *imp. sg.* bē 18, 22 ; *imp. pl.* bēð, 28, 7 ; *pt. sg.* was, 1, 3 ; wass, 9, 30 ; wes, 1, 19 ; *neg. pt. sg.* nas, 43, 31 ; *pt. pl.* (eME. wēron, 1, 6 ; wēron, 4, 5) ; wēren, 16, 16 ; wēre wē, 25, 14 ; wēr, 73, 23 (eME. wāren, 3, 1 ; wāre, 77, 3) ; wǫren, 21, 10 ; wǫre, 77, 17 ; *neg. pt. pl.* nēren, 39, 14 ; nēre, 36, 14 ; *pt. sbj. sg.* wēre, 16, 2 (eME. wāre, 1, 15) ; wǫre, 22, 21 ; *pp.* byn, 114, 16 ; been, 243, 16. Nth. *inf.* bē, 128, 9 ; *pr.* 1 *sg.* am, 174, 14 ; *pr.* 2 *sg.* ert, 157, 14 ; *pr.* 3 *sg.* es. 128, 27 ; essę, 151, 25 ; is, 127, 7 ; issę, 156, 24 ; *neg. pr.* 3 *sg.* neys = ne ys, 128, 5 ; *pr.* 3 *sg.* bēs, 128, 32 ; bēsę, 139, 7 ; *pr. pl.* er, 136, 2 ; ere, 144, 2 ; ār, 173, 32 ; *pr. sbj. pl.* bē, 127, 26 ; *pt. sg.* was, 126, 9 ; *pt. pl.* wāre, 130, 24 ; wār, 138, 28 ; was, 158, 31 (late Nth. weir = wēr, 170, 32) ; *pt. sbj. sg.* wār, 134, 2 ; wāre, 246, 12 ; *pt. sbj. pl.* wāre, 133, 15 ; *pp.* hēne, 136, 18. 8th. *inf.* bēon, 198, 6 ; bēn, 176, 2 (eME. gerund bēonne, 192, 23) ; *pr.* 1 *sg.* (eSth. eom, 176, 4 ; æm, 176, 1) am, 194, 1 ; *pr.* 2 *sg.* (eSth. ært, 182, 30) art, 201, 23 ; *pr.* 3 *sg.* is (ys), 176, 7 ; *pr. pl.* (eSth. sünden, 184, 31) ; *pr.* 1 *sg.* bēo, 176, 4 ; *pr.* 3 *sg.* bið, 178, 21 ; *pr.* 3 *sg.* bið, *shall be*, 183,

11 ; *pr. pl.* (eSth. bēoþ, 176, 19) ; bēþ, 203, 20 ; bēth, 119, 11 ; büþ, 176, 23 ; bið, 178, 20 ; bȳeþ, 215, 23, *pr. sbj.* (eSth. sī, 179, 29 ; bēo, 177, 8) ; *pr. sbj. pl.* (eSth. bēon, 177, 4) ; *imp. sg.* (eSth. bēo 177, 5) ; *pt. sg.* wes = was, 176, 1 ; *neg. pt. sg.* nes, 194, 8 ; nas, 204, 15 ; *pt. pl.* węre, 179, 11 ; węr, 223, 5 ; *pt. sbj. sg.* (eSth. węore, 181, 9) ; węre, 243, 18 ; *pt. sbj. pl.* (eSth. węoren, 182, 9) ; węre, 242, 24 ; *neg. pt. sbj. sg.* (eSth. nēore, 187, 4) ; *pp.* (eSth. ibēon, 176, 3) ; ibē, 203, 14 ; ybē, 236, 20. Kt. *inf.* bīe, 211, 11 ; *pr. pl.* bīeþ, 212, 25 ; bīe yē, 212, 8 ; *pp.* ibȳe, 212, 20 ; *pt. pl.* waren, 212, 17.

benam, *see* benime(n).

benche, *sb.*, OE. benc, *f.* ; *bench*, 58, 6.

bēnd, *sb.*, OE. bend, bēnd ; *tie, ribbon, bend (in heraldry)*, 228, 15.

bēnde(n), *wkv.*, OE. bendan (bēndan) ; *bend, bind, fetter* ; Nth. *inf.* bēnd, 140, 17.

bēnde, *sb.*, OE. bend, bēnd, *f.* ; *bond, fetter*, 180, 14.

bēne, *sb.*, OE. bēn, *f.* ; *prayer, entreaty* ; *pl.* bēnes, 218, 21.

benefȳce, *sb.*, OF. benefice ; *favor, gift, benefit*, 124, 12.

beneme, *see* benime(n).

Benēt, *sb.*, NF. Beneit, OF. Benoit ; *Benet, Benedict*, 155, 24.

Beniamin, *sb.*, Lat. Beniamin ; *Benjamin*, 25, 25.

benime(n), binime(n), *stv.*, OE. beniman-nōm (4) ; *take away* ; *inf.* binime, 177, 20 ; *pr.* 1 *sg.* beneme, 211, 18 ; *pt. sg.* benam, 5, 21 ; *pt. pl.* binōmen, 182, 19 ; *pp.* binume, 183, 26.

benisūn, *sb.*, OF. beneisūn ; *blessing, benison*, 134, 22.

bēode(n), bęom, *see* bęm, będe(n).

bēo(n), beore, *see* bē(n), bęre.

bēonne(n), *stv.*, based on OE. bannan, (bǫnnan), bēon (R) ; *summon, command* ; *pt. pl.* bēonnen, 187, 23.

bēorn, *sb.*, eSth. = Ml. bērn, bern;
OE. beorn, bēorn; *man, hero,
warrior*, 186, 28. Cf. bērn.

bēot, *sb.*, eME. = Ml. bēt; OE. bēot;
threat, boast, promise, 184, 17.

bēot, bēoþ, *see* bēte(n), bē(n).

beovīe(n), *wkv.*, eSth. = Ml. bive(n);
OE. bifian, beofian; *tremble; pt. pl.*
beoveden, 187, 1.

bepēche(n), *wkv.*, OM. bepēcan
(WS. -pǣcan)-pēhte; *deceive; pp.*
bepaht, 1, 4.

bēr, *sb.*, Nth. = Ml. bēre; OM. bēre,
WS. bǣre; *noise, uproar*, 150, 2.

bęrd, *sb.*, OE. beard, bēard; *beard,*
86, 17; bęrdę, 120, 29.

berdene, *sb.*, Kt. = Ml. birþene, bir-
dene; OE. byrðen, *f.*; *burden*, 212,
21.

bęre, *sb.*, OE. bera; *bear (the animal)*,
82, 17. eSth. beore, 196, 3.

bēre, *sb.*, OE. bǣr, *f.*; *bier, litter,*
35, 3.

bēre, *sb.*, OM. gebēru, WS. gebǣru, *f.*;
bearing, deportment, noise, uproar,
36, 20.

bęrebag, *sb.*, based on OE. beran +
ON. baggi; *bag-bearer* (nickname
of Scots), 161, 6.

bęre-blisse, *sb.*, OE. beran + blisse;
bear-bliss; as name, 216, 30.

bęre(n), *stv.*, OE. beran-bǣr (4);
bear; inf. bęren, 22, 20 (eME.
bǣron, 3, 15); *imp. pl.* bęreð,
27, 19; *pr. pl.* bęrynge, 124, 2;
pt. sg. bar, 4, 6; *pt. pl.* bęren,
70, 17; bēre, 35, 19; *pt. sbj. sg.*
bēre, 53, 15; bāre, 2, 5; *pp.* bǫren,
33, 14; bǫre, 66, 11; born, 49, 28.
Nth. *pr.* 3 *sg.* bęres, 127, 19; bęrs,
150, 20; *pt. sg.* barę, 131, 10; *pt.
pl.* bāre, 165, 24; *pp.* born, 132, 6.
Sth. *pr.* 3 *sg.* berð, 198, 24; *pr. pl.*
(eSth.) bereð, 177, 22; *imp. pl.*
bęreð, 199, 22; *pt. sg.* bar, 181, 17;
pt. pl. bęre(n), 205, 9; *pp.* (eSth.
iboren, 179, 16); ibǫre, 46, 7;
ybǫre, 209, 32; ybǫren, 240, 8.

berge(n) = berʒen, berwe(n), *stv.*,
OM. bergan-barg (WS. beorgan-
bearg) (3); *protect, save; inf.* ber-

gen, 14, 7; berwen, 86, 13; *pp.*
borrʒhenn, 10, 19.

berid, berīe(n), *see* birīe(n).

berīe, *sb.*, OE. berige, berīe, *f.*;
berry, 21, 26.

bēring, *sb.*, based on OM. bēr, WS.
bǣr; *bearing, behaviour*, 25, 18.

bērn, *sb.*, OE. beorn, bēorn; *hero,*
126, 7; 149, 25.

bęrn, *sb.*, OE. bearn; *child*, Scotch
bearn, 82, 15.

bernd, *see* bērne(n), *wkv.*

bērne(n), *stv.*, OE. beornan-bǫrn (3);
burn; pt. sbj. sg. burne, 182, 23.

bērne(n), *wkv.*, OM. *bernan, WS.
bærnan; *burn; inf.* bērne, 43, 2; *pp.*
bernd, 58, 27. Sth. *pr. pl.* bērneþ,
218, 7; *pr. ppl.* bērnynde, 217, 24.

berrhless, *sb.*, OE. *beorhels, berhels;
salvation, 10, 13.

bęrst, *see* bęre(n).

berwe(n), *see* berge(n).

Berwīk, *sb.*, *Berwick*, 159, 8.

bęryng, *sb.*, OE. *berung, *f.*; *bearing*;
nativity, 231, 20.

besǣt, besǣtte, *see* besitte(n), be-
sette(n).

bēs(e), *see* bē(n).

besetten, *wkv.*, OE. besettan; *surround, beset*; eME. *pt. sg.* besǣtte
= besette, 5, 22; *pp.* bisett, 12, 25.

besiʒte, *sb.*, OE. *besihð, *besiht, *f.*;
provision, 226, 8.

besitte(n), *stv.*, OE. besittan-sǣt (5);
sit upon, oppress, besiege; eME. *pt.
sg.* besǣt, 2, 13.

besme, *sb.*, OE. besma; *besom. bundle
of rods*, 194, 16.

best, *see* gōd.

bęst, *sb.*, OF. beste; *beast*, 82, 18;
pl. bęstes, 51, 21. eSth. bęast, 195,
12.

beswīke(n), *see* biswīke(n).

beswǭ, *adv.*, Sth. = Ml. beswō; OE.
be + swā; *by so, so that*, 214, 2.

besȳnes, *see* bisīnes.

bet, *adv.* (*adj.*) *comp.*, OE. bet;
better, 31, 14; *quickly*, 239, 5.

betęche(n), beteht, *see* bitęche(n).

bēte(n), *wkv.*, OE. bētan; *mend,
remedy, better; inf.* bēte, 129, 23;

pr. 3 *sg.* bēteð, 16, 22. eSth. *pr.*
3 *sg.* bēot = bēt = bēteð, 180, 4 ; *pp.*
ibet, 179, 11.

bẹ̄te(n), *stv.*, OE. bēatan-bēot (2) ;
beat ; *inf.* bẹ̄te, 152, 6 ; *pp.* bẹ̄tin,
53, 30. eSth. *imp. pl.* bẹ̄aten,
194, 22 ; *pp.* ibēaten, 194, 15.

betere, bettre, bettur, betste, *see*
gōd.

bēþ, *see* bē(n).

beþ, *sb.*, Sth. = Ml. baþ; OE. bæþ;
bath, 218, 6.

bẹ̄ðe(n), *wkv.*, OE. beðian ; *wash,*
foment ; *inf.* bẹ̄ðen, 33, 31.

betōknep, betwē, *see* bitokne(n),
bitwēn.

betwix, bitwix, bitwixen, *adv.*
prep., OM. betwex (betwix), WS.
betweox(betwux); *betwixt,between*;
betwyx, 2, 16; betwux, 7, 15;
betwyxen, 117, 9; bitwix, 130, 3;
bitwixen, 244, 4. Nth. bytwixand,
128, 15.

beutē, *see* beautee.

bevlȳe(n), *stv.*, Sth. = Ml. beflē(n) ;
WS. beflēon-flēah (2) ; infl. by
flēȝen (flīen); *flee from, avoid*;
inf. bevlȳ, 218, 25; *pr.* 3 *sg.*
bevlȳȝþ, 217, 23 ; bevlȳȝt, 219, 17.

Bewis, *sb.*, *Bewis* (Bevis? see note),
62, 6.

bewreyynge, bewreyyng, *sb.*, OE.
bewrēging, f. ; *bewraying, accus-*
ing, 90, 32.

beye(n), beyne, *see* bige(n), bē(n).

bī (bȳ), be, *prep. adv.*, OE. bī ; *by,*
bī, 3, 6 ; be, 3, 3. Kt. bīẹ, 212,
30.

bibūȝe(n), *stv.*, OE. bebūgan-bēah
(2) ; *avoid, surround, reach, at-*
tain; *pt. sg.* bibah, 188, 21.

bicalle(n), *wkv.*, ME. bi + ON. kalla
(OE. ceallian); *call out upon, accuse*;
pr. 3 *sg.* bicalleð, 29, 26.

bicam, *see* bicume(n).

bicause, *see* bycause.

biclūpīe(n), *wkv.*, Sth. = Ml. bi-
clipe(n) ; OE. beclypian ; *summon,*
accuse, 179, 18.

bicume(n), *stv.*, OE. becuman-cōm
(4) ; *become* ; *inf.* bicōmen, 240, 2 ;

pr. 3 *sg.* bicumeð, 16, 14 ; *pt. sg.*
bicam, 24, 20 ; becōm, 126, 18 ;
bicōm, 227, 19 ; *pp.* bicume, 46, 6.

bidde(n), bydde(n), bide(n), bid,
stv., OE. biddan–bæd (5) ; *pray,*
pray for, beg, command, offer, in-
vite, by confusion with bēde(n);
inf. bidden, 16, 27 ; biddenn (O),
9, 29 ; biden, 71, 31 ; bide, 71, 28 ;
bid, 72, 28 ; *pr,* 1 *sg.* bidde, 10, 4 ;
pr. 1 *sg.* biddest, 64, 24 ; *pr.* 3 *sg.*
biddeþ, 40, 14 ; bit, 27, 14 ; *pr. sbj.*
pl. bidden, 196, 20 ; *imp. sg.* bid, 18,
12 ; *imp. pl.* biddeþ, 230, 30 ; *pt. sg.*
badd (O), 8, 18; bad, 21, 3; baddẹ,
64, 10 ; *pt. sg. offer*, bid, 44, 33 ; bid
godday, *bid good day*, 47, 7 ; *pt. pl.*
bēden, 35, 21 ; bēdin, 60, 19; bẹ̄de,
39, 11 ; *pp.* beden, 26, 20 ; bẹ̄de, 40,
5. Nth. *inf.* byd, 140, 11. Sth.
pr. 3 *sg.* bit, 180, 4 ; *pt. sg.* (eSth.
bæd, 185, 18) ; bed, 196, 4.

bidẹ̄lẹ(n), *wkv.*, OE. bedǣlan; *de-*
prive of; *pp.* bidẹ̄lde, 185, 6.

bīde(n), bȳde(n), *stv.*, OE. bīdan
–bād (1) ; *abide, await, expect*; *inf.*
bȳdin, 118, 15 ; *pt. sg.* bọ̄d, 47, 4 ;
bọ̄de, 89, 25.

bidēne, bidēn, *adv.*, origin uncertain ;
by that, thereby, together, also, at
once ; bidēne, 74, 2 ; bidēn, 148, 7 ;
bedēne, 116, 5.

biding, *see* byddynge.

bidlīch, *adj.*, based on OE. biddan,
'to pray'; *that may be implored,*
gracious, 103, 15.

bie, *see* bī.

bīe(n), bīeþ, *see* bē(n).

bifalle(n), *stv.*, OM. befallan (WS.
befeallan)–fēol (R) ; *befall*; *inf.*
bifalle, 38, 20 ; *pr. sbj. sg.* bifalle,
232, 5 ; *pt. sg.* bifeliẹ, 75, 1 ; befellẹ,
106, 8 ; byfyl, 89, 1 ; byfell, 135, 5.
Sth. *pt. sg.* byfūl, 220, 6.

biflēo(n), *stv.*, eME. = Ml. biflē(n);
OE. beflēon -flēah (2) ; *flee, escape*;
inf. biflēon, 180, 30.

bifọren, biforn, bifọr, *prep. adv.*,
OE. beforen ; *before* ; eME. beforen,
4, 30 ; bifọren, 16, 9 ; biforn, 16,
3 ; bifọr, 47, 26 ; bifọọre, 245, 19.

bifọresaide, *pp. or adj.*, OE. beforen, *adv.* + ME. saide ; *foresaid*, 235, 22.

biforn, *see* bifọren.

bigat, *see* biʒete(n).

bige(n) = biʒe(n), bīe(n), *wkv.*, OE. bycgan–bohte ; *buy, atone for* ; *inf.* bigen, 25, 6 ; bȳe, 95, 21 ; *pt. sg.* bouʒte, 58, 26 ; boght, 110, 3 ; *pt. pl.* bohton, 4, 29 ; *pp.* boght, 89, 27. **Nth.** *inf.* bii, 131, 6 ; bȳe, 156, 27. Cf. **Sth.** (biǧǧen). **Kt.** *inf.* beye(n), 244, 17.

biʒēonde, *adv. prep.*, OE. begeondan ; *beyond*, 185, 24.

biget, *see* biʒete(n).

biʒete(n), bigete(n), begēte(n), *stv.*, OE. begetan–gæt (5) ; *receive, obtain* ; *inf.* biʒeten, 185, 21 ; begæton, 7, 2 ; begeten, 25, 20 ; *pt. sg.* begæt, 4, 18 ; bigat, 28, 23 ; bigēte, 49, 16.

biʒetyng, *sb.* < *pr. ppl.*, OM. begetan, WS. begietan ; *begetting, generation*, 101, 18.

biǧǧə(n), *wkv.*, **Sth.** = Ml. biggen, bīe(n) ; OE. bycgan–bohte ; *buy, purchase, atone for* ; *inf.* biggen, 74, 17 (SEMl.), bigge, 178, 9 ; *pr.* 3 *sg.* biʒð, 180, 24.

bigge(n), *wkv.*, ON. byggja ; *build* ; *pt. sg.* bigged, 101, 13.

bigines, *see* biginne(n).

biging, *sb.*, ON. bygging ; *habitation, dwelling*, 161, 6.

biginne(n), *stv.*, OE. beginnan–gann (3) ; *begin* ; *inf.* biginne, 66, 20 ; *pt. sg.* bigon, 181, 20 ; *pt. pl.* begunne, 116, 18 ; *pt. sbj. sg.* begónne, 216, 4 ; *pp.* begunnon, 8, 11 ; bigunnenn (O), 9, 30. **Nth.** *pr.* 3 *sg.* bigines, 148, 17 ; *pt. sg.* begoūth, 166, 7.

biginninge, bigin(n)ing, *sb.*, OE. *beginnung, f.* ; *beginning*, 134, 27 ; byginnyng, 236, 4.

biʒite(n), *stv.*, **Sth.** = Ml. biʒete(n) ; WS. begietan-geat (5) ; *receive, obtain, beget* ; *pr.* 3 *sg.* biʒit = bigiteþ, 198, 21 ; *pt. sg.* biget, 192, 23 ; *pp.* biʒite, 179, 16.

Bigod, *sb.*, *Bigod* ; Roger, Earl of Norfolk, 227, 3.

bigọ(n), *anv.*, OE. begān–beēode ; *go around, occupy, possess* ; *cherish, honor* ; *pp.* bigọn, 62, 19. e**Sth.** *pt. pl.* byʒēode, 222, 11.

bigon, *see* biginne(n).

bigrīpe(n), *stv.*, OE. begrīpan–grāp (1) ; *gripe, chasten, chide* ; *inf.* bigrīpe(n), 19, 18.

biʒð, *see* biǧǧə(n).

bigunnen, *see* biginne(n).

bihāld, *stv.*, **Nth.** = Ml. **Sth.** behọlde(n) ; ON. behaldan (hāldan) –hēold (R) ; *behold* ; *pr. pl.* byhāldes, 145, 17 ; *pt. sg.* bihēldə, 139, 17.

bihāte(n), *stv.*, e**ME.**, **Nth.** = Ml. bihọte(n) ; OE. behātan–hēt (R) ; *promise* ; *pr.* 3 *sg.* bihāteð, 177, 14.

bihēdə(n), *wkv.*, OE. behēdan ; *watch, observe, guard* ; *pt. sg.* bihedde, 187, 22.

bihẹfdīe(n)(hẹvde(n)),*wkv.*, **Sth.** = Ml. behẹvde(n) ; OE. behēafdian ; *behead* ; *pp.* bihẹfdet, 196, 26.

bihēlde, bihēold, *see* bihālde(n), bihọlde(n).

biheste,*sb.*,OE. behǣs, *f.* ; *behest,promise*, 209, 12 ; *pl.* byhestes, 221, 16.

bihēte(n), *stv.*, based on *pt.* hēt ?; *promise* ; *inf.* bihēte, 52, 4. Cf. bihọte(n).

bihiʒt, *see* bihọte(n).

bihīnde, *adv. prep.*, OE. behindan –hīndan ; *behind*, 178, 31.

bihōf, *sb.*, OE. *behōf, cf. behōfian ; behoof, profit, use*. **Sth.** *ds.* bihōve, 200, 7.

bihōfþe, *sb.*, OE. *bihōfð, f.*, cf. OFris. behofte ; *behoof, use*, 204, 30.

bihọlde(n), *stv.*, OM. bihāldan (WS. healdan)–hēold (R) ; *behold, look on*; *inf.* bihọlde, 36, 2 ; *pt. sg.* bihēld, 38, 3 ; *pt. pl.* bihēld, 68, 20. **Nth.** *see* bihāld. e**Sth.** *pt. sg.* bihēold, 196, 22.

bihọte(n), *stv.*, OE. behātan–hēt (R); *promise* ; *pt. sg.* bihēt, 85, 25 ; biheet, 220, 12 ; *pp.* bihọten, 82, 8 ; behọten, 116, 22 ; *pp.* bihiʒt, 59, 12.

bihōve, *see* bihōf.

bihōve(n), *see* behōve(n).

bii (bȳ), *see* bige(n).

bīing, *sb.*, OE. bycging infl. by *vb.*; *buying, atonement, salvation*, 148, 19.

bīke, *sb.*, origin uncertain ; *nest, as of bees*, 128, 26.

biknowe(n), *stv.*, OE. becnāwan -cnēow (R) ; *acknowledge, know* ; *pp.* biknewe, 44, 16.

bilǣfde, *see* bilēve(n).

bilǣve, *see* bilēve(n).

bilai, *see* biliġġe(n).

bilaven, *see* bilēve(n).

bīlde(n), *wkv.*, OE. byldan, bȳldan ; *build* ; *pp.* ibild, 42, 5.

bile, *sb.*, OE. bile ; *bill, beak*, 16, 11.

bilēf, *see* bilēve(n).

bilēȝe(n), bilewe(n), *stv.*, OE. bilēogan–lēag (2) ; *belie, calumniate* ; *pp.* bilowen, 199, 13.

bilēove(n), *see* bilēve(n).

bilēve(n), *wkv.*, OM. belēfan (WS. belīefan) ; *believe* ; *inf.* belēve, 122, 4 ; *pp.* bilēved, 213, 13.

bilēve(n), *wkv.*, OE. belǣfan ; *relinquish, leave, remain* ; *inf.* belēven, 27, 9 ; *pr.* 1 *sg.* bilǣve, 184, 13 ; *imp. sg.* bilēf, 41, 1 ; *pt. sg.* bilǣfde, 185, 2 ; *pt. pl.* bilēvede, 205, 27. Nth. *pt. sg.* bilēvid, 163, 30. eSth. *inf.* bilēofven, 184, 11 ; *pt. pl.* bilaven, 183, 9.

biliġġe(n), *stv.*, Sth. = Ml. bilīe(n) ; OE. bilicgan–læg (5) ; *lie by, beset* ; *pt. sg.* bilai, 188, 10.

bilīve, *see* belȳve.

bilīve(n), *stv.*, OE. belīfan–lāf (later lǣf, lēaf) (1) ; *remain, leave* ; *pt. sg.* bilēf, 24, 32.

bille(n), *wkv.*, OE. *billan ; *bill, peck with beak* ; *pr.* 3 *sg.* billeð, 16, 8.

bilōke(n), *wkv.*, OE. belōcian ; *look at, look around* ; *pr. pl.* bilōken, 20. 1.

biloken, *see* bilūke(n).

bilōng, *adj.*, cf. OE. gelǫng : *depending, belonging*, 21, 22.

bilowen, *see* bilēȝe(n).

bilūke(n), *stv.*, OE. bilūcan–lēac (2) ;

---

shut in, close around ; *pp.* biloken, 178, 25.

biluvīe(n), *wkv.*, Sth. = Ml. biluve(n) ; OE. belufian ; *delighted in, loved* ; *pt. pl.* biluveden, 184, 10.

bimēne(n), *wkv.*, OE. bemǣnan ; *bemoan, lament* ; *pr.* 3 *sg.* bimēneð, 27, 2 ; *pp.* biment, 26, 10.

bimēning, *sb.* < *pr. ppl.*, OE. bemǣnan ; *bemoaning, lamentation*, 35, 6.

biment, *see* bimēne(n).

bīnde(n), *stv.*, OE. bindan (bīndan) –band, bǫnd (3) ; *bind, fetter* ; *inf.* bīnden, 26, 1 ; *pt. sg.* bǫnd, 207, 8 ; *pt. pl.* bŭnden, 26, 24 ; *pp.* bŭnden, 137, 6 ; bōunden, 81, 20. Nth. *imp. pl.* bīndes, 138, 23 ; *pt. pl.* bānd, 140, 19.

binēþe(n), *adv. prep.*, OE. beneoðan ; *beneath*, 41, 20 ; binēþe, 208, 8. eSth. bineoðen, 178, 30.

binime(n), *see* benime(n).

binne, *adv. prep.*, OE. binnan , *within, in*, 82, 28.

binōme, binume, *see* binime(n).

biquēðe(n), *wkv.*, OE. *becwǣðan < cwīðan ; *lament, bewail* ; *inf.* biquēðen, 34, 1.

bir, *sb.*, ON. byrr, 'strong wind' ; *force, speed*, 142, 5.

birǣd, *see* birīde(n).

bird, *see* bire(n)

bīrde, *sb.*, OE. gebyrd, *f.*; *birth* ; bīrde tīme, *birth time*, 17, 11.

bire(n), *wkv.*, OE. (ge)byrian ; *belong to, behoove* ; *pr.* 3 *sg.* birrþ (O), 8, 26 ; bird, 150, 16 ; birrd, 156, 31 ; *pt. sg.* birde, 153, 19.

birēounesse, *sb.*, eME. = Ml. birewnesse ; OE. *behrēowness, *f.*; *commiseration, pity*, 198, 33.

birēowse(n), *wkv.*, eME. = Ml. birewse(n) ; OE. behrēowsian ; *repent* ; *imp. pl.* birēowseð, 196, 6.

birī, *sb.*, OE. byrig, *ds.* of burh ; *castle, city*, 28, 1.

birīde(n), *stv.*, OE. berīdan–rād (1) ; *ride around, surround, besiege* ; *pt. sg.* birǣd for birād, 187, 13.

biriele, *see* birīgeles.

birīe(n) (berīen), *wkv.*, OE. byrgan (byrigean); *bury*; *inf.* birīen, 33, 8; birȳ, 68, 16 ; berīe (Kt.?), 245, 23 ; *imp. pl.* birīeþ, 68, 29 , *pt. pl.* byrīeden, 4, 32 ; birīed, 70, 19. **Nth.** *pt. sg.* berid, 143, 10.

birīgeles, birīele, *sb.*, OE. birigels; *burial*, 34, 27 ; 35, 10.

Birkabeyn, *sb.*, ON. Birkibeinn (a nickname); *Birkabein*, 75, 4.

birrd, birrþ, *see* bire(n).

birst, *pp.* or *adj.*, OE. gebrȳsed < OE. brȳsan ; *bruised*; bētin and birst, *beaten and bruised*, 53, 30.

biscop, *sb.*, eME. = Ml. bischop; OE. biscop ; *bishop*, 1, 5.

biscunīe(n), *wkv.*, Sth. = Ml. bischune(n); OE. bescunian ; *shun, flee from*, 180, 30.

bīse, *sb.*, OF. bise ; *name of north wind*, 87, 9.

bisēche(n), *wkv.*, OE. besēcean–sōhte (sohte) ; *beseech*; *pr.* 1 *sg.* bisēchc, 196, 20; *pr. pl.* bisēchen, 45, 22. **Nth.** *pt. sg.* bisoht, 156, 8. **Sth.** *pr. pl.* bisēcheth, 211, 15.

bisēkeing, *sb.* < *pr. ppl.*, OE. besēcan ; *beseeching, imploring*, 74, 8.

bisэmare, *see* bismere.

bisē(n), *stv.*, ON. besēon–sæh (WS. seah) (5); *oversee, look after*; *inf.* bisēn, 24, 13.

bisett, *see* besette(n).

bisīde, bisīde(s), *adv. prep.*, OE. bī sīde ; *beside, besides*, 57, 5 ; bysīdes, 223, 3.

bisīnes, besȳnes, *sb.*, OE. *bysignes, *f.*; *business, care, trouble*; besȳnes, 144, 20 ; bysȳnes, 224, 24.

bismere, bismare, *sb.*, OE. bismer, *neut. m.*; *insult, evil, scorn*, 55, 18; bismare, 201, 19.

bīsne, *sb.*, OE. bīsen, *f.*; *example, copy*, 10, 5.

bisoht, *see* bisēche(n).

bisschop, *see* biscop.

bistēlэ(n), *stv.*, OE. bestelan–stæl (4); *steal, steal away*; *pt. sg.* bīstal, 188, 1 ; *pp.* bistolen, 176, 17.

bistiзe, *sb.*, OE. *bestīg, *f.* or new *cpd.* ; *path, way, ascent*, 101, 4.

bistolen, *see* bistēle(n).

bistrīde(n), *stv.*, OE. bestrīdan–strād (1) ; *bestride* ; *inf.* bistrīden, 181, 15.

biswīke(n), *stv.*, OE. beswīcan — swāc (1) ; *deceive* ; *inf.* beswīken, 6, 17 · biswīken, 19, 17; *pt. sg.* (eME.) biswāc, 187, 31.

bisȳ, *adj.*, OE. bysig; *anxious, sorrowful, busy*, 66, 15.

bit, *see* bidde(n).

bitache, bitǣchen, *see* bitēche(n).

bitācne(n), *wkv.*, eME. for bitōkne(n); OE. *bītācnian ; *betoken* ; *pp.* bītācnedd (O), 12, 28. **Nth.** *pr.* 3 *sg.* bytākens, 127, 22.

bitagt(e), bitaзt, bitaht, *see* bitēche(n).

bitāke(n), *stv.*, OE. bi (be) + ON. taka–tōk (6); *commit, betake*; *pt. sg.* bitōk, 67, 19 ; bitook, 231, 22 ; *pp.* bitāke, 203, 24.

bitākэns, *see* bitācne(n).

bitaucte, bitaugt, *see* bitēche(n).

bite, *sb.*, OE. bytt, *f.*; *bottle, flagon (originally leather*); bollen as a bite, *swollen as a bottle*, 50, 6.

bitēche(n), bitēache(n), *wkv.*, OE. betǣcean–tǣhte (tǣhte) ; *assign, deliver, commit*; *inf.* bitǣche, 9, 19; bitēche, 43, 22 ; *pt. sg.* bitagte, 24, 11; *pp.* betēht, 5, 7; bitagt, 21, 7; bitaзt, 43, 18; bitauзt, 49, 27. **eSth.** *inf.* bitēachen, 193, 8; *pr.* 1 *sg.* bitache, 190, 22 ; *pp.* bitaht, 193, 31.

bīte(n), *stv.*, OE. bītan-bāt (1); *bite*; *pt. sg.* bōt, 66, 8.

biter, *see* bitter.

biðð, *see* bē(n).

biþэnche(n), biðenke(n), *wkv.*, OE. biðencan-ðōhte (ðohte) ; *think, bethink, conceive*; *inf.* biðenken, 16, 16; *pt. sg.* biðogte, 23, 19; biþoзte, 208, 1 ; *pp.* biþoзt as *adj.*, *thoughtful, discreet*, 36, 21 ; biþoht, 176, 8. **Sth.** biþenche, 176, 6; *pr.* 3 *sg.* biþencð, 177, 9.

bitīde(n), *wkv.*, OE. betīdan; *happen, betide*; *inf.* bitīde, 39, 27; *pr.* 3 *sg.* bitīd, 25, 21 ; *pp.* bitid, 31, 6.

bitilde(n), *wkv.*, OE. beteldan (?);
cover, surround; *pp.* bitild, 192, 26.
bitīme, *adv.* OE. *betīma?; *betimes,
promptly*, 204, 6.
bitōk, *see* bitāke(n).
bitǫkne(n), bitǫckne(n), *wkv.*, OE.
*bitācnian; *betoken*; *pr.* 3 *sg.*
bitǫkneþ, 71, 8; betǫckneþ, 212,
27.
bitook, *see* bitāke(n).
bitray, *wkv.*, Nth. = Ml. bitraischen
(bitraissen, betraien); OE. be(bi) +
OF. trair; *betray*; *pp.* bitrayd,
137, 3.
bitter, bittre, *adj.*, OE. biter; *bitter*,
140, 16; bittre, 194, 16.
bitterlīche, *adv.*, OE. biterlīce;
bitterly, 67, 9.
bittre, *see* bitter.
bitternesse, *sb.*, OE. biterness, *f.*;
bitterness, 202, 14.
biturnīe(n), *wkv.*, Sth. = Ml. bi-
turne(n); OE. *beturnian; *turn
about*; *pt. pl.* biturnde, 208, 7.
bitwēn, betwē(n), *adv. prep.*, OE.
betwēonan; *between, among*, 26, 11;
betwē, 95, 14; bytwēne, 222, 2.
bitwix, bitwixen, *see* betwix.
bive(n), *wkv.*, OE. bifian; *tremble*;
pr. 3 *sg.* biveð, 28, 24. Sth. *inf.*
bivīe, 182, 23. Cf. beovīen.
bivīe(n), *see* bive(n).
bivǫre(n), *adv. prep.* Sth. = Ml. bi-
fǫre(n); OE. beforan; *before*; eSth.
bivoren, 181, 17; bivǫre, 206, 17.
biwāke(n), *wkv.*, OE. *bewacian;
watch over; *inf.* biwāken, 33, 28.
biwēfe(n), *wkv.*, OE. bewǣfan;
clothe; *pt. sg.* biwẹ́fde, 188, 26.
biwēnde(n), *wkv.*, OE. bewendan
(wēndan); *turn away, turn around*;
pt. sg. biwente, 48, 6.
biwēpe(n), *wkv.*, OE. bewēpan;
weep for; *imp. pl.* biwēpeð, 196, 6.
bewīnde(n), *stv.*, OE. bewindan
(wīndan)–wand (wǫnd) (3); *wind
about, surround*; *pp.* biwūnden,
196, 30.
biwreye(n), *wkv.*, OE. *biwrēgan,
cf. wrēgan; *bewray, accuse*; *inf.*
biwreye, 243, 27.

biwūnden, *see* biwīnde(n).
blac, *adj.*, OE. blæc; *black*, 52, 24.
Blais, *sb.*, OF. Blois; *Blois*, 2, 7.
blāme, *sb.*, OF. blâme < blasme;
blame, 120, 20.
blāme(n), *wkv.* OF. blasmer, blâmer;
blame; *inf.* blāme, 159, 14; *pr.* 3
sg. blāmeþ, 202, 2.
blasphēmoūr, *sb.*, OF. blasphemeur
(or); *blasphemer*, 246, 5.
Blauncheflūr, *sb.*, OF. Blancheflur;
Blanchefleur, 36, 15; *gs.* Blauncheflūres, 35, 26.
blawe(n), *stv.*, eME., Nth. = Ml.
blowe(n); OE. blāwan-blēow (R);
blow; *inf.*, blawe, 82, 31; *pp.*
blawenẹ, 144, 7. eSth. *pr.* 3 *sg.*
blāweð, 180, 16.
blē, blee, *sb.*, OE. blēo; *color, com-
plexion*, 52, 1; blee, 231, 25.
blēde(n) *wkv.*, OE. blēdan; *bleed*;
pr. ppl. blēdyng, 221, 23.
bleike, *adj.*, ON. bleikr; *pale*, 79,
9.
blenche(n), *wkv.*, OE. blencan;
blench, flinch; *inf.* blenche, 58, 12;
pt. sg. blenchte, 195, 32.
blēnde(n), *wkv.*, OE. blendan, blēndan; *make blind*; Sth. *pp.* iblende,
125, 33; yblent, 217, 2.
blenke(n), *see* blynke(n).
blesse(n)(earlier blētcen),blisce(n),
wkv., OE. blēdsian, blētsian; *bless,
cross oneself*, blesse hem, *cross themselves*; *inf.* blesse, 123, 7; *pr.* 1 *sg.*
blisce, 128, 19; *imp. sg.* blisce,
104, 14; *imp. pl.* blisceþ, 105, 12;
pt. sg. blessede, 205, 7; *pp.* (eME.
blētced, 7, 31) blesced, 100, 15;
blisced, 132, 19; blessyd, 94, 1;
blissed, 228, 30. Sth. *pp.* yblisced,
72, 21.
blessyng, *sb.*, OE. blētsung,*f.*; *blessing*, 96, 3; blisceing, 69, 22; bliscyng, 101, 17; blissing, 32, 14.
blētcen, *see* blesse(n).
blēþelīche, *see* blīþelike.
blēve(n), *wkv.*, OE. bilǣvan, Kt.
bilēvan; *remain*; Kt. *pp.* yblēved,
217, 6.
blēvinge, *sb.*, Kt. = Ml. blẹ́vinge;

OE. *belǣvung, *f.*; *abiding, existence*, 216, 27.

blin, *see* blinne(n).

blīnd, *adj.*, OE. blind, blīnd ; *blind*, 51, 25; blȳndę, 119, 7.

blinne(n), bline(n), *stv.*, OE. blinnan—blann (blǫnn) (3) ; *cease* ; *inf.* blinne, 55, 30. Nth. *inf.* blin, 130, 7.

blis, blisce, *see* blisse.

blisceing, bliscyng, *see* blessyng.

bliscęþ, *see* blesse(n).

blisfōl, blisful, *adj.*, OE. *blisful ; *blissful, happy*, 219, 3 ; blisful, 192, 30.

blisfullīch, *adj.*, OE. *blisfullīce · *blissfully*, 102, 23.

blisse, blis, *sb.*, OE. bliss, *f.* < blīþs [blīð] ; *bliss, happiness*, 7, 7 ; blis, 38, 4; blisce, 211, 25. eSth. *ds.* blissen, 195, 6.

blissing, *see* blessyng.

blīðe, blȳþe, blīth, *adj.*, blīðe ; *glad, blithe*, 31, 7 ; blīth, 139, 9.

blīþęlīke, blīþeliȝ, *adv.*, OE. blīðelīce ; *gladly, blithely*, 10, 1 ; blīþęliȝ (O), 10, 21 ; blȳþęlȳ, 94, 27. Kt. blēþelīche, 211, 15.

blǫ, *adj.*, ON. blār, cogn. with OE. blāw ; *livid, blue-black*, 52, 24.

blōd, blood, *sb.*, OE. blōd ; *blood*, 28, 21 ; blood, 238, 19. eSth. *ds.* blōde, 189, 32. 1Nth. bludę, 146, 1.

blōdī, blōdȳ, *adj.*, OE. blōdig; *bloody*, 152, 2 ; blōdȳ, 228, 5.

blōdstręm, *sb.*, OE. *blōdstrēam ; *stream of blood*, 187, 2.

blōdȳ, *see* blōdī.

blōme(n), *wkv.*, ON. *blōma ?, cognate with OE. blōstmian ; *bloom· pt. sg.* blōmede, 21, 25.

blǫndinge, *sb.*, based on OF. blandir ; *blandishing, flattery*, 219, 5.

bloodręd, *adj.*, OE. blōdrēad ; *bloodred*, 229, 14.

blowe(n), *stv.*, OE. blāwan-blēow (R) ; *blow* ; *inf.* blowen, 62, 5 ; *imp. sg.* blou, 82, 29 ; *pp.* blowen, 50, 14.

bludę, blȳndę, *see* blōd, blīnd.

blynke(n), *wkv.*, ON. *blinka, Dan. blinke ; *look, wink, blink, wake from sleep* ; *inf.* blinke, 91, 31. 1Nth. *pt. sg.* blenkit, 172, 23.

blȳþe, *see* blīþe.

blȳþęlȳ, *see* blȳþelīke.

blȳve, *adv.*, OE. be + līfe ; *quickly*, 111, 4.

bǫ. *adj.*, OE. bā (bēgen); *both*, 38, 5. Cf. bā.

bōc, *see* bōke.

bochēre, *sb.*, OF. bochier ; *butcher*, 57, 18.

bōcstaf, *sb.*, OE. bōcstæf ; *letter of alphabet* ; bocstaff (O), 10, 7.

bǫd, bǫde, *see* bīde(n).

bǫde, *sb.*, OE. gebod, *neut.*; *command, request, message* ; *pl.* bǫdes, 17, 28. eSth. *pl.* boden, 181, 4.

bodede, *see* bodīe(n).

bǫdeword, *sb.*, OE. *bodword or new cpd.; *message*, 28, 26.

bodī, bodȳ, *sb.*, OE. bodig ; *body*, 17, 23 ; *pl.* bodīs, 68, 16 ; bodīes, 221, 8. Sth. *ds.* bodȳe, 216, 14.

bǫdīe(n), *wkv.*, Sth. = Ml. bǫde(n) ; OE. bodian; *announce, proclaim, speak* ; *pt. sg.* bodede, 186, 23.

bodīlī, bodȳlīch, *adj.*, OE. *bodiglīce ; *bodily*, 146, 16 ; bodȳlȳ, 146, 26. Sth. bodȳlīch, 216, 29.

bǫdyn, *see* bēde(n).

boght, bohton, *see* bige(n).

boistouslȳch, *adv.*, origin uncertain ; *boisterously*, 221, 8.

bōke, bōc (bōk), *sb.*, OE. bōc, *f.*; *book* ; bōc, 9, 1 ; bōke, 15, 9 ; 40, 3 ; 66, 28 ; bōk, 67, 7.

bōld, *sb.*, OE. bold, bōld ; *house, building* ; *pl.* bōldes, 196, 8.

bǫld, *adj.*, OM. bald, bāld, WS. beald ; *bold*, 23, 25.

bollen, *pp.* as *adj.*, OE. belgan, *swollen*, 50, 6.

bolne(n), boln, *wkv.*, ON. bolgna ; *swell*. Nth. *inf.* boln, 151, 18.

bǫn, bǫǫn, *sb.*, OE. bān ; *bone* ; *pl.* bǫǫnys, 113, 18. Nth. bān, 139, 25.

bǫnd, *see* bīnde(n).

bǫnd, *sb.*, ON. band, 1OE. bǫnd ; *bond, durance*, 22, 12.

bǫndā̆ǧe, *sb.*, OF. *bondage, ML.
bondaginnus; *bondage*, 94, 15.

bǫnde, bǫnd, *sb.*, OE. bonda < ON.
bōndi; *bondman, servant*; bǫnde
manēre, *manner of a bondman*, 94,
22. Nth. bǫnd, as in phr. *bond
and free*, 135, 11.

bōne, *sb.*, ON. bōn, *f.*, cogn. with
OE. bēn; *prayer, boon*, 16, 27.
Sth. *pl.* bōnen, 199, 1.

Bonefāce, *sb.*, OF. Boniface; *Boniface of Savoy*, 226, 24.

bōrd, *sb.*, OE. bord, bōrd, *neut.*;
board, plank, table, side of ship;
ds. bōrde, 190, 7.

bōrde, *sb.*. NF. borde, OF. bourde;
jest, 122, 26.

bǫre(n), born, *see* bẹre(n).

borh, *sb.*, OE. borh, *m.*; *bail, security,
payment*, 195, 31.

borrghenn, *see* berge(n).

borwe(n), *wkv.*, OE. borgian; *receive
on pledge, borrow*; *pt. sg.* borwed,
245, 10.

bǫst, bǫstẹ, *sb.*, based on root of
OE. bōgan, ‘boast’?; *boast*, 158,
2; bǫǫst, 242, 1.

bǫsting, *sb.* < *pr. ppl.*; *boasting*, 160,
23.

bǫt, *see* bīte(n).

bōt, bote, *see* bōte, bute.

bōtǝ (bōt), *sb.*, OE. bōt, *f.*; *help,
remedy, salvation*, 18, 12; bōt, 54,
11. lNth. bute, 157, 14.

botel, *sb.*, OF. bouteille; *bottle*, 245, 10.

bǫþe (bǫðe), bǫthe, *adj., prn.*, ON.
bāþir; *both, also*, 37, 30; *pl.* (Sth.)
bǫðen, 21, 13. Cf. bāþe.

bouȝte, *see* bige(n).

bōun, *adj.*, ON. *pp.* būinn; *ready,
prepared*, 139, 16; bōwne, 105, 22.

bōunden, *see* bīnde(n).

bōuntē, būntē, *sb.*, AN. bunté, OF.
bonté; *bounty, goodness*, 97, 13;
būntē, 214, 12.

bōur, *see* būr.

bōurde(n), *wkv.*, OF. bourder; *jest*,
242, 15.

bōuxomnes, *see* buxsumnes.

bōwande, *see* bōwe(n).

bowdraucht, *sb.*, OE. boga + *draht?;

bow-draft, distance a bow will carry,
166, 19.

bōwe(n), *stv.*, OM. būgan–bēg (WS.
bēah) (2); *bow, bend, turn aside,
be obedient*; *pr. ppl.* bōwande, 96,
32. Cf. būȝe(n).

bowes, bōwn, *see* bug, bōun.

box, *sb.*, OE. box; *box*, 245, 8.

Braband, Brabant, *sb.*, OF. Braband,
Brabant; *Brabant*, 161, 23; Brabant, 162, 8.

brād (brādẹ), braid, *adj.*, eME.
Nth. = Ml. brǫd; OE. brād; *broad*;
eME. brād, 190, 9; brādẹ, 122, 11.
lNth. braid, 167, 26.

brǣcon, *see* brẹke(n).

braid, *see* brād, breyde(n).

braie(n), *wkv.*, OF. braire; *bray,
resound harshly*; *pr. ppl.* brayinde,
217, 25.

brastlīe(n), *wkv.*, Sth. = Ml. brast-
le(n); OE. brastlīan; *rustle, crackle,
make a noise*; *pr. pl.* brastlīen, 189,
29.

brāthlȳ, *adv.*, Nth. = Ml. brǫthlȳ;
ON. brāðligr; *violently*, 128, 13.

braunche, *sb.*, OF. branche; *branch*;
pl. braunches, 235, 22.

braydẹ, *see* breid.

brayinde, *see* braie(n).

brẹad, *see* brẹd.

brẹadlẹp = brẹdlẹp, *sb.*, OE. brēad
+ lēap, ‘basket’; *bread basket*, 22,
14.

bred, bredde, *see* brēde(n).

brēdale, *see* brīdale.

brẹd, *sb.*, OE. brēad; *bread*, 21, 12;
brẹad, 22, 15; brẹdẹ, 89, 26; brẹẹd,
243, 1.

brẹde, *sb.*, Sth. = Ml. brēde; WS.
brǣde, OM. brēde; *roast meat*, 180,
23.

brẹde, Nth. brēde sometimes; *sb.*,
OE. brǣdu; *breadth*; on brēd, *in
breadth, stretched out*, 140, 21.

brẹde(n), *wkv.*, OE. brǣdan; *broaden,
expand*; *inf.* brẹde, 133, 17.

brēde(n), *wkv.*, OE. brēdan; *breed*;
pp. bred, 17, 11; bredde, 53, 19.

brẹdwrigtẹ, *sb.*, OE. brēad + wyrhta
(wryhta); *baker, bread-wright*, 22, 13.

brę̄d, *see* brḗd.
brēflī. *adv.*, OF. brief + ME. -lī;
briefly, 130, 6.
breid, braydę, *sb.*, OE. brǣgd; *rapid
movement, cunning, throw, strata-
gem*; at a breid, *rapidly, at a bound*,
60, 3. **Nth.** braydę, 140, 16.
brę̄ken, *stv.*, OE. brecan–brǣc (4);
break, tear up, violate; *inf.* brę̄ken,
203, 11; *pr.* 3 *sg.* brę̄keþ, 222, 6;
pt. sg. brak, 69, 32; brakk, 112, 26;
brēkę, with vowel of *pl.*, 67, 32;
pt. pl. (eME. brǣcon, 3, 13);
brēken, 69, 15; *pp.* brǭken, 18, 1.
Sth. *pr. pl.* brekeð, 179, 2; *ƒt. pl.*
brę̄ken, 186, 31; *pp.* ibrǭken, 203,
11; ībrǭke, 204, 16.
brę̄kynge, *sb.*, OE. brecung, *f.*;
breaking, 146, 8.
Brembre, *sb.*, OM. Brēmel, Brēmber?
(WS. Brǣmel); *Brember*; Nicholus,
233, 1.
brēme, *adj.*, OE. brēme; *famous,
excellent*, 46, 24. **Nth.** brēm, 152, 30.
brēmlī, brēmlȳ, *adv.*, OE. *brēme-
līce*; *fiercely*, 152, 6.
bren, brēnd, *see* brenne(n).
Brenicia, *sb.*, Lat. Bernicia, OE.
Beornica rīce; *Bernicia*, 221, 31.
brenne(n), *wkv.*, ON. brenna; *burn*;
tr. ppl. brennynde, 61, 6; *pt. pl.*
brendon, 3, 25, brenden, 83, 7; *pp.*
brent, 111, 1; brentę, 107, 9. **Nth.**
inf. bren, 151, 32; *pt. pl.* brēnd, 163,
25.
brenstǭn, brimstǭn, *sb.*, OE. *bren-
stān*, cf. ON. brennistein; *brimstone,
sulphur*, 217, 24; brimstǭn, 62, 17.
brent, *see* brenne(n).
brēoste, *see* brēst.
brērę, *sb.*, OE. brēr; *briar*, 235, 24.
brēst (brest), *sb.*, OE. brēost; *breast*,
pl. brēstess (O), 12, 5; *pl.* breste,
41, 20; brest, 54, 12. **eSth.** *pl.*
brēoste, 197, 21.
brēstatter, *sb.*, OE. brēost + ātor,
atter; *breast poison*, 17, 14.
brēstfīlðe, *sb.*, OE. brēost + fȳlð, *f.*;
breastfilth, evil in the heart, 18, 20.
Bretayne, *sb.*, OF. Britaine, Bretaine;
Brittany, 116, 8.

brēthere, brethere(n), *see* brōther.
bretherhǭd, *sb.*, OE. brōðor + hād;
brotherhood, 116, 18.
brēðren, *see* brōther.
brewe(n), brew, breu, *stv.*, OE.
brēowan –brēaw (2); *brew, prepare*;
pp. browen, 57, 25. **Nth.** *inf.* brew,
130, 4; breu, 149, 27.
breyde(n), *stv.*, OE. bregdan–brǣgd
(3); *wrench, move, turn, act*; *inf.*
breyde, 50, 30; *pt. sg.* breyde, 93,
31; braid, 195, 33; *pt. pl.* broiden,
62, 1.
brībōr, *sb.*, OF. bribeur, NF. bribeor;
thief, rascal, 221, 19.
brid, *sb.*, OE. bridd; *bird*; *pl.*
briddes, 198, 23.
brīd, *sb.*, **Nth.** = Ml. brīde; OE. brȳd,
f.; *bride*, 159, 31.
brīdale (MS. briddale), *sb.*, OE.
brȳdealo; *bridal, bride-feast*, 46,
26. **Kt.** brēdale, 219, 8.
brīdel, *sb.*, OE. brīdel; *bridle*, 50,
21.
brȝit, brigt, briht, *adj.*, OE. briht;
bright, 52, 1; *pl.* brigt, 15, 26;
brihte, 178, 19; bryghte, 144, 1;
comp. brihtre, 194, 33.
brimstǭn, *see* brenstǭn.
brin, *stv.*, **Nth.** = Ml. brinne(n);
ON. brinna -brann (3); *burn*; *inf.*
brin, 141, 6.
bringe(n), *wkv.*, OE. bringan–brōhte
(brohte); *bring*; *inf.* bringen, 24,
31; bringe, 41, 13; *pr.* 1 *sg.* bringe,
37, 4; *pr.* 3 *sg.* brinngeþþ (O), 11,
13; *pt. sg.* brohte, 4, 15; broȝte, 38,
25; *pt. pl.* brohten, 2, 2; *pt. sbj.
pl.* brohten, 186, 9; *pp.* brohht (O),
8, 26; broght, 89, 28. **Nth.** *pr.*
3 *sg.* brynges, 145, 3; *sbj. sg.* bring,
157, 8. **Sth.** *pp.* ibroht, 207, 32;
ibroȝt, 38, 23; ybrouȝt, 70, 23.
Bristowe, *sb.*, OE. Brycgstōw, *f.*;
Bristol, 5, 27.
Britayn, Brytayn, *sb.* OF. Britaine;
Britain, 220, 12; Brytayn, 220,
5.
brith, *sb.*, **Nth.** = Ml. birþe; *gebryþ,
cogn. with OE. gebyrd, *f.* or ON.
byrð; *birth*, 130, 4.

Britŏn, Brytŏn, *sb.,* OF. Breton, Briton; *Briton*; *pl.* Britŏns, 220, 13; Brytŏns, 221, 24.

brǫd, *adj.,* OE. brād; *broad,* 47, 3.

brŏde, *sb.,* OE. brŏd, *f.* ꞉ *offspring, brood,* 68, 26.

broght, brogte, *see* **bringe(n).**

brohte(n), brohht, *see* **bringe(n).**

broiden, *see* **breyde(n).**

brǫken, *see* **brēke(n).**

brǫnd, *sb.,* OE. brand, brǫnd [brennan]; *brand,* 61, 26.

brŏther, *sb.,* OE. brŏðor; *brother,* 5, 23; brŏþerr (O), 8, 13; *pl.* (eME. brēthere, 26, 7; brēðren, 196, 21); brethere, 117, 22; bretheren, 116, 20.

brouch, *sb.,* OF. broche; *brooch,* 224, 23.

browen, *see* **brewe(n).**

Bruce, *sb., Bruce*; Robert þē Bruce, 170, 1.

Bruǧhes (MS. Brig, Burghes), *sb.,* OF. Bruges; *Bruges,* 161, 8.

brüke(n), *stv.,* OE. brūcan-brēac(2); *enjoy, brook; inf.* brūkenn (O), 13, 23; brūke, 18₅, 18.

Brut, *sb.,* OF. Brut; *Brutus,* 126, 7.

Brüt, *sb.,* Sth.= Ml. Brit; OE. Bryt; *Briton; gpl.* Brütten, 183, 31; Brütte, 184, 4; *pl.* Brüttes, 184, 30.

Brütlǫnd, *sb.,* OE. Brytenlǫnd (Brytlǫnd); *land of Britain, England,* 183, 26.

Brüttaine, Brütaine, *sb.,* Sth. = Ml. Bretaine; OF. Bretaine, mod. by OE. Bryt, Bryten; *Britain,* 184, 8. Cf. **Britayn.**

Brüttisc, *adj.,* Sth. = Ml. Brittish; OE. Brytisc; *British,* 183, 29.

brȳche, *adj.,* OE. brȳce; *useful, of service,* 96, 17.

bryght, *see* **briȝt.**

brynge(n), *see* **bringe(n).**

brynīge, *sb.,* ON. brynja, OE. byrne; *coat of mail; pl.* brynīges, 3, 7.

Brytayn, *see* **Bretayne.**

Brytŏn, *see* **Britŏn.**

būc, *sb.,* OE. būc; *belly, paunch, abdomen,* 195, 23.

buckler, *sb.,* OF. bucler; *buckler,* p. 282.

büdel, *sb.,* Sth.= Ml. bidel, bēdel; OE. bydel; *beadle,* 194, 22.

bug = buȝ, *sb.,* OE. bŏh(g); *bough; pl.* buges, 21, 24; bōwes, ꝛoꝛ, 14.

būȝe(n), būhe(n), *stv.,* OE. būgan –bēah(2); *bow, turn, go; be obedient; inf.* būȝe, 184, 8; būhen, 193, 26; Sth. *pt. sg.* bēh, 185, 26. Cf. **bōwe(n).**

bulche, *sb.,* OE. *bulce, cogn. with ON. bulki, MnE. bulk; hump, heap, bunch,* 60, 10.

bülde(n), *wkv.,* Sth. = Ml. bilde(n); OE. byldan; *build; imp. pl.* büldeð, 196, 8; *pt. pl.* bülde, 221, 20.

büldyng, *sb.,* Sth. = Ml. bildinge, based on bülde(n); *building,* 220, 3.

bünden, *see* **bīnde(n).**

bündyn, *adj.* < *pp.* ME. bünde(n); *bound,* 169, 29.

büntē, *see* **bōüntē.**

būr, bōūr, *sb.,* OE. būr; *bower, originally the woman's part of the house,* 35, 16; bōūr, 49, 7. eSth. *ds.* būre, 181, 12.

Burch, *see* **burh.**

bürde, *sb.,* Sth.= Ml. birde; OE. *byrdu?; woman,* 191, 11.

burȝewere, *see* **burhwere.**

burgeis, *sb.,* OF. burgeis; *burgess, citizen,* 42, 21.

burh, burch, *sb.,* OE. burh(g), *f.; town, borough,* 6, 27; specifically Burch = *Peterborough,* 1, 2. eSth. *ds.* burhȝe, 187, 17.

burhfolc, *sb.,* OE. *burhfolc; people of the town, citizens,* 187, 26.

burhȝe, *see* **burh.**

burhwere, *sb.* OE. burhwaru; *dweller in a city, citizen; pl.* burhweren, 187, 7; burȝewere, 187, 19.

būrn, *sb.,* OE. burna, burne; *brook, little stream,* 168, 24.

burne, *see* **berne(n).**

bürst, *adj.,* Sth.= Ml. brist; *allied to* OE. byrst, *sb.,* 'bristle'; *bristly clothed with bristles,* 195, 12.

bürþtonge, *sb.*, Sth. = Ml. birþtunge ;
OE. (ge)byrd + tunge ; *birth tongue,
mother tongue,* 224, 16.

busk, *sb.*, OE. *busc ?, cf. Dan. busk,
LL. *buxicum ; *bush, stalk,* 23,
9.

buske(n), *wkv.*, ON. būask, ' get
oneself ready ' ; *prepare, adorn,
disguise, go* ; *imp. sg.* busk, 161, 8 ;
pt. sg. busked, 108, 4.

busshel, *sb.*, OF. buissel ; *bushel* ;
pl. busshels, 242, 8.

busshment, *sb.*, OF. buschement ;
ambush ; *pl.* busshmentz, 233, 19.

but, bute, *see* būte(n), bōte.

būte(n), later but, bōt(e), *prep.
conj.*, OE. būtan ; *but, except, without,* 2, 6 ; būten, 16, 24 ; būte, 17,
24 ; but, 26, 4 ; but if, *except,* 118,
7. eSth. būte ȝif, 199, 33, būte,
without, 177, 28.

butelēr, *sb.*, OF. bouteillier ; *butler,*
21, 19.

butere, *sb.*, OE. butere, Lat. buty-
rum ; *butter,* 3, 27.

būþ, *see* bē(n).

butirflīȝe, *sb.*, OM. buttorflēge (flīge),
WS. -flēoge ; *butterfly,* 36, 25.

buven, *see* abuven.

buxsumnes, bouxomnes, *sb.*, OE.
būhsomnes, *f.* ; *obedience, humility,*
127, 12 ; bouxomnes, 146, 29.

bȳ, *see* bē, bige(n), bē(n).

bycause, *adv. prep.*, OE. bi + OF.
cause ; *because,* 221, 7.

byd(de), byddys, *see* bidde(n).

bȳddynge, byddyng, biding, *sb.*,
OE. *bīddung, *f.* ; *praying, bidding,
command* ; byddyng, 96, 30 ; biding,
138, 25.

bȳden, bȳdin, *see* bīde(n).

bȳe(n), *see* bige(n).

bȳeþ, *see* bē(n).

byfalle(n), byfell, byfūl, byfyl,
see bifalle(n).

bygēoden, byȝēode, *see* bigō(n).

bygynnyng, *see* biginning.

byhālden, *see* bihālde(n),

byheste, byn, *see* biheste, bē(n).

bylēve, *sb.*, OE. *beleafe, gelēafe ;
belief, 125, 34.

bynk, *sb.*, Nth. = Ml. benk ; ON.
bennk ; *bench,* 173, 26.

byrīede(n), *see* birīe(n).

byrthen, *sb.*, OE. byrðen ; *burden,*
2, 5.

byschoprȳke, *sb.*, OE. biscoprice ;
bishopric, 113, 28.

bysīdes, *see* bisīde.

bysȳnes, *see* bisīnəs.

bytāken, *see* bitācne(n).

bytwēne, *see* bitwēn.

bytwixand, *see* bətwix.

C.

caas, *see* cas.

cāble, *sb.*, OF. cable ; *cable,* 86, 26.

cache(n), *wkv.*, NF. cachier ; *catch* ;
inf. cache, 125, 28.

Cādor, *sb.*, OF. Cador ; *Cador,* 190,
17.

čēəsə, *sb.*, eME. = Ml. chēse ; OM.
cēse, WS. cīese ; *cheese,* 3, 27.

čæste, *see* chestə.

Cæstre, *sb.*, eME. = Ml. Chestre,
Chester ; OE. Ceaster, Lat. castra ;
Chester, 5, 19.

Cai, *sb. Kay,* 126, 13.

Caim (Kaim), [Kaïm], *sb.*, OE.
Cain with change of final consonant,
or OF. *Caim ; *Cain,* 68, 10.

caitīf, *sb.*, NF. caitif ; *caitiff, wretch,*
63, 8 ; kaitȳf, 240, 32 ; *pl.* kaytefes,
155, 12.

cakel, *adj.*, ON. *kakel, cf. Swed.
kackla ? ; *cackling* ; kakel, 198, 18.

cakele(n), *wkv.*, ON., cf. Swed.
kackla ? ; *cackle* ; *inf.* kakelen, 198,
21 ; *pr. ppl.* kakelinde, 198, 24 ;
pp. icakeled, 198, 27.

cālende, *sb.*, OE. calend ; *first of the
month* ; þē fortēnde kālende of
Mearch, *the fourteenth day from the
first of March,* 197, 9.

calīs, *sb.*, OF. (Picard) calice ;
chalice, 203, 8.

Calixtes, *sb.*, Lat. Calixtus ; *Calixtus, Pope and Saint,* 209, 19.

calle(n), *wkv.*, ON. kalla ; *call* ; *inf.*
calle, 87, 30 ; *pt. sg.* kalde, 63, 28 ;

kalled, 94, 9; callyd, 105, 21; *pp.*
cald, 135, 8.

Cambria, *sb.*, Lat. Cambria; *Cambria*, 223, 8.

Camelförd, *sb.*, *Camelford*, 109, 21;
ds. Camelförde, 189, 22.

Campaine, *sb.*, NF. Campaine;
Campania, 196, 32.

can = gan, *see* ginne(n).

canceler, *sb.*, NF. canceler, later
displaced by OF. chancelere;
chancellor, 2, 25.

cändel, **candel**, *sb.*, OE. candel
(cändel), cŏndel; *candle*; kandel,
82, 29; *pl.* cändles, 5, 14, candelys,
117, 2.

cändelmasse, **candelmasse**, *sb.*, OE.
Candelmæsse (cändel-); *Candelmas*,
5, 25.

candelys, *see* cändel.

canŏn, *sb.*, OE. canon; *canon, rule*,
245, 29.

canŏn, *sb.*, OF. (Picard) canone;
canon, prebendary; *pl.* canŏns,
210, 3.

Cantelow, *sb.*, *Cantelupe*, Walter of,
Bishop of Worcester, 227, 1.

Cantwarberī, *sb.*, OE. Cantwaraburh
(-byrig, **Kt.** -berig); *Canterbury*,
5, 16; Caunterbirȳ, 231, 24. **Sth.**
Kantebürī, 226, 24.

canunk, *sb.*, ON. kanunkr; *canon,
prebendary*; *gs.* kanunnkess (O), 8,
17.

cäpŏn, *sb.*, OF. capon, AN. capun;
capon; *pl.* cäpŏns, 244, 28.

Carausius, *sb.*, Lat. Carausius;
Carausius, 221, 21.

cäre, *sb.*, OM. caru, WS. cearu; *care,
sorrow*, 39, 2; eME. kare, 177, 21.

cäreful, *adj.*, OE. cearful; *full of
care, careful*; eME. *superl.* karefullest, 188, 27.

carīe(n), *wkv.*, NF. carier; *carry*,
inf. carȳe, 233, 15; *pr. ppl.* cariynge,
245, 14; *pp.* carīed, 239, 3. **Sth.**
pp. ycarīed, 242, 28.

carited = caritēþ, *sb.*, NF. caritēth,
OF. caritē, charitē, Lat. caritatem;
charity, almsgiving, 4, 13.

cariynge, *see* carīen.

carl, *sb.* as *adj.*, ON. karl; *man, male*,
contemptuously, *low, common man*;
carl, 240, 21; carle, 111, 25.

Carliün, *sb.*, AN. Carliun; *Caerleon*;
Karliün, 188, 24.

carlman, *sb.*, ON. karl, OE. man;
male person, man; *pl.* carlmen,
3, 3.

carole, *sb.*, OF. carole; *carol, song*;
karole, 215, 21.

cart, *sb.*, ON. kartr, perh, OE. cræt;
cart; *pl.* cartes, 31, 10.

carȳe, *see* carīe(n).

cas, **cäs**, *sb.*, OF. cas; *case, circumstance*, 68, 9; kas, 98, 7; casę, 106,
30; *pl.* caas, 225, 9; par cas, *by
chance*, 245, 24.

castelweorc, *sb.*, NF. castel + OE.
weorc; *work of building castles,
castle work*; *pl.* castelweorces, 2,
32.

caste(n), *wkv.*, ON. kasta; *cast*;
inf. caste, 41, 19; *pr.* 3 *sg.* casteþ,
100, 22; *pt. sg.* caste, 207, 7; *pp.*
kast, 58, 19; cast, 245, 19. **Nth.**
pr. 3 *sg.* castys, 143, 24; *pp.* casten,
156, 2. **Sth.** *pp.* icaste, 42, 4. Cf.
keste(n).

castel(l), *sb.*, NF. castel; *castle*;
castell, 108, 16; *pl.* castles, 2, 14;
castelęs, 76, 32.

castynge, *sb.* < *pr. ppl.*, ME. casten;
casting, hurling, 124, 29.

castye, *see* caste(n).

cat, *sb.*, OE. catt; *cat*; kat, 202, 28.

catęl, **catellę**, **cateyl**, *sb.*, NF. catel,
OF. chatel; *cattle, property*, 53, 7;
catellę, 117, 27; kateyl, 94, 7.

Cathenēsia, *sb.*, Lat. Cathenesia;
Caithness, 220, 21.

Cätoün, *sb.*, AN. Catun; *Cato*, 216,
15.

cauersyn, **kauersyn**, *sb.*, OF. *cauer-
sin; *money-lender*, 88, 1.

Caunterbirȳ, *see* Cantwarberī.

cause, *sb.*, NF. cause; *cause*. **Nth.**
caus, 136, 26.

caye, *sb.*, OE. cǣg, *f.*, cǣge; *key*,
161, 22.

Cayfas, *sb.*, Lat. Caifas; *Caiaphas*;
gs. Cayfas, 137, 7.

caysēre, *sb.*, ON. keisari ; *emperor* ; kaysēre, 75, 15 ; kaysēr, 162, 9 ; keisēr, 192, 4.

ce = se.

cęęs, *see* cēse(n).

cendel, *sb.*, OF. cendal, sendal ; *rich cloth*, 49, 6.

cergě, *sb.*, OF. cirge ; *wax candle*, 83, 7.

certain, sertaynę, certānę, *adj.*, *adv.*, OF. certein ; *certain* ; sertayne ; 141, 13 ; lNth. certānę, 167, 21.

certānę, *see* certain.

certes, certys, *adv.*, OF. certes ; *certainly*, 38, 11 ; certys, 107, 16 ; sertis, 138, 10.

Cēsar, *sb.*, OF. Cesar ; *Cæsar* ; Julȳ Cēsar, 126, 4.

cęse(n), *wkv.*, OF. cesser ; *cęase, cause to cease* ; *inf.* cęęs, 111, 27.

cetē, *see* citē.

cēte, *sb.*, OF. cēte ; *whale*, 19, 15.

cēthegrande, *sb.*, OF. cetegrande ; NF. cēthegrande ; *whale*, 19, 1.

ch = tf(tsh).

chaffāre, cheffāre, *sb.*, OM. *cēap fare ; *chaffer, trade*, 95, 25. Sth. cheffare, 203, 5.

chāld, *see* cōld.

chalȳs, *sb.*, OF. chalice ; *chalice, communion cup*, 122, 10. Cf. calīs.

chāmbre, *see* chaumbre.

Chānaan, *sb.*, Lat. (Vulgate) Chanaan ; *Canaan*, 24, 29.

chance, *see* chaunce.

chanoun, *sb.*, OF. chanoun, AN. canon ; *canon*, 75, 22. Cf. canōn.

chānge(n), *wkv.*, OF. changer ; *change* ; *pt. sg.* chayngede = chāngede, 224, 28 ; Nth. *pt.* chāngit, 170, 9.

chapēl, *sb.*, OF. chapele ; *chapel*, 230, 9.

char, *see* cher.

charemyngę, *sb.*, based on charmen, OF. charmer ; *enchantment*, 145, 12.

chāre(n), *wkv.*, OE. cerran ; *turn, go* ; *inf.* chāren, 33, 20 ; *pr.* 1 *sg.* chāre, 32, 6.

charǧe, *sb.*, OF. charge ; *charge, wéight*, 145, 5.

charǧe(n), *wkv.*, OF. chargier ; *charge, load, weigh down* ; *pp.* charged, 89, 26.

Charles, *sb.*, OF. Charles, NF. Carl ; *Charles* ; *Charles the Great, Charlemagne*, 126, 15.

chartre, *sb.*, OF. chartre ; *charter*, 85, 24.

chartre, *sb.*, OF. chartre ; *prison*, 21, 7.

charytē, charitē, *sb.*, OF. charitē, NF. caritē ; *charite*, 89, 31 ; charytee, 116, 12 ; charitē, 127, 14. Cf. caritēd.

chāsēr, *sb.*, based on chasse(n) ; *chaser, pursuer* ; *pl.* chāsēris, 169, 5.

chass, *sb.*, OF. chace ; *chase*, 168, 27.

chasse(n), *wkv.*, OF. chacier ; *chase* ; *pr. ppl.* chassand, 169, 2.

chassing, *sb.*, based on OF. chacier ; *chasing, chase*, 168, 29.

chāst(e), *adj.*, OF. chaste ; *chaste*, 120, 3.

chastīe(n), *wkv.*, Sth. = Ml. chaste(n) ; OF. chastier ; *chastise, chasten* ; *imp. pl.* chastī ǧē, 200, 21.

chastīement, *sb.*, OF. chastiement ; *chastisement*, 200, 29.

chastitē, *sb.*, OF. chastetē ; *chastity*, 127, 13.

chaul, *see* chāvel.

chaumberlayn, *sb.*, OF. chamberlene, -lain ; *chamberlain*, 41, 1.

chaumbre, chāmbre, *sb.*, OF. chambre ; *chamber*, 35, 23 ; chaumbre, 49, 2 ; chāmbre, 241, 6.

chaunce, *sb.*, OF. cheance ; *chance*, 90, 20.

chaunǧe, *sb.*, OF. change ; *change*, 128, 7.

chaunǧe(n), *wkv.*, OF. changier ; *change* ; *pr.* 1 *sg.* chaunge, 37, 14 ; *pr. pl.* chaungen, 37, 30 ; *pt. sg.* chaungede, 45, 4 ; *pp.* chaunged, 52, 29. Sth. *pp.* ychaunged, 224, 27.

chāvel, chaul, *sb.*, OM. cafl, WS. ceafl ; *jaw, beak ; talk, chatter* ; chāvel, 19, 15 ; chaul, 60, 17. eSth. chēafle, 201, 7.

chayng̑ede, *see* **chāng̑e(n)**.
chēafle, *see* **chāvel**.
chēapīe(n),*wkv.*,**Sth.** = Ml. chēpe(n);
OE. chēapian; *buy, sell*; *pr.* 3 *sg.*
chēapeð, 203, 5.
chēapild, *sb.*, based on OE. cēap +
hyld; *fond of bargaining, a bar-
gainer*, 203, 5.
cheffare, *see* **chaffāre**.
chēle, *sb.*, OM. cele, WS. ciele; *chill,
cold*, 219, 6.
chēofle(n), *wkv.*, **eME** = Ml. chē-
vle(n); OE. *ceaflian, cf. LG.
kavilen; *chatter, converse aimlessly*;
pr. 3 *sg.* chēofled = chēofleð, 200,
10.
chēoke, *sb.*, **eME.** = Ml. chēke; OE.
cēoce; *cheek*. **Sth.** *pl.* chēoken,
200, 10.
chēose, *see* **chēse(n)**.
chepmon, *sb.*, **Sth.** = Ml. chapman;
OE. cēapman; *merchant, chapman*,
203, 6.
cher, char, *sb.*, OM. cerr, WS. cierr;
turn, time, piece of work; char, 53,
16. **Sth.** *ds.* chere, 192, 9; cherre,
197, 17.
cherche, *see* **chirche**.
chēre,*sb.*, OF. chēre, chiere; *countenance,cheer(with change of meaning)*,
45, 4. **Nth.** chēr, 155, 21.
cherise(n), *wkv.*, OF. cherir, *pr. st.*
cheriss-; *cherish*; *inf.* cherise, 234,
32.
chērl, cherl, *sb.*, OE. ceorl; *husbandman, rustic, churl*, 83, 33.
cherre, *see* **cher**.
chēse, *sb.*, OM. cēse, WS. cīese;
cheese, 84, 23. Cf. eME. **cǣse**.
chēse(n), *stv.*, OE. cēosan –cēas (2);
choose; *inf.* chēse, 233, 13; *pt. sg.*
chēs, 130, 30; *pt. pl.* (eME cusen,
8, 1); chōsen, 76, 7; *pp.* (eME.
cosan, 8, 4); chōsen, 102, 24. **Sth.**
(eSth. *inf.* cheose, 220, 15); *pp.*
icoren, 179, 15; icornee, 212, 26.
cheste, *sb.*, OE. cist, cest, *f.*; *chest,
box*, 241, 5; eME. cæste, (MS.
ceste?) 3, 11.
chēste, chẹst, *sb.*, OE. cēast, *f.*?;
strife, contention; chẹst, 68, 17.

chēsūn, chẹsōn, *sb.*, AN. acheisun,
OF. (-on); *occasion, motive*, 91, 5;
chẹsōn, 145, 26.
chēsynge, *sb.*, OE. *cēosung, *f.*;
choosing, 117, 30.
chewe(n), *stv.*, OE. cēowan –cēaw
(2); *chew*; *pr. sbj.* chewe, 122, 14.
chiloe, *sb.*,OE. *cildse; *childishness,
puerility*, 176, 7.
chīld (chȳld),*pl.* childer (childre),
children; OE. cīld; *child*; eME.
cild, 4, 29; chīldẹ, 163, 20; *pl.*
childer, 24, 21; chyldyr, 116, 4;
gpl. without ending, childer, 69,
12; children, 80, 6. **Sth.***ds.* chīlde,
176, 24; *pl.* children, 202, 18; childern, 225, 6; chyldern, 224, 17.
chīldhẹde,*sb.*, OE. cild,cīld + *hǣde;
cf. OE. cildhād; *childhood*, 214, 2.
Childrīch(e), *sb.*, OE. *Cildrīc;
Childrich, 185, 17.
chirche, *sb.*, OE. cirice; *church*, 72,
30; eME. circe, 3, 32; cherche,
88, 6.
chirchegǫng, *sb.*, OE. cyrice + gang;
church-going, church-service, 34,
18.
chirchepȳrl, *sb.*, **Sth.**= Ml. chirche-
þirl; OE. cyrice + þyrl; *church
window*; *ds.* chircheþürle, 199. 21.
chirch-hay, *sb.*, OE. cirice + hege,
'hedge, enclosure'; *churchyard*,
124, 25.
chǫsen, *see* **chēse(n)**.
chǫst, *sb.*, OE. cēast becoming ceāst?;
dispute, strife, 125, 1.
chyldyr, *see* **chīld**.
chyrche, *see* **chirche**.
chyrcheȝẹrd, -ȝẹrde, -ȝorde,*sb.*, OE.
*ciricegeard (ȝeard); *churchyard*,
88, 6; eME. cyrceiǣrd, 3, 32;
chyrcheȝorde, 124, 32.
chytering, *sb.*, based on chitere(n);
chattering, 224, 15.
chyvalrōūs, *adj.*, OF. chevalereus;
chivalrous, 114, 29.
ciclatūn,*sb.*,AN. ciclatun; *ciclatoun,
sort of rich cloth*, 192, 27.
čīld, čirce, *see* **chīld, chirche**.
čircewīcan, eME. for chirchewīken,
OE. cirice + wīce, *wkf.*, *office of the*

churchwarden; circewīcan, 4, 20.
Cf. **wīken.**

citē (cytē), sitē, *sb.,* OF. citē; *city,*
73, 24; cytē, 106, 3; sitē, 32, 31.
Nth. cetē, 135, 6.

clad, cladde, *see* **clōþe(n).**

clane, *adv.,* OE. clǣne (clāne);
wholly, clean (in dial. English),
183, 9.

clanse(n), *wkv.,* OE. clǣnsian by
shortening; *cleanse; inf.* clanse,
122, 18. Cf. **clense(n).**

Clāre, *sb.,* OF. Clare; *Clare,* Richard
of, 227, 2.

Clārīce, Clārīs, *sb.,* OF. Claris;
Clarice, 36, 31.

clāþ, clāþe, *sb.,* **eME., Nth.** = Ml.
clōþ; OE. clāð; *cloth, garment, pl.
clothes,* 150, 12; *pl.* clāðes, 192,
27.

clause, *sb.,* OF. clause; *clause, sentence,* 155, 29.

clauwe, clawe, *sb.,* OE. clawu; *claw,*
60, 11; clawe, 231, 23.

clay, *sb.,* OE. clǣg; *clay,* 50, 12.

clēf, *see* **clēve(n).**

clēne, clēn, *adj.,* OE. clǣne; *clean,
pure, chaste,* 33, 23. **lNth.** clēn,
157, 3.

clenlīche, *adv.,* **Sth.** = Ml. clenlī;
OE. clǣnlīce; *cleanly,* 219, 31.

clennesse, *sb.,* OE. clǣnness, *f.;
cleanness, chastity,* 232, 11.

clense(n), *wkv.,* OE. clǣnsian;
cleanse; inf. clense, 102, 1. **Nth.**
inf. clens, 156, 10. **Kt.** *pr.* 3 *sg.*
clenzeþ, 217, 16; *pp.* yclenzed,
218, 8.

cleopīen, *see* **clēpe(n).**

clēpe(n), *wkv.,* OE. cleopian (cli-
pian); *call; inf.* clēpe, 222, 26;
pt. sg. clēpede, 41, 1; *pt. pl.* (eME.)
clepeden, 3, 23; *pp.* clēped, 39,
29. **Sth.** *inf.* (eSth. cleopīen, 187,
32); *pr. pl.* clēpīeth, 211, 17;
clēpeþ, 222, 24; *pr. sbj. pl.* clēpīe,
211, 14; *imp. sg.* clēpe, 212, 12;
imp. pl. (eSth. cleopeð, 196, 11);
pt. sg. (eSth. cleopede, 184, 4);
pp. yclēpud, 221, 6; Cf. **Sth.
clūpīe(n).**

cleppe, *sb.,* **Sth.** = Ml. clappe; OE.
*clæppe; cf. MDu. klappe, kleppe;
clapper,* 200, 11.

cleppe(n), *wkv.,***Kt.** = Ml. clippe(n);
OE. clyppan; *embrace; inf.* cleppen,
40, 20; *pr. pl.* cleppen, 39, 7; *pt.
pl.* klepte, 37, 32; **Sth.** *pp.* iclept,
41, 8.

clerc, *see* **clerk.**

clēr(e), *adj.,* OF. cler. clier; *clear,
excellent,* 101, 9.

clərğīe, *sb.,* OF. clergie; *learning,*
216, 12.

clərk, *sb.,* OE. cleric, infl. by OF.
clerc; *clergyman, scholar, clerk*;
clerc, 8, 2. **Sth.** *pl.* clerken, 209,17.

clēve, *sb.,* OE. cleofa; *chamber, den,
house,* 82, 1.

clēve(n), *stv.,* OE. clēofan-clēaf (2) ;
cleave, split; pt. sg. clēf, 51, 24.

clīmbe(n), *str.,*OE.climban (clīmban)
–clamb (clōmb) (3); *climb; inf.*
clīmben, 101, 14; *pr. sbj. pl.*
clīmben, 201, 13.

clive(n), *wkv.,* OE. clifian; *adhere,
cleave, belong; pr.* 3 *sg.* cliveð, 31,
32.

cliver, *adj.,* OE. clibbor?; *tenacious,
bold,* 18, 25.

clōche = cluche, *sb.,* origin uncertain;
clutch, 60, 6.

clōþ, *sb.,* OE. clāð; *garment, pl.
clothes;* clōþþe, 93, 6; clōþes, *bedclothes,* 41, 19.

clōþe(n), *wkv.,* OE. clāðian; *clothe;
pp. sg.* clōþede, 77, 23; *pp.* clōðed,
17, 17; clad, 23, 24. **Sth.** *pp.*
yclōðed, 231, 25.

clōþing, *sb.,* based on OE. clāð;
clothing, 92, 27.

clout, clowt, *see* **clūt.**

cloyster, *sb.* or *adj.,* OF. cloistre;
cloister, 154, 5.

Clūnīe, *sb.,* OF. Clunie; *Cluny,* dep.
Saône-et-Loire, 1, 3.

clūpīe(n), *wkv.,* **Sth.** = Ml. clipen
(clepen) OE. clypian; *cry out,
call; inf.* clūpīe, 206, 3; *pp.*
iclūped, 179, 15.

clūse, *sb.,* OE. clūs, *f.; enclosure,
dam (of a mill),* 201, 1.

clūt, clout, clowt, *sb.*, OE. clūt;
clout, rag; *pl.* clūtes, 81, 22; clout,
57, 8; clowt, 241, 7.

clyf, *sb.*, OE. clif (cleof); *cliff*, 222,
14.

clynke(n), *wkv.*, cf. MDu. clinken;
clink, ring as a bell; *inf.* clynke,
239, 2.

cnāve, *sb.*, OE. cnafa; *boy, servant*,
54, 28; knāve, 82, 11.

cnāwe(n), *see* knawe(n).

cniht, *sb.*, OE. cniht; *knight*, 181, 5.

cnotted, *pp.* as *adj.*, OE. cnottod <
cnottian; *knotted*, 3, 8.

cōf, *adj.*, OE. cāf; *swift, eager, bold*,
17, 17; þē cōve, *the swift one, the
thief* ?, 198, 22.

coine(n), *wkv.*, OF. coigner; *coin*;
8th. *pp.* ycoyned, 242, 7.

cōk, *sb.*, OE. cōc; *cook*; *pl.* cōkes,
49, 9.

cōld, *adj.*, OM. cald, cāld, WS. ceald;
cold, 39, 4; kōld, 77, 19. eKt.
chāld, 218, 6.

cōlīe(n), *wkv.*, Sth. = Ml. cōle(n);
OE. cōlian; *become cool, cool*; *pt. sg.*
cōlede, 195, 17.

cōlter, *sb.*, OE. culter, Lat. culter;
colter, 60, 23.

com, cōm(an), *see* cume(n).

cōm, *see* cōme.

comande(n), *wkv.*, OF. commander;
command; *pr.* 1 *sg.* comand, 69,
22; *pt. sg.* commandede, 222, 26;
cumand, 163, 17; *pp.* comaunded,
235, 2. Nth. *pr. ppl.* comand, 151,
5; *pp.* comand, 140, 20.

comandement, comandment, *sb.*,
OF. comandement; *commandment,
engagement*; comandement, 69, 15;
comandment, 67, 32; cumandment, 163, 14; *pl.* commande-
mentes, 144, 8; comaundement,
234, 4.

comaunde(n), *see* comande(n).

comaundement, *see* comandement.

cōme, *sb.*, OE. *cōme; cf. ON kvāma,
f.; *coming, arrival*, 11, 6. Nth.
cōm, 133, 3.

cōme(n), *see* cume(n).

coming, *see* cume(n).

cōmlyng, *sb.*, OE. *cumelung ?, cf.
OHG. chomeling; *new comer,
stranger*, 225, 13.

comm, *see* cume(n).

commandement, *see* comandement

commūn, comōnẹ, *adj.*, AN. cumun,
OF. comon; *common*, 133, 26; comōnẹ,147,14; in commune, *together*,
all together, 233, 23; *pl.* as *sb.* commūnes, *commons*, 233, 12.

commyxstiōn, *sb.*, OF. commistion,
AN. commistiun, infl. by Lat. com-
mixtio; *commingling*, 224, 13.

cōmon, *see* cume(n).

comōnẹ, comōun, *see* commūn.

compaignȳe, cumpanȳ, *sb.*, OF.
compaignie; *company*, 237, 7.

companȳe(n), *wkv.*, OF. com-
paignier; *accompany, meet together*;
inf. companȳe(n), 234, 11.

compelle(n), *wkv.*, OF. compeller;
compel; *pp.* compelled, 224, 18.

compīle(n), *wkv.*, OF. compiler;
compile; *pp.* compīled, 234, 23.

compleyne(n), *wkv.*, OF. com-
pleindre; *complain*; *pr. pl.* compleynen, 232, 20.

coms, comp, *see* cume(n).

comūne(n), *wkv.*, AN. communier;
commune, converse; *pr. ppl.* comūnyng, 236, 15.

comūnlȳch, comūnlīk, *adv.*, AN.
comun + ME. līche; *commonly*, 93,
15. Nth. comūnlīk, 133, 28.

Comyn, *sb.*, *Comyn*; Jǫn þē, 159,
29.

comvn, *see* cume(n).

con, conne, *see* cunne(n).

conceive(n), *wkv.*, NF. conceivre,
OF. concoivre; *conceive, beget*; *pt.
sg.* conceived, 102, 6; *pp.* conceived,
102, 5.

concepciōn, *sb.*, OF. conception;
conception, conceiving, 133, 10.

concyence, concyens, conscience,
sb., OF. conscience; *conscience*, 144,
9; concyence, 146, 1; consciens,
155, 31.

condiciōn, *sb.*, OF. condicion; *condition*, 220, 14.

cone, *see* cunne(n).

348   GLOSSARY

confederat, *adj.*, Lat. confederatus; *confederate, associated with*, 224, 7.

conferme(n), *wkv.*, OF. confermer; *confirm*; *imp. sg.* conferme, 102, 15.

confiture, *sb.*, OF. confiture; *preserve, confection*, 245, 1.

confort, *sb.*, OF. confort; *comfort*, 160, 3.

conforte(n), *wkv.*, OF. conforter; *comfort*; *pt. pl.* conforted, 101, 6. Nth. *pr.* 3 *sg.* confortes, 151, 2; *pp.* confort, 140, 32.

confounde(n), *wkv.*, OF. confundre; *confound, injure, destroy*; Nth. *pr. pl.* confoundes, 147, 6.

confusion, *sb.*, OF. confusion; *confusion*, 238, 17.

congregacioun(en), *wkv.*, based on AN. congregatiun; *assemble*, 118, 25.

conne(n), *see* cunne(n).

conquerour, *sb.*, OF. conquereur; *conqueror*, 126, 3.

conquest, *sb.*, OF. conqueste; *conquest*, 225, 2.

consail, conseil, *see* conseyl.

consciens, *see* concyence.

conseilie(n), *wkv.*, Sth. = Ml. conseile(n); AN. cunseilier, OF. conseilier; *counsel*; *inf.* conseili. 204, 21; *pt. sg.* conseilede, 206, 16; *pt. pl.* conseilede, 205, 28.

consenti(n), *wkv.*, Sth. = Ml. consente(n); OF. consentir; *consent*; *inf.* consenti, 217, 31.

conseyl, consail, *sb.*, OF. conseil, AN. cunseil; *counsel*; conseyl, 100, 24; conseil, 204, 15; conseille, 236, 7; consayl, 46, 32. Cf. counseil.

Constantin, *sb.*, OE. Constantin; *Constantine*, 190, 18.

construccion, *sb.*, OF. construction; *construction*, 224, 28.

construe(n), *wkv.*, OF. construire; *construe, explain, translate*; *inf.* construe, 224, 19; *pr. pl.* construeþ, 225, 3.

contemplacyone, *sb.*, OF. contemplacion; *contemplation*, 145, 7.

contemplaytyfe, *adj.*, OF. contemplatif; *contemplative*, 146, 18.

contenanss, *see* cuntenaunce.

conteyne(n), *wkv.*, OF. continir, *conteinir; *contain, include*; *pr.* 3 *sg.*; conteyneþ, 221, 28.

contrē, contray (contrei), *sb.*, OF. cuntree; *country*, 37, 16; contree, 239, 14; contray, 221, 31; *pl.* contrays, 220, 6; contreie, 205, 32; cuntrē, 98, 8.

contrycyōn, *sb.*, OF. contricion, AN. contriciun; *contrition*; contrycyōne, 123, 23.

contynúe(n), *wkv.*, OF. continuer; *continue*; *pp.* contynued, 234, 25.

converte(n), *wkv.*, OF. converter; *convert*; *pt. sg.* convertid, 135, 4; convertede, 221, 30; *pp.* converted, 102, 17.

conveye(n), *wkv.*, OF. conveier; *convey*, 230, 19.

cōpe, *sb.*, ON. kāpa, LL. capa; *cope*, 61, 5.

corāg̃eūs, *adj.*, OF. corageus; *courageous*, 206, 1.

coreccion, *sb.*, OF. correction; *correction*, 236, 8.

cōrn (corn), *sb.*, OE. cōrn; *corn, grain*, 3, 27.

cōrnlōnd, *sb.*, OE. corn + lōnd; *corn land*, 225, 32.

Cornwal, Cornwaile, *sb.*, OE. Cornweal; *Cornwall*; *ds.* Cornwale, 188, 32; Cornwalen, *pl.* ?, 188, 9; Cornwaile, 190, 17; Jōhan, 224, 27.

coroune, *sb.*, AN. corune; *crown*, 227, 19. Cf. crōune (crūne).

coroune(n), *wkv.*, OF. coruner; *crown*; *pr.* 3 *sg.* coroūneþ, 216, 30; *pp.* coroūned, 229, 31.

corrupt, *adj.*, OF. corrupt; *corrupt*, 2,8, 22.

cors, *sb.*, OF. cors; *corpse, corse, body*, 118, 13.

corsed, *see* curse(n).

corsur, *sb.*, origin uncertain, cf. corser, N.E.D.; *dealer in horses*, 108, 11.

cos, *sb.*, OE. coss; *kiss*, 196, 21.

cosan, *see* chēse(n).

cosīn, *sb.*, OF. cosin ; *cousin, relative,*
204, 28.

cost, *sb.*, OF. coste ; *expense,* at here
comoūn cost, *at their expense in
common,* 118, 24.

cǫste, *sb.*, OF. coste ; *coast,* 220, 9.

costnīe(n), *wkv.*, ON. kosta extended ?; *cost, expend ; pr.* 3 *sg.*
costneþ, 219, 20.

costome, *see* custome.

cǫte, *sb.* OE. cote ; *cote, cot,* 87, 22.

cǫte, MS. colte, *sb.*, OE. colt ; *colt,*
61, 12.

Cotingham, *sb.*, *Cottingham* (Northampton), 4, 23.

coūnseil, coūnsaylę, *sb.*, AN. cunseil ; *counsel,* 100, 15 ; coūnsaylę,
110, 5 ; counsail, 200, 18.

coūrs, *see* cūrs.

coūrt, *sb.*, OF. curt ; *court,* 50, 17 ;
cūrt, 7, 32 ; courtę, 125, 1.

coūth, coūþest, *see* cunne(n).

covayte(n), *wkv.*, OF. cuveiter ;
covet ; Nth. *inf.* covayte, 147, 27 ;
pr. 2 *sg.* covaytes, 135, 23 ; *pt. sg.*
covayted, 140, 2 ; *pp.* covayt, 139,
32.

cǫve, *see* cǫf.

covenaunt, *sb.*, OF. covenant ; *covenant, agreement* ; at the covenaunt ;
with the agreement, 221, 3.

covent, *sb.*, OF. couvent, covent ;
convent, monastery, order of monks,
111, 29.

covertoūre, *sb.*, OF. coverture ;
covering, bedclothes, 49, 5.

coveytīse, *sb.*, OF. coveitise ; *cove-
tousness,* 54, 14.

coveytoūs, *adj.*, OF. coveitous ;
covetous, 88, 23.

cǫwlte, *sb.*, OF. coulte, cuilte ; *quilt,*
49, 5.

crādel, *sb.*, OE. cradol ; *cradle,* 224,
22.

craft, *sb.*, OE. cræft ; *power, skill,*
craft, 17, 6.

craftīlīk, *adv.*, OE. cræftiglīce ;
powerfully, wonderfully, craftily,
131, 4.

craftȳ, *adj.*, OE. cræftig ; *crafty,*
skilful, 129, 4.

crāke(n), crakke(n), *wkv.*, OE.
cracian ; *crack* ; *pt. sg.* crakede, 82,
12. Nth. *inf.* crak, 160, 24 : *pp.*
crakked, 159, 11.

crāve(n), *wkv.*, OE. crafian ; *crave* ;
inf. crāven, 31, 14 ; crāve, 54, 26 ;
pt. sg. crāvede, 84, 13.

crēatoūr, sb., OF. creatour ; *creator,*
246, 8.

crēatūre, *sb.*, OF. creature ; *creature,*
creation, 62, 26. Nth. *pl.* crēatūrs,
144, 23.

crēde, *sb.*, OE. crēda. Lat. crēdo ;
creed, 16, 25.

creoissen (croissen), *wkv.*, OF.
croiser ; *cross, sign with the cross* ;
imp. pl. creoiseð, 197, 20.

crēpe(n), *stv.*, OE. crēopan-crēap
(2) ; *creep* ; *pr.* 3 *sg.* crēpeð, 17, 6.
Nth. *inf.* crēp, 152, 11.

crī, crȳ, *sb.*, OF. crī ; *cry,* 62, 22.

crīe(n), *wkv.*, OF. crier ; *cry* ; *inf.*
crīe, 36, 6 ; crȳe, 105, 23 ; *pr. pl.*
crīen, 41, 31 ; *pr. sbj.* crīe, 198, 33 ;
pr. ppl. crīende, 60, 15 ; *pt. sg.*
crīed, 104, 10 ; *pt. pl.* crīede, 206,
19.

cripele(n), *wkv.*, based on OE.
cryppel ? ; *go as a cripple* ; *pr. ppl.*
cripelande, 17, 6.

crisme, *sb.*, OF. cresme ; *Chrism,*
sacred oil, 34, 11.

Crissten, *see* Crīsten.

crisstenndōm, *see* cristendōm.

crisstned, *see* cristne(n).

Crīst, *sb.*, OE. Crīst, Lat. Christus,
through OIr. Crīst : *Christ,* 1, 8 ; *gs.*
Crȳstys, 88, 5. Nth. *gs.* Crīstis,
135, 1 ; Sth. *ds.* Crīste, 176, 20.

Cristen, crystyn, *adj.*, *sb.*, OE.
cristen ; *Christian,* 4, 29 ; *pl.*
Crisstene (O), 10, 13, crystyn,
146, 6.

cristendōm, *sb.*, OE. cristendōm ;
Christendom ; Crisstenndōm (O),
8, 14 ; crystendōm, *christianity,*
salvation, 65, 9 ; 94, 24.

Cristenmesse, *sb.*, OE. cristen + OF.
messe ; *Christmas,* 229, 21.

cristientē, *sb.*, OF. chrestianitē,
cristianitē ; *cristendom,* 228, 32.

cristne(n): *wkv.*, OE. cristnian; *christen*; *pp.* crisstnedd (O), 13, 26.

cristninge, *sb.*, based on cristne(n); *christening*, 218, 4.

Cristōfer, *sb.*, OF. Cristopher; *Christopher*, 164, 7.

Cristus, *sb.*, Lat. Christus; *Christ*, 8, 11.

croicę, croycę, *sb.*, OF. crois; *cross*, 133, 1; croycę, 139, 22.

crōked, *pp.* as *adj.*, ME. crōke(n): *crooked*, 241, 32.

cronyclǝ(n). *wkv.*, OF. croniquer, *cronikler; *chronicle, record*; *pp.* cronyclyd, 116, 7.

cros, *sb.*, OIr. cross, through ON. kross; *cross*, 136, 23.

crōūne, crūne, *sb.*, AN. corune; *crown*, 82, 12; crōwne, 105, 19; crūne, 194, 33. Cf. corūne.

crōūne(n),*wkv.*,OF.coruner; *crown*; *pr.* 3 *sg.* crōūneþ, 104, 19.

crōwne, croyce, *see* crōūne, croicǝ.

crūcethūs, *sb.*, origin of first part unknown; *torture house*, 3, 11.

crucyfīǝ(n), *wkv.*, OF. crucifier; *crucify*; *pp.* crucifīede, 145, 23.

crūninge, *sb.*, based on crūne(n); *crowning, reign*, 226, 23.

crȳ, crȳe(n), *see* crī, crīe(n).

crystǝndōm, *see* cristendōm.

crystyn, Crȳstys, *see* Cristen, Crīst.

cū, kū, *sb.*, OE. cū; *cow*; *gs.* kūes, 202, 31.

cumandment, *see* comandment.

cumand, *see* comande(n).

cume(n), *stv.*, OE. cuman–cōm (cwōm) (4); *come*; *inf.* cumen, 1, 17; cume, 39, 16; cȯm, 74, 13; *pr.* 3 *sg.* cumeð, 15, 11; cȯmþ, 89, 12; *pr. pl.* cumen, 19, 13; cume gē, 25, 11; cȯmen, 58, 11; *pr. sbj. sg.* cȯme, 52, 8; *pr. sbj. pl.* cumen, 226, 18; cume, 180, 2; *imp. sg.* cum, 37, 24; *pr. ppl.* cȯminge, 39, 31; *pt. sg.* cȯm, 1, 1; comm (O), 11, 17; cam, 23, 7; kam, 15, 2; *pt. pl.* (eME. cȯmen, 2, 16); cȯme, 63, 30; *pt. sbj. sg.* cȯme, 8, 7; *pt. sbj. pl.* (eME. cōman, 4, 3); cȯmen,

185, 22; *pp.* cumen, 2, 7; cȯmyn, 110, 13. Nth. *pr.* 2 *sg.* cums, 141, 25; *pr.* 3 *sg.* cȯms, 127, 19; *pr. sbj. sg.* cum, 141, 30; *pr. ppl.* cumand, 149, 4; *pp.* cumin, 170, 32. Sth. *ger.* cumene, 214, 24; *pp.* icumen, 183, 23; icume, 40, 31; icȯme, 44, 26; ycȯmen, 73, 20.

cumpaignīe, cumpaynīe, *sb.*, AN. cumpaignie; *company, companionship*, 38, 22; cumpaynīe, 56, 21; cumpanȳ, 117, 15.

cumpanȳ, *see* cumpaignīe.

cumpasse(n), *wkv.*, AN. cumpasser; *compas, surround, protect*; *late ME. inf.* cumpas, 103, 27.

cums, *see* cume(n).

cumyng,*sb.*,OAng.*cumung; *coming*, 141, 23.

cün, *sb.*, Sth.=Ml. kin; OE. cynn; *kin, kind, race*; *ds.* cünne, 184, 12; *gpl.* cünne, 184, 1.

cunne(n), *ptprv.*, OE. cunnen–cūðe; *know, be able, can*; *inf.* kunne, 38, 9; cȯne, 55, 10; *pr.* 1, 3 *sg.* can, 3, 20 (WMl. cȯnnę, 125, 22); cȯn, 168, 19; ˙kan, 243, 27; *pr.* 2 *sg.* kanst, 70, 2; *pr. pl.* cunnen, 4, 9; cȯnnen, 51, 25; kunne, 78, 6; kȯnne, 235, 31; *pr. sbj. sg.* cunne, 14, 6; cune, 18, 10; cȯne, 84, 2; cȯnne, 210, 15; *pt.* 1, 3 *sg.* cūthe, 5, 19; kūðe, 198, 17; kūde, 23, 18; *pt.* 2 *sg.* cōuþest, 49, 29; *pt. pl.* kȯuþen, 76, 4; kūðen, 201, 4; *pt. sbj. sg.* cȯude, 89, 16. Nth. *pt. sg.* cȯuth, 167, 21; kȯuth, 136, 21. Sth. *pr. pl.* cȯnneþ, 225, 7.

cüntenaunce, *sb.*, AN. cuntenance; *countenance, expression*, 38, 4. Nth. cȯntenanss, 170, 9.

cüntesse, *sb.*, AN. cuntesse, OF. contesse; *countess*, 5, 31.

cuntraye, cuntrē, *see* contrē.

cūpe, *sb.*, OE. *cūpe; *basket*, 35, 18; *pl.* cūpen, 35, 15.

cuppe, cupe, *sb.*, OE. cuppa; *cup*, 29, 22; kuppe, 21, 11; cupe, 46, 5.

cur, *sb.*, OF. curre. cure; *chariot*, 192, 26; *ds.* cure, 192, 24.

oúratoūrẹ, *sb.*, OF. curateur ; *curator*, 119, 16.

Curbuil, *sb.*, OF. Corbuil, Corbeil ; *Curbeuil* (*Curbuil*, *Corbeil*) ; William of, Archbishop of Canterbury, 2, 9.

cūrs, *sb.*, OF. curs, cours ; *course*, *attack*, *assault*, *regard* ; 103, 30. Nth. hālden in cūrs, *hold in regard*, 128, 1.

cursednesse, *sb.*, based on curse(n) ; *cursedness*, 246, 2.

curse(n), *wkv.*, OE. cursian ; *curse* ; *inf.* curssen, 66, 12 ; *pt. sg.* cursede, 6, 4 ; *pt. pl.* cursede, 4, 5 ; *pp.* curssed, 68, 10 ; cursed, 121, 12 ; córsed, 61, 12.

cūrsur, *sb.*, Lat. cursor, infl. by OF. coursier ; *courser, runner* ; Cūrsur o Werld, translating cursor mundi, 134, 25.

cūrt, court, *sb.*, OF. curt ; *court*, 7, 32.

curteis, *adj.*, NF. curteis, OF. curtois ; *courteous*, 42, 22.

curteisȳe, curteysȳe, curtesȳ, *sb.*, NF. curteisie ; OF. curtoisie ; *courtesy*, 97, 26 ; córteysȳe, 219, 2 ; curteisȳe, 241, 10 ; kurteisīe, 199, 30.

cusẹn, *see* chēse(n).

cüsse(n), *wkv.*, Sth. = Ml. kisse(n) : OE. cyssan ; *kiss* ; *pt. sg.* cüste, 196, 21.

custome, costome, *sb.*, OF. custume ; *custom*, 89, 5 ; costome, 122, 1.

cut, *sb.*, Celtic origin, cf. Cymr. cwta ' short' ; *cut, lot*, 242, 30.

cùþ, *adj.*, OE. cūð ; *known*, 41, 10.

cūþe(n), *wkv.*, Sth. = Ml. kīðe(n) ; OE. cȳðan ; *make known* ; *pp.* icüd, 198, 8.

cūðlẹchunge, kúðlẹchunge, *sb.*, Sth. = Ml. cuðlēchinge ; OE. *cūðlǣcung, *f.*; cf. cūðlǣcan ; *acquaintance*, 199, 6.

cutted, *pp.* as *adj. pl.*, *slashed*, 120, 23.

cwēad, *see* quẹd.

cwēme(n), *wkv.*, OE. cwēman ; *please* ; *inf.* cwēmen, 179, 6 ; *pp.* cwemmd, (O), 12, 1.

cwēne, cweð, *see* quēne, cwẹþe(n).

cwike, *see* quik.

---

cyrceiǣrd, *see* chirchezẹrd.

cytē, *see* citē.

D.

dǣde, dǣi (dǣis), *see* dēde, dai.

dǣiliht, *sb.*, OE. *dæglēoht (liht) ; *daylight*, 187, 21.

dǣl, dǣre, dǣþ, *see* dẹl, dēre, dẹþ.

daft, *adj.*, OE. (ge)dæft ; *mild, stupid*, 49, 23. See deft.

daggere, *sb.*, ON. daggarðr ; *dagger*, 244, 2.

daghen, dawen, *sb.*, OE. dazung ?, *dazen ; *dawn*, 213, 24.

daz, dazzess, dazen, *see* dai.

dai, *sb.*, OE. dæg–dagas ; *day, dawn* ; (eME. dæi, 1, 14 ; dei, 1, 14) ; dazz (O), 11,9 ; dai, 15, 2 ; day, 37, 11 ; *gs.* (eME. dæies, 3, 3 ; dæis, 3, 26) ; *ds.* (WMl. dawe, 119, 10) ; *pl.* dazzess (O), 12, 10 ; daiges, 33, 29. Nth. *ds.* in expression bryng of daw ; *kill*, 170, 14. eSth. dei, 178, 20 ; *ds.* deie, 193, 5 ; *dpl.* dazen, 188, 9 ; *pl.* dawes, 200, 3. deis dei, *day's dawn*, 192, 15. Kt. deai, 212, 20.

dāl, *sb.*, Nth. = Ml. dǫle ; OE. dāl, *neut.*, *division, part*, 222, 10.

dāle, *sb.*, OE. dæl, *neut.*, Dan. dal, *m. f.* ; *dale*, 57, 23. Sth. (SEMl.) dẹle, 14, 3.

Dalreudīne, *sb.*, *Dalreudine* ; *pl.* 222, 9.

damǎge(n), *wkv.*, OF. *sb.* damage ; *damage* ; *pp.* damaged, 72, 8.

dāme, *sb.*, OF. dame ; *dame*, 82, 2.

damezēle, *sb.*, OF. damisele ; *damsel*, 216, 29.

dammǎge, *sb.*, OF. damage ; *damage, loss*, 95, 24.

dampnāble, *adj.*, CF. damnáble ; *damnable, condemnable*, 237, 16.

dampnācĭōn, *sb.*, OF. damnation ; *damnation, condemnation*, 238, 18.

dampne(n), *wkv.*, OF. damner ; *condemn, damn* ; *pp.* dampned, 92, 5.

Dāne, *sb.*, OF. Dane ; *Dane* ; *pl.* Dānes, 222, 27.

dar, *see* durre(n).

dāre, *wkv.*, OAng. *daran?, cf. Du. Fris. (be)daren; *lurk, lie concealed, be disconsolate*; *inf.* dāre, 157, 19; *pr. ppl.* dāreand, 158, 23.

Dārīs, *sb.*, OF. Daris; *Daris*, 47, 11.

daunce, *sb.*, OF. dance, danse; *dance*, 159, 18.

daunce(n), *wkv.*, OF. dancer, danser; *dance*; *pr. pl.* daunce, 237, 11.

Dāvid, Dāvī, eME. David, *sb.*, OF. David; *David, King of Scotland*, 2, 14; *David, the Psalmist*, *gs.* without ending, 72, 5. Nth. Dāvī, 131, 1.

Dāvȳ, *sb.*, OF. David; *Davy*; Adam, 232, 1.

daw(e), dawes, *see* dai.

dawnsynge, *pr. ppl.* as *sb.*, daunce(n); *dancing*, 120, 21.

day, *see* dai.

dayne(n), *wkv.*, OF. deigner; *deign*; *pt. pl.* daynede, 219, 30.

dēad, deai, dēap, *see* dēd, dai, dēp.

debāte, *sb.*, OF. debat; *strife, debate*, 233, 3.

debrūse(n), *wkv.*, OF. debruisier; *bruise, break in pieces*; *pp.* debrused, 208, 28.

decīple, *see* disciple.

declāre(n), *wkv.*, OF. declarer; *declare*; *pr. ppl.* declāryng, 223, 12.

decollācioūn, *sb.*, AN. decollaciun; *beheading*, 228, 21.

dēd, *adj.*, OE. dēad; *dead*, 1, 18; dēad, 33, 15; dedd, 112, 17; dēed, 240, 14. Nth. dēde, 138, 22.

dēd, dēde, *see* dēp.

dēdbōte, *sb.*, OM. dēdbot. WS. dǣdbōt, *f.*; *atonement, restitution*, 196, 7.

dēde, dēde, *see* dēp, dō(n).

dēde, *sb.*, OM. dēd, WS. dǣd, *f.*; *deed*; dǣde, 4, 7; dēde, 8, 23. Nth. *pl.* dēdis, 127, 23; dēdys, 146, 24.

dēdlȳ, *adj.*, OE. dēadlic; *deadly*, 147, 22.

dēden, deden, *see* dō(n).

dēed, dēel, *see* dēd, dēl.

dēore, *see* dēre.

dees, *sb. pl.*, OF. de, 'die for play'; *dice*, 237, 11.

dēeth, *see* dēp.

dēf, *adj.*, OE. dēaf; *deaf*, 51, 26.

dēf, *see* dūve(n).

defaile(n), *wkv.*, OF. defaillir; *grow feeble, enfeeble, weaken*; *inf.* defailen, 101, 1.

defāme(n), *wkv.*, OF. defamer; *defame*; Nth. *pr.* 3 *sg.* defāmes, 147, 5.

defawte, defaute, *sb.*, OF., defaute; *default, lack*, 119, 15. Nth. defaut, 150, 12.

dēfel, dēfles, *see* dēvel.

defend(en), *wkv.*, OF. defendre; *defend, forbid*; *inf.* defenden, 104, 10; defend, 104, 12; *pp.* deffended, 238, 28.

defens, *sb.*, OF. defense; *defence, protection*, 103, 23.

deffended, *see* defend(en).

defoūle(n), *wkv.*, OF. defouler; *tread under foot, defoul*; *inf.* defoūle, 104, 8.

deft, *adj.*, OE. (ge)dæfte (dēft?); *mild, gentle*, later *skilful, deft*, 14, 19.

degrē, *sb.*, OF. degre; *degree, rank, condition*; bȳ thȳ degrē, *according to thy condition*, 120, 32.

dēh, dei, *see* duge(n), dai.

deie(n), *wkv.*, ON. deyja; *die*; *inf.* deie, 43, 8; deye, 118, 12; dȳe, 65, 13; *pr. pl.* dȳen, 68, 29; *pt. sg.* deide, 77, 5; dȳed, 66, 30. Nth. *inf.* dey, 152, 16; dȳ, 137, 21; *pt. sg.* deyed, 154, 25.

deies, *adv.*, Sth. = Ml. daies; *by day*, 203, 12.

deill, dēl, *see* dēle(n), dēvel.

dēl, *sb.*, OE. dǣl; *deal, part*, 47, 13; (eME. dǣl, 226, 5); never a dēel, *not at all*, 239, 8; deyl, 89, 8.

dēle, *see* dāle.

dēle(n), *wkv.*, OE. dǣlan; *divide, share, deal*; *pp.* dēled. 1Nth. *inf.* deill, 166, 13. Sth. *pp.* idēld, 39, 6.

delīte, *sb.*, OF. delit; *delight*, 144, 29.

delīte(n), *wkv.*, OF. deliter; *delight*; *inf.* delīten, 102, 21. Nth. *pr. pl.* delȳtes, 144, 31.

delivere(n), Sth. **delivrīe(n)**, *wkv.*,
OF. delivrer; *deliver*; *inf.* deliver,
104, 9; *imp. sg.* deliver, 102, 18;
pt. sg. deliverd, 103, 25. **Kt.** *inf.*
delivrī, 211, 23.

delve(n), *stv.*, OE. delfan–dealf (3);
delve, dig, bury; *inf.* delven, 34, 5;
pp. dolven, 15, 1.

delȳte(n), *see* **delīte(n)**.

delyverlȳ, *adv.*, OF. delivre + ME.
lȳ; *promptly*, 172, 26.

dēme, *sb.*, OE. dēma; *judge*; **eSth.**
ds. dēmen, 179, 7.

dēme(n), *wkv.*, OE. dēman; *judge,
deem*; *inf.* dēmenn (O), 11, 11;
dēmen, 58, 6; dēme, 49, 29; *pr.*
3 *sg.* dēmð, 179, 30; *pp.* dempt,
21, 2. **Nth.** *inf.* dēm, 150, 28;
pt. pl. dempt, 132, 8; *pp.* dēmid,
137, 9. **Sth.** *pp.* idēmd, 179, 17;
idēmet, 193, 31.

demēre, *sb.*, NF. demere, OF. de-
moere, demeure; *delay*, 40, 17.

dēmpt, dempt, *see* **dēme(n)**.

den, *sb.*, OE. denn; *den*, 14, 7.

Denemark, Sth. **Denemarch**, *sb.*,
OE. Denemarc, -mearc, f. modified
by ON. -mark; *Denmark*, 75, 2.
Sth. Denemarch, 203, 19.

denne(n), *wkv.*, OE. *dennian; *be
sheltered as in a den, lodge*; *pt. sg.*
dennede, 14, 18.

dēofel, dēovel, *see* **dēvel**.

dēor, dēore(n), *see* **dēr**.

dēorewurðe, *see* **dērworþe**.

dēorlīche, *adv.*, OE. dēorlīce; *in
costly manner*, 196, 30.

dēorling, *sb.*, OE. dēorling; *darling,
beloved*, 186, 26.

dēovlen, dēovles, *see* **dēvel**.

dēp, *adj.*, OE. dēop; *deep*, 53, 9.

departe(n), *wkv.*, OF. despartir, de-
partir; *depart, separate, divide*; *pr.*
3 *sg.* departeþ, 104, 29; *pt. sg.*
departede, 222, 7. **Nth.** *pr. pl.*
departis, 146, 18.

dēr, *sb.*, OE. dēor, *neut.*; *animal,
deer*; *pl.* dēr, 2, 4. **eSth.** *ds.*
dēore, 180, 23; *pl.* dēor, 193, 21;
dēoren, 182, 14.

dēre, dēr, *adj.*, OE. dēore; *dear,*

beloved, costly, 27, 23; (eME. dǣre,
3, 27); dēr, 21, 20.

dēre, *adv.*, OE. dēore; *hardly,
severely*, 54, 19; deere, 238, 20.
Sth. dūre, q.v. **Kt.** dȳere, 217,
29.

dēre, *sb.*, OM. *dere; cf. OE. daru;
injury, harm, 157, 20.

dēre(n), *wkv.*, OE. derian; *injure,
harm, destroy*; *inf.* dēren, 17, 18;
dēre, 82, 18; *pr. sbj. sg.* dēre, 35, 2.
Nth. *p.* 3 *sg.* ders, 149, 30.

dereynīə(n), dereynī, *wkv.*, Sth.
= Ml. dereine(n); OF. derainier;
*defend one's cause, vindicate one's
claim*; *inf.* dereynī, 206, 8.

derf, OE. gedeorf; *trouble, affliction,*
195, 2.

derf, *adj.*, OM. *deorf?, cf. gedeorf-
nes; perh. ON. diarfr; *painful,
grievous*; comp. dervre, 194, 18.

derfe, *adv.*, OE. *deorf, *adj.*, cf.
gedeorfnys; *hardly, severely*, 149,
30.

derflīche, *adv.*, OE. *deorflīce (*see*
derf); *harshly, cruelly*, 191, 26.

derk, *adj.*, OE. deorc; *dark, gloomy,*
49, 7.

derknes, *sb.*, based on OE. deorc,
adj.; *darkness*, 103, 29.

dērne, *adj.*, OM. derne, dērne, WS.
dierne; *secret*, 14, 17; dērn, 16, 14.

dērnelīche, *adv.*, OM. derne (dērne),
WS. dierne + ME. līche; *secretly,*
202, 8.

ders, *see* **dēre(n)**.

dērðe, *sb.*, OM. *dērð, ON. dȳrð, *f.*
[dēore]; *dearth, scarcity*, 27, 13.

dervre, *see* **derf**.

dērwòrþe, dērwòrþ, *adv.*, OE. dēorwurðe; *precious, dear*, 229, 19;
dērworþ, 229, 2. **eSth.** dēore
wurðe, 191, 17.

desalȳ, *adv.*, OE. dysig + ME. lȳ;
dizzily, 172, 30.

desavauntāǧe, *sb.*, OF. desavantage;
disadvantage, 225, 5.

deshonūre(n), *wkv.*, OF. deshonurer;
dishonor; *inf.* deshonūr, 42, 17.

desīre, *sb.*, OF. desīer, infl. by
desirier, *vb.*; *desire*, 104, 20.

despīse(n), despȳse(n), *wkv.*, OF. despiser; *despise*; *inf.* despīsen, 102, 23; despȳse, 121, 13. Nth. *pr.* 3 *sg.* dispȳses, 145, 27.

despīte, *see* dispīte.

destanȳe, *sb.*, OF. destinee; *destiny*, 111, 16.

dester, *sb.*, OF. destre; *right hand*, 48, 24.

destroye(n), *see* destruye(n).

destrucciōn, *sb.*, OF. destrucion; *destruction*, 233, 4.

destruye(n), *wkv.*, OF. destruire; *destroy, disturb*; *inf.* destruye, 220, 20; *pt. sg.* destruyde, 223, 31; *pp.* destruyd, 223, 13; destroyed, 223, 11.

desturbe(n). *wkv.*, OF., destourber; *disturb*; *pp.* disturbed, 103, 6. Nth. *imp. pl.* desturbes, 139, 15.

dēþ, *see* dō(n).

dēþ, *sb.*, OE. dēað; *death*, 19, 30; (eME. dǣþ, 11, 8; dǣþþ (O), 11, 26); dēað, 27, 8; dēth, 57, 28; dēeth, 239, 13; *ds.* dǣþe, 11, 9; dēþe, 42, 23; dēde, 15, 3. Nth. dēd, 128, 7; dēde, 135, 27; *gs.* dēdes, 158, 10. Sth. *ds.* dēðe, 185, 8 (eSth. dēaðe, 191, 26). Kt. *ds.* dīaþe, 214, 14; dīeðe, 179, 17; dȳaþ, 215, 7; *pl.* dȳeaþes, 216, 21.

deu, *sb.*, OE. dēaw; *dew*, 14, 6.

dēvel, devel, divel, *sb.*, OE. dēofol; *devil*; (eME. dēfell (O), 12, 14); devel, 20, 13; divel, 14, 17; dēl, 125, 27; *pl.* (eME. dēovles, 3, 1, dēfless (O), 11, 27); develene, 60, 4. Nth. dēvil, 136, 5; dēvell, 167, 2; *pl.* dēvells, 144, 12. eSth. *pl.* dēofles, 179, 8; *dpl.* dēovlen, 193, 30. Kt. *pl.* dȳevlen, 217, 25.

devīsȳe(n), *wkv.*, OF. devisier; *contrive, devise*; *inf.* devīsȳ, 217, 13.

devōcyōne, *sb.*, OF. devocion, AN. devociun; *devotion*, 124, 3.

deye(n), deyl, *see* deie(n), dēl.

dīadlīche, *adj.*, Kt. = Ml. dēdelī; OE. dēadlīc; *deadly*, 211, 21.

Dīane, *sb.*, Lat. Diana; *Diana*, 193, 20.

dīaþe, *see* dēþ.

diche, *sb.* OE. dīc, *f.*; *ditch*; *as.* diche, 177, 17.

dicht, *see* diȝte(n).

did, dide(n), *see* dō(n).

dīeð(e), *see* dēþ.

diȝte(n), *wkv.*, OE. dihtan; *prepare, set in order*; *inf.* diȝten, 105, 10; dyght, 110, 19; *pp.* dight, 159, 32; dyght, 110, 21; dicht, 171, 5. Sth. *pp.* idihte, 191, 3.

dīgne, *adj.*, OF. digne; *worthy*, 116, 16; dȳgne, 93, 10.

dignitee, *sb.*, OF. dignitē; *dignity*, 240, 5.

dīke, *sb.*, ON. dīki, cogn. with OE. dīc; *dike*, 56, 8.

dille(n), *wkv.*, OE. *dyllen; *render useless*. Nth. *inf.* dill, 132, 24.

dim, *adj.*, OE. dimm; *dim*, 20, 26; *pl.* dimme, 15, 15.

din, *sb.*, OE. dyne, dyn; *din, noise*, 148, 9.

dinge(n), *stv.*, OE. *dingan–dang (3); *beat, strike, ding*; *pt. pl.* dongen, 61, 21.

dint, *sb.*, OE. dynt; *dint, stroke*, 61, 25.

discīple, decīple, *sb.*, OF. disciple; *disciple*, 139, 29; decīple, 210, 22.

disciplīne, *sb.*, OF. discipline; *discipline, correction*, 101, 6.

disclaundre(n), *wkv.*, based on OF. disclaunder, *sb.*; *slander, disgrace*; *pp.* disclaundred, 234, 14.

discord, *sb.*, OF. discorde; *discord, quarrelling*, 219, 6.

discrēt, *adj.*, OF. discret; *discreet*, 234, 24.

disēse, *sb.*, OF. disaise; *disease, trouble*, 236, 26.

dishonōur, *ob.*, OF. deshonur; *dishonor, wrong*, 239, 29.

dispīte, *sb.*, OF. despit; *scorn, despite*, 137, 27.

displēsance, *sb.*, OF. desplesance; *displeasure*, 146, 30.

displēse(n), *wkv.*, OF. displaisir; *displease*; *pr. ppl.* displēsyng, 233, 29.

disprōve(n), *wkv.*, OF. desprover; *disprove*; *pp.* disprōved, 234, 19.

dispȳse(n), *see* despīse(n).
dīst, *see* dō(n).
dīte(n), *wkv.*, OF. diter, dicter; *in-dite*; *inf.* dīte, 70, 2.
divel, *see* dēvel.
dīve(n), *wkv.*, OE. dȳven; *dive*; *pr.* 3 *sg.* dīveð, 20, 11.
dīvers, dȳvers, *adj.*, OF. divers; *divers, different*, 213, 31; dȳvers, 225, 12.
dōand(e), *see* dō(n).
doctōur, *sb.*, OF. doctour; *doctor*, 145, 21.
doghter, doghtres, *see* dohter.
dȯghtȳ, *adj.*, OE. dyhtig, infl. by un-mutated forms; *doughty*, 116, 5.
dohter, *sb.*, OE. dohtor; *daughter*, 5, 30; dowter, 24, 19; doghter, 131, 9; *pl.* douhtres, 75, 12; dou-tres, 87, 2; doghtres, 238, 4; douȝ-tres, 220, 14.
dǭle, *sb.*, OE. dāl; *portion, dole*, 201, 22.
dōlę, *sb.*, OF. doel (duel); *grief, mourning*, 159, 32.
dōle(n), *wkv.*, OF. doler, duiller; *grieve*; *pr.* 3 *sg.* dolęþ, 70, 32.
dolven, *see* delve(n).
dōm, *sb.*, OE. dōm; *judgement, decree, authority, doom, death*, 9, 24; 43, 30; dōmę, 121, 2. Sth. *ds.* dōme, 177, 24.
dōmesday, Sth. dōmesdei, *sb.*, OE. dōm+dæg; *doomsday*, 50, 16. Sth. dōmesdei, 180, 14.
dōmesman, *sb.*, OE. dōm+man; *judge*, 135, 7.
don, *see* dūn.
dō(n), *anv.*, OE. dōn–dyde (dǣde); *do*; *inf.* dōn, 8, 18; dō, 43, 23; dōnę, 226, 15; *pr.* 2 *sg.* dōst, 46, 32; *pr.* 3 *sg.* dōð, 18, 4; dōth, 53, 18; dooth, 238, 15; *pr. pl.* doon, 237, 13; *imp. sg.* dō, 30, 13; *imp. pl.* dōþ, 68, 32; dooþ, 232, 5; *pr. ppl.* dōand, 104, 21; *pt. sg.* dide, 1, 9; did, 51, 18; dēde, 18, 29; *pt.* 2 *sg.* didest, 50, 9; dīst, 50, 22; *pt. pl.* diden, 2, 28; dēden, 23, 4; deden, 26, 19; dēde, 68, 18; *pp.* dōn, 8, 18; dōnę, 109, 1. Nth. *pr.* 3 *sg.*

dōs, 128, 20; dusę, 147, 17; *pr. ppl.* dōande, 144, 3. Sth. *ger.* dōnne, 196, 12; *pr.* 3 *sg.* dēþ, 176, 21; *pr. pl.* dōþ, 178, 2; *imp. pl.* dōn, 176, 23; *pr. sbj. sg.* dō, 177, 16; *pt. sg.* düde, 176, 2; *pt. pl.* düden, 179, 7; düde, 207, 31; *pp.* idōn, 64, 7; idōnę, 123, 9; ydōn, 176, 7; idō, 179, 28; ydō, 204, 3.
Dȯndē, *sb.*, Celtic dun 'hill'+dee 'river name'; *Dundee*, 159, 18.
dȯng, *sb.*, cf. MDu. dunge; *dung*, 219, 11.
dȯngǝ = dunǥon, *sb*, OF. dongōn –jōn; *dungeon*, 63, 22.
dongen, *see* dinge(n).
donward, *see* dūnward.
dor, dorstest *see* durre(n).
dōs, dōþ, *see* dō(n).
Dōuglas, *sb.*, *Douglas*, James of, 174, 29.
douȝter, douhter, *see* dohter.
douhte, *see* duge(n).
dōumb, *see* dumb.
dōun, *see* dūn.
dōune, earlier dūne, *sb.*, OE. dūn, *f.*; *hill, down*, 57, 23; dūne, 182, 13. Sth. *pl.* dūnen, 187, 5.
dōute, dout, *sb.*, OF. doute; *doubt, fear*, 53, 11. Nth. dōut, 160, 28.
dōuteful, *adj.*, OF. doute+ME. ful; *doubtful*, 220, 14.
dōutelęs, *adj.*, OF. doute+ME. lęs; *doubtless*, 238, 10.
dōute(n), *wkv.*, OF. douter; *doubt, fear*; *inf.* douten, 101, 5; *pt. sg.* dōutede, 86, 24; *pt. pl.* douted, 160, 6. Cf. dūte(n).
doutres, *see* dohter.
dōwn, dowter, *see* dūn, dohter.
dȯynge, *sb.*, based on dō(n); *doing, act*, 235, 6.
drāf, *see* drīve(n).
drāge(n), drawe(n), *stv.*, OE. dragan–drōg (6); *drag, draw*; *inf.* drāgen, 31, 26; *pr.* 3 *sg.* drāgeð, 14, 5; *pr. pl.* drāgen, 20, 4; drawe, 224, 7; *pr. sbj. sg.* drawe, 203, 4; *pt. sg.* drōȝ, 43, 13; drouȝ, 57, 28; drou, 86, 21; drōh, 193, 4; *pt. pl.* drowen, 62, 10; *pp.*

drawen, 234, 17. **Nth**. *pr.* 3 *sg.*
draws, 127, 10; drawes, 127, 27;
drawis, 171, 25.

drank, *see* drinke(n).

drāpen, *see* drēpe(n).

drauȝt, *sb.*, OE. *draht?; *draught,*
pull, tendency, 50, 23.

draune, drawe(n), draws, *see*
drāge(n).

drecche(n), *wkv.*, OE. dreccan; *vex,*
torture, delay; *pr.* 3 *sg.* dreccheð,
16, 20.

drēde, drẹd(e), *sb.*, OM. *drēd, *f.* ?,
WS. *drǣd; *dread*, 36, 5. **Sth.**
drẹde, 197, 22; it is nọ̄ drẹde, *there*
is no doubt, without doubt, 238, 25.

drēde(n), *stv.*, OM. drēdan (WS.
drǣdan)–drēd (R); *dread, fear*;
pr. pl. drēden, 104, 28; *imp. pl.*
drēdeð, 30, 23; *pt. sg.* dredde, 53,
25; draddle, 234, 5. **Nth.** *inf.*
drēd, 150, 29; *pr. ppl.* drēdand,
142, 29; *pt. sg.* drēd, 141, 17. **Sth.**
pr. 3 *sg.* drēt = drēdeð, 211, 6; *pr.*
pl. drēdeþ, 218, 15.

drēdlī, *adj.*, cf. OM. drēdan, WS.
drǣdan; *dreadful, fearful,* 48, 8.

drēge(n), drēȝe(n), drēhe(n), drī-
ȝe(n), dreye(n), *stv.*, WS. drēogan–
drēag (2); *endure, carry through,*
accomplish; *inf.* drīȝen, 182, 26;
pr. pl. drēge wē, 26, 16; *pp.* drogen,
32, 18. **Nth.** *inf.* drey, 171, 31.
Sth. *inf.* drēhe, 194, 18.

dreinche(n), *see* drenche(n).

drẹm, *sb.*, OE. drēam, infl. in meaning
by ON. draumr?; *dream*, 21, 13;
drẹmẹ, 91, 32; *gpl.* drẹmes, 23, 16.
Nth. *pl.* drẹmys, 145, 17.

drēme(n), *wkv.*, OM. drēman (WS.
drīeman), infl. in meaning by ON.
dreyma?; *dream*; *inf.* drēmen, 22,
3; *pt. sg.* drempte, 21, 13.

drench, *sb.*, OE. drenc; *drink, potion*;
pl. drenchen, 190, 29.

drenche(n), dreinche(n), *wkv.*, OE.
drencan; *drench, drown*; *inf.*
dreinchen, 82, 5; *pp.* drenched,
80, 27.

drēpe(n), eME. drepe(n), *stv.*, OE.
drepan–drǣp (5); *kill, destroy*; *pr.*

3 *sg.* drẹpeð, 20, 12; *pr. sbj. sg.*;
drẹpe, 80, 13; *pt. pl.* drāpen, 3, 10.

drērī, *adj.*, OE. drēorig; *dreary,*
sorrowful, 133, 4.

dresce(n), *wkv.*, OF. dresser; *make*
straight, direct, prepare, dress; *imp.*
sg. dresce, 103, 19.

drey, *see* drēge(n).

drīe, drī, *adj.*, OE. drȳge; *dry,* 103,
5. **Nth.** drī, 142, 8.

drīf(e), *see* drīve(n).

drīȝe(n), *see* drēge(n).

Drihte(n), Dryhtin, *sb.*, OE. Drihtin; *Lord*, 4, 30; Drihhtīn (O), 8,
20; Drigten, 15, 1; Drigtin, 16,
28. **Nth.** Drightin, 132, 1. **Sth.**
Drihte, 178, 24.

drinc, drink, drynk, *sb.*, OE. drinc;
drinking, 21, 16; drynk, 101, 8.

drinke(n), *stv.*, OE. drincan–dranc
(3); *drink*; *inf.* drinken, 17, 10;
drinke, 60, 19; *pr.* 3 *sg.* drinkeð,
17, 12; *pt. sg.* drank, 52, 28; *pp.*
as *adj.*, drunken, 101, 9. **Sth.** *pp.*
idrunke, 180, 22; ydrónke, 223, 22.

dritchērl, *sb.*, ON. dritr + OE. ceorl;
dirty churl (term of contempt),
85, 30.

drīve(n), *stv.*, OE. drīfan–drāf (1);
drive; *pr.* 3 *sg.* drīveð, 14, 7; *imp.*
pl. drīve ȝē, 203, 5; *pt. sg.* (eME.
drāf, 196, 32) drọ̄f, 87, 10; drọ̄fẹ,
90, 6; *pp.* driven, 25, 5; dryven,
238, 25. **Nth.** *inf.* drīfe, 155, 15;
drīf; *follow,* 168, 12. **Sth.** *pr.* 3
sg. drȳfþ, 219, 23; *pr. pl.* drīveþ,
219, 24; *pp.* ydryve, 220, 8.

drónke, *pp.* as *adj.*, OE. druncen;
drunk, 219, 10.

drónkelẹc, *sb.*, OE. drunken + ME.
lẹc, possibly OE. *lǣc < lāc;
drunkenness, 120, 11.

drónkelewe, *adj.*, OE. druncen +
ME. lewe < ON. legr?; *drunken,*
238, 13.

drónkenessǝ, *sb.*, OE. drunceness, *f.*;
drunkenness, 238, 2.

drọ̄pe, *sb.*, OE. dropa; *drop,* 63, 25.

drou, drouȝ, *see* drāge(n).

drōupe(n), *wkv.*, ON. drūpa; *droop*;
pr. 1 *sg.* drōupe, 157, 19.

drōupening, *pp.* as *sb.*, ME. drūpnen
< ON. drūpna; *drooping, dejection,*
47, 26.

drōvī, *adj.*, extended from OE. drōf;
turbid, troubled, 19, 25.

drowen, *see* drāge(n).

drugte, *sb.*, OE. drūgaõ, *f.*; *drought,*
23, 11.

drunken, *see* drinke(n).

drynke, *see* drinke(n).

drȳve(n), *see* drīve(n).

dubbe(n), *wkv.*, OE. dubbian < OF.
aduber; *dub, adorn; pt.sg.* dubbede,
46, 16.

dubbyng, *sb.*, based on dubbe(n).;
dubbing, that is *creating of a knight,*
229, 27.

duble, *sb.*, OF. duble; *double,* 200, 1.

dubonēre, *adj.*, OF. de bon aire;
gentle, meek, 95, 28.

dūc, *sb.*, OF. duc; *duke,* 43, 27.
Sth. *ds.* duk, 222, 3.

Duche, *adj.*, OF. Duche < MDu.
Dutsch; *Dutch,* 162, 16.

dūde, *see* dō(n).

duelle, duelling, *see* dwelle(n).

duge(n), duȝe(n), *ptprv.*, OE. dugan
-dohte; *avail; pr. sg.* dēh, 197, 1;
pt. sg. douhte, 86, 19.

duȝeõə, duheõe, *sb.*, OE. duguõ, *f.*;
*nobility, body of attendants, people,
dignity, honor,* 181, 7; duheõe,
192, 5.

duke, *see* duc.

dumb (dōumb), *adj.*, OE. dumb;
dumb, 49, 23; dōumb, 81, 18.

dūn, dōun (dōwn), dȯn, *adv.*, OE.
dūn < OIr. dūn, 'hill'; *down,* 6, 29;
dōun, 52, 17; dōwn, 90, 3; dōwnę,
123, 10; dȯn, 128, 13.

dūne, dūnen, *see* dōune.

dūnt, *sb.*, Sth. = Ml. dint (dent); OE.
dynt; *blow, stroke, dint,* 208, 14.

dūnward, dȯnward, *adv.*, OE.
ādūnweard; *downward*; dȯnward,
208, 7.

dure, *sb.*, OE. duru; *door,* 180, 2.

dure, *see* durre(n).

dūre, *adv.*, Sth. = Ml. dēre; lWS.
dȳre, OM. dēre; *dearly, with great
price,* 180, 24.

dūrne, *adv.*, Sth. = Ml. dērne; WS.
dīerne, dyrne (dȳrne); *secretly,*
178, 22.

durre(n), *ptprv.*, OE. durran–dorste;
dare; pr. sg. dar, 53, 18; *pr. pl.*
duren, 27, 15; *pr. sbj. sg.* dure, 18,
8; durre, 109, 23; dȯr, 235, 30;
pt. sg. durste, 2, 3; dorst, 53, 24;
pt. 2 sg. dorstest, 217, 31.

dusę, *see* dō(n).

dūst, dust, *sb.*, OE. dūst, *dust*; dusst
(O), 14, 5.

dūte(n), *wkv.*, OF. dutir, douter;
fear, doubt; pr. 3 sg. dūteþ, 40, 32;
imp. pl. dūte ȝē, 38, 18. Cf.
dōute(n).

dūvelunge, *adv.*, Sth. = Ml. de-
velunge; based on WS. dīevan,
lWS. dȳvan, OM. dēvan; *headlong,
with a plunge,* 196, 26.

dūve(n), *stv.*, OE. dūfan–dēaf (2);
dive, sink; pt. sg. dēf, 196, 26.

dwelle(n), *wkv.*, OE. dwellan;
hinder, delay, dwell; inf. dwelle,
59, 23; duelle, 153, 13; *pr. ppl.*
dwellynge, 117, 12; *pt. sg.* dwellyd,
110, 29. Nth. *inf.* duelle, 153, 13;
pt. sg. dweld, 138, 31.

dwelling, *sb.*, based on dwelle(n);
dwelling, 161, 10.

dwīne(n), *stv.*, OE. dwīnan–dwān
(1); *vanish, perish*; Nth. *inf.*
dwīn, 148, 9.

dȳaþ, dȳeaþ, *see* dēþ.

dyche, *sb.*, OE. dīc, *f.*; *ditch,* 119, 8.

dȳeadlīch, dȳadlīch, *adj.*, OE.
dēadlīc; *deadly,* 216, 19; dȳadlȳch, 217, 15.

dȳed, dȳeaþ, *see* dēd.

dȳe(n), dȳere, *see* deie(n), dēre.

ċȳevlen, *see* dēvel.

dyght(en), *see* diȝte(n).

dȳgne, *see* dīgne.

dyshonōur, *sb.*, OF. deshonur; *dishonor*; dyshonōurę, 114, 8.

dyssayve(n), *wkv.*, OF. decevoir;
deceive; inf. dyssayve, 145, 15.

dyssh, *sb.*, OE. disc; *dish,* 96, 24.

dystresse, *sb.*, OF. destrece, destresse;
distress, 107, 2.

dȳvers, *see* dīvers.

dyvȳnynge, *sb.*, based on devīne(n) ; *divining, divination* ; *pl.* dyvȳn-ynges, 145, 16.

dyvysiŏn, *sb.*, OF. division ; *division*, 236, 4.

E.

ē, *see* ēȝe, þē.

eal, *see* al.

ēalches, ēald, *see* ēch, āld.

ēaren, *see* ēre.

ēarninge, *sb.*, OE. earnung, *f.* ; *merit, earning*, 178, 8.

Ēbrisse, *adj.*, OE. Ēbreisc, Lat. Hebræus + OE. -isc ; *Hebrew*, 25, 26.

Ēbrŏn, *sb.*, Lat. Hebron ; *Hebron*, 33, 8.

ēc, ēke, Sth. ēc, ēch, *adv.*, OM. ēc, WS. ēac ; *also, eke*, 12, 27 ; ēke, 193, 33. Sth. ēc, 176, 11 ; ēch, 176, 3 ; ēke, 197, 21.

ēch, ǣch, *indef. pron.*, OE. ǣlc < ǣghwylc ; *each* ; ǣlc, 4, 24 ; ēch, 39, 16 ; ich, 101, 12 ; ǣch, 226, 14 ; euch, 192, 15. Sth. (eSth. ēlc, 178, 9 ; ēlch, 179, 18 ; *ds.* ēlche, 178, 30, *f. nom. sg.* ēlche, 178, 32) ; *ds.* ēche, 208, 10 ; *fds.* ǣlchere, 189, 5 ; *gs.* ēalches, 179, 1. Kt. ēch, 215, 7 ; *ds.*, ēche, 218, 18.

ēche, *adj.*, OE. ēce ; *eternal*. 18, 2.

ēche, *sb.*, based on OE. ēce, *adj.* ; *eternity*, 191, 22.

ēddī, ēdī, *adj.*, OE. ēadig ; *happy, favorable, good*, 22, 22 ; *wk.* ēdīe, 192, 30.

ēde (ēdest), ēdīe, *see* gŏ(n), ēddī.

ēdmŏdlīche, *adv.*, Sth. = Ml. ēd-mŏdlī ; OE. ēadmōdlīce ; *humbly, graciously*, 202, 26.

Edward, *sb.*, OE. Eadward ; *Edward* ; *Seint, the Confessor*, 204, 31.

eet, *see* ēte(n).

effēr, effēre, *sb.*, OF. afair ; *business, haste* ; *behavior*, 170, 8 ; effēre, 167, 9.

Effraym, *sb.*, Lat. Ephraim ; *Ephraim*, 24, 23.

efft, *see* eft.

efsōnes, *see* eftsōne.

eft (æft), *adv.*, OE. eft ; *afterwards, again* ; efft (O), 10, 3 ; æft, 183, 7. efter, *see* after.

efterward, *see* afterward.

eftsōne, efsōnes, Kt. eftzōne, *adv.*, OE. eft + sōna ; *afterwards, eftsoon* ; efsōnes, 6, 19 ; eftsōne, 207, 27. Kt. eftzōne, 217, 19.

Ēgēas, *sb.*, Lat. Egeas ; *Egeas*, 135, 8.

Egbert, Egbertus, *sb.*, OE. Ecg-berht ; Lat. Egbertus ; *Egbert*, 222, 28 ; Egbertus, 222, 25.

ēȝe, ēge, eiȝe, eie, īȝe, *sb.*, OM. ēge, WS. ēage ; *eye* ; eie, 41, 18 ; eyȝe, 69, 30 ; īȝe, 36, 26 ; *pl.* ēgen, 14, 13 ; eiȝen, 65, 28 ; eiȝenę, 51, 25 ; eyȝen, 67, 14 ; eyne, 85, 28 ; ȳȝen, 68, 30. Nth. ē, 172, 9 ; *pl.* ēghen, 140, 25. Sth. eie, 208, 20 ; *pl.* ēȝen, 178, 19 ; eien, 197, 15 ; ēhnen, 195, 32.

eȝȝwhǣr, *adv.*, OM. ēghwēr (hwǣr), WS. ǣghwǣr ; *everywhere*, 9, 9.

ēghen, ēȝhnen, *see* ēȝe.

eȝte, *see* agte.

eȝtetēnþe, *adj.*, OM. æhtetēoða, WS. eahtetēoða ; *eighteenth*, 226, 22.

eȝtī, *adj.*, OM. æhtig, WS. eahtig ; *eighty*, 103, 10.

ēgir, *adj.*, OF. aigre, egre ; *eager*, 142, 3.

ēgirlȳ, ēgyrlȳ, *adv.*, OF. aigre, egre + ME. lȳ ; *eagerly*, 168, 31.

Egypte, *sb.*, OE. Egipte, later OF. Egipte ; *Egypt*, 27, 28 ; 131, 17.

ēhsihŏe, *sb.*, OM. ēge, (WS. ēage) + sihŏ, *f.* ; *eyesight*, 195, 23.

ehte, *see* agte.

ehte, eiȝte, *adj.*, OM. æhta, WS. eahta ; *eight*, 4, 11 ; eiȝte, 67, 24 ; eyȝte, 222, 25.

ei, *sb.*, OE. ǣg ; *pl.* ægru ; *egg* ; *pl.* eiren, 198, 22.

ei, eie (eiȝe, eyȝe), *see* enī, ēȝe.

eie, *sb.*, OE. ege ; *awe, fear*, 7, 29 ; æie (eME.), 2, 3 ; eyȝe, 53, 29.

eieþürl, *sb.*, Sth. = Ml. eiþirl ; OE. ēagŏyrl ; *window* ; *pl.* eieþürles. 200, 13.

ei3e(n), ei3te, *see* ē3e, ehte.
ei3tetēne, ey3tetēne, *adj.*, OM.
æhtatēne (WS. eahtatīene); *eighteen*, 220, 2.
eihte, *see* agte.
eilīe(n), *wkv.*, OE. eglian; *trouble,
ail, annoy*; *pr. sbj. sg.* eilīe, 203, 2.
eilǫnd, *sb.*, OM. ēgland-lǫnd, WS.
īgland; *island*, 19, 5.
eir, eiren, eis, *see* heir, ei, ænī.
eise, eyse, ēse, *adj.*, OF. aise; *easy,*
55, 27; eyse, 54, 3; ēse, 109, 29.
eiþer (eyþer), aiþer, aiþere, *adj.*,
OM. ēgðer, WS. æghwæðer, ǣgðer;
either, 37, 29; eyþer, 45, 5; aiþer,
39, 3; aiþere, 130, 6. Sth. æiþer,
178, 6; eiðer, 178, 32.
ēke, ēke, *see* ēc.
ēke(n), *wkv.*, OM. ēcan, WS. īecan;
add, increase; *inf.* ēkenn (O), 9,
15; *pp.* ēkedd (O), 9, 9.
ēl, ēle, *see* ēvel.
ēlc, ēlch, ēlche, *see* ēch.
ēlde, *sb.*, OM. eldo, ēldo, WS. ieldo;
age, eld, 15, 11. Sth. ȳlde, 176,
17.
ēlde(n), *wkv.*, OM. eldan, ēldan,
WS. ieldan; *grow old, enfeeble*;
pp. ēlded, 18, 3. Cf. Kt. yēalde(n).
eldere, *see* ǫld.
elecciōn, *sb.*, OF. eleccion, AN.
elecciun; *election*, 232, 24; elexiōn,
115, 26.
Elewsius, *sb.*, Lat. Eleusius; *Eleusius*, 192, 7; Lat. *as.* Elewsium,
195, 2.
elexiōn, *see* elecciōn.
elleft, *adj.*, OE. endleofta, ellefta;
eleventh, 152, 13.
elleovene, *see* enlevene.
elles, ellis, ellys, *adv.*, OE. elles;
else; elless (O), 10, 9; elles, 42,
25; ellis, 235, 30; ellys, 110, 9;
els, 137, 22.
elleswhēre, elleswhare, *adv.*, OE.
elles + hwǣr; *elsewhere*, 236, 30;
elleswhare, 187, 29.
elmesse, *see* almes.
elmessegifte, *sb.*, OE. ælmesse + ME.
gifte; *almsgiving*, 34, 19.
els, *see* elles.

Ēlȳ, *sb.*, OE. Eli; *Ely*, 100, 3. Cf.
Hēlȳ.
ēm, ēmę, *sb.*, OE. ēam; *uncle*, archaic
eam; (eME. ēom, 2, 20), ēmę, 108,
22. eSth. ǣm, 184, 29; *ds.* ǣme,
185, 25.
emparōur, *see* emperōur.
empēre, *sb.*, OF. empire; *empire*,
221, 13.
emperice, emperes, *sb.*, OF. em-
pereris, emperice; *emprèss*, 5, 30;
emperes, 107, 1.
emperōur, *sb.*, OF. empereur, em-
pereor; *emperor*, 96, 9; emparōur,
126, 4; emperōr, 220, 17.
empoisōnyng, *sb.*, based on OF. em-
poisoner; *poisoning*, 245, 30.
empoysōnēre, *sb.*, OF. empoisoneur;
poisoner, 2,6, 1.
emprisōnęment, *sb.*, OF. emprisonne-
ment; *imprisonment*; *pl.* emprisōnementz, 233, 8.
emprisōne(n), *wkv.*, OF. emprisoner;
imprison; *pp.* emprisōned, 233, 29.
en, *see* in.
enarmynge, *pr. ppl.* as *sb.*, OF. en-
armer; *arming*, 233, 6.
end, *see* and.
ēnde, *sb.*, OE. ende, ēnde; *end*; ēnde
(O), 8, 26; ǣnde, 226, 10.
ēndelēs, *adv.*, OE. endelēase; *continually, endlessly*, 153, 15.
ēndelīes, *adj.*, Sth. = Ml. ēndelēs;
OE. endelēas; *endless*; *ds.* ēndelīese,
180, 21.
ēnde(n), *wkv.*, OE. endian; *end*;
Nth. *inf.* ēnd, 149, 19; *pt. pl.* endid,
132, 31; *pp.* ended, 245, 32.
ēndinge, endyng, *sb.*, OE. ēndung,
f.; *ending*, 8, 12; ending, 27, 5;
ēndynge, 215, 13.
endīte(n), *wkv.*, OF. enditer; *indict,
indite*; *pp.* endīted, 234, 13.
enemȳ, enmȳ, *sb.*, OF. enemis;
enemy, 112, 21; *pl.* enmȳs, 158, 30.
endlāng, *adv. prep.* ON. endilang;
along, beside, 166, 18.
ēnes, *adv.*, OE. ǣne extended; *once*,
196, 2.
enfermēr, *sb.*, OF. enfermier; *super-
intendent of infirmary*, 154, 2.

enfourme(n), *wkv.*, OF. enformer ; *inform* ; *pp.* enfourmed, 236, 20.

engel, *sb.*, OE. engel (L. angelus), later displaced by OF. angel, *see* **ãn̄g̃el** ; *angel* ; enngell (O), 12, 32 ; *pl.* engles, 179, 5. **Sth.** *ds.* engle, 198, 17 ; *gpl.* englene, 196, 24.

Engeland (-lǫnde), *sb.*, OE. Englaland (lǫnd) ; *England* ; Engeland, 83, 23 ; Engelǫnd, 223, 3 ; Engelǫnde, 227, 15.

engīn, *sb.*, OF. engin ; *skill, engine*, 45, 19.

engīne(n), *wkv.*, OF. engignier ; *contrive, torture, ensnare, displease* ; *inf.* engīne, 51, 14.

engle, englene, *see* **engel**.

Engelānd, Engeneloande, *sb.*, eME. = Ml. Engeland (lǫnd) ; OE. Englaland ; *England*, 2, 2 ; *ds.* Engeneloande, 226, 1. Cf. Engelānd.

English, Englishe, Englische, Engliss, *adj.* and *sb.*, OE. Englisc ; *English* ; Ennglissh (O), 8, 19 ; *wk.* Ennglisshe, 10, 20 ; Englisch, 222, 27. **Sth.** Engliss = English, 207, 26.

Englyschman, *sb.*, OE. Englisc + man ; *Englishman*, *pl.* Englyschman, 222, 26.

enī, enȳ, *see* **ænī**.

enlǝvene, ellevene, *adj.*, OE. endleofan, elleofan ; *eleven* ; enlevene, 220, 2 ; (eME. elleovene, 186, 17).

enmãng, *prep. adv.*, OE. ongemang ; *among* ; enmãng þis, *meanwhile*, 2, 7.

enmȳs, *see* **enemȳ**.

ennelēpī, *adj.*, **Kt.** = Ml. enlīpī ; OE. ǣnlȳpig ; *single*, 219, 9.

ǫnngel, *see* **engel**.

Ennglissh, *see* **English**.

Ennok, *sb.*, OF. Enoch? ; *Enoch*, 100, 3.

enprīse, *sb.*, OF. emprise ; *enterprise, cleverness*, 57, 17.

ensaumple, ensample, *sb.*, OF. ensample ; *example*, 70, 7 ; ensample, 88, 17 ; ensampel, 148, 24.

entente, entent, *sb.*, OF. entente ; *intent, design, purpose*, 244, 21. **Nth.** entent, 130, 5.

enter, enterit, *see* **entre**(n).

entērlīch, *adv.*, **Sth.** = Ml. entērlī ; OF. entier + ME. līch ; *entirely*, 236, 24.

enterynge, *pr. ppl.* as *sb.*, OF. enterrer ; *interring*, 118, 15.

entrede, *see* **entre**(n).

entremēte(n), *wkv.*, OF. entremetre ; *meddle with, disturb* ; *inf.* entremēten, 202, 1.

entre(n), *wkv.*, OF. entrer ; *enter* ; *inf.* entre, 101, 21 ; *pt. pl.* entrede, 220, 9. **Nth.** *pt. sg.* enterit, 166, 3. **Sth.** *pp.* ientred, 213, 25.

envīe, envȳ, *sb.*, OF. envie ; *envy*, 54, 15 ; anvīe, 211, 20 ; envȳ, 135, 10.

ēode, ēom, *see* **gǭ**(n), **ēm**.

eom, ēorl, *see* **bē**(n), **ērl**.

eorne(n), *stv.*, OM. iornan, WS. iernan (yrnan)-ǫrn (3) ; *run* ; *pr.* 3 *sg.* ēorneð, 196, 16 ; *pt. sg.* orn, 182, 15.

ēorðe, *see* **ērthe**.

ēorðetilie, *sb.*, OE. eorðtilia ; *tiller of the earth, husbandman* ; **Sth.** *pl.* ēorðtilien, 202, 10.

ēou, ēow, *see* **þū**.

Eouwerwīc, Eowerwīk, *see* **Evorwīc**.

epple, *see* **appel**.

er, *see* **ōþer**.

ę̄ː, *sb.*, OE. ēar ; *ear (of corn)* ; *pl.* ę̄res, 23, 8.

ę̄r (ę̄re), *adv.*, OE. ǣr ; *before, ere* ; (eME. ǣr, 4, 26) ; ę̄r, 7, 24 ; ę̄re, 7, 23 ; *superl.* (eME. ǣresst, 13, 30) ; ę̄rest, 197, 18 ; erst, 238, 32.

er, erǝ, ert, *see* **bē**(n).

erand, *see* **ernde**.

ę̄rd, *sb.*, OE. eard, ēard ; *land, country, dwelling, home*, 22, 30 ; eME. ǣrd, 184, 13.

ę̄rde(n), *wkv.*, OE. eardian, ę̄ardian ; *dwell, inhabit* ; *inf.* ę̄rde, 87, 24.

ę̄rę, *see* **ę̄r**.

ę̄re, *sb.*, OE. ēare ; *ear*, 51, 26 ; ǣre, 10, 22 ; *pl.* ę̄ren, 64, 22. **eSth.** *pl.*

ẹaren, 197, 21. **Kt.** ẏare, 214, 23.

ērl, *sb.*, OE. eorl; *earl*, 42, 6; ēorl, 5, 7; ǣorl, 5, 23. **eSth.** *as.* ēorle, 186, 21.

ẹrlīche, ẹrlīch, *adv.*, OE. ǣrlīce; *early*, 57, 11; ẹrlīch, 103, 15.

ẹrn, ẹrnẹ, *sb.*, OE. earn, ēarn; *eagle*, 15, 8; ẹrnẹ, 104, 20.

ernde, erand, *sb.*, OM. ērende, WS. ǣrende; *message, errand, petition*; 22, 9; errnde (O), 11, 5; erand, 70, 10.

erndīe(n), *wkv.*, Sth. = Ml. ernde(n); OE. ǣrendian; *intercede*; *pr. sbj. sg.* erndī, 197, 10.

erndunge, *sb.*, OE. ǣrendung, *f.*; *intercession*, 191, 21.

ẹrnest, *sb.*, OE. earnest,*f.*; *earnestness*, 207, 23.

ērnynge, *sb.*, based on OM. eornan, ēornan; *course, running, stream*, 100, 19.

errnde, *see* ernde.

erre, *see* bē(n).

errōwrẹ, *sb.*, OF. errour; *error*, 145, 21.

erst, *see* ẹr.

ērthe, ērþe, *sb.*, OM. erðe, ērðe, WS. earðe; *earth*, 4, 6; ērþe (O), 10, 16; (eME. ēorðe, 178, 19); an ērþe, *in earth, to burial*, 209, 27. **Nth.** ērth, 132, 28.

ērthelȳ, ērþliȝ, *adj.*, OE. eorðlīc, ēorðlic; *earthly*; ērthelȳ, 144, 6; ērþliȝ, 12, 17.

es, essẹ, *see* bē(n).

Ēsaū, *sb.*, OE. Esau (trisyllabic); *Esau*, 130, 26.

eschāpe(n), *wkv.*, OF. eschaper, NF. escaper; *escape*; **Nth.** *pt. sg.* eschāpit, 167, 32.

eschāping, *sb.*, based on eschāpe(n); *escaping, escape*, 167, 33.

eschewe(n), *wkv.*, NF. eschever, *pr. st.* eschew; *eschew, shun*; *inf.* eschewe; 120, 8.

ẹse, *see* eīse.

ẹselīche, *adv.*, OF. aise (eise) + ME. līche; *easily*, 208, 7.

espȳe, *sb.*, OF. espie; *spy*, 241, 26.

esse, *see* bē(n).

ẹst, ẹstẹ, *sb.*, OE. ēast; *east*; ẹstẹ, 104, 29.

estāt, *sb.*, OF. estat; *estate, state*, 234, 3.

Ẹstren, Ẹstre, *pl.* as *sg.*, OE. Ẹastran(on); *Easter*, 4, 30; Ēstre, 200, 3.

Ẹstūn,*sb.*,OE.*Easton* (Northampton), 4, 23.

ẹstward, *adv.*, OE. ēastweard; *eastward*, 231, 11.

et, *see* at.

ēte(n), eME. eten, *stv.*, OM. etan –ēt (WS. ǣt) (5); *eat*; *inf.* æten, 5, 14; ẹte, 109, 2; *pr. pl.* ẹten, 237, 12; *pt. sg.* ēt, 52, 28; ētẹ, 67, 25. **Sth.** *ger.* ẹtene, 202, 19; *pt. sg.* ę̣t, 238, 28.

etwīte(n), *see* atwīte(n).

ẹðemōded, *adj.*, OE. ēaðmōd extended; *perh.* OM. *ēðe (WS. īeðe)–mōded; *humble, gracious*, 27, 25.

ẹðlẹte, *adj.*, OE. *ēaðlǣte, cf. earfoðlǣte; *lightly esteemed*, 178, 18.

ẹðlūke, *adj.*, OE. ēað + lūcan, 'to pull'?; *easily pulled* (?), 195, 27.

euch, *see* ẹch.

Eugenīe, *sb.*, OF. Eugenīe; *Pope Eugenius III*, 4, 18.

Eustāce, *sb.*, eME. Eustace, OF. Eustace; *Eustace*; eME. Eustace, 7, 1.

Ēve, *sb.*, L. Ēva, OE. Ēfe; *Eve*, 64, 9; *gs.* Ēves, 71, 26.

ẹvel (ẹvyl), ẹvuyl, ēl, *adj. sb.*, **Kt.** = Ml. ivel (ẹvel ?); OE. yfel, Kt. efel; *evil*; ẹvel, 211, 19; ẹvyl, 92, 9; ẹvil, 141, 16; ẹvuylẹ (WMl.), 120, 2; ēl, 125, 28; ēlẹ, 121, 3. Cf. yvel.

ẹven, *adj.*, OE. efen; *even, just*, 234, 18.

ẹven, evne (æfne), *adv. prep.*, OE. efen, efne; *evenly, equally, according to*; eSth. æfne, 183, 16.

ēven, *sb.* OM. ēfen, WS. ǣfen; *evening*, 49, 26.

ẹver (ǣvre), ẹvre, ever, everẹ, *adv.*, OE. ǣfre; *ever*; eME. ǣvre, 3, 22;

ǣvęre, 183, 11; ǣfre, 10, 16;
ever, everę, 121, 3; aver, 187, 19;
ǣvert = ę̄ver te (tō), *ever to this time,
ever yet*, 7, 24. eSth. ę̄vre, 178, 9.
everemǫǫre, *see* evermǫre.
everilc, ǣvric, everī (everȳ), evereuch, *adj. prn.*, OE. ǣfre, ǣlc;
every, every one, 23, 2; ǣvric, 2, 1:
everī, 69, 24. eSth. ǣvrich, 177,
8; evereuch, 195, 1; everich, 212,
14.
everlastand, *pr. ppl.* as *adj.*, OE.
ǣ.re + lǣstan; *everlasting*, 101, 20.
evermāro (-mār), *adv.*, Nth. = Ml.
evermǫre; OE. ǣfre māra; *evermore*, 14, 2; evermār, 129, 16.
evermǫre, evermǫr, *adv.*, OE. ǣfre +
māra; *evermore*; evermǫre, 97, 24;
evermǫr, 30, 2; everemǫǫre, 239,
21.
Everwīk, *see* Evorwīc.
everȳ(che), *see* everilc.
everȳwhęr, everȳwhęrę, *adv.*, OE.
ǣfre + hwǣr, *everywhere*, 95, 11.
ēvesǭng, *sb.*, OM. ēfensang–sǭng,
WS. ǣfensang; *evensong, vespers*,
51, 6.
Evorwīc, Ʒork, *sb.*, OE. Eoferwīc;
York, 5, 7; Euerwīk, 205, 29;
(eSth. *ds.* Eouwerīc, 188, 18; Eouerwīke, 188, 23); Ʒork, 225, 25.
ę̄vuyle, ę̄vyl, *see* ę̄vel.
ę̄vynlȳ, *adv.*, OE. efenlīce; *evenly,
equally, at once*, 169, 17.
examine(n), *wkv.*, OF. examiner;
examine; *pt. sg.* examyned, 111,
7.
excūse(n), *wkv.*, OF. escūser, excūser;
excuse; *inf.* excuse, 236, 22; *pp.*
excusyd, 117, 10.
Execestre, *sb.*, OE. Exanceaster;
Exeter, 2, 12.
exęcūte(n), *wkv.*, OF. execūter;
execute, perform; *pp.* execut, 236,
30.
exęquīs, *sb.*, OF. exequis; *funeral*;
pl. exequīses, 118, 20.
Exton, *sb.*, *Exton*, Nicholus, 234, 26.
extorcyōne, *sb.*, OF. extorcion, AN.
-un; *extortion*, 147, 17.
eyʒe(eyne), eyse, *see* ēʒe, eie, eise.

egyhte (eyʒte), *see* ehte.
eyʒtetēne, *see* eiʒtetēne.
eyþer, *see* eiþer.

F.

fā, *sb.*, Nth. = Ml. fǭ; OE. fāh, fā;
foe; lNth. fais, 168, 32; fayis,
174, 7.
fāce, *sb.*, OF. face; *face*, 64, 13.
fader, *sb.*, OE. fæder; *father*, 7, 17;
faderr (O), 13, 7; *gs.* fader, 69,
23; faderes, 31, 20; fadyrę, 146,
25. Sth. feder, 180, 28 (eSth.
feader, 191, 16).
fērd, færʒest, *see* fērd, fair.
fæste(n), *wkv.*, OE. fæstan; *make fast,
fasten*; eME. *pt. pl.* fæston, 6, 16.
fæstne(n), *wkv.*, OE. fæstnian;
fasten; *pp.* fæstned, 3, 15.
fæu, faght, *see* few, feght.
fāʒę(n), fagen, feyn, *adj.*, OE.
fægen, fægn; *fain, glad*; fāgen =
fāʒen, 19, 12; fāʒe, 44, 1; fayn, 63,
15; feyn, 95, 26; fain, 165, 2.
faht, *see* fiʒte(n).
faile(n), *wkv.*, OF. faillir; *fail*; *pt.
sg.* faylyd, 112, 27; *pt. pl.* failedcn,
103, 8; failed, 103, 5; failede, 222,
30; faylede, 223, 13. Nth. *pr.* 3
sg. failes, 129, 1. Sth. *pr.pl.* faileþ,
223, 6; *pp.* yfayled, 215, 23.
faintes, *sb.*, OF. feintise; *languor,
weakness, cowardice*, 105, 2.
fair, feir, fayer, fāre, *adj.*, OE.
fæger; *fair*; fayer, 75, 6; fāre,
228, 10; *wk.* faire, 47, 8; *pl.* feire,
39, 19; feyre, 91, 11. Sth. feir,
192, 9; væir (eSth.), 181, 10;
vair, 206, 4; *comp.* fehere, 194, 33;
superl. færʒest, 188, 19; vairest,
190, 26.
faire, fair, *adv.* fægere; *fairly, well*,
8, 11. Sth. feire, 193, 10; vaire,
209, 26; fair, 222, 11.
fais, *see* fā.
faiþful, *adj.*, NF. feið (OF. fei) +
ME. ful; *faithful*, 154, 8.
fal, *sb.*, OM. *fall, WS. *feall or ON.
fall; *fall, ruin*, 58, 3.

fal, *see* **falle(n)**.

fale, *see* **fēle**.

falle(n),*stv.*, OM. fallan (WS. feallan)
–fēol (R) ; *fall* ; *happen*; *pr.* 3 *sg.*
falleð, 15, 29; *pr. pl.* fallen, 15,
27 ; falle, 46, 18; *pr. sbj. sg.* falle,
103, 4; *pt. sg.* fēl, 43, 26 ; fellę, 40,
22 ; fil, 243, 8 ; *pt. pl.* fellen, 28,
16. Nth. *inf.* fal, 149, 31 ; *pr.*
3 *sg.* falles, 153, 31 ; *pt. pl.* fell,
126, 11. Sth. *inf.* valle, 182, 2 ;
pr. 3 *sg.* valþ, 218, 20 ; *pt. sg.* vēol
(eSth.), 182, 2 ; fēol (eSth.), 182,
3 : vēl, 206, 4.

falle(n), *wkv.*, OM. fellan, WS.
fīellan (fyllan) by confusion with
fallen < OE. feallen ; *fell, destroy,
kill* ; *inf.* fallen, 183, 8.

fallow, felawe, *see* folȝe(n), **fallowis**.

fallwe(n), *wkv.*, OE. fealwian; *grow
yellow, fade* ; *inf.* fallwen, 100, 20.

fals, *adj.*, OF. fals ; *false* ; *wk.* false,
51, 24. Sth. *pl.* valse, 109, 19.

falsenesse, *sb.*, OF. fals + ME. nesse ;
falsness, 234, 8.

falshęde, *sb.*, OF. fals + ME. hęde ;
falsehood, 203, 23.

falslȳ, *adv.*, OF. fals + ME. lȳ ;
falsely, 234, 13.

familerlīch, *adv.*, OF. familier +
ME. līch ; *familiarly*, 235, 16.

fānd, *see* **fīnde(n)**.

fantum, *sb.*, OF. santosme, fantome ;
phantom, fancy, 128, 5.

fāre, *sb.*, OE. faru, *f.* ; *journey* ; eME.
fare, 3, 26; *behavior, haughtiness,
boasting*, 135, 20.

fāre, *see* **fair**.

fārə(n), eME. faren, *stv.*, OE. faran–
fōr (6) ; *fare, go* ; *inf.* (eME. faren,
1, 10) fāre, 32, 5 ; *pr.* 3 *sing.* fāreð,
17, 21 ; *pr. sbj. sg.* fāre, 16, 26 ;
pt. sg. fōr, 1, 13 ; *pt. pl.* fōren, 35,
4. Nth. *pr.* 1 *sg.* fār, 155, 4
eSth. *inf.* varen, 184, 31 ; *pp.*
ivaren, 181, 10; ifaren, 187, 7.

faste, *aav.*, OE. fæste ; *fast, firmly*,
21, 3 ; fast, 18, 21. Sth. vaste,
205, 21.

faste(n), *wkv.*, OE. fæstan ; *fast,
abstain from food*; *inf.* faste, 56,

27 ; *pr.* 3 *sg.* fasteð, 17, 4 ; *pt. sg.*
fasted, 238, 26. Nth. *pr.* 3 *sg.*
fastes, 145, 6 ; *pp.* fastyt, 171, 17 ;
fast, 131, 23.

fatt, *adj.*, OE. fætt ; *fat*, 101, 8.

faucōun, *sb.*, AN. faucon ; *falcon*;
pl. faucōuns, 48, 25.

fauȝt, *see* **flȝte(n)**.

faurtēnd, *see* **fortēnd**.

fāvōur, *sb.*, OF. favur ; *favor*, 147, 3.

Favresfēld, *sb.*, *Faversham* (Kent),
7, 27.

fay, *sb.*, OF. faye ; *fay, fairy*, 125, 25.

fayer (fayre), *see* **fair**.

fayle, *sb.*, OF. faille ; *fail, failure*,
110, 4.

fȝyle(n), fayn, *see* **faile(n), fāȝen**.

fayrnes, *sb.*, OE. fægernes, *f.* ; *fair-
ness*, 129, 13.

fē, *sb.*, OE. fēo < feoh ; *property,
money, fee*, 76, 21.

feader, feale, *see* **fader, fēle**.

feat (fęat ?), *sb.*, OE. fæt ; *vat, vessel*,
195, 14.

fēaw, *see* **few**.

fēblelīke, *adv.*, OF. fēble + OE.
līce ; *feebly, scarcely*, 77, 21.

feche(n), fecche(n), fette(n), *wkv.*,
OE. fetian, feccan (fettan) ; *fetch,
bring*; *inf.* fechen,31, 11 ; fecchen,
195, 14 ; fette, 59, 27 ; *pr. pl.* fette,
46, 22 ; *pt. pl.* fett, 113, 23 ; *pp.* fet,
62, 2. Nth. *pr.* 3 *sg.* fettes, 127,
18.

fēde(n), feede(n), *wkv.*, OE. fēdan ;
feed; *inf.* fēde, 84, 1 ; feede, 147, 5 ;
pt. 2 *sg.* fedde, 48, 26 ; *pp. pl.* fedde,
53, 21. Nth. *pt. sg.* fedd, 132, 4.
Sth. *inf.* vēden, 201, 30.

feder, feend, *see* **fader, fēnd**.

feer, fęęste, *see* **fēr, fęst**.

fēge(n), *wkv.*, ON. fægja ; *cleanse,
polish* ; *imp. sg.* fęge, 18, 20.

fegtande, fęghte(n), *see* **flȝte(n)**.

fehere, *see* **fair**.

feill, *see* **fēle**.

feinte(n), *wkv.*, OF. *pp.* feint <
feindre ; *faint* ; *inf.* feinte, 231, 3.

feir, feire, *see* **fair, faire**.

feið, *sb.*, NF. feið, feid, OF. fei ;
faith, 25, 27. Cf. **fey**.

fel, fell, *adj.,* OE. fel ; *fierce, cruel* ; *pl.* felle, 74, 25.

fel, fēl, *see* falle(n), felle(n).

fel, felle, *sb.,* OE. fell; *skin, fell,* 17, 4 ; felle, 113, 18 ; *ds.* felle, 59, 29.

fel, felle, *sb.,* ON. fell; *mountain, hill, fell,* 151, 19.

felawe, felaw, felau (fela), *sb.,* ON. fēlagi ; *fellow* ; felaw, 97, 20 ; *pl.* felawes, 90, 9 ; felas, 117, 7. **Nth.** fallow, 171, 9 ; *pl.* felaus, 154, 4 ; fallowis, 170, 19. **eSth.** *pl.* feolahes, 192, 7. **Kt.** *pl.* velaghes, 212, 20.

fēld, *see* fōlde(n).

fēld, fēlc̣e, *sb.,* OE. feld, fēld ; *field* ; *pl.* fēldes, 30, 28 ; *ds.* fēlde, 113, 5. **Sth.** vēld, 182, 5 ; *ds.* vēlde, 206, 8.

fēldest, *see* fēle(n).

fẹle, eME. fele, *adj.,* OE. fela, feola, *sb., adj.* ; *many* ; eME. fele, 10, 6 ; fẹle, 31, 19. **eSth.** feale, 178, 14 ; fale, 176, 10 ; feole, 184, 1 ; vele, 179, 8.

fēle(n), *wkv.,* OE. fēlan ; *feel* ; *pr. pl.* fēlen, 19, 12 ; *pt. sg.* fēlde, 192, 10. **Nth.** *pr.* 3 *sg.* fēlis, 150, 1 ; *pp.* felid < fēlid, 154, 13.

felicitee, *sb.,* OF. felicitē ; *felicity,* 242, 24.

fēlid, *see* fēle(n).

fell, felle, fellen, *see* falle(n), fel.

felle(n), fele(n), *wkv.,* OAng. fellan, WS. fiellan ; *fell, cut down, take down* ; **Nth.** *inf.* fell, 142, 15 ; fel, 149, 28.

felōn, *sb.,* OF. felon, AN. -un, *felon, evil-doer* ; *pl.* felōns, 42, 30.

felōnȳ, *sb.,* OF. felonie ; *felony,* 78, 15.

felūnlȳche, *adv.,* AN. felun + ME. lȳche ; *feloniously, evilly,* 90, 2.

fẹme(n), (in), *wkv.,* OE. fǣman ; *foam* ; *inf.* fẹmin, 195, 13.

fen, *sb.,* OE. fen ; *marsh, fen,* 162, 25.

fen, *sb.,* Arabic, fan ; *fen, section of Arabic canon,* 245, 29.

fēnd, feend, fēndẹ, *sb.,* OE. fēond ; *fiend, devil,* 56, 4 ; fēndẹ, 66, 3 ;

feend, 244, 16 ; *pl.* fēndes, 59, 26. **Sth.** *pl.* fēond (eSth.), 183, 8 ; vēond (eSth.), 198, 14. **Kt.** vȳend, 219, 7.

fenn (fen), *sb.,* OE. fenn ; *fen, marsh* ; *ds.* fenne, 51, 23.

fēol, feolahe, *see* falle(n), felawe.

feole, fēond, *see* fẹle, fēnd.

fēord, *see* fērd.

fēorde(n), *see* fēre(n).

feorrenẹ, *adv.,* Sth. = Ml. ferre(n) ; OE. feorrene ; *afar, far,* 200, 5.

fēouwer, *see* fower.

feowertēne, *see* fowertēne.

Feoverēl (Feoverer), *sb.,* OF. Fevrier ; *February,* 197, 9.

fēowertēne, *see* fowrtēne.

fer, *adv.,* OE. feor ; *far, long,* 33, 13.

fēr (fẹr), *sb.,* OM. fēr, WS. fǣr ; *fear,* 59, 13. **Sth.** *ds.* fẹẹre, 233, 9.

fērd, *see* fēre(n).

fērd, fērde, *sb.,* OM. fērd, WS. fierd, *f.* ; *army,* 5, 25 ; (eME. fǣrd, 5, 6 ; fēord, 6, 28). **Sth.** *ds.* fērde, 185, 7 ; vērde, 185, 5.

fērde, *sb.,* OAng. *fērde?, cf.* MHG. gevǣrde ; *terror, fear,* 142, 30.

ferde(n), *see* fēre(n).

fēre, *sb.,* OE. gefēra ; *companion* ; *pl.* fēres, 34, 31. **Sth.** vēre, 199, 28.

fēre, *see* fīr.

fēre, *sb.,* OE. gefēr, *n.* ; *company* ; in fēre, *together,* 109, 6 ; ī fēre, 40, 18.

fereden, *see* ferīe(n).

fēre(n), *wkv.,* OE. fēran ; *go, follow, act, do* ; *pt. sg.* fēorde, 1, 6 ; fērde, 5, 24 ; ferde, 78, 18 ; *pt. pl.* (eME. fēorden, 2, 16) fērden, 29, 18. **Nth.** *pt. sg.* ferd, 155, 17.

ferie(n), *wkv.,* OE. ferian < ON. ferja ; *ferry, carry* ; *pt. sg.* fereden, 182, 20. **Sth.** *pt. pl.* vereden, 191, 4.

fērlī, *adj.,* OM. fērlīc, WS. fǣrlīc ; *fearful, wonderful,* 151, 14.

fērlīch, fērlȳ, *sb.,* OM. fērlīc, WS. fǣrlīc ; *terror, fear, wonder, miracle,* 36, 8 ; *pl.* fērlȳs, 126, 11.

fērlȳ, fērlīch, *adv.,* OM ſerlīce, WS.
ſǣrlīce ; *fearfully, wonderfully,* 90,
8 ; ſerlīch, 194, 5.

ferre, *adj.,* OE. feorren ; *far,* 144, 26.

fers, *sb.,* OE. fers, later displaced by
OF. vers ; *verse* ; ferrs (O), 9, 16.

fērs, *adj.,* OF. fiers ; *fierce,* 48, 16.

ferst, *see* **first.**

fērþe, *adj.,* OE. fēorða ; *fourth,* 11,
28.

ferthermōre, *adv.,* ME. ferther (<
OE. feor) + mōre, *furthermore,* 233,
10.

ferþynge, ferþyng, *sb.,* OE. fēorðing,
f. ; *farthing,* 94, 30 ; ferthynge,
117, 24.

fest, *adj.,* OE. fǣst ; *fast,* 31, 21.

fest, *sb.,* Kt. = Ml. fist ; OE. fȳst ;
fist, 243, 6.

fęste, fęst, *sb.,* OF. feste ; *feast,* 34,
23 ; fęęste, 238, 7 ; fęst, 116, 23.

festen, *sb.,* Sth. = Ml. faste(n) ; OE.
fǣsten ; *fast, abstaining from food,*
180, 25.

feste(n), *wkv.,* ON. festa, OE. fǣstan ;
fasten, strengthen ; *inf.* fesstenn (O),
12, 5 ; *pr. pl.* festen, 20, 5 ; *imp. sg.*
feste, 18, 20 ; feste, 18, 6. **Nth.**
imp. pl. festes, 138, 21 ; *pt. pl.*
festid, 140, 18 ; fest þai, 138, 27.

festne(n), *wkv.,* OE. fǣstnian ? ;
fasten ; *inf.* fesstnenn (O), 12, 8.
Sth. *pp.* ivestned, 203, 3. Cf.
fæstne(n).

fet, *see* **feche(n).**

fęt, *adj.,* OE. fǣt ; *fat,* 23, 2 ; *pl.*
fette, 23, 5. Cf. **fatt.**

fēte, fētsteppe, *see* **fōt, fōtsteppǝ.**

fęte(n), *wkv.,* OE. fǣttian or OM.
*fǣtan ; *fatten, make fat* ; *inf.* fęte,
84, 22.

feter, *sb.,* OE. fetor, feotor ; *fetter* ;
pl. feteres, 5, 28.

feðere, *sb.,* OE. feðer, *f.* ; *feather* ; *pl.*
feðres, 15, 27 ; *pl.* feþers, 103, 27.

fetles, *sb.,* OE. fǣtels ; *vessel,* 194,
25.

fette, fette(n), *see* **fęt, feche(n).**

fettes, *see* **feche(n).**

fętȳs, *adj.,* OF. fetis, faitis : *shapely,
neat, skilful,* 237, 22.

few, *adj.,* OE. ſēaw ; *few* ; (eME.
fæu, 5, 8). **eSth.** ſēaw, 212, 26.

fey, *sb.,* OF. fei, NF. feið ; *faith,
belief* ; bȳ mȳ fey, 241, 33. Cf.
feið.

feyn, feyr, *see* **faȝen, fayer.**

feyre, *sb.,* OF. feire ; *fair, market* ;
pl. feyres, 120, 25.

fīf, fīve, fīfe, fiffe, *adj.,* OE. fīf ;
five, 31, 17 ; fīve, 64, 26. **Nth.**
fīfe, 167, 11 ; fiffe, 166, 11. **Sth.**
vīf, 218, 17.

fifętēnde, *adj.,* OAng. fīftēgða ; *fifteenth,* 152, 21.

fiffe, *see* **fīf.**

fīfte, fyfte, *adj.,* OE. fīfta ; *fifth,* 12,
2 ; fyfte, 222, 29.

fiftēne, fiftēn, *adj.,* OM. fīftēne,
WS. fīftīene ; *fifteen* ; fyftēne, 116,
4 ; fiftēn, 151, 13. **Nth.** fivętēn,
133, 4.

fiȝte(n), figte(n), *stv.,* OM. fehtan
–fæht, WS. feohtan–feaht (3) ; *fight* ;
inf. fihten, 185, 25 ; fiȝte, 54, 11 ;
pr. 3 sg. figteð, 17, 21 ; *pr. ppl.*
figtande, 17, 21 ; *pt. sg.* faht, 189,
31 ; fauȝt, 50, 25 ; *pt. pl.* fuhten, 5,
8. **Nth.** *pr. ppl.* fegtande, 144, 11 ;
pt. sg. faght, 131, 2 ; *pt. pl.* faght,
126, 15. **Sth.** *inf.* vihte, 189, 12.

fiht, *sb.,* OE. feoht, *f.* ; *fight, battle,*
187, 3 ; *ds.* fihte, 187, 18.

fihte(n), *see* **fiȝte(n).**

filde, *see* **fille(n).**

fīle(n), *wkv.,* OE. fȳlan ; *make foul,
defile* ; *pp.* fīled, 66, 19.

Filip, *see* **Philip.**

fille(n), *wkv.,* OE. fyllan ; *fill, fulfil* ;
inf. fillenn (O), 8, 23 ; *pr. 3 sg.*
filleð, 14, 4 ; *pt. pl.* fylden, 2, 31 ;
pp. pl. filde, 75, 17 ; filled, 245,
16 ; filt, 26, 21 ; ifild (SEMl.), 42,
6. **Nth.** *pp.* fillit, 171, 23. **Sth.**
inf. füllen, 195, 15 ; *pp.* ifüild, 208,
18.

filstne(n), *wkv.,* OE. *fylstnian or
extension of fylstan ; *support, help* ;
pt. sg. filstnede, 15, 3.

filt, *see* **fille(n).**

filðe, fylthe, *sb.,* OE. fȳlð, *f.* ; *filth,*
18, 16 ; fylthe, 144, 10.

fīn, *adj.*, OF. fīn ; *fine*, 31, 18.
fin, *sb.*, OF. fīn ; *end*, 35, 21.
fīnde(n), fȳnde(n), *stv.*, OE. findan
(fĭndan)–fand (fǫnd) (3); *find,
provide for*; *inf.* fīnden, 3, 26;
findenn (O), 9, 5; fȳnde, 91, 9;
pr. 2 sg. fīndes, 29, 32; *pr. 3 sg.*
fīndeð, 20, 18; *pt. sg.* (eME. fānd,
4, 11); fǫnd, 26, 32; fǫndę, 90, 4;
fūnde, 44, 13; *pt. pl.* fūnden, 83,
15; foūnde, 100, 1; *pp.* fūnde, 39, 1.
Nth. *pr. pl.* fīndes, 134, 16; *pp.*
fūndun, 128, 27. **Kt.** *pr. 3 sg.* vīnt
= Ml. fīndeþ, 218, 8; *pt. pl.* fǫnden,
212, 9.
fīr, *sb.*, OE. fȳr, *n.*; *fire*, 17, 16; *ds.*
fīre, 44, 12. **Sth.** fūr, 178, 20; *ds.*
fūre, 177, 19; *pl.* fūr, 189, 29. **Kt.**
vēr, 217, 24; fēre, p. 272.
firmest, *adv.*, OE. fyrmest; *at first,
best*, 18, 21.
firrste, *see* first.
firse(n), firsi(n), *wkv.*, OE. feorsian,
fiersian (fyrsian); *remove*; *inf.* firsin,
194, 14.
first, *sb.*, OE. first, fyrst; *space of
time, time*, 53, 28. **Sth.** dōn ā
fūrst, *place in respite, put off, delay*,
177, 13.
first, *adj.*, OE. fyrest, fyrst; *first*; *wk.*
firrste (O), 10, 5. **Sth.** fūrst, 220,
1. **Kt.** ferst, 212, 3; verst, 203,
17.
fisc, fish, fis, fiss, *sb.*, OE. fisc; *fish*,
fis = fish, 19, 1. **Nth.** fiss, 132, 4;
pl. fisces, 151, 28. **eSth.** fisc, 182,
20; *pl.* fisces, 178, 27.
fishęre, *sb.*, OE. fiscere; *fisher*, 80, 31.
fite(n), *wkv.*, OE. fettian, *fittian;
contend with, abuse, 105, 21.
fīve, fivetēn, *see* fīf, fiftēne.
flǣsh, *see* flęsh.
flah, *see* flē(n).
flamme, flaumme, *sb.*, OF. flamme;
flame, 99, 23; flaumme, 99, 24.
Flandres, Flaundres, *sb.*, OF.
Flandres; *Flanders*, 159, 20;
Flaundres, 237, 7.
flatryng, *sb.*, based on MDu. flat-
teren?; *flattering*, 221, 15.
flaumme, *see* flamme.

flaun, *sb.*, OF. flaon; *pancake*, 84,
24.
Flaundres, *see* Flandres.
flē, fledde, *see* flē(n).
flaye(n), *wkv.*, ON. fleyja; *put to
flight, frighten.*
flēge(n) = flēȝe(n), flīge(n), *stv.*,
OM. flēgan–flēh, WS. flēogan–flēah
(2); *fly as a bird*; *pr. 3 sg.* flēgeð,
15, 19; *pr. pl.* flīe, 51, 23; *pt. sg.*
fliȝte, 36, 25. **Nth.** *pr. 3 sg.* flȳes,
143, 26. **Sth.** *pr. 3 sg.* vlȳȝþ, 219,
22; *pr. ppl.* vlȳinde, 215, 18.
flēh, fleis, fleisch, *see* flē(n), flęsh.
flęm, *sb.*, OE. flēam; *flight*; **Sth.** *ds.*
flęme, 182, 8.
flem, *sb.*, OF. flegme; *slimy matter
in throat, sluggishness of tempera-
ment*, 221, 8.
flēme(n), *wkv.*, OM. flēman, WS.
flīeman; *put to flight*; *pt. pl.*
flēmden, 5, 9. **Nth.** *pp.* flēmid,
158, 28.
Flemmyng, Flemyng, *sb.*, OE.
Fleming; *Fleming*, 223, 2.
flē(n), *stv.*, OM. flēon–flēh (WS.
flēah) (2); *flee*; *inf.* flē, 79, 31;
pr. 3 sg. flēð, 17, 16; *pt. sg.* flēh,
5, 32; *pt. pl.* flugen, 3, 29; flōwe,
208, 3; *wk. pt. pl.* fledde, 233, 8;
wk. pp. pl. fledde, 48, 28. **Sth.** *pt.
sg.* flah, 188, 21.
flēos, *sb.*, eSth. = Ml. flēs; OE.
flēos; *fleece*; *ds.* flēose, 199, 4.
flēs, flęs, flesche, *see* flęsh.
flęschlīch, *adj.*, OE. flǣsclīc; *fleshly,
carnal*, 191, 24.
flęsh, flǫsh, fleisch, flēs, flesse,
flessh, *sb.*, OE. flǣsc; *flesh, animal
food*; (eME. flęsc, 3, 27; flǣsh (O),
12, 7); flęs, 17, 9; fleis, 22, 25;
fleys, 49, 13; fleisch, 50, 8; flęschę,
113, 18; flessh, 241, 3. **Nth.**
flessę, 128, 30. **Kt.** flēs, 213, 7.
flēte(n), *stv.*, OE. flēotan–flēat (2);
float, swim; *pr. 3 sg.* flēt = flēteð,
19, 4; *pr. sbj. sg.* flēte, 80, 29.
flȩt, *sb.*, OE. flett; *floor*; *ds.* flette,
122, 32.
fleys, flīe(n), *see* flęsh, flēge(n).
fliȝte, *see* flēge(n).

fligt, *sb.*, OE. flyht ; *flight*, 15, 14.

floc, *sb.*, OE. flocc ; *flock, troop* ; flocc (O), 9, 24.

flōd, *sb.*, OE. flōd ; *river, flood*, 22, 32 ; *ds.* flōdę, 72, 1. **Sth.** *ds.* vlōde, 182, 18.

flōdȝet, *sb.*, **Sth.** = Ml. flōdȝat ; OE. *flōdgeat ; *floodgate* ; *pl.* flōdȝeten, 201, 16.

flom, *see* flum.

flǭ(n), *sb.*, OE. flān ; *arrow* ; *pl.* flǭn, 208, 12.

flǭ(n), *stv.*, OM. flān (WS. flēan) –flōh (6) ; *flay, skin* ; *inf.* flǭ, 83, 25.

Flǫrīs, *sb.*, OF. Floris ; *Floris*, 35, 18.

florische(n), **florrisse(n)**, *wkv.*, OF. florir, floriss- ; *flourish* ; *inf.* florissen, 105, 4 ; *pr. sbj. sg.* florische, 103, 4.

flǫryn, *sb.*, OF. florin ; *florin*, 242, 7.

flǫte, *sb.*, OF. flote ; *flock, company*, 87, 23.

flour, flourę, *see* flūr.

floūred, *pp.* as *adj.* ; OF. flurir ; *flowered, ornamented*, 117, 2.

flowe, flugen, *see* flē(n).

flum, *sb.*, OF. flum ; *river*, 35, 8 ; flumm (O), 11, 21 ; flóm, 65, 5.

flūr, flour, *sb.*, OF. flūr, flour ; *flower*, 35, 14 ; flour, 49, 3 ; floūrę, 105, 4.

flȳe, *sb.*, OAng. flēge, WS. flēoge ; *fly*, 158, 8.

flȳe(n), *see* flēge(n), flīge(n).

flyghyng, *sb.*, based on flīe(n) ; *flying, flight*, 144, 24.

fnaste(n), *wkv.*, OE. *fnǣstian < fnǣst 'breath' ; *breathe* ; *inf.* fnaste, 81, 23.

fǭ, *sb.*, OE. fā(h), *adj.*; *foe, enemy*, 56, 4. **Sth.** *pl.* fǭn, 230, 22.

fꞷ, *adj.*, ON. fār, cogn. with OE. fēaw ; *few*, 32, 19 ; *pl.* fǭnę, 161, 14 ; lNth. funę, 161, 15.

foangen = fǭnge(n), *stv.*, ON. fanga, replacing in pres. OE. fōn–fēng (R) ; *seize, catch* ; *inf.* foangen, 226, 16.

fodder, *sb.*, OE. fōdor, foddur ; *fodder*; *ds.* foddre, 202, 31.

fōde, *sb.*, OE. fōda ; *food*, 16, 5.

fol, *see* ful.

fōl, *adj.*, OF. fol ; *foolish* ; fole, 204, 11.

fōl, fōlę, *sb.* < *adj.*, OF. fol ; *fool*, 200, 7 ; fōlę, 137, 30 ; lNth. foul, 127, 10.

folc, *see* folk.

fǫlde, *sb.*, OM. fald, fāld (WS. feald?), *f.*; *enclosure for sheep or other animals*, then *the sheep*, 15, 5.

fōlde, *sb.*, OE. folde ; *ground, land*; ā fōlden (eSth. *adv. phr.*) *to the ground, wholly*, 189, 14.

fǭlde(n), *stv.* OM. faldan (fāldan), WS. fealdan–fēold (R) ; *fold, en-wrap* ; *pt. pl.* fēld, 68, 19.

folȝe(n), **folge(n)**, **foleche(n)**, **folwe(n)**, *wkv.*, OE. folgian ; *follow*; *inf.* (eME. follȝehenn (O), 8, 16) ; folgen, 20, 26 ; folwen, 101, 9 ; foluwe, 57, 29 ; *pr. 3 sg.* (eME. follȝehþþ (O), 10, 18) ; folȝeþ, 176, 14 ; folegeð, 20, 18 ; *pt. pl.* (eME. folecheden, 6, 9) ; *pt. sg.* folewede, 57, 27 ; *pr. sbj. pl.* (eME. follȝhe (O), 10, 15). **Nth.** *inf.* fallow, 170, 23 ; *pt. sg.* followit, 167, 17. **Sth.** *inf.* volȝī, 218, 23 ; *pr. 3. sg.* volȝeþ, 219, 21 ; *imp. pl.* voleweð, 198, 18.

folī, folīe, *see* folȳe.

folk, follc, *sb.*, OE. folc ; *folk, people* ; eME. folc, 5, 32 ; follc (O), 8, 22 ; *gpl.* follkess (O), 10, 13. **Sth.** *ds.* volke, 181, 18.

follȝehenn, *see* folȝe(n).

follkess, followit, *see* folk, folȝe(n).

folte(n), *wkv.*, based on OF. folet (folt), 'fool' ; *act like a fool* ; *pp.* folted as *adj.*, *foolish*, 97, 3.

foluwe(n), **folwe(n)**, *see* folȝe(n).

folȳe, folī (folȳ), *sb.*, OF. folie; *folly*, 50, 1 ; folī, 127, 10 ; folȳ, 118, 7.

fōman, *sb.*, OE. fāh + man ; *foeman*, *pl.* fǭmen, 106, 21.

fǭn, *see* fǭ.

fō(n), *stv.*, OE. fōn–fēng (R) ; *seize, take* ; *pt. pl.* fēng, 223, 2 ; **Sth.** *pp.* ifōn, 183, 18.

fǫnd, fonden *see* fīnde(n), funde(n).

fǫnde(n), **fǫndi(n)**, *wkv.*, OE. fandian, fǫndian ; *try, test, prove* ; *inf.* fǫnden, 46, 3 ; fǫndin, 193, 10 ; *pp.* fǫnded, 131, 24.

fǫndynge fōndunge. *sb.*, OE. fandung, fǫndung, *f.*; *temptation*; fǫndyng, 97, 29; *pl.* fǫndunges, 198, 31.

fonne, *sb.* < *adj.*, perh. related to Dan. fonnik, 'clumsy, stupid person'; *fool*, 125, 21.

for, *adv.*, *prep. conj.*, OE. for; *because*, *on account of*, *for*, 1, 18; forr (O), 8, 22. **Sth.** vor þæn; *therefor*, 183, 29.

fōr, *see* fāre(n).

forbāren, *see* forbēre(n).

forbēde(n), *stv.*, OE. for bēodan –bēad (2); *forbid*, *prohibit*; *pr.* 1 *sg.* forbēde, 120, 25; *imp. sg.* forbēdę, 125, 25; *pt. sg.* forbęd, 50, 22; *pp.* forbǫden, 145, 11. **Sth.** *pt. sg.* vorbęad (eSth.), 200, 19; vorbęd, 205, 24.

forbęre(n), eME. forberen, *stv.*, OE. forberan–bær (4); *spare*, *forbear*; *inf.* forbęre, 75, 14; *pt. pl.* forbāren, 3, 31.

forberne(n), *wkv.*, OM. forbærnan, WS. biernan; *burn*, *consume*; *inf.* forbernen, 189, 14; forberne, 184, 9; *pp.* forbernd, 193, 25.

forbisne, *sb.*, OE. forbysen f.; *example*, *parable*, 211, 28.

forblēnde(n), *wkv.*, OE. for+blendan, blēndan; *blind*; *pp.* forrblēndedd (O), 9, 24.

forbǫden, *see* forbēde(n).

forbreide(n), **forbrēde(n),** *wkv.*, OE. forbregdan–brægd (3); *pervert*, *corrupt*; *pr.* 2 *sg.* forbrēdes, 18, 1; *pp.* forbroiden, 17, 3.

forbręke(n), *stv.*, OE. forbrecan –bræc (4); *break in pieces*; *pp.* forbrǫken, *worn out*, 17, 3.

forbrenne(n), *wkv.*, OE. forbernan; *burn up*; *pp.* forbrent, 61, 26.

forbroiden, *see* forbreide(n).

forbrǫken, *see* forbręke(n).

forbȳ, *prep.*, OE. for+bī; *beside*, *in respect to*, 236, 22.

forcursed, *pp.* as *adj.*, OE. for+cursian; *accursed*, 4, 5.

forcūð, *adj.*, OE. forcūð; *cowardly*, *knavish*, 185, 7; *superl.* forcūðest, 185, 31.

fordēme(n), *wkv.*, OE. fordēman; *condemn*, *destroy*; *inf.* fordēme, 184, 2; *pt. sg.* fordēmde, 192, 5.

fordfēorde, *see* forþfēre(n).

forditte(n), *wkv.*, OE. fordyttan; *shut up*; *pp.* fordit, 63, 22.

fordō(n), *anv.*, OM. fordōn–dǣde (WS. dyde); *ruin*, *destroy*; *inf.* fordōn, 184, 3; fordō, 149, 8; *pp.* fordōn, 4, 7; fordōnę, 120, 24. **Sth.** *pt. sg.* fordüde, 195, 20.

fordrēde(n), *stv.*, OM. fordrēdan –drēd, WS. fordrǣdan–drēd (R); *dread*, *fear*; *pp.* fordrēd, 25, 31.

fordrive(n), *stv.*, OE. fordrīvan–drāf (1); *drive away*; *pp.* fordriven, 19, 29.

fordrȯnke, *adj.*, OE. fordruncen; *very drunk*, *drunken*, 239, 12.

fordüde, *see* fordō(n).

foren, *prep.*, OE. foran; *before*, 182, 15.

fōren, *see* fāre(n).

forest, *sb.*, OF. forest; *forest*, *wood*, 169, 21.

forestēr, *sb.*, OF. forestier; *forester*, 147, 17.

forewarde, **forward(e),** forewerde, *sb.*, OM. forewārd, WS. foreweard, *f.*; *precaution*, *agreement*, *bargain*, 6, 19; forward, 27, 12; *instruction*, 28, 8, *pl.* forwardes, 7, 19. **Sth.** forwerde, 212, 4; vorewarde, 104, 5; vorwarde, 204, 13.

forfaite(n), *wkv.*, based on OF. *pp.* or *sb.* forfait; *forfeit*; *inf.* forfait, 235, 18; *pt. sg.* forfaited, 234, 2.

forgaa, *anv.*, **Nth.** = Ml. forgǫ(n); OE. forgān; *forgo*, *pass by*, *dispense with*, *abstain from*; *inf.* forgaa, 144, 22.

forgat, *see* forgete(n).

forġelwe(n), *wkv.*, OE. *forgelwian; *become yellow*, *fade*; *pr.* 2 *sg.* forgelwes, 18, 2.

forgifnes, *sb.*, OE. forgifnes, *f.*; *forgiveness*, 141, 28.

forȝete(n), -gete(n), *stv.*, OM. forgetan–gæt, WS. gietan–geat (5);

forget; *inf.* forʒete, 37, 18; *pr. sbj.*
sg. forʒete, 37, 17; *pt. sg.* forgat, 22,
28; *pp.* forgeten, 23, 6. **Sth.** *inf.*
forʒite, 177, 10; forʒyte, 179, 9;
pr. 3 *sg.* forʒitet, 177, 14; forgüt,
177, 1; *pr. pl.* voryeteþ, 219, 25;
imp. sg. voryet, 217, 21.

forʒife(n), forʒeve(n), foryeve(n),
stv., OM. forgefan–gæf, WS. giefan
–geaf(5); *forgive; pr.* 3 *sg.* forʒeveþ,
124, 16; *pr. sbj. sg.* forrʒife (O), 9,
29; foryeve, 246, 11; *pt. sg.* forʒaf,
74, 6; *pp.* forʒive, 45, 28.

forʒite(n), *see* **forʒete(n).**

forgǫ(n), *anv.,* OE. forgān; *forgo,
give up; inf.* forgǫn, 57, 14.

forgüt, forʒyte, *see* **forʒete(n).**

fochęle(n), *stv.,* OE. forhelan–hæl
(5); *conceal; pt. sg.* forhal, 58, 1;
pp. (eME. forholen, 5, 1); forhǫlen,
29, 29.

forhewe(n), *stv.,* OE. forhēawan
–hēow (2); *hew down, cut to pieces;*
e**Sth.** *pt. sg.* forhēou, 181, 21.

forholen, forhǫlen, *see* **forhęle(n).**

forlēse(n), *stv.,* OE. forlēosan–lēas
(2); *lose; pt. sg.* forlęs, 5, 32; *pp.*
(eME. forloren, 2, 30), forlǫren, 16,
10; forlorn, 50, 2; forlǫre, 213,
16. **Kt.** *pp.* vorlǫre, 218, 24.

forlēte(n), *stv.,* OM. forlētan, WS.
forlætan–lēt (R); *leave, forsake;*
pt. sg. forlēt, 33, 24.

forloren, forlǫren, *see* **forlēse(n).**

formast, *adj.,* OE. formest, modified
by mast<OE. mǣst, māst, ' most ';
foremost, first, 69, 3.

forme, *adj.,* OE. forma; *first,* 71,
18.

forme, fourme, *sb.,* OF. forme;
form, 147, 8.

fornayse, *sb.,* OF. fornaise; *furnace,*
218, 7.

fornime(n), *stv.,* OE. forniman–nōm
(4); *take away, remove; pp.* fornumen, 27, 4.

forǫuten(-yn), *adv.,* OE. *without,*
172, 13; forǫutyn, 173, 7.

forquat = **forwhat,** *adv.,* OE. for
hwæt; *wherefore,* 21, 17.

forr, *see* **for.**

forrēde(n), *wkv.,* OM. forrēdan, WS.
forrǣdan; *deceive, seduce, wrong;*
pp. forrēd, 25, 32; forrad, 56, 22.
e**Sth.** *pr.* 3 *sg.* forrēadeð, 194, 24.

forrǫuth, forrǫwth, *prep. adv.,* cf.
Dan. forud; *before, forward,* 170,
21; torrǫwth, 170, 27.

forrþī, *see* **forþī.**

forsaid, forseid, *adj.* < *pp.,* OE.
foresecgan; *foresaid,* 159, 9. **Sth.**
forseyed, 222, 28.

forsāke(n), *stv.,* OE. forsacan–sōc
(6); *forsake; inf.* forsāke, 56, 26;
pr. 3 *sg.* forsākeð, 16, 17. e**Sth.**
pr. 3 *sg.* vorsakest, 193, 11.

forscalde(n), *wkv.,* OE. for + OF.
escalder; *scald completely; pt. sg.*
forscaldede, 195, 19.

forseid(-seyd), *see* **forsaid.**

forsitte(n), *stv.,* OE. forsittan–sæt
(5); *neglect, delay;* **Sth.** *pt. sbj.
sg.* forsęte, 189, 13.

forsōþ, forsōþe, *adv.,* OE. forsōþ;
forsooth, 42, 28; forsōþe, 47, 27.
Sth. vorzōþe, 215, 10.

forstande(n), *stv.,* OE. forstandan
–stōd (6); *avail, profit; pt. sg.*
forstōd, 6, 17; *pt. sbj. sg.* forstōde,
2, 17.

forstoppe(n), *wkv.,* ON. stoppa,
forstoppa?; stop up, obstruct;
Sth. *pr. pl.* forstoppeð, 201, 12.

forswalʒe(n), *stv.,* OE. forswelgan
–swealh (3); *swallow up, destroy;*
inf. forswalʒe, 188, 16.

forswat, *see* **forswęte(n).**

forswēle(n), *wkv.,* OM. forswēlan,
WS. swǣlan; *burn up; pp.* forswēlde, 188, 13.

forswelte(n), *wkv.,* OE. *forsweltan;
kill, destroy; inf.* forswelten, 194,
29.

forswęre(n), *stv.,* OE. forswerian
–swōr(6); *forswear, commit perjury;*
pp. (eME.) forsworen, 2, 29. **Sth.**
pp. vorswǫre, 207, 11.

forswęrynge, *sb.,* cf. forswęren;
perjury, 147, 21.

forswęte(n), *wkv.,* OE. *forswǣtan;
weary with labor, spoil with sweat-
ing;* **Nth.** *pp.* forswat, 166, 2.

forsworen, *see* forswēre(n).

Fort, *sb.*, *De Fors* or *de Fortibus*;
Willelm of, Earl of Albemarle,
227, 4.

fortēnde, *adj.*, OE. fēowertēoða;
fourteenth, 197, 9. Nth. faurtēnd,
152, 19.

forð, furþ (furþe), *adv.*, OE. forð;
forth, 17, 6; furþ, 99, 16; furþe,
99, 5; furth, 137, 6. Sth. vorð,
185, 1.

forðan, *adv.*, OE. for ðon; *therefore,
thereupon*, 24, 30.

forðcume(n), *stv.*, OE. forðcuman
–cōm (cwōm) (4); *come forth,
appear*; *pp.* forðcumen, 24, 8.

forðe(n), *wkv.*, OE. forðian; *promote, effect, further*; *inf.* forðen,
17, 19; *pp.* forþedd (O), 8, 18.

forþer, *adj.*, OE. furðra; *fore, front*,
231, 23.

forðfare, *sb.*, eME. = Ml. forðfāre;
OE. forðfaru; *departure, death*,
191, 7.

forþfēre(n), *wkv.*, OE. forðfēran; *go
forth*; *die*; eME. *pt. sg.* fordfēorde,
5, 16.

forþī, forþīę, *adv. conj.*, OE. for þȳ;
because, therefore, 1, 2; forrþī (O),
8, 24; forþīę, 154, 18. Sth. vorþī,
198, 19.

forþinke(n), *wkv.*, OE. forðencean
–ðōhte (ðohte); *misthink, dislike,
repent*; *pr. 3 sg.* forþingketh, 212,
23. Sth. forþuncheð, 194, 12.

forþirmār, *adv.*, Nth. = Ml. furþer-
mōr; OE. furðer + mār; *furthermore*, 166, 8.

forðriht, *adv.*, OE. forðriht; *right
forth, straightway*, 183, 16.

forþünche(n), *see* forþinke(n).

forðward, forðwar, *adv.*, OM. forð-
–ward, WS. weard; *continually,
always*, 18, 20; forðwar, 87, 16.

forðweię, *sb.*, OE. forðweg; *departure, journey*, 27, 27.

fortō, *prep.*, OE. for tō; *until*, 221,
32.

fortravale(n), *wkv.*, OE. for + OF.
travailer; *tire out*; Nth. *pp.* fortravalit, 171, 26.

fortune, *sb.*, OF. fortune; *fortune*,
242, 16.

forward(e), *see* forewarde.

forwerpe(n), *stv.*, OE. forweorpan
–wearp (3); *reject, cast away*; *inf.*
forrwerrpenn (O), 9, 23.

forwhȳ, *adv.*, OE. for + hwȳ; *because*,
244, 19.

forwith, *adv.*, ONth. *forwið; *before*,
128, 16.

forwrappe(n), *wkv.*, origin uncertain; *wrap up*; *pp.* forwrapped,
240, 22.

forwrēʒe(n); *wkv.*, OE. forwrēgan;
accuse; *inf.* forwrēʒen, 179, 8.

forwūndīe(n), *wkv.*, Sth. = Ml. for-
wūnde(n); OE. forwundian (wūndian); *wound*; *pp.* forwūnded,
190, 9.

forwurðe(n), *stv.*, OE. forweorðan
–wearð (3); *perish, go wrong*; *inf.*
furwurðen, 193, 31; *pr. 3 sg.* forwurðes, 18, 2; *pp.* forwurðe, 188, 2.

foryeve(n), *see* forʒife(n).

fosterling, *sb.*, OE. fōstorling; *foster-
child*, 190, 8.

fostir, fostyr, *sb.*, OE. fōster; *foster,
nursling*, 173, 12; fostyr, 175, 16.

fostre(n), *wkv.*, OE. fōstrian; *foster*;
pp. fostrid, 53, 21.

fostrild, *sb.*, based on OE. fōstor +
hild; *nurse*, 201, 6.

fōt, *sb.*, OE. fōt; *foot*, 28, 16; on
fōte, *on foot*, 6, 29; *pl.* fēt, 3, 6;
fētę, 138, 19. lNth. fut, 168, 6.

fōtsteppe, *sb.*, OE. fōt + steppe;
footstep; *pl.* fētsteppes, 14, 4.

foul, foul, fowle, *see* fōl, ful, fugel.

fōunde(n), *wkv.*, OE. fundian; *seek,
endeavor*; *proceed*; *pt. sg.* fōunded,
157, 22.

four, fourme, *see* fower, forme.

fourme(n), *wkv.*, OF. former; *form*;
pp. fourmed, 102, 28.

fourtēne, *see* fowrtēne.

fourty, *see* fowertī.

fowertī, *adj.*, OE. fēowertig; *forty*,
33, 29; fowwerrtīʒ (O), 12, 10;
furtī, 214, 6.

fowertiʒþə, *sb.*, OE. fēowertēoðe;
fourteenth, 236, 23. Cf. fortēnde.

fowhel, fōwle, *see* fugel.

fowre, *adj.*, OE. fēower ; *four*, 8, 1 ; foure, 70, 29. eSth. fēouwer, 185, 20.

fowrtēne, fourtēne, *adj.*, OM. fēowertēne, WS. -tīene ; *fourteen*, 33, 2 ; fourtēne, 118, 6. eSth. fēouwertēne, 185, 5.

fowwerrtiȝ, *see* fowertī.

foysyn, *sb.*, OF. foyson ; *plenty, power, success*, 96, 4 ; fuysoune, 141, 31.

frā, *adv. prep.*, eME., Nth. = Ml. friǭ ; *from*, 6, 31 ; 128, 21.

fram, *prep. adv.*, OE. fram, frǫm ; *from*, 4, 18. Sth. vrom, 198, 2 ; vram, 217, 10.

frāme, frame, *sb.*, ON. frami, cogn. OE. fram, ' *valiant* '; *advantage, profit*; eME. frame, 8, 21 ; frāme, 14, 20.

Fraunce, Fraunce, *sb.*, OF. France; *France*, 7, 10 ; Fraunce, 221, 13.

Franche, Frankys, *adj.*, Nth. = Ml., Sth. Frenkish ; ONth. Francisc or Frencisc modified by Franc; *French*, 127, 6 ; Franche, 157, 23.

Fraunce, *see* France.

fraunchīse, *sb.*, OF. franchise; *franchise*, 232, 26.

frayne(n), *see* freine(n).

frē, *adj.*, OE. frēo ; *free*, 74, 17 ; (SEMl.) frēo, 42, 21. eSth. frēo, 187, 19.

frēdōm, frēdam, *sb.*, OE. frēodōm ; *freedom*, 84, 11 ; frēdam, 232, 26.

freend, *see* frēnd.

freine(n), *stwkv.*, OM. *fregnan, WS. frignan–fræġn (3) ; *question, inquire, ask*; *inf.* frayne, 106, 29; *wk. pt. sg.* freinde, 21, 17; freinede, 194, 6.

freis, *adj.*, Nth. = Ml. fresh ; OE. fersc ; *fresh*, 151, 31.

frek, *adj.*, OE. frec ; *bold, insolent*, 157, 23.

frēklȳ, *adv.*, OE. freclīce ; *boldly*, 171, 16.

frēlīch, *adj.*, Sth. = Ml. frēlī ; OE. frēolīc ; *freely*, 232, 26 ; eME. frēolīch, 192, 9.

frēman, *sb.*, OE. frēoman ; *freeman*, 84, 8.

frəmde, *see* fremede.

frǣme, *sb.*, OE. fremu ; *profit, advantage*, 226, 8.

fremede, fremde, *adj.*, OE. fremede, fremde ; *strange, foreign*, 144, 14; fremde, 177, 10.

frǣme(n), *wkv.*, OE. fremman ; *promote, profit, do*; *inf.* frǣme, 78, 12.

French, Frensch, Freynsch, *adj.*, OE. Frencisc ; *French*, 210, 12; Frensch, 225, 3 ; Freynsch, 224, 19.

frenchype, *see* frendschipe.

frēnd, freend, *sb.*, OE. frēond ; *friend* ; frēnde, 76, 10 ; *pl.* (eME. frēond, 6, 12) frēnd, 2, 2 ; freendes, 241, 25.

frendschipe, *sb.*, OE. frēondscipe ; *friendship*; eME. frēontschipe, 192, 8 ; frenchype, 144, 21.

frēo, *see* frē.

frēoboren, *adj.*, eME. = Ml. frēbǭren; OE. frēo + *pp.* boren; *noble born, free born*, 192, 11.

frēolīch, *see* frēlīch.

frēond, *see* frēnd.

frēontschipe, *see* frendschipe.

frēte (frǣte), *sb.*, OM. *frēt, WS. *frǣt, *f.*; *food*, 40, 12.

frǣte(n), *stv.*, OE. fretan–frǣt (5) ; *devour, eat up* ; *pt. sg.* frǣt, 198, 23 ; *pp.* freten, 23, 5.

Freynsch, *see* French.

Frīdai, Frīdæi (Frīdawes), *sb.*, OE. Frigdæg ; *Friday* ; Frīdæi (eME.), 4, 31 ; *pl.* Frīdawes, 200, 2. Sth. Vrīdeie, 199, 33.

friȝte, friȝt, *sb.*, OE. fyrhtu, OM. *fryhtu ; *fright*, 59, 13.

frigtī, *adj.*, OS. *fyrhtig ; *timid*, 28, 15.

frigtīhēd, *sb.*, OM. *fryhtighæd, WS. *fyrhtighæd ; *timidity*, 26, 30.

frigtīlīke, *adv.*, OE. *fyrhtiglīce; *with fear, timidly*, 25, 3.

frith, *sb.*, OE. frīð; *forest, wooḁ*, 162, 25.

friðe(n), *wkv.*, OE. friðian ; *keep in peace, preserve, free* ; *pr. sbj. sg.* friðe, 30, 15.

frǫ, frǫǫ, *adv. prep.*, ON. frā, cogn. with OE. fram, frǫm ; *from*, 15, 3.

frōfre(n), *wkv.*, OE. frōfrian ; *comfort* ; *inf.* frōfrenn (O), 12, 14. Sth. *inf.* vrōvren, 201, 2.

froit, *see* fruit.

frǫtyng, *sb.*, based on OF. froter, 'rub' ; *rubbing, harsh sounding*, 225, 26.

frouȝ, *adj.*, suggests OE. *frōh, perh. ON. frār, 'swift' ; *fickle*, dial. *frough* (*frow*), 57, 30.

fruit, frut (froit), *sb.*, OF. fruit, 27, 23 ; fruyt, 238, 28 ; froit, 148, 26 ; frut, 100, 19 ; frutę, 134, 16.

frumschaft, *sb.*, OE. frumsceaft, *f.* ; *creation*, 191, 16.

frut, frutę, *see* fruit.

frutestęre, *sb.*, OF. fruit + ME. stęre ; *female fruitseller*, 237, 22.

fugel, fuhel, fowlę, fōul, *sb.*, *pl.* fugeles ; OE. fugel (ol) ; *bird, fowl*, 22, 17 ; fōwle, 145, 4 ; fōul, 172, 6, *pl.* fuȝeles, 178, 27 ; fuheles, 193, 22 ; fowheles, 144, 24. Sth. vóȝel ; 215, 18.

fuhten, *see* fiȝte(n).

ful, *adj.*, *adv.*, OE. ful ; *full*, 2, 31 ; fól, 49, 12 ; fullę, *adv.*, 119, 14.

ful, *see* fulle(n).

fūl, fōul, *adj.*, OE. fūl ; *foul*, 3, 6 ; fūlę, 85, 30 ; fōul, 48, 10. Sth. vōul, 217, 25.

fulfille(n), fulfylle(n), *wkv.*, OE. fulfyllan ; *fulfil, complete, satisfy* ; *inf.* fulfillen, 104, 12 ; fulfylle, 95, 6 ; fulfille, 244, 5 ; *pp.* fulfild, 103, 15 ; fulfyllt, 111, 18. Nth. *pr. pl.* fulfill, 144, 9 ; *pr. ppl.* fulfilland, 146, 4.

fulhtne(n), *wkv.*, OE. *fulhtnian ; *baptize* ; *pp.* fullhtnedd (O), 11, 23.

fulle(n), *wkv.*, OE. fullian ; *fill, be full* ; *imp. sg.* ful, 18, 6.

fülle(n), *see* fille(n).

fulluht, *sb.*, OE. fulwiht, fulluht ; *baptism* ; fulluhht (O), 8, 14.

fully, *adv.*, OE. fullīce ; *fully*, 240, 15.

fülste(n), *wkv.*, Sth. = Ml. filste(n) ; OE. fylstan ; *help, assist* ; *inf.* fülste, 191, 15.

fulsum, *adj.*, OE. fulsum ; *plentiful*, 24, 25.

fulsumhęd, *sb.*, OE. *fulsumhǣd ; *plenty, copiousness*, 23, 32.

fultum, *sb.*, OE. fultum ; *help* ; *ds.* fultume, 226, 1.

fünde(n), *wkv.*, OF. fonder ; *found, establish* ; Nth. *inf.* fūnd, 130, 13.

funde(n), fonde(n), *wkv.*, OE. fundian, *seek, go* ; *inf.* fonde, 94, 5.

fünde(n), fūndun, *see* finde(n).

fune, *see* fō (fō).

funtfat, *sb.*, OF. funt + OE. fæt ; *font, baptismal vessel*, 16, 23.

für, fürst, furþ, *see* fir, first, forð.

furþe, *adj.*, OE. fēowerða ; *fourth*, 222, 22.

furtī, *see* fowertī.

furwurðe, *see* forwurðe(n).

fūs, *adj.*, OE. fūs ; *eager, ready*, 132, 13.

füse(n), *wkv.*, Sth. = Ml. fīse(n) ; OE. fȳsan ; *make ready* ; *pt. sg.* füsde, 186, 8.

fut, fuysoūne, *see* fōt, foysyn.

fyfte, fyftēne, *see* fifte, fiftēne.

fylden, *see* fille(n).

fyllynge, fyllyng, *sb.*, OE. *fyllung, *f.*; *filling, refreshment, restoration*, 101, 3.

fy!the, fȳnde(n), *see* filþe, finde(n).

G.

gā, *anv.*, Nth. = Ml. gǭ(n) ; OE. gān ; *go* ; *pr.* 3 *sg.* gāsę, 161, 11 ; *pt. pl.* ȝēde, 140, 22. lNth. *pt. sg.* ȝudę = ȝōdę, 167, 15 ; *pt. pl.* ȝeid = ȝēd, 167, 7. Cf. gǭn.

gabbe, *sb.*, ON. gabb, *n.* ; *jest, imposture*, 37, 9.

Gābriēl, *sb.*, OF. Gabriel ; *Gabriel* ; *gs.* Gābriēles, 199, 7.

gadere(n), *wkv.*, OE. gaderian ; *gather* ; *inf.* gaderen, 24, 6 : gadere, 35, 14 ; *pp.* gadered, 2, 21. Nth. gader, geder, *see* geder. Sth. *inf.* gederen, 202, 6 ; *pr. ppl.* gederinde, 202, 23.

gaderinge, gadering, *sb.,* OE. ga-
derµng, *f.*; *gathering, assembly*;
gadering, 2, 23.

gæde, ȝǣld, *see* gǭ(n), ȝēld.

ȝǣn, *see* ȝēn.

gǣre, ȝǣt, *see* ȝēn, ȝēt.

gaf(e), *see* ȝeve(n), geve(n).

gai, *see* gay.

gain, *wkv.,* Nth. = Ml. gaine(n); ON.
gegna, gagna ; *obtain, gain,* 16ɔ, 7.

galai(y), *sb.,* OF. galei; *galley,* 164,
25; *pl.* galaies, 163, 15.

galiǫte, *sb.,* OF. galiote ; *small galley,*
164, 13.

gall, *sb.,* **ONth.** galla, WS. gealla ;
gall, bitterness, anger, 129, 20.

Galway, Galeway, *sb., Galloway,*
221, 28; Galeway, 222, 14.

galwes, *sb.pl.* regularly; OM. galga,
WS. gealga, infl. by ON. galgi?;
gallows, 86, 3.

galwetrē, *sb.,* OE. galgatrēo ; *gallows
tree,* 86, 11.

gāmen, game, gammyn, *sb.,* OE.
gamen ; *game, sport, jest* ; gāmen,
79, 7; gāme, 1ɔ9, 4. **Nth.** gammyn,
167, 15.

gan, *see* ginne(n).

gange(n), gǭnge(n), *stv.,* OE. gan-
gan-gēng (Ř); *go, move*; *inf.* gangen, 17, 5; gǭnge, 86, 6; *pr. pl.*
gangen, 18, 7. Cf. ȝeonge(n).

ganninde, *see* gǭ(n).

gāpe(n), *wkv.,* ON. gapa, cognate,
OE. geapan; *gape*; *pr.* 3 *sg.* gāpeð,
19, 8.

gāre, *sb.,* **eME.** = Ml. gǭr ; OE. gār,
gāra; *spear*; *pl.* gāren, 186, 15.

gare(n), garris, gart, *see* gēre(n).

garring, *sb.,* based on garren < MHG;
chatter, roar, 224, 15.

gāst, gāstę, *sb.,* **Nth.** = Ml. gǭst ; OE.
gāst; *ghost, spirit,* 131, 24; gāstę,
142, 28.

gast, *sb.,* OE. gāst, short form ; *spirit,
ghost,* 20, 22.

gāstelȳ, *adj.,* **Nth.** = Ml. gǭstlȳ ; OE.
gāstlīc ; *spiritual,* 146, 26.

gat, *see* gete(n).

gāte, gat, *sb.,* ON. gata ; *gait,* dial.
gate, strut, way, manner, 59, 5 ;

gat, 89, 10 ; **gāte,** 89, 23. **Nth.**
gāte, 137, 7 ; lNth. gāt, 167, 21.
Cf. ȝāte.

ȝāte(n) = ȝāte(n), *wkv.,* OE. gēatan
(gǣtan, gētan) ; *grant, concede* ; *pt.
sg.* gatte, 34, 30.

gaud, *sb.,* **Nth.** = Ml. gaude ; OF.
gaude perh.; trick, wile : 16ɔ, 7.

gay, gai, *adj.,* OF. gai; *gay,* 154, 24 ;
gai, 158, 25.

ȝē, ȝear, *see* þū, ȝēr.

ȝēde, ȝēde, *wkv. def.,* OE. geēode,
pt. of OE. gegān ; *see* gǭ(n).

geder, *wkv.,* **Nth.** = Ml. gadere(n) ;
gather; *pt. sg.* gederd, 135, 11 ;
gedird, 138, 32.

gederen, gederinde, *see* gedere(n).

gees, ȝef, *see* gōs, ȝif.

Ȝeffree, *sb.,* OE. Geoffrey ; *Geoffrey*;
gs. Geffrees, 227, ʕ.

gegge, *sb.,* OF. guigue, AN. gigge
(gegge?) ; *maid, frivolous woman,*
35, 19.

gehāten, ȝēld, *see* ȝehāte(n), ȝēld.

ȝēlde(n), gelt, *see* ȝēlde(n), gilt.

ȝenerallȳ, *adv.,* OF. general + ME.
lȳ; *generally,* 146, 15.

gēnge, *sb.,* ON. gengi ; *company, following, army,* 5, 10.

ȝentę, *adj.,* OF. gent ; *gentle, noble,*
111, 22.

ȝentil, *adj.,* OF. gentil ; *noble,* 207, 21.

ȝentilman, *sb.,* OF. gentil + ME.
man ; *gentleman,* 224, 20.

gēr, gēre, *see* ȝēr.

gēre(n), gare(n), *wkv.,* ON. görva
(gerva), cogn. with OE. gearwian,
gerwan ; *prepare, make*; *inf.* gēren,
33, 25 ; *pt. sg.* gart, 125, 29. **Nth.**
inf. ger, 138, 5 ; *pr.* 3 *sg.* garris,
174, 2 ; *pt. pl.* gert, 155, 26 ; *pt.
.sbj. sg.* gert, 141, 7.

ȝerke(n), *wkv.,* **SEMl.** = Ml. ȝarke(n);
OM. garkian, WS. gearcian ; *pre-
pare, inf.* gerken, 27, 31.

gerlǫnd, *sb.,* OF. gerlande ; *garland,*
215, 22.

Ȝermain, *adj. sb.,* OF. Germain ;
German ; *pl.* Germans, 222, 24.

Germānia, *sb.,* Lat. Germania ; *Germany,* 222, 23.

gērn, *adv.*, OE. georne mod. by ON.
    giarn; *eagerly, earnestly*, 154, 18.
Gersen, *sb.*, Lat. Gessen; *Goshen*,
    31, 1.
gersume, *sb.*, OE. gersume < ON.
    gersami; *treasure*, 46, 5.
gert, *see* gēre(n).
gest, *sb.*, ŌM. gest, WS. giest; infl.
    by ON. gestr ; *guest* ; *pl.* gestes, 4,
    12.
ǧest(e), *sb.*, OF. geste ; *story, achieve-
    ment*, MnE. *jest*, 116, 7 ; gest, 132,
    29 ; *pl.* jestes, 130, 1.
gēt, gētę, *see* ʒēt.
gete(n), *stv.*, ON. geta–gat (5), cogn.
    with and later displacing OM.getan,
    WS. gietan ; *get, obtain* ; *inf.* gete,
    50, 11 ; *pt. sg.* gat, 80, 2. **Nth.** *pr.*
    2 sg. gettes, 141, 31 ; *pt. sg.* gat,
    172, 26.
gēte(n), gēte(n), *wkv.*, ON. gǣta ;
    guard, keep, take care of ; **Nth.** *inf.*
    gēt, 155, 25 ; *imp. sg.* gēt, 161 22.
gettes, *see* gete(n).
gēþ, *see* gǭ(n).
ǧēvelīc, *adj.*, OE. ge-efenlīc ; *equal,
    like*, 18, 31.
ǧeven, *see* ʒeve(n).
geve(n), *stv.*, ON. gefa, cogn. with
    and later displacing OM. gefan-gæf,
    WS. giefan-geaf (5) ; *give* ; *pt. sg.*
    gafę, 109, 28.
geyne(n), *wkv.*, ON. gegna ; *gain* ;
    pt. sg. geyned, 54, 29.
ǧhe, ǧif, *see* hē, ʒif.
gife(n), *see* give(n).
gilde, *see* gylde.
gildeday, *see* gyldeday.
gīle, *sb* , OF. guile, AN. gile ; *guile,
    treachery*, 160, 6.
ǧilerī, ǧillerȳ, *sb.*, OF. gillerie ;
    deceit, 101, 17 ; gillerȳ, 147, 15.
gilt, *sb.*, OE. gylt ; *guilt*, 28, 6 ; *ds.*
    gilte, 32, 25. **Kt.** *ds.* gelte, 218, 10.
giltelēęs, *adj.*, OE. gylt + lǣs ; *guilt-
    less*, 238, 9.
ǧin, *sb.*, OF. engin ; *gin, snare, in-
    genuity*; *ds.* ginne, 46, 3 ; gynnę,
    111, 25.
ǧing, *adj.*, **Sth.** = ME. ʒung ; based on
    WS. geong ? ; *young*, 18, 22.

ǧinǧivre, *sb.*, OE. gingifre mod. by
    OF. gingimbre, gingibre ; *ginger*,
    202, 25.
ginne(n), *stv.*, OE. (on)ginnan–gann
    (3) ; *begin* ; *pt. sg.* gan, 21, 6 ;
    can = gan, 106, 14 ; *pt. pl.* gunen,
    31, 26 ; gònnen, 63, 7 ; gunne, 184,
    1 ; gònne, 205, 16. **Nth.** *pt. sg.*
    gun, 135, 6 ; *pt. pl.* gun, 137, 11.
    Sth. *pt. sg.* gon, 181, 7 ; gun, 182,
    16.
gist, *sb.*, **Sth.** = Ml. gest ; WS. giest,
    OM. gest, infl. by ON. gestr and
    gista ; *guest*, 199, 27.
give(n), gyve(n), *stv.*, ON. gefa,
    cogn. with and later displacing OM.
    gefan-gæf, WS. giefan-geaf (5) ;
    give ; *inf.* gifenn (O), 12, 16 ; *pr.*
    2 sg. givest, 50, 5 ; *pr. sbj. sg.* gif,
    112, 12 ; *pp.* given, 55, 16 ; gyven,
    75, 27. **Nth.** *inf.* gife, 130, 31 ;
    gyffe, 145, 16 ; *pr. sbj. pl.* gyfe, 146,
    19.
ǧiven, *see* ʒeve(n).
glad, *adj.*, OE. glæd ; *glad* ; *comp.*
    gladdore, 205, 10. **Sth.** gled, 195,
    26.
glāde(n), *wkv.*, OE. gladian ; *gladden,
    be glad* ; *inf.* glāde, 67, 15 ; glāden,
    102, 11 ; *pt. pl.* glāded, 103, 17.
gladlȳ, *adv.*, OE. glǣdlīce ; *gladly*,
    146, 31. **Sth.** gledlīche, 215, 5.
gladnesse, gladnes, *sb.*, OE. glǣd-
    ness, *f.* ; *gladness*, 44, 7 ; gladnes,
    102, 10.
glas, *sb.*, OE. glæs ; *glass*, 56, 14.
glaȝ, *adj.*, ON. glaðr, cogn. with OE.
    glæd ; *glad, happy* ; *pl.* glāðe, 29, 9.
glē, *sb.*, OE. glēo(w) ; *glee, joy, song*,
    128, 4 ; SEMl. glēo, 36, 29. **Nth.**
    gleu, 149, 28.
gled, *see* glad.
gledīe(n), *wkv.*, **Sth.** = Ml. gladen ;
    OE. gladian ; *gladden* ; *inf.* gledīen,
    199, 28.
gledlīche, *see* gladlȳ.
glēm, *sb.*, OE. glǣm ; *gleam, splendor*,
    228, 11.
glēo, gleu, *see* glē.
gleyve, *sb.*, OF. glaive ; *sword, glaive* ;
    pl. glęyves, 60, 25.

glīde(n), *stv.*, OE. glīdan–glād (1) ;
glide, proceed ; *pr. 3 sg.* glīdeð, 191,
17 ; *pt. pl.* glide, 37, 21.

glifne(n), *wkv.*, cf. Scotch gliff, 'a
glance' ; *glance, look* ; Nth. *pt. sg.*
gliffnit, 172, 2.

glōrie, *sb.*, OF. glorie ; *glory*, 101,
22.

glōrifīe(n), *wkv.*, OF. glorifier ;
glorify ; *inf.* glōrifīen, 104, 12 ; *pp.*
glōrifīde, 139, 23.

glōryōus, *adj.*, OF. glorius ; *glorious,
excellent*, 117, 9.

glòterīe, *sb.*, OF. gluterie ; *gluttony* ;
54, 13.

glòtonȳe, glotonīe, *sb.*, OF. glou-
tonie ; *gluttony*, 49, 16 ; glotonīe,
206, 18.

glouand, *see* glowe(n).

Gloucester, *sb.*, OE. Gleawecester
(Glowe-) ; *Gloucester*, 5, 12 ; Glowchestre, 227, 2.

glōve, *sb.*, OE. glōf, *f.* ; *glove*, 112, 8.
Sth. *pl.* glōven, 190, 11.

Glowchestre, *see* Gloucester.

glowe(n), *stv.*, OE. glōwan–glēow
(R) ; *glow, be radiant with heat* ;
pr. ppl. glowende, 60, 23. Nth.
pr. ppl. glouand, 151, 32.

gnēde, *adj.*, OM. *gnēde, WS. *gnīede ;
stingy, parsimonious, 48, 27.

gnēdelīche, *adv.*, OM. *gnēdelīce,
WS. *gnīedelīce ; *sparingly*, 202, 4.

gō, gōand, *see* gō(n).

God, Godd, *sb.*, OE. god ; *God* ;
Godd (O), 9, 29 ; *ds.* Gode, 16, 21 ;
gs. Godes, 1, 4 ; Goddys, 91, 17.
Nth. *gs.* Goddis, 130, 30 ; *gs.* without ending, God sake, 138, 4 ; *pl.*
goddes, 135, 10. Sth. *group gs.*
God Almiȝttīes, 232, 17.

gōd, good, *adj.*, OE. gōd ; *good*, 2,
3 ; good, 22, 3 ; *comp.* bettre (OE.
betera), 9, 11 ; better, 4, 26 ; bettur,
128, 18 ; *superl.* best, 29, 13. lNth.
gudę, 141, 11. Sth. *comp.* betre,
177, 6 ; *superl.* betste, 177, 27 ;
betst, 179, 22. Kt. guod, 216, 31 ;
wk. guoden, 217, 3.

gōd, *sb.*, OE. gōd, *neut.* ; *property,
wealth, goods*, 3, 2 ; *pl.* gōde, 164,

16 ; gōdes, 104, 20. Kt. *pl.* guodes,
215, 22.

Godard, *sb.*, Godard, 76, 10.

godday, *sb.*, OE. gōd + dæg ; *good-
day*, 47, 7.

goddes, goddis, *see* God.

goddspell (O), later gospell, *sb.*, OE.
godspel ; *gospel*, 8, 19 ; gospellę,
123, 5 ; godspel, 149, 13. Sth. *ds.*
godspelle, 210, 21 ; godespelle,
211, 27.

goddspellbōc (O), *sb.*, OE. godspell-
bōc ; *book of the gospel*, 11, 15.

goddspellwrihhte (O), *sb.*, OE.
godspel + wyrhta (wryhta) ; *gospel-
writer*, lit. *-worker, -maker*, 11, 5.

goddys, *see* God.

gōde(n), *wkv.*, OE. gōdian ; *improve,
endow, enrich* ; *pt. sg.* gōded, 4, 14.

gōdenesse, *see* gōdnesse.

godespelle, *see* goddspell.

gōdleȝȝc (O), *sb.*, ON. gōðleikr, infl.
by OE. gōd ? ; *goodness*, 12, 29.

gōdnesse, *sb.*, OE. gōdness, *f.* ; *goodness, favor*, 11, 15 ; gōdęnesse,
98, 4.

godspelle, *see* goddspell.

Godwine, *sb.*, OE. Godwine ; *Godwin,
earl and father of Harold*, 204, 27.

gōld, *sb.*, OE. gold, gōld ; *gold* ; 2, 5 ;
ds. gōlde, 40, 24.

Golī, *sb.*, OF. Golī ? ; *Goliah*, 131, 2.

Gomore, *sb.*, OE. Gomorre ; *Gomorrah*,
73, 23.

gon, gonne(n), *see* ginne(n).

gō(n), *anv.*, OE. gān–ēode (ȝēode) ;
go ; *inf.* gōn, 25, 24 ; gō, 42, 28 ; gǫn,
227, 23 ; *pr. 2 sg.* gōst, 124, 21 ;
pr. 3 sg. gōð, 16, 7 ; gōþ, 125, 18 ;
gōþ, 244, 23 ; *pr. pl.* gōn, 37, 25 ;
gǫn, 240, 10 ; *pr. sbj. sg.* (eME.
gā, 196, 2) ; *pr. sbj. pl.* gōn, 15, 7 ;
imp. sg. gō, 18, 17 ; *imp. sg.* with
inf. gō tel, *go tell*, 65, 10 ; *imp. pl.*
gōð, 197, 21 ; *pr. ppl.* gōand, 103,
29 ; *pt. 2 sg.* ēdest, 51, 9 ; *pt. sg.*
(eME. gǣde, 3, 9 ; iǣde, 6, 29) ;
gēde, 28, 31 ; ȝet = ȝēd (?), 44, 32 ;
pt. pl. iēden, 3, 28 ; ȝēden, 35, 24 ;
pt. sbj. sg. ēde, 52, 17 ; *pp.* gǫnę,
96, 16 ; gǫn, 228, 22. Nth. gā,

q. v. **Sth.** pr. pl. gọ̄ð, 197, 17;
pr. ppl. (eSth.) ganninde, 189, 16;
pt. sg. (eSth.) ēode, 186, 19; yēde,
210, 22; pt. pl. yēde, 212, 11; pp.
ygọ̄n, 64, 25. **Kt.** inf. guo, 218,
14; pr. 3 sg., gēþ, 215, 19; imp.,
sg. guo, 217, 8; pp. yguo = igʒ̄,
216, 5.

gọ̄ng, sb., OE. gang, gọ̄ng; going,
gang; affair, 51, 8.

gọ̄nge(n), good, see **gange**(n), **gōd**.

goodman, sb., OE. gōd + man; goodman, husbandman, 212, 2.

gōs, sb., OE. gōs; goose; pl. gees, 86,
18.

gospell, see **goddspell**.

gọ̄st, sb., OE. gāst; ghost, spirit, 48, 4.

gọ̄st, see **gọ̄**(n).

gọ̄stlīch, adj., OE. gāstlīc; spiritual,
198, 29.

gọ̄t, sb., OE. gāt; goat, 86, 17.

Gọ̄te, Gọ̄the, sb., OE. Gota; Goth;
pl. Gọ̄tes, 221, 11; Gọ̄thes, 221, 15.

gọ̄th, gọ̄ð, see **gọ̄**(n).

goule(n), wkv., ON. gaula; howl;
pr. pl. goule, 78, 25.

góvernaunce, sb., OF. gouvernance;
government, 234, 23.

governe(n), wkv., OF. governer;
govern, rule; pr. 3 sg. governeþ,
101, 1.

grāce, sb., OF. grace; grace, favor,
16, 28.

grācyous, grācioūs, adj. OF.
gracieus; gracious, 96, 1; grācioūs,
235, 19.

gradde, see **grēde**(n).

grāme, sb., OE. grama; anger, harm,
44, 10.

gramēre, sb., OF. gramaire; grammar,
224, 28.

gramērscōle, sb., OF. gramaire +
OE. scōl, f. mod. by OF. escole;
grammar-school, 224, 28.

grante(n), **grantit**, see **graunte**(n).

grat, see **grēt**.

Gratiānus, sb., Lat. Gratianus;
Gratian, 221, 13.

graunte(n), wkv., OF. granter; grant,
give; pr. sbj. graunte, 45, 22; imp.
sg. grawntẹ, 123, 28; pt. sg.

grauntyd, 107, 28; pt. pl. graunted,
89, 21; grauntede, 222, 12; pp.
graunted, 73, 16. **Nth.** pr. 2 sg.
grauntes, 137, 32; pt. pl. grantit,
170, 15. **Sth.** inf. grantī, 209, 30;
pp. igranted, 45, 30.

grāve, sb., OE. græf, f.; grave, 54,
24. **Nth.** grāvẹ, 143, 11.

grāve(n), stv., OE. grafan-grōf (6);
grave, dig, bury; inf. grāve, 83, 26;
pp. grāven, 33, 15.

grawnte, see **graunte**(n).

grāy, adj., OE. græg; gray, 229, 8.

grayth, adj. ON. greiðr; ready,
quick; superl. graythest, 137, 7.

grayþe(n), see **greiþe**(n).

grēat, see **grēt**.

Grēce, sb., OF. Griece; Greece, 126, 5.

grēde(n), wkv., OM. grēdan, WS.
grǣdan; cry out; inf. grēde, 36, 6.
Sth. pr. pl. grēdeþ, 215, 16; pr.
sbj. pl. grēde wē, 211, 19; pt. sg.
gradde, 205, 21.

grēdī, adj., **Sth.** = Ml. grēdī; WS.
grǣdig, OM. grēdig; greedy, comp.
grēdiure, 202, 13.

grēdīnesse, sb., **Sth.** = Ml. grēdīnesse; WS. grǣdiʒnesse, OM. grēdig-
ness, f.; greediness, 202, 13.

Gregorīe, Gregorȳ, sb., OF. Gre-
gorie, Gregory; Gregorīe, 201, 6.

grēdiure, see **grēdī**.

greiþe(n), **grayþe**(n), wkv., ON.
greiða; prepare, aid; inf. greiþe,
49, 10; grayþe, 65, 12; pp. greyþed,
86, 30.

grēme(n), **Sth.** grēmīe(n), wkv.,
OE. gremian; anger, irritate; inf.
grēme, 78, 13. **eSth.** inf. gremīen,
193, 7.

grēne, adj., OE. grēne; green, 79, 9.

grenne(n), wkv., OE. grennian;
grin, gnash the teeth; inf. grenne,
51, 27; pt. sg. grennede, 61, 13.

grēot, sb., **eME.** = Ml. grēt; OE.
grēot; sand, gravel, grit, 200, 8.

gressẹ, gresẹ, sb., OE. græs, gærs;
grass, 103, 3; gresẹ, 152, 1.

grẹste, see **grēt**.

grẹt, grẹtẹ, adj., OE. grēat; great,
grẹtẹ, 137, 27; eME. grẹat, 193, 8;

comp. grettore, 51, 11 ; gretter, 235, 32 ; *superl.* grettest, 236, 6 ; grḗste, 198, 32. **Kt.** grīat, 212, 1 ; grat, 218, 26.

grēte, *sb.*, ONth. *grēte ; cf. ON. grǣti ; *weeping, sorrow,* 132, 11.

grēte(n), *stv.*, OM. grētan, WS. grǣtan–grēt (R) ; *weep*; *pr. ppl.* grētand, 93, 8 ; *pt. sg.* grēt, 28, 31 ; *pt. pl.* grēten, 77, 18 ; *pp.* grēte, 93, 13.

grēte(n), *wkv.*, OE. grētan ; *greet, salute*; *pr.* 3 *sg.* grēteð, 31, 30 ; *pt. sg.* grette, 78, 23.

grḗtlȳ, *adv.*, OE. grēat + lȳ ; *greatly,* 91, 32.

gretter, grettore, *see* grḗt.

grēve(n), *wkv.*, OF. grever ; *grieve, injure*; *inf.* grēve, 65, 33 ; grēven, 71, 24.

grew, *see* growe(n).

Grey, *sb.*, *Grey, Richard of,* 227, 6.

greythe, *adv.*, ON. grelðr, *adj.* ; *readily, excellently,* 125, 9.

greyþe(n), *see* greiþe(n).

griat, grīhond, *see* grḗt, grȳhond.

grill, gryl, *adj.*, OE. *gril, cf. grillan ; *harsh, fierce,* 50, 5.

grim, grym, *adj.*, OE. grim ; *grim, cruel,* 89, 20.

Grim, *sb.*, OE. Grim ? ; *Grim,* 81, 2.

Grimesbī, *sb.*, ON. OE. Grim + ON. bȳ, 'town'; *Grimsby (Lincolnshire),* 87, 30.

grimlī, *adj.*, OE. grimlīc ; *grim, fearful,* 148, 23.

grin, *sb.*, OE. grin ; *snare*; lof and grin, *some instrument or instruments of torture,* 3, 14.

grīnde(n), *stv.*, OE. grindan (grīndan) –grand (grǫnd) (3) ; *grind*; *inf.* grīnden, 200, 8 ; *pr.* 3 *sg.* grīnt (**Sth.**), 200, 10 ; *pr. sbj. pl.* grīnden, 200, 12 ; *pt. sg.* grūnde, 195, 12 ; *pt. sbj. sg.* grūnde, 200, 8.

grīnstǫn, *sb.*, OE. *grīnd, grīndstān ; *grindstone,* 200, 10.

grip, *sb.*, ON. grīpr ; *raven, vulture,* 82, 16.

grisbittyng, *sb.*, OE. gristbitung, *f.* ; *gnashing of teeth,* 224, 15.

grīse, *sb.*, OM. *grȳs, cf. OE. grȳslīc; *horror, fear.*

grīse(n), *stv.*, OE. (a)grīsan–grās (1) ; *feel horror, terrify*; *inf.* grīse, 54, 20.

grislī, grislȳ, *adj.*, OE. grȳslīc ; *horrible, grisly,* 150, 22 ; grislȳ, 237, 17. **Sth.** grislīch, 182, 12.

grislīche, *adv.*, **Sth.** = Ml. grislī ; OE. grīslīce ; *horribly, grisly,* 61, 13.

grispatīe(n), *wkv.*, **Sth.** = Ml. grispate(n) (baten) ; OE. gristbātian ; *gnash the teeth*; *inf.* grispatīen, 195, 13.

grip, grith, *sb.*, OE. grið ; *peace, security,* 50, 11 ; grith, 80, 18.

griðfulnesse, *sb.*, based on OE. grið ; *peacefulness, security,* 202, 30.

grǒcchyng, *sb.*, based on OF. grouchier ; *grudging, wrong,* 233, 26.

grome, *sb.*, eME. = ME. grǫme ; OE. grama, grǫma ; *anger,* 193, 8.

grǫne(n), *wkv.*, OE. grānian ; *groan, inf.* grǫn, 267.

grǫt, *sb.*, ON. grātr ; *weeping,* 29, 1.

grǫte, *sb.*, OE. grot, *neut.*; *particle, piece,* 61, 18 ; *pl.* grǫtes, 79, 11.

grǫve, earlier grǫf, *sb.*, OE. grāf, *neut.*; *grove,* 241, 33.

growe(n), *stv.*, OE. grōwan–grēow (R) ; *grow*; *pt. sg.* grew, 36, 3. **Nth.** *pr. ppl.*, grouand, 151, 3.

gruchche(n), *wkv.*, OF. grouchier ; *murmur, grudge*; *pt. pl.* gruchchede hī, 212, 18.

grūnd, *sb.*, OE. grund, grūnd ; *bottom, ground,* 19, 25 ; *ds.* grūnde, 20, 11. **Sth.** *ds.* (Lay.) grūnden, 181, 24.

grūnde, *see* grīnde(n).

grūndlīke, *adv.*, OE. *grundlīce, grūndlīce ; *ravenously,* 84, 31.

grūndwall, *sb.*, OAng. grundwall, grūndwall, WS. -weall ; *foundation,* 130, 12.

grȳhond, grīhond, *sb.*, **Kt.** = Ml. graihūnd ; OE. *greyhound,* 219, 21 ; grīhond, 219, 23.

gryl, grym, *see* grill, grim.

ġū, gude, *see* þū, gōd.

gülden, *adj.*, Sth. = Ml. gilden; OE.
  gylden; *golden*; *fs.* güldene, 182, 13.
gülte(n), *wkv.*, Sth. = Ml. gilte(n);
  OE. gyltan; *sin, incur guilt*; *pr.* 3
  sg. gültet, 179, 2.
gun, gunen, *see* ginne(n).
ǧungest, *see* ʒung.
gunnen, *see* ginne(n).
guo, *see* gǫ(n).
guod, gūr, *see* gōd, ʒūre.
gürde(n), *wkv.*, Sth. = Ml. girde(n);
  OE. gyrdan; *gird*; *pp.* igürd, 207, 2.
gūðhẹde, *sb.*, OM. gugoðhãd (*hǣd,
  f.?), WS. geogoðhãd; *youth*, 15, 10.
guyldehalle, *sb.*, ON. gildi + ME.
  halle; *gild hall, guildhall*, 233, 16.
gȳde, *sb.*, OF. guide, ON. gide;
  guide, 108, 13.
gyfe, gyffe, *see* give(n).
gylde, *sb.*, ON. gildi, cogn. with OM.
  geld, WS. gield; *guild*, 116, 18.
gyldeday, *sb.*, ON. gildi + OE. dæg;
  guildday, day of the guild's meeting,
  117, 21.
gyltȳ, *adj.*, OE. gyltig; *guilty*, 107, 4.
ǧynne, *see* ǧin.
gȳsel, *sb.*, OE. gīsel; *hostage*; *pl.*
  gȳsles, 6, 20.
gyterne, *sb.*, OF. guiterne, AN.
  giterne; *guitar*, 237, 10.
gyve, *sb.*, OM. gifu, WS. giefu mod.
  by ON.?; *gift*, 75, 19.
gyve(n), *see* give(n), ʒeve(n).

H.

hā, *see* hāve(n), hē.
ha, *interj.*, OE. ha; *ha*, 102, 12.
habb, habbe(n), habbet, habbeþ,
  hãbeþ, *see* hāve(n).
habitāciōn, *sb.*, OF. habitacion;
  habitation, 239, 27.
hãd, *ʒb.*, eME., Nth. for ME. hǫd;
  OE. hãd; *condition, quality, rank*,
  8, 17.
hǣldə(n),*wkv.*, eSth. = Ml. hēlde(n);
  OM. heldan, hēldan, WS. hieldan
  (hyldan); *incline, tip, heel*; *inf.*
  hǣlden, 181, 24; *pt. sg.* hǣld, 181,
  24.

hæleð, *sb.*, OE. hæleð; *hero, man,
  warrior*; *g. pl.* hæleðe, 188, 6.
hærm, *see* harm.
hǣrne, *sb.*, ON. hjarni; *brain*; *pl.*
  hǣrnes, 3, 9.
hǣþeliʒ, *adv.*, ON. hǣþiliga; *scornfully, contemptuously*, 9, 26.
hǣved, hafd, *see* hẹved.
haf, hafden, hafe, haffdenn, *see*
  hāve(n).
hafved, *see* hẹved.
hai, *sb.*, OM. hẽg, WS. hīeg; *hay*,
  105, 3.
hail(l), hāl, *adj.*, eME., Nth. = Ml.
  hǫl; *whole*; haill, 175, 10; hāl,
  179, 25.
hãlde(n), *stv.*, eME., Nth. = Ml.
  hǫlde(n); OAng. hãldan (WS.
  healdan)–hēold (R); *hold, keep*;
  inf. hãlden, 6, 4; (Nth.) hãlde,
  144, 6; *pr.* 3 *sg.* (Nth.) hãldes,
  128, 25; *imp. sg.* hãld, 190, 24;
  imp. pl. (Nth.) hãldis, 170, 5; *pt.
  sg.* hēold, 4, 10; hēld, 155, 30;
  hild (Nth.), 131, 32: *pt. pl.* hēolden,
  2, 29; *pp.* hãlden, 128, 1. Kt. *pr.*
  3 *sg.* halt, 214, 23. Cf. hǫlde(n).
halechen, *see* hālī.
haleche(n), *see* halʒhe(n).
haleweiʒe, *sb.*, OE. *hǣlewǣge, cf.
  ON. heilivãgr; *balsam*, literally
  health bringer, 190, 29.
halewen, halewyn, *see* hālī.
hãleȳ, *adv.*, OE. hãl + lȳ; *wholly*,
  175, 17.
half, halve, halven, *adj.*, OM. half,
  WS. healf; *half*, 4, 11; halve; *side*,
  60, 13; halven, 58, 8.
half, *sb.*, OE. healf; *half, side*, 185, 20.
halʒhe(n), halwe(n), *wkv.*, OE.
  hãlgian; *hallow, consecrate*; *inf.*
  hallʒhenn (O), 11, 22; *pt. sg.*
  (eME.) halechede, 2, 9; halwede,
  205, 9. Nth. *pr. sbj. sg.* halowe,
  146, 14; *pr. sbj. pl.* halowe, 146,
  23; *pp.* haloud, 139, 23.
hālī, *adj.*, eME., Nth. = Ml. hǫlī;
  OE. hãlig; *holy, pl. saints*; eME.
  hālī, 5, 1; hālīʒ (O), 12, 13; *wk.*
  hallʒhe (O), 8, 19; *pl.* halechen,
  4, 8; halhen, 197, 1; halwen, 117,

2; halewyn, 116, 16; halewen, 228, 28. Nth. hālȳ, 146, 19.

hālīdōm, halȳdōm, *sb.*, OE. hāligdōm; *saintly relic, sacrament,* 6, 20; halȳdōm, 90, 17.

Halidon, *sb.*, *Halidon,* 157, 10.

hāliȝ, *see* hālī.

halle, *sb.*, OE. heall, *f.*; *hall,* 49, 2.

hallerōf, *sb.*, OE. heall + rōf; *hall-roof, roof of the hall,* 181, 23.

hallȝhe, *see* hālī.

haloud, halowe, *see* halȝhe(n).

halpe, *see* helpe(n).

halpenȳ, *sb.*, OE. healf pening; *half penny,* MnE. *ha'peny,* 117, 4.

hals, *sb.*, OM. hals, WS. heals; *neck,* 3, 17.

halse(n), *wkv.* Nth. = Ml. halse(n); OE. hālsian; *conjure, adjure; salute*; *pt. sg.* halsit, 169, 30.

halsing, *sb.*, OE. hālsung, *f.* ; *salutation,* 169, 31.

halt, *adj.*, OE. halt, healt; *halt, lame*; *pl.* halte, 81, 18.

halt, *see* halde(n).

halve, halven, *see* half.

halwen, *see* hālī.

halwe(n), *see* halȝhe(n).

hālȳ, *see* hālī.

halȳdayȩ, *sb.*, Nth. = Ml. hōlīdai; OE. hāligdæg; *holy day, holiday,* 146, 14.

halȳdōm, ham, *see* hālīdōm, hē.

hām, *adv.*, eME., Nth., Ml. hōm; OE. ham; *home* (Scot. *hame*), 8, 7.

hamme, *sb.*, OE. hamm., *f.*; *ham, inner or back part of knee,* 223, 23.

Hamtūn(-ōn), *sb.*, OE. Hamtūn; *Southampton,* 163, 23. Sth. *ds.* Hamtone, 188, 5.

hamzelve, *see* self.

hān, *see* hāve(n).

hānd, *sb.*, Nth. = Ml., Sth. hōnd (hand) ; ONth. hand, hānd ; *hand,* 126, 7. Nth. *pl.* hēnd < ON. hendr, 138, 19. eSth. *ds.* hande, 178, 24.

hāndewerc, *sb.*, OE. handgeweorc ; *handiwork,* 130, 18.

handle(n), *wkv.*, OE. handlian ; *handle* ; *inf.* handlen, 36, 2.

hānge(n), hōnge(n), *wkv.*, OE. hangian ; *hang*; *inf.* hōnge, 242, 27. Nth. *inf.* hāng, 138, 18; *pt. sg.* hānged, 139, 30; *pp.* hānged, 136, 16; hānget, 138, 30.

hap, *sb.*, ON. happ; *fortune, hap,* 90, 4.

happe(n), *wkv.*, ON. happa; *to come about, happen* ; *pt. sg.* happed, 245, 24.

Harald, *sb.*, OE. Harold < ON. Haraldr ; *Harold, son of Godwin,* 203, 22.

hard, *adj.*, OE. heard ; *hard, difficult,* 21, 18.

harde, *adv.*, OM. harde, WS. hearde ; *hard, cruelly,* 21, 4.

hārdī, hardī (hardȳ), *adj.*, ꓌F. hardi ; *hardy, bold,* 23, 25.

hardlīche, *adv.*, OE. heardlīce ; *sorely, stoutly, hardly,* 181, 20.

hardne(n), *wkv.*, OE. *heardnian ; *become hard, harden*; *pr. sbj. sg.* harden, 103, 5.

hare, *see* hē, here.

hāre, *sb.*, OE. hara ; *hare,* 219, 21.

hare(n), *wkv.*, OE. hergian ; *harry, plunder, lay waste,* *pt. sg.* hāred, 132, 22.

harm, *sb.*, OE. harm, hearm ; *harm*; *ds.* harme, 29, 26. eSth. *ds.* hærme, 185, 30. Sth. herm, 202, 33.

harme(n), Sth. harmīe(n), hermīe(n), *wkv.*, OE. harmian ; *harm*; *inf.* harmen, 195, 3. Sth. *inf.* harmȳe, 222, 14; *pr. pl.* harmeþ, 195, 4 ; *pr. sbj. sg.* hermīe, 203, 2.

harpe, *sb.*, OE. hearpe ; *harp,* 237, 10.

harryng, *sb.*, imitative word? ; *snarling,* 224, 15.

hasard, *sb.*, OF. hasard ; *hazard, a game at dice,* 237, 8.

hasardōur, *sb.*, OF. hasardour ; *gambler, player at hazard,* 241, 22.

hasardrȳe, *sb.*, OF. hasardrie ; *gambling,* 246, 4.

haspe, *sb.*, OE. hæpse ; *hasp, clasp,* 61, 7.

hāst(e), *sb.*, OF. hæste ; *haste* ; hāst, 120, 4.

hāstilī, hāstilȳ, *adv.*, OF. hastif+
ME. lī; *hastily*, 138, 22.

Hāstinge, *sb.*, OE. Hæstinga
(ceaster); *Hastings*, 205, 18.

hāstlȳ, *adv.*, OE. haste+ME. lȳ;
hastily, 94, 7.

hāt, *adj.*, eME. Nth. = Ml. hǭt;
OE. hāt; *hot*, 195, 15.

hāteden, *see* hātīe(n).

hāte(n), *stv.*, eME., Nth. = Ml.
hǭte(n); OE. hātan-hēt (heht) (R);
call, command, promise; *pt. sg.* hēt,
41. 2; hehte, 186, 9; hight, 141,
18; hiht, 154, 21; hētę, 189, 13;
pp. (eSth.) ihāte, 191, 13.

hāþ, *see* hāve(n).

hātīe(n), *wkv.*, Sth. = Ml. hāte(n);
OE. hatian; *hate*; *inf.* hātȳe, 218,
26; *pr. pl.* hātīeþ, 214, 18; *pt. pl.*
hāteden, 216, 17.

hatre, *sb.*, OE. hætern, *pl.* of *hæt;
garments, clothes*; *double pl.* hatren,
89, 3.

hātte, *def. v.*, only relic of *Teut.
passive*; OE. hātte–hātton; *is called,
is named*; *was called, was named*;
pt. sg. hātte, 5, 4; *pt. sg.* hyght,
95, 17; hēt, 207, 25.

hatterlīche, hetterlīche, *adv.*, based
on dial. Eng. hetter, 'quick, eager,'
cf. MLG. hetter; *quickly*, 194, 19.

haunte(n), *wkv.*, OF. haunter; *haunt,
practise*; *pt. pl.* haunteden, 237, 8.

Havelok, *sb.*, cf. note; *Havelok*, 77,
13.

hāve(n), eME. haven, *wkv.*, OE.
habban-hæfde; *have, possess*; *inf.*
haven, 5, 22; hafenn (O), 8, 16;
hāven, 18, 13; hān, 240, 29; *pr.
1 sg.* (eME. hafe, 8. 18); *pr.
2 sg.* hāvest, 18, 1; hast, 52, 10;
hāves, 86, 4; *pr. 3 sg.* (eME.
hafeþþ (O), 8, 20) hāveð, 14, 8;
hāþ, 37, 7; hath, 114, 30; *pr. pl.*
hāven, 26, 10; hāve gē, 29, 27;
hān, 70, 6; *pr. sbj. sg.* hāve, 18,
28; *imp. sg.*, 43, 15; hā, 101, 27;
pt. sg. hadde, 2, 20; hefde, 5, 30;
hedde, 7, 7; hāved, 56, 22; hade,
72, 20; had, 90, 16; *pr. 2 sg.*
haddist, 55, 15; *pt. pl.* hadden,

2, 28; hefden, 3, 2; hafden, 4, 21;
hæfden, 6, 33; haffdenn (O), 12, 1;
pt. sbj. sg. hade, 102, 20; *pt. sbj.
pl.* hadde, 243, 19; *pp.* had, 56, 18.
Nth. *inf.* hā, 134, 20; *pr. 2 sg.*
havis, 153, 29; haves, 86, 4; *pr.
pl.* hāve, 129, 10; hāfc, 144, 9.
Sth. (SEMl.) *inf.* habbe, 177, 15;
pr. 1 sg. habbe, 176, 3; habb, 176,
5; *pr. 2 sg.* hest, 216, 6; *pr. 3 sg.*
(eSth. haveð, 177, 16; hefð, 178,
10; hafð, 179, 28; heþ, 216, 7;
hafeð, 183, 18); *pr. pl.* (eSth.
habbeþ, 177, 12; habbet, 179, 12;
habbeoð, 190, 24); habbeþ, 209, 7;
hābeþ, 213, 31; *pr. sbj. pl.* habben,
203, 12; *pt. pl.* hedde, 177, 27.
Kt. *pp.* iheed, 213, 19.

hāvene, eME. havene, *sb.*, OE.
hæfen, *f.*; *haven*; havene, 186, 11;
hāvene, 205, 13; *pl.* hāvenes, 225,
33.

Haverfōrd, *sb.*, OE. *Haverford* (in
Pembroke), 223, 5.

hāves, *see* hāve(n).

hāvyng, *sb.*, based on hāve(n);
behaviour, 170, 17.

hₐwe, *sb.*, OE. haga, *hedge, enclosure,
meadow*, 244, 27.

hawkyng(e), *pr. ppl.* as *sb.*, ME.
hauken, based on OE. hafoc,
'hawk'; *hawking*, 120, 21.

haxte, *see* heӡ.

hayl, *adj.*, ON. heil; *well, sound*;
later in salutation, 139, 22.

hē, hee, *prn. masc.*, OE. hē; *he*, 1,
2; hee, 108, 3; *dat.-acc.* him, 1, 9;
himm (O), 10, 4; hym, 89, 19;
hē't = hē it, 10, 4. Nth. hē, 126,
18; *dat.-acc.* hym, 127, 10. Sth.
hē, 176, 14; hā, 211, 17; *dat.-acc.*
him, 176, 14; *acc.* hine, 181, 10;
hyne, 219, 22.

hēo, ghē (hē), hā, *prn. fem.*,
OE. hēo; *she*, 36, 16; ghē, 24, 21;
hē (SEMl.), 40, 30, footnote; *dat.-
acc.* hire, 5, 32; hir, 64, 11; hur,
106, 13. Later schē, *q.v.* Nth.
scho; *dat.-acc.* here, 126, 18; hir,
128, 10. Sth. hēo (eSth.), 181, 23;
hā, 192, 19; *dat.-acc.* hire, 188, 22;

hare, 197, 4; *as.* (eSth.) hēo, 182,
7 : hā. 192, 19.

sche, *prn. fem.*, OE. sēo; *she*,
64, 12 ; eME. scǣ, 5, 32 ; scho, 128,
10.

it, *prn. neut.*, OE. hit; *it*, 1, 8;
itt (O), 8, 21 ; hit, 36, 3 ; hyt, 88,
13. **Nth.** hit, 128, 5 ; it, 128, 6 ;
yt, 162, 6. **Sth.** hit, 176, 13 ; it,
177, 30; *it* (with expletive force),
there, 79, 1.

hī (hii), **hē, a, is**, *prn. pl.*, OE.
hīe, hēo, hī ; *they*, 2, 16 ; hii, 102, 25 ;
hē, 19, 12 ; it, *npl.* 23, 13 ; 60, 17 ;
gpl. here, 31, 4 ; her, 28, 2 ; *dat.-
acc.* (eME. hēom, 2, 16), hemm (O),
9, 13 ; is = his (hes), 14, 6. **Nth.**
þai, *see* þey. **Sth.** hēo, 182, 9 :
hī (hy), 176, 22 ; hii, 203, 20 ;
dat.-acc. (eSth.), heom, 183, 9 ;
ham, 191, 17 ; hom, 204, 22 ; hem,
212, 8. *apl.* hī, 212, 5 ; *apl.* is, 177,
31 ; his, 212, 19 ; hisę, 216, 7 ; ā,
221, 6.

hęalde(n), *see* hǫlde(n).

hęale, *sb.*, eSth. = Ml. hęle ; OE.
hǣlu, hǣle ; *health, safety* ; tō
wrāðer hęale, *to (her) bad health*,
193, 7.

hęate(n), *wkv.*, **eSth.** = Ml. hęte(n) ;
OE. hǣtan ; *heat* ; *inf.* 195, 15.

hęavet, *see* hęved.

hechele, *sb.*, OE. *hecele ; *hetchel,
heckel*, 61, 17.

hedde, *see* hāve(n).

hēde, *sb.*, OE. *hēde, cf. hēdan, 'to
heed' ; *heed, care*, 70, 22.

hēde(n), *wkv.*, OE. hēdan ; *heed,
guard*; *inf.* hēden, 192, 28.

hedertō, *adv.*, OE. hider + tō ;
hitherto, 223, 28.

hee, *see* hē, hēȝ.

heele = hēle, *sb.*, OE. hēla ; *heel*,
225, 8.

heer, heere, *see* hēr, hēre(n).

hęęste (hefden), *see* hęste, hāve(n).

heet, *see* hōte(n).

hefde(n), *wkv.*, OE. (bi-)hēafdian ;
behead; *pt. sg.* hefdid, 131, 26.

hęfed, *see* hęved.

heffne, hefð, *see* heven, hāve(n).

hēȝ, heg, hey, hȳ, *adj.*, OM. hēh,
WS. hēah ; *high* ; hēg, 14, 14 ;
hey, 62, 23 ; ḥeyȝe, 48, 14 ; hȳe,
108, 28 ; *comp.* heyer, 151, 18 ;
superl. hēgest, 24, 14 ; hēȝestę, 39,
18 ; heiȝ, 231, 24 ; heigh, 242, 24.
Nth. hee, 169, 23 ; high, 139, 21.
Sth. hēȝ, 190, 6 ; hēh, 192, 6 ; hey,
208, 3 ; *fds.* (eSth.) hēȝere, 187, 20 ;
superl. hexte, 184, 12 ; haxte, 184,
26.

hēȝe(n), **heye**(n), *wkv.*, OM. *hēgan,
WS. hēan for *hīen ; *raise high,
exalt* ; *pp.* heyed, 74, 18. **Sth.** *pr.
ppl.* heinde, 192, 4 ; *pt. sg.* hēhede,
196, 22 ; *pp.* iheiet, 197, 11.

hēȝere, *see* hēȝ.

hēȝlīce, hēglīce, hēhlīce, *adv.*, OM.
hēhlīce, WS. hēahlīce ; *highly, with
honor* ; hēglīce, 5, 2 ; hēhlīce, 8, 4.
Kt. heȝlīche, 217, 17.

heȝte, heȝt, *sb.*, OM. hēhðo, WS.
hēahðo; *height* ; heȝt, 104, 27.
Nth. heyt, 151, 21.

hēh, hēhlīce, *see* hēȝ, hēȝlīce.

hehede, *see* hēȝe(n).

hēhrēve, *sb.*, OM. hēhgerēfa, WS.
hēahgerēfa ; *highreeve, prefect*, 192,
22.

hehte, *see* hāte(n).

heiȝ, heigh, *see* hēȝ.

heil, *adj.*, ON. heill, cognate OE.
hǣl [hāl] ; *whole, well*, 15, 30.

heild, *wkv.*, lNth. = Ml. hēlde(n) ;
OAng. heldan, hēldan ; *incline,
incline to*; *pr. pl.* heild, 134, 17.

heilnesse, *sb.*, OM. heil + OE. ness, *f.* ;
happiness, joy, 22, 4.

heinde, heir, *see* hēȝe(n), hēr.

heir, *sb.*, OF. heir ; *heir*, 72, 5 ; eir,
83, 19.

heiward, *sb.*, OE. hege + weard ;
*hayward, guardian of the hedge,
farm bailiff*, 202, 32.

hēld, *see* hālde(n), hǫlde(n).

hēlde(n), *wkv.*, OM. heldan, hēldan,
WS. hieldan; *incline, incline to*;
inf. hēlden, 17, 28 ; *pr. pl.* hēlden,
116, 21 ; *pr. sbj. pl.* hēlde wē,
18, 31.

helden, hele, *see* hālde(n), helle.

hēle, *sb.*, OE. hǣlu: *health, salvation,* 137, 22.

hēle(n), *stv.*, OE. helan-hæl (5); *conceal*; *inf.* hēle, 110, 8; *pr.* 1 *sg.* hęle, 38, 21. eSth. *inf.* heolen, 192, 33; *pp.* ihęled, 199, 32.

hēle(n), *wkv.*, OE. hælan; *heal*; *pr.* 3 *sg.* hęleþ, 104, 17; *pt. sg.* hęled, 132, 9.

hēlēre, *sb.*, Kt. = Ml. hęlęre; based on OE. hǣlan; *healer*, 211, 17.

hęleþ, *see* hęle(n).

Helflēd, *sb.*, cf. note; *Helfled*, 77, 14.

hęlīe(n), *wkv.*, Sth. = Ml. hęle(n); OE. helian; *conceal, cover, protect*; *pp.* ihęled, 199, 32.

helle, *sb.*, OE. hell, *f.*; *hell*, 11, 8; hele, 125, 32.

hellehŏund, *sb.*, OE. hellehund, -hūnd; *hell hound, dog of hell*, 58, 11.

hellepīne, *sb.*, OE. helle + pin, *f.*; *punishment of hell*, 77, 8.

hellewā, eMĒ, for hellewǭ, *sb.*, OE. hell + wā; *woe of hell*, 11, 30.

hellewel, *sb.*, OE. helle + wel; *abyss of hell*, 63, 24.

helm, *sb.*, OE. helm; *helm*, 61, 9. Sth. *ds.* helme, 227, 18; *pl.* helmen (Lay.), 189, 28.

helpe, *sb.*, OE. helpe; *help*, 6, 33; hellpe (O), 8, 25.

helpe(n), *stv.*, OE. helpan-healp (3); *help*; *inf.* helpe, 35, 17; *pr. sbj. sg.* helpe, 226, 14; *imp. sg.* help, 18, 7; *pt. sg.* halpę, 92, 10; help (SEMl.), 45, 25; *pp.* hollpenn (O), 10, 26. Nth. *pr.* 3 *sg.* helps, 128, 22. Sth. *pr. pl.* helpeð, 195, 4; *pr. sbj. pl.* (eSth.) heolpen, 187, 20.

helping, *sb.*, based on helpe(n); *helping, aid*, 129, 25.

helps, *see* helpe(n).

helðe. *sb.*, OE. hǣlþe; *health, safety, salvation*, 30, 24.

Hēlȳ, *sb.*, Lat. (Vulg.) Heli; *Eli, the priest*, 220, 1. Cf. Ēlȳ.

hem, (hemm), *see* hē.

hemself, hemselfe, *see* self.

hen, hęnd, *see* henne, hānd.

hęnde, *adj.*, OE. gehende (-hēnde) [hand]; *near, ready, prompt,*

gracious, 36, 31; as þē hęnde, *as the gracious one, graciously, gently,* 204, 1; *superl.* hęndest, 184, 4.

hēndī, *adj.* OE. hendig; *handy, apt, courteous,* 202, 21.

hēnge(n), *wkv.*, ON. hengja; *hang, cause to hang*; *pt. pl.* hęnged, 3, 6. Nth. *inf.* hing, 140, 22.

hēngen, *see* hō(n).

henne, hen, *sb.*, OE. henn, *f.*; *hen,* 86, 18. Sth. hen, 198, 20; *gs.* henne, 198, 20.

henne, hennes, *adv.*, OE. heonon, infl. by *adverbs* in -es; *hence,* 239, 25; hennes, 123, 22.

Henrī, Henrȳ, *sb.*, OF. Henri; *Henry*; *Henry I,* 1, 1; *Henry, the abbot,* 1, 1; *Henrȳ,* 223, 2.

henten, *wkv.*, OE. hentan; *pursue, catch, seize*; *inf.* hente, 240, 14; *pt. sg.* hente, 90, 7; *pp.* hent, 61, 22. Sth. *pp.* yhent, 245, 7.

hēo, heom, *see* hē.

hēold, hēolde(n), *see* hālde(n), hǭlde(n).

heolen, *see* hęle(n).

heolpen, *see* helpe(n).

hēordemon, *sb.*, eSth. = Ml. hērde-man; OE. heord, *f.* + man; *herdsman*; eSth. *gpl.* hēordemonne, 202, 32.

heore, heorte, *see* here, herte.

heortelīch(e), *adv.*, OE. *heortelīce; *heartily,* 196, 15.

heoū, heovene, *see* hū, hevene.

heovenlīch, *see* hevenlīch.

hęp, *sb.*, OE. hēap; *heap*; *ds.* hępe, 36, 18.

her, *see* hire.

hēr, *sb.*, OM. hēr, WS. hǣr; *hair,* 63, 25.

hēr, heer, *adj. conj.*, OE. hēr; *here,* 6, 22; heer, 239, 6; heerę, 243, 15; hēr befǭren; *before this, already, in respect to this,* 24, 5. lNth. heir = hēr, 166, 10. Kt. hȳer, 218, 1.

herboru, *sb.*, ON. herbergi; *harbor, place of shelter,* 87, 27.

herborwe(n), *wkv.*, ON. herbergja; *harbor, shelter*; *pp.* herborwed, 87, 27.

hercnīe(n), *wkv.*, Sth. = Ml. herk-
ne(n); OE. hercnian, heorcnian;
hearken; *pr. sbj. pl.* hercnen, 200,
12; *imp. pl.* hercneð, 198, 1.

hērde, *sb.*, OE. heord, hēord,*f.*; *herd*,
88, 5.

hērde, *sb.*, OE. heorde; *tow, hards*, or
refuse flax in *pl.* 142, 8.

herde, *see* hēre(n).

here, her, *pers, prn.*, based on OE.
pl. gs. hiora, heora; *their*; her, 2,
15; here, 2, 14; (eME. heore, 5,
26). Nth. þaire, þāre, þēr, *see*
þeʒʒre. Sth. heore (eSth.), 179;
12; hare, 197, 4; hore, 199, 6; hor,
204, 22; here, 220, 5.

hēre, *sb.*, OE. here; *army, war*, 35, 1.

here, hēre, *see* hē, hēre(n).

hēreaftēr, hērefter, *adv.*, OE. hēr
+ æfter; *hereafter*, 70, 5; hērefter,
1, 17.

herede, *see* hēre(n).

herekempe, *sb.*, OE. *herecempa*;
warrior; Sth. *pl.* herekempen, 185,
29.

heremarke, *sb.*, OE. here + mearc,*f.*;
standard of the army; Sth. *pl.*
heremarken, 189, 27.

hēre(n), Sth. herīe(n), *wkv.*, OE.
herian; *praise*; *inf.* hēre, 61, 9;
Sth. *pp.* yherd, 74, 18. eSth. *pr.*
ppl. herīende, 192, 4; *pt. sg.* herede,
195, 25; *pp.* iheret, 197, 11.

hēre(n), *wkv.*, OM. hēran, WS.
hīeran; *hear*; *inf.* hērenn (O), 10,
1; hēre, 52, 27; heere, 237, 17;
pr. sbj. sg. hēre, 14, 1; *imp. pl.*
hēreð, 15, 16; *pt. sg.* hērde, 6, 27;
herde, 21, 17.

hēre(n), *wkv.*, Kt. = Ml. hīre(n); OE.
hŷran; *hire*; *inf.* hēre, 212, 3; *pt.
sg.* hērde, 212, 9.

hēreyn, *adv.*, OE. hēr + in; *herein*,
99, 14.

herīen, *see* hēre(n).

heritāge, *sb.*, OF. heritāge; *heritage*;
221, 4.

herke(n), *wkv.*, OM. *hercian*, cf.
OE. hercnian, 'hearken'; *listen*,
hark; *inf.* herk, 94, 10.

herkne(n),*wkv.*, OE. hercnian, heorc-

nian; *hearken*; *imp. pl.* herkneth,
239, 34.

herm, *see* harm.

hermīe(n), *see* harme(n).

hermīte, *sb.*, OF. hermite; *hermit*;
pl. hermītes, 78, 1.

hērne, *see* hürne.

hērne, *sb.*, ON. hiarni; *brain*; *pl.*
hērnes, 163, 32.

Herōdẹ, Herōd, *sb.*, OF. Herod;
Herod, 131, 15.

Herōdes, *sb.*, Lat. Herodes; *Herod*,
238, 6.

herrte, *see* herte.

herrunge (hērunge), *see* hēryng.

herte,hert, *sb.*, OE. heorte; *heart*, 28,
29; herrte (O), 10, 22; hert, 102,
11. Nth.*pl.* hertys,146, 10. eSth.
heorte, 178, 18; *pl.* herten, 219, 31.

herteblood, *sb.*, OE. heorte + blōd:
heart blood, 246, 9.

hervest,*sb.*, Sth. = Ml. harvest; OE.
hærfest; *harvest*, 205, 11.

hēryng, herrunge, *sb.*, based on
hēre(n); *hearing*, 99, 2; herrunge,
197, 16.

hēryyng, *sb*, OE. herung; *praise*,
102, 20.

hēse, hest (heþ), *see* hēste, hāve(n).

hēste (hẹẹste), hēst, *sb.*, OE. hǣs,
possibly *hǣste,f.*; *command, order*,
41, 4; hẹẹste, 238, 8; hēst, 68, 18.
eSth. hēse, 179, 2; hēste, 223, 4.

hē't, hēt (hēte), *see* hē, hāte(n).

hēt, *see* hatte.

hēte, *sb.*, OE. hǣto; *heat*, 15, 27.
Kt. hēte, 212, 21.

hēte, *wkv.*, ON. hǣta < hōeta; cf. Icl.
hōta, Scotch hoot; *threaten*; *pr.* 3
sg. hētes, 161, 12.

heþ, *see* hāve(n).

hẹþen, hẹþen, *adj.*, OE. hǣðen,
OHG. heiden; *heathen*, 3, 30. Kt.
hēþen, 213, 10.

heðen, heðen, heþen, *adv.*, ON.
heðan; *hence*, 25, 28; heþen, 85, 31.

hẹthing, *sb.*, ON. hǣðing, *f.*; *scorn*,
contempt, 136, 32.

hetilīch,*adv.*, OE. hetelīce; *hatefully*,
spitefully, 227, 24.

hette(n), heu, *see* hōte(n), hew.

hēvalȳ, *adv.*, OE. hefiglīce; *heavily*, 172, 29.

hēved, *sb.*, OE. hēafod, *neut.*; *head*, 17, 23; eME. hēfed, 3, 7; hǣved, 3, 8; *pl.* hēved, 207, 18. eSth. hafd, 182, 5; hafved, 183, 24; hēavet (eSth.), 195, 24.

heveking, *see* hevenẹking.

heven, *see* hevene.

hēve(n), *stv.*, OE. hebban–hōf (6); *raise, heave, transfer* (eME.); *pr. pl.* heven, 189, 27; *pt. sg.* hōf, 181, 14; Sth. *pp.* yhǫve, 223, 5.

hevenblys, *sb.*, OE. heofon + bliss; *bliss of heaven*, 128, 22; hevenẹblis, 228, 23.

hevene, heven, *sb.*, OE. heofone, *wf.* heofon, *m.*; *heaven*, 15, 20; *ds.* heffne (O), 10, 28; heven, 74, 13; hevenẹ, 101, 23; *pl.* hevens, 102, 24. Nth. hevin, 140, 25. eSth. heovene, 177, 3.

heveneblis, *see* hevenblys.

Hevenẹkyng, Heveking, *sb.*, OE. heofone + kyning; *King of Heaven, Lord*, 92, 28. eSth. *ds.* Hevekinge, 178, 7.

hevenlīch, *adj.*, Sth. = Ml. hevenlī; OE. heofonlīc; *heavenly*, 179, 7; heovenlīch, 191, 26.

Hevenlǫverd, *sb.*, OE. heofon + lāford; *Lord of Heaven*, 18, 28.

hevenrīche, heverīche, *sb.*, OE. heafonrīce; *kingdom of heaven*, 14, 14; heverīche, 178, 9.

hevens, *see* hevene.

hēvidlēs, *adj.*, OE. hēafodlēas; *headless*, 164, 32.

hēvīe, hevȳ, *adj.*, OE. hefig; *heavy*; as *sb.*, 35, 20; hevȳ, 144, 21.

hevin (hevyn), *see* hevene.

hevŏ, *see* hāve(n).

hevȳnes, *sb.*, OE. hefignes, *f.*; *heaviness*, 144, 25.

hew (heu), *sb.*, OE. hēow; *hue, color*, 98, 16; heu, 37, 30.

hewe(n), *stv.*, OE. hēawan–hēow (R); *hew, cut down*; *inf.* or *ger.* hewene, 181, 20; *pt. pl.* hewe, 112, 23.

hexte, *see* hēʒ.

hey (heyʒe), heyed, *see* hēʒ, hēʒe(n).

heyer, *see* hēʒ.

heyre, *sb.*, OF. haire; *hair-shirt, hair-cloth*, 241, 7.

heyt, hexst, *see* heʒte, hēʒ.

hī, hii, *see* hē.

hī, hicht, *see* hiʒe, hȳʒe(n), hiʒte(n).

hid, hidde, *see* hīde(n).

hight, hiht, *see* hāte(n).

hīd(e), *sb.*, OE. hȳd, *f.*; *hide, skin*; hīd (for hīde?), 17, 13.

hīde(n), *wkv.*, OE., hȳdan; *hide, conceal*; *inf.* hīde, 158, 5; *pt. sg.* hidde, 36, 10; hydde, 98, 21; *pp.* hid, 29. 22; hidde, 234, 21; es noght at hide, *it is not to be hidden*, 158, 5. Sth. *pp.* yhidde, 236, 3.

hider, hidere, *adv.*, OE. hider; *hither*, 28, 26; hidere, 185, 30.

hiderward, *adv.*, OE. hiderweard; *hitherward, hitherto*, 233, 24.

hīdynge, *sb.*, based on hīde(n); *hiding, hiding place*, 233, 22.

hīe(n), *wkv.*, OE, hīgian; *hasten, hie*; *pr. sbj. pl.* hīen, 201, 13.

hiʒe, hī, hȳ, *sb.*, cf. OE. hīgian; *haste*; Nth. hī, 141, 19; hȳ, 166, 16.

high, *see* hēʒ.

higtes(t), hiht, *see* hǫte(n).

hii, *see* hē.

hiʒte(n), hichte(n), *wkv.*? based on OE. heht < hātan?; *promise*, *pr.* 1 *sg.* hicht, 171, 6.

hil, hille, hyll, OE. hyll, *m.*, hylle, *f.*; *hill*, 14, 14; *ds.* or old *f.* form hille, 14, 1; hyll, 157, 10.

hild, hille, *see* hālde(n), hil.

him, himm, *see* hē.

himmsellfenn, *see* self.

himselven (-seollfenn, -sülf, -sülve), *see* hē, self.

hine, *see* hē.

hīne, *sb.*, OE. hīna, *gpl.* of hīwa; *servant, domestic, one of the household*; dial. Eng. *hind*, 83, 33; hȳn, 51, 16.

hing, hir (hirẹ), *see* hengen, hē.

hīrd, *see* hīred.

hīrde, *sb.*, SEMl. or Sth. = Ml. hērd; WS. hierde, OM. herde, hērde; *shepherd, guardian, keeper*, 15, 5.

hīrdeman, *sb.*. SEMl. or Sth. = Ml. hērdeman; WS. hierdeman, OM.

hērdeman; *herdsman*; *pl.* hīïde-men, 32, 11.

h:re, *sb.*, OE. hȳr, *f.*; *hire*, 164, 32.

hire, *poss. prn.*, OE. *fgs.* hire; *her*, 6, 7. Nth. hir, 129, 6. Cf. hē.

hīred, *sb.*, OE. hīrēd; *court, retinue*; *ds.* hīrede, 186, 5; hīrd, 192, 5.

hīredman, *sb.*, OE. hīrēdmann; *one of the household or court, retainer*; *pl.* hīredmen, 190, 6.

hirte(n), *wkv.*, OF. hurter; *hurt*; *pr. sbj. sg.* hirt, 104, 7.

his, hise, *pos. prn.*, based on OE. *gs.* his; *his*, 1, 7; hiss (O), 12, 15; *pl.* hise, 2, 25; hyse, 75, 17.

hit, *see* hē.

hlāverd (-ord), hō, *see* lǫverd, whō.

hōaten, hōf, *see* hǫte(n), hēve(n\.

hōkerlīche, *adv.*, OE. *hōcorlīce; *mockingly, scornfully*, 194, 5. •

hǫl, *adj.*, OE. hāl; *whole, entire*, 27, 19.

hōld, *adj.*, OE. hold; *faithful, friendly*; *pl.* hōlde, 226, 3.

hǫlde(n), *stv.*, OM. haldan (hāldan), WS. healdan-hēold (R); *hold, possess*; *inf.* hǫlden, 15, 4; *pr. sbj. sg.* hǫlde, 17, 24; *pr. sbj. pl.* hǫlden. 27, 12; *imp. pl.* hǫlde ʒē, 199, 21; *pt. sg.* (eME. hēold, 4, 10); hēld, 2, 12; *pt. pl.* (eME. hēolden, 2, 29); hēlden, 2, 14; *pp.* hǫlden, 22, 12. Nth. eME. hālde(n), *q.v.* eSth. *inf.* hēalden, 177, 31; *pr. sbj. pl.* hēalden, 226, 11. Sth. *pr. pl.* hǫldeþ, 222, 31; *pt. pl.* hülde, 203, 19; *pp.* ihǫlden, 198, 9.

hǫldynge, *pr. ppl.* as *sb.*, based on OM. haldan, hāldan; *holding*, 125, 1.

hǫlī, hǫolȳ, *adj.*, OE. hālig; *holy*, 17, 28; hǫolȳ, 238, 1.

hollpenn, *see* helpe(n).

holouʒ, *adj.*, OE. holh, *pl.* holʒe; *hollow*; *pl.* holouʒ, 223, 22.

holpe(n), *see* helpe(n).

hǫlȳch, *adv.*, Sth. = Ml. hǫllī; OE. hāllīce: *wholly*, 223, 26.

hǫlȳlȳch, *adv.*, OE. hālig + līce; *holily*, 218, 16.

hom, *see* hē.

hǫm, *sb.*, OE. hām; *home*, 24, 32; hǫmę, 98, 10.

hǫm, hǫom, *adv.*, OE. hām; *home, homeward*, 28, 14; hǫom, 242, 22.

homāǧe, *sb.*, OF. homage; *homage*, 161, 24.

hc̨mward, *adv.*, OE. hāmweard; *homeward*, 31, 24; hǫmęward, 108, 3.

homycīde, *sb.*, OF. homicide; *homicide, murder*, 245, 32.

hō(n), *stv.*, OE. hōn-hēng (R); *hang*; *pt. pl.* hēngen, 3, 7.

hond, *see* hūnd.

hǫnd, *sb.*, OE. hand, hǫnd; *hand*, 21, 27; *ds.* hǫnde, 37, 4; *pl.* hǫnd. 65, 26; hǫndenę, 59, 18. Sth. *pl.* hǫnden, 181, 23.

hǫndhabbing, *adj.*, OE. handhæb-bende, *pp.* as *adj.*; *having in hand (stolen property), red-handed*, 42, 30.

hondred, *see* hundred.

hǫɛdselle(n), *wkv.*, OM. *handsellan -sāld, cf. ON. handselja; *promise, betroth*; *pp.* ihǫndsāld, 192, 13.

honeste, *adj.*, OF. honeste; *honest*, 120, 27; oneste, 219, 16.

hǫnge, honger, *see* hānge(n), hunger.

honōrde, *see* honūre(n\.

honōūr, honten, *see* honūr, hun-te(n).

honourd, honōūre, *see* honūre(n).

honūr, honōūr, *sb.*, OF. honur(-our); *honor, praise, pomp*, 39, 17; honōūr, 102, 25.

honūre(n), *wkv.*, OF. honurer; *honor*; *inf.* honūre, 136, 3; *imp. sg.* honōūre, 146, 25; *pp.* honōrdę, 138, 6; honourd, 139, 25.

hònȳ, *adj.*, OE. hunig; *honey*, 128, 26.

hǫolȳ, hǫom, *see* hǫlī, hǫm.

hǫor, hǫr, *adj.*, OE. hār; *hoar*, 241, 14.

hoord, *see* hōrd.

hǫpe, *sb.*, OE. hopa; *hope*, 16, 21.

hǫpe(n), Sth. hǫpīe(n), *wkv.*, OE. hopian; *hope*; *inf.* hǫpen, 103, 24; hope, 103, 27. Nth. *pr.* 1 *sg.* hǫp, 156, 11; *pt. pl.* hǫpid, 143, 18. Sth.

pr. pl. hǫpīeþ, 213, 27; *pr. sbj. sg.*
hopīe (eSth.), 176, 24.

hor, hore, *see* here.

hōrd, hoord, *sb.,* OE. hord (hōrd);
hoard, 226, 21. Sth. *ds.* hōrde,
176, 12; hoord, 242, 12.

hōrderwȳce, *sb.,* OE. hōrdere + wīce,
wkf.; *office of treasurer, treasurer-
ship;* old *dat. sg.* or *pl.* 4, 21. Cf.
wīken.

hōredōm, hōrdom, *sb.,* OE. hōre, *f.*
+ dōm; *adultery, whoredom,* 42,
16; hōrdom, 209, 17.

hōrling, *sb.,* OE. *hōrling, cf. hōring;
adulterer,* 179, 14.

hōrn (horn), *sb.,* OE. horn, hōrn;
horn, 57, 24.

hors, *sb.,* OE. hors; *horse,* 61, 10;
ds. horse, 48, 14; *pl.* horsys, 107,
14. Sth. *pl.* horsen, 184, 27.

hǫsə, *sb.,* OE. hose; *hose, trousers,*
229, 12.

hoselī, hosle(n), *see* hòsle(n).

hòselyɪ̨ge, *sb.,* based on OE. hūslian
or hūsel, *sb.; houseling, administer-
ing the eucharist,* 122, 12.

hòsle(n), *wkv.,* OE. hūslian; *housel,
administer eucharist;* *pp.* hòsled,
75, 26; hòsęlet, 122, 2. Sth. *inf.*
hòselī, 206, 21; *pp.* ihòseled, 121,
31.

hōst, *sb.,* OF. hoiste mod. by host;
host, bread of the sacrament, 122, 14.

hǫst, *sb.,* OF. host; *host, army,* 167, 31.

hǫt, *adj.,* OE. hāt; *hot,* 60, 18; *superl.*
hǫtest, 214, 5.

hǫte(n), *stv.,* OE. hātan–hēt (R);
call, command, promise; *pt. sg.* hēt,
31, 13; *pt. 2 sg.* higtest, 17, 25;
higtes, 17, 27; *pt. pl.* hette, 61, 1;
pp. hǫten, 25, 25. Nth. hāte(n),
q.v. Sth. *pr. 3 sg.* hǫt, 214, 19;
pt. sg. heet, 222, 26; *pp.* (SEMl.)
ihǫten, 32, 32; yhǫten, 73, 28.

hou (hōw, hou3), *see* hū.

hóund, hous (houss), *see* hūnd, hūs.

houre, *see* ūre.

hòuve, *sb.,* OE. hūfe; *cap, covering,
for the head;* hōuve of glas, *a cap
of glass,* i.e. *something ridiculous or
ineffective,* 56, 14.

hǫve(n), *wkv.,* MDu., MLG. hoven?;
tarry, hover; *pr. 3 sg.* hǫveð, 15,
24; *pr. pl.* hǫven, 19, 13; *pt. sg.*
hǫved, 164, 15.

hōw, *see* hū.

Howel, *sb.,* *Howell,* 184, 12.

hows, hōwselę, *see* hūs, hūsel.

hū, hou (hōw), *adv.,* OE. hū; *how,*
9, 11; hou, 66, 25; hōw, 88, 20.
eSth. heōu, 185, 10; hwū, 202, 9;
hou3, 224, 3.

hūde(n), *wkv.,* Sth. = Ml. hīde(n);
OE. hȳdan; *hide;* *pp.* hūd, 178,
21.

Hugo, *sb.,* OF. Hugo; *Hugo,* 4, 23.

hūire, *sb.,* Sth. = Ml. hīre; OE. hyr,
f.; *hire,* 202, 32.

hūl, *sb.,* Sth. = Ml. hyll; OE. hyll;
hill, 208, 6. Cf. hil.

hūl̄de, *see* hǫlde(n).

Humber, Humbre, *sb.,* OE. Humbre,
f. or *indcl.;* *Humber river,* 87, 18;
eME. Humbre, 185, 24.

hūnd, hōund, hond, *sb.,* OE. hund
(hūnd); *hound, dog,* 167, 2 ; hōund,
48, 26; hónd, 219, 25.

hundereth, *adj.,* ON. hundraþ, cogn.
with OE. hundred; *hundred,* 164,
26. Cf. hundred.

hundred, hondred, *adj.,* OE. hundred; *hundred,* 32, 17; hóndred,
220, 4.

hundredfẹald, *.adj.* eSth. = Ml.
hundredfɔld, WS. hundredfealde;
hundredfold; *pl.* hundredfẹalde,
177, 30.

hundrethfāld, *sb.,* Nth. = Ml., Sth.
hundredfǫ̣ld; ON.hundraþ + OAng.
fald, fāld, WS. feald; *hundredfold,*
129, 28.

hunger (eME. hūngər), hongər,
sb., OE. hungor; *hunger,* 3, 19;
hónger, 55, 16.

hungre(n), *wkv.,* ON. hungra, OE.
hyngran; *hunger, be hungry;* *pr.*
3 *sg.* hungreð, 19, 8; hungreth,
78, 26; *pt. sg.* hungrede, 85, 2.

hungrī, *adj.,* OE. hungrig; *hungry,*
24, 8.

hunte, *sb.,* OE. hunta; *hunter,* 14,
17.

hunte(n), *wkv.*, OE. huntian; *hunt*; *inf.* hunten, 14, 1; hönten, 62, 5; *pr.* 3 *sg.* hunteð, 198, 10.

Huntendóneschīre, *sb.*, OE. Huntandūnscir, *f.* ; *Huntingdonshire*, 226, 3.

huntynge, huntyng, *sb.*, OE. huntung, *f.*; *hunting*, 120, 21; huntyng, 106, 25.

hur, hŭrde, *see* hē, hŭre(n).

hure, *sb.*, OF. hure ; *skull-cap*, 229, 10 ; hure gray, *gray cap*, 229, 28.

hŭre(n), *wkv.*, Sth = Ml. hēre(n) ; WS. hīeran (hȳran), OM. hēran ; *hear* ; *pt. sg.* hūrde, 203, 22.

hŭrne, *sb.*, Sth. = Ml. hīrne (hērne); OF. hyrne ; *nook, corner*, 204, 18 ; Kt. ? hērne, 204, 8.

Hurtford, *sb.*, OE. Heorotford ; *Hertford*, 227, 3.

hurtynge, *sb.*, based on OF. hurter ; *hurting, injury*, 147, 4.

hŭs, hōus (hōws), *sb.*, OE. hūs ; *house*, 4, 13 ; hōus, 89, 28 ; hōws, 125, 4 ; hōuss, 171, 1. Sth. *ds.* hūse, 199, 10.

husband, *sb.*, ON. hūsbōndi ; *husband, small farmer*; *pl.* husbandis. 171, 1.

hŭsel, hōwselẹ, *sb.*, OE. hūsel ; *eucharist* ; hōwselẹ, 123, 21.

hŭsewīf, *sb.*, OE. hūswīf ; *housewife*, 202, 7.

hŭslẹfdī, *sb.*, OE. hūs + hlǣdiȝe ; *lady of the house, mistress*, 202, 1.

hŭswīfschipe, *sb.*, OE. *hūswīf + scipe ; *management of a house*, 201, 25.

huyre, *sb.*, WMl. = Ml. hīre, Sth. hŭre ; OE. hȳr, *f.* ; *hire*, 125, 17.

hwām, hwan, hwat, *see* whā.

hwan, *see* whanne.

hwaroof, *see* whērof.

hwatloke, *adv.*, OE. hwætlīce ; *quickly, speedily* ; Sth. *comp.* watloker, 204, 13.

hwatsẹ, *adv.*, OE. hwæt + sǣ; *whatso, whatsoever*, 189, 19.

hwenne, *see* whenne.

hwēr(e), *see* whēr.

hwērfore, *see* whērfọre.

hwēːinne, *adv.*, OM. Kt. hwērinne, WS. hwǣrinnẹ, *wherein*, 218, 7.

hwet, *see* whō.

hwẹtə, *sb.*, eME. = Ml. whẹte ; OE. hwǣːe ; *wheat*, 200, 8.

hweðersẹ, *see* wheðersẹ.

hwī, hwil, hwilem, *see* whī, whīle, whīlem.

hwō (hwọ̄), hwon. *see* whō, whanne.

hwū, hwücche, *see* hū, while.

hȳ, *see* hiȝe, hē.

hȳde(n), *see* hīde(n).

hyder, *see* hider.

hȳe, hȳer, *see* heȝ, hēr.

hyght(e), *see* hātə(n), hātte, họ̄te(n).

hȳȝȝə(n), *wkv.*, OE. hīgian ; *hasten, hie* ; *inf.* hȳȝe, 65, 12. Cf. hīe(n).

hyll, *see* hil.

hym, hymself, *see* hē, self.

hȳn (hȳne), hyne, *see* hīne, hē.

Hyrtlingberī, *sb.*, *Irthlingborough* (Northampton), 4, 23.

hyse, hyt, *see* his, hē.

I.

Ī, ī, *see* ic, in.

Iācōb, *sb.*, Lat. Iacōbus, later displaced by OF. Jacob; *Jacob*, 24, 30.

iǣde, *see* gọ̄(n).

iaf, (iāfen, iāven), *see* ȝeve(n).

ibē, ibēon, *see* bēːn).

ibēaten, *see* bẹte(n).

ibẹre, *sb.*, Sth. = Ml. bēre ; OM. gebēru, WS. gebǣru ; *bearing, conduct, noise, shout* ; *pl.* ibẹren, 183, 31.

ibet, ibild, *see* bẹte(n), bīlde(n).

iblende, *see* blēnde(n).

ibọre (iboren), *see* bẹre(n).

ibroȝt, ibroht, *see* bringeːn).

ibrọ̄ke(n), ibȳe, *see* brọ̄ke(n), bē(n).

ic, ī, ich, *prn.*, OE. ic; *I*, 21, 23 ; icc (O), 8, 18 ; Ī, 3, 20 ; *dat.-acc.* mē, 8, 20 ; mee, 107, 12. Sth. (SEMl.) ich, 36, 23 ; 181, 12. Pl. wē, 4, 9; *dat.-acc.* us, 15, 6 ; uss (O), 11, 13 ; ōus, 66, 5 ; *gpl.* ūre, 28, 6 ; *dual.* witt (O), *we two*, 8, 16 ; *dat.-acc.* unnc (O), 8, 26.

icakeled, *see* cakele(n).
icaste, *see* caste(n).
ich, iclept, *see* ēch, **cleppe (n).**
iclüpəd, *see* clüpīe(n).
icnāwe(n), *stv.*, Sth. = eME., Nth.
 knāwe(n), Ml. knǭwe(n) ; OE.
 gecnāwan–cnēow (R) ; *know* ; *pr.*
 3 *sg.* icnāweð, 180, 15 ; *pp.* icnāwen,
 194, 9.
icnowen, *see* knowe(n).
icome, *see* cume(n).
icoren, icornee, *see* chēse(n),
icüd, *see* cūpə(n).
icume(n), *see* cume(n).
īdel, *sb.*, OE. īdel ; *idleness, vanity* ;
 īdell (O), 9, 27.
īdel, ȳdill, ȳdul, *adj.*, OE. īdel ;
 idle, empty, 51, 8 ; ȳdill, 143, 23 ;
 ȳdul, 125, 19.
idēld, *see* dēle(n).
īdelnessə, *sb.*, OE. īdelness, *f.* ; *idleness*, 101, 16 ; ȳdillnes, 144, 2.
idēmd, idēmet, *see* dēme(n).
idihte, idōn(e), *see* diȝte(n), dō(n).
idrunke, *see* drinke(n).
iēden, *see* gǭ(n).
ientred, *see* entre(n).
ifā, *sb.*, eSth. = Ml. fǭ, OE. gefāh ;
 foe ; *pl.* ifān, 196, 23.   Cf. ifǭ.
ifaren, *see* fāre(n).
ifēre, *sb.*, SEMl. Sth. = Ml. fēre ;
 OE. gefēra ; *companion*, 37, 22.
ifīld, *see* fīlle(n).
ifǭ, *sb.*, OE. gefāh ; *foe* ; *pl.* ifoan =
 ifǭn, 226, 19.
ifōn, *see* fōn.
ifō(n), *stv.*, Sth. = Ml. fō(n) ; OE.
 gefōn -fēng (R) ; *receive, take back* ;
 inf. ifō, 43, 24.
ifüld, ifünde, *see* fülle(n), fīnde(n).
igain, igaines, *see* agein, ageines.
igainsawe, *sb.*, OE. *ongegn + sagu ;
 gainsaying, contradiction, 153, 26.
iȝarket, īȝe, *see* ȝarkīe(n), ēȝe.
iȝēlde(n), *stv.*, OM. geldan (gēldan),
 WS. gieldan–geald (3) ; *yield* ; *pt.
 sg.* iȝǭlde, 206, 31.
iȝēte, iȝīrnd, *see* ȝete(n), ȝērne(n).
iȝive, iȝǭlde, *see* ȝive(n), ȝēlde(n).
igranted, *see* grante(n).
igrāp, *see* igrīpe(n).

igrētinge, *sb.*, OE. gegrēting, *f.* ;
 greeting, 226, 3.
igrīpe(n), *stv.*, Sth. = Ml. grīpe(n) ;
 OE. gegrīpan–grāp (1) ; *seize, grip,
 take hold of* ; *pr. sbj.* igrīpe, 196, 2 ;
 eME. *pt. sg.* igrāp, 182, 4.
igürd, *see* gürde(n).
ihāte(n), *see* hāte(n).
ihēalde(n), *stv.*, eSth. = eME.hālden,
 Ml. hǭlden, WS. healdan–hēold
 (R) ; *hold, possess, keep* ; *inf.* ihēal-
 den, 177, 32.
iheed, iheiet, *see* hāve(n), hēȝe(n).
ihēled, *see* hēle(n).
ihēre(n), *wkv.*, SEMl., Sth. for Ml.
 hēre(n) ; OM. gehēran, WS. hīeran
 (hȳran) ; *hear* ; *inf.* ihēre(n), 42,
 24 ; *imp. pl.* ihērep, 212, 27 ; *pt. sg.*
 iherde, 37, 19 ; *pt. pl.* iherden, 187,
 7 ; *pp.* iherd, 37, 26.   Kt. *imp. sg.*
 yhȳer, 216, 13.
iheret, *see* hēre(n).
ihīerde, *see* ihīere(n).
ihīere(n) = ihēre(n), *wkv.*, Kt. = Ml.
 hīre(n) ; OE. gehȳran ; *hire* ; *pt. sg.*
 ihīerde, 213, 6.
ihǭlden, ihǭndsāld, *see* hǭlde(n),
 hǭndselle(n).
ihoseled, *see* hōsle(n).
ihǭten, *see* hǭte(n).
ihüren, *wkv.*, Sth. = Ml. ihēre(n) ;
 WS. gehīeran (hȳran) ; *hear* ; *inf.*
 ihüre, 203, 15 ; *pr.* 3 *sg.* ihürð, 178,
 33 ; *pp.* ihürd, 203, 17.
iiven, *see* ȝeve(n).
ikenne(n),*wkv.*,Sth. = Ml. kenne(n),
 OE. gecennan ; *learn, know* ; *inf.*
 ikennen, 189, 33.
ikindled, *see* kindle(n).
ikneu, *see* iknowe(n).
iknowe(n), *stv.*, OE. geknāwan
 -knēow (R) ; *know* ; *pt. sg.* ikneu,
 37, 29.
ikǖð, *adj.*, OE. gecūð ; *known*, 48,15.
il, *see* ill.
ilǣd, ilǣred, *see* lēde(n), lēred.
ilǣrde, ilaht, *see* lēre(n), lacche(n).
ilaste(n), *wkv.*, Sth. = Ml. laste(n) ;
 OE. gelǣstan ; *endure, last, fulfil* ;
 pt. sg. ilaste, 208, 23 ; ylaste, 206,
 20.

ilc, ilk, yche, *adj.*, OE. ilca, *m.*, ilce,
f.; *same*, 1, 18; *wk.* yche, 88, 11;
ilke, 196, 25. Sth. ilche, 226,
15.

ilc, ilche, ilk, ilke, yche, *prn.*, OE.
ilc; *each, every*, illc (O), 9, 20;
ilk, 16, 17; ilke a, 61, 18; ilk a,
139, 24.

ileawed, *adj.*, Sth. = Ml. lewed; OE.
*gelæwed, læwed; *unlearned, lay*;
MnE. *lewd*, 226, 3.

ileid, ilēnet, *see* leie(n), lēne(n).

ileosed, ilēred, *see* losīe(n), lēre(n\.

ilēste(n), *wkv.*, OE. gelæstan; *last,
endure*; *pt. sg.* ilēste, 38, 1; *pr.
ppl.* ilēstinde, 226, 9.

ilet, ilēt, *see* lette(n), lēte(n).

ilēve(n). *wkv.*, Sth. = Ml. lēve(n);
OM. gelēvan, WS. gelīevan; *believe,
inf.* ilēve, 177, 25; *pr. pl.* ilēveð,
180, 9.

ilīche, *adj.*, Sth. = Ml. līche, like;
OE. gelīce; *alike*, 178, 10.

ilīcnesse, *sb.*, OE. gelīcnes, *f.*; *likeness*, 196, 23.

ilīke, *adv.*, OE. gelīce; *alike*, 128,
24; lēle ilīke, *loyally*, 128, 25.

ilimpe(n), *stv.*, OE. gelimpan–lamp
(lǫmp) (3); *happen*; *pt. sg.* ilomp.
186, 6; *pp.* ilimpe, 183, 1.

ilk, ilke, *see* ilc.

ill, il, *adj.*, ON. illr; *ill, bad, evil*;
il, 49, 22; *wk.* ille, 37, 19; *pl.*
ylle, 88, 16.

illc, *see* ilc.

ille, *adv.*, ON. illr; *badly*, 50, 9.

ilōme, ilomp, *see* ʒelōme, ilimpe(n).

ilüsd, imād, *see* lüse(n), māke(n).

imætte, *see* imēte(n).

imāked, *see* māke(n).

imānge, *see* omāng.

imēane, *sb.*, OE. gemǣna; *company*,
196, 25.

imelled, *see* melle(n).

imēne, *adv.*, OE. gemǣne; *together*,
197, 17.

imenge(n), *wkv.*, OE. mengan;
mingle, disturb, trouble; *pp.*
imenged, 190, 1; imēng = imēngd,
180, 22.

imet, *see* imēte(n).

imēte(n), *wkv.*, Sth. = Ml. mēte(n);
OE. gemētan; *meet with, find,
obtain*; *inf.* imēten, 180, 11.

imēte(n),*wkv.*,OE. gemǣtan; *appear
in dream*; *pt. sg.* imætte, 181, 13;
pp. imet, 196, 17.

immǫbill, *adj.*, OF. immoble, older
-mueble, -moeble; *immovable*, 147,
24.

in (inn, yn), ī, ine, *prep. adv.*, OM.
in, WS. on (in); *in*, 1, 8; inn (O),
9, 2; ī, 8, 14; ine, 197, 14.

in, *sb.*, OE. inn; *inn, public-house*,
117, 26.

inc, *see* þū.

indifferent, *adj.*, OF. indifferent;
indifferent, unbiased, 235, 26.

ine, inēd, *see* in, nēde(n).

inempnet, *see* nemne(n).

informācion, *sb.*, OF. information;
information, 235, 13.

inʒēong, *sb.*, OE. ingang-gǫng;
entrance, going in, 187, 8.

Ingland, *sb.*, Nth. = Ml., Sth.
England (-lǫnd), OE. Englaiand;
England, 126, 8.

Inglis, *adj.*, Nth. = Ml. Sth. English;
OE. Englisc; *English*, 127, 6.

inguoynge, *sb.*, Kt. = Ml. ingōinge;
based on ingǫn; *entrance, ingoing*,
216, 32.

inn, *see* in, *prep.*

innen, inne, *adv.*, OE. inne, innan;
in, within, 3, 10; innen, 8, 1.

innocent, *adj.*, OF. innocent; *innocent*, 101, 15.

innocent, *adj.* as *sb.*, OF. innocent;
child, innocent, 116, 16; *pl.* innocentys, 147, 6.

inntill, *see* intil.

innwarrdliʒ, *see* inwardliʒ.

inōh, inōg, inouʒ, inow, ynug,
inogh, inohe, ynou, *adj.*, OE.
genōh(g); *enough*, 9, 5; 12, 15;
onōh, 3, 15; inōg, 17, 12; ynug,
24, 28; inouʒ, 50, 25; inow, 86,
22; inogh, 129, 14; inohe, 150,
10; ynou, 205, 29; ynoʒ, 218. 28
ynow, 226, 10; *pl.* inoʒe, 227, 7.

inome, *see* nime(n).

inouʒ, inow, *see* inōh.

inseȝel, *sb.*, OE. insegele ; *seal* ; *pl.*
innseȝȝless (O), 12, 25.

intil(l), **intel**, *adv. prep.*, OM. intil?
cf. Swed. intill ; *into, to* ; inntill (O),
8, 19 ; intel, 227, 9. **Nth.** intil
150, 19 ; intill, 144, 22.

into, *prep. adv.*, OM. in tō, WS.
on tō ; *into, unto*, 4, 15.

inume, **inumen**, *see* nime(n).

inwardlīȝ, **inwardliȩ**, *adv.*, OM.
inwardlīc, WS. inweardlīc ; *earnestly, inwardly* ; innwarrdlīȝ (O),
13, 27 ; inwardliȩ, 156, 8. **Sth.**
inwardlīche, 198, 33.

Ioneck, *sb.*, OF. Yonec ; *Yoneck*,
127, 1.

Iōsēp, **Iōsēph**, *sb.*, Lat. Iōsēph ;
later displaced by OF. Joseph ;
Joseph, 21, 2 ; Iōsēph, 22, 3.

ipeynted, *see* peynte(n).

ipliȝte(n), *wkv.*, OE. *geplihtan ;
plight, engage, pledge ; *pt. sbj. sg.*
ipliȝt, 204, 11.

ipricked, *pp.* as *adj.*, OE. prician ;
pricked, clothed, adorned, 48, 20.

iqueden, irad, *see* queðe(n), rēde(n).

īre, **ȳre**, *sb.* OF. ire ; *ire, anger,*
103, 5 ; ȳre, 103, 8.

irȩadī, *adj.*, OE. *gerǣdig, cf. Swed.
rēdig ; *ready, prepared,* 192, 32.

irēd, *see* rēde(n).

Irelọnd, **Irlọnd**, *sb.*, OE. Īraland,
-lọnd ; *Ireland* ; *ds.* Irelọnd, 227, 9 ;
Irlọnde, 188, 33 ; Ȳrlọnd, 220, 11 ;
Ȳrloande, 226, 2.

īren, **ȳre**, *sb.*, OE. Īren ; *iron,* 3, 16 ;
ȳren, 165, 2 ; *spade* (?), 34, 5 ;
e**Sth.** *ds.* ȳrne, 227, 17.

irēve, *sb.*, OE. gerēfa ; *prefect,
steward, judge, reeve,* 117, 26.

irk, *adj.*, ON. *yrk, cf. Swed. yrka,
' to urge ' ; *distasteful, irksome,*
150, 2.

Irlçnd, *see* Irelọnd.

irreverence, *sb.*, OF. irreverence ;
irreverence, 146, 3.

is, isæh, *see* he, isē(n).

isah, *see* isē(n).

isæid, isæt, *see* iseȝȝe(n), sette(n).

isauved, *see* save(n).

ischende, *see* schende(n).

ischoten, *see* schēte(n).

ischriven, ischryven *see* schrīve(n).

ischrüd, *see* schrüde(n).

isē, iseȝ, *see* isē(n).

iseǧǧe(n), *wkv.*, **Sth.** = Ml. seie(n) ;
OE. gesecgan-sægde (sǣde) ; *say* ;
pp. isæied, 183, 24 ; isēd, 180, 19.

iseghe, iseȝe(n), **iseh, isei**, *see*
isē(n).

iseid, iseyd, *see* seie(n).

iseined, *see* seinīe(n).

isē(n), *stv.*, **Sth.** = Ml. sē(n) ; OE.
gesēon-ȝeseah (5) ; *see, behold* ;
inf. (eSth.) isēon, 176, 18 ; ysē,
65, 17 ; *pr. pl.* isēoð, 199, 22 ; *pr.
sbj. sg.* isē, 207, 20 ; *pt. sg.* iseȝ, 41,
12 ; ysey, 205, 5 ; iseh, 181, 22 ;
isæh (eSth.), 182, 17 ; isah, 182,
12 ; isey, 62, 21 ; isei, 208, 21 ;
ysey, 205, 5 ; *pt. pl.* isēȝen, 179, 9 ;
pt. sbj. pl. iseye, 205, 3 ; *pp.* iseghe,
211, 9 ; ysēn, 221, 7. **Kt.** *inf.* yzȳ,
217, 11 ; *pr. 2 sg.* yziȝt, 217, 29 ;
pr. 3 sg. yzyȝþ, 216, 8 ; yzȳeþ, 217,
1 ; yzēþ, 217, 2.

isent, *see* sēnde(n).

isēon, isēoð, *see* isē(n).

iset, *see* sette(n).

isetnesse, *sb.*, OE. gesetness, *f.* ; *constitution, statute* ; *pl.* isetnesses,
226, 12.

iseyd, iseye, *see* seie(n), isē(n).

islaȝen, *see* slọ(n).

isọld, *see* selle(n).

isọm, *adj.*, OE. gesom ; *united,
gathered,* 185, 32.

isomned, *see* somnīe(n).

ispend, *see* spēnde(n).

Israēl, *sb.*, Lat. Israel ; *Israel,* 31, 29.

isse, issọte, *see* bē(n), schēte(n).

istrēoned, *see* strēone(n).

isūnde, *adj.* OE. gesunde-sūnde ;
sound, well, 190, 28.

isundret, *see* sundrīe(n).

isunken, *see* sinke(n).

iswinch, *sb.*, **Sth.** = Ml. swinc ; OE.
geswinc ; *work, labor, trouble,* 177,
12.

iswọren (iswçrene), *see* swēre(n).

iswunken, *see* swynke(n).

it, itālde, *see* hē, telle(n).

iþank, *sb.*, Sth. = Ml. þank; OE. geðanc; *thought, will, intention*: *ds.* iþanke, 178, 13.

iðenche(n), *wkv.*, Sth. = Ml. þenke(n); OE. geðencean–ðohte; *think*; *inf.* iðenche, 179, 29; iþenche, 214, 23; *pp.* iþoht, 182, 24.

iþōld, iþōled, *see* þōle(n), þōlie(n).

iþraste(n), *wkv.*, OE. geðræsten; *press, force*; *inf.* iþraste, 190, 11.

itīde(n), *wkv.*, OE. getīdan; *happen, betide*; *pr.* 3 *sg.* itīt, Ml. tīdeþ, 180, 3.

itimbbred, *see* timbre(n).

itīmed, *see* tīme(n).

itīt, itōld, *see* itīde(n), telle(n).

itravailed, *see* travaile(n).

iturned, *see* turnīe(n).

Iudas, Lat. Iudas. later displaced by OF. Judas; *Judas*, 27, 11.

Iudēus, *sb., pl.*, OE. Iudēas, L. Iudæus; *The Jews*, 4, 29.

iung, ivaren, *see* ʒung, fāre(n).

ivel, *see* yvel.

ivele, *adv.*, OE. yfele; *badly, evilly*, 17, 5.

ivēng, *see* ivō(n).

ivēre, *sb.*, Sth. = Ml. fēre; OE. gefēra; *companion*, 179, 13; *pl.* ivēren, 187, 31.

ivestned, *see* festne(n).

ivīnde(n), *stv.* Sth. = Ml. fīnde(n); OE. gefindan, (fīnden); *find, provide for*; *pt. sg.* ivōnd, 198, 15.

ivō(n), *stv.*, Sth. = Ml. fō(n); OE. gefōn–fēng (R); *seize*; *pt. sg.* ivēng, 182, 15.

ivōnd, *see* ivīnde(n).

ivōrþīe(n) *wkv.*, Sth. = Ml. fōrðe(n); OE. gefōrðian; *perform, execute*: *pr. sg.* ivōrþe, 184, 17.

iwākīe(n), eSth. iwakīe(n), *wkv.*, Sth. = Ml. wāke(n); OE. gewacian: *awake, rouse from sleep*; *inf.* iwakīen, 182, 22.

iwar, *adj.*, OE. gewar; *aware*; *pl.* iwarre, 199, 3.

iweddet, *see* wedde(n).

iwēnde(n), *wkv.*, Sth. = Ml. wēnde(n); OE. gewendan–wēndan;

turn, wind, go; *pt. sg.* iwende, 182, 18; *pp.* iwend, 198, 11.

iwēne(n), *wkv.*, Sth. (SEMl.) = Ml. wēne(n); OE. gewēnan; *hope, think, ween*; *pr.* 2 *sg.* inwēnest, 54, 29.

iwēpen, *sb.*, OE. wǣpen, *gewǣpen; *weapon*; *pl.* iwēpnen, 187, 17.

iwersed, *see* wersīe(n).

iwhile, *prn.*, OE. gehwilc; *each*; īwhillc (O), 11, 12.

iwil, ywil, *sb.*, OE. gewil; *pleasure, will*, 193, 5; *ds.* iwille, 178, 17; ywil, 176, 14.

iwilnet, *see* wilnīe(n).

iwis, ywis, *adv.*, OE. gewiss; *certainly*, 37, 25; ywys, 111, 3; mid iwisse, *certainly*, 177, 16; tō iwisse, 182, 25.

iwisse, *see* iwis.

iwite(n), *pt. prv.*, OE. gewitan -wiste; *know, wit, learn*; *inf.* iwite, 41, 14; ywyte, 215, 6; *imp. pl.* iwiteð, 197, 18.

iwlaht, *see* wlacīe(n).

iwonne, *see* winne(n).

iwōrded, *see* wōrdīe(n).

iwraht, *see* wūrche(n).

iwrit, *sb.*, Sth. = Ml. writ; OE. gewrit, *neut.*; *writing, book*; *ds.* iwrite, 179, 12.

iwriten, *see* wrīte(n).

iwroʒt, *see* wirke(n).

iwūndet, *see* wūndīe(n).

iwuned, *see* wune(n).

iwurðe(n), *wkv.*, OE. geweorðan (wurðan)–wearð (3); *be, become*; *pr.* 1 *sg.* iwurðe, 194, 17; *pp.* iwurðen, 184, 22.

iwūst, *see* wite(n).

J.

Jāmes, *sb.*, OF. James; *James*, 174, 29.

jangle(n), *wkv.*, OF. jangler; *jangle, dispute, chatter*; *pr. ppl.* jangland, 89, 13.

jāpe, *sb.*, OF. *jape, *jappe?; *joke, trick, jape*, 121, 9.

Jerōm, *sb.*, OF. Jerome; *Jerome*, 151; 13.

jeste, *see* ǧeste.

Jēsù, Jēsus, *sb.*, OF. Jēsus, Jēsu; *Jesus*, 11, 16; Jēsu Crīst, 33, 14; Jēsus, 68, 7.

Jew, *sb.*, OF. Geu, Gieu; *Jew*, 74, 25; *pl.* Jewes, 137, 5; Jews, 136, 15; Juus, 130, 29.

Jǭchim, *sb.*, OF. Joachim; *Joachim*, 131, 8.

Jōb, *sb.*, OF. Job; *Job*, 201, 2.

Jōēl, *sb.*, OF. Joel; *Joel*, 150, 20.

Jǭhan, Jǭhn, Jǭn, *sb.*, OF. Johan; *John*; eME. Johān, 12, 24; Jǭhn, 106, 19; Jǭnẹ, 88, 21; *gs.* Jǭnes, 131, 25; Jǭn, 228, 21.

joliftee, *sb.*, OF. jolivetē, joliftē; *jollity, happiness*, 242, 17.

Jǭn, *see* Jǭhan.

Jǭnas, *sb.*, OF. Jonas; *Jonah*, 73, 30.

Jordan, *sb.*, OF. Jordan: *Jordan*; Jorrdān (O), 11, 21.

jornay, *see* jurnay.

Jorrdān, *see* Jordan.

joye, *sb.*, OF. joie; *joy*, 37, 7.

joyful, *adj.*, OF.joie + ME. ful; *joyful*, 139, 27.

Jùdas, *sb.*, OF. Judas; *Judas*, 77, 28.

jùǧẹ, *sb.*, OF. juge : *judge*, 90, 27.

jùǧement, *sb.*, OF. jugement; *judgement, indictment*, 42, 2.

jùǧǧẹ(n), *wkv.*, OF. jugier; *judge*; *pp.* juged, 102, 5.

Jùliāne, *sb.*, OF. Juliane; *Juliana*, 191, 23.

Julȳ, *see* Cēsar.

jurnay, jurney, *sb.*, OF. jurnee, infl. by *vb.* NF. jurneier; *journey*, 107, 25; jurnay, 114, 30; jórnay, 163, 4.

jùstīce, jùstīs, *sb.*, OF. justice; *justice*, 2, 27; justīs, 131, 4.

justīse, *sb.*, OF. justice; *judge*, 152, 24.

Juus, *see* Jew.

K.

ka, kā, for words beginning with these letters see ca, cā forms.

kam, *see* cume(n).

kan, kane, kanst, *see* cunne(n).

karf, *see* kerve(n).

keccche(n),*wkv.*, Sth. = Ml. cache(n); OF. cachier; *catch*; *pr.* 3 *sg.* kec-cheð, 196, 1; *pr, sbj. pl.* kecchen, 202, 23.

kechyn (kichen), *sb.*, OE. cycene; Lat. coquīna (cocīna); *kitchen*, 99, 13.

keisēr, *see* caysēre.

kēle(n), *wkv.*, OE. cēlan; *cool*; Nth. *inf.* kēle, 156, 12.

kēmbe(n),*wkv.*,OE.cemban,cēmban, ON. kemba; *comb*; *inf.* kēmbe, 39, 20.

kempe, *sb.*, OE. cempa; *soldier*, 185, 7; Sth. *pl.* kempen, 186, 30.

kend, kēnde, *see* kenne(n), kīnde.

kēne, *adj.*, OE. cēne; *bold, keen*, 133, 3.

kenne(n), *wkv.*, OE. cennan; *know, make known, teach*; *inf.* kenne, 51, 25. Nth. *inf.* kenn, 129, 25; *pp.* kend, 174, 28.

kēp, *sb.*, cf. OE. cēpan; *heed, guard*, 53, 7; kēpẹ, 67, 10.

kēpe(n), *wkv.*, OE. cēpan; *keep, preserve*; *inf.* kēpen, 34, 6; *await, receive*, 50, 18; *pr. sbj. pl.* kēpe, 104, 6. Nth. *pr.* 3 *sg.* kēpes, 144, 1.

kēpynge, *sb.*, based on kēpe(n); *keeping, watching*, 103, 2.

kerve(n), *stv.*, OM. cerfan–carf, WS. ceorfan–cearf (3): *carve*; *pt. sg.* karf, 79, 10.

keste(n), *wkv.*, ON. kasta; *cast*; *pt. sg.* kest, 54, 6; *pt. pl.* kesten, 63, 17; *pp.* kest, 61, 6. Cf. caste(n), of which this is a secondary form.

kevel, *sb.*, ON. kefli; *bridle-bit, gag*, 81, 22.

keveringe, *sb.*, based on OF. (re)co-vrir; *recovery, regaining*, 209, 4.

kid, *see* kīðe(n).

kin, kyn, *sb.*, OE. cynn; *kin, kind, species*; *gs.* kinness (O), 12, 32; *ds.* kinne, 47, 6; *pl.* kin, 70, 13; kinnes, 46, 25; kyn, 220, 16. Nth. sēre kin thinges, *several kinds of affairs*, 127, 3.

kīnde, kīnd, kȳnd, *sb.*, OE. cynd, *f.* ;
species, kind, nature, 8, 13 ; kīnd,
65, 4 ; *pl.* kȳndis, 143, 23. Sth.
künde, 198, 20 ; künde trᶒsōns,
kind of treasons, 223, 18. Kt.
kēnde, 218, 9.

kīnde, *adj.,* OE. cynde ; *natural,
native* ; kinde, 22, 11.

kindle(n), *wkv.,* OE. [cynd], dial,
kindle ; *bring forth,' increase* ; *inf.*
kyndle, 237, 25; SEM1. *pp.* ikindled,
born, 14, 8. Nth. *inf.* kindel, 160,
24 ; *pr.* 3 *sg.* kindels, 161, 5.

kinedōm, *sb.,* OE. cynedōm ; *kingdom,*
47, 2.

kinelīch, *adj.,* OE. cynelīc ; *royal* ;
wk. kinelīche, 183, 3.

kinelᶒnd, *sb.,* OE. *cyneland, -lᶒnd ;
royal land, kingdom, 184, 14 ; *ds.*
kinelᶒnde, 189, 10.

kinewurᶞe, *adj.,* WS. *cynewierᶞe
–wurᶞe ; *royal,* 193, 19.

king, eME. kīng ; *sb.,* OE. cyning,
cyng ; *king,* 1, 1 ; *pl.* kinges, 22,
16. eSth. *ds.* kīnge, 181, 2 ; *pl.*
kīngen, 188, 9.

kinne, kinnes, *see* kin.

kinrīc, *sb.,* OE. cynerīc ; *kingdom,*
149, 12.

kire, *sb.,* OE. cyre ; *custom,* 34, 4.

kirke, kyrce (kyrke), *sb.,* ON. kirkja;
Dan. kirke, cogn. with OE. cyrice ;
kirk, church, 16, 15 ; kyrce, 133,
21 ; kyrke, 147, 8. Cf. chirche.

kirkedure, *sb.,* ON. kirkja + OE.
dure ; *church door,* 17, 26.

kisse(n), *wkv.,* OE. cyssan ; *kiss* ; *inf.*
kysse, 110, 27 ; *pr. pl.* kisse, 39, 7 ;
pt. sg. kiste, 28, 10.

kissinge, *sb.,* OM. *cyssung, *f.* ; *kiss-
ing,* 38, 1.

kiste, *sb.,* OE. cyst, *f.*; *choice, selection,
virtue,* 39, 9.

kiste, *see* kisse(n).

kīᶞe(n), *wkv.,* OE. cȳᶞan ; *make
known, show* ; *inf.* kīᶞen, 15, 8 ;
kīþe, 154, 12 ; *pr.* 3 *sg.* kīᶞeᶞ, 17,
6 ; *pp.* kid, 31, 5 ; kyd, 133, 1.

klepte, *see* clᶒpe(n).

klērelȳ, *adv.,* OF. cler, clier + lȳ ;
clearly, 136, 21.

knāve, *see* cnāve.

knawne, *see* knawe(n).

knawe(n), *stv.,* eME., Nth. = Ml.
knowe(n); OE. cnāwan–cnēow (R);
know ; Nth. *inf.* knaw, 127, 28 ;
pr. 3 *sg.* knawes, 137, 2 ; *pp.* knawyn,
170, 28. eSth. *pr.* 3 *sg.* cnāwaᶞ,
179, 21. Kt. *inf.*, knāwe, 218, 25 ;
pr. 3 *sg.* knaweþ, 216, 9. Cf.
knowe(n).

knē, *sb.,* OE. cneo(w) ; *knee; pl.* knēs,
78, 22 ; knēus, 122, 31.

knēle(n), *wkv.,* OM. *cnēolian, MLG.
knēlen ; *kneel* ; *inf.* knēle, 123, 10;
pr. ppl. knēlynge, 122, 32 ; *pt. sg.*
knēled, 66, 29 ; knēlid, 140, 3.

knew(en), *see* knowe(n).

knict, knicht, *see* kniȝt.

knīf, *sb.,* OE. cnīf ; *knife,* 79, 18.

kniȝt, knict, knicht, knight, knyht,
sb., OE. cniht ; *knight,* 46, 16 ;
knict, 75, 5 ; knicht, 75, 7 ; *pl.*
knyhtes, 126, 11 ; kniȝttes, 227,
22 ; knyghtys, 105, 21.

knokke(n), *wkv.,* OE. cnocian, infl.
by ON. knoka?; *knock* ; 1 *sg.*
knokke, 241, 1 ; *pp.* knokked, 163,
29; knᶒked, 163, 32.

knculᶒche(n), *wkv.,* OE. cnāwan,
extended by lǣcan?; *acknowledge,
recognize* ; *inf.* knoulᶒche, 51, 3.

knowe(n), *stv.,* OE. cnāwan–cnēow
(R); *know* ; *pr.* 2 *sg.* knowest, 38,
6 ; *pr.* 3 *sg.* knoweᶞ, 17, 1 ; *imp.*
know, 17, 25 ; *pt. sg.* knew, 41, 21,
pt. pl. knewen, 25, 2 ; *pp.* knowen,
104, 22; knowe, 234, 5. Sth. *pp.*
icnowen, 198, 8 ; yknowe, 230, 32.
Cf. Nth. Kt. knawe(n), knāwe(n).

knowlych(e), *sb.,* der. from *vb.* know-
lᶒche(n); *knowledge,* 95, 14.

knowynge, knowyng, *sb.,* based on
knowe(n) ; *knowing, knowledge,* 98,
30.

knyght, knyht, knyȝt, *see* kniȝt.

ko, kō, kᶒ (words), *see* co, cō, cᶒ.

konne, kouth, kouþen, *see* cun-
ne(n).

krike, *sb.,* OF. crique ; *creek,* 86, 24.

ku, kū (words), *see* cu, cū.

kude, *see* cunne(n).

kŭme, *sb.*, OE. cyme ; *coming*, 183, 20.

kŭnde, *see* kīnde.

kŭnerīche, *sb.*, Sth. = Ml. kinerīke ;
OE. cynerīce ; *kingdom*, 226, 6.

kŭnesman, *sb.*, OE. cynesman ;
kinsman, 207, 15.

kuppe, kurteisīe, *see* cuppe, curteysȳ.

kŭðən, *see* cunne(n).

kwēʌd, *see* quęd.

kweynte, *adv.*, AN. *adj.* queint beside
OF. coint; *famously,skilfully,neatly*,
48, 15.

kyd, *see* kīðe(n).

kyn (kynne), kyng, *see* kin, king.

Kynādius, Kynādyus, *sb.*, Lat. Cynadius? ; *Cynadius*, 221, 32.

kyndle(n), *see* kindle(n).

kynemerk,*sb.*,OE. cyne + ON. merki ;
royal mark, 83, 17.

kyngdōm, *sb.*, OE. cynedōm ; *kingdom* ; kyngdōmę, 105, 11.

kyrce, kyrke, *see* kirke.

kyrtyl, *sb.*, OE. cyrtel ; *kirtle*, 92, 30.

kysse(n), *see* kisse(n).

L.

lābour, *sb.*, OF. labour ; *labor*, 234,
23.

lac, *sb.*, OE. *læc, MDu. lac ; *lack,
fault, deformity*, 60, 12 ; lakk, 112,
25.

lāc, *sb.*, eME., Nth. = Ml. lǭc ; OE.
lāc ; *gift, offering*, 187, 17.

lacche(n), *wkv.*, OE. læccan–læhte ;
seize, catch ; *pt. sg.* lauhte, 87, 29 ;
lauȝt, 50, 21 ; *pp.* lagt, 22, 17.
Sth. *pp.* ilaht, 196, 1.

lāce(n), *stv.*, eME., Nth. = Ml.
lǭke(n) ; OE. lācan–lēolc (lēc) (R);
move, leap, go swiftly; *pt. sg.* læc,
189, 15 ; lęac, 195, 26.

lad, ladden, *see* lęde(n).

lādȳ, *see* lavedȳ.

lēc, *see* lāce(n).

læd, lǣden, *see* lēde(n).

læi, *see* līe(n).

læide, læiden, *see* leie(n).

lǣn, lēt, lǣtenn, *see* lęn, lēte(n).

lǣwed, *see* lewed.

lāf, *pl.* lāves, *sb.*, Nth. = Ml., Sth.
lǭf ; OE. hlāf ; *loaf*, 132, 4.

lāf, layff, *sb.*, Nth. = Ml. lǭf ; OE.
lāf, *f.*; *remainder, what is left*;
layff, 167, 3.   Cf. lāve.

lāferrd, laft, *see* lāverd, lęve(n).

lag, *see* līe(n).

lāge, laȝe, laȝen, lahen, later lawe,
sb., OE. lagu < ON. lög, lagu ;
law, custom, 14, 12 ; lawe, 100, 18 ;
pl. lāges, 17, 27 ; laiges, 33, 30.
eSth. laȝe, 187, 19 ; *pl.* laȝen, 190,
24 ; lahen, 191, 27.

lagt, *see* lacche(n).

lāh, *adj.*, eME., Nth. = Ml. low;
ON. lāgr ; *low, humble*, 192, 20.

lahen, *see* lāge.

lahhe(n), *stv.*, OM. hlæhhan, WS.
hliehhan–hlōh (6) ; *laugh* ; *pt. sg.*
lough, 237, 20 ; *pt. pl.* lōȝen, 36,
29 ; lowe, 46, 8.   Sth. *inf.* lauhwen,
201, 19.

lai, laidest, *see* līe(n), leie(n).

laiges, *see* lāge.

lāke, *sb.*, OE. lacu, *f.* < Lat. lacus ;
lake, 58, 20.

lakk, *see* lac.

lām, *sb.*, Nth. = Ml., Sth. lǭm ; OE.
lām ; *loam*, 132, 15.

lāmb, *sb.*, OE. lamb, lāmb (lǭmb) ;
lamb, Lamb (*Christ*), 12, 27.

Lammasse, *sb.*, OE. hlāmmæsse <
hlāf + mæsse ; *Lammas, feast of first
fruits, Aug.* 1 ; *ds.* 1, 13.

land, eME. lānd (lǭnd), *sb.*, OE.
land, lānd (lǭnd) ; *land*, 1, 1 ; *ds.*
lānde, 3, 29 ; *pl.* lāndes, 1, 15.
Cf. lǭnd.

lāne, *sb.*, Nth. = Ml. lǭn ; OE.
lān (læn), *f.*; *loan, gift, favor*,
142, 1.

lāng, *adj.*, eME., Nth. for Ml. lǫng ;
OE. lāng, lǫng ; *long*, 1, 9.   Cf.
lǫng.

lāng, *adj.*, OE. gelang–lāng ; *dependent, belonging*, dialectal *along of*;
iss lāng (O), *depends on*, 10, 14.

langāǧe, *sb.*, OF. langage ; *language*,
134, 5.   Cf. lǫngāge.

lānge, lāng, *adv.*, eME., Nth. =

Ml. lǫnge; OE. lange; *long*, 7, 8.
Nth. lāng, 139, 32.

lāre, *sb.*, **eME.**, **Nth.** for ME. lǫre;
OE. lār, *f.*; *lore, teaching*, 8, 19.

larǧe, *adj.*, OF. large; *large*, 129,
11; *generous*, 201, 19.

larǧelīche, *see* larǧelȳ.

larǧelȳ, *adv.*, OF. large + ME. lȳ;
largely, charitably, 88, 15. **Sth.**
largelīche, 204, 22.

larǧesse, *sb.*, OF. largesse; *bounty,
largess*, 202, 16.

lārspell, *sb.*, OE. lārspel; *discourse,
sermon, treatise*, 9, 14.

las, lasse (last), *see* lēse(n), lēs.

lasse(n), *wkv.*, based on OE. lǣs,
'less'; *lessen, decrease*; *imp. pl.*
lasseð, 196, 7.

last, lastand, *see* laste(n), *endure*.

laste(n), *wkv.*, ON. lasta; *blame*;
inf. lasten, 195, 22.

last (n), lēste(n), *wkv.*, OE. lǣstan;
last, endure; *pr. ppl.* lestende, 118,
5; *pt. sg.* lastede, 3, 21; *pp.* last,
58, 15. **Nth.** *pr.* 3 *sg.* lastes, 129,
2; *pr. ppl.* lastand, 129, 30. Cf.
lēste(n).

lasten, *see* lēs.

lastunge, *sb.*, OE. *lastung, *f.*; cf.
ME. lasten; *blame*, 198, 10.

lat, late, laten, *see* lēde(n), lēte(n).

lat, *adj.*, OE. læt; *late, slow*; *comp.*
later (eME.), 180, 11; *superl.* lest,
132, 30.

lāte, *adv.*, OE. læte; *late*, 58, 29;
lately, 99, 15.

lātę, *see* lǫte.

lāþ, lath, *adj.*, **eME.**, **Nth.** for ME.
lǫþ, lāth; OE. lāð; *hateful, loathsome, hostile, evil*, 9, 24; lāth, 127,
11; lāð (e**Sth.**), 193, 7; *ds.* as *sb.*
lāðe, 178, 5.

lāðe, *sb.*, ON. hlaða; *barn*, dial. Eng.
lathe, 24, 6.

lāðe(n), lāði(n), *wkv.*, OE. laðian;
be hateful, loathsome; *inf.* lāðin,
194, 15.

lāðie(n), *wkv.*, OE. lāðian; *invite*;
imp. pl., lāðe ȝē, 202, 20.

Latinę, **Latin**, *adj.*, OF. Latin;
Latin, 127, 6; *gpl.* Latīnes, 191, 18.

lau, *adj.*, **Nth.** = Ml. low; OE. lāh;
low; *comp.* lauer, *lower*, 151, 25.

laud, *see* lauid.

lauȝt, lauhte, *see* lacche(n).

lauhwen, *see* lahhe(n).

lauid, *adj.*, **Nth.** = Ml. lewed; OE.
lǣwed; *lay, unlearned*; MnE.,
lewd, 134, 7.

lāve, *sb.*, e**Sth.** = Ml. lᶧve; OE. lāf,
f.; *leaving, remnant*, 190, 12.

lavedȳ, lavedī, lādȳ, *sb.*, OE.
hlᴂfdīge; *lady*, 116, 14; lavedī,
129, 19; *gs.* lādȳes, 108, 22. Cf.
lēvedī.

lāverd, *sb.*, **eME.**, **Nth.** for Ml.
lǫverd, lǫrd; OE. hlāford; *lord*, 5,
26; lāferrd (O), 11, 1; **eME.** *ds.*
lāverde, 194, 13. e**Sth.** hlāvord,
178, 24.

lāves, lawe, *see* lāf, lāge.

lawful, *adj.*, ON. lögfullr; *lawful*,
234, 11.

lawlȳlȳ, *adv.*, based on OE. lāhlīc,
adj.; *lawfully*, 146, 31.

lay, *sb.*, OF. lai; *lay, song, story*,
116, 8.

lay, *see* līe(n).

layd, layff, *see* leie(n), lāf.

layk, *sb.*, ON. leikr, cogn. with OE.
lāc; *play, sport*; *pl.* laykes, 163, 28.

layn, *see* līe(n).

Lāzar, *sb.*, OF. *Lazarus*, 132, 15.

lēac, lēade, *see* lāce(n), lēde(n).

lēafde, *see* lēve(n).

lēafdī, lēare(n), *see* lēvedī, lēre(n).

lēave, lēavė(n), *see* lēve, lēve(n).

lēche (lēche), *sb.*, OM. lēce, .WS.
lǣce; *leech, physician*, 59, 4.

lēche(n), *wkv.*, OM. lēcnian, WS.
lǣcnian, infl. by lēche, *sb.*, *heal,
act as physician*; *inf.* lēche, 131,
30.

lecherīe, lecherȳe, *sb.*, OF. lecherie;
lechery, 54, 13; lecherȳe, 237, 25.

lēchnunge, *sb.*, OE. lǣchnung, *f.*;
healing, remedy, 192, 10.

lēd, *sb.*, OE. lēad; *lead*, 60, 18.

led, *see* lēde(n).

lēdar, *sb.*, OE. lǣdᵉre; *leader*, 166,
20.

ledde(n), leddes, *see* lēde(n).

lēde, *sb.*, OM. lēden (?), WS. lǽden; *language, speech*; orig. Latin < latīnus, 48, 18.

lēde, *sb.*, OE. lēode, *pl.*; *people*, 10, 21. eSth. *pl.* lēodan, 183, 7.

lēde(n), *wkv.*, OE. lǽdan; *lead*; *inf.* lēden, 26, 1; lēde, 39, 12; *pr.* 1 *sg.* lēde, 176, 5; *pr.* 3 *sg.* lat = lēdeð, 56, 7; *pl. sg.* ledde, 28, 1; lad, 101, 3; led, 155, 33; ladde, 185, 2; *pr.* 2 *sg.* leddes, 48, 24; *pt. pl.* lǽd (eME.), 5, 27; ledden, 6, 10; ledde, 57, 23; ladd, 116, 2; *pp.* led, 35, 3; leddę, 90, 24. Nth. *pr. pl.* lēdis, 136, 6. eSth. *inf.* lǽden, 180, 1; *pr. sbj. sg.* lēade, 191, 21; *pp.* yladde, 64, 9; ilǽd, 176, 5; ileid, 211, 2. Kt. *pr.* 3 *sg.* lēdeþ, 219, 20.

lēdene, *sb.*, OE. lǽden, lēden; *language, speech*, 191, 18. Cf. Ml. lēde.

lēdis, *see* lēden.

leef, leeve, *see* lēf.

lęęs, lęęst, *see* lēs.

lęęt, lęf(e), *see* lēte(n), lęve(n).

lęf, *sb.*, OE. lēaf; *leaf*, 51, 22.

lęf, *sb.*, OE. lēaf. *f.*; *permission*, 154, 22. Cf. lęve.

lēf, leef, *adj.*, OE. lēof; *dear, pleasant*, archaic, *lief*, 9, 26; *ds.* lēve, 20, 19; lēve, *wk.* 33, 5; lēfe, 110, 13; leeve, 241, 2; *comp.* lēvere, 22, 21; lēver, 152, 28. 1Nth. leif, 126, 17. eSth. lēof, 178, 17; lēofe, 183, 17; *ds.* lēofen, 183, 25; lēofve, 184, 12; *comp.* lēovre, 177, 5; *superl.* lēofvest, 181, 22.

lefde, *see* lęve(n).

lęfdī, lęghe(n), *see* lęvedī, līe(n), *prevaricate.*

lęfful, *adj.*, OE. lēaf + ful; *allowable, lawful*, 235, 7.

lefte, *see* lęve(n).

leie(n), *wkv.*, OE. lecgan, infl. by *pr.* 3 *sg.*; *lay, place, put aside, banish*; *inf.* leyʒe, 52, 11; lein, 55, 25; leyn, 87, 3; ley, 89, 18; *pt. pl.* lǽiden, 3, 23; lǽide, 7, 5; *pr.* 2 *sg.* leidest, 84, 16; laidest, 103, 6; *pt. pl.* leiden, 189, 28;

leyd, 91, 23; *pp.* leid, 27, 6; layd, 155, 23; Sth. *pp.* ileid, 198, 21; (SEMl.), yleyd, 66, 32.

leien, *see* līe(n).

leif, leiʒen, *see* lēf, līe(n).

leinte, leinten, *see* lēngten.

Leirchestre, *sb.*, OE. Legraceaster; *Leicester*, 227, 2.

lēk, *see* lūke(n).

lęlę, *adj.*, OF. leial; *loyal, leal*, 128, 25.

lēme, *sb.*, OE. lēoma; *light, gleam, brightness*; *pl.* lēmes, 155, 1.

lēme(n), *wkv.*, OE. lēomian; *give light, shine*; *pt. sg.* lēmede, 61, 14.

lemman, *sb.*, OE. lēofman; *dear one, leman*, 43, 15.

lēn, *see* lēne(n).

lęn, *sb.*, OE. lēan; *reward*; eME. lǽn (O), 10, 27.

lēnde(n), *wkv.*, OE. lendan, lēndan; *land, arrive, abide*; *inf.* lēnde, 87, 18. Nth. *pr.* 3 *sg.* lēndes, 143, 5; *pt. sg.* lēnd, 162, 27.

lęne, *adj.*, OE. hlǽne; *lean, not fat*, 17, 5.

lęne(n), *wkv.*, OE. hleonian; *lean, incline*, 122, 30.

lēne(n), *wkv.*, ON. lēna, cogn. with OE. lǽnan; *lend*; *pp.* lēnedd, 8, 20; lent, 59, 8. Nth. *inf.* lēn, 142, 1. Sth. *pr. sbj. sg.* lenne, 179, 33; *pp.* ilēnet, 194, 7.

leng, eME. lēng, *adv. comp.*, OE. leng, lēng; *longer*, 4, 20.

lēngten, later lenten, leinten, *sb.*, OE. lēngten; *spring, season of Lent*, 5, 13; *gs.* lentenes, 121, 23; leinten, 200, 3; leinte, 231, 2.

lengðe, *sb.*, OE. lengð, *f.*; *length*, 20, 24.

lenne, lent, *see* lēne(n).

lenten, *see* lēngten.

lēo, lēoden, *see* lēun, lēde.

lēof, lēofe, lēoſen, *see* lēf.

leoft, left (lift), *adj.*, OE. *lyft, cf. MDu. luft, 'left'; *left (hand)*, 182, 4; lift, 225, 8.

lēofve, lēofvest, *see* lēf.

lēop,lēorne(n),*see* lēpe(n), lērne(n).

lēote(n), *see* lēte(n).

lēoūn, *see* lēūn.

lēovemon, *sb.,* OE. *lēofman(mon); *dear one, leman,* 192, 30.

leovinde, *see* livīe(n).

lēovre, *see* lēf.

lēpe(n), *stv.,* OE. hlēapan–hlēop (R) ; *leap; inf.* lēpe, 36, 17 ; *pt. sg.* lēp, 36, 4; *pt. pl.* lēpen, 37, 31. eSth. *pt. sg.* lēop, 195, 18.

lēr, *sb.,* OE. hlēor; *cheek* ; MnE. *leer; pl.* lēre, 37, 21.

lēred, *pp.* as *adj.,* OE. lǣran; *learned,* 4, 4. eSth. ilǣrde, 226, 3.

lēre(n), *wkv.,* OE. lǣran [lār]; *learn; pr.* 3 *sg.* lēreð, 16, 19; *pt. sg.* lērede, 29, 12 ; *pp.* lēred, 50, 4 ; lērd, 137, 29. Nth. *pr.* 3 *sg.* lēres, 91, 28. Sth. *inf.* lēaren (eSth.), 196, 5 ; *pr.* 3 *sg.* lēareð, 198, 7 ; *pp.* ilēred, 198, 4.

lērne(n), lerne n), *wkv.* OM. lērnian, WS. leornian; *learn; inf.* lērnenn (O), 8, 22 ; *pr.* 3 *sg.* lērne þ þ (O),10,18;*pp.* lerned, 58, 21. eSth. *inf.* lēornen, 192, 15. Sth. *pt. pl.* lurneþ, 225, 4; *pt. sg.* lurnede, 224, 29. Kt. *pr.* 3 *sg.*, lȳerneþ, 218, 25; *imp. sg.* lȳerne, 215, 1 ; *pp.* ylȳerned, 215, 1.

lērningeniht, *sb.,* OE. leorningeniht; *disciple* ; lērninngcnihhtess (O), 12, 13.

lēs, *adj.,* OE. lēas; *false, evil,* 111, 30.

lēs, les, *adj.,* OE. lǣs; *less* ; lęęs, 223, 16; les, 141, 27; lesse, 178, 4 ; lasse, 225, 6 ; *superl.* lęste, 53. 16 ; lēst, 178, 5; *ds.* (eSth.) laste, 190, 11; lęęst, 233, 30. Kt. lēste, 219, 9.

lēs, *sb.,* OE. lēas; *falsehood,* 231, 32; *ds.* lēse, 183, 25.

lescūn, lessōn, *sb.,* AN. lecun (OF. -on); *lesson,*198,13; lessōn,224,19.

lēse(n), *wkv.,* OM. lēsan, WS. līesan; *release, deliver, loose* ; *inf.* lēsenn (O), 11, 27; lēsen, 194, 11; *imp. pl.* lēseð, 201, 16; *pp.* lēsedd (O), 11, 8. Cf. Sth. lūse(n).

lēse(n), *stv.,* OE. lēosan–lēas (2); *lose* ; *inf.* lēse, 53, 25; *pt. pl.* lorn, 67, 1 ; *pp.* loren, 48, 3 ; loren, 52,

12. Nth. *pr. pl.* lēsis, 126, 6. Sth. *pp.* ylore, 95, 16.

lęse(n), *stv.,* OE. lesan–lǣs (5); *gather, collect*; *pt. sg.* las, 56, 12.

lēseþ, lēsedd, *see* lēse(n), *release.*

lęsing, lēsis, *see* lęsynge, lēse(n).

lesse, lessōn, *see* lēs, lesoūn.

lēst, lest, *see* laste(n), lat.

lęste, *see* lęs.

lest, leste, *adv. conj.,* OE. ðȳ lǣs ðe, *later* lǣsþe ; *lest,* 121, 23 ; leste, 202, 23.

lēst, *see* lēte(n).

lęste(n), laste(n), *wkv.,* OE. lǣstan ; *last, endure, continue*; Nth. *inf.* lēst, 168, 11. Sth. *pr. ppl.* lęstinde, 226, 20. Cf. laste(n).

lestende, *see* laste(n).

lęstined, *see* lęste(n).

lestned, *see* listne(n).

lęsynge, lęsing, *sb.,* OE. lēasing; *falsehood,* 111, 13 ; lęsing, 40, 11.

lēte(n), *stv.,* OM. lētan (WS. lǣtan) –lēt (R); *let, permit, loose* ; *leave*; *think*; *inf.* lēten, 6, 13; lǣtenn (O), 9, 26; lēte, 52, 2 ; *pr.* 2 *sg.* lētest, 194, 7 ; lēst, 63, 5 ; *pr.* 3 *sg.* lēteð, 16, 21 ; *imp. sg.* lēt, 18, 16 ; late, 99, 5 ; *pt. sg.* lǣt (eME.), 4, 14; lēt, 12, 4; lēte, 64,14; *pt. pl.* lēte, 35, 28 ; *pp.* let, 61, 30; late, 56, 5. Sth. *inf.* lēoten (eSth.), 193, 21 ; lęten, 201, 1 ; *pr.* 3 *sg.* lęteð,180,6; lęt, 180, 7; *imp. sg.* lęęt, 241, 2; *imp. pl.* lęted = lēteð, 201, 17; *pt. pl.* letten, 186, 15 ; *pp. pl.* ylete, 221, 8.

lęth, *sb.,* OE. lǣððu ; *hatred, enmity,* 127, 13.

lett, OM. *lette, *hindrance, let,* 107, 7.

lette(n), *wkv.,* Nth. = Ml. lette(n); OE. lettan ; *hinder, impede* ; Nth. *pr. pl.* lettys, 146, 17 ; *imp. pl.* lettes, 139, 14; *pt. sg.* lett, 163, 28. Sth. *pp.* ilet, 226, 17.

letten, *see* lęte(n).

letter, *sb.,* OF. lettre, 72, 8 ; *pl.* letters, 71, 22.

lettyng, *sb.,* based on OE. lettan ; *hindrance, delay,* 174, 26.

lēun, lēoūn, *sb.*, AN. leun, liun; *lion*, 14, 1 ; lēoūn, 82, 17 ; lēo, 182, 13. Cf. lȳūn.

lēve, *see* lēf.

Lēve, *sb.*, OE.? ; *Leve*, 82, 2.

lēve, *sb.*, OE. lēaf, *f.*; *permission*, 18, 28. eSth. lēave, 199, 29. Cf. lēf.

lēve, *sb.*, OE. lēafa; *belief, faith*, 20, 22.

levede, *see* live(n).

lēvedī, *sb.*, OE. hlǣfdige; *lady*, 52, 1 ; lēvedy, 117, 1 ; lēfdī, 155, 5; lēfdȳe, 156, 5. Nth. *pl.* lēvedis, 129, 19. eSth. lēafdī, 193, 14. Cf. lavedȳ.

lēveful, *adj.*, OE. lēaffull [(ge)lēafa]; *believing, faithful*, 234, 4.

lēvelīke, *adv.*, OE. lēoflīce; *lovingly, gladly*, 28, 19.

lēve(n), *wkv.*, OE. lǣfan; *leave, permit*; *inf.* lēve, 57, 3; *pr. pl.* lēve wē, 100, 13; *imp. sg.* lēf, 196, 23; *pr. sbj. sg.* lēve, 47, 22 ; *pt. sg.* lafte, 241, 33; *pt. pl.* lefte, 223, 25; *pt. sbj. sg.* lefde, 200, 8; *pp.* laft, 49, 19. Nth. *inf.* lēf, 153, 19. eSth. *inf.* lēaven, 192, 33 ; *imp. pl.* lēaveð, 196, 7; *pt. sg.* lēafde, 191, 27; *pp.* yleft, 225, 10.

lēve(n), *wkv.*, OM. lēfan, WS. līefan [gelēafa] ; *believe*; *pr. 3 sg.* lēveð, 16, 19. Nth. *imp. pl.* lēves, 165, 17 ; *pt. sg.* lifed, 135, 9.

lēver, lēvere, *see* lēf, *adj.*

lēvinge, *sb.*, Kt. = Ml. lēvinge; based on Kt. lēve(n), Ml. lēve(n); *remainder, residue*, 218, 2.

lewe, *adj.*, OE. hlēowe; *warm*, 80, 5.

lewed, *adj.*, OE. lǣwede; *unlearned, lay, as opposed to clerical*, 88, 4.

lewse (= lēswe?),*sb.*,OM. lēs(lēswe), WS. lǣs (lǣswe),*f.* [lesan, 'glean']; OE. lǣs; *pasture land*, dial. Eng. *leasow*, 31, 1.

ley, leyen, *see* leie(n), līe(n).

leyke(n), *stv.*, ON. leika-lēk (R); *play, sport*, 79, 8.

leyʒe, *sb.*, OM. lēg, WS. līeg, *mn.*; *flame*, 61, 14.

leyn, leyʒen, *see* līe(n), leie(n).

Lhoaverd, *see* Lǫverd.

libbe(n), *wkv.*, OE. libban ; *live*; eSth. *inf.* libben, 192, 11 ; libbe, 177, 9; *pr.* 1 *sg.* libbe (SEMl.), 37, 8; *pr. ppl.* libbinde, 217, 21 ; libbynde, 218, 33. Cf. live(n).

līc, *see* līch.

līcam, *sb.*, OE. līchama; *body, corpse*, 132, 16.

līce(n), lict, *see* līke(n), liht.

līch, līchę, *sb.*, OE. līc; *body*, 33, 25 ; līchę, 35, 10; eME. līc, 2, 2.

lichtman,*sb.*,OE.lēoht + man; *bearer of a light, torch-bearer*, 169, 26.

līchūr, līchoūrę, *sb.*, OF. lechur, lichur; *unchaste person, lecher*, 127, 13; līchoūrę, 147, 7.

lid,*sb.*,OE. hlid; *cover, lid*; *pl.* lides, 14, 13.

līde(n), *see* līðe(n).

līen, *sb.*, OE. *līen < lēan; *reward, recompense*, 178, 8.

līe(n), *stv.*, OE. licgan–læg (5); *lie, recline*; *belong to*; *inf.* līen, 3, 17; lȳe, 52, 3; *pr.* 2 *sg.* līst, 48, 11; *pr.* 3 *sg.* līeð, 14, 12 ; līð, 14, 9; *pr. pl.* līen, 4, 19; *pr. sbj. sg.* lȳe, 121, 20; *pt. sg.* lai, 1, 14; lag, 27, 30; lay, 47, 25 ; *pt. pl.* leien, 190, 13; leyen, 79, 14; *pp.* leyn, 53, 9; leiʒen, 58, 20 ; layn, 111, 29. Nth. *pr. pl.* ligges, 153, 17 ; līes, 152, 14. Sth. (SEMl.) *inf.* liǧǧe, 41, 30; *pr.* 1 *sg.* liǧǧe, 52, 24 ; *pt. sg.* (eSth.) læi, 181, 12.

līe(n), *stv.*, OM. lēgan–lēg, WS. lēogan–lēag (2); *lie, prevaricate, deny, be false to*; *inf.* līen, 199, 18; *pr.* 3 *sg.* līeð, 199, 15. Sth. *inf.* līhen, 194, 3; *pr. ppl.* līhinde, 191, 21. Kt. *pr.* 3 *sg.* lēgheþ, 214, 15.

līerne, *see* lērne(n).

līf, OE. līf; *life*, 8, 17 ; liif, 65, 7; lȳfę, 106, 15 ; *gs.* līves, 48, 3 ; *ds.* in *phr.* on līve, *alive*, 33, 1 ; of līve, 41, 32 ; *pl.* līve = lives, 160, 9. eSth. *ds.* līfe, 176, 23 ; lȳve, 215, 12.

life (līfes), līfed,*see* live(n), lēve(n).

lifedæi, *sb.*, OE. lífdæg; *lifeday, life*; *ds.* lífedaȝe, 186, 20.

lífhāli, *adj.*, OE. *líihālig; *holy in life, holy*, 191, 20.

liflāde, *sb.*, OE. líflād, *f.*; *way of life, conduct, life*, 191, 19.

lift, *see* leoft.

lift, *sb.*, OE. lyft; *air, upper region*, 152, 20.

lifte, *wkv.*, ON. lypta, lyfta; *lift*; *pp.* lift, 143, 4.

lifte(n), *wkv.*, ON. lyfta, cf. Icl. lypta < lyfta; *lift*; *pp.* lifted, 101, 20.

liȝe, *adj.*, OF. lige (liege); *liege*, 232, 20.

liȝeaunce, *sb.*, OF. ligence; *allegiance*, 235, 5.

liȝeman, *sb.*, OF. lige (liege) + ME. man; *liegeman*, 233, 31.

liȝȝe(n), *see* līe(n) 'recline.'

liȝht, *see* liht.

lightlȳ, *see* liȝtlī.

Liȝtbern, *sb.*, OE. Lēohtberend, translation of L. Lucifer; *Lucifer*, 68, 5.

liȝtlī, *adv.*, OE. lēohtlíce; *lightly, easily*, 50, 10.

liȝtnesse, liȝtnisse, *sb.*, OE. lihtness, *f.*; *light, brightness*, 66, 32; liȝtnisse, 67, 22.

liȝtyng, *sb.*, OE. lyhting, *f.*; *illumination*, 103, 7.

ligte(n), *wkv.*, OE. líhtan, lihtan; *make light or easy, alight*; *inf.* ligten, 14, 16; *pp.* ligt, 27, 28. **Sth.** *inf.* lihten, 192, 20; *pp.* yliȝt, 65, 3.

līhen, *see* līe(n) *prevaricate*.

lihhtlīke, *see* lihtlīke.

lihinde, *see* līe(n), *prevaricate*.

liht, *sb.*, OM. lēht (lēht, liht), WS. lēoht; *light*; lict, 82, 20; lyhte, 117, 6.

lihte(n), *see* ligte(n).

lihte(n), *wkv.*, OM. lēhtan, WS. lēohtan, līohtan; *light, kindle*; *inf.* lihten, 186, 12; *pt. pl.* lihtede, 5, 14.

lihtlīke, *adv.*, OM. lēhtlíce, WS. lēohtlíce; *lightly, easily*: lihhtlīke (O), 13, 5.

liif, *see* líf.

līk, līch, *adj.*, OE. gelíc; *like*; lȳchę, 98, 20; līkę, 126, 10.

līke(n), *wkv.*, OE. līcian; *please, like*; *pr.* 3 *sg.* līkeð, 193, 9; *pr. sbj. sg.* lȳke, 232, 20; *pt. sg.* līkede, 14, 16; līcede, 176, 13. **Nth.** *pr.* 3 *sg.* līkes, 128, 4.

līm, līme, *sb.*, OE. līm; *lime*, 73, 2.

līm, līmę, *sb.*, OE. lim; *limb, member*, 3, 13; līmę, 60, 12; *ds.* līmę, 50, 15.

līmēl, *adv.*, OM. limmēlum, WS. -mǣlum; *limb by limb*, 193, 25.

limpe(n), *stv.*, OE. limpan—lamp (lǫmp) (ȝ); *happen, be becoming*; *pr.* 3 *sg.* limpeð, 200, 23.

Lincol, *sb.*, OE. Lincolne (Lincolle); *Lincoln*, 1, 5.

līnde, *sb.*, OE. lind, and linde, *f.*; *linden, lime-tree*, 51, 22.

Lindeseye, *sb.*, OM. Lindesēg, WS. Lindesīg, *f.*; *Lindsey, Island of the Lindi*, 87, 19.

līne, *sb.*, OE. līne; *rope, strong cord*, 81, 14.

lippe, *sb.*, OE. lippe; *lip*, 102, 19.

list, *sb.*, OE. lyst; *pleasure, lust*, 20, 16.

līst, līp, *see* līe(n).

liste(n), *wkv.*, OE. hlystan; *listen*; *inf.* lisstenn (O), 10, 22. **Nth.** *imp. pl.* listens, 165, 17. **Sth.** *imp. pl.* lüsteð, 196, 5.

listne(n), *wkv.*, *hlystnan, cf. Swed. lyssna; *listen*; *pr.* 3 *sg.* listneð, 20, 23; *pt. sg.* listnede, 24, 9; lestned, 98, 29. **Sth.** *inf.* lüstnin, 191, 19.

līt, lit, *sb.*, OE. lȳt; *little*; *ds.* līte, 177, 22; lȳte, 215, 20; lite, 40, 32. **Sth.** lüt. *few*, 198, 30; lüte, 209, 12.

lītel, lȳtel, litle, *adj.*, OE. lȳtel; *little*, 2, 17; little (O), 8, 20; lȳtel and lȳtel, *little by little*, 222, 21; lyttill, 145, 2. WMl. luytel, 120, 1. **Sth.** lütel, 180, 15; lȳtel, 222, 20.

līðe(n), *stv.*, OE. līðan—lāð (1); *go, travel*; *inf.* līðe, 182, 13.

līðe(n), līði(n), *wkv.*, ON. hlȳða; *listen*; *imp. pl.* līðeð, 23; līðeð, 196, 6. **Nth.** *imp. pl.* līthes, 157, 9. **Sth.** *inf.*, līðin, 191, 19.

liðerīe(n), *wkv.*, OM. leðrian, WS. līeðrian (lyðrian); *lather, become covered with foam*; *pr. sbj. sg.* liðerī, 194, 20.

līve, līves, *see* līf.

live(n), Sth. livīe(n), *wkv.*, OE. līfian; *live*; *inf.* liven, 4, 20; lyve, 88, 14; *pr.* 3 *sg.* liveth, 31, 31; *pr. pl.* liven, 34, 10; *pt. sg.* livede, 7, 16; *pt. pl.* liveden, 73, 22; lived, 73, 21; *pp.* lyved, 91, 2. Nth. *inf.* life, 130, 32; *pr.* 3 *sg.*, lifes, 165, 18; *pr. ppl.* liffand, 169, 14. Sth. *pr. pl.* livīeð, 196, 18; *pr. ppl.* livīende, 192, 1; leovinde, 194, 24; *pt. sg.* levede, 215, 11.

lō, *interj.*, OE. lā; *lo*, 90, 11.

loand, *see* lōnd.

lob, *sb.*, OE. lobbe, *f.*; *spider*, 103, 9.

lōd, *sb.*, OE. lād, *f.*; *journey, load*, 63, 23.

lōdlīch, lōdlukest, *see* lōþlī.

Lodovīa, *sb.*, Lat. Lodovia; *Lodovia*, 221, 28; see note.

Lodway, *sb.*, *Lodway*, 221, 29.

lof, *sb.* (?), origin uncertain; expression lof and grin, *instruments of torture*, 3, 14. See note.

lof, *sb.*, OE. lof; *praise*; loff (O), 12, 17.

lōf, lōfę, *sb.*, OE. hlāf; *loaf*, 90, 5.

lofe(n), *see* lōve(n).

lōgen, loȝen, lōwe, *see* lahhe(n).

loken, *see* lūke(n).

lōke(n), *wkv.*, OE. lōcian; *look, keep, observe*; *inf.* lōken, 18, 8; *imp. sg.* lōke, 67, 20; lookę, 239, 7; *imp. pl.* lōkeþ, 200, 11; *pr. sbj. sg.* lōke, 10, 7; *pt. sg.* lōkede, 40, 26; *pp.* lōke for lōked in rime, 40, 4. 1Nth. *inf.* luke, 142, 25. Sth. *pr. pl.* lōkeþ, 218, 16; *pr. sbj. pl.* lōkī, 219, 31.

lōking, *pp.* as *sb.*, based on lōke(n); *care, keeping, looking*, 49, 19.

lōmb, *sb.*, OE. lamb, lāmb (lǫmb); *lamb*, 199, 4.

lōme, *adv.*, OE. gelōme; *often, frequently*, 176, 11.

lǫnd, *sb.*, OE. land, lǫnd (lōnd); *land*; loand = lǫnd, 226, 6; *ds.*

lǫnde, 19, 10. Sth. *pl.* lǫnden, 182, 30. Cf. land.

lǫndīe(n), *wkv.*, OE. landian, lǫndian; *land, as a ship*; *pt. pl.* lǫndede, 222, 14.

lǫng, *adj.*, OE. lang; lǫng; *long*; Sth. *fas.* lǫnge, 181, 5.

lǫngāge, *sb.*, OF. langage; *language*, *pl.* longāges, 224, 4.

lǫnge, *adv.*, OE. lange, lǫnge; *long*, 39, 13.

lǫnge(n), *wkv.*, OE. langian, lǫngian; *reach forth, extend, belong*; *inf.* lǫnge, 221, 32; NEM1. *pr.* 3 *sg.* lǫnges, 76, 31.

looke, *see* lōke(n).

Looth, *sb.*, Lat. (Vulgate) Lōth; *Lot*, 238, 3.

lǫrd, *see* lǫverd.

lǫrdeship, *sb.*, OE. hlāfordscipe; *dominion, lordship*, 235, 27.

lǫrding, *see* lǫverding.

lǫrdshipe(n), *wkv.*, based on OE. hlāfordscipe, *sb.*; *have lordship over, rule*; *inf.* lǫrdship, 105, 11.

lǫre, OE. lār, *f.*; *lore, teaching*, 16. 19.

lǫre, *adj.*, based on OE. lār, *sb.*?; *learned*, 88, 4.

lǫren (lǫrn), *see* lēse(n).

Lōrn(e), *sb.*, *Lorne*; Jōhn of, 167, 9; 169, 6.

losīe(n), *wkv.*, Sth. = Ml. lose(n); OE. losian; *lose, be deprived of*; *pp.* ileosed (eSth.), 186, 24.

lost, *see* lust.

lōte, *sb.*, ON. lāt. læti, *n.*; *countenance, manner*, 30, 8; *pl.* lōten, 28, 2. Nth. lāt, 170, 9.

lōð, lōth, *adj.*, OE. lāð; *loath, unwelcome*, 19, 30; lōth, 78, 11.

lōþlī, *adj.*, OE. lāðlīc; *loathly, loathsome*, 62, 11. Sth. lōdlīch, 202, 33; *superl.* lōdlukest, 198, 32.

loud, *adj.*, OE. hlūd; *loud*, 48, 18.

lough, Lōuk, *see* lahhe(n), Lūc.

lōute(n), lōwte(n), *see* lūte(n).

lōvelīch, *adj.*, Sth. = Ml. luvlī; OE. luflīc; *lovely, handsome*, 230, 11.

lōvelǫnging, *sb.*, OE. lufu + langung (lǫngung); *love longing, desire of love*, 97, 30.

lǫve(n), *wkv.*, OE. lofian; *praise*;
eME. *inf.* lofenn (O), 9, 25; *pp.*
loved, 159, 5. Nth. *pt. pl.* lovyt,
175, 18.
lǫverd, lǫrd, *sb.*, OE. hláfweard;
lord, 14, 15; lǫrd, 25, 12; lǫrdę,
106, 28. Nth. *gs.* without ending,
lǫrde fēte, 132, 12. Sth. hláverd,
178, 24; Lhoaverd, 226, 1.
lǫverding, lǫrding, *sb.*, based on
lǫverd; *lording, lord, sir*; lǫverding,
80, 22; lǫrding, 42, 9.
lovīə, lovīynde, *see* luve(n).
lovynge, lovyng, *sb.*, OE. lofung,
f.; *praise, laudation*, 145, 23;
lovyng, 169, 4.
lovyt, *see* lǫve(n).
lowe, *sb.*, OE. hlǽw, hláw-hláwe;
cave, earlier *mound, hill*, 62, 11.
lowe(n), *wkv.*, based on OE. lāg <
ON. lāgr, 'low'; *make low*; *pt. sg.*
lowed, 103, 17.
lowe, lōwte, *see* lahhe(n), lūte(n).
Lowis, *sb.*, OF. Louis < Hlōðwīg;
Louis; Lowis of Bavēre, *Louis of
Bavaria*, 162, 9.
Lùc, Lùk, *sb.*, OF. Luc; *Luke*, 209,
19. Nth. Lōuk, 148, 1.
Lùcīe, *sb.*, OF. Lucie; *Lucy*; Seint,
229, 21.
lūde, *adv.*, OE. hlūde; *loudly, aloud*,
36, 28.
lufe(n), *see* luve(n).
lufrēdene, *sb.*, OM. lufrēden, WS.
lufrǽden, *f.*; *love, friendship*, 154,
12.
lufsum, *adj.*, OE. lufsum; *loveable,
lovely*, 192, 1; *superl.* lufsumest,
193, 24.
lufsumlīche, *adv.*, OE. lufsumlīce;
kindly, graciously, 193, 28.
lüfte, *sb.*, Sth. = Ml. lift; OE. lyft;
air; *ds.* lüfte, 178, 27.
luke, *see* lōke(n).
lüke(n), *stv.*, OM. lūcan-lēc (WS.
lēac) (2); *lock*; *inf.* lūken, 14, 13;
pr. 3 *sg.* lūkeð, 19, 15; *pt. sg.* lèk,
63, 21; *pt. pl.* luken, 189, 28; *pp.*
loken, 77, 32.
Lunden, *sb.*, OE. Lundon (-den);
London; *ds.* Lundene, 2, 8.

Lundenisc, -issc, *adj.*, OE. Lundenisc; *of London*; *wk.* Lundenisce, 2, 8; Lundenissce, 5, 32.
lūrdan, *sb.*, OF. lourdein; *lazy person*,
138, 2.
lurke, *wkv.*, perh. OE. *lūrcian, based
on *lūran; *lurk*; *pr. ppl.* lurkand,
168, 17.
lurnede, lurneþ, *see* lerne(n).
lurnīe(n), *see* lērne(n).
lüse(n), *wkv.*, Sth. = Ml. lēse(n);
WS. līesan (lȳsan); *release, deliver*;
pp. ilüisd, 180, 14. Cf. lēse(n).
lust, *sb.*, OE. lust; *desire, lust*, in
older sense of *pleasure*; lusst (O),
12, 16; lustę, 144, 10; *pl.* lòstes,
216, 28.
lüste(n), *see* liste(n), *listen*.
lüste(n), *wkv.*, OE. lystan; *be pleasing, delight*; *pt. sg.* lüst, 233, 30.
lüstni(n), *see* listne(n).
lüt, *see* līte.
lùte, *sb.*, OF. lut; *lute*, 237, 10.
lütel, *see* lītel.
lüte(n), lōute(n), lōwte(n), *stv.*,
OE. lūtan-lēat (2); *bow, incline the
head, worship*; *inf.* loūte, 53, 17;
lōwte, 145, 24; *pt. pl.* lutten, 25, 3.
lüþer, *see* lythyr.
lüðere, *adv.*, Sth. = Ml. liþere; OE.
lȳðer; *badly, terribly*, 194, 20.
lütle(n), *wkv.*, Sth. = Ml. lītlen,
litlen; OE. lȳtlian; *belittle*, 194,
23.
luve, *sb.*, OE. lufu; *love*, 4, 32.
luve(n), Sth. luvīe(n), *wkv.*, OE.
lufīan; *love*; *inf.* luven, 21, 6;
luve, 37, 7; *pr.* 3 *sg.* luveþ, 37, 6;
pt. sg. luvede, 7, 25; *pt. pl.* luveden,
4, 27; *pp.* luved, 8, 3. Nth. *pr. pl.*
lufes, 144, 2; *pt. pl.* lufit, 170, 18;
pp. lufde, 140, 1. Sth. (SEMl.)
inf. luvīen, 17, 27; luvīe, 47, 23;
pr. ppl. lòvīynde, 219, 27; *pr. sbj.*
sg. luvīe, 191, 20.
luxùrīe, *sb.*, OF., luxurie, luxure;
luxury, wantonness, 238, 2.
luytel, lȳche, *see* lītel, līk.
lȳe(n), *see* līe(n).
lȳenge, *sb.*, based on root of OAng.
lēgan, 'prevaricate'; *lying*, 147, 20.

GLOSSARY

lȳernie(n), lȳfe, see lērne(n), līf.
lȳge, lyghtlȳ, see līge, liȝtlȳ.
lyht, lȳke(n), see liht, līke(n).
lȳkne(n), wkv., OE. *līcnian, cf.
Swed. līkna; liken, make like, compare; inf. lȳkne, 224, 23.
lȳkynge, sb., OE. līcung, f.; liking,
pleasure, 117, 28.
lȳte, lȳtel, see līte, lītel.
lyþ, sb., OE. li‎ð; joint, limb, 50, 15.
lythyr, adj., OE. lȳðre; evil, bad,
111, 30. Sth. liþer, 207, 10.
lyttill, lȳve, see lītel, līf.
lȳun, sb., AN. liun, leun; lion, 48,
16. Cf. lēun.
lyve(n), see live(n).
lyvynge, sb., based on live(n); living,
condition of life, 120, 2.

M.

mā, adv., adj., eME., Nth. for mǭ;
OE. mā; more, 6, 3; comp. māre,
3, 30; mār, 5, 28; superl. mēst,
39, 25; māst, 132, 27. lNth. mair,
167, 16. Sth. superl. mēst, 176,
7; mǣste, 187, 30 (eSth.). Kt.
mēste, 216, 16. Cf. mǭ.
mā, mac, macod, see māke(n).
mad, adj., OE. (ge)mǣd; mad,
angry, 54, 27; madd, 110, 26.
made(n), mæi, see māke(n), may.
mæi(e), see may.
mǣre, adj., OE. mǣre; famous, illus-
trious, 188, 17.
mæssedæi, mǣst, see messedai, mā.
Magdalēn, sb., OF.?; Magdalene,
132, 11.
māȝe, sb., OM. mēge (māge), WS.
mǣge (māge); kinswoman, 177, 5.
māȝe, maȝȝ, see muge(n).
magt, maht, mahte, sb., OM. mæht,
WS. meaht. f.; might. power; magt,
20, 13 mahhte (O), 10, 15. Cf.
miȝt.
mahen, mäi, see muge(n).
mæi, may, sb., OE. mǣg, f. (?); maid,
earlier kinswoman?, 45, 7; may,
47, 8.

maid, see māke(n).
maiden, meiden, maide, sb., OE.
mægden; maiden; meiden, 14, 19;
maide, 36, 5; pl. maidenes, 36, 17.
Sth. meiden, 191, 19; gs. meidenes,
196, 24; gpl. maidene, 190, 26.
maig, see muge(n).
Mailrǭs, sb., Mailros, 223, 3.
maine, sb., OE. mægen, mægn;
might, main, 138, 26.
mainē, meynē, mēnȝē, sb., OF.
maisnee, mainee; household, re-
tainers, 46, 14; meynē, 57, 10;
mēnȝe, 137, 4; mēnȝhē, 167, 30.
mainlēs, adj., OE. mægenlēas; power-
less, 17, 5.
maintēne(n), wkv., OF. maintenir;
aid, maintain; inf. maintēne, 158,
20.
mair, see mā.
mair, sb., OF. maire; mayor, 233, 2.
mairaltee, sb., OF. mairaltē; mayor-
alty, office of mayor, 232, 24.
maister, mayster, maystir, sb., OF.
maistre: master, 54, 28; mayster,
139, 30; maystir, 136, 25. Sth.
meister, 198, 6.
maistrīe, maistrī, sb., OF. maistrīe;
mastery, lordship, dominion, 206,
32. Nth. maistrī, 148, 16.
mak, māke, sb., OE. (ge)maca;
equal, mate, companion, 129, 18.
māke(n), eME. maken, Sth.
makīe(n), wkv., OE. macian; make,
do; inf. māken, 17, 19; pr. 3 sg.
mākeð, 14, 11; pr. ppl. mākand,
101, 8; pt. sg. makede (eME.), 2,
4; makod (eME.), 2, 23; maket
(eME.), 5, 3; mākede, 36, 20;
māde, 21, 12; pt. 2 sg. mākedest,
38, 28; mādest, 56, 14; pt. pl.
makeden (eME.), 7, 19; māden,
56, 24; māde, 204, 26; pp. maked
(eME.), 2, 28; māked, 34, 23;
mād, 117, 17. Nth. inf. māke,
129, 4; māk, 129, 5; pr. 3 sg. mās,
108, 24; (lNth.) pt. sg. maid, 167,
19. Sth. inf. makīen (eSth.), 190,
28; makeȝe (eSth.), 184, 18;
mākīen, 226, 12; imp. pl. mākīeð,
202, 19; pr. ppl. mākand, 101, 8;

pp. imāked, 226, 12; imād, 61, 7; ymad, 203, 23.

Malduit, *sb.*, Malduit; *Malduit or Mauduit*; William, 4, 22.

malisūn, *sb.*, AN. maleisun, malisun; *malediction*, 77, 29.

man, *see* mun(e).

man, mon, *sb.*, OE. man (mǫn); *man*, 2, 27; mon, 43, 28; *gs.* mannes, 3, 16; *ds.* manne, 11, 17; *pl.* men, 1, 16; *gpl.* manne (eME.), 14, 20. **Nth.** man, 127, 22; manę, 145, 28; *gs.* mans, 137, 19; *gpl.* men, 147, 13; mens, 147, 25. **eSth.** *as.* monne, 203, 2; *gpl.* monnes, 185, 13; monnen, 185, 31; *dpl.* monnen, 185, 27.

man, me, *indef. prn.*, OE. man, *sb.*; *one, some*; mann (O), 10, 11; me, 2, 22; men, 87, 9.

man, *see* mune(n).

mān, *sb.*, eME., **Nth.** = Ml. mǭn; OE. gemāna; *companionship, marriage, intercourse*, 192, 17.

manās, *sb.*, OF. manace, menace; *menace*, 94, 32.

manāsinge, *sb.* and *pr. ppl.*, OF. menacier, manacier; *menacing, threat*; *pl.* manasinges, 159, 1.

Manassēn, *sb.*, Lat. *as.* Manassen; *Manasseh*, 24, 23.

māne, *sb.*, **Nth.** = Ml. mǫne; OE. *mane, *mǣne, cf. mǣnan; *moan, complaint*, 165, 8.

maneir, *see* manēre.

manękȳndę, mankȳndę, *sb.*, OE. *mancynd; *mankind*, 145, 15; mankȳnde, 242, 3.

manēr(e), *sb.*, OF. maniere; *manner, sort, kind of*, 64, 21; *pl.* manērs, 92, 14. **lNth.** maneir, 173, 8; manēr, 222, 17.

manheid, *sb.*, **Nth.** = Ml. manhędę; OE. *manhǣd, *f.*; *manhood*, 173, 11.

manī, maniӡ, *adj.*, OE. manig, mǫnig; *many*, 3, 13; maniӡ (O), 9, 8; manīe a, 32, 8; *pl.* manīe, 4, 25; manīge, 25, 20. **eSth.** *gs.* manīes, 177, 12; in menȳe = Lat. in multis, *in general*, 221, 9.

manifǣldlīc, *adj.*, eME. = Ml. manī-

fǫldlī; OM. manigfā̆ldlīc, WS. -feald-; *manifold, numerous*, 5, 3.

maniӡe, *see* manī.

mankę, *sb.*, OE. mancus; *mancus, eighth of a pound*, 178, 14.

mankin, *sb.*, OE. manncynn; *mankind*; mannkinne nēde (O) = OE. manncynna nēd, *need of mankind*, 11, 7; mankin, 18, 27; mankinnę, 56, 2. **Sth.** monciin, 184, 3.

manlȳ, *adv.*, OE. mannlīce; *manfully, boldly*, 112, 22.

maune, *see* man.

manrēd, *sb.*, OM. manrēden, WS. -rǣden; *homage*, 2, 28; manrēdę, 79, 23.

mantel, *sb.*, OF. mantel; *mantel*, 229, 8.

manȳfāldę, *adj.*, **Nth.** = Ml. manīfǫld; *manifold*, 137, 20.

manȳwhat, *indef. prn.*, OE. manig + hwæt; *many things*, 89, 9.

mār, *see* mā.

marcat, *see* market.

marchal, *see* marescal.

marchand, *sb.*, OF. marchand; *merchant*, 106, 26; marchandę, 107, 10.

marchaundȳe, *see* marchaundȳse.

marchaundȳse, *sb.*, OF. marchandise; *merchandise*, 120, 18; *new sg.* marchaundȳe, 95, 22.

Māre, māre, *see* **Mārīe**, mā.

marescal, marchal, *sb.*, OF. marescal; *marshal*, 227, 4; marchal, 230, 31.

marӡen, *see* morwen.

Mārīe, **Māre**, *sb.*, OF. Marie; *Mary*, 14, 19; *gs.* without ending Mārīe dǫle, 201, 22. **Nth.** Māre, 131, 9.

Māriuӡ, *sb.*, Lat. Marius; *Marius, mythical king of Britain*, 220, 18.

market, marcat, *sb.*, OE. market; *market*, 120, 25. **Sth.** *ds.* marcatte, 212, 7.

marre(n), *wkv.*, OM. merran, WS. mierran; *hinder, waste, mar*; *pt. pl.* marryd, 112, 24.

marter, martir, *see* martyr.

Martha, **Marthe**, *sb.*, Lat. **Martha**; *Martha*, 132, 13; Marthe, 201, 20; *gs.* Marthe, 201, 30.

Martin, *sb.*, OF. Martin ; *Martin*, abbot of St. Neot's, I, 11.

martir, martyr, *sb.*, OE. martyr (L) ; *martyr*, martir, 191, 23 ; marter, 116, 16 ; *pl.* martyrs, 3, 5.

mās, *see* **māke(n)**.

masse, *sb.*, OE. mæsse ; *mass*, 51, 6.

massedæi, māst, *see* **messedai, mā**.

mast, *sb.*, OE. mæst; *mast (of a ship)*, 86, 25.

master, *wkv.*, **Nth.** = Ml. maistre(n) ; OF. maistrer ; *master* ; *pt. sg.* masterit, 172, 31.

matēr, *sb.*, OF. matere ; *matter*, 129, 3.

matines, *sb.pl.*, OF. matines; *matins, morning service*, 51, 6.

matremoyne, *sb.*, OF. matrimoine; *matrimony*, 147, 20.

maugrē, mawgrē, *prep.*, OF. maugrē ; *in spite of* ; mawgrē, 136, 30 ; maugrē his, *in spite of him*, 137, 11.

maumet, mawmet, *sb.*, OF. Mahomet; *mahomet*, then *idol*, 141, 27; mawmet, 192, 4.

maumetrȳ, mawmetrȳ, *sb.*, based on maumet; *idolatry*, 135, 9; *pl.* mawmetrȳse, 145, 12.

mawgrē, *see* **maugrē**, *prep.*

mawgrē, *sb.*, OF. maugrē ; *ill-will, displeasure, evil*, 159, 2.

mawmet, *see* **maumet**.

mawmetrȳ, mawmetrȳse, *see* **maumetrȳ**.

Maximian, *sb.*, Lat. Maximianus; *Maximian*, 192, 3.

Maximus, *sb.*, Lat. Maximus ; *Maximus*, 221, 12.

may, mayht, *see* **mai, muge(n)**.

may, *sb.*, OE. mæg ; *relative, kinsman*, 153, 21. **Sth.** mei, 177, 5 ; mæi, 183, 12 (eSth.) ; *ds.* mæie, 184, 16.

mayle, *sb.*, OF. maile ; *coat of mail*, 112, 24.

mayn, *sb.*, OE. mægen; *force, strength, power*, 41, 2.

maynteigne(n), *wkv.*, OF. maintenir; *maintain* ; *inf.* meynteigne, 233, 30 ; *pp.* maynteigned, 234, 1. Cf. **maintēne(n)**.

mayster, maystir, *see* **maister**.

me, mē (mee), *see* **man, ic**.

me, *adv. conj.*, cf. OFris. MDu. men; *but*, 194, 6.

Mearch = March, *sb.*, OF. March, Mars; *March*, 197, 9.

medcyn, *see* **medecīne**.

mēde, *sb.*, OE. mēd, *f.* ; *reward*, 10, 28.

mēde, *sb.*, OM. *mēde, WS. mæde ; *meadow, mead*, 35, 14.

medecīne, *sb.*, OF. medicine ; *medicine*; medcyn, 143, 13.

meete(n), *see* **mēte(n)**.

mei, *see* **may, muge(n)**.

meiden, *see* **maiden**.

meister, meit, *see* **maister, mēte(n)**.

meiðhād, *sb.*, OE. mægðhād ; *virginity*, 192, 17.

mēk, *adj.*, ON. miukr ; *meek* ; mēkę, 92, 16. **eSth.** meok, 195, 13.

mēkelīch, mēkelȳ, *see* **mēklȳ**.

mēke(n), *wkv.*, OM. *mēcan ?, cf. ON. miukr, 'meek'; *make meek*; *pt. sg.* mēked, 96, 23.

mēkenesse, *see* **mēknes**.

mekil(l), *see* **micel**.

mēklȳ, *adv.*, based on mēk ; *meekly*, 96, 30; mēkęlȳ, 146, 30. **Sth.** mēkęlīch, 236, 8.

mēknes, mēkęnesse, *sb.*, based on mēk ; *meekness*, 100, 6; mēkęnesse, 236, 28.

mekyll, *see* **micel**.

mēl, *sb.*, OM. mēl, WS. mæl ; *time, occasion, meal*, 21, 16.

mēld, *wkv.*, **Nth.** = Ml. melde(n); OE. meldian, mēldian ; *declare, accuse* ; **Nth.** *inf.* mēld, 155, 31.

melle(n), *wkv.*, OE. medler, meller; *mix, mingle, meddle*; **Sth.** *pp.* imelled, 221, 24 ; ymelled, 223, 10.

mellyng, *sb.*, based on OF. meller; *mingling*, 224, 13.

membre, *sb.*, OF. membre; *member*, 232, 21. **Nth.** *pl.* membris, 139, 24.

memorīe, *sb.*, OF. memorie; *memory, remembrance*, 119, 2.

menāce(n), *wkv.*, OF. menacier ; *menace, threaten* ; *inf.* menācen, 104, 25.

mēnd, *wkv.*, **Nth.** = Ml. mēnde(n); OF. amender; *correct, amend, aid,* 139, 10.

mēne(n), *wkv.*, OF. mener; *manage, urge on; behave, act;* **Nth.** *pp.* mēnd, 158, 13.

mēne(n), *wkv.*, OE. mǣnan; *mean; indicate, signify; moan, complain; pr.* 1 *sg.* mēne, 20, 21; *pr.* 3 *sg.* mēneþþ (O), 9, 3. **Nth.** *pr.* 3 *sg.* mēnes, 83, 10; *pt. sg.* mēnyt, *moaned,* 167, 12; ment, 156, 16.

mēnes, *sb. pl.*, AN. meien, OF. moien, *adj.*, 'mean, middle'; *means, intermediary,* 236, 10.

mēnȝē, mēnȝhē, *see* mainē.

mennissk, *adj.*, ON. menskr, cogn. with OE. mennisc; *human; wk.* mennisske (O), 12. 4.

menske, *sb.*, ON. mennska; *dignity, honor,* 194, 32.

menske(n), *wkv.*, ON. menska, *sb.*, cogn. with OE. mennisc; *dignify, honor;* **Nth.** *pr.* 3 *sg.* menskes, 129, 27.

ment, menȳ, *see* mēne(n), manī.

mēnynge, *sb.*, OE. *mǣnung, f.*; *meaning;* tō mēnynge, *in meaning,* 222, 28.

mēok, merācle, *see* mēk, mirācle.

merc, *sb.*, OAng. merce, WS. mierce; *mark,* 130, 17.

mercēr, *sb.*, OF. mercier; *mercer,* 198, 28.

mercerȳe, *sb.*, OF. mercerie; *mercery, company of mercers or cloth merchants,* 232, 21.

mercī, mercȳe, *sb.*, OF.merci; *mercy, thanks,* 25, 24; mercȳe, 154, 27.

mercīāble, *adj.*, OF. merciable; *merciful, having mercy,* 104, 23.

mercīful, *adj.*, OF. merci + ME. ful; *merciful,* 104, 17.

Mercii, *sb.*, Lat. Mercii; *Mercians,* 225, 21.

mercȳe, *see* mercī.

mere, *sb.*, OAng. *merre, allied to merran, WS. mierran, 'hinder'; *hindrance,* 128, 17.

merīe, merȳ, *see* mirīe.

Merlin, *sb.*, *Merlin,* 191, 13.

merre(n), *wkv.*, OE. merran; *mar, injure; pr.* 3 *sg.* merriδ, 194, 32.

mersuīnę, *sb.*, OE. mereswin; *sea-pig, porpoise, dolphin,* 151, 27.

merveyle, mervayl, *sb.*, OF. merveille; *marvel,* 90, 19; mervayl, 65, 17.

merȳ, *see* mirīe.

mes, *sb.*, OF. mes; *mess, course at table, feast; pl.* mes, 57, 4.

meschēf, mischēf, *sb.*, OF. meschief; *mischief, trouble;* mischēfę, 118, 3; *pl.* meschēvys, 136, 28. lNth. mischeif, 169, 15.

mēsellfenn, mēself, *see* self.

messāge, *sb.*, OF. message; *message; errand, embassy;* messāge, 206, 6.

messagēr, messanğēr, *sb.*, OF. messager; *messenger; pl.* messagēres, 96, 9; messangērys, 106, 1.

messe, *sb.*, OE. mæsse, messe; *mass,* 9, 2. Cf. **masse.**

messebōc, messebōk, *sb.*, OE. mæssebōc, messebōc; *mass book, missal,* 9, 2; messebōk, 76, 26.

messedai, *sb.*, OE. mæsse (messe) dæg; *massday, as.* 1, 12; massedæi, 1, 19.

messegēre, *sb.*, OF. messe + ON. gervi; *mass garments, things pertaining to the mass,* 76, 24.

messesǫng, *sb.*, OE. mæsse (messe) sǫng; *song of the mass,* 34, 19.

messinge, *sb.*, OF. mes + ME. -inge; *messing, eating together,* 215, 22.

mēst, *see* mā.

mestēr, mistēr, mysteir, *sb ,* OF. mestier; *office, trade, occupation, need, necessity;* mistēr, 139, 10. lNth. it is nā mysteir, *there is no need,* 170, 24.

mēsūre, *sb.*, OF. mesure; *measure,* 147, 16.

mēte, mēt, *sb.*, OE. mete; *meat,* 16, 11: *pl.* mēten, 22, 15. **Nth.** mēt, 171, 3.

mēte(n), *wkv.*, OE. mētan; *meet; inf.* meete, 239, 21; *pr. sbj. sg.* mēte, 138, 20; *pt. sg.* mette, 66, 5; *pt. pl.* mettin, 60, 27; mett, 112, 22. lNth. *inf.* meit = mēt. 170, 2.

mẹte(n), *wkv.*, OE. gemǣtan ; *dream*; *pt. sg.* mette, 227, 12.

mẹte(n), *stv.*, OE. metan–mæt (5) ; *measure, mete*; *pt. sg.* mette, 128, 18.

mẹpynkyþ, *see* þinke(n).

mett, *sb.*, OE. met ; *measure*, 147, 15.

mett, mette, mettin, *see* mẹte(n).

mẹtyng, *sb.*, OE. mǣting, *f.* ; *dream*, 228, 26.

mẹtyng, *sb.*, OE. mētung ; *meeting*, 175, 8.

meynē, *see* mainē.

meynteigne(n), *see* maynteigne(n).

mī, mȳ, *see* mīn.

micel, mycel, michel, miche, mòche, *adj., adv.*, OE. mycel ; *much, great, large* ; mycel (eME.), 4, 12 ; michel, 38, 9 ; michil, 26, 14 ; michelę, 64, 2 ; miche, 65, 17 ; myche, 125, 20 ; mòche, 92, 11 ; **Nth.** (NEMl.) mikell (O), 8, 21 ; mikil, 52, 12 ; mekyll, 112, 20 ; mykelę, 124, 9 ; mikel, 149, 28 ; mekil, 135, 3. **Sth.** müchel, 176, 12 ; *ds.* müchele, 179, 3 ; *fds.* müclere, 185, 11 ; müchelere, 188, 4 ; müche, 181, 23.

Michelmasse, *sb.*, OF. Michael + mæsse ; *Michaelmas*, 209, 19.

mid, midę, mit, *prep. adv.*, OE. mid ; *with*, 1, 6 ; midę, 15, 28 ; mit, 14, 11.

middæi, *sb.*, OE. middæg ; *midday*, 1, 16.

middel, *sb.*, OE. middel ; *middle*, *ds.* midle, 182, 15.

middelērd, *see* midelērd.

middelnicht, *adj.*, OE. middelniht ; *midnight*, 82, 19.

middenẹard, *sb.*, **eSth.** = Ml. middenẹrd ; OE. middaneard ; *middle dwelling, earth*, 180, 18.

mide, *see* mid.

midelērd, *sb.*, OE. *mīddel geard, cf. middan (mid) geard ; *mid-dwelling, abode of man, earth*, 157, 15. **eSth.** middelǣrd, 184, 22.

midewintre, midwinter, *sb.*, OE. middewinter ; *midwinter* ; mide-

wintre dæi, *Christmas day*, 2, 10; midwinter, 7, 31.

midsīde, *sb.*, OE. mid + sīde ; *midside, middle of the side*, 61, 15.

midwinter, *see* midewintre.

Miʒhēl, *sb.*, Lat. Michael, OE. Michahel ; *Michael*, 67, 19.

miʒt, miʒht, myght, *sb.*, OM. mæht, miht, WS. meaht, miht ; *might* ; miʒht, 55, 13 ; myght, 106, 22 ; *pl.* miʒtis, 51, 18 ; myʒtes, 103, 10.

miʒtful, mihtful, *sb.*, ME. miʒt + ful ; *mighty*, 101, 22 ; mihtful, 153, 21.

mightī, *adj.*, OAng. mæhtig, WS. mihtig ; *mighty*, 136, 1.

migte, *see* muge(n).

mihte, mihhte, *see* muge(n).

mihtful, *see* miʒtful.

mikell, mikyll, *see* micel.

milce, *sb.*, OE. milds, milts, *f.* ; *mercy*, 1, 4 ; 176, 8.

mildę, *adj.*, OE. milde ; *mild*, 2, 27 ; *comp.* mȳlder, 92, 17.

mīldelī, mīldelīke, mȳldelȳ, *adv.*, OE. mildelīce, mīldelīce ; *mildly*, 18, 10 ; mȳldelȳ, 97, 25 ; mīldelī, 151, 2.

mīldnes, *sb.*, OE. *mildenes ; *mercy, mildness*, 102, 30.

mīle, *sb.*, OE. mīl, *f.* ; *mile* ; *long time*, 38, 1.

milk, *sb.*, OE. meoluc, milc ; *milk*, 84, 23.

mīn, mī, mȳ, *pos. prn.*, OE. mīn ; *mine*, 8, 13 ; mī, 38, 30 ; mȳ, 52, 18. **eSth.** minne < mīne, 184, 12, *fds.* mīre < mīnre, 182, 4.

mīnde, *adj.*, OE. *gemynde, mȳnde ; *mindful, minded*, 56, 3.

ministre, *sb.*, OF. ministre ; *minister* ; *pl.* mynystyrs, 147, 17 ; *pl.* ministris, 105, 13.

minne, minstre, *see* mīn, mynstre.

minte(n), *wkv.*, OE. myntan ; *think, intend* ; *pt. sg.* mint, 4, 20.

mirācle, eME. miracle, *sb.*, OF. miracle ; *miracle* ; miracle, 5, 3 ; mirācle, 80, 7 ; myrācle, 99, 30. **Nth.** merācle, 131, 31.

mīre, *see* mīn.

mīre, *sb.*, OE. mȳre; *mire*, 164, 31.

mire3þe, myrthe, *sb.*, OE. myrhþ, *f.*; *mirth*, 43, 12; myrthe, 110, 30. Sth. mürhðe, 180, 32; mürðe, 194, 32; *pl.* mürhðen, 196, 17.

mirīe, merīe, merȳ, *adj.*, OE. myrige; *merry, pleasant*, 57, 14; merīe (Kt.?), 245, 22; merȳ, 110, 28. Sth. mürȳe, 244, 15.

mirke, mirk, *adj.*, OE. myrce, ON. myrkr; *dark, murky*, 16, 16; mirk, 77, 7.

mirknes, *sb.* ON. myrkr, cogn. with OE. mirce + ME. -nes; *murkiness, darkness*, 150, 19.

mis, *see* mysse(n).

mischēfe, mischeif, *see* meschēf.

misdēde, Sth. misdēde, *sb.*, OM. misdēd, WS. misdǣd, *f.*; *misdeed*, 21, 9; *pl.* misdēdes, 18, 13. Sth. misdēde, 180, 10.

misdō(n), *anv.*, OE. misdōn; *do amiss, misdo*; *inf.* misdōn, 2, 4; *pt. pl.* mysdēde, 97, 2. Sth. *pt. pl.* misdüde, 179, 10; *pp.* misdō, 206, 30.

miseise, *sb.*, OF. mesaise; *misease, trouble*, 202, 27.

mīself, *see* self.

mislēve(n), *wkv.*, based on OM. lēvan, WS. līevan; *discredit, disbelieve*; *pp.* mislēved, 199, 13.

mislīch, *adj.*, OE. mislīc; *wanting in likeness, miserable* (?), 194, 28.

mislīche(n), *wkv.*, Sth. = Ml. mislīke(n); OE. mislīcian; *dislike, be displeasing*; *pr. 3 sg.* mislīcheð, 176, 13.

miss, *see* mysse.

mist, *sb.*, OE. mist; *mist*, 16, 20. eSth. *ds.* miste, 176, 18.

mistāke(n), *wkv.*, ON. mistaka -tōk (6); *mistake*; *pp.* mistākin, 156, 24.

miste, *see* mist.

mistēr, mysteir, *see* mestēr.

mit, *see* mid.

mīþe(n), *stv.*, OE. mīðan-mað (1); *avoid, conceal*; *inf.* mīþe, 84, 32.

mix, *sb.* as *adj.*, OE. meox, mix; *dunghill*, 194, 25.

mǭ, *adv., adj.*, OE. mā, *adv.*; *more*, 32, 17; *comp.* mǭr, 1, 7; *superl.* mǭst, 29, 8; ðe mǭste, *the greatest*, 19, 2; mǭǭst, 232, 19. eSth. *comp.* moare = mǭre, 226, 5. Cf. mā.

mǭbill, mǭbyll, *adj.*, OF. moble, older mueble, moeble; *moveable*, 147, 24; as *sb. pl.* mǭbylls, 147, 28.

moche, *see* micel.

mōd, *sb.*, OE. mōd; *courage, pride*, 18, 10; mood, 227, 21; *ds.* mōde (eSth.), 181, 11.

mōder, *sb.*, OE. mōdor; *mother*, 7, 8; mooder, 241, 2; mōdur, 128, 28; mōdyre, 146, 25; *gs.* mōder, 220, 16; moodres, 240, 33.

mōdī, *see* mōdȳ.

mōdī3nesse, *sb.*, OE. mōdignes, *f.*; *courage, pride*, 9, 25.

Mōdrēd, *sb.*, OF. Mordret in Wace; *Modred*, 181, 18; *gs.* Mōdrēdis, 182, 5; *ds.* Mōdrēde, 181, 3; Mōdrēd, 184, 3.

mōdur, *see* mōder.

mōdȳ, mōdī, *adj.*, OE. mōdig; *brave, proud*, MnE. *moody*, 48, 1; mōdī, 192, 3.

mōdyre, *see* mōder.

moge (moghte, moht), *see* muge(n).

mōlde, mōld, *sb.*, OE. mōlde; *ground, earth, mould*, 68, 12.

mon, mōn, *see* man, mōne.

monoün, *see* mankin.

mōne, mōn, *sb.*, OE. mōna; *moon*, 1, 15. Nth. mōn, 150, 23.

mǭne, *sb.*, OE. *māne, *mǣne, cf. mǣnan, *wkv.*; *moan*, 58, 14.

monē, *sb.*, OF. moneie; *money*, 162, 31.

monek, *see* munec.

mone(n), *see* mune(n).

mōneliht, *sb.*, OE. mōna + lēoht; *moonlight*, 81, 9.

mōneð, moneþ, *sb.*, OE. mōneð; *month*, 197, 9; *pl.* mōneð, 34, 15; mōneþ, 228, 22.

monk, monke, *see* munec.

monne(n), *see* man.

mōntance, mōuntōuns, *sb.*, OF. montance, AN. muntance; *amount*, 245, 2; mōuntouns, 94, 30.

monument, *sb.*, OF. monument;
monument, 143, 9.

monweored, *sb.*, OE. mannwerod;
band of men; *ds.* monweorede,
189, 8.

mood, mooder, *see* mōd, mōder.

moote, mǫǫst, *see* mōt, mǫ.

mōr, *sb.*, OE. mōr; *moor, waste land*;
1Nth. murę, 169, 22. Sth. *pl.*
mōren, 182, 11.

mǫr(e), *see* mǫ.

moreȝe, moreghen, *see* morwen.

moreȝentīde, moretīde, *sb.*, OE.
morgentīde; *morning, morrow*, 39,
28; moretīd, 39, 16.

moreyn, *sb.*, OF. morine; *murrain,
plague*, 224, 26.

morn, *see* morwen.

mōrne(n), *wkv.*, OE. murnan; *mourn;*
pt. sg. mōrned, 106, 13. Cf.
murne(n).

mornyng, *sb.*, based on OE. morgen;
morning, 103, 4.

mōrnyng, *sb.*, OE. murnung; *mourning*, 92, 1.

Morrē, *sb.*, *Moray*, 158, 26.

Mortęmēr, *sb.*, OF. Mortemer (-en
-Brai); *Mortimer*; Roger, *sixth
Baron Wigmore*, 227, 7.

morð, *sb.*, OE. morð; *death, destruction*, 184, 23.

morwe(n), moreȝe, morn, *sb.*, OE.
morgen; *morning, morrow*, 29, 17;
moreȝe, 40, 15; morn, 49, 26;
marȝen, 181, 7; moreghen, 212, 3;
morghen, 212, 16.

morweslēp, *sb.*, OM. morgen + slēp;
morning sleep, 57, 14.

mǫst, mōste, *see* mǫ, mōt.

mōt, *ptprv.*, OE. mōt–mōste; *may,
must*; *pr. sg.* mōt, 9, 14; mootę,
241, 20; *pr. pl.* mōtenn (O), 13, 23;
mōte, 42, 24; *pr. sbj. sg.* mōte, 13,
31; *pr. sbj. pl.* mōten, 232, 11; *pt.
sg.* mōste, 4, 20; mōst, 53, 17;
pr. 2 sg. mǫstist, 51, 7.

mǫucte, mouhte, mǫun, *see* muge(n).

mǫuntein, *sb.*, QF. montaigne; *mountain*, 101, 14.

mōuntǫuns, *see* mōntance.

mōuþe, mōwe(n), *see* mūþ, muge(n).

mowe(n), *stv.*, OE. māwan–mēow
(R); *mow, cut down*; *inf.* mowen,
176, 22.

mōwne, *see* muge(n).

mōwþe, *see* mūþ.

Mōysēs, *sb.*, OE. Mōysēs < Lat.;
Moses, 104, 22.

müche, müchel(e),   müclere,
müchelere, *see* micel.

müchele(n), *wkv.*, Sth. = Ml. mikel-
le(n); OE. myclian; *enlarge, increase*; *inf.* müchelin, 194, 31.

muge(n), *ptprv.*, OM. *mugan-
mæhte, mihte (WS. meahte, mihte);
have power, be able, MnE. *may,
might*; *inf.* mugen, 22, 26; *pr.* 1,
3 *sg.* mai, 3, 20; maȝȝ (O), 9, 10;
maig, 16, 5; *pr. 2 sg.* mayht, 84, 21;
pr. pl. māȝe, 41, 26; muȝe, 176, 23;
mahen, 191, 18; muwen, 198, 29;
mōwen, 52, 23; mǫuwe, 51, 21;
mōwe, 76, 29; mōun, 78, 31; mōw,
88, 13; mōwnę, 105, 25; *pr. sbj.
sg.* muge, 17, 19; *pt.* 1, 3 *sg.* mihte,
1, 7; myhte, 3, 17; mihhte (O), 8,
21; migte, 14, 17; micte, 75, 8;
moucte, 75, 18; mouhte, 76, 13; *pt.*
2 *sg.* miȝte, 38, 8; miȝt, 43, 16;
myhtes, 3, 25; miȝtest, 43, 12;
mihtest, 183, 6; *pt. pl.* muhten, 6,
8; miȝtten, 227, 25; *pt. sbj. sg.*
muhte, 200, 7. Nth. *pt. sg.* might,
142, 6; mycht, 166, 13; moht, 152,
28; *pt. pl.* moghte, 144, 22. Sth.
pr. 1, 3 *sg.* mei, 176, 16.

müln, *sb.*, Sth. = Ml. miln (mill);
OE. mylen, myln; *mill*; *ds.* mülne,
201, 1.

multiplīe(n), *wkv.*, OF. multiplier;
multiply, prosper; *inf.* multiplīen,
100, 21.

mun, *see* mune(n).

mūnd, *sb.*, OE. mund, mūnd, *f.*; *protector*, 184, 22.

münde, *sb.*, Sth. = Ml. mīnde; OE.
(ge)mynde (mȳnde); *memory, mind*,
199, 1.

muneo, munek, monek, monk, OE.
munuc (-ec); *monk*; mǫnek, 206,
6; mǫnkę, 111, 25; munk, 154, 1;
pl. muneces, 1, 2; munekes, 4,

1 ; mónkes, 75, 22 ; mónękes, 78, 1.

münechene, *sb.*, OE., mynecen, *f.*; *nun*, 188, 27.

mune(n), *ptprv.*, OE. gemunan, munan–munde ; *remember, think of* ; *inf.* móne, *remind*, 55, 12 ; *pr.* 3 *sg.* muneð, 32, 25 ; *pr. sbj. sg.* mune, 33, 6. Nth. *pr. pl.* mun, 158, 32 ; man, 170, 19.

munk, *see* munec.

Muntfort, *sb.*, OF. Mundford ; *Montfort*, Sīmōn of, 227, 2 ; Perres of, 227, 6.

mürcðɔ, murę, *see* mireȝþə, mōr.

murk̄ðen, murkðe, murðe, *see* mireȝþe.

murne(n),*wkv.*,OE.murnan; *mourn*; *inf.* murnen, 21, 17. Nth. *pr. ppl.* murnand, 133, 7. Cf. mōrne(n).

murrē,*sb.*,OF. moree; *dark red, mulberry color*, 231, 25.

mürȳe, *see* mirīe.

mūþ, moūþ, mōwþ, *sb.*, OE. mūð ; *mouth*, 13, 27 ; moūþę, 102, 19; mōwthę, 120, 5 ; mōwþe, 120, 7. eSth. *ds.* mūðe, 197, 14.

muwen, *see* muge(n).

mȳ, *see* mīn.

mycel, myche(l), *see* micel.

mychelnes, *sb.*, OE. micelness, *f. greatness*, 101, 28.

mycht, *see* muge(n).

myddel, *adj.*, OE. midla ; *middle*, 224, 11.

myght, myȝt, muhte, *see* miȝt, muge(n).

mykele, mykyle, *see* micel.

mȳldelȳ, *see* mīldelīke.

mȳlder, *see* mīlde.

myne(n),*wkv.*,OE. mynian, mynnan; *have in mind, think upon* ; Nth. *inf.* myn, 129, 30.

mynstre, minster, *sb.*, OE. mynster; *minster*, 1, 3 ; minster, 7, 27.

mynystyr, *see* ministre.

myrācle, *see* mirācle.

myrthe, *see* mireȝþe.

mys,*adv.*,ON.mis;*badly,amiss*,52,14.

myschaunce, *sb.*, OF. mescheance ; *mischance, ill-fortune*, 91, 22.

myscheif, *see* meschēf.

mysdēde, *see* misdō(n).

mȳselve, *see* self.

mysęse, *sb.*, OF. misaise ; *misease, trouble*, 118, 4. Cf. miseise.

myssawe, *sb.*, OE. *missagu or new cpd. ; *evil speaking*, 146, 29.

mysse, mis, *sb.*, ON. missa; *loss, privation*, 110, 30. Nth. mis, 139, 5.

mysse(n), *wkv.*, OE. missan; *miss* ; *inf.* mysse, 232, 10. Nth. *inf.* mis, 165, 13.

mysseye(n), *wkv.*, OM. *missecgan or new cpd. ; *speak evil of, slander*; *pp.* mysseyd, 97, 6.

mysteir, *see* mestēr.

mysŭse(n), *wkv.*, OF. mesuser ; *misuse* ; *pp.* mysused, 235, 20.

mȳtred, *adj.*, OF. mitre + OE. -ed(e); *mitred*, 229, 30.

N.

nā, *see* nān.

na, *adv.*, OE. nā, by shortening; *no*, 70, 32.

naam, *see* nime(n).

nabbe(n), *see* nảve(n).

nāciōn, *sb.*, OF. nacion(un); *nation*, 133, 31.

nadre, nēvre, *see* neddre, nęvre.

nafd, naght, *see* naht, nảve(n).

naȝle(n), nayle(n), *wkv.*, OE. næglian ; *nail* ; *pp.* naȝȝledd (O), 12, 7 ; nayled, 60, 11.

naht, *adv.*, OE. nāwiht, nāht (naht); *naught, not*, 2, 6 ; naght, 97, 8 ; nat, 97, 31 ; nauȝt, 100, 16. eSth. nawiht, 193, 23; nawt, 193, 17. Cf. noht.

nai, nay, *adv.*, ON. nei, cogn. with OE. nā ; *nay, no*, 25, 13 ; nay, 107, 5.

nāked, *adj.*, OE. nacod ; *naked*, 16, 23 ; nākit, *p.* 292.

nalde, nām, *see* wille(n), nāme.

nam, *see* nime(n).

nāme, nome, eME. name, *sb.*, OE. nama ; *name*, 13, 26. eSth. nome, 191, 17. Nth. nām, 134, 24.

nāmelȳ, nāmelīc, *adv.*, OE. nama + ME. lȳ; *namely, by name*, 91, 3. Nth. nāmelīc, 148, 4.

nāmen, *see* nime(n).

namōre, namoọre, *adv.*, OE. nā + māra; *no more, not at all*, 38, 19 ; namoọre, 239, 22.

nān, nā, *adj. prn.*, eME., Nth. = Ml. nọn ; OE. nān ; *none, no*, 1, 7 ; nā, 2, 22 ; *gs.* nāness, 12, 32. eSth. *as.* nānne, 179, 30 ; nenne, 200, 20.

narwe, naᵣeu, narow, *adj.*, OE. nearu; *narrow, confined, small*, 17, 7 ; nareu, 3, 12 ; narow, 222, 13.

nas, *see* bē(n).

nat, nāt, *see* naht, wite(n).

natheleẹs, *adv.*, OE. nā þȳ (þē) lǣs; *nevertheless*, 243, 17.

naþemọ, *adv.*, OE. nā ðȳ (ðē) mā ; *no more*, 206, 25.

nāþing, *prn.*, Nth. = Ml. nọþing ; OE. nān ðing ; *nothing*, 150, 29.

nauȝt, *see* naht.

nāve(n), *wkv.*, OE. nabban < ne habban ; *not to have*. Nth. *pt. sg.* nafd, 155, 6. Sth. *pr.* 2 *sg.* navest (eSth.), 194, 10 ; *pr.* 3 *sg.* nafð (eSth.), 180, 12 ; nāveð, 200, 25 ; *pr. pl.* nabbeð, 179, 9.

naver, navere, *see* nẹvre.

navð, *see* nāve(n).

nawiht (nawt), *see* naht.

nay, *see* nai.

nayl, *sb.*, OE. nægl, nægel ; *nail*, 86, 28.

nayle(n), *see* naȝle(n).

nẹ, ni, *neg. part.*, OE. ne ; *not*, 1, 7 ; ni, 178, 20.

nẹaver, *see* nẹvre.

neb, *sb.*, OE. nebb ; *beak, face*, 41, 9.

necessarīe, *sb.*, OF. necessaire, *necessairie ; necessary*, 239, 19.

nēd, *see* nēde.

neddre, nadre, *sb.*, OM. nēddre, WS. nǣddre, *f.; adder*, 17, 2 ; *pl.* nadres, by shortening, 3, 10.

nēde, *sb.*, OM. nēd, WS. nīed, *f.; need, desire*, 9, 4 ; nēd (for nēde ?), 18, 5. eSth. *ds.* nēoden, 187, 20 ; nēode, 199, 25. Kt. nȳed, 217, 18 ;

nȳede, 211, 12; *pl.* nīedes, 211, 13.

nēde, *adv.*, OM. nēde, WS. nīede; *necessarily, of necessity*, 9, 17 ; *at need*, 119, 21.

nēde(n), *wkv.*, OM. nēdan, WS. nīedan; *force, compel, urge, to be necessary*; *pr.* 3 *sg.* nēdeð, 18, 23 ; nēdeth, 119, 23. Sth. *pr.* 3 *sg.* nēodeð (eSth.), 202, 4 ; *pr. pl.* nēdeð, 201, 8 ; *pp.* inēd, 201, 11.

nēdes, nēdys, *adv.*, OM. nēdes, WS. nīedes ; *of necessity, needs* ; nēdes, 164, 4 ; nēdys, 91, 24.

nēdful, *adj.*, OE. nēod + ful ; *full of need, necessitous, necessary*, 24, 2 ; nēdfull, 146, 20.

nēdī, *adj.*, OAng. nēdig, WS. nīedig; *needy, oppressed*, 129, 21.

nēdys, *see* nēdes.

nefe, *sb.*, OE. nefa ; *nephew*, 1, 7 ; *pl.* neves, 2, 25.

nefen, *see* nẹvenẹ.

negge(n), neiȝe(n), *wkv.*, OM. genē-gan ; *approach, draw near* ; *inf.* neggen, 17, 15 ; *pr.* 3 *sg.* neiȝeþ, 65, 13 ; *pr. sbj. sg.* negge, 14, 2. Nth. *inf.* negh, 141, 32.

neȝbūr, *sb.*, OM. nēhgebūr, WS. nēahgebūr ; *neighbour*, 101, 17. Nth. neghtẹbou̅rẹ, 147, 19 ; neght-bou̅r, 147, 24. Sth. *pl.* neiheboures, 202, 11.

negh, neghest, *see* negge(n), nēh.

neȝhtẹbou̅re, neghtbou̅r, *see* neȝ-būr.

nēh, nei, niȝ, *adj. adv.*, OM. nēh, WS. nēah ; *near (nigh)*, 1, 3 ; niȝ, 36, 13 ; *wk.* neie, 38, 16 ; neye (*adv.*), 84, 14 ; nȳȝ, 62, 27 ; *comp.* nērẹ (*adv.*), *nearly*, 110, 26 ; *superl.* next, 116, 23. lNth. *comp.* neir, 168, 32 ; *superl.* neghest, 129, 21 ; nexst, 128, 12; neist, 130, 27. Sth. nẹh, 186, 31 ; nei, 206, 5 ; nyȝ, 222, 24.

nēhlēche(n), *wkv.*, OM. nēhlēcan-lēhte, WS. nēahlǣcan-lǣhte; *draw near, approach*, 192, 21.

nei, *see* nēh.

neidweis, *adv.*, lNth. = Ml. nēdwais;

OE. nēod + wæg; *of necessity*, 171, 27.

neiȝe(n), *see* neȝge(n).

neihebour, *see* neȝbūr.

neir, neist, *see* neh.

neiþer, neyther, *indef. prn.*, OE. ne + ǣgðer; *neither*, 45, 1; neyther, 78, 29; neythyr, 109, 26.

nekke, *sb.*, OE. hnecca; *neck*, 44, 31.

nelle, nele, nolde, nalde, *see* wille, *vb.*

nemne(n), *wkv.*, OE. nemnan; *name, call by name*; *pp.* nemmnedd(O), 11, 4; nempned, 228, 29. Sth. *pp.* inempnet, 191, 23.

nenne, *see* nān.

Nēod, Sanct, *sb.*, eME. = Ml. Nēd; OE. Nēot; *St. Neot's, Huntingdonshire*, 1, 11.

nēode, nēode(n), *see* nēde, nēde(n).

neomen, nēore, *see* nime(n), bē(n).

nēre, nēren (nēre), *see* nēh, bē(n).

nērhand, *adj.*, OE. nēar + hand; *near at hand*, 151, 8.

neruhlīche, *adv.*, Sth. = Ml. narulīke; WS. nearulīce; *narrowly, closely, carefully*, 202, 5.

nes, Sth. = Ml. nas, *see* bē(n).

nēse, *sb.*, OE. neosu, *f.* beside nosu, or possibly ON. nös, *f.*; *nose*, 14, 2.

neste, *sb.*, OE. nest; *nest*, 144, 26.

nēt (nēet), *sb.*, OE. nēat, *neut.*; *cow, ox, neat (cattle)*; nēet, 23, 1; nēt, 86, 16.

nevene, nefen, *wkv.*, ON. nefna, cogn. with OE. nemnan; *name, tell, relate*; Nth. *inf.* nefen, 153, 25; *pr.* 3 *sg.* nevenes, 145, 27.

neverþē·es, *adv.*, OE. nǣvre þy lǣs; *nevertheless*, 159, 15.

neves, *see* nefe.

nēvre, nevre, navere, *adv.*, OE. nǣfre < ne ǣfre; *never*, 3, 26; nǣvre (eME.), 3, 5; nǣvere (eME.), 183, 11; nevre, 14, 13; never te, *never yet*, 213, 19; never þē later, *notwithstanding, besides*, 122, 9. Sth. naver, 181, 6; navere, 182, 29; nēver, 195, 31.

newe, newæ, *adj.*, OE. nēowe, OM. nēwe, WS. nīewe; *new*; newæ, 4,

15; newe, 16, 1; as *sb.*, *new love*, 37, 14. Sth. nywe, 209, 1.

newe(n), *wkv.*, OM. nēwan, WS. nīwian; *renew, restore*; *inf.* newe, 125, 11; *pr.* 3 *sg.* neweð, 15, 10; *imp. sg.* newe, 18, 4.

nexst (next, neye), *see* nēh.

neynde, neys, *see* nȳnde, bē(n).

neyther, neythyr, *see* neiþer.

ni, *see* ne.

Nichomēdes, *sb.*, Lat. Nicomedes; *Nichomedes I, king of Bithynia*; *gs.* Nichomēdes, 191, 23.

nīed, niȝ, *see* nēd, nēh.

nigen, nȳne, *adj.*, OE. nigon; *nine*, 33, 31; nȳne, 225, 2.

nigentēne, *adj.*, OM. nigontēne, WS. -tīene (tȳne); *nineteen*, 3, 21.

nigt, niht, niȝht, *sb.*, OE. niht, *night*, 1, 15; nigt, 15, 18; nyȝt, 47, 25; niȝht, 227, 12; *pl.* nihtes, 3, 3; nigtes, 33, 29; nigt, 33, 31; niht, 185, 5.

nihtes, *adv.*, OE. nihtes; *at night, by night*, 203, 13.

nime(n), *stv.*, OE. niman-nōm (4); *take, seize; betake oneself, go*; *inf.* nimen, 46, 30; nim, 57, 12; *pr.* 3 *sg.* nimeð, 16, 15; *pr. sbj. sg.* nime, 226, 16; *pt. sg.* nam, 2, 24; nōm, 40, 24; naam, 213, 7; *pt. pl.* nāmen, 2, 1; nōme, 65, 22; *pt. sbj. sg.* nōme, 50, 26; *pp.* numen, 22, 6; nōme, 53, 7. Sth. *inf.* neomen (eSth.), 193, 2; *pp.* inume, 183, 2; inōme, 42, 30.

Ninian, *sb.*, OE. Ninias, Ninian; *Ninias*, 221, 30.

Ninivē, *sb.*, Lat. Nineve; *Nineveh*, 73, 28.

nis, niste, *see* bē(n), wite(n).

nīþ, nīþe, *sb.*, OE. nīð; *contention, envy, malice*, 9, 24; nīþe, 54, 15.

niðer, *adv.*, OE. niðor; *downwards*, 14, 3.

nīþful, *adj.*, OE. nīþful; *envious*, 9, 25.

nō (noan), *see* nōn.

nō, *adv.*, OE. nā; *not, not at all*, 35, 24.

nǭble, nǭbyll, adj., OF. noble;
noble, 73, 24; nǭbyll, 105, 21;
nǭbill, 139, 5.
nǭbleye, sb., OF. noblei; splendor,
grandeur, 210, 7.
nocht, see noht.
Nōē, sb., Lat. Noe; Noah, 73, 15;
gs. Nōēs, 72, 1.
nǭȝe(n), ptprv., OE. ne + āgan–āhte;
ought not; pr. 2 sg. noȝtest, 44, 20.
nogt (noȝt, noght), see noht.
nogtest, see nǭȝe(n).
nᵌwēr, adv., OE. ne āhwēr; nowhere, 59, 28.
noht, nogt, noght, noȝt, nouȝt,
nout, prn. adv., OE. nāwiht, nāht,
nǒht; nought, not, 1, 8; nohht (O),
9, 16; nogt, 17, 15; nouȝt, 57, 8;
nout, 14, 9; nowt, 82, 22; noȝt,
208, 17. Nth. noght, 128, 14.
noise, sb., OF. noise; noise, 198,
27.
nōk, sb., Ir. niuc?; nook, corner; ferþyng nōkę, value of a farthing, 96,
8.
nolde, see wille, vb.
nome, nōm(e), see name, nime(n).
nǭme, sb., ON. nām, or perh. OM.
*nōm; seizure, pledge, hostage, 28,
12.
nomecǔðe, adj., OE. namcūð; re-
nowned, 197, 8.
nomelīche, adv., OE. nama (nǫma) +
līce; namely, 199, 17.
nǫn, nǫ, adj., OE. nān; none, no;
nǫn, 16, 5; nǫǫn, 212, 23; nǫ, 29,
10. eSth. noan, 226, 16. Cf.
nān.
nōn, sb., OE. nōn; noon, 200, 3;
noonę, 109, 2.
nōntīd, sb., OE. nōntīd; noontide, 5,
14.
nǫǫn, noone, see nǫn, nōn.
nǫǫnys, sb. < adj., OE. ānes < ān;
nonce, occasion, in phr. for the
nǫǫnys, 113, 9.
nǫǫt, see wite(n).
nǫr, adv., OE. nāhwæðer, nāwðer,
nāðer; nor 49, 22.
norisse(n), wkv., OF. nurrir, nuriss;
nourish; pt. sg. norissed, 101, 2.

Norman, adj., sb., OF. Norman, cf.
OE. Norþmann; Norman; pl. Normans, 206, 19; Normannes, 209,
3.
Normandī, Normandȳe, sb., OF.
Normandī; Normandy, 1, 19, Normandȳe, 158, 2.
norð, north, adv., OE. norð; north,
16, 26; north, 55, 21.
Northampton, sb., OE. Norðhamtūn;
Northampton; Jǫhn, 233, 2.
norþeron, adj., OE. norðerne; northern, 224, 11.
Northfolk, sb., OE. Norðfolc; Norfolk; ds. Northfolke, 227. 3.
Norþthümberlǫnd, sb., OE. Norð
hymbraland (lǫnd); Northumber-
land, 221, 32.
Norþümbre, sb., Sth. = Ml. Norþ
himbre; OE. Norðhymbre, pl. adj.;
Northumbrian; pl. Norþümbres,
225, 25.
Norwīc, Norwychę, sb., O.E. Norð
wīc; Norwich, 4, 29; Norwychę,
116, 19.
nǭtarȳe, sb., OF. notarīe; notary,
94, 10.
nóte = nute, sb., OE. hnutu; nut,
77, 22.
notful, adj., OE. notu + ful; useful,
advantageous, 133, 15.
nǭþelēs, nǭðelēas, adv. conj., OE.
nā þȳlǣs; nevertheless, 88, 7. eSth.
nǭðelēasę, 199, 31.
nǭþer, see nouther.
nǭþing, sb., OE. nān + þing; nothing,
38, 18.
nou (now), see nū, noht.
noughtwithstǫndyng, prep. adv.,
OE. nāwiht + wiðstǫnding; notwithstanding, 232, 26.
nougt, see noht.
noumber, sb., OF. nombre; number,
164, 14.
nout, see noht.
nouther, nǭþer, prn. conj., OE.
nāhwæðer, nāwðer; neither, dial.
nawther, 3, 32; noyþer, 58, 12;
nowthirę, 147, 2; nowðer, 194, 3;
nǭþer, 209, 2.
now, see nū.

nǫwiderwardes, *adv.*, OE. nāhwider + wardes; *no whither, in no direction,* 3, 17.

nǫwor, *adv.*, OM. nāhwer, WS. hwǣr; *nowhere,* 15, 7.

nowt, *see* noht.

nowðer (nowthirę, noyþer), *see* nouther.

noye(n), *wkv.*, OF. anoier; *annoy, be troublesome; pr. pl.* noye, 147, 22.

nū, noū, *adv. conj.*, OE. nū; *now,* 4, 28; *since,* 30, 25; noū, 49, 7; now, 89, 30.

Nubīę, *sb.*, OF. Nubīe; *Nubia,* 42, 27.

nül (nültʔ), *see* wille, *vb.*

nüte (nüste), *see* wite(n).

numen, *see* nime(n).

nūþe, nūþen, *adv.*, OE. nū þā; *now then, now,* 37, 30; nūþen, 195, 30.

nȳ, nȳce, *see* nēh, nȳse.

nȳed(e), *see* nēd.

nygh, nyȝt, *see* nēh, niht.

nygun, *sb.*, based on Scand. *hniggu, cf. ON. hnöggr, 'niggardly'; *niggard,* 88, 24.

nȳnde, neynde, *adj.*, OE. nigoða, mod. by ON. niundi?; *ninth,* 147, 23; neynde, 152, 9.

nȳne, *see* nigen.

nȳse, nȳce, *adj.*, OF. nice; *nice,* 121, 9.

nyste, nyte, *see* wite(n).

nywe, *see* newe.

O.

ǫ, *interj.*, OE. ā; *O, oh,* 66, 9.

ǫ (ǫǫ), *adv.*, OE. ā; *ever;* ay and ǫǫ, *ever and aye,* 56, 26.

ō, ǭ, o, *see* on, ǫn, of.

obout, *see* abūten.

oc, *adv.*, OE. ac (oc); *but,* 1, 8. Cf. ac.

occean, *sb.*, OF. occean; *ocean,* 220, 8.

occupīe(n), *wkv.*, OF. occuper; *occupy;* Sth. *inf.* occupīe, 221, 13; *pt. pl.* occupīede, 221, 25; *pp.* occupīed, 223, 14.

Octǫbre, *sb.*, OF. Octobre; *October,* 226, 22.

of, off, o, *prep. adv.*, OE. of; *of, from, off,* 1, 2; off (O), 8, 22; o, 38, 6.

ofdrēde(n), *stv.*, OM. ofdrēdan (WS. drǣdan)-drēd (R); *frighten, terrify; pp.* ofdrēd, 1, 17. Sth. *pp.* ofdrḗd, 177, 19; *pl.* ofdredde, 179, 5.

off, *see* of.

offere(n), *wkv.*, OE. offrian; *offer; inf.* offeren, 117, 2.

offēre(n), *wkv.*, OM. *offēran, WS. *offǣran; *frighten off; pp.* offḗrd, 36, 27.

office, *sb.*, OF. office; *office,* 233, 25; offis, 22, 7; offys, 118, 10.

officēr, offycēr, *sb.*, OF. officier; *officer,* 233, 30; *pl.* offycēres, 117, 29.

cffis, offte, *see* office, ofte.

offycēr, offys, *see* offīcēr, office.

ofrand, *sb.*, OF. offrende; *offering,* 135, 15.

ofrigt, *pp.* as *adj.*, OE. āfyrht, *afryht < āfyrhtan; *affrighted,* 21, 14.

ofsēnde(n), *wkv.*, OE. ofsendan (sēndan); *send for, summon; inf.* ofsēnde, 204, 20.

ofservīe(n), *wkv.*, OE. of+OF. servir; Sth.=Ml. ofserve(n); *deserve, merit; pr. pl.* ofserveþ, 214, 21.

ofslę̄(n), *stv.*, Sth.=Ml. ofslǭ(n); OE. ofslēan-slōh(g) (6); *strike off, kill, slay; pt. sg.* ofslōh, 188, 11; *pp.* ofslaȝe, 190, 3.

ofspring, *sb.*, OE. ofspring; *offspring,* 25, 22. Nth. oxspring = ossspring, 130, 21.

ofte, offte, often, *adv.*, OE. oft; *oft, often;* offte (O), 9, 17; oftyn, 98, 18; offte sīþe, *see* oftesīðe(n).

oftesīðe(n), *adv.*, OE. oft+sīðan; *ofttimes, often;* oftesīðen, 203, 9; offte sīþe (O), 12, 9. Cf. oftsīþys(es).

ofþinche(n), *wkv.*, OE. ofðyncan-ðühte (ðuhte); *displease; repent; pr. 3-sg.* ofþinchet, 176, 10.

oftsīþys, oftesȳthes, *adv.*, OE. oft +
sīðes; *ofttimes, often* ; oftesȳthes,
144, 19. Cf. oftesīþe(n).

ofttȳme, *adv.*, OE. oft + tīma ; *ofttimes*, 235, 5.

oftyn, *see* ofte.

ofwundre(n), *wkv.*, OE. ofwundrian;
become astonished; pp. ofwundred,
1, 16.

ǭg, *see* ǭ3e(n).

o3ain, ogayn, ogaynę, *see* agein.

o3ains (o3ayns), *see* agaynes.

ǭ3e(n), ǭgo(n), owe(n), *ptprv.*,
OE. āgan–āhte ; *have, possess,
own; owe, ought; pr.* 1, 3 *sg.* ǭg, 25,
27; ouh, 198, 1; *reg. pr.* 3 *sg.*
owyth, 113, 30; *pr. pl.* owen, 199,
16; owe, 236, 13; ouwe3ē, 199, 25;
pt. sg. o3te, 43, 8. Cf. āge(n).

ǭ3en, owen, oun, *adj.*, OE. āgen;
own ; eMl. ā3henn, 11, 12; oun,
223, 29; *wk.* oune, 50, 26; ǭ3ene,
38, 12. eSth. ā3e, 177, 6; *ds.*
āhne, 193, 9; *fds.* ā3ere, 183, 3.

o3t (a3t), out, *indef. prn.*, OE.
āwiht, aht, oht ; *ought (aught),
anything*, 38, 6; oucht, 174, 8;
out, 202, 26. Cf. a3t.

o3te, *see* ǭ3e(n).

oht, *adj.*, OE. āht; *brave, valiant*,
181, 1.

ōkerēre, *sb.*, ON. ōkr, cogn. with
OE. wōcor + OE. -ę̄re (ēre); *usurer*,
88, 22; *pl.* okerērs, 88, 1.

ōkeryng,*sb.*, ON. ōkr, cogn. with OE.
wōcor + ME. -ing; *usury*, 88, 12.

ōkyrə, *sb.*, ON. ōkr, cogn. with OE.
wōcor; *usury*, 147, 16.

ǭld, *adj.*, OM. ald, āld, WS. eald ;
old, 16, 14; ǫǫld, 240, 17; *comp. pl.*
eldere, 33, 13. eSth. *comp.* elder,
176, 1; *pl.* elderne, 206, 25. Cf. āld.

olhnunge, *sb.*, OE. ōleccung,
*ōlehnung, f.; *soothing, caressing,
gentleness*, 193, 26.

olie, *sb.*, OF. olie; *oil*, 34, 11.

olle = ullə = wulle, *see* wille, *vb.*

olühne(n), *wkv.*, Sth. = Ml.
olihne(n) ; cf. OE. ōleccan ; *flatter* ;
inf. olühnen, 202, 32.

omāng, *see* amāng.

ǭn, ǭ, ǭnę, *adj.*, OE. ān; *one*, 21, 11;
eME. *as.* ǭnne, 3, 15; *ds.* ǭne, 43,
25; ǭne, 89, 5; ǭn, 25, 19; ǭ, 43,
9; tǭn (< þat ǭn), 26, 4; tǭ, 90,
31. Cf. ān (ā) and the reduced
forms an, a.

on, ō, *prep. adv.*, OE. on; *on, in,-
with*, 1, 12; ō, 3, 28; onn (O), 9,
27; onę, 40, 22.

ǭnde, *sb.*, OE. anda, ǭnda; *indigna-
tion, malice*, 54, 15.

ǭnde, *sb.*, ON. andi, cognate OE.
anda, 'envy'; *breath*, 19, 9.

onderstand, *see* understande(n).

onę, ǭne, *see* on, ǭn.

ǭnelēpī, *see* ǭnlēpȳ.

ǭnes, ǭnis, *adv.*, OE. ān + es; *once*;
ǭnys, 111, 13: with *at, at one,
together, in fellowship*; al ǭnes, for
al at ǭnes, *wholly at one, united*,
239, 34.

oneste, *see* honeste.

on3ēnes, *see* a3ēnes.

onī, onīe, *see* anī.

ǭnlēpȳ, *sb.*, OM. ānlēpig, WS.
ānlīepig; *single, sole*, 215, 11.

onlive, *adv.*, OE. on + *ds.* līfe; *alive*,
86, 10. Cf. līf.

ǭnlȳ, ǭnlȳch, *adv.*, OE. ānlīce; *only*,
94, 32; ǭnlȳch, 94, 24.

ǭnne, onn, *see* ǭn, on.

onnēaþə, onōh, *see* unę̄þe, inōh.

onǭn, *adv.*, OE. on ān; *anon, at
once*, 26, 7.

onont, *adv.*, OE. on-efn; *by, near*,
193, 25.

onsāge, *sb.*, OE. onsagu, *f.; *accusation, charge against a person; pl.*
onsāgen, 21, 9.

onstad, *see* onstede(n).

onstę̄de(n), *stv.*, OE. *onstedan-
stæd, or ON. steðja–stadd (5);
stand, stand by; pt. sg. onstad,
132, 26.

onswere, *see* answere.

onswerīe(n), *see* answere(n).

ontful, *adj.*, OE. *andful, ǫndful;
envious, 199, 18.

onworpə(n), *wkv.*, OE. un-
weorðia(n); *disdain, dishonor,
despise; pt. pl.* onworþede, 216, 18.

ǭnys, ǫǫnys, *see* ǭnes.

ǫǫk = ǭk, *sb.*, OE. āc; *oak,* 242, 2.

ǫǫld, ǫǫth, *see* ǭld, ǭþ.

oother, *see* ǭþer.

ǭpene(n), ǭpne(n), *wkv.*, OE. openian; *open*; *inf.* oppnenn (O), 12, 26; ǭpenen, 199, 29; *imp. pl.* ǭpeneþ, 101, 19; *pt. sg.* openede (eME.), 195, 32; ǭpenede, 62, 15. Nth. *inf.* oppyn, 174, 30.

ǭpenlīc, *adj.*, OE. openlīc; *open, conspicuous,* 153, 28.

ǭpenlīce (eME. openlīce), ǭpenlīche, ǭpenlīk, ǭpenlȳ, *adv.*, OE. openlīce; *openly,* 4, 8. Nth. ǭpenlīk, 131, 29; ǭpenlȳ, 154, 28. Sth. ǭpenlīche, 217, 17.

opon, oppnenn,*see* upon, ǭpene(n).

oppressiōn, *sb.*, OF. oppression; *oppression,* 232, 22.

oppyn, *see* ǭpene(n).

opwexe(n), *wkv.*, OE. *upweaxan; Sth. = Ml. upwaxe(n); *grow up, increase*; *pr. pl.* opwexeþ, 219, 3.

cr, *see* ǭþer.

ǭr, ǭre, *adv. prep.*, ON. ār, cognate OE. ǣr, 'ere'; *ere, before,* 16, 14; ǭre, 97, 23; *superl.* ǭrest, 21, 25.

orchard, *sb.*, OE. orceard < ort + geard; *orchard,* 109, 8.

ōːd, *sb.*, OE. ord, ōrd; *beginning,* 45, 31. eSth. *ds.* ōrde, 178, 29.

ordeine(n), ordeigne(n), ordān, *wkv.*, OF. ordeiner; *ordain, order*; *pt. pl.* ordeinede, 205, 28; *pp.* ordeyned, 117, 10; ordeigned, 236, 27. Nth. *inf.* ordān, 138, 18; *pt. sg.* ordānd, 143, 9; *pt. pl.* ordāned, 137, 10.

crdenaunce, *sb.*, OF. ordenance; *ordering, arrangement*; ordynaunce, 233, 14; *pl.* ordenaunce, 117, 19; ordenaunces, 116, 20.

orderę, *sb.*, OF. ordre; *order, religious order,* 120, 30; ordyrę, 144, 14.

ordeyne(n), *see* ordeine(n).

ordynaunce, *see* ordenaunce.

ordyrę, ǭrę, *see* orderę, ǭr.

ǭre, *sb.*, OE. ār, *f.*; *oar*; *pl.* ǭres, 86, 27.

ǭre, *sb.*, OE. ār, *f.*; *favor, grace,* 63, 10.

oresūn, *see* orisōn.

orf, *sb.*, OE. orf; *cattle, inheritance, property,* 30, 32.

original, *sb. adj.*, OF. original; *origin, original,* 238, 18.

origt, *adv.*, OE. on riht; *aright,* 27, 2.

orisūn, orisōun, *sb.*, OF. orisūn; *prayer, orison*; oresūn, 40, 5; orisōune, 140, 4.

ormēte, *adj.*, OM. ormēte, WS. ormǣte; *immense, immeasurable,* 5, 5.

Ormin, *sb.*, ON. Orm, cogn. with OE. weorm, wyrm; *Ormin, Orm*; Orrmīn (O), 13, 26.

orn, ǭt, *see* ürne(n), wīte(n).

ǭþ, ǭth, ǫǫth, *sb.*, OE. āð; *oath,* 77, 22; ǭth, 78, 10; ǫǫth, 240, 12. eSth. *ds.* ǭþe, 226, 15.

ǭþer, or, er, *conj.*, OE. āghwæðer, āwðer, eME. ouðer; *or*; ǭþerr (O), 13, 28; or, 51, 10; er, 17, 19; or ... or, *either ... or,* 21, 9. Nth. owthire, 144, 2; outhire, 144, 15.

ōþer, oother, ōþor, *adj.*, OE. ōþer; *other, second,* 1, 18; oother, 240, 1; ōþor, 219, 22; tōþer (< þat ōþer), 77, 14; tōthire, 145, 25; *pl.* ōþre, 1, 5; tōðere, 30, 20. eSth. *gs.* ōðres, 177, 6.

ōðerhwūles, *adv.*, OE. ōðer + hwīl, lWS. hwȳl, *at another time,* 199, 23.

ōu, oucht, *see* þū, cȝt.

ōuer, ouh, *see* ūre, čȝe(n).

oule, *sb.*, OE. awul(el), *f.*; *awl*; *pl.* oules, 61, 24.

oun, oune, *see* ōȝe(n).

ōur (ōure), ōus, out, *see* ūre, ic, oȝt.

ōutcaste(n), *wkv.*, OE. ūt + ON. kasta; *outcast*; *pp.* ōutcast, 238, 29.

ōute, ōuterlīche, *see* ūte, ōutrelȳ.

oʊ þe, *see* unne(n).

ouðer, ouðire, *see* ǭðer.

ōutrāgę, *sb.*, OF. outrage < ultrage; *outrage, excess,* 134, 6.

ōutrelȳ, *adv.*, OE. ūtor + līce; *outwardly, utterly, to the uttermost,* 244, 21. Sth. ōuterlīche, 234, 26.

ouwe, *sb.*, OE. eowu; *ewe*, 53, 4.
ouwe, *see* ǭʒe(n).
ōūwer, *see* þū.
ǭver, eME. over (ofer), *prep. adv.*,
OE. ofer; *over*; over (eME.), 1, 13;
ǭver, 237, 12. Nth. ǭvr, 174, 9.
ǭverall, ǭveral, *adv.*, OE. ofer + OM.
Nth. al; *over all, wholly, everywhere*, 136, 12; ǭveral, 202, 2.
ǭvercume(n), *stv.*, OE. ofercuman-
cōm (4); *overcome*; *pr. sbj. sg.*
ǭvercum, 102, 4; *pt. sg.* ǭvercōmę,
207, 6; *pp.* ǭvercumen, 23, 12;
ǭvercóme, 206, 25.
ǭvergǭ(n), *anv.*, OE. ofergān-ēode;
go over, overcome; *inf.* ǭvergǭn,
28, 30.
ǭverheghe(n), *wkv.*, OAng. *ofer-
hēan; *raise too high*; Nth. *pp.*
ǭverheghedę, 143, 27.
ǭverkūð, *adj.*, OE. *ofercūð; *familiar*;
comp. ǭverkūðre, *too familiar*, 200,
22.
ꝯverlōp, *sb.*, ME. ǭver + Scand. *lōp;
cf. MLG. overlōp, cogn. with OE.
*oferhlēap; *omission, skipping*, 155,
28.
ǭverlyttill, *adv.*, OE. *oferlȳtel; *too
little*, 144, 15.
ǭvermanȳ, *adj.*, OE. *ofermanig;
very many, over many, 235, 12.
ǭvermǣst, *adj.*, OE. ofer + mǣst;
overmost, outer, 140, 12.
ǭvermekill, *adv.*, OE. ofermicel, *adj.*,
overmuch, too much, 144, 15.
ǭvernōn, *sb.*, OE. ofernōn : *afternoon*,
208, 24.
ǭverrenne(n), rinne(n), *stv.*, OE.
ofer + ON. renna (rinna) (3); *over-
run, run over, recount*; Nth. *inf.*
ǭverrin, 130, 8; *pr.* 3 *sg.* ǭverrennęs,
134, 26.
ǭversē(n), *stv.*, OE. ofersēon-seah
(5); *observe, see, care for*; eME.
pr. 3 *sg.* oversihð, 178, 19; *pt. sg.*
oversah, 181, 16.
ǭverskyle, *adv.*, OE. ofer + ON.
skil; *beyond reason, without reason*,
96, 23.
ǭvertāke(n), *stv.*, OE. ofer + ON.
taka-tōk (6); *overtake*; *pr.* 3 *sg.*

ǭvertākeð, 29, 25; *pt. sg.* ǭvyrtōkę,
113, 2.
ꝯverðogt, *pp.* as *adj.*, OE. *ofer-
ðencean-ðōhte (ðohte); *amazed,
stupefied*, 26, 27.
ǭverwēnde(n), *wkv.*, OE. ofer-
wendan, wēndan; *turn over, go
over*; *pt. sg.* ǭverwente, 28, 29.
ǭvr, *see* ǭver.
ǭvyrtōke, *see* ǭvertōke.
ōw, oway, *see* þū, awai.
owe(n), *see* ǭʒe(n).
ōwer (ōūwer, ōure), *see* ʒūr.
ǭwer, *adv.*, OM. āhwēr, WS. āhwǣr;
everywhere, anywhere, 3, 31; 4, 2.
owhen, *see* ǭʒe(n).
owthirę, outhirę, *see* ōþer.
owyth, *see* ǭʒe(n).
oxe, *sb.*, OE. oxa; *ox*, 57, 24.
Oxeneford, *sb.*, OE. Oxenaford;
Oxford, 2, 24; *ds.* Oxenfōrde, 8, 5.
oxspring, *see* ofspring.
oyle, oyl, *sb.*, OF. oile; *oil*, 65, 7
Nth. oylę, 143, 12; oyl, 143, 15.
oys, *sb.*, OF. use, uise; *use*, 147, 10.

P.

pade, *sb.*, eME. = Ml. pāde; ON.
padda; *frog, toad*; *pl.* pades, 3, 10.
pāen, *adj. sb.*, OF. paien; *pagan*; *pl.*
pāens, 213, 18.
pāǵe, *sb.*, OF. page; *page*, 98, 25.
pᴀie(n), paye(n), *wkv.*, OF. paier;
satisfy, pay; *inf.* payen, 117, 5; *pt.
sg.* paidę, 212, 15; *pp.* paied, 26,
23; payd, 91, 13; paid, 141, 23.
paine, *see* peyne.
pais, *sb.*, OF. pais, pes; *peace*, 2, 4.
Cf. pęs.
paisible, *adj.*, OF. paisible; *peaceable*, 232, 25.
pal, *sb.*, OE. pæll, Lat. pallium; *pall,
costly cloth*, 38, 24; *pl.* palles, 46, 6.
palais, *sb.*, OF. palais; *palace*, 42, 5.
pᴀle, *adj.*, OF. pale; *pale*, 241, 9.
palefrey, *sb.*, OF. palefreid; *palfrey,
saddle-horse*; *pl.* palefreys, 48, 23.
pāpe, *sb.*, eME., Nth. = Ml. pǭpe;
OE. pāpa; *pope*, 4, 18.

Paradīs, Paradȳs, *sb.*, OF. Paradis
(Parais) ; *Paradise,* 64, 10.

Paraīs, *sb.*, OF. Parais (Paradis) ;
Paradise, 198, 12.

paramoūr, *sb.*, OF. par amour, *adv.
phr.*; *lover, paramour,* 128, 19.

paramūr, *adv.*, OF. par amur
(amour) ; *as a lover, passionately,*
37, 6.

parauntre, *see* **peraventure.**

pardee, *interj.*, OF. par + de(u) ; *pardee,* 239, 10.

pardōn, *sb.*, OF. pardōn; *pardon,*
134, 20.

paresche, *sb.*, OF. paroche ; *parish,*
119, 22.

Paris, Pariss, *sb.*, OF. Paris ; *Paris,*
206, 27 ; Pariss, 163, 9.

parlement, *sb.*, OF. parlement; *parliament, assembly,* 207, 1.

parlūr, *sb.*, OF. parloir, infl. by -ūr
words; *parlor, reception room* ; *pl.*
parlūres, 197, 18.

part, *sb.*, OF. part ; *part,* 38, 10.

parte(n), *wkv.*, OF. parter ; *part* ;
inf. parten, 65, 15; *pr.* 2 *sg.* partest,
241, 23; *pr.* 3 *sg.* parteð, 198, 2 ;
imp. pl. parteþ, 100, 8.

partenēr, *sb.*, OF. parcener, infl. by
part ; *partner* ; *pl.* partenērs, 225,
22.

parting, *pt. ppl.* as *sb.*<parten ; OF.
partir ; *parting,* 43, 14.

partȳ, *sb.*, OF. parti ; *party, side* ; on
þē tō partȳ, *on the one side,* 90, 31.

partȳ, *sb.*, OF. partie ; *part, portion* ;
a partȳ, *in part, partly, in some
measure,* 93, 14.

pas, *see* **passe(n).**

pas, *sb.*, OF. pas ; *pass, pace, passage* ;
92, 20.

pas-e(n), *wkv.*, OF. passer ; *pass*;
inf. passen, 105, 4; *pr.* 3 *sg.* passeth,
239, 6 ; *pr. sbj. sg.* passe, 103, 3 ;
pp. passid, 53, 6. **Nth.** *inf.* pas,
135, 21 ; *pr. pl.* passes, 144, 24 ; *pt.
pl.* passit, 169, 21 ; *pp.* past, 133,
20; passit, 167, 18. **Sth.** *pr. pl.*
passeþ, 223, 19 ; *pp.* ypased, 216,
22.

passiūn, passioūn, *sb.*, OF. passiūn ;

passion, death, martyrdom, 40, 6 ;
passioūn, 139, 15.

pāstee, *sb.*, OF. pastē ; *pasty, pastry* ;
pl. pastees, 84, 24.

pastūre, *sb.*, OF. pasture ; *food, pasture,* 101, 2. ⓔ

paternoster, *sb.*, Lat. pater noster ;
Lord's prayer, 16, 25.

patriarche, *sb.*, OF. patriarche; *patriarch* ; *pl.* patriarches, 212, 32.

patriark, *sb.*, Lat. patriarchus ; *patriarch,* 77, 31.

Paul, *see* **Powel.**

pay, *sb.*, OF. paie ; *satisfaction,*
120, 14 ; *pleasure,* 50, 18.

payen (payd), *see* **paie(n).**

payne, *see* **peyne.**

pēce, *sb.*, OF. piece ; *piece*; *pl.* pēces,
62, 1.

pēęs, *see* **pęs.**

peir, *sb.*, OF. pair ; *pair* ; peirę, 39,
23.

Peitou, *sb.*, NF. Peitowe, OF. Poi-
towe ; *Poitou,* 7, 11.

pelēr, *sb.*, OF. pilleur; *robber,* 161, 1.

peltyēr, *sb.*, OF. peletier ; *furrier,*
116, 18.

penaunce, penance, penaus, *sb.*,
OF. penance ; *penance, suffering,*
56, 27 ; penance, 147, 26 ; penaus,
157, 4 ; penonce, 218, 4.

Pencrych, *sb.*, Welsh ? ; *Pencrych,*
Richard, 224, 29.

penī, penīe, *sb.*, OE. pening, penig ;
penny, 86, 21 ; penīe, 178, 11 ; *pl.*
pęnes, 88, 25 ; pens, 118, 6.

penonce, *see* **penaunce.**

peoddare, *sb.*, cf. Skeat, *Etym. Dict.*,
pedlar ; *pedlar,* Sch. *peddir,* 198,
27.

pēople, pēple, pēpul, pōple, *sb.*,
OF. pueple; *people,* 220, 11 ; pēpul,
119, 12 ; pēpullę, 125, 7 ; pōple,
74, 2 ; puple, 139, 11. **Sth.** pēople,
220, 11.

peraventure, parauntre, *adv.*, OF.
par aventure ; *perchance,* 104, 7 ;
parauntre, 205, 6.

pēre, *sb.*, OE. pere(u) ; *pear,* 127, 19.

pērę, *sb.*, OF. per ; *peer, equal,* 139,
29.

perel, peril(1), *sb.*, OF. peril; *peril*, 92, 10.

perfay, *adv.*, OF. per fei; *through faith, by my faith*, 167, 3.

perfeccyŏnę, *sb.*, OF. perfeccion; *perfection*, 146, 21.

peril 1), see perel.

perisse(n), *wkv.*, OF. perir; *pr. ind.* periss-; *perish*; *inf.* perissen, 100, 25. Sth. *pr. pl.* perisset = perisseþ, 211, 5; *pr. sbj. pl.* perissi, 211, 23.

Perres, Pērs, *sb.*, OF. Peres, Pers; *Pierce*, 88, 18; *gs.* without ending, 89, 14; Perres, 227, 4.

persāve(n), *wkv*, 1Nth. = Ml. percēve(n); OF. perceiver; *perceive*; *pt. sg.* persāvit, 167, 23.

persevere(n), *wkv.*, OF. perseverer; *persevere*; *pr. 3 sg.* persevereth, 238, 15.

persŏne, *sb.*, OF. persone; *person*, 147, 4.

pertsly, *adv.*, OF. (a)pert + ME. ly; *quickly, boldly*, 111, 20.

pęrtrē, *sb.*, OF. pere(u) + trēo; *pear-tree*, 127, 19.

pęs, pęsę, *sb.*, AN. pēs, OF. païs; *peace*; pęsę, 111, 21; pęęs, 233, 4.

pestilence, *sb.*, OF. pestilence; *pestilence*, 239, 17.

petē, see pitē.

Pēter, *sb.*, OF. Peter; *Peter*, 116, 23; *gs.* Pētres, 1, 12.

peyne, paine, *sb.*, OF. peine; *penalty, pain*, 117, 13; paynę, 138, 28; *pl.* paines, 74, 24; paynęs, 137, 20.

peyneble, *adj. adv.*, OF. peineble; *careful, carefully*, 95, 30.

peynte(n), *wkv.*, OF. peint, *pp.* to peindre; *paint, decorate.* Sth. *pp.* ipeynted, 49, 3; ypeynt, 221, 10.

peynted, *adj.* < *pp.*, OF. peint < peindre; *painted*, 221, 11.

peyntynge, *sb.*, based on OF. peint, *pp.* of peindre; *painting*, 221, 7.

peys, *sb.*, NF. peis, OF. pois; *weight*, 91, 26.

peyse(n), *wkv.*, NF. peiser, OF. poiser; *weigh, balance*; *inf.* peyse, 88, 16.

Phăran, *sb.*, Lat. Pharan; *Paran*, 35, 9.

Phăraŏn, -ūn, *sb.*, OF. Pharaon, AN. Pharaun; *Pharaoh*, 22, 1; Phāraūn, 23, 22.

Philip, Filip, *sb.*, OF. Philip; *Philip*, 158, 29; Filip, 159, 21.

philosŏphe, *sb.*, OF. philosophe; *philosopher*, 216, 17.

pich, *sb.*, OE. pic; *pitch*, 62, 17.

Pict, *sb.*, OF. Pict, OE. Peoht, Piht; *Pict*; *pl.* Pictes, 220, 7.

pīk, *sb.*, OE. pīc; *pike, spike*, 61, 16.

pike(n), *wkv.*, ON. *pika, cogn. with OE. pician; *cover with pitch, pitch*; *inf.* pike, 86, 23.

Pīlāte, *sb.*, OF. Pilate; *Pilate*, 137, 8.

pilę, *sb.*, OF. pel; *skin, peel*; pile and piþ, *peel and pith*, i. e. *outside and inside*, 50, 13.

pilēr, *sb.*, OF. piler; *pillar*, 40, 23; pylēr, 122, 30.

pilerināġe, *sb.*, OF. pelerinage; *pilgrimage*, 230, 21.

pilgryme, *sb.*, OF. pelegrin; *pilgrim*, 229, 16.

pilte(n), *wkv.*, OE. *pyltan < Lat. pultare?; *push, thrust, knock, pelt*; *pp.* pilt, 26, 22.

pīne, pīn, *sb.*, OE. *pīn; cf. OE. pīnung, pīnness, or ON. pīna?; *torture, pain*; pīn, 53, 6; *pl.* pīnes, 3, 20. Sth. *pl.* pīnen, 197, 7.

pīne(n), *wkv.*, OE. pīnian; *torture, suffer pain*; *pt. pl.* pīned, 3, 4; pīneden, 4, 30; *pp.* pīned, 3, 5; pȳned, 138, 24. Nth. *pr. 3 sg.* pinnes, 150, 5. Sth. *inf.* pīnīe, 180, 20.

pīning, *sb.*, OE. pīnung, -ing; *torture*, 3, 5.

pinnes, see pīne(n).

pit, pitę, *sb.*, OE. pytt; *pit*, 63, 18; pitę, 50, 8; *pl.* pittes, 152, 12.

pitē, *sb.*, OF. pitee; *pity*, 38, 17; pytē, 106, 9. Nth. petē, 136, 27.

piþ, *sb.*, OE. piða; *pith*, 50, 13.

pittes, see pit.

plāce, *sb.*, OF. place; *place*, 87, 28.

plai, *sb.*, OE. plega; *joy, happiness*, 157, 6.

plaine, *sb.*, OF. plaine ; *plain, level country*, 160, 3.

plante(n), *wkv.*, OE. plantian, OF. planter ; *plant* ; *pt. sg.* plantede, 4, 25.

plāte, *sb.*, OF. plate ; *plate, piece* ; *pl.* plātes, 31, 18.

playinge, *sb.*, based on plegen ; *playing*, 215, 22.

playne, *adj.*, OF. plain ; *flat, even, clear*, 162, 31.

playnlī, *adv.*, OF. plain, *adj.* and *adv.* ; *plainly, clearly, certainly*, 135, 21.

plenērlȳ, *adv.*, OF. plenier + ME. lȳ ; *fully*, 96, 7.

plentē, *sb.*, OF. plentē ; *plenty*, 101, 12 ; plentee, 243, 15

plẹ̄se(n), *wkv.*, OF. plaisir ; *please* ; *pr. sbj. sg.*, plẹ̄se, 119, 17.

Plesseiz, *sb.*, OF. Plesseis ; *Plessis*, Jọ̄han of, 227, 5.

pleye(n), *wkv.*, OE. plegan ; *play* ; *pr. pl.* pleyen, 237, 11.

pleyne(n), *wkv.*, OF. plaindre ; *complain* ; *inf.* pleyne, 238, 30 ; *pt. sg.* pleyned, 233, 27.

pleyt, *see* **plight**.

plight, *see* **plyȝte(n)**.

plight, *sb.*, OE. plight ; *plight, trouble*, 134, 22 ; pleyt, 60, 7.

plihtful, *adj.*, OE. pliht + ful ; *dangerous, perilous*, 153, 19.

plyȝte(n), **plyghte(n)**, *wkv.*, OE. plihtan ; *promise, pledge, plight* ; *inf.* plyghte, 95, 2 ; *pr.* 1 *sg.* plyȝte, 124, 19 ; *pp.* plight, 240, 6.

pōēr, *see* **pōuēr**.

pōke, *sb.*, OE. poca ; *bag*, 81, 30.

polcat, *sb.*, OF. poule, ' hen ' + OE. cætt ; *polecat*, 244, 27.

pollusyōnẹ, *sb.*, NF. pollucion ; *pollution*, 147, 9.

pomp, *sb.*, OF. pompe ; *pomp*, 157, 26.

pọ̄pe, *sb.*, OE. pāpa ; *pope, father*, 77, 31.

pōple, *see* **pēple**.

porchas, *see* **purchas**.

pōre, *see* **pōvre**.

portēr, *sb.*, OF. portier ; *porter*, 35, 13.

porvoie(n), *wkv.*, OF. purveir ; *provide, purvey* ; *inf.* porvoie, 51, 19 ; *pp.* porveid, 208, 10 ; *pl.* purveyde, 233, 4.

pọ̄st, *sb.*, OE. post ; *post* ; *pl.* pọ̄stes, 181, 21.

postel, *sb.*, OE. postol ; *apostle* ; *pl.* posstless (O), 12, 4.

Posthumus, *sb.*, Lat. Posthumus ; *Posthumus* ; Silvius, 220, 2.

pot, *sb.*, OF. pot ; *pot* ; *pl.* pottes, 96, 24.

pothecārīe, *sb.*, OF. apotecaire ; *apothecary*, 244, 24.

potten, *see* **putte(n)**.

pọ̄udre, *sb.*, OF. poudre ; *powder*, 100, 22.

pọ̄uēr, **pọ̄wēr**, **pọ̄ēr**, *sb.*, NF. pouer < poueir ; OF. pouoir ; *power, ability*, upen here pọ̄wēr, *according to their ability*, 116, 21 ; pọ̄uēr, 215 16 ; pọ̄ēr, 204, 14.

Poule, **pọ̄und**, *see* **Powel**, **pūnd**.

pọ̄ure(n), *wkv.*, origin uncertain ; *pour* ; *pt. sg.* pọ̄ured, 245, 11.

pọ̄ustē, *sb.*, OF. poestē, poustē ; *power, ability*, 148, 16.

pōver, *see* **pōvre**.

povert, *sb.*, OF. poverte, beside povertē ; *poverty*, 94, 16.

pọ̄vre, **pōre**, *adj.*, OF. povre : *poor*, 18, 7 ; pōre, 48, 20 ; pōver, 135, 12.

Powel, **Poule**, *sb.*, OE. Pāwel ; *Paul*, 117, 1 ; *ds.* Poule, 109, 22. **Kt.** Paul, 216, 27.

pōwēr, *see* **pōuēr**.

poynt, *sb.*, OF. point ; *point*, 59, 3.

poysōn, *sb.*, OF. poison ; *poison*, 244, 17.

praid, **praies**, *see* **preie(n)**.

praise(n), *see* **preise(n)**.

prangle(n), *wkv.*, OE. *prangan. cf. Goth. praggan ; *fetter* ; *pp.* prangled, 84, 19.

pray, **prayde**, *see* **preie(n)**.

praye, **pray**, *sb.*, OF. preie ; *prey*, 219, 24. Nth. pray, 158, 22.

prāyen, *see* **preie(n)**.

prayēre, *see* **preyēre**.

prayinge, **prayng**, *sb.*, based on OF. preier ; *praying* ; prayng, 222, 18.

prēche(n),*wkv*., OF.prêcher; *preach*; *inf.* prēchen, 200, 20; prēche, 51, 1; *imp. pl.* prēche ȝē, 200, 18. Nth. *pr. ppl.* prēchand, 140, 30; *pt. sg.* prēchid, 136, 12.

prēchūr, *sb.*, OF. prêchur ; *preacher*, 213, 20.

prēchynge, prēching, *pr. ppl.* as *sb* ; *preaching*, 120, 1 ; prēching, 137, 30.

preciōus, precius, *adj.*, OF. precius ; *precious*, 242, 12 ; precius, 139, 26.

prēde, *see* prȳde.

preie(n), preye(n), praye(n), *wkv.*, OF. preier ; *pray* ; *inf.* preien, 58, 30 ; preye, 51, 1 ; *pr.* 1 *sg.* prey, 106, 22 ; pray, 123, 31 ; *pr. pl.* prayen, 236, 26 ; *pt. sg.* preyd, 98, 10 ; praid, 139, 11 ; preyde, 244, 25 ; *pt. pl.* prayde, 223, 20. Nth. *pr.* 3 *sg.* praies, 129, 26.

preise(n), praise(n), *wkv.*, OF. preiser ; *praise, value* ; *inf.* preisen, 198, 4 ; *pt. pl.* preysed, 89, 7 ; *pp.* praised, 134, 4.

prejudȳs, *sc.*, OF. prejudice ; *prejudice*, 117, 18.

prelāt, *sb.*, OF. prelat ; *prelate* ; *pl.* prelātes, 127, 4.

prēost, prēove, *see* prēst, prēve(n).

presand, *see* present.

prēse, *sb.*,NF. prēs, OF. preis; *praise*, 160, 10.

present, *sb.*, OF. present ; *present* ; *pl.* present, 28, 17. Nth. presand, 131, 14.

presse(n), *wkv.*, OF. presser ; *press, pursue*; Nth. *pt. pl.* presit, 175, 11.

prēst, prēste, *sb.*, OE. prēost ; *priest*, 119, 16 ; *pl.* prēostes (eME.), 4, 1 ; *ds.* prēoste (eME.), 197, 22.

prest, *adj.*, OF. prest ; *ready, prompt*, 61, 10.

presūme(n), *wkv.*, OF. presumer ; *presume* ; *pr. pl.* presumen, 236, 2.

prevelȳ, *see* privelȳ.

prēve(n), *wkv.*, OF. pruever, prever, prover ; cf. prōve(n) ; *prove* ; *inf.* prēve, 88, 3. eME. *pr. sbj. sg.* prēove, 199, 18.

preyd, preye(n), *see* preie(n).

preyēre, prayēre, *sb.*, OF. preiēre ; *prayer*, 93, 11 ; prayēre, 139, 19.

preysen, prīce, *see* preise(n), prīs.

prīde, *see* prȳde.

prike(n), *wkv.*, OE. prician (priccan) ; *prick, spur, as a horse* ; *pt. pl.* priked, 161, 1.

prikke, *sb.*, OE. prica ; *prick, point, dot*, 215, 12.

prīme, *sb.*, OF. prīme ; *prime, six in the morning*, 119, 6 ; prīme day, *first hour of the day*, 119, 2.

prince, *sb.*, OF. prince ; *prince* ; *pl.* princes, 101, 20.

principal, pryncipal, *adj.*, OF. principal ; *principal* ; *pl.* principāle, 130, 9 ; pryncipal, 235, 28.

priōr, *sb.*, NF. prior, OF. priur ; *prior*, 1, 11.

prīs, prīce, prīse, *sb.*, OF. prīs ; *prize, price, high esteem, value*, 27, 23 ; prīse, 135, 14 ; prīce, 169, 4 ; *ds.* prȳce, 105, 21 ; blowe þē prīs, *arouse the prize* (as in hunting), 62, 8.

prisse(n), *wkv.*, OF. prisier ; *appraise, value, praise, extol* ; Nth. *inf.* priss, 169, 13.

prisūn, prisōun, prisōn, *sb.*, OF. prison, AN. prisun ; *prison*, 2, 26 ; *pl.* prisūnes, *prisoners*, 21, 8 ; prisōn, 42, 4 ; prisoun, 232, 5.

prisunēr, *sb.*, OF. *prisonier, or based on prisun ; *keeper of prison*, 21, 6.

privē, privee, *adj.*, OF. privē; *privy, secret*, 102, 7 ; pryvē, 9), 19 ; privee, 239, 13.

privelȳ, privilīche, *adv.*, OF. privē + ME. lȳ ; *privily*, 243, 1 ; pryvylȳ, 98, 31 ; prevelȳ, 113, 20. Sth. privilīche, 204, 12.

privileȝe, *sb.*,OF. privilege; *privilege, special grant* ; *pl.* privilegies for -es, 4, 18.

processiūn, *sb.*, AN. processiun, OF. procession ; *procession*, 8, 8.

proclamāciōn (-ōun), *sb.*, OF. proclamacion ; *proclamation*, 233, 18 ; *pl.* proclamāciōuns, 235, 10.

procūre(n), *wkv.*, OF. procurer ; *procure* ; *pp.* procuredę, 147, 9.

professyōn, *sb.*, OF. profession ; *pro-fession*, 110, 8.

profitāble, prcfytāble, *adj.*, OF. profitable ; *profitable*, 234, 22 ; profytāble, 225, 33.

profre(n), *wkv.*, OF. proferer ; *proffer, offer* ; *inf.* profre, 235, 2 ; *pt. pl.* proferd, 162, 19.

profyt, *sb.*, OF. profit ; *profit*, 223, 27.

profytāble, *see* profitāble.

proǧenīe, *sb.*, OF. progenie ; *progeny*, 69, 10.

prǫloug, *sb.*, OF. prologue ; *prologue, announcement*, 134, 23.

propheci, *sb.*, OF. prophecīe ; *pro-phecy*, 131, 5.

prophēte, *sb.*, OF. prophete ; *prophet*, 73, 30.

propǫse(n), *wkv.*, OF. proposer ; *propose, nominate* ; *pt. sg.* propǫsed, 233, 1.

propre, propir, *adj.*, OF. propre ; *proper*, 222, 4 ; propir, 136, 10.

proūd, *see* prūd.

proūt, *adj.*, OE. prūt ; *proud*, 208, 4. Cf. prūd.

prōve(n), *wkv.*, OF. pruever ; *prove* ; *inf.* prōve, 106, 4. **Nth.** *pr.* 2 *sg.* prōves, 137, 12 ; *pr. sbj. pl.* pruf (lNth.), 167, 1. Cf. prēve(n).

prōwę, *sb.*, Oś. prou ; *profit*, 107, 21.

prōwesse, *sb.*, OF. pruesse ; *prowess*, 206, 28.

prūd, proūd, *adj.*, lOE. prūd, cf. ON. prūðr ; *proud*, 31, 16 ; proūd, 48, 16 ; *superl.* proūdeste, 240, 20.

pruf, *see* prōve(n).

prūte, *sb.*, Sth. = Ml. prīde ; OE. prȳte ; *pride*, 209, 13.

pruyde, prȳce, *see* prȳde, prīs.

prȳde, *sb.*, OE. prȳte ; *pride*, 108, 11. WMl. pruyde, 120, 12. Kt. prēde, 211, 20.

pryncipal, *see* principal.

pryvē, *see* privē.

pryvylȳ, *see* privelȳ.

pryvytē, *sb.*, OF. privetē ; *secrecy, secret*, 94, 11.

pūnd, poūnd, *sb.*, OE. pund, pūnd ; *pound* ; *pl.* pūnd, 47, 10 ; poūnd, 94, 20 ; eME. *ds.* pūnde, 178, 11.

pūnde(n), *wkv.*, **Sth.** = Ml. pīnde(n) ; OE. pyndan (pȳndan) ; *impound* ; *dam up, as water* ; *pr.* 3 *sg.* pūnt, 200, 33 ; ☉. *pl.* pūndeð, 201, 12.

punische(n), *wkv.*, OF. punir, puniss- ; *punish* ; **Sth.** *pp.* ypun-issed, 218, 12.

puple, *see* pēp!e.

pur, *prep.*, OF. pur ; *for*, 89, 31.

pùr, *adj.*, OF. pur ; *pure, simple*, 209, 2.

purchas, porchas, *sb.*, OF. pourchas ; *earnings, endeavor* ; porchas, 204, 22.

purgātorīe, *sb.*, OF. purgātorīe ; *pur-gatory*, 217, 11.

pùrifīe(n), *wkv.*, OF. purifier ; *purify* ; *inf.* purifīe, 102, 9.

purpre, *sb.*, OF. purpre ; *purple*, 192, 26.

pursùe(n), *wkv.*, OF. por-poursuir ; *pursue, follow after, take* ; *pt. pl.* pursued, 222, 28.

purveyen, *see* porveie(n).

pūt, *sb.*, **Sth.** = Ml. pit ; OE. pytt ; *pit* ; *ds.* pütte, 182, 7.

pūtfal, *sb.*, OE. *pyttfeall, f.* ; *pitfall, trap*, 223, 24.

Putifar, *sb.*, Lat. Putiphar ; *Potiphar*, 21, 1 ; 24, 17.

putte(n), *wkv.*, OE. potian, perh. OF. bouter, 'thrust' ; *push, thrust, put* ; *inf.* putten, 120, 13 ; *imp. sg.* putt, 102, 14 ; *pr. ppl.* puttyng, 233, 27 ; *pt. sg.* putte, 244, 17 ; put, 136, 29 ; *pt.* 2 *sg.* pōttest, 55, 9. **Nth.** *pr.* 3 *sg.* puttes, 143, 25. **Sth.** *pp.* yput, 222, 20 ; yputt, 223, 11.

pȳked, *pp.* as *adj.*, *piked, pointed*, 120, 23.

pylēr, pȳne(n), *see* pilēr, pīne(n).

pylgrymāǧe, *sb.*, OF. pelerinage, infl. by pilegrim < OF. pelegrin ; *pil-grimage*, 98, 7. Cf. pelerināǧe.

pytē, *see* pitē.

Q.

quā, *see* whō.

quāc, quad, *see* quāke(n), queǫðe(n).

quāke(n), Sth. quākīe(n), *wkv.*, OE. cwacian; *quake, tremble; pt. sg.* quākede, 44, 10. Nth. *inf.* quāc, 152, 8. eSth. *inf.* quakīen, 182, 22.

quᴈlle, *sb.*, Nth. = Ml. whāl; OE. hwæl; *whale,* 151, 27.

quām, *see* whō.

quan (qwan, quane, quanne), *see* whanne.

quantitee,*sb.*,OF.quantitē; *quantity,* 233, 15.

quarēl, *sb.*, OF. quarrel; *quarrel, square bolt,* 215, 18.

quarell, *sb.*, OF. querele; *quarrel,* 106, 5.

quārfor, *see* whērfōre.

quarterne, *sb.*, OE. cweartern, *neut.*; *prison*; *pl.* quarterne, 3, 9.

quārþoru, *see* whērþoru.

quāsā, *see* whōsō.

quat, *see* whō, qu̯e̯ðe(n).

quatkin,*prn.*,OE. hwæt + cynn; *what kind of,* 133, 20.

quatsō, *indef. prn.*, OE. hwætswā; *what so,* 30, 14.

quatsōevere, *indef. prn.*, OE. hwætswā + ǣfre; *whatsoever,* 30, 12.

qu̯e̯d, cwēad, quēad, *sb.*, OE. cwǣd; *evil,* 50, 20; þē quēde, *evil one,* 89, 25. Sth. *ds.* cwēade, 200, 27; kwēad, 217, 8. Kt. *ds.* kwēade, 216, 31.

quedur, quehepir, *see* wheþer.

queintīs, *sb.*, NF. queintise, OF. cointise; *skill, wisdom,* 104, 8. Cf. quointīse.

quelle(n), *wkv.*, OE. cwellan; *kill,* archaic *quell*; *inf.* quelle, 44, 20. Nth. *inf.* qwell, 159, 30.

quēme, *adj.*, OE. cwēme; *pleasant, agreeable,* 76, 28.

quēmə, *sb.*, OE. cwēme; *pleasure,* tō quēme, *for pleasure,* 49, 25.

quen, quhen, *see* whanne.

quenching, *sb.*, based on OE. cwen-can; *quenching,* 18, 18.

quēne, *sb.*, OE. cwēn; *queen*; cwēn (eME.), 6, 6; cwēne, 74, 1; quēne, 42, 14.

qu̯e̯ðe(n), *stv.*, OE. cweðan–cwað (5);

speak, say; pt. sg. quað, 22, 3; quad, 22, 21; quat, 30, 9; quod, 114, 7. Sth. *pt. sg.* cweð, 201, 23; quoð, 193, 30; *pp.* iqueden, 176, 9.

queðersō, *indef. prn.*, Nth. eME. = Ml. wheþersō; OE. hwæðer + swā; *whether so,* 21, 21.

quhā, *see* whō.

quhārthrou, *see* quārþoru.

quhen, *see* whanne.

quhene, *adv.*, OE. hwanone, hwanan; *whence,* 173, 28.

quhīll, quī, *see* whīl, whī.

quiclīche, *adv.*, Sth. = Ml. quiklȳ, OE. *cwiclīce, cf. cwiculīce; *quickly,* 207, 24.

quide, *sb.*, OE. cwide; *what is said, word,* 191, 14.

quik, cwik, *adj.*, OE. cwic; *alive,* 141, 6.

quik, quic, *adv.*, OE. cwice; *quickly,* quyk, 88, 19.

quil, quilc, *see* whīl, whilc.

quil(e), *see* whīle.

quīles,*adv.*, eME., Nth. = Ml. whīles, OE. hwīlum, mod. by *gen. advs.*; *whiles, at times,* 34, 10.

quilke, *see* whīlc.

quīlum, *see* whīlem.

quiste, *sb.*, OE. cwis, *f.* + t; *will, testament,* 75, 27.

quite (quīte?), *adj.*, OF. quite; *quit, free,* 44, 22.

quite(n), *wkv.*, OF. quiter; *requite, pay*; *inf.* quite, 54, 30.

quō, quod, *see* whō, qu̯e̯ðe(n).

quointīse, *sb.*, OF. cointise; *skill, plan, wisdom, ornament,* 208, 1.

quōr, *adv.*, eME., Nth. = Ml. whēr, whōr; OM. hwēr, hwār, WS. hwǣr, *where,* 33, 12.

quōsō, *see* whōsō.

quoynte, *adj.*, OF. coint; *happy, gay,* 57, 6.

quyk, *see* quik.

qwan, *see* whanne.

qwat, *see* whō.

qwell, *see* quelle(n).

qwō, qwōsō, *see* whō, whōsō.

qwyche, *see* which.

R.

rac, *sb.*, cf. Norw. Swed. rak ; *blow, push, beating,* 52, 20.

rachentēge, *sb.*, OM. racentēge, *f.*, WS. racentēage ; *chain, fetter; pl.* rachentēges (eME.), 3, 14.

rad, radde, *see* rēde(n).

rāde,*sb.*,eME.,Nth.=Ml. rǭde; OE. rād,*f.*; *road,* 196, 29.

rādī, *see* rędī.

rēd, rēdesman, *see* rēd, rędesman.

rēflāc, *sb.*, OE. rēaflāc; *robbery, rapine,* 2, 11.

rēvede(n), *see* ręve(n).

rēvęre, *sb.*, OE. rēafęre; *robber,* 4, 4.

rafte, *see* ręv(en).

rāge, *sb.*, OF. rāge; *rage, folly,* 240, 9.

rāge(n), *wkv.*, OF. ragier ; *rage, be wanton*; Nth.*pr.* 3 *sg.* rāges, 127, 30.

ragged, *adj.*, cf. ON. rögg, ' tuft, rag'; *ragged, shaggy,* 60, 9.

rais (raiss), *see* rīse(n).

raised, raises, *see* reise(n).

rāke(n), *wkv.*, ON. raka; *rake or sweep away, destroy*; *inf.* rāken, 24, 4.

Ramesæie, *sb.*, OE. Ramesig (-eg) ; *Ramsey* (Huntingdonshire), 8, 9.

Ramesē,*sb.*, Lat. Rameses; *Rameses,* 32, 32.

ran, *see* renne(n).

ranc, rank, *adj.*, OE. ranc ; *strong, proud, rank,* 23, 9.

Randalę,*sb.*,*Randall*; Schir Thomas, 169, 1.

Randolf, *sb.*, *Randolf,* Earl of Chester, 5, 18.

ransāke(n), *wkv.*, ON. rannsaka, cognate with OE. ærn, 'house', and sacan, ' strive '; *ransack, search*; *inf.* ransāken, 30, 3.

ransōūne(n), *wkv.*, OF. ransonner, ransunner; *ransom*; *pr.* 3 *sg.* ransōūnneþ, 104, 18.

rap, *sb.*, ON. *rap, Dan. rap; *blow, beating,* 52, 20.

rāp, *sb.*, eME., Nth.=Ml. rǭp ; OE. rāp; *rope*; *pl.* rāpes, 6, 29.

rāpe(n), *wkv.*, ON. hrapa ; *hasten*; *imp. pl.* rāpeð, 30, 29.

raplī, *adv.*, ON. *hrap, cf. Dan. rap, ' swift ' + ME. lī ; *quickly,* 155, 26.

rās, *see* rīse(n).

ratch, *sb.*, OE. ræcc ; *hunting dog*; *pl.* ratches, 62, 7.

rað, *adj.*, OE. hræð; *quick*; *comp.* rāþer, 220, 15.

rāðe, rāþe, *adv.*, OE. hraðe; *quickly,* 29, 25 ; raðe (eME.), 180, 11.

ratte,*sb.*,OE. rætt,*f.*; *rat*; *pl.* rattes, 244, 26.

Rauland, *sb.*, OF. Roland?; *Roland,* 126, 15.

raunsūn, *sb.*, OF. raenson, ranson, AN. ransun ; *redemption, ransom,* 94, 25.

raw, *sb.*, Nth.=Ml. Sth. rowe; OE. rāw,*f.*; *row, line, order,* 133, 11. Cf. rowe.

ręaden, ręadeð, *see* rēde(n).

ręaven, ręavīen, *see* ręve(n).

recche(n), reche(n), *wkv.*, OE. reccan, reccean; *tell, expound*; *inf.* rechen, 22, 22 ; *pr.* 1 *sg.* recche, 94, 23 ; *pt. sg.* rechede, 23, 28. Cf. reke(n).

receyve(n),*wkv.*, OF. rece(ï)ver; *receive*; *pr. pl.* receyveth, 122, 11 ; *pr. sbj. pl.* receyve, 122, 5; *pp.* receyved, 111, 6 ; reseyvet, 118, 28. Nth. *inf.* resayve, 139, 28 ; *pr.* 3 *sg.* rescheyves (lNth.), 146, 6.

reche(n), *wkv.*, Sth. = Ml. reke(n) ; OE. rēcan (reccan)–rōhte (rohte) ; *care, reck*; *pr.* 1 *sg.* recche, 94, 23; reiche, 231, 18 ; 3 *sg.* recþ, 180, 13.

ręche(n), *wkv.*, OE. ræcean–ræhte ; *reach*; *inf.* ręche, 43, 21.

reching, *sb.*, based on rechen ; *interpretation,* 21, 22.

recomande(n), *wkv.*, OF. recommander; *call, summon*; *inf.* recomandyn, 118, 31.

record, *sb.*, OF. record ; *record*; *ds.* recorde, 234, 16.

recorde(n), *wkv.*, OF. recorder; *record*; *pt. sg.* recorded, 105, 3.

recrẹaunt, *sb.*, OF. recreant; *recreant, defeated,* 113, 5.

recŏe, rēd, *see* reche(n), rēde(n).

rẹd, redd, *adj.*, OE. réad; *red*; *ds.* rẹde, 47, 10; redde, 112, 11.

rēd, (rẹd), rēde, *sb.*, ON. rēd, WS. rǣd, *f.*; *counsel, advice*; rǣd, 6, 18; rēd, 46, 21; ⅋. rēde, 70, 16. Sth. rẹde, 176, 4.

redde, *see* rẹdī.

rēde(n), *stv.*, OM. ĭēdan (WS. rǣdan)-rēd (R); *counsel, explain, read*; *inf.* rēdenn (O), 9, 10; *pr.* 1 *sg.* rēde, 24, 5; rẹde, 15, 9; *pr. sbj. sg.* rēde, 52, 21; *pt. sg.* rēd, 155, 27. Nth. *inf.* rēd, 126, 2; *pr. ppl.* rēdlande, 144,ᵃ3. Sth. *inf.* rẹde, 206, 23; *pr.* 1 *sg.* rēade (eSth.), 193, 13; *imp. pl.* rẹadeŏ, 200, 19; *pt. sg.* radde, 45, 25; *pp.* rad, 35, 3; irad, 40, 4; irēd (WMl.), 123, 5. Kt. *pr. pl.* rēdeth, 210, 21.

:ǫdesman, *sb.*, Sth. = ME. rēdesman; WS. rǣdesman; *counsellor*; *pl.* rǣdesmen, 226, 5; rẹdesmen, 226, 24.

rẹdī, radī, redde, *adj.*, OE. *rǣdig, extended from OE. rǣde, ' ready'; *ready,* 17, 18; radī, 101, 7; redde, 133, 1ħ

rẹdīlỹ, rẹdīlīche, *adv.*, OE. *rǣdilīce; *readily, quickly,* 239, 5. Sth. (SEMl.), rẹdīlīche, 69, 30.

Rẹdinge, *sb.*, OE. Rēadinge; *pl.* name of people, then of place; *Reading,* Berks., 2, 2.

rẹdnes, *sb.*, OE. rēadness, *f.*; *redness,* 148, 11.

rōdunge, *sb.*, OM. rēding, WS. rǣding, *f.*; *reading,* 192, 3.

Redvērs, *sb.*, OF. Redviers, Reviers; *Redvers,* Baldwin de, 2, 12.

rẹẹs, *sb.*, OE. rǣs; *rush, forward movement,* 111, 24.

rēfe(n), *wkv.*, eME. = Ml. rēven; OE. hrēfan; *roof*; *inf.* rēfen, 4, 14.

refúse(n), *wkv.*, OF. refuser; *refuse*; *pr. sbj. sg.* refuse, 118, 10.

refú⊙ *sb.*, OF. refute; *refuge,* 103, 24.

rezhellbōc, *sb.*, OE. regolbōc; *book of canons or rules,* 8, 16.

regnynge, *sb.*, based on regne(n); *reigning, ruling,* 236, 28.

reiche, *see* reche(n).

rein, *sb.*, OE. regn; *rain,* 186, 6.

reise(n), *wkv.*, ON. reisa, cogn. with OE. rǣran; *raise*; *pr.* 3 *sg.* reiseŏ, 14, 11; *pt. sg.* raised, 132, 16; *pp.* reysed, 117, 6. Nth. *pr.* 3 *sg.* raises, 129, 22.

reke(n), *wkv.*, OE. rēcan, reccanrōhte (rohte); *care, reck*; Nth. *pt. sbj. sg.* roucht, 167, 3.

reke(n), reche(n), *wkv.*, OM. reccean-ræhte (WS. reahte); *stretch, extend, direct one's way*; *go tell, recite*; *pt. pl.* rekened, 89, 5. Cf. recche(n).

religĭūs, *adj.* and *sb.*, OF. religius (ous); *religious,* 199, 5.

relỹ(en), *wkv.*, OF. relier, ralier; *rally*; Nth. *pt. sg.* relỹit, 167, 30.

relygyōn, *sb.*, OF. ĭeligion; *religion,* 112, 4.

rẹm, *sb.*, OF. realme, reaume, reame; *realm,* 225, 16. Cf. rewme.

1ẹm, *sb.*, OE. hrēam; *cry, uproar,* 14, 11.

remedye, remedỹ, *sb.*, OF. remede, perh. *remedie; *remedy,* 235, 28; remedỹ, 145, 13.

remembre(n), *wkv.*, OF. remembrer; *remember*; *pr. ppl.* remembraunt (for -and), 105, 9.

remenaunt, *sb.*, OF. remanant; *remnant, remainder,* 118, 7.

rēnde(n), *wkv.*, OE. rendan, rēndan; *rend, tear*; *pt. sg.* rende, 195, 21.

renne(n), rinne(n), *stv.*, ON. renna (rinna)-rann (3); *run*; *inf.* renne, 50, 30; *pt. sg.* ran, 78, 3. Nth. *imp. sg.* ryn, 141, 30; *pt. pl.* ryn, 141, 5.

rente, *sb.*, OF. rente; *revenue, rent*; *pl.* rentes, 4, 14.

reope(n), *see* rīpe(n).

repaire(n), repāre(n), *wkv.*, OF. repairer; *repair, return*; *pr.* 3 *sg.* repaireth, 245, 17. lNth. *pp.* repārit, 168, 28.

repente(n), *vkv.*, OF. repentir; *repent*; *inf.* repente, 244, 22.

repleet, *adj.*, OF. replet ; *replete, quite full*, 238, 7.

reporte(n), *wkv.*, OF. reporter ; *report* ; *pr. sbj. sg.* report, 239, 7.

represente(n),*wkv.*,OF. representer; *represent*; *pt. sg.* represented, 234, 3.

reprōve(n), *wkv.*, OF. reprover ; *reprove* ; *pt. sbj. sg.* reprōved, 234, 1 ; *pp.* reprŏffede, 145, 21.

rẹquiem,*sb.*, OF. requiem ; *requiem*, 117, 21.

rẹre(n), *wkv.*, OE. rǣran ; *rear, raise, build* ; *inf.*rẹren, 73, 2. Sth. *inf.* rẹre, 210, 2.

resayve, rescheyve, reseyvet, *see* **receyve(n)**.

rẹsōn, rẹsūn, rẹsoūn, *sb.*, OF. reson, AN. resun ; *reason, discourse*, 105, 18 ; rẹsūn, 133, 9 ; rẹsoūn, 91, 6 ; rẹsoūnẹ, 141, 8.

rẹsonāble, *adj.*, OF. raisonable ; *reasonable*, 136, 26.

reste, *sb.*, OE. rest, *f.* ; *rest*, 32, 28. Nth. ryst, 146, 23 ; rystẹ, 144, 5.

reste(n), ryste(n), *wkv.*, OE. restan : *rest* ; Nth. *inf.* ryste, 144, 31 ; *pr.* 3 *sg.* rystes, 144, 28.

restelẹẹs, *adj.*, OE. resteléas infl. by ME. reste ; *restless*, 240, 32.

restọre(n), *wkv.*, OF. restorer ; *restore* ; *inf.* restọre, 95, 24.

rẹsūn, *see* **rẹsōn**.

Reuda, *sb.*, *Reuda*, 222, 3.

reuel, reul, *sb.*, OF. reule ; *rule*, 155, 24; reul, 155, 26.

reuful, *adj.*, OE. *hrēowsul ; *rueful, sorrowful*, 92, 19.

reulīche, *adv.*, OE. hrēowlīce ; *sadly, pitifully*, 60, 8.

reulȳ, *see* **rewelī**.

reuþe, rewðe, reuth, *sb.*, OE. *hrēowð, *f.* ; *sorrow, repentance, ruth*, 37, 19 ; rewðe, 30, 19. Nth. reuth, 129, 17.

rẹve(n), *wkv.*, OE. rēafian ; *rob, plunder* ; *inf.* rẹven, 79, 19 ; *pr.* 3 *sg.* rẹveð, 198, 22 ; *pt. sg.* rǣvede (eME.), 2, 1 ; rẹvede, 7, 4 ; rafte, 55, 4 ; *pt. pl.* rǣveden (eME.), 3, 25 ; *pp.* rafte, 115, 24. Nth. *inf.* rẹve, 144, 12. Sth. *inf.* rẹaven

(eSth.), 197, 2 ; *imp. sg.* rẹavie, 200, 26.

reward, *sb.*, OF. reward, *regard* ; tō þe reward of, *to the regard of, in respect to*, 218, 7.

rewe, *sb.*, OE. rǣw (rāw), *f.* ; *row*; bȳ rewe, *in a row*, 228, 15.

rewelī, reulȳ, *adj.*, OE. hrēowlīc ; *sad, compassionate*, 30, 8 ; reulȳ, 59, 11.

rewe(n), *stv.*, OE. hrēowan-hrẹaw (R) ; *rue, repent* ; *inf.* rewen, 20, 24 ; ruwen, 176, 21.

rewme, *sb.*, OF. realme, reaume ; *realm*, 236, 5. Cf. rẹm.

rewnesse, *sb.*, OE. hrēowness, *f.* ; *pity*, 80, 9.

rewðe, rewthe, *see* **reuþe**.

reyke(n), *wkv.*, ON. reika ; *wander* ; *inf.* reykin, 55, 21.

reysed, *see* **reise(n)**.

rīce, rīche, *adj.*, OE. rīce, later infl. by OF. riche ; *powerful, rich*, 1, 6 ; *superl.* riccheste, 182, 30 ; ricchest, 186, 23.

Richard, *sb.*, OE. Richard ; *Richard*, 206, 31.

rīche, *sb.*, OE. rīce ; *realm* ; Sth. *ds.* rīchen, 183, 13.

richelīke, *adv.*, OE. rīchlīce, mod. by OF. riche ; *richly*, 33, 26.

richesse, *sb.*, OF. richesse ; *wealth, riches*, 215, 17.

richt, *see* **riht**.

rīde(n), *stv.*, OE. rīdan-rād (1) ; *ride* ; *pr. ppl.* rīdend, 4, 3 ; *pt. sg.* rọd, 52, 28 ; rọọd, 229, 6 ; rọdẹ, 106, 25 ; *pt. pl.* ridyn, 112, 25. Sth. *pr. ppl.* rīdinde, 189, 16.

rīfle(n), *wkv.*, OF. rifler ; *rifle, plunder, spoil* ; *pp.* rīfild, 161, 2.

rift, *sb.*, OE. rift ; *veil* ; *ds.* rifte, 188, 26.

rightlȳ, *adv.*, OE. rihtlīce ; *rightly* ; 127, 24.

rightwīs,*adj.*,OE.rihtwīs; *righteous*, 139, 3.

rigolāğe, *sb.*, OF. rigolage ; *sport, struggling, boisterous conduct*, 127, 31.

rigt, rigte, *see* **riht**.

rigte(n),*wkv.*,OE. rihtan; *straighten, correct*; *inf.* rigten, 16, 27; *pr.* 3 *sg.* rigteð, 15, 18.

riȝtful, ryȝtful, *adj.*, OE. *rihtful; *righteous*; ryȝtful, 100, 21 ; ryghtful, 232, 19.

riȝtfulnes, *sb.*, OE. *rihtfulnes, *f.* ; *righteousness*, 101, 4.

riht, rigt, richt, *adj.*, OE. riht ; *right*; rihht(O), 10, 4; rigt, 15, 23 ; richt, 76, 30; right, 127, 11 ; *ds.* rigte, 20, 22 ; be gōde rihte, *ds.*, *by good right*, 7, 3 ; *pl.* ryght, 233, 5.

rihtwīsnesse, *sb.*, OE. rihtwīsnes,*f.* ; *righteousness*, 178, 16.

riif, *see* **rȳfe**.

rīke, *adj.*, **Nth.** = Ml. Sth. rīche ; OE. rīce ; *powerful, mighty, rich*,126, 9.

rīme, rīm, *sb.*, OE. rīm, *neut.* ; *rime, number, song*, 9, 8. **Nth.** rīm, 129, 5.

rīme(n), *wkv.*, OE. rīman ; *number, rime* ; **Nth.** *pr. ppl.* rīmand, 133, 13.

rīne(n), *wkv.*, OE. rignan, rīnan ; *rain* ; *inf.* rīne, 186, 6.

ring, *sb.*, OE. hring ; *ring*, 24, 11 ; rynge, 109, 27 ; *ds.* ringe, 46, 20.

ringe(n), **rynge**(n), *stv.*, OE. ringan –rang (rǫng) (3) ; *ring* ; *inf.* rynge, 123, 11 ; *pt. sg.* rǫng, 238, 32. **Nth.** *pr. pl.* ringes, 76, 25.

rinne(n), *see* **renne**(n).

rīote, rīot, *sb.*, OF. riote ; *riot*, 127, 30 ; rīot, 237, 9.

rīotour, *sb.*, OF. rioteur, riotour ; *brawler, rioter*, 238, 31.

rīpe, *adj.*, OE. rīpe ; *ripe*, 21, 26.

rīpe(n), *stv.*, OE. rīpan–rāp (1) ; *reap* ; *inf.* rīpen, 176, 22. **eSth.** *imp. pl.* reope (< OAng. reopan–rāp), 196, 19.

rīse(n), *stv.*, OE. rīsan–rās (1) ; *rise* ; *imp. sg.* rīs, 82, 28 ; *pt. sg.* rās (eME.), 11, 9 ; rǫs, 15, 3 ; *pt. pl.* risen, 2, 11 ; *pp.* risenn (O), 12, 6. **lNth.** *pt. sg.* raiss = rās, 172, 16.

rīvelīe, *adv.*, ON. rīfr, 'abundant' + ME. līc ; *abundantly, frequently, commonly*, 154, 7.

riveling, *sb.*, OE. rifeling ; *a sort of*

shoe; rughfut riveling (*a nickname of the Scotch*), 161, 5.

rīxe(n), *wkv.*, OE. rīcsian, rīxian ; *rule, reign* ; *inf.* rīxan, 7, 8.

rixlīe(n), *wkv.*, **Sth.** = Ml. rixle(n) ; OE. rīxlian ; *rule* ; **eSth.** *pr.* 3 *sg.* rixleoð, 182, 30.

rō, *sb.*, ON. rō, cogn. with OE. rōw, *f.* ; *rest, quiet*, 51, 19.

robbe(n), *wkv.*, OF. rober ; *rob, plunder* ; *pt. pl.* robbed, 165, 23. **Sth.** *inf.* robbȳ, 205, 25.

robberīe, *sb.*, OF. roberie ; *robbery*, 209, 17.

robbȳ, *see* **robbe**(n).

rǫbe, *sb.*, OF. robe, *robe, clothing* ; *pl.* rǫbes, 49, 4.

Rodbert, *sb.*, OF. Rodberd ; *Robert, Earl of Gloucester*, 5, 11.

rǫde, *sb.*,OE. rād,*f.* ; *riding, journey, road*, 61, 27.

rōde, *sb.*, OE. rōd, *f.* ; *cross, rood*, 4, 31.

rǫde, *see* **rīde**(n).

rōdetrē, *sb.*, OE. rōd,*f.* + trēo ; *cross, rood-tree*, 11, 26.

Rodrīc, *sb.*, OF. Rodric ; *Roderic*, 220, 19.

Roger, *sb.*, OF. Roger ; *Roger*, 227, 3.

Rogingham,*sb.*, *Rockingham* (Northampton), 4, 22.

rohlȳ, *adv.*, OE. *rūhlīce ; *roughly, savagely*, 149, 23.

rolle(n), *wkv.*, OF. roller ; *roll* ; *pr.* 3 *sg.* rolleth, 244, 10.

Romare, *sb.*, NF. Romare, OF. Roumare ; *Romare, William of*, 5, 23.

rǫmaunse, rǫmans, *sb.*, OF. romance ; *romance*, 115, 21 ; rǫmans, 126, 2.

Rōmayn, *adj.*, OF. roumain, NF. rōmain; *Roman*, 221, 27.

Rōme, *sb.*, OE. Rōm, *f.*, L. Rōma ; *Rome*, 4, 17.

Romenel,*sb.*,OF.Romenel ; *Romney*, 186, 9.

ron, *see* **rūn, rūne**.

rōnd, *adj.*, OF. rond, AN. rund ; *round* ; *wk.* rōnde, 126, 14.

rǭng, *see* ringe(n).

rǫǫd, rǭs, *see* rīde(n), rīse(n).

rospe(n), *wkv.*, ON. *raspen, Dan. raspe or OF. raspe ; rasp, scrape, destroy ; inf.* rospen, 24, 4.

rǭste(n), *wkv.*, OF. rostir ; *roast* ; **Nth.** *inf.* rǭst, 171, 3 ; *pt. pl.* rǭstit, 171, 15.

rōte, *sb.*, ON. rōt, *f.* ; *root,* 127, 18.

rǭte(n), *wkv.*, OE. rotian ; *rot, become putrid* ; *pp.* rǭted, 58, 20.

rǭten, rǭtin, *adj.*, ON. rotinn ; *rotten, putrid,* 50, 12.

rǭþ, *sb.*, ON. rāð, cogn. with OM. rēd, WS. rǣd ; *counsel, advise, plan* ; *ds.* rǭþe, 86, 9.

rǭðe(n), *wkv.*, ON. rāða, cogn. with OE. rǣdan ; *advise, counsel* ; *inf.* rǭðe, 75, 23.

rōu, *adj.*, OE. rūh ; *rough, hairy,* 60, 9.

roucht, *see* reke(n).

rōun, *see* rūn, (rūne).

rōunǧe(n), *wkv.*, OF. ronger ; *gnaw, gnash with the teeth,* perh. Scot. *runch* ; **Nth.** *inf.* rōunge, 156, 23.

rōute, rōut, *sb.*, OF. route ; *company, army, rout,* 205, 28. **Nth.** rōut, 138, 32 ; rōwt, 158, 16.

route(n), *wkv.*, ON. rauta ; *roar, snore* ; *pt. sg.* routit, 172, 10.

Rōvecestre, *sb.*, OE. Hrōfesceaster ; *Rochester,* 6, 10.

rowe, *sb.*, OE. rǣw, raw, *f.* ; *row, straight line,* 62, 9.

rowe(n), *stv.*, OE. rōwan–rēow (R) ; *row, go by water, sail* ; *inf.* rowen, 197, 2.

rōwt, *see* rōute.

rüǧ, 8th. = Ml. riǧ (riǧǧe), *sb.*, OE. hrycg ; *back, ridge* ; *ds.* rügge, 207, 9.

rugge(n), *wkv.*, ON. rugga ; *rock, agitate, pull* ; *pt. pl.* rugget, 142, 5.

rughfute, *sb.* as *adj.*, OE. ruh + fōt ; *rough foot,* 161, 5.

rūme(n), *wkv.*, OE. ɪūman ; *make room, enlarge* ; *pt. sg.* rūmde, 186, 16.

rūne, rūn, ron, *sb.*, OE. rūn, *f.* ; *secret, colloquy, counsel,* 178, 33 ; *language, letter, poem* ; rēden rōun, *direct the conversation,* 52, 21. **Nth.** rón, 133, 9.

rūne(n), *wkv.*, OE. rūnian ; *whisper,* archaic *round* ; *pt. sg.* rūnde, 44, 14.

ruwen, *see* rewe(n).

rybawdȳe, *sb.*, OF. ribaudie ; *ribaldry,* 121, 9.

ryche, rycht, *see* rīche, riht.

rȳe, *sb.*, OE. ryge ; *rye,* 158, 4.

rȳfę = rȳf, *adj.*, OE. rīf ; *abundant, frequent,* 106, 21 ; riif, 131, 31.

ryght, *see* riht.

ryghtful, *see* riȝtful.

ryghtwȳse, *see* rightwīs.

ryȝtful, *see* riȝtful.

ryn, *see* renne(n).

rynge, ryngen, *see* ring, ringe(n).

ryste (ryst), *see* reste, reste(n).

rȳsyng, *sb.*, based on OE. rīsan; *rising, getting up,* 173, 2.

rȳve(n), *stv.*, ON. rīfa ; *rive, tear, break* ; *inf.* rȳve, 243, 32.

S.

sā, sacclǣs, *see* swā, seie(n), saklęs.

sacrafīse, *see* sacrifīce.

sacrament, sacrement, *sb.*, OF. sacrement ; *sacrament,* 122, 4 ; sacrement, 146, 7.

sacrifīce, sacrafȳse, *sb.*, OF. sacrifice ; *sacrifice,* 102, 21 ; sacrafīse, 135, 13 ; sacrifīse, 237, 13.

sāde, *adv.*, OE. sǣde ; *sufficiently, fully,* 122, 19.

sadel, sadil, OE. sadol ; *saddle,* 61, 15.

sǣ, *see* sę̄.

sǣcle(n), *wkv.*, OM. sēclian, WS. sīeclian ; *sicken, become sick* ; *pt. sg.* sǣclede, 7, 33.

sǣden, sǣgen, *see* seie(n).

sǣgen, *sb.*, OE. segen (sǣgen), *f.* ; *saying, assertion,* 6, 28.

sǣht, *adj.*, eME. = Ml. saht ; OE. sǣht ; *at peace, reconciled; pl.* sǣhte, 2, 17.

sǣhte, *see* **saght, sahte.**

sǣhtleden, *see* **sahtle(n).**

sæin, sælf, *see* seie(n), self.
sǣrī, *adj.*, OE. sārig; *sad, sorrowful,* 186, 21.
sǣrīnesse, *sb.,* OE. sārigness, *f.;* *sorrow,* 183, 28.
sæt, *see* sitte(n).
sag, sagh, sahh, *see* sē(n).
saght, sahte, *sb.,* OE. sæht, *f.;* *agreement, compact,* 7, 15; sæhte, 7, 17. Nth. saght, 126, 16.
sahtle(n), *wkv.,* OE. sahtlian; *reconcile, make peace; pt. pl.* sahtlede, 6, 13; sahtleden, 6, 15.
saie, saine, *see* seie(n).
saik, *see* sāke.
saint, seint, sainte, seynte, sain, *adj. sb.,* OF. saint, *f.* sainte; *saint;* seint, 58, 25; seynt, 88, 21; seyntę Jǫhn, 106, 19; Seynte Mārīe, 116, 15; Seynt Mārīe, 118, 2. Nth. sain, 148, 1; saint, 160, 21. Sth. sein, 205, 13; seinte, 198, 16. Cf. sanct.
sais, *see* seie(n).
sāke, sāk, *sb.,* OE. sacu; *sake, cause;* for . . . sāke, *on account of,* 58, 16; sāke, *guilt,* 230, 8. Nth. sāk, 131, 16; saik = sāk, 173, 32.
sākelēas, *see* saklēs.
sakerynge, *pr. ppl.* as *sb.,* based on OF. sacrer; *consecration,* 123, 12.
saklēs, *adj.,* OE. saclēas; *innocent, without injury;* sacclǣs (O), 11, 26; saklēs, 139, 6. eSth. sākelēas, 199, 13.
sal, salt, *see* schule(n).
Salamōn, *sb.,* OE. Salamōn; *Solomon,* 72, 4.
sāld(e), *see* selle(n).
salve, *sb.,* OE. sealf, *f.; salve, remedy,* 198, 30.
sāme, *see* schāme(n).
sāme, samę, *sadj.,* ON. samr; *same,* 223, 5; samę, 136, 14; *dat.* sammyn, 170, 22.
sāme(n), sāmyn, *adv.,* ON. saman; *together,* 79, 6; sāme, 109, 5; sāmyn, 137, 18.
samne(n), *wkv.,* OE. samnian; *collect, assemble; pp.* sammnedd (O), 9, 1.
sāmyn, sammyn, *see* sāmen.

sanct, sant, *sb.,* OE. sanct; *saint,* 1, 11; sannt (O.), 8, 17. Nth. sānt, 131, 8. Cf. saint.
sand, *sb* , OE. sand, sǫnd; *sand, land,* 161, 25. Cf. sǫnd.
sānde, *sb.,* OE. sand, sǫnd, *f.; mission, message, messenger; pl.* sāndes, 2, 16. Cf. sǫnde.
sāne, *wkv.,* Nth. = Ml. seine(n); OE. segnian; *sign, mark with sign, bless, pt. sg.* sānyt (1Nth.), 169, 12.
sāng, *sb.,* Nth. = Ml., Sth. sǫng; OE. sang, sǫng; *song,* 127, 5.
sannt, sānt, *see* sanct.
sānyt, *see* sāne.
sār, *adj.,* Nth. = Ml. sǫr; OE. sār; *sore, grievous, sad; superl.* sārest, 149, 32.
Sarasyn, Sarazin, *sb.,* OF. Sarazin; *Saracen, heathen,* 88, 2; *pl.* Sarazins, 126, 16; Sarasynes, 230, 4.
sāre, *adv.,* Nth. for Ml. sǫre; OE. sāre; *sorely,* 77, 4; 109, 10.
sārī, *see* sārȳ.
sārlīc, *adj.,* OE. sārlīc; *sad, mournful,* 188, 18.
sārȳ, *adj.,* Nth. = Ml. sǫrī; OE. sārig, *sorry,* 154, 17.
Sātan, *sb.,* OF. Satan; *Satan,* 155, 7.
Sātanas, Satenas, *sb.,* L. Satanas; *Satan,* 16, 17; Satenas, 153, 10.
sate, sāte, *see* sitte(n).
Saterday, *sb.,* OE. Sæterdæg; *Saturday,* 209, 20.
sattel, *wkv.,* Nth. = Ml. settle(n); OE. setlan; *settle; inf.* sattel, 151, 24.
sau, sauʒ, *see* sawe, sē(n).
Saul, *sb.,* OF. Saul; *Saul,* 131, 1.
sāule (sawle), saul, *sb.,* eME. Nth. = Ml. sowle, OE. sāwel, sāwl, *f.; soul,* 2, 22; sāwle nēde, *soul's need,* 9, 4; sāwle berrhless (O), *soul's salvation,* 10, 24. Nth. saul, 142, 20; sawell, 156, 18; *pl.* sauls, 137, 22. eSth. *pl.* saule, 180, 16; sawlen, 197, 6. Kt. zaule, 216, 14; *pl.* saulen, 211, 24.
saumpul, *sb.,* OF. esample; *example, sample,* 127, 29.
sauve, *see* sāve(n).

sāve, *prep.* and *conj.*, OF. sauf; *save, except*, 73, 15.
sāve(n), *wkv.*, OF. salver, sauver, saver; *save, preserve, observe*; *inf.* sāve, 117, 18; unwȳse tō sāve it, *ignorant in observing it*, 235, 17; *pr. sbj. sg.* sāve, 90, 12; *imp. sg.* sāve, 211, 4; sauve, 211, 22; *pp.* sāved, 74, 7. Nth. *pr. 3 sg.* sāves, 128, 21. Sth. *pp.* isauved, 211, 25.
Savvey, *sb.*, NF. Savei, OF. Savoi, *Savoy*; *ds.* Savveye, Perres of, *Peter, Earl of Richmond*, 227, 4.
savyōūrę, *sb.*, OF. saveour; *savior*, 119, 17.
sawe, *sb.*, OE. sagu; *saying, saw*, 97, 6; *pl.* sawes, 137, 1. Nth. sau, 148, 23.
sawe, *see* sē(n).
sawell, sawle(n), *see* sāule.
sawtērę, *sb.*, OF. sautier < psaltier; *psalter*, 121, 1.
Saxon, *sb.*, OF. Saxon; *Saxon*; *pl.* Saxons, 203, 18; in Saxon, *against the Saxons, or in Saxony, that is England*, 224, 1; West Saxon, *the kingdom of the West Saxons*, 222, 26.
Saxonlȳch, *adv.*, OF. Saxon + līce; *like the Saxon*, 224, 9.
say, saye(n), sayn, *see* seie(n).
scǣ, *see* hē.
scœl, scœrp, *see* schule(n), scharp.
scaft, *sb.*, eME. = Ml. schaft; OE. sceaft; *shaft, arrow, spear*; *pl.* scaftes, 189, 30. Cf. shaft.
scane(n), *wkv.*, OE. scǣnan; *break*; eME. *pr. pl.* scanen, 189, 30.
scarslȳch, *adv.*, OF. escars + Sth. lȳch; *scarcely*, 225, 18.
scatere(n), *wkv.*, ODu. scateren?; *scatter*; *pt. sg.* scatered, 2, 21.
scāðe, *sb.*, ON. skaði; *harm*, 29, 10.
scaw, *see* schewe(n).
sceal, *see* schule(n).
scēld, *sb.*, eME. = Ml. schēld; OM. sceld (scēld), WS. scield; *shield*; *pl.* scēldes, 189, 30.
scēone, *adj.*, WS. scēone, scīene, OM. scēne; *beautiful, bright*, 190, 27.
sceort, *see* schort.

scēove(n), *stv.*, OE. scēofᴀn (scūfan)–scēaf (2); *shove, move with violence*; eSth. *inf.* scēoven, 191, 2.
scerp, schaft, *see* scharp, shafte.
schal(e), schalle, schalt, *see* schule(n).
schāme, *sb.*, OM. scamu (WS. sceamu, scamu); *shame, ignominy*, 42, 17; shāme, 87, 13. eSth. scheome, 195, 30. Sth. ssāme, 207, 16.
schāme(n), *wkv.*, OE. sceamian; *be ashamed, feel shame*; Sth. *imp. pl.* ssāme ʒē, 207, 10.
schāmlīc, *adj.*, OE. sceamlīc; *shameful, base*, 153, 4.
schāp, *sb.*, OM. gescap, WS. gesceap; *shape, image*, 62, 24.
scharp, *adj.*, OM. scarp (WS. scearp); *sharp*, 60, 6; eME. scærp, 3, 12. Sth. scerp, 186, 15.
schāpe, *sb.*, OM. scaða, WS. sceaða; *harm, injury*, 150, 4.
schau, schaues, *see* schewe(n).
schauing, *sb.*, Nth. = Ml. schowinge; OE. scēawung, *f.*; *showing*, 153, 28.
schāve(n), *stv.*, OE. scafan–scōf (6); *shave*; *pp.* schāve, 120, 29.
schawed, *see* schewe(n).
schē, schēawe(n), *see* hē, shewe(n).
schēde(n), *stv.*, OE. scēadan–scēod (R); *separate, divide, shed*; *pt. pl.* schēd, 132, 19.
schēde(n), *wkv.*, OM. *scēdan, based on scēadan, *stv.*; *separate, divide, shed*; *pt. sg.* schedde, 122, 22. Sth. *pt. sg.* ssedde, 208, 30.
schēlde(n), *wkv.*, OM. sceldan, WS. scieldan; *shield, protect*; *imp. sg.* schēldę, 123, 20. Sth. (SEMl.), *inf.* sīlde(n), 15, 6; *pr. 3 sg.* sīldeð, 17, 23; *pr. sbj. sg.* schilde, 64, 3.
schēnde(n), *wkv.*, OE. scendan, scēndan; *injure, disgrace*; *imp. pl.* schēndeð, 195, 30; *pp.* schent, 59, 10. Sth. *pp.* ischende, 125, 34.
scheome, *see* schāme.
scheortlīche, *see* schortlȳ.
schēp, shēp, *sb.*, OM. scēp, WS. scēap; *sheep*, 53, 3; sēp = schēp, 15, 6; schēp, 86, 16.

scheppe(n), *stv.*, OM. sceppan (WS. scieppan)–scōp (6); *shape, fashion, create; pt. sg.* schōp, 49, 17; schōpe, 62, 25; shoope, 245, 13. eSth. *pt. sg.* scōp, 178, 27.

schēte(n), *stv.*, OE. scēotan–scēat (2); *shoot, throw; pp.* schǫte, 61, 16. Sth. *pt. sg.* sscęt, 207, 24; *pp.* ischoten (eME.), 195, 33; issǫte, 208, 20.

schewe(n), *wkv.*, OE. scēawian; *show; inf.* shǣwenn (O), 13, 1; schewe, 44, 15; shewe; 104, 13; *pr.* 1 *sg.* shewe, 227, 11; *pp.* shewed, 91, 1. Nth. *inf.* scaw, 130, 1; schau, 148, 24; schew, 130, 5; *pr.* 3 *sg.* schaues, 150, 15; *pr. ppl.* schewand, 144, 4; *pt. sg.* schawed, 155, 32; *pp.* schawed, 153, 29. eSth. *imp. pl.* schęaweð, 198, 31. Kt. *inf.* ssewȳ, 216, 1; sēawȳ, 217, 16; *pr. pl.* sēaweth, 211, 28; *pt. sg.* sēawede, 213, 8.

schift, *sb.*, OAng. *scift, cf. scíftan; *shift, turn, trick*; at a schift, *suddenly*, 152, 19.

schilde(n), *see* schēlde(n).

schip, ship, *sb.*, OE. scip; *ship*, 73, 18; scip (eME.), 1, 14. Sth. ssip, 205, 15; *pl.* scipen (eSth.), 185, 4; schipes, 221, 17.

schipe(n), *wkv.*, OE. scipian; *take ship, navigate; pt. pl.* schipede, 220, 8.

schipman, *sb.*, OE. scipman; *shipman, sailor*, 163, 13. eSth. *pl.* scipmen, 186, 9.

schir, *see* sīre.

schīre, *sb.*, OE. scīr, *f.*; *shire*, 227, 8.

scho, *see* hē.

schō, *sb.*, OM. scōh (scō), WS. scēoh (scēo); *shoe;* shō, 229, 12; *pl.* schōnę, 120, 23.

schold(e), schollde, *see* schule(n).

schone, *see* schune(n).

schōp, *see* scheppe(n).

schorn, *see* shęre(n).

schort, *adj.*, OM. scort, WS. sceort; *short;* eME. scort, 3, 11; schortę, 145, 2. eSth. sceort, 191, 2; ssort, 215, 10.

schortlȳ, *adv.*, OAng. scortlīce, WS. sceortlīce; *shortly, briefly*, 133, 13. eSth. scheortlīche, 198, 17.

schǫte(n), *see* schēte(n).

schōtynge, *pr. ppl.* as *sb.*, based on OE. scēotan; *shooting*, 120, 19.

schręade, *sb.*, eSth.= Ml. schręde; OE. scręade; *shred, cutting; pl.* schręaden, 202, 8.

schrewe, *see* shrewe.

schrīde(n), *wkv.*, OE. scrȳdan; *clothe, enshroud; inf.* schrīde, 57, 7.

schrif, *see* schrīve(n).

schrift, schryft, *sb.*, OE. scrift; *confession, shrift*, 156, 32; *ds.* scrifte, 18, 19; schryftę, 109, 30. Sth. *ds.* ssrifte, 218, 21.

schrīve(n), schrȳve(n), *stv.*, OE. scrīfan–scrāf (1); *shrive; inf.* schrȳve, 110, 16; *pp.* schriven, 59, 10; shriven, 75, 26; schryvyn, 110, 22. Nth. *pr. sbj. sg.* and *pl.* schrīf, 157, 3. Sth. *pt. sg.* schrǭf, 199, 15; *pt. pl.* ssrive, 206, 20; *pp.* ischriven, 199, 16; ischryve, 121, 30.

schroud, *sb.*, OE. scrūd; *dress, garment, shroud*, 48, 20; 57, 4; *pl.* srūd = shrūd, 31, 15.

schrūde(n), *wkv.*, Sth. = Ml. schrīde(n); OE. scrȳdan; *clothe; inf.* schrūden, 201, 30; *pp.* ischrūd, 199, 4.

schryft, *see* schrift.

schrȳve(n), schryvyn, *see* schrīve(n).

schule(n), shule(n), *pt. prv.* OM. sculan–scel (WS. sceal); *ought, shall; pr.* 1, 3 *sg.* schal, 37, 11; schalę, 123, 22; schallę, 123, 5; *pr.* 2 *sg.* shallt (O), 9, 5; schalt, 49, 8; *pr. pl.* shulenn (O), 9, 23; schullen, 65, 17; schul, 65, 20; schulyn, 116, 21; shǫle wē, 82, 6; *pt.* 1, 3 *sg.* sculde (eME.), 1, 7; shollde (O), 9, 17; schōlde, 68, 15; schōld, 71, 24; *pt.* 2 *sg.* sculdest (eME.), 3, 26; scholdest, 49, 30; scholdist, 55, 23; *pt. pl.* scholde, 46, 13. Nth. *pr.* 1, 3 *sg.* sal, 128, 17; *pr.* 2 *sg.* salt, 18, 15; *pr. pl.* sal, 133, 5; *pt. sg.* suld, 135, 25;

pt. pl. suld, 130, 32 ; *pt. pl.* sulden, 27,32. **Sth**.*pr.*1, 3 *sg*. scæl (eSth.), 176, 21 ; sceal (eSth.), 177, 2 ; ssel, 215, 2 ; *pr.* 2 *sg*. ssalt, 204, 18 ; sselt, 215, 2 ; *pr. pl.* sollen, 212, 1 ; ssolle, 207, 18 ; scule wē, 179, 3 ; *pt.* 1, 3 *sg*. ssolde, 204, 8 ; *pt. pl.* solden, 213, 21 ; *pr.* 2 *sg*. schuldest, 194, 8.

schune(n), **shune**(n), *wkv.*, OE. scunian ; *shun, avoid, abhor* ; *inf.* schóne, 55, 8.

schyl, *sb.*, OM. *scil, cogn. with ON. skil; *reason, excuse*, 117, 14.

scilwīs, *adj.*, ON. skilwīss ; *wise in reason, wise*, 127, 15.

scip, **scipen**, *see* **schip**.

scipman, *see* **schipman**.

Scitia,*sb.*,Lat.Scythia ;*Scythia*,220,8.

sclī, *see* **slīc**, **slyȝ**.

scōle, **skōle**, *sb.*, OE. scōl, *f.*, infl. by OF. escole? ; *school*, 224, 17 ; skōle, 137, 29.

scōp, *see* **scheppe(n)**.

scōre, *sb.*, ON. skor, *f.* ; *score*, 225, 1.

scorn, *sb.*, OF. escorne ; *scorn, derision* ; *pl.* scornes, 218, 13.

scort, *see* **schort**.

Scot, **Skot**, *sb.*, OE. Scottas, *pl.* ; *Scot* ; *pl.* Scottes, 159, 12 ; Skottes, 160,20. **Sth**.*gpl*.Scottene,222,14.

Scotlānd, **Scotlǫnd**, *sb.*, OE. Scotland ; *Scotland*, 2, 15 ; *ds.* Scotlǫnde, 189, 2 ; Scotlǫnd, 220, 21.

Scottene, *see* **Scot**.

Scottysch, **Scottys**, **Scottes**, *adj.*, OE. Scyttisc, infl. by Scot ; *Scottish*, *Scotch*, 221, 28. **Nth**.Skottis, 159, 31 ; Scottes, 160, 7.

scōwkyng, *sb.*, based on root in sculken < ON. *skulka ; cf. Dan. skulke ; *skulking, treacherous relation*, 170, 12.

scrift, *see* **schrift**.

scrīpe(n) = **schrīpe(n)**, *stv.*, OE. scrīðan–scrāð (1) ; *glide, go, fly* ; eME. *inf.* scrīpen, 186, 15.

sculde, **sculen**, *see* **schule(n)**.

scurn, *wkv.*, origin uncertain; *hasten* ; **Nth**. *inf.* scurn, 150, 26.

sē, *see* **sē(n)**, **þē**.

sę̄ (sē), *sb.*, OE. sǣ ; *sea* ; eME. **sæ̈**, 1, 13 ; sę̄, 19, 22 ; *gs.* sę̈ę̈s, 19, 25. **Nth**. sē, 151, 17. **eSth**. sę̄a, 196, 33. **Kt**. see, 211, 1.

sē, *sb.*, OF. sed ; *see (of a bishop), seat, throne*, 68, 4.

sę̄, **se**, *adv.*, OE. sǣ < swǣ ; *so*, 178, 11 ; se (O), 10, 6.

sēa, *see* **sę̄**.

sēaweth, **sēawȳe(n)**, *see* **schewo(n)**.

sēche(n), **seke(n)**, *wkv.*, OE. sēcean –sōhte ; *seek* ; *inf.* sēche, 98, 28 ; sēke, 90, 3 ; *pr.* 3 *sg*. sēkeð, 15, 17 ; *imp. sg.* sēch, 193, 3 ; *pr. ppl.* sēchand (Nth.?), 101, 19 ; sēchyng, 235, 12 ; *pt. sg.* sogt, 23, 23 ; *pp.* sogt, *driven*, 25, 1. **Sth**. *pr. pl.* sēkeð, 196, 13. **Kt**. *pr.* 3 *sg*. zēkþ, 219, 20 ; *pr. sbj. sg.* zēche, 218, 29.

seck, *sb.*, ON. sekkr. cogn. with OE. sæcc, Lat. saccus ; *sack, bag* ; *pl.* seckes, 26, 21.

secunde, *adj. sb.*, AN. secund, OF. second ; *second*, 225, 2.

sēd, *sb.*, OM. sēd, WS. sǣd ; *seed, offspring*, 73, 10.

sēde, **see**, *see* **sę̄(n)**, **seie(n)**.

sę̈ęl, *sb.*, OF. seel ; *seal*, 226, 21.

seen, *see* **sē(n)**.

sefenfāld, *sb.*, **eME**. = Ml. sevenfǫ̈ld ; OM. seofonfāld, WS. –feald ; *sevenfold* ; sefennfāld (O), 12, 29. **eSth**. seovevāld, 195, 4.

seffnde, **seffne**, *see* **sevende**, **seven**.

sę̈ge(n), *wkv.*, OE. *sǣgan < sīgan ; *sink, fall* ; *pr.* 3 *sg*. sę̈geð, 27, 8.

sę̄ȝen, **sę̈ggen**, *see* **sē(n)**, **seie(n)**.

seghen, *see* **sē(n)**.

sę̈grūnd, *sb.*, OE. sǣgrund (grūnd) ; *bottom of the sea*, 19, 19.

seh, *see* **sē(n)**.

seie(n), **saie(n)**, *wkv.*, OE. secgan –sægde ; *say* ; *inf.* seien, 19, 3 ; sei, 2, 5 ; sægen (eME.), 4, 28 ; sǣin (eME.), 4, 9 ; seyn, 119, 1 ; saie, 103,23 ; saynę̈, 111, 28 ; say,120,4 ; *pr.* 1 *sg*. seyȝe, 52, 9 ; *pr.* 2 *sg*. seyst, 112, 7 ; *pr.* 3 *sg*. seyþ, 65, 18 ; seythę̈, 111, 8 ; seið, 179, 23 ; *pr. sbj. sg.* sei, 18, 19 ; *imp. sg.* seię̈, 41, 27 ; *imp. pl.* seið, 30, 30 ; *pt. sg.* sǣde, 6, 5 ;

sēde, 37, 1 ; seide, 21, 19 ; seyd, 65,
30 ; *pt.* 2 *sg.* seidist, 51, 8 ; *pt. pl.*
sǣden (eME.), 1, 17 ; seiden, 25, 4 ;
pp. seid, 33, 9. **Nth.** *inf.* sainę,
160, 1 ; *pr.* 2 *sg.* sais, 138, 6 ; seys,
91, 25 ; *pr.* 3 *sg.* sais, 150, 17 ; *pr. pl.*
sā ӡhē, 174, 14 ; *pt. sg.* sayd, 135,
22 ; *pp.* saydę, 140, 15. **Sth.** *inf.*
seggen, 179, 3 ; siggen, 198, 1 ;
sügge, 181, 6 ; *imp. pl.* siggeð, 197,
22 ; *pr. sbj. sg.* segge, 179, 25 ; *pr.*
sbj. pl. sigge wē, 211, 22 ; *pp.* iseyd,
60, 1 ; yseyd, 66, 31. **Kt.** *inf.* zigge,
215, 6 ; *pr.* 2 *sg.* zayst, 215, 5 ; *pr.*
3 *sg.* zayþ, 215, 8 ; *pt. pl.* sēden,
213, 1 ; *pp.* yzēd, 216, 11.
seiӡ, seiӡe(n), *see* sē(n).
seil, *sb.*, OE. segl ; *sail* ; *pl.* seiles,
205, 16 ; seyl, 86, 27.
sein, *see* saint.
seinie(n), *wkv.*, **Sth.** = Ml. seine(n) ;
OE. segnian ; *sign, marke' with a*
sign, bless ; *pp.* iseined, 226, 20.
seint, seinte, *see* saint.
sēk, *adj.*, OE. sēoc ; *sick*, 59, 9.
e**Sth.** sēoc, 181, 9.
sēke(n), *see* sēche(n).
sēkęnisse, sekęnes, *sb.*, OE. sēocness, *f.* ; *sickness, disease* ; *pl.* sēkenisses, 104, 18 ; sēkęnes, 143, 14.
seker, *see* siker.
sēking, *sb.*, based on OE. sēcan ;
seeking, search, 99, 32.
sekyr, *see* sikere(n).
sēl, *sb.*, OM. sēl, WS. sǣl ; *time,*
occasion ; on sēl, *on occasion, regu-*
larly, 21, 15 ; sēlę, 95, 9.
sēl, *adj.*, OE. sēl ; *good* ; **Sth.** *ds.*,
sēle, 183, 28 ; *gpl.* sēlere, 186, 30.
Sēland, *sb.*, OE. *Sǣland ; *Seland,*
164, 6.
selc, *sb.*, OE. seolc ; *silk*, 38, 24.
selcūth, *adj.*, OE. seldcūð ; *strange,*
wonderful, 127, 5.
sēld, *see* shēld.
sēlde(n), sēldum, *adv.*, OE. selden
(sēlden) ; *seldom*, 134, 3 ; sēlde, 36,
14 ; sēldum, 25, 21.
sēle, *see* sēl.
self, *prn.*, OE. self, *wk.* selfa ; *self* ;
eME. sælf, 8, 2 ; self, 38, 26 ; *wk.*

selve, 68, 4 ; *wk. pl.* selven, 59, 21 ;
combined with *pers. prn.* mēsellfenn
(O), 9, 8 ; mīself, 44, 29 ; þȳself,
119, 24 ; þīselve, 50, 2 ; himmsellf
(O), 11, 23 ; himmsellfenn (O), 13,
1 ; hymself, 92, 8 ; *pl.* hemself, 63,
20 ; hemselfe, 118, 4. **Nth.** þāmselfe, 144, 6 ; þaymęselfe, 146, 28.
Sth. (eSth. seolf, 182, 10 ; seolve,
182, 18 ; seolven, 183, 23) ; sülf,
177, 5 ; *ds.* sülfne, 176, 14 ; combined with *pers. prn.* himsülf, 207,
28 ; *pl.* himsülve, 177, 8. **Kt.** zelve,
217, 9 ; *pl.* ham zelve, 218, 22.
selhða, *sb.*, OM. sēlð, WS. sǣlð, *f.* ;
happiness, felicity, 193, 12.
sē.ī, *adj.*, OM. sēlig, WS. sǣlig ;
happy, good, 24, 10 ; 80, 6.
sęllə(n), *wkv.*, OM. sellan-sālde
(WS. sealde) ; *sell* ; *inf.* selle, 86,
20 ; *pt. sg.* sōlde, 86, 15. **Nth.** *pp.*
sāld, 130, 28 ; saldę, 148, 22. **Sth.**
pp. isǫld, 36, 16.
sellȳ, *adj.*, OE. sellīc < seldlīc ;
strange, marvellous, 47, 27.
selvə, selven, *see* self.
sęm, *sb.*, OE. sēam ; *horse load* ; *pl.*
sęmes, 31, 21
semblaunt, *sb.*, OF. semblant ; *ap-*
pearance, semblance, 42, 8.
semblē, *sb.*, OF. semblē ; *meeting*,
118, 25.
semble(n), *wkv.*, OF. sembler ;
assemble, collect ; *pt. sg.* sembled,
164, 19.
sēmęlȳ, *adj.*, ON. sœmligr ; *agree-*
able, seemly, 116, 6.
sēme(n), *wkv.*, OE. sēman ; *befit,*
suit, seem ; *pr.* 3 *sg.* sēmeþ (O),
9, 19 ; sēmeð, 25, 9 ; *pr. sbj. sg.*
sēme, 50, 1 ; *pt. sg.* sēmyd, 108, 12 ;
pt. pl. sēmede, 221, 9. **Nth.** *pr.*
3 *sg.* sēmes, 145, 6.
sən, *see* sippen.
sē(n), *stv.*, OM. sēon-sæh (WS.
seah) (5) ; *see, look after, care for* ;
inf. sēn, 9, 10 ; seen, 33, 22 ; sēo,
37, 2 ; *pr.* 2 *sg.* sēst, 81, 9 ; sȳst,
124, 11 ; *pr.* 3 *sg.* sēð, 15, 20 ; *pr.*
pl. sēn, 20, 1 ; sēnę, 124, 1 ; *pr. sbj.*
sg. sē, 17, 15 ; *imp. sg.* sē, 102, 5 ;

GLOSSARY

433

pt. sg. sahh (O), 12, 25; sag, 27,
29; sau3, 47, 27; say, 58, 13;
sei3e, 67, 18; sagh, 89, 29; sȳe,
1c8, 29; sawę, 113, 1; *pt. pl.* se3e
< se3en, 41, 24; sei3en, 103, 18;
pt. sbj. sg. sawe, 79, 12; sǫge, 19,
4; *pp.* seyn, 63, 19; sēnę, 85, 4.
Nth. *inf.* sē, 127, 15; *pt. sg.* sey,
132, 26; sagh, 133, 8; *pp.* sēnę,
129, 10. **Sth.** *pr. pl.* sēþ, 209, 7;
pr. sbj. sg. sēo (eSth.), 195, 23; *pt.
sg.* seh, 194, 12; sei3, 229, 29; *pt.
pl.* sȳe, 223, 16. **Kt.** *pr.* 3 *sg.* zȳþ,
219, 26; *pr. ppl.* zȳinde, 216, 8;
pt. pl. seghen, 212, 16; *pp.* yzy3þ,
216, 8.
senche(n), *wkv.*, OE. sencan; *cause
to sink, sink, drown*; *pt.sg.* senchte,
197, 3.
sēnde(n),*wkv.*, OE. sendan (sēndan);
send; *pr.* 3 *sg.* sēndeð, 31, 31;
sēnt, 64, 24; *pr. pl.* sēnden, 27, 16;
pr. sbj. sg. sēnde, 177, 3; *pt. sg.*
sende, 1, 4; sennde (O), 12, 13;
sente, 24, 31; sent, 65, 21; *pt. pl.*
senden, 2, 9; *pp.* sent, 28, 18. **Nth.**
pt. pl. sēnd=sendit, 171, 14. **Sth.**
pr. pl. sēndet for sēndeþ, 177, 22;
pt. sg. senden, 184, 32; *pp.* isent,
42, 1; ysent, 69, 16. **Kt.** *inf.* zēnd,
217, 10.
sēne, *see* sē(n).
Seneca, *sb.*, Lat. Seneca; *Seneca*,
200, 31.
Senek, *sb.*, OF. Senek; *Seneca*, 238,
10.
senne, sēo, *see* sinne, sē(n).
sēoc, *see* sēk.
seolf, seolve, seolven, *see* self.
seolver, *see* silver.
seotel, *sb.*, eME.=Ml. settel; OE.
setl, setol; *seat, settle*, 195, 11.
seoððan, *see* siþþen.
seove(n), seovene, *see* seven.
seoveniht, *see* sevenyht.
seovevāld, *see* sefenfāld.
sēowen, sēp, *see* sowe(n), schēp.
sēr, *adj.*, ON. sēr; *several, various*;
pl. sēre, 126, 2; sērę, 135, 3.
sēr, *adj.*, OE. sēar; *sear*, 59, 9.
Seresberī (Sereberī), *sb.*, OE.

Searoburh (-byrig); based on Lat.
Sorbiodunum; *Salisbury, Old Sa-
rum* (Wiltshire); eME. Rogēr of,
1, 5; 2, 24.
serfullī, *adv.*, OM. *serhfullīc?; cf.
Orm's serrhfull; *sorrowfully*, 48,
8.
serjaunt, serğant, *sb.*, OF. sergant,
-jant; *sergeant, man of law*, 98, 5;
sergant, 212, 12.
serk, *sb.*, ON. serkr, cogn. with OE.
serc; *shirt*, Scotch *sark*, 83, 16.
sermōne(n), *sb.*, OF. sermoner;
preach, 245, 18.
sertaynę, sertis, *see* certain, certes.
servāğe, *sb.*, OF. servage; *service,
servitude*, 94, 16.
servandę, *sb.*, OF. servant, modified
by *pr. ppl.* of serven?; *servant*,
147, 28.
serve(n), *wkv.*, OF. servir; *serve*;
pr.pl. serven, 39, 23; *pt.sg.* servede,
21, 15; *pt. pl.* serveden, 213, 30;
pp. served, 48, 2. **Sth.** *inf.* servī,
195, 2.
serves, *see* servīse.
servīe(n), *see* serve(n).
servīse, servȳs, serves, *sb.*, OF.
service; *service*, 212, 1; servȳs,
144, 27; serves, 120, 4.
sęse(n), sęsi(n), *wkv.*, OF. saiser;
*put in possession of, take possession
of, seize*; *pt. sg.* sęsyd, 115, 23.
sęsǫnd, *sb.*, OE. sǣ+sand (sǫnd);
sea sand, 19, 6.
sesse(n), *wkv.*, OF. cesser; *cease*;
pr. sbj. pl. sesse, 146, 15. Cf.
cęse(n).
sēst, *see* sē(n).
sęsȳde, *sb.*, OE. sǣ+sīde; *seaside*,
222, 12.
sęte, *sb.*, ON. sǣti; *seat*, 105, 10.
sēte, *adj.*, ON. sœta, cogn. with OE.
swēte; *sweet, agreeable, pleasing*,
56, 15.
set, sete, sēte, sēte(n), *see* sitte(n).
Seþ, *sb.*, OE. Seth, Lat. Seth; *Seth*,
64, 9.
sēþ, *see* sē(n).
sethin, seþþen, seþthe, *see* siþþen.
sette(n), *wkv.*, OE. settan; *place*,

set; *pt. sg.* sette, 4, 13; sett, 101, 2; setted, 104, 3; *pt. pl.* setten, 60, 25; sette, 35, 27; *pp.* sett (O), 9, 7; set, 22, 7. **Sth.** *pp.* isæt (eME.), 183, 3; iset, 200, 24.

seurtē, *sb.*, OF. seurté; *surety, pledge*, 114, 15.

seven, seve, *adj.*, OE. seofan; *seven*; *pl.* seffne (O), 11, 15; sevene, 15, 21; seve, 42, 12. **eSth.** seovene, 177, 4; seove, 180, 20. **Kt.** zeve, 218, 20.

sevende, *adj.*, OE. seofoða; *seventh*, 147, 11; seffnde (O), 12, 18; seven = sevend, 71, 9.

seventī, *adj.*, OE. seofontig; *seventy*, 103, 9.

sevenyght, *sb.*, OE. seofon + niht, *pl.*; *seven-night, week, sennight*, 109, 18. **eSth.** seovenihet, 201, 3.

seveþe, *adj.*, **Sth.**, OE. seofoða; *seventh*, 223, 4. Cf. **sevende**.

sex, six, *adj.*, OM. sex, WS. siex, six; *six*; sexe, 15, 21; six, 223, 31.

Sexisch, *adj.*, OE. Sexisc; *Saxon, of the Saxon*; *mas.* Sexisne = Sexischne, 186, 21.

Sexlǫnd, *sb.*, OE. Seaxland(lǫnd); *land of the Saxons*, 185, 16; *ds.* Sexlǫnde, 189, 1.

sexte, *adj.*, OM. sexta, WS. siexta (sixta); *sixth*, 12, 11; syxte, 223, 1.

sextī, sixtī, *adj.*, OAng. sextig, WS. siextig, sixtig (sextig); *sixty*; sextī fōt, *sixty feet*, 151, 22; sixtī, 4, 24. **Kt.** zixtī, 216, 6.

sey(n), *see* **sē(n)**.

seyde, seyȝe, *see* **seie(n)**.

seyl, *see* **seit**.

seylīe(n), *wkv.*, **Sth.** = Ml. seile(n); OE. seglian; *sail*; *pt. pl.* seylede, 221, 2.

seyn, *see* **seie(n), sē(n)**.

seynt, seynte, *see* **saint**.

seyntwarȳ, *sb.*, OF. saintuaire, saintuairie; *sanctuary*, 124, 25.

shadowe, *sb.*, OE. sceadu, *acc.* sceadwe, *f.*; *shadow*, 101, 5.

shadowe(n), *wkv.*, OE. sceadwian; *shadow, shade*; *inf.* shadow, 103, 26.

shǣwe(n), *see* **schewe(n)**.

shafte, *sb.*, OE. sceaft, *f.*; *created thing, creature, creation*; shaftte (O), 12, 32; schaft, 49, 17. Cf. **scaft**.

shallt, *see* **schule(n)**.

shāme, *see* **schāme**.

shanke, *sb.*, OE. sceanca, scanca; *shank, leg*, 229, 14.

shāpe(n), *wkv.*, OM. scapian (WS. sceapian); *shape*; *inf.* shāpe, 243, 17; *pp.* shāped, 77, 27.

shāve(n), *stv.*, OM. scafan (WS. sceafan) –scōf (6); *shave, scrape*; *pp.* shāven, 23, 24.

shēld, *sb.*, OM. sceld (scēld), WS. scield; *shield*, 79, 28; sēld = shēld, 17, 23.

shenke(n), *wkv.*, OE. scencan; *pour out*; *pr. pl.* shenke, 60, 20.

shēp, *see* **schēp**.

shēre(n), *stv.*, OE. sceran–scær (4); *shear, cut, reap*; *inf.* shēren, 30, 27; *pp.* schorn, 57, 26.

shewe(n), *see* **schewe(n)**.

shīlde(n), *see* **schēlde(n)**.

shīne(n), *stv.*, OE. scīnan–scān (1); *shine*; *pr.* 3 *sg.* shȳneð, 228, 12; *pp.* sinen, 14, 10.

shīr, *adj.*, OE. scīr; *bright, clear, pure*, 83, 1.

shō, schole, shollde, *see* **schō, schule(n)**.

shoopþe, *see* **scheppe(n)**.

shrewe, schrewe, *sb.*, OE. scrēawa; *shrew, evil person*; *pl.* shrewes, 97, 2; schrewes, 121, 7.

shriven, *see* **schrīve(n)**.

shrȳn, *sb.*, OE. scrīn; *shrine*; *ds.* shrȳne, 227, 20.

shuldre, *sb.*, OE. sculdor, *pl.* sculdru; *shoulder*, 83, 17; *pl.* shulderis, 103, 26. **Sth.** *pl.* ssóldren, 207, 18.

shulen(n), sholde, *see* **schule(n)**.

shȳne(n), *see* **shīne(n)**.

shȳnyng, *pr. ppl.* as *sb.*, OE. scīnend; *shining, glory*, 103, 19.

sī, *see* **bē(n), þē**.

sib, syb, *adj.*, OE. sibb; *related, friendly*; *pl.* sybbe, 144, 14.

sib, *sb.*, OM. sibb, *f.*, later *neut.*; *peace, concord*, 7, 17.

sic, *see* **swilc**.

side, *sb.*, OE. sīde; *side*, 46, 10; *pl.*
sīden, 76, 6; on sўde, *aside, near
by*, 169, 25.

sigge(n), sight(e), *see* **seie**(n), **siht**.

sign, *sb.*, OF. signe; *sign*, 199, 30.

signefiance, *sb.*, OF. signifiance;
significance, 212, 27.

sigt, **sizt**, *see* **siht**.

sīhe(n), *stv.*, OE. sīgan–sāg(h) (I);
glide, fall, rise; *pr. pl.* sīhen, 196,
27.

siht, **sigt**, **sizt**, **sight**, **sighte**, *sb.*,
OE. gesiht, gesihð,*f.*; *sight*; sigte,
16, 22; syʒt, 47, 27; sizht, 55, 9;
siht, 156, 17; sighte, 242, 10. Kt.
zyʒþe, 215, 12.

sihðe, *sb.*, OE. gesihð,*f.*; *sight, vision*,
197, 14. Cf. **siht**.

sīke(n), *stv.*, OE. sīcan–sāc (I); *sigh,
groan*; *pr.* 3 *sg.* sīkeð, 196, 15.

siker, *adj.*, ON.?, cf. Dan. sikker,
OFris. siker < Lat. securus; *sure,
secure*; seker, 150, 30, **eSth.** *ds.*
sikere, 177, 18.

sikere(n), *wkv.*, cf. OFris. sikura;
make sure, secure; *inf.* sekyr,
110, 4.

sikerliche, **sikerlīke**, **sikerlike**
(lyke), **sycurlў**, *adv.*, ON.?, cf.
Dan. sikker, OFris. siker, Lat.
securus; *certainly, truly*, 16, 22;
sikerlike, 77, 25; sikerlyke, 107,
10; sycurly, 124, 12; **Sth.** sikerlīche, 200, 17.

sīlden, *see* **schelde**(n).

sīlence, *sb.*, OF. silence; *silence*, 199,
26.

silver, *sb.*, OM. siolfor, seolfor; *silver*,
26, 22; sylvre, 2, 5; sylver, 2, 22;
eSth. seolver, 189, 4.

Silvius, *sb.*, Lat. Silvius; *Silvius
Posthumus*, 220, 2.

Sīmōn, *sb.*, OF. Simon; *Simon*,
227, I.

sin, **sinden**, *see* **sippen**, **bē**(n).

sinen, *see* **shīne**(n).

sineginge, *sb.*, OE. syngung, *f.*;
sinning, 18, 11.

sinful, *adj.*, OE. synful; *sinful*, 16,
17.

singe(n), *stv.*, OE. singan–sang (song)
(3); *sing*; Nth. *pr.* 3 *sg.* singes,
76, 26. **Sth.** *pr. ppl.* singinde, 196,
27.

sinʒēre, **sinniēr**, **synnēr**, *sb.*, based
on OE. synnig, 'sinful'; *sinner*;
pl. sinʒēres, 100, 16; sinniērs, 100,
23; synnērs, 100; 25; synʒērs,
104, 2.

singinde, *see* **singe**(n).

sinīgeden, *see* **synne**(n).

sinke(n), *stv.*, OE. sincan–sanc (3);
sink; *inf.* sinken, 20, 10; *pt. pl.*
sònken, 63, 20; suncken, 197, 6.
Sth. *pp.* isunken, 188, 31.

sinndenn, *see* **bē**(n).

sinne, **synne**, *sb.*, OE. syn(n), *f.*;
sin; *pl.* sinnes, 4, 9; synʒes, 104,
26. Nth. syne, 144, 10; *pl.* syns,
137, 19. **Sth.** *pl.* sünnen, 196, 7.
Kt. senne, 211, 20; zenne, 216, 22;
pl. zennes, 218, 12.

sīp, *see* **schip**.

sīre, **sўr**, **syr**, *sb.*, OF. sīre; *sire, sir*;
sīrę, 40, 3; sўr, 108, 30; syr, 110,
13. Nth. sir, 137, 8; schir, 166, 9.

sīse, *sb.*, OF. assise; *session, meeting*,
set yōur sīse, *made your compact*,
57, 15.

sister, **syster**, *sb.*, ON. syster, cogn.
with OE. sweostor, lWS. swystor;
sister, 77, 14; *pl.* systeren, 116, 20;
systeres, 118, 32. Cf. **suster**.

sīte, *sb.*, ON. sўti; *sorrow*, p. 294.

site(n), sitē, *see* **sitte**(n), **citē**.

sīþ, **sīþe**, *sb.*, OE. sīð, *m.*; *time,
occasion*; *ds.* sīþe, 10, 3; *pl.* sīþe,
42, 12. Kt. *pl.* zīþe, 218, 20.

sith(–on), **sīðen**, **siþin**, **sythen**, *see*
siþþen.

siþþen (**seþþen**), **siþþe**, **sīðen**, **siþin**,
sin, *adv.*, OE. siððan; *afterwards,
since*; siððan (eME.), 2, 13; sythen,
4, 32; siþþenn (O), 11, 10; sithon,
3, 31; sīðen, 15, 12; sìþin, 49, 27;
sīþþe, 39, 6; syth, 110, 1; sin, 52, 30;
seþþen, 65, 29. Nth. sethin, 137,
5; sen, 135, 23; syne, 168, 20.
Sth. seoððan (eSth.), 182, 7;
seþthe, 224, 27; sòððen, 196, 28;
süððe, 179, 28; süþthe, 224, 20.

sitte(n), *stv.*, OE. sittan–sæt (5); *sit,*
remain; *inf.* sitten, 3, 17; *pr.* 2 *sg.*
sittest, 62, 23; *pr.* 3 *sg.* sit (sitt) =
sitteþ, 67, 17; *pr. ppl.* sittende, 3,
26; syttyng, 93, 21; *pr. sbj. sg.*
sitte, 199, 11; *imp. pl.* sitteð, 184,
5; sitte ȝē, 201, 29; *pt. sg.* (eME.)
sæt, 183, 27; sat, 52, 14; satę, 89,
11; *pt. pl.* sāte, 89, 2; *pt. sbj. sg.*
sēte, 19, 6; *pp.* sete, 58, 6. Nth.
pr. 3 *sg.* sittes, 62, 27; *pp.* sittyn,
174, 25; *pr. ppl.* sytand, 173, 26.
Sth. *pt. sg.* set, 195, 11; *pt. pl.*
sęten, 201, 2.

six, *see* sex.

sixtēnðe, *adj.*, OE. sixtēoða, infl. by
sixtēne; *sixteenth,* 197, 8.

sixtī, *see* sextī.

skant, *adj.*, ON. scamt, *neut.* of
skammr, 'short'; *scant,* 143, 21.

skarslī, *adv.*, OF. escars + ME. lī;
scarcely, 143, 20.

skīe, *sb.*, ON. skȳ, *n.*; *sky, cloud*; *pl.*
skīes, 15, 21.

skil, *sb.*, ON. skil; *discrimination,*
reason, skill, 49, 18; skill (O), 9,
28; *ds.* skylle, 88, 7.

skōle, Skottis, *see* scōle, Scottysch.

skylle, *see* skil.

skyn, *sb.*, ON. skinn; *skin,* 241, 3.

slad(e), *sb.*, OE. slæd *n.* ; *slade, grass-*
land; eME. *pl.* slades, 187, 5.

slæn, *see* slǭ(n).

slāēr, *sb.*, based on slā, ' strike, kill';
slayer; *pl.* slāērs, 147, 4.

slagen, *see* slǭ(n).

slāke(n), *wkv.*, OE. slacian; *loose,*
set free, slack; *pr.* 3 *sg.* slākeð, 17,
4; *pp.* slāked, 159, 5.

slā(n), *stv.*, ONth. slā (WS. slēan)–
slōh(g) (6); *strike, slay, kill*; *inf.*
slā, 158, 30; slay < *pr.* 3 *sg.* 152,
8; *pr. sbj. sg.* slaa, 147, 2; *pt. sg.*
slogh, 131, 16; *pt. pl.* slogh ȝē, 160,
17; slew, 171, 2; *pp.* slānę, 173, 10.

slaughtre, *sb.*, ON. slähtr, infl. by
slahtra, ' to slaughter'; *slaughter,*
massacre, 233, 8.

slāwe(n), *wkv.*, eME., OE. slāwian;
be slow, neglect; *inf.* slawen, 177,
13.

slay, slayn, *see* slā(n), slǭ(n).

slē, sleeþ, *see* slǭ(n).

sleghþe, *sb.*, ON. slǣgð, *f.* ; *device,*
sleight, 125, 27.

sləip, slę̄(n), slę̨ęn, *see* slēp, slǭ(n).

slēp, *sb.*, OM. slēp, WS. slǣp, Gt.
slēp; *sleep,* 1, 14; *ds.* slēpe, 14, 9.
Nth. sleip, 172, 31.

slēpe(n), Sth. slę̄pe(n), *stv.*, OM.
slēpan (WS. slǣpan)–slēp (R);
sleep; *inf.* slēpen, 3, 18; *ger.* tō
slēpen, 14, 12; *pr. ppl.* slēpinge,
39, 32; *pt. sg.* slēpę, 4, 8. Nth. *pr.*
ppl. slēpand, 154, 29. Sth. *inf.*
slę̄pen, 203, 10.

slēpyng, *sb.* < *pr.* *p.* of slēpe(n);
sleeping, 93, 17.

sleuth, *sb.*, 1Nth. = Ml. slōþ; ON.
slōð; *track,* 166, 21.

sleuþe, *sb.*, OE. slǣwð, *f.* ; *sloth,*
idleness, 209, 13.

sleuthhǔnd, *sb.*, ON. slōð + OE.
hund, hūnd; *sleuth-hound, tracking*
hound, 166, 20.

slewe, sley, *see* slǭ(n), slyȝ.

slī, slīc (slīk), *adj.*, ON. slīkr, cogn.
with OE. swylc; *such*; slī, 128,
16; sclī, 129, 32; slīc, 149, 29.

slī, *see* slyȝ.

slinge(n), *stv.*, OE. slingan–slang
(3); *sling, fling*; *pt. pl.* slóngen,
63, 16; *pp.* sloungen, 61, 19;
slónge, 208, 11.

slǭ(n), slę̄(n), *stv.*, OM. slān, slēan
(WS. slēan)–sloh(g) (6); *strike,*
slay, kill; *inf.* slān (eME.), 184,
9; slǭ (NEMl.), 80, 19; slę̨ęn
(SEMl.), 238, 9; *imp. sg.* slę̄, 120,
16; *pt. sg.* slogh, 163, 25; slōh, 186,
17; slou, 80, 8; slouȝ, 220, 21; *pt. pl.*
slōghen, 5, 9; slowe, 208, 12; slewe,
110, 28; *pp.* slagen, 30, 1; slayn, 53,
6. Sth. *inf.* slę̨ęn, 240, 3; slæn
(eME.), 183, 9; *pr.* 3 *sg.* slę̨ęth,
239, 14; *imp. sg.* slę̄, 233, 21; *pp.*
islaȝen, 186, 26; yslawe, 244, 28;
yslayn, 239, 11. Cf. Nth. slā.

slonge(n), sloungen, *see* slǭ(n).

slouþe, *sb.*, OE. slǣwð, *f.*, infl. by
slāw; *sloth, laziness,* 120, 12.

slowe, *see* slǭ(n).

slycht, *sb.*, ON. slœgð, *f.*; *device, sleight,* 166, 14. Cf. Ml. sleghþe.

sly3, slī (sclī) *adj.*, ON. slœgr (slǣgr), earlier, ME. slēh; *cunning, skilful, sly,* 62, 25. Sth. sley, 206, 6.

slȳlȳ, *adv.*, ON. slœgr + ME. lȳ; *slily,* 242, 29.

slyttyng, *sb.*, OE. *slittung, *f.*, cf. OE. slītan, *stv.*; *slitting, piercing,* 225, 25.

smæt, *see* smīte(n).

smāken,*wkv.*,OE.smæccan,smeccan, or *smacian?; *taste, smack, smell*; *inf.* smāken, *smell,* 33, 27 ; *pr. shj. sg.* smāke, 14, 2.

smal, *adj.*, OE. smæl; *small, thin*; *pl.* smāle, 23, 11.

smart, *see* smerte.

smecchunge, *sb.*, OE. *smeccung,*f.*; *tasting,* 197, 14.

smēch, *sb.*, OM. smēc, WS. *smīec (smīc, smȳc) ; *vapor, smoke*; *ds.* smēche, 176, 18.

smel, *sb.*, *smell,* 62, 18 ; nēse smel, *smell of his nose,* 14, 2.

smelle(n), *wkv.*, based on OE. smel, *sb.*; *smell*; *inf.* smelle, 49, 11.

smeorte, *sb.*, eME. = Ml. smerte ; OE. *smeorte, cf. smeortan; *grief, sorrow,* 179, 25.

smēre(n),*wkv.*,OE. smerian; *smear, anoint*; *inf.* smēren, 33, 26; *pt. pl.* smēred, 34, 8 ; *pp.* smēred, 34, 10.

smērles, *sb.*, OE. smerels ; *ointment,* 34, 7.

smert, earlier smerte, *adv.*, OE. *smeorte, cf. smeortan; *smartly, quickly,* 92, 30.

smerte, smart, *adj.*, OE. *smeorte ; *smart*; Nth. smart, 128, 8.

smertlȳ, *adv.*, OE. *smeortlīce, cf. *vb.* smeortan; *smartly, briskly,* 138, 17.

smīt, *see* smīte(n).

smite, *sb.*, OE. *smite, cf. MLG. smite; *blow, stroke, part,* 69, 24.

smīte(n), *stv.*, OE. smītan–smāt (1); *smear, cast, smite, go*; *pr.* 3 *sg.* smīt = smīteð, 19, 9; *pt. sg.* smŏt, 60, 24; smǫǫt, 239, 15; *pt. pl.*

smiten, 23, 13. Nth. *inf.* smīt, 152, 6. e8th.*pt. sg.* smæt, 182, 5.

smǫke, eME. smoke, *sb.*, OE. smoca ; *smoke,* 62, 16; smoke, 3, 6.

smǫken, eME. smoken, *wkv.*, OE. smocian; *smoke*; *pt. pl.* smoked (eME.), 3, 6.

smǫǫt, smǫt, *see* smīte(n).

˜smoþer, *sb.*, OE.*smorðor, cf. smorian, choke,' smother'; *dense smoke,*62, 16.

smyttyng, *sb.*, OE. *smittung,*f.*, cf. smittian ; *smearing,* 221, 7.

snāke, eME. snake, *sb.*, OE. snaca; *snake,* 3, 10.

snarre, *sb.*, OE. snearu ; *snare; pl.* snarrys, 145, 14.

snell, *adj.*, OE. snell; *quick, active,* 49, 9.

snow, *sb.*, OE. snāw; *snow*; snowę, 102, 10.

sǫ (sō), soche, *see* swǫ, swilc.

socōre, socōur, socūre, *see* sucūr.

soden, *see* suden.

sodenlȳch, sodeynlȳch, *adv.*, OF. soudain + Sth. lȳch ; *suddenly,* 223, 23.

Sodom, *sb.*, OF. Sodom, displacing OE. Sodoma ; *Sodom,* 73, 23.

soffre(n) (sofere(n)), *see* suffre(n).

softe, *adj.*, OE. sēfte, infl. by sōfte, *adv.*; *soft, mild, peaceable,* 2, 27.

softe, *adv.*, OE. sōfte; *softly,* 53, 23.

sǫge, sogt, *see* sē(n), sēche(n).

sǫjorne(n), *wkv.*, OF. sojourner ; *sojourn*; *inf.* sǫjorne, 108, 20.

sǫlās, *sb.*, OF. solas, sollas; *solace,* 216, 27.

solidi, *sb.*, Lat. solidus-i ; *shillings,* 4, 24.

sollen (solden), *see* schule(n).

som, somdęl, *see* sum, sumdęl.

somed, *adv.*, OE. samod, somod ; *together,* 187, 25.

somer, *see* sumer.

somer, *sb.*, OF. somier, sumer; *sumpter horse,* 48, 22.

somnīen, *wkv.*, Sth. = Ml. somne(n) ; OE. samnian, somnian; *assemble*; *pt.sg.*somnede,188, 32; *pp.*isomned, 185, 27.

somonōr, *sb.*, OF. semoneor; *summoner, apparitor*, 117, 32.

somoūne(n), somoūnyn, *wkv.*, OF. somuner; *summon*; *inf.* somoūnyn, 119, 3; *pp.* somoūned, 118, 25; sompned, 233, 13.

son, *see* sune, sunne.

sōn(sōna), *see* sōne.

sǭnd, *sb.*, OE. sand, sǫnd; *sand*, 86; 24; *as.* sǫnde, 105, 24.

sǭnde,*sb.*, OE. sand, sǫnd,*f.*; *sending, messenger*; *dish of food, course at dinner*, 29, 7; *pl.* sǭndes, 25, 5. Sth. *pl.* sǫnde, 186, 5; sǫnden, 192, 13.

sǭnde = shǭnde, *sb.*, OM. scand, scǫnd, WS. sceand, *f.*; *disgrace, ignominy*, 20, 18.

sǭnden, *see* sǭnde, 'sending'.

sone, *see* sune, sunne.

sōne, sōn, *adv.*, OE. sōna; *soon*, 2, 1; sōna, 2, 11; sōn, 155, 18. 1Nth. soyn=sōn, 166, 3.

Sonenday, *see* sunnendai.

sǭngę, *sb.*, OE. sǫng; *song*, 124, 27.

sonken, *see* sinke(n).

sonne, *see* sunne.

sonnebęm, *see* sunnebęm.

sǭpe, *sb.*, OE. sāpe; *soap*, 198, 28.

Sophīe, *sb.*, eSth. = Ml. Sǫphīe; OF. Sophīe; *Sophia*, 196, 28.

sorcerȳę, *sb.*, OF. sorcerie; *sorcery*, 145, 16.

sǭre, *adv.*, OE. sāre; *sorely*, 20, 24.

soreʒen, *see* sorge.

sorful, sorhful, *adj.*, OE. sorhfull; *sorrowful*, 30, 6. eSth. sorhful, 186, 22. Cf. sorowful.

sorge, soreʒe, sorow(e), sorwe, *sb.*, OE. sorh(g), *f.*; *sorrow*, 22, 18; soreʒe, 37, 8; sorwe, 26, 12; sorow, 93, 7; sorowe, 103, 11. Sth. (SEMl.) *pl.* soreʒen, 41, 10; sorʒen, 182, 26; sorghen, 211, 18. Nth. soru, 151, 30; *pl.* sorous, 143, 1. Kt. zorʒe, 215, 13; *pl.* zorʒes, 217, 12.

sorhful, *see* sorful.

sǭrī, sǭrȳ, *adj.*, OE. sārig; *sorry*, 24, 2; sǫrȳ, 240, 21.

scrīnesse, *sb.*, OE. sārigness, *f.*; *sorrow, compassion*, 44, 8.

sorow(e), scrwe, *see* sorge.

sorowful, *adj.*, OE. sorhful, infl. by OE. sorh-sorwe, ME. sorge, sorow; *sorrowful*, 102, 23.

soru, sorous, sorwe, *see* sorge.

sǫrȳ, *see* sǭrī.

sot, sotę, *adj.*, *sb.*, OF. sot; *foolish, fool, sot*; sot, 177, 6; sotę, 126, 18.

sōþ, sōð, sōth, *adj.*, *sb.*, OE. sōð; *true*, archaic *sooth*, 10, 24; sōð, 22, 27; sōth, 52, 16; tō sōþe, archaic *to sooth, in truth*, 10, 10; *comp.*, *pl.* sōðere, 188, 20. 1Nth. suth, 136, 9; sōthę, 146, 2. Kt. zōþ, 216, 3.

sōþefast, *adj.*, OE. sōðfæst; *true*, 149, 11.

sōþenes, *sb.*, OE. *sōðnes, *f.*; *truth*, 102, 7.

sōðere, *see* sōþ.

sōððen, *see* siþþen.

sotlīce, *adv.*, OF. sot + OE. līce; *foolishly*, 2, 21.

soule, *see* sowle.

soulehęale, *sb.*, eME. = Ml. soulehęle; OE. sāwol + hæl, hæle, *f.*; *soul health* or *safety, salvation*, 200, 13.

soulenēde, *sb.*, ME. soule + nede; *need of the soul, salvation*, 51, 5.

soulevōde, *sb.*, Sth. = Ml. soulefōde; OE. sawul + fōda; *soul-food*, 200, 12.

soūn, *sb.*, AN. sun, OF. soun(son); *sound*, 225, 12.

soūne(n), *wkv.*, OF. suner; *sound*; Nth. *pr.* 3 *sg.* soūnes, 146, 2.

soūning, *sb.*, OF. sun, NF. soun + ME. ing(e); *sounding, pronunciation*, 225, 20.

soūth (soūþ), *see* sūð.

soūþeron,*adj.*,OE. sūðerne; *southern*, 224, 11.

sowe(n), *stv.*, OE. sāwan-sēow (R); *sow, plant*; *inf.* sowen, 30, 27; *pt.* *pl.* sēowen (eME.), 176, 22.

sowle, soule, *sb.*, OE. sāwol,*f.*; *soul*; *gs.* sowles, 16, 28; soule drink, *soul drink*, 18, 18. Cf. sāwle, saule.

soyn, *see* sōnę.

spac, spæche, *see* spēke(n), spēche.
spak, spāk, *see* spēke(n).
Spallding, *sb.*, *Spalding* (Lincolnshire), 8, 10.
spāre, *adj.*, OE. spær; *spare, stingy,*
124, 28.
spāre(n), Sth. sparīe(n), *wkv.*, OE.
sparian; *spare*; *pr. sbj. pl.* spāre
þey, 124, 5. Sth. *inf.* sparīen, 202,
7; *imp. pl.* (eSth.), sparīe, 195, 29.
sparkle, *sb.*, OE. spearka, extended;
spark, sparkle; *pl.* sparkles, 61, 25.
Spaygne, *sb.*, OF. Spaine; *Spain,*
46, 1.
spec, *see* spēke(n).
spēce, *sb.*, OF. spece, spice; *spice,*
49, 11. Cf. spīce.
spēche (spēche), *sb.*, OM. spēc, WS.
spæc, *f.*; *speech, language, discourse,*
50, 29; spǣche (O), 10, 20;
spēche (?), 59, 2. Sth. spēche,
199, 7.
special, specyal(l), *adj.*, OF. especial; *special, beloved,* 154, 6;
specyal, 95, 14; specyall, 146, 18;
in special, *especially,* 233, 26.
specialī, *adv.*, OF. especial + ME. lī;
specially, 146, 16. Sth. specialȳch,
225, 25; specialīch, 236, 26.
specialtē, *sb.*, OF. especialtē; *specialty,*
partiality, 174, 2.
specialȳch, *see* specialī.
specyal, *see* special.
spēd, *sb.*, OE. spēd, *f.*; *speed, good
fortune, success,* 24, 10.
spēde(n), *wkv.*, OE. spēdan; *speed,
prosper; inf.* spēden, 29, 15; *pt. sg.*
spedde, 7, 3.
spēk, *sb.*, Nth. = Ml. spēche; OAng.
spēc, WS. spǣc, *f.*; *speech, discourse,*
170, 15.
spēke(n), *stv.*, OE. specan-spæc (5);
speak; inf. spēke, 38, 27; *pr. 3 sg.*
spēkeð, 198, 5; *pr. sbj. pl.* spēken,
197, 15; *imp. pl.* spēke 3ē, 199, 9;
pr. ppl. spēkyng, 98, 29; *pt. sg.*
spac, 6, 2; spak, 42, 21; spake,
105, 18; *pt. pl.* spōken, 76, 7; spāk,
89, 9. eSth. *inf.* speke, 176, 9;
speoken, 193, 17. Sth. *pt. sg.* spec,
199, 6.

spēle(n), *wkv.*, OE. spelian; *spell,
take place of, atone for, spare*; *inf.*
spēle, 63, 4
spell, *sb.*, OE. spell; *speech, narrative,*
MnE. *spell*; eSth. *dpl.* spellen, 184,
1; *pl.* spelles, 184, 6.
spelle(n), *wkv.*, OE. spellian; *narrate,
spell, speak; inf.* spellenn, 9, 4.
Nth. *pr.* 1 *sg.* spell, 134, 7.
spellunge, *sb.*, OE. spellung, *f.*; *conversation, discourse,* 197, 14.
spēnde(n), *wkv.*, OE. āspendan;
spend; Sth. *pp.* ispend, 176, 12.
speoken, *see* spēke(n).
spēre, *sb.*, OE. spere; *spear,* 61, 23.
eSth. *pl.* speren, 189, 29.
spēre(n), *wkv.*, ON. sperra; *fasten;
inf.* spēren, 26, 2; *pp.* sperrd (O),
12, 26; sperd, 21, 3.
spewe(n), *stv.*, OE. spīwan-spāw
(1); *spew, vomit; pr. 3 sg.* speweð,
17, 10.
spīce, *sb.*, OF. espice; *spice; pl.* spīces,
27, 23.
spīcelike, *adv.*, OF. espice + OE.
līce; *with spices,* 33, 27.
spīe, *sb.*, OF. espie; *spy,* 56, 19; *pl.*
spīes, 25, 9.
spīe(n), *wkv.*, OF. espier; *spy, ex-
plore; inf.* spīen, 25, 12.
spille(n), *wkv.*, OE. spillan; *spill,
destroy; inf.*, spylle, 113, 10; *pp.*
spylte, 111, 12. Nth. *inf.* spill,
137, 11. Sth. *pp.* yspild, 219, 18.
spōken, *see* spēke(n).
spōusebrēk, *adj.*, OF. espūse + OAng.
brēce, WS. brǣce; *adulterous,*
132, 7.
spōusīe(n), *see* spūse(n).
sprang, *see* springe(n).
spraule(n), *wkv.*, OE. sprēawlian;
sprawl; pt. pl. sprauleden, 79, 14.
sprēde(n), *wkv.*, OE. sprǣdan;
spread; inf. sprēde, 133, 18; *pt.
pl.* spred, 89, 3; spredden, 228, 18.
sprenge(n), *wkv.*, OE. sprengan;
make to spring, sprinkle; pr. 2 sg.
sprengest, 102, 8; *pr. pl.* sprengen,
189, 29.
springe(n), *stv.*, OE. springan-sprang
(3); *spring; pr. 3 sg.* springeð, 15,

17; *pt. sg.* sprǫngę, 228, 10; *pt.pl.*
sprŏngen, 61, 25. **Nth.** *pt. sg.*
sprāng, 143, 12. **Sth.** *pr. pl.*
springeð, 202, 14.

spulʒe(n), *wkv.*, *spoil, despoil*; *pp.*
spulʒeit, p. 292.

spūse(n), *wkv.*, OF. espouser; *es-*
pouse, betroth, marry; *inf.* spūsen,
46, 20. **Sth.** *inf.* spoūsī, 204, 4.

spylte, *see* spille(n).

squyēre, *sb.*, OF. esquiere; *squire*;
pl. squyērs, 98, 5.

squylēr, *sb.*, OF. escuelier; *scullion*,
99, 13.

srūd, *see* schroūd.

ssalt, ssāme, *see* schule(n), schāme.

sscęt, *see* schēte(n).

ssed = shed, *sb.*, **Sth.** = Ml. shāde;
OE. scead (scæd); *shade, shadow*,
215, 18.

ssedde, *see* schędde(n).

sselt, *see* schule(n).

ssētare = schētare, -ęre, *sb.*, based
on OE. scēotend or *scēotere?;
shooter, bowman; *pl.*(?) ssētare,
208, 19.

ssewȳ, ssip, *see* schewe(n), schip.

ssoldren, *see* shuldre.

ssolle, ssolde, *see* schule(n).

ssort, ssrift, *see* short, shrift.

ssrive, *see* schrīve(n).

stābell, *adj.*, OF. estable; *firm,
stable, brave*; *pl.* stābell, 126, 13..

stāhle(n), *wkv.*, OF. establir; *establish*; *pp.* ystābled, 223, 15.

stābylnes, *sb.*, OF.estable + ME.nes;
stableness, stability, 145, 4.

stad, stæl, *see* stede, stęle(n).

staf, *sb.*, OE. stæf; *staff*, 241, 1.

stāgę, *sb.*, OF. estage; *stage, period*,
127, 32.

stāh, stæl, *see* stīge(n), stęle(n).

stal, stāli, *see* stęle(n).

stalwŏrþe, stalwŏrp, *adj.*, OM. stæl-
werðe, WS. swierðe; *strong, stal-
wart*, 97, 29; stalewurþe, 195, 29;
stalwŏrþ, 221, 16.

stampyng, *sb.*, based on stampe(n);
stamping, pounding, 174, 25.

stān, eME. Nth. for Ml. stǫn, *sb.*,
stone; *pl.* stānes, 3, 12.

standard, *sb.*, OF. estendard; *Battle
of the Standard*, 5, 9.

stande(n), stǫnda(n), *stv.*, OE.
standan (stǫndan)-stōd (6); *stand*;
inf. stanndenn (Ō), 12, 14; stǫnde,
59, 24; stǫnden, 234, 13; *pr. 3 sg.*
stannt (Ō), 9, 3; stant, 14, 1;
stontę, 98, 19; *pt. sg.* stōd, 21, 23;
stōd tō, *incline to*, 51, 4; stōdę,
89, 11; stood, 227, 20; *pt.pl.* stōdę,
190, 25. **1Nth.** *pt. sg.* stud, 168,
17. **Sth.** *pr.* 3 *sg.* stent, 176, 20;
pp. ystǫnde, 336, 18.

stāne(n), *adj.*, OE. stǣnen, infl. by
stān?; *of stone*; in stānene, *in (coffin,
sepulchre) of stone*, 196, 33.

stāne(n), *wkv.*, OE. stǣnan, infl. by
stān; *stone*; **Nth.** *inf.* stān, 132,
8.

stānęstill, *adj.*, OE. stān + still; *stonestill*, 161, 18.

Stanewig, *sb.*, *Stanwick* (Northamp
ton), 4, 24.

Stanfŏrd, *sb.*, *Stamford* (Lincolnshire), 6, 15.

stannt, starck, *see* stānde(n), stark.

stāre(n), *wkv.*, OE. starian; *stare,
glitter, shine*; *pr. ppl.* stārinde, 80,
15. **Nth.** *pr. ppl.*, stāreand, 163,
13.

stark, starck, *adj.*, OE. starc, stearc;
stark, strong, 75, 3; starck, 197, 3.

stāt, *sb.*, OF. estat; *state, condition*;
stātę, 133, 21; stāt, 154, 14; *pl.*
stātes, 236, 2.

staðel, *sb.*, OE. staðol; *foundation*;
ds. staðele, 196, 8.

statūt, *sb.*, OF. statut; *statute*, 236,
26.

stēde, *sb.*, OE. stēda; *steed*; *pl.*
stēdes, 48, 23; stēdys, 107, 15.

stędę, *sb.*, OE. stede, lWS. styde;
place, stead, 32, 30. **Sth.** stüde
(< lWS. styde), 189, 21.

stędefæstlīche, *adv.*, based on OE.
stedefæst; *steadfast*, 226, 11.

stędefast, stedfast, *adj.*, OE. stedefæst; *steadfast*, 20, 21; stedfast,
130, 14. **eSth.** stędefæst, 226, 9.

stędefastnesse, *sb.*, OE. stedefæstnes,
f.; *steadfastness*, 18, 6.

stede(n), *wkv.*, ON. steðja, *pp.*
staddr; *stand, place, press hard*;
pp. stad, 168, 4; 173, 4. Cf. cn-
stede.

stedfast, *see* stędefast.

stefne, *sb.*, OE. stefn. *f.* ; *voice, sound,
commotion*, 183, 30.

steiȝe, *see* stīge(n).

stęke(n), *stv.*, OE. stecan-stæc (5);
stick, fasten itself; *inf.* stęke, 122,
16.

stēl, *sb.*, OM. stēl, WS. stīel; *steel*,
20, 7.

stęlen, eME. stelen, *stv.*, OE. stelan-
stæl; *steal*; *pt. sg.* stæl, 5, 24; stal,
6, 29; *pt. pl.* stāli hī, 6, 8; *pp.*
stǫlen, 22, 11.

stęm, *sb.*, OE. stēam; *steam, vapor*,
83, 4.

stent, steorm, *see* stǫnde(n), storm.

stēorman, *sb.*, eSth. = Ml. stērman;
OE. stēorman; *steersman, pilot*; *pl.*
stēormen, 188, 8.

steortnaket, *adj.*, OE. steort + nacod;
quite naked, 194, 19.

Stęphne, later **Stęphen**, *sb.*, OF.
Stephne; *Stephen*; Stephen of Blois
(Blais), nephew of Henry I, and
king from 1135-54, 2, 7.

steppe(n), *stv.*, OE. steppan (stæp-
pan)-stōp (6); *step*; *pr.* 3 *sg.* steppeð, 14, 5; *pt. pl.* stōpen, 187, 27.

sterfst, sterfþ, *see* sterve(n).

sterin, *see* stire(n).

stērne, *sb.*, ON. stiarna, Dan. stjeıne;
star; *pl.* stērnys, 145, 16.

sterre, *sb.*, OE. steorra; *star*; *pl.*
sterres, 1, 16.

stert, *sb.*, OE. steort; *tail*, 14, 5.

sterte(n), *wkv.*, ON. sterta; *start*;
pt. sg. sterte, 36, 9. Cf. **stirte(n)**.

stertle(n), *wkv.*, based on ON. sterta,
ME. sterten, 'start'; *rush, move
swiftly, startle*; *pr. ppl.* stertlinde,
52, 8.

sterve(n), *stv.*, OE. steorfan-stearf
(3); *die, starve*; *inf.* sterve, 245, 4;
pr. 2 *sg.* sterfst, 216, 11; *pr.* 3 *sg.*
sterfþ, 215, 1; *pr. ppl.* stervinde,
218, 33; *imp. pl.* sterveþ, 216, 10; *pt.
pl.* sturven, 3, 28; storven, 245, 27.

stervinge, *sb.*, OE. *sterfung, *f.*;
death, 217, 22.

stevyn, stevin, *sb.*, OE. stefn; *voice,
constitution*, 135, 25; stevin, 140,
26.

steward, *see* stiward.

stī, *sb.*, OE. stīg; *path, way*, 18, 14.

stīge(n), stīȝe(n), *stv.*, OE. stīgan-
stāg(h) (1); *ascend, go up*; eME.
pt. sg. stāh, 11, 10. **SEMl.** *pt. sg.*
steiȝe, 68, 8.

stile, *sb.*, OE. stīgel, *f.*; *stile*, 160, 8.

stille, *adj. adv.*, OE. stille; *still,
quiet*, 14, 9; stylle, 89, 25.

stilnesse, *sb.*, OE. stilnes *f.*; *quiet*,
201, 25.

stinge(n), *stv.*, OE. stingan-stang
(3); *sting*; *pp.* stŏngen, 61, 23.

stinke(n), *stv.*, OE. stincan-stanc
(3); *smell, stink*; Sth. *pr. ppl.*
stinkinde, 217, 25.

stire(n), styre(n), *wkv.*, OE. styrian;
stir; *inf.* sterin, 53, 2; *pr.* 3 *sg.*
stireð, 14, 9; *pp.* styred, 5, 28.
Sth. *inf.* stüriȩ͑n), 181, 7; *pt. sg.*
stürede, 183, 30.

stirne, *adj.*, OE. styrne; *stern*, 43,
31. Sth. stürne, 204, 17.

stirte(n), *wkv.*, ON. sterta; *start,
leap*; *pr. pl.* stirte, 240, 9; *pt. sg.*
stirte, 82, 10; stirt, 77, 1; *pt. pl.*
stirten, 83, 12.

stīth, *adj.*, OE. stīð; *hardy, strong,
brave*, 128, 11.

stiward, later **steward**, *sb.*, OE.
stīweard < stigweard; *steward*, 27,
31; steward, 115, 22.

stōd(e), *see* stānde(n).

stok, *sb.*, OE. stocc; *stock, stem*, 235,
24.

stǫlen, *see* stęle(n).

stǫn, eME. Nth. stān, *sb.*, OE. stān;
stone, the grave, 15, 2; stǫnȩ, 90, 3.

stǫnchi(en), *wkv.*, OF. estanchier;
stanch, cause to cease; *inf.* stǫnchī,
217, 26.

stǫnde(n), stood, *see* stande(n).

stongen, *see* stīnge(n).

stǫnstille, *adj.*, OE. stān + stille;
still as a stone, stonestill, 201, 29.

stontȩ, *see* stande(n).

stŏpen, *see* steppe(n).

stoppe(n), *wkv.*, ON. stoppa ; *stop* ;
pr. 3 *sg.* stoppeð, 201, 10.

stǭre, *sb.*, OF. estor ; *store, treasure*,
88, 25.

storke, *sb.*, OE. storc ; *stork*, 145, 5.

storm, *sb.*, OE. storm ; *storm, tumult*,
19, 22. eSth. steorm, 196, 31.

storven, *see* sterve(n).

stǫry, *sb.*, OF. estoire, estorie ; *story,
tale*, 111, 8. Nth. *pl.* stǫris, 127,
3. Sth. stǫrẏes, 223, 10.

stound, *see* stŭnd.

stoūpe(n), *see* stŭpe(n).

stoūre, stŏwre, *see* stŭr.

stout, stoute, *adj.*, OF. estout ; *stout,
hardy, bold* ; stoute, 96, 18.

strā, *sb.*, ON. strā, cogn. with OE.
strēaw, strāw ; *straw*, 79, 5.

strāke, *sb.*, Nth. = Ml. strǫk ; OE.
*strāc ; cf. strācian ; *stroke* ; 173, 2.
Cf. strǫok.

strāng, *adj.*, Nth. = Ml., Sth. strǫng ;
OE. strang, strǫng ; *strong* ; *wk.*
strānge, 126, 5.

strānge, *sb.*, OF. estrange ; *strange*,
224, 9.

strāngelẏch, *adv.*, OF. estrange +
Sth. lẏch ; *strangely*, 225, 28.

stranger, *see* strǭng.

strangle(n), *wkv.*, OF. estrangler ;
strangle ; *pp.* strangled, 84, 20.

strātly, *adv.*, lNth. = Ml. streitlī ;
OF. estreit + ME. lī ; *straitly,
seriously*, 173, 4.

straungēr, *sb.*, OF. estranger ;
stranger, 233, 16.

strawe(n), *wkv.*, OE. strēawian,
streawian ; *strew, scatter* ; *inf.*
strawen, 35, 16.

strēam, *see* strēm.

strecche(n), strechche(n), *wkv.*,
OE. streccan–streahte ; *stretch* ; *inf.*
strecchen, 196,4; *pr.*3*sg.*strechcheþ,
221,27; *pt.sg.* (Sth.) strehte, 181,8.

streinþe(n) < strengþe(n), *wkv.*,
based on OE. strengðo ; *strengthen* ;
pt. sg. streinþed, 104, 28.

streite, *adv.*, OF. estreit ; *straitly,
closely, narrowly*, 61, 8.

strēm, *sb.*, OE. strēam ; *stream, river*,
22, 32 ; *pl.*, strēmis, 164, 5. Kt.
strēam, 216, 32 ; strēme, 217, 1.

strencðe, *see* strengþe.

strēng, later string, *sb.*, OE. streng ;
string ; *pl.* strēnges, 3, 8 ; stringes,
62, 10.

strenge(n), *wkv.*, OE. strengan ;
strengthen, make strong, establish ;
pr. sbj. sg. strenge, 196, 12.

strengere, *see* strǭng.

strengthe, strengþe, strenþe, *sb.*,
OE. strengðu, strengð,*f.* ; *strength*,
4, 22 ; strenþe, 149, 13 ; mid
strengþe, *by force*, 204, 10 ; strencðe,
196, 12 ; strengthe, 222, 5.

strēone(n), *wkv.*, eME. = Ml. strē-
ne(n) ; OE. strēonan ; *generate,
beget* ; Sth. *pp.* istrēoned, 198,
25.

strēte, *sb.*, OM. strēt, WS. strǣt,*f.* ;
street, 52, 8.

Stretford-atte-Bowe, Stretforþe-
Bowe, *sb.*, OM. Strētford, WS.
Strǣtford ; *Stratford-atte-Bow*, 230,
31 ; Stretforþe-Bowe, 232, 15.

streyȝt, *adv.*, *pp.* < OE. streccan ;
straight, straightway, 222, 22.

strīf, strẏf, *sb.*, OF. estrīf ; *strife*, 33,
24 ; striif, 126, 5 ; *ds.* strẏfe, 106,
18.

Striflin, *sb.*, *Stirling*, 160, 27.

string, *see* streng.

strogele(n), *wkv.*, origin uncertain,
perhaps *strǫkelen < OE. strāc ;
struggle ; *pr.* 2 *sg.* strŏgelest, 244, 1.

strǫnd, *sb.*, OE. strand, strǫnd ;
strand, shore ; eME. *ds.* strǫnde,
186, 14.

strǫng, *adj.*, OE. strang, strǫng ;
strong, 16, 4 ; *comp.* strengere, 7,
24 ; stranger ; 219, 15. eSth. *fas.*
strǫnge, 181, 19.

strǫok, *sb.*, OE. *strāc ; *stroke*, 228, 3.

stroye(n), *wkv.*, OF. destruire ; *de-
troy* ; Nth. *inf.* stroy, 163, 12.

strucyo, *sb.*, Lat. struthio ; *ostrich,
stork*, 145, 4.

strŭpe(n), *wkv.*, OE. (be)strȳpan ;
strip ; *inf.* strŭpen, 194, 19.

stryf, *see* strīf.

stud, stŭde, *see* stande(n), stēde.

studelfast, *adj.*, OE. *studolfæst, cf.
OHG. studil, ON. stuðill; *steadfast*,
196, 10.

studīe(n), *wkv.*, Sth. = Ml. stude(n);
OE. *studian, cf. OHG. (ga)studian,
OE. studu, *sb.*, 'prop'; *support*,
prop, stop; *imp. pl.* studgī 3ē, 195,
31.

stumble(n), *wkv.*, ON. stumra,
stumla; *stumble*; *pp.* stumbilde,
160, 8.

stūnd, stoūnd, *sb.*, OE. stund, stūnd,
f.; *moment, hour, time*, 19, 26; *ds.*
stoūnde, 100, 2.

stùnde, *adv.*, OE. stūnd, *sb. f.*; *at
once, for the time*, 35, 28.

stūpe(n), stoūpe(n), *wkv.*, OE. stū-
pian; *stoop*; *inf.* stūpen, 196, 4;
pt. sg. stūpede, 43, 27; stoūped,
90, 3.

stūr, stoūrę, sto͞wrę, *sb.*, OF. es-
tour; *strife, battle, tumult*; *pl.*
stūres, 150, 8; stoūrę, 115, 29;
sto͞wrę, 160, 9.

stūrīe(n), *see* stire(n).

stūrne, *see* stirne.

stūrnlīche, *adv.*, Sth. = Ml. sternlī;
WS. styrnlīce,OM.sternlīce; *sternly*,
fiercely, 187, 27.

sturven, *see* sterve(n).

stutte(n), *wkv.*, OE. *stuttan, cf.
MLG. stutten; *cease, stay, stop*; *pt.
sg.* stutte, 195, 27.

styff, styffę, *adj.*, OE. stīf; *strong,
valiant, stiff*; styffę, 115, 29.

stykke, *sb.*, Nth. = Ml. sticche; OE.
stycce; *stick, piece, fragment*, 142,
10.

stylle, *see* stille.

stynte(n), *wkv*, OE. (a)styntan;
cease, stop, stint; *inf.* stynte, 106,
18.

stynting, *sb. < pr. ppl.*; cf. OE.
styntan; *stop, pause*, 167, 19.

styre(n), *see* stire(n).

styrrynge, *sb.*, OE. styryng, *f.*; *stir-
ring, motion, emotion, passion*; ill
styrrynges, *evil passions*, 146, 13.

stywes, *sb. pl.*, OE. *stēawe, cf.
MLG. stouwe, 'fish pond'; *brothels*,
237, 9.

subject, *sb.*, OF. sujet, subject; *subject, vassal*, 235, 23.

subtile, *adj.*, OF. soutil, soubtil; *subtile*; subtiles (OF. *pl.*), 232, 22.

subtillȳ, *adv.*, OF. soutil, subtil +
ME. -lȳ; *carefully, subtilly*, 243, 2.

successiōn, *sb.*, OF. succession; *succession*, 221, 4.

succoūr, *see* sucūr.

sūch, suche, *see* swilc.

sucūr, succoūr, sòcoūr, sòcūrę,
sòcōrę, *sb.*, OF. sucurs; *succor*,
43, 4; sòcour, 102, 27; sòcūrę,
128, 20; sòcōre, 157, 17; succoūr,
168, 15.

sucūrīe(n), *wkv.*, Sth. = Ml. su-
cūre(n); OF. succurre; *succour*;
pr. sbj. sg. sucūrī, 211, 13; *pt. sg.*
sucūrede, 211, 13.

suddanlȳ, *adv.*, OF. sudein + lȳ,
suddenly, 172, 2.

suden, sòden, sudan, *adj.*, OF.
soudein; *sudden*; sòden, 124, 17;
sudan < sudān?, 143, 1.

sudūwīe(n), *wkv.*, OE. suduire; *subdue*; *pt. pl.* suduwede, 222, 31.

suętę(n), *wkv.*, OE. swǣtan; *sweat*;
Nth. *inf.* suętę, 152, 2.

suffrand, *see* suffre(n).

suffraunce, *sb.*, OF. sufraunce; *suffer-
ance, permission*, 236, 1.

suffre(n), sòffre(n), sòfere(n), *wkv.*,
OF. suffrir; *suffer*; *inf.* suffre, 42,
31; *imp. sg.* sòffere, 123, 3; sòfere,
123, 26; *pr. ppl.* suffrand, 104, 21;
pt. sg. suffred, 97, 7; sòffered, 122,
6; sufferd, 137, 26; *pp.* sòffrid, 55,
25. Nth. *inf.* suffer, 137, 20; *pr.
3 sg.* suffers, 139, 6.

sùgę̄ę, *see* seie(n).

sugḡestiōn, *sb.*, OF. suggestion;
suggestion, 235, 13.

sūke(n), *stv.*, OE. sūcan, sūgan, OM.
sēc (WS. sēac); *suck*; *pr. 3 sg.*
sūkeð, 19, 16.

sule(n) (sal, suld), *see* schule(n).

sülf, *see* self.

süllīche, *adv.*, OM. seldlīce, lWS.
syllīce; *strangely*, 193, 6.

sum, sòm, *adj.*, OE. sum; *some one*,
4, 28; *pl.* sume, 3, 11; sòme, 60, 17.

eSth. *gs.* summes, 192, 19; *ds.* summe, 200, 17.

sum, *conj.*, cf. Dan. som, OE. same, sǫme; *so, as, soever*; swā summ (O), *so as, just as*, 8, 17.

sumdēl, sòmdēl, *sb.*, OE. sum + dǣl; *some deal, somewhat*, 78, 21; sòmdēl, 208, 24.

sumer, *sb.*, OE. sumor; *summer, fair weather, as opposed to winter or foul weather*, 19, 23.

sumkin, *prn.*, OE. sum + cynn; *some kind of*; Nth. *pl.* sumkins, 130, 1.

summe, summes, *see* sum.

sumtȳde, *adv.*, OE. sum + tīd, *f.*; *sometimes*, 158, 1.

sumwhat, sumwat, *prn.*, OE. sum + hwæt; *somewhat*, 92, 27; sumwat, 53, 27. Nth. sumquat, 130, 22.

sun, suncken, *see* sune, sinke(n).

sūnd, *adj.*, OE. gesund(sūnd); *sound, healthy*, 15, 30.

Sunday, *see* Sunnendai.

sŭnden, *see* bē(n).

sundrī, *adj.*, OE. syndrig, infl. by sunder; *sundry, separate*, 31, 2.

sundrīe(n), *wkv.*, Sth. = Ml. sundre(n); OE. sundrian; *sunder, separate*; *pt. sg.* sundrede, 201, 21; *pp.* isundret, 195, 24.

sune, sòne, *sb.*, OE. sunu; *son*, 2, 1; sòne, 46, 1; *pl.* sunes, 24, 30; (SEMl.), sunen, 25, 15. Nth. sun, 129, 6; *pl.* sònnys, 174, 19.

sunne, sònne, sòn(e), sun, *sb.*, OE. sunne; *sun*, 1, 15; sònne, 89, 4. Nth. sòne, 150, 18; sòn, 148, 6; sun, 150, 19.

sunnebēm, *sb.*, OE. sunnebēam; *sunbeam*, 83, 5; sònnebēm, 228, 12.

sünnen, *see* sinne.

Sunnendæi, Sunday, *sb.*, OE. sunnandæg; *Sunday*; Sunnendǣi, 7, 31; Sónenday, 71, 9; Sunday, 116, 23.

superflùytee, *sb.* OF. superfluitē; *superfluity, excess*, 237, 15.

suppōse(n), *wkv.*, OF. supposer; *suppose*; *pr. pl.* suppōse, 234, 29.

sustayne(n), *wkv.*, OF. sustenir, infl. by ending teine; *sustain*; Nth. *pt.*

pl. sustaynede, 146, 27. Sth. *inf.* susteinī, 204, 19; susteyne, 220, 11.

susteinī, susteyne, *see* sustayne(n).

sustenance, sustenaunce, *sb.*, OF. soustenance; *sustenance*, 146, 27; sustenaunce, 234, 28.

suster, *sb.*, OE. sweoster, swuster; later displaced by ON. syster; *sister*, 7, 2; *gs.* suster, 180, 28; *pl.* sustren, 196, 21. Cf. sister.

susteyne(n), *see* sustaine(n).

suteli(n), *wkv.*, OE. sweotillian, swutelian; *become manifest, appear*; *inf.* sutelin, 194, 27.

sūð, sūth, sōuth, *adv.*, OE. sūð; *south*, 16, 26; sūth, 78, 5; sōuth, 55, 21.

suth, *see* sōþ.

suthfast, *adj.*, 1Nth. = Ml. sōþfast; OE. sōðfæst; *truthful*, 141, 12.

suthlȳ, *adv.*, Nth. = Ml. sōthlȳ; OE. sōðlīce; *truly*, 174, 14.

sūððe(n), süpthe, süth, *see* sippen.

swā, sā, *adv.*, eME. Nth. for Ml. swō (sǭ); OE. swā; *so, also, yet*, 1, 3; 128, 13; sā, 151, 29. Cf. swō.

Swanborow, *sb.*, *Swanborow*, 77, 14.

swart, *adj.*, OE. sweart; *dark, swart*, 182, 7.

sweche, *see* swilc.

swein, *sb.*, ON. svein, cogn. with OE. swān; *swain, servant*; sweyn, 75, 5; swein, 185, 9; *pl.* sweines, 186, 24.

swelle(n), *stv.*, OE. swellan–swæl (3); *swell*; *inf.* swelle, 49, 13.

swenche(n), swenke(n), swynke(n), *wkv.*, OE. swencan; *fatigue, torment, afflict*; *pt. pl.* swencten, 2, 32.

swēord, *see* swērd.

sweore, *sb.*, OE. sweora; *neck*, 180, 24.

swēp (swēp), *sb.*, OE. *swǣp(?); *scope, meaning*, 22, 22.

swērd, *sb.*, OE. sweord; *sword*, 41, 13; eME. swēord, 181, 17; *ds.* swēorde, 182, 6; *pl.* swēord, 189, 28. eSth. *ds.* swērde, 227, 25.

swēre, *sb.*, OE. swirn, sweora; *neck*, p. 267.

swēre(n), *stv.*, OE. swerian–swor(6); *swear*; *pr. sbj. sg.* swēre, 76, 23; *pt. sg.* swor, 6, 3; *pt. pl.* swore, 90, 13; *pp.* sworen, 2, 29; sworn, 57, 20. Nth. *pr.* 3 *sg.* swēris, 145, 27. Sth. *inf.* swerien (eSth.), 193, 19; *pr. sbj. pl.*, swērien, 226, 11; *pp.* iswōre, 204, 16; iswōrene, 226, 24.

swērie(n), *see* swere(n).

swērynge, *sb.*, OE. *swerung; *swearing*, 145, 28.

swēte, *adj.*, *adv.*, OE. swēte; *sweet*, 33, 27; swetteste, with shortening, 19, 10.

swettnes, *sb.*, OE. swētnes, *f.*, by shortening; *sweetness*, 145, 1.

sweven, *sb.*, OE. swefen; *sleep, dream*; eME. *ds.* swevene, 182, 24.

swevenyng, *sb.*, extension of OE. swefen; *dreaming*, 93, 18.

sweyn, *see* swein.

swicdōm, *sb.*, OE. swicdom; *deceit, fraud*, 1, 6.

swīce(n), *see* swīke(n).

swiche, *see* swilc.

swik, *sb.*, OE. swic, *n. deception*; *ds.* swike, 19, 14.

swike, *sb.*, OE. swica; *traitor, deceiver*; *pl.* swikes, 2, 12.

swikedōm, *sb.*, OE. swicdom; *treachery*; *ds.* swikedome, 183, 5.

swikelhēde, *sb.*, OE. *swicolhǣd; *deception*, 203, 22.

swīke(n), *stv.*, OE. swīcan–swāc (1); *deceive, fail, cease, desist from*; *imp. sg.* swīc, 18, 11; *pt. pl.* swyken, 5, 26; *pp. pl.* swikene, 179, 14.

swilc, swich, sych, such. sòch, *adj.* (*adv. conj.*), OM. swilc, lWS. swylc; *such, so*, 1, 15; swillc (O), 10, 6; swilch, 178, 24; sychę, 125, 29; *pl.* swilce, 4, 7; swilke, 25, 20; sweche, 59, 19; sòche, 114, 9; *wk.* swiche, 39, 12; suche, 36, 20. Nth. swilk, 128, 27; sic, 172, 8. Sth. süch, 203, 23. Kt. *pl.* zuyche, 215, 23.

swīn, swȳn, *sb.*, OE. swīn, *n.*; *swine*,

hog, 86, 17; swȳn, 53, 4. Sth. *gs.* swüines, 180, 23.

swinc, *sb.*, OE. swinc; *labor, trouble*, archaic swink, 4, 11; swinnc (O), 9, 26. Sth. *gs.* swinches, 178, 8.

swinch, *see* swinc.

swīnde(n), *adv.*, OE. swindan (swīndan)–swand (swǫnd) (3); *waste away, vanish, be of no avail*; *inf.* swīnden, 178, 1.

swinnc, *see* swinc.

swire, *sb.*, OE. swira (sweora), ON. sviri; *neck*, 44, 33.

swīthe, swȳðe, *adv.*, OE. swīðe; *very, strongly, greatly, quickly*, 1, 8. Sth. swüðe, 180, 23.

swīðe(n), *stv.*, ON. swīðn, ME. swīðe(n)–swāð (1); *singe, burn*; *pr.* 3 *sg* swīðeð, 15, 25.

swīwike, *sb.*, OE. *swīgwiocu; *week of silence, holy-week*, 200, 3.

swǫ (swō), sǫ (sō), *adv.*, OE. swā (*sā), Dan. saa; *so*, 15, 3; sǫ, 14, 3. Kt. zuǫ, 216, 2.

swolhe(n), *stv.*, OE. swelgan (sweolgan)–swealh (3); *swallow*; *inf.* swolhen, 196, 13.

swōr(e), swore(n), sworn, *see* swēre(n).

swün, swüðe, *see* swīn, swīðe.

swyke(n), *see* swīke(n),

swyle(n), *wkv.*, OE. swilian; *wash, swill*; *inf.* swyle, 96, 24.

swylke, *see* swilc.

swȳn, *see* swīn.

swynke(n), *stv.*, OE. swincan–swanc (3); *labor, work*; *inf.* swynke, 245, 13. Sth. *pp.* iswunken, 202, 18.

sȳ, *sb.*, OE. sige; *victory*, 193, 11.

syb, syche, *see* sib, swilc.

sycurlȳ, sȳe, *see* sikerlīke, sē(n).

sȳde, *see* sīde.

syghe(n), *wkv.*, OE. sīcan, *sīgan?; *sigh*; *pt. sg.* syghed, 109, 10.

syghyng, *sb.* < *pr. ppl.*; OE. sīcan; *sighing*, 92, 1.

sȳgne, *sb.*, OF. seigne, signe; *sign*, 93, 9.

syȝt, *see* siht.

sykernes, *sb.*, ON. ?, cf. Dan. sikker,

OFris. siker (Lat. securus) + ME. -nes; *security*, 94, 26.

syknes, *sb.*, OE. sēocness, *f.*; *sickness*, 90, 22.

sylver(re), *see* silver.

Symeōn, *sb.*, Lat. Simeon; *Simeon*, 26, 4.

symple, *adj.*, OF. simple; *simple*, 235, 16.

syn, syne (syns), *see* si̇ðð∂n, sinne.

syngēr, synnēr, *see* sinʒēre.

syngēre, *sb.*, OE. *sing̊ēre; *singer*, 237, 23.

synne, synʒe, *see* sinne.

synnēr. *see* sinʒēre.

synne(n), sinne(n), *wkv.*, OE. syngian; *sin*; *pp.* synned, 102, 3 Sth. (SEMl.), *pt. pl.* sinīgeden, 26, 13.

sȳr (syr), *see* sīre.

syster, sȳst, *see* sister, sē(n).

syth (sythe), sythen, *see* siþþen.

sytte(n), *see* sitte(n).

syxte, *see* sexte.

T.

t', *see* tō.

tā, taak, *see* tāke(n).

tābell, *sb.*, OF. table; *table*, 126, 14.

tabernācle, *sb.*, OF. tabernacle; *tabernacle, dwelling place*, 104, 5.

tachte, *see* tēche(n).

tācnen, *wkv.*, eME. Nth. for Ml. tōkne(n); OE. *tācnian; *show, betoken*, 12, 31.

tæcen, *see* tāke(n).

tēche(n), *see* tēche(n).

tǣlen = tēle(n), *wkv.*, OE. tǣlan; *blame, curse*; *pr.* 3 *sg.* tæleþþ (O), 9, 25.

tǣr, tǣronne, *see* þēr, þēron.

tagte, *see* tēche(n).

tail, *sb.*, OE. tægel, tægl; *tail, retinue*, 63, 16; *ds.* taile, 207, 11.

tāke(n), eME. taken, *stv.*, ON. takatok (6); *take, seize, begin, touch*; *inf.* tæcen (eME.), 5, 11; tāke, 55, 8; *pr.* 3 *sg.* tākeð, 16, 12; *imp. pl.* taak, 242, 14; *pt. sg.* tōc, 2, 15; tokę, 67, 10; tōc tǭ, *succeed to*, 7,

9; *pt. pl.* tōcan (eME.), 2, 14; tōken, 26, 8; tōke, 89, 14; *pp.* takenn (O), 8, 16; tāke, 58, 18. Nth. *inf.* tā, 166, 21; *pr.* 3 *sg.* tās, 127, 25; tākes, 143, 26; *pr. pl.* tāk wē, 134, 27; *pt. sg.* tuk (lNth.), 167, 31; *pp.* tāne, 136, 15; tākin, 137, 5. eSth. *inf.* taken on, *act, do, take on*, 185, 12; *pt. sg.* tōk, *touch* (?), 211, 7; *pp.* ytāke, 219, 9.

tākening, *see* tākning.

takenn, *see* tāke(n).

tākēr, *sb.*, based on ME. tāken <ON. taka; *taker, protector*, 103, 24.

tākning, tākening, *sb.*, Nth. = Ml. tǭkeninge; OE. tācnung, *f.*; *token, sign, tokening*, 148, 5; tākening, 153, 7.

tākyng, *sb.*, based on tāke(n); *seizure, taking*, 220, 3.

tāld, *see* telle(n).

tāle, *sb.*, OE. talu; *tale, story, number*, 21, 1; at ǭ tāle, *in a case*, 57, 19.

Tambre, *sb.*, OE. Tamar; *Tamar*; *ds.* Tambre, 189, 20. See note.

tāme, *adj.*, OE. tam, ON. tamr; *tame*, 159, 12.

tāne, *see* tāke(n).

tarette, *sb.*, OF. teride; *transport vessel*; *pl.* tarettes, 164, 12.

tarǧe, *sb.*, OF. targe, cogn. with OE. targe; *targe, shield*; *pl.* targes, 207, 31.

tarīe(n), tarǧīe(n), *wkv.*, OM. tergan, WS. tiergan; *delay, tarry*; *inf.* tarīe, 243, 3; targī, 214, 12.

tās, *see* tāke(n).

tatt, *see* þat.

taugtest, tauʒtest, *see* tēche(n).

taverne, *sb.*, OF. taverne; *tavern*; *pl.* tavernes, 120, 17.

tavernēr, *sb.*, OF. tavernier; *innkeeper*, 239, 23.

tawne(n), *wkv.*, OM. *ætēawnian, later *æteawnian by shortening, eME. *atawnen *tawnen; cf. O. awwnen, implying OM ēawnian, eawnian; *show, point out*; *inf.* tawnen, 23, 30.

tayled, *adj.*, based on OE. tægl 'tail'; *tailed, having a tail*, 60, 9.

Taylefēr, *sb.*, OF. Tailefer; *Tail-lefer*, 207, 25.

te, tē, *see* tō, þē or þū.

tēche(n), *wkv.*, OE. tæcan, tæcean-tæhte (tahte); *teach*; *inf.* tēche, 50, 27; *pr.* 3 *sg.* tēcheþ, 124, 10; tæcheþþ(O), 10, 4; *pr. sbj. sg.* tēche, 198, 30; *pt. sg.* tagte, 29, 12; *pt.* 2 *sg.* taugtest, 49, 24; tauʒtist, 55, 11. **Nth.** *pt. sg. wk.* tēchid, 136, 13. **Sth.** *pt. sg.* tachte, 213, 20; *pp.* ytauʒt, 66, 27. **Kt.** *pr.* 3 *sg.* tēkþ, 216, 15.

tēchēr, tēcher, *sb.*, based on tēche(n); *teacher*, 141, 11.

tēchinge, *sb.*, **Kt.** = Ml. tēchinge; OE. tæcung, *f.*; *teaching*, 213, 1.

teday, tee (teʒ), *see* tōday, tē(n).

teʒʒ, *see* þeʒ.

tegǣdere, -gidre, *see* tōgadere.

tēken, *adv. prep.*, OM. tō-ēcan, WS. tō-ēacan; *in addition, besides*; tēkenn (O), 9, 5.

tēkþ, *see* tēche(n).

tel, teld, *see* telle(n).

telę, *sb.*, OE. getæl (*getel), perhaps til? cf. telynge; *number, rime, fortune-telling* (?), 125, 31.

telle(n), *wkv.*, OE. tellan–OM. tālde (WS. tealde); *tell, number, account*; *inf.* tellen, 3, 20; tellenn (O), 9, 14; telle, 107, 26; *pr.* 3 *sg.* telþ, 211, 10; *pr. sbj. sg.* telle, 45, 16; *imp. sg.* tel, 21, 20; telle, 66, 17; *pt. sg.* tōlde, 23, 22; *pt. pl.* tōlden, 26, 29; *pp.* tōọld, 239, 9. **Nth.** *inf.* tell, 116, 12; *pr.* 2 *sg.* tels, 136, 9; *pr.* 3 *sg.* telles, 125, 6; *pt. sg. wk.* teld, 136, 14; *pp.* tāld, 130, 27; *pp. wk.* telld, 154, 14. **Sth.** *pr. pl.* tellęþ, 210, 15; *pp. pl.* itālde (eME.), 185, 28; itọld, 36, 15.

telynge, *sb.*, OE. tilung, teolung, *f.*; *sorcery*, 125, 23.

tēme(n), *wkv.*, OM. tēman (WS. tīeman); *lead, bring forth, instruct*; *inf.* tēmen, 179, 19; tēme, 50, 27.

tempeste, *sb.*, OF. tempeste; *tempest*, 211, 1.

temple, *sb.*, OF. temple; *temple*, 72, 29.

temptāciōun, *sb.*, AN. tentatiun, modified; *temptation, trial*, 103, 29.

tē(n), *stv.*, OE. tēon–OM. tēh (WS. tēah) (2); *draw, lead, go, mount*; *inf.* tee, 232, 13; *pr.* 3 *sg.* tēð, 15, 19; *pt. sg.* teʒ < tēʒ, 41, 11. **Sth.** *inf.* tēon (eSth.), 186, 32; *pt. pl.* tuhen, 192, 25.

tēn, *adj.*, OM. tēn; WS. tīen; *ten*, 17, 4.

tēn, tēnd (tēnde), *see* tēne, tēnþe.

tēnde(n), *wkv.*, OE. tendan, tēndan; *kindle*; *pt. pl.* tenden, 43, 2.

tendirly, *adv.*, OF. tendre + lȳ; *lovingly, tenderly*, 173, 20.

tēne, tēn, *sb.*, OE. tēona; *vexation, injury*, 87, 14. **Nth.** tēne, 144, 20; tēn, 148, 8. **eSth.** tēone, 194, 26.

tenserīe, *sb.*, OF. *tenserie, Lat. tensarium; *special impost, tribute*, 3, 24.

tente, tent, *sb.*, OF. entente; *intention, care, heed*, 99, 17.

tente(n), *wkv.*, OF. tendre; *attend*; **Nth.** *inf.* tent, 134, 13.

tenþe, *adj.*, OM. tēgoða (WS. tēogoða), modified by tēn; *tenth*, 62, 20. **Nth.** tēnde, 152, 11; tēnd, 147, 26.

Tēodbāld, *sb.*, OF. Theodbald; *Theobald*, 5, 17.

tēon, tēone, *see* tē(n), tēne.

teonne, *see* þanne.

tēr, *sb.*, OE. tēar; *tear*; *pl.* tēres, 28, 32. **Kt.** tȳear, 218, 21.

tēr, tērefter, *see* þē, þēr, þērafter.

tēre(n), *wkv.*, OE. *teorian, tirwan; *cover with tar*; *inf.* tēre, 86, 23.

terme, *sb.*, OF. terme; *term, period*, 64, 25.

testament, *sb.*, OF. testament; *testament, command*, 105, 9; *part of the Bible*, 130, 6.

tet, tēth, *see* þat, tōþ.

teythe, *sb.*, OM. tēgoða (WS. tēogoða); *tenth, tithe*, 125, 10.

teythe(n), *wkv.*, OM. tēgoðian, WS. tēogoðian; *tithe*; *inf.* teythe, 125, 12.

teythynge, *sb.*, OM. tēgoðung, *f.*; *tithing*, 125, 14.

tham(e), thaym(e), *see* þey.

thare, *see* þēr.

that (thatt), thē, *see* þat, þē.

theef, thēf, *see* þēf.

thei, theim, them, *see* þey.

thēn, *stv.*, OE. ðēon–OM. ðeh (WS. ðeah) (2); *prosper; inf.* thē, 107, 4.

thēr and compounds, *see* þēr.

theþen, *see* ðeðen.

t'ēves, thēvis, thew, *see* þēf, ðew.

thider, thinc, *see* þider, þinche(n).

thise, *see* þis.

thō, thoro, thorow, *see* þat, þurh.

thossand, *see* þusand.

thoughte, thourgh, *see* þinche(n), þurh.

thow(e), *see* þōh.

thrālī, *adv.*, OE. ðrǣl + līce; *tyrannically*, 132, 18.

thrāng, *sb.*, Nth. = Ml. þrǫng, thrǫng; OE. geðrang; *crowd, throng;* in thrāng, *in durance*, 174, 7.

thrang, *see* þringe(n).

thraw, *sb.*, Nth. = Ml. throw; OE. þrāh, *f.; time, season*, 167, 13.

thrē, *see* þrē.

thrēte(n), thrette(n), *wkv.*, OE. ðrēatan; *threaten;* Nth. *pr.* 3 *sg.* thrētes, 161, 17; *pt. pl.* thrette, 132, 18.

thrēting, *sb.*, OE. ðreatung; *threatening, menace*, 161, 16.

thrette(n), *see* þrēte(n).

thrid, *see* þridde.

thringe(n), *stv.*, OE. ðringan–ðrang (ðrong) (3); *press, throng; pt. sg.* thrāng, 141, 21.

thritte, thrīve(n), *see* þrittī, þrīve(n).

thrōne, *see* trōne.

throte, *see* ðrōte.

throu, *see* þurh.

thrum, *sb.*, OAng. *ðrum, cf. WS. ðrym; *power, multitude;* al on a thrum, *all in a body, with a rush*, 141, 21.

thurgh, thurghe, *see* þurh.

thyfte, *sb.*, OE. ðēofð, possibly ON. ðyfð, ðyſt, *f.; theft*, 147, 11.

thynkande, thynketh, *see* þinche(n), þinke(n).

thynkande, *see* þenche(n), þenke(n).

thynkynge, *sb.*, based on OE. þencan; *thinking*, 146, 17.

thyrde, thys, *see* þridde, þis.

tīde, *sb.*, OE. tid, *f.; time, season, hour;* MnE. *tide;* tȳde, 108, 1; *pl.* tīdes, 212, 29. eSth. *ds.* tīden, 181, 1.

tīde(n), *wkv.*, OE. tīdan; *happen, betide; pp.* tīdę, 159, 24.

tīdende, *see* tīðende.

tīdī, *adj.*, extension of OE. tīd or *tīdig ?; *fit, suitable, neat;* wēl tīdī, *well grown*, 23, 9.

tīding, *sb.*, OE. tīdung, *f.; message, news, tidings*, 65, 24.

til·(l), tyl, tyllę, *prep. conj.*, ONth., possibly Merc. (?), til; *till, to, until*, 2, 26; tyl, 98, 32; tyllę, 107, 23; till, *as long as*, 171, 31.

tile(n), *wkv.*, OE. tilian; *obtain, procure, cultivate, till, aid; inf.* tilen, 16, 5; tylle, 91, 30; *pt. sg.* tilede, 4, 6; *pp.* tiled, 3, 27.

tille(n), *wkv.*, OE. tyllan; *draw, entice; pp.* tilled, 78, 9.

tilðe, *sb.*, OE. tilð, tilðe, *f.; labor*, 178, 1.

tilward, *adv.* Nth. for Ml. tōward; OE. til + weard; *toward*, 148, 20.

tīm, *see* tīme.

timbre(n), timbrin, *wkv.*, OE. timbrian; *build, make, do; inf.* timbrin, 194, 26. Sth. *pp.* itimbbred, 184, 23.

tīme, tȳme, *sb.*, OE. tīma; *time*, 2, 4; tȳme, 52, 30. Nth. tīm, 126, 10.

tīme(n), tīmīe(n), *wkv.*, OE. getīmian; *happen, befall, prosper; inf.* tīmen, 31, 9. Sth. *pp.* itīmed, 188, 15.

tīn, tīne, *see* þīn.

tintreow, *sb.*, OE. tintreg; *torment*, 194, 26.

tīraunt, *sb.*, OF. tirant; *tyrant*, 221, 12.

tire(n), *wkv.*, OE. tirian; *vex, strive; inf.* tire, 44, 34.

tirne(n), *wkv.*, OE. tyrnan; *turn; pt. pl.* tirneden, 83, 16.

tis(s), *see* þis.

tīte, *adv.*, ON. tītt, *neut.* of tīðr, *adj.*; *quickly*, 137, 28.

tīþende, tīþand, tīdende, tīðinge, *sb.*, ON. tīðindi; *message, tidings*; tīþennde (O), 11, 4; tīðing, 31, 6. Nth. tīþand, 154, 30. Sth. tīdende, 185, 14; tīðing, 200, 14. Cf. tidinge.

Tiwesniȝht, *sb.*, OE. Tīwesniht; *Tuesday night*, 228, 27.

tō, *see* þē, þat, ōn.

tō, te, t', *prep. adv.*, OE. tō; *to. for*, 1, 1; t' (O), 9, 10; te, 195, 13; tō (*adv.*) *toward*, 51, 15; tō ðat, *until*, 3, 9.

tō, *adv.*, OE. tō; *too, also*, 176, 11.

tō, *see* twō.

tōbēre(n), *stv.*, OE. tōberan–bær (4); *separate, cause trouble*; *pt. sg.* tōbar, 24, 18.

tōbrast, *see* tōbreste(n).

tōbrēke(n), *stv.*, OE. tōbrecan–bræc (4); *break asunder*; *pr. pl.* tōbreken (eME.), 189, 30; *pt. sg.* tōbrac, 182, 1; *pp.* tōbrōke, 208, 16.

tōbreste(n), *stv.*, OE. tōberstan–bærst (3); *burst asunder*; *pp.* tōbrast, 58, 17.

tōbroke, *see* tōbrēke(n).

tōc, tōcan, *see* tāke(n).

tōdæi, *see* tōday.

tōdǣlen, *see* tōdēle(n).

tōday, *sb.*, OE. tōdæg; *today*, 77, 29. eME. tōdæi, 184, 24; tōdai, 210, 21. Kt. teday, 211, 10.

tōde, *sb.*, OE. tādige, tādie; *toad*, 61, 29.

tōdēle(n), *wkv.*, OE. tōdǣlan; *divide, distribute, scatter*; *pt. sg.* tōdǣide (eME.), 7, 10; tōdēld, 2, 20; tōdēlde, 187, 5; *pp.* tōdēled, 6, 23. Kt. *pr.* 3 *sg.* tōdēlþ, 216, 32; *pr. sbj. pl.* tōdēle wē, 216, 16; *imp. sg* tōdēl, 217, 9.

tōdēlinge, *sb.*, Kt. = Ml. tōdēlinge, based on Kt. tōdēlen; *separation*, 216, 14.

tōdiȝtinge, *sb.*, based on OE. *tōdihtan; *dividing, separation*, 216, 23.

tōdrāȝe(n), *stv.*, OE. tōdragan–drōh (6); *draw asunder, destroy*; eME. *inf.* tōdraȝe, 184, 27; *pt. sg.* tōdrōh, 181, 23.

tōfōre, *adv. prep.*, OE. tōforan; *before*, 102, 3. Sth. tōvōre, 218, 19.

tōfōreniseid, *adj.*, OE. tōforan + Sth. *pp.* iseid; *aforesaid, beforesaid*; *pl.* 226, 8.

tōgadere.-gædere,-gedere,-gidere, *adv.*, OE. tō gǣdere; *together*, 36, 14; tōgædere, 2, 16; tōgedere, 37, 25; tōgider, 30, 32; tōgidre, 53, 21; tegidre, 59, 5. Nth. tōgedir, 135, 11; tōgydre, 234, 9.

tōgǣnes, tōgēanes, *see* tōgēnes.

tōgedere, *see* tōgadere.

tōgederes, tōgedres, *adv.*, OE. tōgædere; *together*, 192, 9; tōgedres, 228, 2.

tōgēnes, tōgǣnes, *prep. adv.*, OE. tōgegnes; *against, opposite*; tōgǣnes (eME.), 5, 6. Sth. tōgēanes (eSth.), 178, 20; tōȝeines, 189, 18. Kt. tōyēnes, 213, 6.

togge(n), togge(n)?, *wkv.*, origin uncertain, cf. MDu. tocken; *draw, pull, tug*; *pp.* togged, 63, 1.

tōgider (-re), tōgydre. *see* tōgadere.

tōhewe(n),*stv.*, OE. tōhēawan–hēow (R); *hew in pieces*; eME. *pp.* tōhauwen, 190, 13.

tōken, *see* tāke(n).

tōkenynge, *sb.*, OE. tācnung, *f.*; *sign, token, tokening*, 110, 11.

tōld, tōlden, *see* telle(n).

tole = tōl, *sb*, OE. tōl; *tool*, p. 282.

tolle(n), *wkv.*, cf. OE. tyllan, 'draw,' perhaps ON. tolla, 'cleave'; *draw, attract*; MnE. *tull*; *pr.* 3 *sg.* tolleð, 20, 17.

tollēre, *sb.*, OE. tollēre; *toll collector*, 88, 18.

tōloken, *see* tōlūke(n).

Tolōus, MS. Tollous, Tullous, *sb*, OF. Tolous, Tulous; *Toulouse*, 106, 7.

tōlūke(n), *stv.*, OE. tōlūcan–lēac (2); *tear asunder*; *inf.* tōlūken, 193, 21; *pt. pl.* tōluken, 197, 6; *pp.* tōloken, 193, 25.

tōmærʒe, tōmarʒen, *see* tōmorwen.
tŏmbestĕre, *sb.*, OE. tumbestēre;
female dancer, 237, 21.
tōmorwen, tōmoruwe, tōmoru, *sb.*,
OE. tōmorgen; *tomorrow*, 81, 5;
tōmoruwe, 49, 8; tōmoru, 128, 6.
eSth. tōmarʒen, 184, 31; tōmærʒe,
184, 7.
tŏn, tong (tonge), *see* ŏn, tunge.
tōniht, tōniht, tōnight, tōnyght,
sb., OM. tō næht, WS. niht; *tonight*,
81, 8; tōniht, 181, 10; tōnight,
239, 11.
tŏōld, *see* telle(n).
top, *sb.*, OE. topp; *top, tuft of hair,
head*, 63, 16.
torche,*sb.*,OF. torche; *torch*,118,13.
tōrēnde(n), *wkv.*, OE. *tōrendan, cf.
OFris. torenda; *rend or tear
asunder*; *pt. pl.* tōrente, 240, 13;
pp. torent, 61, 24.
torment, *sb.*, OF. torment; *torment*;
pl. tormens, 217, 13.
tŏrn, *sb.*, OF. turn; *turn, advantage*,
243, 19.
tornd, *see* turne(n).
Torneie, *sb.*, OE. Đorneg; *Thorney*
(Cambridgeshire), 8, 9.
tŏrnement,*sb.*,OF. tornoiement, AN.
torneiement; *tournement*, 61, 20.
tōsāmen, *adv.*, OE. tō + ON. samen;
together, 23, 13.
tōsnēde(n), *wkv.*, OE. tōsnǣdan,
*snǣðan?; *cut in two*; *pt. sg.* tōsnaðde (for tōsnadde?), 182, 6.
tōsomne, *adv.*, OE. tōsamne(sǫmne);
together, 189, 31.
tōsprēde(n), *wkv.*, OE. tōsprǣdan;
spread apart or about, scatter; *pp.*
tōsprad, 208, 9.
tōtēre(n), *stv.*, OE. tōteran ·tær (4);
tear to pieces; *inf.* tō;ēren, 22, 25;
pr. pl. tōtēre, 237, 18. eSth. tōteoren, 193, 21.
tĕþ, *sb.*, OE. tōð; *tooth*; *pl.* tēð, 50,
21; tēth, 122, 16.
tōpere, tōper, tōthīre, *see* ōper.
toū, *see* þū.
toūmbe, *sb.*, OF. tumbe, tombe;
tomb, 117, 3.
tōūn(e), toūr, *see* tūn, tūr.

toūrne, *see* turne(n).
tŏuward, *see* tōward.
tōvlēote(n), *stv.*, OE. tōflēotan–flēat
(2); *float in different directions, be
dispersed*; eSth.*inf.* tōvlēoten, 201,
14.
tŏvŏre, *see* tōfŏre.
tōwaille, *sb.*, OF. touaille; *towel*,
39, 21.
tōward, *adj. prep.*, OE. tōweard;
towards, 66, 7; tōuward, 188, 5.
tōwraste(n), *wkv.*, OE. tōwrǣstan;
tear or wrest asunder; *pt. pl.* to-
wraste, 60, 17.
tōwrenche(n),*wkv.*,OE.*towrencan;
tear apart; *inf.* tōwrenche, 58, 10.
tōwrŏng,*adj.*,OE. to + ON. vrangr?;
twisted, awry, 15, 13.
tōyēnes, *see* tōgēnes.
toyle(n), *wkv.*, OF. toiller; *pull
about, harass*; *pp.* toyled, 60, 8.
traist, *adj.*, ON. *treystr, cf. treysta,
v.; *strong,confident*;*superl.*traistest,
128, 9.
traistlī, *adv.*, based on traist; *con-
fidently*, 134, 18.
traitŏr, traytŏr, traitoūr, *sb.*, NF.
traitre, *acc.* traitor (OF. traitur);
traitor; traytŏr, 56, 16; traitŏr,
223, 19; *pl.* traitoūrs, 57, 19;
traytoūrs, 57, 16.
translāte(n), *wkv.*, OF. translater;
transfer, translate; *pp.* translāte,
133, 22.
trappe,*sb.*,OE. træppe, treppe; *trap*;
pl. trappes, 103, 25.
trass, *sb.*, OF. trace; *track, trace*,
168, 13.
trāste(n), *wkv.*, lNth. = Ml. traiste(n); ON. treysta; *trust, rely
upon*; lNth. *inf.* trāst, 171, 29.
travail, *sb.*, OF. travail; *labor,
travail, trouble*, 103, 11. Nth.
traveil, 129, 7; travǎle (lNth.),
167, 24.
travaile(n), travale(n), *wkv.*, OF.
travailer; *travail, labor, travel*;
pt. pl. travailleden, 235, 9; *pp.*
itravailed, 212, 19. Nth. *pr. pl.*
travalis, 174, 3; *pr. ppl.* travaland,
173, 31.

travāl̦e, traveil, *see* **travail.**

traysōn, *see* **trēsōn.**

traytōr, traytour, *see* **traitōr.**

trē, *sb.* OE. trēo ; *tree*, 100, 18.

trēcberȳ, *sb.*,OF. trecherie; *treachery*, 78, 14.

tred, *sb.*, OE. tredd ; *tread, track*, 62, 4.

trēde(n), *stv.*, OE. tredan–træd (5); *tread* ; *inf.* tredenn (O), 9, 23 ; *pt. pl.* trǫde, 62, 3 ; *pp.* troden, 240, 16.

trēothe, trēowthe, *see* **trēuthe.**

trēowe, *see* **trewe.**

trēowlīch, *adj.*, eSth. = Ml. treulī; OE. trēowlīc ; *truly, sincerely*, 192, 14.

trēsōn, trēsūn, traysōn, *sb.*, OF. traison, AN. traisun ; *treason*, 1, 19 ; traysōn, 51, 13.

trēsōr, trēsūr, eME. **tresōr,** *sb.*, NF. tresor, OF. tresur ; *treasure* ; tresōr (eME.), 2, 20 ; trēsōr, 242, 16.

trespas, *sb.*, OF. trespas ; *trespass*, 92, 4.

trespasse(n), *wkv.*, OF. trespasser ; *trespass* ; *pr. sbj. sg.* trespasse, 241, 12.

trēuthe, treuthe, *sb.*, OE. trēowðe ; *truth, faith, troth*, 2, 29 ; trewðe, *promise*, 30, 16 ; treuþe, 204, 11 ; *pl.* trēothes, 2, 30.

treuthēde, -ēde, *sb.*, OAng. trēowð-hæd, *f.* ; *truth, fidelity*, 129, 15.

trewe, trew, *adj.*, OE. trēowe ; *true*, 18, 22 ; *guiltless*, 109, 21 ; *superl.* trewest, 76, 9.

trewehēde, *sb.*, OE. trēow + hēde ; *faithfulness, especially religious faith*, 205, 3.

trewelȳ, *adv.*, OE. trēowlīce ; *truly, indeed*, 242, 25.

trewe(n), *wkv.*, OE. trēowian ; *trust, believe* ; *pr.* 3 *sg.* treweð, 21, 1. Cf. **trowe(n).**

trewnesse, *sb.*, OE. trēwness, *f.* ; *trust, confidence*, 37, 20.

trewðe, trewthe, *see* **trēuthe.**

tribulāciōun, *sb.*, AN. tribulatiun ; *tribulation*, 104, 11.

tricherīe, *sb.*, OF. tricherie, triquerie ; *treachery, trickery*, 204, 19.

trinitē, *sb.*, OF. trinitē ; *trinity*, 116, 14.

trist, *sb.*, OF. tristre, triste ; *appointed place, rendezvous*, 173, 18.

trīst, tryst, *sb.*, perhaps OM. *trȳst (tryst), cf.* ON. treista, *vb.* ; *trust, confidence*, 51, 15 ; trystę, 108, 5.

Tristrem, *sb.*, OF. Tristrem ; *Tristrem*, 126, 17.

trofle, *see* **trufle.**

trǫde, troden, *see* **trēde(n).**

trǫne, *sb.*,OF. trone, throne ; *throne*, 157, 11 ; thrǫne, 102, 26.

trotevāle, *sb.* (?), origin uncertain ; *idle talk*, 57, 21.

trouth (trouthe), *see* **trowðe.**

trowe(n), *wkv.*, OE. trēowian ; *believe, trust* ; *inf.* trowwenn (O), 9, 6 ; *pr.* 1 *sg.* trowwe (O), 9, 12 ; trowe, 225, 27 ; *pt. sg.* trowede, 76, 17. **Nth.** *inf.* trow, 141, 26. Cf. **trewe(n).**

trowþe, trouth, *sb.*, OE. trēowð, *f.* ; *truth, honor, covenant, troth* ; trowwÞe (O), 8, 14 ; trouthe, 95, 2. **Nth.** trouth, 135, 4.

trowwe(n), *see* **trowe(n).**

Troye, Troy, *sb.*, OF. Troie ; *Troy*, 220, 3. **Nth.** Troy, 126, 5.

trūandīs, *sb.*, OF. truandise ; *imposture, begging*, 134, 11.

truble(n), *wkv.*, OF. trubler ; *trouble*, *pr. pl.* trublen, 101, 7 ; *pp.* trubled, 102, 22.

trufle, trǒfle, *sb.*, OF. trufle ; *trifle, nonsense* ; trǒfle, 134, 11 ; *pl.* trufles, 218, 13.

trukīe(n), *wkv.*, Sth. = Ml. truke(n) ; OE. trucian ; *fail, be lacking* ; *pr. sbj. sg.* trukīe, 199, 11.

trukne(n), *wkv.*, OE. *trucnian, cf.* trucian ; *fail, be lacking* ; *pr.* 3 *sg.* trukeneð, 192, 14.

trume, *sb.*, OE. truma ; *troop, band*, 186, 31.

trüste(n), *see* **tryste(n).**

trüstī, *adj.*, Sth. = Ml. tristī ; OM. *trystig, cf.* Dan. trӧstig ; *confident of, trusty*, 198, 29.

trystę, *see* **trist.**

tryste(n), *wkv.*, OM. *trystan (?), cf. ON. treysta ; *trust* ; *pr.* 1 *sg.* tryste, 114, 26. **Sth.** *pr.* 3 *sg.* trüsteð, 192, 14 ; *pt. sg.* trüste, 192, 14.

tū, *see* þū.

tuelfte, twelfte, *adj.*, OE. twelfta ; *twelfth*, 152, 15.

tuhen, *see* tē(n).

tühte(n), *wk.*, **Sth.** = Ml. tihte(n) ; OE. tyhtan ; *draw, move* ; *pt. sg.* tühte, 188, 24 ; *pt. pl.* tühten, 189, 20.

tuk, *see* tāke(n).

tūn, tōun, *sb.*, OE. tūn ; *town* ; *ds.* tūne, 3, 26 ; tōun, 52, 19. **Sth.** *ds.* tōune, 210, 8.

tunder, *sb.*, ON. tundr, cognate with OE. tynder ; *tinder*, 20, 7.

tūne(n), *see* **tuyne**(n).

tunge, tònge, eME. tūnge, *sb.*, OE. tunge ; *tongue* ; tūnge, 10, 23 ; tunge, 76, 4 ; tònge, 59, 2. **Nth.** tòng, 134, 4.

tūnscipe, *sb.*, OE. tūnscipe ; *inhabitants of a town*, 4, 3.

tūr, tōur, *sb.*, OF. tur ; *tower*, 6, 28 ; *pl.* tūres, 37, 8 ; tōures, 49, 1 ; tōurs, 152, 4.

turment, *sb.*, OF. turment ; *torment, suffering*, 104, 4.

turmentóur, *sb.*, OF. tormenteour ; *tormentor, persecutor*, 140, 13.

turmentrȳ, *sb.*, OF. tormenterie ; *instruments of torture*, 138, 16.

turne(n). tòrne(n), *wkv.*, OE. turnian ; *turn* ; *inf.* turnnenn (O), 8, 21 ; turn = turne, 68, 2 ; *pr.* 3 *sg.* turrneþþ, 10, 30 ; *pr sbj. sg.* tòurne, 228, 26 ; *imp. sg.* turne, 102, 30 ; *imp. pl.* turneþ, 103, 1 ; *pt. sg.* turned, 45, 8 ; *pt. pl.* turnde, 223, 18 ; *pp.* tòrnd, 55, 26. **Nth.** *pr.* 3 *sg.* turnes, 144, 18 ; *pr. sbj. pl.* turn, 167, 28. **Sth.** *pp.* iturned, 191, 19 ; yturnd, 225, 30.

tus, *see* þus.

tusk, *sb.*, OE. tusc ; *tusk* ; *pl.* tuskes, 195, 12.

tuyne(n), *wkv.*, WMl. = Ml. tīne(n) ; OE. tȳnan ; *enclose, close, shut* ; *imp. sg.* (with excrescent d) tuyndę,

121, 11. **Sth.** *imp. pl.* tūneð, 200, 14.

twā, *adj.*, **Nth.** = Ml. twǫ ; OE. twā ; *two*, 170, 22.

tway, *see* **tweie.**

Twēde, *sb.*, *Tweed*, 159, 8.

tweie, tway, tweien, tweiȝe, *adj.*, OE. twēgen ; *twain, two*, 35, 19 ; tway, 66, 5. **eSth.** tweiȝe, 188, 25 ; tweien, 190, 14.

twelfmonþe, *sb.*, OE. tweolf + mōneð, *twelvemonth, year*, 204, 7.

twelve, *adj.*, OE. twelf, twelve ; *twelve*, 34, 15.

twentī, *adj.*, OE. twēntig ; *twenty*, 4, 10.

twiȝes, twīes, *adv.*, OE. twiga + es ; *twice* ; twiȝȝess (O), 10, 7 ; twīes, 199, 29.

twin, *adj.*, ON. tvinnr ; *two, twin*, 31, 15.

twist, *sb.*, OAng. twist, cf. MDu. twist ; *branch, twig*, 172, 6.

twō, twǫ, *adj.*, OE. twā ; *two*, 22, 29 ; tō, 117, 2. **Nth.** twā, q.v. **Sth.** twǫ, 238, 4.

twȳe, *adv.*, OE. twīa < twīwa ; *twice*, 43, 8.

tȳde, tȳear, *see* tīde, tēr.

tȳene(n), *wkv.*, **Kt.** = Ml. tēne(n) ; WS. tīenan, OM. tēnan ; *harm, irritate, weary oneself* ; *imp. sg.* tȳene, 217, 19.

tyl, tylle, tylle(n), *see* til, tile(n).

tȳme, *see* tīme.

tȳre(n), *wkv.*, ON. tȳna ; *lose* ; **Nth.** *inf.* tȳnę, 166, 21 ; *pp.* tȳnt, 167, 24.

þ, Ð.

ča (þa), þē, *see* þē, þat.

þā, *adv. conj.*, eME. **Nth.** for Ml. þǫ (ðǫ) ; OE. ðā ; *then, when*, 1, 1.

þā, þǣn (þā, þǣn), *see* þat, þē.

þænne, *see* þanne.

þēr (tǣr) and compounds, *see* þēr.

þēre, ťǣrf, *see* þēr, þurve(n).

þæt, *see* þat

þaȝ, þah, *see* þeȝ.

þai (þām), þaimselfe (þaymselfe, þāmselfe), *see* þey, self.

þaire, *see* þeȝȝre.
þān, *see* þē.
þan, ðan, *see* þanne.
þanc, þank, *sb.,* OE. ðanc, ᵭǫnc; *thought, favor, thanks*; *gs.* here þankes, *by the will of them, willingly,* 6, 31; cunnen þanc, *know or feel gratitude, show favor,* 178, 14.
þane, *see* þē.
þanke(n), *wkv.,* OE. þancian, þǫn-cian; *thank*; *inf.* þannkenn (O), 8, 26; *pt. pl.* thankyd, 112, 14; *pp.* þanked, 97, 25.
þanne, ðanne, þan, *conj.,* OE. þanne, þonne; *than*; þanne, 4, 8; ðanne, 14, 11; þan, 3, 31; ðan, 18, 17. eSth. þænne, 176, 22; þen, 176, 1; þeone, 187, 9; teonne, 200, 1.
þar, ðar and compounds, *see* þēr.
þārat, þārbī, *see* þērate, þērbī.
þār, þāre, *see* þeȝȝre.
þāre, *adv.,* Nth. for Ml. þǭre; OE. þāra; *there,* 110, 29.
þārtill, *see* þērtil.
þārwith, þās, *see* þērwyth, þis.
þat, ðat, that, *conj.,* OE. þæt; *that*; ðat, 1, 2; ðatt (O), 8, 24; tatt (O), 8, 21; that, 54, 19; thatt, 146, 23. Sth. tet, 197, 15.
þat, ðat, *dem. prn.,* OE. þæt; *that, the*; ðat, 1, 3; þæt (eME.), 7, 27; þatt (O), 8, 20; tat, 14, 14; *pl. those, the,* þā (eME.), 2, 11; tǭ < þǭ, 5, 2; ðǭ, 21, 8. Nth. (ON.) *pl.* þīr, 148, 26; *sg.* þīr, 149, 29. Sth. þet, 177, 27.
þat, that, *rel. prn., sg.* and *pl.*; OE. þæt, *dem.*; *that, which*; þatt (O), 8, 20; tatt (O), 9, 3; þet (eME.), 7, 19; þat (eME.), 176, 7; þatt (O), 9, 10; *that, that which,* 120, 15. Nth. at < þat, 174, 31. Sth. *ds.* þon, 192, 3.
þauh, *see* þēh.
þay, *see* þey.
þe, ðe, *rel. prn.*; OE. þe; *that, who, which,* 1, 6; ðe, 14, 15. Sth. þe, 176, 10; þa, 179, 4.
þē, ðē, thē, *def. art.,* OE. sē, infl. by þ-forms; *the,* 1, 2; sē (eME.), 1, 13; ðē, 14, 1; tē, 5, 9; thē, 1, 12;

ē in at ē, *at the,* 212, 32. Sth. þ̄ē, 176, 21; sē (eSth.), 177, 26; þēo, 191, 26; *das.* þēne, 181, 5; þēn, 184, 10; þane (SEMl.), 47, 19; *fds.* þēre, 182, 3; tēr, 201, 1; *fas.* þā, 181, 21; *pl.* þēo, 191, 25; *dpl.* þān, 178, 9; vor þēn, *because, therefore,* 183, 29. Kt. sī, 211, 10; ē, 218, 24; *fas.* tǭ < þǭ, 211, 7.
þē, tē, *adv.,* OE. þȳ, instr.; *the* in phrases like *the more*; tē, 9, 11; þē, 122, 9. Cf. nǭþeles.
þeavīe(n), *wkv.,* OE. ðafian; *permit*; *inf.* þeavīen, 194, 31.
þēde, eME. þēd, *sb.,* OE. ðēod, *f.*; *people, nation*; þēd, 9, 6; *pl.* þēde, 11, 11; *pl.* ðēden (SEMl.), 29, 14.
þedyr, *see* þider.
þēf, *sb.,* OE. ðēof; *thief*; theef, 239, 13; *pl.* thēves, 240, 26. Nth. *pl.* thēvis, 175, 13. eSth. *ds.* þēove, 177, 19; *pl.* þēoves, 221, 19. Kt. þȳef, 219, 33.
þeȝ, þeiȝ, þey, þaȝ, *conj.,* OM. þēh (þeh), WS. þēah; *though*; þeȝ, 37, 17; þeiȝ, 58, 5; þey, 59, 15; þaȝ, 125, 21. Sth. þēh, 176, 4; þah, 189, 25; þauh, 199, 9; þeyȝ, 224, 10.
þeȝȝ, þeȝȝm, *see* þey.
þeȝȝre (þēr), þaire (þāre, þēr), *pos. prn.,* based on ON. *gpl.* þeira; *their*; þeȝȝre (O), 9, 4; þēr, 108, 20; thēr, 115, 28. Nth. þaire, 140, 14; þāre, 127, 30; þēr, 126, 6; þēre, 127, 32; þār, 134, 14; þair, 153, 5.
þegn, þeȝn, þein, *sb.* OE. þegn; *soldier, servant, thane, pl.* þeines, 187, 24.
þēh, *see* þeȝ.
þēhwheðer, *adv. conj.,* Sth. = Ml. þohwheþer; WS. þēah hwæðₑre (hweðere); *yet, nevertheless, but,* 180, 9.
þeiȝ, þem, *see* þeȝ, þey.
þen, þēn (þēnₑ), *see* þanne, þē.
þenche(n), þₑnke(n), þinke(n), *wkv.,* OE. ðencean–ðōhte (ðohte); *think*; *inf.* þenche 100, 17; þenke, 51, 5; þynke, 91, 32; þink, 72, 10; *imp. sg.* ðenke, 22, 8; *pt. sg.* þoȝte, 35, 13; ðoht, 29, 10; þoucte, 80,

11; *pt.* 2 *sg.* þohhtesst (O), 8, 21; *pt. pl.* þoght, 105, 18. Sth. *inf.* þenchen, 202, 31; *pr.* 3 *sg.* ðenchet, 178, 22; *pr. sbj. sg.* þenche, 207, 9; *pr. ppl.* þenchinge, 216, 25; *pt.* 2 *sg.* þohtest, 183, 4.

þənchen, *seem,* see þinche(n).

þenchinge, *sb.,* based on OE. þencan, þencean; *thinking,* 216, 25.

þenke, ðenke, see þenche(n).

þennes, *adv.,* OE. ðanon, infl. by -es ending; *thence,* 223, 5.

þēo, see þē, þǭ.

þeone, *see* þanne.

þēos, þēove, *see* þis, þēf.

þēr, *see* þeȝȝre.

þēr, ðēr, thēr, þar, &c., *adv.,* OM. ðēr, WS. ðǣr; *there, where;* þēr, 1, 6; ðēr, 14, 5; thēr, 2, 19; tǣr = þēr, 9, 5; þar, 2, 24; thare, 4, 18. Sth. þēr, 176, 22; þǣre, 179, 10; ðēre, 177, 26.

þēras, *adv.,* OM. ðēr, WS. ðǣr + ME. as, *there where, where,* 197, 5.

þērate, *adv.,* OM. þēr + æt; *thereat,* 64, 12. Nth. þārat. 163, 6.

þērbī, þērbȳ, *adv.,* OM. ðērbī, WS. ðǣrbī; *thereby;* Sth. þērbȳ, 225, 4. Nth. þārbī, 129, 25.

þēre, þēre, *see* þē, þeȝȝre.

þērefter, *adv.,* OM. þērefter, WS. þǣr æfter; *thereafter,* 1, 9. Sth. tȝrefter < þērefter, 197, 16.

ðērfǭre, þarfǭre, *adv., conj.,* OM. þēr + fore; *therfor, therefore,* 19, 11; þarfǭre, 63, 13. Sth. þērfǭre, 180, 24; þērvore, 181, 13; þērvǭre, 215, 7.

þērinne, þǣrinne, thēreynne, þarinne, *adv.,* OM. þēr + inne; *therein,* 3, 12; þǣrinne, 3, 13; þarinne, 3, 32; thēreynne, 121, 20; þrinne, 81, 20.

þērmit, *adv.,* OM. þēr, WS. þǣr + mid; *therewith,* 63, 20.

þerne, *see* þis.

ðērof, þēroffe, thēroffe, thēreof, þarof, &c., *adv.,* OM. þēr + of; *thereof,* 20, 3; þēroffe, 76, 7; thēroffe, 79, 5; thēreof, 106, 9; tharof, 2, 22. Sth. þērof, 185, 18.

ðēron, þēronne (-ǭn), *adv.,* OM. ðēr = on; *thereon;* ðēron, 16, 8; tǣronne, 9, 5.

ðērǭver, *adv.,* OM. ðēr + ofer; *thereover,* 15, 19.

þērþurh, *adv.,* OM. ðēr + ðurh; *therethrough;* þǣrþurh, 7, 2.

þērtil, *adv.,* OM. ðēr + til; *thereto,* 49, 24. Nth. þārtill, 171, 22.

þērtō, þartō, *adv.,* OM. ðēr + to; *thereto;* 87, 17; þartō, 4, 14.

þērvore, *see* þērfore.

þērwyþ, *adv.,* OM. ðēr + wið; *therewith,* 88, 14. Nth. þārwith, 134, 2.

ðēs, þēs, þēos, *see* þis.

þess, *adv.,* OE. ðæs; used adverbially; *so much;* all þess tē bettre, *so much, wholly better by this,* 9, 11.

þesternisse, *sb.,* OE. ðēosterness, *f.;* darkness, 67, 21.

þēstre(n), þestre(n), *wkv.,* OE. ðēostrian; *become dark;* *pt. sg.* þēstrede, 1, 14.

þet, *see* þat.

ðēðen (-in), theþen, *adv.,* ON.ðaðan, ðeðan; *thence,* 23, 1; theþen, 131, 18; þeþin, 137, 8.

ðew, thew, *sb.,* OE. ðēaw; *custom, virtue,* archaic *thews,* 18, 6; *pl.* thewes, 121, 8.

þey, þeȝȝ, thei, þai, *prn. pl.,* ON. þei; *they,* 56, 23; þeȝȝ (O), 9, 26; teȝȝ (O), 10, 14; thei, 60, 5; *dat.-acc.* þeȝȝm (O), 9, 11; þem, 116, 4; them, 105, 22. Nth. þai, 126, 16; *dat.-acc.* þaym, 144, 15; thaym, 144, 4; þām, 127, 8. Sth. þay, 221, 24.

þey, þeyȝ, ðī, *see* þeȝ, þīn.

þider (þedyr), *adv.,* OE. þider, þyder; *thither, to that place,* 5, 22; þedyr, 99, 10; thider, 241, 20. Sth. þüder, 177, 27.

þiderward, *adv.,* OE. ðiderweard; *thitherward,* 189, 24.

ðierf, *see* þurve(n).

þikke, *adv.,* ON. þykkr, cogn. with OE. ðicce; *thickly,* 207, 30.

þilke, þilk, *prn.,* OE. þylc; *such, that,* 37, 11; þilk, 228, 4. Sth. þülke, 204, 13.

þīn, þī, *pos. prn.*, OE. ðīn; *thine*, 8,
18; ðī, 30, 14; tīne, 18, 19.

þinche(n), þinke(n), *wkv.*, OE.
ðyncean–ðūhte (ðuhte); *seem, appear; inf.* ðinche, 178, 6; þenchen
(infl. by þenchen), 103, 9; *pr.* 3 *sg.*
ðinkeð, 32, 19; þincþ (eME.), 176,
5; mēþynkeþ, 109, 20; *pt. sg.* ðugte,
21, 28; þuʒte, 38, 2; þouʒt, 71, 5;
þoght, 90, 24; þouʒht, 228, 7;
thoughte, 237, 19. Nth. *pr.* 3 *sg.*
mē thinc (for thinks?), 133, 15;
pr. ppl. thynkande, 144, 3. Sth.
pr. 3 *sg.* þūncheð, 202, 29; *pt. sg.*
þuhte, 186, 3. Kt. *inf.* þenche, 213,
16.

þing, þyng, eME. þīng, *sb.*, OE.
ðing, *n.*; *thing*, 1, 17; *pl.* þing, 42,
29; þinge, 38, 13; þyng, 88, 11;
þinges, 204, 26.

þink, þinkeð, *see* þenche(n), þin-
che(n).

þinne, *adj.*, OE. þynne; *thin*, 55, 28.

þīr, *see* þat.

ðirl, *sb.*, OE. ðyrel; *perforation, hole,
window*, 17, 7. Sth. *ds.* þürle, 197,
18.

þirst, ðrist, *sb.*, OE. ðurst, infl. by
ðyrstan, ðyrstig; *thirst*, 54, 2;
þrist, 20, 15; þorst, 219, 6.

þis, þys, ðis, this, *prn., pl.* þās, þǭs,
OE. þis, *neut.*; *this*, 1, 1; þiss (O),
8, 24; tiss (O), 11, 2; tis, 16, 13;
thys, 112, 3; SEMl. *f. sg.* þēs,
37, 19; þys, 88, 7; *pl.* þās (eME.),
1, 19; ðēs, 23, 16; ðise, 24, 3;
þēse, 50. 5. Sth. *mns.* þēs, 177, 17;
mgs. þeos, 185, 6; *mds.* þissen, 184,
13; *mas.* þisne, 183, 22; þerne, 217,
3; *fns.* þēos (eSth.), 198, 11; *fds.*
þissere, 184, 24; *pl.* þēos (eSth.),
199, 25; þēose, 221, 11; *pl.* þǭs,
212, 11.

þīself, þȳself, *see* self.

þisne, þissen, þissere, *see* þis.

ðǭ, *adv.*, eME., Nth. þā (ða); OE.
ða; *then, when, since, because*, 14,
16. Sth. þēo, 201, 3; þǭ, 203, 22.

þoght(e), þoʒte, *see* þenche(n),
þinche(n).

þogt, *see* þoht.

þoh, ðog, þoʒ, þogh, thowe, þof,
conj., ON. þō, earlier þōh; *cogn.*
with OM. ðēh, WS. ðēah; *though*;
þohh (O), 11, 3; ðog, 16, 4; þoʒ, 50,
7; þogh, 114, 23; thowe, 111, 26;
þoþ = þo þe (?), 2, 17. Nth. þof,
128, 23; þofe, 146, 2. Cf. þeʒ.

þohhtesst, *see* þenke(n).

þoht, ðogt, þouht, *sb.*, OE. ðōht,
ðoht; *thought*; þohht (O), 8, 23;
ðogt, 23, 15; *pl.* þouhtes, 201, 8.

þoht, *see* þenche(n).

þohwethere, þoþwethere, *adv. conj.
prep.*, ON. þō (þōh) hwæðere, hweðere; *notwithstanding, nevertheless*,
2, 15; þoþwethere, 4, 13; þoþwæthere, 7, 14.

þǭl(e), þǭlede, *see* þǭle(n).

þǭlemōdenesse, *see* þǭlmōdnesse.

þǭle(n), eME. þole(n), *wkv.*, OE.
þolian; *bear, suffer, endure; inf.*
þolen (eME.), 6, 8; þolenn (O), 9,
12; þǭle, 45, 1; *pr.* 2 *sg.* þǭlest, 43,
10; *pt. pl.* þoleden, 4, 9; *pp.* þǭlede,
40, 6. Nth. *inf.* þǭl, 148, 8; *pr.* 3
sg. þǭles, 150, 11. Sth. (SEMl.)
inf. þǭlīe, 43, 6; þǭlȳe, 217, 14;
pp. iþǭled, 212, 21.

þǭlmōdnesse, *sb.*, OE. ðolmōdnes,
f.; *patience, long suffering, endur-
ance*, 96, 27; þǭlemōdenesse, 232, 8.

þǭlȳe, þon, *see* þǭle(n), þat.

þonk, *sb.*, OE. ðanc (ðonc); *thought,
gratitude, favor; ds.* þonke, 183, 14.

þonke(n), *wkv.*, OE. ðancian, ðon-
cian; *thank; pr.* 1 *sg.* þonke, 38,
29; *pt. sg.* þonkede, 47, 8.

ðǭr, *adv.*, OE. ðar; *there, where*, 21,
15; tǭr bifǭren, *lit. before there*,
but *before it or them.*

ðǭrbī, *adv.*, OE. ðar + bī; *thereby*, 23,
10.

ðǭre, þǭre, *adv.*, OE. þāra, emphatic
form of þær; *there*, 16, 17.

ðǭrfōre, þǭrfōre, *adv.*, OE. ðar + fore;
therefore, 22, 18.

ðǭrof, ðǭroffen, *adv.*, OE. ðar + of;
thereof, 27, 20; ðǭroffen, 32, 19).

þo rst, porte, *see* þirst, purve(n).

ðǭrtil, *adv.*, OE. ðar + til; *thereto*,
31, 19.

þoru (þoruȝ), *see* þurh.
þorútlíke, *adv.*, OE. þurhūt + líce ;
thoroughly, through and through,
85, 28.
þǭs, *see* þis.
þoþ (and compounds), *see* þoh.
þosand, þossand, *see* þúsend.
þou, þoucte, *see* þú, þenche(n).
þought, þouȝt, *see* þinche(n).
þousande, þousond, þouzen, *see*
þúsend.
þous, *see* ðus.
þral, *sb.*, ON ðrǽl ; *thrall, slave,*
servant, 55. 2.
ðraldóm, *sb.*, ON. ðrǽldómr ; *thral-*
dom, 30, 2.
þrasten, *wkv.*, OE. ðrǽstan ; *press,*
force ; *pt. sg.* þraste, 60, 23.
þrē, ðrē, *adj.*, OE. ðrēo ; *three,* 56,
23; thrē, 1, 15. **Kt.** þrī, 216,
21.
þrēnge(n),*wkv.*,OE.*þrengan ; *press,*
force ; *pt. pl.* þrēngden, 3, 12.
þrēohād, *sb.*, based on OE. ðrī, ðrēo ;
trinity, 197, 11.
þretēnd, *adj.*, OAng. ðrēotēðe, infl.
by ðrēotēne ; *thirteenth,* 152, 16.
ðrētēne, *adj.*, OM. ðrēotēne, WS.
ðrēotīene, -tēne ; *thirteen,* 5, 15.
þrī, *see* þrē.
þridde, *adj.*, OE. ðridda ; *third,* 8,
15. **Nth.** thrid, 137, 23 ; thyrde,
143, 27.
ðríes, *adv.*, OM. ðriga < ðrīe + es ;
thrice, 14, 10.
þrin, *adj.*, ON. þrinnr ; *threefold,*
triple, 87, 1.
þrinne,ðrist, *see* þērinne, þirst.
þríste, *adj.*, OE. ðrīste ; *bold,* 176,
19.
ðríste(n), *wkv.*, ON. ðrýsta ; *thrust* ;
pt. pl. ðrīsten, 23, 14; *pp.* þríste,
84, 18.
ðrittī, *adj.*,OE. ðrītig, ðrittig ; *thirty,*
32, 17. **Nth.** thritte, 132, 10.
þrittuðe, *adj* , OE. ðrītigoðe ; *thir-*
tieth, for *thirty*?, 197, 4.
þríve(n), *stv.*, ON. ðrīfa, ME. þríven-
þrǭf (1) ; *thrive* ; *inf.* thríve, 80,
20 ; *pr. sbj. sg.* þríve, 54, 7 ; *pp.*
þriven, 51, 17.

þrǭ (þrō?), *adj.*, ON. þrár ; *bold,*
strong, 51, 17.
þrof, *see* þērof.
ðrǭte, *sb.*, OE. ðrotu ; *throat,* 19, 9.
eME. throte, 3, 16.
þrou, *see* þurh.
þruh, *sb.*, OE. þruh ; *coffin,* 197, 1.
þryft,*sb.*,ON. þrift ; *thrift, prosperity,*
90, 13.
þú, thú, þou, tú, ú, *prn.*, OE. þú ;
thou, 3, 25 ; þou, 48, 13; tú, 17,
25 ; tou, 49, 24 ; ú, 37, 2 ; ou, 50,
11 ; *das.* ðē, 31, 31 ; tē, 8, 18 ; *pl.*
gē, 16, 13 ; ȝē, 38, 18 ; yē, 78, 25 ;
gpl. gūre, 29, 30 ; *dapl.* gū, 28, 4 ;
yū, 78, 24 ; ȝōw, 88, 19. **Nth.** *pl.*
ȝhē (ȝē), 166, 10 ; yuu, 131, 7. **Sth.**
das. ēow (eSth.), 177, 26 ; ēou,
(eSth.), 184, 6 ; ū, 193, 11 ; ōw,
194, 24 ; ou, 197, 20 ; ȝew, 226,
20 ; *d. dual,* inc, 195, 3.
þüder, *see* þider.
þüderward, *adv.*, Sth. = Ml. þiderward ; lWS. ðyderweard ; *thither-*
ward, 206, 2.
þugte, þuȝte, þuht, *see* þinche(n).
þülke, *see* þilke.
þumbe, eME. þumbe, *sb.*, OE. þuma ;
thumb ; *pl.* þúmbes, 3, 7.
þünche(n), *see* þinche(n).
þurh, ðurg, þur, þurch, þurgh,
þurghe, þurghe, þureȝ, þoru,
þoruȝ, thorow, *prep. adv.*, OE.
þurh ; *through, on account of,* 1, 4 ;
þur, 5, 3 ; þurrh (O), 8, 14 ; ðurg,
14, 2 ; þurch, 64, 19 ; þurgh, 95,
15 ; þureȝ, 42, 29 ; þoruȝ, 61, 23 ;
þoru, 76, 2 ; thorow, 105, 23. **Nth.**
thoro, 131, 5 ; thurgh, 140, 10 ;
throu, 166, 5. **Sth.** þurh, 177, 17.
þurhlōke(n), *wkv.*, OE. *þurhlōcian ;
look through, examine ; *inf.* þurrhlōkenn (O), 9, 20.
þurhsēke(n), *wkv.*, OE. þurhsēcan-
sōhte (sohte) ; *seek out,seek through* ;
inf. þurrhsēkenn (O), 9, 20.
ðurhsē(n), *stv.*, OE. ðurhsēon-seah
(5) ; *see through, penetrate with the*
sight ; *pr.* 3 *sg.* ðurhsihð, 179, 1.
þürl, þurrh, *see* þirl, þurh.
þurrhlōkenn, *see* þurhlōke(n).

þurrhsēkenn, *see* þurhsēke(n).

Þursday, *sb.*, OE. Đunresdæg; *Thursday*, 231, 20.

þurve(n), *ptprv.*, OE. ðurfan–ðurfte (ðorfte); *need*; *pr.* 3 *sg.* ðærf (eME.), 177, 21; *pr. sbj. sg.* ðierf (eSth.), 177, 19; *pt. sg.* þorte, 59, 13; þurt, 96, 22.

ðus, ðūs, *adv.*, OE. ðus; *thus, in this manner*, 16, 22; tus, 16, 15. Kt. þous, 215, 19.

þūsend, þōūsand, *sb.*, OE. þūsend, *neut.*; *thousand*, 3, 18; þōūsandе, 64, 26; þōūsond, 215, 11; þōūzen, 219, 13; thōsand, 126, 6; thōssand, 132, 3. **Sth.** þūsende, 185, 28.

þusgāt, *adv.*, OE. þus + gate; *in this way*, 150, 25.

þūstre, *sb.*, **Sth.** = Ml. þīstre; OE. ðīestre (ðȳsstre), beside ðēostre; *darkness*, 178, 20.

þūstre, *adj.*, **Sth.** = Ml. þīstre; WS. ðīestre, ðȳstre; *dark*, 178, 21.

þwartōver, *adj.*, ON. þvert + ME. ōver; *crossing, extending*, 221, 27.

þwertūt, *adv.*, ON. þwert, *neut.* of þwerr + ūt; *thoroughly, completely*; þwerrtūt (O), 9, 23.

þȳef, þyng, *see* þēf, þing.

þynke(n), *see* þenche(n), þinche(n).

þys, *see* þis.

U.

ū, üfel, ülle, *see* þū, yvel, willǝ.

uglīnes, *sb.*, ON. uggligr + ME. -ness; *ugliness*, 148, 12.

um, *prep.*, ON. um, cogn. with OE. ymbe; *round, about, after*; um wīle, *at times, now and then*, 3, 23.

ümbe, *adv. prep.*, **Sth.** = Ml. imbe?; OE. ymbe; *round about, after*, 183, 30.

umbethynke(n), *wkv.*, ON. um + OE. beðencean; *consider, meditate*; *imp. sg.* umbethynke, 146, 13.

umbilappe(n), *wkv.*, ON. um + OE. *belappen?, cf. OE. læppa; *surround, cover*; *pt. pl.* umbilappid, 142, 23.

ämbridei, *sb.*, **Sth.** = Ml. emberdai,

OE. ymbrendæg; *emberday, one of three fast days occurring in each season*; *pl.* ümbridawes, 200, 2.

umsette(n), *wkv.*, ON. *umsetta, cogn. with OE. ymbsettan; *surround, beset*; *pt. pl.* umsette, 132, 17.

unavȳsedlȳ, *adv.*, based on OF. avis, *sb.*; *unadvisedly*, 146, 30.

unbāld, *adj.*, eME. = Ml. unbǫld; OM. unbāld, WS. unbeald; *timid, unbold*, 183, 29.

unbīnde(n), -bȳnde(n), *stv.*, OE. onbindan (unbīndan)–band (bǫnd) (3); *unbind*; *inf.* unbīnde, 91, 10; *pt. sg.* unbǫnd, 26, 31; *pt. pl.* unbōūnden, 83, 14; *pp.* unbūnde, 39, 2.

unblēndyde, *adj.*, OE. un + *pp.* of OE. blēndan; *unmixed, unblended*, 144, 10.

unboht, *adj.* < *pp.*, OE. bycgan; *unbought, unatoned for*, 178, 3.

unbǫnd, *see* unbōūnden, unbūndе, *see* unbīnde(n).

uncerteyn, *adj.*, OE. un + OF. certein; *uncertain*, 102, 7.

unclǫþe(n), *wkv.*, OE. un + clāðian; *unclothe*; *pt. sg.* unclǫþede, 85, 7.

uncomlī, *adj.*, based on OE. cyme(?); *uncomely*, 52, 6.

uncost, *sb.*, ON. kostr, 'choice, virtue'; *vice*, 18, 11.

uncūð, *see* unkūð.

undēp, *adj.*, OE. undēop; *not deep*, 3, 12.

under, *prep. adv.*, OE. under; *under*; unnderr (O), 8, 17.

underfō(n), *stv.*, OE. underfōn–fēng (R); *receive*; *imp. sg.* underfēng, 196, 24; *pt. sg.* underfēng, 2, 8; *pp.* underfången (eME.), 2, 19; underfǫnge, 213, 25. **Sth.** *imp. pl.* undervō ʒē, 203, 7; *pt. sg.* undervēng, 210, 9; *pt. pl.* undervēngen, 187, 10.

undergete(n), ʒete(n), *stv.*, OM. undergetan (WS. gietan)–gæt (WS. ʒeat(5)); *obtain, get, perceive*; *pt. pl.* undergǣton (eME.), 2, 2ᴿ; *pp.* underʒete, 39, 14.

undergọ̄(n), *anv.*, OE. undergān(?) ; *undergo, take care of* (?) ; *pr. sbj. sg.* undergọ̄, 231, 19.

underling, *sb.*, OE. underling ; *inferior, subject*, 183, 17.

undernime(n), *stv.*, OE. underniman–nōm (4) ; *take, take unawares* ; *pp.* undernumen 24, 7 ; undernómen, 55, 19.

understande(n), **-stọ̄nde**(n), *stv.*, OE. understandan–stōd (6) ; *understand, receive* ; *inf.* unnderrstanndenn (O), 9, 10 ; understọ̄nd, 72, 13 ; undyrstọ̄nde, 90, 15 ; undurstọ̄nde, 106, 1 ; *pr.* 3 *sg.* understont, 198, 9 ; *imp. sg.* understand, 216, 13 ; *imp. pl.* understọ̄ndeþ, 206, 26 ; *pt. sbj. sg.* understōde, 204, 2. **Nth.** *pr.* 3 *sg.* understandes, 134, 8. **Kt.** *inf.*, ōnderstọ̄nde, 218, 26 ; *pr. sbj. pl.*, ōnderstọ̄nde, 218, 23.

undertāke(n), *stv.*, OE. under + ON. taka–tōk (6) ; *undertake* ; *pt. sbj. sg.* undertōke, 76, 12.

underþēde(n), *wkv.*, OM. underþēdan, WS. þīedan (þēodan) ; *make subject* ; *inf.* underþēden, 1, 3.

undertōke, *see* undertāke(n).

undervēng, undervō(n), *see* underfō(n).

undevọ̄cyọ̄ne, *sb.*, OE. un + OF. devocion ; *lack of devotion*, 146, 9.

undirstāndynge, *sb.*, OE. understanding, *f.* ; *intelligence, understanding*, 145, 6.

underwrīte(n),*stv.*,OE.underwrītan–wrāt (1) ; *subscribe, sign* ; *pp.* undirwriten, 116, 20.

undō(n), *anv.*, OE. ondōn, undōn ; *undo* ; *inf.* undōn, 23, 18.

undren, *sb.*, OE. undern ; *time from nine to twelve, morning*, 28, 13.

undühtī, *adj.*, OE. *undyhtig ; *unprofitable, unavailing*, 192, 5.

unẹ̄ře, unēaþe, *adj.*, *adv.*, OE. unēaðe ; *difficult, with difficulty*, 181, 11. **Kt.** unēaþe, 215, 1.

unẹ̄ðes, *see* unnẹ̄ðes.

unfēre, *adj.*, OE. unfēre ; *disabled, infirm*, 132, 9.

unfọ̄lde(n), *stv.*, OM. unfaldan (fāl-

dan), WS. fealdan–fēold (R) ; *unfold, open* ; *pt. sg.* unfēld, 65, 28.

unforʒolde, *adj.*, **eME.** based on OE. forʒildan ; *unrequited*, 178, 3.

unfrīð, *sb.*, OE. unfrið ; *discord, lack of peace*, 2, 10.

unhelþe, *sb.*, OE. unhǣlð, *f.* ; *illness, lack of health*, 176, 16.

unhōld, *adj.*, OE. unhold (hōld) ; *disloyal, unfriendly, ungracious*, 177, 12.

unhonestē, *sb.*, OE. un + OF. honestē ; *dishonesty*, 146, 29.

unimẹ̄te, *adj.*, **Sth.** = Ml. unimēte ; OM. ungemēte, WS. ungemǣte ; *immeasurable, unnumbered*, 181, 18.

unisẹ̄lī, *adj.*, **Sth.** = Ml. unsẹ̄lī ; WS. ungesælig, OM. ungesēlig ; *unhappy, unfortunate*, 199, 15.

unkevele(n), *wkv.*, OE. un + ON kefla ; *ungag* ; *pt. pl.* unkeveleden, 83, 14.

unkīnde,*adj* , OE. uncynde ; *strange, unkind, foreign*, 29, 14.

unkọ̄nning, *adj.*, based on cunne(n); *uncunning, ignorant*, 235, 16.

unkūð, *adj.*, OE. uncūð ; *unacquainted*, 16, 25 ; uncūð, 19, 14.

unkȳndelȳ, *adv.*, OE. *uncyndelīce, uncȳndelīce ; *unnaturally*, 238, 3.

unlahe, *sb.*, OE. unlagu ; *violation of law, injustice, sin* ; **Sth.** *pl.* unlahen, 196, 8.

unlẹ̄ffullīch, *adv* , OE. ungelēaffullīce ; *unfaithfully, wrongly*, 236, 19.

unlẹ̄veful, *adj.*, OE. ungelēafful ; *unfaithful*, 235, 6.

unlīch (-lȳch), *adj.*, **Sth.** = Ml. unlīk ; OE. unlīc ; *unlike*, 194, 2.

unlust, *sb.*, OE. unlust ; *displeasure*, 54, 17.

unmēð, *adj.*, OM. *unmēð, *sb.*, WS. mǣð ; *unmeasured*, 192, 4.

unmēþ (mẹ̄þ), *sb.*, OM. unmēþ, WS. -mǣþ ; *lack of moderation, error, blame*, 43, 5.

unmyghttȳ, *adj.*, OE., unmihtig ; *feeble, impotent*, 146, 28.

unnc, *see* ic.

unnēdeful, *adj.*, OE. *unnēodful;
unnecessary, 235, 6.

unneile(n), *wkv.*, OE. *onnæglian;
unnail, loose from nails; *pt. sg.*
unneilede, 230, 13.

unne(n), *ptprv.*, OE. unnan–ūðe;
grant, favor; *pr. sbj. sg.* unne, 8,
11; *pr. sbj. pl.* unnen, *wish*, 183,
8; *pt. sg.* ouþe, 55, 15.

unnēðes, unēðes, *adv.*, OE. unēaðe
+ es; *with difficulty, scarcely*, 17, 8.

unnit, *sb.*, OE. unnytt; *vanity,
frivolity*; unnitt (O), 9, 27.

unnkerr (O), *pos. prn.*, OE. uncer;
our (dual), *of us two*, 9, 26.

unnüt, *adj.*, Sth. = Ml. unnit; OE.
unnytt; *useless*, 176, 5.

unprēnāble, *adj.*, ME. un + OF.
prenable; *impregnable, improper,
wrong*, 233, 28.

unricht, *see* unriht.

unrīde, *adj.*, OE. ungerȳde; *rough,
violent*, 19, 7.

unrīht, unricht, *sb.*, OE. unriht;
wrong, evil, 179, 4; unricht, 212,
23.

unryghtwȳselȳ, *adv.*, OE. unriht-
wīslīce; *unrighteously*, 144, 16.

unschāpe, *adj.*, OE. un + sceapen,
pp.; *unformed, unpleasant, out-
landish*, 225, 26.

unschill, *sb.*, OE. *unscil; *indiscre-
tion, evil purpose*, 132, 23.

unselhðe, *sb.*, OM. unsēlhð, WS.
sǣlhð, *f.*; *unhappiness, misfortune*,
29, 28.

unsēlī, *adj.*, OM. unsēlig, WS. sǣlig;
unhappy, unfortunate, 29, 27.

unsēmlȳ, *adj.*, based on ON. sœmr;
unfitting, unseemly, 52, 5.

unshaþīʒnesse, (eME.), *sb.*, as if OE.
*unsceaðigness *f.*; *innocence*; unn-
shaþīʒnesse (O), 12, 1.

unshewed, *pp.* as *adj.*, ME. un +
shewed; *unshown, hidden*, 231, 28.

unstrǫng, *adj.*, OE. unstrang-
strǫng; *weak, infirm*, 15, 14.

untellendlīce, *adj.*, OE. *un-
tellendlīc?; *unspeakable*, 3, 4.

unþanc, unþank, *sb.*, OE. unðanc;
ingratitude, displeasure; *gs.* here

unþankes, *contrary to their pleasure,
unwillingly*, 6, 32; unþanc his, *contrary to his wish*, 62, 10.

unðēau, *sb.*, OE. unðēaw; *bad
manners, vice*, 200, 21.

untīd, *sb.*, OE. untīd, *adj.*, perh. *sb.*;
unseasonableness; *evil*, 50, 24.

untiʒht, *sb.*, OE. *untyht? < tyht,
'usage, right' (?); *evil, vice*, 55,
11.

untill, *prep.*, OE. un + til; *unto,
until*, 163, 3.

untrewe, *adj.*, OE. untrēowe; *untrue,
awry*, 16, 2.

untwǣme(n), *wkv.*, eME. = Ml.
untwǣme(n); OE. untwǣman; *not
to divide or be divided*; *pp.* un-
twǣmet, *undivided*, 197, 11.

unwar, *adj.*, OE. unwær; *unaware,
unprepared*, 223, 23.

unwarc, *sb.*, OE. *unweorc; *idleness,
evil*; *pl.* unwarces, 134, 10.

unwēlde, *adj.*, OM. *unwelde (wēlde),
WS. *unwielde, ungewīelde; *not
subject to control, weak, impotent*,
15, 12.

unweommet, *adj.*, OE. unwemmed;
unspotted, pure, 192, 16.

unwilles, *adv.*, OE. unwilles < un-
will; *against one's will*; al hire
unwilles, *against her will*, 192, 13.

unwīse, *adv.*, OE. unwīse; *unwisely*,
40, 21.

unwitynglȳ, *adv.*, OE. unwitende +
lȳ; *without knowledge, unwittingly*,
238, 4.

unwraste, *adv.*, OE. unwrǣste;
badly, wickedly, 187, 30.

unwraste, unwrest, *adj.*, OE. un-
wrǣst; *infirm, weak*, 54, 10; *miserable, foul*, 81, 22; *evil*, 199, 14.

unwurð, *adj.*, OE. unweorð (wurð);
not worth, valueless, 193, 33.

unwytyng, *adj.*, OE. unwitende;
unwitting, unintentional, 236, 22.

up, *prep. adv.*, OE. up; *up, upon,
above*, 2, 26; 29, 32; up snowe,
according to, like snow, 102, 10.

upbęrȩr, *sb.*, OE. up + ME. bȩrȩr,
based on bȩre(n), *stv.*; *upbearer,
supporter*, 233, 1.

upbrayd, upbreyd, *sb.*, OE. up+
brægd (bræd); *upbraiding,* upbrayd, 155, 22; upbreyd, 97, 7.

upen, *see* upon.

uplǫndysch, *adj.,* based on OE.
uppeland (lǫnd); *up country,
rural,* 224, 23.

upnime(n), *stv.,* OE. upniman-nōm
(4); *take up, raise; pt. sg.* upnōm,
43, 27.

upon, upponn, upen, opon, *prep.
adv.,* OE. ŭp+on; *upon,* 30, 19;
upponn (O), 9, 21; uppō = uppon,
10, 5; opon, 71, 23; upen, *according to,* 116, 21. Nth. opon, 132, 20.
Sth. uppen, 181, 14.

uppard, *see* upward.

uppen, uppō, *see* upon.

uprais, *see* uprīse(n).

upriȝt, upryght, *adj.,* OE. upriht;
upright, 46, 15; upryght, 239, 12.

uprīse(n), *stv.,* OE. uprīsan-rās (1);
uprise, rise up; inf. uprīse, 137,
23. Nth. *pt. sg.* uprais = uprās,
132, 25.

uprīsyng, *pr. ppl.* as *sb.; uprising,*
132, 24.

upryght, *see* upriȝt.

upsterte(n), *wkv.,* OE. up + ON.
sterta; *upstart; pt. sg.* upsterte,
89, 23.

upstey, *see* upstīe(n).

upstīe(n), *stv.,* ON. upstīgan-stē (1);
ascend, rise; pt. sg. upstey = upstē,
132, 25.

upstǫnde(n), *stv.,* OE. upstandan
(stǫndan)-stōd (6); *stand up; inf.*
upstǫnde, 111, 20.

upward, uppard, *adv.,* OE. upweard;
upward; uppard, 196, 22.

ūre, hōure, *sb.,* OF. hure, ure; *hour,*
212, 19; hōure, 239, 9.

ūre, ūr, ōur, *prn.,* OE. ūre (ūser);
our, 4, 9; ūr, 25, 12; ōure, 66, 1;
ōwer, 38, 22.

ūre, *see* ic.

ürne(n), *stv.,* Sth. = Ml. rinne(n);
WS. iernan (yrnan)-orn (3); *run;
pt. sg.* orn, 182, 15.

us, uss, *see* ic.

usāge, *sb.,* OF. usage; *usage,* 246, 6.

ūse, *sb.,* OF. use; *use; pl.* uses, 235,
25.

ūse(n), *wkv.,* OF. user; *use; inf.*
use, 120, 20. Sth. *pr. pl.* useþ,
223, 18; *pp.* yused, 224, 26.

ūt, ōut, *adv. prep.,* OE. ūt; *out,* 1,
10; ōut, 51, 16.

ūtcume(n), *stv.,* OE. ūtcuman-cōm
(cwōm) (4); *come out; pt. pl.*
utcōmen, 23, 1.

ūte, ōute, *adv.,* OE. ūte; *out,* 6, 27;
ōute, 48, 4.

ūten, *adv. prep.,* OE. ūtan; *without,
beyond,* 32, 22.

ūtgǫ(n), *anv.,* OE. *ūtgān-ēode; *go
out; pt. sg.* ūtyēde, 212, 3.

ūðe, *sb.,* Sth. = Ml. īþe; OE. ȳð, *f.;
wave; †l.* ūðen, 182, 17.

Uðer, *sb.,* Uther (*father of Arthur*);
gs. Uðeres, 190, 25.

ūtnume, *pp.* as *adj. adv.,* based on
OE. niman; *exceptionally,* 192, 9.

ūtyēde, üvele, *see* ūtgǫ(n), yvel.

uvenan, *adv., prep.,* OE. ufenan;
upon, 189, 6.

V.

væie, *adj.,* Sth. = Ml. feie, faie;
OE. fæge; *fated, doomed,* 189, 19.

væir, vair, *see* fair.

væisīð, *sb.,* Sth. = Ml. fæisīþ; OE.
fæge + sīð; *fated journey, death;
væisīð makeȝe, make the fated
journey, die,* 184, 18.

vair, vaire, *see* fair, faire.

Valays, *sb.,* NF. Valeis, OF. Valois;
Valois, 158, 29.

valē, *sb.,* OF. valee; *valley,* 166, 4.

valeie, *sb.,* OF. valee, AN. valeie;
valley, 208, 17.

Valentiniānus, *sb.,* Lat. Valentinianus; *Valentinianus,* 221, 14.

valle(n), *see* falle(n).

vals, *see* fals.

valsīen, *wkv.,* Sth. = Ml. falsen;
OF. falser; *deceive, damage, injure;
pr. ppl.* valsinde, 200, 30.

valþ, *see* falle(n).

vāne < vaine, *sb.,* OF. veine; *vein;
pl.* vānys, 171, 23.

vanitē, *see* vanytē.

vantwarde, *sb.*, OF. avantewarde (garde); *vanguard,* 208, 15.

vanysshe(n), *wkv.,* OF. *vanir, vaniss-,* cf. vanouir; *vanish; pr.* 1 *sg.* vanysshe, 241, 3.

vanytē, vanitē, *sb.,* OF. vanitē; *vanity,* 121, 12; vanitē, 128, 3.

vāren, *see* fāre(n).

Vaspāsian, *sb.,* Lat. Vespasianus; *Vespasian;* Vaspāsian hys, *Vespasian's,* 220, 7.

vaste, *see* faste.

vaynẹ, *adj.,* OF. vain; *vain,* 136, 8.

vayrhēde, *sb.,* Kt. = Ml. fayrhẹde; OE. *fægerhẹd, *f.*; *beauty,* 219, 4.

vēden, vēl, *see* fēde(n), falle(n).

velaghe, *see* felawe.

velaȝrēde, *sb.,* Kt. = Ml. felaȝrēde; ON. fēlagi + ME. rēde; *fellowship, company,* 219, 3.

vēld, velde, vele, *see* fēld, fẹle.

vengeaunce, vengeance, *sb.,* OF. venjance; *vengeance,* 103, 6; vengeance, 135, 16.

venge(n),*wkv.,* OF. venger; *avenge; inf.* venge, 167, 14.

vẹniel (vẹnyal), *adj.,* OF. venial; *venial,* 217, 16.

venim,*sb.,* OF. venin; *venom,* 17, 10.

vēol, vēond, *see* falle(n), fēnd.

vēondlīch, *adj.,* Sth. = Ml. fēndlīc; OE. fēondlīc; *hostile, fiendlike,* 187, 1.

vēr, vērde, vēre, *see* fīr, fērde, fēre.

vereden, *see* ferie(n).

Vergilius,*sb.,* Lat. Vergilius; *Vergil,* 221, 5.

verīe(n), *see* ferīe(n).

vermyn, *sb.,* OF. vermine; *vermin,* 244, 30.

verrailȳ, *adv.,* OF. verai + ME. lȳ; *verily, truly,* 136, 4.

verrament, *adv.,* OF. veraiment; *truly, verily,* 109, 16.

verrē, verray, *adj. adv.,* OF. verai; *very, verily,* 122, 21; verray, 237, 24.

verst, *see* first, *adj.*

vertū, vertūe, virtū, *sb.,* OE. vertu;

virtue, *favor,* 64, 19; vertue, 146, 12; *pl.* virtues, 217, 17; vertus, 144, 9.

vestiment, *sb.,* OF. vestiment; *vestment,* 203, 7.

vīce, vȳce, *sb.,* OF. vice; *vice, defect, sin; pl.* vīces, 104, 7.

vīf, viis, vihte, vihte(n), *see* fīf, vīs, fiht, flȝte(n).

vīl, *adj.,* OF. vil; *vile; pl.* vīle, 144, 6.

vileynȳe, vyleynȳe, *sb.,*OF.vileinie; *villainy,* 238, 21; vyleynȳe, 219, 2.

villāgẹ, *sb.,* OF. village; *village,* 239, 25.

vīllīche, *adv.,* OF. vil + Sth. līche; *vilely,* 204, 28.

vīnt, *see* finde(n).

violence, *sb.,* OF. violence; *violence,* 147, 16.

vīolent, *adj.,* OF. violent; *violent,* 245, 6.

virgīnẹ, *sb.,* OF. virgine; *virgin,* 74, 15.

virtu, *see* vertū.

vīs, vȳsẹ, *sb.,* OF. vis; *face, look;* viis, 66, 8; vȳsẹ, *view,* 121, 14.

visāgẹ, vysegẹ, *sb.,* OF. visage; *visage,* 240, 24; vysege, 98, 21.

visiōn, visiōun, *sb.,* OF. vision, AN. visiun; *vision, dream,* 209, 15; visioun, 232, 4.

vittaillēr, *sb.,* OF. vittailier; *victualer; pl.* vittaillērs, 236, 1.

vlẹ(n), *stv.,* Sth. = Ml. flẹ(n); OE. flēan–flōh (9) (6); *flay; pp.* vlaȝe, 217, 30.

vlōd(e), *see* flod.

vlȳgþ, vlȳinde, *see* flēge(n).

voȝel, *see* fugel.

voicẹ, *sb.,* OF. vois; *voice,* 105, 12.

volẹ, *see* folk.

volewen, volȝī, volȝeþ, *see* folȝe(n).

volk, *see* folk.

vōllīche, *adv.,* Sth. = Ml. fullīke (lī); OE. fullīce; *fully,* 218, 1.

vor, *see* for.

vorarnīe(n), *wkv.,* Sth. = Ml. forarne(n); OE.*forarnian; *ride hard, weary by riding; pp.* vorarned, 208, 27.

vorbēde(n), *see* forbēde(n).

vorbērne(n), *wkv.*, Sth. = Ml. for-
bērne(n) ; OE. forbernan ; *burn up* ;
pr. 3 *sg.* vorbērnþ, 218, 11.

vorbīsne, *sb.*, Sth. = Ml. forbīsne ;
OE. forbīsn, *f.* ; *example, parable,*
199, 19.

vōre, *sb.*, Sth. = Ml. fōre ; OE. fōr,
f. ; *journey, expedition,* 185, 11.

vorewarde, vorwarde, *see* forewarde.

vorlōre, *see* forlēsen.

vorlōrenesse, *sb.*, Sth. = Ml. for-
lorennesse ; OE. forlorenness, *f.* ;
lost condition, 198, 15.

vorprıkīe(n), *wkv.*, Sth. = Ml. for-
prike(n) ; OE. for + prician ; *spur,
violently* ; *pp.* vorpriked, 208, 27.

vorsāke(n), *see* forsake(n).

vorswoluwe(n), *stv.*, Sth. = Ml.
forswelwe(n) (swolwe(n)) ; OE.
forswelgan–swealg (ʒ) ; *swallow
up, devour* ; *pr.* 3 *sg.* vorswoluweð,
198, 25.

vorswōre, *see* forswēre(n).

vort(e), *prep. conj.*, Sth. = Ml. fort ;
OE. for tō ; *until,* 197, 15 ; vorte,
206, 30.

vorð, *see* forþ.

vorþenchinge, *sb.*, Sth. = Ml. for-
þenchinge ; OE. *forðencung ? ;
repentance, 218, 1.

vorþī, *see* forþī.

vorwarde, *see* forewarde.

vorwoūndie(n), *wkv.*, Sth. = Ml.
forwūnde(n) ; OE. forwundian
(wūndian) ; *wound badly* ; *pp.*
vorwoūnded, 208, 27.

voryeteþ, voryet, *see* forʒete(n).

vorzōþe, *see* forsōþe.

voūche(n), *wkv.*, OF. voucher ;
vouch, vow ; with sāfe, sāve, *to
grant* ; *pr.* 1 *sg.* I voūche it sāve, *I
grant it,* 138, 8.

voūl, *see* fūl.

voūlhēde, *sb.*, Kt. = Ml. foūlhēde ;
OE. fūl + Kt. hēde ; *foulness,* 219,
12.

vōwę, *sb.*, OF. vou ; *vow,* 107, 27.

vram, Vrīdei, *see* fram, Frīdai.

vrīlıche, *adv.*, Kt. = Ml. frēlȳ ; OE.

frīlīce (frēolīce) ; *freely, nobly,
willingly,* 215, 4.

vrom, vrōvren, *see* fram, frōfre(n).

vȳce, vȳend, *see* vīce, fēnd.

vyleynȳe, *see* vileynȳe.

vȳse, vyseǧe, *see* vīs, viseǧe.

W.

wā, *sb.*, eME. Nth. = Ml. wǭ ; OE.
wā ; *woe,* 79, 4. Cf. wāwe.

wāde(n), wayd, *wkv.*, OE. wadan,
infl. by ON. vaða ; *go, wade* ; lNth.
inf. wayd = wād, 166, 19.

wāding, *sb.*, OE. wadung, infl. by
ON. vaða ; *wading,* 168, 2.

wǣ, *sb.*, OAng. wǣ, WS. wā ; *woe,
sorrow,* 186, 19.

wæi, wǣl, *see* wei, wēl.

wēlde(n), *see* węlde(n).

wēron, (-en), *see* bē(n).

wærse, wæs, *see* werse, (bēn).

wæt, wæx, *see* whō, waxe(n).

wāferēre, *sb.*, OF. wafre, *wafrier ;
seller of wafers, confectioner, 237,
23.

wāfullīc, *adv.*, Nth. = Ml. wǫfullī ;
based on OE. wā ; *woefully,* 153,
14.

waię, *see* wei.

wain, wayn, *sb.*, OE. wægn ; *wain,
wagon,* 31, 10 ; wayn, 59, 1.

waite(n), *wkv.*, OF. waiter ; *watch,
wait, heed* ; *inf.* waiten, 80, 19.
Nth. *inf.* wait, *watch to injure,
injure,* 159, 16. Sth. *pt. pl.* weytede, 223, 20.

wājoūr, *sb.*, OF. wageure, gageure ;
wager, 89, 18.

wāke(n), *wkv.*, OE. wacian ; *wake,
watch* ; *inf.* wāken, 34, 2 ; wāke,
56, 27 ; *pr.* 3 *sg.* wākeð, 15, 5 ; *pp.*
wāked, 34, 22. Nth. *pr.* 3 *sg.*
wākes, 145, 6 ; *pr. ppl.* wākand,
154, 29.

wāke(n), *stv.*, OE. wacan–wōc (6) ;
wake, awake ; *inf.* wāke, 74, 3 ;
pt. sg. wōc, 23, 15.

wākīe(n), *wkv.*, OE. wācian ; *weaken,
fail* ; Sth. *inf.* 183, 14.

wăkne(n), *wkv.*, OE. wacian; *waken*; Nth. *pt. sg.* wāknyt, 172, 30. Sth. *pp.* ywākened, *be born*, 66, 16.

wal, *sb.*, OM. wall, WS. weall; *wall*, 122, 30. Sth. *ds.* walle, 177, 17.

walawǭ, *interj.*, OE. wā lā wā; *woe, alas*, 48, 9.

wǎld, *sb.*, eME. Nth. for Ml. wǫld; OM. wald, wāld, WS. weald, *mn.*; *power*; *ds.* wālde, 11, 27.

wald, walde, *see* wille.

wǎldǝ(n), *stv.*, eME. = Ml. wǫlden; OM. waldan (wāldan), WS. wealdan –wēold (R); *wield, have power over*; *inf.* wālden, 183, 7.

wǎldend, *sb.*, OM. wāldend, WS. wealdend; *ruler, governor*, 184, 21.

wǎle, *interj.*, OE. wālā; *woe, alas*, 182, 27.

Wǎles, *sb.*, OE. Wealas < Wealh; *Wales*, 222, 20.

Walingfǒrd, *sb.*, OE. Wealenga-ford; *Wallingford* (Berkshire), 6, 30.

walke(n), *stv.*, OE. walcan (wealcan) –wēolc (R); *walk*, earlier *roll, toss*; *pr.* 1 *sg.* walke, 240, 32; *pr.* 3 *sg.* walkeð, 17, 9; *pr. pl.* walken, 123, 32; *pt. sbj. sg.* walked, 240, 26. Nth. *pr. pl.* walkes, 150, 6.

walle, *see* wal.

walle(n), *stv.*, OM. wallan (WS. weallan)–wēol (R); *boil, well up*; *pt. sg.* wēl, 62, 16. Sth. *pr. ppl.* wallinde, 195, 18; *pt. sbj. sg.* wēolle, 195, 16.

walm, *adj.*, OE. *wealm, cf. OM. welm, WS. wielm; *welling, boiling*, 195, 15.

Walrī, *sb.*, OF. Waleri (Wace), Valerie; *Walry*, (St. Valerie), 205, 13.

Walschman, *sb.*, OM. Welisc, WS. Wielisc + man; *Welshman*; *pl.* Walschmen, 224, 4.

walspēre, *sb*, OE. wælspere; *battle-spear*, 190, 9.

Walter, *sb.*, OF. Waltere, Teut. Wald-here; *Walter*; Wallterr, *Orm's brother*, 8, 13; Walter, 227, 1.

Waltevile, *sb.*, *Waltville*, Hugo of, 4, 23; William de, 8, 2.

Waltham, *sb.*, OM. *Walðham, WS.

*Wealðham; *Waltham in Essex*, 210, 1.

Walwaine, Walwain, *sb.*, OF. Walwain, Gawain; *Walwain*, 181, 17. Nth. Wawān, 126, 13.

wāmbe, *sb.*, eME. = Ml. wǫmb (wōmb); OE. wamb, wāmb, *f.*; *stomach, womb*, 180, 25. Cf. wǫmbe.

wan, *see* winne(n), whanne.

wandrēme = wandrēm, *sb.*, OE. wan + drēam; *lack of joy, trouble, distress*, 108, 23.

wandrēþ, *sb.*, ON. vandræði; *misery, trouble*, 148, 8.

wǎne, *sb.*, ON. vān, *f.*, ' hope, expectation '; *hope, store, quantity or number*, 164, 25. lNth. wayn, 166, 2.

wǎne, *adj.*, OE. wana; *wanting, lacking*, 117, 25.

wanne, *see* whanne.

wante(n), *wkv.*, ON. vanta; *want, be lacking*; *pr. sbj. sg.* wante, 27, 20; *pt. sg.* wantede, 24, 27.

wǎr, wǎr(e), *see* bē(n), whēr.

war, *adj.*, OE. wær; *aware, wary, on guard*, 5, 13. Nth. war, 155, 6.

warc, *see* werk.

ward, *see* wurþen.

ward, *adv.*, OM. ward, WS. weard; *toward*; tō Gode ward, *toward God*, 16, 21; 17, 9.

warde, ward, *sb.*, OM. ward, WS. weard, *f.*; *custody, keeping*, 67, 28; warde, *charge, maturity*, 121, 27.

ware, *sb.*, OE. waru; *goods, wares, merchandise*, 178, 12.

wǎre, *see* bē(n).

wǎre(n), *wkv.*, OE. warian; *beware, take precaution, defend*; Nth. *pr. sbj. sg.* warre, 128, 12; *imp. pl.*, wǎr, 160, 20. Sth. *inf.* wārīen, 202, 32.

wāren, *see* bē(n).

wǎre(n), *wkv.*, OE. *warian; *spend*; *inf.* wāre, 95, 26.

warēse, *see* whērsǭ.

waresoūn, *sb.*, AN. warisun, OF. warison; *protection, treasure*, 105, 28.

warevōre, *see* whērfōre.

Warewīk, *sb.*, OE. Wǣringwīc ;
Warwick, 227, 5.

warī, *sb.*, OE. wearg, werig; *felon,
villain* ; Sth. *pl.* warīen, 184, 26.

wārīen, *see* wāre(n).

warīe(n), *wkv.*, OE. wergian; *curse,
condemn* ; *inf.* warīen, 200, 16 ; *pr.
sbj. sg.* warīe, 78, 4 ; *pp.* warīed, 78,
5. Nth. *pt. sg.* waryit, 173, 16.

warlau, *sb.*, OE. *wǣrloga ; *sorcerer,
traitor, devil* ; *pl.* warlaus, 135, 18.

warld, *see* werld.

warm, *adj.*, OE. wearm, warm; *warm* ;
warme, 89, 4.

warme(n), *wkv.*, OM. warmian, WS.
wearmian ; *warm* ; *pr. pl.* warmen,
20, 9.

warnden, *see* werne(n).

warne(n), *wkv.*, OE. wearnian; *warn,
guard* ; *inf.* warne, 122, 13 ; *pp.*
warned, 54, 21 ; *pt. sg.* warnede,
189, 5.

warp, *see* werpe(n).

warpe(n), *wkv.*, ON. varpa ; *throw* ;
inf. warpen, 195, 15.

warraying, *see* werrīe(n).

warre, *see* wāre(n).

warsæ, *see* whērsǭ.

wart, warth, warrþ, *see* wurþe(n).

warþoru, *see* whērþoru.

waryit, *see* warīe(n).

washe(n), wassə(n), *stv.*, OE. was-
can—wōsc (6, R) ; *wash* ; *inf.*wasshe,
101, 28 ; wassen, 29, 3 ; wasse, 39,
22 ; *pt. sg.* weis, 29, 1 ; *pt. pl.*
wyschen, 109, 5. Nth. *inf.* was,
132, 12.

was(s), *see* bē(n).

wāst, *adj.*, OF. wast ; *waste, empty,*
171, 1.

wāsten, *wkv.*, OF. wāster ; *waste* ;
Nth. *inf.* wāst, 134, 10.

wat, wāt, *see* whō, wite(n).

water, wattir, *sb.*, OE. wæter : *water,
stream,* 19, 2 ; wattir, 166, 5 ; *pl.*
waters, 100, 19. Sth. weter, 195,
18 ; *ds.* wetere, 178, 26 ; wettre,
196, 31.

waterkinn, *sb.*, OE. wæter + cvnn ;
kin by water, i. e. *baptism,* 11, 22.

watloker, *see* whatlīche.

wattir, *see* water.

wāvere(n), *wkv.*, ON. vafra ; *waver,
loiter* ; Nth. *pr. ppl.* wāverand, 169,
26 ; *pt. sg.* wāveryt, 167, 20.

waw, *sb.*, OE. wāg; *wall* ; *ds.* wawę,
79, 13.

Wawān, *see* Walwaine.

wāwe, *sb.*, OE. wāwa ; *woe, misery,*
180, 29 ; *pl.* wāwenn (O), 12, 16.

wax, *sb.*, OE. weax ; *wax,* 117, 6.

waxe(n), *stv.*, OE. weaxan—wōx and
wēx (6, R) ; *wax, grow, increase* ;
inf. waxen, 193, 12 ; *pr.* 3 *sg.*
waxeð, 17, 17 ; *pr. sbj. sg.* wax,
103, 5 ; *pr. ppl.* waxand, 103, 29 ;
pt. sg. wæx (eME.), 5, 18 ; wēx, 24,
29 ; wax, 92, 13 ; *pt. pl.* wēxen, 23,
8 ; *pp.* waxen, 21, 24.

way, wąye, *see* wei.

wayd, *see* wāde(n).

wayn, wē, *see* wāne, wain, ic.

wē, *interj.*, OE. wǣ, cogn. with ON.
wei ; *woe,* 66, 9.

wēalde(n), *see* wēlde(n).

wəchdēde, *sb.*, OM. wæcce (*wecċe)
+ dēde ; *watching, vigil,* 34, 13.

weche, *sb.*, OE. wæcche, *f.* ; *watch,
vigil,* 34, 20.

wed, *sb.*, OE. wedd ; *pledge, surety* ;
tō wedde, *for security, for a pledge,*
26, 6.

wedde(n), *wkv.*, OE. weddian ; *wed,
pledge* ; *pt. sg.* weddyd, 116, 1.
eSth. *pp.* iweddet, 194, 1.

weddir, *sb.*, OE. weðer ; *wether,
sheep,* 169, 29.

wēde, *sb.*, OM. wēde, WS. wǣde ;
clothing, weeds ; *pl.* wēden, 31, 17 ;
wēdes, 48, 21.

Wedęnysday, *see* Wodnesdei.

weder, weddir, *sb.*, OE. weder ;
storm, weather, 19, 28 ; *gs.* wederes,
185, 6.

weder, wedir, wheder, and compounds, *see* wheþer.

wedlāc, *sb.*, eME. = Ml. wədlǭk ; OE.
wedlāc ; *wedlock,* 192, 19.

wee, weel, *see* whī, wēl.

wēf, *sb.*, OE. wǣfan (?) ; *whiff, breath,*
51, 28.

weʒe(n), *stv.*, OE. wegan–wæg (5) ; *weigh, estimate* ; *inf.* weʒen, 178, 7.

weghtę, *sb.*, OE. gewiht, gewihte ; *weight*, 147, 15.

wei, way, weię, *sb.*, OE. weg ; *way* ; *ds.* weie, 14, 3 ; waię, 100, 24 ; waye, 65, 22 ; weiʒę, 52, 13 ; wæi (eME.), 186, 16 ; *adv. gs.* ways, 136, 18; wayis,167, 15 ; weies, 178, 16 ; weis, 193, 27.

weilawei,*interj.*, ON. vei + lā + vei, cognate with OE. wā lā wā ; *woe, alas*, 22, 24.

weile, *interj.*, ON. vei + OE. lā; *woe*, 48, 9.

weil(l), weint, *see* **wēl, wēnde(n).**

weir, *see* **bē(n).**

weis, *see* **wei, washe(n).**

wēl, wǣl, wēlę, well, *adv.*, OE. wel (wēl) ; *well, truly, very* ; wēl, 1, 3 ; wǣl, 4, 17 ; well, 9, 17 ; wellę, 14, 14; wēlę, 70, 2 ; weel, 239, 7 ; swiðe wēl, *very often*,192, 8. lNth. weil, 167, 27; weill, 168, 12 ; weyl, 89, 7.

wēl, *see* **walle(n).**

welcome, *see* **wilcume.**

wēlde(n),*wkv.*,OM. weldan, wēldan, WS. wieldan ; *rule over, wield, rule* ; *inf.* wēlden, 24, 15 ; wēlde, 121, 28 ; wēlden, *obtain*, 193, 29 ; *pr.* 3 *sg.* wēldeð, 192, 1.

wēlde(n), *stv.*, Sth. = Ml. wǫlden; WS. wealdan (wēaldan)–wēold (R) ; *wield, have power over* ; eME. *inf.* wēalden, 177, 31 ; *pr.* 1 *sg.* wælde, 176, 2.

wēlę, *sb.*, OE. wele ; *weal, happiness*, 63, 2. eSth. *pl.* weolen, 193, 12.

wēle, *see* **wēl.**

welked, *pp.* as *adj.*, cf. MDu. welken, 'to wither' ; *withered*, 241, 9 ; *pl.* welkede, 23, 11.

well, wellę, *see* **wēl.**

welle, *sb.*, OM. welle, WS. wielle,*j.*; *well*, 15, 17.

wellegründ,*sb.*,OM. well,*f.* + gründ ; *bottom of a well*, 15, 29.

welðe, *sb.*, OE. *welð,*f.* ; *wealth*, 31, 22.

wen, *see* **whanne.**

wēn, wēnd(e), *see* **wēne(n).**

wēnden,*wkv.*, OE. wendan, wēndan ; *turn, wend, go* ; *inf.* wēnden, 14, 3 ; wēnde, 70, 30 ; wēnd, 114, 19 ; *pr. sbj. sg.* wēnde, 178, 30 ; *pt. sg.* wende, 4, 26 ; *pt. pl.* wenden, 6, 31 ; wenten, 69, 2 ; *pp.* wennd (O), 8, 19 ; went, 26, 9. **Nth.** *imp. pl.* wēndis, 139, 13. **Sth.** *pr.* 3 *sg.* weint < wēndeð, 196, 16 ; wēnt, 215, 9 ; *pp.* ywent, 215, 9.

wēndingę, *sb.*, OE. wendung, wēndung, *f.*; *wending, turning, journey*, 215, 7.

wēne, *sb.*, OE. wēn, *f.* wēna, *m.*; *thought, hope, expectation*, 42, 13.

wēne(n), *wkv.*, OE. wēnan ; *think, ween* ; *pr.* 2 *sg.* wēnest, 50, 7 ; *pr.* 3 *sg.* wēneð, 177, 17 ; *pr. pl.* wēnen, 20, 2 ; *imp. sg.* wēn, 193, 23 ; *pt.sg.* wēnde, 7, 2 ; *pt. pl.* wēnden, 2, 19. **Nth.** *pr.* 2 *sg.* wēnis, 128, 9 ; *pr.* 3 *sg.* wēnes, 83, 11 ; *pt. pl.* wēnd, 155, 10.

weng, wyng, *sb.*, ON. vengr ; *wing* ; *pl.* wenges, 145, 5 ; wynges, 144, 1.

Wenhevēr, *sb.*, OF. Wenhaver ; *Wenhavere, Guenevere*, 181, 22 ; *ds.* Wenhavēren, 185, 10.

weolcne, *sb.*, OE. wolcne, *f.*; *sky, welkin*, 182, 31.

weolde, *see* **wille(n).**

weole, weolen, *see* **wēle.**

wēolle, *see* **walle(n).**

wēopmon, *sb.*, eSth. = Ml. wepman ; OM. wēpman, WS. wǣpman ; *man, male*, 199, 8.

weorch, wēorde, *see* **werk, wōrd.**

wēorę, wēoren, *see* **bē(n).**

weork, *see* **werk.**

weorldmon, *sb.*, OE. weoroldmann (mǫnn) ; *man upon earth, man of affairs*: *ds.* weorldmonne, 183, 15.

weorre, *adj. comp.*, ON. verri ; *worse*, 200, 30.

wēp, *sb.*, OE. *wēp ?, beside wōp ; *weeping*, 30, 8 ; *ds.* wēpe, 93, 15.

wēpe(n), *stv.*, OE. wēpan–wēop (R) ; *weep* ; *inf.* wēpe, 56, 9 ; *pr. ppl.*

wēpinge, 38, 14; wēpeand, 64, 16;
pt. sg. wēp, 57, 16; wēpę, 67, 9;
wōp, 70, 31; *pt. pl.* wēpen, 37, 32;
wōpen, 70, 28. Sth. *pr. pl.* wēpeþ,
215, 15.

wēpen, wepen, *sb.*, OM. wēpn, wēpen,
WS. wǣpen; *weapon*; wepne, 79,
29. Sth. *pl.* wēpnen, 184, 31.

wēr, wẹr, *see* bē(n).

wer, wẹr, *see* whēr.

wer, *see* werre.

wer, were, *sb.*, OE. wer; *man, husband*; *ds.* were, 177, 7; were,
194, 6.

werc, *see* werk.

werd, *sb.*, Nth. = Ml. werld; OE.
werold; *world*, 129, 9.

werdlȳ, *adj.*, Nth. = Ml. werldlī;
OE. weoroldlīc; *worldly*, 146, 19.

were, *adj.*, ON. verri, cogn. with
OM. wersa, WS. wiersa; *worse*,
128, 18.

wẹre, wēre, *see* bē(n), werre, whēr.

wẹre, *sb.*, origin unknown; *doubt*,
92, 2. 1Nth. weyr (cf. Scotch
weir), 173, 7.

wērefọre, *see* whērefọre.

wẹre(n), *wkv.*, OE. werian; *defend,
protect, keep off, drive away, go
away, wear*; *inf.* wẹren, 17, 20.
Sth. *inf.* wẹrien, 226, 12.

wẹre(n), *wkv.*, OE. werian; *wẹar*;
inf. wẹre, 61, 3; *pr. 3 sg.* wẹreð,
16, 20.

wẹren, *see* bē(n).

wērī, *see* wērȳ.

werk, eME. weork, *sb.*, OE. weorc,
n.; *work*; werrc (O), 8, 24; *pl.*
weorkes (eME.), 4, 26; werkes,
103, 18; werkys, 109, 25; werke,
105, 14. Nth. warc, 129, 30; *pl.*
werks, 152, 4; eSth. *ds.* weorche,
176, 11.

werkman, *sb.*, OE. weorcman; *work-
man*; *pl.* werkmen, 212, 3.

werld, werlde, world, warld, *sb.*,
OE. weorold, *f.*; *world, age, eternity*;
werlde, 17, 1; werld, 18, 3; world,
56, 3. Kt. wordle, 211, 24; *pl.*
wordles, 213, 31.

werne(n), *wkv.*, OM. *wernan, WS.

wiernan; *refuse, deny*; *pt. pl.*
werneden, 26, 15; warnden, 187, 8.

wēron, *see* bēn.

werpe(n), *stv.*, OE. weorpan–wearp
(3); *cast, throw*; *pt. sg.* warp,
197, 5.

werrais, werrc, *see* werrīe(n), werk.

werre, *sb.*, OF. werre, guerre; *war*,
5, 18. Nth. wer, 149, 31; wẹre,
157, 22; *pl.* wers, 149, 29.

werrīe(n), werre(n), *wkv.*, OF.
werreier; *make war on*; *inf.* werrīen, 2, 15; werre, 221, 17; *pt. sg.*
werrede, werred, 223, 31. Nth.
pr. 3 sg. werrais, 127, 14.

werrïour, *sb.*, OF. werreor; *warrior*,
223, 26.

wers, *see* werre.

werse, wers, *adj.*, comp. to ivel;
OM. werse, WS. wierse (wyrse);
worse, 3, 22; wærse, 5, 20; *superl.*
worste, 242, 13. Nth. wers, 127,
20. Sth. würse, 190, 1.

wersīe(n), *wkv.*, Kt. = Ml. werse(n),
wurse(n); OE. wyrsian; *make
worse*; *pp.* iwersed, 226, 17.

wẹrþe, *see* wurþe(n), bē(n).

wẹrȳ, wērī, *adj.*, OE. wērig; *weary*,
161, 9; wērī, 182, 21.

wes, westen, *see* bē(n), wite(n).

west, *adj.*, OE. west; *west*, 222, 6.

Westmynstre, *sb.*, OE. Westmynster;
Westminster, 236, 27.

wet = whet, *see* whō.

wēt, *adj.*, OM. wēt, WS. wǣt; *wet*,
28, 32. Sth. wẹt, 182, 21.

wēte (wẹte), *sb.*, OM. wēte, WS.
wǣte, *f.*; *moisture, water*, 15, 28.

weter(e), wettre, *see* water.

wēxe(n), weyȝe, *see* waxe(n), wei.

weyl, *see* wēl.

weyr, weyten, *see* wẹre, waite(n).

w3-words, *see* wh- forms.

whā, *rel. prn.*, eME. Nth. = Ml.
whō; OE. hwā; *who*; Nth. *da.*
whaym, 145, 23. eSth. hwām,
194, 7; *dpl.* hwān, 179, 6. Cf.
whō.

whæt, *see* whō.

whanne, wanne, whan, wan,
whenne, *adv. conj.*, OE. hwanne;

when; wanne,♦14, 8; quan, 24, 8;
quane, 31, 27; whan, 45, 19; wan,
48, 5; hwan, 75, 20; whenne, 119,
7; when, 47, 16; ȝwanne, 55, 11;
qwan, 117, 25; wen, 128, 9; hwenne,
177, 11. eSth. hwon, 197, 20.
Nth. quen, 128, 20; quhen, 168, 4.
whar, whare, and compounds, *see*
wh**ē**r, and compounds.
whareb**ȳ**, *adv.*, OE. hw**ǣ**r + b**ī**,
whereby, 119, 9.
wharef**ǫ**re, *see* wh**ē**rf**ǫ**re.
wh**ā**rt**ō**, *adv.*, OE. hw**ǣ**r, hw**ā**r + t**ō**;
whereto, 141, 25.
wh**ā**se, *indef. prn.*, eME., Nth. for
wh**ō**se; OE. hw**ā** sw**ā**, hw**ā** sw**ǣ**;
whoso, whosoever, 9, 14.
wh**ā**sw**ā**, *see* wh**ō**s**ǫ**.
what, wat, see wh**ō**.
wha**ð**er, *see* whe**þ**er.
whatl**ī**che, *adv.*, OE. hw**æ**tl**ī**ce;
swiftly, quickly; *comp.* watloker,
more especially, 204, 13.
whaym, *see* wh**ā**.
whederward, *adv.*, OE. hw**æ**ð**e**r +
weard; *whitherward*, 99, 18;
whydyrward, 96, 14.
whenne, when, see whanne.
whens, *adv.*, OE. hw**ǫ**nan + es;
whence, 106, 27.
wh**ē**r, wh**ē**r**ę**, whar**ę**, w**ē**r**ę**, *adv.*
conj., OM. hw**ē**r, hw**ā**r, WS. hw**ǣ**r;
where; ȝw**ē**re, 48, 17; w**ē**re, 52, 13;
whare, 36, 21; w**ā**re, 131, 11; whar,
182, 9; w**ę**r, 206, 12; wh**ǫ**re, 135, 6.
Kt. hw**ē**r, 218, 14.
wh**ē**reas, *adv.*, Sth. = Ml. wh**ē**ras;
WS. hw**ǣ**r + ME. as; *whereas*,
where, 237, 10.
wh**ē**rf**ǫ**re, wharęf**ǫ**re, hw**ē**rfore,
adv., OM. hw**ē**rfore, WS. hw**ǣ**rfore;
wherefore, 119, 16.
Nth. quars**ǫ**r, 155, 9. eSth. hw**ē**r-
fore, 193, 11; warev**ǫ**re, 209, 31.
Kt. w**ē**ref**ǫ**re, 213, 9.
wh**ē**rof, *adv.*, OM. hw**ē**r (WS. hw**ǣ**r)
+ of; *whereof*, 202, 4.
wh**ē**rs**ǫ**, *adv.*, OM. hw**ē**rsw**ā**, WS.
hw**ǣ**rsw**ā**; *whereso, wheresoever*;
warsæ (eME), 4, 6; warese, 7, 4.
wh**ē**r**þ**oru, *adv.*, OM. hw**ē**r (WS.

hw**ǣ**r) + **þ**urh; *wherethrough*; Nth.
quar**þ**oru, 156, 3; quh**ā**rthrou, 169,
3. Sth. war**þ**oru, 208, 30; wh**ę**r-
þurȝ, 226, 16.
wh**ę**r**þ**urȝ (-thourgh), *see* wh**ē**r**þ**oru.
wh**ę**te, *sb.*, OE. hw**æ**te; *wheat*, 158,
4.
whe**þ**er, whethir, *prn., adv.*, OE.
hw**æ**þer; *whether*; wedir, 52, 17;
ȝwider, 60, 2; whethir, 137, 31;
wha**ð**er, 188, 30; whether, *which of*
two, 234, 19. Nth. quedur, 127,
26; quehe**þ**ir, 169, 32; wydur, 128,
14; whethir, 137, 31.
whe**ð**ers**ę**, *adv.*, OE. hw**æ**ð**e**r + s**ǣ**;
whetherso, 200, 7.
wh**ī**, wh**ȳ**, *adv.*, OE. hw**ȳ**; *why*, 10,
11; w**ȝȳ**, 48, 11; ȝw**ī**, 48, 19. Nth.
qu**ī**, 155, 9. Sth. w**ī**, 179, 15. Kt.
wee, 212, 8.
whil**c**, wil**c**, which, *indef. interrog.*,
later *rel. prn.*, OE., hwil**c**; *which*;
wil**c**, 14, 3; quilke, 30, 30; ȝhwilk,
54, 3; which**ę**, 72, 7; which, 101,
21; whych, 88, 3; **þ**ē which, 104,
17; qwyche, 118, 6. Nth. quilk,
130, 32; **þ**ē whilke, 145, 14; wylke,
144, 22. Sth. *ds.* whilche, 180,
10; hw**ü**cche, 195, 13; w**ü**ch, 203,
21.
whilche, *see* whil**c**.
wh**ī**l**ę**, w**ī**l**ę**, *adv.*, OE. hw**ī**l; *while*;
w**ī**le, 3, 22; qu**ī**le, 21, 5; w**ȝī**le, **ȝ**3,
28; ȝw**ī**le, 59, 8. Nth. qu**ī**l, 156,
6; quh**ī**ll, 170, 27. Sth. wule, 206,
20.
wh**ī**lem, wh**ī**len, wh**ī**lum, wh**ī**lom,
adv., OE. hw**ī**lum < hw**ī**l; *whiles*,
once; qu**ī**lum, 26, 13; hw**ī**len, 191,
6; hwilem, 213, 29; wh**ī**lom, 237,
7. Nth. qu**ī**lum, 128, 23.
whilke, *see* whil**c**.
wh**ī**ls, *adv.*, based on wh**ī**l; *whiles*,
135, 2.
wh**ī**t, wh**ȳ**t, *adj.*, OE. hw**ī**t; *white*;
wh**ȳ**t**ę**, 102, 9; *pl.* wh**ī**te, 228,
16.
Whits**ǫ**nd, *sb.*, OE. Hw**ī**tsand?
Wissant (near Calais), 185, 3.
wh**ō**, *indef., inter.*, later *rel. prn.*;
OE. hw**ā**; *who*; h**ō**, 37, 6; ȝw**ō**,

50, 4; qwō, 117, 29; *da.* whōm, 94, 23. **Nth.** quā, 128, 31; quhā, 166, 18; *da.* quām, 29, 32; 126, 10. **Sth.** hwǭ, 197, 19; wǭ, 207, 19; *neut.* wat, 4, 28; what, 35, 13; 3wat, 49, 22. **Nth.** quat, 127, 16; qwat, 118, 3. **Sth.** wet, 176, 23; whet, 179, 1; hwet, 194, 6.

whōmsǭ, *see* whōsǭ.

whǭre, *see* whēr.

whōsǭ, *indef. prn.,* OE. hwāswā; *whoso*; wuāswa (eME.), 2, 5; wōsǭ, 20, 18; qwōsǭ, 117, 5. **Nth.** quāsā, 129, 13. **Sth.** whāswā (eSth.), 189, 13; *da.* whǭmsǭ, 233, 28.

whych, *see* which.

whydyrward, *see* whederward.

whȳt, wī, *see* whīt, whī.

wīaxe, wīax, *sb.,* OE. wīg + cax, *f.*; *battle-ax,* 181, 19.

wicche, *sb.,* OE. wicche, *f.*; *witch*; *pl.* wicches, 20, 14.

wicci, wicke, *see* wikke.

wicht, *adj.,* OE. *wiht, adj.,* cf. MLG. wicht; *brave, valiant,* 75, 6.

wicked, wikked, *adj.,* based on ME. wicke; *wicked, evil,* 100, 15; wykked, 88, 2.

wickedness, wikkednesse, *sb.,* based on wikke, q.v.; *wickedness,* 101, 28; wikkednesse, 246, 3. **Nth.** wiknes, 153, 8.

wid, widūten, *see* wiþ, wiþūten.

wīde, *adv.,* OE. wīde; *wide, widely,* 19, 8.

wīf, *sb.,* OE. wīf; *wife*; wiif, 65, 6; *ds.* in phr. tō wīfe (wīve), 7, 2; wȳefe, 147, 27; *pl.* wīves; wȳve (in rime), 59, 17; so *ns.* wȳve for wȳf, 121, 22; wīve, 188, 27. **Sth.** *ds.* wīfe, 176, 24.

wi3t, *see* wiht.

wi3t, wyght, *sb.,* OE. wiht [wegan]; *weight,* 42, 12; wyghtę, 117, 8.

wiht, wi3t, *sb.,* OE. wiht; *person, wight, creature*; wihht (O), 12, 26; wi3t, 36, 3; *pl.* wihte, 178, 22.

wiis, wike, *see* wīs, wikke.

wike, wyke, *sb.,* OE. wiocu; *week,* 200, 1; wyke, 107, 11. Cf. wuke.

wīken, *sb.,* OE. wīce, *wf.*; *office, duty, charges*; wīkenn (O), 9, 19.

wikke, wike, wyk, *adj.,* based on OE. wīcan(?); *wicked, evil*; wicci, 6, 18; wikke, *unpleasant,* 51, 28; wike, 77, 28; wicke, 85, 13; wyk, 88, 20. **Nth.** *pl.* wike, 153, 5. Cf. wicked.

wikkedęhęd, *sb.,* based on wikke, q.v.; *wickedness,* 50, 24.

wiknes, wikkednesse, *see* wickednes.

wil, wyl, *sb.,* OE. will; *pleasure, will,* 20, 13; wyl, 117, 14.

wilc, *see* whilc.

wilcume, welcome. *adj.* < *sb.,* OE. wilcuma, later infl. by wēl (wel); *welcome,* 181, 3; welcôme, 114, 24.

wīlde, *adj.,* OE. wilde, wīlde; *wild,* 48, 12.

wilde (wile), *see* wille(n).

wīle, *see* whīle.

wīles, *adv.,* OE. hwīle + es; *whiles, while,* 16, 20.

wilfull, *adj.,* OE. *wilfull, cf. wilfullīce; *voluntary, wilful,* 147, 9.

will, *adj.,* ON. villr, cogn. with OE. wild; *wild, bewildered, despairing,* 166, 2.

will, *see* wille(n).

Willam, *see* Willelm.

wille, wylle, *sb.,* OE. willa; *will, desire, wish,* 8, 18; wylle, 89, 32; after wille, *according to desire,* 205, 16; *pl.* wyllis, 219, 31.

wille, *adv.,* ON. willr, *adj.,* cogn. with OE. wilde, 'wild'; *wildly, wrongly,* 15, 7.

wille(n), wile, wole, *anv.,* OE. wille-wolde; *wish, will*; *inf.* wilenn (O), 10, 3; *pr.* 1, 3 *sg.* wile, 10, 11; wille, 14, 7; wǒle, 110, 16; ǒlle, 203, 21; wǒl, 242, 31; wyll, 106, 20; *pr.* 2 *sg.* wyltę, 111, 15; wǒlt, 204, 17; willes, 195, 2; *pr. pl.* willen, 4, 28; wilen, 29, 16; wylle, 88, 8; wol wē, 242, 18; *pt. sg.* wolde, 1, 2; wollde (O), 8, 22; wulde, 16, 13; wōlde, 36, 1; wōld, 68, 12; wold, 71, 5; wilde, 75, 16; *pt.* 2 *sg.*

wuldes, 19, 3; woldest, 38, 10; woldyst, 111, 28. Nth. *pr. sbj. sg.* will, 141, 29; *pt. pl.* wald, 126, 16; wold, 138, 11; *wk.* wilde, 75, 16. Sth. *pr.* 1, 3 *sg.* wüle, 177, 15; ülle, 193, 2; *pr.* 2 *sg.* wült, 192, 33; *pr. pl.* wülleð, 177, 10; willeþ, 211, 28; *pt. sg.* weolde (eSth.), 187, 18; walde, 192, 12. Neg. forms: *pr.* 1, 3 *sg.* nelle < nille < ne wille, 45, 26; nele, 180, 1; *pt.* 2 *sg.* noldest, 38, 7; *pt. sg.* nalde, 192, 20. Sth. *pr.* 1, 3 *sg* nül, 192, 32; *pr.* 2 *sg.* nült, 193, 2. Kt. *pr.* 1, 3 *sg.* nele, 216, 7.

Willelm, William, Willam, *sb.*, NF. Willelm; *William*; Sanct Willelm, *William of Norwich*, 5, 4; William, 116, 15; *gs.* Willyams, 117, 3; Willam, 203, 22.

willesfõl, *adj.*, OE. willa, *m.*, will, *neut.* + ful; *wilful, headstrong*, 206, 3.

William, *see* Wellelm.

wilnīe(n), *wkv.*, Sth. = Ml. wilne(n); OE. wilnian; *desire, wish for*; *inf.* wilnin (Ml. ?), 193, 28; wylnī, 217, 14; *imp. pl.* wilnīe 3ē, 199, 5; *pr. sbj. pl.* wilnen, 202, 11; *pt. pl.* wylnede, 216, 18; *pp.* iwilnet, 195, 26.

wimman, wummon, womman, *sb.*, OE. wīfman, wimman; *woman*, 7, 6; wymman, 53, 19; wummon, 194, 16; *pl.* wimmen, 3, 3; wymmen, 220, 16; wummen, 202, 18; women, 235, 8; *gpl.* wymmones, 121, 5. Nth. womman, 132, 7; *pl.* womene, 144, 32. Sth. *gpl.* wimmonen, 181, 22; wimmonne, 188, 19; wyfman, 218, 6.

win, *sb.*, OE. winn; *labor, contention, strife*, 18, 27; *ds.* winne, *gain, acquisition*, 47, 5.

wīn, wȳn, *sb.*, OE. wīn < Lat. vīnum; *wine*, 22, 3; wȳn, 53, 8.

Winchestre, -chæstre, -cestre, *sb.*, OE. Wintunceaster; *Winchester*; Wincestre (eME.), 6, 1; Winchestre, 187, 9; Winchæstre, 188, 16; *ds.* Winchestren, 187, 31.

wīnd, wȳnd, *sb.*, OE. wind, wīnd; *wind*, 50, 14; wȳndę, 100, 22; *pl.* wīndes, 185, 6.

wīndə(n), *stv.*, OE. windan (wīndan)—wand (wǭnd) (3); *wind, wrap, go*; *inf.* wīnden, 34, 1; *pt. sg.* wǭnd, 182, 5; *pp.* wounden, 81, 21. Sth. *pp.* ywǫnden, 229, 8.

wingę, *see* weng.

wīnȝẹrd, winyard, *sb.*, OE. wīngeard; *vineyard* (by infl. of vīne); wīniærd (eME.), 4, 25; *ds.* winyarde, 212, 4; wynyarde, 212, 5.

winiærd, *see* wīnȝẹrd.

winnan, *see* winne(n).

winne, *sb.*, OE. wynn, *f.*; *pleasure, joy*, 55, 24. Sth. wünne, 190, 31; *pl.* wünnen, 193, 12.

winne(n), wynne(n), *stv.*, OE. winnan-wann (3); *strive, contend, win*; *inf.* winnan (eME.), 5, 6; winnenn (O), 10, 24; *pr. pl.* winnen, 19, 23; *pt. sg.* wan, 4, 23; *pt. pl.* wǫnne, 203, 21; *pp.* wune, 100, 12. Nth. *inf.* wyne, 146, 31. Sth. *pp.* iwǫnne, 204, 23; ywǫnne, 216, 6.

winter, wintre, *sb.*, OE. winter; *winter*, 19, 23; *gs.* winteris, 47, 25; *pl.* wintre (eME.), 3, 22; winter, 64, 26.

wīntrē, *sb.*, OE. wīntrēo; *vine, wine-tree*, 21, 23.

winyard (wynyard), *see* wīnȝẹrd.

wirche(n), wirke(n), *wkv.*, OE. wyrcan-worhte; *work*; *inf.* wirchen, 80, 17; wirche, 72, 29; wirrkenn (O), 8, 24; *pt. sg.* wrohte, 4, 13; *pp.* wrohht (O), 11, 2; wrouȝt, 55, 1; wroght, 109, 25. Nth. *inf.* wyrke, 143, 24; *pp.* wroght, 130, 16. Sth. *inf.* würchen, 192, 29; *pr. pl.* würcheð, 196, 10; *imp. sg* würch, 194, 18; *pp.* iwroȝt (SEMl.) 38, 24; iwraht, 192, 2.

Wirechestre, *sb.*, OE. Wigraceaster; *Worcester*, 227, 1.

wirking, *sb.*, OE. wyrcung, *f.*; *working, doing, pain*, 139, 2.

wirm, worm, *sb.*, OE. wyrm; *serpent, worm*, 17, 1; *pl.* wormes, 49, 14.

wirrkenn, *see* wirche(n).

wirschip, *sb.*, **Nth.** = Ml. wurschipe ; OE. weorðscipe ; *worship*, 129, 29.

wis, *see* **wisse(n)**.

wīs, wiis, wȳs, *adj.*, OE. wīs ; *wise*, 23, 17 ; wiis, 72, 15 ; wȳs, 91, 28 ; *superl.* wīseste, 182, 31.

wis, wiss, *adv.*, OE. wiss ; *certainly* ; wiss (O), 12, 6 ; tō wis, *certainly*, 62, 12.

wisdōm, wisdōmę, *sb.*, OE. wīsdōm ; *wisdom*, 55, 10 ; wisdōmę, 103, 14.

wīse, *sb.*, OE. wīse ; *wise, manner, respect*, 8, 15. **Nth.** wiss, 170, 22. **Sth.** *ds.* wīsen, 189, 5.

wiss, wisselīch, *see* **wīse, wisslīke**.

wisse(n), *wkv.*, OE. wīsian, wissian ; *guide, show, point out* ; *inf.* wisse, *to be guided*, 49, 20 ; *pr.* 3 *sg.* wisseð, 192, 1. **Nth.** *ps. sbj. sg.* wis, 143, 6.

wisslike, *adv.*, OE. wisslīce ; *certainly* ; wisslike, 11, 9. **Sth.** wisselīch, 231, 19.

wiste, wit, *see* **wite(n)**, *ic.*

wīt, *see* **wīte(n)**.

wit, wyt, *sb.*, OE. witt ; *wit, intelligence* ; witt (O), 8, 20 ; wyt, 49, 18 ; wytt, 106, 16 ; witę, 50, 4 ; *pl.* wyttes, 218, 17.

wīteȝe, *sb.*, OE. wītega ; *wise man, prophet*, 188, 17.

wite(n), *ptprv.*, OE. witan–wiste ; *know* ; *inf.* witenn (O), 10, 11 ; wi:en, 14, 17 ; wytt, 106, 16 ; *pr.* 1, 3 *sg.* wǭt, 23, 16 ; ǭt, 83, 19 ; wǫǫt, 242, 23 ; *pr.* 2 *sg.* wǭst, 52, 16 ; wǫǫst, 243, 14 ; *pr. sbj. sg.* wite, 194, 8 ; *pt. sg.* wiste, 1, 6 ; wist, 49, 22 ; wyste, 53, 8 ; *pt.* 2 *sg.* wistist, 56, 1 ; *pt. pl.* wisten, 26, 25 ; wist, 71, 16. **Nth.** *pr.* 1, 3 *sg.* wāt, 128, 14. **Sth.** *pr.* 1, 3 *sg.* wāt (eSth.), 178, 22 ; me wȳt, *one knows*, 210, 19 ; *pr. pl.* wüteð, 199, 27, *pt. sg.* wüste, 186, 4 ; *pp.* iwüs⁺, *observcd, kept*, 201, 8. **Kt.** *pt. pl.* westen, 216, 19. **Neg.** forms : *pr.* 1, 3 *sg.* nǫǫt, 243, 20 ; nāt (eME.), 180, 26 ; *pr. pl.* nyteþ, 217, 5 ; *pt. sg.* niste, 36, 7. **Sth.** *pr. pl.* nüte wē, 196, 19 ; *pt. sg.* nüste, 179, 13.

wite(n), *wkv.*, OE. witian ; *keep, guard* ; *inf.* wite, 39, 13 ; *pr. sbj. sg.* wite, 10, 10. **Sth.** *inf.* witīe, 204, 30 ; *pr.* 3 *sg.* wīt < witeð, 178, 28 ; *imp. sg.* wite, 190, 23.

wīte(n), *stv.*, OE. wītan–wāt (1) ; *go, depart* ; **Nth.** *inf.* wīt, 151, 24.

wīte(n), *wkv.*, OE. wītian ; *blame* ; *inf.* wīte, 44, 21 ; *pr.* 2 *sg.* wītest, 55, 17.

witer, *see* **witter**.

witerlȳ, *see* **witterlīke**.

wið, wiþþ, wid, wyd, wyþ, *prep. adv.*, OE. wið ; *against, with, according to*, 2, 4 ; wiþþ (O), 8, 23 ; wid, 6, 2 ; wyd, 6, 26 ; wyþ, 89, 18 ; wið þan, *with that*, 187, 20.

wiþal, wiþalle, wyþal, *adv. phr.*, OE. wiþ + OM. all ; *withal, entirely*, 54, 30 ; wiþalle, 38, 19 ; wyþal, 89, 29.

wiþdrāȝe(n), drawe(n), *stv.*, OE. wiðdragan–drōg (6) ; *withdraw* ; *pt. sg.* withdrow, 80, 5 ; *pp.* wiþdrāȝe, 44, 2.

withdraweynge, *sb.*, based on OE. *wiðdragan ; *withdrawing, purloining*, 147, 12.

withdrow, *see* **wiþdrāȝe(n)**.

wiðe, *sb.*, OE. wiðer ? ; *conflict*, 190, 1.

wiþerward, *adj. adv.*, OE. wiðerweard ; *adverse, contrary*, 228, 4.

wiþerwyne, *sb.*, OE. wiðerwinna ; *adversary, enemy* ; *pl.* wiþerwynes, 230, 3.

wiþinnen, wyþynne, *adv.*, OE. wiðinnan ; *within* ; wiþþinnenn (O), 12, 10 ; wyþynne, 100, 9.

wiþnime(n), *stv.*, OE wið + nimannōm (4) ; *take away* ; *pp.* wiþnumen, 103, 12.

wiþoutyn (withōwttenę, wiþōwte), *see* **wiþūten**.

withstande(n), -stǫnde(n), *stv.*,OE. wiðstandan (stǫndan)–stōd (6) ; *withstand* ; *pt. sg.* withstōd ; *stood by*, 48, 6.

withtāke(n), *stv.*, OE. wið + ON. taka–tōk (6) ; *blame, reprove* ; *pr. ppl.* withtākand, 144, 4.

wiððan, *adv.*, OE. wið ðām (ðon); *provided that*, 30, 15; *with* Þan, 81, 7.

wiþūte(n), widūten, wiþūte, wiþoūte(n), *adv. prep.*, OE. wiðūtan; *without, except*; wiþþūtenn (O), 11, 26; widūten, 6, 9; wiþūte, 37, 9; wiþoutyn, 100, 5; withoūwttene, 145, 26; withoūwte, 204, 15.

witīe(n), *see* wite(n).

witne(n), *wkv.*, ON. vitna; *testify, prove*; *pr.* 3 *sg.* witneð, 202, 3.

witnesse, wyttnes, *sb.*, OE. witness, *f.*; *witness*, 228, 20. Nth. wyttnes, 147, 19.

witnesse(n), *wkv.*, based on witnesse, *sb.*; *witness*; *pr.* 3 *sg.* wytnesset, 215, 14; *pr. sbj. sg.* witnesse, 226, 21.

witt, *see* ic.

witter, witer, *adj.*, ON. vitr; *knowing, wise, clear*, 30, 10; witer, 189, 6.

witterlīke, witterlȳ, wytterlȳ, witterlīche, *adv.*, ON. vitr + OE. līce; *surely, evidently*, 29, 32; witterlȳ, 71, 7; wytterlȳ, 111, 7. Sth. witterlīche, 200, 17.

wittȳ, *adj.*, OE. witig, wittig; *wise, skilful, witty*, 170, 16.

witunge, *sb.*, OE. *witung, f.*; *guarding, caretaking*, 203, 9.

wīve, *see* wīf.

wīve(n), *wkv.*, OE. wīfian; *marry, take a wife*; *inf.* wīven, 193, 18; *pr. sb. sg.* wīve, 193, 18.

wlacīe(n), *wkv.*, OE. wlacian; *become lukewarm or tepid*; *pp.* iwlaht, 195, 18.

wlaffyng, *sb.*, cf. MDu. blaffen, 'stammer'; *stammering*, 224, 15.

wlech, *adj.*, Sth. = Ml. wlach; OE. wlæc; *lukewarm, tepid*, 195, 18.

wlite, *sb.*, OE. wlite, wlita, *wk.*; *face, form*, 28, 32; wliten (< OE. wlita–wlitan?), 29, 1.

wǭ, *see* whō.

wǭ, *sb.*, OE. wā; *woe*, 23, 4.

woane, wōc, *see* wune, wāke(n).

wǭcnesse, *sb.*, OE. wācnes, *f.*; *weakness, meanness of condition*, 198, 15.

wōd, *adj.*, OE. wōd; *mad, angry*, 44, 9; wōdę, 97, 3.

wode, *see* wude.

wōdelukest, *adv.*, OE. wōdlīce; *most madly*, 195, 16.

Wodnesdei, Wedęnysday, *sb.*, OE. Wōdnęsdæg; *Wednesday*; *pl.* Wodnesdawes, 200, 2; Wedęnesday, 228, 21.

węȝ, *sb.*, OE. wāg(h); *wall*, 216, 24.

wogh, *sb.*, OE. wōh; *evil, wrong*, 131, 15.

woke, *see* wuke.

wol, wold, *see* wille(n).

wǭld, *sb.*, OM. wald, wāld, WS. weald; *power, meaning*, 23, 26; hāven . . . on wǭld, *have in power, obtain*, 55, 22.

wǭld, *sb.*, OM. wāld, WS. weald; *woodland*; *ds.* wǭlden, 182, 10.

wolde, *see* wille, *vb.*

wǭlde(n), *stv.*, OM. waldan, wāldan (WS. wealdan)–wēold (R); *have power over, control, possess*; wǭlden, 18, 2.

wole, wollde, wolt, *see* wille, *vb.*

wolle, *see* wulle.

wǫmbe, *sb.*, Sth. = Ml. wōmbę; OE. wamb, wāmb, *f.*; *stomach, womb*, 207, 12.

womman (women, womene), *see* wimman.

won (woned), *see* wune(n).

won, *sb.*, OE. wan; *lack*; *ds.* wone, 199, 13.

wond, wǫnd, *see* wūnde, wīnde(n).

wone, *see* wune.

wǫnd, *sb.*, OE. *wand ?*, ON. vöndr; *wand, rod*, 55, 29.

wǫnde(n), *wkv.*, OE. wandian (wǫndian); *turn aside, refrain from, alter*; *inf.* wǫrde, 114, 9.

wonder, *see* wunder.

wǫndrīe(n), *wkv*, Sth. = Ml. wandre(n); OE. wandrian, wǫndrian; *wander*; wǫndrīen, 182, 11.

wǫne, *sb.*, perhaps ON. vän, *f.*; *hope, thought*; *pl.* wǫnys, 113, 12.

would, *see* wune(n).

wǫng, *sb.*, OE. wang, wǫng; *plain*; *pl.* wǫnges, 76, 32.

wǫnge, *sb.*, OE. wange, wǫnge ; *cheek* ;
pl. wǫnges, 156, 32.

wonne, *see* winne(n).

wont, *see* wune(n).

wonȳ, *see* wune(n).

wȯnynge, wonyng, *sb.*, OE. wunung,
f. ; *dwelling, home*, 221, 5.

wǫnys, *see* wǫne.

woodnesse, *sb.*, OE. wōdnes, *f.* ;
madness, 238, 14.

wǫǫst (wǫǫt). *see* wite(n).

wōp, *sb.*, OE. wōp ; *weeping*, 215,
21.

wōp, wōpen, *see* wēpe(n).

wōpned, *pp.* as *adj.*, ON. vāpna,
cogn. with OE. wǣpnian ; *armed,
weaponed*, 35, 1.

wōrd, *sb.*, OE. word, wōrd ; *word* ;
wōrd (O), 8, 23 ; *pl.* wōrdes, 243,
24. Nth. *pl.* wurdes, 136, 8. eSth.
ds. wēorde, 176, 3 ; *pl.* wōrd, 176,
9 ; wōrden, 188, 20.

wōrdīe(n), *wkv.*, Sth. = Ml. wō.-
de(n) ; OE. wōrdian ; *utter words* ;
pp. iwōrded, 198, 4.

wordle, wǫre(n), *see* werld, bē(n).

wǫrī, *adj.*, OE. wārig ; *dirty, stained
with seaweed*, 180, 22.

world, *see* werld.

worldlich, *adj.*, Sth. = Ml. worldlī ;
OE. woruldlīc ; *worldly*, 194, 2.

worm, *see* wirm.

worschipe, worssippe, *see* wurschipe.

worschype, *see* wurschepe(n).

worste, worþ, *see* werse, wurþ.

worþe(n), *see* wurþe(n).

worþingniȝht, *sb.*, OE. weorðung +
niht ; *worthing-night, feast of purification* ?, 230, 5.

worþis, worthit, *see* wurþe(n).

worþnesse, *sb.*, OE. weorðness, *f.* ;
dignity, honor, 226, 7.

worþsippe, *see* wurschipe.

worthȳ, *see* wurþī.

woruldwele, *sb.*, eME., OE. weoruld-
wela ; *worldly wealth*, 180, 31.

wōsǫ, *see* whōsǫ.

wǫst, wot, *see* wite(n).

wouȝ, *adj.*, OE. wōh ; *bad, evil*,
58, 2.

wōunde, *see* wŭnde.

wōunden, *see* wīnde(n).

wōunde(n), *wkv.*, OE. wundian
(wūndian) ; *wound* ; *pp.* wōunded,
65, 31.

wōunder, *see* wunder.

wrac, *sb.*, OE. wrǣc ; *misery, punishment, wrack*, 60, 16.

wrāke, *sb.*, OE. wracu ; *vengeance*,
141, 17.

wrancwīs, *adj.*, eME. = Ml. wrǫng-
wīs ; ON. rangr + ME. wīs ; *unjust,
wrong* ; *ds.* wrancwīse, 177, 24.

wrāng, *see* wrǫng.

wrāngwīsliȩ, wrāngwȳsȩlȳ, *adv.*,
ON. wrangr + ME. wīs + lī ; *wrongly,
unjustly*, 155, 33 ; wrāngwȳsȩlȳ,
147, 13.

wrappe(n), *wkv.*, origin uncertain ;
wrap ; *inf.* wrappa, 241, 7.

wrastelynge, *pr. ppl.* as *sb.*, OE.
wrǣstlian ; *wrestling*, 120, 19.

wrastlīe(n), *wkv.*, Sth. = Ml. wrast-
le(n) ; OE. wrǣstlian ; *wrestle* ; *pt.
pl.* wrastlede, 207, 8.

wrāt, *see* wrīte(n).

wrāth (wrāðer, wrāðest), *see* wrǫþ.

wraþþe, *sb.*, OE. wrǣðo, wrǣððo ·
wrath, 46, 11.

wraþþe(n), *wkv.*, OE. wrāðian ; *make
wroth, become angry* ; *inf.* wraþþe,
104, 25. Sth. *pr. sbj. sg.* wraðōī,
192, 32.

wraðōīe(n), *see* wraþþe(n).

wrecce, wrecche, *see* wreche

wreccehȩd, wrecchȩde, wrechēd-
hȩd, *sb.*, based on OE. wrecca +
ME. hȩde ; *wretchedness, misery*, 3,
30 ; wrecchȩde, 209, 16.

wrecchȩde, *see* wreccehȩde.

wrechche, *see* wreche.

wrēche (wrȩche), *sb.*, OM. wrēc,
WS. wrǣc, *f.* ; *vengeance*, 59, 6.

wreche, wretche, wrecche, *sb.*, OE.
wrecca ; *wretch*, 49, 7 ; wretche,
49, 23 ; *pl.* wrechen, 195, 7.

wreche, *adj.*, OE. wrecc ; *wretched*,
48, 11 ; wrecce, 2, 32 ; wretche, 49.
23 ; wrechche, 215, 3.

wrechidnes, *sb.*, based on OE. wrecc ;
wretchedness, 144, 20.

wreie(n), *wkv.*, OE. wrēgan; *accuse,
betray*, cf. archaic (*be*)*wray*; *pr.
sbj. sg.* wreie, 38, 15 ; *pt. sg.* wreide,
1, 2.

wrēke(n), *stv.*, OE. wrecan–wrǣc(5);
avenge; *pp.* wrǫken, 160, 18.

wrench, *sb.*, OE. wrenc ; *guile, deceit,
artifice, trick* ; *ds.* wrenche, 207, 10.

wrengðe, *sb.*, as if OM. wrengð, WS.
wriengð, *f.*; *distortion*, 16, 10.

wretche, *see* wreche.

wrēþe, wreth, *sb.*, OE. wrǣð, *f* ,
wrǣðu, *indcl.*; *wrath*, 69, 16. Nth.
wrēth, 127, 14. Kt. wrēþe, 211, 21.

wreðð̄e(n), *wkv.*, OE. wrǣðan; *anger,
get angry* ; *inf.* wreðð̄en, 194, 5 ; *pt.
sg.* wreðð̄ede, 193, 3.

wrigtelēslīke, *adv.*, cf. OE. gewyrht ;
*in manner without desert, wrong-
fully*, 22, 12.

wrīgtful, *adv.*, OE. wyrht + ful ;
deservedly, 26, 12.

wrihte, *sb.*, OE. wryht, *f.* ; *thing done,
merit, blame*; wrihhte (O), 11, 26.

wringe(n), *stv.*, OE. wringan–wrang
(wrǫng) (3) ; *wring, twist, press*;
inf. wringe, 59, 18 ; *pt. sg.* wrǫng,
21, 28.

writ, *sb.*, OE. writ ; *writing, writ*;
writt (O), 13, 30; writ, 46, 28.

wrīte(n), *stv.*, OE. wrītan–wrāt (1) ;
write ; *inf.* wrītenn (O), 10, 3 ; *pr.
sbj. sg.* wrīte, 10, 7 ; *pt. sg.* wrāt
(eME.), 12, 24 ; wrǫt, 71, 19;
wrǫot, 245, 29 ; *pp.* writenn, 10, 8 ;
writen, 71, 25 ; wryten, 119, 6 ;
write, 69, 23 ; wryte, 90, 21. Sth.
pp. iwriten, 179, 29 ; ywrite, 72, 20.

wrīteing, *sb.*, OE. wrīting, *f.*; *writing*,
72, 26.

wrīþe(n), *stv.*, OE. wrīðan–wrāð (1) ;
twist, turn, bind, writhe ; *pr. ppl.*
wrīþinde, 55, 29 ; *pt. pl.* wrythen,
3, 8.

wroght(e), wroht(e), wrohht, *see*
wirche(n).

wrǫken, *see* wrēke.

wrǫng, *adj., sb.*, ON. vrang ; *twisted,
awry, wrong*, 16, 3 ; *ds.* wrǫnge, 58,
23. Nth. wrāng, 127, 11.

wrǫng, *see* wringe(n`.

wrǫot, wrǫt, *see* wrīte(n).

wrǫþ, wrǫthe, *adj.*, OE. wrāð ; *wroth,
angry, bad*, 35, 20 ; wrǫthe, 112, 16;
tō wrǫþer hēle, *to bad health, evil
fate*, 62, 30. Nth. wrāth, 127, 12.
eSth. tō wrāðer hēale, 193, 7 ;
superl. wrāðest, 189, 7.

wrǫþər, *see* wrǫþ.

wrouʒt, *see* wirche(n).

wrȳte(n), *see* wrīte(n).

wrythen, *see* wrīþe(n).

wū, *adv.*, Sth. = Ml. hū ; OE. hwū,
hū ; *how*, 209, 16.

wuāswā, wüch, *see* whōsǫ, whilc.

wude, *sb.*, OE. wudu < widu ; *wood,
forest* ; wòde, 51, 9.

wuke, *sb.*, OE. wucu < wiocu ; *week*;
pl. wukes, 34, 26 ; wòke, 118, 5.
Cf. wike.

wulde, wüle, wülleð, *see* wille, *vb.*

wule, *see* whīle.

wulf, *sb.*, OE. wulf ; *wolf*, 82, 17 ;
pl. wulves, 199, 4.

wulle, *sb.*, OE. wull, wulle, *f.*; *wool* ;
wòlle, 86, 16.

wulvine, *sb.*, OE. wylfen, *f.*, mod. by
wulf ; *she-wolf*, 82, 17.

wumme, *interj* , OE. wā mē ; *woe is
me*, 195, 33.

wummon, wummen, *see* wimman.

wünde, wöunde, *sb.*, OE. wund, *f.*;
wound, 20, 12 ; *pl.* wöundes, 60,
28. Nth. wònd, 146, 1. Sth. *pl.*
wòndes, 221, 7 ; wünden, 190, 10.

wunder, *sb.*, OE. wundor, -er, *neut.*;
wonder, prodigy, miracle ; wònder,
68, 22; wounder, 173, 13; as *adv.*,
wònder, *wondrously*, 159, 26 ; *pl.*
wunder, 2, 28 ; 3, 20.

wunderlīc, *adj.*, OE. wunderlīc ;
wonderful, marvelous, *pl.* 5, 3 ;
superl. wunderlukeste, 178, 12.

wündī, *adj.*, OE. *wyndig, perh.
*wendig, 1WS. wyndig, wȳndig, cf.
MLG. wendich ; *averse*, 193, 2.

wündīe(n), *wkv.*, Sth. = Ml. wün-
de(n), OE. wundian, wündian;
wound; *pp.* iwündet, 192, 10.

wune, wone, *sb.*, OE. wuna ; *custom,
habit, dwelling* ; *pl.* wunes, 29, 5 ;
wòn, 62, 13. Sth. *pl.* woanes, 202, 8.

wune, *adj.*, OE. gewuna; *accustomed, wont*, 22, 2.

wune, *see* winne(n).

wune(n), *wkv.*, OE. wunian; *inhabit, dwell, remain*; *inf.* wunen, 19, 24; wune, 43, 12; wòne, 220, 22; *pr.* 3 *sg.* wuneð, 19, 19; *pr. pl.* wunen, 34, 17; *pr. ppl.* wònyng, 222, 17; *pt. sg.* wunede, 33, 1; *pp.* wuned, 39, 25; wòned, 48, 13; wònt, 48, 25; wunt, 98, 6. **Nth.** *pr. pl.* wòn, 134, 10. **Sth.** *inf.* wunīen, 180, 29; wònȳ, 220, 10; *pr. pl.* wuneð, 180, 16; wòneþ, 222, 24; *pr. sbj. sg.* wunnīe, 191, 9; *pp* iwuned, 178, 1; ywòned, 225, 6.

wünlīch, *adj.*, **Sth.** = Ml. winlīc; OE. wynlīc; *pleasant, winsome*, 183, 19.

wünne, *see* winne.

wunnīe, *see* wune(n).

wünsum, *adj.*, **Sth.** = Ml. winsum; OE. wynsum; *winsome, pleasant*, 195, 17.

würchen, *see* wirche(n).

wurd, *see* wōrd.

wurrþenn, *see* warþe(n).

wurschepe(n), -schipe(n), *wkv.*, based on OE. weorðscipe; *honor, worship,*; *pp.* wurscheped, 97, 16.

wurschipe, worschipe, wurtscipe, *sb.*, OE. weorðscipe; *dignity, honor, worship*; wurscipe, 1, 12; wurtscipe, 4, 16; wòrschipe, 116, 14; wurð-schipe, 199, 22. **Sth.** wòrþsippe, 215, 17.

würsǝ, *see* werse.

wurð, *adj.*, OE. weorð, wurð; *worth, of value, honored, good*; wurth, 158, 8; wòrþ, 215, 16.

wurð, wurth, *sb.*, OE. weorð, wurð; *worth, dignity*; *pl.* wurðes, 195, 7.

wurþe(n), worþe(n), *stv.*, OE. weorðan (wurðan)–wearð (3); *become, be*; *inf.* wurrþenn (O), 10, 19; wurðen, 32, 27; wērþe (SEMl.), 68, 14; *pr.* 2 *sg.* wurðest, 188, 16; *pr.* 3 *sg.* wurðeð, 15, 30; *pr. sbj. sg.* wurðe, 17, 20; wurð, 21, 22; wòrþe, 48, 10; wòrþ, 218, 24; *pt. sg.* ward, 1, 15; warth, 1, 18; warrþ (O), 11,

17; wart, 5, 12; wurð, 21, 26; *pt. pl.* wurðe, 2, 16; wurthen, 6, 9. **Nth.** *pr.* 3 *sg.* wòrþis, 171, 24; *wk. pt.* wòrthit, 171, 27.

wurþe(n), *wkv.*, OE. weorðian; *honor*; *pr. pl.* wurðen, 34, 16.

wurþī, worthȳ, *adj.*, OE. weorðig; *worthy*, 18, 8; wurrþī (O), 10, 19; wurþȳ, 97, 15; wòrthȳ, 111, 23; wurthī, 138, 11; *superl.* wòrthīest, 232, 19.

wurðing, *sb.*, OE. weorðung, *f.*; *honor, ornament*, 24, 12.

wurðlīc, wurðlī, wurðlīche, *adj.*, OE. weorðlīc; *valuable, of worth*, 18, 31; wurðlī, 48, 21; wurthlī, 143, 7. **Sth.** wurðlīche, 183, 6.

wüste, wüte(n), *see* wite(n).

wychecraft, wychecraftǝ, *sb.*, OE. wiccecræft; *witchcraft*, 49, 21; wychecraftǝ, 125, 23.

wyd, wydur, *see* wiþ, wheþer.

wydewe, *sb.*, OE. widuwe; *widow*; *pl.* wydewes, 59, 18.

wȳefe, wȳf, wȳfe, *see* wīf.

wyfman, *see* wimman.

wyghtǝ, wyk, *see* wiȝt, wikke.

wyke, *see* wike.

wykked, wyl, *see* wikked, wil.

wȳl, *sb.*, OE. wīl; *wile, deceit*, 58, 10.

wylke, wylle, *see* whilc, wille(n).

wyllis, *see* wille, *vb.*

wylnȳ (wylnede), *see* wilnīe(n).

wylnynge, *sb.*, OE. wilnung, *f.*; *desire*, 216, 25.

wymman, wȳn, *see* wimman, wīn.

wyne, wynne, *see* winne(n).

wȳnd, wȳndǝ, *see* wīnd.

wynke(n), *wkv.*, OE. wincian; *wink, close the eyes, sleep*; **Nth.** *pt. sg.* wynkit, *winked*, 171, 32.

wynne, *see* winne.

wynne(n), *see* winne(n).

wyrke, wȳs, *see* wirche(n), wīs.

wysche(n), *see* washe(n).

wyste, *see* wite(n).

wyt, wytt, *see* wit.

wyte, wytene, *see* wite(n).

wyþ (wyth and compounds), *see* wiþ.

wyþhòlde(n), *stv.*, OM. wiðhāldan (WS. healdan)–hēold (R); *with-*

hold; *inf.* wyþhǭlde, 94, 29; *pt. sg.*
wyþhēlde, 96, 8.

wytnessebē̆ryng, *sb.*, OE., witnes, *f.*
+ bering; *witness-bearing*, 236, 16.

wytnesset, *see* witnesse(n).

wytterlȳ, *see* witterlīke.

wyttnes, *sb.*, OE. witnes; *witness*,
147, 19.

wȳve, *see* wīf.

ȝ.

ȝǣn, ȝaff, *see* ȝēn, ȝeve(n).

ȝāld, ȝald, *see* ȝēlde(n).

ȝāre, ȝārew, ȝārew, ȝārewe, *see*
ȝāru.

ȝarkīe(n), *wkv.*, **Sth.** = Ml. ȝarke(n);
OE. gearkian; *prepare, make ready*;
pt. sg. ȝarkede, 206, 16; *pp.* iȝarket,
195, 19.

ȝarnand, *see* ȝērne(n).

ȝāru, ȝārew, ȝāre, *adj.*, OE. gearu-
gearwe; *ready*, eMnE. *yare*; eME.
ȝaru, 187, 21; ȝarew, 195, 31; *pl.*
ȝarewe, 184, 31; ȝāre, 205, 11.

ȝāte, *sb.*, OM. gat, WS. geat, *n.*;
gate, 59, 1.

ȝāve, *see* ȝeve(n).

ȝē, ȝēare, *see* þū, ȝēr.

ȝēd(e), ȝēden, *see* gā, gǭ(n).

ȝef, ȝeft, *see* ȝif, ȝeve(n), ȝyft.

ȝehāte(n), *stv.*, eME. = Ml. hǭte(n);
OE. gehātan–hēt (heht) (R); *call*;
pp. gehāten, 1, 11; ȝehātenn (O),
11, 14.

ȝeid, ȝeit, *see* gā, ȝēt.

ȝeie(n), *wkv.*, ON. geyja, ‘bark’;
shout (mockingly); *inf.* ȝeien, 194,
22.

ȝel, *sb.*, OM. *gell, WS. *giell, cf.
gellan, giellan, ‘to yell’; *yell*, 62,
14.

ȝēld, *sb.*, OM. gēld, WS. gield (gyld);
payment of money, tribute; *pl.*
gǣldes (eME.), 3, 23; *pl.* gēldes,
7, 5.

ȝēlde(n), *stv.*, OM. geldan (gēldan),
WS. gieldan–gāld, WS. geald (3);
recompense, yield, pay tribute; *inf.*
ȝēldenn (O), 11, 12; ȝēlde, 90, 28;
pr. 3 *sg.* ȝēldeþ, 104, 26; *imp. sg.*

ȝēldę, 102, 15; yēld, 212, 13; *imp.*
pl. ȝēldeþ, 195, 31; *pt. sg.* gę̄ld
(SEMl.), 24, 24; ȝę̄ldę, 47, 14; *pp.*
yǭlde, 217, 17. **Nth.** *inf.* ȝēld, 129,
28; yeild, 134, 18; *pt. sg.* yāld,
132, 31; ȝald < ȝāld, 169, 31.
Sth. *pr.* 3 *sg.* ȝēlt, 198, 5; *pp.*
iȝōlde, 47, 9.

ȝēldyng, ȝēldęing, *sb.* < *prp.* OM.
geldan, gēldan; *yielding, payment*
of debt, recompense, 104, 2; *pl.*
ȝēldęinges, 104, 16.

ȝelle(n), *stv.*, OM. gellan–gall, WS.
giellan–geal (3); *yell*; *inf.* ȝelle,
59, 25. **Nth.** *inf.* yel, 151, 29.
Sth. *pr. pl.* yelleþ, 215, 16.

ȝelōme, ilōme, *adv.*, OE. gelome;
frequently, 177, 23.

ȝēlt, *see* ȝēlde(n).

ȝēme, *sb.*, OM. gēme, WS. gīeme;
care, heed, 68, 27.

ȝēme(n), *wkv.*, OM. gēmen, WS.
gīeman; *care for, guard*; ȝēme, 49,
27; yēme, 76, 3; yēmen, 84, 10.

ȝēn, ȝę̄n, *prep. adv.*, OE. gegn;
against; ȝǣn (O), 9, 21.

ȝę̄ne(n), *wkv.*, OE. *gǣnan?, cf. OE.
gānian; *yawn*; *pt. sg.* ȝę̄nede, 61, 13.

ȝengþe, *sb.*, based on OE. geong,
OM. gung; *youth*, 104, 20.

ȝeond, *see* ȝond.

ȝeong, *see* ȝung.

ȝeonge(n), *stv.*, OE. geongan (R);
go, move; *inf.* ȝeongen, 182, 16;
ȝynge, p. 317. Cf. gange(n).

ȝeornlīche, *adv.*, OE. geornlīce;
earnestly, 192, 16.

ȝēorne, ȝeove(n), *see* ȝērne, ȝeve(n).

ȝēr, gēr (gēar), *sb.*, OM. gēr, WS.
gēar, *neut.*; *year*, 9, 2; gēar, 1, 1;
gǣr, 1, 18; *ds.* gāre, 1, 13; *pl.* gēr,
22, 29; gēre, 24, 8; gēres, 24, 25;
ȝēres, 57, 2; yērys, 115. 25. **Nth.**
gērę, 143, 18; *pl.* gērę, 165, 10; yeir,
132, 10. **Sth.** ȝę̄r, 199, 33; *pl.*
ȝę̄r, 180, 20. **Kt.** yēar, 215, 11.

ȝērde, *sb.*, OE. geard, *f.*; *rod*, MnE.
yard (*a measurement*); **Sth.** *pl.*
ȝę̄rden, 194, 21.

ȝērę, *see* ȝēr.

ȝernd, *see* ȝērne(n).

ӡērne, *adv.*, OM. gerne, WS. georne; *earnestly, yearningly*, 8, 22. eSth. ӡēorne, 177, 25.

ӡērne(n), *wkv.*, OM. gernan, WS. giernan; *desire, yearn for*; *inf.* ӡērne, 121, 1; *pt. 2 sg.* ӡernndesst (O), 8, 24; *pp.* ӡernd, 58, 23. Nth. *pr.* 3 *sg.* yērnes, 126, 1; *pr. ppl.* ӡarnand, 166, 11. Sth. *pr.* 1 *sg.* ӡīrne, 202, 20; *pp.* iӡīrnd, 192, 24. Kt. *pr.* 3 *sg.* ȳernþ, 219, 21.

ӡerre(n), *stv.*, OE. georran-gear (3); *resound, roar, babble*; *pt. pl.* ӡurren, 187, 2.

ӡesceaft, *sb.*, eSth. = Ml. shaft; OE. gesceaft *f.*; *created thing, creature*, 178, 28.

ӡēt, gēt (gǣt), ӡēte (ӡete), ӡit, *adv. conj.*, OM. gēt, WS. gīᵉt; *yet*, 8, 15; gēt, 2, 20; gǣt, 3, 30; ӡēte, 38, 6; ӡete, 40, 31; ӡit, 41, 18; yēte, 80, 2. Sth. ӡȳet (eSth.), 176, 5; ӡüt (lWS. gȳt), 203, 20; ӡüte, 210, 16.

ӡēt, *see* gǫ(n).

ӡēte(n), *stv.*, OE. gēotan-gēat (2); *pour*; *pt. sg.* ӡēt, 194, 21; *pt. pl.*, ӡǫten, 60, 18.

ӡǝte(n), *stv.*, OE. geetan-ǣt (5); *eat*; *pp.* iӡēte, 205, 30.

ӡette(n), *wkv.*, OM. gētan (*gettan), WS. gēatan; *grant, give*; *pt. sg.* ӡettede, 192, 12.

ӡeve(n), ӡive(n), *stv.*, OM. gefan *gifan (WS. giefan)-gaf (WS. geaf (5); *give*; *inf.* gyven, 1, 9; iiven, 6, 5; geven, 32, 14; ӡive, 35, 21; ӡeve, 38, 10; yive, 79, 24; yeven, 81, 6; ӡyve, 88, 11; *pr.* 1 *sg.*, ӡeve, *care for*, 195, 3; *pr.* 3 *sg.* yeveth, 78, 30; *pr. sbj. sg.* ӡife, 13, 21; ӡive, 41, 32; *imp. sg.* ӡif, 74, 27; yif, 85, 22; *imp. pl.* ӡeveþ, 99, 17; *pt. sg.* iaf, 1, 10; ӡaff (O), 11, 25; gaf, 29, 8; yaf, 77, 22; ӡāve, 90, 14; *pt. pl.* iāfen, 2, 26; iāven, 6, 27; *pp.* given, 34, 11; yeven, 242, 16. Sth. *inf.* ӡeoven (Ml.?), 185, 23; ӡieven, 178, 8; ӡiven, 199, 19; *pr.* 3 *sg.* ӡivet, 178, 15; ӡifð, 180, 24; yefþ, 214, 12; *pr. sbj. sg.*

ӡeove (Ml.?), 196, 11; *imp. sg.* yef, 212, 14; *pt. sg.* ӡef, 204, 31; ӡaf, 220, 21; *pp.* iӡive, 206, 7. Kt. *pr.* 3 *sg.* yefþ, 214, 12.

ӡeveðe, *adj.*, OE. gifeðe; *given, granted*, 186, 25.

ӡǝw (ӡhē), *see* þū.

ӡhwilk, *see* whilc.

ӡieven, *see* ӡeve(n).

ӡif, ӡiff, ӡef (gef), *conj.*, OE. gif; *if*, 101, 4; ӡiff (O), 10, 11; gif = ӡif, 4, 20; ӡef, 119, 17; gef, 19, 4; yif, 76, 12; yef, 154, 19; yf, 144, 17.

ӡīrnen, *see* ӡērne(n).

ӡisterdai, *sb.*, OE. geostrandæg, gistrandæg; *yesterday*, 103, 2.

ӡit, *see* ӡēt.

ӡive, *sb.*, Sth. = Ml. geve, give, gift; OM. *gefu, gifu, WS. giefu *f.*; *gift*, 178, 18. Cf. ӡyft.

ӡive(n), *see* ӡeve(n).

ӡǭ, *adv.*, ON. jā, cogn. with OM. gē, WS. gēa; *yea, yea*, 99, 6. Cf. yǭ.

ӡōle, *sb.*, ON. jōl, cogn. with OE. gēol; *Yole*, MnE. *Yule*?, 95, 17.

ӡon, ӡone, *prn.*, OM. gon, WS. geon; *yon*; ӡone, 98, 25.

ӡond, *prep. adv.*, OM. gond, WS. geond; *around, among, through*; ӡēond (eSth.), 182, 11; ӡont, 192, 25.

ӡong, ӡonger, *see* ӡung.

ӡōngling, *sb.*, OM. ӡungling, WS. geongling; *youth, young man*, 44, 3.

ӡont, *see* ӡond.

ӡǭre, *adv.*, OM. gāra, WS. gēara; *long since, yore, of old*, 42, 15.

ӡork, *see* Eouwerwīc.

ӡǭten, *see* ӡete(n).

ӡoūre, *see* ӡūr.

ӡoūþe, youthe, *sb.*, OM. gugoð, WS. geoguð, *f.*; *youth*, 55, 19; youthe, 240, 28. Sth. ӡuheðe, 192, 10.

ӡoᵚw, ӡude, *see* þū, gā(n).

ӡuheðe, *see* ӡoūþe.

ӡung (iung), gong, yung, *adj.*, OM. gung, WS. geong; *young*; *wk.* iunge, 7, 11; ӡōng, 53, 28; *wk.* yunge, 86, 31; *pl.* yunge, 76, 3; *comp.* ӡōnger, 66, 18; *superl.* gungest, 24,

32; yóngeste, 244, 9. eSth. *pl.*
ȝeonge, 188, 12.

ȝūr, gūr, ȝōur, yōur, *poss. prn.*, OE.
ēower; *your*; *sg.* gūr, 28, 4; gūre,
25, 18; yōur, 57, 15; ȝoūre, 57, 17;
yōwre, 235, 15. Sth. ōwer, 194,
24; oūwer, 201, 12; oūre, 197, 18.

ȝurren, *see* ȝerre(n).

ȝūt, ȝwat, *see* ȝēt, whō.

ȝwanne, ȝwēre, *see* whanne, whēr.

ȝwī, ȝwider, *see* whī, whider.

ȝwīle, ȝwīlene, *see* whīle, whīlen.

ȝwō, *see* whō.

ȝyēt, *see* ȝēt.

ȝyft, ȝeft, *sb.*, OM. geft, WS. gift;
gift, 89, 22; *pl.* ȝeftes, 221, 15. Cf.
ȝive.

ȝyng, *adj.*, Sth. = Ml. ȝung; WS.
geong; *young*, 176, 4.

ȝynge, *see* ȝeonge(n).

ȝys, *adv.*, OM. *gese < *gēswā, WS.
gēa + swā; *yes*, 114, 22.

ȝyve, ȝyve(n), *see* ȝeve(n).

Y.

yaf, yāld, *see* ȝeve(n), ȝēlde(n).

ȳare, *see* ēre.

yáre, *adv.*, OM. gāre, WS. gēare;
readily, archaic *yarely*, 107, 16.

ybē, yblent, *see* bē(n), blēnde(n).

yblēved, *see* blēve(n).

yblisced, *see* blesse(n).

ybōre, ybōre(n), *see* bēre(n).

ybrouȝt, *see* bringe(n).

ycarīed, *see* carīe(n).

ychaunged, *see* chaunge(n).

yche, yclenzed, *see* ilc, clense(n).

yclēpud, *see* clēpe(n).

yclc̄ped, *see* clōpe(n).

ycome, *see* cume(n).

ycoyned, *see* coine(n).

ȳdill, ȳdel, *see* īdel.

ȳdillness, *see* īdelnesse.

ydō, ydōn, *see* dōn.

Ȳdoine, *sb.*, OF. Idoine; *Idoine*,
127, 2.

ydronke, *see* drinke(n).

ydryve(n), *see* drīve(n).

ȳdul, yē, *see* īdell, þū.

yȳ, *adv.*, OM. gǣ, WS. gēa; *yea, yes*,
241, 7.

yēalde(n), *wkv.*, Kt. WS. ealdian,
grow old; *pr. 3 sg.* ȝēaldeþ, 219, 1.
Cf. ēlde(n).

yēar, yēde, *see* ȝēr, gǭ(n).

yef (yf), yefþ, *see* ȝif, ȝeve(n).

yeild, yeir, *see* ȝēlde(n), ȝēr.

yel, yelleþ, *see* ȝelle(n).

yēld, *see* ȝēlde(n).

yēme(n), *see* ȝēme(n).

yēr, *see* ȝēr.

yȳrd, *sb.*, OE. geard, gēard; *yard*,
86, 18.

yēre, *see* ȝēr.

yērnes, (yērneþ), *see* ȝērne(n).

ȳesyȝte, *sb.*, OM. ēge + sihte = sihðe,
f.; *eyesight*, 124, 20.

yēte, yeve(n), *see* ȝēt, ȝeve(n).

yfayled, yfel, *see* faile(n), yvel.

yȝen, ygǭn (yguo), *see* ēȝe, gǭ(n).

yhent, yherd, *see* hente(n), hēre(n).

yhidde, *see* hidde(n).

yhōten, yhōve, *see* hōte(n), hēve(n).

yhȳer, *see* ihēre(n).

yif, yiven, *see* ȝif, ȝeve(n).

yknowe, *see* knowe(n).

ylad, yladde, *see* lēde(n).

ylaste(n), ȳlde, *see* laste(n), ēlde.

yleft, *see* lōve(n).

ylēste(n), *wkv.*, Kt. gelēstan, WS.
gelǣstan; *endure, last*; Kt. *inf.*
ylēste, 215, 13.

ylet, yleyd(-id), *see* lēte(n), leie(n).

yliȝt, *see* ligte(n).

ylle, ylōre, *see* ille, lēse(n).

ȳlǭnd, *sb.*, Sth. = Ml. eilǭnd, īlǭnd;
WS. īegland (-lǭnd); *island*, 220,
1. Cf. eilond.

ylȳerned, *see* lērne(n).

ymad, *see* make(n).

ymelled, *see* melle(n).

ymäȝe, *sb.*, OF. image; *image*, 145, 23.

yn, *see* in.

Ȳnde, *sb.*, OF. Inde; *India*, 240, 26.

ynesche, *adj.*, OE. *gehnesce; *soft,
tender, gentle*, 144, 14.

Yngland, *see* Ingland.

ynime(n), *stv*, OE. geniman-nōm
(4); *seize, take*; *pt. sg.* ynam, 73,
13; *pp.* ynōmen, 65, 4.

ynkurlȳ, *adv.*, based on ON. einkar + ME. lī; *specially, particularly*, 172, 1.

ynne, *see* -inne(n).

ynoȝ, ynomen, *see* inōh, ynime(n).

ynou, ynough, ynow, ynug, *see* inōh.

yǫlde, yongeste, *see* ȝēlde(n), ȝung.

yōur, yōure, *see* ȝūr.

youthe, *see* ȝoūþe.

ypased, *see* passe(n).

ypeynt, ypeynted, *see* peynte(n).

ypocrisȳe, *sb.*, OF. ipocrisie; *hypocrasy*, 219, 5.

ypocrite, *sb.*, OF. ipocrite; *hypocrite*; *pl.* ypocrittes, 146, 10.

ypunissed, *see* punische(n).

yput(t), *see* putte(n).

ȳre (ȳren), *see* īren.

Ȳrisch, *adj.*, OE. *Īrisc; *Irish*, 222, 11.

Ȳrloande (-lǫnd), *see* Īrelǫnde.

ȳrne, *see* īren.

yrokked, *pp.* as *adj.*, ON. (Dan.) rokka; *rocked*, 224, 22.

Ȳryschman, *sb.*, OE. *Īriscman ; *Irishman* ; *pl.* Ȳryschmen; 221, 3.

ys, *see* bē(n).

Ȳsaāc, *sb.*, OE. Isaac; *Isaac*, 130, 23.

Ȳsambrāse, *sb.*, OF. Isambrace; *Isambrace*, 127, 1.

yschilt, *pp.* OE. scilian ; *separated, divided, p.* 267.

ysē, *see* isē(n).

yselþe, *sb.*, Sth. = Ml. selþe ; OE. gesǣlð, *f.*; *happiness, prosperity, wealth, advantage*, 176, 15.

ysēn (ysey), *see* isē(n).

ysent, *see* sēnde(n).

ysey, yseyd, *see* seie(n), isē(n).

yslawe, yslayn, *see* slǫ(n).

Ysotę, *sb.*, OF. Isolde ; *Iseult*, 126, 17.

yspild, yspylt, *see* spille(n).

ystābled, *see* stāble(n).

ystǫnde, *see* stānde(n).

yt, ytāke(n), *see* hē, tāke(n).

ytauȝt, *see* tēche(n).

yū (yuu), yung, *see* þū, ȝung.

yused, *see* ūse(n).

yvel (yfel), yvil, *adj.*, *sb.*, OE. yfel; *evil, bad* ; yfel, 2, 11 ; yvil, 58, 22 ; *ds.* yfele, 176, 19; *pl.* yvele, 3, 1; *pl.* as *sb.* ivels, 101, 5. Sth. *ds.* üvele, 177, 2.

ywākened, *see* wākne(n).

ywent, *see* wēnde(n).

ywil, *see* iwil.

ywonden, *see* wōūnde(n).

ywoned, *see* wune(n).

ywonne, *see* winne(n).

ywrite, ywys, *see* wrīte(n), iwis.

ywrouȝt, *see* wirche(n).

ywyte(n), *see* iwite(n).

yzēd, *see* seie(n).

yzēþ, yzȳ, yzȳeþ, yzyȝþ, *see* isē(n).

yziȝt, yzī, *see* isē(n).

Z.

zaule, *see* sāule.

zayst (zayþ), *see* seie(n).

zēche (zekþ), *see* sēche(n).

zelve, *see* self.

zēnd, *see* sēnde(n).

zenne, *see* sinne.

zeve, ziğğe, *see* sēve(n), sīþ.

zīþ, zixtī, *see* seie(n), sixtī.

zǫmtȳme, *adv.*, Kt. = Ml. sumtīme; OE. sumtīma ; *sometime*, 215, 15.

zǫng, *sb.*, Kt. = Ml. sǫng ; OE. sang, sǫng; *song*; *pl.* zǫnges, 215, 23.

zorȝe (zorȝen), zōþ, *see* sorȝe, sōþ.

zorȝe(n), *wkv.*, Kt. = Ml. sorȝe(n) ; OE. sorgian; *grieve, sorrow*; *pr. pl.* zorȝeþ, 215, 16.

zōþlīche, *adv.*, Kt. = Ml. sōþlīche (līke) ; OE. sōðlīce ; *truly*, 218, 24.

zuǫ, zuyche, *see* swǫ, swilc.

zyȝþe, zȳinde (zȳþ), *see* siht, sē(n).

zyker, *adj.*, Kt. = Ml. siker, cf. Dan. sikker, OFris. siker ; *certain, sure*, 219, 28.

zȳþ, *see* sē(n).

NOV DISCHA 1967

NOV 1 2 1993